KU-528-149

WITHDRAWN

SOURCEBOOK ON PUBLIC INTERNATIONAL LAW

Tim Hillier, LLB, MA, Senior Lecturer in law,
De Montfort University, Leicester

Cavendish
Publishing
Limited

London • Sydney

LIVERPOOL JOHN MOORES UNIVERSITY
Aldham Roberts L.R.C.
TEL. 0151 231 3701/3634

First published in Great Britain 1998 by Cavendish Publishing Limited,
The Glass House, Wharton Street, London WC1X 9PX.
Telephone: 0171-278 8000 Facsimile: 0171-278 8080
e-mail: info@cavendishpublishing.com
Visit our Home Page on http://www.cavendishpublishing.com

© Hillier, T 1998

All rights reserved. No part of this publication may be reproduced, stored in a
retrieval system, or transmitted, in any form or by any means, electronic,
mechanical, photocopying, recording, scanning or otherwise, except under the
terms of the Copyright Designs and Patents Act 1988 or under the terms of a
licence issued by the Copyright Licensing Agency, 90 Tottenham Court Road,
London W1P 9HE, UK, without the permission in writing of the publisher.

Hillier, Tim
Sourcebook on Public International Law – (Sourcebook series)
I Title II Series
341

ISBN 1 85941 050 2

Printed and bound in Great Britian

Books ar   )n or before
)w.

SOURCEBOOK ON PUBLIC

Books are to be returned on   T
the last date below

Cavendish
Publishing
Limited

LIVERPOOL JMU LIBRARY

3 1111 01003 7339

CONTENTS

Contents

TABLE OF CASES

TABLE OF STATUTES

TABLE OF INTERNATIONAL CONVENTIONS
AND OTHER DOCUMENTS

CHAPTER 1

INTRODUCTION

States and law faculties of higher educational institutions are encouraged to include international law as a core subject in their curricula. They are also encouraged to introduce courses in international law for students studying law, political science, social sciences and other relevant disciplines; they should study the possibility of introducing topics of international law in the curricula of schools at the primary and secondary levels. They should also consider introducing public international law courses geared towards career training and the establishment of clinical programmes in various areas of international law. Co-operation between institutions at the university level among developing countries, on the one hand, and their co-operation with those of developed countries, on the other, should be encouraged.[1]

On 17 November 1989 the UN General Assembly passed Resolution 44/23 by which it declared the period 1990–99 the United Nations Decade of International Law. Among the purposes of the Decade are the promotion of the acceptance of and respect for the principles of international law and the encouragement of the teaching, study, dissemination and wider appreciation of international law. The adoption of the resolution by the 183 member states of the United Nations indicates the ever-increasing significance of international law.

The purpose of this Sourcebook is to provide a clear and comprehensive guide to the major topics of international law. It has been the author's aim to include all the up-to-date material necessary for the reader to achieve the level of discussion expected of a good student during classes and for the preparation for examinations. It is hoped that this Sourcebook can be used both as a textbook and as a cases and materials book. International law is a subject for which a Sourcebook is particularly appropriate: the sources of its rules are numerous and diverse and many of these sources are not always readily available in the standard law library. The Sourcebook has been written so as to provide an entire and comprehensive undergraduate course in public international law, although it should also prove useful to those who simply wish to find a particular source.

This chapter provides a general introduction to the subject of international law by examining the definition, nature and scope of the subject. It is also useful at this stage to place modern international law in its historical context by tracing its development over the last three centuries.

A new and very small sovereign state was admitted as a member of the United Nations in the 1970s. Within the United Nations the *de facto* position is that each sovereign state is equal and has one vote in the United Nations General Assembly, even though beneath that technical equality the usual hierarchy exists with the richest and most powerful states exerting the most influence. The newly appointed representative from the newly independent state did not initially

---

1   Resolution adopted by the United Nations General Assembly – Resolution 51/157 United Nations Decade of International Law (A/RES/51/157 16 December 1996).

grasp that the quality was supposed only to be formal. Consequently he or she spoke at length on every topic which fell for debate to the obvious chagrin of the representatives of the larger and greater states. At last, in considerable frustration, he was taken off into the office of a delegate of one of the great states, upon the wall of which hung a large map of the world. The 'Important Delegate' explained to the unimportant new representative his position by showing the vast area of the map covered by such states as the US, Canada, Ghana, and even New Zealand, when compared to the tiny dots which represented the new delegate's country. The new delegate's immediate response was to ask a question – 'who drew that map?[2]

The question 'who drew that map?' can partially be answered by an investigation of the historical development of international law. Closely linked to the question of 'who' are the questions of 'how' and 'why' which will also be addressed in this chapter. With a grasp of the theoretical underpinnings, the 'map' of international law, investigated in subsequent chapters, will be more understandable.

1.1 Historical development

The modern system of international law is a product, roughly speaking, of only the last four hundred years. It grew to some extent out of the usages and practices of modern European states in their intercourse and communications, while it still bears witness to the influence of writers and jurists of the sixteenth, seventeenth, and eighteenth centuries, who first formulated some of its most fundamental tenets. Moreover, it remains tinged with concepts such as national and territorial sovereignty, and the perfect equality and independence of states, that owe their force to political theories underlying the modern European state system, although, curiously enough, some of these concepts have commanded the support of newly emerged non-European states.

But any historical account of the system must being with earliest times, for even in the period of antiquity rules of conduct to regulate the relations between independent communities were felt necessary and emerged from the usages observed by these communities in their mutual relations. Treaties, the immunities of ambassadors, and certain laws and usages of war are to be found many centuries before the dawn of Christianity, for example in ancient Egypt and India, while there were historical cases of recourse to arbitration and mediations in ancient China and in the early Islamic world, although it would be wrong to regard these early instances as representing any serious contribution towards the evolution of the modern system of international law.[3]

The Law of Nations, or International Law, may be defined as the body of rules and principles of action which are binding upon civilised states in their relations with one another. Rules which may be described as international law are to be found in the history of both the ancient and medieval worlds; for ever since men began to organise their common life in political communities they have felt the need of some system of rules, however rudimentary, to regulate their inter-community relations. But as a definite branch of jurisprudence the system which

---

2   Mansell, Meteyard and Thomson, *A Critical Introduction to Law*, 1995, London: Cavendish Publishing at p 1.

3   IA Shearer, *Starke's International Law*, 11th edn, 1994, London: Butterworths at p 7.

we now know as international law is modern, dating only from the 16th and 17th centuries, for its special character has been determined by that of the modern European state system, which was itself shaped in the ferment of the Renaissance and the Reformation.[4]

The origin of the international community in its present structure and configuration is usually traced back to the Peace of Westphalia (1648), which concluded the ferocious and sanguinary Thirty Years War. However, it was not then that international intercourse between groups and nations started. From time immemorial there had been consular and diplomatic relations between different communities, as well as treaties of war and peace and treaties of alliance; reprisals had been regulated for many years, and during the Middle Ages a body of law on the conduct of belligerent hostilities had gradually evolved. A peace treaty going back to approximately 3100 BC has come to light – concluded in the Sumerian language between Eannatum, the victorious ruler of the Mesopotamian city state of Lagash, and the representatives of Umma, another Mesopotamian city state, which had been defeated. And yet all these relations were radically different from current international dealings, for the body politic itself was different.[5]

It can be seen that there is widespread agreement that the modern system of international law developed from Western European origins. With the gradual break up of the Holy Roman Empire after 1648, states such as England, the Netherlands, France and Spain became strong and independent from any superior authority. Without the influence of Papal or Imperial laws, new rules were developed to govern inter-state relations. These rules owed much to doctrines of canon law and of Roman law. The basis of the system was the consensus of equal, independent sovereign states and the rules could therefore be created by express agreement or develop out of a continued common practice. Holding such a view of the development of international law has important consequences both for the nature and definition of international law[6] and for the sources of international law.[7] However, while the perception of modern international law as a phenomenon of medieval Western European origins tends to be the prevailing one there are those who take a different view:

> As all the introductory historical sections of the leading textbooks agree, it was not until this time[8] that there appeared, in the shape of nation states possessing unlimited sovereignty, those subjects of international law which, together with the simultaneously and universally blossoming theoretical study of constitutional and international law, provided the doctrinal bases for a legally ordered system of states. At this time the only open question was the date when the international law of the modern era was supposed to have begun. After some hesitation, a willingness was expressed to go back a good century before Grotius, to Charles VII's Italian Campaign of 1649, to Machiavelli and Bodin, to the

---

4   JL Brierly, *The Law of Nations, An Introduction to the International Law of Peace*, 6th edn, 1963, Oxford: Oxford University Press at p 1.

5   Antonio Cassese, *International Law in a Divided World*, 1986, Oxford: Oxford University Press at p 34.

6   See, for example, the views expressed by Hall, Westlake and Oppenheim at p 9.

7   Discussed in Chapter 3.

8   ie the modern era – post 1648.

overseas expansion of the European maritime powers and to the theories of the Spanish late scholastics. Everything lying further back, even in the cases where important development factors were recognised, was consciously left out of consideration ... It was evident from a comparatively early point that the basic requirements for an international legal order were fully present in the European society of states not just at the beginning of the modern era, but, at the latest, by the end of the 13th century. It was recognised that the concepts of law and legal validity underlying European international law, the justifications which were always necessary when an action entailed intervention in a foreign area, the duty to participate in common sanctions against disturbers of the peace, and other basic ideas all went back to the early era of the ancient Greek *polis*, ie to the sixth century before Christ. It was further recognised that, not merely in the modern eras but at all times, international legal practice was accompanied by the theoretical ideas and claims of theologians, philosophers, historians and, later, lawyers. What this means is that, although the theory of the modern era became vastly more detailed over what had hitherto been customary, it hardly contained anything in principle that was new. Since the beginning of the 1930s, following in the footsteps of historical and archaeological research, the history of international law finally began to explore the wider world beyond Europe. First of all the history of international law turned to the ancient Near East – which also includes Egypt – and to later international legal developments in the region, in particular, those brought into being from the sixth decade of the seventh century onwards by the formation and spread of Islam. The most incisive changes to the picture handed down by the 19th century may, however, be expected from the efforts which only began in recent decades to uncover international legal developments which, of their own volition, appeared in the world outside Europe and away from the Mediterranean. As yet, no more than a start has been made. It is nevertheless possible, even given the gaps in our knowledge, to accept that there is, beyond the world of the Near East and Europe (which understandably claimed the attention of early researchers), evidence of international law scattered over the earth in abundance.[9]

The end of World War I is almost unanimously considered as the end of an epoch in the history of the law of nations. It is also generally accepted that this caesura was more profound than those of 1648 or 1815, which marked previous transformations of international law, adopted it to the changing character of the state system which was fashioned and conditioned by the sequence of Spanish, French and British supremacy. It is generally accepted that by 1919 the classical system of international law had given way to a different system, often called 'new' or 'modern' international law. However, terminological confusion may result from the ambiguity inherent in the words 'new' and 'modern'. Historians customarily see 'modern times' as beginning at the end of the 15th century, and the new type of international law which developed from this juncture, the 'classical' system, is often called 'modern international law'. In the interest of avoiding confusion the author prefers to use the term 'post-classical' to denote the type of international law which began to evolve in 1919. Together with the classical system, it forms part of modern – in contrast to medieval – international law.

---

9   Wolfgang Prieser, 'History of the Law of Nations' in R Bernhardt (ed), *Encyclopedia of Public International Law*, Vol II, 1995, pp 717–18.

In the wake of World War II and as a consequence of a new balance of forces and deep structural changes in the state system, post-classical international law was again significantly modified. What began in 1919 entered into a second stage in 1945 – a stage, however, which both continued and developed the traits of the first post-classical period. In comparison with the law of preceding centuries, the two latest stages belong together and justify their classification within a coherent post-classical system.

The basic and characteristic feature of the classical system was its close commitment to the modern sovereign state as the sole subject of international law. Deriving from this basic structure, two other elements helped to form the shape of the classical system: the unorganised character of the international community, composed of a multitude of sovereign states as legally equal, if *de facto* unequal members; and the acceptance of war as the ultimate instrument of enforcing law and safeguarding national honour and interest.

Starting in 1919, a different system of international law developed, based on a new concept of the nation state which, by force of circumstances, was more receptive to the idea of some restrictions of its sovereign rights (eg in the field of minority protection) and more sensitive to the rights of the human individual and his legal protection. For the first time in history, an attempt was made to organise the international community within a League of Nations, which was intended to become a universal framework for regulating the peaceful intercourse of nations and for preventing armed conflict. War as an instrument of national policy was intended to be restricted by the League Covenant, and subsequently outlawed by the Kellogg-Briand Pact (1928).[10]

1.2   Definitions and the nature of public international law

International law is the body of rules which are legally binding on states in their intercourse with each other. These rules are primarily those which govern the relations of states, but states are not the only subjects of international law. International organisations and, to some extent, also individuals may be subjects of rights conferred and duties imposed by international law. International law in the meaning of the term as used in modern times began gradually to grow from the second half of the Middle Ages. As a systematised body of rules, it owes much to the Dutch jurist Hugo Grotius, whose work, *De Jure Belli ac Pacis, Libri iii*, appeared in 1625, and became a foundation of later development.

That part of international law that is binding on all states, as is far the greater part of customary law, may be called *universal* international law, in contrast to particular international law which is binding on two or a few states only. General international law is that which is binding upon a great many states. *General* international law, such as provision of certain treaties which are widely, but not universally, binding and which establish rules appropriate for universal application, has a tendency to become universal international law.

One can also distinguish between those rules of international law which, even though they may be of universal application, do not in any particular situation give rise to rights and obligations *erga omnes*, and those which do. Thus, although all states are under certain obligations as regards the treatment of aliens, those

---

10 William G Grewe, in R Bernhardt (ed), *Encyclopaedia of Public International Law*, Vol II, 1995 pp 839–40.

obligations (generally speaking) can only be invoked by the state whose nationality the alien possesses: on the other hand, obligations deriving from the outlawing of acts of aggression, and of genocide, and from the principles and rules concerning the basic rights of the human person, including protection from slavery and racial discrimination, are such that all states have an interest in the protection of the rights involved.[11] Rights and obligations *erga omnes* may even be created by the actions of a limited number of states. There is, however, no agreed enumeration of rights and obligations *erga omnes* and the law in this area is still developing, as it is in the connected matter of a state's ability, by analogy with the *actio popularis* (or *actio communis*) known to some national legal systems, to institute proceedings to vindicate an interest as a member of the international community as distinct from an interest vested more particularly in itself. The International Court of Justice has held that proceedings in defence of legal rights or interests require those rights or interests to be clearly vested in those who claim them (even though they need not necessarily have a material or tangible object damage to which would directly harm the claimant state), and that the *actio popularis* 'is not known to international law as it stands at present'.[12] Although the notion of *actio popularis* is in some respects associated with that of rights and obligations *erga omnes*, the two are distinct and, to the extent that they are accepted, each may exist independently of the other.

International law is sometimes referred to as 'public international law' to distinguish it from private international law. Whereas the former governs the relations of states and other subjects of international law amongst themselves, the latter consists of the rules developed by states as part of their domestic law to resolve the problems which, in cases between private persons which involve a foreign element, arise over whether the court has jurisdiction and over the choice of the applicable law: in other terms, public international law arises from the juxtaposition of states, private international law from the juxtaposition of legal systems. Although the rules of private international law are part of the internal law of the state concerned, they may also have the character of public international law where they are embodied in treaties. Where this happens the failure of a state party to the treaty to observe the rule of private international law prescribed in it will lay it open to proceedings for breach of an international obligation owed to another party. Even where the rules of private international law cannot themselves be considered as rules of public international law, their application by a state as part of its internal law may directly involve the rights and obligations of the state as a matter of public international law, for example where the matter concerns the property of aliens, or the extent of the state's jurisdiction.[13]

The title and subject matter of this book is *Public International Law*. For convenience we shall use the terms public international law and international law interchangeably. The subject has also been known as the Law of Nations and the Law of War and Peace. International law must be distinguished from municipal, internal or domestic law. As a starting point, international law can be said to apply only between those entities that can claim international

---

11 *Barcelona Traction* case (Second Phase) [1970] *ICJ Rep* at p 32.

12 *South West Africa* cases (*Ethiopia and Liberia v South Africa*) (Second Phase) [1966] *ICJ Rep* at p 47.

13 *Oppenheim's International Law*, edited by Jennings and Watts, 9th edn, 1992, Longman at pp 4–7 (footnotes omitted).

personality, whilst municipal law is the internal law of states and regulates the conduct of individuals and other legal persons within the jurisdiction. Public international law should also be distinguished from private international law. Private international law, or the conflict of laws, is the term used to describe the body of rules of municipal law that regulates legal relations with a foreign element such as, for example, contracts of sale between persons in different countries or marriages between persons from different legal systems.

It can be argued that the functions of international law are different from the functions of municipal law. In the main, international law is not concerned with the rights and duties of individuals, except where states have agreed that this should be so. International law plays a major role in facilitating international relations. It is clearly of considerable importance in the drafting of diplomatic documents and treaties, as well as, in appropriate instances, in the drafting and application of internal legislation. It should also be remembered that law can never be totally separated from questions of political reality. In international law, the political and the legal are extremely closely intertwined. International law cannot exist in isolation from the political factors operating in the sphere of international relations.

On another level, international 'law' needs to be distinguished from international 'non-law'. Reference is sometimes made to international comity or international usage to indicate those norms of behaviour that are outside the rules of law, properly called. Some writers argue that the problem is resolved with the adoption of a comprehensive definition of law, while others deny that a definition is either possible or desirable. To some extent the problem of identifying the rules of international law is dealt with in Chapter 3, but at this early stage it may be useful to refer to some of the various concepts and definitions of the subject that have been offered.

International law, as its name implies, is a form of law. In your law studies, you have come across various other forms of law – contract law, land law, LA Law. Well, international law is no different in principle from any other form of law. However, since none of you will have anything but the most infantile ideas about the theoretical nature of law in general, it's not really very exciting of me to say that international law is law like any other law.

It'll probably never have occurred to you, and maybe no one has ever told you, that law is an aspect of the systematic structure of a society. There's been a great deal of discussion down the centuries about just how law fits into the general structural system of society. Some really heavy names have had all sorts of seriously weird ideas about that – Plato and Confucius and Moses and Nietzsche and Hitler – people like that. But the long and the short of it all is that society is not quite like a poem, and society is not quite like a motor-car, but society is a bit like both of them.

Society is like a poem because it's a creation *of* human consciousness, *for* human consciousness. Society is a work of the imagination, like literature. But society is also a bit like a machine, such as a car, because it's designed to process specific inputs into specific outputs, following a structured system. And the structured system determines the relationship of the output to the input. And the result of it all is that society, like a motor-car, is designed to travel from A to B, namely, from the past to the future.

Well, one input into society is the activity of individual human consciousness, imagination and reason. And the output is social consciousness which then re-enters individual consciousness and pre-existing social consciousness. So there's a systematic loop – with the individual human being making society, as society makes society and the individual. *Society and the individual make society and the individual.* Our first slogan.

A poem works because there are conventions of vocabulary and grammar and syntax, and there are great semantic force-fields in which the poem is placed, force-fields of associative meaning and shared meaning. So the poem is an output from the poet and an input into the reader into which the reader also puts an input. A poem does not exist in quite the same way that a particular table exists: it is any number of resultants formed from all the interacting inputs and outputs.

In the case of a particular society, the society creates great semantic force-fields for itself, as an integral part of its self-creating as a society – religion, mythology, morality, philosophy, art and so on. And then systematic principles of society's functioning – social vocabulary and grammar and syntax, as it were – determine the specific outputs of the given society, determine the interactive effect between society and its members, and between the society and other societies.

The totality of the systematic processes of society is presented to society in what we call a constitution. The constitution of a society is a bit like the personality of a human person: it's a structured summation of a particular functioning identity, evolving over time, forming itself over time. The constitution forms the society as the society forms its constitution. *Society is a system constituting itself as a system.* Another slogan.

One aspect of the constitution of a society is its legal constitution. This is a specifically organised set of social sub-systems which process social material in a particular way. The constitution of a society carries the society from its past to its future. The society continues over time and space because it continues in the consciousness of its members and of those who observe it. And the continuation over time and space of a society is achieved by ordering the willing and acting of the members of society in accordance with the constitution of the society.

The law, made under the legal constitution, organises legal relations – that's to say, it organises the interactive willing and acting of two or more members of society. If you and I are bound by a legal relation – say, a right or a duty – then, if we will and act in conformity with the legal relation, we act in the way society wanted us to act. The legal relation socialises our behaviour, or, to put it another way, the legal relation universalises the particularity of our behaviour in the social interest.

But, of course, there are not only two people involved in a legal relation. A legal relation involves many other people in its implementation. A legal relation is really the focus of a network of legal relations. And legal relations necessarily involve what is called *accountability*.

Accountability means that society watches the way in which its legal relations take effect. It monitors them socially – social accountability; and it monitors them legally – legal accountability, including the monitoring through legal proceedings. Accountability means that the implementation of legal relations feeds back into the total social process, being judged in terms of society's values, leading perhaps to protest or dissent, leading perhaps to a change in the law.

So law is an intensely dynamic thing, flowing from the past of society into its future, tending to make the future of society into what society has willed in the past that its future should be. That's why some of us define the law as specifically retained acts of social willing. *The law is an ever-changing set of retained acts of social willing.* Our third slogan.

So society is a purposive enterprise, inventing purposes for itself in the form of values, organising itself to achieve its purposes.

One way in which society acts is through economic action, that's to say, through transforming material reality and ideal reality in ways which society values as conducive to its survival and prospering. And that's an important social function of law. The law is used to make economic transformation possible. The law of property, contract, money, corporate law – and so on – are sets of legal relations which are designed to organise particular forms of social transformation, especially economic transformations.

So that's what all society is and what all law is. And that means that we now already know what international society is and what international law is.

International law is, simply, the law of international society. The whole human race seeks its survival and prosperity through transforming the world in accordance with its values. The whole human race uses social processes to cause its future to be in accordance with what it wills that its future should be.[14]

1.2.1   The traditional view

The view expressed in the most recent edition of Oppenheim represents a retreat from the traditional conception of international law as the law of nations, exclusively the province of nation states. For example, Hall in 1890 wrote:

> International law consists in certain rules of conduct which modern civilised states regard as being binding on them in their relations with one another with a force comparable in nature and degree to that binding the conscientious person to obey the laws of the country, and which they also regard as being enforceable by appropriate means in case of infringement.[15]

Four years later Westlake stated, 'international law is the body of rules prevailing between states'.[16]

Oppenheim was even more explicit when he wrote, 'states solely and exclusively are the subjects of international law'.[17]

In 1927, the Permanent Court of International Justice was called upon to decide a dispute between France and Turkey. In the course of the judgment the court found it necessary to set down the parameters of international law:

> International law governs relations between independent states. The rules of law binding upon states therefore emanate from their own free will as expressed in conventions or by usages generally accepted as expressing principles of law and established in order to regulate the relations between these co-existing independent communities or with a view to the achievement of common aims.[18]

---

14   Philip Allott, 'New International Law – The First Lecture of the Academic Year 20—' in *Theory and International Law: An Introduction*, 1991, London: BIICL at pp 108–10.

15   WE Hall, *A Treatise on International Law*, 3rd edn, 1890, Oxford: Clarendon Press.

16   Westlake, *International Law*, 1894, Cambridge: Cambridge University Press.

17   Oppenheim, *International Law*, 1st edn, 1905, London: Longmans.

18   The *Lotus* case PCLJ Ser A, No 10 (1927).

1.2.2   The modern view

Although international law may have developed as a system of rules governing the relations between sovereign states, it has developed beyond that. The establishment of the League of Nations after the First World War marked a shift in approach to international relations which received further impetus with the setting up of the United Nations Organisation in 1945. The Nuremberg War Crimes Tribunal in 1946 raised questions of the international obligations of individuals and the *Universal Declaration of Human Rights* 1948 suggested the possibility of individual international rights. In the wake of the United Nations, a number of other super-national organisations were established, all raising questions of their status within the community of nation states. In 1949 the International Court of Justice was asked by the General Assembly of the United Nations for its opinion on matters arising out of the assassination of a UN representative in Jerusalem. In the course of its judgment the court stated:

> ... [the United Nations Organisation] is a subject of international law and capable of possessing international rights and duties, and ... has capacity to maintain its rights by bringing international claims.[19]

It was becoming clear that it was no longer adequate to discuss international law in terms of a system of rules governing exclusively the relations between states.[20] Later definitions reflected this fact:

> International law can no longer be adequately or reasonably defined or described as the law governing the mutual relations of states, even if such a basic definition is accompanied by qualifications or exceptions designed to allow for modern developments; it represents the common law of mankind in an early stage of development, of which the law governing the relations between states is one, but only one, major division.[21]

Some definitions continued to stress the primacy of states, for example:

> 'International law' is a strict term of art, connoting that system of law whose primary function it is to regulate the relations of states with one another. As states have formed organisations of themselves, it has come also to be concerned with international organisations and an increasing concern with them must follow from the trend which we are now witnessing towards the integration of the community of states. And because states are composed of individuals and exist primarily to serve the needs of individuals, international law has always had a certain concern with the relations of the individual, if not to his own state, at least to other states ... even the relations between the individual and his own state have come to involve questions of international law ... *Nevertheless, international law is and remains essentially a law for states* and thus stands in contrast to what international lawyers are accustomed to call municipal law ... [22]

Other definitions give greater acknowledgment to non-state entities:

> International law is the body of rules of conduct, enforceable by external sanction, which confer rights and impose obligations primarily, though not

---

19   *Reparation for Injuries Suffered in the Service of the United Nations* case [1949] *ICJ Rep* at p 174.

20   See also Chapter 5.

21   C Jenks, *The Common Law of Mankind*, 1958, London: Stevens.

22   C Parry in M Sorensen (ed), *Manual of Public International Law*, 1968, London: Macmillan (emphasis added)

exclusively, upon sovereign states and which owe their validity both to the consent of states as expressed in custom and treaties and to the fact of the existence of an international community of states and individuals. In that sense international law may be defined more briefly (though perhaps less usefully), as the law of the international community.[23]

1.2.3 Contemporary theories

Although the early development of international law owes considerable debt to natural law concepts, much of the discussion about its nature over the last 100 years has been held within the broad church of legal positivism. Analysis of international law tended to concentrate on the activities of states and the identification of positive legal rules. Underlying the theories was a firm view that international law was based on the consensus of states to be bound. After the Second World War, world events increasingly undermined this view of law. The independence of former colonies raised the issue of the extent to which new states could be truly taken to consent to existing rules of international law.

> International law (or more precisely public international law) is an autonomous system of law that is distinct from the national legal systems of specific states. International law operates in the international system and represents its normative subsystem.
>
> In literature one may find different definitions of the international system. Some of them are so wide that they encompass, in effect, all of human society. In the present context there is no need to analyse these definitions.
>
> What is then the international system in which international law is a component part?
>
> That system encompasses states, international (inter-state) organisations, various associations of states (eg the non-aligned movement and the Group of 77), nations and peoples struggling for their independence, and also certain state-like formations (eg free cities and the Vatican). That, then, is the inter-state system. It includes not only the subjects that have been listed but also relations among them (international relations in the narrow sense of the word), international legal and other social norms (norms of international morality, international comity, international customs) and also mutual interactions among all the components of the international system and between that system itself and its components. Such a system does indeed exist. Lenin noted that 'we are living not merely in a state but in a system of states'.
>
> What is important for international legal science is that aside from other components the concept of 'international system' also includes international law. It follows that international law must be viewed in its mutual interaction with them, while international relations must be studied in their interaction with international law and not independently of it ...
>
> The basic task of international law is to contribute to a normal functioning of the international system and to ensure peace and a resolution of international problems through legal means, on the basis of agreements among sovereign and equal states.[24]

---

23 Hersch Lauterpacht, *Collected Papers*, Vol 1, 1970, Cambridge: Cambridge University Press.
24 G Tunkin (ed), *International Law: a textbook*, 1982, Moscow: Progress Publishers.

The onset of the Cold War and the dominance of the two super-powers brought into question the extent to which the behaviour of the United States and the Soviet Union was guided by positive legal rules. In the 1950s the American Realists turned their attention from analysing municipal legal systems to international law. They found that law was not determined by legal rules nor by precedents but that judicial decision making was an intuitive act motivated by a desire to do justice in a particular context. International law needs to be studied in the context of international society and not merely as a collection of legal rules capable of being understood on their own.

Another approach, often referred to as 'sociological jurisprudence', involved an attempt to move away from simple analysis of rules to consider international law as an integral part of the diplomatic and political process. Notable here is the work of Myres McDougal whose policy-oriented approach sees law as a process of decision-making rather than a system of rules and obligations. McDougal has been criticised for minimising the legal content of the study of international law, and later writers, such as Richard Falk, while adopting the general approach of McDougal, have sought to place greater emphasis on the importance of legal rules and structures.

> Two criticisms are often advanced against international law. One group of critics has accused international law of being too political in the sense of being too dependent on states' political power. Another group has argued that the law is too political because founded on speculative utopias. The standard point about the non-existence of legislative machineries, compulsory adjudication and enforcement procedures captures both criticisms. From one perspective, this criticism highlights the infinite flexibility of international law, its character as a manipulable facade for power politics. From another perspective, the criticism stresses the moralistic character of international law, its distance from the realities of power politics. According to the former criticism, international law is too apologetic to be taken seriously in the construction of international order. According to the latter, it is too utopian, to identical effect.

> International lawyers have had difficulty answering these criticisms. the more reconstructive doctrines have attempted to prove the normativity of the law, its autonomy from politics, the more they have become vulnerable to the charge of utopianism. The more they have insisted on the close connection between international law and state behaviour, the less normative their doctrines have appeared ...

> Many of the doctrines which emerged from the ashes of legal scholarship at the close of the First World War explained the failure of pre-war international doctrines by reference to their apologist character ... Writings by Hersch Lauterpacht, Alfred Verdross and Hans Kelsen among others, created an extremely influential interpretation of the mistakes of pre-war doctrines. By associating the failure of those doctrines with their excessive closeness to state policy and national interest and by advocating the autonomy of international legal rules, these jurists led the way to the establishment of what could be called a *rule approach* to international law, stressing the law's normativity, its capacity to oppose state policy as the key to its constraining relevance.

> The approach insists on an objective, formal test of pedigree (sources) which will tell which standards qualify as legal rules and which do not. If a rule meets this test, then it is binding. Though there is disagreement between rule approach lawyers over what constitutes the proper test, there is no dispute about its

importance. The distinctions between hard and soft law, rules and principles, regular norms and *jus cogens*, for instance, are suspect: these only betray political distinctions with which the lawyer should not be too concerned. Two well-known criticisms have been directed against this approach. First, it has remained unable to exclude the influence of political considerations from its assumed tests of pedigree. To concede that rules are sometimes hard to find while their content remains, to adopt HLA Hart's expression 'relatively indeterminate' is to undermine the autonomy which the rule approach stressed. Second, the very desire for autonomy seems suspect. A pure theory of law, the assumption of a *Volkerrechtsgemeinschaft* or the ideal of the wholeness of law – a central assumption in most rule approach writing – may only betray forms of irrelevant doctrinal utopianism. They achieve logical consistency at the cost of applicability in the real world of state practice.

The second major position in contemporary scholarship uses these criticisms to establish itself ... Roscoe Pound's programmatic writings laid the basis for the contemporary formulation of this approach by criticising the attempt to think of international law in terms of abstract rules. It was, rather, to be thought of 'in terms of social ends'.

According to this approach – the *policy approach* – international law can only be relevant if it is firmly based in the social context of international policy. Rules are only trends of past decision which may or may not correspond to social necessities. 'Binding force' is a juristic illusion. Standards are, in fact, more or less effective and it is their effectiveness – their capacity to further social goals – which is the relevant question, not their formal 'validity'.

But this approach is just as vulnerable to well-founded criticisms as the rule approach. By emphasising the law's concreteness, it will ultimately do away with its constraining force altogether. If law is only what is effective, then by definition, it becomes an apology for the interests of the powerful. If, as Myres McDougal does, this consequence is avoided by postulating some 'goal values' whose legal importance is independent of considerations of effectiveness, then the (reformed) policy approach becomes vulnerable to criticisms which it originally voiced against the rule approach. In particular, it appears to assume an illegitimate naturalism which – as critics stressing the liberal principle of the subjectivity of value have noted – is in constant danger of becoming just an apology of some states' policies.

The rule and the policy approaches are two contrasting ways of trying to establish the relevance of international law in the face of what appear as well-founded criticisms. The former does this by stressing the law's normativity, but fails to be convincing because it lacks concreteness. The latter builds upon the concreteness of international law, but loses the normativity, the binding force of its law. It is hardly surprising, then, that some lawyers have occupied the two remaining positions: they have either assumed that international law can neither be seen as normatively controlling nor widely applied in practice (the sceptical position), or have continued writing as if both the law's binding force as well as its correspondence with developments in international practice were a matter of course (idealist position). The former ends in cynicism, the latter in contradiction ...

The difficulty in choosing between a rule and a policy approach is the difficulty of defending the set of criteria which these put forward to disentangle 'law' from other aspects of state behaviour. For the rule approach lawyer, the relevant criteria are provided by his theory of sources. For the policy approach, the corresponding criteria are provided by his theory of 'base-values', authority or some constellation of national or global interest and need, because it is these criteria which claim to provide the correct description of social processes themselves. To decide on the better approach, one would have to base oneself on some non-descriptive (non-social) theory about significance or about the relative justice of the types of law rendered by the two – or any alternative – matrices. Such a decision would, under the social concept of law and the principle of the subjectivity of value, be one which would seem to have no claim for objective correctness at all. It would be a political decision ...

The formality of international law makes it possible for each state to read its substantive concept of world society as well as its view of the extent of sovereign freedoms into legal concepts and categories. This is no externally introduced distortion in the law. It is a necessary consequence of a view which holds that there is no naturally existing 'good life', no limit to sovereign freedom which would exist by force of some historical necessity. If this kind of naturalism is rejected – and since the Enlightenment, everybody has had good reason to reject it – then to impose any substantive conception of communal life or limits of sovereignty can appear only as illegitimate constraint – preferring one state's politics to those of another.

It is impossible to make substantive decisions within the law which would imply no political choice. The late modern turn to equity in the different realms of international law is, in this sense, a healthy admission of something that is anyway there: in the end, legitimising or criticising state behaviour is not a matter of applying formally neutral rules but depends on what one regards as politically right, or just.[25]

International law is not rules. It is a normative system. All organised groups and structures require a system of normative conduct – that is to say, conduct which is regarded by each actor, and by the group as a whole, as being obligatory, and for which violation carries a price. Normative systems make possible that degree of order if society is to maximise the common good – and, indeed, even to avoid chaos in the web of bilateral and multilateral relationships that that society embraces. Without law at the domestic level, cars cannot safely travel on the roads, purchases cannot be made, personal safety cannot be secured. Without international law, safe aviation could not be agreed, resources could not be allocated, people could not safely choose to dwell in foreign lands. Two points are immediately apparent. The first is that this is humdrum stuff. The role of law is to provide an operational system for securing values that we all desire – security, freedom, the provision of sufficient material goods. It is not, as is commonly supposed, only about resolving disputes. If a legal system works well, then disputes are in large part *avoided*. The identification of required norms of behaviour, and techniques to secure routine compliance with them, play an important part. An efficacious legal system can also *contain* competing interests, allowing those who hold them not to insist upon immediate and unqualified vindication. Of course, sometimes dispute resolution will be needed; or even norms to limit the parameters of conduct when normal friendly relations have broken down and dispute resolution failed. But these last elements are only a small part of the overall picture.

The second point is that, in these essentials, international law is no different from domestic law. It is not, as some suppose, an arcane and obscure body of rules whose origin and purpose are shrouded in mystery. But, if the social purpose of

25 Martti Koskenniemi, 'The Politics of International Law', in (1990) 1/2 *EJIL* 4 at pp 9–13, 31.

international law and domestic law is broadly similar, there are important differences arising from the fact that domestic law operates in a vertical legal order, and international law in a horizontal legal order. Consent and sovereignty are constraining factors against which the prescribing, invoking, and applying of international law norms must operate.

...

There is a widely held perception of international law as 'rules' – rules that are meant to be impartially applied but are frequently ignored. It is further suggested that these rules are ignored because of the absence of effective centralised sanctions – and, in turn, that all of this evidences that international law is not 'real law' at all.

The view that international law is a body of rules that fails to restrain states falls short on several counts. In the first place, it assumes that law is indeed 'rules'. But the specialised social processes to which the word 'law' refers include many things besides rules. Rules play a part in law, but not the only part. I remain committed to the analysis of international law as process rather than rules and to the view I expressed many years ago, when I said:

> When ... decisions are made by authorised persons or organs, in appropriate forums, within the framework of certain established practices and norms, then what occurs is legal decision-making. In other words, international law is a continuing process of authoritative decisions. This view rejects the notion of law merely as the impartial application of rules. International law is the entire decision-making process, and not just the references to the trend of past decisions which are termed 'rules'. There inevitably flows from this definition a concern, especially where the trend of past decision is not overwhelmingly clear, with policy alternatives for the future.[26]

Thus 'rules' are just accumulated past decisions. And, if international law was just 'rules', then international law would indeed be unable to contribute to, and cope with, a changing political world. To rely merely on accumulated past decisions (rules) when the context in which they were articulated has changed – and indeed when their content is often unclear – is to ensure that international law will not be able to contribute to today's problems and, further, that it will be disobeyed for that reason.

The rejection of the perception of law as 'rules' entails a necessary consequence. It means that those who have to make decisions on the basis of international law – judges, but also legal advisers and others – are not simply 'finding the rule' and then applying it. That is because the determination of what is the relevant rule is part of the decision-makers' function; and because the accumulated trend of past decisions should never be applied oblivious of context. Although this reality has been regarded as anathema by many traditionalists, it was well understood by Sir Hersch Lauterpacht. He rejected the notion that the judicial function meant finding the appropriate rule in an impartial manner. The judge, he argued, does not 'find rules' but he 'makes choices' – and choices 'not between claims which are fully justified and claims which have no foundation at all but between claims which have varying degrees of legal merit'.[27]

---

26 R Higgins, 'Policy Considerations and the International Judicial Process' (1968) 17 *ICLQ* 58 at pp 58–59.

27 H Lauterpacht, *The Development of International Law by the International Court*, 1958, London: Stevens at p 399.

The reason why some insist that international law is 'rules', and that all international lawyers have to do is identify them and apply them, are not hard to find. They are an unconscious reflection of two beliefs, deeply held by many international lawyers. The first is that, if international law is regarded as more than rules, and the role of the authorised decision-maker as other than the automatic applier of such rules, international law becomes confused with other phenomena, such as power or social or humanitarian factors. The second reason is that it is felt by many that only by insisting on international law as rules to be impartially applied will it be possible to avoid the manifestation of international legal argument for political ends.

I want to deal with each of these reasons in turn, and tell you why I do not agree with them. To seek to contrast law with power (in which task the perception of law as 'rules' plays an essential task) is fundamentally flawed. It assumes that law is concerned only with the concept of authority and not with power or control. International law *is* indeed concerned with authority – and 'authority' not just in the sense of binding decisions, but in the broader sense of jurisdictional competence, and more. Myres McDougal has explained:

> By authority is meant expectations of appropriateness in regard to the phases of effective decision processes. These expectations specifically relate to personnel appropriately endowed with decision-making power; the objectives they should pursue; the physical, temporal and institutional features of the situations in which lawful decisions are made; the values which may be used to sustain decision, and so forth ... [28]

So far, so good. But it is not the case, as is frequently supposed, that international law is concerned with authority alone, and that 'power' stands somehow counterpoised to authority, and is nothing to do with law, and indeed inimical to it. This view – which banishes power to the outer darkness (that is to say, to the province of international relations) – assumes that authority can exist in the total absence of supporting control, or power. But this is a fantasy. The authority which characterises law exists not in a vacuum, but exactly where it intersects with power. Law, far from being authority battling against power,[29] is the interlocking of authority with power. Authority cannot exist in the total absence of control. Of course, there will be particular circumstances when power overrides authority. On such occasions we will not have decision-making that we can term lawful. But that is not to say that law is about authority only, and not about power too; or that power is definitionally to be regarded as hostile to law. It is an integral element of it.

What then of the other argument – that a perception of international law as other than neutral rules inevitably leads to bias and partiality? A classical statement of this view was made by Judges Fitzmaurice and Spender in the *South West Africa* cases in 1962, when they wrote:

> We are not unmindful of, nor are we insensible to, the various considerations of a non-judicial character, social humanitarian and other ... but these are matters for the political rather than for the legal area. They cannot be allowed

---

28 M McDougal, H Lasswell, and M Reisman, 'The World Constitutive Process of Authoritative Decision' (1966) 19 *Journal of Legal Education* 253 at p 256.

29 For expression of this view, see G Shwarzenberger, 'The Misery and Grandeur of International Law', inaugural lecture 1963; see also M Bos, *A Methodology of International Law*, 1984, Amsterdam: North-Holland, esp Chapter XI.

to deflect us from our duty of reaching a conclusion strictly on the basis of what we believe to be the correct legal view.[30]

This formulation reflects certain assumptions: that 'the correct legal view' is to be discerned by applying 'rules' – the accumulated trend of past decisions, regardless of context or circumstance – and that 'the correct legal view' has nothing to do with applying past decisions to current contexts by reference to objectives (values) that the law is designed to promote.

The classical view, so brilliantly articulated by Fitzmaurice but shared by very many others, is that international law can best perform its service to the community exactly by distancing itself from social policy. As the International Court of Justice put it in 1966: 'Law exists, it is said, to serve a social need; but precisely for that reason it can do so only through and within the limits of its own discipline. Otherwise, it is not a legal service that would be rendered.' [31] Of course, the International Court of Justice thought it self-evident as to where law does draw 'the limits of its own discipline'. But what is self-evident to one is merely question begging to another.

Reference to 'the correct legal view' or 'rules' can never avoid the element of choice (though it can seek to disguise it), nor can it provide guidance to the preferable decision. In making this choice one must inevitably have consideration for the humanitarian, moral, and social purposes of the law. As I have written elsewhere:

> Policy consideration, although they differ from 'rules', are an integral part of that decision making process which we call international law; the assessment of so-called extralegal considerations is part of the legal process, just as is reference to the accumulation of past decisions and current norms. A refusal to acknowledge political and social factors cannot keep law 'neutral', for even such a refusal is not without political and social consequence. There is no avoiding the essential relationship between law and politics.[32]

Because I believe there is no avoiding the essential relationship between law and policy, I also believe that it is desirable that the policy factors are dealt with systematically and openly. Dealing with them systematically means that all factors are properly considered and weighed, instead of the decision-maker unconsciously narrowing or selecting what he will take into account in order to reach a decision that he has instinctively predetermined is desirable. Dealing with policy factors openly means that the decision-maker himself is subjected to the discipline of facing them squarely (instead of achieving unconsciously desired policy objectives by making a particular choice, which is then given the label of 'the correct legal rule'). It also means that the choices made are open to public scrutiny and discussion.

All this being said, there is still a problem we have to address. If international law is not the mere application of neutral rules in an impartial fashion, but requires choices to be made between alternative norms that could, in the context, each be applicable, then do we really have something other than a justification of the end by the means? This is the serious question, made the more so by the

---

30 *South West Africa* cases [1962] *ICJ Rep* at p 466.

31 *South West Africa* cases [1966] *ICJ Rep* 6 at para 49.

32 Higgins, 'Integrations of Authority and Control: Trends in the Literature of International Law and Relations', in B Weston and M Reisman (eds), *Towards World Order and Human Dignity*, 1976, New York: Free Press.

events of the early 1980s. During the administration of President Reagan, the United States engaged in various acts of foreign policy which were designed not only to secure national goals but to secure certain objectives perceived as being in the interests of international order and justice. In particular, there occurred military interventions to remove totalitarian rulers and to allow a democratic freedom of choice to the peoples of the countries concerned. We may cite military action in Nicaragua in 1983, in Grenada in 1983, and in Panama in 1989. There has also been military action to punish perceived terrorism: here we may cite the US bombing of Libya in 1986. Each of these actions occasioned significant debate, among Americans and friends of the United States as much among others. There were widely differing views as to the lawfulness of these various actions under international law. The Legal Adviser to the Department of state and the scholars who supported the military interventions very much emphasised the social purposes of international law in their analysis of what was and was not permitted under the United Nations Charter and under customary international law.

My intention is not to enter the fray on the substance of these matters ... Rather, I ask this question: if one shares the belief in the preferability of democracy over tyranny, and if one is committed to the policy-science approach to international law, whereby trends of past decisions are to be interpreted with policy objectives in mind, does it necessarily follow that one would have viewed all these actions as lawful? I think not.

In the first place, I do not believe that the policy-science approach requires one to find every means possible if the end is desirable. Trends of past decisions still have an important role to play in the choices to be made, notwithstanding the importance of both context and desired outcome. Where there is ambiguity or uncertainty, the policy-directed choice can properly be made. Some will say that, in a decentralised legal order, to allow one party to interpret the law to achieve desirable outcomes merely will allow another, less scrupulous party to claim to do the same. I am not greatly impressed with that argument. There is no escaping the duty that each and every one of us has to test the validity of legal claims. We will each know which are intellectually supportable and which are not, and it is a chimera to suppose that, if only international law is perceived as the application of neutral rules, it will then be invoked only in an unbiased manner. But it is in the common interest that some prohibitions should be absolute (for example, the prohibitions against some kinds of weaponry);[33] and it is in the common interest that other kinds of limitation on conduct should be regarded as compelling, even if, on any single occasion, that prevents the achievement of an outcome otherwise to be regarded as desirable.

That being said, it is still quite wide of the mark to suggest, as some do, that, in the absence of third-party determination, the policy-science approach means simply whatever the policy-maker wants. It really carries matters no further for critics to say that this approach 'can lead to international law being used by states as a device for *post facto* justifying decisions without really taking international law into account'.[34] This simply begs the question of what international law is. Such a comment merely presupposes that there is a 'real' international law that all men of good faith can recognise – that is, rules that can

---

33 See Chapter 14 and 'the Legality of the Use by the state of Nuclear Weapons in Armed Conflict' [1966] *ICJ Rep* at p 1.

34 GJH Van Hoof, *Rethinking the Sources of International Law*, 1983, Deventer: Kluwer at p 43.

be neutrally applied, regardless of circumstance and context. And that is where the debate began.

Of course the debate on legal theory is not only about whether international law is 'rules' or 'process'. But this is a critical aspect. Emphasis on rules is associated with, but not limited to, legal positivists – that is to say, those who conceive of law as commands emanating from a sovereign. Austin, the founding father of legal positivism, put it thus: 'Every positive law, or every law simply and strictly so called, is set by a sovereign individual or a sovereign body of individuals, to a person or persons in a state of subjection to its authority.'[35] Kelsen, seeking to give meaning to positivism in a horizontal, decentralised international legal order, where command and sovereignty are notably lacking, proposed the existence of a *Grundnorm* – the highest fundamental norm from which all others derived their binding force.[36]

Some leading scholars have sought to reconcile the 'rule' and 'process' approaches. Yet others, while showing an interest in these matters, have sought to avoid taking positions, insisting that they will merely address the substantive problems of international law on a pragmatic level. My view is that, superficially attractive though 'reconciliation' or 'synthesis' or 'middle views' may seem (as writers frequently want to claim to offer these attractive middle ways), they avoid or blur the essential questions rather than provide an answer to them. And pragmatism itself entails certain assumptions about legal philosophy, no matter how much it seeks to cut clear of the argument.[37]

More recently, and coinciding with the rise of the critical legal studies movement, there has been an increase in interest in international legal theory. Writers such as Anthony Carty, David Kennedy and Philip Allott have all made valuable contributions to this area of study by re-examining the nature of international law. A major reason for the increase in interest has been the perceived decline in the influence of the sovereign state, particularly in the light of events in the Balkans and elsewhere in Eastern Europe. Characteristic of the new approach is the view that the traditional ideal of international law is based on contradictory premises. Social conflict is resolved by political means and law is just one of the political weapons available. Such theorists argue that a universal definition of law is not possible and instead maintain that the study of law should involve analysis of the way in which states behave and the way in which they justify their behaviour.

'Critical' international legal studies constitute a so-called post-modern approach to international law. This is to assert that the discipline is governed by a particular, historically conditioned discourse which is, in fact, quite simply, the translation onto the international domain of some basic tenets of liberal political theory. It opposes itself to the positivist international law, as representative of an actual consensus among states. The crucial question is simply whether a positive system of universal international law actually exists, or whether particular states

---

35 J Austin, *Lectures on Jurisprudence or the Philosophy of Positive Law*, 5th edn, 1885, London: John Murray at p 34.

36 H Kelsen, *General Theory of Law and State*, trans A Wedberg, 1949, Cambridge, Mass: Harvard University Press at p 113.

37 Rosalyn Higgins, *Problems and Processes, International Law and How We Use it* (1994), Oxford: Oxford University Press at pp 1–8. The book is a revised version of Rosalyn Higgins' General Course in International Law delivered to the Hague Academy of International Law.

and their representative legal scholars merely appeal to such positivist discourse so as to impose a particular language upon others *as if it were a universally accepted legal discourse*. So post-modernism is concerned with unearthing difference, heterogeneity and conflict as reality in place of *fictional* representations of universality and consensus ...

... There is a contradiction within international legal practice which consists in a virtually unending process of reification[38] of the discourse of state consent into actually existing, constraining rules independent of states, which have only to be identified for problems of authority in relations between states to be resolved. In practice this leads to sterile and acrimonious attempts to 'demonstrate' that 'the other side' has 'consented' to a viewpoint which one prefers, an elusive exercise, given that the starting point will usually be a conflict of interest which supposes that neither party is 'consenting' to what 'the other' wishes.

The critical approach, far from denying the very existence of international law, allows a way out of this impasse precisely because it recognises the character of liberalism as a tradition. It does this by means of two devices. It recognises the absence of a central international legal order as an impartial point to which state actors can refer, ie the simple meaning to be given to the phrase 'the disappearance of the referent'.[39] At the same time it favours a mature anarchy in international relations, the recognition of states as independent centres of legal culture and significance, which have to be understood, in relation to one another, as opposing to one another very fragile, because invariably partial, understanding of order and community.

The role of the international lawyer in such an acutely relativised, self-reflective culture is now, more than ever, crucial. It is his function to resist phoney, reified, would-be universalist legal discourse in favour of the recognition of the inevitably restrictive and exclusive nature of individual state discourse. Above all this calls for the development of a new critical standard which is concerned with penetrating through the cultural symbols of pseudo-universalisation thrown up by individual state to assert themselves against one another. It is not the ambition of the critical international lawyer to substitute another pseudo-impartial legal order, but to facilitate the development of the process of inter-state/inter-cultural dialogue and understanding which may allow a coming together, however temporary and fragile. What is called for is scholarly work of legal translation, itself attempting to be impartial, to stand outside the circles of meaning projected by individual states.[40]

1.3   Is international law really law?

One particular aspect of the discussion about international law has been the questioning by some writers of the very claim made to legal status. Much of the debate surrounding international law's status as law can be traced to the

---

38   Reification means simply to consider or to make an abstract idea or concept real or concrete.

39   Referent means the object or idea to which a word or phrase refers. A major thesis of post-modernism, very closely linked to the concept of reification is that words have, to a very significant extent, lost any outside referents, that concepts merely refer to one another in a process of mutual differentiation within language.

40   Anthony Carty, 'Critical Legal Law: Recent Trends in the Theory of International Law' (1991) 2 *EJIL* 66 at pp 66–68.

positivist legacy of John Austin. In his major theoretical work, *The Province of Jurisprudence Determined*, he wrote:

Laws properly so called are a species of commands ... And hence it inevitably follows, that the law obtaining between nations is not positive law: for every positive law is set by a given sovereign to a person or persons in a state of subjection to its author ...

The positive moral rules which are laws improperly so called, are laws set or imposed by general opinion: that is to say, by the general opinion of any class or any society of persons. For example, some are set or imposed by the general opinion of persons who are members of a profession or calling: others by that of persons who inhabit a town or province: others, by that of a nation or independent political society: others, by that of a larger society formed of various nations ...

The body by whose opinion the law is said to be set, does not command; expressly or tacitly, that conduct of the given kind shall be forborne or pursued. For, since it is not a body precisely determined or certain, it cannot, as a body, express or intimate a wish. As a body, it cannot signify a wish by oral or written words, or by positive or negative deportment. The so called law or rule which its opinion is said to impose, is merely the sentiment which it feels, or is merely the opinion which it holds, in regard to a kind of conduct ...

The law obtaining between nations is law (improperly so called) set by general opinion. The duties which it imposes are enforced by moral sanctions: by fear on the part of nations, or by fear on the part of sovereigns, of provoking general hostility, and incurring its probable evils, in case they shall violate maxims generally received and respected.[41]

HLA Hart also questioned the nature of international law contrasting the 'clear standard cases' of law constituted by the legal systems of modern states with the 'doubtful cases' exemplified by primitive law and international law.[42]

Many serious students of the law react with a sort of indulgence when they encounter the term 'international law', as if to say, 'well, we know it isn't *really* law, but we know that international lawyers and scholars have a vested interest in calling it law'. Or they may agree to talk about international law *as if* it were law, a sort of quasi-law or near-law. But it cannot be true law, they maintain, because it cannot be enforced: how do you enforce a rule of law against an entire nation, especially a superpower such as the United States or the Soviet Union?

I THE 'ENFORCEMENT' ARGUMENT

One intriguing answer to these serious students of the law is to attempt to persuade them that enforcement is not, after all, the hallmark of what is meant, or what should be meant, by the term 'law'. As Roger Fisher observed, much of what we call 'law' in the domestic context is also unenforceable. For example, where the defendant is the United States, such as in a case involving constitutional law, how would the winning private party enforce his or her judgment against the United States? Upon reflection, we see that the United States, whenever it loses a case ... only complies with the court's judgment because it wants to. The winning party cannot hold a gun to the head of the

---

41 Austin, *The Province of Jurisprudence Determined*, 1955, London: Weidenfeld and Nicholson, at pp 133, 140, 141.

42 See *The Concept of Law*, 1961, Oxford: Clarendon Press at p 3.

United States to enforce compliance, even if there were a natural meaning to the term 'head of the United States'. We can go even further than Professor Fisher did: every criminal law prosecution is a case of an individual pitted against the state (or the 'people' of the state). What is to stop the state from saying, 'you were acquitted by the jury, but that was a travesty of justice, so we're going to imprison you anyway'? How does the defendant, in handcuffs, stop the state from going ahead? In some countries, at some times, we have heard of dictators or military regimes proceeding with the imprisonment and execution of defendants who were acquitted by their own courts. In terms of power, there is nothing to stop the United States from disregarding adverse judgments of its own courts. In this sense, therefore, a great deal of what we normally call 'law' in the United States is unenforceable by private parties against the state.

It is no objection to this line of reasoning, by the way, to dismiss it as far-fetched. If one objects that the United States, in any event, routinely complies with adverse judgments of its own courts, then the international lawyer can answer that the same is true of rules of international law. As Louis Henkin put it, 'almost all nations observe almost all principles of international law and almost all of their obligations almost all of the time'.

But a more substantial critique of Professor Fisher's analogy between cases involving the government as a party and international law cases is that *most* domestic litigation, after all, does not involve the government as a party. Most cases involve one citizen against another ('citizen' including artificial persons such as corporations), and to *those* cases the law is enforced by the full sovereign powers of the state against the losing litigant. This majority of cases, then, tends to define what we mean by 'law'; it constitutes the paradigmatic instance of law. Therefore, the argument goes, the minority of cases that do involve the state or the United States as a party are, in a sense, parasitic upon the paradigmatic instance. We tend to regard this latter minority of cases as 'law' only because they share certain attributes with the generality of cases. But if we look hard at this minority of cases where the government is a party, we must concede that they are not really 'law' because, at bottom, they are unenforceable. They only appear to be law when looked at uncritically. In short, this line of argument concedes Professor Fisher's major premise – that international law cases are similar to domestic cases where the government is a party – but denies his minor premise, that such cases are instances of 'law'. Hence, international law is no more 'law' than constitutional law or even criminal law. As John Austin stated, both constitutional and international law are merely 'positive morality'.

... Let us then consider a second line of reasoning against the proposition that enforcement is the hallmark of law. This argument is not associated with any particular writer, because it relies on early conceptions of law and also on the philosophy of law itself. If we consider what law is not, we soon realise it is not a rationale for the application of force. It is not a system of 'might makes right' in the sense that the state constantly has to compel people, at gunpoint, to behave in a certain way. If you look through a volume of cases, or even a volume of statutes or annotations, you will find that most of the matters therein concern the working-out of private arrangements in a complex society. Most of 'law' concerns itself with the interpretation and enforcement of private contracts, the redress of international and negligent harms, rules regarding sales of goods and sales of securities, rules relating to the family and the rights of members thereof, and other such rules, norms, and cases. The rules are obeyed not out of fear of the state's power, but because the rules by and large are perceived to be right, just, or appropriate. No state could possibly compel people to obey all these rules at gunpoint; there would not be enough soldiers and policemen to hold the guns (a sort of extreme Orwellian vision of society), they would have to sleep sooner or later, and then anarchy might break out.

... If law is not, by and large, a body of rules that are enforced at gunpoint, what is an individual rule of law? Is it, as the 19th century positivists maintained, a command of the state that is backed by the state's enforcement power? To be sure, some 'laws' might be just that: a dictator issues a command for his personal indulgence or whim, and if he has sufficiently satisfied his close advisors and the military in other areas, they will probably enforce his command. But most laws will not have this characteristic. Indeed, looking at the matter more microscopically, what is it that forces a judge to decide the case before her on the basis of precedent and statutes? Is another judge holding a gun to her head? Does she examine whether the law will be enforced to see whether it is law? How does she know, in advance of her own decision, what will be enforced?

This point came up in the famous case of *Marbury v Madison*,[43] famous to generations of American law students but often misinterpreted. In that case, Chief Justice Marshall's 'bottom line' was that the Supreme Court has no original jurisdiction to issue writs of *mandamus*. In short, there was no power to enforce that which the plaintiff demanded. If 'law' were coincident with enforceability, then, since under Marshall's reasoning there was not power of enforcement in the Supreme Court because it lacked jurisdiction, nothing Marshall said in his opinion would have had any legal significance. To put it another way, lacking a 'remedy', the plaintiff would have no 'right', not even a right to get a decision from the Court on the question of 'right'.

But Marshall took an entirely different tack. He began with the question: does the plaintiff have a right? He then asked the second question: if the plaintiff has a right, does he have a remedy? And his third question was, if the plaintiff has a remedy, can the relief issue form this Court? By putting the questions in this order, Marshall did the opposite of what the positivists would require. By dealing first with the question of 'right', Marshall was able to address that question wholly apart from whether there was a remedy or whether the remedy was available from the Supreme Court. As all law students know, Marshall answered his own question that there was indeed a right, and secondly, there being a right meant that the plaintiff had a remedy. By going through this reasoning, Marshall was able to establish the groundwork for his path-breaking assertion of judicial review of questions of constitutionality. He held that, in the face of a right and remedy, the congressional statute purporting to grant that remedy to the Supreme Court as a matter of original jurisdiction violated the Constitution. Marshall would not have been able to make his assertion of judicial review if he had begun and ended his opinion with the simple sentence, 'we have no jurisdiction; case dismissed'. Hence, we see that in a case where by the Court's own admission it lacked jurisdiction and the power of enforcement, nevertheless the Court was able to establish a point of fundamental substantive significance.

Marshall's persuasiveness was dependent upon a consensus at the time he wrote his opinion that there could be such a thing as a 'right' without a legal remedy. This was part of a larger conviction in those days that the 'law' itself was not something that only works when a policeman is standing by ready to enforce it physically. Law indeed is something that is opposed to force. Right is not the

---

43   5 US (1 Cranch) 137 (1803).

same thing as might. In Continental countries, the word for 'law' is, as translated, the word 'right'. In law, there is a fundamental element of right, of justice, dating back to Cicero's and St Thomas' equation of 'right reason' with the natural law (the latter being those reasonable rules that accommodate the peaceful affairs of persons in a society).

Under this argument that we are developing, the relation of force to law, of might to right, is a contingent and not a necessary relation. We can imagine a society under law where there is no force. People obey the laws, and no one disobeys. There is no need, in this idyllic utopia, for enforcement, because there is universal willing compliance. Surely we cannot claim that such a society does not have 'law'. It is clear that the society is one that is under law, and that the contingent use of force is simply not necessary. To take an example closer to home, suppose that in some state of the Union there has not been a kidnapping since that state entered the Union. Would we say that the law against kidnapping in that state is not a law? Certainly no one would argue that if a law is so successful that it never needs enforcement, it is not a law. Thus, we can conclude from this hypothetical that enforcement is not intrinsic to, is not necessary to, the idea of law.

But you might object that enforcement must potentially be present, even if it is not invoked. In other words, in the state that has no kidnapping, it is nevertheless true that if someone commits this crime – or even contemplates committing it – the potential for enforcement is ever-present. It is this potential for enforcement, after all, that the positivists insist upon when they draw our attention to the necessary connection between a rule of law and its enforcement.

To take care of this objection, we may simply modify our previous hypothetical of the idyllic utopia. Assume not only that they have never had a need to enforce their laws, but also that they have no enforcement machinery – no police, no jails, no sheriffs, no marshals. They can still have a system of laws, as complex as you please, even without the potential for enforcement.

You might now object that we cannot prove something about the nature of law, an all-too-human institution, by postulating the existence of a utopia where the inhabitants never break the law. Can we modify our utopia to make it seem more realistic? Suppose occasionally someone breaks the law, but is ostracised from society. Suppose one who breaches a contract is considered a moral renegade who should not be entrusted with any further business dealings. These expressions of sharp social disapproval, and occasionally of ostracism, may work to discourage the few people who would disobey the law. They may not always work, but they may be potent enough to deter most of the people (a minority to begin with) who might consider breaking the law. Thus, our non-perfect utopia now consists of a regime where almost all of the laws are obeyed almost all of the time, where occasional disobedience is met with sharp social disapproval, and where occasionally, despite the 'mechanism' of social disapproval, occasional violations of the law occur. Is this not, nevertheless, a legal system?

A positivist might happen to object to this concept as follows: the idea of social disapproval, and sometimes social ostracism, is the same thing as a sanction. It constitutes a way of enforcing the law. Hence, by introducing this social-disapproval factor into this utopia, we have simply underscored the original point – that law (except in idyllic utopias which do not exist) depends upon potential enforcement.

But if that is the positivist's position, then the international lawyer should gladly concede the point. For international law recognises that the social-disapproval factor operates as a sanction. A nation among the community of nations which violates the law, for example, by disregarding a treaty obligation, would certainly be subject to social disapproval by the other nations. in this sense, international law is really 'law'.

Now it is perhaps the positivist's turn to beat a hasty retreat. The positivist may now want to retract the equation of social disapproval with 'sanction', for fear of including international law under the term 'law'. Instead, the positivist will retreat to the original position that physical or even violent enforcement is necessary to make law 'law', and hence international law is not 'law'. We may, however, suspect that the positivist is reshaping definitions in order to exclude the international case, rather than to arrive at a general definition of law. Consistent with this position, the positivist will have to argue that any legal system in which social disapproval functions as the sole sanction (for example, in a peaceful tribal society) does not have 'law'. 'Law' is present only when, in addition to social disapproval, there is physical coercion stemming from the sovereign power of the state. But what if there is no need for physical coercion? The positivist must then conclude that there is no law.

Such a position would be difficult to defend, for if there is a society where people are so law-abiding that they get along only with the social-disapproval sanction, that society manifests a rather good case of 'law'. It is strange to insist that, for there to be law, physical coercion must also be used even if there is no need for it.

Yet even the serious student of law may not be satisfied with the preceding argument in its entirety. We want to ask what happens if the need for physical coercion should arise. In the international system, at least, we have states which occasionally break the rules of international law and which seem not to be deterred by expressions of social disapproval from other states. This is a reality of international life. Therefore, unlike the tribal society where social disapproval may constitute an effective sanction, international society needs a physical sanction to underscore its rules, otherwise, the rules will occasionally be flouted. Perhaps they will be ignored most often when the 'chips are down', which is exactly when they most need to be enforced. How can we call such a system, dependent for its support on so feeble a mechanism as social approval, a 'legal' system?

It is hard to discern the logic behind the preceding objection, even while it is easy to understand it. We all recognise, and regret, that rules of international law are flouted on occasion, and we are all too aware of the fact that an outraged world public opinion simply is incapable of discouraging the violation. Should our conclusion then be that the rules of international law are not 'law' as we know the term, because as we know the term the 'law' involves the concept of physical enforcement? Yet, even in asking this, we acknowledge that physical enforcement is not a necessary characteristic of law (our 'utopian' examples). And we also acknowledge that, even in domestic cases, where the state is one of the parties, we cannot meaningfully speak of physical enforcement (Professor Fisher's argument). These two arguments destroy most of the logical force of our position that international law is not really law, and yet, we may cling to that position.

Some early writers on the law of nations attempted to meet the enforcement objection head-on, by asserting that rules of international law are indeed enforced by the mechanism of war. A nation that violates the rules will be the object of a 'just war' initiated precisely to punish the transgressing nation and to enforce the validity of the rules. This argument today sounds like an archaic ploy, for we know enough about wars to have learnt that the 'transgressing' state may occasionally win if it has the physical power to do so. Physical might bears no necessary connection to international right. Interestingly, the concept of a 'just war' has become, if possible, even more archaic under the collective security mechanisms of the League of Nations and its successor the United Nations. These bodies, in principle at least, are designed to stamp out acts of aggression wherever they occur. In other words, they are not set up for the purpose of enforcing international law, but simply for the purpose of enforcing international peace. It follows that if the peace is unjust, it will be enforced anyway. The United Nations seems to call for a 'cease fire' in disregard of the merits of the local conflict, and it appears to be concerned less with enforcing international law than with enforcing a prohibition against the use of force no matter what the justification.

Yet there is something in the notion of a 'just war' that may help us to fashion a more compelling case for the proposition that international law is really 'law' than the other arguments we have examined ... what I will label as reciprocal-entitlement violation is a mechanism akin to the old 'just war' notion that underlies a realistic enforcement mechanism for international law.[44]

Some writers argue that much of the scepticism about international law could be equally applied to municipal law:

... the problem of the ultimate foundation of the binding character of law is in no way peculiar to international law.. It is a general legal problem, and arises just as much with regard to national law as it does for international law. No better illustration of this could be given than the one which is to be found in Salmond's *Jurisprudence*. A man is told he cannot ride his bicycle along a certain footpath. he asks why, and is told because it is forbidden by a certain by-law. He asks what is the authority for the by-law, and is told that it is made under an Act of Parliament. But if he asks what is the authority for the Act of Parliament, and what is the source of the rule that Acts of Parliament have the force of law, there is, and can be, no final answer. As Salmond says, no statute can confer this authority on Parliament, for that would be to assume the power that has to be accounted for. Whence would the statute itself derive its validity? No doubt the legal force of Acts of Parliament derives from the Constitution, written or unwritten. But then it must be asked what it is that gives the Constitution legal force? In some countries the Constitution itself has been enacted: but what gave that enactment validity? If those who enacted it had the legal, as distinct merely from the physical, power to do so, whence did they derive it, what is the rule of law that conferred the power on them, and whence did it derive its validity? And so on. Ultimately there can be no answer, or there can only be a series of answers, no one of which can be absolutely final.

The reason why the difficulty is less obtrusive in the national than in the international field, is that in the national field the interim terms in the series afford a sufficiently satisfying practical basis for the obligatory force of the law to make the average person feel it unnecessary to go further – for instance, it is usually enough that the law has been enacted by the proper method, without enquiring what it is that confers legal force on enactment by that particular method. In the international field, however, there are no interim terms of quite the same kind. The absence of any patent and obvious source of obligation, such as might exist if there were an international legislature, deprives the international

---

44 Anthony D'Amato, 'Is International Law Really "Law"?' (1985) 79 *Northwestern University Law Review* at p 1300.

jurist of any manifest point at which he can rest, and which he can regard as a satisfactory terminal point beyond which there is no practical necessity to go.

In such a position as this, the international lawyer might well take a leaf out of the mathematician's book when the latter is faced with an infinite regress. One mathematical pronouncement on the subject[45] is to this effect: that when the object of any search begins to recede in the repetitive fashion of a regress:

> ... you may rest assured that you are battering against a boundary of *possible* human knowledge – *a boundary which manifests itself in that form.*

The mathematician knows that, if this is the position, no useful purpose will be served, nor will any additional knowledge be gained, by going beyond the first and second, or, at most, the third term of the series; for with the third term, the regress is invariably entered. The international lawyer would be justified in adopting the same view. For those who favour the *consent* theory, for instance, there would be little practical object in going beyond the proposition that there is an overriding principle of customary international law, not itself deriving from consent, but having the consequence that the general consent of states to a rule, once given or shown to exist, makes that rule binding on each state, irrespective of its subsequent wishes. For those who see law in the hallmark of society – the maxim *ubi societas ibi jus* – and who consequently postulate the necessity for the existence of law in any society, there would be no need to go beyond a proposition to the effect that if law is a necessity of the international (or any other) order, this implies that the law must be binding, or it cannot serve its purpose. If law is *necessary*, that necessity must lie precisely in the need for obligatory rules as between members of a society, and it would involve an inherent contradiction to propound law as necessary, if it was not also necessarily binding. This way of putting the matter has considerable attractions.[46]

The international community, as a society whose members – or at least whose 'basic members' – are sovereign states, cannot possess a *corpus* of law similar to that of domestic law. The latter is created and imposed on the members of each national society by an authority which is juridically superior to them; in other words, the structure of the domestic legal systems is institutionalised and the law – or at least a major part of it – is derived from institutional machinery. In the international society, on the other hand, the states, precisely because they are sovereign, are not subject to a hierarchical authority regarded as juridically imposed upon them as superior. The international community is therefore a non-institutionalised society, that is to say endowed with only those institutions – the international organisations – which the 'basic members' have been pleased to create by agreement among themselves, institutions which they can, if they so desire, liquidate. International law, therefore, can only be composed – at bottom – of rules which the sovereign states themselves establish in order to regulate the relations between them.'[47]

Other writers accept the nature of international law as law and cast doubt on the positivist use of municipal law as a model for law in general. Such writers

45   JW Dunne, *Nothing Dies*, 1946, London: Faber & Faber at p 32.

46   GG Fitzmaurice, 'The Foundations of the Authority of International Law and the Problem of Enforcement' (1956) 19 *MLR* 1 at pp 9–11.

47   Luigi Condorelli (Professor of International Law at the University of Geneva), in *International Law: Achievements and Prospects*, 1991, Bedjaoui (ed) London: Martinus Nijhoff and UNESCO, at p 179.

argue that municipal law governs legal persons within a state, and such law is derived from a legal superior. International law operates on a different plane.

International law is a law of co-ordination, not, as is the case of most internal law, a law of sub-ordination. By law of co-ordination we mean to say that it is created and applied by its own subjects, primarily the independent states (directly or indirectly), for their own common purposes.[48]

The young reader embarking on the study of international law is aware that 'law' is a body of rules which a human community, a society or an entity sets up in order to govern respective relationships at a given time. Such a reader knows that, over the long term, the content of such law varies, particularly in terms of the type of regulation exercised over the relationships considered (law of subordination or equality, of constraint or freedom, such as feudal law, capitalist or liberal law, socialist law, colonial law, and so forth) or, of course, in terms of the subject areas and sectors of life to be regulated (civil, penal, commercial, aerial, medical law, and so forth), or again in terms of the countries or areas of civilisation (Roman law, Anglo-Saxon law, Islamic law, Chinese law, and so on). What informs the inquiry of the student as he sets out on what for him are the fresh fields of international law is therefore less the concept of 'law', on which he has already acquired some ideas, than the fact – which calls for some explanation – that it is termed 'international'.

Just as what is known as 'municipal' law is the set of rules governing the relationships of individuals, juridical persons, groups and entities among themselves within a given state, the law known as 'international' consists of a body of norms, in written form or otherwise, intended to discipline the relationships of states among themselves. Thus, in principle, it regulates the conduct of states and not that of individuals. states are still almost the only protagonists on the international stage. To be more precise, we should be speaking here of international 'public' law but the shorter expression is preferred in ordinary speech and we shall maintain its use here. The fundamental characteristic of this international law is thus that its function is to regulate the relations between states, in other words between entities known to be sovereign and which, in principle, assert their full independence of any legal order. This at once raises the problem (which lends international law its specificity and colour) of how these states which affirm their sovereignty can be subject to international law. If one postulates at the outset that there is no higher authority than the state, how can the norm of international law be produced for and applied by such a sovereign state? As might be expected, there is only one possible answer to this question, namely that, historically, it has not been possible for international law to be anything other than a law resting largely on the consent, whether express or tacit, of states and that this situation is bound to continue for a long time to come. This determines the true nature and real tonality of international law. It is more a law of co-ordination (between the sovereign jurisdictions of individual states) than a law of subordination such as municipal law, which regulates its subjects, where necessary through coercion exercised by the state apparatus.[49]

The implication here is that international law and municipal law are two different species of law. This issue will be further referred to in the context of the monist-dualist debate discussed in Chapter 2. It should be noted here,

---

48 Rosenne, *Practice and Methods of International Law*, 1984, Dobbsferry, New York: Oceana at p 2.

49 Mohammed Bedjaoui (Judge of the International Court of Justice), *International Law: Achievements and Prospects*, 1991, London: Martinus Nijhoff and UNESCO at p 2.

however, that not all municipal law can be considered to be a 'law of subordination', derived from a legal superior. One only has to consider the development of public law in Britain to see an area of municipal law which is created and applied by its own subjects. Many of the rules of public law place restraints on government action although it is the government, as majority party in the House of Commons, that arguably has the power to make the law as it chooses.

Other writers have countered arguments about the validity of international law by pointing to the behaviour of states. For example, Brierly has written:

> The best evidence for the existence of international law is that every actual state recognises that it does exist and that it is itself under obligation to observe it. states may often violate international law, just as individuals often violate municipal law, but no more than individuals do states defend their violations by claiming that they are above the law.[50]

The fact is that states, the principal subjects of international law, do recognise a system of legal rules which they refer to as international law. Louis Henkin summed up the position:

> ... almost all nations observe almost all principles of international law and almost all of their obligations almost all of the time.[51]

> ... the reality of international law, that is to say, the actual use of rules described as rules of international law by governments, is not to be questioned. All normal governments employ experts to provide routine and other advice on matters of international law and constantly define their relations with other states in terms of international law. Governments and their officials routinely use rules which they have for a very long time called the 'law of nations' or ' international law'. It is not the case that resort to law is propagandist – though it sometimes is. The evidence is that reference to international law has been a part of the normal process of decision-making.[52]

When Iraq invaded Kuwait in August 1990, Saddam Hussein did not argue that there was no system of law preventing Iraq acting in the way it did. Rather he sought to justify military action on the basis of compliance with the rules of international law. Of course, the fact that states refer to and justify their actions in the language of international law is not conclusive proof that it exists. It may be argued that states behave according to pure self-interest and only refer to international law for purposes of legitimisation. Schwarzenberger has written that the primary function of law is to assist in maintaining the supremacy of force and the hierarchies established on the basis of power, and to give this overriding system the respectability and sanctity law confers. But this is not to deny international law's status of law. It can and has been argued that municipal law exists to maintain the position of the ruling class. The actions of states cannot always be explained in terms of immediate self-interest. Even when extreme pragmatism governs state action and the result is the use of armed force, ultimately it is the rules of international law that are used to make the peace.

---

50 Brierly, *The Outlook for International Law*, 1944, Oxford: Oxford University Press at p 5.

51 Henkin, *How Nations Behave*, 2nd edn, 1979, New York: Columbia University Press at p 47.

52 Brownlie, 'The Reality and Efficacy of International Law' (1981) LII *BYIL* 1.

International law receives a bad press because it is the breakdowns that make the news – but just because a law is broken does not mean that it does not exist.

1.4   The enforcement of international law

International law is not imposed on states in the sense that there is no international legislature. As has been seen, the traditional Western view is that international law is founded essentially on consensus. As will be seen in Chapter 3, it has traditionally been created in two ways: by the practice of states (custom) and through agreements entered into by states (treaties). Once international rules are established they have an imperative character and cannot be unilaterally modified at will by states. Unlike municipal law, however, there is no uniform enforcement machinery. The full details of the various ways in which states are made to conform to their international obligations will be discussed throughout the book. The aim here is simply to introduce the range of mechanisms available.

1.4.1   The United Nations

Under Chapter VII of the Charter of the United Nations, the UN Security Council may take enforcement measures where it has determined the existence of a threat to the peace, breach of the peace, or act of aggression. This topic will be dealt with in more detail in Chapter 13. Suffice it to say at this stage that the measures available to the Security Council range from the use of economic sanctions, as in the case of the severance of air links with Libya as a result of the Lockerbie bombing in 1992, to the use of armed force in the case of Iraq. The Security Council's main role is in maintaining international peace and security rather than in enforcing international law, but the two functions will often overlap.

1.4.2   Judicial enforcement

Reference has already been made to judgments of the International Court of Justice, which is the judicial organ of the United Nations. Its main role is to resolve legal disputes between states and its judgments are binding on the parties to the dispute. In addition to the ICJ there are a number of specialised international tribunals dealing with particular areas of the law and it is not uncommon for states to establish *ad hoc* tribunals to resolve differences. The whole issue of the peaceful settlement of disputes will be dealt with in more detail in Chapter 12.

1.4.3   Loss of legal rights and privileges

A common enforcement method used by states is the withdrawal of legal rights and privileges. The best known example is the severing of diplomatic relations, but sanctions falling short of this may include trade embargoes, the freezing of assets, and suspension of treaty rights. The adoption of such measures, and indeed the mere threat of them, can very often prove effective in enforcing international obligations.

1.4.4 Self-help

In very limited situations, international law does countenance self-help in the sense of use of armed force. It is a fundamental rule of international law that the first use of armed force is prohibited but a right of self defence does exist and again the actual use or threat of action in self defence may be effective in enforcing international obligations. The law relating to the use of force, including the right of self defence, is discussed in Chapter 13.

Two further points can be made about enforcement. First, an important aspect of law is its role in helping to predict future action. The action of individuals and states is generally predicated on a presumption that the law will be observed. Although the existing laws may be criticised and reforms demanded, it is in the general interest that law is upheld. An important factor influencing the observance of international law is therefore reciprocity. For example, it is in a state's own interests to respect the territorial sovereignty of other states as they will in turn respect *its* territorial sovereignty. Over 300 years ago Grotius could state:

> ... law is not founded on expediency alone. There is no state so powerful that it may not some time need the help of others outside itself, either for the purposes of trade or even to ward off the forces of may foreign nations untied against it ...
> All things are uncertain the moment men depart from law.

The final point involves public opinion. Allusion has already been made to the role of law in the legitimisation of action. states are ever keen to show that their actions are compatible with international law and fear criticism based on the fact that they are failing to observe its rules. One only has to look at the role played by organisations such as Amnesty International in publicising abuses of international human rights law to recognise the effect that informed public opinion can have on state practice. Of course, no system of law can prevent atrocities being carried out. Just as municipal criminal law does not necessarily prevent the occurrence of murder and rape, international law cannot necessarily prevent genocide. It is worth considering whether multiracial elections would have taken place in South Africa if there existed no system of international law. For, arguably, it was the international law prohibition of apartheid, and the United Nations sanctions that were imposed on South Africa for its breach of the prohibition, that led to the demise of the white minority regime. The issue of human rights and apartheid will be further considered in Chapter 15.

CHAPTER 2

THE RELATIONSHIP BETWEEN MUNICIPAL LAW AND INTERNATIONAL LAW

2.1 Introduction

International law is not confined to regulating the relations between states, and the scope of international law is no longer limited to the rules of warfare and the conduct of diplomatic relations. Matters of social concern such as health, education and economics fall within the ambit of international law and a growing body of rules sets down rights and duties for individuals. Even if it were still correct to speak in terms of international law being a system of rules governing the conduct of states, the fact remains that states are abstract entities which can only act through individuals. State actions are performed by individuals and it therefore follows that international rules have to be applied by individuals. Individual conduct within a state is the subject of municipal law and thus it can be seen that there is potential for the rules of international law to come into contact with rules of municipal law.

This chapter is concerned with the relationship that exists between international law and municipal law. That relationship gives rise to two main areas of discussion:

1   The theoretical question as to whether international law and municipal law are part of a universal legal order ('monism') or whether they form two distinct systems of law ('dualism');

2   The practical issue of what rules govern the situation where there appears to be a conflict between the rules of international law and the rules of municipal law: This may occur either:

(a) before an international court; or

(b) before a municipal court

2.2 The theoretical issue

Historically there have been two main schools of thought: monism and dualism. Their ideas are outlined here but it should be noted that many modern writers doubt the utility of the monism/dualism dichotomy. Furthermore, courts faced with practical problems involving potential conflicts between the rules of international law and municipal law rarely refer to the theoretical issues. It is, however, instructive when considering actual court decisions to question their theoretical underpinnings.

> The relationship between international law and municipal law has been the subject of much doctrinal dispute. At opposing extremes are the 'dualist' and 'monist' schools of thought. According to the former, international law and the internal law of states are totally separate legal systems. Being separate systems, international law would not as such form part of the internal law of a state: to the extent that in particular instances rules of international law may apply within a state they do so by virtue of their adoption by the internal law of the state, and apply as part of that internal law and not as international law. Such a view avoids any question of the supremacy of the one system of law over the other

since they share no common field of application: and each is supreme in its own sphere.

On the other hand, according to the monistic doctrine, the two systems of law are part of one single legal structure, the various national systems of law being derived by way of delegation from the international legal system. Since international law can thus be seen as essentially part of the same legal order as municipal law, and superior to it,[1] it can be regarded as incorporated in municipal law, giving rise to no difficulty of principle in its application as international law within states.

These differences in doctrine are not resolved by the practice of states or by such rules of international law as apply in this situation. International developments, such as the increasing role of individuals as subjects of international law, the stipulation in treaties of uniform internal laws and the appearance of such legal orders as that of the European Communities, have tended to make the distinction between international law and national law less clear and more complex than was formerly supposed at a time when the field of application of international law could be regarded as solely the relations of states amongst themselves. Moreover, the doctrinal dispute is largely without practical consequences, for the main practical questions which arise – how do states, within the framework of their internal legal order, apply the rules of international law, and how is a conflict between a rule of international law and a national rule of law to be resolved? – are answered not be reference to doctrine but by looking at what the rules of various national laws and of international law prescribe.[2]

2.2.1 Monism

Monism considers international law and municipal law to be both part of the same body of knowledge – law. They both operate in the same sphere of influence and are concerned with the same subject matter and thus can come into conflict. If there is a conflict, it is international law that prevails. Some, like Kelsen, argue that this is because international law is a higher law from which the state derives its authority and thus its ability to make municipal laws:

> Since the basic norms of the national legal orders are determined by a norm of international law, they are basic norms only in a relative sense. It is the basic norm of the international legal order which is the ultimate reason of validity of the national legal orders too.[3]

Others, including Lauterpacht, argue on natural law grounds that international law prevails because it protects individuals, and the state itself is only a collection of individuals. It is supported by the natural law doctrine that authority and legal duty are both subject to the universality of natural law. A recent articulation of this view is to be found in the writing of Philip Allott:

> Every legal power in every society in the world is connected with every other legal power in every other society in the world through the international law of

---

1 There is an alternative theory which, while being monistic, asserts the supremacy not of international but of municipal law.

2 *Oppenheim's International Law*, Vol 1, 9th edn, 1992, London: Longman at pp 53–54.

3 Kelsen, *General Theory of Law and the State*, 1945, Cambridge, Mass: Harvard University Press at pp 367–68.

the international society, the society of all societies, from which all law-making power is delegated.[4]

2.2.2 Dualism

The dualist doctrine developed in the 19th century partly because of the development of theories about the absolute sovereignty of states and partly alongside the development of legal positivism. Dualist doctrine considers international law and municipal law to be two separate legal orders operating and existing independently of one another. International law is the law applicable between sovereign states and is dependent on the common will of states for its authority; municipal law applies within the state regulating the activities of its citizens and has as the source of its authority the will of the state itself. On this basis neither system has the power to create or alter rules of the other. Since both systems may deal with the same subject matter it is possible for conflicts between the two systems to arise. Where there is a conflict between the two systems, a municipal court following the dualist doctrine would apply municipal law. This might lead to a state being in breach of its international obligations, but that would be a matter for an international tribunal.

2.2.3 A third way?

Both monism and dualism take the view that international law and municipal law can deal with the same subject matter. A third school of thought can be identified which, while subscribing to the dualist concept of two separate legal orders, argues that the two orders deal with different subject matters. Foremost among the advocates of this doctrine are two former judges at the World Court: Sir Gerald Fitzmaurice and Dionisio Anzilotti. In an opinion given in a case in 1939 Anzilotti stated:

> It is clear that, in the same legal system, there cannot at the same time exist two rules relating to the same facts and attaching to these facts contradictory consequences ... It is for instance impossible that the relations between the two states should be governed at one and the same time by a rule to the effect that, if certain conditions are fulfilled, the Court has jurisdiction and by another rule to the effect that, if certain conditions are fulfilled, the Court has no jurisdiction – by a rule to the effect that in certain circumstances the state concerned may have recourse to the Court and by another to the effect that in the same circumstances the state has no right to do so, etc, etc. In cases of this kind, either the contradiction is only apparent and the two rules are really co-ordinated so that each has its own sphere of application and does not encroach on the sphere of application of the other, or else one prevails over the other, ie, is applicable to the exclusion of the other.[5]

Anzilotti seemed to support the view that the two sets of rules, international law and municipal law, each had its own sphere of application. In an earlier case he had indicated how international tribunals should deal with rules of municipal law:

> From the standpoint of International Law and of the Court which is its organ, municipal laws are merely facts which express the will and constitute the

---

4   Allott, *Eunomia: New Order for a New World*, 1990, Oxford: Oxford University Press at p 308.
5   *The Electricity Company of Sofia and Bulgaria*, Ser A/B, No 77 (1939).

activities of states, in the same manner as do legal decisions or administrative measures.[6]

In a lecture to the Hague Academy of International Law, Fitzmaurice made the point even more forcefully:

The controversy [between monism and dualism] turns on whether international law and internal law are two separate legal orders, existing independently of one another – and, if so, on what basis it can be said that either is superior to one or supreme over the other; or whether they are both part of the same order, one or the other of them being supreme over the other within that order. The first view is the dualist view, the second monist ... A radical view of the whole subject may be propounded to the effect that the entire monist-dualist controversy is unreal, artificial and strictly beside the point, because it assumes something that has to exist for there to be any controversy at all – and which in fact does not exist – namely a common field in which the two legal orders under discussion both simultaneously have their spheres of activity ... In order that there can be controversy about whether the relations between two orders are relations of co-ordination between self-existent independent orders, or relations of subordination of the one to the other, or of the other to the one – or again whether they are part of the same order, but both subordinate to a superior order – it is necessary that they should both be purporting to be, and in fact be, applicable in the same field – that is, to be the same set of relations and transactions. For instance ... it would be idol to start a controversy about whether the English legal system was superior to or supreme over the French or vice versa, because these systems do not pretend to have the same field of application ... There is indeed no basis on which it is even possible to start an argument, because, although these legal systems may in a certain sense come into conflict in particular cases, thus giving rise to problems of what is called Conflict Law, or Private International Law, each country has its own conflict rules whereby it settles such problems arising before its own courts. Ultimately therefore, there can be no conflict between any two systems in the domestic field, for any apparent conflict is automatically settled by the domestic conflict rules of the forum. Any conflict between them in the international field, that is to say on the inter-governmental plane, would fall to be resolved by international law, because in that field international law is not only supreme, but in effect the only system there is. Domestic law does not, as such, apply at all in the international field. But the supremacy of international law in that field exists, not because of any inherent supremacy of international law as a category over national law as a category, but for other reasons. It is, rather, a supremacy of exactly the same order as the supremacy of French law in France, and of English law in England – ie a supremacy not arising from content, but from the field of operation – not because the law is French but because the place, the field, is France. The view here suggested is neither dualist nor monist: it is precisely the view put forward in the following passage from Anzilotti, who is often miscalled a dualist in this respect:

It follows from the same principle that there cannot be conflict between the rules belonging to different juridical orders, and, consequently, in particular between international and internal law. To speak of conflict between international law and internal law is as inaccurate as to speak of the conflict between the laws of different states: in reality the existence of a conflict between norms belonging to different juridical orders cannot be confirmed except from a standpoint outside both the one and the other.

---

6   *Certain German Interests in Polish Upper Silesia*, Ser A, No 7, p 39 (1926).

The logic of this cannot be contraverted, and in actual fact, the necessity for a common field of operation as the basis of any discussion as to the relations between two legal orders, is recognised by modern protagonists of the monist-dualist controversy. This can be seen from the following sentence in an article by a writer of the monist school, reading: 'Two normative systems with binding force *in the same field* must form part of the same order' – [italics added]. This may be true, or at least it is capable of discussion, if the two orders in question are binding in the same field, but not otherwise. Consider again a sentence such as the following one, taken from one of the most eminent and justly celebrated modern exponents of the positivist-monist view: 'International law and national law cannot be mutually different and mutually independent systems ... if ... both systems are considered to be valid for the same space and at the same time.' Everything here depends of course on the 'if' – which surely assumes the very point that has to be proved. What calls for question is precisely the phrase 'valid for the same space at the same time'. Had this passage said 'valid simultaneously for the same class of relations', it would not have been open to question, though only because international and national law do not in fact govern the same set of relations. To say this is not to deny the validity of the monist view, but only its relevance in this particular connexion. Equally, the relevance of the dualist view is denied. Recognising, as they evidently do, that only relations between legal orders that operate in the same field can usefully and meaningfully be discussed, the protagonists of the monist-dualist controversy seem to be driven to trying to create the necessary common field – though it is more particularly the monists who seek to do this, since the dualists can rest quite content with the existence of two orders, provided they operate in separate fields. The endeavour to create a common field takes the form in effect of denying the existence or reality of the state, or reducing it to the sum total of the individuals composing it. For instance, the same eminent authority, evidently aware of the difficulty that must arise unless there is a common field, has suggested the following solution:

> The mutual independence of international and national law is often substantiated by the alleged fact that the two systems regulate different subject matters. National law, it is said, regulates the behaviour of individuals, international law the behaviour of states. We have already shown that the behaviour of states is reducible to the behaviour of individuals representing the state. Thus the alleged difference in subject matter between international and national law cannot be a difference between the kinds of subjects whose behaviour they regulate ...

Formally, therefore, international and domestic law as systems can never come into conflict. What may occur is something strictly different, namely a conflict of obligations, or an inability for the state on the domestic plane to act in a manner required by international law. The supremacy of international law in the international field does not in these circumstances entail that the judge in the municipal courts of the state must override local law and apply international law. Whether he does or can do this depends on the local law itself, and on what legislative or administrative steps can be or are taken to deal with the matter. The supremacy of international law in the international field simply means that if nothing can be or is done, the state will, on the international plane, have committed a breach of international law obligations, for which it will be internationally responsible, and in respect of which it cannot plead the condition of domestic law by way of absolution. International law does not therefore in any way purport to govern the content of national law in the national field – nor does it need to. It simply says – and this is all it needs to say – that certain things are valid according to international law, and that if a state in the application of its domestic law acts contrary to international law in these respects, it will commit a breach of its international obligations.[7]

2.3 The practical issue

2.3.1 Municipal law before international tribunal

There is ample judicial and arbitral authority for the rule that a state cannot rely upon the provisions or deficiencies of its municipal law to avoid its obligations under international law. One of the earliest authorities is the decision in the *Alabama Claims Arbitration* (1872).[8] During the American Civil War, a number of ships were built in England for private buyers. The vessels were unarmed when they left England but it was generally known that they were to be fitted out by the Confederates in order to attack Union shipping. They were so fitted and caused considerable damage to American shipping. The US sought to make the UK liable for these losses on the basis that it had breached its international obligations as a neutral during the War. The UK argued that under English law as it stood there was no way in which it could prevent the sailing of the vessels. The arbitrator rejected the UK argument and had no hesitation in upholding the supremacy of international law. Similar rulings were made in the *Serbian Loans Case* (1929). In the Draft Declaration on the Rights and Duties of States 1949 prepared by the International Law Commission, Article 13 states:

> Every state has the duty to carry out in good faith its obligations arising from treaties and other sources of international law, and it may not invoke provisions in its constitution or its laws as an excuse for failure to perform this duty.[9]

Similarly, Article 27 of the Vienna Convention on the Law of Treaties 1969 provides:

> A party may not invoke the provisions of its internal law as justification for its failure to perform a treaty.

Although international tribunals will uphold the supremacy of international law over municipal law this should not be taken to mean that municipal law is of no relevance. Municipal law, and in particular domestic legislation, has an important role to play. Very often an international tribunal will have cause to examine domestic legislation closely to discern the practice of states. International tribunals have also looked to municipal law when considering 'the general principles of law' indicated as source of international law in Article 38(1)(c) of the Statute of the International Court of Justice, although it should be pointed out that the court will look at municipal law in general rather than any single system of municipal law.

Barcelona Traction, Light and Power Company Limited Case (Second Phase)[10]

38 In this field international law is called upon to recognise institutions of municipal law that have an importance and extensive role in the international

---

7 'The General Principles of International Law Considered from the Standpoint of the Rule of Law', 1957, 92 *Hague Recueil* at p 70ff – footnotes omitted.

8 Moore, 1 *Int Arb* 495.

9 *YBILC* 1949 p 286.

10 *Belgium v Spain* [1970] *ICJ Rep* at p 3.

field. This does not necessarily imply drawing any analogy between its own institutions and those of municipal law, nor does it amount to making rules of international law dependent upon categories of municipal law. All it means is that international law has to recognise the corporate entity as an institution created by states in a domain essentially within their domestic jurisdiction. This in turn requires that, whenever legal issues arise concerning the rights of states with regard to the treatment of companies and shareholders, as to which rights international law has not established its own rules, it has to refer to the relevant rules of municipal law. Consequently, in views of the relevance to the present case of the rights of the corporate entity and its shareholders under municipal law, the Court must devote attention to the nature and interrelation of those rights ...

50 In turning now to the international legal aspects of the case, the Court must, as already indicated, start from the fact that the present case essentially involves factors derived from municipal law – the distinction and the community between the company and the shareholder – which the Parties, however widely their interpretations may differ, each take as the point of departure of their reasoning. If the Court were to decide the case in disregard of the relevant institutions of municipal law it would, without justification, invite serious legal difficulties. It would lose touch with reality, for there are no corresponding institutions of international law to which the Court could resort. Thus the Court has, as indicated, not only to take cognizance of municipal law but also refer to it. It is to rules generally accepted by municipal legal systems which recognise the limited company whose capital is represented by shares, and not to the municipal law of a particular state, that international law refers. In referring to such rules, the Court cannot modify, still less deform them.

Another manner in which municipal law may be of importance in a case before an international tribunal arises from the doctrine of opposability. This doctrine allows one state to invoke against, or 'oppose' to, another state a rule of its own municipal law. As a general principle, provided that the rule of municipal law is not contrary to rules of international law it may be legitimately opposed in order to defeat the international claims of the other state. Thus, in the *Anglo-Norwegian Fisheries* case (1951)[11] the ICJ held that a Norwegian law delimiting an exclusive fishery zone along almost 1,000 miles of coastline was not contrary to international law and therefore could be successfully opposed to defeat British claims to fish in the disputed waters.

2.3.3   *International law in municipal courts*

2.3.3.1 Transformation and incorporation

Before considering a number of examples of the treatment of international law by municipal courts it is necessary to explain briefly the concepts of transformation and incorporation. If, as the dualist theory maintains, international law and municipal law constitute two distinct legal systems, a practical consequence is that before any rule of international law can have effect within domestic jurisdiction it requires express and specific 'transformation' into municipal law by the use of the appropriate constitutional machinery, such

---

11 [1951] *ICJ Rep* at p 116.

as a municipal statute. A different view, and one reflecting the monist position, is that rules of international law automatically become part of municipal law as a result of the doctrine of 'incorporation'.

Put at its simplest, transformation doctrine views rules of international law as being excluded from municipal law unless specifically included; the incorporation doctrine holds that rules of international law are included as part of municipal law unless they are specifically excluded.

2.3.3.2 British practice

Customary international law

As far as the rules of customary international law are concerned the English courts have generally adopted the doctrine of incorporation. Provided that they are not inconsistent with Acts of Parliament or prior authoritative judicial decisions, then rules of customary international law automatically form part of English law: customary international law is incorporated into English law. The 18th century lawyer, Blackstone, wrote:

> The law of nations, wherever any question arises which is properly the object of its jurisdiction, is here adopted in its full extent by the common law, and it is held to be a part of the law of the land.[12]

In *Buvot v Barbuit* (1737)[13] Lord Talbot declared that 'the law of nations in its full extent was part of the law of England'. Lord Talbot's statement was followed in a series of 18th and early 19th century cases. Cynics may suggest that the reason for this view was that at the time the international community was small and Britain had a major impact on the formation of customary international law.

Some doubt was thrown on the incorporation doctrine by the decision in *R v Keyn (The Franconia)* (1876).[14] *The Franconia*, a German ship, collided with a British ship in the English Channel three miles off the British coast. The defendant was prosecuted for manslaughter of a passenger on board the English ship who drowned as a result of the collision and was found guilty. However, the question whether an English court had jurisdiction to hear the case was reserved for the Court of Crown Cases Reserved which decided by a seven to six majority that it did not. Cockburn CJ found that under international law, events occurring on board a foreign ship while it was on the high seas were governed by the law of the foreign state. It was only when the foreign ship came into the ports or waters of another state that the ship and those on board become subject to the local law. Unless, therefore, the defendant at the time of the offence was on British territory or on board a British ship, an English Court would have no jurisdiction. The question for the court was whether the collision had occurred in British territory. It found that according to English law, the three mile belt of sea surrounding Great Britain was not British territory. The court could also not find any clear rule of international law stipulating

---

12   Blackstone, *Commentaries*, IV, Chapter 5.

13   (1737) Cas t Talbot 281.

14   (1876) 2 Ex D 63.

jurisdictional rights over a three mile territorial sea and therefore found that there was no basis for jurisdiction over Keyn. The case led to the passing of the Territorial Waters Jurisdiction Act 1878 which gave the English courts jurisdiction over the territorial sea. Some have argued that the judgment of Lord Cockburn supports the transformation doctrine. In the course of his judgment he discussed what the position would have been had the court been able to discern a clear rule of international law recognising a three mile territorial sea. He argued that even if unanimity could be found among states on the adoption of a three mile territorial sea it would amount to a new law and the courts were not able to usurp the role of Parliament in creating new law. However, other writers have confined the case to its particular facts and argued that the decision was only concerned with the existence or not of any jurisdiction over the territorial sea and did not amount to a rejection of the rule that international law is part of the law of England.

The confusion was not resolved in the case of *West Rand Central Gold Mining Co v R* (1905),[15] Lord Alverstone CJ stated:

> It is quite true that whatever has received the common consent of civilised nations must have received the assent of our country, and that to which we have assented along with other nations in general may properly be called international law, and as such will be acknowledged and applied by our municipal tribunals when legitimate occasion arises for those tribunals to decide questions to which doctrines of international law may be relevant. But any doctrine so invoked must be one really accepted as binding between nations, and the international law sought to be applied must, like anything else, be proved by satisfactory evidence, which must shew either that the particular proposition put forward has been recognised and acted upon by our own country, or that it is of such a nature, and has been so widely and generally accepted, that it can hardly be supposed that any civilised state would repudiate it. The mere opinions of jurists, however eminent or learned, that it ought to be so recognised, are not in themselves sufficient. They must have received the express sanction of international agreement, or gradually have grown to be part of international law by their frequent practical recognition in dealings between various nations ... *Barbuit's Case*, *Torquet v Bath* and *Heathfield v Chilton* are cases in which the Courts of law have recognised and given effect to the privilege of ambassadors as established by international law. But the expressions used by Lord Mansfield when dealing with the particular and recognised rule of international law on this subject, that the law of nations forms part of the law of England, ought not to be construed so as to include as part of the law of England opinions of text-writers upon a question as to which there is no evidence that Great Britain has ever assented, *a fortiori* if they are contrary to the principles of her laws as declared by her Courts. The cases of *Wolff v Oxholm* (1817) and *R v Keyn* are only illustrations of the same rule – namely, that questions of international law may arise, and may have to be considered in connection with the administration of municipal law.

The incorporation doctrine was further qualified by the Privy Council in *Chung Chi Cheung v The King* (1939)[16] where Lord Atkin stated:

---

15 [1905] 2 KB 391.
16 [1939] AC 160.

It must always be remembered that, so far, at any rate, as the courts of this country are concerned, international law has no validity save in so far as its principles are accepted and adopted by our own domestic law. There is no external power that imposes its rule upon our own code of substantive law or procedure.

The Courts acknowledge the existence of a body or rules which nations accept amongst themselves. On any judicial issue they seek to ascertain what the relevant rule is, and having found it, they will treat it as incorporated into the domestic law, so far as it is not inconsistent with rules enacted by statutes or finally declared by their tribunals.

The issue of the relationship of customary international law to English law was raised again in the important case of *Trendtex Trading Corporation v Central Bank of Nigeria* (1977).[17] The case concerned issues of state immunity which will be further discussed in Chapter 8. In the course of their judgments all three members of the Court of Appeal accepted the incorporation doctrine, Shaw LJ stating, 'What is immutable is the principle of English law that the law of nations ... must be applied in the courts of England'. The case also raised the question of the relationship between the doctrine of precedent and customary international law. The court had to consider whether *stare decisis* applies to rules of United Kingdom law that incorporate rules of customary international law so that a change in international law can only be recognised within the limits of that doctrine. Earlier cases seemed to suggest that the doctrine of precedent prevailed and that the courts could not recognise a change in the rules of customary international law if it conflicted with an earlier decision of the English courts. The majority in *Trendtex* rejected this view, Lord Denning stating:

> ... a decision of this court – as to what was the ruling of international law 50 or 60 years ago – is not binding on this court today. International law knows no rule of *stare decisis*. If this court today is satisfied that the rule of international law on a subject has changed from what it was 50 or 60 years ago, it can give effect to that change – and apply the change in our English law – without waiting for the House of Lords to do it.

The most recent confirmation of the incorporation doctrine applying to customary international law is to be found in the Court of Appeal judgments in *Maclaine Watson v Department of Trade* (1989). Their view was not contradicted in the House of Lords (1990) although their Lordships found that the case concerned the application of treaty rights rather than rules of customary international law.

Taken as a whole, the authorities would seem to support the incorporation doctrine and thus it can be said that customary international law will be applied by the English courts subject to two main conditions:

1   If there is a conflict between customary international law and an Act of Parliament, the Act of Parliament prevails. It should be noted that, as a general rule of statutory interpretation, the courts will try to interpret statutes so as to avoid a conflict with international law. This does not of course apply if the statute is clear and unambiguous.

---

17   [1977] QB 578.

2   If there is a conflict between customary international law and a binding judicial precedent laying down a rule of English law, the judicial precedent prevails. But following the *Trendtex* case the English courts may now depart from earlier judicial precedent which lays down a rule of international law if the international law has changed in the meantime.

One final point about the incorporation doctrine is that since customary international law is considered to be part of English law it does not need to be proved as fact by expert evidence, unlike the position with regard to rules of foreign municipal law. The British courts will take judicial notice of international rules, and may of their own volition refer to textbooks and other sources for evidence thereof.

Treaties

The British practice regarding treaties is different from that regarding customary law. The main reason for this is that the conclusion and ratification of treaties are matters for the executive, coming as they do under the scope of the prerogative. Parliament has no say in the making of treaties. If they were to have direct effect, the Crown could alter the law without recourse to Parliament: therefore it is established that treaties only become part of English law if an enabling act of Parliament has been passed. This point has been reiterated by the courts in a number of cases and should be familiar to those who have studied the doctrine of Parliamentary supremacy and the effect of British membership of the European Union.

Recent discussion of the place of treaties in English law took place in the House of Lords in *Department of Trade v Maclaine Watson* (1990).[18] The question for the courts was whether a member state of an international organisation could be sued directly for the liabilities of the organisation. As has already been stated the Court of Appeal saw the matter as raising issues of customary international law. The House of Lords viewed the matter differently – they saw it as an issue of treaty rights, and explicitly confirmed that a treaty to which the United Kingdom is a party cannot automatically alter the laws of the UK. Only if a treaty is transformed into UK law by statute can it be enforced by the courts in this country; hence the need for the European Communities Act 1972 to transform the Treaty of Rome.

> A treaty is a contract between the governments of two or more sovereign states. International law regulates the relations between sovereign states and determines the validity, the interpretation and the enforcement of treaties. A treaty to which Her Majesty's government is a party does not alter the laws of the United Kingdom. A treaty may be incorporated into and alter the laws of the United Kingdom by means of legislation. Except to the extent that a treaty becomes incorporated into the laws of the United Kingdom by statute, the courts of the United Kingdom have no power to enforce treaty rights and obligations at the behest of a sovereign government or at the behest of a private individual.[19]

---

18   [1990] 2 AC 418.
19   *International Tin Council* case [1990] 2 AC 418 *per* Lord Templeman.

The usual way in which treaties are transformed into English law is by the passing of an enabling act to which a schedule is attached containing the provisions of the treaty to be enacted. For example the Diplomatic Privileges Act 1964 enacts the Vienna Convention on Diplomatic Relations 1961. Where the treaty is contained in a schedule it is an integral part of the Act and any interpretation of the statute will involve interpretation of provisions of the treaty. Full discussion of the international law rules on treaty interpretation is to be found in Chapter 4. The issue here is the rules of interpretation that the English courts use when considering the provisions of a treaty. The leading case is *Fothergill v Monarch Airlines Ltd* (1980).[20] In that case the House of Lords was called upon to interpret the provisions of the Warsaw Convention for the Unification of Certain Regulations concerning International Air Travel 1929 which formed part of the Carriage by Air Act 1961. The House of Lords held that it was entitled to use the rules of treaty interpretation found in the Vienna Convention on the Law of Treaties 1969 even though such rules conflicted with the English rules of statutory interpretation.

On some occasions, Parliament may pass legislation to give effect to the terms of a treaty without enacting the treaty itself in a schedule. In such cases the question arises as to the extent to which the courts can have regard to the treaty in interpreting the statute. The leading case here is *Salomon v Commissioners of Customs and Excise* (1967)[21] in which the Court of Appeal had to interpret the Customs and Excise Act 1952. The Act was intended to give effect to the Convention on Valuation of Good for Customs Services 1950, although no specific mention was made of the Convention in the Act. The court set down three principles to be applied in such cases. First, if the terms of the statute are clear and unambiguous, the court must give effect to them even if they conflict with the treaty provisions. Secondly, if the provisions of the statute are not clear and are capable of more than one meaning, the treaty can be used as an aid to interpretation and a presumption operates that Parliament cannot have intended to legislate contrary to international law. Thirdly, the court may refer to the treaty in such cases even if there is no reference to it anywhere in the statute. Extrinsic evidence can be brought to show that the statute was intended to give effect to the treaty. It must be noted that the rules regarding European law are different and reference should be made to the House of Lords decision in *R v Secretary of State for Transport ex p Factortame (No 2)* (1990)[22] for a discussion of the relationship between English statute and European law.

Finally, there is the situation where an act of Parliament, while not intended to give effect to any specific treaty, deals with the same subject matter as a treaty to which the UK is a party. Again, it should be noted that there are specific rules dealing with the position of European law and reference should be made to textbooks on Constitutional law and European law for the position with regard to conflict between statute and law derived from the Treaty of Rome. In other situations the rules are fairly straightforward. The courts will

---

20   [1981] AC 251.
21   [1967] 2 QB 116.
22   [1991] 1 AC 603.

always give effect to clear and unambiguous words contained in a statute even if they conflict with a treaty to which the UK is a party. Therefore in *R v Secretary of State for the Home Department ex p Brind* (1991)[23] the House of Lords upheld the broadcasting ban on certain 'terrorist' organisations introduced under the provisions of the Broadcasting Act 1981 even though it was argued that it breached provisions of the European Convention on Human Rights 1950 to which the UK is a party. However, where there is some ambiguity in the statute the courts will endeavour to interpret it so as to conform with the UK's international obligations. Similarly, if the common law is uncertain the courts should approach the issue on the basis that any decision should be in conformity with international obligations. Thus in *Derbyshire County Council v Times Newspapers Ltd* (1992),[24] the Court of Appeal was asked to decided whether a local authority could sue for libel. The court held that it could not and in the course of his judgment Balcombe LJ expressed the view that since the domestic law was uncertain the court could take into account the provisions of Article 10 of the European Convention on Human Rights.

2.3.3.3 The practice of other states

It is impossible to discern any uniform practice among states, although a number of similarities in approach can be identified. The majority of states with a common law system adopt an approach similar to that in Britain. Those states which have a written constitution do have the opportunity to make the situation clear by making specific reference to the status of international law. For example, although US practice concerning customary law is similar to Britain, the US Constitution provides:

> ... all treaties made or which shall be made with the authority of the United states, shall be the supreme law of the land and the Judges in every state shall be bound thereby, anything in the Constitution or Law of any state to the contrary notwithstanding.[25]

To mitigate the effects of this rule, the US courts have distinguished 'self-executing treaties' which automatically become law and 'non-self-executing treaties' which require legislation by Congress to become law. Discussion of the distinction between self-executing and non-self-executing treaties has taken up much American court time and the implication of the various cases is that the distinction depends on the political content of the treaty. Where a treaty involves political questions the issue should be left to Congress but where a treaty contains provisions which are capable of enforcement as between private parties then it will be regarded as self-executing. Treaties in conflict with the US Constitution are not regarded as binding.

The constitutions of Austria, Germany and Italy all declare that the generally recognised rules of international law form part of the domestic system. For example, Article 25 of the Basic Law of Germany states:

---

23   [1991] 1 AC 696.

24   [1992] QB 770.

25   US Constitution Article VI, s 2.

... the general rules of public international law are an integral part of federal law. They shall take precedence over the laws and shall create rights and duties for the inhabitants of the federal territory.

The courts in all three states have found that while such provision may apply to customary international law, the provisions of treaties do not automatically become part of municipal law. A different approach is taken by the Dutch constitution which provides that international treaties to which the Netherlands is a party become part of municipal law and prevail over incompatible provisions of Dutch law. No mention is made of the rules of customary international law and the Dutch courts have not considered international custom to be automatically part of Dutch law. As a general observation it can be said that few municipal courts have upheld the priority of international law over municipal law.

2.3.4   The relationship between international law and European law

An area of developing interest is the relationship between European law and international law although it has not yet been subject to the same degree of analysis as that given to the relationship between international law and municipal law. It is generally accepted that the European Union has a separate legal personality under international law and that European law constitutes a distinct legal order. Article 177 of the Treaty of Rome allows the European Court of Justice to rule on questions of the validity of European law and this can involve discussion of the relationship between it and international law. According to Article 228 of the Treaty of Rome, treaties concluded by the EU are binding on its institutions and on member states. They are regarded as forming an integral part of European law. Rules of customary international law will be upheld and applied by the European Court provided they are not incompatible with provisions of European law. A particular point which arises in respect of the EU is the extent to which a member state can rely on a rule of international law as a defence against it failing to fulfil obligations under European law. Article 234 of the Treaty of Rome provides that Community law leaves unaffected the treaty rights and obligations entered into between member states and non-member states if the conclusion of such agreements predates Community competence.

The monist conception is more in line with the ECJ's conception of the European Community legal system,[26] and it has applied it in its consideration of the relationship between international agreements and community law.

The ECJ has applied a very extensive interpretation of Article 177 in the context of international agreements. A Council Decision or Regulation concluding an international agreement (in the sense of internal EC acceptance) is one of the

---

26   See K Meessen, 'The Application of Rules of Public International Law within Community Law' (1976) 13 *CMLR* 485–501, pp 500–1; J Groux and P Manin, *The European Communities in the International Order* (Brussels, EC Commission, European Perspective Series, 1985); Hancher, 'Constitutionalism, the Community Court and International Law' (1994) 25 *NYIL* at pp 276–77.

'acts' of a Community institution for the purposes of Article 177(1)(b).[27] So too are the decisions of an Association Council since they give effect and the Association Council is entrusted with responsibility for the implementation of the agreement.[28] Therefore, the ECJ has jurisdiction to rule on the 'validity' and 'interpretation' of those acts under the preliminary reference procedure.[29] In the *SPI and SAMI* case the ECJ ruled that jurisdiction also extended to an agreement, the GATT, to which the EC had succeeded as a matter of law and so there was no Community act at all.[30]

In the *International Fruit Co* case it was submitted that validity extended to 'validity under international law'.[31] The ECJ accepted this. Thus the validity of a measure, 'may be affected by reason of the fact that it was contrary to a rule of international law'.[32] The 'rule of international law' could be derived from an international agreement, customary international law, or be a general principle of international law.[33] However, only rules deriving from international agreements have been argued before the ECJ. Moreover, the ECJ has in fact never held a community measure invalid because it was contrary to international law. As the Court of the Community it is institutionally disposed to uphold the validity of community measures against rules in international agreements.[34] However, where an international agreement can be given effect without having to invalidate a community measure, then the ECJ has been more receptive.[35] It is also interesting to note two arguments of the Commission in cases decided in 1982. In *Kupferberg* it submitted that, 'As a subject of international law particularly dependent on the proper functioning of the international legal order the Community has no interest in impeding that process by an *a priori* restrictive attitude to the direct effect of international agreements'.[36] At the same time,

---

27 Case 181/73, *Haegeman v Belgium* [1974] ECR 449 pr 4 (hereinafter *Haegeman*); Case 104/81, *Hauptzollamt Mainz v Kupferberg* [1982] ECR 3641 (hereinafter *Kupferberg*). Often a '*sui generis* decision' is used. 'If the agreement contains provisions which are capable of having direct effect, or which, if promulgated as internal legislation within the Community, would take the form of a regulation, the Council act concluding the agreement will often take the form of a Regulation. Otherwise, the *sui generis* decision is used', I Macleod: *A Manual of Law and Practice*, 1996, Oxford: Oxford University Press at p 81.

28 Case C-192/89, *Sevince v Staatssecretaris van Justitie* [1990] ECR I-3461 prs 9–10 (hereinafter *Sevince*); Case 30/88, *Greece v Commission* [1989] ECR 63 pr 13; Case 351/95, *Selma Kadiman v Freistaat Bayern* on the interpretation of Article 7 of Decision 1/80 of the EEC/Turkey Association Council.

29 For a claim of alleged illegality of a bilateral fishing agreement concluded between the EC and Canada see Case T-194/95, *Area Cova and Others v Council*.

30 Joined Cases 267 and 269/81, *Amministrazione delle Finanze dello Stato v SPI and SAMI* [1983] ECR 801. The succession by the Community is thus treated as having the same effect as an act of the Community. See AG Reisch in 'The *SPI and SAMI* case'; TC Hartley, 'International Agreements and the Community Legal System: Some Recent Developments' (1983) 8 *EL Rev* at pp 383–92.

31 Joined Cases, 21 and 24/72, *International Fruit Company NV v Produktschap voor Groentend en Fruit* [1972] ECR 1219 (hereinafter *IFC* case).

32 *IFC* case, para 5.

33 See Article 38 of the ICJ.

34 This partially explains why the ECJ's restrictive interpretation of *locus standi* under Article 173. See TC Hartley, *The Foundations of European Community Law*, 3rd edn, 1994, Oxford: Clarendon Press at pp 361–92.

35 See P Craig and G De Burca, *EC Law – Texts, Cases and Materials*, 1995, Oxford: Oxford University Press at pp 171–72.

36 *Kupferberg*, p 3654.

however, the Commission argued in the *Polydor* case that 'the concept of direct effect, as developed in Community law, must not as such be transposed to the field of the Community's international relations'.[37]

In the *International Fruit Co* case the ECJ stated two conditions that would have to be satisfied before a Community measure could be held invalid due to its incompatibility with international law. First, the Community must be bound by the provision of international law concerned. Secondly, the provision of international law must have direct effect in Community law. We consider these conditions in turn.

The Community must be bound by the provision of international law concerned: the binding nature of Treaties concluded by the Community

Treaties concluded by the Community and one or more states or international organisations, 'shall be binding on the institutions of the Community and on member states' (Article 228(7)).[38] As a consequence of this, 'it is incumbent upon the Community institutions, as well as upon the member states, to ensure compliance with the obligations arising from such agreements'.[39] When the member states ensure respect for such obligations they are fulfilling obligations in relation to the Community as well as to the non-member country concerned.[40] This obligation to the Community explains the ECJ's view that when an international agreement to which the EC is a party comes into force its provisions 'form an integral part of Community law',[41] and of the 'community legal system'.[42] So too the Decisions of an Association Council.[43] This integration into community law means that the provisions have, for the purposes of community law, a community nature or character. Given this character, the interpretation and effect of such provisions should not vary between member states, for example, by having direct effect in some but not others.[44] Similarly it should not be dependent on whether the application of the provisions is the responsibility of the Community institutions or the member states.[45]

The requirements of consistent and 'uniform application throughout the Community',[46] is ensured by the ECJ, through its jurisdiction to interpret the provisions of such agreements.[47] However, it is important to be clear that the ECJ has no direct jurisdiction under the EC Treaty to interpret an international

---

37 Case 270/80, *Polydor Ltd v Harlequin Record Shops Ltd* [1982] ECR 329, p 343 (hereinafter *Polydor*).

38 Formerly Article 228(2).

39 *Kupferberg*, pr 11.

40 *Ibid*, p 12.

41 *Haegeman*, pr 5. Internal implementation does not appear to be necessary as a matter of principle.

42 *Kupferberg*, pr 13.

43 *Sevince*, pr 9; *Greece v Commission* [1989] ECR 63 pr 13.

44 The concept appears elsewhere in EC law, for example, over regulations not being transposed by national laws and thereby losing their community character, Case 39/72, *Commission v Italy* [1973] ECR 101.

45 *Kupferberg*, pr 14; Case 12/86, *Demeril v Stadt Schwabisch Gmund* [1987] ECR 3719 pr 10 (hereinafter *Demeril*).

46 *Kupferberg*, pr 14.

47 See also *Sevince*, pr 11. Jurisdiction to interpret an international agreement could arise by way of a preliminary ruling or in a direct action, see Opinion 1/91 (First EEA Opinion), pr 38.

agreement as between the EC and a non-member state party.[48] It only has jurisdiction to interpret an international agreement 'where its interpretation is relevant to the question of the validity of an act of a Community institution or to the question of the interpretation to be given for such an act'.[49] Its interpretation of the provisions concerned is 'for the purposes of [their] application in the Community'[50] and 'in so far as that agreement is an integral part of the Community legal order'.[51] That interpretation is obviously not binding on the non-member state, though in practice it may be very influential.[52] An international agreement could confer jurisdiction on the ECJ to interpret it for the purposes of its application in non-member countries.[53] The original EEA Agreement did this. However, the ECJ has taken the view that such jurisdiction would only be compatible with the EC Treaty if the ECJ's judgments have binding effect.[54] Alternatively, an international court could be established or given jurisdiction to interpret an international agreement to which the EC is a party. The decisions of such a court would be binding on the community institutions, including the ECJ.[55] Such a system or courts is, in principle, compatible with Community law:

> The Community's competence in the field of international relations and its capacity to conclude international agreements necessarily entails the power to submit to the decisions of a court which is created or designated by such an agreement as regards the interpretation and application of its provisions.[56]

As well as being bound as a treaty, the ECJ has also accepted that the EC can become bound by an international agreement by a process of substitution or replacement for the member states.[57] This has been the case with the

---

48 Only states can be parties before the ICJ. A third state could refer a dispute over the interpretation of a Community agreement to the ICJ. Presumably a member state could also do in relation to the interpretation of the Agreement itself rather than matters of EC competence. Under Article 219 EC only the ECJ is to have jurisdiction over EC matters, see Opinion 1/91 (First EEA Opinion), pr 35, and the discussion in Opinion 2/94 (ECHR). A dispute over CFSP could also go to the ICJ although this is unlikely.

49 AG Warner, in *Haegeman*, p 473.

50 *Kupferberg*, pr 45.

51 Opinion 1/91 (First EEA Opinion), pr 39.

52 In effect the position of the ECJ is the same position as that of a national court interpreting an international agreement.

53 Opinion 1/91 (First EEA Opinion), pr 59. Note also the 1971 Protocol to the Brussels Convention on Jurisdiction and the Enforcement of Judgments in Civil and Commercial Matters (1968) which provides for the ECJ to have jurisdiction to interpret the Convention. Only member states are parties. See C-389-92, *Mund and Fester v Hatrex International Transport* [1994] ECR 1-467.

54 Opinion 1/91 (First EEA Opinion), pr 61. The agreement was changed to make the judgments of the ECJ binding, see Opinion 1/92 (Second EEA Opinion) [1992] ECR I-2821 See also Case C-188/91, *Deutsche Shell AG v Hauptzollamt Hamburg-Harburg* [1993] ECR I-363.

55 Opinion 1/91 (First EEA Opinion), pr 39.

56 Opinion 1/91 (First EEA Opinion), pr 40. See Schermers 29 *CML Rev*, 991–1010. This would be of significance in relation to the jurisdiction of the European Court of Human Rights to interpret the ECHR in relation to the EC. See the discussion in Opinion 2/94 (ECHR).

57 There are a number of possible explanations for this process including an analogy with Article 228 or the transfer of sovereignty from the member state to the EC with the consent of the third parties concerned. See Cheyne, 'International Agreements and the European Community Legal System' (1994) 18 *EL Rev* at pp 581–98.

GATT,[58] and two customs conventions.[59] Thus in the *International Fruit Co* case the ECJ found that the provisions of the GATT agreement were binding on the Community.[60] The ECJ appears to treat such agreements as an integral part of the Community legal order in the same way as agreements expressly adopted by the EC.[61] The ECJ has not accepted that the EC has succeeded to the European Convention on Human Rights.[62]

In the 1990s the EC has increasingly been faced with questions of state succession to treaties. German reunification, the disintegration of the USSR[63] and of Yugoslavia, the separation of Czechoslovakia and the agreed secession of Eritrea from Ethiopia raised a series of issues for which Community practice has to develop. The results were inevitably variable and pragmatic with the 1978 Vienna Convention on Succession of States in Respect of Treaties providing analogous rules which have served 'as a useful point of reference but no more'.[64] The international law rules of state succession are themselves far from clear.

In *Demirel* the UK and Germany argued that in the case of a mixed agreement the ECJ's jurisdiction only extends to those parts of the agreement which are within EC competence. Arguably, it does not extend to those parts of the agreement which are within member state competence.[65] The ECJ responded that the question did not arise because Article 238 empowered the Community to guarantee commitments towards non-member countries in all fields covered by the Treaty. That obviously included the provisions on the free movement of workers that were in issue in the case. It made no difference to this conclusion that it was for member states to lay down rules which were necessary for giving effect in their territory to the provisions of an international agreement or the decisions adopted by an Association Council.[66] The ECJ recalled its ruling in

---

58 *IFC* case. The ECJ has also held that it has exclusive competence to interpret the GATT for the purposes of EC law, *SIOT v Ministero delle Finanze* [1983] ECR 731 (hereinafter *SIOT*).

59 The Convention on the Nomenclature for the Classification of Goods in Customs Tariffs and the Convention Establishing the Customs Co-operation Council. See Case 38/75, *Douaneagent der NV Nederlandse Spoorwegen v Inspecteur der Invoerrechten en Accijzen* [1975] ECR 1439.

60 See also Joined Cases 267 and 269/81 *Amministrazione delle Finanze dello Stato v SPI and SAMI* [1983] ECR 801.

61 See Cheyne, 'International Agreements and the European Community Legal System', p 5878; G Bebr, 'Agreements Concluded by the Community and their Possible Direct Effect: from *International Fruit Company* to *Kupferberg*' (1983) 20 CMLR 35–73, p 43; Case C-69/89, *Nakajima All Precision Co v Council* [1991] ECR I-2069 concerning the GATT Anti-dumping Code to which the EC is a party. ELM Volker, 'The Direct Effect of International Agreements in the Community's Legal Order', *Legal Issues of European Integration*, 1983/1, 131–45, pp 142–43, expresses a contrary view.

62 See Cases 50-52/82, *Administrateur des Affaires Maritimes, Bayonne v Dorca Marina* [1982] ECR 3949. Opinion 2/94 (ECHR) would seem to reinforce that view.

63 On the application of the Community's anti-dumping procedures to a successor state see Case T-164/94, *Ferchimex SA v Council* [1995] ECR II-2681.

64 See PJ Kuyper, 'The Community and State Succession in Respect of Treaties', in D Curtin and T Heukels (eds), *Institutional Dynamics of European Integration: Essays in Honour of HG Schermers*, Vol II, 1994, Dordrecht: Nijhoff at p 640. See also HG Schermers and NM Blocker, *International Institutional Law*, 3rd edn, 1995, The Hague: Nijhoff at pp 986–88.

65 *Demirel*, see p 3725 (Germany) and p 3729 (UK).

66 *Demirel*, pr 10.

Kupferberg that the obligation of member states to lay down such rules was a community obligation.[67]

Pre-existing international commitments and the EC legal order

Article 234 protects third states by providing for the continuing effect of pre-existing international agreements:

> The rights and obligations arising from agreements concluded before the entry into force of this Treaty between one or more member states on the one hand, and one or more third countries on the other, shall not be affected by this Treaty.

Those international agreements with third states do not become part of the EC legal order. Whether the agreement has direct effect will depend on the national law of the member state concerned rather than on EC law.[68] The agreements do not become binding on the EC,[69] subject to the rare possibility of succession. Article 234 continues by providing that if there are incompatibilities between the international agreements and the EC Treaty then the member state concerned 'shall take all appropriate steps to eliminate the incompatibilities concerned'. Member states are to 'assist each other to this end' and, 'where appropriate, to adopt a common attitude'.[70] This obligation should not be interpreted to the point of requiring member states to denounce agreements with third states.[71] The number of cases in which member states seek to rely on Article 234 is increasing steadily.

Article 234 will effectively provide a member state with a defence when they would otherwise be in breach of their obligations under the EC Treaty.[72] For example, in the *Levy*[73] and *Minne*[74] cases the effect of Article 234 was that Article 5 of the Equal Treatment Directive 76/207 could not be relied upon to prevail over the national provisions adopted to comply with an ILO Convention of 1948. The institutions of the Community are bound not to impede the performance of those obligations by the member state concerned.[75] The third paragraph of Article 234 emphasises the common advantages to member states of EC membership. This would be consistent with an interpretation of Article 234 which only allows member states to rely on it when it has an obligation to a third state that is relevant. A member state should not be able to rely on Article 234 to

---

67 *Ibid*, pr 11. See TC Hartley, 'International Agreements and the Community Legal System: Some Recent Developments' (1983) 8 *EL Rev* 383–92, p 389.

68 See Case 812/79, *Attorney General v Burgoa* [1980] ECR 2787, pr 10 (hereinafter *Burgoa*).

69 *Ibid*, at 2808.

70 A particular problem that can arise is where one member state interprets similar international obligations in a different way to other member states, see JM Grimes, 'Conflicts Between EC Law and International Treaty Obligations: A Case Study of the German Telecommunications Dispute' (1994) 35 *Harv ILJ* 535–64, pp 554–5.

71 See Grimes, 'Conflicts Between EC Law and International Treaty Obligations'. See also Opinion 1/76 (*Rhine Navigation* case), pr 2, on Article 234 justifying participation in an international agreement.

72 See R Churchill and N Foster, 'European Community Law and Prior Treaty Obligations of Member States: *The Spanish Fisherman's* cases' (1987) 36 *ICLQ* 504–24.

73 Case C-158/91, *Ministère public et direction du travail et l'emploi v Levy* [1993] ECR I-4287.

74 Case C-13/93, *Office nationale de l'emploi v Minne* [1994] ECR I-371.

75 *Burgoa*, at 2808.

gain a benefit or advantage.[76] Article 234 cannot be relied upon in intra-community relations if the rights of non-member states are not involved.[77]

The direct effect of international agreements

The concept of direct effect has been of fundamental importance in the development of the European Community Law system. The EC Treaty does not contain the concept of 'direct effect'. There is a similar sounding concept of 'direct applicability' in Article 189 EC but that only refers to Regulations. The subject matter is similar to, but more extensive than, the international law concept of 'self-executing treaties'.[78] The ECJ uses the terms 'directly effective' and 'directly applicable' interchangeably.[79] This work uses the term 'directly effective'. If a provision of an international agreement is directly effective, as a matter of EC law, then it grants natural and legal persons rights that must be upheld by the national courts of the member states.[80] One or more of the provisions of an international agreement can have direct effect even if the other provisions of the same agreement do not have direct effect.[81]

In accordance with *Van Gend En Loos*[82] and subsequent case law, the general test for direct effect of community law measures is threefold:

1   The provision must be clear and unambiguous.

2   It must be unconditional.

3   Its operation must not be dependent on further action being taken (by the community or by national authorities or international bodies such as an Association Council).

These strict criteria were intended to make the doctrine more acceptable to states. In practice, although these tests appeared rigorous when first introduced, over time they have been considerably relaxed in their application. To an extent they are not even applied as successive tests anymore. For internal measures direct effect may now be regarded as the norm rather than the exception. The test is essentially a practical one. If a provision lends itself to judicial application it will be held to be directly effective. Only when direct effect would create serious practical problems will the provision be held not to be directly effective. This supports the view that the test has become little more than one of justiciability:'
A rule can have direct effect whenever its characteristics are such that it is

---

76   See Case 10/61, *Commission v Italian Republic* [1962] ECR 1, at 10; Case 812/79, *Attorney General v Burgoa* [1980] ECR 2787; Case C-158/91, *Ministère public et direction du travail et l'emploi v Levy* [1993] ECR I-4287.

77   Cases C-241/91P and C-242/91P, *Radio Telefis Eireann (RTE) and Independent Television Publications v Commission* [1995] ECR I-743. On the replacement by Community regulations of social security conventions concluded between member states see Case C-475/93, *Jean-Louis Thevenon and Others v Landesversicherrungsanstalt* [1995] ECR I-3813.

78   See J Jackson, 'Status of Treaties in Domestic Legal Systems' (1992) 86 *AJIL* 310–40.

79   In Case C-58/93, *Yousfi v Belgian State* [1994] ECR I-1353, A-G Tesauro considered the alleged distinction between direct applicability and direct effect and stated that 'the difference between the expressions used, at least in the case law, is merely terminological and non-substantive', pp 1357–58.

80   See Bebr, 'Agreements Concluded by the Community'; Volker, *op cit*; Bourgeois, 'Effects of International Agreements in European Community Law' (1984) 82 *MichLRev* 1250–73.

81   So *Polydor* and *Kupferberg* concerned the same agreement with Portugal.

82   Case 26/62 [1963] ECR 1.

capable of judicial application'.[83] It is possible that only part of an EC law can have direct effect.

This jurisprudence on direct effect of EC measures is important because there has been substantial legislative implementation of international agreements within Community law by means of Regulations and Directives. If a provision in such a measure has direct effect there may be no need to consider as a separate issue whether the international agreement concerned can have direct effect in its own right. This issue is particularly important, however, if no internal implementation measures have been taken.

Does the general test for direct effect apply to international agreements?

Formally, the answer appears to be yes.[84] According to the ECJ's well-established jurisprudence:

> A provision in an international agreement concluded by the Community with non-member countries must be regarded as being directly applicable when, regard being had to its wording and the purpose and nature of the agreement itself, the provision contains a clear and precise obligation which is not subject, in its implementation or effects, to the adoption of any subsequent measure.[85]

The decisions of an Association Council must satisfy the same conditions as those applicable to the provisions of the agreement itself.[86] However, the result of the practical application of this test has been that direct effect of international agreements has been the exception rather than the norm. This is the reverse of the situation with internal EC measures. We need to consider closely the ECJ's approach to the interpretation of international agreements.

How does the ECJ approach the interpretation of international agreements?

The ECJ has rarely referred expressly to the generally accepted rules of interpretation in international law in the Vienna Convention on the Law of Treaties (1969).[87] According to the ECJ, to determine the effect in the community legal system of the provisions of an international agreement, its 'international origin' has to be taken into account.[88] Parties to an agreement can '[i]n conformity with principles of public international law' expressly specify the

---

83 See P Pescatore, 'The Doctrine of Direct Effect – An Infant Disease of Community Law' (1983) *ELRev* 155–77.

84 *Ibid*, pp 171–74.

85 *Demirel*, pr 14; Case C-18/90, *Office National de l'Emploi v Kziber* [1991] ECR I-199, pr 15. N Neuwahl suggests that it is 'not clear whether these criteria are sufficient in the case of an international agreement', 'Individuals and the GATT: Direct Effect and Indirect Effects of the General Agreement on Tariffs and Trade in Community Law', in N Emiliou and D O'Keeffe (eds), *The European Union and World Trade Law – After the GATT Uruguay Round*, 1996, Chichester: Wiley at p 319.

86 *Sevince*, prs 14–15.

87 Examples are Opinion 1/91 (First EEA Opinion), pr 14, and C-432/92, *R v Ministry of Agriculture, Fisheries and Food, ex p Anastasiou*, [1994] ECR I-3087, both referring to Article 31 VCLT. The Vienna Convention on the Law of Treaties between States and International Organisations or between International Organisations (1986) contains broadly analogous rules. The EC is not a party. See P Manin, 'The European Communities and the Vienna Convention on the Law of Treaties between States and International Organisations or between International Organisations' (1987) 24 *CMLR* 457–81.

88 *Kupferberg*, pr 17.

effect of the provisions of an agreement in their respective legal orders.[89] In practice they rarely do this and, in default, the question can come before the ECJ.[90] It is then a question of interpretation of the agreement concerned.

The general approach of the ECJ to the interpretation of international agreements is to examine its provisions in the light of the general structure of the agreement and any amending or additional Protocols to it.[91] Simultaneously, 'The spirit, the general scheme and the general terms of the ... agreement must be considered'.[92] In *Haegeman* the ECJ clearly read the international agreement concerned in the light of the EC provisions concerned. There was no reference to GATT or to the international backgrounds.

The aims and context of the agreement must also be considered, and its provisions analysed in the light of its object and purpose.[93] The considerations which lead to a certain interpretation in a Community context do not necessarily apply in the context of an international agreement. The ECJ has stressed on many occasions that the EC Treaty creates a new and unique legal order notwithstanding that it was concluded in the form of an international legal agreement.[94] The Treaty constitutes the constitutional charter of a Community based on the rule of law.[95] Member states have limited their sovereign rights. Community law has primacy over the law of the member state and many of its provisions have direct effect.[96] The Treaty pursues certain aims and objectives, and in particular, 'by establishing a common market and progressively approximating the economic policies of the member states, seeks to unite national markets into a single market having the characteristics of a domestic market'.[97] The provisions of the Treaty are not an end in themselves. They are only means to attaining the objectives of the EC and 'making concrete progress towards European unity'.[98] The interpretation and application of the Treaty, even against the same provisions in an international agreement, uses 'different approaches, methods and concepts in order to take account of the nature of each Treaty and its particular objectives'.[99] Stress is also often placed on the institutional structure of the Treaty system and that the Community has at its disposal instruments to achieve the uniform application of EC law and the progressive abolition of legislative disparities.[100]

---

89 *Ibid*. Presumably the parties could not all specify that an agreement does or does not have direct effect.

90 *Kupferberg*, pr 17.

91 *Haegeman*, pr 10. AG Warner at 469 stated that the expressions in question must be interpreted in the context of the association agreement read as a whole and against the background of the provisions of the EEC Treaty. This suggests a broader framework than just the EC. In Opinion 1/91 (First EEA Opinion) the ECJ's interpretation of some of the Protocols to the EEA Agreement were very significant for its opinion.

92 IFC Case pr 20; Case C-280/93, *Germany v Council* [1994] ECR I-4973, pr 105; Case 87/75, *Conceria Daniele Bresciani v Amministrazione delle Finanze Stato* [1976] ECR 129 pr 16 (hereinafter *Bresciani*).

93 *Kupferberg*, pr 23.

94 Opinion 1/91 (First EEA Opinion) pr 21.

95 *Ibid*.

96 *Ibid*.

97 *Polydor*, pr 16.

98 Opinion 1/91 (First EEA Opinion), pr 17.

99 Opinion 1/91 (First EEA Opinion), pr 51.

100 *Polydor*, pr 20; Opinion 1/91 (First EEA Opinion), pr 21.

By contrast, the various classes of international agreements to which the EC is a party pursue different and more limited objectives than the EC.[101] In contrast to the EC Treaty, such an international agreement 'merely creates rights and obligations as between the Contracting Parties and provides for no transfer of sovereign rights to the inter-governmental institutions which it sets up'.[102] This is the case with free trade and co-operation agreements. Similarly with association agreements[103] but, to the extent that they seek to prepare the associating state for membership, they are closer on the spectrum to the EC Treaty than mere free trade and co-operation agreements.[104] In *Bresciani* it was important that the international agreement concerned was intended to promote the development of the associated states.[105] The function of the provisions concerned is important and whether it is the same as that performed by similarly worded provisions of the EC Treaty.[106] In any event the result is the same in that the interpretation given to the provisions of the EC Treaty cannot be applied by way of simple analogy to the provisions of other kinds of international agreements even if the wording is similar or even identical.[107] 'Such similarity of terms is not a sufficient reason for transposing to the provisions of the Agreement', the case law of the Community.[108] This is important because many of the EC's international agreements reproduce the language of the EC Treaty. For example, the provisions of the EEA Agreement are textually identical to the corresponding provisions of EC law.[109] Similarly, each of the different classes of EC agreements, for example, free trade, partnership and co-operation, Europe agreements tend to use identical provisions. Thus, the interpretation of any one agreement has significance for others in the same class, and sometimes for agreements in other classes.[110]

In a small number of cases the ECJ held that provisions of association agreements can have direct effect.[111] So too can the Decisions of an Association Council which are directly connected with the agreement to which they give effect. In

---

101 Reference is often made to the Preamble or the first article of those agreements to determine their objectives and purpose: see, for example, *Polydor*, pr 10; Case C-280/93, *Germany v Council* [1994] ECR I-4973 pr 106.

102 Opinion 1/91 (First EEA Opinion), pr 20.

103 See Opinion 1/91 (First EEA Opinion), pr 15; *Polydor*, pr 18–20.

104 In *Demirel* the Commission analysed the Association agreement concerned as 'a combination of an association for the purposes of development and an association prior to accession', p 3730. Also, 'The concept of association has a very wide scope and covers various forms of relationship', p 3730.

105 *Bresciani*, pr 22.

106 See Case 17/81, *Pabst & Richarz KZ v Hauptzollamt Oldenburg* [1982] ECR 1331, pr 26. For an important decision on the interpretation of 'changes having equivalent effect' in bilateral or multilateral agreements concluded by the Community see Case C-125/94, *Aprile Srl en liquidation v Amministrazione delle Finanze dello Stato* [1995] ECR I-2919.

107 *Kupferberg*, pr 30; *Polydor*, pr 14; Opinion 1/91 (First EEA Opinion), pr 22; Case C-312/91, *Metalsa Srl v Italy* [1993] ECR I-3751.

108 *Polydor*, pr 15.

109 Opinion 1/91 (First EEA Opinion), pr 22.

110 In the *Polydor* case the UK submission noted that the provision in issue appeared in seven free trade agreements with EFTA countries, all of the Community's agreements with Mediterranean countries, and in the GATT, p 340. See also Case C-103/94, *Zoulika Krid v Caisse Nationale d'Assurances Vieillesse des Travailleurs Salaries* [1995] ECR I-719.

111 For example, *Haegeman, Bresciani*.

Kupferberg (1982) the same reasoning was extended, in principle, to free trade agreements.[112] The ECJ proceeded from one of the general rules of international law that there must be *bona fide* performance of every agreement.[113] It observed that in the absence of specific provisions on implementation in the agreement itself, international law did not specify the legal means appropriate for the full execution of a party's commitments under an agreement. It was a matter of discretion for the party concerned.[114] Accordingly, that the legal system of one party accorded direct effect to the provisions of an agreement, while the other party's legal system did not, was simply a reflection of how the parties exercised their discretion as to methods of implementation. Such a situation did not in itself constitute a lack of reciprocity in the implementation of the agreement. In the context of an agreement on development, an imbalance in the obligations of the parties may be inherent in the special nature of the agreement itself.[115] Similarly, that the parties have established a special institutional framework for consultations and negotiations on implementation is not in itself a justification for excluding the possibility of direct effect in principle.[116] Provisions in an international agreement which set out a programme to be achieved would not normally satisfy the standard conditions for direct effect. However, this 'does not prevent the decisions of Council of Association which give effect in specific respects to the programmes envisaged in the Agreement from having direct effect'.[117] The non-publication of a decisions of an Association Council will also not serve to deprive a private individual of the rights which that decision confer on him.[118] Finally, the existence of 'safeguard clauses' which enable parties to derogate from certain provisions of the agreement is also not itself sufficient to exclude the possibility of direct effect in principle.[119] In principle then, neither the nature nor structure of a Free Trade Agreement prevented it from having direct effect in the community legal system.[120]

The direct effect of the decisions of an Association Council cannot be affected by the fact that under those decisions the rights concerned are to be established any national rules. Such provisions 'merely clarify the obligation of the member states to take such administrative measures as may be necessary for the implementation of those provisions, without empowering the member states to make correctional or restrict the application of the precise and unconditional right which the decisions of the Council of Association grant ...'[121]

. . .

---

112 *Kupferberg*, pr 22. See Bebr, 'Agreements Concluded by the Community and their Possible Direct Effect'.

113 *Ibid*, pr 18. Article 26 of the VCLT provides that 'Every treaty in force is binding upon the parties to it and must be performed by them in good faith'.

114 This is clearly correct. For example, the UK has not incorporated the European Convention on Human Rights.

115 *Bresciani*, pr 23.

116 *Kupferberg*, prs 19–20. Similarly in *Fediol*, pr 21.

117 *Sevince*, pr 21.

118 *Ibid*, pr 24. Non-publication would prevent the decision being applied adversely to an individual, *ibid*.

119 *Kupferberg*, pr 21; *Sevince*, prs 19–20 in the context of an Association Agreement.

120 Interestingly, AG Rozes has taken a different view, stressing the lack of reciprocity, the flexibility of the provisions, the limited objectives of the agreement, and the difference in the wording of the provisions concerned.

121 *Sevince*, pr 22.

Vertical and horizontal direct effect

Another preliminary question concerns the nature of direct effect in terms of vertical and horizontal direct effect. Vertical effect concerns the relationship between an individual or other private legal person and the state.[122] For example, in cases concerning the direct effect of international agreements, the disagreement is often between the state (customs authorities, tax authorities) and an individual or a company. However, the 'state' has a particular community law meaning in this context (*Foster v British Gas plc*)[123] and therefore covers 'emanations of the state' which for other purposes would be considered as private bodies.[124] Horizontal effect concerns the relationship between one individual or private legal person and another individual or private legal person. Again, given the wide community interpretation of the state, this would be more accurately expressed as one 'non-state emanation' and another 'non-state emanation'. For our purposes, the important question is whether the direct effect of international agreements is limited to vertical direct effect. Provisions of the Community Treaties can have both horizontal and vertical effect.[125] Many provisions of the EC Treaties have been held to be directly effective both vertically and horizontally. The fact of their being addressed to states has been no bar to their horizontal effects. The same argument can be applied to international agreements. In all of the cases considered by the ECJ to date the argument has been one of the vertical direct effect of an international agreement, for example, against a customs authority. However, the *Polydor* case (1982) represented an example of an attempt to rely on the direct effect of a Treaty against a private party.

Finally, [as] Regulations and Directives are often used to implement international agreements it is important to note the possibility of them have direct effect. Regulations can have both vertical and horizontal direct effect, Directives, however, can have vertical direct effect, but not horizontal direct effect.[126] Secondary legislation implementing an international agreement must, as far as possible, be interpreted in a manner that is consistent with it.[127, 128]

2.3.5 The relationship between regional international law and universal international law

Since 1945, particularly in the areas of human rights and environmental protection, there has been a growth in the number of treaties setting down rules applicable to particular regions of the world. Specific treaties are discussed in subsequent chapters but it is worth highlighting here the potential problems which have yet to be fully resolved. In the event of a conflict between the

---

122 In a general sense, this regulation of the indiviudal-state relationship is one familiar to constitutional lawyers.

123 Case C-188/89, *Foster v British Gas* [1990] ECR I-3133. It does not matter in which capacity the state is acting.

124 For example, in the context of international personality or state immunity.

125 Case 43/75, *Defrenne v SABENA* [1976] ECR 455.

126 Case 152/84. *Marshall v Southampton & SWHAHA (Teaching)* [1986] ECR 723; Case C-91/92, *Paulo Faccini Dori, Recreb Sri* [1994] ECR I-3325.

127 See Case C-64/94, *Commission v FRG* [1996] ECR.

128 D McGoldrick, *International Relations Law of the European Union*, 1997, London: Longman at pp 117–33.

regional rule and the rule of universal application, which rule is to prevail? As will be seen in Chapter 3, the problem may be resolved by use of one of the principles: *lex posterior derogat priori* (a later law repeals an earlier law), *lex posterior generalis non derogat priori speciali* (a later law, general in character, does not derogate from an earlier law which is special in character), or the principle *lex specialis derogat generali* (a special law prevails over a general law). However, such principles are not always easily applicable to specific circumstances and it is not always clear which is the special law and which is the general law. It will only be as state practice builds up that it will be possible to state with any degree of certainty the relationship between rules of international law of limited regional application and those rules which have universal, global application.

CHAPTER 3

SOURCES OF INTERNATIONAL LAW

3.1   Introduction

The term 'sources of law' has generated considerable debate among writers and is capable of conveying more than one meaning.

In English jurisprudence at least, the classic scheme of the sources of law is that of Salmond, who divided them first into those which are 'formal' and those which are 'material' – those imparting to a given rule the force of law and those from which its substance is drawn. He further subdivided 'material sources' into 'legal' and 'historical' sources – those which the law itself acknowledges, such as statute and judicial precedent in England, and those which, though possibly no less influential, are not so acknowledged, as, for instance, the Roman legal system from which, via judicial precedent, many English rules are derived. Finally, in a footnote, Salmond distinguished a category of 'literary' sources, consisting in 'the sources of our knowledge of the law, or rather the original authoritative sources of our knowledge, as opposed to later commentary and literature'.[1]

Though its primary distinction between 'formal' and 'material' sources, however difficult of application in practice, still commands some general acceptance, Salmond's scheme has been much criticised. The alternatives to it which have been proffered have not, however, fared much better. Indeed Sir Carleton Allen, Salmond's chief critic, is regarded by Professor Paton as advocating the abandonment of the search for the sources of law in favour of an enquiry, into first, its validity and, second, the origins of the materials from which it is fashioned, on the ground that the multiplicity of theories has utterly confused the term 'source'.[2]

The traditional notion of sources in international law: terminology

International lawyers appear to have persisted longer in the search for 'sources'. Whether this is because they have displayed a greater capacity for the clear definition of terms is perhaps questionable. But their terminology is, in any case, slightly different from Salmond's.

In an endeavour to introduce some order into the words used, Professor Corbett essayed 40 years ago to distinguish different elements relevant to the discussion. He laid it down thus:

1   The *cause* of international law is the desire of states to have the mutual relations which their social nature renders indispensable regulated with the greatest possible rationality and uniformity.

2   The *basis* of the rules of international law as a system and of the rules of which it is composed is the consent of states.

3   The origins of the rules of international law, which may also be called '*the sources*' of that law – though the word 'source' has such a history of confusion behind it that it might well be abandoned – are the opinions, decisions or acts constituting the starting point from which their more or less gradual establishment can be traced.

---

1   Salmond, *Jurisprudence*, 10th edn, 1947, London: Sweet & Maxwell at pp 151–56.
2   Paton, *Jurisprudence*, 3rd edn, 1964, Oxford: Clarendon Press at pp 159–60.

4   The records or *evidence* of international law are the documents or acts proving the consent of states to its rules. Among such records or *evidence*, treaties and practice play an essential part, though recourse must be had to unilateral declarations, instructions to diplomatic agents, laws and ordinances, and, in a lesser degree, to the writings of authoritative jurists. Custom is merely that general practice which affords conclusive proof of a rule.[3]

Amongst the interesting features of this series of propositions is, first, that the term but not ostensibly the concept of 'sources' of law is condemned, though both term and concept are narrower than Salmond would have made them; and, secondly, the introduction of the term 'evidence'. This last is something more, it is clear, than Salmond's 'literary sources'.

Even writers in English have not adhered to these golden rules, as is testified by John Basset Moore, who usually had a pretty turn of phrase. For, in the Introduction to his great series of *International Adjudications* he wrote:

> Being desirous to deal with the substance of things, and, by avoiding as far as possible wars of epithets, to save a great cause from needless injury and attrition, I have placed the words 'source' and 'evidence' [in the title to a section on the influence of arbitral decisions on the law] in the alternative, thus leaving it to their partisans, who may often agree except in terminology, the unchallenged enjoyment of the title they prefer.[4]

Oppenheim endeavoured to resolve the confusion between 'source' and 'cause' by tracing the former term to its own source, in the meaning of spring or well, which:

> ... has to be defined as the rising from the ground of a spring of water. When we see a stream of water and want to know whence it comes, we follow the stream upwards until we come to the spot where it rises naturally from the ground. On that spot, we say, is the source of the stream of water. We know very well that this source is not the cause of the existence of the stream of water ...[5]
>
> ...
>
> If we apply the conception of source in this meaning to the term 'source of law' the confusion of source with cause cannot arise. Just as we see streams of water running over the surface of the earth, so we see, as it were, streams of rules running over the area of law. And if we want to know whence these rules come, we have to follow these streams upwards until we come to the beginning; where we find that such rules do not rise from a spot on the ground as water does; they rise from facts in the historical development of a community. Thus in Great Britain a good many rules rise each year from Acts of Parliament. 'Source of law' is therefore the name for an historical fact out of which rules of conduct rise into existence and legal force.[6]

Romantic and evocative though I find this image, I must avow that it is unhelpful to me for at least two reasons. First, I feel that the assertion that an Act of Parliament is, or is simply, 'an historical fact' would stand, and would not

---

3   Corbett, 'The Consent of States and the Sources of the Law of Nations' (1925) *BYIL* VI at pp 20, 29–30.

4   *International Adjudications*, Modern Series (1929), Vol I, p xii.

5   Oppenheim, *International Law*, Vol I, 8th edn, 1955, London: Longman at p 24.

6   Oppenheim, *International Law*, Vol I, 8th edn, 1955, *ibid* at p 25.

withstand, closer examination. And secondly, though I can see that an Act of Parliament would be both a 'literary source' in Salmond's sense and an item of 'evidence' in Professor Corbett's, and that this circumstance would not exclude its inclusion in other categories established by those authors (since these categories are not necessarily on the same plane or not mutually exclusive), I am troubled by the possible effect of Professor Corbett's cursory assignment of custom to the category of *evidence*.

To say this is perhaps to be obscure unless it is first explained that Oppenheim goes on almost immediately to say that 'Custom is the oldest and original source of international law', to define it as 'a clear and continuous habit of doing certain actions [which] has grown up under the aegis of a conviction that these actions are, according to international law, obligatory or right', and to distinguish it from mere usage, a habit which has grown up without any such conviction.[7] Professor Corbett is no doubt more logical here: he says, in effect, custom merely proves or illustrates – or indeed merely provides evidence – that the conduct it reflects is obligatory. Therefore, in his system it cannot be a 'source' – an origin. Oppenheim says or implies in somewhat circular fashion that a custom is already considered as binding before it becomes such, but it is for him a source. But perhaps I misunderstand Professor Corbett here. Perhaps what he terms *practice* is Oppenheim's custom, and presumably he would concede *practice* to be both source and evidence in his sense. The alternative, which is not to be excluded, is that Professor Corbett has in fact carried out his threat and excised 'source' in all but name from his system: certainly it is difficult to regard *practice*, however, defined, as involving no more than 'the opinions, decisions or acts constituting the starting-point'.

However, this may be, it is well – a point sometimes overlooked by students of international law – to see briefly how writers in other languages and other countries regard the matter of terminology. A fair and accurate summary seems, if one may say so, to be provided by Professor Sorensen, who says that in usual legal language the sources of international law are those things which indicate the actual or concrete content of that system. Admittedly, certain authors prefer to avoid the term altogether or substitute alternative lines of enquiry for an enquiry after sources. Among these he includes Professor Corbett, thus confirming in some measure the suspicion we have already aired. But there is no harm in retaining the word if one makes sure how it is intended to be used. And it should not be used in relation to the question why international law is in general binding: that is the problem of 'basis', upon which designation Professor Corbett and many others agree,[8] or of 'source' in the singular. Nor should it be used in connection with the question what are the 'material sources' of international law in the sense of the elements and influences determining its content, be they the practical interests and needs of states or the idealistic urgings of the social conscience or the ideologies prevailing at any particular time.[9] [10]

Clive Parry makes reference to Oppenheim's *International Law* and cites passages from the eighth edition which was published in 1955. The view

---

7 Oppenheim, *International Law*, Vol I, 8th edn, 1955, *ibid* at pp 25–26.

8 *Cf* Brierly, *The Basis of Obligation in International Law*, 1958, Oxford: Clarendon Press.

9 Sorensen, *Les Sources du Droit International*, 1946, Copenhagen: E Munksgaard.

10 Clive Parry, *The Sources and Evidences of International Law*, 1965, Manchester: Manchester University Press at pp 1–5.

taken by the editors of the ninth edition (published in 1992) is slightly different:

There is much discussion of the meaning to be attributed to such terms as 'source', 'cause', 'basis' and 'evidence' of international law.[11] There is, however, an unavoidable degree of flexibility and overlap in the use of such terms, and little practical purpose is served in attempting to define them too precisely or to differentiate them too rigidly. Nevertheless, the concept of a 'source' of a rule of law is important, since it enables rules of law to be identified and distinguished from other rules (in particular rules *de lege ferenda*) and concerns the way in which the legal force of new rules of conduct is established and in which existing rules are changed.

The causes of a rule of law are generally to be found in particular social and historical circumstances in the development of a community, which suggest the need for a rule of conduct in a particular sense. The source of a rule of law is, by contrast, to be found in the process by which it first becomes identifiable as a rule of conduct with legal force and from which it derives its legal validity.

The sources of international law must not be confused with the basis of international law; this, as we have seen, is to be found in the common consent of the international community. The sources of law, on the other hand, concern the particular rules which constitute the system, and the processes by which the rules become identifiable as rules of law. The sources of the rules of law, while therefore distinct from the basis of the law, are nevertheless necessarily related to the basis of the legal system as a whole.

We should at this point also note the distinction between the formal and the material sources of international law. The former – with which we are more concerned here – is the source from which the legal rule derives its legal validity, while the latter denotes the provenance of the substantive content of that rule. Thus, for example, the formal source of a particular rule may be custom, although its material source may be found in a bilateral treaty concluded many years previously, or in some state's unilateral declaration.[12]

The attempt is often made to distinguish between the basis, the causes, the sources, the formal and material sources, and the evidence of sources of international law. These and similar distinctions may be useful, within limits, so long as their importance is not exaggerated and so long as they are not permitted to conceal the essential identity of the subject matter which they are intended to elucidate. The basis – the primary cause – of international law is the fact of the existence of an international society composed of human beings organised as sovereign states. Its more immediate cause (or, as it is occasionally referred to, its objective source) is the interdependence, in its manifold manifestations, of these sovereign states; the need to safeguard their interests and their independent existence by means of binding rules of law; and the necessity to protect the individual human being who is the ultimate unit of all law, in so far as such protection, both of nationals and aliens, is rendered relevant by reference to the existence of separate sovereign states ...

---

11 On the different meanings of these terms see Corbett (1925) *BYIL* 6 at pp 20–30; Fitzmaurice in *Symbolae Verzijl*, 1958, p 153; Parry, *The Sources and Evidences of International Law*, 1965, Manchester: Manchester University Press .

12 Jennings and Watts (eds), *Oppenheim's International Law*, 9th edn, 1992, London: Longman at p 23.

The more direct sources of international law are the agencies, human or other, by means of which it is expressed and rendered binding.[13]

Some writers have gone further to argue that the whole idea of 'sources' of international law is flawed. For example, O'Connell has written:

Sometimes the word 'source' is used to indicate the basis of international law; sometimes it is confused with the social origin and other 'causes' of the law; at others it is indicative of the formal law-making agency and at others again it is used instead of the term evidence of the law... As a figurative association the word 'source' is misleading and should be discarded.[14]

3.2 Article 38 of the Statute of the International Court of Justice

1   The Court, whose function is to decide in accordance with international law such disputes as are submitted to it, shall apply:

(a)   international conventions, whether general or particular, establishing rules expressly recognised by the contesting states;

(b)   international custom, as evidence of a general practice accepted as law;

(c)   the general principles of law recognised by civilised nations;

(d)   subject to the provisions of Article 59, judicial decisions and the teachings of the most highly qualified publicists of the various nations, as subsidiary means for the determination of rules of law.

2   This provision shall not prejudice the power of the Court to decide a case *ex aequo et bono*, if the parties agree thereto.[15]

The traditional starting point for any discussion of the sources of international law has been Article 38 of the Statute of the International Court of Justice. Apart from a few formal changes the Statute is similar to the Statute of the Permanent Court of International Justice. The Permanent Court of International Justice (PCIJ) was created in 1920 under the auspices of the League of Nations and the Statute was drafted by an 'Advisory Committee of Jurists' appointed by the Council of the League of Nations. The role and procedures of the International Court are discussed in Chapter 12.

The search for the thing which, by the highest compulsive force as it were, gives to the content of the rules of international law their character as law, whither should it be directed? The traditional approach leads one to turn to Article 38(1) of the Statute of the International Court of Justice – formerly the same article in the Statute of the Permanent Court of International Justice. Quite why this should be the approach is not wholly clear. That article, says Brierly, is 'a text of the highest authority',[16] which is to state the proposition to be proved. The article does not even say that it purports to be a list of sources otherwise than by implication. For it simply states that the Court 'whose function it is to decide in accordance with international law such disputes as are submitted to it, shall

---

13   E Lauterpacht (ed), *International Law – Collected Papers of Hersch Lauterpacht*, Vol 1, 1970, Cambridge: Cambridge University Press at p 51.

14   O'Connell, *International Law*, Vol 1, 1970, London: Stevens.

15   Article 38 of the Statute of the International Court of Justice.

16   Brierly, *Law of Nations*, 6th edn, 1963, Oxford: Clarendon Press at p 56.

apply' that which it prescribes. One of the matters so prescribed is 'the writings of the most highly qualified publicists ... as a subsidiary means for the determination of rules of law', a formulation which suggests less a formal source than what Salmond would have called no more than legal literature – not even a literary source. Another item echoes, or is echoed by, Professor Corbett: namely 'international custom as evidence of a general practice accepted by law' – not a source at all according to him, if he admits any sources at all.[17]

Article 38 does not actually use the term 'sources' but rather describes how the Court is to decide disputes which come before it for settlement. Law is not necessarily simply defined in terms of how courts decide disputes. Article 38 does not refer to resolutions of the United Nations or other international organisations yet such resolutions may play an extremely important role in international society and may arguably constitute a source of law. A question that will be considered at the end of this chapter is the extent to which Article 38 is to be regarded as a comprehensive list of the sources of international law.

Another question that arises is whether Article 38 para 1 creates a hierarchy of sources. It is argued that there is no rigid hierarchy, but those drafting the article intended to give an order and in practice the Court may be expected to observe the order in which they appear. (a) and (b) are obviously the important sources, and the priority of (a) is explicable by the fact that this refers to a source of mutual obligation of the parties – source (a) is thus not primarily a source of rules of general application, although as we shall see, treaties may provide evidence of the formation of custom. It may be useful here to note what Lauterpacht has written on the issue:

> The order in which the sources of international law are enumerated in the statute ... is, essentially, in accordance both with correct legal principle and with the character of international law as a body of rules based on consent to a degree higher than is law within the state. The rights and duties of states are determined, in the first instance, by their agreement as expressed in treaties – just as, in the case of individuals, their rights are specifically determined by any contract which is binding upon them. When a controversy arises between two or more states with regard to a matter regulated by treaty, it is natural that the parties should invoke and that the adjudicating party should apply, in the first instance, the provisions of the treaty in question.[18]

3.3 Treaties

Treaties represent a source of law whose importance has grown since 1945. In this chapter we are only concerned with treaties as a source of law. Chapter 4 deals with the mechanics of treaty making and enforcement in more detail. Treaties may be bipartite/bilateral or multipartite/multilateral and they may create particular or general rules of international law. A distinction is often drawn between **law-making treaties** (*traité-lois*) and **treaty contracts** (*traité contracts*). The essence of the distinction lies in the fact that **treaty contracts**,

---

17 Clive Parry, *The Sources and Evidences of International Law*, 1965, Manchester: Manchester University Press at p 5.

18 Lauterpacht, *International Law*, Collected Papers, Vol 1, p 87.

being agreements between relatively few states, can only create a particular obligation between the signatories, an obligation which is capable of fulfilment, eg an agreement between France, Germany and the UK to develop and build a new fighter jet. **Law-making treaties** create obligations which can continue as law, eg an agreement between 90 states to outlaw the use of torture. There has been a great increase in the number of law-making treaties throughout this century. One reason for this growth is the increase in the number of states and the fact that many new states have a lack of faith in any rules of customary international law in which they have not played a part in creating. The term 'law-making' can lead to confusion and it should be used with care – strictly speaking no treaty can bind non-signatories. Even a multipartite treaty only binds those states which are party to it. The mere fact that a large number of states are party to a multilateral convention does not make it binding on non-parties although its existence may be evidence of customary international law as was discussed in the *North Sea Continental Shelf* cases (1969).[19] For this reason sometimes the term law-making is replaced by 'normative'. Normative treaties bind signatories as treaties, but may also provide evidence of rules of custom which bind all states. Examples of normative treaties would include treaties operating a general standard setting instrument – eg International Covenant on Civil and Political Rights 1966; and treaties creating an internationally recognised regime – eg the Antarctic Treaty 1959.

Customary law and treaty law have equal authority. However if there is a conflict between the two it is the treaty that prevails. This point is illustrated by the *Wimbledon* case (1923).[20] In that case the PCIJ, while recognising that customary international law prohibited the passage of armaments through the territory of a neutral state into the territory of a belligerent state, upheld the Treaty of Versailles Article 380, which provided that the Kiel canal was to be free and open to all commercial vessels and warships belonging to states at peace with Germany. In stopping a vessel of a state with which it was at peace, Germany was in breach of treaty obligations. It should, however, be noted that there is a presumption against the replacement of custom by treaty – treaties will be construed to avoid conflict with rules of custom unless the treaty is clearly intended to overrule existing custom.

3.4 Custom

In any society rules of acceptable behaviour develop at an early stage and the international community is no exception. As contact between states increased, certain norms of behaviour crystallised into rules of customary international law. Until comparatively recently the rules of general international law were nearly all customary rules.

---

19 *Federal Republic of Germany v Denmark; Federal Republic of Germany v The Netherlands* [1969] *ICJ Rep* 3.

20 *PCIJ Rep*, Ser A, No 1.

3.4.1 Definitions of international custom

Custom in international law is a practice followed by those involved because they feel legally obliged to behave in such a way. Custom must be distinguished from mere usage, such as acts done out of courtesy, friendship or convenience rather than out of obligation or a feeling that non-compliance would produce legal consequences. Article 38 circumscribes customary law as 'international custom, as evidence of a general practice accepted as law.' The Court cannot apply custom, only customary law and subpara 1(b) arguably reverses the logical order of events since it is general practice, accepted as law, which constitutes evidence of a customary rule. Judge Hudson of the International Law Commission listed the following criteria for the establishment of a customary rule:

(a) concordant practice by a number of states with reference to a type of situation falling within the domain of international relations;

(b) continuation or repetition of the practice over a considerable period of time;

(c) conception that the practice is required by, or consistent with, prevailing international law; and

(d) general acquiescence in the practice by other states.[21]

How then is custom distinguished from behaviour which involves no legal obligation? The traditional view is that a rule of customary international law derives its validity from the possession of two elements: a material element and a psychological element. The material element refers to the behaviour and practice of states; whereas the psychological element, usually referred to as the *opinio juris sive necessitatis* or simply *opinio juris*, is the subjective conviction held by states that the behaviour in question is compulsory and not discretionary. Any alleged rule of customary law must therefore be checked as to its material and its psychological element.

ASYLUM CASE[22]

The Colombian government has finally invoked 'American international law in general'. In addition to the rules arising from agreements which have already been considered, it has relied on an alleged regional or local custom peculiar to Latin-American states.

The Party which relies on a custom of this kind must prove that this custom is established in such a manner that it has become binding on the other Party. The Colombian government must prove that the rule invoked by it is in accordance with a constant and uniform usage practised by the states in questions, and that this usage is the expression of a right appertaining to the state granting asylum and a duty incumbent on the territorial state. This follows from Article 38 of the Statute of the Court, which refers to international custom 'as evidence of a general practice accepted as law'.

In support of its contention concerning the existence of such a custom, the Colombian government has referred to a large number of ... treaties ...

---

21 UN Doc A/CN4/16 3/3/50 at p 5.

22 *Asylum* case (*Columbia v Peru*) [1950] *ICJ Rep* 266.

Finally, the Colombian government has referred to a large number of particular cases in which diplomatic asylum was in fact granted and respected. But it has not shown that the alleged rule ... was invoked or – if in some cases it was in fact invoked – that it was, apart from conventional stipulations, exercised by the states granting asylum as a right appertaining to them and respected by territorial states as a duty incumbent on them and not merely for reasons of political expediency. The facts brought to the knowledge of the Court disclose so much uncertainty and contradiction, so much fluctuation and discrepancy in the exercise of diplomatic asylum and in the official views expressed on various occasions, there has been so much inconsistency in the rapid succession of conventions on asylum, ratified by some states and rejected by others, and the practice has been so much influenced by considerations of political expediency in the various cases, that it is not possible to discern in all this any constant and uniform usage, accepted as law, with regard to the alleged rule of unilateral and definitive qualification of the offence.

The Court cannot therefore find that the Colombian government has proved the existence of such a custom. But even if it could be supposed that such a custom existed between certain Latin-American states only, it could not be invoked against Peru which, far from having by its attitude adhered to, has, on the contrary, repudiated it by refraining from ratifying the Montevideo Conventions of 1933 and 1939, which were the first to include a rule concerning the qualification of the offence in matters of diplomatic asylum.

NORTH SEA CONTINENTAL SHELF CASES[23]

70   The Court must now proceed to the last stage in the argument put forward on behalf of Denmark and the Netherlands. This is due to the effect that even if there was at the date of the Geneva Convention no rule of customary international law in favour of the equidistance principle, and no such rule was crystallised in Article 6 of the Convention, nevertheless such a rule has come into being since the Convention, partly because of its own impact, partly on the basis of subsequent state practice – and that this rule, being now a rule of customary international law binding on all states, including therefore the Federal Republic, should be declared applicable to the delimitation of the boundaries between the Parties' respective continental shelf areas in the North Sea.

71   In so far as this contention is based on the view that Article 6 of the Convention has had the influence, and has produced the effect described, it clearly involves treating that Article as a norm-creating provision which has constituted the foundation of, or has generated a rule which, while only conventional or contractual in its origin, has since passed into the general *corpus* of international law, and is now accepted as such by the *opinio juris*, so as to have become binding even for countries which have never, and do not, become parties to the Convention. There is no doubt that this process is a perfectly possible one and does from time to time occur: it constitutes indeed one of the recognised methods by which new rules of customary international law may be formed. At the same time this result is not lightly to be regarded as having been attained.

---

23   *Federal Republic of Germany v Denmark; Federal Republic of Germany v The Netherlands* [1969] *ICJ Rep* 3.

72 It would in the first place be necessary that the provision concerned should, at all events potentially, be of a fundamentally norm-creating character such as could be regarded as forming the basis of a general rule of law. Considered *in abstracto* the equidistance principle might be said to fulfil this requirement. yet in the particular form in which it is embodied in Article 6 of the Geneva Convention, and having regard to the relationship of that Article to other provisions of the Convention, this must be open to some doubt. In the first place, Article 6 is so framed as to put second the obligation to make use of the equidistance method, causing it to come after a primary obligation to effect delimitation by agreement. Such a primary obligation constitutes an unusual preface to what is claimed to be a potential general rule of law. Without attempting to enter into, still less pronounce upon on question of *jus cogens*, it is well understood that, in practice, rules of international law can, by agreement, be derogated from in particular cases, or as between particular parties – but this is not normally the subject of any express provision, as it is in Article 6 of the Geneva Convention. Secondly, the part played by the notion of special circumstances relative to the principle of equidistance as embodied in Article 6, and the very considerable, still unresolved controversies as to the exact meaning and scope of this notion. must raise further doubts as to the potentially norm-creating character of the rule. Finally, the faculty of making reservations to Article 6, while it might not of itself prevent the equidistance principle being eventually received as general law, does add considerably to the difficulty of regarding this result as having been brought about (or being potentially possible) on the basis of the Convention: for so long as this faculty continues to exist, and is not made the subject of any revision brought about in consequence of a request made under Article 13 of the Convention – of which there is at present no official indication – it is the Convention itself which would, for the reasons already indicated, seem to deny to the provisions of Article 6 the same norm-creating character as, for instance, Articles 1 and 2 possess.

73 With respect to the other elements usually regarded as necessary before a conventional rule can be considered to have become a general rule of international law, it might be that, even without the passage of any considerable period of time, a very widespread and representative participation in the convention might suffice of itself, provided it included that of states whose interests were specially affected. In the present case, however, the Court notes that, even if allowance is made for the existence of a number of states to whom participation in the Geneva Convention is not open, or which, by reason for instance of being land-locked states, would have no interest in becoming parties to it, the number of ratifications and accessions so far secured is, though respectable, hardly sufficient. That non-ratification may sometimes be due to factors other than active disapproval of the convention concerned can hardly constitute a basis on which positive acceptance of its principles can be implied. The reasons are speculative, but the facts remain.

74 As regards the time element, the Court notes that it is now over ten years since the Convention was signed, but that it is even now less than five years since it came into force in June 1964, and that when the present proceedings were brought it was less than three years, while less than one had elapsed at the time when the respective negotiations between the Federal Republic and the other two Parties for a complete delimitation broke down on the question of the application of the equidistance principle . Although the passage of only a short period of time is not necessarily, or of itself, a bar to the formation of a

new rule of customary international law on the basis of what was originally a purely conventional rule, an indispensable requirement would be that within the period in question, short though it might be, state practice, including that of states whose interests are specially affected, should have been both extensive and virtually uniform in the sense of the provision invoked – and should moreover have occurred in such a way as to show a general recognition that a rule of law or legal obligation is involved.

75 The Court must now consider whether state practice in the matter of continental shelf delimitation has, subsequent to the Geneva Convention, been of such a kind as to satisfy this requirement ... Some fifteen cases have been cited in the course of the present proceedings, occurring mostly since the signature of the 1958 Geneva Convention, in which continental shelf boundaries have been delimited according to the equidistance principle – in the majority of the cases by agreement, in a few other, unilaterally – or else the delimitation was foreshadowed but has not yet been carried out ... even if these various cases constituted more than a very small proportion of those potentially calling for delimitation in the world as a whole, the Court would not think it necessary to enumerate or evaluate them separately, since there are, *a priori*, several grounds which deprive them of weight as precedents in the present context.

76 ... Over half the states concerned, whether acting unilaterally or conjointly, were or shortly became parties to the Geneva Convention, and were therefore presumably, so far as they were concerned, acting actually or potentially in the application of the Convention. From their action no inference could legitimately be drawn as to the existence of a rule of customary international law in favour of the equidistance principle. As regards those states, on the other hand, which were not, and have not become parties to the Convention, the basis of their action can only be problematical and must remain entirely speculative. Clearly, they were not applying the Convention. But from that no inference could justifiably be drawn that they believed themselves to be applying a mandatory rule of customary international law. There is not a shred of evidence that they did and ... there is no lack of other reasons for using the equidistance method, so that acting, or agreeing to act in a certain way, does not of itself demonstrate anything of a juridical nature.

77 The essential point in this connection – and it seems necessary to stress it – is that even if these instances of action by non-parties to the Convention were much more numerous than they in fact are, they would not, even in the aggregate, suffice in themselves to constitute the *opinio juris* – for, in order to achieve this result, two conditions must be fulfilled. Not only must the acts concerned amount to a settled practice, but they must also be such, or be carried out in such a way, as to be evidence of a belief that this practice is rendered obligatory by the existence of a rule requiring it. The need for such a belief, ie the existence of a subjective element, is implicit in the very notion of the *opinio juris sive necessitatis*. The states concerned must therefore feel that they are conforming to what amounts to a legal obligation. The frequency, or even habitual character of the acts is not in itself enough. There are many international acts, eg in the field of ceremonial and protocol, which are performed almost invariably, but which are motivated only by considerations of courtesy, convenience or tradition, and not by any sense of legal duty.

78 In this respect the Court follows the view adopted by the Permanent Court of Justice in the *Lotus Case*, as stated in the following passage, the principle of which is, by analogy, applicable almost word for word, *mutatis mutandis*, to the present case (PCIJ Ser A, No 10, p 28, (1927)):

Even if the rarity of the judicial decisions to be found ... were sufficient to prove ... the circumstances alleged ... it would merely show that states had often, in practice, abstained from instituting criminal proceedings, and not that they recognised themselves as being obliged to do so; for only if such abstention were based on their being conscious of having a duty to abstain would it be possible to speak of an international custom. The alleged fact does not allow one to infer that states have been conscious of having such a duty; on the other hand ... there are other circumstances calculated to show that the contrary is true.

Applying this *dictum* to the present case, the position is simply that in certain cases – not a great number – the states concerned agreed to draw or did draw the boundaries concerned according to the principle of equidistance. There is no evidence that they so acted because they felt legally compelled to draw them in this way by reason of a rule of customary law obliging them to do so – especially considering that they might have been motivated by other obvious factors ...

81   The Court accordingly concludes that if the Geneva Convention was not in its origins or inception declaratory of a mandatory rule of customary international law enjoining the use of the equidistance principle for the delimitation of continental shelf areas between adjacent states; neither has its subsequent effect been constitutive of such a rule; and that state practice up-to-date has equally been insufficient for this purpose ...

It should be noted that in recent years a number of writers have criticised this traditional view of customary law. In an article written in 1982, Sir Robert Jennings, former President of the ICJ criticised the traditional view on the basis that it was outworn and inadequate and commented:

... most of what we perversely persist in calling customary international law is not only not customary law, it does not even faintly resemble a customary law.[24]

Critics of the traditional view argue that although the ICJ speaks in terms of state practice and *opinio juris*, increasingly its conclusions are determined by the application of legal rules that are largely treated as self-evident. The interpretation of state practice and *opinio juris* is never a straightforward automatic operation but involves a choice, usually justified on grounds of relevance, between conflicting facts and statements. Advocates of the non-traditional view, such as Martti Koskenniemi and Bruno Simma, argue that the study of international law must involve discussion of the way in which that choice is to be made. There is considerable merit to this view and an attempt will be made here to look critically at the way in which the ICJ deals with alleged rules of international custom.

---

24   'The Identification of International Law' in Cheng, *International Law: Teaching and Practice*, 1982, London: Stevens.

3.4.2 The material element

3.4.2.1 State practice

State practice includes any act, articulation, or other behaviour of a state which discloses the state's conscious attitude concerning a customary rule or its recognition of a customary rule. In 1950 the International Law Commission listed the following classical forms of 'Evidence of Customary International Law':

- treaties;
- decisions of national and international courts;
- national legislation;
- diplomatic correspondence;
- opinions of national legal advisers;
- practice of international organisations.

The list was not intended to be exhaustive but to provide a basis for discussion.[25]

There is some disagreement as to whether, for the purpose of the formation of customary law, state practice should consist merely of concrete actions, or whether it may also include abstract verbal, ie written or oral, statements of state representatives, or their votes, at diplomatic conferences, or in UN bodies. Judge Read's dissenting opinion in the *Anglo-Norwegian Fisheries* case (1951), explained the restricted view of state practice in more detail:

> Customary law is the generalisation of the practice of states. This cannot be established by citing cases where coastal states have made extensive claims ... Such claims may be important as starting points, which, if not challenged, may ripen into historic title in the course of time ... The only convincing evidence of state practice is to be found in seizures, where the coastal state asserts its sovereignty over the water in question by arresting a foreign ship.[26]

Dr Thirlway gives a similar view:

> The fact that the practice is 'against interest' gives it more weight than the mere acceptance of a theoretical rule in the course of discussion by state representatives at a conference, and considerably more weight than the assertion of such a rule ... Claims may be made in the widest of general terms; but the occasion of an act of state practice contributing to the formation of custom must always be some specific dispute or potential dispute.
>
> The mere assertion *in abstracto* of the existence of a legal right or legal rule is not an act of state practice ... Such assertions can be relied on as supplementary evidence both of state practice and of the existence of the *opinio juris*.[27]

Such views regard abstract statements as less, or not at all, relevant, apparently due to a reluctance to accept the notion that one body or conference could make law. However, states themselves do regard comments at conferences as

---

25 (1950) *ILC Yearbook* at pp 368–72.
26 *Anglo-Norwegian Fisheries* case [1951] *ICJ Rep* at p 116.
27 *International Customary Law and Codification*, 1972, Leiden: AW Sijthoff at p 64.

constitutive of state practice and the courts do refer to abstract statements when identifying a customary rule. Also the term 'practice' in Article 38 is general enough to cover any act or behaviour of a state and it is not clear in what respect verbal acts originating from a state could not be considered behaviour of a state. It is also the case that the traditional evidence of state practice – diplomatic notes, instructions to state representatives – are often abstract and verbal. It could be argued that the restricted view of state practice is more compatible with a time when means of communication were much slower and there was less interaction between states. In the past, too, there has been a difficulty in obtaining evidence of state practice in situations not involving concrete actions. It is submitted that today such difficulties are no longer as great. Satellite communication and the development of techniques of information gathering and storage have made the collection of evidence of what states say far easier.

Of course, when using statements as evidence of state practice it is necessary to look at the context and the manner in which they were made. Consideration must be given to whether they were made *de lege lata* (about the law that is in force) or *de lege ferenda* (about the law which it is desired to establish), 'against' or 'not against interest', or as trading ploys. Statements made *de lege lata* and against national interest are likely to provide more compelling evidence than those made *de lege ferenda* or supporting national interest. It is not always easy to discover a state's true motives behind statements. It may be argued that it is unnecessary to look at motives, since whatever a state feels or believes when making a statement, other states may come to rely on the statement and the original state may become estopped from altering its position.

A further question concerns whether written texts such as conventions, ILC drafts, resolutions, etc can be regarded as state practice. There seems no difficulty in regarding treaties as state practice, providing it is remembered that state practice must be accompanied by *opinio juris* for the creation of customary law. In the *North Sea Continental Shelf* cases the ICJ stated that 'a very widespread and representative participation in the convention might suffice of itself' for a conventional rule to generate customary law – but it seems clear that *opinio juris* has to be demonstrated beyond mere contractual obligation in such cases. Mere participation in a conference and votes on single draft rules possess little value as practice, although votes on the draft text are of much more use but usually only when accompanied by statements and explanations.

In the end, one of the main problems in evaluating the evidence for state practice is trying to ascertain what states actually do – their practice is not always consistent. For example if one were looking at the law relating to military intervention in the internal affairs of other states does one look at USSR practice in Afghanistan in 1980 which was denounced by the USA or at USA practice in Grenada in 1983 which was denounced by the USSR; how does one reconcile a reluctance to intervene militarily in 'Yugoslavia' with military action taken against Iraq? It is exactly this point that the critics of the traditional view of custom wish to explore further. They are concerned to try to identify the basis on which the ICJ and others applying international law make decisions about conflicting state practice.

One final point should be made here. Although discussion has been of 'state practice' this should not be taken to mean that it is only the behaviour of states which is of interest. The practice of international organisations and even of individuals may well be taken into account in the attempt to establish the existence of a rule of customary international law.

3.4.2.2 The extent of the practice

The formation and existence of a customary rule requires general state practice. In the *North Sea Continental Shelf* cases the ICJ postulated that 'state practice ... should ... have been extensive'. The term 'general' indicates that common and widespread practice is required, although universal practice is not necessary. It seems also that practice must be representative in the sense that all the major political and socio-economic systems should be involved in the widespread practice. This marks a shift away from the position before the First World War when Professor Westlake could argue that to prove the existence of a rule of custom:

> ... it is enough to show that the general consensus of opinion within the limits of European civilisation is in favour of the rule.[28]

If practice is not widespread or general it may still give rise to a local or regional customary rule/special rule, as was argued, unsuccessfully, in the *Asylum* case (1950). In that case, the ICJ held that before state practice could be acknowledged as law, it had to be in accordance with a constant and uniform usage practised by the states in question. The case concerned political asylum – after an unsuccessful rebellion in Peru one of the leaders was granted asylum in the Colombian embassy in Lima. Columbia sought a guarantee of safe conduct of the leader out of Peru which was refused. Columbia took the matter to the ICJ and asked for a ruling that Columbia, as the state granting asylum, was competent to qualify the offence for the purposes of granting asylum – it argued for the ruling on the basis of treaty provisions and American law in general – ie local/regional international custom. The court found that it was impossible to find any constant and uniform usage accepted as law. There was too much fluctuation and inconsistency.[29]

However inconsistency *per se* is not sufficient to negate the crystallisation of a rule into customary law – the inconsistency must be analysed and assessed in the light of such factors as subject matter, the identity of the states practising the inconsistency, the number of states involved and whether or not there are existing rules with which the alleged rule conflicts.

The practice of specially affected states is also often significant – for example in the *North Sea Continental Shelf* cases it was coastal states with a continental shelf which were specially affected; the practice of landlocked states was not significant. However, it is not true to say that if all affected states follow a particular practice then a rule of customary law comes into effect, since the practice of non-affected states may be sufficiently inconsistent to prevent the

---

28   Westlake, *International Law*, Part I, 1904, Cambridge: Cambridge University Press.
29   For a successful assertion of a local/special custom see the *Right of Passage* case [1960] *ICJ Rep* 6.

formation of a rule. It may be said that what is most significant is the adherence to a rule by all those states who had the opportunity to engage in such practice.

3.4.2.3 The practice of dissenting states and persistent objectors

If, and when, certain patterns of practice are emerging, or have emerged, states may wish to diverge or dissent from such practice. States may dissent from a customary rule from its inception onwards. The feasibility of such dissent was acknowledged by the ICJ in the *Anglo-Norwegian Fisheries* case (1951). The case concerned the manner in which Norway calculated its territorial sea and the Court found that Norway was not bound by the existing general rules of customary law relating to the matter. A persistent objector is not bound by the eventual customary rule if the state fulfils two conditions:

1   The objections must have been maintained from the early stages of the rule onwards, up to its formation and beyond.

2   The objections must have been maintained consistently, since the position of other states that may have come to rely on the position of the objector, has to be protected. The objector should not be able to rely on his own inconsistencies. Thus if a state objects and at other times invokes the rule, it will no longer be entitled to be regarded as a persistent objector. In all cases the persistent objector bears the burden of proving its exceptional position.

It may be that states dissent from a customary rule after its formation. Their position is untenable because other states have come to rely on the 'subsequent objector' originally conforming to the rule. Also, general customary law is binding on all states and cannot be the subject of any right of unilateral exclusion exercisable at will by any one state in its own favour. It should be noted, however, that a large number of subsequent objections may lead to desuetude or modification of the rule. It should also be noted that acquiescence over a period of time to an apparent breach of a general customary rule will lead to the result that the apparent breach cannot be challenged by those states acquiescing in it.

There has been some discussion regarding the situation of newly independent states. Such states have not participated in the creation of customary rules already in force when they come into existence, nor have they had any opportunity to oppose the rule's formation. It is open to the new state to contest the validity of customary rules or dispute their interpretation but it has no right to refuse to observe such rules, save in regard to those states which have expressly agreed to their waiver. When a new state begins to enter into relations with other states it must be taken to accept the rules of international law which are then in force. When a state applies for membership of the UN it must declare its acceptance of the principles of the Charter, the first purpose of which is the settlement of disputes 'in conformity with the principles of justice and international law' (Article 1(1)).

3.4.2.4 Duration of practice

In the *North Sea Continental Shelf* cases, the ICJ held that:

> Even without the passage of any considerable period of time, a very widespread and representative participation in the (practice) might suffice of itself ... Although the passage of only a short period of time is not necessarily, of itself, a

bar to the formation of a new rule of customary law ... within the period in question, short though it might be, state practice ... should have been both extensive and virtually uniform.

There is no set time limit and no demand that the behaviour should have existed since time immemorial. The relative unimportance of time was highlighted by the ICJ in the *North Sea Continental Shelf* cases. The cases involved the Federal Republic of Germany, Denmark and Holland and a dispute over the continental shelf. Denmark and Holland argued that the equidistance principle which was contained in the Convention on the Continental Shelf 1958 was customary law. The two states had argued that even if no customary rule existed at the time of the Convention, a rule had since come into being, partly as a result of the impact of the Convention, and partly on the basis of subsequent state practice. The Court was therefore required to look at the time requirement and it ruled, in rejecting their argument, that although the passage of only a short period of time is not necessarily, or of itself, a bar to the formation of a new rule of customary international law, an indispensable requirement would be that the practice of states whose interests are specially affected, should have been extensive and virtually uniform.

The length of time required to establish a rule of customary international law will therefore depend on other factors pertinent to the alleged rule. If, for example, the rule is dealing with subject matter about which there are no previously existing rules, then the duration of practice required is less than if there is an existing rule to be overturned. Time has also become less important as international communication has improved – it is much easier to assess a state's response to an alleged rule than it was in the past.

3.4.3   *The psychological element*

In addition to the material element an alleged rule of customary international law also requires a psychological element, otherwise known as *opinio juris sive necessitatis*. State practice must occur because the state concerned believes it is legally bound to behave in a particular way – customary law must be distinguished from mere usage. The Statute of the International Court refers to 'a general practice accepted as law'. The essential problem then becomes one of burden and standard of proof. The position is probably as follows – the proponent of a custom has to establish a general practice and, having done this, must show that the general practice is due to a feeling of legal obligation. In many cases the International Court has been willing to assume the existence of an *opinio juris* on the basis of evidence of a general practice, or the previous determinations of the Court or other international tribunals (for example in the *Gulf of Maine* case (1984)). However, in a significant minority of cases the Court has adopted a more rigorous approach and has called for more positive evidence of the recognition of the validity of the rules in question. The first occasion where such an approach was taken was in the *Lotus* case (1927) where the Court said:

Even if the rarity of the judicial decisions to be found among the reported cases were sufficient to prove in point of fact the circumstances alleged by the agent for the French government, it would merely show that states had often, in practice, abstained from instituting criminal proceedings, and not that they recognised themselves as being obliged to do so; for only if such abstention were based on their being conscious of a duty to abstain would it be possible to speak of an international custom. The alleged fact does not allow one to infer that the states have been conscious of having such a duty; on the other hand ... there are other circumstances calculated to show that the contrary is true.

More recently the ICJ stated:

> For a new customary rule to be formed, not only must the acts concerned amount to a settled practice, but they must be accompanied by the *opinio juris sive necessitatis*.[30]

The generally held view of customary law, which has been endorsed by the International Court of Justice,[31] is that the creation of a rule of customary international law postulates:

> ... two constitutive elements: (1) a general practice of states and (2) the acceptance by states of the general practice as law.[32]

> ...

The precise definition of the *opinio juris*, the psychological element in the formation of custom, the philosophers' stone which transmutes the inert mass of accumulated usage into the gold of binding legal rules, has probably caused more academic controversy than all the actual contested claims made by states on the basis of alleged custom, put together. A present-day writer may be understandably reluctant to call upon his readers to devote further time to this juridical squaring of the circle, but it is impossible to discuss the future of customary law without some study of the elements which are regarded as going to its making.

The simple equation of the *opinio juris* with the intention to conform to what is recognised, at the moment of conforming, as an existing rule of law has been exposed to the objection of Kelsen and others which, on its own terms, is unanswerable – that it necessarily implies a vicious circle in the logical analysis of the creation of custom. As a usage appears and develops, states may come to consider the practice to be required by law before this is in fact the case; but if the practice cannot become law until states follow it in the *correct* belief that it is required by law, no practice can ever become law, because this is an impossible condition. Nor does the avenue of escape indicated by the tag *communis error facit jus*, ie the argument that the belief, even the mistaken belief, of states in the existence of a rule of law requiring them to act, or refrain from acting, in a certain way, is sufficient to create the rule believed in, have many adherents.

The extreme opposite view, the theory that the establishment of international custom does not require *opinio juris* at all, but that established usage is sufficient without evidence of states of mind, has also comparatively few supporters.[33] As Professor Zemanek has observed,[34] while the requirement of *opinio juris* does

---

30 ICJ in *Nicaragua v US (Merits)* case (1986).

31 See particularly *Continental Shelf* cases [1969[*ICJ Rep* at p 44.

32 Schwarzenberger, *A Manual of International Law*, 1967, London: Stevens at p 32.

33 See for example, Kelsen, 'Théorie du droit international coutumier', *Revue internationale de la théorie du droit*, 1939, p 253ff; Guggenheim, *Lehrbuch des Volkerrechts*, 1948, pp 46–47; *Les deux éléments de la coutume en droit international*, Etudes en l'honneur de G Scelle, Vol 1, p 275; 'Principes de droit international public', 80 *Receuil des Cours*, 1952–I, at pp 70–72.

34 'Die Bedeutung der Kodifizierung des Volkerrechts für deine Anwerdung', in *Festschrift Verdross*, 1971, p 565 at p 574.

undoubtedly give rise to many problems in practice, particularly with regard to proof of its existence, to assert that it is wholly unnecessary is to 'throw out the baby with the bathwater'. Furthermore, it is admittedly difficult to distinguish between usage which has not (apart from cases, such as the *Right of Passage* case before the International Court of Justice,[35] in which the question is largely or entirely one of generality or consistency of practice), without allowing the psychological element in the creation of custom to creep back into the discussion by a devious route and under another name.[36]

A proposal for an interpretation of the traditional concept of the *opinio juris* which would not be subject to objection that it creates a *circulus inextricabilis* was advanced by Mr IC MacGibbon in 1957.[37] Mr MacGibbon starts by drawing attention to the importance of distinguishing between customary rules expressed as rights and customary rules expressed as obligations, and argues that the *opinio juris is* principally, if not wholly, of importance from the latter standpoint.

> It is only with difficulty that it can be conceived that a practice motivated by reasons of convenience or self-interest would have been initiated or evolved under the conviction on the part of the states participating that such a practice was in conformity with the law, far less that it was enjoined by the law, although such consideration may well apply to the formation of a customary obligation. To hold otherwise would be to suppose that the assertion of a claim, far from being made as of right or in a state of indifference as to whether or not it was in conformity with law, was made as a matter of duty.[38]

The distinction is of course a valid one, and it is perfectly correct that a state can hardly be supposed to believe that customary international law requires it to *assert* a certain claim, as opposed to requiring it to admit or recognise the claim of some other state, made in conformity with existing law. But the distinction as expressed by Mr MacGibbon is in fact an oversimplification of the problem: for the state which asserts a claim will be guided by what it believes to be the law in fixing the *extent* of its claim. The *opinio juris* in the traditional sense does therefore have a real existence and meaning on the side of the state which asserts a right, in that it claims as much and no more as it believes to be due to it,[39] that is to say, it does not *make* its claim because it believes that international law requires it to do so, but because it *limits* its claim because it believes that international law requires it to do so.[40]

The orthodox view is that a rule of customary law has two constitutive elements: (i) *corpus*, the material or objective element, and (ii) *animus*, the psychological or subjective element. The *corpus* of a rule of customary law is the existence of a usage (*consuetudo*) embodying a rule of conduct. The *animus* consists in the

---

35 *Right of Passage over Indian Territory (Merits)*, [1960] *ICJ Rep* at p 6.

36 *Cf* Tunkin, 'Remarks on the Juridical Nature of Customary Norms of International Law' (1961) 49 *Cal LR* p 419 at p 476, with reference to Guggenheim's paper (*op cit* n 28 above).

37 'Customary International Law and Acquiescence', 33 *BYIL* at p 115.

38 MacGibbon, *op cit* at pp 127–28.

39 Of course in practice a state may, and probably will, claim more than it thinks it is entitled to, in the form of a sort of percentage to allow for objections, but this does not affect the point made above.

40 HWA Thirlway, *International Customary Law and Codification*, 1972, Leiden: AW Sijthoff at pp 47–49.

conviction on the part of states that the rule embodied in the usage is binding (*opinio juris*). This view finds expression in Article 38(1)(b) of the Statute of the International Court of Justice which speaks of the Court applying 'international custom, being evidence of a general practice accepted as law'.

There is a school of thought, the principal exponent of which at present is doubtless Professor Guggenheim, which disputes the reality and consequently the requirement of the subjective element of *opinio juris*. But both the Permanent Court of International Justice and the International Court of Justice have in a number of cases stressed the importance of the subjective element of *opinio juris*. indeed, it should be perhaps pointed out that by the so-called 'psychological' element of *opinio juris*, it is intended to mean not so much the mental process or inner motive of a state when it performs or abstains from certain acts, but rather the *acceptance* or *recognition* of, or *acquiescence* in, the *binding character* of the rule in question implied in a state's action or omission. It is not without reason that the Statute of the World Court speaks of 'international custom, being evidence of a general practice *accepted* as law'.

However, Article 38(1)(b) of the Statute would have been even more correct if it had said 'international custom as evidenced by a general practice accepted as law', for it is not the custom or customary rule of international law which is evidence of the general practice, but rather the general practice accepted as law that provides evidence of the customary rule.

Indeed, it may be permissible to go further and say that the role of the usage in the establishment of rules of international customary law is purely evidentiary; it provides evidence on the one hand of the contents of the rule in question and on the other hand of the *opinio juris* of the states concerned. Not only is it unnecessary that the usage should be prolonged, but there need also be no usage at all in the sense of repeated practice, provided that the opinio juris of the states concerned can be clearly established. Consequently, international customary law has in reality only one constitutive element, the *opinio juris*. Where there is *opinio juris*, there is a rule of international customary law. It is true that in the case of a rule without usage, objection might be taken to the use of the term custom or customary. But whether in such a case one speaks of international customary law or an unwritten rule of international law becomes purely a matter of terminology.

It should, however, be pointed out that in municipal law it would ordinarily not be possible to have a legally binding custom without usage; for in municipal law it is not the *opinio juris* of individual subjects of the legal system that is decisive but the *opinio juris generalis* of the community, locality, trade or profession concerned as a whole. To this *opinio juris generalis* the general law of the community gives its blessing and lends the weight of its own authority. Such *opinio juris generalis* can normally be established and ascertained only through a general and usually also prolonged practice.

But in international law, the possibility of international customary law without usage becomes obvious if it is remembered that in international society states are their own law-makers. From the analytical point of view, the binding force of all rules of international law ultimately rests on their consent, recognition, acquiescence or the principle of estoppel. If states consider themselves bound by a given rule as a rule of international law, it is difficult to see why it should not be treated as such insofar as these states are concerned, especially when the rule does not infringe the right of a third state not sharing the same *opinio juris*. The *Asylum* case and the *Right of Passage* case have shown that it is possible for such *opinio juris* to exist among a limited number of states or even between two states so that, besides rules of universal international customary law, one finds also local and even bipartite international customary law.

From this point of view, there is no reason why an *opinio juris communis* may not grow up in a very short period of time among all or simply some members of the United Nations with the result that a new rule of international law comes into being among them. And there is also no reason why they may not use an Assembly resolution to 'positivise' their new common *opinio juris* ...

... when a General Assembly resolution proclaims principles recognised, albeit not long since, by members of the United Nations as principles of international law, and is adopted unanimously, it represents the law as generally accepted in the United Nations. In such an event, the binding force of these principles comes not from the resolution, but from their acceptance by member states as part of international law. They are, therefore, binding even before the resolution, although the resolution helps to establish their existence and contents.[41]

Discussion of custom usually takes place in the context of discourse about sources. For a positivist (and most international lawyers are more or less positivists today), what this means is process: we seek to identify the types of procedure which, if carried out by authorised actors, create law for members of the society in question ...

... What characterises [custom], above all, is its very lack of formality. So to discuss customary law in terms of elements, steps in its creation, and so on is to impose on it a framework which in a sense falsifies its nature. The problem is exacerbated by the modern jurist's unfamiliarity with customary law outside the international sphere. Not so very long ago, the general custom of the realm, the region, or the municipality was an important source of law throughout Europe, as well as in other places; but it came to be replaced by statute law and (to a greater or lesser extent) judicial precedent. True, customary law lingers on in parts of Africa and elsewhere, but even there it has become somewhat subordinated to the modern, 'Western' approach. So most commentators about the sources of international law slip easily into a formalistic mode of analysis without stopping to ask themselves whether the technique is suitable to the phenomenon under consideration. It is submitted that, *mutatis mutandis*, the study of domestic customary law societies, past and present, can afford useful insights into the nature of customary law ...

There is another methodological trap of which one should beware. Because in modern municipal societies jurisdiction is compulsory, it is at least feasible (if not wholly correct) to think of law in terms of what a judge will do; and in few areas is this more marked than in the doctrine of sources, where the question is often reduced to an investigation of what processes a judge would regard as capable of creating binding law. But it should not be forgotten that, in the international system, where jurisdiction is not compulsory, adjudication is the exception, not the rule. The more typical decision-maker is the government official, engaged either in advising his or her own government, or in negotiating with others. The difference in the observational standpoint has the following consequence for our topic. At least in theory, if the status of an alleged rule as customary law is challenged before a tribunal, the judge or arbitrator has to decide whether the processes for the creation of custom had been completed by the critical date.

---

41 Bin Cheng, 'United Nations Resolutions on Outer Space: "Instant" International Customary Law?', in Bin Cheng (ed), *International Law: Teaching and Practice*, 1982, London: Stevens at pp 249–52.

Government decision-makers, however, need not be so objective; whilst they may well want to find out how much support the practice has attracted up until now, if it is one which they wish to follow on its merits they will probably do so, even if the rule has not yet 'crystallised'...

Some identify the subjective element in custom as the state's will (or several or all states' will) that the practice become a rule of law: in other words, with consent to the (would-be) rule. Proponents of this, voluntarist, approach tend to equate the creation of custom with tacit agreement: just as treaties are the written, formal expression of states' will, so custom is its informal manifestation. Others reject the voluntarist thesis, preferring to regard the subjective element as a *belief* – a belief in the legally permissible or obligatory character (as the case may be) of the conduct in question: *opinio juris sive necessitatis*, or *opinio juris* as it is known for short.

The jurisprudence of the World Court has certainly failed to still the controversy, and proponents of both theories can cite judgments which expressly or impliedly support (or appear to support) their contentions ...

OPINIO JURIS SIVE NECESSITATIS

Literally, the phrase means 'belief (or opinion) of law or of necessity'. This does not make much sense in English, and in fact its clumsiness as a piece of Latin arouses the suspicion that it is not Roman at all. The present writer has not found it in the *Digest* or other classical writings on Roman law, and although the Glossators and post-Glossators have not been exhaustively combed through, the expression does not appear to have much of a pedigree in Roman law. The first person to use the complete phrase seems to have been Geny in 1919,[42] though, as Guggenheim noted,[43] one finds parts of the phrase or something like it in the writings of the German historical school in the late 18th and early 19th centuries. We shall return to the historical school later. So far as specifically international law is concerned, the expression does not seem to have been used by any of the so-called 'fathers' of international law, and the earliest use of the concept – though not the precise phrase – that the present writer has found in this context is in Rivier in 1896.[44] The idea was quickly adopted by many others, however.

It is quite common to dress up legal maxims and the like in Roman robes in order to give them an air of respectability, though only too often the toga can muffle thought. In this case, the robes seem not even to be genuine, and it is submitted that the linguistic incoherence of the phrase *opinio juris sive necessitatis* reflects a certain incoherence of the thought behind it.

What does *opinio juris sive necessitatis* mean, or what should it mean, in the context of international law? At this point, it may be helpful to offer a working translation or definition. It is *a belief in (or claim as to) the legally permissible or*

---

42 *Méthode d'interpretation et sources en droit privé positif,* 2nd edn, 1919, Paris: Librairie générale de droit et de jurisprudence at pp 319–24, 360.

43 'Contribution à l'histoire des sources du droit des gens' (1958–II) 94 *Recueil des Cours* pp 1, 52; *id,* 'L'origine de la notion de la *opinio juris sive necessitatis comme deuxième élément de la coutume dans l'histoire du droit des gens',* in *Hommage d'une génération de juristes au Président Basdevant,* 1960 at p 258.

44 *Principe du droit des gens,* Vol 1 p 35. But there are perhaps earlier hints of this in Savigny, *System des heutigen Römischen Rechts,* Vol 1, 1840, Heidelberg: Mohr at pp 32–34.

obligatory nature of the conduct in question,[45] *or of its necessity.* We shall return later to the part of the definition which refers to necessity.

On the subject of belief, it may also be convenient at this juncture to refer to an observation made by Virally,[46] and echoed by D'Amato[47] and Akehurst,[48] amongst others. We cannot know what states believe, it is suggested. First of all states, being abstractions or institutions, do not have minds of their own; and in any case, since much of the decision-making within governments takes place in secret, we cannot know what states (or those who direct or speak for them) really think, but only what they say they think. There may be something of an exaggeration here. In some instances, we can discover their views because the opinions of their legal advisers or governments are published.[49] Furthermore, it will be suggested later that the express or presumptive understandings and beliefs of the international community about the rules of international law are in certain circumstances relevant. We should not speak of a *psychological* element in custom, but of a *subjective* one, for it is more a question of the *positions* taken by the organs of state about international law, in their internal processes[50] and in their interaction with other states, than of their *beliefs*. This viewpoint is not unrelated to the well-known observation of McDougal that the customary process is one of claim and response, where the legal claims and the responses thereto can be implied in the conduct concerned without necessarily being expressed ...

45　The bipolar nature of legal relations means that if X has a legal right (eg to compensation), Y will have a duty to pay; and if X has a liberty (eg of innocent passage through Y's territorial sea), Y will have no right to complain and an obligation not to interfere with that passage. These ideas can be expressed in terms of obligatoriness and permissibility. *Cf* Mendelson 'State Acts and Omissions as Explicit or Implicit Claims', in *Le Droit international au service de la paix, de la justice et du développement*, 1991, Mélanges Michel Virally at p 373. It is hard to follow MacGibbon's suggestion that the role of *opinio juris* should be limited to positive conduct.

46　'The Sources of International Law' in Sorensen (ed), *Manual of Public International Law*, 1968, London: Macmillan at pp 116, 133–4.

47　*The Concept of Custom in International Law*, 1971, Ithaca: Cornell University Press at pp 35–39. This volume, which enjoyed a considerable vogue, particularly in the United States, for some years after its publication, propounds a number of unconventional ideas, but unfortunately not a few of them seem unfounded or overstated. Reasons of space preclude a complete examination here, but among these questionable ideas are the following. (1) The equation or substitution of *opinio juris* with a theory of articulation, whereby if any entity, be it a state, international organisation, or scholar, has articulated what it, he or she considers to be a new rule of customary law, and that articulation is followed at any time thereafter by an act of state practice – apparently even a single one – then that will found the rule, even if the state which performed the act made no connection between its own conduct and the articulation by another – so long as it was aware of it, or had reason to be (pp 74–87). (2) So far as concerns the material element, the author appears to consider that treaty promises constitute (without more) qualifying state practice, but unilateral acts, such as legislation, cannot – a strange reversal (pp 89–91). (3) A mechanistic form of reasoning (pp 91–8) leads him to suggest that just two precedents can constitute a (*semble general*) customary rule. This seems far too crude. *A fortiori* the suggestion that, in litigation, a single precedent might well suffice. (4) The legal significance of protest is downgraded (pp 98–102) in a manner belied by the practice of states and the decisions of international tribunals.

48　'Custom as a Source of International Law' (1974–75) *BYIL* 47 p 1 at pp 36–37.

49　Though admittedly this is done only on a partial and selective basis and often only long after the event, and though it must also be conceded that the opinion of a legal adviser does not invariably become that of the government.

50　Including the communication of governments to national legislatures and courts, and the express or implicit *prises de position* about rules of international law by national courts and legislatures in the exercise of their functions.

Summary and conclusions

1   A state's consent to a rule will be a sufficient explanation of its being bound by it, and its refusal at the formative stage of a rule a reason why it is (probably) not bound. But the voluntarist approach does not provide a satisfactory explanation of the whole of customary law. In particular, it does not provide a convincing reason why states who have not truly participated in the formation of a rule should be bound by it – though undoubtedly they are.

2   *Opinio juris sive necessitatis*, for its part, is a phrase of dubious provenance and uncertain meaning. The concept was originally used by the historical school of jurisprudence to explain the content of substantive national law, and was transferred to the context of international law around the turn of the present century. It does have a role to perform in explaining why certain types of conduct constitute mere comity or otherwise do not count as precedents. It is not certain, however, that these functions could not be as well or better performed by using the language of claim and response.

3   In any case, there seems analytically to be no particular reason to insist on proof of the presence of *opinio juris* in the standard type of case, where there is a constant, uniform and unambiguous practice of sufficient generality, clearly taking place in a legal context and unaccompanied by disclaimers, with no evidence of opposition at the time of the rule's formation by the state which it is sought to burden with the customary obligation, or by another state or group of states sufficiently important to have prevented as general rule coming into existence at all.

The adoption of the present thesis would bring doctrine more into line with the practice of states and of international tribunals than the mechanical repetition of the necessity of the two elements. As a matter of theory, too, it is submitted that this approach could be justified in terms of the creation of legitimate expectations. This is not the place for a complete explanation of this author's theory of legitimate expectations which underlie the sources of international law. Perhaps it will suffice for the present to say that if a state actually consents to a rule, a legitimate expectation will be created that it will comply with it, just as a disclaimer or persistent dissent at the appropriate time will prevent such an expectation being created. And where there is a constant and uniform practice of sufficient generality, in a legal context, it seems legitimate for members of the community to expect all others to continue to observe that practice. And finally, as a matter of policy, the solution proposed seems a reasonable one. If a relevant practice is sufficiently widespread, it ought to become law, because otherwise the convoy will have to move at the pace of the slowest. To require proof of consent – or even *opinio juris* on the part of each and every state – seems excessive and unnecessary. At the same time, the sovereignty and the reasonable interests of states can be safeguarded. If a sufficient number of like-minded states object to a new practice, they can prevent it from ever becoming general law. And in addition, the individual state can individually opt out, at the formative stage, by becoming a persistent objector. By these means, customary law can continue to make a useful contribution to the formation of international law; and given that the treaty process has disadvantages as well as advantages, it is essential that custom continues to make that contribution.[51]

---

51 M Mendelson, 'The Subjective Element in customary International Law' (1995) 66 *BYIL* at pp 177, 178–81, 194–96, 207–8.

3.4.4 *Treaties as evidence of customary law*

The issue here is the extent to which a multilateral treaty can be used as evidence of customary international law. It is a general rule of international law which is confirmed in Article 34 of the Vienna Convention on the Law of Treaties 1969 that treaties cannot bind third parties without their consent. If a state wishes to enforce the provisions of a treaty against a non-party it is necessary to argue that the provisions of the treaty are valid as rules of customary international law. Two possible situations arise:

1   Where the treaty is intended to be declaratory of existing customary international law;

2   Where the treaty is constitutive of new law.

If the treaty on its face purports to be declaratory of customary international law or if it can be established that it was intended to be declaratory of customary international law, then it may be accepted as valid evidence of the state of the customary rule. If the treaty at the time of its adoption was constitutive of new rules of law, then the party relying on the treaty as evidence of customary law will have the burden of establishing that the treaty has subsequently been accepted into custom.

The ICJ in the *North Sea Continental Shelf* cases recognised that it is possible for a treaty to contain norm-creating provisions which become accepted by the *opinio juris* and bind non-parties just as much as parties to the convention but the court did lay down a series of conditions:

1   The convention provision must be of a fundamentally norm-creating character such as could be regarded as forming the basis of a general rule of law;

2   There must be widespread and representative participation in the convention particularly of those states whose interests are specifically affected;

3   There must be *opinio juris* reflected in extensive state practice virtually uniform in the sense of the provision invoked.

The following point should also be noted:

> Since treaties and custom are on the same footing, it follows that the relations between rules generated by the two sources are governed by those general principles which in all legal orders govern the relations between norms deriving from the same source: *lex posterior derogat priori* (a later law repeals an earlier law), *lex posterior generalis non derogat priori speciali* (a later law, general in character does not derogate from an earlier law which is special in character), and *lex specialis derogat generali* (a special law prevails over a general law).[52]

3.5   General principles of law

> The general object, then, of inserting the phrase ['general principles of law recognised by civilised nations'] in the statute seems to have been, essentially, to make it clear that the Court was to be permitted to reason, though not to

---

52   Cassese, *International Law in a Divided World*, 1986 Oxford: Clarendon Press at p 180.

legislate, and by, for instance, the application of analogies from the law within the state, to avoid ever having to declare that there was no law applicable to any question coming before it. This was a problem which troubled the Continental jurists who assisted in the drafting of the Statute, but did not trouble the Anglo-Saxons, who of course expected judges to reason without express instructions.[53]

The prevailing view as to the meaning of Article 38(1)(c) is that it authorises the Court to apply the general principles of municipal jurisprudence, in particular of private law, in as far as they are applicable to the relations of states. It is not thought to refer to principles of international law itself, which are to be derived from custom or treaty. International tribunals will often refer to 'well-known' or 'generally recognised' principles such as the principle of the independence and equality of states. Such principles do not come within Article 38(1)(c).

> [General principles] are, in the first instance, those principles of law, private and public, which contemplation of the legal experience of civilised nations leads one to regard as obvious maxims of jurisprudence of a general and fundamental character – such as the principle that no one may be judge in his own cause, that a breach of legal duty entails the obligation of restitution, that a person cannot invoke his own wrong as a reason for release from legal obligation, that the law will not countenance the abuse of a right, that legal obligations must be fulfilled and rights must be exercised in good faith, and the like.[54]

No decision of the Court, or indeed the Permanent Court, has yet been based explicitly upon a principle or rule of law drawn from the 'general principles of law recognised by civilised nations' referred to in Article 38, para 1(c) of the Statute.[55] It is comparatively rare for a state to base a claim before the Court on such principles, so that it is correspondingly infrequent for the Court to have occasion to refer to them for the purposes of its decision. Even where referred to

---

53 Clive Parry, *The Sources and Evidences of International Law*, 1965, Manchester: Manchester University Press at p 83.

54 Lauterpacht, *International Law*, Vol 1, 1970, Cambridge: Cambridge University Press at p 69.

55 A member of the Court has however gone on record, in an extra-judicial capacity, to the following effect:

'The silence observed in this matter by them International Court of Justice or other international tribunals must [not] be misinterpreted as any neglect of the importance of examining the common grounds of national systems. However, as far as my experience goes, basic principles common to national legal systems are not normally disputed. The *jus gentium* applied by the Roman *praetor peregrinus* is still a reality. The main question is, however, how a generally accepted principle can provide an appropriate solution in the actual case under consideration. Studies of national legislations which have been submitted to the Court in the past are very helpful in clarifying the concepts and solutions found in national law, but usually they cannot offer precise criteria for the application and interpretation of international law in the given case. The presentation of the various solutions of national legislations paraphrasing the basic principle involved, would often not be in conformity with the style of a judgment, the reasoning of which must proceed in a continuous chain of thought and argument to the operative part. I admit, however, that it would be welcomed not only by the parties but also by the international legal world if the reasoning of judgments and advisory opinions were to explain that the Court had examined, by comparative methods, the assertion – sometimes boldly stated – that a general principle of law, having a specified meaning and significance, forms part of binding general international law': Mosler, 'To what extent does the variety of legal systems of the world influence the application of general principles of law within the meaning of Article 38(1)(c) of the Statute of the International Court of Justice?', *International Law and the Grotian Heritage*, 1985, The Hague: TMC Asser Instituut at p 180.

by a party to proceedings, the general principles tend to be employed as something of a makeweight or last resort, a supplementary argument in case the contentions based on customary law or treaties fail to convince: with the result that the Court hardly ever needs to refer to them. On the other hand, individual Members of the Court invoke general principles more frequently: Judge Ammoun was particularly attached to them, though he had strong objections to the use in the Statute of the term 'civilised nations'.

...

It is fairly well established that the general principles contemplated by Article 38, para 1(c) of the Statute are at least primarily those which reveal themselves in the consistent solutions to a particular problem adopted in the various systems of municipal law – what Mr Elihu Root called, during the discussions of the 1920 Committee of Jurists, those which were 'accepted by all nations *in foro domestico*'.[56] It is necessary, though not always easy, to distinguish these principles from, on the one hand, what Sorensen has called *'les principes fondamentaux de la structure du droit international'*[57] ... and from, on the other hand, mere arguments from analogy by reference to institutions or rules found in one or more systems of municipal law. These discussions were the subject of much argument between the parties in the *Right of Passage* case.[58]

The general principles of law recognised by civilised nations' form part of the law to be applied by the permanent forum of the family of nations, the International Court of Justice ...

[Article 38 of the Statute of the International Court of Justice] is the same as Article 38 of the Statute of the Permanent Court of International Justice, except for an alteration in the numbering of the paragraphs and sub-paragraphs[59] and the addition of a few words of no great practical importance in the introductory phrase. The mention of 'general principles of law recognised by civilised nations' (*'les principes generaux de droit reconnus par les nations civilisées'*) as part of the law to be applied by the Permanent Court of International Justice at once provoked considerable discussion among writers, in which the most divergent views on the character of such principles were expressed.

Some writers consider that the expression refers primarily to general principles of international law and only subsidiarily to principles obtaining in the municipal law of the various states.[60] Others hold that it would have been

---

56　*Procès-verbal* of the Committee, p 335.

57　*Les Sources du droit international*, p 116. The interpretation of Article 38(1)(c) as restricted to principles derivable from municipal law recognition does not of course signify the exclusion of other general principles form the corpus of law applicable by the Court. Mosler, following Anzilotti, observes that the more basic principles need no transformation into international law, whereas the principles commonly accepted in municipal systems do need to be so transformed, hence the inclusion of Article 38(1)(c) in the Statute: *'Bedeutungswandel in der Anwendung "der van den zivilisierten Staaten annerkannten allgemeinen Rechtgrundsatze"'*, *Pensamiento juridico y sociedad internacional*, 1986, Madrid: Melanges Treyol Serra at pp 7–76.

58　H Thirlway, 'The Law and Procedure of the International Court of Justice 1960–1989' Part Two (1990) 61 *BYIL* at pp 110, 114.

59　In the Statute of the PCIJ the paragraphs were not numbered, while the sub-paragraphs were numbered by arabic figures. The present Art 38 1(c) was, therefore, referred to, under the old statute, as Art 38 I 3, or often Art 38 3. For the sake of convenience, the new numbering will be used in this work even when referring to the Statute of the PCIJ.

60　Anzilotti, (1929) 1 *Cours de Droit International* at p 117. Hudson, *The PCIJ 1920–42*, 1943, New York: Macmillan at p 611. Castberg *'La methodologie du droit international public,'* (1933) 43 *Recueil La Haye* p 313 at p 370 *et seq*. Morellie *'La théorie générale du procès international'*, 61 *ibid*, p 253 at p 344 *et seq*.

redundant for the Statute to require the Court to apply general principles of international law, and that, therefore, this provision can refer only to principles obtaining in municipal law.[61] Some writers even maintain that the expression is intended to refer exclusively to principles of private law.[62]

A difference of opinion also exists as to whether 'the general principles of law recognised by civilised nations' are or are not principles of natural law. While certain authors think they are, others deny categorically that they have any connection with natural law. A leading exponent of the modern doctrine of natural law believes, however, that while they are not actually principles of natural law, they are derived from it.[63]

Nor do authors agree as to whether 'general principles of law' are part of the international legal order, simply because it is a legal order, or because there exists a rule of customary international law according to which such principles are applicable in international relations. Moreover, some writers maintain that 'general principles of law' do not form part of the law to be applied by the World Court by virtue of the enabling provision in its Statute.

The greatest conflict of views concerns the part played in international law by these 'general principles'. While some writers regard them merely as a means for assisting the interpretation and application of international treaty and customary law, and others consider them as no more than a subsidiary source of international law, some modern authors look upon 'general principles' as the embodiment of the highest principles – the 'superconstitution' of international law.

Interesting though this discussion of the character of such 'general principles' may be in the theory of international law, it is even more important to know what they in fact represent. For this reason, the purpose of the present study is not to ascertain what they ought to be theoretically, or how they should be classified, but is primarily intended to determine what they are in substance and the manner in which they have been applied by international tribunals.

As an introduction to this study, the genesis of Article 38(1)(c) of the Statute of the World Court may usefully be examined. In February 1920 at its second meeting, the Council of the League of Nations appointed an Advisory Committee of Jurists for the purpose of preparing plans for the establishment of

---

61 Strupp, 'Le droit de juge international de statuer selon l'équité' 33 ibid (1930) p 357 at pp 474–75. Scerni, I principi generali di diretto riconosciuti dala nazioni civili, 1932, p 13 et seq.

62 Cf Lauterpacht, Private Law Sources and Analogies of International Law, 1927, Cambridge: Cambridge University Press at p 71: 'Those general principles of law are for the most practical purposes identical with general principles of private law.' See also ibid, p 85. For a criticism of this exclusive approach, see Le Fur, 'Règles générales du droit de la paix' (1935) 54 Recueil La Haye p 5 at pp 206–07. In his The Function of Law in the International Community, 1933, Lauterpacht admitted that they included also general principles of public law, general maxims and principles of jurisprudence.

Graspin, Valeur internationale des principaux generaux du droit, 1934, pp 64–66. Ripert 'Règles du droit civil applicables aux rapports internationaux (1933) 44 Recueil La Haye at p 569. Ripert believed that they were principles of municipal law (jus civile of the Romans): he seemed to have allowed it subsequently to assume its modern meaning of private law by tracing the evolution of the meaning of the term in France (p 583). His main object, however, was to ascertain which principles of private law were really principles applicable in all legal systems (p 569) and he did not appear to maintain that the latter were exclusively to be found in private law.

63 Le Fur, 'La coutume et les principes generaux du droit comme sources du droit international public', (1936) 3 Recueil Geny p 362 at p 368. The relevant passage was almost textually reproduced in the same authors 'Règles generales etc' loc cit p 205.

the Permanent Court of International Justice provided for in Article 14 of the Covenant of the League of Nations. This Advisory Committee held its meetings from June 16 to July 24, 1920 and was able to present its Report together with the Draft Statute of the Court to the Council of the League at its eighth session (July 30–August 5, 1920).

Before the Advisory Committee actually met, a Memorandum was submitted to it by the Secretariat of the League of Nations, together with a number of draft schemes prepared by states and individuals, relating to the establishment of a World Court. In so far as the law to be applied by the Court was concerned, it will be found that none of these drafts took a positivist[64] or voluntarist[65] view. Besides treaties and established rules, the Court was according to these various drafts directed to apply 'general principles of law,'[66] 'general principles of law and equity,'[67] 'general principles of justice and equity,'[68] or even 'rules which, in the considered opinion of the Court, should be the rules of international law'.[69]

It was, therefore, quite in line with these drafts, which may be considered as a fair indication of the general opinion on the subject, that, when the question of the law to be applied by the Court came up for discussion in the Advisory Committee of Jurists, Baron Descamps, Chairman of the Committee, proposed that, after conventions (clause 1) and commonly recognised custom (clause 2), the Court should apply 'the rules of international law as recognised by the legal conscience of civilised nations' (clause 3), or, as they were described in the original French version of the proposal *'les règles de droit international telles que les reconnaît la conscience juridique des peuples civilisés.'*

Mr Elihu Root, the American member of the Committee, whilst not objecting to the application by the Court of conventions and recognised custom (ie clauses 1 and 2 of the Descamps proposal) said that he 'could not understand the exact meaning of clause 3'. He wondered whether it was possible to compel states to submit their disputes to a court 'which would administer not merely law but also what it deems to be the conscience of civilised peoples'.

It may be apposite to point out here that although some words, which are identically spelt in French and English, can be literally transposed from one language into the other, others carry subtle but important differences in meaning in the two languages so that literal transposition becomes impossible. Thus the word *'conscience'*, which exists in both English and French, while it often conveys the same meaning in both languages, does not invariably do so. 'Conscience' has

---

64 As used in this work, 'positivism' denotes that school of thought which consider that law 'properly so called' consists only of rules derived from a 'determinate source' or, in other words, rendered 'positive' by means of a formal process.

65 As used in this work 'voluntarism' denotes that school of thought which emphasises the element of will in the formation of legal norms, either the will of the state, in the form of a command, or the will of the subjects, as manifested by consent.

66 Draft scheme of Denmark, Norway and Sweden, Art 27 II.

67 German Draft Scheme, Art 35. Clovia Bevilaqua's Draft scheme, Art 24 II. Bevilaqua's second category of rules is in fact customary international law.

68 Article 42 of the Swiss Draft Scheme establishes the following three categories: conventions, principles of international law, and the general principles of justice and equity. Article 12 of the Draft of the *Union Juridique Internationale* directs the court to apply 'law, justice and equity'.

69 Draft Scheme of Denmark, Norway and Sweden, Art 27 II (Alternative) Danish Draft Scheme, Art 15 II, Norwegian Draft Scheme, Art 15 II, Swedish Draft Scheme, Art 17 II, Draft Scheme of the Five Neutral Powers (Denmark, Norway, Netherlands, Sweden, Switzerland), Art 2 II.

acquired in current English usage a primarily moral and introspective connotation – the sense of what is *morally* right or wrong possessed by an individual or a group *as regards things for which the individual himself,* or the group collectively, *is responsible.*

In French *'conscience'* denotes also 'the sense of what is right or wrong', but not necessarily what is *morally* right or wrong. For instance, the French speak of *'liberté de conscience'* for 'freedom of belief', thus distinguishing *'conscience réligeuse'* from *'conscience morale'.* It follows that *'conscience juridique'* is equally distinguishable from *'conscience morale'.* It is a familiar expression with French jurists, meaning 'the sense of what is juridically right or wrong'.

Furthermore, although *'conscience'* in French also implies the passing of judgment upon human actions and motives, it does not invariably mean an introspective judgment upon one's own actions and motives. Thus *'conscience publique'* in French merely means 'the people's sense of what is right or wrong' without necessarily implying self-judgment.

For these reasons, the phrase *'la conscience juridique des peuples civilisés'* which figured in the Descamps proposal may be translated into English as 'the sense common to all civilised peoples[70] of what is juridically right or wrong', or as 'the *opinio juris communis* of civilised mankind'.

The literal translation of the phrase by 'the conscience of civilised nations' would seem to have a different meaning in English, namely 'the moral sense of right or wrong possessed by each civilised nation as regards things for which it is responsible'. And, since 'conscience' in English denotes an essentially moral quality, the original English translation of the Descamps proposal which spoke of the 'legal conscience of civilised nations', is, if not self-contradictory, at least as difficult to understand, as, indeed, Mr Root found it.

The reason why Mr Root at first objected to the Descamps proposal was certainly more substantial than one arising from a linguistic misunderstanding but a proper understanding of the original proposal is nevertheless important.

An examination of the various proposals put forward and opinions expressed during the discussion, concerning the rules of law to be applied by the Court, discloses five distinct views:

(1) First, a group of proposals refrained from indicating to the Court which rules of law it was to apply.

(2) Secondly, the various Scandinavian drafts and that of the five neutral powers inspired by the Swiss Civil Code directed the Court to apply conventions and recognised rules of international law, and, in default of such rules, to apply what, in its considered opinion, the rule of international law on the subject

---

70 It should be noticed that the original proposal of Descamps referred to *'peuples civilisés'*, ie 'civilised peoples' or 'civilised mankind'. This is important, because the expressions 'civilised nations' and *'nations civilisés'* which are now found in the English and French text of Art 38 1(c) originate from Root's amendment to the Descamps proposal. This amendment referred to 'civilised nations' which was the English translation used by the Committee of Jurists for Descamps' *'peuples civilisés'.* In fact, the earlier translation of the Root amendment also used *'peuples civilisés'* in the French version. Looked at from this angle, the word 'nation' in Art 38 1(c) should be understood not in its politico-legal sense, as it is used in the 'League of Nations' 'United Nations' or 'International Law' but in its more general sense of a people, as for instance, the Scottish nation, the French nation, the Maori nation, etc. Some further support for this view may be found in the fact that, at certain stages of the drafting of the article, the word nation in clause 3 was written with a small n, while the same word in clause 4 in the sense of a country was written with a capital N.

ought to be. The latter part of this proposal was regarded as conferring on the Court a legislative power, and, since all the members of the Committee were in agreement that a Court should not legislate, this formula did not find any favour.

(3)   Thirdly, there was the proposal of Baron Descamps, which was supported by M Loder and M Hagerup and received no serious opposition except from Mr Elihu Root. In order to appreciate how much this view coincides with the fifth view which was that of Lord Phillimore's, it must be realised that, in his proposal, Baron Descamps defined international custom as *'pratique commune des nations, acceptée par elles comme loi'*. As such, his conception of custom was much more restrictive than Lord Phillimore's. According to the Descamps formula, both the *consuetudo* and the *opinio juris*, the two constitutive elements of a custom, have to be common to all nations. Adopting so stringent a view of international custom, it is not surprising that Baron Descamps should classify another portion of international law under a third heading, *'les règles de droit international telles que les reconnait la conscience juridique des peuples civilisés'*. While he conceived these as rules of objective justice, he limited the formula to what the *opinio juris communis* of the civilised world considered as rules of international law. These rules of objective justice Baron Descamps also called 'general principles of law', and, as an illustration of the principles he had in mind, he cited the case of the application of the principle of *res judicata* in the *Pious Fund* case by the Permanent Court of Arbitration.

(4)   Fourthly, there was the original view of Mr Root who seemed ready to admit only clauses 1 and 2 of the Descamps proposal, and even entertained some doubt as to clause 2 concerning the application by the Court of commonly recognised custom. The position originally adopted by this distinguished American statesman, who had contributed so much to the establishment of the Permanent Court of International Justice, was, however, actuated more by an earnest wish to see the Statute accepted by all countries than by a strict adherence to juridical principles. In this connection, it should be borne in mind that, at the time, the Advisory Committee had agreed in principle that the compulsory jurisdiction of the Court should be accepted by all the members of the League of Nations by the very fact of adhering to the Statute of the Court. Mr Root rightly linked this aspect of the question with the rules concerning the application of law. However unconnected they may be from a juridical standpoint, their relation is certainly real and substantial from the point of view of states called upon to submit to the jurisdiction of the Court. A restrictive formula with regard to the law to be applied would, in Mr Root's opinion, have facilitated the acceptance of the step forward in the field of jurisdiction. He was, therefore, disposed to accept the Descamps proposal in respect of all the Court's jurisdiction other than its compulsory jurisdiction. He was even disposed to accept it, where the Court had compulsory jurisdiction, so long as the dispute concerned the extent and nature of reparation for breach of an obligation, or the interpretation of judgments, but he was not prepared to accept it where the dispute concerned questions of international law in general.

(5)   Finally, there was Lord Phillimore's amended text of the Descamps proposal, elaborated in conjunction with Mr Root, which was in fact the text adopted by the Advisory Committee. On closer examination, Lord Phillimore's views were not so different from Baron Descamps. His attitude with regard to the rules concerning the law to be applied was even more liberal than that of Baron Descamps; for he was ready to allow that, in the absence of treaty law,

the Court should apply the rules of international law in force 'from whatever source they may be derived'. But, even on the assumption that, by this formula, Lord Phillimore intended the only alternative to treaty law to be customary law, his conception of international custom was much more liberal than that of Baron Descamps; for he declared that 'generally speaking, all the principles of common law are applicable to international relations. they are in fact part of international law.' He considered the example cited by Baron Descamps to illustrate *'les règles de droit international telles que les reconnait la conscience juridique des peuples civilisés'*, namely the principle of *res judicata* as one of the principles of common law. 'This', he said, 'is a principle which has the same character of law as any formulated rule'. In other words, there are principles of international law in force which have not yet assumed the form of formulated rules. Indeed when questioned by Baron Descamps Lord Phillimore agreed that international law as understood by him resembled natural law. Theoretical niceties apart, there is, therefore, little practical difference between the views of Baron Descamps who held that international law included certain principles of objective justice and the views of Lord Phillimore who held that international law included all the principles of common law, which itself resembled natural law. Furthermore, Lord Phillimore declared himself generally in agreement with M Ricci-Busatti who has said that the Court should apply 'general principles of law'. It is indeed, in this formula that the views of Baron Descamps and Lord Phillimore found their common denominator.

When, therefore, at the 15th meeting of the Committee (3 July 1920) the formula 'the general principles of law recognised by civilised nations' in lieu of the original clause 3 was actually proposed by Mr Root, who had in collaboration with Lord Phillimore prepared an amended text to the Descamps proposal, it was immediately agreed to by Baron Descamps and the rest of the committee. This is the origin of the present Article 38(1)(c) of the Statute of the International Court of Justice.[71]

DRAFT CODE OF GENERAL PRINCIPLES OF LAW

Article 1   Good faith shall govern relations between states.

In particular, every state shall fulfil its obligations and exercise its rights in good faith.

Article 2   A state is responsible for any failure on the part of its organs to carry out the international obligations of the state, unless the failure is due to *vis major*.

Vis major, in order to relieve a state of its obligations, must be of such a nature as to make it impossible for the state to fulfil that obligation, and this impossibility must not be imputable to the state itself.

Article 3   Responsibility involves an obligation on the part of the state concerned to make integral reparation for the damage caused, in so far as it is the proximate result of the failure to comply with the international obligation.

The state shall, wherever possible, make restitution in kind. If this is not possible, a sum corresponding to the value which restitution in kind would bear shall be paid. Whenever restitution in kind, or

---

71   Bin Cheng, *General Principles of Law as applied by International Courts and Tribunals*, 1993, Cambridge: Cambridge University Press at pp 1–14.

payment in lieu of it, does not cover the entire loss suffered, damages shall be paid in order that the injured party is fully compensated.

The damage suffered shall be deemed to be the proximate result of an act if it is the normal and natural consequence thereof, or if it would have been foreseen by a reasonable man in the position of the author of the act, or if it is the intended result of the act.

Article 4   Any claim by one state against another shall be deemed invalid if the claimant state has, by its own negligence, failed to present the claim for so long as to give rise to a danger of mistaking the truth.

Article 5   Every tribunal has the power, in the first instance, to determine the extent of its jurisdiction, in the absence of express provision to the contrary.

Article 6   The jurisdiction of a tribunal extends to all relevant matters incidental to the principal question in respect of which it is competent, in the absence of express provisions to the contrary.

Article 7   Parties to a dispute are disqualified from acting as judges or arbitrators in such a dispute.

Where a judge or arbitrator is the national of, or has been selected by, one of the parties to the dispute, he shall not consider himself as an agent of that party, but must decide the case submitted to him impartially without fear or favour.

Article 8   In judicial proceedings, the tribunal shall ensure that both parties have an adequate and equal opportunity to be heard.

Article 9   The above provision shall not affect the right of the tribunal to decide by default, if one of the parties, without valid reason, fails to appear before the tribunal, or to defend his case.

In such an event the tribunal must decide according to the merits of the case, after satisfying itself that it has jurisdiction.

Article 10   The tribunal shall, within the limits of its jurisdiction, examine points of law *proprio motu*, without being limited to the arguments of the parties.

Article 11   Parties to a case must abstain from any act which might aggravate or extend the dispute and, in particular, from any measure calculated to have a prejudicial effect in regard to the carrying out of the decision to be given.

Article 12   The decision of an international tribunal is final. Any question which has been resolved by a valid and final decision may not be reopened between the same parties.

Article 13   The decision of an international tribunal is binding only upon the parties to the dispute.

Decisions on incidental or preliminary questions are only binding upon the parties to the dispute.

Article 14   A judgment may be annulled:

(a) if the tribunal which gave the judgment lacked jurisdiction or exceeded its jurisdiction;

(b) if the tribunal, or any member thereof is proved to have been guilty of fraud or corruption in connection with the particular case; or

(c) if the tribunal failed to give both parties an equal and adequate opportunity to be heard.

Article 15 A judgment may be revised on the grounds of:

(a) manifest and essential error;

(b) after-discovered evidence; or

(c) fraud of the parties or collusion of witnesses.

Article 16 A tribunal may annul or revise its own judgment, either *proprio motu*, or on the application of one of the parties, for any of the reasons mentioned in the two preceding Articles provided that it still has jurisdiction over the dispute.[72]

3.5.1 Some examples

A number of decisions of the International Court help illustrate the nature of 'general principles'. In the *Chorzow Factory (Jurisdiction)* case, the Permanent Court enunciated the principle that:

> ... one party cannot avail himself of the fact that the other has not fulfilled some obligation, or has not had recourse to some means of redress, if the former party has, by some illegal act, prevented the latter from fulfilling the obligation in question, or from having recourse to the tribunal which would be open to him.[73]

Later on in the same case, the Court observed:

> ... that it is a principle of international law, and even a general conception of law, that any breach of an engagement involves an obligation to make reparation.[74]

In a number of cases the International Court has made use of the doctrine of estoppel as recognised by a number of municipal legal systems. Perhaps the clearest example came in the *Temple* case involving Thailand (formerly Siam) and Cambodia, formerly part of French Indo-China. The two states were in dispute over a section of the frontier. Cambodia successfully relied on a map of 1907 which the predecessor French authorities had produced at the request of the Siamese Government. The map clearly showed the Temple area as part of French Indo-China. The Siamese authorities, far from protesting at the error, had thanked the French for preparing the map and requested a number of copies. Furthermore, in 1930, a Siamese prince paid a state visit to the disputed area and was officially received there by the French authorities. Together, these two events were seen by the International Court as conclusive and it found that Thailand was precluded by its conduct from denying the frontier indicated on the map.[75]

Other principles considered by the Court have included the right to bring class actions (*actio popularis*)[76] and the doctrine of corporate personality in the *Barcelona Traction, Light and Power Company Limited* case.[77]

---

72 Bin Cheng, *General Principles of Law as applied by International Courts and Tribunals*, 1993, Cambridge: Cambridge University Press at Appendix I.

73 *Chorzow Factory (Jurisdiction)* case PCIJ Ser A, No 9 (1927).

74 *Chorzow Factory (Merits)* case (1928) PCIJ Ser A, No 17 (1928).

75 *Temple of Preah Vihear* [1962] ICJ Rep at p 1.

76 *South West Africa* case [1950] ICJ Rep at p 128.

77 [1970] ICJ Rep at p 3.

3.5.2 Equity

Amongst these general principles it could be argued that equity, in the sense of justice and fairness, is included and in a number of cases it has been used indirectly to affect the way in which substantive law is applied. The application of equity as a general principle should not be confused with Article 38(2) which states that if both parties to a dispute agree, the court can decide a case *ex aequo et bono*, ie the court can apply equity in precedence to all other legal rules.

> During the period under review [1960–1989] there has been a striking increase in references to equity in the work of the Court – not only in the pleadings of the parties, but in the judgments themselves; so much so that one observer has felt able to declare that 'after 50 years of hesitation the World Court has clearly accepted equity as an important part of the law that it is authorised to apply'.[78] Concepts of equity have certainly had a very extensive influence in one particular domain – that of the delimitation of maritime areas; but it is probably premature to see in the decisions of the Court even in that specific field the application of any consistent and mature theory of equity. In matters unconnected with maritime delimitation, equity has been referred to and applied sporadically, but in ways which paradoxically are easier to reconcile with classical concepts of equity than the specialised use of it in disputes of maritime areas.[79]

The ICJ itself has on a number of occasions indicated that it considers the principles of equity to constitute an integral part of international law. In the *Diversion of Water from the Meuse* case (1937), Judge Hudson declared:

> What are widely known as principles of equity have long been considered to constitute a part of international law, and as such they have often been applied by international tribunals.[80]

Over 40 years later the ICJ confirmed this view in the *Continental Shelf (Tunisia/Libyan Arab Jamahiriya)* case (1982):

> Equity as a legal concept is a direct emanation of the idea of justice. The court whose task is by definition to administer justice is bound to apply it ... [The Court] is bound to apply equitable principles as part of international law, and to balance up the various considerations which it regards as relevant in order to produce an equitable result.

For a particularly full discussion of the place of equity within international law readers are referred to the judgment of Judge Weeranmantry in the *Case Concerning Maritime Delimitation in the Area Between Greenland and Jan Mayen (Denmark v Norway)*(1993).

3.6   Judicial decisions

In the event of the court being unable to solve a dispute by reference to treaty law, custom or general principles, Article 38 provides a subsidiary means of

---

78   Sohn, *The Role of Equity in the Jurisprudence of the International Court of Justice*, 1984, *Mélanges Georges Perrin* (1984) at p 311.

79   H Thirlway, 'The Law and Procedure of the International Court of Justice 1960–1989' Part One (1989) 60, *BYIL* (1989) at p 49.

80   PCIJ Ser A/B, No 70.

judicial decisions and the teachings of the most highly qualified publicists of the various nations be employed – although the increase of treaty law has led to a decline in the use of the subsidiary source.

Judicial decisions may be applied subject to the provisions of Article 59 which states:

> The decision of the Court has no binding force except between the parties and in respect of that particular case.[81]

In other words, there is no *stare decisis* in international law. Nevertheless the ICJ does look at earlier decisions and take them into account. Value is seen in judicial consistency. But caution should be exercised when looking at a particular decision. Decisions are by majority. In the event of even division a decision may have been made by the President using a casting vote. Some dissenting judgments may be made more for political than for legal reasons. Arbitration decisions depend for their weight on the subject matter involved and the agreement between the states to submit the dispute to arbitration. The procedure of international tribunals is considered in more detail in Chapter 12.

Article 38 does not limit the judicial decisions that may be applied to international tribunals. If a municipal court's decision is relevant it may be taken into account – the weight attached will depend on the standing of the court – eg the US Supreme Court is held in high regard, particularly in disputes on state boundaries; similarly the decisions of the English Prize Courts contributed to the growth of prize law – the law relating to vessels captured at sea during war. Municipal court decisions may also be evidence of state practice for the purpose of establishing the rules of customary international law.

3.7   The teachings of the most highly qualified publicists of the various nations

Historically, writers have performed a major role in the development of international law. The significance of jurists such as Grotius, Suarez and Gentilis has already been discussed in Chapter 1. Even today states make plentiful reference to academic writings in their pleadings before the Court. Writers have played an important part in the development of international law for two main reasons, the comparative youth of a comprehensive system of international law and the absence of any legislative body. In the formative period writers helped to determine the scope and content of international law. However as the body of substantive law has increased so the influence of writers has decreased – although writers still have an important role in developing new areas of law, eg marine pollution. Who are the most qualified writers is a matter for subjective assessment – as usual in these matters death is often seen as an important qualification! It should be noted that the Court itself does not usually make reference to specific writers.

---

81   Article 59 of the Statute of the ICJ.

3.8 Other possible sources

Over the last 30 years there has been increasing support for the view that Article 38 should not be understood as a comprehensive and complete list of the sources of international law. On the one hand, examples can be found from the more recent decisions of the ICJ which seem to be based on rules of law not readily falling within the triad of sources created by the statute. On the other hand it is argued that international law does not simply consist of the decisions of the ICJ. Indeed, between 1966 and 1980 the work load of the court decreased dramatically following the decision in the *South West Africa* case, Second Phase (1966).[82] The decision was heavily criticised by the newly independent states who were already distrustful of what they perceived as a European and American bias within the Court. Rather than submit disputes to the ICJ they preferred to seek remedies through the political organs of the UN. As the work of the UN has increased it can be seen to have had a profound effect on the behaviour of states which cannot be ignored in any analysis of international law. For both these reasons, it is argued that the discussion of the sources of international law can no longer be confined to the provisions of Article 38. Support for this view can be found among the judges of the ICJ:

> We cannot reasonably expect to get very far if we try to rationalise the law of today solely in the language of Article 38 of the Statute of the International Court of Justice, framed as it was in 1920. It too needs urgent rethinking and elaboration ... To use Article 38 as it stands, as we constantly do still, for the purposes of analysing and explaining the elements and categories of the law today has a strong element of absurdity.[83]

It is therefore necessary to consider a number of other sources of international law.

3.9 Resolutions of international organisations

The exact status of resolutions of international organisations, in particular resolutions of the United Nations General Assembly, has long been an area of controversy. Nonetheless it is certainly true that the resolutions passed by the UN General Assembly have a far more significant role to play in the formation of international law than was envisaged in 1945, let alone in 1920 when Article 38 was drafted. When discussing the effect of resolutions it may be useful to consider the categories suggested by Sloan, who identifies three main categories of resolution:

- Decisions

By virtue of Article 17 of the UN Charter, the General Assembly may take decisions on budgetary and financial matters which are binding on the members. Failure to abide by budgetary decisions can ultimately lead to suspension and expulsion from membership. In addition, Article 2(5) of the Charter provides that:

---

82 [1966] *ICJ Rep* at p 6.

83 Jennings, 'The Identification of International Law' in *International Law, Teaching and Practice*, Bin Cheng (ed), 1982, at p 9.

All members shall give the United Nations every assistance in any action it takes in accordance with the present Charter, and shall refrain from giving assistance to any state against which the United Nations is taking preventive or enforcement action.

Thus arguably, resolutions that commit the UN to taking 'action' can be binding on member states.

• Recommendations

Article 10: The General Assembly may discuss any questions or any matters within the scope of the present Charter ... and ... may make recommendations to the members of the United Nations or to the Security Council or to both on any such questions or matters.

The essence of 'recommendations' is that they are non-binding. They cannot, therefore, instantly create binding rules of international law in themselves. However, recommendations can be used as evidence of state practice and thus go towards the creation of customary rules of international law.

• Declarations

Declarations are a species of General Assembly resolutions based on established practice outside the express provisions of Chapter IV of the Charter ... While the effect of declarations remains controversial, they are not recommendations and are not to be evaluated as such.[84]

Since 1945 the General Assembly has adopted a number of resolutions which have been termed declarations and have expressed principles of international law. Such declarations have often been adopted by unanimous vote or by consensus (ie without voting). The most comprehensive was Declaration on Principles of International Law concerning Friendly Relations and Co-operation among states (GA Resolution 2625 (XXV) (1970)). Other significant declarations have been the Declaration on the Granting of Independence to Colonial Territories and Peoples (GA Resolution 1514 (XV) (1960)); Declaration of Legal Principles Governing the Activities of States in the Exploration and Use of Outer Space (GA Resolution 1962 (XVIII) (1963)). Certain other resolutions, although not designated as 'declarations' have affirmed principles of international law. One example is the resolution entitled Affirmation of the Principles of International Law Recognised by the Charter of the Nuremberg Tribunal (GA Resolution 95 (I) (1946)). It should also be noted that some 'declarations' by the General Assembly are not intended to express legal rights and obligations, an important example being the Universal Declaration of Human Rights (GA Resolution 217 (III)) which is expressly stated to proclaim 'a common standard of achievement'.

It seems to be almost universally accepted today, therefore, that in certain situations UN resolutions can be used to establish binding rules of international law. Whether a particular resolution will be regarded as valid international law will depend on a number of criteria including the context in which the resolution was passed, voting behaviour and analysis of the provisions concerned. In *Texaco Overseas Petroleum Co v Libya* (1978),[85] an arbitration which

---

84 Sloan, 'General Assembly Resolutions Revisited' (1987) 58 *BYIL* 93.

85 (1978) 17 ILM at pp 1–37.

arose after Libya had nationalised the property of two American oil companies, the arbitrator, Professor Dupuy, had cause to discuss the international law relating to nationalisation of foreign owned property. In particular, he referred to the General Assembly Resolution on Permanent Sovereignty over Natural Resources 1962 (GA Res 1803 (XVII)) and the Charter of Economic Rights and Duties of States, 1974 (GA Res 3281 (XXIX)). Resolution 1803 had been adopted by 87 votes to 2, with 12 abstentions. France and South Africa had voted against the resolution and the Soviet bloc, Burma, Cuba and Ghana had abstained. The resolution recognised the right to expropriate foreign owned property where it was carried out for reasons of public utility, security or national interest and where compensation is paid. Arbitrator Dupuy, who had been appointed by the President of the ICJ commented:

> On the basis of the circumstances of adoption ... and by expressing an *opinio juris communis*, Resolution 1803 (XVII) seems to this Tribunal to reflect the state of customary law existing in this field ... The consensus by a majority of states belonging to the various representative groups indicates without the slightest doubt universal recognition of the rules therein incorporated. [86]

He then turned to consider the status of the Charter of Economic Rights and Duties of States 1974. This resolution was adopted by 120 votes to 6 with 10 abstentions. The states voting against were Belgium, Denmark, the Federal Republic of Germany, Luxembourg, the UK and the USA; those abstaining were Austria, Canada, France, Ireland, Israel, Italy, Japan, the Netherlands, Norway and Spain. The provisions of the Charter were much more favourable to the developing states. Arbitrator Dupuy found that there were several factors which mitigated against recognising the Charter as a source of international law:

> In the first place, Article 2 of this Charter must be analysed as a political rather than a legal declaration concerned with the ideological strategy of development and, as such, only supported by non-industrial states ... The absence of any connection between the procedures of compensation and international law and the subjection of this procedure solely to municipal law cannot be regarded by the Tribunal except as a *de lege ferenda* formulation, which even appears *contra legem* in the eyes of many developed countries. [87]

Since it now seems to be accepted that resolutions are capable of constituting rules of international law, debate now is focused on whether such resolutions constitute a source of law in their own right or whether they merely provide evidence of customary law or general principles of law. One resolution which has been the subject of much analysis is the Declaration on Outer Space which was passed in 1962. The main aim of the resolution was to establish a legal regime for outer space which incorporated the principles that space exploration was to be carried out for the benefit of all mankind, that 'outer space and celestial bodies' were not to be the subject of national appropriation, and that the use and exploration of outer space was to be carried out for peaceful purposes only. During the discussions leading to the adoption of the resolution

---

86   *Ibid*, p 30.
87   *Ibid*, p 32.

delegates to the General Assembly considered the legal effect of declarations in general and support was offered for the view that a declaration of legal principles, adopted unanimously could be, in effect, legally binding. A significant number of states expressed the view that the binding nature of such declarations was based on the fact that the declaration constituted state practice and also the necessary *opinio juris* to create a rule of custom. Such resolutions constituted, in the words of Bin Cheng, 'instant customary law'.[88] In the *Nicaragua* case (1986) the ICJ expressed the view that UN Resolutions could constitute *opinio juris* which together with evidence of state practice could constitute a rule of custom. Until the provisions of Article 38 of the Statute of the ICJ are amended it seems likely that international tribunals will continue to refer to resolutions in terms of evidence of international custom. Whether that is an accurate description of the procedure remains open to doubt.

3.10   Resolutions of regional organisations

Regional organisations, for example, the European Union, the Council of Europe, the Organisation of American States, and the Organisation for African Unity can, via their internal measures, demonstrate what they, as a regional group, consider to be the law. This is especially important in the area of human rights law, which is discussed in Chapter 15.

3.11   The International Law Commission and codification

The major difficulty with customary law is that it is diffuse and often lacks precision. In the light of this, attempts have been made to codify international law, an early example of which is provided by the Hague Conferences of 1899 and 1907 which did much to codify the laws relating to dispute settlement and the use of armed force. The codification and development of international law was a concern of the founders of the UN and that concern is reflected in Article 13(1) of the UN Charter which provides:

> The General Assembly shall initiate studies and make recommendations for the purpose of:
>
> (a) promoting international co-operation in the political field and *encouraging the progressive development of international law and its codification'* (emphasis added).

In 1947, under the auspices of the UN, the International Law Commission was set up and charged with the task of progressively developing and codifying international law. The ILC is made up of 34 members from around the world who remain in office for five years each and who are appointed from lists supplied by national governments. The members of the ILC sit as individuals rather than as state representatives. Generally the Commission works on its own initiative. Draft articles are prepared and sent for comments, a conference may then be convened at which the draft articles are discussed with the aim of producing a finished convention which can then be opened for signature. Conferences can last for some time – the Third Law of the Sea Conference had

---

88   Bin Cheng, 'UN Resolutions on Outer Space: Instant International Customary Law?' (1965) 5 *Indian Journal of International Law* 23.

its opening session in New York in 1973 and the Law of the Sea Convention was finally opened for signature in December 1982. Ratified conventions are clearly a source of law, while the drafts are often highly persuasive statements of present state practice in a particular area of law.

Although the ILC is the most important international body engaged in the development and codification of international law, there do exist a number of other public organisations which are involved in the same mission. Such organisations generally specialise in particular areas of law – eg the UN Commission on International Trade Law (UNCITRAL); the International Labour Organisation (ILO); the United Nations Educational, Scientific and Cultural Organisation (UNESCO). Additionally there are also some private, independent bodies engaged in the development of the law eg the International Law Association and the Institut de Droit International are two of the best known today, while the various Harvard Research drafts produced before the Second World War are still of value today.

3.12 'Soft law'

A recent development in the study of the sources of international law has been the claim that international law consists of norms of behaviour of varying decrees of density or force. On the one hand there are rules, usually contained in treaties, which constitute positive obligations binding states objectively. On the other hand, there are international instruments which, while not binding on states in the manner of treaty provisions, nonetheless constitute normative claims and provide standards or aspirations of behaviour. Such instruments can have an enormous impact on international relations and the behaviour of states but would not be considered law in the positivist sense. A growing body of writers has argued that both types of norms should be considered law and the distinction between the two is indicated by the terms 'hard law' and 'soft law'. The concept of soft law has been used significantly in the area of environmental protection which is discussed more fully in Chapter 17.

One particular benefit of soft law is that it allows states to participate in the formulation of standards of behaviour which they may not feel, at the time of formulation, ready to implement fully. For example, the Universal Declaration of Human Rights 1948 might be considered to be soft law since it was expressed to be non-binding and instead set down aims for achievement. Since that time it can be argued that most, if not all, its provisions have transformed into rules of hard law. Another example might be the Charter of Economic Rights and Duties of States 1974 which has already been mentioned. This has undoubtedly had an effect on the behaviour of states but is certainly a long way from hardening into a binding rule of law. It is clear that within soft law there will be varying degrees of hardness. Other examples of soft law would include the Final Act of the Conference on Security and Co-operation in Europe 1975 (the Helsinki Declaration) which was expressed to be non-binding, the OECD Guidelines for Multinational Enterprises and the Gleneagles Agreement on the Sporting Boycott of South Africa. All undoubtedly have some legal effects without being creating legally binding obligations.

3.13 *Jus cogens* or peremptory norms

Having discussed the distinction between hard and soft law it seems appropriate to turn to consideration of a duality of levels within hard law itself. Many municipal systems distinguish between *jus cogens*[89] (rules or principles of public policy which cannot be derogated from by legal subjects, often referred to as *ordre public*) and *jus dispositivum* (norms which can be replaced by subjects in their private dealings). The idea that there are certain non-derogable fundamental norms in international law is not new. Even before the First World War many writers had expressed the view that treaties which contravened certain fundamental norms would be void. The doctrine of international *jus cogens* was heavily influenced by natural law theories. Unlike the positivists who argued that sovereign states enjoyed an almost complete freedom of contract, natural lawyers argued that states were not completely free in their treaty-making powers. They argued that there were certain fundamental principles underpinning the international community which all states were obliged to respect.

In preparing the draft articles on the Law of Treaties the ILC gave considerable thought to the doctrine of *jus cogens*. The ILC supported the idea that treaties conflicting with peremptory norms of international law would be void but it proposed no clear criteria by which such norms could be identified. An attempt at definition was made at the Vienna Conference and the result was seen in Article 53 of the Vienna Convention on the Law of Treaties 1969 which provides:

> A treaty is void if, at the time of its conclusion, it conflicts with a peremptory norm of general international law. For the purposes of the present Convention, a peremptory norm of general international law is a norm accepted and recognised by the international community of states as a whole from which no derogation is permitted and which can be modified only by a subsequent norm of general international law having the same character.

The identical provision was included in the Vienna Convention on the Law of Treaties Between States and International Organisations or Between International Organisations 1986. The doctrine of *jus cogens* is further reflected in the Draft Articles on State Responsibility prepared by the ILC which propose the notion of an international crime resulting from the breach by a state of an international obligation 'essential for the protection of fundamental interests of the international community'.[90] Support for the existence of peremptory norms is also to be found in a number of judgments of the ICJ, notably in the *Nicaragua* case (1986) where the Court identified the prohibition on the use of force as being 'a conspicuous example of a rule of international law having the character of *jus cogens*'. Other activities that have been identified as contravening *jus cogens* include slave trading, piracy and genocide.

Although it seems to be undisputed that international law recognises the concept of *jus cogens*, what is less clear is the way in which rules of *jus cogens*

---

89 See also the more detailed discussion in Chapter 4.
90 (1976 – II) *YBILC* 73.

may be created. Since *jus cogens* has the status of a higher law binding all states it should not be possible for rules of *jus cogens* to be created by a simple majority of states and then imposed on a political or ideological minority. During discussions at the Vienna Conference on the Law of Treaties a number of states stressed the need for universal acceptance of norms of *jus cogens* while the Austrian delegate argued that rules could only be regarded as having the status of *jus cogens* if there was 'the substantial concurrence of states belonging to all principal legal systems'[91] and the US representative argued that such a norm 'would require, as a minimum, the absence of dissent by any important element of the international community'.[92] It therefore seems that the creation of a rule of *jus cogens* must, at the very least, meet the requirements of the establishment of a rule of customary law. As the Russian jurist, Gennady Danilenko, has written:

> As 'higher law' *jus cogens* clearly requires the application of higher standards for the ascertainment of the existence of community consensus as regards both the content and the peremptory character of the relevant rules. Only such an approach may ensure the required universality in the formation and subsequent implementation of rules designed to reflect and to protect the fundamental interests of the World Community.[93]

91 UNCLOT I at p 388.

92 UNCLOT II at p 102.

93 'International *Jus Cogens*: Issues of Law-Making' (1991) 2 *EJIL* at p 65.

CHAPTER 4

THE LAW OF TREATIES

The significance of treaties as a source of international law has already been discussed in Chapter 3. This chapter is concerned with the mechanics of treaties: how they are concluded, interpreted, observed, and terminated.

4.1 Introduction

Prior to 1969, the law of treaties consisted of customary rules of international law. Many of the rules relating to treaties between states were codified in the Vienna Convention on the Law of Treaties 1969 (VCT 1969) which was concluded on 23 May 1969 and entered into force on 27 January 1980, following receipt of the 35th ratification. The VCT 1969 is an early and important example of the codifying work of the International Law Commission. Additionally of interest is the Vienna Convention on Succession of States in Respect of Treaties 1978 (VCS 1978), concluded on 23 August 1978 and not yet in force, and the Vienna Convention on the Law of Treaties between States and International Organisations or between International Organisations 1986 (VCIO 1986), concluded on 21 March 1986, also not yet in force. The VCIO 1986 repeats most of the substantive rules contained in VCT 1969 and applies to those treaties which involve international organisations. In this chapter reference will generally only be made to the relevant provisions of the VCT 1969. The VCT 1969 is not retroactive and only applies to treaties concluded after 27 January 1980. The rules of customary law still have an important role and it is important to decide the extent to which the Vienna Conventions codify existing customary law and the extent to which they introduce new rules of law. When studying the law of treaties it is therefore important to be clear as to which rules are contained in the various Vienna Conventions and which rules are to be found in international custom.

At its first session in 1949, the International Law Commission included the law of treaties in its provisional list of topics selected for codification.[1] The ILC then completed a special report on reservations to treaties in 1951,[2] and participation in general multilateral treaties.[3, 4]

VIENNA CONVENTION ON THE LAW OF TREATIES[5]

The States Parties to the present Convention,

Considering the fundamental role of treaties in the history of international relations,

---

1   (1949) *YBILC* at p 281.

2   (1951) *YBILC* ii at pp 125–131.

3   (1963) *YBILC* ii at pp 217–223.

4   See further on multilateral treaties UN Doc A/35/312. For ILC Draft Articles and commentary, see (1966) *YBILC* ii at pp 173–274. For VCIO Draft Articles see (1982) *YBILC* ii pt 2 at pp 9–77.

5   UKTS No 58 (1980), Cmnd 7964; 1155 UNTS 331; (1969) 81 ILM 679; (1969) 63 AJIL 875. The Convention entered into force on 27 January 1980.

Recognising the ever-increasing importance of treaties as a source of international law and as a means of developing peaceful co-operation among nations, whatever their constitutional and social systems,

Noting that the principles of free consent and of good faith and the *pacta sunt servanda* rule are universally recognised,

Affirming that disputes concerning treaties, like other international disputes, should be settled by peaceful means and in conformity with the principles of justice and international law,

Recalling the determination of the peoples of the United Nations to establish conditions under which justice and respect for the obligations arising from treaties can be maintained,

Having in mind the principles of international law embodied in the Charter of the United Nations, such as the principles of the equal rights and self-determination of peoples, of the sovereign equality and independence of all states, of non-interference in the domestic affairs of states, of the prohibition of the threat or use of force and of universal respect for, and observance of, human rights and fundamental freedoms for all,

Believing that the codification and progressive development of the law of treaties achieved in the present Convention will promote the purposes of the United Nations set forth in the Charter, namely, the maintenance of international peace and security, the development of friendly relations and the achievement of co-operation among nations,

Affirming that the rules of customary international law will continue to govern questions not regulated by the provisions of the present Convention,

Have agreed as follows:

PART I
INTRODUCTION

Article 1   Scope of the present Convention

The present Convention applies to treaties between states

Article 2   Use of terms

1   For the purposes of the present Convention:

(a) 'treaty' means an international agreement concluded between states in written form and governed by international law, whether embodied in a single instrument or in two or more related instruments and whatever its particular designation;[6]

(b) 'ratification', 'acceptance', 'approval' and 'accession' mean in each case the international act so named whereby a state establishes on the international plane its consent to be bound by a treaty;

---

6   Article 2(1) VCIO 1986 provides: 'For the purposes of the present Convention:

(a) "treaty" means an international agreement governed by international law and concluded in written form:

(i) between one or more states and one or more international organisations; or

(ii) between international organisations,

whether that agreement is embodied in a single instrument or in two or more related instruments and whatever its particular designation.'

(c) 'full powers' means a document emanating from the competent authority of a state designating a person or persons to represent the state for negotiating, adopting or authenticating the text of a treaty, for expressing the consent of the state to be bound by a treaty, or for accomplishing any other act with respect to a treaty;

(d) 'reservation' means a unilateral statement, however phrased or named, made by a state, when signing, ratifying, accepting, approving or acceding to a treaty, whereby it purports to exclude or to modify the legal effect of certain provisions of the treaty in their application to that state;

(e) 'negotiating state' means a state which took part in the drawing up and adoption of the text of the treaty;

(f) 'Contracting State' means a state which has consented to be bound by the treaty, whether or not the treaty has entered into force;

(g) 'party' means a state which has consented to be bound by the treaty and for which the treaty is in force;

(h) 'third state' means a state not party to the treaty;

(i) 'international organisation' means an intergovernmental organisation.

2   The provisions in paragraph 1 regarding the use of terms in the present Convention are without prejudice to the use of those terms, or to the meanings which may be given to them, in the internal law of any state.

Article 3   International agreements not within the scope of the present Convention

The fact that the present Convention does not apply to international agreements concluded between states and other subjects of international law, or between such other subjects of international law, or to international agreements not in written form, shall not affect:

(a) the legal force of such agreements;

(b) the application to them of any of the rules set forth in the present Convention to which they would be subject under international law independently of the Convention;

(c) the application of the Convention to the relations of states as between themselves under international agreements to which other subjects of international law are also parties.

Agreements not in writing may nonetheless be legally binding although not under the provisions of VCT – see *US v Gonzales* (1986) 80 AJIL p 653, where a telephone conversation created an arrangement with another government.

Article 4   Non-retroactivity of the present Convention

Without prejudice to the application of any rules set forth in the present Convention to which treaties would be subject under international law independently of the Convention, the Convention applies only to treaties which are concluded by states after entry into force of the present Convention with regard to such states.

Article 5   Treaties constituting international organisations and treaties adopted within an international organisation

The present Convention applies to any treaty which is the constituent instrument of an international organisation and to any treaty adopted within an international organisation without prejudice to any relevant rules of the organisation.

PART II
CONCLUSION AND ENTRY INTO FORCE OF TREATIES
SECTION 1 CONCLUSION OF TREATIES

Article 6   Capacity of states to conclude treaties

Every state possesses capacity to conclude treaties.

Article 7   Full powers

1   A person is considered as representing a state for the purpose of adopting or authenticating the text of a treaty or for the purpose of expressing the consent of the state to be bound by a treaty if:

   (a)   he produces the appropriate full powers; or

   (b)   it appears from the practice of the states concerned or from other circumstances that their intention was to consider that person as representing the state for such purposes and to dispense with full powers.

2   In virtue of their functions and without having to produce full powers, the following are considered as representing their state:

   (a)   Heads of state, Heads of Government and Ministers for Foreign Affairs, for the purpose of performing all acts relating to the conclusion of a treaty;

   (b)   heads of diplomatic missions, for the purpose of adopting the text of a treaty between the accrediting state and the state to which they are accredited;

   (c)   representatives accredited by states to an international conference or to an international organisation or one of its organs, for the purpose of adopting the text of a treaty in that conference, organisation or organ.

Article 8   Subsequent confirmation of an act performed without authorisation

An act relating to the conclusion of a treaty performed by a person who cannot be considered under Article 7 as authorised to represent a state for that purpose is without legal effect unless afterwards confirmed by that state.

Article 9   Adoption of the text

1   The adoption of the text of a treaty takes place by the consent of all the states participating in its drawing up except as provided in paragraph 2.

2   The adoption of the text of a treaty at an international conference takes place by the vote of two-thirds of the states present and voting, unless by the same majority they shall decide to apply a different rule.

Article 10   Authentication of the text

The text of a treaty is established as authentic and definitive:

   (a)   by such procedure as may be provided for in the text or agreed upon by the states participating in its drawing up; or

   (b)   failing such procedure, by the signature, signature *ad referendum* or initialling by the representatives of those states of the text of the treaty or of the Final Act of a conference incorporating the text.

Article 11   Means of expressing consent to be bound by a treaty

The consent of a state to be bound by a treaty may be expressed by signature, exchange of instruments constituting a treaty, ratification, acceptance, approval or accession, or by any other means if so agreed.

Article 12   Consent to be bound by a treaty expressed by signature

1   The consent of a state to be bound by a treaty is expressed by the signature of its representatives when:

(a)   the treaty provides that signature shall have that effect;

(b)   it is otherwise established that the negotiating states were agreed that signature should have that effect; or

(c)   the intention of the state to give that effect to the signature appears from the full powers of its representative or was expressed during the negotiation.

2   For the purposes of para 1:

(a)   the initialing of a text constitutes a signature of the treaty when it is established that the negotiating states so agreed;

(b)   the signature *ad referendum* of a treaty by a representative, if confirmed by his state, constitutes a full signature of the treaty.

Article 13   Consent to be bound by a treaty expressed by an exchange of instruments constituting a treaty

The consent of states to be bound by a treaty constituted by instruments exchanged between them is expressed by that exchange when:

(a)   the instruments provide that their exchange shall have that effect; or

(b)   it is otherwise established that those states were agreed that the exchange of instruments should have that effect.

Article 14   Consent to be bound by a treaty expressed by ratification, acceptance or approval

1   The consent of a state to be bound by a treaty is expressed by ratification when:

(a)   the treaty provides for such consent to be expressed by means of ratification;

(b)   it is otherwise established that the negotiating states were agreed that ratification should be required;

(c)   the representatives of the state has signed the treaty subject to ratification; or

(d)   the intention of the state to sign the treaty subject to ratification appears from the full powers of its representative or was expressed during the negotiation.

2   The consent of a state to be bound by a treaty is expressed by acceptance or approval under conditions similar to those which apply to ratification.

Article 15   Consent to be bound by a treaty expressed by accession

The consent of a state to be bound by a treaty is expressed by accession when:

(a)   the treaty provides that such consent may be expressed by that state by means of accession:

(b)   it is otherwise established that the negotiating states were agreed that such consent may be expressed by that state by means of accession; or

(c)   all the parties have subsequently agreed that such consent may be expressed by that state by means of accession.

Article 16   Exchange or deposit of instruments of ratification, acceptance, approval or accession

Unless the treaty otherwise provides, instruments of ratification, acceptance, approval or accession establish the consent of a state to be bound by a treaty upon:

    (a)   their exchange between the Contracting States;

    (b)   their deposit with the depositary; or

    (c)   their notification to the Contracting States or to the depositary, if so agreed.

Article 17   Consent to be bound by part of a treaty and choice of differing provisions

1   Without prejudice to Articles 19 to 23, the consent of a state to be bound by part of a treaty is effective only if the treaty so permits or the other Contracting States so agree.

2   The consent of a state to be bound by a treaty which permits a choice between differing provisions is effective only if it is made clear to which of the provisions the consent relates.

Article 18   Obligation not to defeat the object and purpose of a treaty prior to its entry into force

A state is obliged to refrain from acts which would defeat the object and purpose of a treaty when:

    (a)   it has signed the treaty or has exchanged instruments constituting the treaty subject to ratification, acceptance or approval, until it shall have made its intention clear not to become a party to the treaty; or

    (b)   it has expressed its consent to be bound by the treaty, pending the entry into force of the treaty and provided that such entry into force is not unduly delayed.

SECTION 2

RESERVATIONS

Article 19   Formulation of reservations

A state may, when signing, ratifying, accepting, approving or acceding to a treaty, formulate a reservation unless:

    (a)   the reservation is prohibited by the treaty;

    (b)   the treaty provides that only specified reservations, which do not include the reservation in question, may be made; or

    (c)   in cases not falling under sub-paras (a) and (b), the reservation is incompatible with the object and purpose of the treaty.

Article 20   Acceptance of and objection to reservations

1   A reservation expressly authorised by a treaty does not require any subsequent acceptance by the other Contracting States unless the treaty so provides.

2   When it appears from the limited number of the negotiating states and the object and purpose of a treaty that the application of the treaty in its entirety between all the parties is an essential condition of the consent of each one to be bound by the treaty, a reservation requires acceptance by all the parties.

3   When a treaty is a constituent instrument of an international organisation and unless it otherwise provides, a reservation requires the acceptance of the competent organ of that organisation.

4   In cases not falling under the preceding paragraphs and unless the treaty otherwise provides:

(a)   acceptance by another Contracting State of a reservation constitutes the reserving state a party to the treaty in relation to that other state if or when the treaty is in force for those states;

(b)   an objection by another Contracting State to a reservation does not preclude the entry into force of the treaty as between the objecting and reserving states unless a contrary intention is definitely expressed by the objecting state;

(c)   an act expressing a state's consent to be bound by the treaty and containing a reservation is effective as soon as at least one other Contracting State has accepted the reservation.

5   For the purposes of paras 2 and 4 and unless the treaty otherwise provides, a reservation is considered to have been accepted by a state if it shall have raised no objection to the reservation by the end of a period of 12 months after it was notified of the reservation or by the date on which it expressed its consent to be bound by the treaty, whichever is later.

Article 21   Legal effects of reservations and of objections to reservations

1   A reservation established with regard to another party in accordance with Articles 19, 20 and 23:

(a)   modifies for the reserving state in its relations with that other party the provisions of the treaty to which the reservation relates to the extent of the reservation; and

(b)   modifies those provisions to the same extent for that other party in its relations with the reserving state.

2   The reservation does not modify the provisions of the treaty for the other parties to the treaty *inter se*.

3   When a state objecting to a reservation has not opposed the entry into force of the treaty between itself and the reserving state, the provisions to which the reservation relates do not apply as between the two states to the extent of the reservation.

Article 22   Withdrawal of reservations and of objections to reservations

1   Unless the treaty otherwise provides, a reservation may be withdrawn at any time and the consent of a state which has accepted the reservation is not required for its withdrawal.

2   Unless the treaty otherwise provides, or it is otherwise agreed:

(a)   the withdrawal of a reservation becomes operative in relation to another Contracting State only when notice of it has been received by that state;

(b)   the withdrawal of an objection to a reservation becomes operative only when notice of it has been received by the state which formulated the reservation.

Article 23   Procedure regarding reservations

1   A reservation, an express acceptance of a reservation and an objection to a reservation must be formulated in writing and communicated to the Contracting States and other states entitled to become parties to the treaty.

2   If formulated when signing the treaty subject to ratification, acceptance or approval, a reservation must be formally confirmed by the reserving state when expressing its consent to be bound by the treaty. In such a case the reservation shall be considered as having been made on the date of its confirmation.

3   An express acceptance of, or an objection to, a reservation made previously to confirmation of the reservation does not itself require confirmation.

4   The withdrawal of a reservation or of an objection to a reservation must be formulated in writing.

SECTION 3
ENTRY INTO FORCE AND PROVISIONAL APPLICATION OF TREATIES

Article 24   Entry into force

1   A treaty enters into force in such manner and upon such date as it may provide or as the negotiating states may agree.

2   Failing any such provision or agreement, a treaty enters into force as soon as consent to be bound by the treaty has been established for all the negotiating states.

3   When the consent of a state to be bound by a treaty is established on a date after the treaty has come into force, the treaty enters into force for that state on that date, unless the treaty otherwise provides.

4   The provisions of a treaty regulating the authentication of its text, the establishment of the consent of states to be bound by the treaty, the manner or date of its entry into force, reservations, the functions of the depositary and other matters arising necessarily before the entry into force of the treaty apply from the time of the adoption of its text.

Article 25   Provisions application

1   A treaty or a part of a treaty is applied provisionally pending its entry into force if:

(a)   the treaty itself so provides; or

(b)   the negotiating states have in some other manner so agreed.

2   Unless the treaty otherwise provides or the negotiating states have otherwise agreed, the provisional application of a treaty or a part of a treaty with respect to a state shall be terminated if that state notifies the other states between which the treaty is being applied provisionally of its intention not to become a party to the treaty.

PART III
OBSERVANCE, APPLICATION AND INTERPRETATION OF TREATIES
SECTION 1
OBSERVANCE OF TREATIES

Article 26   *Pacta sunt servanda*

Every treaty is binding upon the parties to it and must be performed by them in good faith.

Article 27   Internal law and observance of treaties

A party may not invoke the provisions of its internal law as justification for its failure to perform a treaty. This rule is without prejudice to Article 46.

SECTION 2
APPLICATION OF TREATIES

Article 28   Non-retroactivity of treaties

Unless a different intention appears from the treaty or is otherwise established, its provisions do not bind a party in relation to any act or fact which took place or any situation which ceased to exist before the date of the entry into force of the treaty with respect to that party.

Article 29   Territorial scope of treaties

Unless a different intention appears from the treaty or is otherwise established, a treaty is binding upon each party in respect of its entire territory.

Article 30   Application of successive treaties relating to the same subject-matter

1   Subject to Article 103 of the Charter of the United Nations, the rights and obligations of states parties to successive treaties relating to the same subject-matter shall be determined in accordance with the following paragraphs.

2   When a treaty specifies that it is subject to, or that it is not to be considered as incompatible with, an earlier or later treaty, the provisions of that other treaty prevail.

3   When all the parties to the earlier treaty are parties also to the later treaty but the earlier treaty is not terminated or suspended in operation under Article 59, the earlier treaty applies only to the extent that its provisions are compatible with those of the later treaty.

4   When the parties to the later treaty do not include all the parties to the earlier one:

   (a)   as between state parties to both treaties the same rule applies as in para 3;

   (b)   as between a state party to both treaties and a state party to only one of the treaties, the treaty to which both states are parties governs their mutual rights and obligations.

5   Paragraph 4 is without prejudice to Article 41, or to any question of the termination or suspension of the operation of a treaty under Article 60 or to any question of responsibility which may arise for a state from the conclusions or application of a treaty, the provisions of which are incompatible with its obligations towards another state under another treaty.

SECTION 3
INTERPRETATION OF TREATIES

Article 31   General rule of interpretation

1   A treaty shall be considered in good faith in accordance with the ordinary meaning to be given to the terms of the treaty in their context and in the light of its object and purpose.

2   The context for the purpose of the interpretation of a treaty shall comprise, in addition to the text, including its preamble and annexes:

   (a)   any agreement relating to the treaty which was made between all the parties in connection with the conclusion of the treaty;

   (b)   any instrument which was made by one or more parties in connection with the conclusion of the treaty and accepted by the other parties as an instrument related to the treaty.

3   There shall be taken into account, together with the context:

   (a) any subsequent agreement between the parties regarding the interpretation of the treaty or the application of its provisions;

   (b) any subsequent practice in the application of the treaty which establishes the agreement of the parties regarding its interpretation;

   (c) any relevant rules of international law applicable in the relations between the parties.

4   A special meaning shall be given to a term if it is established that the parties so intended.

Article 32 Supplementary means of interpretation

Recourse may be had to supplementary means of interpretation, including the preparatory work of the treaty and the circumstances of its conclusions, in order to confirm the meaning resulting form the application of Article 31, or to determine the meaning when the interpretation according to Article 31:

   (a) leaves the meaning ambiguous or obscure; or

   (b) leads to a result which is manifestly absurd or unreasonable.

Article 33 Interpretation of treaties authenticated in two or more languages

1   When a treaty has been authenticated in two or more languages, the text is equally authoritative in each language, unless the treaty provides or the parties agree that, in case of divergence, a particular text shall prevail.

2   A version of the treaty in a language other than one of those in which the text was authenticated shall be considered an authentic text only if the treaty so provides or the parties so agree.

3   The terms of the treaty are presumed to have the same meaning in each authentic text.

4   Except where a particular text prevails in accordance with para 1, when a comparison of the authentic text discloses a difference of meaning which the application of Articles 31 and 32 does not remove, the meaning which best reconciles the texts, having regard to the object and purpose of the treaty, shall be adopted.

SECTION 4

TREATIES AND THIRD STATES

Article 34 General rule regarding third states

A treaty does not create either obligations or rights for a third state without its consent.

Article 35 Treaties providing for obligations for third states

An obligation arises for a third state from a provision of a treaty if the parties to the treaty intend the provision to be the mans of establishing the obligation and third state expressly accepts that obligation in writing.

Article 36 Treaties providing for rights for third states

1   A right arises for a third state from a provision of a treaty if the parties to the treaty intend the provision to accord that right either to the third state, or to a group of states to which it belongs, or to all states, and the third state assents thereto. Its assent shall be presumed so long as the contrary is not indicated, unless the treaty otherwise provides.

2   A state exercising a right in accordance with paragraph 1 shall comply with the conditions for its exercise provided for in the treaty or established in conformity with the treaty.

Article 37   Revocation or modification of obligations or rights of third states

1   When an obligation has arisen for a third state in conformity with Article 35, the obligation may be revoked or modified only with the consent of the parties to the treaty and of the third state, unless it is established that they had otherwise agreed.

2   When a right has arisen for a third state in conformity with Article 36, the right may not be revoked or modified by the parties if it is established that the right was intended not to be revocable or subject to modification without the consent of the third state.

Article 38   Rules in a treaty becoming binding on third states through international custom

Nothing in Articles 34 to 37 precludes a rule set forth in a treaty from becoming binding upon a third state as a customary rule of international law, recognised as such.

PART IV
AMENDMENT AND MODIFICATION OF TREATIES

Article 39   General rules regarding the amendment of treaties

A treaty may be amended by agreement between the parties. The rules laid down in Part II apply to such an agreement except in so far as the treaty may otherwise provide.

Article 40   Amendment of multilateral treaties

1   Unless the treaty otherwise provides, the amendment of multilateral treaties shall be governed by the following paragraphs.

2   Any proposal to amend a multilateral treaty as between all the parties must be notified to all the Contracting States, each one of which shall have the right to take part in:

(a)   the decision as to the action to be taken in regard to such proposal;

(b)   the negotiation and conclusion of any agreement for the amendment of the treaty.

3   Every state entitled to become a party to the treaty shall also be entitled to become a party to the treaty as amended.

4   The amending agreement does not bind any state already a party to the treaty which does not become a party to the amending agreement; Article 30, para 4(b), applies in relation to such state.

5   Any state which becomes a party to the treaty after the entry into force of the amending agreement shall, failing an expression of a different intention by that state:

(a)   be considered as a party to the treaty as amended; and

(b)   be considered as a party to the unamended treaty in relation to any party to the treaty not bound by the amending agreement.

Article 41   Agreements to modify multilateral treaties between certain of the parties only

1   Two or more of the parties to a multilateral treaty may conclude an agreement to modify the treaty as between themselves alone if:

(a) the possibility of such a modification is provided for by the treaty; or

(b) the modification in question is not prohibited by the treaty and:

(i)   does not affect the enjoyment by the other parties of their rights under the treaty or the performance of their obligations;

(ii) does not relate to a provision, derogation from which is incompatible with the effective execution of the object and purpose of the treaty as a whole.

2   Unless in a case falling under para 1(a) the treaty otherwise provides, the parties in question shall notify the other parties of their intention to conclude the agreement and of the modification to the treaty for which it provides.

PART V
INVALIDITY, TERMINATION AND SUSPENSION OF THE OPERATION OF TREATIES
SECTION 1
GENERAL PROVISIONS

Article 42 Validity and continuance in force of treaties

1   The validity of a treaty or of the consent of a state to be bound by a treaty may be impeached only through the application of the present Convention.

2   The termination of a treaty, its denunciation or the withdrawal of a party, may take place only as a result of the application of the provisions of the treaty or of the present Convention. The same rule applies to suspension of the operation of a treaty.

Article 43 Obligations imposed by international law independently of a treaty

The invalidity, termination or denunciation of a treaty, the withdrawal of a party from it, or the suspension of its operation, as a result of the application of the present Convention or of the provisions of the treaty, shall not in any way impair the duty of any state to fulfil any obligation embodied in the treaty to which it would be subject under international law independently of the treaty.

Article 44 Separability of treaty provisions

1   A right of a party, provided for in a treaty or arising under Article 56, to denounce, withdraw from or suspend the operation of the treaty may be exercised only with respect to the whole treaty unless the treaty otherwise provides or the parties otherwise agree.

2   A ground for invalidating, terminating, withdrawing from or suspending the operation of a treaty recognised in the present Convention may be invoked only with respect to the whole treaty except as provided in the following paragraphs or in Article 60.

3   If the ground relates solely to particular clauses, it may be invoked only with respect those clauses where:

(a) the said clauses are separable from the remainder of the treaty with regard to their application;

(b) it appears from the treaty or is otherwise established that acceptance of those clauses was not an essential basis of the consent of the other party or parties to be bound by the treaty as a whole; and

(c) continued performance of the remainder of the treaty would not be unjust.

4   In cases falling under Articles 49 and 50 the state entitled to invoke the fraud or corruption may do so with respect either to the whole treaty or, subject to para 3, to the particular clauses alone.

5   In cases falling under Articles 51, 52 and 53, no separation of the provisions of the treaty is permitted.

Article 45   Loss of a right to invoke a ground for invalidating, terminating, withdrawing from or suspending the operation of a treaty

A state may no longer invoke a ground for invalidating, terminating, withdrawing from or suspending the operation of a treaty under Articles 46 to 50 or Articles 60 and 62 if, after becoming aware of the facts:

(a)   it shall have expressly agreed that the treaty is valid or remains in force or continues in operation, as the case may be; or

(b)   it must by reason of its conduct be considered as having acquiesced in the validity of the treaty or in its maintenance in force or in operation, as the case may be.

SECTION 2

INVALIDITY OF TREATIES

Article 46   Provisions of internal law regarding competence to conclude treaties

1   A state may not invoke the fact that its consent to be bound by a treaty has been expressed in violation of a provision of its internal law regarding competence to conclude treaties as invalidating its consent unless that violation was manifest and concerned a rule of its internal law of fundamental importance.

2   A violation is manifest if it would be objectively evident to any state conducting itself in the matter in accordance with normal practice and in good faith.

Article 47   Specific restrictions on authority to express the consent of a state

If the authority of a representative to express the consent of a state to be bound by a particular treaty has been made subject to a specific restriction, his omission to observe that restriction may not be invoked as invalidating the consent expressed by him unless the restriction was notified to the other negotiating states prior to his expressing such consent.

Article 48   Error

1   A state may invoke an error in a treaty as invalidating its consent to be bound by the treaty if the error relates to a fact or situation which was assumed by that state to exist at the time when the treaty was concluded and formed an essential basis of its consent to be bound by the treaty.

2   Paragraph 1 shall not apply if the state in question contributed by its own conduct to the error or if the circumstances were such as to put that state on notice of a possible error.

3   An error relating only to the wording of the text of a treaty does not affect its validity; Article 79 then applies.

Article 49   Fraud

If a state has been induced to conclude a treaty by the fraudulent conduct of another negotiating state, the state may invoke the fraud as invalidating its consent to be bound by the treaty.

Article 50   Corruption of a representative of a state

If the expression of a state's consent to be bound by a treaty has been procured through the corruption of its representative directly or indirectly by another negotiating state, the state may invoke such corruption as invalidating its consent to be bound by the treaty.

Article 51   Coercion of a representative of a state

The expression of a state's consent to be bound by a treaty which has been procured by the coercion of its representative through acts or threats directed against him shall be without any legal effect.

Article 52   Coercion of a state by the threat or use of force

A treaty is void if its conclusion has been procured by the threat or use of force in violation of the principles of international law embodied in the Charter of the United Nations.

Article 53   Treaties conflicting with a peremptory norm of general international law (*jus cogens*)

A treaty is void if, at the time of its conclusions, it conflicts with a peremptory norm of general international law. For the purposes of the present Convention, a peremptory norm of general international law is a norm accepted and recognised by the international community of states as a whole as a norm from which no derogation is permitted and which can be modified only by a subsequent norm of general international law having the same character.

SECTION 3

TERMINATION AND SUSPENSION OF THE OPERATION OF TREATIES

Article 54   Termination of or withdrawal from a treaty under its provisions or by consent of the parties

The termination of a treaty or the withdrawal of a party may take place:

    (a)   in conformity with the provisions of the treaty; or

    (b)   at any time by consent of all the parties after consultation with the other Contracting States.

Article 55   Reduction of the parties to a multilateral treaty below the number necessary for its entry into force

Unless the treaty otherwise provides, a multilateral treaty does not terminate by reason only of the fact that the number of the parties falls below the number necessary for its entry into force.

Article 56   Denunciation of or withdrawal from a treaty containing no provision regarding termination, denunciation or withdrawal

1   A treaty which contains no provision regarding its termination and which does not provide for denunciation or withdrawal is not subject to denunciation or withdrawal unless:

    (a)   it is established that the parties intended to admit the possibility of denunciation or withdrawal; or

    (b)   a right of denunciation or withdrawal may be implied by the nature of the treaty.

2   A party shall give not less than 12 months' notice of its intention to denounce or withdraw from a treaty under para 1.

Article 57 Suspension of the operation of a treaty under its provisions or by consent of the parties

The operation of a treaty in regard to all the parties or to a particular party may be suspended:

(a) in conformity with the provisions of the treaty; or

(b) at any time by consent of all the parties after consultation with the other Contracting States.

Article 58 Suspension of the operation of a multilateral treaty by agreement between certain of the parties only

1   Two or more parties to a multilateral treaty may conclude an agreement to suspend the operation of provisions of the treaty, temporarily and as between themselves alone, if:

(a) the possibility of such suspension is provided for by the treaty; or

(b) the suspension in question is not prohibited by the treaty and:

(i)   does not affect the enjoyment by the other parties of their rights under the treaty or the performance of their obligations;

(ii) is not incompatible with the object and purpose of the treaty.

2   Unless in a case falling under para 1(a) the treaty otherwise provides, the parties in question shall notify the other parties of their intention to conclude the agreement and of those provisions of the treaty the operation of which they intend to suspend.

Article 59 Termination or suspension of the operation of a treaty implied by conclusion of a later treaty

1   A treaty shall be considered as terminated if all the parties to it conclude a later treaty relating to the same subject-matter and:

(a) it appears from the later treaty or is otherwise established that the parties intended that the matter should be governed by that treaty; or

(b) the provisions of the later treaty are so far incompatible with those of the earlier one that the two treaties are not capable of being applied at the same time.

2   The earlier treaty shall be considered as only suspended in operation if it appears from the later treaty or is otherwise established that such was the intention of the parties.

Article 60 Termination or suspension of the operation of a treaty as a consequence of its breach.

1   A material breach of a bilateral treaty by one of the parties entitles the other to invoke the breach as a ground for terminating or suspending its operation in whole or in part.

2   A material breach of a multilateral treaty by one of the parties entitles:

(a) the other parties by unanimous agreement to suspend the operation of the treaty in whole or in part or to terminate it either:

(i)   in the relations between themselves and the defaulting state; or

(ii) as between all the parties;

(b) a party specially affected by the breach, to invoke it as a ground for suspending the operation of the treaty in whole or in part in the relations between itself and the defaulting state;

(c)   any party other than the defaulting state to invoke the breach as a ground for suspending the operation of the treaty in whole or in part with respect to itself if the treaty is of such a character that a material breach of its provisions by one party radically changes the position of every party with respect to the further performance of its obligation under the treaty.

3   A material breach of a treaty, for the purposes of this article, consists in:

(a)   a repudiation of the treaty not sanctioned by the present Convention; or

(b)   the violation of a provision essential to the accomplishment of the object and purpose of the treaty.

4   The foregoing paragraphs are without prejudice to any provision in the treaty applicable in the event of a breach.

5   Paragraphs 1 to 3 do not apply to provisions relating to the protection of the human person contained in treaties of a humanitarian character, in particular to provisions prohibiting any form of reprisals against persons protected by such treaties.

Article 61   Supervening impossibility of performance

1   A party may invoke the impossibility of performing as treaty as a ground for terminating or withdrawing from it if the impossibility results from the permanent disappearance or destruction of an object indispensable for the execution of the treaty. If the impossibility it temporary, it may be invoked only as a ground for suspending the operation of the treaty.

2   Impossibility of performance may not be invoked by a party as a ground for terminating, withdrawing from or suspending the operation of a treaty if the impossibility is the result of a breach by that party either of an obligation under the treaty or of any other international obligation owed to any other party to the treaty.

Article 62   Fundamental change of circumstances

1   A fundamental change of circumstances which has occurred with regard to those existing at the time of the conclusion of a treaty, and which was not foreseen by the parties, may not be invoked as a ground for terminating or withdrawing from the treaty unless:

(a)   the existence of those circumstances constituted an essential basis of the consent of the parties to be bound by the treaty; and

(b)   the effect of the change is radically to transform the extent of obligations still to be performed under the treaty.

2   A fundamental change of circumstances may not be invoked as a ground for terminating or withdrawing from a treaty:

(a)   if the treaty establishes a boundary; or

(b)   if the fundamental change is the result of a breach by the party invoking it either of an obligation under the treaty or of any other international obligation owed to any other party to the treaty.

3   If, under the foregoing paragraphs, a party may invoke a fundamental change of circumstances as a ground for terminating or withdrawing from a treaty it may also invoke the change as a ground for suspending the operation of the treaty.

Article 63   Severance of diplomatic or consular relations

The severance of diplomatic or consular relations between the parties to a treaty does not affect the legal relations established between them by the treaty except in so far as the existence of diplomatic or consular relations is indispensable for the application of the treaty.

Article 64   Emergence of a new peremptory norm of general international law (*jus cogens*)

If a new peremptory norm of general international law emerges, any existing treaty which is in conflict with that norm becomes void and terminates.

SECTION 4
PROCEDURE

Article 65   Procedure to be followed with respect to invalidity, termination, withdrawal from or suspension of the operation of a treaty

1   A party which, under the provisions of the present Convention, invokes either a defect in its consent to be bound by a treaty or a ground for impeaching the validity of a treaty, terminating it, withdrawing from it or suspending its operation, must notify the other parties of its claim. The notification shall indicate the measures proposed to be taken with respect to the treaty and the reasons therefor.

2   If, after the expiry of a period which, except in cases of special urgency, shall not be less than three months after the receipt of the notification, no party has raised any objection, the party making the notification may carry out in the manner provided in Article 67 the measure which it has proposed.

3   If, however, objection has been raised by any other party, the parties shall seek a solution through the means indicated in Article 33 of the Charter of the United Nations.

4   Nothing in the foregoing paragraphs shall affect the rights or obligations of the parties under any provisions in force binding the parties with regard to the settlement of disputes.

5   Without prejudice to Article 45, the fact that a state has not previously made the notification prescribed in para 1 shall not prevent it from making such notification in answer to another party claiming performance of the treaty or alleging its violation.

Article 66   Procedures for judicial settlement, arbitration and conciliation

If, under para 3 of Article 65, no solution has been reached within a period of twelve months following the date on which the objection was raised, the following procedures shall be followed:

(a)   any one of the parties to a dispute concerning the application or the interpretation of Articles 53 to 64 may, by a written application, submit it to the International Court of Justice for a decision unless the parties by common consent agree to submit the dispute to arbitration;

(b)   any one of the parties to a dispute concerning the application or the interpretation of any of the other articles in Part V of the present Convention may set in motion the procedure specified in the Annex to the Convention by submitting a request to that effect to the Secretary General of the United Nations.

Article 67 Instruments for declaring invalid, terminating, withdrawing from or suspending the operation of a treaty

1   The notification provided for under Article 65, para 1 must be made in writing.

2   Any act declaring invalid, terminating, withdrawing from or suspending the operation of a treaty pursuant to the provisions of the treaty or of para 2 or 3 of Article 65 shall be carried out through an instrument communicated to the other parties. If the instrument is not signed by the Head of State, Head of Government or Minister for Foreign Affairs, the representative of the state communicating it may be called upon to produce full powers.

Article 68 Revocation of notifications and instruments provided for in Articles 65 and 67

A notification or instrument provided for in Articles 65 or 67 may be revoked at any time before it takes effect.

SECTION 5

CONSEQUENCES OF THE INVALIDITY, TERMINATION
OR SUSPENSION OF THE OPERATION OF A TREATY

Article 69 Consequences of the invalidity of a treaty

1   A treaty the invalidity of which is established under the present Convention is void. The provisions of a void treaty have no legal force.

2   If acts have nevertheless been performed in reliance on such a treaty:

(a)   each party may require any other party to establish as far as possible in their mutual relations the position that would have existed if the acts had not been performed;

(b)   acts performed in good faith before the invalidity was invoked are not rendered unlawful by reason only of the invalidity of the treaty.

3   In cases falling under Articles 49, 50, 51 or 52, para 2 does not apply with respect to the party to which the fraud, the act of corruption or the coercion is imputable.

4   In the case of the invalidity of a particular state's consent to be bound by a multilateral treaty, the foregoing rules apply in the relations between that state and the parties to the treaty.

Article 70 Consequences of the termination of a treaty

1   Unless the treaty otherwise provides or the parties otherwise agree, the termination of a treaty under its provisions or in accordance with the present Convention:

(a)   releases the parties from any obligation further to perform the treaty;

(b)   does not affect any right, obligation or legal situation of the parties created through the execution of the treaty prior to its termination.

2   If a state denounces or withdraws from a multilateral treaty, paragraph 1 applies in the relations between that state and each of the other parties to the treaty from the date when such denunciation or withdrawal takes effect.

Article 71 Consequences of the invalidity of a treaty which conflicts with a peremptory norm of general international law

1   In the case of a treaty which is void under Article 53 the parties shall:

   (a) eliminate as far as possible the consequences of any act performed in reliance on any provision which conflicts with the peremptory norm of general international law; and

   (b) bring their mutual relations into conformity with the peremptory norm of general international law.

2   In the case of a treaty which becomes void and terminates under Article 64, the termination of the treaty:

   (a) releases the parties from any obligations further to perform the treaty;

   (b) does not affect any right, obligation or legal situation of the parties created through the execution of the treaty prior to its termination; provided that those rights, obligations or situations may thereafter be maintained only to the extent that their maintenance is not in itself in conflict with the new peremptory norm of general international law.

Article 72 Consequences of the suspension of the operation of a treaty

1   Unless the treaty otherwise provides or the parties otherwise agree, the suspension of the operation of a treaty under its provisions or in accordance with the present Convention:

   (a) releases the parties between which the operation of the treaty is suspended from the obligation to perform the treaty in their mutual relations during the period of the suspension;

   (b) does not otherwise affect the legal relations between the parties established by the treaty.

2   During the period of the suspension the parties shall refrain from acts tending to obstruct the resumption of the operation of the treaty.

PART VI
MISCELLANEOUS PROVISIONS

Article 73 Cases of state succession, state responsibility and outbreak of hostilities

The provisions of the present Convention shall not prejudice any question that may arise in regard to a treaty from a succession of states or from the international responsibility of a state or from the outbreak of hostilities between states.

Article 74 Diplomatic and consular relations and the conclusion of treaties

The severance or absence of diplomatic or consular relations between two or more states does not prevent the conclusion of treaties between those states. The conclusion of a treaty does not in itself affect the situation in regard to diplomatic or consular relations.

Article 75 Case of an aggressor state

The provisions of the present Convention are without prejudice to any obligation in relation to a treaty which may arise for an aggressor state in consequence of measures taken in conformity with the Charter of the United Nations with reference to that state's aggression.

PART VII
DEPOSITARIES, NOTIFICATIONS, CORRECTIONS AND REGISTRATION

Article 76 Depositaries of treaties

1 The designation of the depositary of a treaty may be made by the negotiating states, either in the treaty itself or in some other manner. The depositary may be one or more states, an international organisation or the chief administrative officer of the organisation.

2 The functions of the depositary of a treaty are international in character and the depositary is under an obligation to act impartially in their performance. In particular, the fact that a treaty has not entered into force between certain of the parties or that a difference has appeared between a state and a depositary with regard to the performance of the latter's functions shall not affect that obligation.

Article 77 Functions of depositaries

1 The functions of a depositary, unless otherwise provided in the treaty or agreed by the Contracting States, comprise in particular:

(a) keeping custody of the original text of the treaty and of any full powers delivered to the depositary;

(b) preparing certified copies of the original text and preparing any further text of the treaty in such additional languages as may be required by the treaty and transmitting them to the parties and to the states entitled to become parties to the treaty;

(c) receiving any signatures to the treaty and receiving and keeping custody of any instruments, notifications and communications relating to it;

(d) examining whether the signature of any instrument, notification or communication relating to the treaty is in due and proper form and, if need be, bringing the matter to the attention of the state in question;

(e) informing the parties and the states entitled to become parties to the treaty of acts, notifications and communications relating to the treaty;

(f) informing the states entitled to become parties to the treaty when the number of signatures or of instruments of ratification, acceptance, approval or accession required for the entry into force of the treaty has been received or deposited;

(g) registering the treaty with the Secretariat of the United Nations;

(h) performing the functions specified in other provisions of the present Convention.

2 In the event of any difference appearing between a state and the depositary as to the performance of the latter's functions, the depositary shall bring the question to the attention of the signatory states and the Contracting States or, where appropriate, of the competent organ of the international organisation concerned.

Article 78 Notifications and communications

Except as the treaty or the present Convention otherwise provide, any notification or communication to be made by any state under the present Convention shall:

(a) if there is no depositary, be transmitted direct to the states for which it is intended, or if there is a depositary, to the latter;

(b) be considered as having been made by the state in question only upon its receipt by the state to which it was transmitted or, as the case may be, upon its receipt by the depositary;

(c) if transmitted to a depositary, be considered as received by the state for which it was intended only when the latter state has been informed by the depositary in accordance with Article 77, para 1(e).

Article 79 Correction of errors in texts or in certified copies of treaties

1 Where, after the authentication of the text of a treaty, the signatory states and the Contracting States are agreed that it contains an error, the error shall, unless they decided upon some other means of correction, be corrected:

(a) by having the appropriate correction made in the text and causing the correction to be initialed by duly authorised representatives;

(b) by executing or exchanging the instrument or instruments setting out the correction which it has been agreed to make; or

(c) by executing a corrected text of the whole treaty by the same procedure as in the case of the original text.

2 Where the treaty is one for which there is a depositary, the latter shall notify the signatory states and the Contracting States of the error and of the proposal to correct it and shall specify an appropriate time limit within which objection to the proposed correction may be raised. If, on the expiry of the time limit:

(a) no objection has been raised, the depositary shall make and initial the correction in the text and shall execute a *procès-verbal* of the rectification of the text and communicate a copy of it to the parties and to the states entitled to become parties to the treaty.

(b) an objection has been raised, the depositary shall communicate the objection to the signatory states and to the Contracting States.

3 The rules in paras 1 and 2 apply also where the text has been authenticated in two or more languages and it appears that there is a lack of concordance which the signatory states and the Contracting States agree should be corrected.

4 The corrected text replaces the defective text *ab initio,* unless the signatory states and the Contracting States otherwise decide.

5 The correction of the text of a treaty that has been registered shall be notified to the Secretariat of the United Nations.

6 Where an error is discovered in a certified copy of a treaty, the depositary shall execute a *procès-verbal* specifying the rectification and communicate a copy of it to the signatory states and to the Contracting States.

Article 80 Registration and publication of treaties

1 Treaties shall, after their entry into force, be transmitted to the Secretariat of the United Nations for registration or filing and recording, as the case may be, and for publication.

2 The designation of a depositary shall constitute authorisation for it to perform the acts specified in the preceding paragraph.

PART VIII

FINAL PROVISIONS

Article 81 Signature

The present Convention shall be open for signature by all states Members of the United Nations or of any of the specialised agencies or of the international Atomic Energy Agency or parties to the Statute of the International Court of Justice, and by any other state invited by the General Assembly of the United nations to become a party to the Convention, as follows: until 30 November 1969, at the Federal Ministry for Foreign Affairs of the Republic of Austria, and subsequently, until 30 April 1970, at the United Nations Headquarters, New York.

Article 82 Ratification

The present Convention is subject to ratification. The instruments of ratification shall be deposited with the Secretary General of the United Nations.

Article 83 Accession

The present Convention shall remain open for accession by any state belonging to any of the categories mentioned in Article 81. The instrument of accession shall be deposited with the Secretary General of the United Nations.

Article 84 Entry into force

1   The present Convention shall enter into force on the thirtieth day following the date of deposit of the thirty-fifth instrument of ratification or accession.

2   For each state ratifying or acceding to the Convention after the deposit of the thirty-fifth instrument of ratification or accession, the Convention shall enter into force on the thirtieth day after deposit by such state of its instrument of ratification or accession.

Article 85 Authentic texts

The original of the present Convention, of which the Chinese, English, French, Russian and Spanish texts are equally authentic, shall be deposited with the Secretary General of the United Nations.

In witness whereof the undersigned Plenipotentiaries, being duly authorised thereto by their respective Governments, have signed the present Convention.

Done at Vienna, this twenty-third day of May, one thousand nine hundred and sixty-nine.

ANNEX

1   A list of conciliators consisting of qualified jurists shall be drawn up and maintained by the Secretary General of the United Nations. To this end, every state which is a Member of the United Nations or a party to the present Convention shall be invited to nominate two conciliators, and the names of the persons so nominated shall constitute the list. The term of a conciliator, including that of any conciliator nominated to fill a casual vacancy, shall be five years and may be renewed. A conciliator whose term expires shall continue to fulfil any function for which he shall have been chosen under the following paragraph.

2   When a request has been made to the Secretary General under Article 66, the Secretary General shall bring the dispute before a conciliation commission constituted as follows:

The state or states constituting one of the parties to the dispute shall appoint:

(a) one conciliator of the nationality of that state or of one of those states, who may or may not be chosen from the list referred to in para 1; and

(b) one conciliator not of the nationality of that state or of any of those states, who shall be chosen from the list.

The state or states constituting the other party to the dispute shall appoint two conciliators in the same way. The four conciliators chosen by the parties shall be appointed within sixty days following the date on which the Secretary General receives the request.

The four conciliators shall, within sixty days following the date of the last of their own appointments, appoint a fifth conciliator chosen from the list, who shall be chairman.

If the appointment of the chairman or of any of the other conciliators has not been made within the period prescribed above for such appointment, it shall be made by the Secretary General within 60 days following the expiry of that period. The appointment of the chairman may be made by the Secretary General either from the list or from the membership of the International Law Commission. Any of the periods within which appointments must be made may be extended by agreement between the parties to the dispute.

Any vacancy shall be filled in the manner prescribed for the initial appointment.

3   The Conciliation Commission shall decide its own procedure. The Commission, with the consent of the parties to the dispute, may invite any party to the treaty to submit to it its views orally or in writing. Decisions and recommendations of the Commission shall be made by a majority vote of the five members.

4   The Commission may draw the attention of the parties to the dispute to any measures which might facilitate an amicable settlement.

5   The Commission shall hear the parties, examine the claims and objections, and make proposals to the parties with a view to reaching an amicable settlement of the dispute.

6   The Commission shall report within twelve months of its constitution. Its report shall be deposited with the Secretary General and transmitted to the parties to the dispute. The report of the Commission, including any conclusions stated therein regarding the facts or questions of law, shall not be binding upon the parties and it shall have no other character than that of recommendations submitted for the consideration of the parties in order to facilitate an amicable settlement of the dispute.

7   The Secretary General shall provide the Commission with such assistance and facilities as it may require. The expenses of the Commission shall be borne by the United Nations.

4.2   Definitions

VCT 1969 only applies to written agreements between states, VCIO 1986 deals with written agreements between states and International Organisations or between International Organisations. Although both Conventions only apply to

LIVERPOOL JOHN MOORES UNIVERSITY
LEARNING & INFORMATION SERVICES

written agreements, this should not be taken to mean that agreements not in writing have no effect in international law – such unwritten agreements will still be regarded as treaties and will be governed by the customary law on treaties – subject to difficulties of proof of content.

> There is no precise nomenclature for international treaties: 'treaty', 'convention', 'agreement' or 'protocol' are all interchangeable. Furthermore the meaning of most of the terms used in the law of treaties is extremely variable, changing from country to country and from Constitution to Constitution; in international law it could even be said to vary from treaty to treaty: each treaty is, as it were, a microcosm laying down in its final clauses the law of its own existence in its own terms. The uncertainty in wording is a result of the relativity of treaties ...

> Despite the terminological jumble, a definition is needed if only to delimit the scope of the rules to be discussed. The broader the definition, the fewer the rules applying to all cases it covers. It is precisely because the rules common to written agreements between states are comparatively numerous that the Vienna Convention dealt with them alone. In order to convey the general sense of the problem, a somewhat broader definition will be presented and discussed here, although the greater part of this study is restricted to the Vienna Convention, which covers the most homogeneous and richest part of the subject. The suggested definition is as follows: 'A treaty is an expression of concurring wills attributable to two or more subjects of international law and intended to have legal effects under the rules of international law.'[7]

> The restriction of the use of the term 'treaty' in the draft articles to international agreements expressed in writing is not intended to deny the legal force of oral agreements under international law or to imply that some of the principles contained in later parts of the Commission's draft articles ... may not have relevance in regard to oral agreements.[8]

An example of an oral agreement is to be found in the case involving the *Legal Status of Eastern Greenland* (1933).[9] The case arose from a dispute between Norway and Denmark over claims to sovereignty in Eastern Greenland. Denmark based its claim on the fact that during negotiations between government ministers, the Danish minister suggested to M Ihlen, the Norwegian Foreign Minister, that Denmark would raise no objection to Norwegian claims to Spitzbergen if Norway would not oppose Danish claims to Greenland at the Paris Peace Conference. A week after this conversation, in further negotiations, M Ihlen declared that Norway would 'not make any difficulty' concerning the Danish claim. The PCIJ found that the Spitzbergen question was interdependent on the Greenland issues and as such the Court found that a binding agreement existed between the two states.

4.2.1 Unilateral agreements

The matter was discussed in the *Nuclear Tests* cases (1974).[10] The cases arose out of opposition by New Zealand and Australia to atmospheric nuclear testing

---

7   Paul Reuter, *Introduction to the Law of Treaties*, 1989, London; Pinter Publishers at p 23.

8   (1966–II) *YBILC* at p 189.

9   PCIJ Ser A/B, No 53 (1933).

10   [1974] *ICJ Rep* at p 253.

carried out by France in the South Pacific. Australia and New Zealand brought proceedings before the ICJ but before any decision was made France indicated its intention not to hold any further tests in the region. The ICJ found that in the light of the French declaration it was no longer appropriate for it to give a decision on the merits of the case. In the course of its judgment, the ICJ declared:

> It is well recognised that declarations made by way of unilateral acts, concerning legal or factual situations, may have the effect of creating legal obligations. Declarations of this kind may be, and often are, very specific. When it is the intention of the state making the declaration that it should be bound according to its terms, that intention confers on the declaration the character of a legal undertaking, the state being thenceforth legally required to follow a course of conduct consistent with the declaration.

4.2.2 Subjects of international law

Only those with international personality can be parties to treaties – effectively this means states and international organisations. Whilst the majority of treaties are concluded between states, it should already be clear that it is possible for international organisations to undertake treaty obligations. It is not possible under international law for private individuals or companies to enter into treaties. The nature and requirements of the subjects of international law are dealt with in detail in Chapter 5.

Agreements between states themselves create no problem here but a number of marginal cases are becoming increasingly common. Instead of states themselves the parties to an agreement may be other legal entities such as municipalities or public institutions. In such situations the question arises as to whether such bodies have the power to commit their state, and if they do not, the degree to which it can it be said that they have concluded a treaty. On the whole the problem is dealt with by application of the principles of agency and is resolved by looking at the extent to which the particular body can be implied to be acting as agent for the state concerned. Another problem arises in the case of agreements between states and entities which do not yet qualify as states (for example, national liberation organisations or provisional governments) but have been accorded some measure of international personality. In 1982 the Palestine Liberation Organisation issued a communication in which it purported to accede to the Geneva Conventions 1949 and additional Protocols dealing with the laws of war. Switzerland, as depository of the treaties, declined to accept the accession and sent a note to state parties declaring:

> Due to the uncertainty within the international community as to the existence or the non-existence of a state of Palestine and as long as the issue has not been settled in an appropriate framework, the Swiss government, in its capacity as depository ... is not in a position to decide whether this communication can be considered as an instrument of accession ... The unilateral declaration of application of the four Geneva Conventions and of the additional Protocol I made on 7 June 1982 by the Palestine Liberation Organisation remains valid.[11]

---

11 Embassy of Switzerland, Note of Information sent to States Parties to the Convention and Protocol, 13 September 1989.

While the Peace Treaty between Israel and Jordan (as in the case of the Camp David Agreements between Israel and Egypt) is clearly a treaty between states governed by international law in the sense of the 1969 Vienna Convention on the Law of Treaties, the legal nature of the agreements between Israel and the PLO is a matter of dispute. Some authors argue that '[t]he PLO's lack of status as a state precludes characterisation of the Declaration as a treaty or international convention, and hence as a hard law instrument in the traditional sense'.[12] It is suggested that it is 'rather an agreement between the state of Israel and the PLO, 'representing the Palestinian people' and that '[b]ecause the Declaration of Principles accepts some, but not all, elements of Palestinian statehood, Palestine may be considered a 'quasi-state' for purposes of the agreement; that is an entity enjoying certain prerogatives ordinarily reserved to states, but not fulfilling all of the traditional prerequisites for statehood'.[13] the same author concludes that, although the agreement is 'a soft law document in the traditional sense', it nevertheless is 'an agreement with considerable binding force' which 'appears on close analysis to embody a solid, substantive accord'.[14] Other authors have also expressed doubts (at least) on whether the Israel-PLO agreements are international instruments.[15]

> In the above view there is some confusion on two different issues which need to be distinguished in the analysis. The first issue concerns the law to be applied to the agreement, in particular, whether it is an agreement concluded under international law. The second issue is whether, or to what extent it is a legally binding or non-binding agreement, and what the legal consequences are.

> With regard to the first issue, it is correct that the PLO is not a state in the sense of international law and that it also does not represent any existing state of 'Palestine'. The establishment of a 'state of Palestine' was proclaimed with the Algiers Declaration of 15 November 1988 and it was recognised by many former communist states and developing countries which entered into diplomatic relations with the representatives of this state. However, this 'state of Palestine' does not fulfil one of the essential criteria under international law for the existence of a state because there is no effective sovereign control over the territory and population claimed to form the basis of the 'state of Palestine'.

> This does not mean that the Israel-PLO agreements cannot be treaties under international law. It is true that the 1969 Vienna Convention on the Law of Treaties only applies to treaties concluded between states. But that does not affect, as expressly acknowledged in Article 3 of the Convention, the legal validity of, and the application of international law rules on the law of treaties to, agreements concluded between states and other 'subjects of international law'. Independently of the attitude taken by Israel towards the PLO in the past, in international practice the latter has become recognised as a national liberation movement with the right to self-determination, which, although it does not exercise effective territorial jurisdiction, is a partial subject of international law with the capacity to maintain diplomatic relations with states and international

---

12 'The Israel-PLO Declaration of Principles: Prelude to a Peace?' (1994) 34 *Va J Int L* 435–69 at p 452.

13 *Ibid*, p 465.

14 *Ibid*, p 467.

15 See, for example, YZ Blum, 'From Camp David to Oslo' (1994) 28 *Israel LR* 211 at pp 212–13.

organisations recognising it and to conclude treaties. As a partial subject of international law, the PLO is not equal to a state, but that does not affect the validity of a treaty it concludes with a state.

Yehuda Blum argues that, even if one would be prepared to recognise that national liberation movements could have the status as subjects under international law, 'it does not necessarily follow that agreements entered by them become international agreements; partial and limited subjects of international law logically have only partial capacities under that law'.[16] This argument is not convincing for the following reasons. If the Israel-PLO agreements are not international agreements under public international law, then they must be governed by some national legal system, as in the case of so-called 'state contracts' concluded by a host state and a foreign company (unless, as more frequently in the past, a reference in the contract is made to international law as the governing law, which does not necessarily elevate the contract to the level of a treaty in the international law sense). Quite apparently, this would lead to absurd results.

Moreover, there are two clear indications in the agreements themselves that the parties consider them to be international agreements. First, there is express reference in some provisions that certain action has to be taken 'in accordance with international law'. Second ... the methods of disputes settlement provided for in the agreements are the typical ones of international law dispute settlement procedures. An additional argument can be found in the facts that the United Nations has endorsed the Israel-PLO Accord, that other states have signed as witnesses and that a multilateral international framework has been created in support of the Middle East peace process, all of which does not lend support to the view that the agreements are non-international ones. The agreements made between Israel and the PLO included the recognition by Israel of the PLO as the representative of the Palestinian people, and thereby are clearly governed by international law.

The second issue is: what kind of agreements are these under international law? Although the DOP is entitled 'Declaration' its content reveals that the parties did not want to enter into a mere 'gentleman's agreement' or just intended a declaration of policy. There is, furthermore, no reason to consider the text could be qualified as non-binding on the grounds that it lacks precision, in the sense that Judge Lauterpacht argued in his declaration attached to the judgment of the International Court of Justice in the *Sovereignty of Certain Frontier Land* case, namely that 'the ... provisions ... must be considered as void and inapplicable on account of uncertainty and unresolved discrepancy'.[17] First, the view held by some authors that the vagueness of treaty provisions may lead to the conclusion that these provisions are not legally binding is in itself incorrect. If the parties intended to conclude a treaty, then it is binding as a whole, even if some parts contain broad or unclear language. Vague provisions may give the parties a broad margin of discretion, but as Bernhardt notes, that is not to say that they are without legal significance and binding substance.[18] Secondly, even if one would like to take the contrary view, the detailed nature of many of the obligations laid down in the Israel-PLO agreements (especially after the DOP) clearly show that

16   YZ Blum, 'From Camp David to Oslo' (1994) 28 *Israel LR* 211 at p 213.

17   [1959] *ICJ Rep* 209 at p 231.

18   See R Bernhardt, 'Treaties' (1984) 7 *EPIL* 459–64 at p 461.

the provisions are sufficiently clear and that the parties intended to enter into binding commitments and not merely concluded a non-binding agreement. This is less true with regard to the agreement to negotiate later on the permanent status. It is generally accepted that an obligation to take part in negotiations and to conduct them in good faith, may form the valid and practical object of an international undertaking.[19, 20]

4.2.3 An intention to produce legal effects

An analogy may be drawn with the requirement in municipal contract law of an intention to be bound. Agreements will not be legally enforceable as treaties if it can be shown that one or more of the parties did not intend that the agreement should create binding legal obligations. So, for example, the Final Act of the Helsinki Conference on Security and Co-operation in Europe 1975 provided that it was to be 'not eligible for registration [as a treaty] under Article 102 of the Charter of the United Nations' and throughout the conference it was understood by the participants that the Final Act would not be legally binding. Such agreements may create 'soft law' as discussed in Chapter 3.

4.2.4 Legal effects under public international law

Perhaps the most important requirement of a treaty is that it is an agreement 'governed by international law'. In 1962 the ILC started a detailed study of the law of treaties and the Special *Rapporteur*, Sir Humphrey Waldock, stated in his first report to the ILC that:

> The element of subjection to international law is so essential a part of an international agreement that it should be expressly mentioned in the definition. There may be agreements between states, such as agreements for the acquisition of premises for a diplomatic mission or for some purely commercial transaction, the incidents of which are regulated by the local law of one of the parties or by a private law system determined by reference to conflict of laws principles. Whether in such cases the two states are internationally accountable to each other at all may be a nice question; but even if that were held to be so – it would not follow that the basis of their international accountability was a treaty obligation.[21]

An illustration of this point is provided by the *Anglo-Iranian Oil Co* case (1952).[22] In that case, which arose after Iran had nationalised the oil industry, the UK sought to rely on an agreement made in 1933 between the Anglo-Iranian Oil Co and the government of Iran. The UK argued that the agreement was a treaty and therefore was binding on Iran. The argument was rejected by the ICJ which found that the agreement was nothing more than a concessionary contract between a government and a foreign corporation.

---

19 Judge De Visscher in his dissenting opoinion to the ICJ's Advisory Opinion of 11 July 1950 on *South West Africa* [1950] *ICJ Rep* 186 at p 188.

20 P Malanczuk, 'Some Basic Aspects of the Agrements between Israel and the PLO from the Perspective of International Law (1996) 7 *EJIL* 485 at pp 488–91.

21 Sir Humphrey Waldock [1962] 2 *Yearbook of the International Law Commission* 32.

22 [1952] *ICJ Rep* p 1.

4.2.5 Designation

It should also be noted that the particular designation of the agreement does not govern its validity as a treaty – agreements may be entitled Conventions, Accords, Final Acts, Statutes, Exchange of Notes, Protocols – they are all to be regarded as treaties for these purposes. The designation given may however be of relevance in indicating the nature of the transaction. For example an 'agreement' is usually less formal than a 'treaty' and the term 'convention' will generally indicate a multilateral agreement.

4.3 Conclusion and entry into force of treaties

4.3.1 Accrediting of negotiators

Once a state has decided to create a treaty, it is necessary to appoint representatives to conduct the negotiations. It is necessary that such representatives should be fully accredited and given sufficient authority to conduct negotiations, and conclude and sign the final treaty. As a general rule such authority is contained in a formal document known as 'Full Powers' or often *'Pleins Pouvoirs'*. Full Powers can be dispensed with if practice between the negotiating states shows an intention to consider them as read and a gradual reduction in the use of Full Powers by states can be identified in the recent conduct of international relations.

In the case of multilateral agreements which are generally concluded at international conferences, the practice is for a committee to be set up to investigate the validity of the accreditation of all delegates.

Article 7 of the VCT reflects the rules in customary international law and in the *Legal Status of East Greenland* case (1933) the special position of foreign ministers as representatives for the purpose of entering into international agreements was expressly recognised by the Permanent Court.

If an unauthorised person were to enter into an agreement, his/her actions would be without legal effect unless subsequently confirmed by the state. Article 8 of the VCT 1969 provides a further safeguard against abuse by enabling a state to denounce an agreement entered into by an unauthorised person.

4.3.2 Negotiation and adoption

Negotiations concerning a treaty are conducted either through *pourparlers* in the case of bilateral treaties or at a diplomatic conference in the case of multilateral treaties. The negotiators will maintain contact with their governments and usually, before actually signing a treaty, they will obtain a new set of instructions indicating the manner of signature. The procedure at diplomatic conferences runs to a standard pattern with the appointment of committees and *rapporteurs* to manage the conference as efficiently as possible.

The aim of negotiation is the production of an agreed text of a treaty. The text is adopted by the consent of the parties. Article 9 of the VCT 1969 provides that the adoption of a treaty text at an international conference requires a two-thirds majority of those present and voting, unless a two-thirds majority decides otherwise. A common practice over recent years has been for the final text of multilateral treaties to be adopted by a meeting of the relevant international organisation, for example, the UN General Assembly.

4.3.3 Authentication, signature and exchange

When the text of the treaty has been agreed upon and adopted, the treaty is ready for signing. Signing the treaty, which is usually a formal occasion, serves to authenticate the text. Signing is, therefore, essential to the validity of the treaty unless other methods of authentication have been agreed.

4.3.4 Effect of signature

The effect of signature depends upon whether the treaty is subject to ratification, acceptance or approval. If this is the case, then the signature means no more than that the delegates have agreed a text and have referred it to their governments for approval and ratification. Thus in the *North Sea Continental Shelf* cases (1969), although the Federal Republic of Germany had signed the Continental Shelf Convention 1958 it was not bound by its provisions since it had not ratified it. For this reason, Denmark and Holland had to base their arguments on rules of customary international law. In keeping with the general requirement of good faith, Article 18 of the VCT 1969 provides that where a state signs a treaty which is subject to ratification there is an obligation to do nothing to defeat the object of the treaty until the state has made its intentions clear. Sometimes the treaty will provide that it is to operate on a provisional basis as from the date of signature.

If the treaty is not expressed to be subject to ratification or is silent on the matter the treaty is binding as from the date of signature (Article 12 of the VCT 1969).

4.3.5 Ratification

The next stage, if necessary, is for the delegates to refer the treaty back to their governments for approval. Ratification is the approval by the head of state or government of the signature to the treaty. Article 2 of the VCT 1969 defines ratification as the international act whereby a state establishes on the international plane its consent to be bound by a treaty. Ratification does not have retroactive effect, so states are only bound from the date of ratification, not the date of signature.

It used to be thought that ratification was always essential, but that is no longer the case. Nowadays, it is a question of the intention of the parties as to whether ratification is a mandatory requirement.

It should be noted that the method by which ratification is actually accomplished is a matter for individual states. In the UK, although treaties are signed and ratified under the royal prerogative without the need for reference to Parliament, the practice is to lay the text of any treaty before both Houses of Parliament for 21 days before ratification (this practice is known as the *Ponsonby Rule*).

Generally, ratification has no effect until some notice of it is given to the other parties to the treaty. In the case of bilateral treaties, ratifications are simply exchanged between the parties. This is clearly impractical in the case of multilateral treaties, so multilateral treaties usually provide for the deposit of all ratifications with one central body – in nearly all cases this function is performed by the Secretariat of the United Nations.

4.3.6   Accessions and adhesions

When a state has not signed a treaty it can only accede or adhere to it. Accession indicates that a state is to become a party to the whole treaty, whereas adhesion only involves acceptance of part of a treaty. Strictly speaking states can only accede or adhere to a treaty with the consent of all the existing parties. In practice, the consent of existing parties to accession is often implied.

4.3.7   Entry into force

When a treaty is to enter into force depends upon its provisions, or upon what the parties may otherwise have agreed. Treaties may be operative on signature, or on ratification. Multilateral treaties usually provide for entry into force only after the deposit of a specific number of ratifications, for example, Article 19 of the International Convention on the Elimination of all Forms of Racial Discrimination 1986 provides:

> This Convention shall enter into force on the thirtieth day after the date of the deposit with the Secretary General of the United Nations of the twenty-seventh instrument of ratification or instrument of accession.

VCT 1969 itself entered into force after the receipt by the Secretary General of the 35th ratification. Sometimes a precise date for the entry into force of a treaty is given irrespective of the number of ratifications received.

4.3.8   Registration and publication

Article 102 of the United Nations Charter provides that all treaties entered into by members of the United Nations shall 'as soon as possible' be registered with the Secretariat of the United Nations and be published by it. A similar provision was laid down in Article 18 of the League of Nations Covenant. Failure to so register and publish the treaty will mean that the treaty cannot be invoked in any UN organ. Most significantly this would mean that a state would be unable to rely on an unregistered treaty in proceedings before the ICJ. This provision was included to try to combat the use of secret treaties which were considered to have a detrimental effect on international relations. Article 80 of the VCT 1969 provides that treaties shall, after their entry into force, be transmitted to the Secretariat of the UN for registration or filing and recording, as the case may be, and for publication.

In fact a considerable proportion of treaties are not registered. Paul Reuter suggests that statistical research based on the League of Nations and the United Nations Treaty Series shows that 25% of treaties have not been registered. Although the effect of non-registration of treaties has been discussed on a number of occasions before the ICJ, it is not possible to draw any definite conclusions.

4.4   Reservations

It can frequently happen that a state, while wishing to become a party to a treaty, considers that it can do so only if it can exclude or modify one or more particular provisions contained in the treaty. Ideally, such a state will be able to convince the other parties to amend the text of the treaty to incorporate its specific wishes. However, often this will not be possible and the regime of reservations allows a state, in certain circumstances, to alter the effect of the treaty in respect of its own obligations while preserving the original treaty intact as between the other parties.

4.4.1 Definitions

The growth of reservations to treaties coincides with the growth in multilateral conventions. With regard to bilateral treaties, the two parties to the treaty may disagree over the precise terms of the treaty which is to bind them. If this is the case, they may re-negotiate the terms until they achieve full agreement. There will be no treaty in existence until both sides agree on the terms. From this it follows that there can be no question of reservations to a bilateral treaty. In the case of multilateral treaties, it may not always be possible to get the full agreement of all the negotiating parties to every provision of the treaty. The general practice is for the text of such treaties to be adopted by two-thirds majorities. In the event of such a vote, those parties in the minority are in something of a dilemma: they can either refuse to become parties to the whole treaty, or they can accept the whole treaty even though they disagree with one or more of its provisions. The regime of reservations provides something of a compromise: those in the minority can become parties to the treaty without accepting all of the provisions therein.

Reservations should be distinguished from so-called 'interpretative declarations' whereby a state indicates the view which it holds about the substance of the treaty. Interpretative declarations are not intended as an attempt to derogate from the full legal effect of provisions of the treaty. In practice, the distinction between reservations and interpretative declarations may not always be clear cut. In *Belios v Switzerland* (1988) the European Court of Human Rights had to consider the nature of a declaration made by Switzerland when it ratified the European Convention on Human Rights. Switzerland argued against a finding of the Commission that the declaration was a mere interpretative declaration which did not have the effect of a reservation. The Court found that the declaration was a reservation and in the course of its judgment said:

> The question whether a declaration described as 'interpretative' must be regarded as a 'reservation' is a difficult one ... In order to establish the legal character of such a declaration, one must look behind the title given to it and seek to determine the substantive content.

4.4.2 Validity of reservations

The formerly accepted rule for all kinds of multilateral treaty was that reservations were valid only if the treaty concerned permitted reservations and if all the other parties accepted the reservation. On this basis a reservation constituted a counter-offer which required the acceptance of the other parties, failing which the state making the counter-offer would not become a party to the treaty.

During the period of the League of Nations the practice with regard to multilateral conventions was inconsistent. In 1927 the Committee of Experts for the Progressive Codification of International Law, the League of Nations' equivalent of the International Law Commission, adopted a policy based on the absolute integrity of treaties and argued that reservations to treaties would not be effective without the full acceptance of all parties. At the same time, the members of the Pan-American Union (the forerunner of the Organisation of American states) adopted a more flexible policy including the following key elements:

(a) as between states which ratify a treaty without reservations, the treaty applies in the terms in which it was originally drafted and signed;

(b) as between states which ratify a treaty with reservations and states which accept those reservations, the treaty applies in the form in which it may be modified by the reservations; and

(c) as between states which ratify a treaty with reservations and states which, having already ratified, do not accept those reservations, the treaty will not be in force.

A small number of states, principally from Eastern Europe, adhered to the view that every state had a sovereign right to make reservations unilaterally and at will, and to become a party to treaties subject to such reservations, even if they were objected to by other Contracting States.

Matters came to a head following the unanimous adoption of the Convention on the Prevention and Punishment of the Crime of Genocide by the UN General Assembly in 1948. Article 9 of the Convention provided that disputes or cases arising under the Convention should be compulsorily within the jurisdiction of the ICJ. A number of states wished, for reasons of their own, to avoid being subject to the ICJ's compulsory jurisdiction, but the Convention contained no express provision allowing for reservations. The General Assembly therefore requested an advisory opinion from the ICJ on certain key questions:

1 Could a reserving state be regarded as being a party to the Convention while still maintaining its reservation if the reservation is objected to by one or more of the parties to the Convention but accepted by others?

2 If the answer to question 1 is in the affirmative, what is the effect of the reservation as between the reserving state and:

(a) the parties which object to the reservation?

(b) those which accept it?

The Court in the *Reservations to the Convention on Genocide* case (1951) ruled, by seven votes to five, in response to question 1 that a state which has made and maintained a reservation which has been objected to by one or more of the parties to the Convention but not by others, can be regarded as being a party to the Convention if the reservation is compatible with the object and purpose of the Convention; otherwise, that state cannot be regarded as being a party to the Convention.

In response to question 2, again by a seven:five majority, the ICJ found that:

(a) if a party to the Convention objects to a reservation which it considers to be incompatible with the object and purpose of the Convention, it can consider that the reserving state is not a party to the Convention;

(b) if, on the other hand, a party accepts the reservation as being compatible with the object and purpose of the Convention, it can in fact consider that the reserving state is a party to the Convention.

This judgment was not initially well-received. It was felt that the compatibility test was too subjective and that the result of the decision would be further uncertainty. The International Law Commission reported in 1951, after the Court had given its decision, and recommended a return to the traditional view that reservations required the unanimous consent of the parties to a treaty. However views did gradually change. By 1959 the UN General Assembly had adopted the ICJ's position and in 1962 the International Law Commission decided in favour of the compatibility test. That position was the one adopted by the VCT 1969 and represents customary international law. The relevant provisions are found in Articles 19–23. Article 19 provides that, in general, reservations are always permitted except in three instances:

(a) when the treaty explicitly forbids reservations;

(b) when the treaty does not permit the type of reservation being made;

(c) when the reservation is incompatible with the object and purpose of the treaty.

Some treaties provide mechanisms for deciding on compatibility of reservations – for example Article 20 of the Convention on the Elimination of Racial Discrimination 1966 provides that a reservation shall be considered incompatible if at least two-thirds of the state Parties to the Convention object to it.

Article 20 provides as follows:

1   A reservation expressly authorised by a treaty does not require any subsequent acceptance by the other Contracting States unless the treaty so provides.

2   When it appears from the limited number of negotiating states and the object and purposes of a treaty that the application of the treaty in its entirety between all the parties is an essential condition of the consent of each one to be bound by the treaty, a reservation requires acceptance by all the parties.

3   When a treaty is a constituent instrument of an international organisation and unless it otherwise provides, a reservation requires the acceptance of the competent organ of that organisation.

4   In cases not falling under the preceding paragraphs and unless the treaty otherwise provides:

   (a)   acceptance by another Contracting State of a reservation constitutes the reserving state a party to the treaty in relation to that other state if or when the treaty is in force for those states;

   (b)   an objection by another Contracting State to a reservation does not preclude the entry into force of the treaty as between the objecting and reserving states unless a contrary intention is definitely expressed by the objecting state;

   (c)   an act expressing a state's consent to be bound by the treaty and containing a reservation is effective as soon as at least one other Contracting State has accepted the reservation.

5   For the purposes of paras 2 and 4 and unless the treaty otherwise provides, a reservation is considered to have been accepted by a state if it shall have raised no objection to the reservation by the end of a period of twelve months after it was notified of the reservation or by the date on which it expressed its consent to be bound by the treaty, whichever is later.

Article 21 spells out the legal effects of reservations and sets down three main rules:

1   A reservation modifies the provisions of the treaty to which it relates as regards the reserving state in its relations with other parties and as regards the other parties in their relations with the reserving state.

2   A reservation does not modify the provisions of the treaty for the other parties to the treaty *inter se*.

3   When a state objecting to a reservation has not opposed the entry into force of the treaty between itself and the reserving state, the provisions to which the reservation relates do not apply as between the two states to the extent of the reservation.

Rule 3 was illustrated in the *English Channel Arbitration* (1979) between France and the UK. During the course of the arbitration it was necessary to consider the effect of reservations to Article 6 of the Continental Shelf Convention 1958 to which the UK had objected. VCT 1969 does not apply to the Continental Shelf Convention so the issue had to be decided in accordance with customary law. France argued that the combined effect of reservations and objections was to render Article 6 completely inapplicable as between Britain and France, whereas the UK sought to argue that the effect was to render the article applicable *in toto*. The Court of Arbitration rejected both arguments and held that the combined effect of the reservation and the objection to it was to render Article 6 'inapplicable as between the two countries to the extent, but only to the extent, of the reservations'.

VCT 1969 further provides that reservations and acceptances/objections to reservations must be in writing.

4.5   Application of treaties

4.5.1   The observance of treaties

The doctrine of *pacta sunt servanda*, the rule that treaties are binding on the parties and must be performed in good faith, is a fundamental principle of international law. The rule is included in the VCT 1969 by Article 26 which provides that 'every treaty in force is binding on the parties to it and must be performed in good faith'. As was mentioned in Chapter 1, the principle is derived from the *jus gentium* of the Roman legal system. There has been some discussion as to the question of whence the rule derives its authority and the precise status of the rule. The principle is certainly one of customary international law evidenced by widespread state practice and *opinio juris*. The fact that it is a recognised rule of customary international law enables the VCT 1969 itself to be binding. Arguably, *pacta sunt servanda* constitutes a higher rule of customary law since it is difficult to envisage how a system of international law could operate without it. In this sense it might be viewed as constituting one of the true sources of international law in the sense of a *Grundnorm* as identified by Kelsen. It could also be validly claimed to constitute a rule of *jus cogens*.

4.5.2 Non-retroactivity

Article 28 of the VCT 1969 reflects the customary rule of non-retroactivity of treaties. The provisions of a treaty do not bind a party in relation to any act or fact which took place or any situation which ceased to exist before the treaty entered into force for that state, unless a different intention appears from the treaty or is otherwise established. The rule applies to the VCT 1969 itself which has no application to any treaty entered into before the VCT 1969 came into force. Where treaties are the subject of ratification it is necessary to remember the rule expressed in Article 18 of the VCT 1969 which provides that states, having signed a treaty, should not act in any way to defeat the object and purpose of the treaty until it has made a clear final decision with regard to ratification. It should also be noted that treaties can apply to continuing situations. Although a situation may have arisen before a treaty came into force, it will be governed by the provisions of the treaty if it continues to exist after the treaty comes into force.

4.5.3 Territorial application

The general rule, reflected in Article 29 of the VCT 1969, is that, unless some other intention is made clear, a treaty applies to the entire territory of each party. The issue of territorial application arises where parties to a treaty have overseas territorial possessions, and the presumption is that a treaty applies to all the territory for which Contracting States are internationally responsible. Thus, unless the contrary is explicitly indicated, treaties to which the UK is a party apply to the British colonies and all territory for which the UK is internationally responsible, for example the Channel Islands and the Isle of Man.

4.5.4 Successive treaties

The problem of a later treaty inconsistent with an earlier one is a complex issue, but Article 30 of the VCT 1969 sets out general rules that deal with the majority of cases. As far as UN members are concerned, the UN Charter prevails over any other international agreement which conflicts with it. Otherwise, the basic rules are:

(a) a prior treaty prevails over a later one in any instance of apparent disagreement when the later one specifies that it is subject to, or not incompatible with, the earlier one;

(b) where all the parties to the earlier treaty are also parties to the later treaty, the earlier (if still in effect) applies only to the extent that its provisions are compatible with those of the later treaty;

(c) when the parties to the two treaties are not identical, the earlier applies between states that are parties to both only to the extent that the earlier is not incompatible with the later, while as between a state which is party to both treaties and a state which is a party to only one of the treaties, the treaty to which both are parties governs their mutual rights and obligations.

4.5.5 Treaties and third parties

The general rule expressed in the maxim, *pacta tertiis nec nocent nec prosunt*, is that treaties cannot bind third parties without their consent. The rule is affirmed in Article 34 of the VCT 1969. However, situations in which the rights and duties of third parties are involved have occasionally been created by treaties which are said to establish objective regimes, creating rights and obligations valid universally (*erga omnes*). *Erga omnes* is not a term used in VCT 1969 but Article 36 does provide:

> 1   A right arises for a third state from a provision of a treaty if the parties to the treaty intend the provision to accord that right to a third state, or to a group of states ...

The International Law Commission considered that this provided the legal basis for establishing rights valid *erga omnes* and did not propose any special provision on treaties creating so-called objective regimes such as the Antarctic Treaty 1959. Certainly there is less difficulty where a treaty creates rights for third parties than the situation where a treaty purports to impose obligations on non parties. The subject of *erga omnes* obligations will be considered in more detail in connection with human rights law and environmental protection in Chapters 15 and 17. There are a number of examples of treaties establishing rights for third parties particularly with respect to rights over territory. The Constantinople Convention 1888 was for a long time considered to give a right of passage through the Suez Canal to states that were not parties to the agreement, as did the Treaty of Versailles 1919 with respect to the Kiel Canal.

> The Vienna Convention's five articles dealing directly with treaties and third parties are narrowly drawn and limited in their application. Article 34 commences with a restatement of the classic *pacta tertiis* rule which underscores principles of sovereignty and equality. There is no concession to the various claimed exceptions, nor do the subsequent articles shed any light on possible inroads to the rule. 'The principle enunciated in Article 34, namely that treaties did not have effects with respect to third states was thus absolute.'[23] The decision not to enunciate any exceptions meant that there was also no attempt to provide a juridical basis for any such exceptions.
>
> After the uncompromising stance of Article 34, the following articles deal separately with the imposition of obligations upon third states and the bestowal of rights. The connecting factors are the intentions of the parties and third party assent, which reinforce a narrow, contractual view of treaties. Articles 35 and 36 assume that the parties' intentions and the third party's consent can be accurately determined, and will coincide. If they do not, no obligation can have been imposed, nor right bestowed.
>
> A distinction is drawn between rights and obligations for the purpose of the means of manifesting third party consent. A third party must expressly consent in writing to an obligation, but may impliedly consent to the acceptance of a right. However, as has been seen through the examination of many of the claims, rights and obligations cannot be treated as invariably distinct for they are often interrelated. Rights and obligations are interlocked in the formation of a bargain where all involved have duties to perform and expectations arising. Especially is

---

23   P Reuter [1982] 1 *YBILC* 26.

this so where conditions are attached to the claiming of a right. There is no logical reason for according primacy to either concept; rather they should be treated together.

The International Law Commission, and subsequently the Conference at Vienna, preferred a rigid construction of treaty law so as more easily to gain agreement on a text. The inflexibility is repeated in the subsequent Vienna Convention on International Organisations which, apart form the inclusion of international organisations as parties and third parties to treaties, adopts the same starting point. The narrowness of Articles 34–38 in both Conventions might give the impression that international law has receded from its earlier acceptance of exceptions to the general rule. In fact, a closer examination of both the Conventions, and of developments external to the law of treaties, demonstrates that this has not been the case.

...

The effect of treaties on third parties cannot be determined merely by the formal application of specified rules of treaty law. Indeed, in some instances these rules are inadequate for the changing claims of both parties and non-parties. Instead third party claims must be analysed to determine their relevant factual context, the appropriate policies, and the applicable law. Certain exceptions to the *pacta tertiis* rule can be summarised as falling under the following heads: acquiescence in the conduct of parties and non-parties; application of a special principle of law outweighing the general third party rule; the existence of some situation that displaces the application of treaty law. There is a realisation that the *pacta tertiis* rule should not be applied inflexibly to produce inequity. While the *pacta tertiis* rule formally applies to all states and produces an appearance of equality, in fact it favours stronger states. Such states could conclude (and have concluded) agreements in their own interests which were presented as being to further overall community goals and, as such, binding on weaker states. A number of peace settlements and other territorial arrangements in the 19th and early 20th centuries can perhaps be categorised in this way. At the same time the rule could be cited against weaker powers.

The manipulation of the *pacta tertiis* rule by stronger states and the recognition that one of the major exceptions to it worked primarily to their benefit, has perhaps led to a current tendency to ensure as many states as possible are included in a treaty relationship rather than having more powerful states in effect dictate settlements in the name of the public benefit. Sensitivity to the sovereignty of weaker states favours the inclusion of all interested parties in a treaty arrangement. An example is the package of treaties constituting the Afghanistan settlement.[24] While the United States and the Soviet Union were parties to the arrangement through the Agreement on the Interrelationships for the Settlement of the Situation relating to Afghanistan, so too were Afghanistan and Pakistan. The settlement was not limited to the superpowers and imposed upon the others. The same is true of the Cambodia peace settlement. Devices to include as many parties as possible are also seen in widely phrased accession clauses, and in the use of Protocols allowing for adherence or accession. While presenting problems of juridical analysis, the aim is to provide certainty and stability by including interested or essential (state) participants in the treaty scheme. it may be that traditional treaty analysis which divides states into parties

---

24   Geneva, 4 April 1988 (1988) 27 *ILM* 581.

and non-parties will not work with these devices whose operation should not be frustrated by the technicalities of international law.

The mechanisms described above operate on the assumption of the *pacta tertiis* rule and use it to create interlocking treaty relationships. On the other hand this process disadvantages weaker states where stronger states refuse to accept the invitation to join a treaty regime. There is another development which impacts in the opposite way. There has been a growing use of less formal ways of creating international obligations, primarily through collective actions of international organisations as expressed through their resolutions. Although the formal position remains that General Assembly resolutions are not binding, it is now widely accepted that legitimate expectations as to future behaviour may be engendered by them, which only an unwise or excessively formalistic decision-maker would ignore. The *pacta tertiis* rule has become less relevant with this change: if even those voting in favour of a resolution are not formally bound by it, then 'third' parties are that much further removed form any commitments. However, in a practical sense, it may be very difficult for those states which abstained or dissented form a resolution (third parties) to remain aloof from its consequences. Developing states have favoured the passing of resolutions expressing their interests through their voting majority in the General Assembly and support claims as to their normative effect. Thus there may be a claim that the principles enunciated in General Assembly resolutions relating to the existence of a common heritage of peoples have become opposable even to third parties to a treaty in which the concept is incorporated, for example, the United Nations Convention on the Law of the Sea. Subsequent state conduct and acquiescence may once again play a decisive role in determining obligations flowing from General Assembly resolutions. In considering the current status of the *pacta tertiis* rule exclusive consideration of treaty-making processes distorts the current international prescriptive process. There are instrumentalities for change and development of international law which may not satisfy rigorous application of the traditional criteria for determining normative effect, and which consequently cause juridical inconsistency, but which cannot be disregarded. Any analysis of the classic third party rule is inevitably entwined with this change in the prescriptive process.[25]

It should not be forgotten that the provisions contained in treaties might bind non-parties as rules of customary international law either in situations where the treaty is itself a codification of existing international law or where the treaty leads to the gradual development of new rules of custom.

4.6   Amendment and modification

Prior to VCT 1969 the customary law rule was that a treaty could not be revised without the consent of all the parties, although there was evidence that by 1969 state practice had already begun to depart from the rule. The ILC, when considering the draft convention on treaties, noted the enormous increase in the number of multilateral treaties and the fact that obtaining the consent of all the parties would not always be possible (there are parallels here with the discussions about reservations). The VCT 1969 now draws a distinction between 'amendments' and 'modifications'. Amendment, covered by Article 40, denotes

---

25   C Chinkin, *Third Parties in International Law*, 1993, Oxford: Clarendon Press, at pp 134–35, 142–44.

a formal change in a treaty intended to alter its provisions with respect to all the parties. Modification, dealt with in Article 41, indicates an *inter se* agreement concluded between certain of the parties only, and intended to alter the provisions of the treaty between themselves alone. Modification is only allowed if:

(1) it is permitted by the treaty;

(2) it is not prohibited by the treaty;

(3) it does not affect the other parties to the treaty;

(4) it is not incompatible with the treaty.

More usually amendment or modification is achieved in the case of multilateral treaties by another multilateral treaty which comes into force only for those states which agree to the changes.

4.7   Treaty interpretation

23 The Court recalls that, according to customary international law as expressed in Article 31 of the Vienna Convention on the Law of Treaties of 23 May 1969, a treaty must be interpreted in good faith in accordance with the ordinary meaning to be given to its terms in their context and in the light of its object and purpose. Under Article 32, recourse may be had to supplementary means of interpretation such as the preparatory work and the circumstances in which the treaty was concluded.[26]

4.7.1 Aims and goals of interpretation

There is a measure of disagreement among jurists as to the aims of treaty interpretation. There are those who assert that the primary, and indeed only, aim of treaty interpretation is to ascertain the intention of the parties – this is generally referred to as the *subjective approach*. On the other hand, there are those who start from the proposition that there must be a presumption that the intention of the parties are reflected in the text of the treaty which they have drawn up, and that the primary aim of interpretation is to ascertain the meaning of this text – generally referred to as the *objective* or *textual approach*. Finally, there are those who maintain that the decision-maker must first ascertain the object and purpose of a treaty and then interpret it so as to give effect to that object and purpose – the *teleological* or *object and purpose approach*.

It should be noted straight away that these three schools of thought are not mutually exclusive and a tribunal will probably draw on all three views to some extent when attempting to interpret a treaty. It should also be noted that some writers have argued that it is impossible to discern any general rules or principles governing treaty interpretation, instead what is found is a series of *ex post facto* rationalisations of decisions reached for other reasons.

---

26 *Case Concerning Oil Platforms (Islamic Republic of Iran v United States of America) (Preliminary Objection)* Judgment of ICJ of 12 December 1996.

4.7.2 The Vienna Convention on the Law of Treaties 1969 Section 3

Section 3 of the VCT 1969 adopts a composite position. Article 31 states that treaties 'shall be interpreted in good faith in accordance with the ordinary meaning to be given to the terms of the treaty in their context and in the light of their object and purpose'.

4.7.2.1 Good faith

The principle of good faith underlies the most fundamental norm of treaty law – *pacta sunt servanda*. If the parties to a treaty are required to perform the obligations of a treaty in 'good faith', it is logical to interpret the treaty in 'good faith'.

4.7.2.2 Ordinary meaning

The ordinary meaning does not necessarily result from a strict grammatical analysis. In order to arrive at the ordinary meaning account will need to be taken of all the consequences which reasonably flow from the text. It is also clear that the ordinary meaning of a phrase cannot be ascertained divorced from the context the phrase has in the treaty as a whole. In the *Employment of Women During the Night* case (1932), Judge Anzilotti said:

> I do not see how it is possible to say that an article of a convention is clear until the subject and aim of the convention have been ascertained, for the article only assumes its true import in this convention and in relation thereto. Only when it is known what the contracting parties intended to do and the aim that they had in view is it possible to say either that the natural meaning of terms used in a particular article corresponds with the real intention of the parties, or that the natural meaning of the terms used falls short of or goes further than such intention.[27]

This view can be contrasted with the decision of the ICJ given in the advisory opinion in the *Competence of the General Assembly for the Admission of a State to the UN* case (1950)[28] where the Court said that:

> the first duty of a tribunal which is called upon to interpret and apply the provisions of a treaty is to endeavour to give effect to them in their natural and ordinary meaning in the context in which they occur. If the relevant words in their natural and ordinary meaning make sense in their context, that is an end of the matter.

4.7.2.3 Special meaning

Paragraph 4 of Article 31 provides that a special meaning shall be given to a term if it is established that the parties so intended. In the *Eastern Greenland* case, the PCIJ stated:

> The geographical meaning of the word 'Greenland', ie the name which is habitually used in maps to denote the whole island, must be regarded as the ordinary meaning of the word. If it is alleged by one of the parties that some unusual or exceptional meaning is to be attributed to it, it lies on that party to establish its contention.[29]

---

27 PCIJ Ser A/B, No 50 (1932).

28 [1950] *ICJ Rep* at p 8.

29 PCIJ Ser A/B, No 53 (1933).

4.7.2.4 The context and the object and purpose

The context, for the purposes of interpretation, includes the text, its preamble and annexes and any agreement relating to the treaty made between all the parties, or made by some of the parties and accepted by the other, in connection with the conclusion of the treaty. The text of the treaty must be read as a whole. The preamble to the treaty will often provide assistance in ascertaining the object and purpose of a treaty.

4.7.2.5 Supplementary means of interpretation

Although Article 32 talks of 'supplementary means of interpretation', in practice international tribunals do tend to blur any differences between Article 31 and Article 32 and the preparatory work often referred to by the French term *travaux préparatoires* is regarded as a considerable aid. In the *Employment of Women* case the PCIJ referred to the *travaux préparatoires* to confirm the clear meaning of the text. One possible restriction on the use of *travaux préparatoires* as an aid to interpretation arises where some of the parties to the dispute have not been involved in the preparatory work leading to the treaty. So, for example, in the *River Oder* case (1929) the PCIJ refused to allow reference to the preparatory work of the Treaty of Versailles 1919 on the grounds that several of the parties to the dispute had not taken part in the work of the Conference which had prepared the treaty.

4.8   Multilingual treaties

Treaties are often drafted in two or more languages. In the case of bilateral treaties, the normal practice is that the treaty texts should be drawn up in the two languages of the parties, both texts being equally authentic. Multilateral conventions may be concluded in many languages: conventions concluded under the auspices of the UN will be drawn up in Arabic, Chinese, English, French, Russian and Spanish; the treaty by which Greece became a member of the European Union was concluded in eight languages. A more common practice is to conclude a treaty in two or three widely spoken languages and for these two or three texts to be equally authentic, and for a number of official translations to be deposited with the signed original. If a number of texts are equally authentic, they may be read in conjunction in order to ascertain the meaning of the convention.

4.9   Validity of treaties

The VCT 1969 represents both codification of existing rules of customary international law and also the progressive development of international law. Part V of the Convention which deals with invalidity, termination and suspension represents more a 'progressive development' of the law than simple codification. In looking at the grounds of invalidity contained in the VCT 1969, it should be borne in mind that the customary law rules on validity may well not be as rigid or as settled.

4.9.1 Non-compliance with municipal law requirements

A state cannot plead a breach of its constitutional provisions as to the making of treaties as a reason for invalidating an agreement. For example, where the representative of the state has had her/his authority to consent on behalf of the state made subject to a specific restriction which is ignored, the state will still be bound by that consent except where the other negotiating states were aware of the restriction on authority prior to the expression of consent.

4.9.2 Error

Unlike the role of mistake in municipal contract law, the scope of error in international law is very limited. In practice, given the number of people and the character of states involved in the negotiation and conclusion of treaties, errors are not very likely to occur.

Article 48 declares that a state may only invoke an error in a treaty as invalidating its consent to be bound, if the error relates to a fact or situation which was assumed by that state to exist at the time when the treaty was concluded and formed an essential basis of its consent to be bound. The ground is not open to the state if it contributed to the error by its own conduct or the circumstances were such as to put it on notice of a possible error, or if the error related only to the wording of the text of the treaty.

4.9.3 Fraud and corruption

Where a state consents to be bound by a treaty as a result of the fraudulent conduct of another negotiating state, that state may under Article 49 of the VCT 1969 invoke the fraud as invalidating its consent to be bound. Fraud itself is not defined in the VCT 1969 and since there are no examples of treaties being invalidated as a result of fraud there is a lack of international precedents as to what constitutes fraudulent conduct.

If a state's consent to a treaty has been procured through the corruption of its representative, directly or indirectly by another negotiating state, the former state is entitled to claim that the treaty is invalid under Article 50 of the VCT 1969.

4.9.4 Coercion

4.9.4.1 Coercion of state representatives

Article 51 of the VCT 1969 provides that the expression of a state's consent to be bound by a treaty which has been procured by the coercion of its representative through acts or threats directed against him/her shall be without any legal effect. It has long been an accepted rule of customary international law that duress exercised against a representative concluding a treaty has been a ground for invalidating the treaty.

4.9.4.2 Coercion of a state

There was considerable discussion about Article 52. In the 19th century force had often been seen as a legitimate extension of diplomacy and treaties procured by force were not uncommon. The concept that a treaty may be void if its conclusion has been procured by threat or use of force is therefore of recent origin. At the Vienna Conference discussion centred on the exact definition of 'force'. A group of 19 African, Asian and Latin American states sought to define 'force' as including any economic or political pressure. The vast majority of Western states opposed such a definition, arguing that it would seriously undermine the stability of treaty relations given the width of possible interpretations of pressure. In the event, the 19 states did not push the issue to a vote, although the Conference adopted a declaration which called upon states to refrain from economic and political coercion when negotiating and concluding treaties.

It should be noted that it is acceptance of the treaty that must be coerced. A peace treaty which is signed as a matter of choice between two independent states is valid even though its terms may have been influenced by a prior use of force.

There have been few recent examples of treaties brought about by the use of coercion. One of the best known cases involved the treaty between Germany and Czechoslovakia under which a German Protectorate was established in former Czechoslovakian territory. The treaty was signed by President Hacha of Czechoslovakia in Berlin at 2.00am after he had allegedly been subject to considerable personal threats and told that, if he did not sign, German bombers could destroy Prague within two hours.

4.9.5 Unequal treaties

Many non-Western states take the view that treaties not concluded on the basis of the sovereign equality of all parties are invalid. Thus, treaties between economically powerful states and much weaker states under which the latter grants extensive privileges or facilities to the former should be set aside. For example, the 19th century treaties between the UK and China under which China ceded Hong Kong Island and Kowloon and leased the New Territories to the UK was challenged by the Chinese government on the basis that they were not concluded between two equal states. On the whole, Western writers have regarded the concept of unequal treaties as too vague to be implemented.

4.9.6 Jus cogens

In the ILC's preparation of the Vienna Convention considerable discussion took place about whether there were in international law certain rules so fundamental and of such universal importance that a state would not be entitled to derogate from them even by agreement with another state in a treaty. The ILC concluded that such rules did exist, for example, the prohibition on the unlawful use of force and the use of genocide.

> *Jus cogens*
>
> The concept that a treaty concluded in violation of a norm of *jus cogens* is null and void is highly controversial. Any analysis of the concept requires an investigation into the relevance in international law of private law analogies and into the extent to which, if at all, there exists an objective notion of international public policy consisting of legal rules from which states are not permitted to derogate by way of international agreement.
>
> But first, you may ask, what is *jus cogens*? Suy defines it as 'the body of those general rules of law whose non-observance may affect the very essence of the

legal system to which they belong to such an extent that the subject of law may not, under pain of absolute nullity, depart from them in virtue of particular agreements'.[30] From this definition it will be noted that the concept of *jus cogens* is wholly general in nature and applicable to any system of law. It is not a concept which has been specially developed within the framework of public international law; on the contrary, it derives from, and is deeply embedded in, particular systems of private law.

The origin of the notion of *jus cogens* has been traced back to Roman law. The maxim *jus publicum privatorum pactis mutari non potest* is to be found in the *Digest*. The *jus publicum* was to be understood in a wide sense as embracing not only public law in the strict sense (that is to say, the law governing relations between individuals and the state) but also rules from which individuals were not permitted to depart by virtue of particular agreements.

The pervading influence of this general notion can be recognised by the development of such concepts as *ordre public* and *öffentliche Ordnung* in French and German law respectively, and by the gradual establishment in common law of the principle that certain types of contract are, by their very nature, injurious to society and therefore contrary to public policy. The genesis of this principle in English law can be traced back to Elizabethan times, although it was only in the 18th century that its foundations were effectively laid in a series of decisions proclaiming, in somewhat vague and indeterminate language, the nullity of contracts injurious to the public good or *contra bonos mores*.[31]

It will, then, be seen that every developed national system of law has devised its own concept of public policy. In civil law jurisdictions the notion of *ordre public* is essentially variable and relative, evolving in accordance with the political, social and economic circumstances of the time. In English law it is less variable; certain defined heads of public policy have been established by the courts, and although these heads can be moulded to fit the new conditions of a changing world, it is rarely possible for the courts to establish new heads of public policy.[32]

Thus there has gradually evolved over the years, in practically all systems of municipal law, the principle that the will of the parties to conclude contracts is not unfettered but is subject to certain restraints essential to the continued existence of an ordered society. What the nature of these restraints is will vary according to the political, economic or social climate in the country concerned. Certain restraints may be imposed by statute, others may have been developed by the jurisprudence of the courts. So far as restraints imposed by statute are concerned, political and economic factors may lead to the imposition of new controls on the freedom of individuals to contract, thus in England, the Resale Prices Act 1964 rendered void (subject to an exemption procedure) any term or condition of a contract for the sale of goods by a supplier to a dealer in so far as it provided for the establishment of minimum prices for the resale of the goods.

Notwithstanding the close connection between *jus cogens* and public policy, the two concepts do not entirely coincide, at least if public policy is conceived of in the narrower sense as being confined to the circumstances in which the municipal courts will refuse to enforce a contract. *Jus cogens* is the sum of

30   Suy in *The Concept of* Jus Cogens *in International Law*, 18 (1967).

31   Cheshire and Fifoot, *Law of Contract*, 8th edn, 1972, London: Butterworths at pp 318–25.

32   *Janson v Driefontein Consolidated Mines* [1902] AC 484 at p 492; *Fender v St John-Mildmay* [1938] AC 1 at p 40; see, however, McCardie J in *Naylor Benzon Ltd v Krainische Ind Ges* [1918] 1 KB 331 at p 349 and *Shaw v Director of Public Prosecutions* [1962] AC 220.

absolute, ordering, prohibiting municipal law proscriptions, in contrast to *jus dispotivium*, that is to say, legal prescriptions which can, and do, yield to the will of the parties.

...

It now remains to consider the most controversial aspect of them all: if, on the balance of conflicting considerations, one is constrained to admit the existence of *jus cogens* in international law, what is its content? What are these peremptory norms of general international law from which states are not permitted to derogate by treaty?

Let us begin by taking the more obvious candidates. I have already discussed the extreme case of a treaty which purports to abolish both retrospectively and prospectively the rule *pacta sunt servanda* between the contracting parties; however improbable such a treaty may be, it is difficult to see how its validity could be sustained. But leaving aside treaties whose object and purpose is to deny the fundamental principle underlying the law of treaties itself, what other categories of treaty could be regarded as being inconsistent with rules of *jus cogens*?

The Commission's commentary gives three examples:

(a)   A treaty contemplating an unlawful use of force contrary to the principles of the Charter.

(b)   A treaty contemplating the performance of any other act criminal under international law.

(c)   A treaty contemplating or conniving at the commission of acts, such as trade in slaves, piracy or genocide, in the suppression of which every state is called upon to co-operate.

There would be little disposition among jurists to deny the nullity of a treaty contemplating an unlawful use of force contrary to the principles of the Charter; but, given the pervasive influence of the modern propaganda machine designed to stand everything on its head, it is of course necessary to distinguish a treaty of this nature from a perfectly valid treaty for the organisation of collective self-defence in the event of an armed attack or the threat of an armed attack.

The second example given by the Commission in part overlaps the first, since a treaty between states A and B for the initiation of a war of aggression against state C would, as already indicated, fall foul of both prohibitions. But the second example would presumably also cover the other instance cited by Fitzmaurice – that is to say, a treaty whereby two states agree not to take any prisoners of war and to execute all captured personnel, during future hostilities between them. In this connection, Schwelb aptly reminds us that the four Geneva Conventions of 1949 on the Protection of War Victims all contain denunciation clauses providing that each of the parties shall be at liberty to denounce the Convention; but the denunciation clauses specifically state that denunciation 'shall in no way impair the obligations which the parties to the conflict shall remain bound to fulfil by virtue of the principles of the law of nations, as they result from the usages established among civilised peoples, from the laws of humanity and the dictates of the public conscience'. Schwelb concludes that this is a reference to something akin to *jus cogens* since, if a single state cannot release itself from their provisions by the act of denouncing the Conventions, it appears to follow that two or more states cannot derogate from these principles by agreements amongst themselves. In this he is probably right, given the particular content of the Geneva Conventions. But it does not follow that the inclusion of such a provision would constitute conclusive evidence of the *jus cogens* character of the rules embodied in that Convention since its purpose may be simply to preserve the operation of the rules as rules of customary international law. In the final analysis, it is the *content* of the rules which will be decisive in the determination of whether or not they have the attributes of *jus cogens*.

The third example given by the Commission opens up the floodgates of controversy. The majority of jurists would no doubt go along with the Commission in asserting that the rules prohibiting trade in slaves, piracy or genocide have become norms of *jus cogens* from which states are not free to derogate by treaty. But a word of caution is necessary here. It is right to recall that general multilateral Conventions (even those recently concluded) which prohibit or outlaw slavery and the slave trade and genocide contain normal denunciation clauses. If a state can release itself easily from the conventional obligations it has undertaken in these fields, can it be said that the prohibitions are in the nature of *jus cogens*? Of course, it may be said that the rule prohibiting slavery and the slave trade and the rule prohibiting genocide are rules of general international law which apply independently of the treaties embodying them. More to the point, it is clear that a treaty between two member states of the United Nations contemplating genocide or slavery would be wholly contrary to Articles 55 and 56 of the Charter and would therefore be unenforceable by virtue of Article 103, which provides that, in the event of conflict between the obligations of member states under the Charter and obligations under any other international agreement, Charter obligations prevail. The explanation for the existence of normal denunciation clauses in general multilateral conventions which contain asserted norms of *jus cogens* is, as Schwelb indicates, that 'the idea of international *jus cogens* has not yet penetrated into the day-to-day thinking and action of governments'.[33]

Other examples have been suggested: Barberis mentions treaties contrary to the rules of international law relating to the white slave traffic.[34] Verdross goes much wider in asserting that 'all rules of general international law created for a humanitarian purpose' constitute *jus cogens*.[35] Apart from the difficulty of delimiting what is and what is not a humanitarian purpose, this seems to go much too far. It implies that all human rights provisions contained in international treaties have the character of *jus cogens*. Given that even the United Nations Covenant on Civil and Political Rights is geared only towards 'achieving *progressively* the full realisation of the rights recognised in the present Covenant by all appropriate means',[36] it would be unwise to take at face value the suggestion that *jus cogens* embraces all human rights provisions, despite the fact that, in the Commission's commentary, certain members are recorded as having given treaties violating human rights as examples of treaties which would contravene a rule of *jus cogens*.[37]

---

33 Schwelb, 'Some aspects of international *jus cogens* as formulated by the International Law Commission' (1967) 61 *AJIL* at p 948.

34 Berberis, '*La liberté de traiter des états et le jus cogens*' (1970) ZaoRV pp 19–45 at p 35.

35 Verdors, '*Jus dispositivum* and *jus cogens* in international law' (1966) 60 *AJIL* pp 55–63 at p 59.

36 Article 2(I).

37 [1966] *ILC Rep* at p 77.

Scheuner[38] suggests three categories of norms of *jus cogens*: firstly, rules protecting the foundations of law, peace and humanity, such as the prohibition of genocide, slavery or the use of force; secondly, rules of peaceful co-operation in the protection of common interests, such as freedom of the seas; and thirdly, rules protecting the most fundamental and basic human rights (to which might, as Crawford suggests,[39] be added the basic rules for the protection of civilians and combatants in time of war). There would be little dispute with the first and, subject to what is said above about human rights provisions, the third of these three categories; but the second category is, as Crawford implies, very doubtful.[40] Jimenez de Arechaga would embrace within the first of Scheuner's three categories rules prohibiting racial discrimination, terrorism or the taking of hostages;[41] and Brownlie tentatively puts forward as candidate rules the principle of permanent sovereignty over natural resources and the principle of self-determination.[42]

Marek, in an attempt to find an underlying principle, advances the superficially attractive proposition that a treaty violative of *jus cogens* is any treaty in which two or more states undertake to commit acts which would be illegal if committed by a single state.[43] But even this appears to go too wide; it would seem to exclude the possibility of *inter se* modification of a multilateral treaty, even although *inter se* modification is permissible under certain conditions.

...

Whatever their doctrinal point of departure, the majority of jurists would no doubt willingly concede to the sceptics that there is little or no evidence in positive international law for the concept that nullity attaches to a treaty concluded in violation of *jus cogens*. But they would be constrained to admit that the validity of a treaty between two states to wage a war of aggression against a third state or to engage in acts of physical or armed force against a third state could not be upheld; and, having made this admission, they may be taken to have accepted the principle that there may exist norms of international law so fundamental to the maintenance of an international legal order that a treaty in violation of them is a nullity.

Some (among whom may be counted your author) would be prepared to go this far, but would immediately wish to qualify this acceptance of the principle involved by sketching out the limits within which it may be operative in present-day international law. In the first place, they would insist that, in the present state of international society, the concept of an 'international legal order' of hierarchically superior norms binding all states is only just beginning to emerge. Ideological differences and disparities of wealth between the individual states

---

38 Scheuner, 'Conflict of treaty provisions with a peremptory norm of general international law and its consequences' (1967) *Zeitschrift für ausländisches öffentliches Recht und Volkerrecht* at p 526.

39 Crawford, *The Creation of States in International Law*, 1979, Oxford: Oxford University Press at p 81.

40 *Ibid.*

41 Jimenez de Arechaga, 'International law in the past third of a century' (1978) 159 *Recueil des Cours* at p 64.

42 Brownlie, *Principles of Public International Law*, 1979, Oxford: Oxford University Press at p 513. But note that there is considerable controversy over the content of these principles, even as *jus dispositivum*; the suggestion that they may constitute rules of *jus cogens* is accordingly far-fetched.

43 Marek, '*Contribution à l'étude du jus cogens en droit international*' in *Hommage à Paul Guggenheim*, 1968, Geneva: Faculté de droit de l'Université de Genève pp 426–59 at p 452.

which make up the international community, combined with the contrasts between the objectives sought by them, hinder the development of an overarching consensus upon the content of *jus cogens*. Indeed, it is the existence of these very differences and disparities which constitute the principal danger implicit in an unqualified recognition of *jus cogens*; for it would be only too easy to postulate as a norm of *jus cogens* a principle which happened neatly to serve a particular ideological or economic goal. In the second place, they would test any assertion that a particular rule constitutes a norm of *jus cogens* by reference to the evidence for its acceptance as such by the international community as a whole, and they would require that the burden of proof should be discharged by those who allege the *jus cogens* character of the rule. Applying this test, and leaving aside the highly theoretical case of a treaty purporting to deny the application of the principle of *pacta sunt servanda*, it would seem that sufficient evidence for ascribing the character of *jus cogens* to a rule of international law exists in relation to the rule which requires states to refrain in their international relations from the threat of force against the territorial integrity or political independence of any other state. There is ample evidence for the proposition that, subject to the necessary exceptions about the use of force in self-defence or under the authority of a competent organ of the United Nations or a regional agency acting in accordance with the Charter, use of armed or physical force against the territorial integrity or political independence of any state is now prohibited. This proposition is so central to the existence of any international legal order of individual nation states (however nascent that international legal order may be) that it must be taken to have the character of *jus cogens*. Just as national legal systems begin to discard, at an early stage of their development, such concepts as 'trial by battle', so also must the international legal order be assumed now to deny any cover of legality to violations of the fundamental rule embodied in Article 2(4) of the Charter.

Beyond this, uncertainty begins, and one must tread with considerable caution. The dictates of logic, and overriding considerations of morality, would appear to require that one should characterise as *jus cogens* those rules which prohibit the slave trade and genocide; but the evidence is ambivalent, since the treaties which embody these prohibitions contain normal denunciation clauses. Of course, it may be argued that the presence or absence of normal denunciaton clauses should not be taken as being decisive; denunciation clauses are regularly embodied in treaties for traditional, rather than practical, reasons. In any event, it is likely that the prohibitions may now be taken to form part of general international law binding all states regardless of whether they are parties to the treaties embodying them. The unenforceability of any treaty contemplating genocide or the slave trade is further assured by the fact that such a treaty would contravene the Charter of the United Nations, which prevails in the event of a conflict.

To sum up, there is a place for the concept of *jus cogens* in international law. Its growth and development will parallel the growth and development of an international legal order expressive of the consensus of the international community as a whole. Such an international legal order is, at present, inchoate, unformed and only just discernible. *Jus cogens* is neither Dr Jekyll nor Mr Hyde; but it has the potentialities of both. If it is invoked indiscriminately and to serve short-term political purposes, it could rapidly be destructive of confidence in the security of treaties; if it is developed with wisdom and restraint in the overall interest of the international community it could constitute a useful check upon the unbridled will of individual states.

This was the conclusion presented in the first edition of this book, published more than 10 years ago. It is a conclusion which the author considers is still valid.

But he would wish to add the following. In the 14 years which have elapsed since the adoption of the Convention, there has been continued and continuing disputation among scholars as to the content and significance of *jus cogens*, not only in the context of the law of treaties, but also in other contexts. We have already seen how the notion of *jus cogens* has been used by way of analogy to sustain a distinction between so-called 'international crimes' and 'international delicts' within the framework of the law of state responsibility.[44] The question has also been raised whether, and if so to what extent, *jus cogens* may, despite all the difficulties, be applicable to problems of territorial status – that is to say, whether an entity has been created or extinguished in circumstances of such illegality that international law may, exceptionally, treat an effective entity as not a state (or, conversely, a non-effective entity as continuing to be a state).[45] There has also been speculation about how far, if at all, prescription can be operative if the norm violated is one of *jus cogens*;[46] it is at any rate clear from the Convention (Article 45) that acquiescence is not admissible in the case of conflict of a treaty with an existing or emerging norm of *jus cogens*.

It is of course only right that there should be a thorough and sustained examination by scholars of the implications of *jus cogens* in the law of treaties and also in other branches of international law. What is, however, significant is that, during the past 14 years, there have been few, if any, instances in state practice where the validity of a treaty has been seriously challenged on the ground that it conflicted with a rule of *jus cogens*. The mystery of *jus cogens* remains a mystery. To borrow another analogy from English literature,[47] it has some of the attributes of the Cheshire cat which had the disconcerting habit of vanishing and then reappearing to deliver further words of wisdom. *Jus cogens* will undoubtedly continue to exercise its influence on the development of international law in the foreseeable future. How far that influence will extend to the actual practice of states remains to be seen, although there must now be a consciousness among the legal advisers to foreign ministries that international law does impose certain limitations upon the freedom of states to enter into treaties regardless of their object or content.[48]

Jurists have from time to time attempted to classify rules, or rights and duties, on the international plane by use of terms like 'fundamental' or, in respect to rights, 'inalienable' or 'inherent'. Such classifications have not had much success, but have intermittently affected the interpretation of treaties by tribunals. In the recent past some eminent opinions have supported the view that certain overriding principles of international law exist, forming a body of *jus cogens*.

The major distinguishing feature of such rules is their relative indelibility. They are rules of customary law which cannot be set aside by treaty or acquiescence but only by the formation of a subsequent customary rule of contrary effect. The least controversial examples of the class are the prohibition of the use of force,[49]

---

44 See Chapter 10.

45 Crawford, *The Creation of States in International Law*, 1979, Oxford: Oxford University Press at p 82.

46 Brownlie, *Principles of Public International Law*, 1979,Oxford: Oxford University Press at p 514.

47 Lewis Carroll, *Alice's Adventures in Wonderland*, 1978, London: Methuen, Chapter VI.

48 IM Sinclair, *The Vienna Convention on the Law of Treaties*, 2nd edn, 1984, Manchester: Manchester University Press at pp 202–03, 215–18, 222–24.

49 McNair, *Law of Treaties*, 1961, Oxford: Clarendon Press at pp 214–15; Dept of State Memo (1980) 74 *AJIL* at p 418; judgment of the ICJ in the *Case Concerning Military and Para-military Activities in and against Nicaragua (Merits)* [1986] *ICJ Reps* 100–01 (para 190).

the law of genocide, the principle of racial non-discrimination,[50] crimes against humanity, and the rules prohibiting trade in slaves and piracy.[51] In the *Barcelona Traction* case (Second Phase),[52] the majority judgment of the International Court, supported by 12 judges, drew a distinction between obligations of a state arising *vis-à-vis* another state and obligations 'towards the international community as a whole'. The Court said:

> Such obligations derive, for example, in contemporary international law, from the outlawing of acts of aggression, and of genocide, as also from the principles and rules concerning the basic rights of the human person, including protection from slavery and racial discrimination.

Other rules which probably have this special status include the principle of permanent sovereignty over natural resources[53] and the principle of self-determination.[54]

The concept of *jus cogens* was accepted by the International Law Commission and incorporated in the final draft of the Vienna Convention on the Law of Treaties in 1966, Article 50, which provided that: '... a treaty is void if it conflicts with a peremptory norm of general international law from which no derogation is permitted and which can be modified only by a subsequent norm of general international law having the same character.' The Commission's commentary makes it clear that by 'derogation' is meant the use of agreement (and presumably acquiescence as a form of agreement) to contract out of rules of general international law. Thus an agreement by a state to allow another state to stop and search its ships on the high seas is valid, but an agreement with a neighbouring state to carry out a joint operation against a racial group straddling the frontier which would constitute genocide, if carried out, is void since the prohibition with which the treaty conflicts is a rule of *jus cogens*. After some controversy, the Vienna Conference on the Law of Treaties reached agreement on a provision (Art 53) similar to the draft article except that, for the purposes of the Vienna Convention on the Law of Treaties, a peremptory norm of general international law is defined as 'a norm accepted and recognised by the international community of states as a whole and which can be modified only by a subsequent norm of general international law having the same character'. Charles de Visscher[55] has pointed out that the proponent of a rule of *jus cogens* in relation to this article will have a considerable burden of proof.

Apart form the law of treaties the specific content of norms of this kind involves the irrelevance of protest, recognition, and acquiescence: prescription cannot

---

50 Judge Tanaka, diss op, *South West Africa* cases (Second Phase) [1966] *ICJ Rep* at 298; Judge Ammoun, sep op, *Barcelona Traction* case (Second Phase) [1970] *ICJ Rep* at 304; Judge Ammoun, sep op, *Namibia* opinion [1971] *ICJ Rep* at 78–81. The principle of religious non-discrimination must have the same status as also the principle of non-discrimination as to sex.

51 This statement in the third edition of the work (p 513) was quoted by the Inter-American Commission of Human Rights in the *Case of Roach and Pinkerton*, Decision of 27 March 1987 (OAS General Secretariat) 33–36.

52 [1970] *ICJ Rep* at 3 at p 32. See also *In re Koch*, ILR 30, 496 at 503; *Assessment of Aliens* case, ILR 43, 3 at 8; *Tokyo Suikosha* case (1969) 13 *Japanese Ann of IL* 113 at 115.

53 Declaration on Permanent Sovereignty over Natural Resources, Un GA Res 1803 (XVII) of 14 December 1962 adopted by 87 votes to 2 with 12 abstentions.

54 Judge Ammoun, sep op, *Barcelona Traction* case (Second Phase) [1970] *ICJ Rep* at p 304.

55 *Théories et réalistes en droit international*, 4th edn, 1970, Paris: Pedane at pp 295–96.

purge this type of illegality. Moreover, it is arguable that *jus cogens* curtails various privileges, so that, for example, an aggressor state would not benefit from the rule that belligerents are not responsible for damage caused to subjects of neutral states by military operations. Many problems remain: more authority exists for the category of *jus cogens* than exists for its particular content, and rules do not develop in customary law which readily correspond to the new categories. However, certain portions of *jus cogens* are the subject of general agreement, including the rules to the use of force by states, self-determination, and genocide. Yet even here many problems of application remain, particularly in regard to the effect of self-determination on the transfer of territory. If a state uses force to implement the principle of self-determination, is it possible to assume that one aspect of *jus cogens* is more significant than another. The particular corollaries of the concept of *jus cogens* are still being explored.[56]

4.9.7 The effect of invalidity

Article 69 of the VCT 1969 provides that where the invalidity of a treaty is established, the treaty is void and its provisions have no legal effect. If acts have been performed in reliance on a void treaty then states may require other parties to establish, as far as possible, the position with regard to their mutual relations that would have existed if the acts had not been performed. Acts performed in good faith in reliance on a treaty before its invalidity was invoked are not rendered unlawful by reason only of the invalidity of the treaty. Article 71 deals with the specific consequences arising where a treaty conflicts with *jus cogens*. In such a situation the parties to the void treaty are under an obligation to bring their mutual relations into conformity with the peremptory norm. Where the treaty becomes void and terminates as a result of the development of a new rule of *jus cogens* under Article 64, the parties are released from any obligations further to perform the treaty, but rights and obligations created through the treaty prior to its termination are unaffected provided that such rights or obligations do not themselves conflict with the new peremptory norm.

The answer to one question remains unclear: when a cause of invalidity arises, does it operate automatically, in the sense that anyone called upon to apply the treaty may judge whether or not it is valid, or is an international act of denunciation required on the part of the state that seeks to invoke the invalidity. The position at customary international law seems to be that where the invalidity results from error or fraud then an act of denunciation is required, but on questions of coercion or violation of *jus cogens* there seems to be no real agreement. In practice, however, it will usually be the case that the question of invalidity will arise when a party to the treaty wishes to absolve itself from the obligations contained in it. It is therefore likely that some public act of denunciation will occur. Article 65 of the VCT 1969 provides that a party which seeks to impeach the validity of a treaty must notify the other parties and, providing no objection is received within three months of giving notice, that party may consider the treaty as void. If objections are made there is a duty on the disputants to reach a peaceful settlement. The issue of peaceful settlement of disputes is dealt with in Chapter 12.

---

56 Brownlie, *Principles of Public International Law*, 4th edn, 1990, Oxford: Oxford University Press at pp 512–15.

4.10 Termination, suspension of and withdrawal from treaties

4.10.1 By consent

Articles 54 to 59 of the VCT 1969 provide for various situations where a treaty may be terminated or suspended or where a party may withdraw from a treaty by consent. The most straightforward situation will arise where the treaty either makes provision for termination, denunciation or withdrawal or where all parties consent to a change. Where a treaty makes no provision for termination, denunciation or withdrawal then the rule is that withdrawal and denunciation will not be allowed unless it is established that the parties intended to admit its possibility, or a right of termination and denunciation can be implied by the nature of the treaty. In such a case a party wishing to denounce or withdraw from a treaty should give a minimum of 12 months' notice. The operation of a treaty may be suspended if provided for in the treaty or if all parties consent. In the case of multilateral conventions, two or more parties may conclude an agreement to suspend the treaty as between themselves provided such suspension is not prohibited by the treaty and provided that it is not incompatible with the object and purpose of the treaty. If such an agreement to partially suspend a treaty is concluded there is a duty on the two or more states to inform the other parties to the treaty.

4.10.2 Material breach

It has always been a rule of customary law that the breach of an important provision of a treaty by one party entitles the other parties to regard that agreement as at an end. The main question that arises is how important a breach needs to be before it will justify the termination of a treaty. A material breach will entitle the other parties to a treaty to terminate or suspend a treaty in whole or in part. In the case of multilateral treaties, those not in breach might decide to terminate or suspend the treaty only in respect of the party in breach. It is clear that a party responsible for a material breach cannot itself rely on that breach to terminate a treaty.

4.10.3 Supervening impossibility of performance

Article 61 of the VCT 1969 introduces a rule analogous to the doctrine of frustration in municipal contract law. If a treaty becomes impossible to perform as a result of the permanent disappearance or destruction of an object indispensable for the execution of the treaty, that impossibility may be invoked as a reason for terminating or suspending the treaty. Where the impossibility is only temporary, it may only be invoked as a ground for suspension of the treaty. An example of the operation of Article 61 would be the case of a treaty governing rights pertaining to a river. The treaty could be terminated if the river dried up permanently. The impossibility of performance cannot be invoked by a party, where the impossibility results form the conduct of that party.

Linked to impossibility of performance is the doctrine of *force majeure*. The doctrine will be discussed in more detail in Chapter 9 since it can provide a general defence to international responsibility. The requirements of *force majeure* are that it must be irresistible, unforeseeable and external to the party relying on it. It may therefore exist under conditions which fall short of absolute material impossibility of performance. At the Vienna Conference on the Law of Treaties Mexico proposed that *force majeure* should be included in Article 61 but the proposal was rejected. It therefore seems to be the case that although *force majeure* may provide a defence for states accused of breaching treaty obligations, it will not result in the termination of the treaty. However, since a material breach of a treaty can result in the termination of that treaty, it may be argued that the ultimate effect of *force majeure* will be the same as a material impossibility of performance.

4.10.4 Fundamental change of circumstances

A fundamental change of the circumstances existing at the time the treaty was concluded has traditionally been a ground for withdrawal or termination. The rule is often referred to as the doctrine of *rebus sic stantibus*. Before the First World War a number of treaties were brought to an end by states relying on fairly minor changes. Since that time the law has been tightened up and it is clear that any change must be such as to alter radically the circumstances on the basis of which a treaty was concluded. In the *Fisheries Jurisdiction* case (1973) the ICJ declared that:

> ... international law admits that a fundamental change in the circumstances which determined the parties to accept a treaty, if it has resulted in a radical transformation of the extent of the obligations imposed by it, may, under certain conditions, afford the party affected a ground for invoking the termination or suspension of the treaty. This principle, and the conditions and exceptions to which it is subject, have been embodied in Article 62 of the Vienna Convention on the Law of Treaties, which may in many respects be considered as a codification of existing customary law on the subject ...[57]

The conditions and exceptions which are indicated by Article 62 are that the change of circumstances must not have been foreseen at the time of the conclusion of the treaty; the existence of the circumstances must have constituted an essential basis of consent and the effect of the change is to transform radically the nature and extent of the obligations still to be performed under the treaty. A fundamental change of circumstances may not be invoked with regard to a treaty establishing a boundary, nor if the change is the result of a breach of any international obligation owed to any other party to the treaty by the party invoking it.

4.10.5 Other possible grounds

Article 63 of the VCT 1969 provides that severance of diplomatic relations will not in itself affect treaty relationships, unless of course it amounts to a fundamental change of circumstances. There are a number of views as to the effect on a treaty of the outbreak of war. The VCT 1969 contains no provision relating to war, and it is certain that treaties governing war and peace, for

---

57 [1974] *ICJ Rep* 3.

example the UN Charter and the Geneva Conventions 1949 are not terminated or suspended by war. The most sensible view seems to be that expressed by the New York state Court of Appeals in *Techt v Hughes* (1920): '... treaty provisions compatible with a state of hostilities, unless expressly terminated, will be enforced, and those incompatible rejected'.

4.10.6 *The effect of termination or suspension*

Article 70 of the VCT 1969 provides that termination of a treaty releases the parties form any obligation further to perform the treaty but does not affect rights and obligations or situations created prior to termination. The effect of suspension is to release the parties from their obligations for the period of suspension.

CASE CONCERNING THE GABCIKOVO-NAGYMAROS PROJECT (HUNGARY/SLOVAKIA)[58]

The case concerned a dispute between Hungary and Slovakia (successor state to Czechoslovakia) arising from a 1977 treaty between Hungary and Czechoslovakia which provided for the two states to undertake a joint project for the construction of a system of locks, flood protection schemes and hydroelectric plants on the river Danube. The project had the aims of improving navigation, producing of electricity and protecting against flooding. The parties also undertook to ensure that the quality of the water in the Danube was not impaired as a result of the project. Following the political changes in Eastern Europe and the growth of environmental concern, particularly in Hungary, the parties agreed to slow down the speed of work on the project in 1983. In 1989, Hungary decided to abandon all work on the project and the dispute commenced. In the course of its judgment the ICJ had to consider a number of important aspects of the law relating to treaties as well as issues of state responsibility and environmental protection.

92   During the proceedings, Hungary presented five arguments in support of the lawfulness, and thus the effectiveness, of its notification of termination. These were the existence of a state of necessity; the impossibility of performance of the Treaty; the occurrence of a fundamental change of circumstances; the material breach of the Treaty by Czechoslovakia; and, finally, the development of new norms of international environmental law. Slovakia contested each of these grounds.

93   On the first point, Hungary stated that, as Czechoslovakia had 'remained inflexible' and continued with its implementation of Variant C, 'a temporary state of necessity eventually became permanent, justifying termination of the 1977 Treaty'.

Slovakia, for its part, denied that a state of necessity existed on the basis of what it saw as the scientific facts; and argued that even if such a state of necessity had existed, this would not give rise to a right to terminate the Treaty under the Vienna Convention of 1969 on the Law of Treaties.

---

58   Judgment of 25 September 1997 available at:
http://www.icj-cij.org/idocket/ihs/ihsframe.htm.

94   Hungary's second argument relied on the terms of Article 61 of the Vienna Convention, which is worded as follows:

Article 61 Supervening impossibility of performance

1   A party may invoke the impossibility of performing a treaty as a ground for terminating or withdrawing from it if the impossibility results from the permanent disappearance or destruction of an object indispensable for the execution of the treaty. If the impossibility is temporary, it may be invoked only as a ground for suspending the operation of the treaty.

2   Impossibility of performance may not be invoked by a party as a ground for terminating, withdrawing from or suspending the operation of a treaty if the impossibility is the result of a breach by that party either of an obligation under the treaty or of any other international obligation owed to any other party to the treaty.'

Hungary declared that it could not be 'obliged to fulfil a practically impossible task, namely to construct a barrage system on its own territory that would cause irreparable environmental damage'. It concluded that:

By May 1992 the essential object of the Treaty – an economic joint investment which was consistent with environmental protection and which was operated by the two parties jointly – had permanently disappeared, and the Treaty had thus become impossible to perform.

In Hungary's view, the 'object indispensable for the execution of the Treaty', whose disappearance or destruction was required by Article 61 of the Vienna Convention, did not have to be a physical object, but could also include, in the words of the International Law Commission, 'a legal situation which was the *raison d'être* of the rights and obligations'.

Slovakia claimed that Article 61 was the only basis for invoking impossibility of performance as a ground for termination, that para 1 of that Article clearly contemplated physical 'disappearance or destruction' of the object in question, and that, in any event, para 2 precluded the invocation of impossibility 'if the impossibility is the result of a breach by that party ... of an obligation under the treaty'.

As to 'fundamental change of circumstances', Hungary relied on Article 62 of the Vienna Convention on the Law of Treaties which states as follows:

Article 62 Fundamental change of circumstances

1   A fundamental change of circumstances which has occurred with regard to those existing at the time of the conclusion of a treaty, and which was not foreseen by the parties, may not be invoked as a ground for terminating or withdrawing from the treaty unless:

(a)   the existence of those circumstances constituted an essential basis of the consent of the parties to be bound by the treaty; and

(b)   the effect of the change is radically to transform the extent of obligations still to be performed under the treaty.

2   A fundamental change of circumstances may not be invoked as a ground for terminating or withdrawing from a treaty:

(a)   if the treaty establishes a boundary; or

(b)   if the fundamental change is the result of a breach by the party invoking it either of an obligation under the treaty or of any other international obligation owed to any other party to the treaty.

3   If, under the foregoing paragraphs, a party may invoke a fundamental
      change of circumstances as a ground for terminating or withdrawing from a
      treaty it may also invoke the change as a ground for suspending the
      operation of the treaty.

Hungary identified a number of 'substantive elements' present at the conclusion
of the 1977 Treaty which it said had changed fundamentally by the date of
notification of termination. These included the notion of 'socialist integration', for
which the Treaty had originally been a 'vehicle', but which subsequently
disappeared; the 'single and indivisible operational system', which was to be
replaced by a unilateral scheme; the fact that the basis of the planned joint
investment had been overturned by the sudden emergence of both states into a
market economy; the attitude of Czechoslovakia which had turned the
'framework treaty' into an 'immutable norm'; and, finally, the transformation of
a treaty consistent with environmental protection into 'a prescription for
environmental disaster'.

Slovakia, for its part, contended that the changes identified by Hungary had not
altered the nature of the obligations under the Treaty from those originally
undertaken, so that no entitlement to terminate it arose from them.

96   Hungary further argued that termination of the Treaty was justified by
      Czechoslovakia's material breaches of the Treaty, and in this regard it
      invoked Article 60 of the Vienna Convention on the Law of Treaties, which
      provides:

**Article 60   Termination or suspension of the operation of a treaty as a
consequence of its breach**

1   A material breach of a bilateral treaty by one of the parties entitles the other
      to invoke the breach as a ground for terminating the treaty or suspending its
      operation in whole or in part.

2   A material breach of a multilateral treaty by one of the parties entitles:

      (a)   the other parties by unanimous agreement to suspend the operation of
            the treaty in whole or in part or to terminate it either:

            (i)   in the relations between themselves and the defaulting state, or

            (ii)   as between all the parties;

      (b)   a party specially affected by the breach to invoke it as a ground for
            suspending the operation of the treaty in whole or in part in the relations
            between itself and the defaulting state;

      (c)   any party other than the defaulting state to invoke the breach as a
            ground for suspending the operation of the treaty in whole or in part
            with respect to itself if the treaty is of such a character that a material
            breach of its provisions by one party radically changes the position of
            every party with respect to the further performance of its obligations
            under the treaty.

3   A material breach of a treaty, for the purposes of this article, consists in:

      (a)   a repudiation of the treaty not sanctioned by the present Convention; or

      (b)   the violation of a provision essential to the accomplishment of the object
            or purpose of the treaty.

4   The foregoing paragraphs are without prejudice to any provision in the treaty
      applicable in the event of a breach.

5   Paragraphs 1 to 3 do not apply to provisions relating to the protection of the
      human person contained in treaties of a humanitarian character, in particular

to provisions prohibiting any form of reprisals against persons protected by such treaties.

Hungary claimed in particular that Czechoslovakia violated the 1977 Treaty by proceeding to the construction and putting into operation of Variant C, as well as failing to comply with its obligations under Articles 15 and 19 of the Treaty. Hungary further maintained that Czechoslovakia had breached other international conventions (among them the Convention of 31 May 1976 on the Regulation of Water Management Issues of Boundary Waters) and general international law.

Slovakia denied that there had been, on the part of Czechoslovakia or on its part, any material breach of the obligations to protect water quality and nature, and claimed that Variant C, far from being a breach, was devised as 'the best possible approximate application' of the Treaty. It furthermore denied that Czechoslovakia had acted in breach of other international conventions or general international law.

97   Finally, Hungary argued that subsequently imposed requirements of international law in relation to the protection of the environment precluded performance of the Treaty. The previously existing obligation not to cause substantive damage to the territory of another state had, Hungary claimed, evolved into an *erga omnes* obligation of prevention of damage pursuant to the 'precautionary principle'. On this basis, Hungary argued, its termination was 'forced by the other party's refusal to suspend work on Variant C'.

Slovakia argued, in reply, that none of the intervening developments in environmental law gave rise to norms of *jus cogens* that would override the Treaty. Further, it contended that the claim by Hungary to be entitled to take action could not in any event serve as legal justification for termination of the Treaty under the law of treaties, but belonged rather 'to the language of self-help or reprisals'.

98   The question, as formulated in Article 2, para 1 (c), of the Special Agreement, deals with treaty law since the Court is asked to determine what the legal effects are of the notification of termination of the Treaty. The question is whether Hungary's notification of 19 May 1992 brought the 1977 Treaty to an end, or whether it did not meet the requirements of international law, with the consequence that it did not terminate the Treaty.

99   The Court has referred earlier to the question of the applicability to the present case of the Vienna Convention of 1969 on the Law of Treaties. The Vienna Convention is not directly applicable to the 1977 Treaty inasmuch as both states ratified that Convention only after the Treaty's conclusion. Consequently only those rules which are declaratory of customary law are applicable to the 1977 Treaty. As the Court has already stated above (see para 46), this is the case, in many respects, with Articles 60 to 62 of the Vienna Convention, relating to termination or suspension of the operation of a treaty. On this, the parties, too, were broadly in agreement.

100   The 1977 Treaty does not contain any provision regarding its termination. Nor is there any indication that the parties intended to admit the possibility of denunciation or withdrawal. On the contrary, the Treaty establishes a long-standing and durable regime of joint investment and joint operation. Consequently, the parties not having agreed otherwise, the Treaty could be terminated only on the limited grounds enumerated in the Vienna Convention.

101   The Court will now turn to the first ground advanced by Hungary, that of the state of necessity. In this respect, the Court will merely observe that, even if a state of necessity is found to exist, it is not a ground for the termination of a treaty. It may only be invoked to exonerate from its responsibility a State which has failed to implement a treaty. Even if found justified, it does not terminate a treaty; the treaty may be ineffective as long as the condition of necessity continues to exist; it may in fact be dormant, but – unless the parties by mutual agreement terminate the Treaty – it continues to exist. As soon as the state of necessity ceases to exist, the duty to comply with treaty obligations revives.

102   Hungary also relied on the principle of the impossibility of performance as reflected in Article 61 of the Vienna Convention on the Law of Treaties. Hungary's interpretation of the wording of Article 61 is, however, not in conformity with the terms of that Article, nor with the intentions of the Diplomatic Conference which adopted the Convention. Article 61, para 1, requires the 'permanent disappearance or destruction of an object indispensable for the execution' of the Treaty to justify the termination of a treaty on grounds of impossibility of performance. During the conference, a proposal was made to extend the scope of the article by including in it cases such as the impossibility to make certain payments because of serious financial difficulties (Official Records of the United Nations Conference on the Law of Treaties, First Session, Vienna, 26 March–24 May 1968, Doc A/CONF.39/11, Summary records of the plenary meetings and of the meetings of the Committee of the Whole, 62nd Meeting of the Committee of the Whole at pp 361–65). Although it was recognised that such situations could lead to a preclusion of the wrongfulness of non-performance by a party of its treaty obligations, the participating states were not prepared to consider such situations to be a ground for terminating or suspending a treaty, and preferred to limit themselves to a narrower concept.

103   Hungary contended that the essential object of the Treaty an economic joint investment which was consistent with environmental protection and which was operated by the two contracting parties jointly had permanently disappeared and that the Treaty had thus become impossible to perform. It is not necessary for the Court to determine whether the term 'object' in Article 61 can also be understood to embrace a legal regime as in any event, even if that were the case, it would have to conclude that in this instance that regime had not definitively ceased to exist. The 1977 Treaty and in particular its Articles 15, 19 and 20 actually made available to the parties the necessary means to proceed at any time, by negotiation, to the required readjustments between economic imperatives and ecological imperatives. The Court would add that, if the joint exploitation of the investment was no longer possible, this was originally because Hungary did not carry out most of the works for which it was responsible under the 1977 Treaty; Article 61, para 2 of the Vienna Convention expressly provides that impossibility of performance may not be invoked for the termination of a treaty by a party to that treaty when it results from that party's own breach of an obligation flowing from that treaty.

104   Hungary further argued that it was entitled to invoke a number of events which, cumulatively, would have constituted a fundamental change of circumstances. In this respect it specified profound changes of a political nature, the Project's diminishing economic viability, the progress of environmental knowledge and the development of new norms and prescriptions of international environmental law (see para 95 above).

The Court recalls that, in the *Fisheries Jurisdiction* case ([1973] *ICJ Rep* at p 63, para 36), it stated that:

> Article 62 of the Vienna Convention on the Law of Treaties, ... may in many respects be considered as a codification of existing customary law on the subject of the termination of a treaty relationship on account of change of circumstances.

The prevailing political situation was certainly relevant for the conclusion of the 1977 Treaty. But the Court will recall that the Treaty provided for a joint investment programme for the production of energy, the control of floods and the improvement of navigation on the Danube. In the Court's view, the prevalent political conditions were thus not so closely linked to the object and purpose of the Treaty that they constituted an essential basis of the consent of the parties and, in changing, radically altered the extent of the obligations still to be performed. The same holds good for the economic system in force at the time of the conclusion of the 1977 Treaty. Besides, even though the estimated profitability of the Project might have appeared less in 1992 than in 1977, it does not appear from the record before the Court that it was bound to diminish to such an extent that the Treaty obligations of the parties would have been radically transformed as a result.

The Court does not consider that new developments in the state of environmental knowledge and of environmental law can be said to have been completely unforeseen. What is more, the formulation of Articles 15, 19 and 20, designed to accommodate change, made it possible for the parties to take account of such developments and to apply them when implementing those treaty provisions.

The changed circumstances advanced by Hungary are, in the Court's view, not of such a nature, either individually or collectively, that their effect would radically transform the extent of the obligations still to be performed in order to accomplish the Project. A fundamental change of circumstances must have been unforeseen; the existence of the circumstances at the time of the Treaty's conclusion must have constituted an essential basis of the consent of the parties to be bound by the Treaty. The negative and conditional wording of Article 62 of the Vienna Convention on the Law of Treaties is a clear indication moreover that the stability of treaty relations requires that the plea of fundamental change of circumstances be applied only in exceptional cases.

105 The Court will now examine Hungary's argument that it was entitled to terminate the 1977 Treaty on the ground that Czechoslovakia had violated its Articles 15, 19 and 20 (as well as a number of other conventions and rules of general international law); and that the planning, construction and putting into operation of Variant C also amounted to a material breach of the 1977 Treaty.

106 As to that part of Hungary's argument which was based on other treaties and general rules of international law, the Court is of the view that it is only a material breach of the Treaty itself, by a state party to that treaty, which entitles the other party to rely on it as a ground for terminating the Treaty. The violation of other treaty rules or of rules of general international law may justify the taking of certain measures, including countermeasures, by the injured state, but it does not constitute a ground for termination under the law of treaties.

107 Hungary contended that Czechoslovakia had violated Articles 15, 19 and 20 of the Treaty by refusing to enter into negotiations with Hungary in order to

adapt the Joint Contractual Plan to new scientific and legal developments regarding the environment. Articles 15, 19 and 20 oblige the parties jointly to take, on a continuous basis, appropriate measures necessary for the protection of water quality, of nature and of fishing interests.

Articles 15 and 19 expressly provide that the obligations they contain shall be implemented by the means specified in the Joint Contractual Plan. The failure of the parties to agree on those means cannot, on the basis of the record before the Court, be attributed solely to one party. The Court has not found sufficient evidence to conclude that Czechoslovakia had consistently refused to consult with Hungary about the desirability or necessity of measures for the preservation of the environment. The record rather shows that, while both parties indicated, in principle, a willingness to undertake further studies, in practice Czechoslovakia refused to countenance a suspension of the works at Dunakiliti and, later, on Variant C, while Hungary required suspension as a prior condition of environmental investigation because it claimed continuation of the work would prejudice the outcome of negotiations. In this regard it cannot be left out of consideration that Hungary itself, by suspending the works at Nagymaros and Dunakiliti, contributed to the creation of a situation which was not conducive to the conduct of fruitful negotiations.

108 Hungary's main argument for invoking a material breach of the Treaty was the construction and putting into operation of Variant C. As the Court has found in para 79 above, Czechoslovakia violated the Treaty only when it diverted the waters of the Danube into the bypass canal in October 1992. In constructing the works which would lead to the putting into operation of Variant C, Czechoslovakia did not act unlawfully.

In the Court's view, therefore, the notification of termination by Hungary on 19 May 1992 was premature. No breach of the Treaty by Czechoslovakia had yet taken place and consequently Hungary was not entitled to invoke any such breach of the Treaty as a ground for terminating it when it did.

109 In this regard, it should be noted that, according to Hungary's Declaration of 19 May 1992, the termination of the 1977 Treaty was to take effect as from 25 May 1992, that is only six days later. Both parties agree that Articles 65 to 67 of the Vienna Convention on the Law of Treaties, if not codifying customary law, at least generally reflect customary international law and contain certain procedural principles which are based on an obligation to act in good faith. As the Court stated in its Advisory Opinion on the Interpretation of the Agreement of 25 March 1951 between the WHO and Egypt (in which case the Vienna Convention did not apply):

> Precisely what periods of time may be involved in the observance of the duties to consult and negotiate, and what period of notice of termination should be given, are matters which necessarily vary according to the requirements of the particular case. In principle, therefore, it is for the parties in each case to determine the length of those periods by consultation and negotiation in good faith.' ([1980] *ICJ Rep* at p 96, para 49.)

The termination of the Treaty by Hungary was to take effect six days after its notification. On neither of these dates had Hungary suffered injury resulting from acts of Czechoslovakia. The Court must therefore confirm its conclusion that Hungary's termination of the Treaty was premature.

110 Nor can the Court overlook that Czechoslovakia committed the internationally wrongful act of putting into operation Variant C as a result of

Hungary's own prior wrongful conduct. As was stated by the Permanent Court of International Justice:

> It is, moreover, a principle generally accepted in the jurisprudence of international arbitration, as well as by municipal courts, that one party cannot avail himself of the fact that the other has not fulfilled some obligation or has not had recourse to some means of redress, if the former party has, by some illegal act, prevented the latter from fulfilling the obligation in question, or from having recourse to the tribunal which would have been open, to him. (Factory at Chorzow, Jurisdiction, Judgment No 8, PCIJ Ser A, No 9 p 31 (1927).)

Hungary, by its own conduct, had prejudiced its right to terminate the Treaty; this would still have been the case even if Czechoslovakia, by the time of the purported termination, had violated a provision essential to the accomplishment of the object or purpose of the Treaty.

111 Finally, the Court will address Hungary's claim that it was entitled to terminate the 1977 Treaty because new requirements of international law for the protection of the environment precluded performance of the Treaty.

112 Neither of the parties contended that new peremptory norms of environmental law had emerged since the conclusion of the 1977 Treaty, and the Court will consequently not be required to examine the scope of Article 64 of the Vienna Convention on the Law of Treaties. On the other hand, the Court wishes to point out that newly developed norms of environmental law are relevant for the implementation of the Treaty and that the parties could, by agreement, incorporate them through the application of Articles 15, 19 and 20 of the Treaty. These articles do not contain specific obligations of performance but require the parties, in carrying out their obligations to ensure that the quality of water in the Danube is not impaired and that nature is protected, to take new environmental norms into consideration when agreeing upon the means to be specified in the Joint Contractual Plan.

By inserting these evolving provisions in the Treaty, the parties recognised the potential necessity to adapt the Project. Consequently, the Treaty is not static, and is open to adapt to emerging norms of international law. By means of Articles 15 and 19, new environmental norms can be incorporated in the Joint Contractual Plan.

The responsibility to do this was a joint responsibility. The obligations contained in Articles 15, 19 and 20 are, by definition, general and have to be transformed into specific obligations of performance through a process of consultation and negotiation. Their implementation thus requires a mutual willingness to discuss, in good faith, actual and potential environmental risks.

It is all the more important to do this because as the Court recalled in its Advisory Opinion on the Legality of the Threat or Use of Nuclear Weapons, 'the environment is not an abstraction but represents the living space, the quality of life and the very health of human beings, including generations unborn' ([1996] *ICJ Rep* at para 29; see also para 53 above).

The awareness of the vulnerability of the environment and the recognition that environmental risks have to be assessed on a continuous basis have become much stronger in the years since the Treaty's conclusion. These new concerns have enhanced the relevance of Articles 15, 19 and 20.

113 The Court recognises that both parties agree on the need to take environmental concerns seriously and to take the required precautionary

measures, but they fundamentally disagree on the consequences this has for the joint Project. In such a case, third-party involvement may be helpful and instrumental in finding a solution, provided each of the parties is flexible in its position.

114 Finally, Hungary maintained that by their conduct both parties had repudiated the Treaty and that a bilateral treaty repudiated by both parties cannot survive. The Court is of the view, however, that although it has found that both Hungary and Czechoslovakia failed to comply with their obligations under the 1977 Treaty, this reciprocal wrongful conduct did not bring the Treaty to an end nor justify its termination. The Court would set a precedent with disturbing implications for treaty relations and the integrity of the rule *pacta sunt servanda* if it were to conclude that a treaty in force between states, which the parties have implemented in considerable measure and at great cost over a period of years, might be unilaterally set aside on grounds of reciprocal non-compliance. It would be otherwise, of course, if the parties decided to terminate the Treaty by mutual consent. But in this case, while Hungary purported to terminate the Treaty, Czechoslovakia consistently resisted this act and declared it to be without legal effect.

115 In the light of the conclusions it has reached above, the Court, in reply to the question put to it in Article 2, para 1(c), of the Special Agreement (see para 89), finds that the notification of termination by Hungary of 19 May 1992 did not have the legal effect of terminating the 1977 Treaty and related instruments.

4.11 Dispute settlement

One of the main purposes of international law is to provide a framework for the peaceful settlement of disputes and Article 33 of the UN Charter places an obligation on states to settle their disputes by peaceful means. Clearly this provision applies to disputes between parties to a treaty. Article 66 VCT 1969 deals with the specific question of disputes arising out of questions of validity, termination, withdrawal from or suspension of the operation of a treaty. If parties have not been able to settle the dispute themselves within a period of 12 months then two procedures come into operation. In the case of disputes about the application or interpretation of a rule of *jus cogens* the parties to the dispute may submit it to the ICJ for a decision. Disputes arising for other reasons are to be submitted to a conciliation procedure operated by the Secretary General of the UN and detailed in an annex to the VCT 1969.

4.12 State succession

State succession involves the replacement of one state by another in the responsibility for the international relations of territory and has been a particularly controversial and unsettled area of law. In 1978 the Vienna Convention on the Succession of States in Respect of Treaties was signed. The VCS has yet to enter into force, although the basic rules are thought to reflect customary international law. As far as newly independent states are concerned, the VCS operates the 'clean slate' rule. In other words, a newly de-colonised state:

... is not bound to maintain in force, or become a party to, any treaty by reason only of the fact that at the date of the succession of states the treaty was in force in respect of the territory to which the succession of states relates.[59]

The only exception to this rule is in respect of treaties establishing boundaries or concerning other territorial matters, eg treaties establishing objective regimes. This reflects general international practice with regard to the sanctity of boundaries and is in line with Article 62(2) of the VCT 1969 which provides that a fundamental change of circumstances cannot be invoked as a ground for terminating a treaty that establishes a boundary.

Of course, successor states may wish to become parties to treaties which had been in force with respect to the territory in question. In such a situation, a successor state may become a party by giving notice of succession. This rule will not apply where the application of the treaty to the successor state would be incompatible with the object and purpose of the treaty.

VCS 1978 was adopted when questions of state succession mainly arose as a result of de-colonisation. Recent events in Central and Eastern Europe have raised new questions and it is not yet possible to identify clearly a body of common state practice. Generally, the problem has been dealt with during negotiations leading to recognition of new states and in the drafting of new constitutions. In the case of German unification, many of the problems were dealt with in the Unification Treaty 1990 between the Federal Republic of Germany and the German Democratic Republic. Under the terms of unification the GDR ceased to exist as a state and its territory was integrated into the FRG. As far as treaties to which the FRG is a party are concerned, the principle of moving treaty frontiers applies in that all treaties remain in force 'unless it appears that application of the treaty to the new territory would be incompatible with the object and purpose of the treaty or would radically change the conditions for its operation' (Article 15 of the VCS 1978). As far as treaties to which the GDR was a party are concerned the position is more difficult. In the case of a union between two states which results in a new successor state the VCS 1978 provides for the continuation of the treaties of both states to the extent that application of the treaties to the successor state is compatible with the object and purpose of the treaties, and does not radically change the conditions for its operation. Such treaties continuing in force shall in general only apply in respect of the part of the territory of the successor state in respect of which the treaty was in force at the date of succession. The situation envisaged here is exemplified by the short-lived union of Egypt and Syria in the United Arab Republic, where the two states continued, in practice, to live a separate existence. The rules applicable to that situation do not seem to apply easily to the German situation. The preferred view seems to be that when states become dissolved, *prima facie*, no treaties pass to the successor state. and this rule applies where formerly sovereign territory is integrated into an existing state. Thus treaties concluded by former sovereign parts of the Indian, American and Australian federal states have been discontinued. Clearly, the option remains for the successor state to choose expressly to be bound by such treaties, but succession is not regarded as automatic.

---

59   Article 16 of the VCS 1978.

With regard to those states which were formerly part of the Soviet Union, Russia has been regarded as a continuation of the Soviet Union and the other former Soviet republics have been regarded as successor states, except in the case of the Baltic republics of Latvia, Estonia, and Lithuania, which are regarded as the continuation of states which existed up until Soviet annexation in 1940. The Baltic states do not regard themselves as bound by treaties entered into by the former Soviet Union. The treaty obligations of the other former Soviet republics have been dealt with on a case-by-case basis. The same formula has been used in relation to the division of the former Czechoslovak Republic into the Czech Republic and the Republic of Slovakia and in the case of the break-up of the former Socialist Republic of Yugoslavia. The problem is complicated with regard to Yugoslavia since while the Belgrade regime of Serbia and Montenegro considers itself to be the continuation of former Yugoslavia and refers to itself as the Republic of Yugoslavia, this claim is not recognised by the rest of the international community. The issue of succession to treaties is currently being considered by the ICJ in the *Case Concerning the Application of the Convention on the Prevention and Punishment of the Crime of Genocide*, in which proceedings have been brought by the government of Bosnia and Herzegovina against Serbia and Montenegro. Both parties regard themselves as parties to the Genocide Convention although Serbia and Montenegro has not deposited an instrument of succession. There have recently been discussions within the Council of Europe on the whole question of treaty succession and it has been suggested that matters could be clarified if there was an obligation on the depositories of treaties to contact successor states to ascertain their position with regard to the treaty obligations of those formerly responsible for the territory.

17 The proceedings instituted before the Court are between two states whose territories are located within the former Socialist Federal Republic of Yugoslavia. That Republic signed the Genocide Convention on 11 December 1948 and deposited its instrument of ratification, without reservation, on 29 August 1950. At the time of the proclamation of the Federal Republic of Yugoslavia, on 27 April 1992, a formal declaration was adopted on its behalf to the effect that:

> The Federal Republic of Yugoslavia, continuing the state, international legal and political personality of the Socialist Federal Republic of Yugoslavia, shall strictly abide by all the commitments that the Socialist Federal Republic of Yugoslavia assumed internationally.

This intention thus expressed by Yugoslavia to remain bound by the international treaties to which the former Yugoslavia was party was confirmed in an Official Note of 27 April 1992 from the Permanent Mission of Yugoslavia to the United Nations, addressed to the Secretary General. The Court observes, furthermore, that it has not been contested that Yugoslavia was party to the Genocide Convention. Thus, Yugoslavia was bound by the provisions of the Convention on the date of the filing of the Application in the present case, namely, on 20 March 1993.

18 For its part, on 29 December 1992, Bosnia-Herzegovina transmitted to the Secretary General of the United Nations, as depositary of the Genocide Convention, a Notice of Succession in the following terms:

> The Government of the Republic of Bosnia and Herzegovina, having considered the Convention on the Prevention and Punishment of the

Crime of Genocide, of 9 December 1948, to which the former Socialist Federal Republic of Yugoslavia was a party, wishes to succeed to the same and undertakes faithfully to perform and carry out all the stipulations therein contained with effect from 6 March 1992, the date on which the Republic of Bosnia and Herzegovina became independent.

On 18 March 1993, the Secretary General communicated the following Depositary Notification to the parties to the Genocide Convention:

On 29 December 1992, the notification of succession by the Government of Bosnia and Herzegovina to the above-mentioned Convention was deposited with the Secretary General, with effect from 6 March 1992, the date on which Bosnia and Herzegovina assumed responsibility for its international relations.

19 Yugoslavia has contested the validity and legal effect of the Notice of 29 December 1992, contending that, by its acts relating to its accession to independence, the Republic of Bosnia-Herzegovina had flagrantly violated the duties stemming from the 'principle of equal rights and self-determination of peoples'. According to Yugoslavia, Bosnia-Herzegovina was not, for this reason, qualified to become a party to the convention. Yugoslavia subsequently reiterated this objection in the third preliminary objection which it raised in this case.

The Court notes that Bosnia-Herzegovina became a Member of the United Nations following the decisions adopted on 22 May 1992 by the Security Council and the General Assembly, bodies competent under the Charter. Article XI of the Genocide Convention opens it to 'any member of the United Nations'; from the time of its admission to the Organisation, Bosnia-Herzegovina could thus become a party to the Convention. Hence the circumstances of its accession to independence are of little consequence.

20 It is clear from the foregoing that Bosnia-Herzegovina could become a party to the Convention through the mechanism of state succession. Moreover, the Secretary General of the United Nations considered that this had been the case, and the Court took note of this in its Order of 8 April 1993 ([1993] *ICJ Rep* at p 16, para 25).

21 The Parties to the dispute differed as to the legal consequences to be drawn from the occurrence of a state succession in the present case. In this context, Bosnia-Herzegovina has, among other things, contended that the Genocide Convention falls within the category of instruments for the protection of human rights, and that consequently, the rule of 'automatic succession' necessarily applies. Bosnia-Herzegovina concluded therefrom that it became a party to the Convention with effect from its accession to independence. Yugoslavia disputed any 'automatic succession' of Bosnia-Herzegovina to the Genocide Convention on this or any other basis.

22 As regards the nature of the Genocide Convention, the Court would recall what it stated in its Advisory Opinion of 28 May 1951 relating to the Reservations to the Convention on the Prevention and Punishment of the Crime of Genocide.

In such a convention the Contracting States do not have any interests of their own; they merely have, one and all, a common interest, namely, the accomplishment of those high purposes which are the *raison d'être* of the Convention. Consequently, in a convention of this type one cannot speak of individual advantages or disadvantages to states, or of the maintenance of a perfect contractual balance between rights and duties. ([1951] *ICJ Rep* at p 23.)

The Court subsequently noted in that Opinion that:

The object and purpose of the Genocide Convention imply that it was the intention of the General Assembly and of the states which adopted it that as many states as possible should participate. The complete exclusion from the Convention of one or more states would not only restrict the scope of its application, but would detract from the authority of the moral and humanitarian principles which are its basis. (*Ibid*, p 24.)

23   Without prejudice as to whether or not the principle of 'automatic succession' applies in the case of certain types of international treaties or conventions, the Court does not consider it necessary, in order to decide on its jurisdiction in this case, to make a determination on the legal issues concerning state succession in respect to treaties which have been raised by the Parties. Whether Bosnia-Herzegovina automatically became party to the Genocide Convention on the date of its accession to independence on 6 March 1992, or whether it became a party as a result, retroactive or not, of its Notice of Succession of 29 December 1992, at all events it was a party to it on the date of the filing of its Application on 20 March 1993. These matters might, at the most, possess a certain relevance with respect to the determination of the scope *ratione temporis* of the jurisdiction of the Court, a point which the Court will consider later (paragraph 34 below).

24   Yugoslavia has also contended, in its sixth preliminary objection, that, if the Notice given by Bosnia-Herzegovina on 29 December 1992 had to be interpreted as constituting an instrument of accession within the meaning of Article XI of the Genocide Convention, it could only have become effective, pursuant to Article XIII of the Convention, on the 90th day following its deposit, that is, 29 March 1993.

Since the Court has concluded that Bosnia-Herzegovina could become a party to the Genocide Convention as a result of a succession, the question of the application of Articles XI and XIII of the Convention does not arise. However, the Court would recall that, as it noted in its Order of 8 April 1993, even if Bosnia-Herzegovina were to be treated as having acceded to the Genocide Convention, which would mean that the Application could be said to be premature by nine days when filed on 20 March 1993, during the time elapsed since then, Bosnia-Herzegovina could, on its own initiative, have remedied the procedural defect by filing a new Application. It therefore matters little that the Application had been filed some days too early. As will be indicated in the following paragraphs, the Court is not bound to attach the same degree of importance to considerations of form as they might possess in domestic law.[60]

117   The Court must first turn to the question whether Slovakia became a party to the 1977 Treaty as successor to Czechoslovakia. As an alternative argument, Hungary contended that, even if the Treaty survived the notification of termination, in any event it ceased to be in force as a treaty on 31 December 1992, as a result of the 'disappearance of one of the parties'. On that date

---

60   *Case Concerning the Application of the Convention on the Prevention and Punishment of the Crime of Genocide (Bosnia-Herzegovina v Yugolslavia) (Preliminary Objections)* Judgment of 11 July 1996.

Czechoslovakia ceased to exist as a legal entity, and on 1 January 1993 the Czech Republic and the Slovak Republic came into existence.

118 According to Hungary, 'there is no rule of international law which provides for automatic succession to bilateral treaties on the disappearance of a party' and such a treaty will not survive unless another state succeeds to it by express agreement between that state and the remaining party. While the second paragraph of the Preamble to the Special Agreement recites that 'the Slovak Republic is one of the two successor States of the Czech and Slovak Federal Republic and the sole successor State in respect of rights and obligations relating to the Gabcikovo-Nagymaros Project', Hungary sought to distinguish between, on the one hand, rights and obligations such as 'continuing property rights' under the 1977 Treaty, and, on the other hand, the Treaty itself. It argued that, during the negotiations leading to signature of the Special Agreement, Slovakia had proposed a text in which it would have been expressly recognised 'as the successor to the Government of the CSFR' with regard to the 1977 Treaty, but that Hungary had rejected that formulation. It contended that it had never agreed to accept Slovakia as successor to the 1977 Treaty. Hungary referred to diplomatic exchanges in which the two parties had each submitted to the other lists of those bilateral treaties which they respectively wished should continue in force between them, for negotiation on a case-by-case basis; and Hungary emphasised that no agreement was ever reached with regard to the 1977 Treaty.

119 Hungary claimed that there was no rule of succession which could operate in the present case to override the absence of consent.

Referring to Article 34 of the Vienna Convention of 23 August 1978 on Succession of States in respect of Treaties, in which 'a rule of automatic succession to all treaties is provided for', based on the principle of continuity, Hungary argued not only that it never signed or ratified the Convention, but that the 'concept of automatic succession' contained in that Article was not and is not, and has never been accepted as, a statement of general international law.

Hungary further submitted that the 1977 Treaty did not create 'obligations and rights ... relating to the regime of a boundary' within the meaning of Article 11 of that Convention, and noted that the existing course of the boundary was unaffected by the Treaty. It also denied that the Treaty was a 'localised' treaty, or that it created rights 'considered as attaching to [the] territory' within the meaning of Article 12 of the 1978 Convention, which would, as such, be unaffected by a succession of States. The 1977 Treaty was, Hungary insisted, simply a joint investment. Hungary's conclusion was that there is no basis on which the Treaty could have survived the disappearance of Czechoslovakia so as to be binding as between itself and Slovakia.

120 According to Slovakia, the 1977 Treaty, which was not lawfully terminated by Hungary's notification in May 1992, remains in force between itself, as successor State, and Hungary.

Slovakia acknowledged that there was no agreement on succession to the Treaty between itself and Hungary. It relied instead, in the first place, on the 'general rule of continuity which applies in the case of dissolution'; it argued, secondly, that the Treaty is one 'attaching to the territory' within the meaning of Article 12 of the 1978 Vienna Convention, and that it contains provisions relating to a boundary.

121 In support of its first argument Slovakia cited Article 34 of the 1978 Vienna Convention, which it claimed is a statement of customary international law,

and which imposes the principle of automatic succession as the rule applicable in the case of dissolution of a state where the predecessor state has ceased to exist. Slovakia maintained that state practice in cases of dissolution tends to support continuity as the rule to be followed with regard to bilateral treaties. Slovakia having succeeded to part of the territory of the former Czechoslovakia, this would be the rule applicable in the present case.

122 Slovakia's second argument rests on 'the principle of *ipso jure* continuity of treaties of a territorial or localised character'. This rule, Slovakia said, is embodied in Article 12 of the 1978 Convention, which in part provides as follows:

Article 12 Other territorial regimes

2   A succession of states does not as such affect:

(a)   obligations relating to the use of any territory, or to restrictions upon its use, established by a treaty for the benefit of a group of states or of all states and considered as attaching to that territory;

(b)   rights established by a treaty for the benefit of a group of states or of all states and relating to the use of any territory, or to restrictions upon its use, and considered as attaching to that territory.

According to Slovakia, '[this] article [too] can be considered to be one of those provisions of the Vienna Convention that represent the codification of customary international law'. The 1977 Treaty is said to fall within its scope because of its 'specific characteristics ... which place it in the category of treaties of a localised or territorial character'. Slovakia also described the Treaty as one 'which contains boundary provisions and lays down a specific territorial regime' which operates in the interest of all Danube riparian States, and as 'a dispositive treaty, creating rights in rem, independently of the legal personality of its original signatories'. Here, Slovakia relied on the recognition by the International Law Commission of the existence of a 'special rule' whereby treaties 'intended to establish an objective regime' must be considered as binding on a successor state (Official Records of the United Nations Conference on the Succession of States in respect of Treaties, Vol III, Doc A/CONF.80/16/Add.2 at p 34). Thus, in Slovakia's view, the 1977 Treaty was not one which could have been terminated through the disappearance of one of the original parties.

123 The Court does not find it necessary for the purposes of the present case to enter into a discussion of whether or not Article 34 of the 1978 Convention reflects the state of customary international law. More relevant to its present analysis is the particular nature and character of the 1977 Treaty. An examination of this Treaty confirms that, aside from its undoubted nature as a joint investment, its major elements were the proposed construction and joint operation of a large, integrated and indivisible complex of structures and installations on specific parts of the respective territories of Hungary and Czechoslovakia along the Danube. The Treaty also established the navigational regime for an important sector of an international waterway, in particular, the relocation of the main international shipping lane to the bypass canal. In so doing, it inescapably created a situation in which the interests of other users of the Danube were affected. Furthermore, the interests of third states were expressly acknowledged in Article 18, whereby the parties undertook to ensure 'uninterrupted and safe navigation on the international fairway' in accordance with their obligations under the Convention of 18 August 1948 concerning the Regime of Navigation on the Danube.

In its Commentary on the Draft Articles on Succession of States in respect of Treaties, adopted at its 26th session, the International Law Commission identified 'treaties of a territorial character' as having been regarded both in traditional doctrine and in modern opinion as unaffected by a succession of states (Official Records of the United Nations Conference on the Succession of States in respect of Treaties, Vol III, Doc A/CONF.80/16/Add.2 at p 27, para 2). The draft text of Article 12, which reflects this principle, was subsequently adopted unchanged in the 1978 Vienna Convention. The Court considers that Article 12 reflects a rule of customary international law; it notes that neither of the parties disputed this. Moreover, the Commission indicated that 'treaties concerning water rights or navigation on rivers are commonly regarded as candidates for inclusion in the category of territorial treaties' (ibid, p 33, para 26). The Court observes that Article 12, in providing only, without reference to the Treaty itself, that rights and obligations of a territorial character established by a treaty are unaffected by a succession of States, appears to lend support to the position of Hungary rather than of Slovakia. However the Court concludes that this formulation was devised rather to take account of the fact that, in many cases, treaties which had established boundaries or territorial regimes were no longer in force (ibid, pp 26–37). Those that remained in force would nonetheless bind a successor State.

Taking all these factors into account, the Court finds that the content of the 1977 Treaty indicates that it must be regarded as establishing a territorial regime within the meaning of Article 12 of the 1978 Vienna Convention. It created rights and obligations 'attaching to' the parts of the Danube to which it relates; thus the Treaty itself cannot be affected by a succession of states. The Court therefore concludes that the 1977 Treaty became binding upon Slovakia on 1 January 1993.

124 It might be added that Slovakia also contended that, while still a constituent part of Czechoslovakia, it played a role in the development of the Project, as it did later, in the most critical phase of negotiations with Hungary about the fate of the Project. The evidence shows that the Slovak government passed resolutions prior to the signing of the 1977 Treaty in preparation for its implementation; and again, after signature, expressing its support for the Treaty. It was the Slovak Prime Minister who attended the meeting held in Budapest on 22 April 1991 as the Plenipotentiary of the Federal Government to discuss questions arising out of the Project. It was his successor as Prime Minister who notified his Hungarian counterpart by letter on 30 July 1991 of the decision of the government of the Slovak Republic, as well as of the government of the Czech and Slovak Federal Republic, to proceed with the 'provisional solution' (see para 63 above); and who wrote again on 18 December 1991 to the Hungarian Minister without Portfolio, renewing an earlier suggestion that a joint commission be set up under the auspices of the European Communities to consider possible solutions. The Slovak Prime Minister also wrote to the Hungarian Prime Minister in May 1992 on the subject of the decision taken by the Hungarian government to terminate the Treaty, informing him of resolutions passed by the Slovak government in response.

It is not necessary, in the light of the conclusions reached in para 123 above, for the Court to determine whether there are legal consequences to be drawn from the prominent part thus played by the Slovak Republic. Its role does, however, deserve mention.

In the absence of consistent state practice, state succession in respect of treaties has long been a rather uncertain field of international law. For example, while the 1978 Vienna Convention on Succession of States in Respect of Treaties provided, in accordance with the advice given by the International Law Commission, that a new state is bound by the international agreements binding on the predecessor state,[61] the 1987 Restatement (Third) of the Foreign Relations Law of the United States took the opposite view. Meanwhile scholars involved in the drafting of these instruments readily acknowledge that these standards were very open to criticism.[62] One of the foremost authorities on the subject even observed that 'state succession is a subject altogether unsuited to the process of codification'.[63]

State practice during the 1990s strongly supports the view that obligations arising from a human rights treaty are not affected by the succession of states.[64] This applies to all obligations undertaken by the predecessor state, including any reservations, declarations and derogations made by it. The continuity of these obligations occurs *ipso jure*. The successor state is under no obligation to issue confirmations to anyone.[65] Consent from other states is not required. Individuals residing within a given territory therefore remain entitled to the rights granted to them under a human rights treaty. They cannot be deprived of the protection of these rights by virtue of the fact that another state has assumed responsibility for the territory in which they find themselves. It follows that human rights treaties have a similar 'localised' character as treaties establishing boundaries and other territorial regimes.[66]

---

61 Article 34(1) of the Vienna Convention on Succession of States in Respect of Treaties, adopted 22 August 1978, not yet in force.

62 See, eg I Sinclair, 'Some Reflections on the Vienna Convention on Succession of States in Respect of Treaties', in *Essays in Honour of Erik Castren*, 1979, 149, 153.

63 DP O'Connell, 'Reflections on the State Succession Convention' (1979) 39 *ZAoRV* at p 725.

64 For a more cautious conclusion see MN Shaw, 'State Succession Revisited' (1994) 5 *Finnish Yearbook of International Law* 34, 38 ('one is on the verge of widespread international acceptance of the principle that international human rights treaties continue to apply within the territory of a predecessor state irrespective of a succession'). Disagreeing, Bosw, 'State Succession with Regard to Treaties' (1995) 111 *Mededelingen van de Nederlandse voor International Recht* 18.

65 As a matter of fact, while a notification of continuing adherence to a human rights treaty may not be strictly required, in practice such a step may be gratefully accepted by the depository and the other state parties because it resolves any ambiguities that exist.

66 Menno T Kamminga, 'State Succession in Respect of Human Rights Treaties' (1996) 7 *EJIL* 469 at pp 469, 482.

CHAPTER 5

THE SUBJECTS OF INTERNATIONAL LAW

5.1 Introduction

International personality means capacity to be a bearer of rights and duties under international law. Any entity which possesses international personality is an international person or a subject of international law, as distinct from a mere object of international law.[1]

A subject of international law is considered to be an entity capable of possessing international rights and duties and endowed with the capacity to take certain types of action on the international plane. The terms international legal person or legal personality are commonly used when referring to such entities.[2]

The subjects of law in any legal system are not necessarily identical in their nature or in the extent of their rights, and their nature depends upon the needs of the community. Throughout its history, the development of international law has been influenced by the requirements of international life, and the progressive increase in the collective activities of states has already given rise to instances of action upon the international plane by certain entities which are not states.[3]

A subject of the law is an entity capable of possessing international rights and duties and having the capacity to maintain its rights by bringing international claims.[4]

The principal question we are concerned with here is – to whom does international law apply? In order to be a subject of international law an entity must have international personality – it must be capable of possessing international rights and duties and as a consequence must have the capacity to maintain such rights by bringing international claims. A subject of international law owes responsibilities to the international community and enjoys rights, the benefits of which must be claimed, and which, if denied, may be enforced to the extent recognised by the international legal system, via legal procedures, ie the entity will have procedural capacity.

Since the law of nations is based on the common consent of individual states, and not of individual human beings, states solely and exclusively are the subjects of international law.[5]

Reparation for Injuries Suffered in the Service of the United Nations Case[6]

On 17 September 1948, Count Bernadotte, a Swedish national, was killed, allegedly by a private gang of terrorists, in west Jerusalem, at the time

---

1   Schwarzenberger and Brown, *Manual of International Law*, 6th edn, 1976, London: Stevens at p 42.

2   Henkin *et al*, *International Law: Cases and Materials*, 1993, St Paul's, Minn: West Publishing at p 228.

3   ICJ in *Reparation* case [1949] *ICJ Rep* p 174 at p 178.

4   Brownlie, *Principles of Public International Law*, 1990, Oxford: Oxford University Press at p 58.

5   Oppenheim, *International Law*, 1912, London: Longman.

6   Advisory Opinion [1949] *ICJ Rep* at p 174.

controlled by Israel. Count Bernadotte was the Chief United Nations Truce Negotiator in the area. In the course of deciding what action to take in respect of his death, the United Nations General Assembly sought the advice of the ICJ. Israel was admitted to the United Nations on 11 May 1949, shortly after the Court gave its opinion.

Opinion of the Court

The first question asked of the Court is as follows:

In the event of an agent of the United Nations in the performance of his duties suffering injury in circumstances involving the responsibility of a state, has the United Nations, as an Organisation, the capacity to bring an international claim against the responsible *de jure* or *de facto* government with a view to obtaining the reparation due in respect of the damage caused (a) to the United Nations, (b) to the victim or to persons entitled through him? ...

The subjects of law in any legal system are not necessarily identical in their nature or in the extent of their rights, and their nature depends upon the needs of the Community. Throughout its history, the development of international law has been influenced by the requirements of international life, and the progressive increase in the collective action of states has already given rise to instances of action upon the international plane by certain entities which are not states. This development culminated in the establishment in June 1945 of an international organisation whose purposes and principles are specified in the Charter of the United Nations. But to achieve these ends the attribution of international personality is indispensable.

The Charter has not been content to make the Organisation created by it merely a centre 'for harmonising the actions of nations in the attainment of their common ends' (Article 1, para 4). It has equipped that centre with organs, and has given it special tasks. It has defined the position of the Members in relation to the Organisation by requiring them to give it every assistance in any action undertaken by it (Article 2, para 5), and to accept and carry out the decisions of the Security Council; by authorising the General Assembly to make recommendations to the Members; by giving the Organisation legal capacity and privileges and immunities in the territory of each of its Members; and by providing for the conclusion of agreements between the Organisation and its Members. Practice – in particular the conclusions of conventions to which the Organisation is a party – has confirmed the character of the Organisation, which occupies a position in certain respects in detachment from its Members, and which is under a duty to remind them, if need be, of certain obligations. It must be added that the Organisation is a political body, charged with political tasks of an important character, and covering a wide field namely the maintenance of international peace and security, the development of friendly relations among nations, and the achievement of international co-operation in the solution of problems of an economic, social, cultural or humanitarian character (Article 1); and in dealing with its Members it employs political means. The 'Convention on the Privileges and Immunities of the United Nations' of 1946 creates rights and duties between each of the signatories and the Organisations (see in particular section 35). It is difficult to see how such a convention could operate except upon the international plane and as between parties possessing international personality.

In the opinion of the Court, the Organisation was intended to exercise and enjoy, and is in fact exercising and enjoying, functions and rights which can only be explained on the basis of the possession of a large measure of international personality and the capacity to operate upon an international plane. It is at present the supreme type of international organisation, and it could not carry out the intentions of its founders if it was devoid of international personality. it must be acknowledged that its Members, by entrusting certain functions to it, with the attendant duties and responsibilities, have clothed it with the competence required to enable those functions to be effectively discharged.

Accordingly, the Court has come to the conclusions that the Organisation is an international person. That is not the same thing as saying that it is a state, which it certainly is not, or that its legal personality and rights and duties are the same as those of a state. Still less is it the same thing as saying that it is 'a super-state', whatever that expression may mean. It does not even imply that all its rights and duties must be upon the international plane, any more than all the rights and duties of a state must be upon that plane. What it does mean is that it is a subject of international law and capable of possessing international rights and duties, and that it has the capacity to maintain its rights by bringing international claims.

The next question is whether the sum of the international rights of the Organisation comprises the right to bring the kind of international claim described in the Request for this Opinion. That is a claim against a state to obtain reparation in respect of the damage caused by the injury of an agent of the Organisation in the course of the performance of his duties. Whereas a state possesses the totality of international rights and duties recognised by international law, the rights and duties of an entity such as the Organisation must depend upon its purposes and functions as specified or implied in its constituent documents and developed in practice. The functions of the Organisation are of such a character that they could not be effectively discharged if they involved the concurrent action, on the international plane, of 58 or more Foreign Offices, and the Court concludes that the Members have endowed the Organisation with the capacity to bring international claims when necessitated by the discharge of its functions ...

... It cannot be doubted that the Organisation has the capacity to bring an international claim against one of its Members which has caused injury to it by a breach of its intentional obligations towards it. The damage specified in Question I(a) means exclusively damage caused to the interests of the Organisation itself, to its administrative machine, to its property and assets, and to the interests of which it is the guardian. It is clear that the Organisation has the capacity to bring a claim for this damage. As the claim is based on the breach of an international obligation on the part of the Member held responsible by the Organisation, the Member cannot contend that this obligation is governed by municipal law, and the Organisation is justified in giving its claim the character of an international claim.

When the Organisation has sustained damage resulting from a breach by a Member of its international obligations, it is impossible to see how it can obtain reparation unless it possesses capacity to bring an international claim. It cannot be supposed that in such an event all the Members of the Organisation, save the defendant state, must combine to bring a claim against the defendant for the damage suffered by the Organisation.

In dealing with the question of law which arises out of Question I(b) ... the only legal question which remains to be considered is whether, in the course of bringing an international claim of this kind, the Organisation can recover 'the reparation due in respect of damage caused ... to the victim ...'

The traditional rule that diplomatic protection is exercised by the national state does not involve the giving of a negative answer to Question I(b).

In the first place, this rule applies to claims brought by a state. But here we have the different and new case of a claim that would be brought by an Organisation.

In the second place, even in inter-state relations, there are important exceptions to this rule, for there are cases in which protection may be exercised by a state on behalf of persons not having its nationality.

In the third place, the rule rests on two bases. The first is that the defendant state has broken an obligation towards the national state in respect of its nationals. The second is that only the party to whom an international obligation is due can bring a claim in respect of its breach. This is precisely what happens when the Organisation, in bringing a claim for damage suffered by its agent, does so by invoking the breach of an obligation towards itself. Thus, the rule of the nationality of claims affords no reason against recognising that the Organisation has the right to bring a claim for the damage referred to in Question I(b). On the contrary, the principle underlying this rule leads to the recognition of this capacity as belonging to the Organisation, when the Organisation invokes, as the ground of its claim, a breach of an obligation towards itself.

Nor does the analogy of the traditional rule of diplomatic protection of nationals abroad justify in itself an affirmative reply. It is not possible, by a strained use of the concept of allegiance, to assimilate the legal bond which exists, under Article 100 of the Charter, between the Organisation on the one hand, and the Secretary General and the staff on the other, to the bond of nationality existing between a state and its nationals.

The Court is here faced with a new situation. The questions to which it gives rise can only be solved by realising that the situation is dominated by the provisions of the Charter considered in the light of the principles of international law ...

The Charter does not expressly confer upon the Organisation the capacity to include, in its claim for reparation, damage caused to the victim or to persons entitled through him. The Court must therefore begin by enquiring whether the provisions of the Charter concerning the functions of the Organisation, and the part played by its agents in the performance of these functions, imply for the Organisation power to afford its agents the limited protection that would consist in the bringing of a claim on their behalf for reparation for damage suffered in such circumstances. Under international law, the Organisation must be deemed to have those powers which, though not expressly provided in the Charter, are conferred upon it by necessary implication as being essential to the performance of its duties. This principle of law was applied by the Permanent Court of International Justice to the International Labour Organisation in its Advisory Opinion No 13 of 23 July 1926 (Ser B, No 13, p 18) and must be applied to the United Nations.

Having regard to its purposes and functions already referred to, the Organisation may find it necessary, and has in fact found it necessary, to entrust its agents with important missions to be performed in disturbed parts of the world. Many missions, from their very nature, involve the agents in unusual dangers to which ordinary persons are not exposed. For the same reason, the injuries suffered by its agents in these circumstances will sometimes have occurred in such a manner that their national state would not be justified in bringing a claim for reparation on the ground that diplomatic protection, or, at any rate, would not feel disposed to do so. Both to ensure the efficient and independent performance of these missions and to afford effective support to its agents, the Organisation must provide them with adequate protection ...

In order that the agent may perform his duties satisfactorily, he must feel that this protection is assured to him by the Organisation, and that he may count on it. To ensure the independence of the agent, and, consequently, the independent action of the Organisation itself, it is essential that in performing his duties he need not have to rely on any other protection than that of the Organisation (save of course for the direct and immediate protection due from the state in whose territory he may be). In particular, he should not have to rely on the protection of his own state. If he had to rely on that state, his independence might well be compromised, contrary to the principle applied by Article 100 of the Charter. And lastly, it is essential that – whether the agent belongs to a powerful or to a weak state; to one more affected or less affected by the complications of international life; to one in sympathy or not in sympathy with the mission of the agent – he should know that in the performance of his duties he is under the protection of the Organisation. This assurance is even more necessary when the agent is stateless ...

The obligations entered into by states to enable the agents of the Organisation to perform their duties are undertaken not in the interest of the agents, but in that of the Organisation. When it claims redress for a breach of these obligations, the Organisation is invoking its own right, the right that the obligations due to it should be respected. On this ground, it asks for reparation of the injury suffered, for 'it is a principle of international law that the breach of an engagement involves an obligation to make reparation in an adequate form'; as was stated by the Permanent Court in its Judgment No 8 of 26 July 1927 (Ser A, No 9, p 21). In claiming reparation based on the injury suffered by its agent, the Organisation does not represent the agent, but is asserting its own right, the right to secure respect for undertakings entered into towards the Organisation.

Having regard to the foregoing considerations, and to the undeniable right of the Organisation to demand that its Members shall fulfil the obligations entered into by them in the interest of the good working of the Organisation, the Court is of the opinion that in the case of a breach of these obligations, the Organisation has the capacity to claim adequate reparation, and that in assessing this reparation it is authorised to include the damage suffered by the victim or by persons entitled through him.

The questions remains whether the Organisation has 'the capacity to bring an international claim against the responsible *de jure* or *de facto* government with a view to obtaining the reparation due in respect of the damage caused (a) to the United Nations, (b) to the victim or to persons entitled through him when the defendant state is not a member of the Organisation.

In considering this aspect of Question I(a) and (b), it is necessary to keep in mind the reasons which have led the Court to give an affirmative answer to it when the defendant state is a Member of the Organisation. It has now been established that the Organisation has capacity to bring claims on the international plane, and that it possessed a right of functional protection in respect of its agents. Here again the Court is authorised to assume that the damage suffered involves the responsibility of a state, and it is not called upon to express an opinion upon the various ways in which that responsibility might be engaged. Accordingly the question is whether the Organisation has capacity to bring a claim against the defendant state to recover reparation in respect of that damage or whether, on the contrary, the defendant state, not being a member, is justified in raising the objection that the Organisations lacks the capacity to bring an international claim. On this point, the Court's opinion is that 50 states, representing the vast majority of the members of the international community, had the power, in conformity with international law, to bring into being an entity possessing objective international personality and not merely personality recognised by them alone, together with the capacity to bring international claims ...[7]

(The Court answered Question I(a), unanimously, and I(b), by 11 votes to four, in the affirmative.)

Question II is as follows:

In the event of an affirmative reply on point I(b), how is action by the United Nations to be reconciled with such rights as may be possessed by the state of which the victim is a national?'

The affirmative reply given by the Court on point I(b) obliges it now to examine Question II. When the victim has a nationality, cases can clearly occur in which the injury suffered by him may engage the interest of both his national state and of the Organisation. In such an event, competition between the state's right of diplomatic protection and the Organisation's right of functional protection might arise, and this is the only case with which the Court is invited to deal.

In such a case, there is no rule of law which assigns priority to the one or to the other, or which compels either the state or the Organisation to refrain from bringing an international claim.

... The Court sees no reason why the parties concerned should not find solutions inspired by goodwill and common sense, and as between the Organisation and its Members it draws attention to their duty to render 'every assistance' provided by Article 2, para 5, of the Charter.

Although the bases of the two claims are different, that does not mean that the defendant state can be compelled to pay the reparation due in respect of the damage twice over. International tribunals are already familiar with the problem of a claim in which two or more national states are interested, and they know how to protect the defendant state in such a case.

The risk of competition between the Organisation and the national state can be reduced or eliminated either by a general convention or by agreements entered into in each particular case. There is no doubt that in due course a practice will be developed, and it is worthy of note that already certain states whose nationals have been injured in the performance of missions undertaken for the Organisation have shown a reasonable and co-operative disposition to find a practical solution.

The question of reconciling action by the Organisation with the rights of a national state may arise in another way; that is to say, when the agent bears the nationality of the defendant state.

The ordinary practice whereby a state does not exercise protection on behalf of one of its nationals against a state which regards him as its own national does not constitute a precedent which is relevant here. The action of the Organisation is in fact based not upon the nationality of the victim but upon his status as agent of the Organisation. Therefore it does not matter whether or not the state to which the claim is addressed regards him as its own national, because the question of nationality is not pertinent to the admissibility of the claim.

In law, therefore, it does not seem that the fact of the possession of the nationality of the defendant state by the agent constitutes any obstacle to a claim brought by

---

7   It may be argued that this is incorrect: how can third parties be affected by treaty obligations?

the Organisation for a breach of obligations towards it occurring in relation to the performance of his mission by that agent.

(The Court answered Question II by 10 votes to five.)

5.2 The subjects of international law

5.2.1 Independent states

States are the principal subjects of international law. Of the term 'state' no exact definition is possible, but so far as modern conditions go, the essential characteristics of a state are well settled.[8]

The normal criteria which the government apply for recognition as a state are that it should have, and seem likely to continue to have, a clearly defined territory with a population, a government who are able of themselves to exercise effective control of that territory, and independence in their external relations. Other factors, including some United Nations resolutions, may also be relevant.[9]

The traditional definition of a state for the purposes of international law is the one to be found in the Montevideo Convention on the Rights and Duties of States 1933:

MONTEVIDEO CONVENTION ON THE RIGHTS AND DUTIES OF STATES 1933[10]

Article 1

The state as a person of international law should possess the following qualifications:

    (a)   a permanent population;

    (b)   a defined territory;

    (c)   government; and

    (d)   capacity to enter into relations with other states.

Article 2

The federal state shall constitute a sole person in the eyes of international law.

Article 3

The political existence of the state is independent of recognition by the other states. Even before recognition the state has the right to defend its integrity and independence, to provide for its conservation and prosperity, and consequently to organise itself as it sees fit, to legislate upon its interests, administer its services, and to define the jurisdiction and competence of its courts.

The exercise of these rights has no other limitation than the exercise of the rights of other states according to international law.

---

8   Starke, *Introduction to International Law*, 11th edn, 1994, London: Butterworths at p 95.

9   Minister of state, British Foreign and Commonwealth Office (1986) 57 *BYIL* 507.

10 Done at Montevideo, Uruguay on 26 December 1933. Entered into force on 26 December 1934. Parties: Brazil, Chile, Colombia, Costa Rica, Cuba, Dominican Republic, Ecuador, El Salvador, Guatemala, Haiti, Honduras, Mexico, Nicaragua, Panama, United States, Venezuela.

Article 4

States are juridically equal, enjoy the same rights, and have equal capacity in their exercise. The rights of each one do not depend upon the power which it possesses to assure its exercise, but upon the simple fact of its existence as a person under international law.

Article 5

The fundamental rights of states are not susceptible of being affected in any manner whatsoever.

Article 6

The recognition of a state merely signifies that the state which recognises it accepts the personality of the other with all the rights and duties determined by international law. Recognition is unconditional and irrevocable.

Article 7

The recognition of a state may be express or tacit. The latter results from any act which implies the intention of recognising the new state.

Article 8

No state has the right to intervene in the internal or external affairs of another.

Article 9

The jurisdiction of states within the limits of national territory applies to all the inhabitants.

Nationals and foreigners are under the same protection of the law and the national authorities and the foreigners may not claim rights other or more extensive than those of the nationals.

Article 10

The primary interest of states is the conservation of peace. Differences of any nature which arise between them should be settled by recognised pacific means.

Article 11

The contracting states definitely establish as the rule of their conduct the precise obligation not to recognise territorial acquisitions or special advantages which have been obtained by force whether this consists in the employment of arms, in threatening diplomatic representations, or in any other effective coercive measures. The territory of a state is inviolable and may not be the object of military occupation nor of other measures of force imposed by another state directly or indirectly or for any motive whatever even temporarily.

Article 12

The present Convention shall not affect obligations previously entered into by the High Contracting Parties by virtue of international agreements.

Article 13

The present Convention shall be ratified by the High Contracting Parties in conformity with their respective constitutional procedures. The Minister of Foreign Affairs of the Republic of Uruguay shall transmit authentic certificated copies to the governments for the aforementioned purpose of ratification. The instrument of ratification shall be deposited in the archives of the Pan American Union in Washington, which shall notify the signatory governments of said deposit. Such notification shall be considered as an exchange of ratifications.

Article 14

The present Convention will enter into force between the High Contracting Parties in the order in which they deposit their respective ratifications.

Article 15

The present Convention shall remain in force indefinitely but may be denounced by means of one year's notice given to the Pan American Union, which shall transmit it to the other signatory governments. After the expiration of this period the Convention shall cease in its effects as regards the party which denounces but shall remain in effect for the remaining High Contracting Parties.

Article 16

The present Convention shall be open for the adherence and accession of the states which are not signatories. The corresponding instruments shall be deposited in the archives of the Pan American Union which shall communicate them to the other High Contracting Parties.

An alternative view of statehood is offered by Schwarzenberger and Brown who argue that an entity must satisfy a minimum of three conditions before it can be considered an independent state. Those conditions are:

(1) the entity must possess a stable government which does not recognise any outside superior authority;

(2) the government must rule supreme within a territory which has more or less settled frontiers;

(3) the government must exercise control over a certain number of people.

James Crawford[11] identifies five 'exclusive and general legal characteristics of states':

1. In principle, states have plenary competence to perform acts, make treaties, and so on, in the international sphere: this is one meaning of the term 'sovereign' as applied to states.

2. In principle states are exclusively competent with respect to their internal affairs, a principle reflected by Article 2(7) of the United Nations Charter. This does not of course mean that they are omnicompetent, in international law, with respect to those affairs: it does mean that their jurisdiction is *prima facie* plenary and not subject to the control of other states.

3. In principle states are not subject to compulsory international process, jurisdiction, or settlement, unless they consent, either in specific cases or generally, to such exercise.

4. States are regarded in international law as 'equal', a principle also recognised by the Charter (Article 2(1)). This is in part a restatement of the foregoing principles, but it may have certain other corollaries. It does not mean, for example, that all states are entitled to an equal vote in international organisations; merely that, in any international organisation not based on equality, the consent of all the Members to the derogation from equality is required.

5. Finally, any derogations from these principles must be clearly established: in case of doubt an international court or tribunal will decide in favour of the freedom of action of states, whether with respect to external or internal affairs, or as not having consented to a specific exercise of international jurisdiction, or to a particular derogation from equality. This presumption – which is of course rebuttable in any case – is important in practice, as well as

---

11   James Crawford, *The Creation of States in International Law*, 1979, Oxford: Clarendon Press at p 32.

providing a useful indication of the status of the entity in whose favour it is invoked. It will be referred to throughout this study as the *Lotus* presumption – its classic formulation being the judgment of the Permanent Court in *Lotus*.

These five principles, it is submitted, constitute in legal terms the hard core of the concept of statehood, the essence of the special position in customary international law of states. It follows from this, as a rule of interpretation, that the term 'state' in any document *prima facie* refers to states having these attributes; but this is of course subject to the context. Courts will tend towards strictness of interpretation of the term 'state' as the context predicates plenitude of functions – as, for example, in Article 4(1) of the United Nations Charter. Conversely, if a treaty or other document is concerned with a specific issue, the word 'state' may be construed liberally – that is, to mean 'state for the specific purpose' of the treaty or document.[12]

5.2.1.1 Population and territory

States are aggregates of individuals and accordingly a permanent population living within a defined territory is regarded as a requirement of statehood. But there are no limits as to size of population or territory – eg Liechtenstein has a population of under 30,000, and Monaco has a territory of less than two square kilometres. It is not a requirement that the population should hold the nationality of the state in question, merely that they should live there with some degree of permanence. As far as territorial boundaries are concerned, there is no requirement for absolutely settled borders merely some identification of the state with a portion of the earth's surface.

In order to say a state exists ... it is enough that this territory has a sufficient consistency, even though its boundaries have not yet been accurately delimited, and that the state actually exercises independent public authority over that territory.[13]

... both reason and history demonstrate that the concept of territory does not necessarily include precise delimitation of the boundaries of that territory. The reason for the rule that one of the necessary attributes of a state is that it shall possess territory is that one cannot contemplate a state as a kind of disembodied spirit. Historically, the concept is one of insistence that there must be some portion of the earth's surface which its people inhabit and over which its government exercises authority. No one can deny that the state of Israel responds to this requirement.[14]

There is for instance no rule that the land frontiers of a state must be fully delimited and defined, and often in various places and for long periods they are not, as is shown by the case of the entry of Albania into the League of Nations.[15]

On the other hand, it is possible to cite a few situations where statehood was refused on the basis of unsettled frontiers, the classic example being that of Lithuania, which was refused membership of the League of Nations until border disputes with neighbouring states were settled.

---

12   Crawford, *op cit* at pp 32–33 (footnotes omitted).

13   German-Polish Mixed Arbitral Tribunal in *Deutsche Continental Gas-Gesellschaft v Polish State* (1929) 5 AD 15.

14   Philip Jessup – US representative to the UN Security Council, 1948.

15   ICJ in *North Sea Continental Shelf* case [1969] *ICJ Rep* at p 132.

5.2.1.2 Government

> The shortest definition of a state for present purposes is perhaps a stable political community, supporting a legal order, in a certain area. The existence of effective government, with centralised administrative and legislative organs is the best evidence of a stable political community.[16]

> Finland did not become a definitely constituted state until a stable political organisation had been created, and until the public authorities had become strong enough to assert themselves throughout the territories of the state without the assistance of foreign troops.[17]

There is a strong case for regarding the possession of effective government as the single most importance criterion of statehood since, arguably, all the other requirements depend upon it. But the actual application of the criterion has been far from straightforward – see, for example, the events surrounding the independence of the Belgian Congo in 1960. More recently the extent to which the state of the Lebanon has had any effective government has been in serious doubt. Moves in the General Assembly of the United Nations have also questioned the requirement of possession of effective government. It is worth noting General Assembly Resolution 1514 (XV) Declaration on the Granting of Independence to Colonial Countries and Peoples which declares that inadequacy of political, economic, social or education preparedness *should never serve as a pretext for delaying independence.*

> The following conclusions suggest themselves. First, to be a state, an entity must possess a government or a system of government in general control of its territory, to the exclusion of other entities not claiming through or under it.

> Second, international law lays down no specific requirements as to the nature and extent of this control, except, it seems, that it include some degree of maintenance of law and order.

> Third, in applying the general principles to specific cases, the following must be considered: (i) whether the statehood of the entity is opposed under title of international law; if so, the requirement of effectiveness is likely to be more stringently applied; (ii) whether the government claiming authority in the putative state, if it does not effectively control it, has obtained authority by consent of the previous sovereign and exercises a certain degree of control; (iii) in the latter case at least, the requirement of statehood may be liberally construed; (iv) finally, there is a distinction between the creation of a new state on the one hand and the subsistence or extinction of an established state on the other. There is normally no presumption in favour of the status of the former, and the criterion of effective government therefore tends to be applied more strictly.[18]

5.2.1.3 Capacity to enter into international relations/independence/ sovereignty

Most writers seem to be agreed that the capacity to enter international relations listed in Article 1 of the Montevideo Convention could be better expressed as

---

16 Brownlie, *Principles of International Law*, 1990, Oxford: Oxford University Press at p 73.

17 League of Nations Commission of Jurists in the Aaland Islands Dispute (1920).

18 Crawford, *The Creation of States in International Law*, 1979, Oxford: Oxford University Press at p 45.

'independence' or 'sovereignty' in the sense of having full control over domestic and foreign affairs. The concept of 'capacity to enter into international relations' brings with it a degree of circularity – who has capacity to enter into legal relations? states; what are states? Those entities with capacity to enter into international relations.

> Independence ... is really no more than the normal condition of states according to international law; it may also be described as sovereignty (*suprema potestas*), or external sovereignty, by which is meant that the state has over it no other authority than that of international law.'[19]

Examples can be found where the international community formed the opinion that an alleged state did not have a sufficient degree of independence for full statehood, eg Manchukuo.

There are a number of situations which are not regarded, in international practice, as derogating from formal independence, although if extended far enough, they may derogate from actual independence:

(a) *Constitutional restrictions upon freedom of action*

Provided no outside state has the power to alter the constitution, the fact that the state in question is constitutionally restricted is not seen as a derogation from formal independence, eg the Constitution of the Republic of Cyprus binds the Republic permanently to accept the stationing of foreign (Greek, Turkish and British) military forces on its territory.

(b) *Treaty obligations*

The *Wimbledon* case confirmed the principle that treaty obligations do not derogate from formal independence.

(c) *The existence of foreign military bases*

For example, Cyprus, Germany, United Kingdom.

(d) *The possession of joint organs for certain purposes*

For example, Customs Unions. Of course it is possible for states to unite totally as Syria and Egypt did in the 1950s to form the United Arab Republic and as East and West Germany, North and South Yemen have done more recently – in this case, of course, two states become a single state.

(e) *Membership of international organisations*

Even if the international organisation has some degree of coercive authority, eg the EEC, the United Nations, this is not seen as derogating from formal independence.

Customs Regime between Germany and Austria Case[20]

Article 88 of the Treaty of Saint-Germain 1919 provided:

> The independence of Austria is inalienable otherwise than with the consent of the Council of the League of Nations. Consequently, Austria undertakes in the

---

19 Judge Anzilotti in the *Customs Regime between Germany and Austria* case PCIJ Ser A/B, No 41 (1931).
20 PCIJ Ser A/B, No 41 (1931).

absence of the consent of the said Council to abstain from any act which might directly or indirectly or by any means whatever compromise her independence ...

In 1922 an additional protocol was signed at Geneva which contained similar provisions relating to Austrian economic independence. In 1931 Germany and Austria reached preliminary agreement on a customs union between the two states. The proposal caused widespread international concern and as a result the Council of the League of Nations had requested an Advisory Opinion from the PCIJ whether the proposed customs union would be contrary to the Treaty and Protocol. The court found that the proposed union did not contravene the 1919 Treaty but a majority of eight judges to seven found that the proposed union did contravene the 1922 Protocol. In a separate opinion Judge Anzilotti (who found the proposed union incompatible with both the Treaty and the Protocol) gave some thought to the meaning of independence in international law:

> The conception of independence, regarded as the normal characteristic of states as subjects of international law, cannot be better defined than by comparing it with the exceptional and, to some extent, abnormal class of states known as 'dependent states'. These are states subject to the authority of one or more other states. The idea of dependence therefore necessarily implies a relation between a superior state (suzerain, protector, etc) and an inferior or subject state (vassal, protégé, etc); the relation between the state which can legally impose its will and the state which is legally compelled to submit to that will. Where there is no such relation of superiority and subordination, it is impossible to speak of dependence within the meaning of international law.

> It follows that the legal conception of independence has nothing to do with a state's subordination to international law or with the numerous and constantly increasing states of *de facto* dependence which characterise the relation of one country to other countries.

> It also follows that the restrictions upon a state's liberty, whether arising out of ordinary international law or contractual engagements, do not as such in the least affect its independence. As long as these restrictions do not place the state under the legal authority of another state, the former remains an independent state however extensive and burdensome those obligations may be.

Admission of Liechtenstein to the League of Nations[21]

Liechtenstein sought admission to the League of Nations. Membership was open to 'any fully governing state, Dominion or Colony ... provided that it shall give effective guarantees of its sincere intention to observe its international obligations, and shall accept such regulations as may be prescribed by the League in regard to its military, naval and air forces and armaments' (Article 1(2) LN Covenant). Liechtenstein's application was rejected in view of the following report.

---

21 Report of the 5th Committee to the First Assembly of the LN, 6 December 1920, 1 *Hackworth* 48–49.

The government of the Principality of Liechtenstein has been recognised *de jure* by many states. It has concluded a number of Treaties with various states ...

The Principality of Liechtenstein possesses a stable government and fixed frontiers ...

There can be no doubt that juridically the Principality ... is a sovereign state, but by reason of her limited area, small population and her geographical position, she has chosen to depute to others some of the attributes of sovereignty. For instance she has contracted with other Powers for the control of her Customs, the administrations of her Posts, Telegraphs and Telephone Services, for the diplomatic representation of her subjects in foreign countries, other than Switzerland and Austria, and for final decisions in certain judicial cases.

Liechtenstein has no army.

For the above reasons, we are of opinion that the Principality of Liechtenstein could not discharge all the international obligations which would be imposed upon her by the Covenant.

5.2.1.4 Permanence

A state which has only a very brief life may nevertheless leave an agenda of consequential legal questions on its extinction.[22]

There is no requirement that a state should endure for a specific minimum period – there are examples of states existing for a very short period but they have achieved full statehood, eg Mali Federation 20 June 1960 – 20 August 1960; British Somaliland 26 June 1960 – 30 June 1960.

5.2.1.5 Legality

In recent years the view has increasingly been put forward that, in addition to the criteria already mentioned, international law does not permit the creation of states in violation of fundamental principles of international law/in violation of *jus cogens*.

Self-determination

While discussion of the political principle of self-determination has a long history, the process of establishing it as a principle of international law is of more recent origin. It was discussed in the early days of the League of Nations and the Mandate system was to some degree a compromise between outright colonialism and principles of self-determination. In the period 1920–22 many of the treaties concluded by the Soviet Union enshrined self-determination as a legal right. However the biggest impetus to recognition of self-determination as a legal principle came with the United Nations Charter:

The purposes of the United Nations are:

2   To develop friendly relations among nations based on respect for the principle of equal rights and self-determination of peoples (Article 1).

With a view to the creation of conditions of stability and well-being which are necessary for peaceful and friendly relations among nations based on respect for the principle of equal rights and self-determination of peoples ... (Article 55).

---

22   Brownlie, *Principles of Public International Law*, 4th edn, 1979, Oxford: Oxford University Press at p 77.

All members shall refrain in their international relations from the threat or use of force against the territorial integrity or political independence of any state, or in any other manner inconsistent with the purposes of the United Nations (Article 2(4)).

While it clearly enunciated the principle of self-determination, it left unclear the precise legal ramifications and this fact was seized upon by many Western jurists to deny that self-determination was in any way a legally enforceable right. In 1952 the General Assembly stated (in Resolution 637A (VII)) that 'the right of peoples and nations to self-determination is a prerequisite to the full enjoyment of all fundamental human rights' and is recommended that the United Nations' members 'shall uphold the principle of self-determination of all peoples and nations' while promoting 'realisation of the right of self-determination' for the peoples of colonial territories. Again the resolution left unclear the precise legal implications of the principle.

In 1960 General Assembly Resolution 1514 (XV) entitled Declaration on the Granting of Independence to Colonial Countries and Peoples was adopted 89:0 with nine abstentions (Australia, Belgium, Dominican Republic, France, Portugal, South Africa, Spain, UK, US):

The General Assembly ...

Declares that:

2   All peoples have the right to self-determination; by virtue of that right they freely determine their political status and freely pursue their economic, social and cultural development ...

3   Inadequacy of political, economic, social or educational preparedness should never serve as a pretext for delaying independence ...

6   Any attempt at the partial or total disruption of the national unity and the territorial integrity of a country is incompatible with the purposes and principles of the Charter of the United Nations.

In 1966 two conventions on human rights were signed – the International Covenant on Civil and Political Rights and the International Covenant on Economic, Social and Cultural Rights. Both entered into force in 1966 and at present over 90 states have ratified them. The Covenants have a common Article 1 which states:

1   All peoples have the right of self-determination. By virtue of that right they freely determine their political status and freely pursue their economic, social and cultural development.

Subsequently the Declaration of Principles of International Law Concerning Friendly Relations (General Assembly Resolution 2625 (XXV)) confirmed the principle that self-determination is a right belonging to all peoples and that its implementation is required by the UN Charter in the case of alien subjugation or foreign domination. The Declaration went further in recognising that peoples resisting forcible suppression of their claim to self-determination are entitled to seek and receive support in accordance with the purposes and principles of the Charter.

The principle of self-determination of peoples is rightly considered to be a successor to the political principle of nationality, which became widely recognised in 19th century Europe and related to the emergence of nation states.

Since then, hardly any political or legal principles have been as highly praised and supported by some and as strongly denied by others as has that of self-determination.

After World War I the principle received a new boost. In 1917, in the famous Decree of Peace, Lenin wrote:

> If any nation whatsoever is retained within the boundaries of a given state by coercion, and despite its expressed desire it is not granted the right by a free vote ... with the complete withdrawal of the forces of the annexing or generally more powerful nation, to decide without the slightest coercion the question of the form of state existence of this nation, then it is an annexation ...

President Wilson was an ardent proponent of the principle. In his 'Fourteen Points' he enunciated that 'peoples and provinces must not be bartered from sovereignty to sovereignty as if they were chattels or pawns in a game', and that territorial questions should be decided 'in the interest of the population concerned'.

But at the same time Secretary of state Lansing wrote in a note of 30 December 1918:

> The more I think about the President's declaration as to the right of 'self-determination', the more convinced I am of the danger of putting such ideas into the minds of certain races. It is bound to be the basis of impossible demands on the Peace Congress and create trouble in many lands ... The phrase is simply loaded with dynamite. It will raise hopes which can never be realised. It will, I fear, cost thousands of lives.

Senator Moynihan quotes Frank P Walsh, to whom President Wilson himself had acknowledges that when he had uttered the words on the right to self-determination he had done so without any knowledge that nationalities existed which were coming to them day after day.

Already at that time proponents of the principles interpreted it not only differently, they also interpreted it as being not simply an end in itself but as a means of achieving different ends. For Lenin this principle was subordinated to interests of socialism and was considered as a stage and condition of the final merger of all nations into one socialist society. Hurst Hannum is quite right that it 'should be underscored that self-determination in 1919 had little to do with the demands of the peoples concerned, unless those demands were consistent with the geopolitical and strategic interests of the Great Powers'.

By the turn of the millennium the principle of the self-determination of peoples has travelled the long road from its original political slogan to being one of the fundamental principles of international law. But as Hannum writes: 'Yet the meaning of and the content of that principle remain as vague and imprecise as when they were enunciated by President Woodrow Wilson and others in Versailles.'[23]

In the 1990s the self-determination of peoples is once more not only a topical subject for dissertations, but has become a slogan of political struggle in different parts of the world. If after the First World War the principle was applied only to Eastern European nations which had hitherto been parts of the Ottoman and

---

23 H Hannum, *Autonomy, Sovereignty, and Self Determination: The Accommodation of Conflicting Rights*, 1990, Philadelphia: University of Pennsylvania Press at p 28.

Austro-Hungarian empires, and in the 1960s determined outcomes of the anti-colonial struggle in Africa and Asia, at the end of the 1980s came the turn of the Russian (Soviet) Empire.

All Soviet republics, while seeking independence from the USSR or demanding more autonomy from the centre, vigorously claimed the right to self-determination. But even before these republics could achieve their independence, different ethnicities living in their territories where they constituted minorities (for example, Tartars and Chechens in Russia; Crimeans in Ukraine; Crimean Tartars in their turn in the Crimean peninsula, which was their historical motherland; and Ossetians and Abkhazians in Georgia) started to use the same slogan in the furtherance of their claims.

It seems that the chain of fission is a law not only of the physical worlds but of the social world as well. When a society breaks up, not only are other societies affected by way of example, but newly born states themselves often start a new round of disintegration.

The birth and existence of the Soviet Union had a twofold effect on world society. On the one hand, it was a source of expansion of communist ideas and a resource for different left wing organisations all over the world. On the other hand, the Soviet experience served as a warning for different peoples, averting them from repeating this social experiment.

In the same vein, recent and even some current events in the former Soviet Union as well as in the former Yugoslavia, though certainly providing a source of inspiration for many secessionist movements in other counties should, at the same time, sound as a warning.

Generalisations, of course, should always be made cautiously, because seemingly identical events may have their roots in different reasons and lead to different results. But there may have been something symbolic in the picture I observed in Geneva in autumn 1992 at the time when Georgians and Abkhazians were killing each other in the Caucasus, when ethnic cleansing was in progress in the territories of the former Yugoslavia, and the UN Human Rights Committee, of which I was a member, considered emergency reports of Bosnia-Herzegovina, Croatia, and Yugoslavia (Serbia and Montenegro) on their implementation of such basic human rights as the right to life and freedom from torture and other inhuman forms of treatment. Looking out of the windows of the Palais des Nations one could see the 179 flags of the UN member states fluttering in the cold autumn wind. At that moment I did not feel especially proud of seeing so many new member states' flags, but thought more of the cost of every flag in human lives and suffering. And this notwithstanding the fact that in 1991-92 I was myself actively involved in the process of the dissolution of the Soviet Union as Deputy Foreign Minister of Estonia.

No one doubts any more that the principle of the self-determination of peoples is a legal principle and many declare it to be a *jus cogens* norm of international law. What is much less clear is the content of the principle and its relation to other principles of international law having the same legal force. This last aspect is especially important because such grandiose events like those which have taken place in the erstwhile USSR and in Eastern Europe are never governed only by one principle or norm of international law. Different principles and norms, all being expressions of different real values and interests, if taken in isolation, may often indicate opposite outcomes. Therefore the task of an international lawyer is to apply these principles and norms creatively to concrete events, taking into account not only these legal principles but also important extra-legal factors and possible outcomes as well.

The right of peoples to self-determination is not only one of fundamental principles of international law governing inter-state relations. It is at the same time a very important human rights norm and therefore rightly belongs to both Covenants on human rights. The Vienna Declaration and Programme of Action adopted by the World Conference on Human Rights in June 1993 emphasises that the Conference considers the denial of the right of self-determination as a violation of human rights and underlies the importance of the effective realisation of this right.

This is so because, first, its so-called internal aspect, that is the right of all peoples freely (there are some limitations of even this freedom as I will show later) to determine their political status and to pursue their economic, social and cultural development is the entitlement of all peoples to democracy. Second, even its external aspect, that is the right of peoples freely (so far as this freedom does not infringe upon the freedom of other peoples) to determine their place in the international community of states, is becoming more and more influenced by other human rights norms.

When this principle of self-determination as a legal norm started its development in the context of the process of decolonisation, this link between self-determination and human rights meant that individuals could not be free if the peoples to which they belonged were under an alien yoke.

But the process of development of the principle of respect for human rights – one of the most rapidly and radically evolving principles of international law – has influenced many international law principles and norms and the principle of self-determination of peoples has not remained unaffected either because, as was said in the 1970 Friendly Relations Declaration, all principles of international law and each principle should be construed in the context of other principles. Though in the Friendly Relations Declaration the principle of respect for human rights was still absent, there is no doubt that the following developments in international law have confirmed the place of this principle amongst the fundamental principles of international law. The Final Act of the Conference on Security and Co-operation in Europe contains the principle of respect for human rights and fundamental freedoms and also stresses that all principles should be interpreted whilst taking the others into account.

The principle of respect for human rights has been particularly dramatically developed in the framework of the Helsinki process. The Document of the Copenhagen Conference on the Human Dimension of 1990 not only speaks of concrete rights and freedoms and elaborates respective monitoring mechanisms, but for the first time gives the parameters of a society conducive to the protection of individual rights. And for the first time an international document states *expressis verbis* that freedom of choice by peoples of their political, social, economic and cultural systems is not absolute. Peoples are free to establish their respective political, social and economic systems so far as these systems guarantee respect for international standards of human rights. the states' parties to the Conference on the Human Dimension of the CSCE confirmed that:

> ... they will respect each other's right freely to choose and develop, *in accordance with international human rights standards* [emphasis added], their political, social, economic and cultural systems. In exercising this right, they will ensure that their laws, regulations, practices and policies conform with their obligations under international law and are brought into harmony with the provisions of the Declaration on Principles and other CSCE commitments.

One may at first assume that such a clause limits the freedom of choice of peoples with regard to the formulation of their respective economic, social and political systems. In reality, however, it does not curb peoples' right to self-determination but, on the contrary, strengthens the principle by placing limits on rulers or other antidemocratic forces in a society.

The link between principles of the self-determination of peoples and respect for human rights – or maybe it would be better to say the filling of the principle of self-determination with humanitarian content – found further development in the processes of the dissolution of the USSR and Yugoslavia and especially in the reaction of the world community of states to these processes.

On 16 December 1991, the Council of the European Communities adopted a Declaration on 'Guidelines on the Recognition of New states in Eastern Europe and in the Soviet Union'. This document establishes the criteria and conditions for the recognition of new states which, following the historic changes in the region, have constituted themselves on a democratic basis, have accepted the appropriate international obligations and have committed themselves in good faith to a peaceful process and to negotiations. The Declaration refers specially to the principles of self-determination as a basis for recognition.

Application of the principle of the self-determination of peoples is strongly influenced (or one may say, balanced) also by the principles of the inviolability of frontiers and territorial integrity of states. 'The sovereignty, territorial integrity and independence of states within the established international system, and the principle of self-determination of peoples, both of great value and importance, must not be permitted to work against each other in the period ahead', states a report prepared by the Secretary General of the UN, Dr Boutros-Ghali. The principles of the self-determination of peoples, the inviolability of frontiers and the territorial integrity of states are inseparable and support each other, which means that they should be balanced in the same way as justice and order need to be balanced in any society. One cannot have justice without order, while order without justice is not only inhuman but it also does not last long. Max Kampelman rightly observes that '[t]he inviolability of existing boundaries is an integral part of this process [of self-determination], not because the boundaries are necessarily sound or just, but because respect for them is necessary for peace and stability'.

The principle of the self-determination of peoples developed in the UN mainly in the context of the process of decolonisation. Though no document confines the principle for the decolonisation of colonies of overseas parent states (so-called 'salt water' colonialism), it was natural that at that time this aspect of the principle became the most prominent, and for some states even the only one.[24] Therefore Hector Gross Espiell wrote:

> The United Nations established the right of self-determination as a right of peoples under colonial and alien domination. The right does not apply to peoples already organised in the form of a state which are not under colonial and alien domination, since Resolution 1514 (XV) and other United Nations

---

24 India made the following reservation to article 1 of the Covenant on Civil and Political Rights: 'With reference to Article 1 of the International Covenant on Civil and Political Rights, the government of the Republic of India declares that the words "the right of self-determination" appearing in [that Article] apply only to the peoples under foreign domination and that these words do not apply to sovereign independent states or to a section of a people or nation – which is the essence of national integrity' (UN Doc CCPR/C/Rev 3, 12 May 1992, p 18). France, Germany and the Netherlands strongly objected to this reservation by India (*ibid*, pp 39–40).

instruments condemn any attempt aimed at partial or total disruption of the national unity and the territorial integrity of the country.

It seem to me that, there are two flaws in this approach. First, that the principle applies only to peoples under colonial or alien domination and, second, the assumption that application of this principle to a sovereign (even multi-ethnic) state would inevitably be fraught with the disruption of its national unity or territorial integrity.

In the colonial context, the principle meant the independence of colonies from their parent state. However, the attitude of states[25] as well as that of international bodies clearly shows that the principle of the self-determination of peoples has a universal application and is an ongoing right of all peoples. Outside the colonial context, however, the meaning of the principle becomes less clear and more controversial.[26]

The historic roots of the principle of self-determination include the American Declaration of Independence and the decree of the French Constituent Assembly of May 1790, which refers both to the Rights of Man and to the rights of peoples. In the course of the 19th century European history the principle of nationality was influential and it was the *alter ego* of the principle of self-determination. These concepts, together with the concept of the protection of national minorities, were prominent in the deliberations of the Allied Supreme Council at Versailles in 1919. It is obvious that the concept of self-determination was not as yet accepted as a general principle. Thus the concept of racial equality was excluded form the Covenant of the League of Nations. Moreover, the Mandates System and the famous Minorities Treaties were conspicuous in their application only in certain cases. The special application of such institutions to defeated or newly established states only testified to the absence of a general recognition of the 'principle of equal rights and self-determination of peoples'. However, once the principle had been recognised as such, it was in the long run difficult – in terms both of morality and logic – to maintain that it only applied within the Americas and Europe. Thus, during and after the Second World War it was more and more accepted that self-determination was a universally applicable standard.

No doubt there has been continuing doubt and difficulty over the definition of what is a 'people' for the purpose of applying the principle of self-determination. None the less, the principle appears to have a core of reasonable certainty. This core consists in the right of a community which has a distinct character to have this character reflected in the institutions of government under which it lives. The concept of distinct character depends on a number of criteria which may appear in combination. Race (or nationality) is one of the more important of the relevant criteria, but the concept of race can only be expressed scientifically in terms of more specific features, in which matters of culture, language, religion, and group psychology predominate. The physical *indicia* of race and nationality may evidence the cultural distinctiveness of a group but they certainly do not inevitably condition it. Indeed, if the purely ethnic criteria are applied exclusively many long-standing national identities would be negated on academic grounds – such as, for example, the United States. In any case the

---

25 For example, the German objection to the Indian reservation to article 1 of the Covenant on Civil and Political Rights states: 'The right of self determination as enshrined in the Charter of the United Nations and as embodied in the Covenants applies to all peoples and not only to those under foreign domination' (UN Doc CCPR/Rev 3, p 39).

26 Rein Mullerson, *International Law, Rights and Politics*, 1994, London: Routledge at pp 5–64.

community of states has been prepared to recognise both new states and the existence of legitimate claims by units of self-determination either by institutional procedures within the United Nations or on the basis of general recognition. Bangladesh, for example, was recognised as a state on the basis of general recognition by existing states. Provisions in written constitutions may acknowledge the relevance of self-determination to the affairs of multinational societies.

It is my opinion that the heterogeneous terminology which has been used over the years – the references to 'nationalities', 'peoples', 'minorities', and 'indigenous populations' – involves essentially the same idea. Nor is this view based upon a theoretical construction. Once a member of a people or community is expressing political claims in public discourse in Geneva, New York, Ottawa, of Canberra, and using the available stock of concepts so to do, it seems to me that the type of political consciousness involved is broadly the same. The external participation of culturally distinct groups in the political process is essentially the same as that of individual states in respect of the Law of Nations. By this I mean that in order to obtain recognition of the claim to cultural identity, or to statehood, the claimant must accept the terms of the dialogue. This may sound rather obvious but it is in this context that I want to make the point that the opposition which appears in the sources between the definition of indigenous population 'by themselves' and their definition 'by others' is a false dichotomy.

At this point I would like to stress that in practice the claim to self-determination does no necessarily involve a claim to statehood and secession. There are various models of 'self-government' or 'autonomy' but neither is a term of art. It is true that some models, such as Trusteeship, are related to the purpose of an ultimate transition to independence. However, there are a variety of other models, including that of 'Associated state' (as in the case of the Cook Islands and New Zealand), the regional autonomy of Austrians in the South Tyrol, the Cyprus Constitution of 1960, and the various arrangements within the Swiss and other confederations. There can be little doubt that federalism as a system provides a special capacity and a flexibility in facing cultural diversity. Federalism is probably better able than any other system to provide a regime of stable autonomy which provides group freedoms within a wider political cosmos and keeps the principle of nationality in line with ideas of mutuality and genuine coexistence of peoples.[27]

It now seems an accepted rule of international law that an entity created in defiance of the principle of self-determination cannot be considered a state. There remains the problem, however, of what constitutes a 'people' capable of exercising the right of self-determination. In this context it is worth considering and contrasting the position of the Scots, the Irish, the Croats, the Kurds, the Palestinians, the Basques, the people of Yorkshire, etc, etc. We shall return to the issue of self-determination when looking at the international law of human rights.

5.2.1.6 State succession

The transfer of territory from one state to another takes place in at least five ways:

---

27 Ian Brownlie, 'The Rights of Peoples in Modern International Law', in Crawford (ed), *The Rights of Peoples*, 1988, Oxford: Oxford University Press at pp 4–6.

(a) cession;

(b) annexation;

(c) emancipation;

(d) formation of union;

(e) federation.

In all five situations one sovereign substitutes itself for another – there is a disruption of legal continuity.

5.2.2 Non self-governing territories/dependent states

There still exists, although the number is dwindling, a number of territories which have limited/restricted powers of control over their own affairs and can therefore not be considered as fully independent states. The question arises as to whether they possess any degree of international personality prior to full independence.

5.2.2.1 Colonies

Traditionally international law has not regarded colonies as possessing any international personality, because the control of the colony's foreign relations rested entirely in the hands of the colonial power. We have already seen when looking at the law of treaties that there is a presumption that treaties will apply to a colonial power and its colonial possessions. However with the development of the principle of self-determination, international law has come to recognise that for certain purposes 'pre-independent states' and national liberation movements may have some degree of international personality. For example, in 1974 the Palestine Liberation Organisation was accorded observer status at the United Nations, a position previously reserved solely for the representatives of sovereign states that were not at the time members of the United Nations. The head of the PLO was subsequently invited to address the UN General Assembly and PLO representatives have attended various UN conferences and meetings. Similarly the General Assembly recognised the South West African People's Organisation (SWAPO) as the sole representative of the people of Namibia. However, the exact nature of the personality of liberation movements is far from clear and in the case of *Tel-Oren v Libyan Arab Republic* 765 F 2d 774 (1984) a United States Court of Appeal declined to accept a case against the PLO in part on the ground that the PLO's obligations under international law were unclear.

Declaration on the Gaining of Independence to Colonial Territories and Peoples[28]

The General Assembly ... Declares that:

1   The subjection of peoples to alien subjugation, domination and exploitation constitutes a denial of fundamental human rights, is conntrary to the Charter of the United Nations and is an impediment to the promotion of world peace and co-operation;

---

28 GA Resolution 1514 (XV), 14 December 1960 – adopted by 89 votes to nil, with nine abstentions. The abstaining states were Australia, Belgium, Dominican Republic, France, Portugal, South Africa, Spain, the UK and the USA.

2   All peoples have the right to self-determination; by virtue of that right they freely determine their political status and freely pursue their economic, social and cultural development;

3   Inadequacy of political, economic, social or education preparedness should never serve as a pretext for delaying independence;

4   All armed action or repressive measures of all kinds directed against dependent peoples shall cease in order to enable them to exercise peacefully and freely their right to complete independence, and the integrity of their national territory shall be respected;

5   Immediate steps shall be taken, in Trust and Non-Self-Governing Territories or all other territories which have not yet attained independence, to transfer all powers to the peoples of those territories, without any conditions or reservations, in accordance with their freely expressed will and desire, without any distinction as to race, creed or colour, in order to enable them to enjoy complete independences and freedom;

6   Any attempt aimed at the partial or total disruption of the national unity and the territorial integrity of a country is incompatible with the Purposes and Principles of the Charter of the United Nations;

7   All states shall observe faithfully and strictly the provisions of the Charter of the United Nations, the Universal Declaration of Human Rights and the present Declaration on the basis of equality, non-interference in the internal affairs of all states, and respect for the sovereign rights of all peoples and their territorial integrity

5.2.2.2 Protectorates

There are three situations where protection may be given by a foreign state:

(a) Protection may be exercised over a territory which did not have international personality before the protectorate was created. This occurred in the late 19th century in respect of a number of European states. In such situations the territory in question will only gain full international personality when it is clear that they are acting independently of the protecting state. For example, Kuwait became a British protectorate in 1899 and was gradually given increased control over its own affairs. Its independence was only formally acknowledged by the UK in 1961, but it is clear that Kuwait had achieved statehood and international personality before that time.

(b) Protection may be exercised over an already existing state. The arrangement will usually be covered by agreement between the protecting and the protected state and such protection does not usually affect the legal personality of the protected state. For example, Morocco was an independent state until the start of the 20th century when it was divided into three parts: Tangier became an international city, and the rest of Morocco was divided into a Spanish and a French zone. Foreign relations were completely within Spanish and French control, and France and Spain could conclude treaties on behalf of Morocco. Nevertheless in the *Rights of US Nationals in Morocco* case,[29] the ICJ held that during the period of the protectorate Morocco had retained its international personality.

---

29   [1952] *ICJ Rep* at p 176.

(c) In a few specific cases one state may exercise a protective power over a much smaller state without that smaller state losing its international personality, although the extent of that personality may be limited, eg San Marino, Monaco.

5.2.2.3 Mandates and Trust Territories

The Mandate system was introduced by the League of Nations to provide for the administration of the colonies and dependencies of the losing states in the First World War 'inhabited by peoples not yet able to stand by themselves under the strenuous conditions of the modern world'.[30] The territories concerned were divided into three classes:

Class A Territories were those parts of the Turkish Empire which were thought to be closest to independence and were put under the control of Britain or France. Only Iraq achieved independence under the Mandate system, Palestine (to the extent that it has), Transjordan, Syria and Lebanon only achieved independence as a result of the Second World War.

Class B Territories comprised peoples 'especially those of Central Africa, (who) are at such a stage that the Mandatory must be responsible for the administration of the territory under conditions which will guarantee freedom of conscience and religion, subject only to the maintenance of public order and morals, the prohibition of abuses such as the slave trade, the arms traffic and the liquor traffic, and the prevention of the establishment of fortifications or military or naval bases and of military training of the natives for other than police purposes and the defence of the territory, and will also secure equal opportunities for the trade and commerce of other Members of the League'.[31] Included in the Class B Territories were Tanganyika, British and French Togoland, the British and French Cameroons, Rwanda. The territories concerned only gained independence after transfer to the UN Trusteeship system.

Class C Territories included certain territories 'which, owing to the sparseness of their population, or their small size, or their remoteness from the centres of civilisation, or their geographical contiguity to the territory of the Mandatory, and other circumstances, can be best administered under the laws of the Mandatory as integral portions of its territory, subject to ... safeguards in the interests of the indigenous population'. Included in the Class C Mandates were Namibia, Samoa, and New Guinea.

When the League of Nations was disbanded to be succeeded by the United Nations a replacement was needed for the Mandate system and an entirely new 'trusteeship system' was established under Chapter XI of the UN Charter. Those territories held under Mandate were placed under the trusteeship system which would involve the conclusion of a trusteeship agreement between the administering authority and the United Nations. The main object of the system was 'to promote the political, economic, social and educational advancement of

---

30 Article 22, para 4 of the Covenant of the League of Nations 1919.

31 Article 22, para 5 of the League of Nations Covenant 1919.

32 Article 22, para 6 of the League of Nations Covenant 1919.

the inhabitants of the trust territories, and their progressive development towards self-government or independence as may be appropriate to the particular circumstances of each territory and its peoples and the freely expressed wishes of the people concerned'.[33]

The traditional view of Mandates and trusteeships was that, as long as they subsisted over a particular territory, that territory could not be regarded as having international personality. However, paralleling the situation with regard to colonies, increasingly the view has been expressed that Trust Territories do possess some degree of separate status and international personality, similar to that accorded to organisations such as the PLO.

> Namibia, even at the periods when it had been reduced to the status of a German colony or was subject to the South African Mandate, possessed a legal personality which was denied it only by the law now obsolete ... It nevertheless constituted a subject of law ... possessing national sovereignty but lacking the exercise thereof.[34]

All of the trust territories have now become independent states and the UN is considering the future role of the Trusteeship Council.

5.2.3 International organisations

> Accordingly, the Court has come to the conclusion that the [United Nations] Organisation is an international person. That is not the same thing as saying that it is a state, which it certainly is not, or that its legal personality and rights and duties are the same as those of a state ... What it does mean is that it is a subject of international law and capable of possessing international rights and duties, and that it has capacity to maintain its rights by bringing international claims.[35]

> Whilst ... specific acknowledgement of the possession of international personality is extremely rare, it is permissible to assume that most organisations created by a multilateral inter-governmental agreement will, so far as they are endowed with functions on the international plane, possess some measure of international personality in addition to the personality within the system of municipal law of the members ... Possession of international personality will normally involve, as a consequence, the attribution of power to make treaties, of privileges and immunities, of power to undertake legal proceedings: it will also pose a general problem of dissolution, for in the nature of things, the personality of all such organisations can be brought to an end.[36]

It is clear that international organisations are capable of possessing international personality and of being subjects of international law. The functions, rights and duties of such organisations are governed by what Starke refers to as international constitutional law. Institutions will be defined by reference to their legal functions and responsibilities and the constitutions of such institutions will set out their powers, objects and purpose – analogies can perhaps be drawn with municipal company law and a company's memorandum and articles of association. In that major respect international organisations differ from states

---

33 Article 76 of the UN Charter.
34 Judge Ammoun in the *Namibia* case [1971] *ICJ Rep* at 68.
35 ICJ in the *Reparations* case [1949] *ICJ Rep* at 174.
36 Bowett, *The Law of International Institutions*, 4th edn, 1982, London: Stevens at p 339.

in that their powers are limited and problems of sovereignty and jurisdiction do not arise. Almost everything is within the competence of states whereas anything not expressly within the powers of an international organisation is *prima facie ultra vires* – although certain powers may be implied, as in the *Reparations* case.

The criteria of legal personality of international organisations may be summarised as follows:

(1) a permanent association of states, with lawful objects equipped with organs to carry out those objects;

(2) a distinction between the organisation and its member states;

(3) the existence of legal powers exercisable on the international plane and not solely within the national system of one or more states.

As far as international organisations are concerned the principal questions to be decided are:

(1) the extent to which the organisation can conclude treaties;

(2) the privileges and immunities to which the organisation is entitled;

(3) the capacity of the organisation to bring international claims. It should however be noted at this point that only states have *locus standi* in contentious cases before the International Court of Justice.

5.2.4 *Individuals*

[An individual] is a person in international law, though his capacities may be different from and less in number and substance than the capacities of states. An individual, for example, cannot acquire territory, he cannot make treaties, and he cannot have belligerent rights. But he can commit war crimes, and piracy, and crimes against humanity and foreign sovereigns and he can own property which international law protects, and he can have claims to compensation for acts arising *ex contractu* or *ex delicto*.[37]

Any individual who commits a crime against the peace and security of mankind is responsible for such crime.[38]

---

37 O'Connell, *International Law*, Vol 1, 1970, London: Stevens at pp 108–09.

38 Article 3 of the Draft Code of Offences Against the Peace and Security of Mankind (1987) *ILC Ybk* Vol II, part II, 13.

CHAPTER 6

RECOGNITION AND LEGITIMATION

6.1 Introduction

It has already been seen that an important requirement of statehood is the capacity to enter into international legal relationships. This inevitably concerns the attitude of other states and in particular raises the question of recognition. Do other states recognise the new entity as a state? What are the implications if they do recognise it? What are the implications if they do not?

6.2 The theoretical issue

As is so often the case with international law, discussion of recognition has led to the development of two competing theories. The principal question which the two theories attempt to answer is whether recognition is a necessary requirement for or merely a consequence of international personality.

6.2.1 The constitutive theory

Underlying the constitutive theory is the view that every legal system requires some organ to determine with finality and certainty the subjects of the system. In the present international legal system that organ can only be the states, acting severally or collectively, and their determination must have definitive legal effect.

The constitutive theory developed in the 19th century and was closely allied to a positivist view of international law. According to that view the obligation to obey international law derives from the consent of individual states. The creation of a new state would create new legal obligations and existing states would need to consent to those new obligations. Therefore the acceptance of the new state by existing states was essential. A further argument prevalent during the late 19th century was based on the view of international law as existing between 'civilised nations'. New states could not automatically become members of the international community, it was recognition which created their membership. This had the further consequence that entities not recognised as states were not bound by international law, nor were the 'civilised nations' so bound in their dealings with them. Oppenheim stated the position thus:

> The formation of a new state is ... a matter of fact and not law. It is through recognition, which is a matter of law, that such a new state becomes subject to international law.[1]

Recognition is therefore seen as a requirement of international personality. A major criticism of this theory is that it leads to confusion where a new state is recognised by some states but not others. Lauterpacht attempted to get round this problem by alleging an international legal duty to recognise:

---

1   Oppenheim's *International Law*, Vol 1, 8th edn, 1955, London: Longmans at p 544.

To recognise a community as a state is to declare that it fulfils the conditions of statehood as required by international law. If those conditions are present, existing states are under a duty to grant recognition ... in granting or withholding recognition states do not claim and are not entitled to serve exclusively the interests of their national policy and convenience regardless of the principles of international law in the matter. Although recognition is thus declaratory of an existing fact, such declaration, made in the impartial fulfilment of a legal duty, is constitutive, as between the recognising state and the community so recognised, of international rights and duties associated with full statehood. Prior to recognition such rights and obligations exist only to the extent to which they have been expressly conceded or legitimately asserted, by reference to compelling rules of humanity and justice, either by the existing members of the international society or by the people claiming recognition.[2]

However, although states do make reference to the presence or absence of the factual characteristics of statehood when granting or refusing recognition, in the last resort their decision will normally be based on political expediency – there is no real evidence that states themselves feel that there is a legal duty to recognise when the other requirements of statehood have been satisfied. The question has recently arisen with respect to the territory of former Yugoslavia. In June 1991 Slovenia and Croatia declared their independence. The European Union and its member states did not recognise the two states immediately. In December 1991 Foreign Ministers of EU member states adopted 'Guidelines on the recognition of new states in Eastern Europe and in the Soviet Union'. This provided that recognition would be accorded to those new states which agreed to respect five conditions. The five conditions included matters such as respect for human rights, guarantees for minorities, respect for the inviolability of frontiers, acceptance of commitments to regional security and stability and to settle by agreement all questions concerning state succession. Slovenia, Croatia and Bosnia-Herzegovina agreed to the conditions and were formally accorded recognition in early 1992. It is clear that the conditions set down by the European Union exceeded the normal requirements of statehood. The implication would therefore seem to be that the EU viewed recognition as a political measure which was not required by any international obligation. It remains to be seen whether European practice will continue to use these conditions in all decisions on the recognition of new states or whether the application of the conditions will be restricted to the particular situation in the Balkans and Eastern Europe.

6.2.2 The declaratory theory

An early example of the declaratory theory is to be found in two provisions of the Montevideo Convention:

The political existence of the state is independent of recognition by other states. Even before recognition the state has the right to defend its integrity and independence ... and to organise itself as it sees fit. The exercise of these rights has no other limitation than the exercise of the rights of other states according to international law – Article 3.

---

2   Lauterpacht, *Recognition in International Law*, 1978, New York: AMS Press at p 6.

The recognition of a state merely signifies that the state which recognises it accepts the personality of the other, with all the rights and duties determined by international law – Article 6.

For the adherents to the declaratory theory the formation of a new state is a matter of fact, not law. Recognition is a political act by which the recognising state indicates a willingness to initiate international relations with the recognised state and the question of international personality is independent of recognition. However, the act of recognition is not totally without legal significance because it does indicate that the recognising state considers that the new entity fulfils all the required conditions for becoming an international subject.

The declaratory theory is more widely supported by writers on international law today and it accords more readily with state practice, as is illustrated by the fact that non-recognised 'states' are quite commonly the object of international claims by the very states which are refusing recognition, for example Arab states have continued to maintain that Israel is bound by international law although few of them, until recently, have recognised Israel.

6.3   Non-recognition

The legal regime established by the Covenant of the League of Nations 1919 and the Kellogg-Briand Pact 1928 was the basis for the development of the principle that 'acquisition of territory or special advantages by illegal threat or use of force' would not create a title capable of recognition by other states. The principle achieved particular significance as a result of the Japanese invasion of Manchuria in 1931. The US Secretary of State, Stimson, declared that the illegal invasion would not be recognised as it was contrary to the Kellogg-Briand Pact which outlawed the use of war as an instrument of national policy. Thereafter the doctrine of not recognising any situation, treaty or agreement brought about by non-legal means was often referred to as the Stimson Doctrine.

However, state practice before the Second World War did not seem to support the view that the Stimson Doctrine contained a binding rule of international law. The Italian conquest of Abyssinia (Ethiopia) was recognised as was the German take-over of Czechoslovakia. After 1945 the principle was re-examined and the draft Declaration on the Rights and Duties of States prepared by the ILC emphasised that territorial acquisitions achieved in a manner inconsistent with international law should not be recognised by other states. Similarly the Declaration on Principles of International Law 1970 adopted by the UN General Assembly included a provision to the effect that no territorial acquisition resulting from the threat or use of force shall be recognised as legal. There have been a number of occasions where the Security Council of the United Nations has called on states not to accord recognition to situations which have arisen as a result of unlawful acts:

The Security Council, deeply concerned about the situation in Southern Rhodesia
...

6   Calls upon all states not to recognise this illegal authority and not to entertain any diplomatic or other relations with it.[3]

---

3   Security Council Resolution, 20 November 1965.

Recognition in such situations would itself be a breach of international law.

6.4 Recognition of governments

Although the practice of states is far from establishing the existence of a legal duty to recognise an entity which has established the factual characteristics of statehood, with regard to governments the position is even more difficult. The problem of recognition of governments will arise when a new regime has taken power:

(a) unconstitutionally;

(b) by violent means; or

(c) with foreign help,

in a state whose previous and legitimate government was recognised by other states. Recognition in such circumstances may appear an endorsement of the new regime, and the recognising state may not wish to offer such endorsement or approval. Alternatively, it may be impractical not to acknowledge a factual situation, in which case the recognising state may wish to indicate that recognition is inevitable once a given set of facts arise. Two approaches can therefore be identified: an *objective* approach, whereby recognition will occur if a given set of facts have occurred, or a *subjective* test, whereby recognition will depend on whether or not the new regime is going to act properly in the eyes of the recognising state.

One possible resolution of the problem of when to recognise is to avoid recognition altogether. In 1930, the Mexican Foreign Minister, Señor Estrada, rejected the whole doctrine of recognition on the ground that 'it allows foreign governments to pass upon the legitimacy or illegitimacy of the regime existing in another country, with the result that situations arise in which the legal qualifications or national status of governments or authorities are apparently made subject to the opinion of foreigners'. Henceforward, the Mexican government refused to make declarations granting recognition of governments. This Estrada Doctrine, as it came to be known, denies the need for explicit and formal acts of recognition; all that needs to be determined is whether the new regime has in fact established itself as the effective government of the country.

Although slow at first to catch on, the Estrada Doctrine has come to be followed by an increasing number of states. In 1977, the United States announced that it would no longer issue formal declarations of recognition, the only question in future would be whether diplomatic relations continued with the new regime or not. Following the US practice the UK has also de-emphasised recognition and there is now no formal recognition of new regimes, although the Foreign Office will still have to decide whether or not a new regime has effective control when considering matters such as trade and diplomatic relations.

6.5 *De facto* and *de jure* recognition

A distinction has sometimes been made in cases where governments have been accorded recognition between *de facto* and *de jure* recognition. Recognition of an entity as the *de facto* government can be seen as an interim step taken where there is some doubt as to the legitimacy of the new government or as to its long-term prospects of survival. For example, the UK recognised the Soviet government *de facto* in 1921 and *de jure* in 1924. In some situations, particularly where there is a civil war, both a *de facto* and a *de jure* government may be recognised, as for example during the Spanish Civil War when the Republican government continued to be recognised as the *de jure* government, but as the Nationalist forces under General Franco took increasingly effective control of Spain, *de facto* recognition was accorded to the Nationalist government. Eventually the Nationalist government obtained full *de jure* recognition.

6.6   Collective recognition

COLLECTIVE RESPONSES TO THE UNILATERAL DECLARATIONS OF INDEPENDENCE OF SOUTHERN RHODESIA AND PALESTINE: AN APPLICATION OF THE LEGITIMISING FUNCTION OF THE UNITED NATIONS[4]

I   INTRODUCTION

The proclamation in 1988 of the independent state of Palestine has underlined once again a major function which the United Nations has assumed by default, namely that of collective legitimisation, and its corollary, collective illegitimisation. A comparison with the attempted creation of another controversial state this century – that of Rhodesia – sheds light on this significant development of the United Nations.

It will be recalled that on 11 November 1965 a European minority under the leadership of Ian Smith unilaterally declared the independence of the British colony of Southern Rhodesia. The purported new state of Rhodesia had serious claims to fulfil the traditional criteria of statehood. If possessed a defined territory, permanent population and a government clearly manifesting its effectiveness both in terms of authority over the population, and in terms of independence from external control.

Twenty-three years later, on 15 November 1988, the Palestine National Council, at its 19th Extraordinary Session in Algiers, adopted the decision to declare 'in the name of God and on behalf of the Palestinian Arab people, the establishment of the state of Palestine in the land of Palestine with its capital at Jerusalem'. Whilst there clearly was an identifiable population, there was no *elected* government, and an apparent lack of effective control over defined territory.

In terms therefore of the traditional criteria for recognition of statehood, the contrasts between the two cases may seem to be evident. Yet in the former, the 'State of Rhodesia' was effectively denied recognition and entry into the international community by the United Nations until its accession to independence in 1980 as the State of Zimbabwe on the basis of majority rule. In the latter case, the proclamation of an independent State of Palestine was officially acknowledged by the General Assembly of the United Nations in December 1988, and granted recognition by close to 100 states.[5]

---

4   Vera Gowlland-Debbas (1990) *BYIL* LXI at pp 135–55.

5   Keesing's *Record of World Events* (1988) 34 at para 36321.

This apparent paradox may be explained by reference to an underlying common denominator: in effect in both these cases the traditional criteria of statehood, in particular the principle of effectiveness, were overridden by the legitimising principle of self-determination of peoples, the United Nations acting as the 'dispenser of approval or disapproval' of these unilateral claims to independent status in accordance with their conformity or non-conformity with this principle.

The political and moral impact of this United Nations function of legitimisation has been underlined by a number of commentators.[6] In briefly reviewing the collective responses to these two unilateral proclamations of independent statehood, the present article seeks to demonstrate, however, that in both cases the United Nations went well beyond a political or moral function. For in its unanimous condemnation of the UDI, and its legitimisation of a Palestinian state, it is contended that the United Nations majority resorted to a series of pronouncements having a quasi-legal function: the collective defence of the right to self-determination, a norm now considered as of fundamental concern to the international community, and which has proved to be the cornerstone of subsequent claims to full sovereignty in both the legal and the material sense.

II   THE UNILATERAL DECLARATIONS OF INDEPENDENT STATEHOOD UNDER INTERNATIONAL LAW

(a) The background

The origins of the two unilateral declarations are by now sufficiently well-known to be recalled only briefly.

The constitutional relationship between the territory of Southern Rhodesia and the United Kingdom differed from that of other more classic colonies as a result of its particular circumstances. Instigated by Cecil Rhodes, the British had in 1888 first acquired a sphere of influence in the territory and had then secured exclusive mineral rights from the local chief, following this up by occupation in 1890 and conquest in 1894. The origins of the Southern Rhodesian crisis that was to erupt in November 1965 can be traced to the initial British policy of entrusting local administration to a chartered company, and then to the gradual delegation of powers to the European settlers, leading to the grant to this minority of a considerable measure of internal self-government (Constitutions of 1923 and 1961).[7] Whilst there was no formal system of *apartheid* in existence and legislation was not overtly based on racist lines, deliberate white Rhodesian governmental policies ensured that African participation in the political process and the rate of African political advancement were kept to a minimum. As a result, whilst Southern Rhodesia's two northern neighbours acceded to independence in 1964 as Zambia and Malawi, the United Kingdom, under pressure from the

---

6   Claude, 'Collective Legitimisation as a Political Function of the United Nations' (1966) 20 *International Organisation* 367–79; Virally, *L'Organisation mondiale*, 1992, Paris: Armand Colin, at pp 430–31 and 454–56; *id 'Le Rôle des organisations dans l'attenuation et le règlement des crises internationles'* (1976) 14 *Politique Etrangère* pp 529–62. With a passing reference to Rhodesia and the PLO he states: 'La composition multilatérale de l'organisation internationale, la finalité d'"intérêt-général" ... confère aux actes de ses organes une autorité morale spécifique. Par la-même, elle est en mesure de conférer ou de réfuser le label de la légitimitée aux situations crées par les états ou d'autres acteurs internationaux, ou a leurs aspirations ... Les conséquences practiques de l'éxercice de cette fonction n'ont pas besoin d'être longuement commentées', *ibid*, pp 540–41.

7   See Palley, *The Constitutional History and Law of Southern Rhodesia 1888–1965, with special reference to Imperial Control*, 1966, Oxford: Clarendon Press.

international community not to abandon this large unenfranchised black majority, denied the territory independence so long as the white minority refused to give certain guarantees for their political advancement.[8]

It was the resentment of white Rhodesians over this, following the failure of negotiations with the United Kingdom to obtain independence by constitutional means, that led to a unilateral declaration of independence on 11 November 1965 by which the 'government of Rhodesia' purported to enact a constitution for an independent sovereign state. Significantly, the 'Independence Proclamation', whilst echoing the 1776 American Declaration of Independence, omitted the assertion that 'all men are created equal', and made no reference to 'the consent of the governed'.[9]

Palestine, it will be recalled, as one of the territories detached from the Turkish Empire, had been placed under the League of Nations Mandate system with Great Britain designated as the Mandatory Power. Article 22 of the Covenant of the League provided that the Mandates should be governed by the principle 'that the well-being and development of such peoples form a sacred trust of civilisation', and with respect to Class A Mandates, which included Palestine, provided for the provisional recognition of 'their existence as independent nations ... subject to the rendering of administrative advice and assistance by a Mandatory'. After the Second World War, however, Great Britain, finding itself, in the face of the inherent contradictions of the Mandate and the growing tension in the territory, unable to establish political institutions leading towards self-government, placed the matter in April 1947 in the hands of the General Assembly of the United Nations. The result was the adoption of Resolution 181 (II) on 29 November 1947 recommending a 'Plan of Partition with Economic Union' which provided for the establishment of independent Arab and Jewish states and of a special international regime for the City of Jerusalem. This was never implemented. The consequences are only too well known. Following the 1948-9 Arab-Israeli conflict, the newly proclaimed State of Israel appropriated territories not assigned to it under the Partition Plan, and Egypt and Jordan ended up administering the Gaza Strip and the West Bank respectively,[10] both of which territories were occupied by Israel following further hostilities in 1967.

There were several milestones leading to the declaration of an independent Palestinian state: the formation of the Palestine Liberation Organisation by the National Congress of Palestine in 1964; the recognition of the PLO as the sole and legitimate representative of the Palestinian people by the 8th Arab Summit in Rabat in October 1974; the Palestinian uprising, the *intifadah* begun in the

---

8   For a further analysis of the question of Southern Rhodesia see Gowlland-Debbas, *Collective Responses to Illegal Acts in International Law: United Nations Action in the Question of Southern Rhodesia*, 1990, Dordrecht: Martinus Nijhoff.

9   Rhodesia Proclamation No 53 of 1965. Text in Windrich, *The Rhodesia Problem. A Documentary Record 1923-1973*, 1975, London/Boston: Routledge/Kegan Paul at pp 210–11.

10   On the origins of the Palestine problem and the legal issues raised see Boyle, 'Creating the State of Palestine' (1987–88) 4 *Palestine Yearbook of International Law* pp 15–43; Cattan, *Palestine and International Law. The Legal Aspects of the Arab-Israeli Conflict*, 1973, London: Longma; Kassim 'Legal Systems and Development in Palestine' (1984) I *Palestine Yearbook of International Law* pp 19–35; WT and SV Mallinson, *The Palestine Problem in International Law and World Order*, 1986, London: Longman; Pellet, *'La Déstruction de Troie n'aura pas lieu'* (1987–88) 4 *Palestine Yearbook of International Law* pp 44–84.

occupied territories in December 1987; and King Hussein's decision on 31 July 1988 to give up legal and administrative links with the West Bank.[11]

In contrast to the Rhodesian 'Independence Proclamation', the 'Declaration of Independence' of Palestine was made, *inter alia*:[12]

> By virtue of the natural, historical and legal right of the Palestinian Arab people to its homeland, Palestine ...

> ... on the basis of the international legitimacy embodied in the resolutions of the United Nations since 1947, and

> through the exercise by the Palestinian Arab people of its right to self-determination, political independence and sovereignty over its territory ...

The Declaration also affirmed the establishment in the State of Palestine of, *inter alia*, a democratic parliamentary system and full equality of rights, and affirmed respect for the principles of the UN Charter.

(b) The Unilateral Declarations of Independence and the Criteria of Statehood

Under international law, such unilateral declarations of independence can only be considered as a claim to personality and a request for recognition. Actually to attain that end, fulfilment of the international legal criteria for independent statehood has traditionally been required (as a preliminary step or a determining factor in the achievement of international personality, depending on whether one argues from the constitutive or declaratory viewpoints of the effects of recognition).[13] In particular, the need for effective governmental control has been underlined.[14] Debate relating to the fulfilment of these criteria by Rhodesia and Palestine has been waged on both sides. This debate can be summarised as follows.

1 Southern Rhodesia and the criteria of statehood

In 1965 the purported new State of Rhodesia had serious claims to fulfil these criteria. the first two conditions regarding territorial boundaries and permanent population did not come into question. With respect to the criteria of effectiveness and independence, it appeared that the domestic effectiveness of the Smith regime, a regime given the judicial blessing by the Rhodesian courts,[15] was assured. It wielded effective control over the organs of government, successfully set up new governmental institutions under new constitutional arrangements, issued passports and introduced decimal currency and UDI

---

11 Text in (1988) 27 *International Legal Materials*, pp 1637–54. Regarding the prior status of the West Bank, see Kassim, *loc cit* above pp 27–28; Pellet, *loc cit* p 60.

12 For the English text of the Declaration of Independence and accompanying political communique, see (1988) 27 *International Legal Materials*, pp 1660–71, and UN Doc A/43/827 and S/20278, Ann III (1988). See also Flory, *'Naissance d'un Etat Palestinien'* (1989) 93 *Revue generale de droit international public*, pp 385–407.

13 See Article 1 of the Montevideo Convention on the Rights and Duties of States of 1933, League of Nations Treaty Series, Vol 19, p 165, which states: 'The state as a person of international law should possess the following qualifications: (a) a permanent population; (b) a defined territory; (c) government; and (d) capacity to enter into relations with other states'. See also the *American Law Institute, Restatement (Third) of the Foreign Relations Law of the United States*, 1987, Vol 1, para 201, St Paul, Minnesota.

14 For example, Brownlie, *Principles of Public International Law*, 4th edn, 1990, Oxford: Clarendon Press at p 73; Crawford, *The Creation of States in International Law*, 1979, Oxford: Clarendon Press at pp 36 ff; Thierry, *Combacau, Sur and Vallee, Droit International Public*, 1984, Paris: Editions Montchrestien at pp 198–211.

15 *Archion Ndhlovu and others v The Queen*, Appellate Division, High Court of Rhodesia, 13 September 1968; [1968] (4) SALR 515.

stamps. There was no serious challenge at the time from within, the threat of guerrilla warfare having initially been contained. Southern Rhodesia's independence from the United Kingdom was also clearly demonstrated in the face of that state's futile attempts to assert its sovereignty, whilst refusing at the same time to use force against 'kith and kin'. Finally, Southern Rhodesia's dependence on South Africa's support was said not to affect its legal independence. These arguments concerning statehood were bolstered by the fact that the regime maintained itself in power for over 14 years, despite considerable external pressures.

On the other hand, serious doubts were expressed at the time, which in retrospect proved to be only too well founded, concerning the 'reasonable prospects of permanency' of a regime which denied political participation to the majority in the territory on a racially discriminatory basis, and the stability of a state, the independence of which had been opposed by the entire international community.[16]

2 Palestine and the criteria of statehood

The greater part of this debate has arisen from the request of Palestine for a change from its observer status to full membership of certain of the specialised agencies (so far, the WHO and UNESCO), since the constituent instruments of these organisations make admission to full membership contingent on 'statehood'.[17] This discussion has not at the time of writing been conclusive, compromise resolutions being adopted in both organisations which effectively shelved the admission for an indeterminate period.

However, certain conclusions regarding statehood may be drawn from this stage of the debate. Not surprisingly, the representative from Israel considered that 'the declaration from Algiers proclaims a so-called independent Palestinian state, with no territory, no borders and with Jerusalem, my home town and the capital of Israel, as its declared capital. That declaration has no meaning in reality.'[18] Other states such as Canada, Australia, the United States, Spain (speaking in the name of the European Community) and Norway also declared that, in their view, the proclaimed Palestinian state did not conform with the criteria of international law for the recognition of statehood.

The French Foreign Minister in a more nuanced statement declared:

> Si cette reconnaissance par la France d'un Etat palestinien ne soulève aucune difficulté de principe, il est toutefois contraire à sa jurisprudence de reconnaître un Etat qui ne dispose pas d'un térritoire défini.[18]

16 For arguments and references, see Gowlland-Debbas, *op cit* above (n 4, pp 205–15).

17 Letters dated 1 and 27 April 1989 from Mr Yasser Arafat in his capacity as President of the State of Palestine and Chairman of the Executive Committee of the PLO, to the Directors-General of WHO and UNESCO (WHO Doc A42/INF Doc/3 and UNESCO Doc 25 C/106, Annex 1). The application for admission to the WHO, for example, refers to 'the desire of the State of Palestine to become a full member of the WHO in accordance with Article 6 of the Constitution' (which provides that 'states ... may apply to become Members and shall be admitted as Members when their application has been approved by a simple majority vote of the Health Assembly'), and undertakes 'to fulfil all duties and responsibilities arising from the full membership of the State of Palestine in WHO'.

18 UN Doc A/43/PV 79 at p 32 and letter from the Permanent Representative of Israel to the Director General of the WHO, 21 April 1989 reproduced in WHO Doc A42/INF Doc/3.

19 *Le Monde*, 18 November 1988. See also the statement by the President of the French Republic, underlining 'le principe de l'éffectivité, qui implique l'éxistence d'un pouvoir responsable et indépendant s'éxerçant sur un térritoire et une population. Ce n'est pas encore le cas ...': *ibid*, 24 November 1988.

The Federal Department of Foreign Affairs of Switzerland, with respect to a communication of 21 June 1989, from the Permanent Observer of Palestine to the UN concerning the participation of Palestine in the four 1949 Geneva Conventions and 1977 Additional Protocols, informed the contracting parties that:

> due to the uncertainty within the international community as to the existence or the non-existence of a State of Palestine and as long as the issue has not been settled in an appropriate framework, the Swiss government, in its capacity as depositary of the Geneva Conventions and their additional protocols, is not in a position to decide whether this communication can be considered as an instrument of accession in the sense of the relevant provisions of the Conventions and their additional protocols ...[20]

As for writings on the subject, in a recent article concerning the admission of Palestine to the specialised agencies, one author was led to conclude: 'It is very doubtful that 'Palestine' currently qualifies as a state under international law.'[21]

The case for fulfilment of the criteria of statehood is, however, convincing. In so far as the requirement of population is concerned, it is hard to dispute the existence of a Palestinian people with its own separate cultural identity. This existence has been recognised in a number of international instruments,[22] numerous General Assembly resolutions[23] and state unilateral and collective declarations.[24] It has also been argued that the *intifidah* 'has shown that even 20 years of occupation cannot destroy the aspirations of a people'.[25]

As for a defined territory, it has been pointed out that the declaration of independence and political communiqué of 15 November 1988, combined with recognition of the right of Israel to exist, have now served to remove past ambiguities. These decisions accept the convening of an International Conference on the basis of Security Council Resolution 242 (1967) which, together with General Assembly Resolution 181 (II), would delimit the frontiers of the State of Palestine within the confines of the Palestinian territory occupied since 1967. It may be added that though the Proclamation purports to establish Jerusalem as the capital of an independent Palestinian State (contrary to the *corpus separatum* established by Resolution 181), this has clearly been limited to Arab Jerusalem. It

---

20 Note of information dated 13 September 1989.

21 Kirgis, 'Admission of "Palestine" as a Member of a Specialised Agency and Witholding the Payment of Assessments in Response' (1990) 84 *American Journal of International Law*, pp 218–30 at pp 219 and 230, although he concludes that this does not necessarily determine its eligibility for admission to the specialised agencies or to the United Nations, since these also take into account other factors than that of statehood under customary international law, such as the ability to carry out the ongoing obligations of membership (*ibid*, pp 220–21).

22 An explanatory memorandum dated 12 May 1989 from six Afro-Asian States (UNESCO Doc 131 EX/43, pp 1–2) refers to Article 16 of the Treaty of Sèvres (1920) and the Treaty of Lausanne (1923) and the Mandate over Palestine entrusted to the United Kingdom on the basis of Article 22 of the League Covenant.

23 GA Res 181 of 29 November 1947 on the partition of Palestine and relevant resolutions adopted since 1967 recognising the right to self-determination of the Palestinian people.

24 The Declaration of Venice (12 June 1980) of the Heads of State, Heads of Government and Ministers of Foreign Affairs in the name of the European Community, in which it is explicitly mentioned that 'the Palestinian people, which is conscious of existing as such ...' should exercise in full its right to self-determination (cited in UNESCO Doc 131 EX/43 p 2). See also the declaration of the President of the French Republic: 'D'ores et déjà émerge la nation paléstinienne, identifiée comme telle aux yeux des autres nations du monde': *Le Monde*, 24 November 1988.

25 UN Doc A/43 PV 80, Austria, p 21; Flory, *loc cit* p 397; Pellet, *loc cit* pp 60–61.

can also be contended that a new state may exist despite undefined boundaries[26] – witness the creation of Israel in 1948, admitted to the United Nations on 11 May 1949 despite not only undefined frontiers but also claims relating to its territory as a whole. Furthermore, it may be argued that as a result of the withdrawal of Jordanian administration, there is an absence of other valid claims to this territory since (in accordance with the well-established principle of international law concerning non-acquisition of territory through the use of force) Israel cannot be said to have acquired sovereignty over the territories which it presently occupies.

As for the requirement of effectiveness, it has been argued that the state is endowed with legitimate and representative political powers, namely, an Executive Committee entrusted by the Palestinian National Council (the supreme body of the PLO) with governmental functions, exercising responsibility outside the Palestinian territory in full independence and, inside the territory, carrying out certain (clandestine) functions (social, educational, cultural, etc by the intermediary of clandestine popular committees) since it is temporarily deprived of exercising territorial authority. It must be pointed out, however, that despite allusions to precedents such as the Czechoslovak and Polish National Committees (1917–18) and the French Committee of National Liberation (1943), the status of the Palestinian government remains difficult to define, since the Executive Committee is only entrusted with governmental functions pending the constitution of a provisional Palestinian government and there is a deliberate intention to avoid the term 'government-in-exile'.

However, whilst in these two cases of Rhodesia and Palestine states continue to give lip service to the traditional criteria of statehood, it is remarkable that in both cases these should have been considered irrelevant by the United Nations majority, as reflected in the collective response by the organisation to the two declarations of independence. The reason may be sought in the United Nations function of legitimisation.

III   THE UNITED NATIONS FUNCTION OF LEGITIMISATION

The concept of legitimacy plays an important role in international society. Moreover, whereas the function of legitimisation was once exclusively assumed by individual states through the medium of state recognition, the institutionalisation of state relations has provided a means for the international community as a whole to pronounce on the legitimacy of new situations.

It has been pointed out quite rightly that legitimacy is not to be defined necessarily with legality. It has been stated: '*Même si la distinction n'est pas absolue, il convient cependant de tenir pour légitime ce qui est conforme a une valeur alors qu'est légal ce qui est conforme au droit.*'[27] Indeed, legitimacy affirmed within a moral or political framework may serve to counter the existing legal order. In turn, however, where this process is successful, what was previously only legitimate may well become identified with a new legality. The function of legitimisation has thus been closely associated to the doctrine of collective non-recognition traced back to the 1932 Stimson Doctrine but revived in modern form. The Doctrine is envisaged as a collective response to an act or situation contrary to

---

26   See, eg, *North Sea Continental Shelf* cases, in which the Court stated that 'there is no rule that the land frontiers of a State must be fully delimited or defined ...' [1969] *ICJ Rep* at p 32; Brownlie, *op cit* at p 73.

27   Verhoven, *La Reconnaissance international dans la practique contemporaine. Les Rélations publiques internationales*, 1975, Paris: Editions A Pedone at p 587.

international law and consisting in the withholding of legitimisation, the function of legitimisation being used here in a negative fashion to prevent the consolidation of illegal but otherwise effective changes which would have had, under traditional international law, a law-creating function.

This evolution has been well illustrated in contemporary international society where, under the impetus of the so-called new states, the political process set in motion by the UN majority on the basis of a proclaimed new legitimacy has resulted – largely though not exclusively by means of the passage of General Assembly declaratory resolutions – in the establishment of new rules of conduct for states.

In this sense, therefore, the function of legitimisation – and its corollary, that of illegitimisation – assumed by the political organs of the United Nations may no longer be exclusively analysed within a political context of upholding what is moral, or just, but applied within the framework of a new *legal* order, considered to be more in conformity with contemporary notions of justice and community interests, and which has seen the erosion of the monolithic structure of traditional international law by a hierarchisation (or relativisation) of norms resulting from novel concepts: those of '*jus cogens*' (endorsed by the 1969 Vienna Convention on the Law of Treaties), of 'obligations *erga omnes*' (enunciated by the International Court in the *Barcelona Traction* case) and of 'international crimes' (introduced into the Draft Articles on State Responsibility of the International Law Commission). The process of legitimisation – and illegitimisation – by the United Nations has therefore also become a legal process, as a tool in the collective defence of those norms of the new legal order which are considered fundamental to the international community.

Whilst not explicitly stated in the Charter, this UN function has evolved through the practice on the basis of (a) declaratory resolutions affirming the existence of certain fundamental rules, eg the prohibition of the use of force in international relations and the right to self-determination, and (b) resolutions determining or characterising certain situations or acts – in particular those relating to territorial changes effected through the use of force, and to the birth of new entities – as valid or invalid, as the case may be, a change being considered legitimate only if carried out in conformity with such rules. Unarguably, therefore, the function of legitimisation has become part of the legal process, despite its evident political impetus, in the sense that a whole number of legal consequences (underlined by the International Court of Justice) flow from these declaratory resolutions and from determinations which have 'operative design',[28] thus impinging on and modifying the prior legal situation.

Nowhere is this so evident as in the role played by the United Nations in the promotion of the fundamental right to self-determination. Under the vehicle of Resolution 1514 (XV) on the Declaration of Independence to Colonial Countries and Peoples, and subsequent General Assembly resolutions, the principle, formulated as the right of a majority of a people not yet constituted into a state to

---

28 *Legal Consequences for States of the Continued Presence of South Africa in Namibia (South West Africa) notwithstanding Security Council Resolution 276* [1971] *ICJ Rep* at p 50 ('It would not be correct to assume that because the General Assembly is in principle vested with recommendatory powers, it is debarred from adopting, in specific cases within the framework of its competence, resolutions which make determinations or have operative design'). See the by now classic work of Casteneda, *Legal Effects of United Nations Resolutions*, 1969, London: Columbia University Press.

determine its external and internal political status, was gradually given shape and expanded to include colonialism in all its forms and manifestations. It was to find its way into treaty law and judicial pronouncements, and is now considered to form part of the body of rights fundamental to the international community, breaches of which are deemed to warrant a different and more serious legal response.

Placed within the context of the right to self-determination, the questions of Southern Rhodesia and Palestine were to constitute important precedents in this process.

IV   THE COLLECTIVE RESPONSES TO THE UNILATERAL DECLARATIONS OF INDEPENDENCE

Action with respect to Southern Rhodesia had been initiated in 1961 at the international level as a result of the concern of the UN majority over the progressive evolution towards independence of a territory placed under a local administration of settlers and based on racial discrimination and a denial of political and other rights to the African majority. In seeking the means to oppose and eradicate this system before it could slide into the formal *apartheid* system of its Southern neighbour, and to substitute for it the only goal acceptable, that of self-determination for its people, the UN majority sought to ground international jurisdiction on the international status of Southern Rhodesia. In 1962, this status was determined by the General Assembly, over the protests of the United Kingdom but in the light of international standards and criteria, to be that of a non-self-governing territory under Chapter XI of the Charter (General Assembly Resolution 1747 (XVI)), and hence a self-determination unit to which could be applied the body of law on decolonisation which had progressively been shaped. In this context, it is easy to understand why the UN opposed efforts by the European minority in 1965 to perpetuate colonialism in another form by unilaterally declaring the independence of a state based on minority rule and discrimination.

It is contended that the United Nations went well beyond a verbal condemnation in determining, on the basis of a series of quasi-judicial pronouncements (Security Council Resolutions 216, 217 (1965)),[29] that this unilateral declaration of independence made by a racist minority, as well as the situation arising from it, was not only unconstitutional but also *illegal and invalid under international law* as it ran counter to the rights of the majority.

The United Nations then called for collective sanctions in the form of a dual response: (1) The refusal to validate the purported changes in the status of the territory, by the initiation of a policy of collective non-recognition (one of the most significant revivals of the pre-war Stimson Doctrine) (Security Council Resolutions 216, 217 (1965), 277 (1970)); and (2) the imposition, for the first time in UN history, of a panoply of economic, financial and diplomatic sanctions under Article 41 of the Charter on the basis of a determination that the illegality of the situations resulting from the unilateral declaration of independence constituted a threat to international peace and security under Chapter VII of the Charter (Security Council Resolutions 232 (1966), 253 (1968)). As a corollary, UN resolutions affirmed the legitimacy of the National Liberation Movements of Southern Rhodesia, entailing their right to representation in the international

---

29   See also 277 (1970); 288 (1970); 328 (1973).

arena, recognition of the legitimacy of their struggle by all means at their disposal and their right to assistance by third parties.

Thus whilst seemingly prepared to concede to Rhodesia a certain degree of effectiveness, the United Nations nevertheless denied independence to that entity irrespective of the traditional indicia of statehood. It is evident that the United Nations was here distinguishing between ordinary recognition problems predicated on the existence of statehood, and where questions of legality do not arise, and this type of collective non-recognition of a situation based on a determination that an act contrary to international law has occurred. This becomes apparent from an analysis of the function, content and legal effects of this policy, duplicated in the call for non-recognition of South Africa's continued presence in Namibia, and the proclaimed independence of the South African bantustans. For behind the apparent object of an independent State of Rhodesia, what states were called on not to recognise was in fact the illegal and invalid situation created by the UDI. Hence efforts to argue from the existence or non-existence of the criteria of statehood in this situation obscured the true function of non-recognition – the refusal to validate the act of UDI and its consequences, considered contrary to international law and thus null and void.

Whilst, after the adoption of Resolution 181 (II), and the subsequent establishment of a State of Israel, the Palestine question was not immediately associated with the decolonisation process, the Palestinians initially being looked upon as refugees and treated within the context of an individual right of return, the General Assembly after 1969 shifted its perspective to acknowledge their status as a people belonging to a self-determination unit. At the same time the United Nations sought to illegitimatise all Israeli actions contrary to this right.

Thus in a number of resolutions the Assembly affirmed the following: (1) the legitimate inalienable right of the Palestinian people to self-determination, including the right to establish their own independent state; (2) the legitimacy of its representatives – the PLO – granted observer status in the General Assembly and a right to participate on an equal footing with member states in Security Council debates on the Middle East, as well as in all conferences on the Middle East held under the auspices of the UN; and (3) the illegality under international law and UN resolutions of Israel's occupation of Arab territories since 1967, including Jerusalem, considered contrary to the *jus ad bellum* (the principle of the inadmissibility of the acquisition of territory by force) as well as the *jus in bello*) (the 1949 Geneva Conventions), and the consequent invalidity of all legislative and administrative measures and actions taken by Israel purporting to alter their character and status, in particular, the so-called 'Basic Law' on Jerusalem, the establishment of settlements, the destruction of homes and property and the policy of deportations. However, the right of all states in the region to exist within secure and internationally recognised boundaries was also affirmed.

The Assembly's response to the decision of the Palestine National Council of 15 November 1988 in the form of General Assembly Resolution 43/177 acknowledging the proclamation of an independent State of Palestine must therefore be taken in the same vein as, but acting in an opposite direction to, the Assembly's response to the Southern Rhodesian unilateral declaration of independence. This proclamation is considered in the preamble to be in line with Resolution 181 (II) and *'in exercise of the inalienable right of the Palestinian people ...'*. The resolution *'affirms* the need to enable the Palestinian people to exercise their sovereignty over their territory occupied since 1967' and decides that, effective as of 15 December 1988, the designation 'Palestine' should be used in place of the designation 'Palestinian Liberation Organisation' in the United Nations system.[30]

Not surprisingly, controversy arose over the legal significance of this 'acknowledgment'. The United States declared that by this resolution the General Assembly had expressly withheld the attribution of statehood from 'Palestine' since it was specified that the change of designation of the PLO to 'Palestine' was 'without prejudice to the observer status and functions of the PLO within the United Nations system'.[31] Japan, Australia and the United Kingdom, among others, expressed reservations on the fact that the draft resolution presupposed the establishment of the State of Palestine.[32]

However, it is clear that the function of this resolution was to recognise and affirm the intrinsic legality of a situation – the declaration of independence – considered to be in conformity with General Assembly Resolution 181 and other resolutions recognising the right to self-determination of the Palestinian people, including the right to a state of its own, and the consequent intrinsic illegality, despite its effectiveness, of the Israeli occupation which was preventing the state of Palestine from exercising authority over this territory. The Assembly was not concerned with cognition, in the sense of affirmation of the existence of the criteria of statehood, but with a process of legitimisation. In a sense, by implicitly acknowledging that the conditions for the establishment of a Palestinian State had now been met, several years after the adoption of Resolution 181, the Assembly may be said to have been asserting its competence, assumed on a number of occasions, and upheld by the Court as a discretionary right,[33] to determine the forms and procedures by which the right to self-determination was to be realised. It may be seen, therefore, as the crowning of the decolonisation process in Palestine.

The debate surrounding the adoption of this resolution supports this view. Arafat reiterated in the General Assembly that the independent state of Palestine had been declared by virtue, *inter alia*, of 'our belief in international legitimacy'.[34] Several member states spoke in similar vein. Egypt, amongst others, stated: 'We are thus called upon to adopt resolutions consistent with the norms of international legitimacy and the purposes and principles enshrined in the UN Charter'.[35] It was argued that 'some of the legal pretexts used to justify

---

30 The resolution, one of three adopted on Palestine on 15 December 1988, was carried by 104–2 (Israel and the United States) with 36 abstentions. The General Assembly took no vote at its 44th session in 1989 on a draft resolution, the operative paragraph of which would have decided 'that the designation Palestine shall be construed, within the United Nations, as the State of Palestine, without prejudice to the acquired rights of the Palestine Liberation Organisation in accordance with the relevant United Nations resolutions and practice' (UN Doc A/44/L50). The decision to defer consideration of the draft resolution occurred as a result of an appeal by the President of the General Assembly following a United States threat to withhold its assessed contribution to the budget of the UN, which the President of the General Assembly insisted was 'an obligation under the Charter'. See Kirgis, *loc cit* p 220 for the view that there are no legal grounds in this case justifying US withholding of its contributions.

31 A/43/PV 82, United States pp 46–47.

32 See A/43/PV 82, Australia, p 81, Japan, p 82, United Kingdom, p 83, Canada, p 86, France, p 87. Kirgis states: 'The United Nations did not thereby recognise a Palestinian state, nor did it call the PLO a provisional government' (*loc cit* p 220).

33 *Western Sahara* case [1975] *ICJ Reps* at p 36.

34 A/43/PV 78 pp 23, 27, 32–33.

35 See A/43/PV 78, p 48. See also Saudi Arabia, p 72; Iraq, p 87; A/43/PV 80, Sudan, p 6.

non-recognition of the State of Palestine are clearly no longer part of the spirit of our age'.[36] Even those states which had not yet recognised the State of Palestine stated that they nevertheless welcomed the proclamation as the exercise of the right to self-determination, including the establishment of a state of its own, by the Palestinian people through its legitimate representatives, differing only in the view that recognition of statehood could take place only within the context of a comprehensive Middle East settlement.[37]

There have been similar claims to establish a state on the basis of legitimacy. Indeed the declaration of independence of a Palestinian State reflects the wording of the Declaration on the Establishment of the State of Israel made also 'by virtue of our Natural and Historic Right and on the Strength of the Resolution (181)'.[38]

Another significant precedent was admission of Namibia to membership of, *inter alia*, the International Labour Organisation despite the clear absence of the traditional criteria of statehood, on the basis that the ILO was not prepared to allow the legitimate rights of the Namibian people to be frustrated by the illegal occupation of South Africa, in the absence of which Namibia would have qualified for independent statehood. The Resolution reads:[39]

Noting that Namibia is the only remaining case of a former Mandate of the League of Nations where the former mandatory Power is still in occupation,

Considering that an application for membership in terms of Article I is prevented only by the illegal occupation of Namibia by South Africa, the illegal nature of this occupation having been confirmed by the International Court of Justice in its Advisory Opinion of 21 June 1971,

Affirming that the International Labour Organisation is not prepared to allow the legitimate rights of the Namibian people to be frustrated by the illegal actions of South Africa,

Making it clear that in now granting the application for membership it does not overlook the wording of Article I and believes that in the near future the illegal occupation of Namibia by South Africa will be terminated,

Decides to admit Namibia to membership in the Organisation, it being agreed that, until the present illegal occupation of Namibia is terminated, the United Nations Council for Namibia, established by the United Nations as the legal administering authority for Namibia empowered, *inter alia*, to represent it in international organisations, will be regarded as the government of Namibia for the purpose of the application of the Constitution of the Organisation.

As has been pointed out,[40] the ILO was, by the adoption of this resolution, exercising its function of legitimisation. Whilst General Assembly Resolution

---

36 A/43/PV 78, Iraq, p 87.

37 A/43/PV 79, Sweden, p 74; A/43/PV 80, Chile pp 18–20, Austria pp 21–22, New Zealand, p 132, Canada, pp 172–76. A/43/PV 82, Australia, p 81, Japan, p 82, France, pp 87–88.

38 Quoted in Dugard, *Recognition and the United Nations*, 1987, Cambridge: Grotius Publications at pp 60–61.

39 ILO, 64th Session (Geneva, June 1978) Provisional Record, No 24 pp 19–20.

40 Osieke, 'Admission to Membership in International Organisations: the *Case of Namibia*', (1980) 51 *BYIL* pp 189–229 at pp 214–15. Referring to this resolution Osieke concludes: 'Here then lies the justification, the *raison d'être*, for the admission of Namibia as a member of the ILO. By regarding the rights of the Namibian people as subsisting irrespective of the illegal ...

43/177 was not related to admission of the State of Palestine, it nevertheless appeared to be implying much the same thing.

V   LEGAL CONSEQUENCES OF LEGITIMISATION

Security Council Resolution 277 (1970) calling for collective non-recognition of an independent State of Rhodesia was clearly a mandatory resolution adopted by the Council on the basis of powers conferred under Chapter VII. General Assembly Resolution 43/177 on Palestine, on the other hand, can place no corresponding obligation on member states to acknowledge the proclamation or *a fortiori* to recognise the State of Palestine, in the absence of admissions procedures,[41] though naturally it has determinative effect on the status of the entity for internal purposes (the change of appellation in particular).

However, the characterisation by the Organisation of the situation could not remain without legal effect. In the case of Southern Rhodesia, there existed, beyond the conventional obligation, a general international law duty on the part of states not to recognise a situation determined to be contrary to a fundamental norm – that of self-determination – and hence invalid. It could therefore be argued along the same lines that acknowledgment by the Assembly of the proclamation of an independent State of Palestine, a proclamation determined in this case to be in conformity with that right, could not similarly remain without legal effects.

This means, at the very minimum, that recognition by states of this entity cannot be held to be illegal in the sense of premature recognition. This is not to say that in recognition of statehood, the traditional criteria have been totally replaced, but that where this concerns certain postulated legal rules considered essential for the international community, different considerations operate depending on whether a situation of legality or illegality is involved and whether the object is the upholding of the maxim *ex injuria non oritur* over its rival principle *ex factis jus oritur* or the law-creating influence of facts.[42]

As a legal mechanism, this process of legitimisation, which attempts to override considerations of effectiveness, may be criticised for creating an unbridgable gap between the facts and the law. However, just as the lack of legal title may serve to weaken a situation of fact, assumption of legal title may serve to strengthen it. It is undeniable that the ostracism and diplomatic isolation of the European minority regime in Rhodesia and denial to it of international personality had a

---

40   [cont] occupation of their territory by South Africa, and by refusing to recognise the illegal acts committed by South Africa or to allow that country to benefit from such acts, the Conference appears to have resorted to the principle *ex injuria jus non oritur* according to which 'an illegality cannot as a rule, become a source of legal right to the wrongdoer' (*ibid*, p 217).

41   Even where admission to the United Nations is involved, there has been controversy as to the effects of such admission on recognition of the entity as a state. The majority of authors agree that in the case of ordinary recognition problems, ie where a question of legality does not arise, it is not a function of the United Nations to grant or withhold recognition, since admission to the United Nations is only predicated on the existence of statehood for purposes of the Charter, and other considerations, such as ability to fulfil the obligations of membership, may be relevant. Dugard has, however, convincingly argued that admission to the United Nations constitutes or confirms the existence of a state. (It is generally agreed, however, that membership of an international organisation does not impose an obligation of recognition on member states of that organisation.)

42   Lauterpacht, *Recognition in International Law*, 1947, London: Cambridge University Press, at pp 426–27. Dugard points out that criteria such as effective government and independence are no longer insisted on in matters of admission to the United Nations where they run counter to developments in international law regarding the right of self-determination (*op cit*, p 72).

constitutive effect to the extent that it undermined its effectiveness: it is enough to think of the corollary of UN policy, had Rhodesia been accepted into the United Nations under a white minority regime in 1965. The application of a similar process of legitimisation to Namibia, where the maintenance of the fiction of a United Nations territory contributed to undermining the effectiveness of South Africa's hold over the territory, has had a similarly successful outcome.

Whilst, therefore, in the case of Palestine the UN may be accused of perpetuating a legal fiction, it may be argued that acknowledgement of the legitimacy of the proclamation of an independent Palestinian state, coupled with individual state recognition, may likewise serve to create the very effectiveness that is said to be lacking and contribute towards consolidation of its status. Cassese states that traditionally international law has provided that only those claims and situations which are effective can produce legal effects, in other words, international legitimacy. [43] Today, however, there is evidence that only those claims and situations which are legitimate can produce legal effects and hence be effective.

United Nations collective responses in terms of denial of legal effects to acts or situations in breach of certain norms deemed fundamental, by a determination that such acts are both illegal and invalid, and by the application, in consequence, of a policy of collective non-recognition, have had an extensive and consistent basis.[44] The contrary process of legitimisation of the proclamation of an independent Palestinian State is in line with and strengthens this practice. This practice has been considered as important evidence in the process of identifying and shaping fundamental norms, recognised as essentially dynamic concepts, the content of which evolves in accordance with the changing requirements of the international community.

This tendency to entrust to political organs the task of validating or invalidating claims and situations by means of legal judgments has been contested, but it may be said that it is in keeping with the contemporary tendency to reject, at the international level, municipal law concepts of separation of powers, as the Nicaragua case underlined.[45] It is in keeping with the concept formulated by the International Law Commission, in relation to the defence of fundamental norms, of the need for collective action within an institutionalised framework. Finally, it is in keeping with a noticeable tendency of the contemporary international community to promote a more dynamic and hence interventionist international law, concerned no longer merely with jurisdictional issues but with the evolution, if not transformation, of the international system.

---

43 Cassese, *International Law in a Divided World*, 1986, Oxford: Clarendon Press at pp 26–27.

44 In addition to the cases of Southern Rhodesia, the occupation of Arab territories by Israel, Namibia, and the independence of the South African bantustans already referred to above, one can cite the cases of the declaration of a Turkish Cypriot Republic (SC Res 541 (1983) and 550 (1984)); and the condemnation by the General Assembly in GA Res 35/169B of all partial agreements and separate treaties violating the recognised rights of the Palestinian people (alluding to the Treaty of Peace between Israel and Egypt of 1980). (See also the reaction to the Iraqi invasion of Kuwait in August 1990.)

45 See [1984] *ICJ Rep*, para 92 where the Court refers to Nicaragua's statement regarding the US arguments as to the delineation of powers between the Security Council and the Court.

6.7 The legal effects of recognition in municipal law: UK practice

Since recognition is basically a political act, it is a decision for the executive branch of government and in the UK it is the Foreign Office which will answer questions about the status of entities which purport to have international personality. Such answers are usually given by means of an executive certificate. As has already been noted, in 1980 the British government announced that it was no longer intending to accord formal recognition to governments, although it would continue to recognise states. Of course the substantive question of whether or not an entity is a government and thus entitled to the consequent immunities and privileges still remains but the courts will no longer have the benefit of an executive certificate to assist them. In *The Republic of Somalia v Woodhouse Drake and Carey SA* (1993)[46] Hobhouse J had to decide whether the interim government of Somalia, which was in a state of civil war at the time, was entitled to bring proceedings as the legitimate government of that state. In the course of his judgment Hobhouse J identified four questions which the courts would consider when deciding whether a regime existed as the government of a state:

(1) had the regime come to power by constitutional means?

(2) what was the degree, nature and stability of administrative control exercised by the regime over the territory of the state?

(3) did the British government maintain any form of relationship with the regime?

(4) what was the extent of international recognition of the regime?

The status of international organisations raises a particular problem. Parliament passed the International Organisations Act 1968 which allows domestic legal personality to be conferred on international organisations by means of an Order in Council. As has already been seen, international organisations are established by agreement between states. The House of Lords confirmed in *Maclaine Watson v Department of Trade and Industry* (1990)[47] that the courts have no power to adjudicate on or enforce rights arising out of transactions entered into by sovereign states between themselves and that treaties do not automatically become part of English law.

There are a number of consequences of recognition and non-recognition and these will be illustrated here by reference to a number of important decisions made by the English courts.

6.7.1 Locus standi

Perhaps one of the most important consequences of recognition is that it gives the recognised entity *locus standi* in the courts. In the *City of Berne v The Bank of England* (1804)[48] the court refused to allow the revolutionary government of

---

46 [1993] QB 54.

47 [1989] 3 All ER 523.

48 (1804) 9 Ves Jun 347.

Berne to bring an action against the Bank of England because the government was not recognised by the UK. A number of cases have arisen where recognition has been accorded to both a *de facto* and a *de jure* government. Since the British government declared that it would no longer accord formal recognition to governments the problem may not arise in the same way in the future but nonetheless the cases are of historic interest and do shed some light on the way the courts deal with the whole problem of the status of foreign governments. In *Haile Selassie v Cable and Wireless Ltd (No 2)* (1939)[49] the Emperor of Abyssinia (Ethiopia) was suing a British company for money owed under contract. At the time the action was brought, the British government recognised Haile Selassie as the *de jure* sovereign but recognised the Italian authorities as the *de facto* government. At first instance it was held that since the case concerned a debt recoverable in England and not the validity of acts done in Ethiopia, it was the *de jure* sovereign that was entitled to sue. The defendants appealed. Before the appeal was heard the UK government extended *de jure* recognition to the Italian authorities. A basic principle of recognition is that it operates retroactively to the date when the authority of the government was first accepted as being established. The Court of Appeal therefore found that the *de jure* recognition of the Italian government of Ethiopia was deemed to operate from the date of *de facto* recognition. Since that occurred prior to the commencement of the action for the debt, Haile Selassie was deprived of any *locus standi* in the case.

In *Gur Corporation v Trust Bank of Africa* (1986)[50] the Court of Appeal had to consider the status of the Republic of Ciskei, one of the homelands established by the government of South Africa. At first instance, Steyn J considered whether Ciskei had *locus standi* and asked the Foreign Office for its attitude to Ciskei. The Foreign Office replied that Ciskei was not recognised as an independent state and Steyn J therefore found that it had no *locus* to be joined as a party to the dispute. The issue was taken to the Court of Appeal who investigated the establishment of Ciskei. The court found that the British government continued to regard South Africa as internationally responsible for the territory of Ciskei. Furthermore it found that the government of the 'Republic of Ciskei' had been established under the South African Status of Ciskei Act 1981. It therefore held that the government of the Republic of Ciskei was a subordinate body set up by the Republic of South Africa to act on its behalf and it therefore had *locus standi* in the present case.

The question of recognition was raised more recently in *Arab Monetary Fund v Hashim* (1990).[51] The case was brought by the Arab Monetary Fund which was an international organisation created by treaty. The UK was not a party to the treaty and no Order in Council had been made with respect to the AMF under the provisions of the International Organisations Act 1968. In those circumstances the Court of Appeal found that the AMF could not bring the action. The decision was overturned by the House of Lords on the basis not that

---

49   [1939] Ch 182.

50   [1986] 3 WLR 583.

51   [1991] 2 WLR 729.

it was an international organisation and therefore entitled to sue irrespective of recognition but that it had been incorporated in Abu Dhabi law and therefore could be regarded as an Abu Dhabi corporation. The decision was more based on pragmatism than strict legal principles and followed a line of reasoning which had been used in the earlier case of *Carl Zeiss Stiftung v Rayner and Keeler Ltd (No 2)* (1967).

6.7.2 Effectiveness of legislative and executive acts

A further consequence of recognition is that the courts will give effect to the legislative and executive acts of foreign governments. The classic example of this rule is the case of *Luther v Sagor* (1921).[52] The plaintiffs in the case had owned a timber factory which had been nationalised by the government of the Soviet Union in 1919. The defendants had bought a quantity of timber produced at the factory from the Soviet government in 1920. The plaintiffs claimed the timber on the basis that the nationalisation of the factory by the Soviet government should be ignored. When the case was heard at first instance, the Soviet government was not recognised by the UK, and the court therefore found in favour of the plaintiffs. By the time the case was heard by the Court of Appeal, the Soviet government had been accorded *de facto* recognition. The Court found that recognition would operate from the date when the Soviet government had taken effective control which was accepted as being December 1917. The nationalisation decree was therefore the act of a sovereign government and would have to be given effect to in the UK courts. On that basis the appeal was allowed.

In the *Arantzazu Mendi* (1939)[53] the House of Lords had to consider the rival claims of *de facto* and *de jure* government. The *Arantzazu Mendi* was a private ship registered in Bilbao, Spain. In the summer of 1937 following the capture of the region by Nationalist forces, the Republic government issued a decree requisitioning all ships registered in Bilbao. In early 1938 the Nationalist authorities issued a similar decree. While the *Arantzazu Mendi* was in London the Republican government issued a writ to obtain possession of the ship in accordance with its requisition decree. This was opposed by the owners of the ship who accepted the Nationalists' requisition. The Nationalists argued that since they had been recognised as the *de facto* government over the areas they actually controlled and since they controlled the region around Bilbao, the courts must give effect to their requisition decree and dismiss the Republican action. The House of Lords accepted this view, basing their finding on the fact that the Nationalist government was in effective control of the area and therefore was entitled to be regarded as the government of a sovereign state.

In the early 1950s two cases raised again the distinctions between the *de facto* and *de jure* recognition and the question of retroactivity. *Gdynia Ameryka Linie v Boguslawski* (1953)[54] concerned recognition of the Polish government in 1945. During the Second World War the Polish government in exile was recognised as

---

52 [1921] 1 KB 456.

53 [1939] AC 256.

54 [1953] AC 70.

the *de jure* government of Poland. On 28 June 1945 the communist provisional government took effective control of the country and was recognised as the *de jure* government on 5 July. The case concerned the effect of executive action taken by the Polish government in exile on 3 July. The House of Lords emphasised the general principle of retroactivity which would normally mean that all acts of the communist government would be given effect to as from 28 June. However the acts of the government in exile with respect to issues under their control remained effective up until the withdrawal of recognition on 5 July. Therefore the action taken by the government in exile on 3 July would be effective. A similar result obtained in *Civil Air Transport Inc v Central Air Transport Corporation* (1953).[55]

6.7.3 Sovereign immunity

One of the underlying principles of international law has been the doctrine of sovereign equality and the consequence that one sovereign cannot exercise authority over another. The practical application of the doctrine means that the many activities carried out by a foreign state cannot be the subject of municipal court proceedings. For example, in *Kuwait Airways Corporation v Iraqi Airways Company* (1995) an English court dismissed a claim by Kuwait Airways arising out of the confiscation of civilian aircraft as a result of an Iraqi government directive on the grounds that the directive was an exercise of sovereign authority and was therefore entitled to immunity. The law relating to sovereign immunity is discussed in detail in Chapter 8.

---

55 [1953] AC 70.

CHAPTER 7

TERRITORIAL RIGHTS

7.1   Introduction

Territory is a tangible attribute of statehood and within that particular geographical area which it occupies a state enjoys and exercises sovereignty. Territorial sovereignty may be defined as the right to exercise therein, to the exclusion of any other state, the functions of a state. A state's territorial sovereignty extends over the designated land mass, sub-soil, the water enclosed therein, the land under that water, the territorial sea (the nature and extent of the territorial sea will be discussed in Chapter 10) and the airspace over the land mass and territorial sea (airspace will be considered in Chapter 11). It has already been seen in Chapter 5 that territory is undoubtedly a basic requirement of statehood.

The fundamental nature of territory and sovereignty over territory can be appreciated when an attempt is made to identify the causes of wars and international disputes throughout history – 99 per cent of them could be classified ultimately as territorial disputes. As Philip Allott has written:

> Endless international and internal conflicts, costing the lives of countless human beings, have centred on the desire of this or that state-society to control this or that area of the earth's surface to the exclusion of this or that state-society.[1]

Rights and duties with respect to territory have therefore had a central place in the development of international law, and the principle of respect for the territorial integrity of states has been one of the most fundamental principles of international law. It should be pointed out, however, there is a growing body of international law which operates outside concepts of exclusive territorial rights. As the need for interdependence has grown and as technology has presented increasing problems as well as benefits so international law has responded by developing concepts such as the 'common heritage of mankind' and rules regional and global protection of human rights and environmental rights. These matters will be dealt with in more detail in Chapters 15 and 17. It is also important to note that title to territory in international law is more often than not relative rather than absolute. Thus, resolving a territorial dispute is a question of deciding who has the better claim rather than accepting one claim and dismissing another.

7.2   Basic concepts

7.2.1   Terra nullius[2]

Terra nullius (sometimes *res nullius*) consists of territory which is capable of being acquired by a single state but which is not yet under territorial sovereignty. In the age of European imperialism there was a tendency for the

---

1   Allott, Eunomia, *New Order for a New World*, 1990, Oxford: Oxford University Press at p 330.
2   *Terra nullius* may be contrasted with *res communis* – ie territory not capable of being claimed by any single State, for example, the high seas and outer space.

Western writers to consider as *terra nullius* those territories inhabited by non-Europeans which were not organised on the lines of European states. Such a view was firmly rejected by the ICJ in the *Western Sahara Case*.

Western Sahara case[3]

Western Sahara was colonised by Spain in 1884 and was known as Spanish Sahara. In 1960 it was added to the UN General Assembly list of non-self-governing territories and from 1963 onwards it was considered by the UN Special Committee on Decolonisation. In 1966 the General Assembly asked Spain, in consultation with Mauritania and Morocco to 'determine at the earliest possible date ... the procedures for the holding of a referendum under United Nations auspices with a view to enabling the indigenous population of the territory to exercise freely its right to self-determination'.[4] Spain accepted the principle of self-determination but it was not until 21 August 1974 that it announced that it would hold a referendum under UN auspices in the first half of 1975. At this point both Morocco and Mauritania claimed the territory of Western Sahara on the basis of 'historic title' predating the Spanish colonisation of the area. On 13 December 1974 the General Assembly reaffirmed the right of Spanish Sahara to self-determination and decided to ask the ICJ for an advisory opinion on the following questions:

I   Was Western Sahara (Rio de Oro and Sakiet El Hamra) at the time of colonisation by Spain a territory belonging to no-one (terra nullius)? If the answer to the first question is in the negative,

II   What were the legal ties between this territory and the Kingdom of Morocco and the Mauritian entity?[5]

Opinion of the Court

79   Turning to Question I, the Court observes that the request specifically locates the question in the context of 'the time of colonisation by Spain', and it therefore seems clear that the words 'Was Western Sahara ... a territory belonging to no one (*terra nullius*)?' have to be interpreted by reference to the law in force at that period. The expression '*terra nullius*' was a legal term of art employed in connection with 'occupation' as one of the accepted legal methods of acquiring sovereignty over territory. 'Occupation' being legally an original means of peaceably acquiring sovereignty over territory otherwise than by cession or succession, it was a cardinal condition of valid 'occupation' that the territory should be *terra nullius* – a territory belonging to no-one – at the time of the act alleged to constitute the 'occupation (*cf* Legal Status of Eastern Greenland, PCIJ, Series A/B, No 53, pp 44f and 63f). In the view of the Court, therefore, a determination that Western Sahara was a *terra nullius* at the time of colonisation by Spain would be possible only if it were established that at that time the territory belonged to no-one in the sense that it was then open to acquisition through the legal process of 'occupation'.

80   Whatever differences of opinion there may have been among jurists, the state practice of the relevant period indicates that territories inhabited by tribes or peoples having a social and political organisation were not regarded as *terra*

---

3   Advisory Opinion [1975] *ICJ Rep* at p 12.
4   GA Res 2229, GAOR, 21st Session, Supp 16, p 72 (1966).
5   Mauritania was not a state in 1884.

nullius. It shows that in the case of such territories the acquisition of sovereignty was not generally considered as effected unilaterally through 'occupation' of *terra nullius* by original title but through agreements concluded with local rules. On occasion, it is true, the word 'occupation' was used in a non-technical sense denoting simply acquisition of sovereignty; but that did not signify that the acquisition of sovereignty through such agreements with authorities of the country was regarded as 'occupation' of a *'terra nullius'* in the proper sense of these terms. On the contrary, such agreements were regarded as derivative roots of title, and not original titles obtained by occupation of *terra nullius*.

81   In the present instance, the information furnished to the Court shows that at the time of colonisation Western Sahara was inhabited by peoples which, if nomadic, were socially and politically organised in tribes and under chiefs competent to represent them. It also shows that, in colonising Western Sahara, Spain did not proceed on the basis that it was establishing its sovereignty over *terra nullius*. In its Royal Order of 26 December 1884, far from treating the case as one of occupation of *terra nullius*, Spain proclaimed that the King was taking Rio de Oro under his protection on the basis of agreements which had been entered into with the chiefs of local tribes ...

90   ... Morocco's claim to 'legal ties' with Western Sahara at the time of colonisation by Spain has been put to the Court as a claim to ties of sovereignty on the ground of an alleged immemorial possession of the territory ...

91   In support of this claim Morocco refers to a series of events stretching back to the Arab conquest of North Africa in the seventh century AD, the evidence of which is, understandably, for the most part taken from historical works ... Stressing that during a long period Morocco was the only independent state which existed in the north-west of Africa, it points to the geographical contiguity of Western Sahara to Morocco and the desert character of the territory. In the light of these considerations, it maintains that the historical material suffices to establish Morocco's claim to a title based 'upon continued display of authority' on the same principles as those applied by the Permanent Court in upholding Denmark's claim to possession of the whole of Greenland.

92   This method of formulating Morocco's claims to ties of sovereignty with Western Sahara encounters certain difficulties. As the Permanent Court stated in the case concerning the *Legal Status of Eastern Greenland*, a claim to sovereignty based upon continued display of authority involves 'two elements each of which must be shown to exist: the intention and will to act as sovereign, and some actual exercise or display of such authority' (*ibid*, p 45f). True, the Permanent Court recognised that in the case of claims to sovereignty over areas thinly populated or unsettled countries, 'very little in the way of actual exercise of sovereign rights (*ibid*, p 46) might be sufficient in the absence of a competing claim. But, in the present instance, Western Sahara, if somewhat sparsely populated, was a territory across which socially and politically organised tribes were in constant movement and where armed incidents between these tribes were frequent. In the particular circumstances outlined in para 87 and 88 above, the paucity of evidence of actual display of authority unambiguously relating to Western Sahara renders it difficult to consider the Moroccan claim as on all fours with that of Denmark in the *Eastern Greenland* case. Nor is the difficulty cured by introducing the argument of geographical unity or contiguity. In fact, the information before

the Court shows that the geographical unity of Western Sahara with Morocco is somewhat debatable, which also militates against giving effect to the concept of contiguity. Even if the geographical contiguity of Western Sahara with Morocco could be taken into account in the present connection, it would only make the paucity of evidence of unambiguous display of authority with respect to Western Sahara more difficult to reconcile with Morocco's claim to immemorial possession.

93   In the view of the Court, however, what must be of decisive importance in determining its answer to Question II is not indirect inferences drawn from events in past history but evidence directly relating to effective display of authority in Western Sahara at the time of its colonisation by Spain and in the period immediately preceding that time (cf *Minquiers and Ecrehos*, Judgment [1953] *ICJ Rep* at p 57) ...

162 The materials and information presented to the Court show the existence at the time of Spanish colonisation, of legal ties of allegiance between the Sultan of Morocco and some of the tribes living in the territory of Western Sahara. They equally show the existence of rights, including some rights relating to the land which constituted legal ties between the Mauritanian entity, as understood by the Court, and the territory of Western Sahara. On the other hand, the Court's conclusion is that the materials and information presented to it do not establish any tie of territorial sovereignty between the territory of Western Sahara and the Kingdom of Morocco or the Mauritanian entity. Thus the Court has found no legal ties of such a nature as might affect the application of Resolution 1514 (XV) in the decolonisation of Western Sahara and, in particular, of the principle of self-determination through the free and genuine expression of the will of the peoples of the Territory (cf paras 54–59 above[6])

7.2.2   Intertemporal law

In many disputes the rights of the parties may derive from legally significant acts concluded a long time ago at a time when particular rules of international law may well have been different to what they are today. It has long been accepted as a principle of international law that in such cases the situation must be appraised or the treaty interpreted in the light of the rules of international law as they existed at the time. This principle was re-affirmed by Judge Huber in the *Island of Palmas* case[7] when he stated that:

> Both parties are also agreed that a juridical fact must be appreciated in the light of the law contemporary with it, and not of the law in force at the time when a dispute in regard to it arises or falls to be settled. The effect of discovery by Spain is therefore to be determined by the rules of international law in force in the first half of the sixteenth century.

Some confusion was caused by the fact that Judge Huber went on to note that while the creation of particular rights was dependent upon the international law of the time, the continued existence of such rights depended upon their according with the evolution of the law. One possible implication of this would be that states would constantly have to re-establish title to territory on a basis

---

6   See Chapter 5 on Subjects of International Law.
7   (1928) 2 RIAA 829.

approved by international law at the time. The potential problem would seem to be resolved by acknowledging the fact that title to territory in international law involves assessing the relative strength of competing claims. Creation of title is to be assessed according to contemporary law and creation coupled with effective occupation is likely to defeat most other rival claims apart, perhaps, from claims based on self-determination.

7.2.3   Critical date

The date on which a dispute over territory 'crystallises' is known as the 'critical date'. In many disputes a certain date will assume particular significance in deciding between rival claims. The choice of the critical date or dates will lie with the tribunal deciding the dispute and will usually depend on the particular facts. Once a date is chosen subsequent events relating to territorial claims will be ignored. Thus in the *Island of Palmas* case[8] the United States claimed the island as successor to Spain under a treaty of cession dated 10 December 1898. That date was chosen as the critical date and the case was decided on the basis of the nature of Spanish rights at that time. In the *Minquiers and Ecrehos* case[9] France and the United Kingdom submitted two different critical dates but the ICJ did not specifically choose between the two. Since that case tribunals have made little reference to the choice of critical date.

7.3   Title to territory

Traditionally, writers have referred to five means by which territory and title to territory may be acquired:

1   occupation of *terra nullius;*
2   prescription;
3   conquest;
4   accretion;
5   cession.

These five modes will be discussed here, but it is important in this matter to note the words of Ian Brownlie:

> A tribunal will concern itself with proof of the exercise of sovereignty at the critical date or dates, and in doing so will not apply the orthodox analysis to describe its process of decision. The issue of territorial sovereignty, or title, is often complex, and involves the application of various principles of the law to the material facts. The result of this process cannot always be ascribed to any single dominant rule of 'mode of acquisition'. The orthodox analysis does not prepare the student for the interaction of principles of acquiescence and recognition with the other rules.[10]

---

8   (1928) 2 RIAA 829.

9   *France v United Kingdom*, [1953] *ICJ Rep* at p 47.

10   Brownlie, *Principles of Public International Law*, 1990, Oxford: Oxford University Press at p 132.

7.3.1 Occupation of terra nullius

Occupation is preceded by discovery. Discovery alone is insufficient to establish title; it can only serve to establish a claim which in a reasonable period of time must be completed by effective occupation. Published discovery can obviously establish a better claim in time, but is ineffective against proof of continuous and peaceful display of authority by another state.

The exact nature of effective occupation and title to territory was considered in the *Island of Palmas* case. Under the Treaty of Paris 1898, which brought to an end the Spanish-American War of 1898, Spain ceded the Philippines to the United States. The United States based its claim, as successor to Spain, principally on discovery. There was evidence that Spain had discovered the island in the 17th century, but there was no evidence of any actual exercise of sovereignty over the island by Spain.

Island of Palmas case (1928)[11]

Under the terms of the Treaty of Paris 1898, which ended the Spanish-American War of 1898, Spain ceded the Philippines to the United States. In 1906, a United States official visited Palmas, believing it to be part of the territory of the Philippines, and found the Dutch exercising sovereignty. There followed a protracted dispute between the US and the Netherlands which was finally submitted to arbitration in 1928.

Award of the arbitrator

Sovereignty in the relations between states signifies independence. Independence in regard to a portion of the globe is the right to exercise therein, to the exclusion of any other state, the functions of a state. The development of the national organisation of states during the last few centuries and, as a corollary, the development of international law, have established this principle of the exclusive competence of the state in regard to its own territory in such a way as to make it the point of departure in settling most questions that concern international relations. The special cases of the composite state, of collective sovereignty etc, do not fall to be considered here and do not, for that matter, throw any doubt upon the principle which has just been enunciated. Under this reservation it may be stated that territorial sovereignty belongs always to one, or in exceptional circumstances to several states, to the exclusion of all others. The fact that the functions of a state can be performed by any state within a given zone is, on the other hand, precisely the characteristic feature of the legal situation pertaining in those parts of the globe which, like the high seas or lands without a master, cannot or do not yet form the territory of a state.

Territorial sovereignty is, in general, a situation recognised and delimited in space, either by so-called natural frontiers as recognised by international law or by outward signs of delimitation that are undisputed, or else by legal engagements entered into between interested neighbours, such as frontier conventions, or by acts of recognition of states within fixed boundaries. If a dispute arises as to the sovereignty over a portion of territory, it is customary to examine which of the states claiming sovereignty possesses a title – cession, conquest, occupation etc – superior to that which the other state might possibly

---

11 *Netherlands v United States* (1928) 2 RIAA 829, Permanent Court of Arbitration – sole arbitrator: Huber.

bring forward against it. However, if the contestation is based on the fact that the other Party has actually displayed sovereignty, it cannot be sufficient to establish the title by which territorial sovereignty was validly acquired at a certain moment; it must also be shown that the territorial sovereignty has continued to exist and did exist at the moment which for the decision of the dispute must be considered as critical. This demonstration consists in the actual display of state activities, such as belongs only to the territorial sovereign.

Titles of acquisition of territorial sovereignty in present-day international law are either based on an act of effective apprehension, such as occupation or conquest, or, like cession, presuppose that the ceding and the cessionary Powers, or at least one of them, have the faculty of effectively disposing of the ceded territory. In the same way natural accretion can only be conceived of as an accretion to a portion of territory where there exists an actual sovereignty capable of extending to a spot which falls within its sphere of activity. It seems therefore natural that an element which is essential for the constitution of sovereignty should not be lacking in its continuation. So true is this, that practice, as well as doctrine, recognises – though under different legal formulae and with certain differences as to the conditions required – that the continuous and peaceful display of territorial sovereignty (peaceful in relation to other states) is as good as title. The growing insistence with which international law, ever since the middle of the 18th century, has demanded that the occupation shall be effective would be inconceivable, if effectiveness were required only for the act of acquisition and not equally for the maintenance of the right. If the effectiveness has above all been insisted on in regard to occupation, this is because the question rarely arises in connection with territories in which there is already an established order of things. Just as before the rise of international law, boundaries of lands were necessarily determined by the fact that the power of a state was exercised within them, so too, under the reign of international law, the fact of peaceful and continuous display is still one of the most important considerations in establishing boundaries between states.

Territorial sovereignty, as has already been said, involves the exclusive right to display the activities of a state. This right has as corollary a duty: the obligation to protect within the territory the rights of other states, in particular their right to integrity and inviolability in peace and in war, together with the rights which each state may claim for its nationals in foreign territory. Without manifesting its territorial sovereignty in a manner corresponding to circumstances, the state cannot fulfil this duty. Territorial sovereignty cannot limit itself to its negative side, ie to excluding the activities of other states; for it serves to divide between nations the space upon which human activities are employed, in order to assure them at all points of the minimum of protection of which international law is the guardian.

Although municipal law, thanks to its complete judicial system, is able to recognise abstract rights of property as existing apart from any material display of them, it has none the less limited their effect by the principles of prescription and the protection of possession. International law, the structure of which is not based on any super-state organisation, cannot be presumed to reduce a right such as territorial sovereignty, with which almost all international relations are bound up, to the category of an abstract right, without concrete manifestations ...

The principle that continuous and peaceful display of the functions of state within a given region is a constituent element of territorial sovereignty is not only based on the conditions of the formation of independent states and their boundaries (as shown by the experience of political history) as well as on an international jurisprudence and doctrine widely accepted; this principle has further been recognised in more than one federal state, where a jurisdiction is established in order to apply, as need arises, rules of international law to the interstate relations of the state members. This is more significant, in that it might well be conceived that in a federal state possessing a complete judicial system for interstate matters – far more than in the domain of international relations properly so-called – there should be applied to territorial questions the principle that, failing any specific provision of law to the contrary, a *jus in re* once lawfully acquired shall prevail over *de facto* possession however well established ...

Manifestations of territorial sovereignty assume, it is true, different forms, according to conditions of time and place. Although continuous in principle, sovereignty cannot be exercised in fact at every moment on every point of a territory. The intermittence and discontinuity compatible with the maintenance of the right necessarily differ accordingly as inhabited or uninhabited regions are involved, or regions enclosed within territories in which sovereignty is incontestably displayed or again regions accessible from, for instance, the high seas. It is true that neighbouring states may by convention fix limits to their own sovereignty, even in regions such as the interior of scarcely explored continents where such sovereignty is scarcely manifested, and in this way each may prevent the other from any penetration of its territory. The delimitation of Hinterland may also be mentioned in this connection.

If, however, no conventional line of sufficient topographical precision exists or if there are gaps in the frontiers otherwise established, or if a conventional line leaves room for doubt, or if, as, eg, in the case of an island situated in the high seas, the question arises whether a title is valid *erga omnes*, the actual and continuous and peaceful display of state sovereignty is in case of dispute the sound and natural criterion of territorial sovereignty ...

The title alleged by the United States of America as constituting the immediate foundation of its claim is that of cession, brought about by the Treaty of Paris, which cession transferred all rights of sovereignty which Spain may have possessed ... concerning the island of Palmas (or Miangos).

It is evident that Spain could not transfer more rights than she herself possessed ... the United States bases its claim, as successor of Spain, in the first place on discovery ...

It is admitted by both sides that international law underwent profound modifications between the end of the Middle Ages and the end of the 19th century, as regards the rights of discovery and acquisition of uninhabited region or regions inhabited by savages or semi-civilised peoples. Both Parties are also agreed that a juridical fact must be appreciated in the light of the law contemporary with it, and not of the law in force at the time when a dispute in regard to it arises or falls to be settled. The effect of discovery by Spain is therefore to be determined by the rules of international law in force in the first half of the 16th century ...

If the view most favourable to the American argument is adopted – with every reservation as to the soundness of such view – that is to say, if we consider as positive law at the period in question the rule that discovery as such, ie the mere fact of seeing land, without any act, even symbolical, of taking possession, involved *ipso jure* territorial sovereignty and not merely an 'inchoate title,' a *jus ad rem*, to be completed eventually by an actual and durable taking of possession within a reasonable time, the question arises whether sovereignty yet existed at the critical date, ie the moment of conclusion and coming into force of the Treaty of Paris.

As regards the question which of different legal systems prevailing at successive periods is to be applied in a particular case (the so-called intertemporal law), a distinction must be made between the creation of rights and the existence of rights. The same principle which subjects the act creative of a right to the law in force at the time the right arises, demands that the existence of right, in other words its continued manifestation, shall follow the conditions required by the evolution of law. International law in the 19th century, having regard to the fact that most parts of the globe were under the sovereignty of states members of the community of nations, and that territories without a master had become relatively few, took account of a tendency already existing and especially developed since the middle of the 18th century, and laid down the principle that occupation, to constitute a claim to territorial sovereignty, must be effective, that is, offer certain guarantees to other states and their nationals. It seems therefore incompatible with this rule of positive law that there should be regions which are neither under the effective sovereignty of a state, nor without a master, but which are reserved for the exclusive influence of one state, in virtue solely of a title of acquisition which is no longer recognised by existing law, even if such a titles ever conferred sovereignty. For these reasons, discovery alone, without any subsequent act, cannot, at the present time, suffice to prove sovereignty over the island of Palmas (or Miangos); and in so far as there is no sovereignty, the question of an abandonment properly speaking of sovereignty by one state in order that the sovereignty of another may take its place does not arise.

If on the other hand the view is adopted that discovery does not create a definitive title of sovereignty, but only an 'inchoate' title, such a title exists, it is true, without external manifestation. However, according to the view that has prevailed, at any rate since the 19th century, an inchoate title of discovery must be completed within a reasonable period by the effective occupation of the region claimed to be discovered. This principle must be applied in the present case, for the reasons given above in regard to the rules determining which of successive legal systems is to be applied (the so-called intertemporal law). Now, no act of occupation nor, except as to a recent period, any exercise of sovereignty at Palmas by Spain has been alleged. But even admitting that the Spanish title still existed as inchoate in 1898 and must be considered as included in the cession under Article III of the Treaty of Paris, an inchoate title could not prevail over the continuous and peaceful display of authority by another state, for such display may prevail even over a prior, definitive title put forward by another state ...

In the last place there remains to be considered title arising out of contiguity. Although states have in certain circumstances maintained that islands relatively close to their shores belonged to them in virtue of their geographical situation, it is impossible to show the existence of a rule of positive international law to the effect that islands situated outside territorial ,waters should belong to a state from the mere fact that its territory forms the *terra firma* (nearest continent or island of considerable size). Not only would it seem that there are no precedents sufficiently frequent and sufficiently precise in their bearing to establish such a rule of international law, but the alleged principle itself is by its very nature so uncertain and contested that even Governments of the same state have on different occasions maintained contradictory opinions as to its soundness. The principle of contiguity, in regard to islands, may not be out of place when it is a question of allotting them to one state rather than another, either by agreement between the Parties, or by a decision not necessarily based on law; but as a rule establishing *ipso jure* the presumption of sovereignty in favour of a particular state, this principle would be in conflict with what has been said as to territorial sovereignty and as to the necessary relation between the right to exclude other states from a region and the duty to display therein the activities of a state. Nor is this principle of contiguity admissible as a legal method of deciding questions of territorial sovereignty; for it is wholly lacking in precision and would in its application lead to arbitrary results. This would be especially true in a case such as that of the island in question, which is not relatively close to one single continent, but forms part of a large archipelago in which strict delimitations between the different parts are not naturally obvious.

There lies, however, at the root of the idea of contiguity one point which must be considered also in regard to the island of Palmas (or Miangas). It has been explained above that in the exercise of territorial sovereignty there are necessarily gaps, intermittence in time and discontinuity in space. This phenomenon will be particularly noticeable in the case of colonial territories, partly uninhabited or as yet partly unsubdued. The fact that a state cannot prove display of sovereignty as regards such a position of territory cannot forthwith be interpreted as showing that sovereignty is inexistent. Each case must be appreciated in accordance with the particular circumstances ...

As regards groups of islands, it is possible that a group may under certain circumstances be regarded as in law, a unit, and that the fate of the principal part may involve the rest. Here, however, we must distinguish between, on the one hand, the act of first taking possession, which can hardly extend to every portion of territory, and, on the other hand, the display of sovereignty as a continuous and prolonged manifestation which must make itself felt through the whole territory.

As regards the territory forming the subject of the present dispute, it must be remembered that it is a somewhat isolated island, and therefore a territory clearly delimited and individualised. It is moreover an island permanently inhabited, occupied by a population sufficiently numerous for it to be impossible that acts of administration could be lacking for very long periods. The memoranda of both Parties assert that there is communication by boat and even with native craft between the island of Palmas (or Miangas) and neighbouring regions. The inability in such a case to indicate any acts of public administration makes it difficult to imagine the actual display of sovereignty, even if the sovereignty be regarded as confined within such narrow limits as would be supposed for a small island inhabited exclusively by natives ...

[The Court then considered the Dutch claim.]

The Netherlands found their claim to sovereignty essentially on the title of peaceful and continuous display of state authority over the island. Since this title would in international law prevail over a title of acquisition of sovereignty not followed by actual display of state authority, it is necessary to ascertain in the first place, whether the contention of the Netherlands is sufficiently established by evidence, and, if so, for what period of time.

In the opinion of the Arbitrator the Netherlands have succeeded in establishing the following facts:

1   The island of Palmas (or Miangas) is identical with an island designated by this or a similar name, which has formed, at least since 1700, successively a part of two of the native states of the island of Sangi (Talautse Isles).

2   These native states were from 1677 onwards connected with the East Indian Company, and thereby with the Netherlands, by contracts of suzerainty,

Loan Receipt
Liverpool John Moores University
Library Services

Borrower Name: Chenge,Owen
Borrower ID: **********0326

Sourcebook on public international law /
31111010037339
Due Date: 13/09/2013 23:59

Total Items: 1
07/08/2013 16:38

Please keep your receipt in case of
dispute.

which conferred upon the suzerain such powers as would justify his considering the vassal state as part of his territory.

3   Acts characteristic of state authority exercised either by the vassal state or by the suzerain Power in regard precisely to the Island of Palmas (or Miangas) have been established as occurring at different epochs between 1700 and 1898, as well as in the period between 1898 and 1906.

The acts of indirect or direct display of Netherlands sovereignty at Palmas (or Miangas), especially in the 18th and early 19th centuries are not numerous, and there are considerable gaps in the evidence of continuous display. But apart from the consideration that the manifestations of sovereignty over a small and distant island, inhabited only by natives, cannot be expected to be frequent, it is not necessary that the display of sovereignty should go back to a very far distant period. It may suffice that such display existed in 1898, and had already existed as continuous and peaceful before that date long enough to enable any Power who might have considered herself as possessing sovereignty over the island, or having a claim to sovereignty, to have, according to local conditions, a reasonable possibility for ascertaining the existence of a state of things contrary to her real or alleged rights.

The decisions of the international tribunals indicate that for a claim to territory based on occupation to succeed two elements must be satisfied: the claiming state must have the intention to act as sovereign (the *animus occupandi*) and also must be able to point to some actual, physical manifestation of this sovereignty. The intention is a matter of inference from all the facts – merely raising a flag is not enough. The second element is satisfied by some concrete evidence of possession or control or some symbolic act of sovereignty – it depends on the nature of the territory involved.

Clipperton Island Arbitration[12]

Award of the arbitrator

In fact, we find, in the first place, that on 17 November 1858 Lieutenant Victor Le Coat de Kerweguen, of the French Navy, commissioner of the French Government, whilst cruising about one-half mile off Clipperton, drew up, on board the commercial vessel L'Amiral, an act by which, conformably to the orders which had been given to him by the Minister of Marine, he proclaimed and declared that the sovereignty over the said island beginning from that date belonged in perpetuity to His Majesty the Emperor Napoleon III and to his heirs and successors. During the cruise, careful and minute geographical notes were made; a boat succeeded, after numerous difficulties, in landing some members of the crew; and on the evening of 20 November, after a second unsuccessful attempt to reach the shore, the vessel put off without leaving in the island any sign of sovereignty. Lt de Kerweguen officially notified the accomplishment of his mission to the Consulate of France at Honolulu, which made a like communication to the Government of Hawaii. Moreover, the same consulate had published in English in the journal The Polynesian, of Honolulu, on 8 December, the declaration by which French sovereignty over Clipperton had already been proclaimed.

---

12 *France v Mexico* (1932) 26 AJIL 390 – arbitrator: King Victor Emmanuel III of Italy. Clipperton is a coral reef less than three miles in diameter situated in the Pacific Island 670 miles southwest of Mexico.

Thereafter, until the end of 1887, no positive and apparent act of sovereignty can be recalled either on the part of France or on the part of any other Powers. The island remained without population, at least stable, and no administration was organised there. A concession for the exploitation of guano beds existing there, which had been approved by the Emperor on 8 April 1858, in favour of a certain Mr Lockhart, and which had given rise to the expedition of Lt de Kerweguen, had not been followed up, nor had its exploitation been undertaken on the part of any other French subjects.

Towards the end of 1897 ... France stated ... that three persons were found in the island collecting guano ... and that they had, on the appearance of the French vessel, raised the American flag. Explanations were demanded on this subject from the United States, which responded that it had not granted any concession to the said company and did not intend to claim any right of sovereignty over Clipperton ...

About a month after this act of surveillance had been accomplished by the French Navy ... Mexico, ignoring the occupation claimed by France and considering that Clipperton was territory belonging to her for a long time, sent to the place a gun boat, La Democrata, which action was caused by the report, afterwards acknowledged to be inaccurate, that England had designs on the island. A detachment of officers and marines landed from the said ship on 13 December 1897, and again found the three persons who resided on the island at the time of the preceding arrival of the French ship. it made them lower the American flag and hoist the Mexican flag in its place ... After that the Democrata left on 15 December

On 8 January, France, having learned of the Mexican expedition, reminded that power of its rights over Clipperton ...

According to Mexico, Clipperton Island ... had been discovered by the Spanish Navy and, by virtue of the law then in force, fixed by the Bull of Alexander VII, had belonged to Spain, and afterwards, from 1836, to Mexico as the successor to the Spanish state.

But according to the actual state of our knowledge, it has not been proven that this island ... had been actually discovered by the Spanish navigators ... However, even admitting that the discovery had been made by Spanish subjects, it would be necessary, to establish the contention of Mexico, to prove that Spain not only had the right, as a state, to incorporate the island in her possessions, but also had effectively exercised the right. But that has not been demonstrated at all. The proof of an historic right of Mexico's is not supported by any manifestation of her sovereignty over the island, a sovereignty never exercised until the expedition of 1897, and the mere conviction that this was territory belonging to Mexico, although general and of long standing, cannot be retained.

Consequently, there is ground to admit that, when in November 1858, France proclaimed her sovereignty over Clipperton, that island was in the legal situation of *territorium nullius*, and therefore, susceptible of occupation.

The question remains whether France proceeded to an effective occupation, satisfying the conditions required by international law for validity of this kind of territorial acquisition. In effect, Mexico maintains, secondarily to her principal contention which has just been examined, that the French occupation was not valid, and consequently her own right to occupy the island which must still be considered as *nullius* in 1897.

In whatever concerns this question, there is, first of all, ground to hold as incontestable, the regularity of the act by which France in 1858 made known in a clear and precise manner, her intention to consider the island as her territory.

On the other hand, it is disputed that France took effective possession of the island, and it is maintained that without such a taking of possession of an effective character, the occupation must be considered as null and void.

It is beyond doubt that by immemorial usage having the force of law, besides the *animus occupandi*, the actual, not the nominal, taking of possession is a necessary condition of occupation. This taking of possession consists in the act, or series of acts, by which the occupying states reduces to its possession the territory in question and takes steps to exercise exclusive authority there. Strictly speaking, and in ordinary cases, that only takes place when the state establishes in the territory itself an organisation capable of making its laws respected. But this step is, properly speaking, but a means of procedure to the taking of possession, and, therefore, is not identical with the latter. There may also be cases where it is unnecessary to have recourse to this method. Thus, if a territory, by virtue of the fact that it was completely uninhabited, is, from the first moment when the occupying state makes its appearance there, at the absolute and undisputed disposition of that state, from that moment the taking of possession must be considered as accomplished, and the occupation is thereby completed ...

It follows from these premises that Clipperton Island was legitimately acquired by France on 17 November 1858. There is no reason to suppose that France has subsequently lost her right by *derelicto*, since she never had the *animus* of abandoning the island, and the fact that she has not exercised her authority there in a positive manner does not imply the forfeiture of an acquisition already definitively perfected.

For these reasons, we decide, as arbiter, that the sovereignty over Clipperton Island belongs to France, dating from 17 November 1858.

Legal Status of Greenland case *(Norway v Denmark)*[13]

The case concerned the competing claims of Norway and Denmark. On 10 July 1931 Norway officially claimed sovereignty over the territory on the basis of occupation of *terra nullius*. Denmark objected on the basis that Danish sovereignty had existed over the area since the early part of the 18th century. The Permanent Court upheld the Danish claim.

... a claim to sovereignty based not upon some particular act or title such as a treaty of cession but merely upon continued display of authority, involves two elements each of which must be shown to exist: the intention and will to act as sovereign, and some actual exercise or display of such authority.

Another circumstance which must be taken into account by any tribunal which has to adjudicate upon a claim to sovereignty over a particular territory, is the extent to which the sovereignty is also claimed by some other Power. In most of the cases involving claims to territorial sovereignty which have come before an international tribunal, there have been two competing claims to the sovereignty, and the tribunal has had to decide which of the two is the stronger. One of the peculiar features of the present case is that up to 1931 there was no claim by any Power other than Denmark to the sovereignty over Greenland. Indeed, up till 1921, no Power disputed the Danish claim to sovereignty.

It is impossible to read the records of the decisions in cases as to territorial sovereignty without observing that in many cases the tribunal has been satisfied with very little in the way of the actual exercise of sovereign rights, provided that

---

13 *Norway v Denmark PCIJ* Ser A/B, No 53 (1933).

LIVERPOOL JOHN MOORES UNIVERSITY
Aldham Roberts L.R.C.
TEL. 0151 231 3701/3634

the other state could not make out a superior claim. This is particularly true in the case of claims to sovereignty over areas in thinly populated or unsettled countries ...

The conclusion to which the Court is led is that, bearing in mind the absence of any claim to territorial sovereignty by another Power, and the Arctic and inaccessible character of the uncolonised parts of the country, the King of Denmark and Norway displayed during the period from the founding of the colonies by Hans Egede in 1721 up to 1814 his authority to an extent sufficient to give his country a valid claim to sovereignty and that his rights were not limited to the colonised areas ... the result of all the documents connected with the grant of the [trading, hunting, and mining] concession is to show that, on the one side, it was granted upon the footing that the King of Denmark was in a position to grant a valid monopoly on the east coast and that his sovereign rights entitled him to do so, and, on the other, that the concessionaires in England regarded the grant of a monopoly as essential to the success of their projects and had no doubt as to the validity of the rights conferred ...

The concessions granted for the erection of telegraph lines and the legislation fixing the limits of territorial waters in 1905 are also manifestations of the exercise of sovereign authority.

In view of the above facts, when taken in conjunction with the legislation she had enacted applicable to Greenland generally, the numerous treaties in which Denmark, with the concurrence of the other contracting Party, provided for the non-application of the treaty to Greenland in general, and the absence of all claim to sovereignty over Greenland by any other Power, Denmark must be regarded as having displayed during this period of 1814 to 1915 her authority over the uncolonised part of the country to the degree sufficient to confer a valid title to the sovereignty.

Minquiers and Ecrehos case[14]

The Minquiers and the Ecrehos are two groups of rocks and islets which lie between Jersey and the French coast. The islets were claimed by both France and the UK, each state tracing its title back to the Middle Ages. On 6 December 1951 the UK filed a special agreement at the ICJ between France and itself asking the court to determine the question of which state had the better title.

Judgment of the Court

Both parties contend that they have respectively an ancient or original title to the Ecrehos and the Minquiers, and that their title has always been maintained and was never lost. The present case does not therefore present the characteristics of a dispute concerning the acquisition of *terra nullius*.

The United Kingdom government derives the ancient title invoked by it from the conquest of England in 1066 by William, Duke of Normandy. By this conquest England became united with the Duchy of Normandy, including the Channel Islands, and this union lasted until 1204 when King Philip Augustus of France drove the Anglo-Norman forces out of Continental Normandy. But his attempts to occupy also the Islands were not successful, except for brief periods when some of them were taken by French forces. On this ground the United Kingdom Government submits the view that all of the Channel islands, including the Ecrehos and the Minquiers, remained, as before, united with England, and that

---

14 *France v United Kingdom* [1953] *ICJ Rep* at p 47.

this situation of fact was placed on a legal basis by subsequent Treaties concluded between the English and French Kings ...

The French Government derives the original title invoked by it from the fact that the Dukes of Normandy were the vassals of the Kings of France, and that the Kings of England after 1066, in their capacity as Dukes of Normandy, held the Duchy in the fee of the French Kings ...

The Court considers it sufficient to state as its view that even if the Kings of France did have an original feudal title also in respect of the Channel Islands, such a title must have lapsed as a consequence of the events of the year 1204 and the following years. Such an alleged original feudal title of the Kings of France in respect of the Channel Islands could today produce no legal effect, unless it had been replaced by another title valid according to the law of the time of replacement. What is of decisive importance, in the opinion of the Court, is not indirect presumptions deduced from events in the Middle Ages, but the evidence which relates directly to the possession of the Ecrehos and Minquiers groups ...

The Parties have further discussed the question of the selection of a 'critical date' for allowing evidence in the present case. The United Kingdom submits that, although the Parties have for a long time disagreed as to the sovereignty over the two groups, the dispute did not become 'crystallised' before the conclusion of the Special Agreement of 29 December 1950, and that therefore this date should be considered as the critical date, with the result that all acts before that date must be taken into consideration by the Court. The French government, on the other hand, contends that the date of the Convention of 1839 should be selected as the critical date, and that all subsequent acts must be excluded from consideration.

At the date of the Convention of 1839, no dispute as to the sovereignty over the Ecrehos and Minquiers groups had yet arisen. The Parties had for a considerable time been in disagreement with regard to the exclusive right to fish oysters, but they did not link that question to the question of sovereignty over the Ecrehos and the Minquiers. In such circumstances there is no reason why the conclusion of that Convention should have any effect on the question of allowing or ruling out evidence relating to sovereignty. A dispute as to sovereignty over the groups did not arise before the years 1886 and 1888, when France for the first time claimed sovereignty over the Ecrehos and the Minquiers respectively. But in view of the special circumstances of the present case, subsequent acts should also be considered by the Court, unless the measure in question was taken with a view to improving the legal position of the Party concerned. In many respects activity in regard to these groups had developed gradually long before the dispute as to sovereignty arose, and it has since continued without interruption and in a similar manner. In such circumstances there would be no justification for ruling out all events which during this continued development occurred after the years 1886 and 1888 respectively ...

In 1826 criminal proceedings were instituted before the Royal Court of Jersey against a Jerseyman for having shot at a person on the Ecrehos. Similar judicial proceedings in Jersey in respect of criminal offences committed on the Ecrehos took place in 1881, 1891, 1913 and 1921. On the evidence produced the Court is satisfied that the ... Jersey authorities took action in these cases because the Ecrehos were considered to be within the Bailiwick. These facts show therefore that Jersey courts have exercised criminal jurisdiction in respect of the Ecrehos during nearly a hundred years.

Evidence produced shows that the law of Jersey has for centuries required the holding of an inquest on corpses found within the Bailiwick where it was not clear that death was due to natural causes. Such inquests on corpses found at the

Ecrehos were held in 1859, 1917 and 1948 and are additional evidence of the exercise of jurisdiction in respect of these islets ...

The Court, being now called upon to appraise the relative strength of the opposing claims to sovereignty over the Ecrehos in the light of the facts considered above, finds that the Ecrehos group in the beginning of the 13th century was considered and treated as an integral part of the fief of the Channel Islands which were held by the English King, and that the group continued to be under the dominion of that King, who in the beginning of the 14th century exercised jurisdiction in respect thereof. The Court further finds that the British authorities during the greater part of the 19th century and in the 20th century have exercised state functions in respect of the group. The French government, on the other hand, has not produced evidence showing that it has any valid title to the group. In such circumstances it must be concluded that the sovereignty over the Ecrehos belongs to the United Kingdom ...

It is established that contracts of sale relating to real property in the Minquiers have, as is the case of the Ecrehos, been passed before the competent authorities of Jersey and registered in the public registry of deeds of the island. Examples of such registration of contracts are given for 1896, 1909 and some later years.

In 1909 Jersey customs authorities established in the Minquiers a custom-house with the arms of Jersey. The islets have been included by Jersey authorities within the scope of their census enumerations, and in 1921 an official enumerator visited the islets for the purpose of taking the census.

These various facts show that Jersey authorities have in several ways exercised ordinary local administration in respect of the Minquiers during a long period of time ...

The evidence thus produced by the United Kingdom government shows in the opinion of the Court that the Minquiers in the beginning of the 17th century were treated as a part of the fief of Noirmont in Jersey, and that British authorities during a considerable part of the 19th century and in the 20th century have exercised state functions in respect of this group ...

In such circumstances, and having regard to the view expressed above with regard to the evidence produced by the United Kingdom government, the Court is of the opinion that the sovereignty over the Minquiers belongs to the United Kingdom.

7.3.2 Prescription and acquiescence

... the submission is that (if one excludes adverse holding or negative prescription) the situations described under the rubric of prescription by the writers, on analysis, fall into three categories: cases of immemorial possession; competing acts of sovereignty (*Island of Palmas* case); and cases of acquiescence. The first two categories are not really cases of prescription, but, as to the third, it may be said that acquiescence is a form of prescription and that the question ends as a matter of terminology. However, the doctrine is so tangled that it would be a help if the more candid and unambiguous label were used. And, of course, this would make clear the position of adverse holding in the law. However, it is important to notice that, whilst it is intended as an aid to understanding, the threefold analysis offered is not necessarily reflected neatly by life. In some cases it is not entirely clear whether there has been an occupation by one claimant of a *res nullius* followed later on by competing acts by another state, or whether there have been contemporaneously competing acts from the outset. Again, in either case, a court will take acquiescence into account; in other words the second and third categories may overlap in practice. In conclusion, one may doubt whether there is any role in the law for a doctrine of prescription as such.[15]

Brownlie's warning should be taken seriously and it can be read in conjunction with his comments referred to earlier regarding the dangers of too zealously looking for a single dominant mode of acquisition.[16] Nevertheless, reference is made, by states, by writers and by international tribunals[17] to prescription and it is necessary to have some understanding as to what is meant by it.

> Acquisitive prescription is the means by which, under international law, legal recognition is given to the right of a state to exercise sovereignty over land or sea territory in cases where that state has, in fact, exercised its authority in a continuous, uninterrupted, and peaceful manner over the area concerned for a sufficient period of time, provided that all other interested and affected states (in the case of land territory, the previous possessor, in the case of sea territory neighbouring state and other states whose maritime interests are affected) have acquiesced in this exercise of authority. Such acquiescence is implied in cases where the interested and affected state have failed within a reasonable time to refer the matter to the appropriate international organisation or international tribunal or – exceptionally in cases where no such action was possible – have failed to manifest their opposition in a sufficiently positive manner through the instrumentality of diplomatic protests. The length of time required for the establishment of a prescriptive title on the one hand, and the extent of the action required to prevent the establishment of a prescriptive title on the other hand, are invariable matters of fact to be decided by the international tribunal before which the matter is eventually brought for adjudication.[18]

Prescription can validate an otherwise doubtful title. It depends on public control and the implication that other states see the effective control and acquiesce to the assumption of sovereignty. Protests by other states can defeat a claim based on prescription. Traditionally it was thought that in order to be effective, protests had to involve the threat or use of armed force. As the use of armed force gradually became restricted by international law, so diplomatic protest came to suffice. There remains some discussion as to the precise requirements of effective protest. Some writers have argued that diplomatic protest must, within a reasonable time, be followed by reference of the matter to the UN or the ICJ.

The issue of protest was raised in relation to the dispute between Argentina and the UK over sovereignty over the Falklands Islands (Malvinas). In 1982 the British Foreign Secretary stated that Britain's claim to the Falkland Islands rested partly on principles of prescription.[19] According to Argentinean

---

15 Brownlie, *Principles of Public International Law*, 4th edn, 1990, Oxford: Oxford University Press at p 159.

16 *Ibid* at p 132.

17 See the Chamizal Arbitration (*US v Mexico*) (1911) 5 *AJIL* 782 where the International Boundary Commission considered a US argument based on prescription. The Commission made no decision as to whether prescription was a principle recognised by international law finding on the facts that there was no basis on which the US could found a claim on prescription.

18 Johnson (1950) 27 *BYIL* 332 at pp 353.

19 (1983) 54 *BYIL* 461.

accounts, the Falkland Islands were first discovered by Spain in 1520. Britain claims they were first discovered by Britain in 1592. The islands remained unoccupied until 1764 when a French settlement was established on East Falkland. This settlement was sold to Spain two years later and was maintained by Spain until 1811. Meanwhile a British settlement had been established in West Falkland in 1766. The British settlers were expelled by Spain in 1770 but returned in 1771 only to withdraw completely in 1774, leaving behind the Union flag and a plaque affirming British ownership of the island. Argentina became independent in 1816 and the Falkland Islands remained unoccupied until 1820 when the Argentinean government took possession of them claiming sovereignty as successor to Spain. The occupation of the islands was advertised in *The Times*, London. Between 1820 and 1829 Argentina performed a number of sovereign acts in relation to the Falklands, and it was only in 1829, when a political and military commander was appointed, that Britain protested to the Argentinean government. In 1831 the Argentinean commander of the Falklands seized three American ships for unlawful sealing in Argentinean waters. In retaliation the US destroyed the settlement on East Falkland and declared the islands to be free of all government. In 1833 the British purported to exercise rights of sovereignty over the islands by expelling the remainder of the Argentinean garrison, and the islands remained in continuous British possession until 2 April 1982 when an Argentinean force invaded the islands. The Argentinean government formally protested against Britain's occupation of the islands in 1833, 1834, 1841, and 1842. In 1849 Argentina sent a note to the British government indicating that it intended to make no further protest in respect of Britain's occupation since to do so seemed to be pointless. Nevertheless, Argentina pointed out that in no way should their lack of protest be taken to indicate acquiescence. Argentina resumed its protest in 1884 and they have continued on a regular basis ever since. The Foreign Affairs Committee of the House of Commons was unable to reach a categorical conclusion on the legal validity of either Britain's or Argentina's claim to the Falklands.[20] Clearly, it was the view of the British Foreign Secretary in 1982 that Argentina's failure to protest between 1849 and 1884 amounted to acquiescence to Britain's claims to the Falklands.

The main issue regarding prescription therefore seems to be the question of whether a claim based on it will only succeed with evidence of positive acquiescence, or whether such a claim can only be defeated by evidence of positive protest. Traditionally, claims based on prescription were substantiated by evidence of open, continuous, effective and peaceful occupation, which would seem to suggest that only active and effective protest will defeat such a claim. However, this view would seem to legitimise the claims of powerful states against the weak and may be incompatible with modern views of international law. The preferred view seems to be that of Brownlie, who points out that claims based on prescription rely on the acquiescence of other states:

---

20 See Fifth Report of the Foreign Affairs Committee of the House of Commons, Session, 1983–84, *HC Papers* 268–I, Vol I, pp xiv–xvii; Misc 1 (1985) Cmnd 9447.

If acquiescence is the crux of the matter (and it is believed that it is) one cannot dictate what its content is to be, with the consequences that the rule that jurisdiction rests on consent may be ignored, and failure to resort to certain organs is penalised by loss of territorial rights.[21]

Such a view would cast doubts on Britain's claims to the Falklands if they are based solely on prescription. However, the UK government has relied heavily on principles of self-determination to strengthen its case further. The extent and implementation of a right to self-determination will be discussed in Chapter 15. It has also been suggested that Britain would have been better basing its claim on conquest and subsequent annexation in 1833. As will be discussed in 7.3.3 (below), such a claim would have been valid under principles of intertemporal law. However, for largely political reasons Britain has not seen fit to found its claim on such a basis.

There is no prescribed time period necessary for a claim based on prescription to succeed; much will depend on the circumstances of the case, although in the *British Guiana v Venezuela Boundary Arbitration* (1899)[22] the arbitrators were instructed by treaty that adverse holding or prescription during a period of 50 years would establish a good title.

7.3.3 Conquest/annexation

The third traditional mode of acquisition is of historic interest only. Under the Kellogg-Briand Pact 1928[23] war was outlawed as an instrument of national policy. In 1932 the US declared that it would not recognise 'any situation, treaty, or agreement which may be brought about contrary to the covenants and obligations of the Pact of Paris of 27 August 1928'[24] and specifically would not recognise the state of Manchukuo as it resulted from the conquest of Manchuria by the Japanese. Article 2(4) of the UN Charter prohibits states from using or threatening force against the territorial integrity or political independence of any state, and the Declaration on Principles of International Law Concerning Friendly Relations and Co-operation Among States in Accordance with the Charter of the United Nations[25] states that 'No territorial acquisition resulting from the threat or use of force shall be recognised as legal'. Prior to the First World War, however, the use of armed force was not illegal and it was possible for territory to change hands following its use. Conquest itself was not sufficient to give title to territory and gave rise only to rights of belligerent occupation. In order to give effective title, physical occupation had to be combined with an intention to occupy as sovereign. This intention was usually evidenced by a formal declaration of annexation by the conquering state. Such a declaration of annexation would only be effective when hostilities had ceased. In practice, examples of title created by conquest are rare, because the annexation of

---

21 Brownlie, *Principles of Public International Law*, 4th edn, 1990, Oxford: Oxford University Press at p 157.

22 92 British and Foreign State Papers 160 (1899–1900).

23 See Chapter 13.

24 I Hackworth, *Digest of International Law*, 1940, Washington: US Govt Print Off at p 334.

25 Resolution 2625 (XXV) 24 October 1970.

territory after a war was usually confirmed by an express ceding of the territory from conquered to conqueror in the subsequent peace treaty.

Since 1945 there have been a number of cases in which territory has been occupied as a result of the use of force. The most notable recent example is, of course, Iraq's invasion and annexation of Kuwait in August 1990. Although Iraq sought to justify its action on the basis of historic claims to the territory, such claims were rejected by the international community and in Resolution 662 the UN Security Council declared that: '... annexation of Kuwait by Iraq under any form and whatever pretext has no legal validity, and is considered null and void.'[26]

The situation with regard to the territory taken by Israel during the course of the 1967 Six Day War remains more complicated. Until 1947, Palestine had been the subject of a League of Nations mandate which was administered by Britain. In 1947 the UN recommended partition of Palestine into a Jewish and an Arab state. The partition plan proved to be unworkable, and in May 1948 Israel declared itself an independent state. There followed a period of war which was ended by a number of armistice agreements concluded between Israel and each of its neighbours. Under these agreements Israel retained more territory than would have been allocated to the Jewish state under the partition plan. There were a number of violations of the armistice agreements, the most major one being in 1956, when Israel invaded the Egyptian Sinai peninsula but later withdrew to the 1949 borders. In 1967 Israel again invaded the Sinai peninsula together with East Jerusalem, the West Bank and the Golan Heights. This time the territory was not returned despite UN Security Council Resolution 242 which called for the withdrawal of Israeli armed forces from territories occupied in the conflict. The territory taken from Egypt in the Sinai Peninsula was returned following the peace treaty between the two states in 1979. Israeli civilian law was extended to east Jerusalem in 1967 and to the Golan Heights (which had previously been part of Syria) in 1981. The extension of Israeli law has been declared invalid by the UN, and the prevailing opinion is that Israel continues to be in belligerent occupation of the territory taken in 1967. Apart from its claims on East Jerusalem, Israel has not made any express claim to title to the territory occupied in 1967 but argues that the traditional rules relating to belligerent occupation do not apply. Those rules will be discussed in Chapter 14. Final clarification of the territorial status of much of the area awaits implementation of the PLO-Israel Accords of 1991 and conclusion of peace treaties between Israel and its neighbours.

Some doubts about the clarity of the law relating to conquest are created by the Indian invasion of Goa in 1961. Goa was a Portuguese colony at the time, although India maintained that it was an integral part of India and, as such, the invasion amounted to an act of self-determination. The invasion was criticised by a number of states, but the Security Council was unable to agree on a clear policy. Following the Portuguese revolution in 1974, the new government recognised the Indian title to Goa. It is clear that today Goa forms part of the territory of India. There remains some doubt, however, as to who had title to

---

26 SC Resolution 662 (1990) adopted on 9 August 1990.

the territory between 1961 and 1974 and the precise effect of Portuguese recognition of Indian claims. The suggestion is that it is the recognition itself which makes good India's title to Goa and not the initial use of force. What is prohibited under international law is the unlawful use of force, and force used to obtain self-determination may be regarded as lawful. The whole question of the use of force will be discussed in Chapter 13.

7.3.4 Cession

The possibility of cession of territory under the provision of a peace treaty has already been mentioned in 7.3.2 (above). Cession involves a complete transfer of sovereignty by the owner state to some other state, and may involve a part or all of the owner state's territory. Traditionally there was no bar on the extent to which one state could cede territory to another, although today, a treaty which purported to provide for the cession of territory in conflict with principles of self-determination would violate *jus cogens* and therefore be invalid. It should be noted that the principle *nemo dat quod non habet* applies in international law just as in municipal law: it is not possible for a state to cede what it does not possess.

Cession need not only arise in cases of transfer of territory from losing to victorious state following a war. In the past, land has been ceded in an exchange agreement, for example Britain and Germany exchanged Heligoland and Zanzibar by a treaty made in 1890, and in 1867 Russia ceded Alaska to the United States in exchange for payment.

7.3.5 Accretion

It is possible for states to gain or lose territory as a result of physical change. Such changes are referred to as 'accretion' and 'avulsion'. Accretion involves the gradual increase in territory through the operation of nature, for example, the creation of islands in a river delta. Avulsion refers to sudden or violent changes, such as those caused by the eruption of a volcano. The distinction between avulsion and accretion can be significant in boundary disputes which will be discussed at 7.4 (below).

7.3.6 Other possible modes of acquisition

As has already been stated, issues of title to territory are complex and will usually involve the application of a number of principles. In practice, cases rarely fall neatly into one of the five categories mentioned, and claims to territory will be based on a combination of factors. In addition to the five modes of acquisition that have been discussed, a number of others have been suggested from time to time. Among those that can be clearly identified are 'adjudication', 'disposition by joint decision' and 'continuity and contiguity'.

7.3.6.1 Adjudication

In certain situations, territory may accrue to one state by virtue of a decision of an international tribunal. This is most likely to occur in the context of boundary disputes. Thus in the *Frontier Dispute* case (1985), Burkina Faso and Mali agreed to submit their boundary dispute to a chamber of the ICJ and agreed to accept that tribunal's finding.

7.3.6.2 Disposition by joint decision

Following both World Wars, the victorious states assumed powers of disposition with regard to the territory of the defeated states. More often that not, such dispositions were subsequently confirmed by the provisions of a peace treaty and thus may be thought to come within the concept of cession. However, it is believed that such dispositions remain valid irrespective of any subsequent treaty, and are today justified on the basis of the entitlement of the international community to impose collective sanctions on aggressor states.

7.3.6.3 Continuity and contiguity

The two principles of continuity and contiguity relate to occupation. Under the principle of continuity, an act of occupation in a particular area extends sovereignty so far as it is necessary for the security and natural development of the area of claim. Thus, for a long period, France claimed that its eastern border should follow the west bank of the River Rhine. A more modern example, although not expressed as such, would be Israel's wish to claim the strategically significant Golan Heights from Syria. Connected to the principle of continuity is the hinterland doctrine, under which coastal settlements were deemed to extend over the area of immediate hinterland.

The principle of contiguity involves the extension of sovereignty to all areas that are geographically pertinent to the area of claim. The possibility of such a principle was rejected by Max Huber in the *Island of Palmas* case. It is in respect of the polar regions that the principle has been most used. Both the Soviet Union and Canada have made claims in respect of the Arctic based on the sector principle, which is itself an adaptation of the contiguity principle. Other Arctic states have not followed this example, and a major argument against any territorial claims to the Arctic is that since the area consists almost entirely of frozen sea it constitutes a part of the high seas and is therefore not capable of national appropriation. As regards Antarctica, both Chile and Argentina have made claims based on the contiguity principle, although such claims have not gone unopposed. Under the Antarctic Treaty 1959, all claims to national sovereignty were suspended, and it is argued that Antarctica now constitutes part of the common heritage of mankind, incapable of national appropriation. There will be further discussion of the regime pertaining in Antarctica in Chapter 17.

7.4   Boundaries

Disputes over territory may often arise in the context of boundary disputes, and a number of principles exist which may be of assistance in the determination of borders between states. Sometimes a boundary will be evidenced by some physical barrier, but more often than not the border is an invisible line, and where relations between neighbouring states are friendly, agreement will be reached to enable free movement of officials across the border and joint exploitation of resources which straddle the borderland. For example, as a result of modern surveying techniques, the border between France and the UK in the Channel Tunnel has been pinpointed with immense accuracy, yet agreement between the two states has been reached to provide for customs officials from one state to operate in the other, and for the police of one state to carry out arrests in the Tunnel *environs* of the other state.

Two particular aspects of boundaries will be considered here. The first relates to boundary disputes which arise following decolonisation. The principle which is commonly applied is known as *uti possidetis juris*. The principle was first applied during the break up of the Spanish Empire in South America, when the newly independent states agreed that their boundaries would conform to those set down by the former colonial power. The principle was adopted by the Organisation of African Unity in 1964 when it declared that colonial boundaries existing at independence constituted a tangible reality which all member states pledged themselves to respect. The principle was recognised by the ICJ in the *Frontier Dispute* case (1986) and is reflected in the Vienna Convention on the Succession of States in Respect of Treaties 1978, which provides that treaties establishing boundaries are an exception to the general rule that successor states start with a clean slate in respect of treaties entered into by their predecessors. Further confirmation of the universal nature of the principle came when the EC Arbitration Commission on Yugoslavia (1993) declared that it applied to newly independent states formerly part of a federation. The extent to which the principle has worked in practice with regard to Bosnia is, of course, the subject of much debate.

The other aspect of boundaries to be considered relates to those boundaries formed by rivers. There are a number of well recognised principles which operate in regard to river boundaries in the absence of any express agreement. As far as non-navigable rivers are concerned, the boundary will follow the median line between the two banks. If the river is navigable, the boundary follows the median line of the principal navigation channel, known as 'the Thalweg'. Of course, rivers can be subject to physical changes, and the effect of such changes depends on whether they are a result of accretion or avulsion. Where physical change is gradual (accretion) the boundary will reflect the changes. However, where avulsion occurs the boundary will follow its original course.

7.5 Rights of foreign states over territory

It is a general rule of international law that states have exclusive sovereignty over their territory. However, there are a number of exceptions to this general rule where a foreign state(s) may be granted certain rights over the territory of another independent sovereign state. Such situations include leases – for example the 99-year lease granted by China to the UK in respect of the New Territories and Kowloon – and servitudes.

Servitudes occur where territory belonging to one state is made to serve the interests of territory belonging to another state. The state enjoying the benefit may be entitled to do something on the territory concerned, for example, exercise a right of way, or take water for irrigation. Alternatively, the state on whom the burden falls may be obliged to refrain from doing something, for example, an obligation not to fortify.

Servitudes are normally created by treaty, although very occasionally they have been created as a result of long usage. For example, in the *Rights of Passage* case (1960), the ICJ recognised that Portugal had a right of passage across Indian territory between its Daman and Goa, and that such a right for peaceful purposes existed on the basis of a local customary law between India and Portugal. Such problems as arise will generally involve issues of state succession. The term is adapted from Roman Law, where servitudes ran with the land and bound successors in title. The question then arises as to whether this is also true of international law. There have been a number of instances where international tribunals have held the successor states bound. In the *Free Zones of Upper Savoy and District of Gex* case (1932) the PCIJ held that France was obliged to perform a promise made by Sardinia to maintain a customs-free zone in territory which France had subsequently acquired from Sardinia.

It remains unclear exactly what type of obligation survives changes of sovereignty. For example, under the Lease-Lend Agreement 1940, the UK granted USA military bases on certain British islands in the West Indies. The USA considered that its rights would lapse when the islands became independent. Also of relevance is the North Atlantic Fisheries Arbitration (1910), in which a panel of arbitrators had to consider the effect of a 1818 treaty between UK and USA which stated that 'the inhabitants of the US shall have, for ever, in common with the inhabitants of the UK, the liberty to take fish of every kind from the seas off the Newfoundland coast'. The arbitrators held that this provision did not create a servitude which prevented UK making regulations limiting the fishing rights of all persons, including US nationals, in the area concerned. Arguments have followed as to the precise nature of the decision and it is pointed out that the arbitrators drew a distinction between express grant of sovereign rights and purely economic rights. By this the tribunal implicitly accepted a class of limited servitudes. Clearly with regard to some benefits, such as the right to take water from neighbouring states, it seems more appropriate that they should run with the land rather than be personal to the present title holder.

Servitudes can exist for the benefits of more than just one state. For example, the *Aaland Islands* case (1920) concerned an agreement made in 1856 between Russia, France and Britain under which Russia agreed not to fortify islands lying near Stockholm in the Baltic. Sweden was not part of the treaty. In 1918 the islands became part of Finland, which began fortifying the islands. Sweden complained to the League of Nations and a Committee of Jurists decided that Sweden could claim the benefit of the 1856 treaty. Finland had succeeded to Russia's obligations, and the treaty was designed to preserve the balance of power: therefore all states directly interested could invoke it.

It has been suggested that a similar interpretation should be placed on treaties governing the Panama and Suez Canals. Servitudes are particularly important with regard to rivers and canals. There is a customary rule that foreign ships can be excluded from internal waters, and this is especially hard on land-locked states. Since 1815 most major rivers have been open to navigation – either to all states, riparian states, or ships of all states party to a particular treaty. In 1888 the Convention of Constantinople opened the Suez Canal to all nations. In 1901 and 1903 similar agreements dealt with the Panama Canal. Egypt succeeded to Turkey's obligations, and although the Suez Canal Company was nationalised in 1956, in 1957 Egypt publicly declared that it would keep the canal open to all nations. It was widely understood that Egypt breached its international obligations when it attempted to close the canal to Israeli shipping. It is believed that the 1888 treaty internationalises and institutionalises the use of the canal: the canal is effectively an easement across Egyptian territory.

7.6 Loss of state territory

To the five modes of acquiring sovereignty over territory correspond five modes of losing it – namely, cession, dereliction,[27] operations of nature, subjugation, prescription. But there is a sixth mode of losing territory – namely, revolt. No special details are necessary with regard to the loss of territory through subjugation, prescription, and cession, but the operations of nature, revolt, and dereliction require discussion.

Operations of nature as a mode of losing territory correspond to accretion as a mode of acquiring it. Just as through accretion a state may be enlarged, so it may be diminished through the disappearance of land and other operations of nature. And the loss of territory through operations or nature takes place *ipso facto* by such operations. Thus, if an island near the shore disappears through volcanic action, the extent of the maritime belt of the littoral state concerned is thereafter to be measured from the shore of the continent, instead of from the shore of the former island. Thus, further, if through a piece of land being detached by the current of a river from one bank and carried over to the other bank, the river alters its course and now covers part of the land on the bank from which such piece became detached, the territory of one of the riparian states may be decreased through the boundary line being *ipso facto* transferred to the new middle or mid-channel of the river.

Revolt followed by secession has been accepted as a mode of losing territory to which there is no corresponding mode of acquisition.[28] The question at what time a loss of territory through revolt is consummated cannot be answered once and for all, since no hard and fast rule can be laid down regarding the time when a state which has broken off from another can be said to have established itself safely and permanently. It is perhaps now questionable whether the term revolt is entirely a happy one in this legal context. It would seem to indicate a particular kind of political situation rather than a legal mode of the loss of territorial sovereignty ...

Dereliction (or abandonment or relinquishment) as a mode of losing territory corresponds to occupation as a mode of acquiring it. Dereliction frees a territory from the sovereignty of the present state-owner. It is effected through the owner-state completely abandoning territory with the intention of withdrawing from it for ever, thus relinquishing sovereignty over it. Just as occupation requires first, the actual taking of possession (*corpus*) of territory, and, secondly, the intention (*animus*) of acquiring sovereignty over it, so dereliction requires, first, actual abandonment of a territory, and, secondly, the intention of giving up sovereignty

---

27 The forfeiture of an inchoate title is not the same as the dereliction of territory which has been definitely acquired, whether by occupation or otherwise.

28 Thus the Netherlands fell away from Spain in 1579, Belgium from the Netherlands in 1830, the USA from Great Britain in 1776, Brazil from Portugal in 1822, the former Spanish South American States from Spain in 1810, Greece from Turkey in 1830, Cuba from Spain in 1898, and Panama from Colombia in 1903. There were a number of other instances in Europe during, and at the end of, the First World War.

over it. Actual abandonment alone does not involve dereliction as long as it must be presumed that the owner has the will and ability to retake possession of the territory. Thus, for instance, if an uprising forces a state to withdraw from a territory, such territory is not derelict as long as the former possessor is able, and makes efforts, to retake possession. It is only when a territory is really derelict that any state may acquire it through occupation. History knows of several such cases. But very often, when such occupation of derelict territory occurs, the former owner protests, and tries to prevent the new occupist from acquiring it. The cases of the Island of Santa Lucia and of Delagoa Bay may be quoted as illustrations:

(a) In 1639 Santa Lucia, one of the Antilles Islands, was occupied by England, but in the following year the English settlers were massacred by the natives. No attempt was made by England to retake the island, and France, considering it no man's land, took possession of it in 1650. In 1664 an English force under Lord Willoughby attacked the French, drove them into the mountains, and held the island until 1667, when the English withdrew, and the French returned from the mountains. No further step was made by England to retake the island, but it nevertheless asserted for many years to come that it had not abandoned the island *sine spe redeundi*; and, that, therefore, France in 1650 had no right to consider it no man's land. Finally, however, England resigned its claims in the Peace Treaty of Paris 1763.

(b) In 1823 England occupied, in consequence of a so-called cession from native chiefs, a piece of territory at Delagoa Bay which Portugal claimed as part of the territory owned by her at the Bay, maintaining that the chiefs concerned were rebels. The dispute was not settled until 1875, when the case was submitted to the arbitration of the President of France. the award was given in favour of Portugal, since the interruption of the Portuguese occupation in 1823 was not to be considered an abandonment of a territory over which Portugal had exercised sovereignty for nearly 300 years.[29, 30]

---

29 See Hall, para 34. The text of the award is reprinted in Moore, *International Arbitrations*, V, 1898, Washington: United States Department of State at p 4984.

Dereliction is again a traditional term which no longer entirely happily fits the kind of situation where a state, for example, renounces a claim, thus in effect recognising another claim to title. There are several modern examples which it is appropriate to describe here but which cannot altogether be described as a 'loss' of territorial sovereignty. Thus: (a) In 1972 Columbia and the USA signed a treaty whereby the USA renounced all claims to sovereignty over three groups of small reefs in the Caribbean, Quita Sueno Bank and the Cays on Roucador and Serranca Banks. In return Colombia guaranteed the continuation of certain fishing. (Quita Sueno is submerged at high tide and in the view of the USA was not subject to any claim of sovereignty by any government.) See *Bulletins of the State Department* (2 October 1972), p 387; (b) Under an agreement entering into force on 1 September 1972 the USA recognised the sovereignty of Honduras over the Swan Islands, which has been in the possession of the USA since 1893. See *Bulletin of the State Department* (18 September 1972) at p 326; (c) In a Exchange of Notes of 29 June 1976 (TS No 8 (1977); Cmnd 6713) between the Government of the Seychelles and the Government of the UK, certain conditions were expressed concerning the return to the Seychelles of the islands of Aldabra, Descroches and Farquar'; (d) Kiribati (the former Gilbert Islands) became independent on 12 July 1979. Under the Kiribati Act 1979, a constitution for the new state was contained in an Order in Council made under the Act. In Schedule 2 to the constitution the territories of Kiribati include the islands Canton and Endorbury, whose status has formerly been a matter of dispute between the UK and the USA. There was an agreement drawn up and signed at the time of the independence negotiations by which the USA renounced sovereignty over those islands.

30 *Oppenheim's International Law*, 9th edn, Vol 1, 1996, London: Longman at pp 716–18.

CHAPTER 8

JURISDICTION

8.1 Introduction

State jurisdiction concerns essentially the extent of each state's right to regulate conduct or the consequences of events. In practice jurisdiction is not a single concept. A state's jurisdiction may take various forms. Thus a state may regulate conduct by legislation; or it may, through its courts, regulate those differences which come before them, whether arising out of the civil or criminal law; or it may regulate conduct by taking executive or administrative action which impinges more directly on the course of events, as by enforcing its laws or the decisions of its courts. The extent of a state's jurisdiction may differ in each of these contexts.[1]

Jurisdiction concerns both international law and the internal law of each state. The former determines the permissible limits of a state's jurisdiction[2] in the various forms it may take, while the latter prescribes the extent to which, and the manner in which, the state in fact asserts its jurisdiction.[3] Much of the law relating to jurisdiction has developed through the decisions of national courts applying the laws of their own states. Since in many states the courts have to apply their national laws irrespective of their compatibility with international law, and since courts naturally tend to see the problems which arise primarily from the point of view of the interests of their own state, the influence of national judicial decisions has contributed to the uncertainty which surrounds many matters of jurisdiction and has made more difficult the development of a coherent body of jurisdictional principles.

International problems of jurisdiction arise almost exclusively where a state, either directly or through proceedings in its courts, seeks to assert its authority over persons, property or circumstances which (at least arguably) are or occur abroad. In such cases the questions which usually arise concern the actual or constructive location of the persons, property of circumstances in question; if

---

1   See also Basdevant and others, *Dictionnaire de la terminologie du droit international* (1960) pp 354–57 for a useful description of several senses of 'jurisdiction', including some of the 'competence' aspects.

The meaning of 'jurisdiction' has had to be considered in several cases before the European Commission and Court of Human Rights since Article 1 of the European Convention on Human Rights obliges each state party to secure the rights in question to 'everyone within its jurisdiction'. That provision has been held to apply in various circumstances where a state has exercised authority or control in a manner relevant to the exercise of the right in question.

To the extent that jurisdiction is a matter of the limits to the exercise of authority, it may be noted that questions of jurisdiction may arise not only in relation to states but also in relation to other entities which exercise authority internationally, such as international organisations, and, perhaps less clearly, multinational corporations.

2   In the *Lotus* case the PCIJ, while stating that international law generally left states 'a wide measure of discretion' in the application of their laws and the jurisdiction of their courts added that that discretion was 'limited in certain cases by prohibitive rules' and that it was 'required of a State ... that it should not over-step the limits which international law places upon its jurisdiction': PCIJ, Ser A, No 10, at p 19.

3   As to so-called 'organic' jurisdiction of states and international organisations (ie jurisdiction over their organs as such) see Seyersted (1965) *ICLQ* 14 at pp 31–82, 493–527.

their location is abroad, the extent to which the laws of the forum state are to be construed so as to apply extra-territorially;[4] and, if they are so construed, whether the exercise of the jurisdiction involves any infringement of the rights of other states, or of generally accepted limits to national jurisdiction.

Jurisdiction is not coextensive with state sovereignty, although the relationship between them is close; a state's 'title to exercise jurisdiction rests in its sovereignty'.[5] That jurisdiction is based on sovereignty does not mean that each state has in international law a sovereign right to exercise jurisdiction in whatever circumstances it chooses. The exercise of jurisdiction may impinge upon the interests of other states. What one state may see as the exercise of its sovereign rights of jurisdiction another state may see as an infringement of its own sovereign rights of territorial or personal authority. In practice, however, it is only in relatively few cases that overlapping claims to jurisdiction cause serious problems, usually where the states concerned attach importance to the assertion of their competing claims, and more often in criminal cases (where the element of public authority is more evident)[6] than in civil cases. Usually the coexistence of overlapping jurisdiction is acceptable and convenient; and forbearance by states in the exercise of their jurisdictional powers avoids conflict in all but a small (although important) minority of cases.

Although it is usual to consider the exercise of jurisdiction under one or other of more or less widely accepted categories, this is more a matter of convenience than of substance. There is, however, some tendency now to regard these various categories as parts of a single broad principle according to which the right to exercise jurisdiction depends on there being between the subject matter and the state exercising jurisdiction a sufficiently close connection to justify that state in regulating the matter and perhaps also to override any competing rights of other states.[7, 8]

International jurisdiction is an aspect or an ingredient or a consequence of sovereignty (or of territoriality or of the principle of non-intervention – the difference is merely terminological): laws extend so far as, but no further than, the sovereignty of the state that puts them into force, nor does any legislator normally intend to enact laws which apply to or cover persons, facts, events or conduct outside the limits of his state's sovereignty. This is a principle or, perhaps one should say, an observation of universal application. Since every state enjoys the same degree of sovereignty, jurisdiction implies respect for the corresponding rights of other states. To put it differently, jurisdiction involves both the right to exercise it within the limits of a state's sovereignty and the duty to recognise the same right of other states.

---

4   This is essentially a matter of domestic law and the interpretation of the relevant provisions of statute or common law.

5   PCIJ, Ser A, No 10, at p 19. See also Lord Macmillan in *The Christina* [1938] AC 485, 496–97: 'It is an essential attribute of the sovereignty of this realm, as of all sovereign independent states, that it should possess jurisdiction over all persons and things within its territorial limits and in all cases, civil and criminal, arising within these limits.'

6   An added complication may arise where one state wishes to punish as criminal conduct which another does not regard as involving an offence.

7   See Mann, *Hague Recueil*, 111 (1964), i, pp 43–51, 82ff; Brownlie, *Principles of International Law*, 4th edn, 1990, Oxford: Oxford University Press at pp 298, 306–07. The adoption by the ICJ in the *Nottbohm* case [1955] *ICJ Rep* at p 4 of the principle of a 'genuine link' has been of some influence in the present context.

8   *Oppenheim's International Law*, Vol 1, 9th edn, 1996, London: Longman at pp 456–58.

Or to put the same idea in positive and negative form, the state has the right to exercise jurisdiction within the limits of its sovereignty, but is not entitled to encroach upon the sovereignty of other states ...

Since in the present world sovereignty is undoubtedly territorial in character, in assessing the extent of jurisdiction the starting point must necessarily be its territoriality such as it was developed over the centuries and defined by the Huber-Storyan maxims: as a rule jurisdiction extends (and is limited) to everybody and everything within the sovereign's territory and to his nationals wherever they may be.

It is difficult to believe that these elementary propositions of public international law will be contested. On the contrary, the principle as defined is universal in the sense that *prima facie* it applies to all legislation and all state intervention derived or sanctioned by the competent authority, ie the legislator himself as well as those judicial and executive authorities controlled and empowered by him. Accordingly, there is no room for distinguishing between criminal, public and private laws. The suggestion that the doctrine applies to criminal and public law as well as the prerogative rights of the state such as taxation, but 'that there are no rules of international law limiting the legislative jurisdiction of states in questions of what might loosely be described as private law'[9] is untenable: a legislator who was to invalidate all marriages not celebrated in church and declare the children of such marriages illegitimate would act *ultra vires* and could not expect his statute or the judgments of his courts giving effect to it to be internationally recognised. It may well be that 'the cases in which a state violates international law, eg by applying its own substantive law to a given situation must be extremely rare'.[10] The point is that if such a rare case were to occur it would constitute an international wrong; the very absence of examples in the legislative, though not judicial, practice of states is likely to contribute to the proof of this rule. This remains as first stated by Lord Russell of Killowen in 1896[11] and since then frequently reaffirmed in the Anglo-American world; normally no state was allowed to apply its legislation:

> ... to foreigners in respect of acts done by them outside the dominions of the sovereign power enacting. That is a rule based on international law, by which one sovereign power is bound to respect the subjects and the rights of all other sovereign powers outside its own territory.

When this statement of the rule refers to legislation, it contemplates, of course, not only statutes or common law, but also all judicial and executive acts giving effect to the sovereign's will. International law, therefore, employs the term 'legislation' in a very wide sense indicating regulations rather than merely enactment.[12]

A number of different categories and types of jurisdiction should be identified from the outset. First, it is necessary to distinguish between 'prescriptive jurisdiction', which indicates the power to prescribe rules, and 'enforcement jurisdiction', which refers to the power to enforce rules. It is also useful to

---

9   Akehurst (1972–73) *BYIL* 145 at p 187.

10   Kahn-Freund, 143 *Hague Recueil* (1974–III) at p 176.

11   *The Queen v Jameson* [1896] 2 QB 425, 430.

12   Mann, 'The Doctrine of International Jurisdiction Revisited after Twenty Years', in *Further Studies in International Law*, 1990, Oxford: Clarendon Press (reprinted from a course given to the Hague Academy (1984 ii *Hague Recueil*, 186, 9–98) at pp 4–5.

distinguish between 'legislative', 'executive' and 'judicial jurisdiction'. 'Legislative jurisdiction' refers to the power of the state to make binding laws within its territory. Clearly, there are limits on the 'legislative supremacy' of a state. A state which adopts laws that are contrary to international law will render itself liable for the breach of international law on the international plane, although the internal constitutional position may be such that the municipal courts have to give effect to the municipal law. 'Executive jurisdiction' refers to the capacity of the state to act within the borders of another state. Since states possess territorial sovereignty, it follows that generally state officials may not exercise their functions on foreign soil without the express consent of the host state. 'Judicial jurisdiction' refers to the power of the municipal courts to try cases in which a foreign factor is present. It is the exercise of judicial jurisdiction which has received most discussion.

International law concerns itself with the propriety of the exercise of jurisdiction; exercise itself is a matter for the discretion of the state concerned. Jurisdiction has primarily and historically been exercised on a territorial basis, but there are occasions when states exercise jurisdiction outside their own territory. The PCIJ in the *Lotus* case (1927) confirmed that:

> A state may not exercise its power in any form in the territory of another state. In this sense jurisdiction is certainly territorial; it cannot be exercised by a state outside its territory except by virtue of a permissive rule derived from international custom or from a convention.

However, the Court went on to suggest that this rule really only applied to enforcement jurisdiction; a state could exercise prescriptive jurisdiction in its own territory in respect of acts which occurred abroad provided that there was no positive rule of international law prohibiting such an exercise of power.

It should be recognised that much of the discussion of jurisdiction involves the identification of principles rather than the assertion of rigid rules of law. In this context, the words of Sir Gerald Fitzmaurice in the *Barcelona Traction* case (1970) are of relevance:

> It is true that under present conditions international law does not impose hard and fast rules on states delimiting spheres of national jurisdiction in such matters ... but leaves to states a wide discretion in the matter. It does, however, (a) postulate the existence of limits – though in any given case it may be for the tribunal to indicate what these are for the purposes of that case; and (b) involve for every state an obligation to exercise moderation and restraint as to the extent of the jurisdiction assumed by the courts in cases having a foreign element, and to avoid undue encroachment on a jurisdiction more properly appertaining to, or more appropriately exercisable by, another state.

In addition to jurisdiction exercised on a territorial basis, there are a number of other relevant principles which can be identified and which have received varying degrees of international acceptance.

> An analysis of modern national codes of penal law and penal procedure, checked against the conclusions of reliable writers and the resolutions of international conferences or learned societies, and supplemented by some exploration of the jurisprudence of national courts, discloses five general principles on which a more or less extensive penal jurisdiction is claimed by states at the present time. These five general principles are: first, the territorial principle, determining

jurisdiction by reference to the place where the offence is committed; second, the nationality principle, determining jurisdiction by reference to the nationality or national character of the person committing the offence; third, the protective principle, determining jurisdiction by reference to the national interest injured by the offence; fourth, the universality principle, determining jurisdiction by reference to the custody of the person committing the offence; and fifth, the passive personality principle, determining jurisdiction by reference to the nationality of national character of the person injured by the offence. Of these five principles, the first is everywhere regarded as of primary importance and of fundamental character. The second is universally accepted, though there are striking differences in the extent to which it is used in the different national systems. The third is claimed by most states, regarded with misgivings by a few, and generally ranked as the basis of an auxiliary competence. The fourth is widely, though by no means universally accepted as the basis of an auxiliary competence, except for the offence of piracy, with respect to which it is the generally recognised principle of jurisdiction. The fifth, asserted in some form by a considerable number of states and contested by others, is admittedly auxiliary in character and is probably not essential for any state if the ends served are adequately provided for by another principle.[13]

The commentary to the Harvard Research Draft Convention on Jurisdiction with Respect to Crime 1935 identified five general principles, namely:

(a) the territorial principle;

(b) the passive personality principle;

(c) the nationality principle;

(d) the protective principle; and

(e) the universality principle.

Discussion of the application of these principles will form the main part of this chapter. Before looking at them in detail, it is necessary to consider some issues raised by the assertion of civil jurisdiction. One final introductory point needs to be made: this chapter is concerned with the exercise of jurisdiction by states on the municipal plane. Questions of jurisdiction also arise on the international plane and the subject of international criminal jurisdiction will be discussed in Chapter 9.

8.2   Civil jurisdiction

The rules relating to the exercise of civil jurisdiction have tended to be more flexible than those relating to criminal jurisdiction. Some writers have argued that there in fact exist no clear rules of customary international law governing the exercise of civil jurisdiction, although there are an increasing number of treaties dealing with the matter. The traditional rule in the common law countries was that courts would have jurisdiction over civil disputes if the defendant was present in the territory, no matter for how short a period. Civil law countries have tended to operate on the basis that the defendant is habitually resident within the territory where jurisdiction is to be assumed. The position within the European Union is governed by the Brussels Convention on

---

13 Dickinson, 'Introductory Comment to the Harvard Draft Convention on Jurisdiction with Respect to Crime 1935' (1935) 29 *AJIL*, Supp 443.

Jurisdiction and Enforcement of Judgments in Civil and Commercial Matters 1968. This provides the general rule that persons domiciled in a contracting state must be sued in the courts of that state alone, although there are two main exceptions to this rule. The Brussels Convention is incorporated into English law by the Civil Jurisdiction and Judgments Act 1982. The 1982 Act has since been amended to incorporate the Lugano Convention 1989, which extends the Brussels Convention regime to those states which are members of the European Free Trade Association.

As far as matrimonial cases are concerned, the generally accepted ground for exercising jurisdiction is the domicile or habitual residence of the party bringing the action, and this rule is reflected in the Hague Convention on the Recognition of Divorces and Legal Separations 1970.

For a full discussion of the rules relating to the exercise of civil jurisdiction reference should be made to a textbook on private international law. As far as public international law is concerned, disputes about jurisdiction have usually arisen when a state has attempted to exercise criminal jurisdiction over non-nationals or in respect of actions that have occurred outside the state's own territory.

8.3   Territorial principle

The ability of a state to exercise jurisdiction over crimes committed within its territory is an essential attribute of sovereignty, and the territorial principle has received universal recognition.

According to the territorial principle, events occurring within a state's territorial boundaries and persons within that territory, albeit temporarily, are subject to local law and the jurisdiction of the local courts. The principle has practical advantages in terms of availability of witnesses.

Application of the territorial principle will usually be straightforward where the crime has been committed wholly within the territory. However, it is not always possible to decide on the exact location of the crime. The activities constituting the offence may have taken place in more than one state, for example, suppose X fires a gun in state A killing someone in state B. Which state can claim territorial jurisdiction? Under what is known the 'subjective territoriality principle', state A has jurisdiction, since that is where the offence was commenced. Under the 'objective territoriality principle', state B has jurisdiction, since that is where the offence was completed and had its effect. Both principles are recognised by international law and thus, in the example, both state A and state B would have concurrent jurisdiction.

An example of the subjective territorial principle is found in *Treacey v DPP* (1971).[14] The appellant had written and posted in the Isle of Wight a letter addressed to Mrs X in Germany which demanded money with menaces. Mrs X received the letter in Germany but informed the British police. Treacey was convicted of blackmail and his conviction was upheld by a majority in the House of Lords. Lord Diplock stated that:

---

14   [1971] AC 537.

There was no principle of international comity to prevent Parliament from prohibiting under pain of punishment persons who are present in the United Kingdom, and so owe local obedience to our law, from doing physical acts in England, notwithstanding that the consequences of those acts take effect outside the United Kingdom.

In *DPP v Doot* (1973),[15] the respondents were convicted of conspiracy to import cannabis into the UK. The House of Lords held that the English courts had jurisdiction over the case, even though the actual conspiracy took place abroad, since the offence continued to occur in England when the conspiracy was carried out. Lord Wilberforce stated:

> The present case involves 'international elements' – the accused are aliens and the conspiracy was initiated abroad – but there can be no question here of any breach of any rules of international law if they are prosecuted in this country. Under the objective territorial principle ... or the principle of universality (for the prevention of narcotics falls within this description) or both, the courts of this country have a clear right, if not a duty, to prosecute in accordance with our municipal law.'

It should be noted that recently, the English courts have moved away from a strict application of the subjective or objective territorial principle. Thus in *Somchai Liangsiriprasert v Government of the USA* (1990)[16] Lord Griffiths commented:

> The English courts have decisively begun to move away from definitional obsessions and technical formulations aimed at finding a single *situs* of a crime by locating where the gist of the crime occurred or where it was completed. Rather, they now seem by an examination of relevant policies to apply the English criminal law where a substantial measure of the activities constituting a crime take place in England, and restrict its application in such circumstances solely in cases where it can seriously be argued on a reasonable view that these activities should, on the basis of international comity, be dealt with by another country.

A controversial example of the application of the objective territorial principle is provided by the *Lotus* case (1927). The case arose following a collision on the high seas between a Turkish and a French ship. As a result of the collision the Turkish vessel sank and a number of crew members and passengers drowned. The French ship put into port in Turkey and a number of French crew members were arrested and subsequently tried and convicted of manslaughter. France raised objections to the exercise of jurisdiction by Turkey and the dispute was submitted to the PCIJ. Turkey argued that ships on the high seas formed part of the territory of the state whose flag they fly. They therefore argued that jurisdiction could be exercised on the basis of the objective territorial principle, since the consequences of the French act had occurred on Turkish territory. The PCIJ found in favour of Turkey by the casting vote of the President of the Court. The decision has been criticised for the suggestion it makes that states have a wide measure of discretion to exercise jurisdiction which is only limited to the extent that there are specific prohibitive rules. In other words, the onus is on the

---

15   [1973] AC 807.
16   [1990] 3 WLR 606.

one disputing jurisdiction to provide evidence of a rule restricting jurisdiction. The better view today seems to be that it is the one asserting jurisdiction that must show a relevant permissive rule of international law. It is also important to note that the view that a ship forms part of the territory of the flag state is no longer correct. Questions of jurisdiction on board ships will be discussed in Chapter 10 and jurisdiction on board aircraft will be dealt with in Chapter 11.

Where is cyberspace?[17] The answers seem to approach the metaphysical: it is everywhere and nowhere; it exists in the smallest bursts of matter and energy, and is called forth only by the presence of man through the intercession of an Internet Provider. If the answers are useless, it only shows that we are asking the wrong question. We want to ask first: what is cyberspace? Here, at least a functional answer is possible. Functionally, cyberspace is a place. It is a place where messages and webpages are posted for the whole world to see, if they can find them.[18] It is no further than your own computer terminal, but never closer than your image in a mirror.

Unfortunately, when the common law confronts cyberspace the usual mode of analysis is analogy: not 'What is cyberspace?' but 'What is cyberspace like?' The answers are prosaic: a glorified telephone, a bookstore, a bulletin board. At the common law there is nothing new under the sun.[19] I propose that we must look at cyberspace through the lens of international law in order to properly give cyberspace a home in our laws.[20]

The thesis of this paper is that there exists at international law a category which I call an 'international space'. Currently there are three such international spaces: Antarctica, outer space, and the high seas. For jurisdictional analysis, cyberspace should be treated as a fourth international space.

After all, in cyberspace, jurisdiction is the overriding conceptual problem for domestic and foreign courts alike. Unless conceived of as an international space, cyberspace takes all of the traditional principles of conflicts-of-law and reduces them to absurdity. Whereas a thorny jurisdictional problem might traditionally involve two, three, even six or seven conflicting jurisdictions, the universe of laws which can apply to a simple homespun webpage is all of them. Jurisdiction

---

17 The term 'cyberspace' is sometimes treated as a synonym for the internet, but is really a broader concept. For example, we know exactly how the internet began, but not at what point the connections between a few domestic computers metamorphosed into a global virtual community that we now call cyberspace. I prefer the term because it emphasises that it can be treated as a place. William Gibson is credited with coining the term in his novel 'Neuromancer.' Gibson's concept included a direct brain-computer link that gave the user the illusion of vision, moving about in the data 'matrix' to obtain information. William S Byassee, 'Jurisdiction of Cyberspace: Applying Real World Precedent to the Virtual Community', 30 Wake Forest L Rev 197, 198 n 5.

18 In his book Wyrms, science fiction author Orson Scott Card describes a most remarkable place called Heffiji's house, which could have been a metaphor for cyberspace. Heffiji had a sign on her house reading 'Answers' that lured many curious people. She asked questions of all her visitors and wrote the answers down on scraps of paper. These scraps of paper were scattered all around her enormous house. Unfortunately she had no brain, so she could not learn anything. She did, however, know where she had put the pieces of paper, and you could learn anything from her if you asked the right question.

19 Ecclesiastes 1:9. Solomon could well have been speaking of cyberspace when he wrote, 'For a dream comes with much business, and a fool's voice with many words'. Ecclesiastes 5:3.

20 It is hornbook custom to cite The Paquete Habana for the proposition that 'international law is part of our law': The Paquete Habana, 175 US 677 (1900). With apologies to Voltaire: if The Paquete Habana did not exist, it would be necessary to invent it.

in cyberspace requires clear principles, and better principles rooted in international law, so that courts in all nations may be persuaded to the same conclusions.

I   Principles of jurisdiction

There are three types of jurisdiction generally recognised in international law. These are the jurisdiction to prescribe, the jurisdiction to enforce, and the jurisdiction to adjudicate.[21] The jurisdiction to prescribe is the right of a state to make its law applicable to the activities, relations, the status of persons, or the interests of persons in things.[22] This paper deals almost exclusively with the jurisdiction to prescribe. However, it is useful here to note the distinction between the jurisdiction to prescribe a rule of law for a particular action and the jurisdiction to enforce that rule. This paper will not discuss extradition.

Under international law, there are six generally accepted bases of jurisdiction, usually listed in the order of preference:

1   Subjective territoriality
2   Objective territoriality
3   Nationality
4   Protective principle
5   Passive nationality
6   Universality

These bases of jurisdiction are theories under which a state may claim to have jurisdiction to prescribe a rule of law over an activity. Even where one of the bases of jurisdiction is present, the exercise of jurisdiction must still be reasonable.[23]

Subjective territoriality is by far the most important of the six. If an activity takes place within the territory of the forum state, then the forum state has the jurisdiction to prescribe a rule for that activity. The vast majority of criminal legislation in the world is of this type.

Objective territoriality is invoked where the action takes place outside the territory of the forum state, but the primary effect of that activity is within the forum state. The classic case is that of a rifleman in Canada shooting an American across Niagara Falls in New York. The shooting takes place in Canada; the murder – the effect – occurs in the United States. United States would have the jurisdiction to prescribe under this principle. This is sometimes called 'effects jurisdiction'. This has obvious implications for cyberspace, as will be discussed below.

Nationality is the basis for jurisdiction where the forum state asserts the right to prescribe a law for an action based on the nationality of the actor. Under Dutch law, for example, a Dutch national 'is liable to prosecution in Holland for an offence committed abroad, which is punishable under Netherlands law and which is also punishable under the law of the country where the offence was committed'.[24] Many other civil law countries have similar laws, notably France.

---

21   Restatement (Third) of Foreign Relations, SS 401.
22   *Ibid*, SS 402.
23   Restatement SS 403.
24   *Public Prosecutor v Y*, Supreme Court, 1957 (1961) 24 *Int L Rep* 265, 265.

Passive Nationality is a theory of jurisdiction based on the nationality of the victim. Often passive and 'active' nationality are invoked together to establish jurisdiction. A state has more interest in prosecuting an offence when both the offender and the victim are nationals of that state. This principle is rarely used for two reasons. First, it is offensive to insist that foreign laws are not sufficient to protect your citizens abroad. One of the complaints that sparked the Boxer rebellion in China in 1901 was the privilege of foreigners to be tried only by their own laws. There actually was a US District Court for China during this period. Second, the victim is not being prosecuted. You need to seize the actor in order to have a criminal prosecution.

The Protective Principle is often seen as the ugly stepchild of Objective Territoriality. This principle expresses the desire of a sovereign to punish actions committed in other places solely because it feels threatened by those actions. This principle is invoked where the 'victim' would be the government or sovereignty itself. For example, in *United States v Rodriguez*, 182 F Supp 479 (SD Cal 1960), the defendants were charged with making false statements in immigration applications while they were outside the United States. This principle is disfavoured for the obvious reason that it can easily offend the sovereignty of another nation. Such cases are usually referred to the State Department, not the Justice Department.

The final basis of jurisdiction is Universal jurisdiction, sometimes referred to as 'universal interest' jurisdiction. Historically this was the right of any sovereign to catch and punish pirates. This has expanded during the past century and a half to include more of *jus cogens*: slavery, genocide, and hijacking (air piracy).[25] Although this may at first glance seem extendible to net piracy in the future, to computer hacking and viruses, this is unlikely given the traditionally tortoise-like development of the universal jurisdiction. Just as important, universal jurisdiction traditionally covers only very serious crimes.[26] Because it covers serious crimes, all nations have due-process-like problems with convictions under this principle.

The general mode international conflicts-of-law analysis is to weigh the interests of competing states in determining whether there is jurisdiction to prescribe. Although subjective territoriality usually trumps other interests, a strong state interest in protecting its nationals can outweigh a weak state interest in prosecuting the crime on its own soil.

It is not always clear what it means for an individual defendant if the state lacks the jurisdiction to prescribe law. Under some domestic legal systems, a defendant will be released if the court purported to convict the defendant where there was no jurisdiction to prescribe. In the United States, this question is nastily intertwined with due process analysis and presumptions about the intent of Congress to violate international law. The court will construe US law, where possible, to conform to international law. I will not attempt to extricate it here. At a minimum under international law, a claim will accrue to the state whose sovereignty is offended by the conviction of its national.

---

25 *Jus cogens*, 'compelling law' means a peremptory norm of general international law from which no derogation is permitted.

26 See, eg, US Constitution, Art I, Sec 8 (granting Congress the right 'To Define and Punish Piracies and Felonies committed on the High Seas, and Offenses against the Law of Nations').

II   The theory of the uploader and the downloader

Man interacts with cyberspace in two primary ways: we put information in cyberspace; we take information from cyberspace. Both actions are limited and concrete, and can be performed in the safety and comfort of one's own home. At law in cyberspace, then, there are two distinct actors: the uploader and the downloader.[27] Under this theory, the uploader and the downloader act like spies in the classic information drop – the uploader puts information into a location in cyberspace, and the downloader accesses it at a later time. Neither need be aware of each other's identity. Unlike the classic information drop, however, there need not be any intent to communicate at all: a webpage is just a *vox clamantis in deserto*.[28] Some pages are accessed by thousands of random people all over the world, while others languish as untrodden paving stones in the infinite paths of cyberspace.

In both civil and criminal law, most actions taken by uploaders and downloaders present no jurisdictional difficulties. A state can forbid, on its own territory, the uploading and downloading of material it considers harmful to its interests. A state can therefore forbid anyone from uploading a gambling site from its territory, and can forbid any one within its territory from downloading, ie interacting,[29] with a gambling site in cyberspace.

Two old American cases demonstrate how this theory would play out. *The Schooner Exchange* (1812) held that a French war vessel was not subject to American law, although it was in an American port.[30] A webpage would be ascribed the nationality of its creator, and not subject to the law of wherever it happened to be downloaded.

The *Cutting* case (1887) provides an example of how an uploader should be viewed in a foreign jurisdiction which is offended by material uploaded into cyberspace. Mr Cutting published an article in Texas which offended a Mexican citizen. When Mr Cutting visited Mexico he was incarcerated on criminal libel charges. The Secretary of State instructed the American ambassador to inform the Mexican government that 'the judicial tribunals of Mexico were not competent under the rules of international law to try a citizen of the United States for an offence committed and consummated in his own country, merely because the person offended happened to be a Mexican'.[31] As a general proposition, where uploading certain material is a crime, it is an offence 'committed and consummated' in the state where the uploader is located.

III   Rejecting territoriality: the trouble with Minnesota

There is no doubt that what many states want to do is altogether more troubling: states want to exercise jurisdiction over uploaders (and to a lesser extent,

---

27 I am here ignoring direct communication over the internet, involving e-mail. This will be dealt with later. Suffice it to say now that these direct communications do not present the same conflict-of-laws problems as general postings to the world.

28 The voice of one crying out in the desert. Matthew 3:3; Isaiah 40:3. Whether cyberspace is preparing the way for the Lord is beyond the scope of this paper.

29 Interacting may involve considerably more than downloading, but it always involves the act of downloading.

30 *The Schooner Exchange v McFaddon* (1812) 11 US (7 Cranch) 116. We can ignore for now the question of whether the ship's status as a war vessel was dispositive. The 'temporary presence' doctrine was elaborated in later cases.

31 Letter, Secretary of State to United States Ambassador to Mexico, Department of State, Washington, 1 November 1887.

downloaders) outside their own territorial boundaries. Minnesota is apparently the first jurisdiction (it is no coincidence that this is a jurisdiction not traditionally involved with foreign relations) to attempt a general exercise of such jurisdiction. Minnesota's Attorney General, Hubert Humphrey III, has issued a memorandum stating that 'Persons outside of Minnesota who transmit information via the internet knowing that information will be disseminated in Minnesota are subject to jurisdiction in Minnesota courts for violations of state criminal and civil laws'.[32]

Their concerns are no doubt sincere, but the memorandum is somewhat less than sincere. Of course everybody 'knows' that all information in cyberspace will be downloaded in Minnesota. It is totally foreseeable. Minnesota's rule makes all of cyberspace subject to Minnesota law. Naturally, if every state took this approach (and under Minnesota's guidelines, there is no reason why every state could not) the result would be unbearable, especially for multinational corporations with attachable assets lying all over the world. Much more sensible is the opinion of the Florida Attorney General that 'the resolution of these matters must be addressed at the national, if not international, level'.[33]

The Minnesota Attorney General has laid out a simple syllogism, of the sort that is always suspect: anyone who 'being without the state, intentionally causes a result within the state prohibited by the criminal laws of this state' is subject to prosecution in Minnesota.[34] This simple approach, appealing at first, dissolves upon a sufficiently textured international legal analysis.

An interesting question for strict constructionists, which need not detain us here, is whether, under the federal system, Minnesota has any obligations under international law. As a practical matter, Minnesota, as well as all states and nations, will be constrained by international law. One can observe that the Supreme Court always interprets Congressional mandates, where possible, in accordance with international law, and that presumption is surely stronger against state legislatures. Indeed, most provisions of US foreign relations law are designed to keep international questions in federal hands. Treaties, of course, are the 'supreme law of the land', superior to any state law (US Constitution, Art VI). At any rate, considerations of comity, which are underdeveloped and often thinly conceived in relations between the United States, will be important if Minnesota attempts to assert this jurisdiction internationally.[35]

Minnesota's approach has several problems. First, Minnesota has ignored the presumption against extraterritorial application of US laws. It seems that the Minnesota Attorney General was under the impression that, because the mode of analysis for conflicts-of-law is the same for conflicts between American states as for a conflicts between an American state and a foreign country, the results will also always be the same. Of course they will not. The sovereignty of individual American states is not as easily offended (or defended) as the sovereignty of

---

32 Memorandum of Minnesota Attorney General.

33 Florida Attorney General, Formal Opinion: AG 95–70 (October 18, 1995).

34 Minnesota Statute SS 609.025 (1994) (cited in Memorandum of the Minnesota Attorney General).

35 Comity is the respect courts accord one another and the laws of other sovereigns. Like *forum non conveniens*, it is (in common law countries) a judge-made doctrine for declining jurisdiction. Civil law countries invoke comity more with statute than *sua sponte* court action. See generally Brian Pearce, *The Comity Doctrine as a Barrier to Judicial Jurisdiction: A US–EU Comparison* (1994) 30 Stan J Int L 525.

nation states. To put it another way, courts will accord France's interest in its sovereignty greater weight than Delaware's. This is especially true of French courts. Under the theory of international spaces, outlined below, Minnesota has no jurisdiction to prescribe law over objects in cyberspace because, under the federal system, Minnesota has no 'nationality' to assert. Nationality is, well, national, and the jurisdiction predicated thereon is federal.[36] Minnesota is not accustomed to dealing with international law, and it shows.

Second, Minnesota has conflated *in personam* jurisdiction with the jurisdiction to prescribe law. The former is subject to the 'minimum contacts'[37] analysis; the latter is not. A nexus with Minnesota territory sufficient to establish *in personam* jurisdiction over a defendant may not be sufficient to give Minnesota the jurisdiction to prescribe a rule of law for the action. Indeed, Minnesota courts may have *in personam* jurisdiction over a defendant but may, according to their own choice-of-law statutes, choose to apply foreign law in the case at hand. In criminal cases, where there is no jurisdiction to prescribe a rule of law, there is no jurisdiction at all.[38]

Minnesota has chosen to rely on 'effects' jurisdiction or 'objective territoriality', where it is the territoriality of the object state, rather than (or in addition to) that of the subject actor, which prescribes the rule of law. The 1965 Restatement (Second) of Foreign Relations described objective territoriality as the following:

A state has jurisdiction to prescribe a rule of law attaching legal consequences to conduct that occurs outside its territory and causes and effect within its territory if either:

(a) the conduct and its effect are generally recognised as constituent elements of a crime or tort under the law of states that have reasonably developed legal systems;[39] or

(b) (i) the conduct and its effect are constituent elements of activity to which the rule applies;

(ii) the effect within the territory is substantial;

(iii) it occurs as a direct and foreseeable result of the conduct outside the territory; and

(iv) the rule is not inconsistent with the principles of justice generally recognised by states that have reasonably developed legal systems. *The Restatement (Second) of Foreign Relations SS 18.*

Minnesota's rule misses the texture of this description. None of these cyberspace 'crimes' can meet part (a) of the test, because none of these are traditional crimes, generally recognised, and because the act of uploading is not currently a constituent element of any crime anywhere. Part (b) of the test is where the action is. It speaks of substantial effect and principles of justice generally recognised. Moreover, considerations of comity always play a major role in a basis of jurisdiction so offensive to foreign sovereignty. Objective territoriality is

---

36 This is not to say that federal courts may not turn to the state of residence of the criminal for the substantive law. This paper is about international jurisdiction, not federal jurisdiction.

37 *International Shoe v Washington* 326 US 310 (1945).

38 For example, an American court cannot convict a Swiss citizen for violation of Swiss law. *Habeas corpus* review would be swift and sweet for the defendant. The remedy here is extradition.

39 The older language was 'civilised nations'. No doubt in American and European courts it still means 'civilised nations' with all that implies.

not a blanket to be thrown over cyberspace, but is appropriate only in unusual circumstances. Minnesota needs to find another basis for asserting general jurisdiction over actions in cyberspace.

IV   Rejecting territoriality: 'the law of the server'

Another poor approach to jurisdiction in cyberspace is to treat the location of the server where webpages are 'located' as the place of a criminal action for the purposes of territorial jurisdiction. Under this theory, a webpage 'located' on a server at Stanford University is subject to California law. Where the uploader is also in the forum state, or is a national of the forum state residing abroad, this approach is consistent with the theory of jurisdiction in international spaces.

But where the uploader is in a foreign jurisdiction,[40] this analysis displays fatal shortcomings. To say that a webpage is 'located' at the server means redefining downloading and uploading as a communication between two physical places, the location of the uploader and the 'location' of the webpage. This would territorialise cyberspace through its servers, creating exactly the kind of jurisdictional mayhem that the theory of international spaces seeks to avoid. As a practical matter, we know that data sent from an uploader to even a nearby server can travel in data packets through nodes around the world.

One could envision a system in which we accept the theory of the uploader and the downloader, but insist on exercising territorial jurisdiction over webpages 'located' at a server. Under the theory of the uploader and the downloader, the act of uploading is performed entirely at the computer terminal of the uploader, within one and only one state. Naturally, if that state is the same state as the server, then asserting jurisdiction over a webpage based on a territorial theory about the 'location' of the server rather than on the location of the uploading will produce no difference except in doctrine.

The effects of this doctrine will appear only when the uploader and the server are in different states. In that case, in order to say that the law of the server applies to the webpage, one must assert that the act of uploading had an effect in the forum state substantial enough to provide a basis for jurisdiction under the theory of objective territoriality or 'effects' jurisdiction. The theory of objective territoriality certainly can provide the basis for jurisdiction to prescribe in cyberspace under unusual circumstances, but it will not do as a general rule for ascribing criminal liability to foreign uploading, because all states have an equal interest here. Objective territoriality requires a special, unique interest.

The natural response is to point to the computer files which create a webpage and say that it would be false to claim that the webpage was anywhere else but on the server. This narrow approach ignores the interactivity of cyberspace in four important ways. The first problem can be best stated a question: can one say that a webpage really exists until it is accessed and constituted on the screen of the downloader? Surely the gif[41] file containing pornography cannot create offence until compiled and displayed on the downloader's machine. This is more than a metaphysical oddity. It is not hard to figure out who put garbage into

---

40   With today's technology, one can easily access an internet account from any other server in the world, by use of 'telnet' and 'rlogin' commands over the UNIX platform. In the future, this will presumably be easier. Indeed, it is not a farfetched idea to have a universal server utilising hard drive space around the world for storage, the way a single hard drive stores data on all over its dozens of sectors. We might as well start analysing it this way now.

41   The term 'gif file' refers to pictures saved in the Compuserve format, denoted by the file extension 'gif'. The 'g' is usually hard.

cyberspace, but it is very difficult to say what happens to it once it is there. If the webpage is located at Stanford, how does it 'travel' to Bolivia? Is the Bolivian coming to Stanford? Talk about asking the wrong questions!

Second, constituent parts of a webpage are often called from other servers, with the source code for the page consisting mostly of images called up from other places. We do not know what the future will bring, but we can only suppose that 'sites' consisting of data pulled from around the world at the downloader's request will become more common. Complexity will likely increase, not decrease.

Third, a webpage consists in large part of links to other pages which may be 'located' in other countries. Even if the data is not called up by the webpage itself, links to other data are presented to the downloader for him to (in today's mouse technology) click on. It becomes irrational to say that a webpage with links to gambling and pornography 'located' in 20 different countries is subject to the law of any and all of those countries. A government could criminalise the creation of links to certain sites, but this would create jurisdictional bedlam.[42] Of course as computer technology develops, the future will only create more interactivity and more absurdities. I would like to believe that this analysis of cyberspace would fail the Restatement test of reasonableness.[43]

Fourth, such interactivity is also supplemented by randomness and anonymity. This is often overlooked. In his article, 'Jurisdiction of Cyberspace: Applying Real World Precedent to the Virtual Community', William Byassee argues persuasively that territoriality should refer only to the 'physical components of the cyberspace community', who are the 'sender and recipient'.[44] The terms 'sender' and 'recipient', are terms implying intent of two (and only two) parties to communicate with each other. This is not the same as the 'uploader and downloader'. The downloader and the uploader do not know who the other is, or where the other is. For the downloader, the files are on his computer.

The substantive results of this analysis would lead to a considerable amount of seemingly random criminal liability, without really adding anything to a state's ability to control the content of cyberspace under the theory of international spaces. Persons travelling around cyberspace need to know what set of laws applies to their actions. If we reject the territorialisation of cyberspace, and accept the theory of the uploader and the downloader, we must reject the broad form of the 'law of the server'.

By contrast, under the theory of international spaces developed below, the rules are clear. The state where a server is located retains jurisdiction over the acts performed on that state's territory: the creation of the internet account for the foreign *persona non grata*, and the tolerance of that account (and the offensive

---

42 Picture a computer screen full of links, each one subject to the laws of at least one other jurisdiction, and the webpage itself subject to the law of its server on top of all that. Among other things, one shudders to consider the first amendment analysis of a law criminalising the HTML command, <a href = 'www.university.edu/~homepage'>. Or the random link.

43 1987 Restatement SS 403(1) 'Even when one of the bases for jurisdiction ... is present, a state may not exercise jurisdiction to prescribe law with respect to a person or activity having connections with another state when the exercise of such jurisdiction is unreasonable'.

44 William Byassee, 'Jurisdiction of Cyberspace: Applying Real World Precedent to the Virtual Community' (1995) 30 *Wake Forest L Rev* 197.

content) by whatever powers-that-be (typically a sysop)[45] who can exercise some control over the server. The rule of nationality in cyberspace means that American nationals and US corporations[46] cannot circumvent US law by uploading from foreign jurisdictions, assuring the American government a distinct slice of control over content in cyberspace.[47]

The theory of international spaces, then, converts the 'law of the server' into the law of the sysop. It may be a law of vicarious liability, of dubious wisdom, but it would be a law concerning only a sovereign and its territorial jurisdiction over a sysop, which presents no problems at international law. A sysop could be criminally liable for the content over which he has some measure of control, regardless of the nationality or location of the uploader, but an uploader would only be criminally liable if he was located within the territory of the forum state, or was a national of that forum state.

Fortunately for the future of sysops, this result has two drawbacks. First, it may prove impossible to determine where the material was uploaded from, or the nationality of the uploader. Second, this would create a two-class system of servers in cyberspace, those 'located' within the territory of the forum state and those without, while all are equally accessible. National governments are likely to make very little use of the 'law of the sysop', and instead concentrate on regulating downloaders and uploaders.

V   The theory of international spaces

A   Overview

The theory of international spaces begins with one proposition: nationality, not territoriality, is the basis for the jurisdiction to prescribe in outer space, Antarctica, and the high seas. This general proposition must be assembled through observations. In outer space, the nationality of the registry of the vessel, manned or unmanned, is the relevant category. In Antarctica, the nationality of the base governs.[48] Other informal arrangements (USA provides all air traffic control in Antarctica, for instance)[49] weigh heavily in decisions about jurisdiction.

---

45 Sysop means 'system operator,' but is often referred to as a system administrator, with no apparent thought to the inconsistency. System administrators often have very little control over the system, and indeed can often barely keep it running. They are the Dutch boys with their fingers in the dykes; they do not control the weather.

46 The ascribed nationality of corporations is a study in itself. The US government is particularly willing to ascribe nationality liberally to its corporations acting abroad. For an example, see the case of *Dresser France and the Soviet Pipeline* 'Judge Backs US Bid to Penalize Company on Soviet Pipeline Sale', *NY Times*, 25 August 1982 at A1.

47 As a relic of cyberspace's beginnings in the worldwide scientific community, the primary language in cyberspace is English – which helps to explain why Americans are so interested in regulating all of cyberspace. This is changing as cyberspace becomes 'inhabited' by ordinary people around the world. As this happens, the ability of a government to regulate its nationals, and thereby most of what appears in cyberspace in the national language, will surely seem much more valuable than territorial jurisdiction. The history of the printing press is perhaps illustrative. Ordinary publishing began as a trans-European Latin-language venture in the 16th century. By the end of the 17th century, international book commerce had given way to broad national vernacular markets. Benedict Anderson, 1983, *Imagined Communities: Reflections on the Origin and Spread of Nationalism*, London: Verso at p 25.

48 There is a special provision in the Antarctic Treaty for exchanges of scientists and observers. These individuals are subject only to their own national law. Antarctic Treaty, Art VIII (1).

49 See, eg *Beattie v United States* (1984) 756 F 2d 91. The court permitted a lawsuit claiming negligence of US Air Traffic controllers at McMurdo Station, Antarctica.

On the high seas, the nationality of the vessel is the primary rule, the 'law of the flag'. There is an emerging, competing view that at sea there is really 'floating island' jurisdiction, a subspecies of territorial jurisdiction, or even a full sixth principle – not nationality at all.[50] This theory posits that vessels at sea are really 'floating islands', and that the jurisdiction predicated upon them is territorial in nature.[51] The Supreme Court has weighed in against this interpretation, pointing out that stepping on a US vessel is not entering the United States.[52] The 'floating island' theory appears to derive from the obsolete notion that vessels must somehow possess territoriality because 'the right of protection and jurisdiction ... can be exercised only upon the territory'.[53]

One approach is to treat these three areas as *sui generis* treaty regimes. Some scholars see international law as no more than the sum of various international agreements – a purely positivist approach. This approach has the veneer of theoretical consistency, but only if we are unwilling to recognise an evolving organic international system.

Such a thin conception of international law is, at any rate, out of touch with the real treatment of the respective international regimes in American courts. It is usual for American courts to treat these regimes as analogs. *Smith v United States* is typical in this regard:

> ... Antarctica is just one of three vast sovereignless places where the negligence of federal agents may cause death or physical injury. The negligence that is alleged in this case will surely have its parallels in outer space ... Moreover, our jurisprudence relating to negligence of federal agents on the sovereignless high seas points unerringly to the correct disposition in this case. *Smith v United States* (J Stevens, dissent) 507 US 197, 122 L Ed 2d, 548, 556–57 (1993).[54]

---

50 Christopher Blakesley, 'Criminal Law: United States Jurisdiction Over Extraterritorial Crime' (1982) 73 *J Crim L* 1109, 1110, n 6.

51 There actually was a floating island. Fletcher Ice Island (T-3) is 99% ice, seven miles wide, four miles across, and 100 feet thick. No mere iceberg. It was sighted by an American in 1947, and has been occupied by the US since 1952. Fletcher Ice Island meanders around the Arctic Ocean. In 1961, for example, it was grounded on the Alaskan coastline near Point Barrrow. In 1970, it was in the Baffin Sea, 305 miles from Greenland (Denmark) and 200 miles from Ellesmere Island (Canada). That year, Mario Jaime Escamilla was convicted of involuntary manslaughter in a US Federal Court for the shooting death of Bennie Lightsey while both were on Fletcher Ice Island. Bizarrely, the Court of Appeals reversed and remanded the case on procedural grounds, after first noting that it was 'unable to decide' the jurisdictional issue. *United States v Escamilla* 467 F 2d 341, 344 (4th Cir 1972). That is to say: in the only recorded case of a floating island, the court was unable to endorse the 'floating island' theory as a basis for jurisdiction.

52 *United States ex rel Claussen v Day*, 279 US 398 (1929).

53 Henry Glass, *Marine International Law* (1885) at pp 526–27.

54 Justice Stevens went on to claim that a theory of 'personal sovereignty' held in Antarctica. 'As was well settled at English common law before our Republic was founded, a nation's personal sovereignty over its own citizens may support the exercise of civil jurisdiction in transitory actions arising in places not subject to any sovereign.' He cited *Mostyn v Fabrigas*, 98 ER 1021, 1032 (KB 1774). The reader will soon note that it is the physicality of these 'sovereignless regions', above any relevant legal characteristic, which makes the assertion of a similar regime for cyberspace somewhat intrepid. It is precisely this *Pennoyer v Neff* view of sovereignty, presence, and power which we must learn to move beyond.

In *Hughes Aircraft*,[55] the US Court of Federal Claims held that US patent law did not apply to foreign spacecraft in outer space relying 'perhaps most dispositively' on the decision in *Smith v United States* that barred the application of the Federal Tort Claims Act to claims arising in Antarctica.[56] The governing treaties are also similar in their conception and design.[57]

The next theoretical and conceptual hurdle is physicality. These three physical spaces are nothing at all like cyberspace, a nonphysical space. The physical/nonphysical distinction, however, is only one of so many distinctions which could be made between these spaces. After all, one could hardly posit three more dissimilar physicalities – the ocean, a continent, and the sky. What makes them analogs is not any physical similarity at all, but their international, sovereignless quality. These three, like cyberspace, are international spaces. Lest it be forgotten, Antarctica, the high seas, and outer space are only habitable under special circumstances, and the respective regimes resemble each other most where these 'places' are truly uninhabitable.[58]

As a fourth international space, the default rules for cyberspace should resemble the rules governing the other three international spaces, even in the absence of a regime-specific organising treaty, which the other three international spaces have.

B   Evolution of international law

International law is neither a code nor an international common law. Its sources are many and varied, relying heavily on tradition and custom. The statute of the International Court of Justice is illustrative:

1   The Court, whose function is to decide in accordance with international law such disputes as are submitted to it, shall apply:

   (a) international conventions, whether general or particular, establishing rules expressly recognised by the contesting states;

   (b) international custom, as evidence of a general practice accepted as law;

   (c) the general principles of law recognised by civilised nations;

   (d) ... [J]udicial decisions and the teachings of the most highly qualified publicists of the various nations, as a subsidiary means for the determination of rules of law.

Article 38, Stat ICJ

Under this scheme, treaties are only one, albeit the primary, source of law. Customary international law, the grounds for the decision in *The Paquete Habana*, is often the most important part of international law. Treaties generally codify customary law, rather than create new law. This contrasts greatly with civil law systems, in which the code is paramount, and with common law systems, in which statutes and judicial decisions together form the core of the law.

---

55   *Hughes Aircraft v United States* (1993) 29 Fed Cl 197, 231.

56   *Smith v United States* (1993) 507 US 197, 122 L Ed 2d 548.

57   The Outer Space Treaty was based directly on the Antarctic Treaty. See section C, *infra*.

58   Aristotle would be pleased with the symmetry. We have international regimes for uninhabitable earth, uninhabitable air, and uninhabitable water. Cyberspace completes the four elements as fire, which except for Hell is by its nature uninhabitable.

International law, then, is not a model of positive law. Elements of natural law, including notably *jus cogens*, are mixed into positive law and custom without a grand conceptual framework or metanarrative.[59]

Two concepts of particular importance in the disputes over international spaces demonstrate the point: *res nullius* and *res communis*. The debate over the seabed in international waters, Antarctica, and the moon revolved around the possibility of a nation asserting territorial jurisdiction. Under the theory that these things were *res nullius* (a thing of no one), a theory grounded in Roman law and also Lockean concepts of natural law, any state could assert sovereignty, if the traditional tests of the validity of a territorial claim were met.[60] Other nations, especially third world nations, asserted that these areas were *res communis* (a common thing). This argument is echoed in lofty provisions in treaties such as the Seabed Treaty, Outer Space Treaty, and the Antarctic Treaty calling these places the 'common heritage of mankind'. *Res communis* owes its origin to Roman law, natural law theories, and arguments of customary international law – not to mention general principles of equal sovereignty embodied in the League of Nations and United Nations charters.[61]

Given the nature of international law, it is entirely appropriate for a paper to urge the recognition of a general principle of law derived from custom, treaty, and existing general principles of international law.

C   *The case for international spaces*

1   *History*

The history of international space begins at sea. Admiralty law and the law of the high seas owe their modern incarnation to Grotius[62] in the 17th century.[63] The Law of the Sea remains the dominating voice in this discussion of international spaces, and the oceans have long been by far the most important of the international spaces.

While postulated by the ancient Greeks as an opposite for the northern ocean, the southern continent, Antarctica, was not discovered until about 1820. Antarctica did not become the subject of serious international attention until the 1950s, especially during the International Geophysical Year (1957–58).

Outer space has even a stranger history. Visible since time immemorial, outer space remained a mystery until roughly the time of Grotius, when Copernicus, Galileo, and Newton began to understand what it was. It was not until 1957, however, that Sputnik introduced man to the third international space.

---

59 For an excellent and delightful analysis of what it means for international law to lack a metanarrative, see Barbara Stark, 'What We Talk About When We Talk About War' (1996) 32 *Stan J Int L*.

60 Claiming 'undiscovered' islands (with or without natives) requires a mix of history and presence. The Falkland Islands have been disputed by Britain and Spain (and Spain's successor in interest, Argentina) on largely these grounds. One could summarise the theory as follows: Anything not nailed down is mine. Anything I can pry up is not nailed down.

61 As we can see, *res communis* won the day.

62 Hugo Grotius, *De Iure Belli Ac Pacis* [On the Law of War and Peace], 1853, Cambridge: Cambridge University Press.

63 The Roman *mare nostrum* 'our sea' for the Mediterranean was the result of two centuries of no real conflicts-of-law, the *Pax Romana*. Modern international law really begins with the Peace of Westphalia (1648) which endorsed one theory that the sovereign state is the sole building block of the political world. Today this is so ingrained that every individual 'has' a nationality just as he or she has a gender. Benedict Anderson, 1983, *Imagined Communities: Reflections on the Origin and Spread of Nationalism*, London: Verso at p 14.

Cyberspace emerged during the 1970s and 1980s as the apparatus of the internet took root, but it was not until the early 1990s that an explosion in users and uses, including commercial uses, introduced a worldwide virtual community to a new, fourth, international space.

In each international space, international conflict has been a prime mover in forming treaty regimes. For example, it is cynically suggested by some that Grotius was interested in international law at sea only as Dutch naval power was waning. Certainly naval warfare has a long history of increasing importance in international law.

Concerns over the Antarctic pie during the Cold War led to the treaty regime which, in effect, froze[64] the national claims to polar wedges. These competing national claims will be discussed in greater detail below. Some regard the 1982 Falklands war as a war over Antarctic resources.

Humanity's entrance into outer space was attended at its outset by international conflict, primarily surrounding the Cold War, though also encompassing the ambitions of lesser powers such as France.

Similar pressures will soon come to bear in cyberspace. Computer viruses and the 'munitions' status of cryptography[65] ensure that international confrontation will enter cyberspace even if human beings cannot. Cyberspace is as much a space for traditional public international law as for private international law.

2   *Jurisdiction in Antarctica*

The Antarctic Treaty does not itself prescribe a complete system of jurisdiction. Instead, questions relating to the exercise of jurisdiction in Antarctica were included in the illustrative list of matters which may be taken up by Antarctic Treaty consultative meetings.[66] So far no measures dealing specifically with jurisdictional questions have been adopted.[67] The treaty does make some minor provisions, however. The treaty provides for open observation of all bases and the exchange of scientific personnel between these bases. Article VIII SS 1 provides that such observers and scientific personnel be subject to jurisdiction based solely on their nationality, and not on either strict territorial jurisdiction or 'floating island' jurisdiction (ie the notion that the nationality of the base would grant jurisdiction to that state over all persons thereon).

Subsequent treaties have addressed nationality more directly. The Convention for the Conservation of Antarctic Seals (1972) provides expressly in Article 2 that, 'each Contracting Party shall adopt for its nationals and for vessels under its flag such laws, regulations and other measures, including a permit system as appropriate, as may be necessary to implement this convention'. It does not endorse a territorial or universalist approach.

One reason for avoiding questions of territorial jurisdiction in Antarctica is that seven nations have made overlapping claims to various polar wedges of Antarctic territory (Argentina, Chile, the United Kingdom, France, Norway, Australia, and New Zealand). All of these claims are suspended while the treaty

---

64   'Suspended' rather than 'froze' is more accurate, but 'froze' seems to be the universal formulation, apparently because, as with this author, the pun never fails to satisfy.

65   See Stephen Levy, Cyberpunks, *Wired Magazine* 1.2 May/June 1993.

66   Antarctic Treaty Article IX SS 1(e).

67   Sir Arthur Watts, *International Law and the Antarctic Treaty System* (1992) Cambridge: Grotius at p 169.

is operational.[68] Several nations, including the United States and the Soviet Union, deny all claims and, during the Cold War, both superpowers made a point of maintaining bases in all seven claimed areas. The United States accomplished this the easy way, by maintaining a base at the South Pole.

It is essential that we recognise that Antarctica is not just governed by a set of treaties, but by a regime or system. This is acknowledged in several treaties themselves. For example, the Convention on the Regulation of Antarctic Mineral Resource Activities (1988) Article 2.11 reads: 'This Convention is an integral part of the Antarctic Treaty system, comprising the Antarctic Treaty, the measures in effect under that Treaty, and its associated separate legal instruments ...' It is the established practice of the parties to the various treaties to consider them as part of a single whole.[69]

To date there are 40 signatories to the Antarctic Treaty, and all those involved in Antarctica are signatories. For this reason, it is somewhat academic whether the regime applies to non-treaty parties. However, commentators make the argument that the Antarctic Treaty system constitutes an 'objective regime, such that it is valid for, and confers rights and imposes obligations upon third states'.[70] Although the Treaty does not by its own terms apply *erga omnes*, general acquiesce can establish a regime. In addition, the Vienna Convention (which makes clear that a single treaty does not create obligations on third state without its consent – Article 34) does not strictly apply because it was adopted in 1969. It is reasonable to conclude that the Antarctic Treaty Regime has, like the law of the sea, ripened into full international customary law.

There are several American cases dealing with Antarctica, which illustrate the texture of international law in action, lessons clearly lost on the Minnesota Attorney General.

Beattie v United States is a fascinating case about international law, comity, and international spaces. The facts are tragic: an Air New Zealand jet crashed into Mount Erebus, Antarctica, on 28 December 1979, killing all 257 passengers and the crew. Families of the passengers sued the United States government, claiming negligence by the US air traffic controllers at McMurdo Station, Antarctica. The question before the court was whether, under the Federal Tort Claims Act (FTCA), Antarctica fell under the 'foreign country' exception to the waiver of sovereign immunity under the FTCA. The court held that, for these narrow purposes, Antarctica was not a foreign country, and allowed the lawsuit to proceed.[71] In allowing the suit, it cannot have escaped the American court's notice that this accident 'in terms of loss of human life and family bereavement was the worst disaster to strike New Zealand since the end of the 1939–45 war.'[72]

---

68   The treaty was originally to run for 30 years, from 1961 to 1991. It was renewed in 1991, and will likely be renewed indefinitely.

69   Watts, *supra* n 67 at 292.

70   *Ibid*, at 295.

71   The holding that Antarctica was not a 'foreign country' is really limited to the FTCA in this instance, and is not at all a statement about Antarctica's legal status. *Smith v United States* held that Antarctica was a foreign country, and did not allow the suit to go forward. Her husband was a carpenter who fell into a crevasse on a recreational hike from McMurdo station to Scott Base, a New Zealand outpost. *Beattie* was not overruled.

72   *Mahon v Air New Zealand Ltd*, Privy Council, 1 AC 808; [1984] 3 All ER 201 (opinion by Lord Diplock). The Mount Erebus disaster was the subject of parallel case in New Zealand, and was appealed out of Wellington to the Privy Council in London for a hearing on a matter unrelated to international jurisdiction.

Environmental Defense Fund v Massey[73] contains an exposition on the domestic presumption against extraterritorial application of US law. Again, it deals with the McMurdo base, which is an American base near the Ross Ice Shelf. As is typical, the court notes that 'Antarctica is generally considered to be a "global common" and frequently analogised to outer space'.

In declining to apply the presumption, the court holds that 'where there is no potential for conflict between our laws and those of other nations, the purpose behind the presumption [against extraterritoriality] is eviscerated, and the presumption against extraterritoriality applies with significantly less force'. The court would also likely endorse the corollary, that where, as in cyberspace, the potential for conflicts of law is tremendous, the presumption against extraterritoriality is very forceful.

These cases show that domestic law has absorbed the notion of an international regime in Antarctica, analogised to outer space.

3   Jurisdiction in outer space

In outer space, the fundamental document is the Treaty on Principles Governing the Activities of States in the Exploration and Use of Outer Space, Including the Moon and Other Celestial Bodies (1967). The treaty was adopted pursuant to a United Nations General Resolution which contains verbatim much of the text of the Treaty.[74] The Resolution and the Treaty are explicit that states have jurisdiction over objects bearing their registry. Remarkably, this was a unanimous Resolution of the General Assembly.[75]

There is also no doubt that the Treaty for Outer Space was based on the Antarctic Treaty. The Hearings before the Committee on Foreign Relations (US Senate) 1967 actually includes a copy of the Antarctic Treaty. In the hearings, the committee noted that the Outer Space Treaty was specifically based on the Antarctic Treaty.[76]

Article II of the Treaty states that outer space, including the moon, is not subject to claims of sovereignty. Therefore, no territorial jurisdiction is possible. Article III provides that all activities shall be in accordance with international law. This article assures us that international law is not merely a terrestrial phenomenon, but includes all non-sovereign spaces, whether on this earth or beyond it.

The treaty skirts many jurisdictional problems through Article VI which declares that all activities are to be authorised by a state. States are to assure 'national activities' are carried out in conformity with the Treaty. Article VII makes states responsible for damage caused by objects they launch or cause to be launched – the state of registry and the state of the launcher (nationality of the item, and territoriality of the launcher/uploader). Jurisdiction as set forth in Article VIII is then an easy matter: the national registry of an object gives jurisdiction over that object and over any personnel thereof. This national status functions like the 'temporary presence' doctrine announced in *The Schooner Exchange* and *Brown v*

---

73 *Environmental Defense Fund v Massey* (1993) 986 F 2d 528.

74 UN General Resolution 1962 (XVIII) 13 December 1963.

75 Aside from being extremely rare, this unanimous Resolution represents a new multinational approach to new worlds. It is a significant improvement over the Treaty of Tordesillas 1494, in which the Pope divided the whole unclaimed world between the Spanish and the Portuguese.

76 Hearings before Committee on Foreign Relations (US Senate) 1967 p 80.

Duchesne.[77] When the objects return to earth, their special national status for jurisdictional purposes is not affected.[78]

Therefore we can observe that jurisdiction in outer space, as in Antarctica, is predicated on the nationality principle.

4   *Jurisdiction in cyberspace: the vessel of nationality*

Making nationality work as a principle in cyberspace requires an analysis appropriate to cyberspace. It is too easy to fall into the trap of asking how nationality would play out on the high seas, or in Antarctica, and then trying to make direct analogies to cyberspace. As we have seen, the nationality principle is firmly entrenched in these areas, but it plays out differently in each.

For example: if we are applying the 'law of the flag' from maritime law, we can get bogged down in the analysis of how the nationality of a ship is determined. There is, of course, an international regime in place which determines the registry of a ship, and there are such things as 'flags of convenience', under which US nationals may fly a Panamanian flag and be then subject only to Panamanian law at sea.[79] The obvious question might be: 'So, what is the nationality of a vessel in cyberspace?' But then we are at a loss to find a ship or plane in cyberspace. This, again, is asking the wrong question. We must ask first, what is the vessel of nationality in cyberspace, ie, what carries nationality into cyberspace?

Registry will not suffice; it does not exist. International treaties may at a later date specify that all files be 'registered' with a nationality.[80] Until such time, however, we must discover the default rules. Before there was registry at sea, there was still nationality. It was what Justice Stevens recently referred to as the 'personal sovereignty' of the nation over its citizens.[81] In cyberspace, persons bring nationality into cyberspace through their actions. An uploader marks a file or a webpage with his nationality. We may not know 'where' a webpage is, but we know who is responsible for it. The nationality of items in cyberspace is determined by the nationality of the person or entity who put them there, or perhaps by the one who controls them.

This analysis is relatively painless with webpages. The webpage is my paradigm, because the world wide web will surely prefigure the future of cyberspace in being a place where complicated 'sites' are maintained by individuals and organisations. Generally determining the nationality of a page will be no problem. The creator of a webpage is usually listed on the web page, and is typically and individual or an organisation. Webpages are now created by

---

77 *Brown v Duchesne* 60 US 183 (1857).

78 *Hughes Aircraft v United States* 29 Fed Cl 197 (1993). In this case, an invention under US patent was on board a foreign spacecraft in the United States preparing for launch. It was held to be not subject to US law because of the 'temporary presence' doctrine. The court made the usual analogies to Antarctica as well.

79 This is not entirely true. For American tort law, for example, courts insist that passengers be aware of the nationality of the ship. Trying to squeeze this analogy into cyberspace will produce headaches.

80 Will there be a cyberspace convention? George Trudeau has the best answer. In one Doonesbury cartoon strip from the early 1980s, a white, elderly, wealthy New Yorker is talking to her maid about the glories of Harlem in the 1930s. This young black woman is, needless to say, somewhat incredulous. 'Take heart,' says the elderly woman, 'Harlem will rise again.' 'Yes, Ma'am' the maid replies, 'So will Jesus. But I ain't waitin' up nights.'

81 *Smith v United States*, 507 US 197, 122 L Ed 548, 556–57 (J Stevens, dissent).

individuals and companies for others, which makes us ask who 'owns' the page – the creator or the person on whose behalf it is maintained? International law is not displeased with either answer. If a nation wants to, it can ascribe nationality to all webpages maintained 'on behalf of' its citizens, as well as any webpages created (ie, uploaded) by its citizens. Either solution essentially solves the conflict-of-laws problem, by reducing the conflict to two states at the most. Courts will have to make their own judgments about what level of connection between a cyberspace item and an individual is reasonable for the nationality of that person to dictate the jurisdiction to prescribe law. The theory of international spaces turns cyberspace from a place of infinitely competing jurisdictions or Elysian fields of anarchy into a place where normal jurisdictional analysis can continue.

Here is how it might work: a webpage uploaded from Moldova by a Moldovan citizen, but commissioned by a US citizen, which contains pornography violating the 'Internet Decency Act' could subject that US citizen to prosecution (whether American due process is satisfied is another inquiry altogether). Or the Moldovan could be subject to his own uploading laws. Also, a US citizen in Moldova is not immune from US law because he uploads from Moldova (into cyberspace) rather than from the United States. What the United States cannot do is to prescribe a law for a webpage created and uploaded by a Moldovan without any reasonable (ie, recognisable at international law as a basis for the jurisdiction to prescribe) connection to an American national, merely because, in the Minnesota Attorney General's words, it is 'downloadable' in the United States.

Of course, cyberspace is more than the world wide web. There are bulletin boards, USENET groups, and electronic mail (e-mail). These items contain messages sent by individuals. These persons may be anonymous, but anonymity is as much a practical problem for any municipal law as for international law. Once a person is identified, his nationality will provide the basis for the jurisdiction to prescribe rules for his actions in cyberspace. So, for example, the American government may make it illegal to post to alt.sex.bestiality (a USENET group), but this cannot provide the basis for holding a Korean citizen in Korea (without connection to a United States national) criminally liable for posting to alt.sex.bestiality.

A problem arises when cyberspace fades into normal telecommunications. Not all e-mail is in cyberspace. Cyberspace is a virtual community, and international law applies because it is world-readable. We have a different situation when private e-mail is sent from one individual to another across jurisdictional lines. An e-mail from an Arizonan to an Italian is always subject to Arizona law, but could also be subject to Italian law. After all, a telephone call would be. In this case, the Arizonan, in the language of American jurisprudence, 'purposely availed himself' of the benefits of the Italian jurisdiction. This private one-time e-mail definitely falls short of an item in cyberspace, to mere international communication.

Naturally, we need a clearer definition of when we enter cyberspace. Is a message sent 'cc:otherfolks' to several jurisdictions subject to all of those jurisdictions? Can a message intended to defame a Mexican citizen, as in the 1887 *Cutting* case, and actually e-mailed to that citizen, be saved from liability by also sending it to a hundred other individuals? When is it international enough to be cyberspace? What is the line between a postcard and a 'message in a bottle'? This will resolve itself, ultimately, to the intent to cause an effect in a given country. The burden, however, will be on the prosecuting state to prove that an item in cyberspace was targeted to that state, giving that state a special interest above that of other states. We cannot forget either the test of reasonableness of the jurisdiction to prescribe, which (as with all of these issues) will be litigated in the courts of the prosecuting state. Because of the nature of cyberspace, the great potential for conflicts of law, a fairly strong connection between the e-mailer and the target state will be necessary to assert the jurisdiction to prescribe for the target state based on the principle of objective territoriality.

VI   Jurisdiction in cyberspace: a preview

In this final section of the paper, I believe it would be useful to discuss how the theory of international spaces affects two up-and-coming topics in cyberspace law. This is necessarily brief and general, but should describe the outlines of future litigation.

A   Copyright law

Copyright is currently a 'hot topic' in cyberspace law. As the world wide web is full of written information, it will be the source of considerable copyright litigation. Unlike courts hearing criminal cases, courts of general jurisdiction may hear civil cases in which a foreign state has the jurisdiction to prescribe law, and will apply that foreign law. Two American cases, *Religious Technology Center v Netcom*, No C95-20091 RMW (ND Cal, 3 March 1995) and *Playboy Enterprises Inc v Frena*, 839 F Supp 1552 (Md Fla 1993), avoided international jurisdictional problems. Both were cases brought by American nationals against American nationals, all of whom were clearly subject to American territorial jurisdiction. As the adage goes, there can be no conflict of laws unless there is an actual conflict. Either case would be much more interesting if one of the parties had not been subject to US territorial and national jurisdiction. Fair Use doctrine is not a question of international law.

We can, of course, propose a hypothetical situation. What if Scientology's religious books were copyrighted in the United States, but not in Latvia.[82] Now there is a web site uploaded by a Latvian on which is posted a link to a file containing the religious work. All the downloader need do is click on the link, and the copyrighted work will appear on his computer.

At its greatest extent, American copyright law could reach a webpage created by an American, and uploaded in Latvia. It could also reach a webpage created for an American, by a Latvian citizen, and uploaded in Latvia. As a matter of international law, however, the United States would not have jurisdiction to prescribe copyright law for a webpage uploaded by a Latvian in Latvia whose only connection with the United States was a wish that Americans should download this material. In this situation, there is no American nationality on which to predicate such jurisdiction, nor is there territorial jurisdiction. Objective territoriality, or 'effects' jurisdiction is *per se* unreasonable without considerably more.[83] An American court should throw out this suit for want of jurisdiction or

---

82 We are lucky to have law in Latvia, incidentally. There are plenty of places of uncertain national jurisdiction, including: The Transdniester Republic (Transdnistrovia), Chechnya, Nagorno-Karabakh, Western Sahara, the Spratly Islands, the Palestinian 'occupied territories,' Svalbard, Abkhazia, North Cyprus, the Kashmir, the Republika Srbska (in Bosnia-Herzegovina), parts of the Rub'al Khali (Empty Quarter), and territory within the city of Rome belonging to Knights of Malta and enjoying certain extraterritorial rights.

83 How much more? Probably quite a bit, given how hostile Latvian courts would be to such a proposition. Comity would play a huge role here. Because the harm is a private harm, one could argue that there is never a substantial enough copyright violation to cause the state to invoke this extraordinary jurisdiction. Certainly, the harm would have to far exceed a 'normal' copyright violation.

apply Latvian law based on the Latvian nationality of the uploader and controller, and dismiss.

B   Libel

A recent case in the Supreme Court of Western Australia[84] allowed a US national to sue an Australian defendant over a bulletin board (BBS) posting which the US national claimed was defamatory. This would make sense with traditional conflict-of-laws rules, if the publication were in a newspaper in Australia. The analysis is fairly straightforward: if the place of the tort (*lex loci delicti*) was Australia, then Australia has the jurisdiction to prescribe a rule for that action under the principle of subjective territoriality. Under the theory of international spaces, the tort would have to be defined as the uploading of tortious material from Australian territory, in order for Australian law to apply under the principle of subjective territoriality. Australian law probably does not do so, yet.

However, in this case the *lex loci delicti* of the tort of libel is actually in cyberspace. The libel appeared in cyberspace. It was 'published' in cyberspace. In order for a libel to take place, the uploader and the downloader need to be brought together, as they only can in cyberspace. Under the nationality principle, Australia has the jurisdiction to prescribe a law for libels committed by Australian nationals in cyberspace. Australia could permit a US national to sue an Australian in that instance.

If it was the American who had libelled the Australian, the situation is reversed. The Australian could sue the American in Australian courts, but those courts would have to apply US law to the American's action in cyberspace. If US law does not so provide, an Australian may not have the right to sue an American national for libel committed in cyberspace.

VII   Conclusion

This survey of international law and the treatment of the jurisdiction to prescribe in 'vast sovereignless regions' supports the theory of international spaces. Antarctica, outer space, the high seas, and cyberspace, are four international spaces, whose unique character for jurisdictional purposes is the lack of any territorial jurisdiction. In these four places, nationality is, and should be, the primary principle for the establishment of jurisdiction. Such a rule will provide predictability and international uniformity. It strikes a balance between anarchy and universal liability, and it works. Recognition of cyberspace as an international space is more than overdue. It is becoming an imperative.

I will conclude with a hypothetical situation, which may serve as a warning to national courts not yet aware of the international character of cyberspace.

A Danish citizen posts lurid photographs on his personal web page. The government in Copenhagen has not seen fit to forbid the uploading of such material. Indeed, Danish courts may already have deemed such a law unconstitutional. The Dane is visiting a cousin in the United States over Thanksgiving weekend. Learning of his arrival, the FBI telephones a magistrate, giving her the URL[85] and requesting a warrant for his arrest. The magistrate

---

84   *Rindos v Hardwick* No 940164 (31 March 1994) The opinion is unpublished. The details I have on the case come from Jeremy Stone Weber: Note: Defining Cyberlibel: A First Amendment Limit for Libel Suits Against Individuals Arising from Computer Bulletin Board Speech 46 Case W Res 235 (1995).

85   Uniform Resource Locator. This is the set of words (usually preceded by http://) that represents an internet address, which is otherwise just a series of numbers.

soon downloads the offensive material, obscene under *Miller*[86] in any state in the union, and prohibited by the Internet Decency Act, and issues the warrant. The FBI makes the arrest on Thursday.

On Monday morning, the appointed lawyer for the somewhat melancholy Dane files a petition seeking a writ of *habeas corpus*. My client is a Danish national, argues the lawyer, and he uploaded the pornography while in Denmark. The United States has no jurisdiction to prescribe a law for this action under either the nationality principle or the territoriality principle. The Internet Decency Act should be construed to conform to international law, in the absence of an express Congressional intent to violate international law.

Faced with a statute that explicitly proscribes indecent material on the internet, the judge must decide whether to continue to hold the man who has been in jail for three days already. This paper is intended to provide the Dane's lawyer with his argument, and the judge with an answer. [87]

8.4   Protective or security principle

Under this principle, a state can claim jurisdiction over offences committed outside its territory which are considered injurious to its security, integrity or vital economic interests. The principle remains ill-defined and there are uncertainties about how far it can extend. There remains a considerable danger of abuse. Nevertheless, a large number of states have used the principle to a greater or lesser extent. The Commentary to the Harvard Research Draft Convention stated:

> In view of the fact that an overwhelming majority of states have enacted such legislation [relying on the protective principle], it is hardly possible to conclude that such legislation is necessarily in excess of competence as recognised by contemporary international law.

It has been suggested that the principle was applied in the case of *Joyce v DPP* (1946)[88] which involved the trial for treason of the Nazi propagandist William Joyce, also known as Lord Haw-Haw. Joyce was born in the United States, but in 1933 he fraudulently acquired a British passport by declaring that he had been born in Ireland. In 1939 he left Britain and began work for German radio broadcasting propaganda to Britain. The House of Lords had to decide whether the British courts had jurisdiction to try him for treason. They decided that jurisdiction did exist. Lord Jowitt LC answered the question as to whether the English courts could have jurisdiction to try an alien for a crime committed abroad by stating:

> There is, I think, a short answer to this point. The statute in question deals with the crime of treason committed within or ... without the realm ... No principle of comity demands that a state should ignore the crime of treason committed against it outside its territory. On the contrary a proper regard for its own

---

86   *Miller v California* (1971) 413 US 15. It is my opinion that William Byassee is right, and downloading obscene material from cyberspace is protected under the first amendment by *Stanley v Georgia*, 394 US 557 (1969). See William Byassee, *supra* note 1.

87   Darrel Menthe, *Jurisdiction in Cyberspace: The Theory of International Spaces* (1997) http://www.leland.stanford.edu.80/class/law449/papers/menthe.htm

88   [1946] AC 347.

security requires that all those who commit that crime, whether they commit it within or without the realm, should be amenable to its laws.

The House of Lords also found that jurisdiction could be based on the fact that Joyce owed allegiance to the British Crown. Although he was not a British national and the act of treason had occurred outside the United Kingdom, Joyce had availed himself of a British passport and could thereby be deemed to owe allegiance to the Crown and be liable for breach of that allegiance.

The protective personality principle is most often used in cases involving currency, immigration and economic offences. For example, s 170 of the UK Customs and Excise Management Act 1979 creates jurisdiction over acts done abroad, whether committed by UK nationals or not, to further the fraudulent evasion of import restrictions and duties.

8.4.1 The effects doctrine

A development which is linked to the protective principle and to the objective territorial principle is the emergence of a particular type of extra-territorial jurisdiction known as the 'effects doctrine'. According to this doctrine, States claim jurisdiction over acts committed abroad which produce harmful effects within the territory. The rationale behind the effects doctrine is the need to protect national economic interests. The effects doctrine has been particular significant in the area of US anti-trust or anti-cartel law. In the *Alcoa* decision (*US v Aluminium Co of America* (1945))[89] the US Second Circuit Court of Appeals stated that:

Any state may impose liabilities, even upon persons not within its allegiance, for conduct outside its borders that has consequences within its borders which the state reprehends.

The court suggested that jurisdiction would be founded if two conditions were met: the performance of a foreign agreement must be shown to have had some effect in the US, and secondly, this effect must have been intended. The decision provoked widespread opposition outside the US. In *British Nylon Spinners Ltd v Imperial Chemical Industries Ltd* (1953),[90] the English Court of Appeal was willing to issue an injunction preventing compliance with an order of the US courts made as a result of the application of the effects doctrine.

In the face of widespread opinion that the *Alcoa* decision contravened international law, application of the effects doctrine was modified in *Timberlane Lumber Co v Bank of America* (1976)[91] in which it was stated that the courts had to take into account the economic interests of other nations and the nature of the relationship between the defendants and the US. US courts would only exercise extra-territorial jurisdiction if the interests of the US and the effects on US foreign trade were sufficiently strong *vis-à-vis* the interests of other states. In spite of this modification, application of the doctrine continues to be criticised and a number of states have taken action themselves to protect their national

---

89   (1945) 148 F 28 147.

90   [1953] 1 Ch 19.

91   [1976–97] ILR 66.

companies. For example, under the UK Protection of Trading Interests Act 1980 the Secretary of State can prohibit the production of documents or information to a foreign state's courts if that foreign state is indulging in extra-territorial action relating to the control and regulation of international trade. Furthermore, a UK national or resident can sue in an English court for recovery of damages paid under the judgment of a foreign court in such a situation.

In practice little use has been made of such counter-legislation and the US seems further to have moderated its position such that jurisdiction will only be asserted if the main purpose of an anti-trust agreement is to interfere with US trade and such interference actually occurs. It is submitted that implemented in this way the effects doctrine would be little different in practice from the objective territorial principle and the traditional passive personality principle.

There has been discussion as to the extent to which the effects doctrine has been applied by the European Court. In the *Dyestuffs* case (*ICI v Commission* (1972))[92] the court exercised jurisdiction over ICI, for the purposes of the case a national of a non-EEC country, to control the activities of a price-fixing cartel which had been established outside the EEC but which was having effects within the EEC. The European Commission and the Advocate General had supported jurisdiction on implementation of the effects doctrine, although this position had been criticised by a number of member states. The Court, however, sought to justify the exercise of jurisdiction on the fact that ICI was operating through subsidiaries within the EEC. In the *Woodpulp* case (*Ahlstrom Osakeyhtio v Commission* (1988))[93] the Court went further in exercising jurisdiction over 41 woodpulp producers and two trade associations, all of which were non-EEC nationals. The court stated:

> An infringement of Article 85, such as the conclusion of an agreement which has the effect of restricting competition within the Common Market, consists of conduct made up of two elements, the formation of the agreement, decision or concerted practice and the implementation thereof. If the applicability of prohibitions laid down under competition law were made to depend on the place where the agreement, decision or concerted practice was formed, the result would obviously be to give undertakings an easy means of evading those prohibitions. The decisive factor is therefore the place where it is implemented.

The Court went on to state that it was immaterial to the exercise of jurisdiction whether the producers in the case operated through intermediaries or subsidiaries within the Community and further claimed that the exercise of jurisdiction in the case was covered by the territoriality principle. Critics of the decision, such as Dr Francis Mann, have argued that the decision goes further than the *Alcoa* case and is incompatible with the rules of international law. Others have sought to suggest that the decision is only an extension of the objective territorial principle. It seems accurate to state that the effects doctrine *per se* cannot be supported by any of the sources of international law, although supporters of the effects doctrine point to the dictum of the PCIJ in the *Lotus* case as authority for the view that any assertion of jurisdiction is lawful unless it is specifically prohibited.

---

92 [1972] ECR 619.
93 [1988] ECR 5193.

8.5 Nationality principle

Most civil law systems claim a wide jurisdiction to punish crimes committed by their nationals, even on the territory of a foreign state. Those states which make little use of the nationality principle do not appear to protest about its use elsewhere. Although a state may not enforce its laws within the territory of another state, it can punish crimes committed by nationals extra-territorially when the offender returns within the jurisdiction. Jurisdiction based on nationality is less usual in common law countries, although there may be exceptions with regard to serious offences. For example, under English law, the courts have jurisdiction over British nationals who have committed murder or manslaughter, bigamy or treason outside the territory of the UK. It should also be noted that s 70 of the Army Act 1955 provides for the jurisdiction of the UK military legal system over UK military personnel wherever they are stationed. The specific jurisdictional issues raised by foreign troops will be considered in more detail in Chapter 8.

As a general rule, international law sets no limits on the right of a state to extend its nationality to whomsoever it pleases. In the *Nationality Decrees in Tunis and Morocco* case (1923)[94] the PCIJ stated that:

> In the present state of international law, questions of nationality are, in the opinion of the Court, in principle within the [jurisdiction of the state].

This position was confirmed in Article 1 of the Hague Convention on the Conflict of Nationality Laws 1930, which provides that:

> It is for each state to determine under its own law who are its nationals. This law shall be recognised by other states in so far as it is consistent with international conventions, international custom and the principles of law generally recognised with regard to nationality.

In the *Nottebohm* case (1955)[95] the ICJ stated:

> According to the practice of states, to arbitral and judicial decisions and to the opinions of writers, nationality is a legal bond having as its basis a social fact of attachment, a genuine connection of reciprocal rights and duties. It may be said to constitute the juridical expression of the fact that the individual upon whom it is conferred ... is in fact more closely connected with the population of the state conferring nationality than with that of any other state.

Thus the general rule is that there should be some genuine link between a state and the person to whom it grants nationality. The two most important bases upon which nationality is founded are descent from parents who are nationals (*jus sanguinis*) and birth within the territory of the state (*jus soli*). It is also possible for individuals to change nationality, for example by marriage or by naturalisation based on residence. The issue of nationality is considered in more detail in the context of nationality of claims in Chapter 9.

94　(1923) PCIJ Ser B, No 4.

95　[1955] *ICJ Rep* at p 4.

8.6 Passive personality

Under this principle, jurisdiction is claimed on the basis of the nationality of the actual or potential victim. In other words, a state may assert jurisdiction over activities which, although committed abroad by foreign nationals, have affected or will affect nationals of the state. The Harvard Research Draft Convention on Jurisdiction with Respect to Crime 1935 did not list the passive personality principle as a basis of jurisdiction and the commentary to the Draft Convention indicated that state practice with regard to the principle was inconclusive. The principle was rejected by all six dissenting judges in the *Lotus* case. It is argued that in most cases jurisdiction based on the passive personality principle could also be justified on the protective and the universality principle.

The commonly cited example of the principle is the *Cutting* case (1886). Cutting, a US national, had published defamatory statements amounting to a criminal offence against a Mexican national under Mexican law, even though the publication had taken place in Texas. Cutting was convicted of the offence, *inter alia* on the ground that Mexico was entitled to exercise jurisdiction on the basis of the passive personality theory. This view was strongly contested by the US and eventually Cutting was released, although Mexico claimed that the release was due only to the fact that the victim of the defamation withdrew from the action.[96]

The prevailing view has until recently been that the passive personality principle should not be regarded as a proper basis for exercising jurisdiction. The main ground of objection to the principle is the fact that it seems to base jurisdiction solely on the fortuitous fact of the victim's nationality, which may very often be irrelevant to the commission of the offence itself. However, within the last 10 years the US has begun to alter its practice and it remains to be seen the effect this will have on state practice around the world. The first major indication of the change concerned the Achille Lauro affair, in which the United States sought extradition from Italy of the leader of the group which had hijacked the Achille Lauro in 1985. The sole link between the US and the hijacking was that the hijackers had killed Leon Klinghoffer, a US national. Further confirmation of the US change in attitude was provided by the decision of the Court of Appeal, District of Columbia, in *United States v Yunis* (1991).[97] Yunis, a Lebanese national, was charged with hostage-taking and piracy in connection with the hijacking in 1985 of a Royal Jordanian Airline aircraft on which US citizens were travelling. The Court of Appeals upheld the decision of the lower court which found that the passive personality principle did authorise states to assert jurisdiction over offences committed against their citizens abroad. Chief Judge Mikva stated:

> Under the passive personality principle, a state may punish non-nationals for crimes committed against its nationals outside its territory, at least where the state has a particularly strong interest in the case.

---

96 *Moore's Digest*, Vol II (1906) Washington: US Govt at p 228.

97 (1989) 83 *AJIL* 94.

Yunis unsuccessfully argued that the passive personality principle could only apply where the victims were chosen precisely because they were nationals of a particular state, which was not the case here. The court did also base jurisdiction on the universality principle, and it is suggested that in both this case and in the Achille Lauro incident jurisdiction could, and probably should, have been based on the universality principle alone given the nature of the offences involved. The universality principle is discussed at 8.7 (below). The most recent US decision involving the passive personality was made by the Supreme Court in *United States v Alvarez-Machain* (1992).[98] Dr Alvarez-Machain was a Mexican national who was accused of participating in the torture and murder of a US special agent in the Drug Enforcement Agency. The torture and murder had taken place in Mexico. Although there was an extradition treaty between Mexico and the US, Alvarez-Machain was abducted by US agents and flown to the US. At first instance the District Court upheld Mexican complaints that it lacked jurisdiction to hear the case. The decision was upheld in the Court of Appeals, and the US government appealed to the Supreme Court. It held that the US courts had jurisdiction to try the accused as long as the manner in which he was brought to the court did not breach any treaty obligations between the two states. The court examined the extradition treaty and found that the abduction of Alvarez-Marchain did not contravene any express or implied provisions of the treaty. It therefore held that the US courts had jurisdiction. The court ignored the possibility of the abduction being prohibited by customary international law and the decision seems to provide further evidence of the use of the passive personality principle, since the only connection the US had with the case was the fact that the victim of the crime was a US national. It remains possible to argue that jurisdiction in this case could have been based on the universality principle, since the offence involved allegations of torture.

8.7 Universality principle

It has been seen that so far all the bases of jurisdiction have in some way involved a connection with the state asserting jurisdiction. Events have taken place within the territory of the jurisdictional state or they have been committed by or against nationals or in some other way impinge on the interests of the state claiming jurisdiction. International law further recognises that where an offence is contrary to the interests of the international community, all states have jurisdiction irrespective of the nationality of the victim and perpetrator and the location of the offence. The rationale behind the universality principle is that repression of certain types of crime is a matter of international public policy.

The origins of universal jurisdiction can be traced to the fight against piracy. Customary international law provides that any state can exercise jurisdiction over pirates, provided the alleged pirate is apprehended on the high seas or within the territory of the state exercising jurisdiction. Clearly the nature of piracy makes it difficult, if not impossible, for jurisdiction to be based on any of the other principles: the offence is, by definition, committed outside the territory

---

98 [1992] 95 ILR 355.

of any particular state; the nationality of the pirates would not always be possible to ascertain; and those apprehending the pirates would very often not have been the victims of the act of piracy. The rule of customary international law was affirmed in the Convention on the High Seas 1958, Article 19, and is included in Article 105 of the Law of the Sea Convention 1982.

Piracy under international law (or piracy *jure gentium*) must be distinguished from piracy under municipal law. Offenders that may be characterised as piratical under municipal law may not fall within the definition of international law and thus are not susceptible to universal jurisdiction. Piracy *jure gentium* was defined in Article 15 of the High Seas Convention 1958:

Piracy consists of any of the following acts:

(1) Any illegal acts of violence, detention or any act of depredation, committed for private ends by the crew or the passengers of a private ship or private aircraft, and directed:

(a) on the high seas, against another ship or aircraft, or against persons or property on board such a ship or aircraft;

(b) against a ship, aircraft, persons, or property in a place outside the jurisdiction of any state;

(2) Any acts of voluntary participation in the operation of a ship or of an aircraft with knowledge of facts making it a pirate ship or aircraft;

(3) Any act of inciting or of intentionally facilitating an act described in sub-para 1 or sub-para 2 of this article.

The law relating to piracy and the more general issue of jurisdiction on board ships will be considered in more detail in Chapter 10.

A number of other offences have since joined piracy in being regarded as capable of being subject to universal jurisdiction. One of the earliest offences to be so recognised was slave trading. By the second half of the 19th century it was widely accepted that customary international law prohibited the slave trade, and a number of states began to assert jurisdiction over offences connected with slavery on the basis of the universality principle. For example, s 26 of the UK's Slave Trade Act 1873 provides that the English courts have jurisdiction over certain slavery offences irrespective of where or by whom they are committed. The Slavery Convention 1926 further provides for universal jurisdiction over such offences. Since 1945, universal jurisdiction has been provided for in a number of treaties on matters of international concern, for example, torture, drug trafficking, attacks on diplomats, hostage taking and the hijacking and sabotage of aircraft. Jurisdiction over offences relating to aircraft will be discussed in more detail in Chapter 11.

There has been some discussion of the basis of jurisdiction over war crimes and other breaches of the laws of war. Many writers consider that the exercise of jurisdiction over war crimes is a further example of the universality principle and the classic example given is the *Eichmann* case (1961).[99] Adolph Eichmann was head of the Jewish Office of the German Gestapo and, as such, had been responsible for the carrying out of Hitler's 'Final Solution'. In 1960 he was

---

99 [1961] 36 ILR 5.

abducted by Israeli agents in Argentina and brought to Israel where he was charged with war crimes, crimes against humanity and crimes against the Jewish people. During the course of his trial in Jerusalem, his lawyers made objections to Israeli jurisdiction. It was argued that Eichmann had been a German national at the time of the offences which had been carried out elsewhere than on the territory of Israel against persons who were not Israeli nationals. At the time of the offences, of course, Israel did not exist as a state. The Jerusalem District Court found that it did have jurisdiction, stating that:

> The abhorrent crimes defined in the [Israeli Nazi and Nazi Collaborators (Punishment) Law 1951] are not crimes under Israeli law alone. These crimes, which struck at the whole of mankind and shocked the conscience of nations, are grave offences against the law of nations itself (*delicta juris gentium*). Therefore, so far from international law negating or limiting the jurisdiction of countries with respect to such crimes, international law is, in the absence of an International Criminal Court, in need of the judicial and legislative organs of every country to give effect to its criminal interdictions and to bring the criminals to trial. The jurisdiction to try crimes under international law is universal.[100]

Brownlie argues, correctly it is submitted, that a distinction needs to be drawn between such cases where what is being punished is the breach of international law (*delicta juris gentium*) and the true application of the universality principle where international law merely provides that states have a liberty to assert jurisdiction over certain specific acts which are not themselves necessarily breaches of international law. The distinction may be important since the strict application of the universality principle would seem to depend upon the municipal law of the state asserting jurisdiction whereas jurisdiction over international crimes involves interpretation of the provisions of international law. Thus in the *Barbie* case (1983)[101] the French court found that it had jurisdiction over crimes against humanity committed by Klaus Barbie on the basis of the provisions of the relevant international agreements which were not subject to the usual statutory limitations of French law. The subject of war crimes and crimes against humanity will be discussed in more detail in Chapter 14.

8.8 Double jeopardy

It has already been seen that very often it will be the case that more than one state has jurisdiction over a particular act. In such situations the question of double jeopardy arises: if a person is acquitted or convicted in one state, can that person subsequently be prosecuted for the same offence in another state? There is no unequivocal answer: the Harvard Draft Convention does provide that no state should prosecute or punish an *alien* who has been prosecuted in another state for much the same crime. But no reference is made to *nationals* who have been prosecuted in another state. The English courts have generally held that an acquittal or conviction by a court of competent jurisdiction outside England is a bar to indictment for the same offence before any court in England. However, before a plea of *autrefois convict* or *acquit* can be sustained it must be

---

100 [1961] 36 ILR 5 at para 12.
101 [1983] 78 ILR 78.

shown that the defendant stands in jeopardy of punishment for a second time. Thus in *R v Thomas* (1984) the defendant could be tried in England for an offence for which he had already been tried and convicted in Italy since he had been tried and convicted in his absence and there appeared little likelihood of his actually serving his sentence in Italy.

8.9 Extradition

The term extradition denotes the process whereby, under treaty or upon a basis of reciprocity, one state surrenders to another state at its request a person accused or convicted of a criminal offence committed against the laws of the requesting state, such requesting state having jurisdiction. The rationale behind the law and practice of extradition is as follows:

(a) a desire not to allow serious crimes to go unpunished. Frequently a state in whose territory a criminal has taken refuge cannot prosecute the offence because of a lack of jurisdiction. It will therefore surrender the criminal to a state that can try and punish the offence;

(b) the state on whose territory the offence has been committed is the best able to try the offence because of the availability of evidence etc.

Extradition developed in the 19th century through the use of bilateral treaties, and the principle was accepted that there was no right to extradite, although there is also no rule forbidding the surrender of offenders. In England, extradition is governed by the Extradition Act 1989. Extradition is more principally a matter for municipal law although a number of general principles can be discerned.

Before extradition can be ordered two conditions must be satisfied:

1 there must be an extraditable person;

2 there must be an extradition crime. Such crimes are usually listed in the extradition agreement and very often political crimes, military offences and religious offences are not extraditable. Obviously the definition of such crimes is an area for much argument and there have been a number of cases involving arguments about the extent to which acts of terrorism constitute political crimes.

A usual requirement is that of double criminality: the act should be a crime in both states. Furthermore, it is a general principle that a state should not try an offender for any offence other than the one for which he was extradited.

A particular question that has been raised in the *Lockerbie* case (1992) is whether, in situations where more than one state has jurisdiction over an offence, a state can insist on the extradition of a defendant from a state which is willing to prosecute the offence itself. The matter was not considered by the ICJ when Libya made its request for provisional measures of protection, but it is likely to be raised when the merits of the case are heard.

8.10 Asylum

Linked to the question of extradition is asylum. It involves two elements: shelter and a degree of active protection. It may be either territorial asylum, granted by a state on its territory, or extra-territorial asylum, granted in consular premises, diplomatic missions, etc. The general view is that every state has a right to grant territorial asylum subject to the provisions of any extradition treaty in force. The granting of territorial asylum is regarded as an aspect of state territorial sovereignty. A more important question is whether there ever exists any duty to grant asylum. The right to grant extra-territorial asylum is more controversial and needs to be established in each case, since it involves a derogation from territorial sovereignty.

Article 14, Universal Declaration of Human Rights 1948 provides that:

1   Everyone has the right to seek and enjoy in other countries asylum from persecution.

2   This right may not be invoked in the case of prosecutions genuinely arising from non-political crimes or from acts contrary to the purposes and principles of the United Nations.

A resolution of the UN General Assembly, the Declaration on Territorial Asylum, which was adopted on 14 December 1967 recommended a number of practices and standards:

1   a person seeking asylum from persecution should not be rejected at the frontier – the individual case should be considered properly. This is generally known as the principle of *non-refoulement*;

2   if a state finds difficulty in granting asylum, international measures should be taken to try and alleviate the burden;

3   asylum should be respected by all other states.

The preamble to the declaration made clear that the grant of asylum to persons fleeing persecution is a peaceful and humanitarian act that cannot be regarded as unfriendly by any other state. It now seems to be accepted that the principle of *non-refoulement* is part of customary international law and is a fundamental rule of refugee law. Refugees are defined as those having a well-founded fear of persecution. What has yet to be settled is how the phrase 'well-founded fear of persecution' is to be construed. In particular it is not clear whether the test is an objective or a subjective fear; whether it depends solely on the refugee's own perceptions or whether the views of the receiving or the alleged persecuting state are significant. There are a number of treaties dealing with the rights of refugees, in particular the Refugee Convention 1951 as amended by the Protocol 1967.

As far as extra-territorial asylum is concerned, there exists no general right to grant diplomatic asylum. This point was confirmed by the ICJ in the *Asylum* case (1950).[102] Exceptionally extra-territorial asylum may be granted:

(a) as a temporary measure to individuals in physical danger;

(b) where there is a binding local customary rule that diplomatic asylum is permissible;

(c) under special treaty.

---

102 [1951] *ICJ Rep* at p 1.

8.11   Illegal seizure of offenders

Article 16 of the Harvard Draft Convention provided that no state should have jurisdiction over an offender who had been brought within its territory as a result of measures which themselves breached international law. However, the article appears to be more in the nature of *lege ferenda* than of *lex lata*. state practice seems to establish that the illegal seizure of offenders in the territory of another state is not of itself a bar to the exercise of jurisdiction. In the *Eichmann* case (1961)[103] the defendant was unlawfully seized by Israeli agents in Argentina and transported to face trial in Israel. In *United States v Yunis* (1991),[104] the US courts found that they had jurisdiction although Yunis, a Lebanese national, had been lured onto a yacht in the Mediterranean by FBI agents and then arrested once the yacht entered the high seas. In both cases there was in existence no formal extradition arrangements between the countries involved and thus some writers have argued that seizure of offenders would negate any claim to jurisdiction if extradition would have been possible. However, in the *United States v Alvarez-Marchain* (1992)[105] the Supreme Court held that the US courts had jurisdiction in spite of the fact that Dr Alvarez-Machain had been seized by US drug enforcement agents in Mexico although an extradition treaty was in force between the US and Mexico. In *R v Plymouth Justices, ex p Driver* (1986)[106] the British police wished to interview Driver, who was in Turkey. No extradition arrangements existed between the UK and Turkey and the police therefore asked the Turkish authorities for assistance. As a result Driver was detained and transported to Britain where he was charged with murder. He argued that the English courts had no jurisdiction, but the Divisional Court held that once a person was lawfully in custody within the jurisdiction the courts had no power to inquire into the circumstances by which that person came into the jurisdiction.

Of course, while the manner in which a defendant is brought before the court may not be a ground for denying jurisdiction, it is possible that the manner in which a defendant is seized may involve other breaches of international obligations. In general, the seizure of defendants by government agents acting outside the territory will amount to a breach of the principle of non-intervention in the domestic affairs of another state and will give rise to international liability. In the *Eichmann* case,[107] the Argentinean authorities made strong protests to Israel about the capture of Adolph Eichmann although the dispute between the two states was resolved before the case came to trial.

---

103 [1961] 36 ILR 5.
104 [1991] 30 ILM 403.
105 [1992] 95 ILR 363.
106 [1986] 1 QB 95.
107 [1961] 36 ILR 5.

8.12 The wrongful exercise of jurisdiction

As was stated at the beginning of this chapter, international law is concerned with the propriety of the exercise of jurisdiction. The exercise of jurisdiction over aliens and with respect to events occurring outside the territory may well constitute interference in the domestic affairs of another state. In general, international law prohibits such intervention and it therefore follows that a wrongful exercise of jurisdiction may give rise to liability to another state even in the absence of any intention to harm that other state.

CHAPTER 9

IMMUNITIES FROM NATIONAL JURISDICTION

9.1 Introduction

As was seen in Chapter 7, the principal basis for jurisdiction is territorial. States are recognised as having authority over people, things and events within their own territory and therefore may exercise jurisdiction over them. However, international law does recognise that certain people, things and events are entitled to immunity from the enforcement of local law. It should be noted that immunity is from enforcement rather than from the law itself. It is these exceptions to territorial enforcement which are the subject of this chapter. Traditionally there have been two beneficiaries of the exception: foreign states and foreign diplomats. More recently international organisations have also been accorded certain immunities.

Today, immunity from jurisdiction may be enjoyed by:

(a) foreign states and heads of foreign states (including public ships of foreign states);

(b) armed forces of foreign states;

(c) diplomatic representatives and consuls of foreign states;

(d) international organisations.

An initial point that should be noted is the distinction to be drawn between the related concepts of 'immunity' and 'non-justiciability'. Where an issue is non-justiciable the municipal court has no competence to assert jurisdiction at all. A non-justiciable matter is one that cannot be the subject of judicial proceedings before a municipal court. Immunity arises where the municipal court would ordinarily have jurisdiction but because of the identity of one of the parties involved the court will refrain from exercising that jurisdiction. One of the consequences of the distinction is that it is possible for immunities to be waived but the courts will never be able to consider matters which are non-justiciable. This chapter is principally concerned with immunities.

9.2 State immunity

9.2.1 The basis of state immunity

The traditional view of immunity was set out by Chief Justice Marshall of the United States Supreme Court in *Exchange v McFaddon* (1812).[1] The case concerned a ship, the Exchange, whose ownership was claimed by the French government and by a number of US nationals. The US Attorney General argued that the court should refuse jurisdiction on the ground of sovereign immunity. Chief Justice Marshall stated:

> The full and absolute territorial jurisdiction being alike the attribute of every sovereign, and being incapable of conferring extraterritorial power, would not

---

1   (1812) 7 Cranch 116.

seem to contemplate foreign sovereigns nor their sovereign rights as its objects. One sovereign being in no respect amenable to another; and being bound by obligations of the highest character not to degrade the dignity of his nation, by placing himself or its sovereign rights within the jurisdiction of another, can be supposed to enter a foreign territory only under an express licence, or in the confidence that the immunities belonging to his independent sovereign station, though not expressly stipulated, are reserved by implication, and will be extended to him.

State immunity developed from the personal immunity of sovereign heads of state. At an international level all sovereigns were considered equal and independent. It would be inconsistent with this principle if one sovereign could exercise authority over another sovereign. The immunity of sovereigns is expressed in the maxim *par in parem non habet imperium*. In medieval times ruler and state were regarded as synonymous, and sovereignty was regarded as a personalised concept. By the time of *Exchange v McFaddon* it was clear that sovereign had a representative character and that actions taken on behalf of the sovereign, or in the name of the sovereign, were capable of attracting the same immunities.

State immunity can also be linked to the prohibition in international law on one state interfering in the internal affairs of another. In *Buck v AG* (1965),[2] the Court of Appeal was called upon to discuss the validity of certain provisions of the Constitution of Sierra Leone and refused on the basis that it lacked jurisdiction. In the course of his judgment, Diplock LJ stated:

> The only subject-matter of this appeal is an issue as to the validity of a law of a foreign independent sovereign state ... As a member of the family of nations, the Government of the United Kingdom observes the rules of comity, *videlicet* the accepted rules of mutual conduct as between state and state which each state adopts in relation to other states and expects other states to adopt in relation to itself. One of those rules is that it does not purport to exercise jurisdiction over the internal affairs of any other independent state, or to apply measures of coercion to it or its property, except in accordance with the rules of public international law. One of the commonest applications of this rule ... is the well known doctrine of sovereign immunity ... the application of the doctrine of sovereign immunity does not depend upon the persons between whom the issue is joined, but upon the subject-matter of the issue.

The question arises as to whether immunity arises *ratione personae* or *ratione materiae*. This quotation would seem to support the view that immunity applies only *ratione materiae*, but other writers are not so sure:

> ... does [immunity] apply *ratione personae* or *ratione materiae*? The answer is probably both. Immunity applies *ratione personae* to identify the categories of persons, whether individuals, corporate bodies or unincorporated entities, by whom it may *prima facie* be claimable; and *ratione materiae* to identify whether substantively it may properly be claimed ... [3]

---

2   [1965] Ch 745.

3   Sinclair, 'The Law of Sovereign Immunity; Recent Developments' (1980) 167 *Hague Recueil* 113.

It seems better to suggest a twofold test: first, is the entity concerned entitled to immunity (*ratione personae*) and then, if the answer is yes, is the act itself one which carries immunity (*ratione materiae*).

9.2.2 Absolute and restrictive immunity

The traditional doctrine of state immunity was absolute in that immunity attached to all actions of foreign states. With the rise of industrialisation during the 19th century, States became more involved in commercial activities, particularly in the area of railways, shipping and postal services. The emergence of the Communist states in the first half of the 20th century and the increasing use of nationalisation as a tool of economic development resulted in a massive growth in the commercial activity of states. It became increasingly common for private individuals and corporations to enter into contracts with foreign state trading organisations. Should a dispute subsequently arise the foreign state trading organisation would be able to rely on the doctrine of sovereign immunity and deny the other party the protection of municipal law. This situation led to calls for the modification of the absolute immunity of states and it was suggested that a distinction could be drawn between the public acts of states (acts *jure imperii*) and private acts (trading and commercial acts – acts *jure gestionis*). Under a restrictive view of immunity it would only be acts *jure imperii* that would attract immunity. In *Dralle v Republic of Czechoslovakia* (1950)[4] the Supreme Court of Austria carried out a comprehensive survey of state practice and concluded that in the light of the increased commercial activity of states the classic doctrine of absolute immunity had lost its meaning and was no longer a rule of international law. In 1952 the US State Department issued the Tate Letter which stated that immunity would only be given to public acts and no longer to private acts. This restrictive approach was supported by four justices of the Supreme Court in *Alfred Dunhill of London Inc v Republic of Cuba* (1976)[5] and the doctrine of restrictive immunity was confirmed in the US Foreign Sovereign Immunities Act 1976.

It should be noted that the doctrine of absolute immunity still applies to Heads of State and is usually extended to such members of their family that form part of their household.

9.2.3 The British position

British practice with regard to state immunity has undergone a series of changes. In the mid-19th century the authorities seemed to conflict and there was certainly some evidence of a restrictive view being taken. For example, in *De Haber v Queen of Portugal* (1851),[6] the Lord Chief Justice seemed to favour a restrictive view of immunity when he said:

> ... an action cannot be maintained in an English court against a foreign potentate for anything done or omitted to be done by him *in his public capacity* as

---

4   [1950] 17 ILR 165.
5   425 US 682 (1976).
6   (1851) 17 QB 171.

representative of the nation of which he is head ... no English Court has jurisdiction to entertain any complaints against him in that capacity (at p 207 – emphasis added).

The case seen for a long time as the main authority on state immunity was *The Parlement Belge* (1880).[7] In that case, which concerned a mail ship owned and controlled by the King of Belgium and crewed by the Royal Belgian Navy, the Court of Appeal held that it lacked jurisdiction 'over the person of any sovereign ... of any other state, or over the public property of any state which is destined to its public use'. Forty years later, the Court of Appeal in *The Porto Alexandre* (1920)[8] relied on *The Parlement Belge* to find that immunity attached to a ship which had been requisitioned by the government of Portugal and used to carry cargo belonging to a private company. It was argued that the ship was engaged on an ordinary commercial undertaking, but the court held that that was not capable of displacing the rule of absolute immunity laid down in *The Parlement Belge*. The doctrine of absolute immunity was seen at its most extreme in *Krajina v The Tass Agency* (1949).[9] In that case, Krajina claimed damages for a libel contained in the Soviet Monitor which was published by the London office of the Tass news agency. The Soviet Ambassador to the United Kingdom certified that Tass was a department of state of the Soviet Union and the Court of Appeal accordingly decided that it was entitled to immunity. The decision provoked widespread criticism and led to the setting up of a government committee to consider the whole question of state immunity. The committee found that the UK did accord a greater immunity than that granted by many other states but was unable to agree on the question of the degree of immunity required by international law. The courts continued to apply the absolute doctrine, although in *Rahimtoola v Nizam of Hyderabad* (1958)[10] Lord Denning, in a dissenting judgment, put the case strongly for adopting a restrictive approach.

By the 1970s a significant number of states had adopted the restrictive approach, and following lengthy discussions the Council of Europe promulgated the European Convention on state Immunity 1972 which the United Kingdom signed. Its provisions were incorporated into English law by the State Immunity Act 1978 which entered into force on 22 November 1978. Before the Act came into force the British courts had already shown a change in approach in two notable cases: *The Philippine Admiral* (1977)[11] and *Trendtex Trading Corporation Ltd v Central Bank of Nigeria* (1977).[12] The latter case was notable for the judgment of Lord Denning, to which reference has already been made in Chapter 2. In that case the Court of Appeal held that restrictive immunity was now firmly established as a rule of customary international law and it could therefore be incorporated into the common law without need for Act of Parliament. This point was confirmed by the House of Lords in *I Congreso*

---

7   (1880) 5 PD 197.
8   (1920) p 30.
9   [1949] 2 All ER 274.
10 [1958] AC 379.
11 [1977] AC 373.
12 [1977] 2 WLR 356.

del Partido (1981),[13] a case which concerned matters occurring before the State Immunity Act came into force.

The State Immunity Act 1978 provides in s 1 that states are immune from the jurisdiction of the courts of the United Kingdom except as provided in the Act. The Act contains 10 provisions which create exceptions to the main rule. Probably the most important exception is provided in s 3:

(1) A state is not immune as respects proceedings relating to

    (a)   a commercial transaction entered into by the state; or

    (b)   an obligation of the state which by virtue of a contract (whether a commercial transaction of not) falls to be performed wholly or partly in the United Kingdom.

Subsection 3(3) lists those transactions which will be considered commercial:

    (a)   any contract for the supply of goods or services;

    (b)   any loan or other transaction for the provision of finance and any guarantee or indemnity in respect of any such transaction or of any other financial obligation; and

    (c)   any other transaction or activity (whether of a commercial, industrial, financial, professional or other similar character) into which a state enters or in which it engages otherwise than in the exercise of sovereign authority;

but neither paragraph of subsection (1) above applies to a contract of employment between a state and an individual.

The principle established by the Act is the classical one: it is the foreign[13] state that is immune from the jurisdiction of the courts.[14] The Act does not speak of a sovereign state. On the existence of a state (and of many other international facts) the Secretary of State's certificate is conclusive evidence;[15] the question whether an unrecognised state is entitled to immunity will, therefore, not come up for judicial decision and it is quite possible that in a given case the Secretary of State's certificate may, in effect, be able to answer that question in the affirmative and thus, contrary to traditional learning, withdraw a point of law from judicial decision – an unfortunate and, possibly, objectionable[16] result. The beneficiaries of immunity, however, comprise a number of defendants other than a state. Their definition invites a few comments.

1   The reference to a state includes, of course, its sovereign, 'in his public capacity'[17] (who and whose family shall enjoy the benefit of the Diplomatic Privileges Act 1964[18] as well as the government and its departments.[19] No serious difficulties are likely to arise in respect of these defendants.

---

13   [1981] 2 All ER 1064.

14   This includes a Commonwealth state.

15   Section 1 of the State Immunity Act 1978.

16   Section 21.

17   If and so far as the Foreign and Commonwealth Office purports to decide a question of law there may be a violation of Art 6 of the European Convention on Human Rights.

18   Section 14(1)(a).

19   Section 20.

2   Immunity is also enjoyed by an *entity*, ie, a body capable of suing and being sued, which is not distinct from, that is to say, is a part of, the executive organs of the government.[20] This is to be distinguished from a *separate entity*, ie, a body capable of suing and being sued and distinct from the executive organs of the government; such entity is immune only in certain circumstances to be considered later.

The Act, therefore, does not attach significance to the question whether under its own law the entity is a body corporate, a legal person, or not. It is possible that the entity meets the test of the prescribed procedural status, although it is not a body corporate in the English sense. The Act accepts the decision of a majority in the Court of Appeal[21] according to which a legal entity is entitled to immunity if in substance it is a department of state. The frequently difficult question of whether or not a body is a corporate one has become irrelevant.

Whether the entity which is capable of suing and being sued is 'distinct from the executive organs of the government' is a question of fact and depends on foreign law, *viz* the status which the foreign law confers upon the entity rather than the factual situation. If the entity is intended by the legislator to be distinct, then the fact that it acts in accordance with the directions of the government does not matter. Conversely, if the entity is not intended by the law to be distinct, its actual independence of government organs cannot deprive it of immunity.

It is distinctness from executive organs that matters. Accountability to Parliament or parliamentary organs such as a Public Accounts Committee is immaterial. And the distinctness, it is believed, must be of an organisational character in the sense that the test is provided by the existence of the right of executive organs to give directions about the conduct of the entity's daily business. Political independence is a different and irrelevant point: the entity may have to observe the general lines of the government's policy, yet be distinct from its executive organs. In practice it will probably be helpful to ask whether in substance the entity is a department of government or carries on its business independently, albeit in line with general government policy.

3   Constituent Territories of a federal state have been dealt with somewhat oddly. As a rule they are treated as if they were a separate entity except that s 12 relating to services of process and judgments in default of appearance applies to them in any case. An Order in Council, however, may provide for other provisions to apply as they apply to a state.[22] This creates uncertainty and exposes a legal question to political influence and pressure, but in view of an unsatisfactory provision of the European Convention[23] the British legislator probably had to adopt some such solution.

A corporation which is 'part and parcel' of a department or an arm of the government of a constituent territory, such as the New Brunswick Development Corporation was found to be in relation to the Province of New Brunswick,[24] is not specifically mentioned in the Act and would appear to be disentitled to

---

20 Section 14(1),

21 *Baccus SA v Nacional del Trigo* [1957] 1 QB 438 (Jenkins and Parker LJJ, Singleton LJ dissenting). Noted (1957) *Modern Law Review* 20 at p 273.

22 Section 14(5).

23 Article 28; see SI 1979/457 relating to Austria's constituent territories.

24 *Mellenger v New Brunswick Development Corporation* [1971] 1 WLR 604; *cf Swiss-Israel Trade Bank v Government of Malta* [1972] 1 Lloyd's Rep 497. On both cases see comment (1973) *Modern Law Review* 38 at p 18.

immunity. *Ex hypothesi* it is not and cannot be an entity which is part of the central government and therefore covered by s 14(1). And s 14(5) and (6) as summarised above only refers to the immunity of the constituent territory itself (for instance, 'as if it were a separate entity'), but does not touch a separate entity or a corporation created by the constituent territory. Nor can such an entity be treated as if it were a department of the constituent territory's government. The wording is so clear that a body corporate which is separate and distinct cannot be put on the same level as its creator. Different reasoning was possible and was in fact adopted under the common law, but it is not supported by the accepted canons of statutory interpretation. Nor is there any cause for regretting that such a body as the New Brunswick Development Corporation no longer enjoys immunity in this country. International law did not at any time confer such a privilege upon it.

Exceptions to immunity

The Act includes 10 provisions which create exceptions to the rule of immunity established by the first section. Many of them and certainly those which in practice are the most important ones are founded upon the existence of a 'commercial transaction' or of 'commercial purposes'. They adopt the distinction between acts *jure imperii* and acts *jure gestionis*, which in 1951 the Inter-Departmental Committee had rejected as unacceptable. What is more, to a large extent they refrain from a definition, but leave it to the courts to work out the distinction. In fact 'commercial purposes' is defined in s 17(1) in somewhat circular terms, namely by reference to the definition of 'commercial transaction', in s 3. It is a field which has yielded a large harvest in foreign jurisdictions. Both the Brussels and the European Conventions as well as the recent legislation adopted by the United States of America have accepted exceptions based on the commercial character of the activity. There can be no question of foreign legal developments being a source of law governing the interpretation of an English statute. Yet where the English statute intends to codify the law in a manner consistent with international law, comparative material will have persuasive material of varying strength in construing terms that are now accepted to be common to most countries and expressive of the present state of public international law.

Another general point which requires emphasis is that it would be unjustifiable to subject ss 2 to 11 of the Act to a narrow construction on the ground that they contain exceptions to the principle laid down in s 1. The European Convention precluded any such argument by enumerating in Articles 1 to 14 the circumstances in which a state is not entitled to immunity and by providing in Article 15 for immunity 'if the proceedings do not fall within' the former group. In England it has frequently been a technique of statutory interpretation to say that an exception does not derogate from the principle to a greater extent than the words strictly require, that, in other words, in case of doubt the principle rather than the exception should be held to apply.[25] But this is not invariably so and should certainly not be so in the present case. What the legislator described as exceptions represents a very broad sector of state activity. Its limits should be so drawn as to fit the legislative purpose behind each provision rather than the drafting technique that the legislator followed. The so-called exceptions are a far-

---

25 Such suggestions have frequently been made. See, eg Cockburn LJ in *Sowerby v Smith* [1884] LR 9 CP 524 at 532 where he said that a certain provision 'being in derogation of the freehold given by the Act ... must, I think, be construed most strictly'.

reaching group of provisions which are not subordinate, but equal to, on the same level as the so-called principle. Hence the rule usually applicable to the construction of exceptions does not fit.

The 10 exceptions and their principal implications are as follows:

1   The state which 'has submitted to the jurisdiction of the courts of the United Kingdom' is disentitled to immunity. Submission may come about in four different ways.[26]

First by prior written agreement – an important change in the law of the United Kingdom. Whether there is an agreement and how it is to be construed will be a matter for the proper law of the contract.[27] The Act states that submission of an agreement to English law is not tantamount to submission to English jurisdiction. On the other hand, if English law applies, a clause such as that authorising an English solicitor to accept service or process ought to be treated as a submission. Whether the agreement is in writing is likely to be a matter for English law, which would have no difficulty in holding that the exchange of telex or cable messages or a written reference to an unsigned document such as the identifiable printed form of a contract constitutes sufficient writing. Whether a state which repudiates the agreement to submit remains subject to jurisdiction is likely to come up for judicial decision, it is submitted that the question should be answered in the affirmative.[28]

Secondly, submission may occur 'after the dispute giving rise to the proceedings has arisen'. Here no formality would seem to be required. Once there is a dispute (and it may not always be easy to define its beginning) even an oral statement accepting jurisdiction will be sufficient; a submission in proceedings actually pending does not seem to be required.

If the state 'has intervened or taken any step in the proceedings' then it is 'deemed to have submitted'; this is the third method. If one accepts the law relating to the Arbitration Act 1950, an unconditional appearance will not be regarded as a step in the proceedings,[29] nor will the claim to immunity so be regarded, as the Act expressly states.

The fourth case is the obvious one in which the state itself has instituted the proceedings. In such event the state is exposed to a counter-claim which 'arises out of the same legal relationship or facts as the claim'. It is not necessary that a court in the United Kingdom has (local) jurisdiction in respect of the cross-claim made by the defendant. It is possible, therefore, that the defendant may pursue a claim which he could not pursue by writ.

2   The second exception will in practice be the most important one. According to s 3 the state does not enjoy immunity 'as respects proceedings relating to (a) *a commercial transaction* entered into by the state, or (b) an obligation of the state which by virtue of a contract (whether a commercial transaction or not)

---

26   Section 2.

27   This is the effect of the decision of the House of Lords in *Nova (Jersey) Knit Ltd v Kammgarnspinnerei* [1977] 1 WLR 713 where the agreement required by s 1(1) of the Arbitration Act 1975 was considered to be subject to German Law.

28   The analogy of such cases as *Heyman v Darwins* [1942] AC 356 and of the established practice of the International Court of Justice (see, eg *Fisheries Jurisdiction* case (*United Kingdom v Iceland*) [1973] *ICJ Rep* at p 3) may prove helpful.

29   Section 4.

falls to be performed wholly or partly in the United Kingdom', provided that the latter rule does not apply 'if the contract (not being a commercial transaction) was made in the territory of the state concerned and the obligation in question is governed by its administrative law'.

The rule laid down by sub-para (b) will be readily understood. It is likely to cover many cases. The legal problem which primarily causes difficulty is whether the requirement of total or partial performance in the United Kingdom is to be determined by English law or by the proper law of the contract which, so it must be assumed, is intended by the legislator to govern the existence as well as the construction of the contract, though not its commercial character. The difficulty thus alluded to has arisen in many contexts and is a famous one in the conflict of laws;[30] it led only recently to a decision of the European Court of Justice.[31] It is suggested, though with much hesitation, that it would be so artificial to subject the construction of the contract and the determination of the place of performance to different legal systems that there will be no alternative but to allow the proper law to prevail in both respects.

Nor will sub-para (a) cause much difficulty in the majority of cases, for the Act defines 'commercial transaction' in the widest terms so as to comprise all contracts (except contracts of employment) and any other transaction into which a state enters 'otherwise than in the exercise of sovereign authority'.

In effect, therefore, not only concession agreements but practically every other type of contract will be within the exception, including those contracts which have given trouble to tribunals as well as scholars. The legislator has decided in favour of the objective test of the nature of the transaction and completely disregarded the Inter-Departmental Committee which in 1951 thought[32] that the principle of *jure gestionis* (now adopted as an exception) was not one 'which, even if justified by international law ... could be incorporated into our law as a principle'. The Act of 1978 has provided a definition and made it quite clear that all the contracts which in 1951 were apparently thought to be acts done *jure imperii* are commercial transactions. Government loans, shoes for the army, warships, guns, aeroplanes – all these are the subject matter of commercial transactions in respect of which immunity cannot be claimed. As mentioned above, even a mining concession agreement, though not a contract within the category of contracts mentioned in (b), would be a commercial transaction, because it would be 'any other transaction' ... into which a state enters', unless 'the parties to the dispute are states or have otherwise agreed in writing'. A substantial limitation, however, is due to the fact that before immunity or its absence falls to be considered an English court must have (territorial) jurisdiction, and this will frequently be a serious hurdle for the plaintiff. A very important point must be emphasised: the denial of immunity is independent of the nature of the act from which the claim arises. If the transaction or activity into which a state enters or in which it engages is a commercial one, the state is disentitled to immunity even in cases in which, for instance, the breach of contract arises from an act done in the exercise of sovereign authority. All that matters is the

---

30 Cf Mann, *The Legal Aspect of Money*, 3rd edn, 1971, Oxford: Oxford University Press at pp 206–08.

31 *Etablissements A De Bloos v Etablissements Bouyet SA* [1977] 1 CMLR 60.

32 Paragraph 5.

character of the transaction or activity carried on by the state as opposed to the facts on which the claim or the defence is founded.[33] These facts may even constitute an act of state. As the law stands, its validity probably may not be questioned for reasons which have nothing to do with the Act of 1978, but if the court is concerned only with its effects upon what is a commercial transaction it is not precluded from considering them either by the rule of immunity or by the alleged sacrosanctity of the act of state.[34]

The puzzling feature of s 3 lies in the fact that, according to the definition, the term 'commercial transaction' includes 'any ... activity ... in which [the state] engages otherwise than in the exercise of sovereign authority'. The state is not immune 'as respects proceedings relating to' such an activity. It is submitted that the definition is such as to render it possible to sue a foreign state in respect of a tort other than those mentioned in ss 5 to 7 which has been committed in England, such a tort providing the court with (territorial) jurisdiction according to Order 11 rule 1(h) of the Rules of the Supreme Court. In this somewhat unexpected manner torts do come within the scope of the Act in such a case as *Krajina v The Tass Agency*,[35] but also other cases involving, for instance, claims for damages for fraud or conspiracy. The same applies to cases in which confidential information has been imparted to a foreign state, but misused by it or its agent – a by no means inconceivable situation. The only activity which cannot in any circumstances be a commercial activity is one exercised by virtue of sovereign authority – a phrase which, it is submitted, only qualifies the word 'activity', not the words 'any other transaction'. The term will have to be construed according to English law.[36] In other words the classification of facts alleged to satisfy a conception used by the English legislator must be provided by English law, however alien to English notions they may be. Even if by Soviet law the publication of *The Soviet Monitor* is an act of sovereign authority, this is unlikely to be so under English law.[37] According to the Report of the Inter-Departmental Committee, in 1951 an Italian court decided that the publication in Italy, by a Brazilian state, of a magazine strictly for the purpose of encouraging immigration to Brazil, was not an act done *jure imperii* in respect of which Brazil was entitled to immunity.[38] An English court ought to hold similarly that the publication of such a paper is not an act done in the

---

33 The decision of Robert Goff J in *I Congeso del Partido* [1978] 1 All ER 1169 on this point could not even under the old law easily be supported. It is certainly contrary to the construction which the Act requires.

34 Cf the decsion of the Court of Appeal in *Buttes Gas & Oil Co v Hammer* [1975] QB 557.

35 [1949] 2 All ER 274.

36 The Head of New Scotland Yard who upon request sends a report on the Church of Scientology of California to the Federal Republic of Germany's Federal Criminal Office acts in exercise of sovereign authority and is immune in Germany: German Federal Supreme Court, 26 September 1978, *Neue Juristische Wochenschrift*, 1978, p 1101.

37 In *Yessenin-Volpin v Novosti Press Agency, Tess Agency and the Daily World* (1978) 443 F Sup 849 also (1978) *International Legal Materials* 17 at p 720, a United States district court decided that, although by publishing newspapers the defendants engaged in commercial activity, a libel published in the newspaper was not 'in connection with a commercial activity' for the newspapers were committing 'acts of inter-governmental co-operation'. The decision should not be followed for this reason, among others, that it classifies the terms of a US statute according to Soviet law and practice.

38 Paragraph 18.

exercise of sovereign authority. It would be different, for instance, if a foreign state were to send a diplomatic note to the Foreign and Commonwealth Office; a libel contained in it could not be pursued by proceedings here if the defendant state raised the plea of immunity. The argument here put forward and based on the words 'proceedings relating to ... any ... activity ... in which [the state] engages otherwise than in the exercise of sovereign authority' cannot be met by a reference to ss 5 to 7, which deal with certain torts committed in England. Section 3 comprises torts wherever committed, provided the English court has (territorial) jurisdiction in respect of claim or counter-claim. A tort committed abroad may yet have been committed in England if the damage has occurred here. Furthermore, the fact that certain torts are specifically mentioned does not necessitate the conclusion that other torts are not caught by the wide terms of s 3.

It must be made clear, however, that an activity may be in the exercise of sovereign authority even if it is lawful. Property taken by force may be taken by way of sovereign authority.

The width of the exception allowed by s 3 is likely to be fully recognised only in years to come in the light of experience which practice will bring forth and which at this stage is hard to perceive and foresee.

3   The third exception relates to a *contract of employment* between the foreign state and an individual who is (only) a national of the United Kingdom or habitually resident there, provided that either the contract was made or the work is wholly or partly performed here (s 4). It is open to the parties to agree otherwise in writing, and if the employment is for work in an office, agency or establishment, maintained in the United Kingdom, the state cannot claim immunity except if, at the time when the contract was made, the individual was habitually resident in that state.

Once again the question whether a contract was made and what its terms are must be decided by the proper law. But whether it constitutes a contract of employment, ie a contract of service rather than a contract for services, whether it was made in the United Kingdom or where the individual's habitual residence was – these are questions governed by English law. The question where a contract is made is, as one knows only too well, a particularly difficult one and it is at first sight not easy to understand where the letter of acceptance is posted. Immunity and acceptance of an offer are so different in character that to make the former subject to the latter is a little incongruous.

The section is a narrow one and may support results which will not necessarily appear justifiable. If Nigeria makes in London a contract which is governed by English law and by which a citizen and resident of the United States of America agree to serve on an oil rig on the high seas it would appear that the employer is entitled to immunity in an English court, the (territorial) jurisdiction of which may follow from Order 11.

4   The next exception applies to the case in which the foreign state causes in the United Kingdom *injury to a person or to property*: s 5. The provision and its application are fairly obvious and will only in the most exceptional cases give rise to any problems of construction. One such problem is due to the fact that the section requires the damage to or loss of property to have been caused by an act or omission in the United Kingdom, but does not require the property to be situate there. Suppose a London merchant deposits goods in a warehouse in state X on the understanding that they will be released to him or his order upon production of an authority signed by the merchant and

countersigned by the Trade Delegation in London. The Trade Delegation is contractually bound, but refuses to countersign. The loss of the goods is said to be caused by the failure of the Trade Delegation to act in London. It would seem that in such circumstances state X is not entitled to immunity in an action for damages.

5   The fifth exception, established by s 6, is in certain respects particularly interesting. Sub-sections 1 to 3 deprive the foreign state of immunity in regard to *immovable property* in the United Kingdom, any interest of the state in property of whatever kind and wherever situate if it arises by way of succession, gift or *bon vacantia*, or any interest in an estate of deceased persons, insolvent persons and others and in a trust. In the vast majority of cases the property or the estate will be in the United Kingdom. In such a case the exception is clearly justified and necessary and largely supported by earlier law. In some cases the exception would also seem to apply if the property or estate or trust is situate abroad, but they cannot often occur in an English court.

While the cases thus alluded to may seem fairly clear and even familiar, there is buried among them one particular set of facts which, one may be sure, the legislator did not contemplate but which, it is submitted, may be covered by them. It unfortunately happens quite frequently that states cause the dissolution of corporations and take over their assets and liabilities, sometimes for purposes of a confiscatory character, and that such measures are believed to protect the corporation and its property from the jurisdiction of foreign courts or arbitrators. These are instances of a universal succession and should in future come within the ambit of s 6(2), so that the state can be made personally liable in respect of the 'deceased' corporation's contracts. Such proceedings would appear to relate 'to any interest of the state in movable or immovable property, being an interest arising by way of succession ...' These are words which do not need to be limited to proprietary interests, but may be said to comprise liabilities for the discharge of which the property is, in a loose sense, a security.[39] Even where the state takes only the assets of the dissolved corporation and purports to leave its liabilities unprovided for, *ordre public* would require it to be held liable and for the reasons given it should not be entitled to immunity.[40]

Sub-section 4 reads as follows:

> A court may entertain proceedings against a person other than a state notwithstanding that the proceedings relate to property:
>
> (a) which is in the possession or control of a state; and
>
> (b) in which a state claims an interest,

---

39   *Cf* the French principle of the *patrimoine* of which Charbonnier, *Droit Civil*, Vol 3 section 2 has said: *'c'est la charactéristique de la succession au patrimoine (in universum jus) ... que d'être, tout à la fois et indivisiblement, succession à l'actif et au passif'*, and he quotes the maxim: *bona non sunt nisi deducto aere alieno*.

It is believed that, for the reasons given in the text, *Thai-Europe Tapioca Service Ltd v Government of Pakistan* [1975] 1 WLR 1485 should today be decided differently. On universal succession generally see *Metliss v National Bank of Greece* [1958] AC 509 and *Adams v National bank of Greece* [1961] AC 255.

40   On *ordre public* in case of universal succession see *Metliss'* case in the Court of Appeal [1957] 2 QB 33 at p 48 *per* Romer LJ; and *Adams'* case [1961] AC 255 at p 289 *per* Lord Denning.

if the state would not have been immune had the proceedings been brought against it, or in a case within para (b) above, if the claim is neither admitted nor supported by *prima facie* evidence.

If one ignores ships, which are separately dealt with in the Act, this is the case of the Bank of England with which the state has deposited gold[41] or of Sotheby's who hold a painting sent to them by the state for sale. If proceedings are brought against the Bank of England or Sotheby's by a plaintiff who claims to be the owner or entitled to immediate possession, no Continental court, so it appears, would ever have thought of immunity coming into play, because this is conceived as a personal privilege of the defendant who, if he holds property for a state and cannot bring it before the court by interpleader proceedings, must make his own arrangements with it, but cannot confront the plaintiff with the immunity of the third party. In this country, however, the unfortunate idea grew up and was repeatedly sanctioned by the House of Lords[42] that indirect possession or control by a state involved its 'indirect interpleading' and entitled the defendant actually in possession to immunity. This, one notices with satisfaction, has been abolished in the sense that the defendant can only claim it if the state in an action against it directly could do so. One is thus directed to look again at s 3 and finds that the outcome depends on whether the proceedings relate to any transaction or activity into which the state has entered or in which it has engaged otherwise than in the exercise of sovereign authority. It would seem, therefore, that in the circumstances of the *Dollfus Mieg & Cie* case the plaintiff could not today succeed, because the state which had deposited the gold with the Bank of England had done so and, indeed, had obtained the gold in the exercise of sovereign authority, so that an action against the states which were the bailors would be stayed. If, on the other hand, the plaintiff has purchased identifiable gold bars from the state which has deposited them with the Bank of England but refuses to release them he is entitled to succeed in regard to any plea of immunity. Property which has been confiscated without compensation or, indeed, which has been taken without colour of legality cannot be recovered from the state. Accordingly it cannot be recovered from the defendant in England who is in possession of it. *Rahimtoola v Nizam of Hyderabad*[43] is now a more doubtful case. Lord Denning, whose approach is much to be preferred to that of his colleagues, put forward the attractive and, indeed, convincing thought that the facts pointed to 'an international transaction' or, as Upjohn J had said in the Court of First Instance, an 'intergovernmental transaction' between the Finance Minister of Hyderabad and the Foreign Secretary of Pakistan, a 'transaction more in the nature of a treaty than a contract or trust'.[44] On this basis the court had to deal with a transaction entered into in the exercise of sovereign authority, with the result that Pakistan or its agent, the defendant, could claim immunity and so could the Westminster Bank if the debt due from it could be said to be property in the possession or control of Pakistan or in which Pakistan claimed an interest. This condition, probably, was under the old law and would now be fulfilled, though, as Lord Denning pointed out, it remains

---

41   *United States of America v Dollfus Mieg & Cie* [1952] AC 582.
42   For the first time in *The Christina* [1938] AC 485.
43   [1958] AC 379.
44   At pp 422, 423.

very difficult to understand (and none of the other Law Lords satisfactorily explained) why in the *Dollfus Mieg* case the claim for damages in respect of the converted 13 gold bars was allowed to proceed, while the debt due from the Westminster Bank to the Nizam of Hyderabad as beneficial owner could not be pursued. The conclusion is not entirely fortunate: two of the most regrettable decisions of the House of Lords in the field of sovereign immunity would appear to have been sanctioned by the legislator who at the same time has done nothing to eliminate the logical inconsistency between them.

The sub-section, it will be noted, makes a curious distinction between property which is in the possession or control of a state and property in which a state claims an interest. In the former case the state will have to prove that it is in possession or control, but in the latter case the claim to immunity, unless admitted, will succeed if it is supported 'by *prima facie* evidence'. Two things have to be said about this provision. The claim to an interest in property as a basis for immunity seems to originate with Lord Wright who used the phrase in *The Christina*[45] when he spoke of interests 'lesser than a proprietary interest or even than a possessory interest'. But he probably treated them merely as illustrations of control,[46] while the section under discussion draws a sharp distinction. It is a serious question whether in a statutory text an imprecise phrase used in a judicial opinion should not be given a strict meaning. If so, 'an interest' could only denote an equitable interest as understood by the general law of England. However this may be, the effect is that from the state's point of view it may be more advantageous to allege 'an interest' rather than 'possession or control'. Moreover, the idea that *prima facie* evidence is sufficient and strict proof is not required, though it comes from an Admiralty case,[47] used to have universal validity. It is now clearly confined to the single case of a claim to 'an interest' in property other than ships.

6 Exception 6 relates to industrial property rights in the United Kingdom. No immunity exists where the proceedings relate to any such right belonging to the foreign state and protected in the United Kingdom or to the infringement by the state of any such right belonging to someone else or to a passing-off in the United Kingdom: s 7.

These provisions, the statutory definition of which is much more detailed and precise, are unlikely to prove troublesome and do not require comment at this stage.

7 Similar remarks apply to the seventh exception. A state which is a member of a corporate or unincorporated body and involved in proceedings brought by such body or its other members cannot claim immunity: s 8. The only point which deserves emphasis is that the section applies not only to bodies created in the United Kingdom, but also to such body as 'is controlled from or has its principal place of business in the United Kingdom'. In some very special circumstances it may be possible to bring an action here against a foreign state as a member of a corporation which is formed under such state's own law, but controlled from the United Kingdom.

---

45 [1938] AC 485 at p 507.

46 This was how he was understood by Earl Jowitt in the *Dollfus Mieg & Cie* case [1952] AC 582 at p 604.

47 *Juan Ysmael & Co Inc v Indonesian Government* [1955] AC 72, noted in (1955) 18 *Modern Law Review* at p 184.

8   The eighth exception is designed to overturn a most unfortunate and at the same time wholly avoidable decision of the House of Lords.[48] Where a state has agreed to arbitration, it is without immunity 'as respects proceedings in the courts of the United Kingdom which relate to the arbitration': s 9. It will be noted that the section is not limited to arbitration in the United Kingdom. English awards made against a foreign state can be turned into judgments of an English court (though this should rarely be necessary or useful) and a foreign award can be made enforceable here, though not enforced except as mentioned below. The section also gives jurisdiction to the court to make interlocutory orders for the security of costs, discovery, etc such as are provided for in the Arbitration Act 1950.

9   Exception 9 is of great practical importance in that it excludes immunity in respect of *ships* used or intended to be used for 'commercial purposes': s 10. The principle as expressed in sub-s 2 extends to cargo and other property belonging to or in the possession or control of the state or in which it claims an interest (sub-ss 4 and 5). But the whole section is applicable only in Admiralty proceedings or in proceedings which could be brought in Admiralty (sub-s 1); in such proceedings ss 3 to, that is to say, exceptions two, three and four discussed above, do not apply if the defendant state is a party to the Brussels Convention, for the Act does not intend to interfere with the latter as a self-contained code.

The main point to be made in connection with s 10 arises from the term 'commercial purposes' which occurs in many sections and which in the present context has very special significance. It is to be contrasted with 'commercial transaction' in s 3 which is determined by its objective nature rather than its possibly subjective purpose, in the same way as the American Foreign Sovereign Immunities Act 1976 which takes 'commercial activity' as a test and defines it 'by reference to the nature of the course of conduct or particular transaction or act rather than by reference to its purpose'.

The starting point would seem to be clear: the meaning of 'commercial purposes' should be construed according to English notions. The plaintiff has to prove the facts, but it is for English law to say whether they establish 'commercial purposes' in the English sense.

In answering this question it will be necessary to distinguish clearly between ships and cargo.

As regards a ship the state is disentitled to immunity if the ship belongs to it (in the wide sense referred to above) and is used or intended to be used for commercial purposes. Cargo does not enjoy immunity if the cargo belongs (again in the extended sense mentioned above) to the state and both the cargo and the ship are used or intended to be used for commercial purposes. The last-mentioned two words, therefore, are crucial. A warship which happens to be used for carrying motor-cars for civilian use cannot be immune, but if a trading ship carries ammunition for military purposes both the ship and the cargo are immune, at least if there is no commercial cargo on board. Cement carried in a trading ship may be immune: the result depends on the purpose for which it will be used. If the consignee intends to sell the cement to the military administration, but is not contractually bound to do so, the non-commercial purpose does not in a legally relevant sense exist. If the consignee

---

48   *Duff Development Co v Kelantan* [1924] AC 797, on which see Cohn (1958) 34 *BYIL* at p 260, and Mann (1967) 42 *BYIL* at p 17, also (1973) *Studies in International Law* at p 276.

has sold an identifiable quantity being part of the cargo of cement for the building of military barracks, immunity extends to such quantity and it would probably be no counter-argument that one must not look beyond the consignee; what matter are the ultimate purposes in so far as they can be proven. Shoes for the army (to revert to an often-discussed example) are cargo for a non-commercial purpose, but if they are consigned to a private merchant who only hopes to sell them to the army, the purpose remains non-commercial. If the consignee is the state itself and intends to use the cargo for the business of a state monopoly such as a tobacco or alcohol monopoly, this is a commercial purpose, though the consignee may regard it as a public purpose. Conversely, if there exists in England a monopoly for the production and sale of certain goods (as at present is not the case) this would not prove that the similar goods carried in a foreign ship are not intended for commercial purposes: a state monopoly as such is not by any means a non-commercial venture.

10   The last exception (s 11) does not require more than mention, for it is unlikely to fall often for consideration. No immunity can be claimed by a defendant state in proceedings brought to recover value added tax, customs duty or any agricultural levy or rates in respect of premises occupied for commercial purposes.[49]

9.2.4   The current legal position

It is difficult to state the current position with regard to state immunity with any clear certainty. Most writers stress the trend towards the restrictive approach in the practice of states without going as far as to claim it as an unopposed rule of customary international law. Even if the restrictive view is accepted as reflecting customary law there remains the problem of clearly distinguishing between acts *jure imperii* and acts *jure gestionis*. One aspect of the distinction is whether the deciding factor should be the nature of the activity in issue or whether it is the purpose of the transaction which is more significant. Certainly the US and the UK cases seem to favour a distinction based on the nature of the transaction involved and in the *Empire of Iran* case (1963)[50] the German Constitutional Court stated:

As a means of determining the distinction between *actus jure imperii* and *jure gestionis* one should refer rather to the nature of the state transaction or the resulting legal relationships, and not to the motive or purpose of the state activity.

In 1986 the ILC published its Draft Articles on Jurisdictional Immunities of States and Their Property, and these have since been revised in the light of the comments of states. The draft articles provide for the immunity of states subject to a number of exceptions. 'State' is defined in Article 3 and includes the organs of government, political subdivisions of the state, State agencies and representatives of the state acting in an official capacity. Of particular interest in the context of the discussion about acts *jure imperii* and acts *jure gestionis* is Article 3(2) which provides:

---

49   FA Mann, 'The State Immunity Act 1978' (1979) 43–62 *BYIL* at pp 48–58.
50   (1963) 45 ILR 57.

In determining whether a contract for the sale or purchase of goods or the supply of services is commercial, reference should be made primarily to the nature of the contract, but the purpose of the contract should also be taken into account if, in the practice of that state, that purpose is relevant to determining the non-commercial character of the contract.

The latest draft was published in 1991 and the 6th Committee of the UN General Assembly is currently debating whether to recommend that the General Assembly convenes an international conference to produce a convention on the matter.

9.3   Foreign armed forces

Members of the armed forces usually enjoy limited immunities from local jurisdiction while in the territory of a foreign state. Obviously such immunities only apply where the forces are present with the consent of the host state. The nature and extent of the immunities generally depend on the circumstances under which they were admitted, although simple admission itself can produce legal consequences. The receiving state impliedly agrees not to exercise jurisdiction in such a way as to impair the integrity and the efficiency of the force. The general rule is that the commander of visiting forces has exclusive jurisdiction over offences committed within the area where the force is stationed or while members of the force are on duty. Usually the status and immunities of foreign troops will be the subject of specific agreement. Thus under the North Atlantic Treaty Agreement 1951 the sending state has the primary right to exercise jurisdiction over NATO troops stationed abroad in other member states.

9.4   Diplomatic immunity

VIENNA CONVENTION ON DIPLOMATIC RELATIONS[51]

The States Parties to the present Convention

Recalling that the peoples of all nations from ancient times have recognised the status of diplomatic agents,

Having in mind the purposes and principle of the Charter of the United Nations concerning the sovereign equality of states, the maintenance of international peace and security, and the promotion of friendly relations among nations,

Believing that an international convention on diplomatic intercourse, privileges and immunities would contribute to the development of friendly relations among nations, irrespective of their differing constitutional and social systems,

Realising that the purpose of such privileges and immunities is not to benefit the individuals but to ensure the efficient performance of the functions of diplomatic missions as representing states,

---

51 Adopted 16 April 1961 by the UN Conference on Diplomatic Intercourse and Immunities held in Vienna (UN Doc A/CONF 20/13). The Convention entered into force on 24 April 1964.

Affirming that the rules of customary international law should continue to govern present questions not expressly regulated by the provisions of the present Convention,

Have agreed as follows:

Article 1

For the purpose of the present Convention, the following expressions shall have the meanings hereunder assigned to them:

    (a) the 'head of the mission' is the person charged by the sending state with the duty of acting in that capacity;

    (b) the 'members of the mission' are the head of the mission and the members of the staff of the mission;

    (c) the 'members of the staff of the mission' are the members of the diplomatic staff, of the administrative and technical staff and of the service staff of the mission;

    (d) the 'members of the diplomatic staff' are the members of the staff of the mission having diplomatic rank;

    (e) a 'diplomatic agent' is the head of the mission or a member of the diplomatic staff of the mission;

    (f) the 'members of the administrative and technical staff' are the members of the staff of the mission employed in the administrative and technical service of the mission;

    (g) the 'members of the service staff' are the members of the staff of the mission in the domestic service of the mission;

    (h) a 'private servant' is a person who is in the domestic service of a member of the mission who is not an employee of the sending state;

    (i) the 'premises of the mission' are the buildings or parts of the buildings and the land ancillary thereto, irrespective of ownership, used for the purposes of the mission including the residence of the head of the mission.

Article 2

The establishment of diplomatic relations between states, and of permanent diplomatic missions, takes place by mutual consent.

Article 3

1   The functions of a diplomatic mission consist *inter alia* in:

    (a) representing the sending state in the receiving state;

    (b) protecting in the receiving state the interests of the sending state and of its nationals, within the limits permitted by international law;

    (c) negotiating with the government of the receiving state;

    (d) ascertaining by all lawful means conditions and developments in the receiving state, and reporting thereon to the government of the sending state;

    (e) promoting friendly relations between the sending state and the receiving state, and developing their economic, cultural and scientific relations.

2   Nothing in the present Convention shall be construed as preventing the performance of consular functions by a diplomatic mission.

Article 4

1   The sending state must make certain that the *agrement* of the receiving state has been given for the person it proposes to accredit as head of mission to that state.

2   The receiving state is not obliged to give reasons to the sending state for a refusal of *agrement*.

Article 5

1   The sending state may, after it has given due notification to the receiving state concerned, accredit a head of mission or assign any member of the diplomatic staff, as the case may be, to more than one state, unless there is express objection by any of the receiving states.

2   If the sending state accredits a head of mission to one or more other states it may establish a diplomatic mission headed by a *charge d'affaires ad interim* in each state where the head of mission has not his permanent seat.

3   A head of mission or any member of the diplomatic staff of the mission may act as representative of the sending state to any international organisation.

Article 6

Two or more states may accredit the same person as head of mission to another state, unless objection is offered by the receiving state.

Article 7

Subject to the provisions of Articles 5, 8, 9, and 11, the sending state may freely appoint the members of the staff of the mission. In the case of military, naval or air attaches, the receiving state may require their names to be submitted beforehand, for its approval.

Article 8

1   Members of the diplomatic staff of the mission should in principle be of the nationality of the sending state.

2   Members of the diplomatic staff of the mission may not be appointed from among persons having the nationality of the receiving state, except with the consent of that state which may be withdrawn at any time.

3   The receiving state may reserve the same right with regard to nationals of a third state who are not also nationals of the sending state.

Article 9

1   The receiving state may at any time and without having to explain its decision, notify the sending state that the head of the mission or any member of the diplomatic staff of the mission is *persona non grata* or that any other member of the staff of the mission is not acceptable. In any such case, the sending state shall, as appropriate, either recall the person concerned or terminate his functions with the mission. A person may be declared *persona non grata* or not acceptable before arriving in the territory of the receiving state.

2   If the sending state refuses or fails within a reasonable period to carry out its obligations under para 1 of this article, the receiving state may refuse to recognise the person concerned as a member of the mission.

Article 10

1   The Ministry for Foreign Affairs of the receiving state, or such other ministry as may be agreed, shall be notified of:

(a) the appointment of members of the mission, their arrival and their final departure or the termination of their functions with the mission;

(b) the arrival and final departure of a person belonging to the family of a member of the mission and, where appropriate, the fact that a person becomes or ceases to be a member of the family of a member of the mission;

(c) the arrival and final departure of private servants in the employ of persons referred to in sub-para (a) of this paragraph and, where appropriate, the fact that they are leaving the employ of such persons;

(d) the engagement and discharge of persons resident in the receiving state as members of the mission or private servants entitled to privileges and immunities.

2   Where possible, prior notification of arrival and final departure shall also be given.

Article 11

1   In the absence of specific agreement as to the size of the mission, the receiving state may require that the size of a mission be kept within limits considered by it to be reasonable and normal, having regard to circumstances and conditions in the receiving state and to the needs of the particular mission.

2   The receiving state may equally, within similar bounds and on a non-discriminatory basis, refuse to accept officials of a particular category.

Article 12

The sending state may not, without the prior express consent of the receiving state, establish offices forming part of the mission in localities other than those in which the mission itself is established.

Article 13

1   The head of the mission is considered as having taken up his functions in the receiving state either when he has presented his credentials or when he has notified his arrival and a true copy of his credentials has been presented to the Ministry for Foreign Affairs of the receiving state, or such other ministry as may be agreed, in accordance with the practice prevailing in the receiving state which shall be applied in a uniform manner.

2   The order of presentation of credentials or of a true copy thereof will be determined by the date and time of the arrival of the head of the mission.

Article 14

1   Heads of mission are divided into three classes, namely:

(a) that of ambassadors or nuncios accredited to Heads of State, and other heads of mission of equivalent rank;

(b) that of envoys, ministers and internuncios accredited to Heads of State;

(c) that of *charge d'affaires* accredited to Ministers of Foreign Affairs.

2   Except as concerns precedence and etiquette, there shall be no differentiation between heads of mission by reason of their class.

Article 15

The class to which the heads of their missions are to be assigned shall be agreed between states.

Article 16

1 Heads of mission shall take precedence in their respective classes in the order of the date and time of taking up their functions in accordance with article 13.

2 Alterations in the credentials of a head of mission not involving any change of class shall not affect his precedence.

3 This article is without prejudice to any practice accepted by the receiving state regarding the precedence of the representative of the Holy See.

Article 17

The precedence of the members of the diplomatic staff of the mission shall be notified by the head of mission to the Ministry for Foreign Affairs or such other ministry as may be agreed.

Article 18

The procedure to be observed in each state for the reception of heads of mission shall be uniform in respect of each class.

Article 19

1 If the post of head of the mission is vacant, or if the head of the mission is unable to perform his function, a *charge d'affaires ad interim* shall act provisionally as head of the mission. The name of the *charge d'affaires ad interim* shall be notified, either by the head of the mission or, in case he is unable to do so, by the Ministry for Foreign Affairs of the sending state to the Ministry of Foreign Affairs of the receiving state or such other ministry as may be agreed.

2 In cases where no member of the diplomatic staff of the ministry is present in the receiving state, a member of the administrative and technical staff may, with the consent of the receiving state, be designated by the sending state to be in charge of the current administrative affairs of the mission.

Article 20

The mission and its head shall have the right to use the flag and emblem of the state on the premises of the mission, including the residence of the head of the mission, and on his means of transport.

Article 21

1 The receiving state shall either facilitate the acquisition on its territory, in accordance with its laws, by the sending state of premises necessary for its mission or assist the latter in obtaining accommodation in some other way.

2 It shall also, where necessary, assist missions in obtaining suitable accommodation for their members.

Article 22

1 The premises of the mission shall be inviolable. The agents of the receiving state may not enter them, except with the consent of the head of the mission.

2 The receiving state is under a special duty to take all appropriate steps to protect the premises of the mission against any intrusion or damage and to prevent any disturbance of the peace of the mission or impairment of its dignity.

3 The premises of the mission, their furnishings and other property thereon and the means of transport of the mission shall be immune from search, requisition, attachment or execution.

Article 23

1   The sending state and the head of the mission shall be exempt from all national, regional or municipal dues and taxes in respect of the premises of the mission, whether owned or leased, other than such as represent payment for specific services rendered.

2   The exemption form taxation referred to in this article shall not apply to such dues and taxes payable under the law of the receiving state by persons contracting with the sending state or the head of the mission.

Article 24

The archives and documents of the mission shall be inviolable at any time and wherever they may be.

Article 25

The receiving state shall accord full facilities for the performance of the functions of the mission.

Article 26

Subject to its laws and regulations concerning zones entry into which is prohibited or regulated for reasons of national security, the receiving state shall ensure to all members of the mission freedom of movement and travel in its territory.

Article 27

1   The receiving state shall permit and protect free communication on the part of the mission for all official purposes. In communicating with the government and the other missions and consulates of the sending state, wherever situated, the mission may employ all appropriate means, including diplomatic couriers and messages in code or cipher. However, the mission may install and use a wireless transmitter only with the consent of the receiving state.

2   The official correspondence of the mission shall be inviolable. Official correspondence means all correspondence relating to the mission and its functions.

3   The diplomatic bag shall not be opened or detained.

4   The packages constituting the diplomatic bag must bear visible external marks of their character and may contain only diplomatic documents or articles intended for official use.

5   The diplomatic courier, who shall be provided with an official document indicating his status and the number of packages constituting the diplomatic bag, shall be protected by the receiving state in the performance of his functions. He shall enjoy personal inviolability and shall not be liable to any form of arrest or detention.

6   The sending state or the mission may designate couriers *ad hoc*. In such cases the provisions of para 5 of this article shall also apply, except that the immunities therein mentioned shall cease to apply when such a courier has delivered to the consignee the diplomatic bag in his charge.

7   A diplomatic bag may be entrusted to the captain of a commercial aircraft scheduled to land at an authorised port of entry. He shall be provided with an official document indicating the number of packages constituting the bag but he shall not be considered to be a diplomatic courier. The mission may send one of its members to take possession of the diplomatic bag directly and freely from the captain of the aircraft.

Article 28

The fees and charges levied by the mission in the course of official duties shall be exempt from all dues and taxes.

Article 29

The person of a diplomatic agent shall be inviolable. He shall not be liable to any form of arrest or detention. The receiving state shall treat him with due respect and shall take all appropriate steps to prevent any attack on his person, freedom, or dignity.

Article 30

1 The private residence of a diplomatic agent shall enjoy the same inviolability and protection as the premises of the mission.

2 His papers, correspondence, and, except as provided in para 3 of Article 31, his property, shall likewise enjoy inviolability.

Article 31

1 A diplomatic agent shall enjoy immunity from the criminal jurisdiction of the receiving state. He shall also enjoy immunity from its civil and administrative jurisdiction, except in the case of:

(a) a real action relating to private immovable property situated in the territory of the receiving state, unless he holds it on behalf of the sending state for the purposes of the mission;

(b) an action relating to succession in which the diplomatic agent is involved as executor, administrator, heir or legatee as a private person and not on behalf of the sending state;

(c) an action relating to any professional or commercial activity exercised by the diplomatic agent in the receiving state outside his official functions.

2 A diplomatic agent is not obliged to give evidence as a witness.

3 No measures of execution may be taken in respect of a diplomatic agent except in the cases coming under sub-paras (a), (b) and (c) of para 1 of this article, and provided that the measures concerned can be taken without infringing the inviolability of his person or of his residence.

4 The immunity of a diplomatic agent from the jurisdiction of the receiving state does not exempt him from the jurisdiction of the sending state.

Article 32

1 The immunity from jurisdiction of diplomatic agents and of persons enjoying immunity under Article 37 may be waived by the sending state.

2 Waiver must always be express.

3 The initiation of proceedings by a diplomatic agent or by a person enjoying immunity from jurisdiction under Article 37 shall preclude him from invoking immunity from jurisdiction in respect of any counterclaim directly connected with the principal claim.

4 Waiver of immunity from jurisdiction in respect of civil or administrative proceedings shall not be held to imply waiver of immunity in respect of the execution of the judgment, for which a separate waiver shall be necessary.

Article 33

1 Subject to the provisions of para 3 of this article, a diplomatic agent shall with respect to services rendered for the sending state be exempt from social security provisions which may be in force in the receiving state.

2   The exemption provided for in para 1 of this article shall also apply to private servants who are in the sole employ of a diplomatic agent, on conditions:

    (a)   that they are not nationals of or permanently resident in the receiving state; and

    (b)   that they are covered by the social security provisions which may be in force in the sending state or a third state.

3   A diplomatic agent who employs persons to whom the exemption provided for in para 2 of this article does not apply shall observe the obligations which the social security provisions of the receiving state impose upon employers.

4   The exemption provided for in paras 1 and 2 of this article shall not preclude voluntary participation in the social security system of the receiving state provided that such participation is permitted by that state.

5   The provisions of this Article shall not affect bilateral or multilateral agreements concerning social security concluded previously and shall not prevent the conclusion of such agreements in the future.

Article 34

A diplomatic agent shall be exempt from all dues and taxes, personal or real, national, regional or municipal, except:

    (a)   indirect taxes of a kind which are normally incorporated in the price of goods or services;

    (b)   dues and taxes on private immovable property situated in the territory of the receiving state, unless he holds it on behalf of the sending state for the purposesof the mission;

    (c)   estate, succession or inheritance duties levied by the receiving state, subject to the provisions of para 4 of Article 39;

    (d)   dues and taxes on private income having its source in the receiving state and capital taxes on investments made in commercial undertakings in the receiving state;

    (e)   charges levied for specific services rendered;

    (f)   registration, court or record fees, mortgage dues and stamp duty, with respect to immovable property, subject to the provisions of article 23.

Article 35

The receiving state shall exempt diplomatic agents from all personal services, from all public service of any kind whatsoever, and from military obligations such as those connected with requisitioning, military contributions and billeting.

Article 36

1   The receiving state shall, in accordance with such laws and regulations as it may adopt, permit entry of and grant exemption from all customs duties, taxes, and related charges other than charges form storage, cartage and similar services, on:

    (a)   articles form official use of the mission;

    (b)   articles for the personal use of a diplomatic agent or members of his family forming part of his household, including articles intended for his establishment.

2   The personal baggage of a diplomatic agent shall be exempt from inspection,

unless there are serious grounds for presuming that it contains articles not covered by the exemptions mentioned in para 1 of this article, or articles the import and export of which is prohibited by the law or controlled by the quarantine regulations of the receiving state. Such inspection shall be conducted only in the presence of the diplomatic agent or of his authorised representative.

Article 37

1   The members of the family of a diplomatic agent forming part of his household shall, if they are not nationals of the receiving state, enjoy the privileges and immunities specified in Articles 29 to 36.

2   Members of the administrative and technical staff of the mission, together with members of their families forming part of their respective households, shall, if they are not nationals of or permanently resident in the receiving state, enjoy the privileges and immunities specified in Articles 29 to 35, except that the immunity from civil and administrative jurisdiction of the receiving state specified in para 1 of Article 31 shall not extend to acts performed outside the course of their duties. They shall also enjoy the privileges specified in Article 36, para 1, in respect of articles imported at the time of their first installation.

3   Members of the service staff of the mission who are not nationals of or permanently resident in the receiving state shall enjoy immunity in respect of acts performed in the course of their duties, exemption from dues and taxes on the emoluments that receive by reason of their employment and the exemptions contained in Article 33.

4   Private servants of members of the mission shall, if they are not nationals of or permanently resident in the receiving state, be exempt from dues and taxes on the emoluments they receive by reason of their employment. In other respects, they may enjoy privileges and immunities only to the extent admitted by the receiving state. However, the receiving state must exercise its jurisdiction over those persons in such a manner as not to interfere unduly with the performance of the functions of the mission.

Article 38

1   Except in so far as additional privileges and immunities may be granted by the receiving state, a diplomatic agent who is a national of or permanently resident in that state shall enjoy only immunity from jurisdiction, and inviolability, in respect of official acts performed in the exercise of his functions.

2   Other members of the staff of the mission and private servants who are nationals of or permanently resident in the receiving state shall enjoy privileges and immunities only to the extent admitted by the receiving state. However, the receiving state must exercise its jurisdiction over those persons in such a manner as not to interfere unduly with the performance of the functions of the mission.

Article 39

1   Every person entitled to privileges and immunities shall enjoy them from the moment he enters the territory of the receiving state on proceeding to take up his post or, if already in its territory, from the moment when his appointment is notified to the Ministry for Foreign Affairs or such other ministry as may be agreed.

2   When the functions of a person enjoying privileges and immunities have

come to any end, such privileges and immunities shall normally cease at the moment when he leaves the country, or on expiry of a reasonable period in which to do so, but shall subsist until that time, even in case of armed conflict. However, with respect to acts performed by such a person in exercise of his functions as a member of the mission, immunity shall continue to subsist.

3   In the case of the death of a member of the mission, the members of his family shall continue to enjoy the privileges and immunities to which they are entitled until the expiry of a reasonable period in which to leave the country.

4   In the event of the death of a member of the mission not a national or permanently residing in the receiving state or a member of his family forming part of his household, the receiving state shall permit the withdrawal of movable property of the deceased, with the exception of any property acquired in the country the export of which was prohibited at the time of his death. Estate, succession and inheritance duties shall not be levied on movable property the presence of which in the receiving state was due solely to the presence there of the deceased as a member of the mission or as a member of the family of a member of the mission.

Article 40

1   If a diplomatic agent passes through or is in the territory of a third state, which has granted him a passport visa if such visa was necessary, while proceeding to take up or to return to his post, or when travelling to his own country, the third state shall accord him inviolability and such other immunities as may be required to ensure his transit or return. The same shall apply in the case of any members of his family enjoying privileges or immunities who are accompanying the diplomatic agent or travelling separately to join him or to return to their country.

2   In circumstances similar to those specified in para 1 of this article, third states shall not hinder the passage of members of the administrative and technical or service staff of a mission, and of members of their families, through their territories.

3   Third states shall accord to official correspondence and other official communications in transit, including messages in code or cipher, the same freedom and protection as is accorded by the receiving state. They shall accord to diplomatic couriers, who have been granted a passport visa if such visa was necessary, and diplomatic bags in transit the same inviolability and protection as the receiving state is bound to accord.

4   The obligations of third states under paras 1, 2, and 3 of this article shall also apply to the persons mentioned respectively in those paragraphs, and to official communications and diplomatic bags, whose presence in the territory of the third state is due to *force majeure*.

Article 41

1   Without prejudice to their privileges and immunities, it is the duty of all persons enjoying such privileges and immunities to respect the laws and regulations of the receiving state. They also have a duty not to interfere in the internal affairs of that state.

2   All official business with the receiving state entrusted to the mission by the sending state shall be conducted with or through the Ministry of Foreign Affairs of the receiving state or such other ministry as may be agreed.

3   The premises of the mission must not be used in any manner incompatible

with the functions of the mission as laid down in the present Convention or by other rules of general international law or by any special agreements in force between the sending state and the receiving state.

Article 42

A diplomatic agent shall not in the receiving state practise for personal profit in any professional or commercial activity.

Article 43

The function of a diplomatic agent comes to an end, *inter alia*:

(a) on notification by the sending state to the receiving state that the function of the diplomatic agent has come to an end;

(b) on notification by the receiving state to the sending state that, in accordance with para 2 of Article 9, it refuses to recognise the diplomatic agent as a member of the mission.

Article 44

The receiving state must, even in case of armed conflict, grant facilities in order to enable persons enjoying privileges and immunities, other than nationals of the receiving state, and members of the families of such persons irrespective of their nationality, to leave at the earliest possible moment. It must, in particular, in case of need, place at their disposal the necessary means of transport for themselves and their property.

Article 45

If diplomatic relations are broken off between two states, or if a mission is permanently or temporarily recalled:

(a) the receiving state must, even in the case of armed conflict, respect and protect the premises of the mission, together with its property and archives;

(b) the sending state may entrust the custody of the premises of the mission, together with its property and archives, to a third state acceptable to the receiving state;

(c) the sending state may entrust the protection of its interests and those of its nationals to a third state acceptable to the receiving state.

Article 46

A sending state may with the prior consent of a receiving state and at the request of a third state not represented in the receiving state, undertake the temporary protection of the interests of the third state and of its nationals.

Article 47

1   In the application of the provisions of the present Convention, the receiving state shall not discriminate between states.

2   However, discrimination shall not be regarded as taking place:

(a) where the receiving state applies any of the provisions of the present Convention restrictively because of a restrictive application of that provision to its mission in the sending state;

(b) where by custom or agreement states extend to each other more favourable treatment than is required by the provisions of the present Convention.

Article 48

The present Convention shall be open for signature by all States Members of the United Nations or of any of the specialised agencies or Parties to the Statute of the International Court of Justice, and by any other state invited by the General Assembly of the United Nations to become a Party to the Convention, as follows:

... until 31 October 1961 at the Federal Ministry of Foreign Affairs of Austria and subsequently, until 31 March 1962, at the United Nations Headquarters in New York.

Article 49

The present Convention is subject to ratification. The instruments of ratification shall be deposited with the Secretary General of the United Nations.

Article 50

The present Convention shall remain open for accession by any state belonging to any of the four categories mentioned in Article 48. The instruments of accession shall be deposited with the Secretary General of the United Nations.

Article 51

1   The present Convention shall enter into force on the thirtieth day following the date of deposit of the twenty-second instrument of ratification or accession with the Secretary General of the United Nations.

2   For each state ratifying or acceding to the Convention after the deposit of the twenty-second instrument of ratification or accession, the Convention shall enter into force on the thirtieth day after deposit by such state of its instrument of ratification or accession.

Article 52

The Secretary General of the United Nations shall inform all states belonging to any of the four categories mentioned in Article 48:

(a)   of signatures to the present Convention and of the deposit of instruments of ratification and accession, in accordance with Articles 48, 49 and 50.

(b)   of the date on which the present Convention will enter into force in accordance with Article 51.

Article 53

The original of the present Convention, of which the Chinese, English, French, Russian and Spanish texts are equally authentic, shall be deposited with the Secretary General of the United Nations, who shall send certified copies thereof to all states belonging to any of the categories mentioned in Article 48.

IN WITNESS WHEREOF the undersigned Plenipotentiaries, being duly authorised thereto by their respective Governments, have signed the present Convention.

DONE AT VIENNA, this eighteenth day of April one thousand nine hundred and sixty-one.

The rules concerning diplomatic relations have always been an important aspect of international law and arguably form one of the most accepted areas of the law. In the *US Diplomatic and Consular Staff in Tehran* case (1980) the ICJ confirmed the fundamental nature of the law on diplomatic immunity:

The rules of diplomatic law, in short, consitutute a self-contained regime which, on the one hand, lays down the receiving state's obligations regarding the facilities, privileges and immunities to be acceded to diplomatic missions and, on the other, foresees the possible abuse by members of the mission and specifies the means at the disposal of the receiving state to counter any such abuse. These means are, by their nature, entirely efficacious, for unless the sending state recalls the member of the mission objected to forthwith, the prospect of the almost immediate loss of his privileges and immunities, because of the withdrawal by the receiving state of his recognition as a member of the mission, will in practice compel that person, in his own interest, to depart at once. But, the principle of the inviolabilitiy of the persons of diplomatic agents and the premises of diplomatic missions is one of the very foundations of this long-established regime, to the evolution of which the traditions of Islam made a substantial contribution. The fundamental character of the principle of inviolability is, moreover, strongly underlined by the provisions of Articles 44 and 45 of the Convention of 1961. Even in the case of armed conflict or in the case of a breach of diplomatic relations, those provisions require that both the inviolability of the members of a diplomatic mission and of the premises, property and archives of the mission must be respected by the receiving state. Naturally, the observance of this principle does not mean – and this the applicant government expressly acknowledges – that a diplomatic agent caught in the act of committing an assault or other offence may not, on occasion, be briefly arrested by the police of the receiving state in order to prevent the commission of the particular crime. But such eventualities bear no relation at all to what occurred in the present case.[52]

9.4.1   The basis of diplomatic immunity

There have been three principal theories justifying diplomatic immunity:

(a) personal representation;

(b) extra-territoriality; and

(c) functional necessity

Personal representation

This theory dates back to the time when diplomatic relations involved the sending of personal representatives of the sovereign. Immunity attaching to diplomatic representatives was seen as an extension of sovereign immunity.

Extra-territoriality

This theory was founded on the belief that the offices and homes of the diplomat were to be treated as though they were the territory of the sending state. In 1758 Emmercich de Vattel wrote, 'an ambassador's house is, at least in all common cases of life, like his person, considered as out of the country'. The theory always rested on a fiction and is now no longer respected.

Functional necessity

The preferred rationale for the privileges and immunities attaching to diplomats is that they are necessary to enable them to perform diplomatic functions. Modern diplomats need to be able to move freely and be unhampered as they report to their governments. They need to be able to report in confidence and to negotiate on behalf of their governments without fear of let or hindrance.

---

52 *United States Diplomatic and Consular Staff in Tehran Case; United States v Iran* [1980] *ICJ Rep* at p 3.

Diplomatic immunity is not for the benefit of individuals, but to ensure the efficient performance of the functions of diplomatic missions as representing states.

9.4.2 The international law on diplomatic relations

Until the end of the 1950s, the source of diplomatic law was customary international law. In 1957 the ILC undertook to produce a draft convention on diplomatic relations. This draft formed the basis for the Vienna Convention on Diplomatic Relations 1961 (referred to in this chapter as the Vienna Convention) which was signed on 18 April 1961 and entered into force on 24 April 1964. The Convention was widely regarded as codifying existing rules of customary law and the vast majority of states are party to it. The Convention emphasises the functional necessity of diplomatic immunity and the main functions of a diplomatic mission are set down in Article 3. These functions include representing the sending state in the receiving state; protecting the interests of the sending state; negotiating with the receiving state; reporting on conditions and developments within the receiving state; and generally promoting and developing friendly relations between sending and receiving states. The Vienna Convention became part of UK law by virtue of the Diplomatic Privileges Act 1964.

The first point to be noted is that there is no right to diplomatic relations. Such relations exist only by consent, and a receiving state may declare any member of a diplomatic mission *persona non grata*, in which case the sending state must withdraw the diplomatic agent or face the withdrawal of immunity. This rule is now to be found in Article 9 of the Vienna Convention 1961. Declaring members of a mission *persona non grata* amounts to a unilateral act on the part of the receiving state. More usually, disputes about diplomatic staff are resolved by agreement, and rather than declaring individuals to be *persona non grata*, the receiving state will ask that the sending state withdraws particular members of its mission. The sending state will normally comply with such a request.

9.4.3 The diplomatic mission

The premises of the diplomatic mission, which include the embassy buildings and compound together with the residence of the head of the mission, are inviolable by virtue of Article 22 of the Vienna Convention. This is not to say that the premises of the diplomatic mission constitute part of the territory of the sending state, but does mean that they are inaccessible to agents of the receiving state without the consent of the head of the mission. In observing this rule, the English courts refused to issue a writ of *habeas corpus* with regard to a Chinese dissident who was being held against his will in the Chinese embassy in London in what was known as the Sun Yat Sen incident. Similarly, the inviolability of the diplomatic mission prevented the arrest of those suspected of shooting WPC Fletcher from within the Libyan Embassy in London in 1984.

The inviolability of the diplomatic mission also means that the receiving state is under a duty to afford all reasonable protection to it. It was a failure adequately to protect the US Embassy in Tehran which led to the *US Diplomatic and Consular Staff in Iran* case (1980). On 4 November 1979, following the revolution in Iran, a number of Iranian nationals seized the US Embassy and took the personnel inside hostage. Although the ICJ found that the initial hostage taking could not be attributed to the Iranian government, it had been aware of the threat posed to the embassy and had the means available to provide adequate protection. The court therefore found that Iran's failure to prevent the seizure of the embassy amounted to a breach of its international obligations.

9.4.4   Diplomatic personnel

The Vienna Convention provides for varying degrees of immunity which are dependent on the status of the person concerned. There are five main categories of person each attracting differing degrees of immunity:

- the head of the mission (the ambassador or *charge d'affaires*);
- the members of the diplomatic staff;
- the members of the administrative and technical staff;
- the members of the service staff;
- private servants.

The appointment of the head of the mission requires the consent of the receiving state and details of all other members of the mission must be given to the receiving state if immunity is to be invoked. The receiving state can set limits on the size of a particular mission or refuse, on a non-discriminatory basis, to accept officials of a particular category.

The head of the mission and the members of the diplomatic staff are also referred to as diplomatic agents, and they receive the highest degree of immunity. Article 29 of the Vienna Convention provides that the person of a diplomatic agent shall be inviolable. He or she shall not be subject to any form of arrest or detention, and the receiving state has a duty to ensure his or her protection. Article 31 further provides that diplomatic agents enjoy complete immunity from the criminal jurisdiction of the receiving state and extensive immunity from civil and administrative jurisdiction. These immunities extend to the families of diplomatic agents if they are not nationals of the receiving state.

Members of the administrative and technical staff and their families, provided they are not nationals of the receiving state, enjoy similar immunities to diplomatic agents apart from the fact that their immunity from civil and administrative jurisdiction does not extend to acts performed outside the course of their duties.

Members of the service staff who are not nationals of the receiving state enjoy immunity in respect of acts performed in the course of their duties. Private servants who are not nationals of the receiving state only enjoy exemption from local taxation, unless there is specific agreement which extends their immunities.

The immunities granted to diplomatic personnel can be seen to be quite extensive although Article 41 provides that all persons enjoying such immunities are under a duty to respect the laws and regulations of the receiving state. From time to time a particular instance of law-breaking by a diplomatic agent receives widespread publicity and there are calls for the immunities to be restricted. It is always possible for immunity to be waived by the sending state under Article 32 of the Vienna Convention. Furthermore, in cases of serious abuse of immunity it is possible for the receiving state to declare the diplomatic agent *persona non grata*.

9.4.5 Diplomatic communications

As has already been indicated, one of the functions of a diplomatic mission is to report on conditions and developments within the receiving state. This function can only be achieved if diplomatic staff enjoy a reasonable freedom of movement and communication. Article 26 of the Vienna Convention provides that all members of the diplomatic mission shall enjoy freedom of movement subject to restrictions imposed on grounds of national security.

Article 24 provides that the archives and documents of the mission shall be inviolable. Perhaps the area of diplomatic law which has led to the greatest amount of debate concerns the diplomatic bag. Article 27 requires the receiving state to allow and protect freedom of communication for the mission and states that the official correspondence of the mission shall be inviolable. Paragraph 3 provides that 'the diplomatic bag shall not be opened or detained'. Apart from the requirement that the bag shall be externally marked and only used for diplomatic documents or articles intended for official use, there is no indication as to what constitutes the diplomatic bag. In practice the 'bag' has ranged from a small package to collection of large crates. There have been allegations of the use of diplomatic bags to smuggle drugs and weapons. In 1964 a crate purporting to be an Egyptian diplomatic bag was opened at Rome airport and inside was found a bound and drugged Israeli. In 1984 a former Nigerian minister was kidnapped in London and placed in a crate. The crate was taken to Stansted Airport by a Nigerian diplomat, but since the crate did not itself contain any external diplomatic markings it was opened and Mr Dikko was released. A number of states have since argued that it is permissible to subject the diplomatic bag to electronic or other similar screening, although this has not been universally accepted. Certainly the Draft Articles on the Diplomatic Courier and Diplomatic Bag 1989 adopted by the ILC provides for the absolute inviolability of the diplomatic bag. In practice it seems that a state has limited scope for protest when its diplomatic bags are opened to reveal weapons, drugs or other non-official articles. The lesson for customs and other officials of the receiving state seems therefore to be that a diplomatic bag should only be opened when there is 100 per cent certainty of finding prohibited items.

9.5 Consular immunity

The primary function of consulates, vice consulates, and consular posts is to represent and deal with nationals of the sending state. They enjoy certain immunities, but not as extensive as those enjoyed by diplomatic agents. The law relating to consular relations is contained in the Vienna Convention on Consular Relations 1963 which entered into force in 1967.

As in the case of diplomatic relations, consular relations can only exist by agreement between the two states and by virtue of Article 23 of the Convention it is possible for the receiving state to declare a consular official *persona non grata*. The Convention provides for the inviolability of the consular premises and the consular archives and documents. Consular staff are entitled to freedom of movement, subject to the requirements of national security, and to freedom of communication. Consular officials do not, however, enjoy complete immunity from the local criminal jurisdiction. Although they are not liable to arrest or detention, save in the case of a grave crime, they can be subjected to criminal proceedings. Their immunity from civil and administrative jurisdiction only extends to acts performed in the exercise of consular functions. Members of the consular staff's family do not enjoy significant immunities.

9.6 International organisations

International organisations operate in particular states and will often require the same immunities and privileges as diplomatic missions if they are to carry out their functions effectively. Unfortunately there is no general law applicable to the relations between international organisations and host states. Such immunities and privileges as particular international organisations enjoy must therefore be the subject of specific agreement between the organisation and the host state. Very often the privileges and immunities are provided for in the constituent charter of the organisation or in subsequent supplementary agreements. The position of the UN is dealt with in the Convention on the Privileges and Immunities of the UN 1946.

With the growth in the number of international organisations and the consequent increase in the number of agreements dealing with their immunities and privileges there has been some debate as to whether there exist any rules of customary international law governing the matter. The Third Restatement of the Foreign Relations Law of the United States seems to suggest that there is, stating that international organisations are entitled to:

> ... such privileges and immunities as are necessary for the fulfilment of the purposes of the organisation, including immunity from legal process and from financial controls, taxes and duties.

However, the English courts in the *International Tin Council* cases (1987–89) took the view that customary international law gave no such entitlement to international organisations. The position does not seem to be clear and the subject is currently being examined by the ILC.

CHAPTER 10

STATE RESPONSIBILITY

10.1 Introduction

A corollary of binding legal obligations is legal responsibility for a breach of those obligations. This chapter is concerned with the general rules of international law which determine whether a state is in breach of its international obligations. These rules are often referred to as second-level rules in that, while they seek to determine the consequences of a breach of a legal obligation, they do not concern themselves with the nature and content of that obligation. The obligation will be found in the law of the sea, the law of treaties etc. However, in common with the majority of textbooks, reference will be made in this chapter to the particular content of the rules relating to the treatment of foreign nationals. The rules relating to the settlement of disputes arising from breaches of international obligations are dealt with in Chapter 12.

In recent years, the area of state responsibility has been the subject of much work by the ILC who have produced a set of Draft Articles on State Responsibility. Although these articles have yet to be adopted into a binding international convention, they do form the starting point for most discussions about the topic.

10.2 The Draft Articles on State Responsibility

A   Introduction

51   At its first session, in 1949, the Commission selected state responsibility among the topics which it considered suitable for codification. In response to General Assembly Resolution 799 (VIII) of 7 December 1953 requesting the Commission to undertake, as soon as it considered it advisable, the codification of the principles of international law concerning state responsibility, the Commission, at its seventh session in 1955, decided to begin the study of state responsibility and appointed FV Garcia Amador as Special *Rapporteur* for the topic. At the next six sessions of the Commission, from 1956 to 1961, the Special *Rapporteur* presented six successive reports, dealing on the whole with the question of responsibility for injuries to the persons or property of aliens.[1]

52   The Commission at its fourteenth session in 1962 set up a sub-committee whose task was to prepare a preliminary report containing suggestions concerning the scope and approach of the future study.

53   At its fifteenth session in 1963, the Commission, after having unanimously approved the report of the sub-committee, appointed Mr Roberto Ago as Special *Rapporteur* for the topic.[2]

---

1   (1976) *ILC Yearbook*, Vol II, New York: United Nations at p 229.

2   *Ibid*, p 229 *et seq*.

54   The Commission, from its twenty-first (1969) to its thirty-first sessions (1979) received eight reports from the Special *Rapporteur*.[3]

55   The general plan adopted by the Commission at its twenty-seventh session, in 1975, for the draft articles on the topic 'state responsibility' envisaged the structure of the draft articles as follows: Part One would concern the origin of international responsibility; Part Two would concern the content, forms and degrees of international responsibility; and a possible Part Three, which the Commission might decide to include, could concern the question of the settlement of disputes and the implementation of international responsibility.[4]

56   The Commission at its thirty-second session, in 1980, provisionally adopted on first reading Part One of the draft articles, concerning 'the origin of international responsibility'.[5]

57   At its thirty-first session (1979), the Commission, in view of the election of Mr Ago as a Judge to the International Court of Justice, appointed Mr Willem Riphagen Special *Rapporteur* for the topic.

58   The Commission, from its thirty-second (1980) to its thirty-eighth sessions (1986), received seven reports from Mr Willem Riphagen,[6] for Parts Two and Three of the topic.[7]

59   At its thirty-ninth session in 1987 the Commission appointed Mr Gaetano Arangio-Ruiz as Special *Rapporteur* to succeed Mr Willem Riphagen, whose term of office as a Member of the Commission expired on 31 December 1986. The Commission, from its fortieth (1988) to its forty-eighth (1996) sessions, received eight reports from Mr Gaetano Arangio-Ruiz.[8]

---

3   For the eight reports of the Special *Rapporteur* see: 1969, Vol II, doc A/CN4/217 and Add 1, pp 125–156. *Yearbook* ... 1970, Vol II, doc A/CN4/s 33, pp 177–98. *Yearbook* 1971, Vol II, (Part One) doc A/CN4/246 and Adds 1–3, p 199. *Yearbook* 1972, Vol II, doc A/CN4/264 and Add 1, p 71. *Yearbook* 1976, Vol II (Part One) doc A/CN4/291 and Adds 1 and 2 pp 3–55. *Yearbook* 1977, Vol II (Part One) doc A/CN4/302 and Adds 1–3. *Yearbook* 1978 Vol II (Part One) doc A/CN4/318 and Adds 1–4 doc A/CN4/318/Adds 5–7.

4   *Yearbook* 1975, Vol II pp 53–59 doc A/CN4/Rev 1 paras 38–51.

5   *Yearbook* 1980, Vol II (Part Two) pp 26–63 doc A/35/10 Chap III.

6   For the seven reports of the Special *Rapporteur*, see: *Yearbook* ... 1980, Vol II (Part One), p 107, doc A/CN4/330; *Yearbook* ... 1981, Vol II (Part One), p 79, doc A/CN4/334; *Yearbook* ... 1982, Vol II (Part One), p 22, doc A/CN4/354; *Yearbook* ... 1983, Vol II (Part One), p 3, doc A/CN.4/366; and Add 1; *Yearbook* ... 1984; Vol II (Part One), p 1, doc A/CN4/380; *Yearbook* ... 1985, Vol II (Part One), p 3, doc A/CN4/389; and *Yearbook* ... 1986, Vol II (Part One), p 1, doc A/CN4/397; and Add 1.

7   At its thirty-fourth session (1983) the Commission referred draft articles 1 to 6 of Part Two to the Drafting Committee. At its thirty-seventh session (1985) the Commission decided to refer articles 7 to 16 of Part Two to the Drafting Committee. At its thirty-eighth session (1986) the Commission decided to refer draft articles 1 to 5 of Part Three and its annex to the Drafting Committee.

8   For the eight reports of the Special Rapporteur, see *Yearbook* ... 1986, Vol II (Part One), p 6, doc A/CN4/416 and Add 1; *Yearbook* ... 1990, Vol II (Part One), doc A/CN4/425 and Add 1; *Yearbook* ... 1991, Vol II (Part One), doc A/CN4/440 and Add 1; doc A/CN4/444 and Adds 1–3; doc A/CN4/453 and Add 1 and Corr 1, 2, 3 and Adds 2 and 3; doc A/CN4/461 and Adds 1 and 2; doc A/C.4/469 and Corr 1 (English only) and Adds 1 and 2 and A/CN4/476 and Corr 1 (English only) and Add 1. At its forty-first session (1989) the Commission referred to the Drafting Committee draft articles 6 and 7 of Chapter Two (legal consequences deriving from an international delict) of Part Two of the draft articles. At its forty-second session (1990) the Commission referred draft articles 8, 9 and 10 of Part Two to the Drafting Committee. At its forty-fourth session (1992) the Commission referred to the the Drafting Committee draft articles 11 to 14 and 5 *bis* for inclusion in Part Two of the draft articles. At ...

60   At the conclusion of its forty-seventh session, the Commission had provisionally adopted for inclusion in Part Two, draft Articles 1 to 5[9] and Articles 6 (Cessation of wrongful conduct), 6 *bis* (Reparation), 7 (Restitution in kind), 8 (Compensation), 10 (Satisfaction), 10 *bis* (Guarantees of non-repetition),[10] 11 (Countermeasures) by an injured state), 13 (Proportionality) and 14 (Prohibited countermeasures).[11] It had furthermore received from the Drafting Committee a text for Article 12 (Conditions relating to resort to countermeasures), on which it deferred action.[12] At its forty-seventh session the Commission had also provisionally adopted for inclusion in Part Three, Article 1 (Negotiation), Article 2 (Good offices and mediation), Article 3 (Conciliation), Article 4 (Task of the Conciliation Commission), Article 5 (Arbitration), Article 6 (Terms of reference of the Arbitral Tribunal), Article 7 (Validity of an arbitral award) and Annex, Article 1 (The Conciliation Commission) and Article 2 (The Arbitral Tribunal).

B   *Consideration of the topic at the present session*

61   At its present session the Commission had before it the eighth report of the Special *Rapporteur*, Mr Arangio-Ruiz.[13]The report dealt with problems relating to the regime of internationally wrongful acts singled out as 'crimes' based on Article 19 of Part One as well as some other issues to which he deemed it necessary to call the attention of the Commission. The Commission considered the report at its 2436th meeting on 5 June 1996.

62   At the 2438th meeting of the Commission on 7 June 1996, Mr Arangio-Ruiz announced his resignation as Special *Rapporteur*.

63   The Drafting Committee completed the first reading of draft articles of Parts Two and Three on state responsibility. The Commission considered the Report of the Drafting Committee at its 2452nd to 2459th meetings from 3 to 12 July 1996.[14]

64   At its 2473rd meeting, on 26 July 1996 the International Law Commission decided, in accordance with Articles 16 and 21 of its Statute, to transmit the draft articles set out in Section D of the present chapter, through the Secretary General, to governments for comments and observations, with the request that such comments and observations be submitted to the Secretary General by 1 January 1998.[15]

---

8   [cont] its forty-fifth session (1993) the Commission referred to the Drafting Committee draft articles 1 to 6 of Part Three and Annex thereto. At its forty-seventh session (1995) the Commission referred to the Drafting Committee articles 15 to 20 of Part One dealing with the legal consequences of internationally wrongful acts characterised as crimes under article 19 of Part One of the draft articles and new draft article 7 to be included in Part Three of the draft.

9   For the text of Articles 1 to 5 (para 1) with commentaries see *Yearbook* 1985 Vol II (Part Two) p 24 *et seq.*

10   For the text of Article 5, para 2 and articles 6, 6 *bis*, 7, 8, 10 and 10 *bis*, with commentaries, see *Official Records of the General Assembly*, Forty-eighth Session, Supplement No 10 (A/48/10), p 132 *et seq.*

11   For the text of articles 11, 13 and 14, see *ibid*, Forty-ninth Session, Supplement No 10 (A/49/10), footnote 362. Article 11 was adopted by the Commission on the understanding that it might have to be reviewed in the light of the text that would eventually be adopted for article 12 (see *ibid*, para 352).

12   See *ibid*, para 352.

13   A/CN4/476 and A/CN4/476/Add 1 and Corr 1 (English only) and Add 1.

14   For the report of the Drafting Committee see document A/CN4/L 524.

15   *ILC Report* 1996.

DRAFT ARTICLES ON THE ORIGIN OF STATE RESPONSIBILITY

CHAPTER I
GENERAL PRINCIPLES

Article 1   Responsibility of a state for its internationally wrongful acts

Every internationally wrongful act of a state entails the international responsibility of that state.

Article 2   Possibility that every state may be held to have committed an internationally wrongful act

Every state is subject to the possibility of being held to have committed an internationally wrongful act entailing its international responsibility.

Article 3   Elements of an internationally wrongful act of a state

There is an internationally wrongful act of a state when:

  (a)   conduct consisting of an action or omission is attributable to the state under international law; and

  (b)   that conduct constitutes a breach of an international obligation of the state.

Article 4   Characterisation of an act of a state as internationally wrongful

An act of a state may only be characterised as internationally wrongful by international law. Such characterisation cannot be affected by the characterisation of the same act as lawful by internal law.

CHAPTER II
THE 'ACT OF THE STATE' UNDER INTERNATIONAL LAW

Article 5   Attribution to the state of the conduct of its organs

For the purposes of the present articles, conduct of any state organ having that status under the internal law of that state shall be considered as an act of that state concerned under international law, provided that organ was acting in that capacity in the case in question.

Article 6   Irrelevance of the position of the organ in the organisation of the state

The conduct of an organ of the state shall be considered as an act of that state under international law, whether that organ belongs to the constituent, legislative, executive, judicial or other power, whether its functions are of an international or an internal character, and whether it holds a superior or a subordinate position in the organisation of the state.

Article 7   Attribution to the state of the conduct of other entities empowered to exercise elements of the government authority

1   The conduct of an organ of a territorial governmental entity within a state shall also be considered as an act of that state under international law, provided that organ was acting in that capacity in the case in question.

2   The conduct of an organ of an entity which is not part of the formal structure of the state or of a territorial governmental entity, but which is empowered by the internal law of that state to exercise elements of the governmental authority, shall also be considered as an act of the state under international law, provided that organ was acting in that capacity in the case in question.

Article 8 Attribution to the state of the conduct of persons acting in fact on behalf of the state

The conduct of a person or group of persons shall also be considered as an act of the state under international law if:

(a) it is established that such persons or group of persons was in fact acting on behalf of that state; or

(b) such person or group of persons was in fact exercising elements of the governmental authority in the absence of the official authorities and in circumstances which justified the exercise of those elements of authority.

Article 9 Attribution to the state of the conduct of organs placed at its disposal by another state or by an international organisation

The conduct of an organ which has been placed at the disposal of a state by another state or by an international organisation shall be considered as an act of the former state under international law, if that organ was acting in the exercise of elements of the governmental authority of the state at whose disposal it has been placed.

Article 10 Attribution to the state of conduct of organs acting outside their competence or contrary to instructions concerning their activity

The conduct of an organ of a state, of a territorial governmental entity or of an entity empowered to exercise elements of the governmental authority, such organ having acted in that capacity, shall be considered as an act of the state under international law even if, in the particular case, the organ exceeded its competence according to internal law or contravened instructions concerning its activity.

Article 11 Conduct of persons not acting on behalf of the state

1 The conduct of a person or group of persons not acting on behalf of the state shall not be considered as an act of the state under international law.

2 Paragraph 1 is without prejudice to the attribution to the state of any other conduct which is related to that of the persons or groups of persons referred to in that paragraph and which is to be considered as an act of the state by virtue of Articles 5 to 10.

Article 12 Conduct of organs of another state

1 The conduct of an organ of a state acting in that capacity which takes place in the territory of another state or in any other territory under its jurisdiction shall not be considered as an act of the latter state under international law.

2 Paragraph 1 is without prejudice to the attribution to a state of any other conduct which is related to that referred to in that paragraph and which is to be considered as an act of that state by virtue of Articles 5 to 10.

Article 13 Conduct of organs of an international organisation

The conduct of an organ of an international organisation acting in that capacity shall not be considered as an act of a state under international law by reason only of the fact that such conduct has taken place in the territory of that state or in any other territory under its jurisdiction.

Article 14 Conduct of organs of an insurrectional movement

1 The conduct of an organ of an insurrectional movement which is established in the territory of a state or in any other territory under its administration shall not be considered as an act of that state under international law.

2   Paragraph 1 is without prejudice to the attribution to a state of any other conduct which is related to that of the organ of the insurrectional movement and which is to be considered as an act of that state by virtue of Articles 5 to 10.

3   Similarly, para 1 is without prejudice to the attribution of the conduct of the organ of the insurrectional movement to that movement in any case in which such attribution may be made under international law.

Article 15 Attribution to the state of the act of an insurrectional movement which becomes the new government of a state or which results in the formation of a new state

1   The act of an insurrectional movement which becomes the new government of a state shall be considered as an act of that state. However, such attribution shall be without prejudice to the attribution to that state of conduct which would have been previously considered as an act of the state by virtue of Articles 5 to 10.

2   The act of an insurrectional movement whose action results in the formation of a new state in part of the territory of a pre-existing state or in a territory under its administration shall be considered as an act of the new state.

CHAPTER III

BREACH OF AN INTERNATIONAL OBLIGATION

Article 16 Existence of a breach of an international obligation

There is a breach of an international obligation by a state when an act of that state is not in conformity with what is required of it by that obligation.

Article 17 Irrelevance of the origin of the international obligation breached

1   An act of a state which constitutes a breach of an international obligation is an internationally wrongful act regardless of the origin, whether customary, conventional or other, of the obligation.

2   The origin of the international obligation breached by a state does not affect the international responsibility arising from the internationally wrongful act of that state.

Article 18 Requirement that the international obligation be in force for the state

1   An act of the state which is not in conformity with what is required of it by an international obligation constitutes a breach of that obligation only if the act was performed at the time when the obligation was in force for that state.

2   However, an act of the state which, at the time when it was performed, was not in conformity with what was required of it by an international obligation in force for that state, ceases to be considered an internationally wrongful act if, subsequently, such an act has become compulsory by virtue of a peremptory norm of general international law.

3   If an act of the state which is not in conformity with what is required of it by an international obligation has a continuing character, there is a breach of that obligation only in respect of the period during which the act continues while the obligation is in force for that state.

4   If an act of the state which is not in conformity with what is required of it by an international obligation is composed of a series of actions or omissions in respect of separate cases, there is a breach of that obligation if such an act may be considered to be constituted by the actions or omissions occurring within the period during which the obligation is in force for that state.

5   If an act of the state which is not in conformity with what is required of it by an international obligation is a complex act constituted by actions or omissions by the same or different organs of the state in respect of the same case, there is a breach of that obligation if the complex act not in conformity with it begins with an action or omission occurring within the period during which the obligation is in force for that state, even if that act is completed after that period.

Article 19   International crimes and international delicts

1   An act of state which constitutes a breach of an international obligation is an internationally wrongful act, regardless of the subject-matter of the obligation breached.

2   An internationally wrongful act which results from the breach by a state of an international obligation so essential for the protection of fundamental interests of the international community that its breach is recognised as a crime by that community as a whole constitutes an international crime.

3   Subject to para 2, and on the basis of the rules of international law in force, an international crime may result, *inter alia*, from:

   (a)   a serious breach of an international obligation of essential importance for the maintenance of international peace and security, such as that prohibiting aggression;

   (b)   a serious breach of an international obligation of essential importance for safeguarding the right of self-determination of peoples, such as that prohibiting the establishment or maintenance by force of colonial domination;

   (c)   a serious breach on a widespread scale of an international obligation of essential importance for safeguarding the human being, such as those prohibiting slavery, genocide and apartheid;

   (d)   a serious breach of an international obligation of essential importance for the safeguarding and preservation of the human environment, such as those prohibiting massive pollution of the atmosphere or the seas.

4   Any internationally wrongful act which is not an international crime in accordance with para 2 constitutes an international delict.

Article 20   Breach of an international obligation requiring the adoption of a particular course of conduct

There is a breach by a state of an international obligation requiring it to adopt a particular course of conduct when the conduct of that state is not in conformity with that required of it by that obligation.

Article 21   Breach of an international obligation requiring the achievement of a specified result

1   There is a breach by a state of an international obligation requiring it to achieve, by means of its own choice, a specified result if, by the conduct adopted, the state does not achieve the result required of it by that obligation.

2   When the conduct of the state has created a situation not in conformity with the result required of it by an international obligation, but the obligation allows that this or an equivalent result may nevertheless be achieved by subsequent conduct of the state, there is a breach of the obligation only if the state also fails by its subsequent conduct to achieve the result required of it by that obligation.

Article 22 Exhaustion of local remedies

When the conduct of a state has created a situation not in conformity with the result required of it by an international obligation concerning the treatment to be accorded to aliens, whether natural or juridical persons, but the obligation allows that this or an equivalent result may nevertheless be achieved by subsequent conduct of the state, there is a breach of the obligation only if the aliens concerned have exhausted the effective local remedies available to them without obtaining the treatment called for by the obligation or, where that is not possible, an equivalent treatment.

Article 23 Breach of an international obligation to prevent a given event

When the result required of a state by an international obligation is the prevention by means of its own choice, of the occurrence of a given conduct, there is a breach of that obligation only if, by the conduct adopted, the state does not achieve that result.

Article 24 Moment and duration of the breach of an international obligation by an act of the state not extending in time

The breach of an international obligation by an act of the state not extending in time occurs at the moment when that act is performed. The time of commission of the breach does not extend beyond that moment, even if the effects of the act of the state continue subsequently.

Article 25 Moment and duration of the breach of an international obligation by an act of the state extending in time

1   The breach of an international obligation by an act of the state having a continuing character occurs at the moment when that act begins. Nevertheless, the time of commission of the breach extends over the entire period during which the act continues and remains not in conformity with the international obligation.

2   The breach of an international obligation by an act of the state, composed of a series of actions or omissions in respect of separate cases, occurs at the moment when that action or omission of the series is accomplished which establishes the existence of the composite act. Nevertheless, the time of commission of the breach extends over the entire period from the first of the actions or omissions constituting the composite act not in conformity with the international obligation and so long as such actions or omissions are repeated.

3   The breach of an international obligation by a complex act of the state, consisting of a succession or actions or omissions by the same or different organs of the state in respect of the same case, occurs at the moment when the last constituent element of that complex act is accomplished. Nevertheless, the time of commission of the breach extends over the entire period between the action or omission which initiated the breach and that which completed it.

Article 26 Moment and duration of the breach of an international obligation to prevent a given event

The breach of an international obligation requiring a state to prevent a given event occurs when the event begins. Nevertheless, the time of commission of the breach extends over the entire period during which the event occurs.

CHAPTER IV
IMPLICATION OF A STATE IN THE INTERNATIONALLY WRONGFUL ACT OF ANOTHER STATE

Article 27   Aid or assistance by a state to another state for the commission of an internationally wrongful act

Aid or assistance by a state to another state, if it is established that it is rendered for the commission of an internationally wrongful act carried out by the latter, itself constitutes an internationally wrongful act, even if, taken alone, such aid or assistance would not constitute the breach of an international obligation.

Article 28   Responsibility of a state for an internationally wrongful act of another state

1   An internationally wrongful act committed by a state in a field of activity in which that state is subject to the power of direction or control of another state entails the international responsibility of that other state.

2   An internationally wrongful act committed by a state as the result of coercion exerted by another state to secure the commission of that act entails the international responsibility of that other state.

3   Paragraphs 1 and 2 are without prejudice to the international responsibility, under the other articles of the present draft, of the state which has committed the internationally wrongful act.

CHAPTER V
CIRCUMSTANCES PRECLUDING WRONGFULNESS

Article 29   Consent

1   The consent validly given by a state to the commission by another state of a specified act not in conformity with an obligation of the latter state towards the former state precludes the wrongfulness of the act in relation to that state to the extent the act remains within the limits of that consent.

2   Paragraph 1 does not apply if the obligation arises out of a peremptory norm of general international law. For the purposes of the present draft articles, a peremptory norm of general international law is a norm accepted and recognised by the international community of states as a whole as a norm from which no derogation is permitted and which can be modified only by a subsequent norm of general international law having the same character.

Article 30   Countermeasures in respect of an internationally wrongful act

The wrongfulness of an act of a state not in conformity with an obligation of that state towards another state is precluded if the act constitutes a measure legitimate under international law against that other state, in consequence of an internationally wrongful act of that other state.

Article 31   *Force majeure* and fortuitous event

1   The wrongfulness of an act of state not in conformity with an international obligation of that state is precluded if the act was due to an irresistible force or to an unforeseen external event beyond its control which made it materially impossible for the state to act in conformity with that obligation or to know that its conduct was not in conformity with that obligation.

2   Paragraph 1 shall not apply if the state in question has contributed to the occurrence of the situation of material impossibility.

Article 32   Distress

1   The wrongfulness of an act of a state not in conformity with an international obligation of that state is precluded if the author of the conduct which constitutes the act of that state had no other means, in a situation of extreme distress, of saving his life or that of persons entrusted to his care.

2   Paragraph 1 shall not apply if the state in question has contributed to the occurrence of the situation of extreme distress or if the conduct in question was likely to create a comparable or greater peril.

Article 33   State of necessity

1   A state of necessity may not be invoked by a state as a ground for precluding the wrongfulness of an act of that state not in conformity with an international obligation of the state unless:

   (a)   the act was the only means of safeguarding an essential interest of the state against a grave and imminent peril; and

   (b)   the act did not seriously impair an essential interest of the state towards which the obligation existed.

2   In any case, a state of necessity may not be invoked by a state as a ground for precluding wrongfulness:

   (a)   if the international obligation with which the act of the state is not in conformity arises out of a peremptory norm of general international law; or

   (b)   if the international obligation with which the act of the state is not in conformity is laid down by a treaty which, explicitly or implicitly, excludes the possibility of invoking the state of necessity with respect to that obligation; or

   (c)   if the state in question has contributed to the occurrence of the state of necessity.

Article 34   Self-defence

The wrongfulness of an act of a state not in conformity with an international obligation of that state is precluded if the act constitutes a lawful measure of self-defence taken in conformity with the Charter of the United Nations.

Article 35   Reservation as to compensation for damage

Preclusion of the wrongfulness of an act of a state by virtue of the provisions of Articles 29, 31, 32 or 33 does not prejudge any question that may arise in regard to compensation for damage caused by that act.

Part Two – Content, forms and degrees of international responsibility

CHAPTER I – GENERAL PRINCIPLES

Article 36   Consequences of an internationally wrongful act

1   The international responsibility of a state which, in accordance with the provisions of Part One, arises from an internationally wrongful act committed by that state, entails legal consequences as set out in this Part.

2   The legal consequences referred to in para 1 are without prejudice to the continued duty of the state which has committed the internationally wrongful act to perform the obligation it has breached.

Article 37   *Lex specialis*

The provisions of this Part do not apply where and to the extent that the legal consequences of an internationally wrongful act of a state have been determined by other rules of international law relating specifically to that act.

Article 38   Customary international law

The rules of customary international law shall continue to govern the legal consequences of an internationally wrongful act of a state not set out in the provisions of this Part.

Article 39   Relationship to the Charter of the United Nations

The legal consequences of an internationally wrongful act of a state set out in the provisions of this Part are subject, as appropriate, to the provisions and procedure of the Charter of the United Nations relating to the maintenance of international peace and security.

Article 40   Meaning of injured state

1   For the purposes of the present articles, 'injured state' means any state a right of which is infringed by the act of another state, if that act constitutes, in accordance with Part One, an internationally wrongful act of that state.

2   In particular, 'injured state' means:

(a)   if the right infringed by the act of a state arises from a bilateral treaty, the other state party to the treaty;

(b)   if the right infringed by the act of a state arises from a judgment or other binding dispute settlement decision of an international court or tribunal, the other state or States Parties to the dispute and entitled to the benefit of that right;

(c)   if the right infringed by the act of a state arises from a binding decision of an international organ other than an international court or tribunal, the state or states which, in accordance with the constituent instrument of the international organisation concerned, are entitled to the benefit of that right;

(d)   if the right infringed by the act of a state arises from a treaty provision for a third state, that third state;

(e)   if the right infringed by the act of a state arises from a multilateral treaty or from a rule of customary international law, any other state party to the multilateral treaty or bound by the relevant rule of customary international law, if it is established that:

(i)   the right has been created or is established in its favour;

(ii)   the infringement of the right by the act of a state necessarily affects the enjoyment of the rights or the performance of the obligations of the other States Parties to the multilateral treaty or bound by the rule of customary international law; or

(iii)   the right has been created or is established for the protection of human rights and fundamental freedoms;

(f)   if the right infringed by the act of a state arises from a multilateral treaty, any other state party to the multilateral treaty, if it is established that the right has been expressly stipulated in that treaty for the protection of the collective interests of the States Parties thereto.

3   In addition, 'injured state' means, if the internationally wrongful act constitutes an international crime, all other states.

CHAPTER II – RIGHTS OF THE INJURED STATE AND OBLIGATIONS OF THE STATE WHICH HAS COMMITTED AN INTERNATIONALLY WRONGFUL ACT

Article 41   Cessation of wrongful conduct

A state whose conduct constitutes an internationally wrongful act having a continuing character is under the obligation to cease that conduct, without prejudice to the responsibility it has already incurred.

Article 42   Reparation

1   The injured state is entitled to obtain from the state which has committed an internationally wrongful act full reparation in the form of restitution in kind, compensation, satisfaction and assurances and guarantees of non-repetition, either singly or in combination.

2   In the determination of reparation, account shall be taken of the negligence or the wilful act or omission of:

(a)   the injured state; or

(b)   a national of that state on whose behalf the claim is brought;

which contributed to the damage.

3   In no case shall reparation result in depriving the population of a state of its own means of subsistence.

4   The state which has committed the internationally wrongful act may not invoke the provisions of its internal law as justification for the failure to provide full reparation.

Article 43   Restitution in kind

The injured state is entitled to obtain from the state which has committed an internationally wrongful act restitution in kind, that is, the re-establishment of the situation which existed before the wrongful act was committed, provided and to the extent that restitution in kind:

(a)   is not materially impossible;

(b)   would not involve a breach of an obligation arising from a peremptory norm of general international law;

(c)   would not involve a burden out of all proportion to the benefit which the injured state would gain from obtaining restitution in kind instead of compensation; or

(d)   would not seriously jeopardize the political independence or economic stability of the state which has committed the internationally wrongful act, whereas the injured state would not be similarly affected if it did not obtain restitution in kind.

Article 44   Compensation

1   The injured state is entitled to obtain from the state which has committed an internationally wrongful act compensation for the damage caused by that act, if and to the extent that the damage is not made good by restitution in kind.

2   For the purposes of the present article, compensation covers any economically assessable damage sustained by the injured state, and may include interest and, where appropriate, loss of profits.

Article 45   Satisfaction

1   The injured state is entitled to obtain from the state which has committed an internationally wrongful act satisfaction for the damage, in particular moral

damage, caused by that act, if and to the extent necessary to provide full reparation.

2   Satisfaction may take the form of one or more of the following:

(a)   an apology;

(b)   nominal damages;

(c)   in cases of gross infringement of the rights of the injured state, damages reflecting the gravity of the infringement;

(d)   in cases where the internationally wrongful act arose from the serious misconduct of officials or from criminal conduct of officials or private parties, disciplinary action against, or punishment of, those responsible.

3   The right of the injured state to obtain satisfaction does not justify demands which would impair the dignity of the state which has committed the internationally wrongful act.

Article 46   Assurances and guarantees of non-repetition

The injured state is entitled, where appropriate, to obtain from the state which has committed an internationally wrongful act assurances or guarantees of non-repetition of the wrongful act.

CHAPTER III – COUNTERMEASURES

Article 47   Countermeasures by an injured state

1   For the purposes of the present articles, the taking of countermeasures means that an injured state does not comply with one or more of its obligations towards a state which has committed an internationally wrongful act in order to induce it to comply with its obligations under Articles 41 to 46, as long as it has not complied with those obligations and as necessary in the light of its response to the demands of the injured state that it do so.

2   The taking of countermeasures is subject to the conditions and restrictions set out in Articles 48 to 50.

3   Where a countermeasure against a state which has committed an internationally wrongful act involves a breach of an obligation towards a third state, such a breach cannot be justified under this chapter as against the third state.

Article 48   Conditions relating to resort to countermeasures

1   Prior to taking countermeasures, an injured state shall fulfil its obligation to negotiate provided for in Article 54. This obligation is without prejudice to the taking by that state of interim measures of protection which are necessary to preserve its rights and which otherwise comply with the requirements of this chapter.

2   An injured state taking countermeasures shall fulfil the obligations in relation to dispute settlement arising under Part Three or any other binding dispute settlement procedure in force between the injured state and the state which has committed the internationally wrongful act.

3   Provided that the internationally wrongful act has ceased, the injured state shall suspend countermeasures when and to the extent that the dispute settlement procedure referred to in para 2 is being implemented in good faith by the state which has committed the internationally wrongful act and the dispute is submitted to a tribunal which has the authority to issue orders binding on the parties.

4   The obligation to suspend countermeasures ends in case of failure by the state which has committed the internationally wrongful act to honour a request or order emanating from the dispute settlement procedure.

Article 49   Proportionality

Countermeasures taken by an injured state shall not be out of proportion to the degree of gravity of the internationally wrongful act and the effects thereof on the injured state.

Article 50   Prohibited countermeasures

An injured state shall not resort by way of countermeasures to:

(a)   the threat or use of force as prohibited by the Charter of the United Nations;

(b)   extreme economic or political coercion designed to endanger the territorial integrity or political independence of the state which has committed the internationally wrongful act;

(c)   any conduct which infringes the inviolability of diplomatic or consular agents, premises, archives and documents;

(d)   any conduct which derogates from basic human rights; or

(e)   any other conduct in contravention of a peremptory norm of general international law.

CHAPTER IV – INTERNATIONAL CRIMES

Article 51   Consequences of an international crime

An international crime entails all the legal consequences of any other internationally wrongful act and, in addition, such further consequences as are set out in Articles 52 and 53.

Article 52   Specific consequences

Where an internationally wrongful act of a state is an international crime:

(a)   an injured state's entitlement to obtain restitution in kind is not subject to the limitations set out in sub-paras (c) and (d) of Article 43;

(b)   an injured state's entitlement to obtain satisfaction is not subject to the restriction in para 3 of Article 45.

Article 53   Obligations for all states

An international crime committed by a state entails an obligation for every other state:

(a)   not to recognize as lawful the situation created by the crime;

(b)   not to render aid or assistance to the state which has committed the crime in maintaining the situation so created;

(c)   to co-operate with other states in carrying out the obligations under sub-paras (a) and (b); and

(d)   to co-operate with other states in the application of measures designed to eliminate the consequences of the crime.

Part Three – Settlement of disputes

Article 54   Negotiation

If a dispute regarding the interpretation or application of the present articles arises between two or more states parties to the present articles, they shall, upon the request of any of them, seek to settle it amicably by negotiation.

Article 55   Good offices and mediation

Any state party to the present articles, not being a party to the dispute may, at the request of any party to the dispute or upon its own initiative, tender its good offices or offer to mediate with a view to facilitating an amicable settlement of the dispute.

Article 56   Conciliation

If, three months after the first request for negotiations, the dispute has not been settled by agreement and no mode of binding third party settlement has been instituted, any party to the dispute may submit it to conciliation in conformity with the procedure set out in annex I to the present articles.

Article 57   Task of the Conciliation Commission

1   The task of the Conciliation Commission shall be to elucidate the questions in dispute, to collect with that object all necessary information by means of inquiry or otherwise and to endeavour to bring the parties to the dispute to a settlement.

2   To that end, the parties shall provide the Commission with a statement of their position regarding the dispute and of the facts upon which that position is based. In addition, they shall provide the Commission with any further information or evidence as the Commission may request and shall assist the Commission in any independent fact-finding it may wish to undertake, including fact-finding within the territory of any party to the dispute, except where exceptional reasons make this impractical. In that event, that party shall give the Commission an explanation of those exceptional reasons.

3   The Commission may, at its discretion, make preliminary proposals to any or all of the parties, without prejudice to its later recommendations.

4   The recommendations to the parties shall be embodied in a report to be presented not later than three months from the formal constitution of the Commission, and the Commission may specify the period within which the parties are to respond to those recommendations.

5   If the response by the parties to the Commission's recommendations does not lead to the settlement of the dispute, the Commission may submit to them a final report containing its own evaluation of the dispute and its recommendations for settlement.

Article 58   Arbitration

1   Failing a reference of the dispute to the Conciliation Commission provided for in Article 56 or failing an agreed settlement within six months following the report of the Commission, the parties to the dispute may, by agreement, submit the dispute to an arbitral tribunal to be constituted in conformity with annex II to the present articles.

2   In cases, however, where the dispute arises between States Parties to the present articles, one of which has taken countermeasures against the other, the state against which they are taken is entitled at any time unilaterally to submit the dispute to an arbitral tribunal to be constituted in conformity with annex II to the present articles.

Article 59   Terms of reference of the arbitral tribunal

1   The arbitral tribunal, which shall decide with binding effect any issues of fact or law which may be in dispute between the parties and are relevant under any of the provisions of the present articles, shall operate under the rules laid down or referred to in annex II to the present articles and shall submit its

decision to the parties within six months from the date of completion of the parties' written and oral pleadings and submissions.

2   The tribunal shall be entitled to resort to any fact-finding it deems necessary for the determination of the facts of the case.

Article 60   Validity of an arbitral award

1   If the validity of an arbitral award is challenged by either party to the dispute, and if within three months of the date of the challenge the parties have not agreed on another tribunal, the International Court of Justice shall be competent, upon the timely request of any party, to confirm the validity of the award or declare its total or partial nullity.

2   Any issue in dispute left unresolved by the nullification of the award may, at the request of any party, be submitted to a new arbitration before an arbitral tribunal to be constituted in conformity with annex II to the present articles.

Annex I   The Conciliation Commission

1   A list of conciliators consisting of qualified jurists shall be drawn up and maintained by the Secretary General of the United Nations. To this end, every state which is a member of the United Nations or a party to the present articles shall be invited to nominate two conciliators, and the names of the persons so nominated shall constitute the list. The term of a conciliator, including that of any conciliator nominated to fill a casual vacancy, shall be five years and may be renewed. A conciliator whose term expires shall continue to fulfil any function for which he shall have been chosen under para 2.

2   A party may submit a dispute to conciliation under Article 56 by a request to the Secretary General who shall establish a Conciliation Commission to be constituted as follows:

(a)   The state or states constituting one of the parties to the dispute shall appoint:

(i)   one conciliator of the nationality of that state or of one of those states, who may or may not be chosen from the list referred to in para 1; and

(ii)   one conciliator not of the nationality of that state or of any of those states, who shall be chosen from the list.

(b)   The state or states constituting the other party to the dispute shall appoint two conciliators in the same way.

(c)   The four conciliators appointed by the parties shall be appointed within 60 days following the date on which the Secretary General receives the request.

(d)   The four conciliators shall, within 60 days following the date of the last of their own appointments, appoint a fifth conciliator chosen from the list, who shall be chairman.

(e)   If the appointment of the chairman or of any of the other conciliators has not been made within the period prescribed above for such appointment, it shall be made from the list by the Secretary General within 60 days following the expiry of that period. Any of the periods within which appointments must be made may be extended by agreement between the parties.

(f)   Any vacancy shall be filled in the manner prescribed for the initial appointment.

3   The failure of a party or parties to participate in the conciliation procedure shall not constitute a bar to the proceedings.

4   A disagreement as to whether a Commission acting under this annex has competence shall be decided by the Commission.

5   The Commission shall determine its own procedure. Decisions of the Commission shall be made by a majority vote of the five members.

6   In disputes involving more than two parties having separate interests, or where there is disagreement as to whether they are of the same interest, the parties shall apply para 2 in so far as possible.

Annex II   The arbitral tribunal

1   The arbitral tribunal referred to in Articles 58 and 60, para 2 shall consist of five members. The parties to the dispute shall each appoint one member, who may be chosen from among their respective nationals. The three other arbitrators including the chairman shall be chosen by common agreement from among the nationals of third states.

2   If the appointment of the members of the tribunal is not made within a period of three months from the date on which one of the parties requested the other party to constitute an arbitral tribunal, the necessary appointments shall be made by the President of the International Court of Justice. If the President is prevented from acting or is a national of one of the parties, the appointments shall be made by the Vice-President. If the Vice-President is prevented from acting or is a national of one of the parties, the appointments shall be made by the most senior member of the Court who is not a national of either party. The members so appointed shall be of different nationalities and, except in the case of appointments made because of failure by either party to appoint a member, may not be nationals of, in the service of or ordinarily resident in the territory of a party.

3   Any vacancy which may occur as a result of death, resignation or any other cause shall be filled within the shortest possible time in the manner prescribed for the initial appointment.

4   Following the establishment of the tribunal, the parties shall draw up an agreement specifying the subject matter of the dispute, unless they have done so before.

5   Failing the conclusion of an agreement within a period of three months from the date on which the tribunal was constituted, the subject matter of the dispute shall be determined by the tribunal on the basis of the application submitted to it.

6   The failure of a party or parties to participate in the arbitration procedure shall not constitute a bar to the proceedings.

7   Unless the parties otherwise agree, the tribunal shall determine its own procedure. Decisions of the tribunal shall be made by a majority vote of the five members.

10.3   Fault

There has been some debate as to whether the responsibility of states for unlawful acts or omissions requires an element of fault or whether liability is strict. The ILC Draft Articles provide no assistance in the matter and there are a number of conflicting authorities. Brownlie has argued that the nature of liability will depend on the precise nature of the particular obligation in issue and suggests that the discussions of the ILC tend to support this view.

10.3.1 Objective or risk responsibility

The view that seems to attract majority support is that an objective test should be applied to the actions of states. Provided that the acts complained of can be attributed to the state then it will be liable if those acts constitute a breach of international law regardless of any question of fault or intention. There are certain defences available but the burden of establishing them will be placed upon the defence once the fact of the breach of an obligation is established. The most cited example of the objective test is to be found in the judgment of Verzijl in the *Caire Claim* (1929). Caire was a French national who was asked to obtain a large sum of money by a major in the Mexican army. He was unable to obtain the money and was subsequently arrested, tortured and killed by the major and a number of soldiers. France successfully pursued a claim against the Mexican government which was heard by the French-Mexican Claims Commission. The principal question for the Commission was whether Mexico could be responsible for the actions of individual military personnel who were acting without orders and against the wishes of their commanding officer and independently of the needs and aims of the revolution. Verzijl gave support to the objective responsibility of the state according to which a state is responsible for the acts of its officials and organs even in the absence of any fault of its own. He continued by finding a state to be responsible:

> ... for all the acts committed by its officials or organs which constitute offences from the point of view of the law of nations, whether the official or organ in question has acted within or exceeded the limits of his competence ... [provided that] they must have acted at least to all appearances as competent officials or organs, or they must have used powers of methods appropriate to their official capacity.[16]

Similarly in the *Jessie* case (1921) the British-American Claims Arbitral Tribunal held the United States responsible for the action of its revenue officers who had boarded and searched a British ship on the high seas. The officers had acted in good faith, mistakenly believing that they were empowered to carry out the search by virtue of municipal law and an agreement between the UK and the USA. The tribunal laid down the principle that:

> Any government is responsible to other governments for errors in judgement of its officials purporting to act within the scope of their duties and vested with powers to enforce their demands.[17]

10.3.2 Subjective responsibility

A number of writers, most notably Hersch Lauterpacht, have argued that the responsibility of states depended on some element of fault. Such fault is often expressed in terms of intention to harm (*dolus*) or negligence (*culpa*). A number of cases are commonly cited to support the subjective view. The *Home Missionary Society Claim* (1920) arose following a rebellion in the British

---

16   (1929) RIAA 575.
17   (1921) RIAA 57.

protectorate of Sierra Leone. During the course of the rebellion property belonging to the Home Missionary Society was destroyed or damaged and a number of missionaries were killed. The US brought a claim on behalf of the Missionary Society against the UK. The tribunal dismissed the claim and noted that:

> It is a well established principle of international law that no government can be held responsible for the act of rebellious bodies of men committed in violation of its authority, where it is itself guilty of no breach of good faith, or of no negligence in suppressing insurrection.[18]

Those advocating the objective doctrine have argued that the *Home Missionary Society Claim* was concerned with a specific question of state responsibility for the acts of rebels (which is discussed at 9.3.3) and that the case cannot be used to establish a general rule.

Another case which has been cited in support of subjective responsibility is the *Corfu Channel (Merits)* case (1949).[19] The case arose following the sinking by a mine of a British warship in Albanian territorial waters. The UK brought a claim against Albania arguing firstly that Albania itself had laid the mines. However, it adduced little evidence on this point and its main argument was that the mines could not have been laid without the knowledge or connivance of the Albanian authorities. The ICJ found that the laying of mines could not have been achieved without the knowledge of the Albanian government. This being so, Albania's failure to warn British naval vessels of the risk of mines gave rise to international responsibility. In the course of its judgment the Court stated that:

> It cannot be concluded from the mere fact of the control exercised by a state over its territory and waters that that state knew, or ought to have known, of any unlawful act perpetrated therein, nor yet that it necessarily knew, or should have known, the authors. This fact, by itself and apart from other circumstances, neither involves *prima facie* responsibility nor shifts the burden of proof.

Lauterpacht subsequently remarked that 'the *Corfu Channel* case ... provided an instructive example of the affirmation of the principle that there is no liability without fault'.[20] However it is worth noting that the Soviet judge in the case understood the decision to be an application of the objective responsibility doctrine and dissented from it on that ground. He argued that responsibility could only arise on the basis of *culpa*, a more exacting test than mere fault since it requires a wilful and malicious act or a culpably negligent act, ie guilt rather than mere inadvertence or carelessness. Brownlie has stated that liability in the case arose out of the particular legal obligation of Albania identified by the Court 'not to allow *knowingly* its territory to be used for acts contrary to the rights of other states' (emphasis added).

It is submitted that much of the confusion arising from questions of the nature of responsibility arise from the tendency to equate objective responsibility with the municipal law doctrine of strict liability and to regard

---

18 (1920) RIAA 42.

19 [1949] *ICJ Rep* at p 4.

20 Oppenheim, *International Law*, 8th edn, London: Longman.

strict liability as an absolute liability from which no exculpation is possible. It has already been indicated that objective responsibility does admit the possibility of defences. Discussion about the nature of responsibility highlights the dangers of discussing the topic in isolation from the substantive 'first level' rules of international law. It is for this reason that writers such as Philip Allott have criticised the whole concept of a separate category of 'state responsibility'. In an article written in 1988 he wrote:

> In the terms of legal analysis, wrongdoing gives rise to a liability in the offender owed to others who have rights which may be enforced by legal processes. Liability is not a consequence of some intervening concept of responsibility. It is a direct consequence flowing from the nature of the wrong ... and the nature of the actual wrongful act in the given case.[21]

In individual cases what is important is the particular obligation which has been breached. As Brownlie has stated:

> It must always be borne in mind that the rules relating to state responsibility are to be applied in conjunction with other, more particular rules of international law, which prescribe duties in various precise forms. Indeed, the basic concept of responsibility is a necessary but not a sufficient condition for breaches of particular legal duties ... The relevance of fault, the relative 'strictness' of the obligation, will be determined by the content of each rule ... it would be pointless to embark on an examination of a question, framed in global terms, whether state responsibility is founded upon fault (ie *culpa* or *dolus*) or strict liability: the question is unreal.[22]

10.4 Imputability

As has already been stated, international law is concerned with the responsibility of international persons and in the main that will mean states. Because, ultimately, a state can act only through individuals, and individuals may act for reasons of their own distinct from the intentions of their state, it becomes necessary to know which actions of which persons may be attributed, or imputed, to the state. A state will only be liable for acts which can be attributed or imputed to it, it is not liable for all the private actions of its nationals.

10.4.1 Organs of the state

Article 5 of Part I of the ILC Draft Articles provides that:

> ... conduct of any state organ having that status under the internal law of that state shall be considered as an act of the state concerned under international law, provided that organ was acting in that capacity in the case in question.

and Article 6 states that:

> The conduct of an organ of the state shall be considered as an act of that state under international law, whether that organ belongs to the constituent, executive, judicial or other power, whether its functions are of an international or

---

21 (1988) 29 *Harvard International Law Journal* 1.

22 *The System of the Law of Nations: State Responsibility*, Part I, 1983, Oxford: Clarendon Press at p 40.

an internal character and whether it holds a superior or a subordinate position in the organisation of the state.

This reflects the customary law position that a state is liable for the actions of its agents and servants whatever their particular status. Thus, when, in July 1985, French secret agents sank the Greenpeace ship Rainbow Warrior, France became internationally liable and the tribunal was not concerned with the issue of whether this act of state terrorism was ordered at a high or low level within the French government (*Rainbow Warrior Arbitration* (1987)).[23]

Article 7 extends responsibility to quasi-governmental organisations, ie those organs which, although not part of the formal structure of government, exercise elements of governmental authority, when they act in a governmental capacity. The Commentary to the Draft Articles gives as an example the case of a railway company to which certain police powers have been granted.

Where one state or an international organisation has made available its representatives to another state, as, for example, where it sends members of its medical agencies to assist in an epidemic or natural disaster, responsibility for their actions lies with the receiving state. This is often provided for in the agreement under which such assistance is given and it is also reflected in Article 9 of the Draft Articles. The Commentary to Article 9 gives the specific example of the UK Privy Council acting as the highest court of appeals for New Zealand.

10.4.2 Individuals

Article 8 of the Draft Articles provides that:

> The conduct of a person or a group of persons shall also be considered as an act of the state under international law if:
>
> (a) it is established that such person or group of persons was in fact acting on behalf of that state; or
>
> (b) such person or group of persons was in fact exercising elements of the governmental authority in the absence of official authorities and in circumstances which justified the exercise of those elements of authority.

In the *US Diplomatic and Consular Staff in Tehran* case (1980),[24] the ICJ considered the status of the students who initially took possession of the US Embassy in Tehran:

> No suggestion has been made that the militants, when they executed their attack on the Embassy, had any form of official status as recognised 'agents' or organs of the Iranian state. Their conduct in mounting the attack, overrunning the Embassy and seizing its inmates as hostages cannot, therefore, be regarded as imputable to that state on that basis ... Their conduct might be considered as itself directly imputable to the Iranian state only if it were established that, in fact, on the occasion in question the militants acted on behalf of the state, having been charged by some competent organ of the Iranian state to carry out a specific operation.

---

23   (1987) 26 ILM 1346.

24   [1980] *ICJ Rep* at p 3.

However, the Court went on to find that the status of the students changed during the occupation of the Embassy. On 17 November 1979, the Ayatollah Khomeini issued a decree which declared that the premises of the Embassy and the hostages would remain as they were until the US handed over the Shah for trial.

The ICJ commented:

> The approval given to these facts by the Ayatollah Khomeini and other organs of the Iranian state, and the decision to perpetuate them, translated continuing occupation of the Embassy and detention of the hostages into acts of that state. The militants, authors of the invasions and jailers of the hostages, had now become agents of the Iranian state for whose acts the state itself was internationally responsible.

In *Yeager v Iran* (1987)[25] the Iran-US Claims Tribunal had to consider the status of 'revolutionary guards' who had detained Mr Yeager for a number of days. Iran argued that the conduct of the 'guards' was not attributable to it. The tribunal stated:

> ... attributability of acts to the state is not limited to acts of organs formally recognised under internal law. Otherwise a state could avoid responsibility under international law merely by invoking its internal law. It is generally accepted under international law that a state is also responsible for acts of persons, if it established that those persons were in fact acting on behalf of the state. An act is attributable even if a person or group of persons was in fact merely exercising elements of governmental authority in the absence of official authorities and in circumstances which justified the exercise of those elements of authority.

On the facts, the Tribunal found that the actions of the 'guards' were attributable to the Iranian state.

The rule enunciated in Article 8 will generally apply to activities taking place within the territory of the responsible state. Where the actions complained of take place outside the territory of the responsible state, it appears that a slightly stricter test will be applied. This can be seen in the decision of the ICJ in the *Military and Paramilitary Activities in and against Nicaragua (Merits)* case (1986).[26] One aspect of the case was whether the activities of the contras who, Nicaragua argued, were recruited, organised, financed and commanded by the US government, could be attributed to the US. The contras were acting outside US territory and the Court took the view that:

> US participation, even if preponderant or decisive, in the financing, organising, training, supplying and equipping of the contras, the selection of military or paramilitary targets, and the planning of the whole of its operation, is still insufficient of itself ... for the purpose of attributing to the US the acts committed by the contras ... For this conduct to give rise to the legal responsibility of the US, it would have to be proved that the state had effective control of the military or paramilitary operations in the course of which the alleged violations were committed.

---

25 (1987) 17 Iran-US Claims Tribunal Reports 92.

26 [1986] *ICJ Rep* at p 14.

In general, a state will not be liable for the acts of private individuals which cannot be attributed to it and this is confirmed in Article 11 of the Draft Articles. However, responsibility may still arise if it is shown that there existed a duty to exercise due diligence and that diligence was not exercised. It was seen in Chapter 7 that states are under a duty to protect the premises of diplomatic missions within their territory. Therefore a failure to provide adequate protection will give rise to responsibility should a diplomatic mission be attacked by a group of private individuals. It was for this reason that the Irish government admitted responsibility for the sacking by private individuals of the British Embassy in Dublin in 1972.

10.4.3 Ultra Vires *acts*

The mere fact that a state organ or official acts outside municipal law or express authority does not automatically mean that a state will not be responsible for their actions. Article 10 of Part I of the Draft Articles provides that:

> The conduct of an organ of a state, of a territorial government entity empowered to exercise elements of the governmental authority, such organ having acted in that capacity, shall be considered as an act of the state under international law even if, in the particular case, the organ exceeded its competence according to international law or contravened instructions concerning its activity.

An act may be attributed to a state even where it is beyond the legal capacity of the official involved, providing, as Verzijl noted in the *Caire Claim*,[27] that the officials 'have acted at least to all appearances as competent officials or organs or ... have used powers or methods appropriate to their official capacity'. In the words of the Commentary to the ILC Draft Articles, 'the state cannot take refuge behind the notion that, according to the provisions of its legal system, those actions or omissions ought not to have occurred or ought to have taken a different form'.

In the *Union Bridge Company Claim* (1924)[28] a British government official wrongly appropriated neutral property during the Boer War. The arbitration tribunal held Britain liable and commented:

> That liability is not affected either by the fact that [the official appropriated the property] under a mistake as to the character and ownership of the material or that it was a time of pressure and confusion caused by war, or by the fact, which, on the evidence, must be admitted, that there was no intention on the part of the British authorities to appropriate the material in question.

The *Youman's Claim* (1926)[29] arose from a situation in which Mexican troops, who were sent to protect US nationals besieged by rioters, joined in the attack in which the US nationals were killed. The Mexican authorities argued that since the soldiers had acted in complete disregard of their instructions Mexico could not be responsible for the deaths. The tribunal recognised that a state might not be responsible for the malicious acts of officials acting in a personal capacity but held that a state would almost invariably be responsible for wrongful acts

---

27 (1929) RIAA 575.
28 (1924) RIAA 138.
29 (1926) RIAA 110.

committed by soldiers under the command of an officer. The soldiers in this case had been under the immediate supervision and in the presence of their commanding officer.

The ILC recognised that there was a distinction between action by officials in a private capacity and those done in an official capacity, but provided little assistance on how the distinction was to be made. It will therefore depend on the facts of the particular event. It would appear that in the case of high level officials there is a greater presumption that their acts are within the scope of their authority and Brownlie suggests that in the case of military leaders and cabinet ministers it is inappropriate to use the dichotomy of official and personal acts. An analogy may be drawn with the rules relating to diplomatic immunity: diplomatic agents enjoy the highest level of immunity from jurisdiction whereas lower level diplomatic staff will only attract immunities in respect of activities carried out in the exercise of their official functions. An example of the distinction is seen in the *Mallen Claim* (1927).[30] Mallen, the Mexican consul in Texas was twice assaulted by the Deputy Constable of Texas. On the first occasion the constable had met Mallen in the street, had threatened to kill him and had slapped his face. On the second occasion, the constable had boarded a train on which Mallen was travelling, attacked him and then demanded the train stop so that he could take Mallen to jail. The tribunal found that the first assault had been a private act and no responsibility on the part of the US could arise. However on the second occasion it was clear that the constable had taken advantage of his official position. It was established that the constable had shown his official badge to assert his authority and the tribunal pointed out that a private individual would not have been able to take Mallen to jail. It therefore held the US responsible for the second assault since the constable had been acting with apparent authority even though his behaviour was wholly unreasonable and had been motivated by a private vendetta.

10.4.4 Insurrectionaries

Article 11 of the Draft Articles makes it clear that the conduct of a person or persons not acting on behalf of the state will not be considered as an act of the state under international law. It therefore follows that the actions of rebels and insurrectionaries will not normally be considered as acts of the state and this is provided for in Article 14. However, the state is required to show due diligence, and may be liable if it has provided insufficient protection for aliens (the special protections for diplomatic and consular staff should be noted in this context).

Where an insurrectionary movement is successful and the revolutionaries take over the government, the new government will be liable for the actions of the insurrectionaries before they took power. In the *Bolivar Railway Company Claim* (1903) the tribunal held Venezuela liable for the acts of successful revolutionaries committed before they had taken power. The conclusion was justified on the grounds that:

> Nations do not die when there is a change of their rulers or in their forms of government ... The nation is responsible for the obligations of a successful

---

30 (1927) RIAA 173.

revolution from its beginning, because in theory, it represented *ab initio* a changing national will, crystallising in the finally successful result ... success demonstrates that from the beginning it was registering the national will.[31]

In *Short v Iran* (1987) the Iran-US Claims Tribunal considered the claim of an American national who had been evacuated from Iran three days before the Islamic revolutionary government took office. He was evacuated on the orders of his American employers because of the worsening situation in Iran at the time and he sought compensation from the new government of Iran for loss of salary arising out of what he alleged to be his expulsion from Iran. The tribunal stated:

> Where a revolution leads to the establishment of a new government the state is held responsible for the acts of the overthrown government insofar as the latter maintained control of the situation. The successor government is also held responsible for the acts imputable to the revolutionary movement which established it, even if those acts occurred prior to its establishment, as a consequence of the continuity existing between the new organisation of the state and the organisation of the revolutionary movement.[32]

The tribunal, however, went on to point out that the same rules of attributability apply to revolutionary movements as apply to states. In other words, it must be established that the acts complained of are the acts of agents of the revolutionaries and not the acts of mere supporters.

10.5 International crimes

A distinction is sometimes drawn between international crimes and international delicts. Article 19 of Part I of the ILC Draft Articles provides that all breaches of international obligations are internationally wrongful acts. But an internationally wrongful act which results from the breach by a state of 'an international obligation so essential for the protection of fundamental interests of the international community that its breach is recognised as a crime by that community as a whole' constitutes an international crime. All other wrongful acts are international delicts. Article 19(3) lists some examples of specific international crimes:

- serious breaches of the law on peace and security;
- serious breaches of the right to self-determination;
- serious breaches of international duties on safeguarding the human being (eg slavery, genocide, apartheid);
- serious breaches of obligations to protect the environment.

The Commentary to the Draft Articles makes clear that an international crime is not the same as a crime at international law. It is states who are responsible for international crimes, whilst individuals bear responsibility for crimes at international law.

---

31   (1903) RIAA 445.
32   (1988) *AJIL* 140.

10.5.1 The International Law Commission and the Draft Code of Crimes against the Peace and Security of Mankind

It was recognised by the Nuremberg War Crimes Tribunal that 'international law imposes duties and liabilities upon individuals as well as upon states'. The International Law Commission has now produced a set of Draft Articles dealing with the international criminal responsibility of individuals.

A   Introduction

30   The General Assembly, in Resolution 177 (II) of 21 November 1947, requested the Commission to: (a) formulate the principles of international law recognised in the Charter of the Nürnberg Tribunal and in the Judgment of the Tribunal; and (b) prepare a Draft Code of Offences against the Peace and Security of Mankind, indicating clearly the place to be accorded to the principles mentioned in (a) above. The Commission, at its first session in 1949, appointed Mr Jean Spiropoulos Special *Rapporteur*.

31   On the basis of the reports of the Special *Rapporteur*, the Commission: (a) at its second session, in 1950, adopted a formulation of the principles of international law recognised in the Charter of the Nürnberg Tribunal and in the Judgment of the Tribunal and submitted these principles, with commentaries, to the General Assembly; and (b) at its sixth session, in 1954, submitted a Draft Code of Offences against the Peace and Security of Mankind, with commentaries, to the General Assembly.

32   The General Assembly, in Resolution 897 (IX) of 4 December 1954, considering that the Draft Code of Offences against the Peace and Security of Mankind as formulated by the Commission raised problems closely related to those of the definition of aggression, and that the General Assembly had entrusted a Special Committee with the task of preparing a report on a draft definition of aggression, decided to postpone consideration of the Draft Code until the Special Committee has submitted its report.

33   On the basis of the recommendations of the Special Committee, the General Assembly, in Resolution 3314 (XXIX) of 14 December 1974, adopted the definition of aggression by consensus.

34   The General Assembly, however, did not take action on the Draft Code, until on 10 December 1981 it invited, in Resolution 36/106, the Commission to resume its work with a view to elaborating the Draft Code and to examine it with the required priority in order to review it, taking duly into account the results achieved by the process of the progressive development of international law.[33]

35   The Commission, at its thirty-fourth session, in 1982, appointed Mr Doudou Thiam Special *Rapporteur* for the topic. The Commission, from its thirty-fifth session, in 1983, to its forty-third session, in 1991, received nine reports from the Special *Rapporteur*.[34]

---

33   *Yearbook* ... 1983, Vol II (Part One), p 137, doc A/CN4/364; *Yearbook* ... 1984, Vol II (Part One), p 89, doc A/CN4/377; *Yearbook* ... 1985, Vol II (Part One), doc A/CN4/387; *Yearbook* ... 1986, Vol II, doc A/CN4/398; *Yearbook* ... 1987, Vol II (Part One); doc A/CN4/404; *Yearbook* ... 1988, Vol II (Part One), doc A/CN4/411; *Yearbook* ... 1989, Vol II (Part One), doc A/CN4/419 and Add 1 and Corr 1 and 2 (Spanish only); *Yearbook* ... 1990, Vol II (Part One), doc A/CN4/430 and Add 1; *Yearbook* ... 1991, Vol II (Part One), doc A/CN4/435 and Add 1 and Corr 1.

34   See *Yearbook* ... 1991, Vol II (Part Two), para 173.

36   At its forty-third session, in 1991, the Commission, provisionally adopted on first reading the draft articles of the Draft Code of Crimes against the Peace and Security of Mankind.[35] At the same session, the Commission decided, in accordance with Articles 16 and 21 of its Statute, to transmit the draft articles, through the Secretary General, to Governments for their comments and observations, with a request that such comments and observations be submitted to the Secretary General by 1 January 1993.[36] The Commission noted that the draft it had completed on first reading constituted the first part of the Commission's work on the topic of the Draft Code; and that the Commission would continue at forthcoming sessions to fulfil the mandate the General Assembly had assigned to it in para 3 of Resolution 45/41, of 28 November 1990, which invited the Commission, in its work on the Draft Code, to consider further and analyse the issues raised in its report concerning the question of an international criminal jurisdiction, including the possibility of establishing an international criminal court or other international criminal trial mechanism.[37]

37   At its forty-sixth session, the General Assembly in its Resolution 46/54 of 9 December 1991 invited the Commission, within the framework of the Draft Code to consider further and analyse the issues raised in the Commission's report on the work of its forty-third session (1991)[38] concerning the question of an international criminal jurisdiction, including proposals for the establishment of an international criminal court or other international criminal trial mechanism, in order to enable the General Assembly to provide guidance on the matter.

38   At its forty-fourth and forty-fifth sessions, in 1992 and 1993, the Commission had before it the Special *Rapporteur*'s tenth and eleventh reports on the topic,[39] which were entirely devoted to the question of the possible establishment of an international criminal jurisdiction. The work carried out by the Commission at its forty-fourth (1992), forty-fifth (1993) and forty-sixth sessions on that question culminated in the adoption, at the forty-sixth session in 1994, of a draft statute of an international criminal court which the Commission submitted to the General Assembly with the recommendation that it convene an international conference of plenipotentiaries to study the draft statute and to conclude a convention on the establishment of an international criminal court.[40]

39   At its forty-sixth session in 1994, the Commission had before it the Special *Rapporteur*'s twelfth report on the topic,[41] which was intended for the second reading of the Draft Code and focused on the general part of the draft dealing with the definition of crimes against the peace and security of mankind, characterisation and general principles. It also had before it the comments and observations of governments[42] on the Draft Code adopted on first reading at that session.[43] After considering the twelfth report, the Commission decided at

---

35 *Ibid*, para 175. The Commission noted that it had already started to discharge this mandate and its work on this aspect of the topic was reflected in paras 106 to 165 of its report *(ibid)*.

36 *Yearbook ... 1990*, Vol II (Part Two) (A/45/10), Chap II, sect C.

37 A/CN4/442 and A/CN4/449 and Corr 1 (English only).

38 See *Official Records of the General Assembly*, Forty-ninth Session, Supplement No 10 (A/49/10), Chap II A.

39 A/CN4/460 and Corr 1.

40 In document A/CN4/448 and Add 1

41 *Yearbook ... 1991*, Vol II (Part Two), Chap IV.

42 A/CN4/404 and Corr 1 (English and Russian only).

43 A/CN4/L 522 and Corr 1 (English only), 2 (French only) and 3 (Spanish only).

its 2350th meeting to refer draft Articles 1 to 15, as dealt with in that report, to the Drafting Committee.

40 At its forty-seventh session, the Commission had before it the thirteenth report of the Special *Rapporteur*.[44] This report was prepared for the second reading of the Draft Code and focused on the crimes against the peace and security of mankind set out in Part II. After consideration of the thirteenth report, the Commission decided at its 2387th meeting to refer to the Drafting Committee Articles 15 (Aggression), 19 (Genocide), 21 (Systematic or mass violations of human rights) and 22 (Exceptionally serious war crimes) for consideration as a matter of priority on second reading, in the light of the proposals contained in the Special *Rapporteur*'s thirteenth report and of the comments and proposals made in the course of the debate in plenary. This was done on the understanding that, in formulating those articles, the Drafting Committee would bear in mind and at its discretion deal with all or part of the elements of the following draft articles as adopted on first reading: 17 (Intervention), 18 (Colonial domination and other forms of alien domination), 20 (Apartheid), 23 (Recruitment, use, financing and training of mercenaries) and 24 (International terrorism). The Commission further decided that consultations would continue as regards Articles 25 (Illicit traffic in narcotic drugs) and 26 (Wilful and severe damage to the environment).

41 As regards Article 26 concerning wilful and severe damage to the environment, the Commission decided at its 2404th meeting to establish a working group that would meet at the beginning of the forty-eighth session to examine the possibility of covering in the draft Code the issue of wilful and severe damage to the environment, while reaffirming the Commission's intention to complete the second reading of the draft Code at that session in any event.

42 The Drafting Committee began its work on the second reading of the draft articles at the forty-seventh session of the Commission and completed its work at the present forty-eighth session.

43 At the forty-eighth session, the working group examining the issue of wilful and severe damage to the environment met and proposed to the Commission that the issue of wilful and severe damage to the environment be considered either as (i) a war crime, or (ii) a crime against humanity, or a separate crime against the peace and security of mankind.

44 The Commission at its 2431st meeting decided by a vote to refer to the Drafting Committee only the text prepared by the Working Group for inclusion of wilful and severe damage to the environment as a war crime.

45 The Commission considered the report of the Drafting Committee[45] at its 2437th to 2454th meetings from 6 June to 5 July 1996 and adopted the final text of a set of 20 draft articles constituting the Code of Crimes against the Peace and Security of Mankind.

46 The Draft Code was adopted with the following understanding: 'with a view to reaching consensus, the Commission has considerably reduced the scope of the Code. On first reading in 1991, the Draft Code comprised a list of 12 categories of crimes. Some members have expressed their regrets at the reduced

---

44 The General Assembly unanimously affirmed the principles of international law recognised by the Charter of the Nürnberg Tribunal and the Judgment of the Tribunal in Resolution 95 (I) of 11 December 1946.

45 Agreement for the prosecution and punishment of the major war criminals of the European Axis (hereinafter Nürnberg Charter), 82 UNTS 279.

scope of coverage of the Code. The Commission acted in response to the interest of adoption of the Code and of obtaining support by governments. It is understood that the inclusion of certain crimes in the Code does not affect the status of other crimes under international law, and that the adoption of the Code does not in any way preclude the further development of this important area of law.'

B   *Recommendation of the Commission*

47   The Commission considered various forms which the Draft Code of Crimes against the Peace and Security of Mankind could take; these include an international convention, whether adopted by a plenipotentiary conference or by the General Assembly; incorporation of the Code in the statute of an international criminal court; or adoption of the Code as a declaration by the General Assembly.

48   The Commission recommends that the General Assembly select the most appropriate form which would ensure the widest possible acceptance of the Draft Code.

...

D   *Articles on the Draft Code of Crimes against the Peace and Security of Mankind*

Article 1   Scope and application of the present Code

1   The present Code applies to the crimes against the peace and security of mankind set out in Part II.

2   Crimes against the peace and security of mankind are crimes under international law and punishable as such, whether or not they are punishable under national law.

Article 2   Individual responsibility

1   A crime against the peace and security of mankind entails individual responsibility.

2   An individual shall be responsible for the crime of aggression in accordance with Article 16.

3   An individual shall be responsible for a crime set out in Articles 17, 18, 19 or 20 if that individual:

   (a)   intentionally commits such a crime;

   (b)   orders the commission of such a crime which in fact occurs or is attempted;

   (c)   fails to prevent or repress the commission of such a crime in the circumstances set out in Article 6;

   (d)   knowingly aids, abets or otherwise assists, directly and substantially, in the commission of such a crime, including providing the means for its commission;

   (e)   directly participates in planning or conspiring to commit such a crime which in fact occurs;

   (f)   directly and publicly incites another individual to commit such a crime which in fact occurs;

   (g)   attempts to commit such a crime by taking action commencing the execution of a crime which does not in fact occur because of circumstances independent of his intentions.

Article 3 Punishment

An individual who is responsible for a crime against the peace and security of mankind shall be liable to punishment. The punishment shall be commensurate with the character and gravity of the crime.

Article 4 Responsibility of states

The fact that the present Code provides for the responsibility of individuals for crimes against the peace and security of mankind is without prejudice to any question of the responsibility of states under international law.

Article 5 Order of a government or a superior

The fact that an individual charged with a crime against the peace and security of mankind acted pursuant to an order of a government or a superior does not relieve him of criminal responsibility, but may be considered in mitigation of punishment if justice so requires.

Article 6 Responsibility of the superior

The fact that a crime against the peace and security of mankind was committed by a subordinate does not relieve his superiors of criminal responsibility, if they knew or had reason to know, in the circumstances at the time, that the subordinate was committing or was going to commit such a crime and if they did not take all necessary measures within their power to prevent or repress the crime.

Article 7 Official position and responsibility

The official position of an individual who commits a crime against the peace and security of mankind, even if he acted as head of state or government, does not relieve him of criminal responsibility or mitigate punishment.

Article 8 Establishment of jurisdiction

Without prejudice to the jurisdiction of an international criminal court, each state party shall take such measures as may be necessary to establish its jurisdiction over the crimes set out in Articles 17, 18, 19 and 20, irrespective of where or by whom those crimes were committed. Jurisdiction over the crime set out in Article 16 shall rest with an international criminal court. However, a state referred to in Article 16 is not precluded from trying its nationals for the crime set out in that Article.

Article 9 Obligation to extradite or prosecute

Without prejudice to the jurisdiction of an international criminal court, the state party in the territory of which an individual alleged to have committed a crime set out in Articles 17, 18, 19 or 20 is found shall extradite or prosecute that individual.

Article 10 Extradition of alleged offenders

1   To the extent that the crimes set out in Articles 17, 18, 19 and 20 are not extraditable offences in any extradition treaty existing between states parties, they shall be deemed to be included as such therein. States Parties undertake to include those crimes as extraditable offences in every extradition treaty to be concluded between them.

2   If a State Party which makes extradition conditional on the existence of a treaty receives a request for extradition from another State Party with which it has no extradition treaty, it may at its option consider the present Code as the legal basis for extradition in respect of those crimes. Extradition shall be subject to the conditions provided in the law of the requested state.

3   State Parties which do not make extradition conditional on the existence of a treaty shall recognise those crimes as extraditable offences between themselves subject to the conditions provided in the law of the requested state.

4   Each of those crimes shall be treated, for the purpose of extradition between States Parties, as if it had been committed not only in the place in which it occurred but also in the territory of any other state party.

Article 11   Judicial guarantees

1   An individual charged with a crime against the peace and security of mankind shall be presumed innocent until proved guilty and shall be entitled without discrimination to the minimum guarantees due to all human beings with regard to the law and the facts and shall have the rights:

   (a)   in the determination of any charge against him, to have a fair and public hearing by a competent, independent and impartial tribunal duly established by law;

   (b)   to be informed promptly and in detail in a language which he understands of the nature and cause of the charge against him;

   (c)   to have adequate time and facilities for the preparation of his defence and to communicate with counsel of his own choosing;

   (d)   to be tried without undue delay;

   (e)   to be tried in his presence, and to defend himself in person or through legal assistance of his own choosing; to be informed, if he does not have legal assistance, of this right; and to have legal assistance assigned to him and without payment by him if he does not have sufficient means to pay for it;

   (f)   to examine, or have examined, the witnesses against him and to obtain the attendance and examination of witnesses on his behalf under the same conditions as witnesses against him;

   (g)   to have the free assistance of an interpreter if he cannot understand or speak the language used in court;

   (h)   not to be compelled to testify against himself or to confess guilt.

2   An individual convicted of a crime shall have the right to his conviction and sentence being reviewed according to law.

Article 12   *Non bis in idem*

1   No one shall be tried for a crime against the peace and security of mankind of which he has already been finally convicted or acquitted by an international criminal court.

2   An individual may not be tried again for a crime of which he has been finally convicted or acquitted by a national court except in the following cases:

   (a)   by an international criminal court, if:

      (i)   the act which was the subject of the judgment in the national court was characterised by that court as an ordinary crime and not as a crime against the peace and security of mankind; or

      (ii)   the national court proceedings were not impartial or independent or were designed to shield the accused from international criminal responsibility or the case was not diligently prosecuted;

   (b)   by a national court of another state, if:

(i)   the act which was the subject of the previous judgment took place in the territory of that state; or

(ii)   that state was the main victim of the crime.

3   In the case of a subsequent conviction under the present Code, the court, in passing sentence, shall take into account the extent to which any penalty imposed by a national court on the same person for the same act has already been served.

Article 13   Non-retroactivity

1   No one shall be convicted under the present Code for acts committed before its entry into force.

2   Nothing in this article precludes the trial of anyone for any act which, at the time when it was committed, was criminal in accordance with international law or national law.

Article 14   Defences

The competent court shall determine the admissibility of defences in accordance with the general principles of law, in the light of the character of each crime.

Article 15   Extenuating circumstances

In passing sentence, the court shall, where appropriate, take into account extenuating circumstances in accordance with the general principles of law.

PART II   CRIMES AGAINST THE PEACE AND SECURITY OF MANKIND

Article 16   Crime of aggression

An individual who, as leader or organiser, actively participates in or orders the planning, preparation, initiation or waging of aggression committed by a state shall be responsible for a crime of aggression.

Article 17   Crime of genocide

A crime of genocide means any of the following acts committed with intent to destroy, in whole or in part, a national, ethnic, racial or religious group, such as:

(a)   killing members of the group;

(b)   causing serious bodily or mental harm to members of the group;

(c)   deliberately inflicting on the group conditions of life calculated to bring about its physical destruction in whole or in part;

(d)   imposing measures intended to prevent births within the group;

(e)   forcibly transferring children of the group to another group.

Article 18   Crimes against humanity

A crime against humanity means any of the following acts, when committed in a systematic manner or on a large scale and instigated or directed by a government or by any organisation or group:

(a)   murder;

(b)   extermination;

(c)   torture;

(d)   enslavement;

(e)   persecution on political, racial, religious or ethnic grounds;

(f)   institutionalised discrimination on racial, ethnic or religious grounds involving the violation of fundamental human rights and freedoms and resulting in seriously disadvantaging a part of the population;

(g) arbitrary deportation or forcible transfer of population;

(h) arbitrary imprisonment; forced disappearance of persons;

(i) rape, enforced prostitution and other forms of sexual abuse;

(j) other inhumane acts which severely damage physical or mental integrity, health or human dignity, such as mutilation and severe bodily harm.

Article 19 Crimes against United Nations and associated personnel

1 The following crimes constitute crimes against the peace and security of mankind when committed intentionally and in a systematic manner or on a large scale against United Nations and associated personnel involved in a United Nations operation with a view to preventing or impeding that operation from fulfilling its mandate:

(a) murder, kidnapping or other attack upon the person or liberty of any such personnel;

(b) violent attack upon the official premises, the private accommodation or the means of transportation of any such personnel likely to endanger his or her person or liberty.

2 This article shall not apply to a United Nations operation authorised by the Security Council as an enforcement action under Chapter VII of the Charter of the United Nations in which any of the personnel are engaged as combatants against organised armed forces and to which the law of international armed conflict applies.

Article 20 War crimes

Any of the following war crimes constitutes a crime against the peace and security of mankind when committed in a systematic manner or on a large scale:

(a) any of the following acts committed in violation of international humanitarian law:

(i) wilful killing;

(ii) torture or inhuman treatment, including biological experiments;

(iii) wilfully causing great suffering or serious injury to body or health;

(iv) extensive destruction and appropriation of property, not justified by military necessity and carried out unlawfully and wantonly;

(v) compelling a prisoner of war or other protected person to serve in the forces of a hostile power;

(vi) wilfully depriving a prisoner of war or other protected person of the rights of fair and regular trial;

(vii) unlawful deportation or transfer or unlawful confinement of protected persons;

(viii) taking of hostages;

(b) any of the following acts committed wilfully in violation of international humanitarian law and causing death or serious injury to body or health:

(i) making the civilian population or individual civilians the object of attack;

(ii) launching an indiscriminate attack affecting the civilian population or civilian objects in the knowledge that such attack will cause excessive loss of life, injury to civilians or damage to civilian objects;

(iii) launching an attack against works or installations containing dangerous forces in the knowledge that such attack will cause excessive loss of life, injury to civilians or damage to civilian objects;

(iv) making a person the object of attack in the knowledge that he is *hors de combat*;

(v) the perfidious use of the distinctive emblem of the red cross, red crescent or red lion and sun or of other recognised protective signs;

(c) any of the following acts committed wilfully in violation of international humanitarian law:

(i) the transfer by the occupying power of parts of its own civilian population into the territory it occupies;

(ii) unjustifiable delay in the repatriation of prisoners of war or civilians;

(d) outrages upon personal dignity in violation of international humanitarian law, in particular humiliating and degrading treatment, rape, enforced prostitution and any form of indecent assault;

(e) any of the following acts committed in violation of the laws or customs of war:

(i) employment of poisonous weapons or other weapons calculated to cause unnecessary suffering;

(ii) wanton destruction of cities, towns or villages, or devastation not justified by military necessity;

(iii) attack, or bombardment, by whatever means, of undefended towns, villages, dwellings or buildings or of demilitarised zones;

(iv) seizure of, destruction of or wilful damage done to institutions dedicated to religion, charity and education, the arts and sciences, historic monuments and works of art and science;

(v) plunder of public or private property;

(f) any of the following acts committed in violation of international humanitarian law applicable in armed conflict not of an international character:

(i) violence to the life, health and physical or mental well-being of persons, in particular murder as well as cruel treatment such as torture, mutilation or any form of corporal punishment;

(ii) collective punishments;

(iii) taking of hostages;

(iv) acts of terrorism;

(v) outrages upon personal dignity, in particular humiliating and degrading treatment, rape, enforced prostitution and any form of indecent assault;

(vi) pillage;

(vii) the passing of sentences and the carrying out of executions without previous judgment pronounced by a regularly constituted court, affording all the judicial guarantees which are generally recognised as indispensable;

(g) in the case of armed conflict, using methods or means of warfare not justified by military necessity with the intent to cause widespread, long-term and severe damage to the natural environment and thereby gravely prejudice the health or survival of the population and such damage occurs.[46]

10.5.2 An international criminal court

At the same time as work has been carried out on the preparation of a draft code of international crimes, the ILC has also been preparing a draft statute for an international criminal court. It is proposed that an international diplomatic conference be held in Rome in 1998 to discuss and adopt a convention on an international criminal court.[47] The hope is that the establishment of such a court would render unnecessary in future the establishment of *ad hoc* tribunals such as the ones dealing with events in Rwanda and in former Yugoslavia.

10.6 State responsibility for the treatment of aliens

As was indicated in 10.1 a state may suffer injury indirectly when the victim of wrongful behaviour is one of its nationals. Not every injury suffered by a foreign national abroad will constitute an international wrong. The injury will only give rise to issues of state responsibility if it can in some way be linked to the foreign state. As was indicated in 10.4 a state will not generally be liable for the acts of private individuals but responsibility will arise if the state can be shown to have connived at or failed to take adequate measures to prevent injuries to foreigners, or if, after the event, the foreign authorities fail to make an adequate attempt to provide justice.

Where the respondent state is involved in the wrongful act itself, either through its organs or officials, it is appropriate to talk of *prima facie* breaches of international law. The state of the injured national has the right to intervene on the diplomatic level to insist that the respondent state remedy the wrong it has committed. The matter is on the international plane from the start, even if it only gives rise to state responsibility if the respondent state fails to provide adequate redress through local remedies.

10.6.1 Standard of treatment

One area of considerable controversy is the standard of treatment to be accorded to foreign nationals. A state will only be responsible for treatment of aliens which falls below this standard. There are two conflicting views. Most Western states adhere to the concept of an international minimum standard of treatment. Every state is under a duty to treat aliens within its territory in accordance with this standard. This is so even if municipal law imposes a lower standard of treatment with respect to home nationals. This view was applied in

---

46 *ILC Report* 1996 Chapter II.

47 By its Resolution 51/207 of 17 December 1996, the General Assembly took note of the report of the Preparatory Committee on the Establishment of an International Criminal Court (A/51/22), and decided that the Preparatory Committee shall meet from 11 to 21 February, 4 to 15 August and 1 to 12 December 1997, and from 16 March to 3 April 1998, in order to complete the drafting of a widely acceptable consolidated text of a convention, to be submitted to the diplomatic conference of plenipotentiaries to be held in 1998.

the *Neer Claim* (1926)[48] by the US-Mexican Claims Tribunal and in the *Chevreu* case (1931)[49] by an Anglo-French arbitral tribunal. Proponents of the international minimum standard have sought to argue that the concept is inextricably linked to the international law of human rights which is discussed in Chapter 15.

The opposing view is that foreign nationals are only entitled to be treated in the same manner as home nationals. This national standard would imply that the only thing to guard against is discrimination against foreign nationals. Article 9 of the Montevideo Convention on the Rights and Duties of States 1933 reflected this view by providing that 'foreigners may not claim rights other or more extensive than those of the nationals'. The national standard has been most strongly advocated by the developing states in the context of nationalisation of foreign owned property. This topic is discussed in Chapter 16.

It seems clear that it is not possible to discern a general rule of international law relating to treatment of aliens. Much depends upon the particular rights being asserted. What is more certain is that it is for international law to decide which standard operates in a particular case and this is related to the general principle that provisions of municipal law cannot be used as a defence to breaches of international obligations.

10.7 *Locus standi* and the right to bring claims

The general rule is that it is only injured states which are able to bring international claims against other states for a breach of some international obligation. The principle was strictly applied in the second phase of the *South West Africa* case (1966)[50] when the ICJ held that Liberia and Ethiopia had no legal interest in South Africa's treatment of the inhabitants of Namibia. Although both states had been original members of the League of Nations and therefore had certain rights under the Mandate agreement between the League and South Africa, the Court held that enforcement of the Mandate was a matter for the League alone and individual members suffered no injury and therefore had no independent right to bring claims arising out of breaches of its provisions. Article 5(1) of the ILC Draft Articles on State Responsibility, Part II (1985) provides that an injured state is any state a right of which is infringed by the act of another state if such an act constitutes an internationally wrongful act. Article 5(2) lists a number of situations in which injury will have occurred and this includes breaches of treaty obligations, both bilateral and multilateral, together with breaches of customary international law. Thus, for example, breaches of the European Convention on Human Rights by a State Party may be pursued by any other State Party to the Convention and there is no requirement that the victim of the human rights abuse should be a national of the claiming state.

---

48   (1926) RIAA 60.
49   (1931) RIAA 575.
50   [1966] *ICJ Rep* at p 6.

Article 5(3) of the Draft Articles goes further by providing that if the internationally wrongful act constitutes an international crime (see 9.4) then 'injured state' means all other states. This idea of collective responsibility is one of the most controversial areas of state responsibility and Article 5(3) cannot in any way be said to express an existing rule of international law. The concept of international crimes and *erga omnes* obligations is of particular relevance to claims arising out of human rights abuses, breaches of humanitarian law and environmental damage and will be further discussed in Chapters 14, 15 and 17.

10.8 Nationality of claims

Where a state has suffered directly from an internationally wrongful act such as the breach of a treaty obligation owed to it there will be little difficulty in establishing its right to bring an international claim. However, states may also suffer indirectly. Internationally wrongful acts can occur in respect of the treatment of individuals or corporations. In such situations, the claiming state needs to establish its right to make a claim on behalf of the individual or corporation that has suffered injury. It should be noted that what is being discussed here is the right to bring claims; whether or not a state will actually bring a claim depends on many other considerations, discussion of which is outside the ambit of this book.

10.8.1 Individuals

States may often raise diplomatic protests about the treatment of individuals by foreign states and such protests are not confined to activities involving their own nationals. However, for a state to make specific representation involving claims to reparation and compensation arising from injuries to an individual or group of individuals, or damage to their property, it must be able to show that these individuals are in fact its nationals. The basic rule is that the victim must be a national of the plaintiff state at the time the damage was caused and remain so until the claim is decided. This rule was applied by the PCIJ in the *Panevezys-Saldutiskis* case (1939), the Court stating that:

> In taking up the case of one of its nationals, by resorting to diplomatic action or international judicial proceedings on his behalf, a state is in reality asserting its own right, the right to ensure in the person of its nationals respect for the rules of international law. This rule is necessarily limited to intervention on behalf of its own nationals, because, in the absence of a special agreement, it is the bond of nationality between the state and the individual which alone confers upon the state the right of diplomatic protection.[51]

As indicated by the Court, the general rule can be waived with the consent of the respondent state.

Problems may arise when the individual concerned has dual nationality. Article 4 of the Hague Convention on Certain Questions Relating to the Conflict of Nationality Laws (1930) provides that a state may not exercise protection in respect of one of its nationals against a state whose nationality such person also

---

51 PCIJ Reports Ser A/B, No 76 (1939).

possesses. However, state practice has not always accorded with this provision and its utility was doubted when the Iran-US Claims Tribunal (1984) had to consider a number of individuals who had dual Iranian-US nationality. Article 4 is probably good law when an individual has equal connections with both states of which he or she is a national. However, tribunals will look to see whether the individual has closer or more effective links with one state when deciding questions of the right to exercise diplomatic protection. A state will be able to bring a claim on behalf of its national even if he or she is a national of the respondent state provided that the claimant state can establish the closer, more effective links with the individual concerned. This concept of an effective link was approved by the ICJ in the *Nottebohm* case (1955).[52] In that case the government of Liechtenstein instituted proceedings on the basis that Guatemala had acted unlawfully towards the person and property of Friedrich Nottebohm, a citizen of Liechtenstein. Guatemala disputed Liechtenstein's right to bring the case. Mr Nottebohm had been born in Germany in 1881. In 1905 he had gone to Guatemala and taken up residence there. He continued to travel to Germany and other countries on business and retained his German nationality. He made a few visits to Liechtenstein where his brother lived. While visiting his brother in 1939 he applied for and obtained Liechtenstein nationality. He subsequently had obtained a Guatemalan visa for his Liechtenstein passport and returned to Guatemala. The essential question for the Court was whether the nationality conferred on Nottebohm in 1939 could be relied upon as against Guatemala in justification of the commencement of proceedings. The Court acknowledged that the granting of nationality was a matter of municipal law but found that the right to exercise diplomatic protection of nationals was a matter of international law which the ICJ was entitled to determine. The Court stated that:

> According to the practice of states, to arbitral and judicial decisions and to the opinions of writers, nationality is a legal bond having as its basis a social fact of attachment, a genuine connection of existence, interests and sentiments, together with the existence of reciprocal rights and duties. It may be said to constitute the juridical expression of the fact that the individual upon whom it is conferred ... is in fact more closely connected with the population of the state conferring nationality than with that of any other state. Conferred by a state, it only entitles that state to exercise protection *vis-à-vis* another state, if it constitutes a translation into juridical terms of the individual's connection with the state which has made him its national.

The Court found that Nottebohm had little real connection with Liechtenstein, whereas he had been settled in Guatemala for 34 years and had an intention to remain there. His connection with Guatemala was therefore far stronger than any connection with Liechtenstein and consequently Liechtenstein was not entitled to extend its protection over him *vis-à-vis* Guatemala.

In the same year as the *Nottebohm* case the Italian-US Conciliation Commission considered the *Merge Claim*. The claimant had both US and Italian nationality and the tribunal found that:

> The principle, based on the sovereign equality of states, which excludes diplomatic protection in the case of dual nationality, must yield before the

---

52 [1955] *ICJ Rep* at p 4.

principle of effective nationality wherever such nationality is that of the claiming state.

This *dictum* was subsequently approved and found to be an expression of customary international law by the Iran-US Claims Tribunal.

10.8.2 *Corporations and their shareholders*

Prima facie, a corporation has the nationality of the state where it was incorporated. The problem arises in the fact that companies may be incorporated in states with which they have very little connection. The right of states to bring claims on behalf of shareholders was discussed in the *Barcelona Traction* case (1970).[53] The Barcelona Traction, Light and Power Company was a holding company incorporated in Canada in 1911 to develop and establish an electricity company in Spain. It created three subsidiary companies in Canada, most of whose shares it owned; and a number of operating and concessionary companies in Spain. The case arose following action taken by Spain which resulted in the company being declared bankrupt. Belgium sought to bring a claim based upon the allegation that most of Barcelona Traction's shares were owned by Belgian nationals and companies, mainly by a company called Sidro, the principal shareholder in which was another company called Sofina in which Belgian interests were again predominant. Spain argued that the injury had been done to the company rather than its shareholders and therefore Belgium lacked *locus standi* to bring the claim. The Court found that although shareholders had suffered it was only as a result of wrongs done to the company. The Court adopted the municipal law concept of the corporate veil and the distinction to be drawn between the personality of the company and its individual shareholders. As far as diplomatic protection was concerned, the Court stated that:

> The traditional rule attributes the right of diplomatic protection of a corporate entity to the state under the laws of which it is incorporated and in whose territory it has its registered office. These two criteria have been confirmed by long practice and by numerous international instruments.

It went on to acknowledge that there were situations where some further degree of connection was necessary but that no absolute test of 'genuine connection' existed in international law. It further suggested that there may be situations where:

> If in a given case it is not possible to apply the general rule that the right of diplomatic protection of a company belongs to its national state, considerations of equity might call for the possibility of protection of the shareholders in question by their own national state.

However, such a situation did not arise in the *Barcelona Traction* case and therefore the Court rejected the Belgian claim. Such situations may arise where the company itself no longer exists or more commonly where it is the national state of the company that actively injures the company.

---

53   [1970] *ICJ Rep* at p 3.

10.9 Exhaustion of local remedies

An important rule applicable to indirect injuries to states is that a claim will not be admissible on the international plane unless the individual or corporation has exhausted the remedies provided by the local state. The rule is justified by political and practical considerations. It allows the local state to redress any wrong that has been committed before the matter reaches the level of international dispute settlement. In the *Norwegian Loans* case (1957)[54] Judge Lauterpacht commented that:

> The requirement of exhaustion of local remedies is not a purely technical or rigid rule. It is a rule which international tribunals have applied with a considerable degree of elasticity.

In particular, international tribunals are only concerned with effective local remedies. The rule was considered in the *Ambatelios Arbitration* (1956)[55] which arose following a contractual dispute between a Greek national and the UK. Mr Ambatelios failed to call a vital witness and also failed to take advantage of the opportunity of taking the case to the Court of Appeal. The Commission of Arbitration found that it was up to the defendant state to prove the existence in its municipal law of effective remedies which have not been used. The Commission stated that:

> Local remedies include not only reference to the courts and tribunals, but also the use of the procedural facilities which municipal law makes available to litigants before such courts and tribunals. It is the whole system of legal protection, as provided by municipal law, which must have been put to the test before a state, as the protector of its nationals, can prosecute the claim on the international plane.

An individual or corporation does not need to exhaust all appeal mechanisms if such appeals are clearly going to prove futile. In the *Finnish Shipowners Arbitration* (1934)[56] the UK objected to the Finnish claim on the basis that the Finnish nationals had failed to appeal against a decision of the UK's Admiralty Transport Arbitration Board. The international arbitrator accepted the Finnish argument that in the particular case the Court of Appeal would have been unable to overturn the finding of fact made by the Arbitration Board and that an appeal would therefore have made no difference. Finland was therefore within its rights to pursue the claim on the international plane.

It should be emphasised that the requirement of the exhaustion of local remedies only applies to indirect wrongs and is not relevant where the claimant state has suffered direct injury. Thus the rule did not apply in the *Aerial Incident of 27 July 1955* case (1956)[57] which arose following the shooting down of an Israeli aircraft over Bulgaria. There may be some confusion where a claim arises following injury to nationals which is in breach of treaty provisions. A breach of a treaty obligation would normally be considered to amount to a direct wrong, but where the treaty is invoked on behalf of nationals the local remedies rule

---

54   [1957] *ICJ Rep* at p 9.
55   (1956) 12 RIAA 83.
56   (1934) RIAA 1479.
57   [1956] *ICJ Rep* at p 127.

will generally still apply. The point was considered by the ICJ in the *Elettronica Sicula SpA (ELSI)* case (1989).[58] The US brought a claim against Italy following the nationalisation of ELSI, an Italian corporation wholly owned by two US corporations. Italy claimed that local remedies had not been exhausted while the US argued that the rule did not apply since it was claiming compensation for the two US companies on the basis of the Treaty of Friendship, Commerce and Navigation 1948 between the US and Italy. It therefore sought to argue that the breach of treaty amounted to a direct international wrong. The ICJ found, however, that the principal issue in the case was the injury suffered by the US corporations and it was not possible to separate this from the direct wrong of the breach of treaty. It stated that the parties to treaties could expressly agree that the local remedies rule would or would not apply, but, in the absence of any relevant agreement, where a claim was partly based on injury suffered by nationals, the rule would be presumed to apply. Having dealt with the general issues involved the Court then found that in the particular case local remedies had been exhausted.

10.10 Defences and justifications

In certain circumstances, a breach of an international obligation imputable to a state may not give rise to international responsibility. Chapter V of the ILC's Draft Articles, Part I indicates a number of circumstances which will 'preclude wrongfulness' and thus provide a defence to international claims. State responsibility will not arise in the following situations:

(i)   where the defendant state was coerced into committing the wrongful act by another state;

(ii) where the defendant state had acted with the consent of the harmed state;

(iii) where the defendant state was merely taking permissible counter-measures. Actions involving the use of armed force are excluded from this category of defence.

(iv) where the defendant state's officials acted under *force majeure* or extreme distress and were not wilfully seeking the harm caused. The standard of proof in such cases is high.

The Draft Articles also allow two justifications for wrongful action: necessity and self defence. Necessity will only justify wrongful action if the act was the only means of safeguarding an essential state interest against a grave and imminent peril, and that the act did not seriously impair an essential interest of the state to whom the obligation was owed. For example, in 1967, the Liberian tanker the Torrey Canyon went aground off the UK coast, outside territorial waters, spilling large quantities of oil. After several salvage attempts, the UK finally bombed the ship to burn and disperse the oil. The ILC took the view that this action was justified by necessity. Self-defence justifies an otherwise wrongful act if the measures adopted in self-defence are taken in conformity with the UN Charter. The topic of self-defence will be further discussed in Chapter 13. Neither justification will be available in the case of a violation of a peremptory norm of international law (*jus cogens*).

---

58   [1989] *ICJ Rep* at p 15.

49   The Court will now consider the question of whether there was, in 1989, a state of necessity which would have permitted Hungary, without incurring international responsibility, to suspend and abandon works that it was committed to perform in accordance with the 1977 Treaty and related instruments.

50   In the present case, the parties are in agreement in considering that the existence of a state of necessity must be evaluated in the light of the criteria laid down by the International Law Commission in Article 33 of the Draft Articles on the International Responsibility of States, that it adopted on first reading. That provision is worded as follows:

Article 33   State of necessity

1   A state of necessity may not be invoked by a state as a ground for precluding the wrongfulness of an act of that state not in conformity with an international obligation of the state unless:

(a)   the act was the only means of safeguarding an essential interest of the state against a grave and imminent peril; and

(b)   the act did not seriously impair an essential interest of the state towards which the obligation existed.

2   In any case, a state of necessity may not be invoked by a state as a ground for precluding wrongfulness:

(a)   if the international obligation with which the act of the state is not in conformity arises out of a peremptory norm of general international law; or

(b)   if the international obligation with which the act of the state is not in conformity is laid down by a treaty which, explicitly or implicitly, excludes the possibility of invoking the state of necessity with respect to that obligation; or

(c)   if the state in question has contributed to the occurrence of the state of necessity. (*Yearbook of the International Law Commission*, 1980, Vol II, Part 2 at p 34.)

In its Commentary, the Commission defined the 'state of necessity' as being:

The situation of a state whose sole means of safeguarding an essential interest threatened by a grave and imminent peril is to adopt conduct not in conformity with what is required of it by an international obligation to another state (*ibid*, para 1.)

It concluded that 'the notion of state of necessity is ... deeply rooted in general legal thinking' (*Ibid*, p 49, para 31).

51   The Court considers, first of all, that the state of necessity is a ground recognised by customary international law for precluding the wrongfulness of an act not in conformity with an international obligation. It observes moreover that such ground for precluding wrongfulness can only be accepted on an exceptional basis. The International Law Commission was of the same opinion when it explained that it had opted for a negative form of words in Article 33 of its Draft:

In order to show, by this formal means also, that the case of invocation of a state of necessity as a justification must be considered as really constituting an exception and one even more rarely admissible than is the case with the other circumstances precluding wrongfulness ... (*ibid*, p 51, para 40).

Thus, according to the Commission, the state of necessity can only be invoked under certain strictly defined conditions which must be cumulatively satisfied; the state concerned may not be the sole judge of whether those conditions have been met.

52   In the present case, the following basic conditions set forth in Draft Article 33 are relevant: it must have been occasioned by an 'essential interest' of the state which is the author of the act conflicting with one of its international obligations; that interest must have been threatened by a 'grave and imminent peril'; the act being challenged must have been the 'only means' of safeguarding that interest; that act must not have 'seriously impaired an essential interest' of the state towards which the obligation existed; and the state which is the author of that act must not have 'contributed to the occurrence of the state of necessity'. Those conditions reflect customary international law.

The Court will now endeavour to ascertain whether those conditions had been met at the time of the suspension and abandonment, by Hungary, of the works that it was to carry out in accordance with the 1977 Treaty.

53   The Court has no difficulty in acknowledging that the concerns expressed by Hungary for its natural environment in the region affected by the Gabcikovo-Nagymaros Project related to an 'essential interest' of that state, within the meaning given to that expression in Article 33 of the Draft of the International Law Commission.

The Commission, in its Commentary, indicated that one should not, in that context, reduce an 'essential interest' to a matter only of the 'existence' of the state, and that the whole question was, ultimately, to be judged in the light of the particular case (see *Yearbook of the International Law Commission*, 1980, Vol II, Part 2, p 49, para 32); at the same time, it included among the situations that could occasion a state of necessity, 'a grave danger to ... the ecological preservation of all or some of the territory of a state' (*ibid*, p 35, para 3); and specified, with reference to state practice, that: 'It is primarily in the last two decades that safeguarding the ecological balance has come to be considered an 'essential interest' of all States.' (*ibid*, p 39, para 14.)

The Court recalls that it has recently had occasion to stress, in the following terms, the great significance that it attaches to respect for the environment, not only for states but also for the whole of mankind:

The environment is not an abstraction but represents the living space, the quality of life and the very health of human beings, including generations unborn. The existence of the general obligation of states to ensure that activities within their jurisdiction and control respect the environment of other states or of areas beyond national control is now part of the corpus of international law relating to the environment.' (Legality of the Threat or Use of Nuclear Weapons, Advisory Opinion, *ICJ Reports* 1996, pp 241–42, para 29.)

54   The verification of the existence, in 1989, of the 'peril' invoked by Hungary, of its 'grave and imminent' nature, as well as of the absence of any 'means' to respond to it, other than the measures taken by Hungary to suspend and abandon the works, are all complex processes.

As the Court has already indicated (see para 33 *et seq* above), Hungary on several occasions expressed, in 1989, its 'uncertainties' as to the ecological impact of putting in place the Gabcikovo-Nagymaros barrage system, which is why it asked insistently for new scientific studies to be carried out.

The Court considers, however, that, serious though these uncertainties might have been they could not, alone, establish the objective existence of a 'peril' in the sense of a component element of a state of necessity. The word 'peril' certainly evokes the idea of 'risk'; that is precisely what distinguishes 'peril' from material damage. But a state of necessity could not exist without a 'peril' duly established at the relevant point in time; the mere apprehension of a possible 'peril' could not suffice in that respect. It could moreover hardly be otherwise, when the 'peril' constituting the state of necessity has at the same time to be 'grave' and 'imminent'. 'Imminence' is synonymous with 'immediacy' or 'proximity' and goes far beyond the concept of 'possibility'. As the International Law Commission emphasised in its commentary, the 'extremely grave and imminent' peril must 'have been a threat to the interest at the actual time' (*Yearbook of the International Law Commission*, 1980, Vol II, Part 2, p 49, para 33). That does not exclude, in the view of the Court, that a 'peril' appearing in the long term might be held to be 'imminent' as soon as it is established, at the relevant point in time, that the realisation of that peril, however far off it might be, is not thereby any less certain and inevitable.

The Hungarian argument on the state of necessity could not convince the Court unless it was at least proven that a real, 'grave' and 'imminent' 'peril' existed in 1989 and that the measures taken by Hungary were the only possible response to it.

Both parties have placed on record an impressive amount of scientific material aimed at reinforcing their respective arguments. The Court has given most careful attention to this material, in which the parties have developed their opposing views as to the ecological consequences of the Project. It concludes, however, that, as will be shown below, it is not necessary in order to respond to the questions put to it in the Special Agreement for it to determine which of those points of view is scientifically better founded.

55 The Court will begin by considering the situation at Nagymaros. As has already been mentioned (see para 40 above), Hungary maintained that, if the works at Nagymaros had been carried out as planned, the environment and in particular the drinking water resources in the area would have been exposed to serious dangers on account of problems linked to the upstream reservoir on the one hand and, on the other, the risks of erosion of the riverbed downstream.

The Court notes that the dangers ascribed to the upstream reservoir were mostly of a long-term nature and, above all, that they remained uncertain. Even though the Joint Contractual Plan envisaged that the Gabcikovo power plant would 'mainly operate in peak-load time and continuously during high water', the final rules of operation had not yet been determined (see para 19 above); however, any dangers associated with the putting into service of the Nagymaros portion of the Project would have been closely linked to the extent to which it was operated in peak mode and to the modalities of such operation. It follows that, even if it could have been established which, in the Court's appreciation of the evidence before it, was not the case, that the reservoir would ultimately have constituted a 'grave peril' for the environment in the area, one would be bound to conclude that the peril was not 'imminent' at the time at which Hungary suspended and then abandoned the works relating to the dam.

With regard to the lowering of the riverbed downstream of the Nagymaros dam, the danger could have appeared at once more serious and more pressing, in so far as it was the supply of drinking water to the city of Budapest which would have been affected. The Court would, however, point out that the bed of the

Danube in the vicinity of Szentendre had already been deepened prior to 1980 in order to extract building materials, and that the river had from that time attained, in that sector, the depth required by the 1977 Treaty. The peril invoked by Hungary had thus already materialised to a large extent for a number of years, so that it could not, in 1989, represent a peril arising entirely out of the project. The Court would stress, however, that, even supposing, as Hungary maintained, that the construction and operation of the dam would have created serious risks, Hungary had means available to it, other than the suspension and abandonment of the works, of responding to that situation. It could, for example, have proceeded regularly to discharge gravel into the river downstream of the dam. It could likewise, if necessary, have supplied Budapest with drinking water by processing the river water in an appropriate manner. The two parties expressly recognised that that possibility remained open even though – and this is not determinative of the state of necessity – the purification of the river water, like the other measures envisaged, clearly would have been a more costly technique.

56   The Court now comes to the Gabcikovo sector. It will recall that Hungary's concerns in this sector related on the one hand to the quality of the surface water in the Dunakiliti reservoir, with its effects on the quality of the groundwater in the region, and on the other hand, more generally, to the level, movement and quality of both the surface water and the groundwater in the whole of the Szigetkwz, with their effects on the fauna and flora in the alluvial plain of the Danube (see para 40 above).

Whether in relation to the Dunakiliti site or to the whole of the Szigetkz, the Court finds here again, that the peril claimed by Hungary was to be considered in the long term, and, more importantly, remained uncertain. As Hungary itself acknowledges, the damage that it apprehended had primarily to be the result of some relatively slow natural processes, the effects of which could not easily be assessed.

Even if the works were more advanced in this sector than at Nagymaros, they had not been completed in July 1989 and, as the Court explained in para 34 above, Hungary expressly undertook to carry on with them, early in June 1989. The report dated 23 June 1989 by the *ad hoc* Committee of the Hungarian Academy of Sciences, which was also referred to in para 35 of the present judgment, does not express any awareness of an authenticated peril even in the form of a definite peril, whose realisation would have been inevitable in the long term when it states that:

> The measuring results of an at least five year monitoring period following the completion of the Gabcikovo construction are indispensable to the trustworthy prognosis of the ecological impacts of the barrage system. There is undoubtedly a need for the establishment and regular operation of a comprehensive monitoring system, which must be more developed than at present. The examination of biological indicator objects that can sensitively indicate the changes happening in the environment, neglected till today, have to be included.

The report concludes as follows:

> It can be stated, that the environmental, ecological and water quality impacts were not taken into account properly during the design and construction period until today. Because of the complexity of the ecological processes and lack of the measured data and the relevant calculations the environmental impacts cannot be evaluated.

The data of the monitoring system newly operating on a very limited area are not enough to forecast the impacts probably occurring over a longer term. In order to widen and to make the data more frequent a further multi-year examination is necessary to decrease the further degradation of the water quality playing a dominant role in this question. The expected water quality influences equally the aquatic ecosystems, the soils and the recreational and tourist land-use.

The Court also notes that, in these proceedings, Hungary acknowledged that, as a general rule, the quality of the Danube waters had improved over the past 20 years, even if those waters remained subject to hypertrophic conditions.

However 'grave' it might have been, it would accordingly have been difficult, in the light of what is said above, to see the alleged peril as sufficiently certain and therefore 'imminent' in 1989.

The Court moreover considers that Hungary could, in this context also, have resorted to other means in order to respond to the dangers that it apprehended. In particular, within the framework of the original Project, Hungary seemed to be in a position to control at least partially the distribution of the water between the bypass canal, the old bed of the Danube and the side-arms. It should not be overlooked that the Dunakiliti dam was located in Hungarian territory and that Hungary could construct the works needed to regulate flows along the old bed of the Danube and the side-arms. Moreover, it should be borne in mind that Article 14 of the 1977 Treaty provided for the possibility that each of the parties might withdraw quantities of water exceeding those specified in the Joint Contractual Plan, while making it clear that, in such an event, 'the share of electric power of the Contracting Party benefiting from the excess withdrawal shall be correspondingly reduced'.

57 The Court concludes from the foregoing that, with respect to both Nagymaros and Gabcikovo, the perils invoked by Hungary, without prejudging their possible gravity, were not sufficiently established in 1989, nor were they 'imminent'; and that Hungary had available to it at that time means of responding to these perceived perils other than the suspension and abandonment of works with which it had been entrusted. What is more, negotiations were under way which might have led to a review of the Project and the extension of some of its time-limits, without there being need to abandon it. The Court infers from this that the respect by Hungary, in 1989, of its obligations under the terms of the 1977 Treaty would not have resulted in a situation 'characterised so aptly by the maxim *summum jus summa injuria*' (*Yearbook of the International Law Commission*, 1980, Vol II, Part 2 at p 49, para 31).

Moreover, the Court notes that Hungary decided to conclude the 1977 Treaty, a Treaty which whatever the political circumstances prevailing at the time of its conclusion was treated by Hungary as valid and in force until the date declared for its termination in May 1992. As can be seen from the material before the Court, a great many studies of a scientific and technical nature had been conducted at an earlier time, both by Hungary and by Czechoslovakia. Hungary was, then, presumably aware of the situation as then known, when it assumed its obligations under the Treaty. Hungary contended before the Court that those studies had been inadequate and that the state of knowledge at that time was not such as to make possible a complete evaluation of the ecological implications of the Gabcikovo-Nagymaros Project. It is nonetheless the case that although the principal object of the 1977 Treaty was the construction of a System of Locks for the production of electricity, improvement of navigation on the Danube and protection against flooding, the need to ensure the protection of the environment had not escaped the parties, as can be seen from Articles 15, 19 and 20 of the Treaty.

What is more, the Court cannot fail to note the positions taken by Hungary after the entry into force of the 1977 Treaty. In 1983, Hungary asked that the works under the Treaty should go forward more slowly, for reasons that were essentially economic but also, subsidiarily, related to ecological concerns. In 1989, when, according to Hungary itself, the state of scientific knowledge had undergone a significant development, it asked for the works to be speeded up, and then decided, three months later, to suspend them and subsequently to abandon them. The Court is not, however, unaware that profound changes were taking place in Hungary in 1989, and that, during that transitory phase, it might have been more than usually difficult to co-ordinate the different points of view prevailing from time to time.

The Court infers from all these elements that, in the present case, even if it had been established that there was, in 1989, a state of necessity linked to the performance of the 1977 Treaty, Hungary would not have been permitted to rely upon that state of necessity in order to justify its failure to comply with its treaty obligations, as it had helped, by act or omission to bring it about.

58   It follows that the Court has no need to consider whether Hungary, by proceeding as it did in 1989, 'seriously impair[ed] an essential interest' of Czechoslovakia, within the meaning of the aforementioned Article 33 of the Draft of the International Law Commission a finding which does not in any way prejudge the damage Czechoslovakia claims to have suffered on account of the position taken by Hungary.

Nor does the Court need to examine the argument put forward by Hungary, according to which certain breaches of Articles 15 and 19 of the 1977 Treaty, committed by Czechoslovakia even before 1989, contributed to the purported state of necessity; and neither does it have to reach a decision on the argument advanced by Slovakia, according to which Hungary breached the provisions of Article 27 of the Treaty, in 1989, by taking unilateral measures without having previously had recourse to the machinery of dispute settlement for which that Article provides.

59   In the light of the conclusions reached above, the Court, in reply to the question put to it in Article 2, para 1(a), of the Special Agreement (see para 27), finds that Hungary was not entitled to suspend and subsequently abandon, in 1989, the works on the Nagymaros Project and on the part of the Gabcikovo Project for which the 1977 Treaty and related instruments attributed responsibility to it.

10.11 Remedies for international wrongs

In the *Chorzow Factory* case (1928) the PCIJ was called upon to consider the consequences of the illegal expropriation by Poland of a factory in Upper Silesia. In the course of its judgment the Court stated that:

The essential principle contained in the notion of an illegal act – a principle which seems to be established by international practice and in particular the decisions of arbitral tribunals – is that reparation must, as far as possible, wipe out all the consequences of the illegal act and re-establish the situation which would, in all probability, have existed if that act had not been committed.[59]

59   PCIJ Ser A, No 17 (1928).

It seems to be accepted law that the first consideration, following a breach of an international obligation, should be the restoration of the *status quo* that existed before the wrongful act was committed. Territorial disputes can often readily be settled by means of restitution and in the *Temple of Preah Vihear* case (1962)[60] Thailand was ordered to return to Cambodia objects it had illegally taken from the temple in Cambodia. Where restitution is not physically possible, or even in cases where it is not politically possible, compensation can be paid. The aim of any monetary compensation should be to wipe out the consequences of the illegal act. Compensation should cover all damage which has flowed from the unlawful act, subject to principles of remoteness.

In some cases, monetary compensation will not be an appropriate remedy. In such cases, reparation can be made by satisfaction, which may involve apologising, acknowledging guilt, or accepting the award of a declaratory judgment. For example, in the *Rainbow Warrior* case, the French government did belatedly apologise to the victims of the sinking of the ship.

It was formerly thought that compensation would only be available for actual injury or damage suffered. This view was largely based on the fact that very often states would accept apologies or acknowledgements of guilt as sufficient reparation where no actual physical damage had been caused. However, it is now believed that compensation can be awarded for non-material damage. In the *I'm Alone* case (1933) the *I'm Alone*, a ship registered in Canada, was sunk by US coastguards. The international tribunal found that the ship was almost wholly owned by US nationals and therefore found that no compensation ought to be paid in respect of the loss of the ship or its cargo. However the US was ordered to formally apologise to the Canadian government and to pay $25,000 compensation as acknowledgment of the wrong done to Canada.

---

60   (1933) RIAA 1609.

CHAPTER 11

LAW OF THE SEA

11.1 Introduction

The law of the sea is that law by which states regulate their relations in respect of the marine territory subject to coastal state jurisdiction and those areas of the sea and sea bed beyond any national jurisdiction. The law is an amalgam of treaty and customary rules. It should be noted that the law of the sea is distinct from admiralty or maritime law which is concerned with relations between private persons involved in the transport of passengers or goods by sea.

The law has developed considerably since the end of the Second World War. The 1950s saw a dramatic rise in the number of claims and disputes involving the sea and technological advances together with changes in fishing methods led to a realisation that there was a need for a clarification of the law. The ILC was requested to work on producing a codification of the law of the sea and their work resulted in the subsequent emergence of four conventions governing much of the law. The four conventions marked the first successful occasion in which the ILC was involved in an attempt to codify an area of international law. Many of the conventions' provisions reflected rules of customary international law although some provisions represented a new development and thus did not bind non-parties. The four conventions were adopted at the first and second Geneva Conferences on the Law of the Sea of 1958 and 1960 (UNCLOS I and II). The conventions were:

- Convention on the Territorial Sea and the Contiguous Zone (TSC) which entered into force on 10 September 1964;
- Convention on the Continental Shelf (CSC) which entered into force on 10 June 1964;
- Convention on Fishing and the Conservation of the Living Resources of the High Seas (FC) which entered into force on 20 March 1966;
- Convention on the High Seas (HSC) which entered into force on 30 September 1962.

UNCLOS III convened in 1973 to reach agreement on a Law of the Sea Convention which would deal with many new areas of concern including the exclusive economic zone (EEZ) and the deep sea bed. The Conference did not convene to discuss any pre-existing draft convention but had its origins in the Sea Bed Committee which had been established by the UN General Assembly in 1967. Advances in technology during the 1960s opened up for the first time the possibility of exploiting the rich resources of the deep sea bed and discussions about the regime for the deep sea bed took up much of the discussion at UNCLOS III. Because of the big difference in views between developing and developed states it was thought that there was little use in adopting provisions of a new treaty by majority vote. The success of any new convention would depend upon the acceptance of the major maritime states who could be outvoted by other participants at the conference. The procedure adopted at UNCLOS III was therefore to look for consensus in an attempt to obtain maximum support for the whole convention. The outcome of UNCLOS III was the Law of the Sea Convention 1982 (LOSC) which entered into force on 16 November 1994, 12 months after Guyana became the 60th state to ratify it. Many of the provisions of LOSC reflect customary international law and thus will bind non-parties, but some parts of the Convention are much more controversial and have yet to gain the acceptance of many of the major maritime powers.

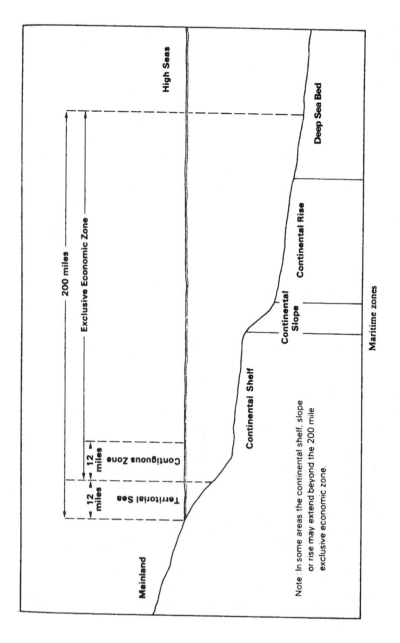

Much of the law of the sea is concerned with the rights enjoyed by states in particular maritime zones. The principle zones that can be identified are:

- the territorial sea over which the coastal state enjoys many of the rights which attach to land territory. The regime of the territorial sea is discussed at 11.4;
- the exclusive economic zone (EEZ) and the contiguous zone which refers to an area of sea beyond the territorial sea over which the coastal state enjoys limited rights. The EEZ is discussed at 11.5.
- the continental shelf which refers to the area of sea bed not covered by deep ocean. The continental shelf is discussed at 11.6;
- the high seas which is constituted by all those areas of sea not included in the territorial sea or EEZ. The regime of the high seas is discussed at 11.7.

11.2 Baselines

In determining the extent of a coastal state's territorial sea and other maritime zones it is obviously necessary to establish from what line on the coast the outer limits are to be measured. This line is referred to as the baseline. The waters on the landward side of the baseline are internal waters and are an integral part of the territory of the coastal state. None of the provisions of the law of the sea applies to internal waters and a state enjoys full territorial sovereignty over them. The rules for delimiting baselines are to be found in Articles 3–11 and Article 13 of the TSC and in Articles 4–14 and Article 16 of the LOSC. The rules there stated are deemed to represent customary international law.

The starting point for drawing the baseline is the low-water line along the coast (Article 3 of the TSC and Article 5 of the LOSC) and this will be used wherever the coastline is relatively straight and unindented. Different rules apply to:

- coastlines which are heavily indented or fringed with islands;
- bays;
- river mouths;
- harbour works;
- low-tide elevations;
- islands;
- reefs.

There is a general rule that where states depart from the use of the low-water line as a baseline, such departures should be clearly indicated on charts and due publicity should be given to the baseline adopted.

11.2.1 Straight baselines

Where the coastline is heavily indented or fringed with islands it may be impractical for the baseline to follow exactly the low-water mark along the coast. For example, much of the Norwegian coastline is heavily indented by fjords and it is fringed with many small islands and rocky reefs. It would be possible to draw a baseline which followed the low water mark but this would prove difficult and it would mean that ascertaining the outer limit of the territorial sea and other maritime zones would be confusing. Therefore Norway adopted the practice of drawing straight baselines connecting the outer-lying rocks and mouths of fjords along its coast. From the 1930s onwards the UK protested about this Norwegian practice and in 1949 the dispute was referred to the ICJ. In the *Anglo-Norwegian Fisheries* case (1951) the ICJ held that the Norwegian system of straight baselines was in conformity with international law. The court made it clear that the coastal state does not have an unfettered discretion as to how to draw the baseline and there was a requirement that such baselines follow the general direction of the coast. If a state does use straight baselines it must indicate the fact on charts and give due publicity to them.

Both Article 4 of the TSC and Article 7 of the LOSC permit the drawing of straight baselines where the coastline is 'deeply indented and cut into, or if there is a fringe of islands along the coast in its immediate vicinity'. Both conventions make it clear that such baselines should not depart from the general direction of the coast and the sea inside the baseline must be sufficiently closely linked to the land domain to be subject to the regime of internal waters. A further condition is that straight baselines cannot be used to cut off from the high seas the territorial sea of another state. There was an attempt at UNCLOS I to introduce a maximum length for a single straight baseline of 15 miles but the proposal did not obtain widespread agreement. In the *Norwegian Fisheries* case the ICJ approved one baseline which was 44 miles long.

The normal rule remains the drawing of baselines using the low-water mark and states are under no obligation to use straight baselines. Both TSC and LOSC make clear that the drawing of straight baselines should be limited to exceptional geographical circumstances. More than 50 states have in fact drawn straight baselines along part of their coasts. Not all of these states follow the rules or spirit of the law. For example, Colombia has a straight baseline of 131 miles in length which encloses a smooth coast with no indentations and Vietnam has connected an island 74 miles from its coast to an islet which is 161 miles away although it has been objected to by a number of other states. Prescott, who has carried out a survey of state practice has stated that:

> It would now be possible to draw a straight baseline along any section of coast in the world and cite an existing straight baseline as a precedent.[1]

However, the fact that a number of states have gone beyond what is permitted by the rules of international law does not mean that new customary rules emerge. As the ICJ stated in the *Norwegian Fisheries* case:

> The delimitation of sea areas has always an international aspect; it cannot be dependent merely upon the will of the coastal state as expressed in its municipal law. Although it is true that the act of delimitation is necessarily a unilateral act, because only the coastal state is competent to undertake it, the validity of the delimitation with regard to other states depends upon international law.[2]

Reference should be made to the discussion of customary international law at 3.2.2 on the nature of state practice and the effect of objections to it.

---

1 'Straight and archipelagic baselines' in Blake, 1987, *Maritime Boundaries and Ocean Resources*, London: Croom Helm.

2 [1951] *ICJ Rep* at p 116.

11.2.2 Bays

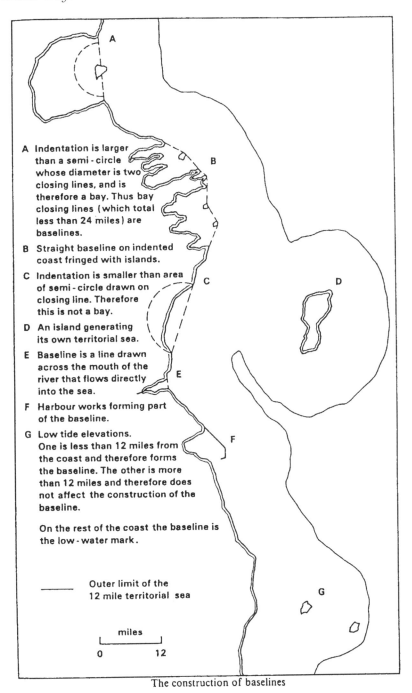

A Indentation is larger than a semi-circle whose diameter is two closing lines, and is therefore a bay. Thus bay closing lines (which total less than 24 miles) are baselines.

B Straight baseline on indented coast fringed with islands.

C Indentation is smaller than area of semi-circle drawn on closing line. Therefore this is not a bay.

D An island generating its own territorial sea.

E Baseline is a line drawn across the mouth of the river that flows directly into the sea.

F Harbour works forming part of the baseline.

G Low tide elevations. One is less than 12 miles from the coast and therefore forms the baseline. The other is more than 12 miles and therefore does not affect the construction of the baseline.

On the rest of the coast the baseline is the low-water mark.

—— Outer limit of the 12 mile territorial sea

miles

0   12

The construction of baselines

International law has always recognised that bays have a close connection with land and that it is more appropriate for them to be considered internal waters rather than territorial sea. Customary international law therefore has long accepted that straight baselines can be drawn across the mouths of bays. The difficulty was in determining the amount of indentation required for a bay, and the maximum length of a closing line. Article 7 of the TSC established clear rules which are repeated in Article 10 of the LOSC. To establish whether an indentation is a bay, a line should be drawn across the natural entrance points of the indentation. A semi-circle should then be drawn with the line forming the diameter. The area of this semi-circle should be measured and compared with the area of the total indentation. If the area of water is greater than the semi-circle then the indentation is a bay. A closing line can then be drawn. If the closing line does not exceed 24 miles it will constitute the baseline. If the closing line is greater than 24 miles a closing line of 24 miles is drawn to enclose the greatest amount of water possible and the line forms the baseline. With respect to any part of the bay which remains unenclosed the baseline will be the low-water mark. A problem which has remained unresolved is how the natural entrance points to a bay are established. In *Post Office v Estuary Radio* (1968)[3] the UK Court of Appeal had to decide whether the Thames estuary was a bay in a case involving pirate radio broadcasting. The estuary's status as a bay depended upon where the closing line was drawn. No two points were obviously the entrance points to the estuary although the Court of Appeal found in favour of the Post Office's contention that the entrance points could be located at a point which would mean the estuary satisfied the test of a bay set down in TSC.

These rules pertaining to bays do not apply where straight baselines are used nor do they apply to historic bays. Historic bays are not dealt with in either TSC or LOSC but have long been a feature of customary international law although it is clear that the regime attaching to historic bays depends upon the particular circumstances of each case. In some situations a state may enjoy full sovereignty over an historic bay, in others it may only enjoy exclusive fishing rights. In *El Salvador v Nicaragua* (1917)[4] the Central American Court of Justice held that the Gulf of Foncesa, which is surrounded by Nicaragua, Honduras and El Salvador and which is about 19 miles across at its mouth was 'an historic bay possessed of the characteristics of a closed sea' over which the three states held joint sovereignty. In 1973 Libya claimed the Gulf of Sidra as an historic bay and drew a closing line across it which is 296 miles in length. Several states objected to Libya's claims and the USA sent a naval squadron into the area to emphasise the point that it considered the Gulf to constitute high seas. In 1981 US shot down two Libyan aircraft flying over the Gulf and there seems little evidence that the bay is a historic bay.

The general rules applying to bays do not apply where the bay is bordered by more than one state, for example Lough Foyle which is bordered by Ireland and the UK. Such situations will normally be resolved by agreement between

---

3   [1968] 2 QB 740.
4   (1917) *AJIL* 674.

the states concerned but the general view seems to be that the baseline follows the low-water mark and no closing line is drawn.

11.2.3 River mouths

Both Article 13 of the TSC and Article 9 of the LOSC provide that if a river flows directly into the sea, the baseline shall be a straight line across the mouth of the river between points on the low water line of its banks. No limit is placed on the length of such a closing line. The rule applies only to rivers which flow directly into the sea. It does not apply to rivers which flow into the sea via estuaries although this is not always an easy distinction. Estuaries occur where the river valley becomes flooded by the sea and the mouth of the river takes on a characteristic funnel shape. Estuaries are treated as bays as was seen in *Post Office v Estuary Radio* (1968).[5] Sometimes a river will carry down solid material which, if they cannot be removed by the action of the tides, form alluvial deposits at the mouth of the river. As the deposits build up the river will divide and sub-divide as it flows into the sea and a delta will be formed. If the river enters the sea via a delta, baselines will be calculated by the low-water line or by straight baselines.

11.2.4 Harbour works

Article 8 TSC provides that the outermost permanent harbour works such as piers and breakwaters which form an integral part of the harbour system are to be regarded as forming part of the coast and can therefore act as the baseline. This provision is repeated in Article 11 of the LOSC, although LOSC makes it clear that harbour works must be attached to the coast. Off-shore installations and artificial islands are not to be considered as harbour works.

11.2.5 Low-tide elevations

Article 11(1) of the TSC and Article 13(1) of the LOSC define a low-tide elevation as a naturally formed area of land which is surrounded by and above water at low tide but submerged at high tide. Such elevations are sometimes referred to as drying rocks. Where a low-tide elevation is situated wholly or partly at a distance not exceeding the breadth of the territorial sea from the mainland or an island, the low-water line on that elevation may be used as the baseline for measuring the breadth of the territorial sea. Where the elevation is situated beyond the limits of the territorial sea, it cannot be used for the purposes of drawing baselines. Low-tide elevations are also often used in the drawing of straight baselines.

11.2.6 Islands

Article 10(1) of the TSC and Article 121(1) of the LOSC define an island as a naturally formed area of land surrounded by water which is above water at high tide. There is no condition as to size nor habitation, although as regards isolated islands which are incapable of sustaining habitation the rules on

---

5   [1968] 1 QB 740.

acquisition of territory discussed in Chapter 6 may be relevant. The general rules applying to baselines will apply to islands and this clearly poses no problems in the case of large islands such as Britain. With the development of the regimes of the continental shelf and EEZ the significance of small islands vastly increased. It is accepted that every island, no matter how small, is capable of possessing a territorial sea but doubts have been expressed as to whether small islands have continental shelves or EEZs. Article 121(2) of the LOSC provides that islands will possess baselines for all maritime zones, but an exception is made in the case of rocks which are incapable of sustaining human habitation or economic life of their own. Such islands can only serve as the baseline for the territorial sea and contiguous zone and not for the continental shelf and EEZ. In practice most uninhabitable island rocks lie immediately offshore and will be dealt with under the provisions relating to straight baselines and archipelagic states. Regimes applying to rocks which lie a long way offshore, such as Rockall which lies 240 miles west of the Outer Hebrides, tend to be or have been the subject of specific agreement or dispute resolution.

11.2.7 Reefs

A reef is formed by a ridge of rocks or coral which lies near the surface of the sea. An atoll is a reef which forms in the shape of a horseshoe or ring, usually enclosing an island. Reefs and atolls may be permanently submerged or, if exposed at low tide, may be situated from the mainland at a distance greater than the breadth of the territorial sea. They would therefore not come within the definition of low-tide elevations and could not therefore be used for the purposes of drawing baselines. However, there are strong ecological reasons for holding that the sea on the land side of the reef, the lagoon, has the status of internal waters.

There was discussion about the status of reefs at UNCLOS I but no provisions were included in TSC. The emergence during the 1960s of many independent states in the Caribbean and the Indian and Pacific Oceans possessing reefs disclosed a need to establish clear rules with respect to reefs and atolls. Article 6 of the LOSC provides that:

> ... in the case of islands situated on atolls or of islands having fringing reefs, the baseline for measuring the breadth of the territorial sea is the seaward low-water line of the reef.

The provision suggests that the rules will only apply to reefs which are exposed at low tide although the ILC draft prepared for UNCLOS I provided that 'the edge of the reef as marked on charts should be accepted as the low-water line'. It also remains unclear as to whether there is any limit to how far from an island a fringing reef can lie, although most geographical works refer to fringing reefs as lying near the shore of an island, with corals growing out from the shore to a depth of about 50 metres. Fringing reefs are to be distinguished from barrier reefs which lie at some distance from the shore. Thus Article 6 would not apply to the Great Barrier Reef which in places is 150 miles from the coast of Australia. The environmental concerns relating to the Great Barrier Reef have partly been dealt with under the World Heritage Convention 1975 which is discussed in Chapter 17.

11.2.8 Archipelagos

Archipelago is the term used to refer to a group of islands and a question arises as to whether the baseline should follow the low-water mark of every island or whether straight baselines can be used to connect the outermost parts of the group of islands to enclose the archipelago. The question was discussed at UNCLOS I but no final agreement was reached although Article 4 of the TSC did allow the use of straight baselines in the case of coastal archipelagos, ie groups of islands fringing a coast. In 1957 Indonesia announced that its territorial sea would henceforth be measured from straight baselines drawn between the outermost points on the islands forming the Republic of Indonesia. The waters within the baselines would be regarded as internal waters although the peaceful passage of foreign vessels through them would be guaranteed. A similar measure was adopted by the Philippines. A number of states protested but the issue was not authoritatively settled. The concern of the major maritime states was that many of the archipelagic states straddled important shipping lanes and they feared that the adoption of straight baselines and creating large areas of internal water might lead to a considerable loss of navigational freedom.

During the 1960s a number of archipelagic states achieved independence and it became clear that there was a need for some agreement on the drawing of baselines in respect of such states. A new regime was introduced in Part IV LOSC. The new regime allows straight baselines to be drawn between the outermost points of the islands but would only apply in the case of 'archipelagic states'. An archipelagic state is defined in Article 46 as a state constituted wholly by one or more archipelagos. This definition does not include mainland states with non-coastal archipelagos, for example Portugal which possesses the archipelago of the Azores, lying 900 miles west of Lisbon. Nor would it apply to the Azores themselves since they do not constitute a state on their own. The definition would seem to include states such as the UK and New Zealand although they would not consider themselves to be archipelagic states. In any event Article 47 of the LOSC merely provides that archipelagic states may draw straight baselines; it imposes no obligation to do so.

A number of conditions are set down regarding the drawing of straight baselines. They can only be drawn round the archipelago in such a way as the ratio of land to water is not more than 1:1 and not less than 1:9. This condition would itself exclude the UK and New Zealand and also the very widely scattered archipelagos. The baselines must not exceed 100 miles in length and must not depart from the general configuration of the archipelago.

11.3   Internal waters

Internal waters are those which lie on the landward side of the baseline from which the territorial sea and other maritime zones are calculated. As has already been seen, internal waters may include bays, estuaries and ports and waters enclosed by straight baselines. Internal waters constitute an integral part of the coastal state and the coastal state enjoys full sovereign rights over them. There is no right of innocent passage through internal waters such as exists through the territorial sea. Two particular aspects of a coastal state's sovereignty over internal waters have given rise to much discussion: the right of access to ports and other internal waters; and the exercise of jurisdiction over foreign ships in ports. It should also be noted that a special regime applies to archipelagic waters.

11.3.1 Rights of access to ports and other internal waters

The rules of sovereignty over internal waters mean that there is no general right in customary law for foreign ships to enter a coastal state's ports. This point was confirmed by the ICJ in the *Nicaragua* case (1986). Although coastal states will normally allow the entry of foreign merchant ships into their ports, there is no indication that such practice is supported by sufficient *opinio juris* to create a rule of customary international law. The only situation in which a foreign ship would be entitled as of right to enter internal waters would be where it was in distress and seeking safety. Such a situation would give rise to application of the general defences to state responsibility discussed at 9.9. It is clear that there are no general rights of entry to foreign warships.

Normally states will nominate those of their ports which are open to international trade and will so designate such ports of entry for customs and immigration purposes. Customary international law allows states to close their international ports to protect their vital interests and it is for the state itself to define what constitutes its vital interests. States also have a wide discretion to prescribe conditions for access to their ports. It is usual for states to enter into bilateral treaties, usually known as Treaties of friendship, navigation and commerce (FCN Treaties), which will set down rights and conditions of access to internal waters and ports. Among EU member states access to internal waters is governed by the general rules relating to freedom of movement and the free movement of goods.

Questions relating to the access of foreign ships will also arise in respect of navigable rivers and canals which also constitute internal waters. Access here will generally be much more restricted although as was mentioned at 6.6 most international rivers and canals, ie those which flow through the territory of more than one state, will be subject to specific international agreement.

11.3.2 Exercise of jurisdiction over foreign ships in internal waters

Since internal waters constitute an integral part of the territory of a state, application of the territorial rules of jurisdiction would imply that a state is entitled to enforce its laws against all ships and those on board within its internal waters, subject to the rules of sovereign and diplomatic immunity. However, since ships are more or less self-contained units and are subject to the laws of the flag state at all times, coastal states will usually only enforce their laws in cases where their particular interests are involved. Local jurisdiction will be asserted when the offence affects the peace or good order of the port, for example in the case of customs or immigration offences.

11.3.3 Archipelagic waters

The concept of archipelagic waters was created at UNCLOS III to deal with the situation arising where archipelagic states made use of straight baselines to enclose the archipelago. Although archipelagic waters form an integral part of the territory of the archipelagic state in the same manner as internal waters, they are subject to certain rights enjoyed by foreign states which are set out in Articles 51 to 53 of the LOSC. These articles provide that existing agreements and traditional rights must be respected and that foreign ships enjoy a right of innocent passage through the archipelagic waters, although the archipelagic state may designate reasonable sea lanes. Within the archipelagic baselines, a state may draw closing lines across river mouths, bays and ports on individual islands and thereby create internal waters.

11.4   Territorial sea

Throughout the history of modern international law it has been accepted that coastal states enjoy certain rights in the seas adjoining their coasts. A distinction has long been made between the freedom of the high seas over which no claims to sovereignty could be made and territorial waters over which coastal states enjoyed particular rights and undertook certain duties. What was not settled was the question of the breadth of the territorial waters and the precise nature of the rights and duties which existed there. There was also a question as to whether states automatically possessed a territorial sea or whether it had to be specifically and expressly claimed. Debate on these issues continued during the first half of this century and the question did not begin to be settled until the 1950s.

11.4.1 The breadth of the territorial sea

The breadth of the territorial sea has been a matter of controversy throughout history. Early writers used criteria of visibility whilst Grotius and other 17th and 18th century writers suggested that territorial waters extended up to a point at which those waters could be controlled by a shore-based cannon. There were differences as to whether this rule meant that territorial sea followed parallel to the coast or only existed where cannon were actually mounted. Towards the end of the 18th century it was suggested that it made more sense for states to adopt a three-mile limit along the whole of the coast rather than to depend on the existence in particular places of coastal batteries. The three-mile limit was chosen as a matter of reasonableness and convenience, contrary to a popular myth it was not chosen as the actual range of cannon. The three-mile rule gained widespread and rapid approval although it was never unanimously accepted, for example, the Scandinavian countries consistently claimed four miles. During this century there have been repeated attempts to reach agreement on the breadth of the territorial sea which have failed. At UNCLOS II a six-mile territorial sea with an additional six-mile fishing limit was proposed but failed to be adopted by a single vote. By the time UNCLOS III was convened many states were claiming territorial seas of 12 or more. Article 3 of the LOSC sets the limit of the territorial sea at 12 miles. Since there has been no state which has persistently objected to 12-mile limits and a large number of states, including the UK, have now adopted the 12-mile limit, it would be fair to assume that the 12-mile limit has now been accepted as indicative of customary international law on the matter.

11.4.2 Delimitation of maritime boundaries

A major cause of disputes between states is the delimitation of maritime boundaries. Problems can arise in determining the extent of one state's territorial sea or disputes may arise between adjacent or opposite states as to how maritime territory is to be apportioned. It is extremely difficult to set down any universally accepted rules since each case will usually depend very much on its own particular facts. Very often maritime boundaries will be agreed between neighbouring states in specific bilateral agreements. There are however a number of guidelines that can be identified.

In the case of delimitation between opposite states the normal practice has been to agree upon the median line. Practice in delimiting the boundary between adjacent States has been less consistent. Considerable use has been made of the equidistance principle which involves drawing a median line outwards from the boundary on the shore. Other criteria have been used, for example, by drawing a line perpendicular to the general direction of the coast. Some maritime boundaries follow the line of latitude passing through the point where the land boundaries meet the sea. In all cases it is possible that special circumstances, such as the presence of offshore islands or the general configuration of the coast, or claims based on an historic title will demand the adoption of some other boundary line by agreement between the states. These general principles are reflected in Article 12 of the TSC and Article 15 of the LOSC.

11.4.3 The right of innocent passage

The principal restriction on the exercise of sovereignty by the coastal state over its territorial sea is the customary rule of international law allowing foreign ships the right of innocent passage. The right clearly has two aspects which can be discussed further:

Passage: this includes not only actual passage through the territorial sea, but also stopping and anchoring in so far as this is incidental to ordinary navigation or rendered necessary by *force majeure* or distress. This point is reflected in Article 14(3) of the TSC. Article 18 of the LOSC expressly extend the distress provision to cover cases where one ship seeks to assist another ship, person or aircraft in distress. Apart from permitted stopping and anchoring, passage must be continuous and expeditious and foreign ships have no right to hover or cruise around the territorial sea. All submarines must navigate on the surface.

Innocence: for a long time the criterion of innocence lacked any clear definition. In 1930 the Hague Conference which was convened to consider codification of the law of the territorial sea adopted a text which read: 'Passage is not innocent when a vessel makes use of the territorial sea of a coastal state for the purpose of doing any act prejudicial to the security, to the public policy or to the fiscal interests of that state.' It was not possible, however, for a convention to be agreed.

The definition of innocent passage received full discussion in the *Corfu Channel* case (1949) which concerned the passage through the Corfu Channel of British warships. The ICJ considered that the manner of passage was the decisive criterion, holding that as long as the passage was conducted in a fashion which presented no threat to the coastal state it was to be regarded as innocent. Innocence itself was regarded as incapable of objective determination.

There was much discussion of various definitions in the lead up to UNCLOS I and a compromise was reached with Article 14(4) of the TSC. A more precise definition has been achieved in Article 19 of the LOSC.

One particular issue which has raised controversy has been the extent to which the passage of foreign warships can ever be considered innocent. State practice is inconclusive and although in the majority of cases foreign warships request and are given prior authorisation for passage by the coastal state it is unclear whether this is a simple act of courtesy or amounts to sufficient *opinio juris* to create a binding rule of customary international law. A related problem arises with regard to nuclear powered vessels and ships carrying hazardous materials. The general rule would seem to be that such vessels do have a right of innocent passage although there are a number of conventions which set down requirements of notification and documentation. This topic will be discussed further in Chapter 17.

11.4.4 The right to deny and suspend passage

The territorial sea is subject to the sovereignty of the coastal state, and the only right which foreign ships have, apart from any specific treaty provision, is the right of innocent passage. Consequently once a ship ceases to be innocent, or steps outside the scope of passage, it may be excluded from the territorial sea. It also follows that a coastal State has the right to suspend or deny passage altogether where the passage of any ship would be prejudicial to peace, good order or security. Coastal states may also require ships to confine their passage to a particular sea lane.

11.4.5 Straits

A strait is a narrow stretch of water connecting two more extensive areas of sea. It is not defined in any of the law of the sea conventions but reference is made to particular rules which apply in the case of straits. Where straits form part of the high seas then all states will enjoy freedom of navigation. Problems arise where the strait forms part of the territorial sea. As has already been seen coastal states are able to suspend innocent passage through their territorial sea in certain situations. If the strait connects two areas of the high seas such suspension of passage through the strait would affect the freedom of navigation on the high seas. The rule therefore developed and was reflected in Article 16(4) of the TSC that innocent passage could not be suspended in straits used for international navigation connecting one part of the high seas with another.

By the time of UNCLOS III the extension of the breadth of the territorial sea in many cases to 12 miles and the creation of other rights for coastal states led to the issue of straits being considered again. The result is to be found in Part III LOSC which concerns straits used for international navigation. The most significant development is the introduction of a new concept of transit passage. It has been argued by the majority of maritime states that the right of transit passage is now part of customary international law.

The rules on transit passage do not oust those applicable under long-standing conventions which regulate passage through particular straits, for example the Montreux Convention 1936 which concerns the Turkish straits of the Dardenelles and the Bosphorus.

11.5 The exclusive economic zone (EEZ) and the contiguous zone

Following the Second World War an increasing number of states made claims to extend their authority over ships in waters beyond the territorial sea. Such zones were known as 'contiguous zones' and the rights within them had to be positively established in each case. In 1958 contiguous zones were given more widespread recognition in Article 24 of the TSC. This allowed states to claim contiguous zones up to a maximum of 12 miles (the territorial sea distance was still generally accepted as three miles at this time) for customs, fiscal, immigration and sanitary purposes. With the extension of the territorial sea, LOSC extended the limits of the contiguous zone to 24 miles and this is generally accepted to be the customary law position.

The contiguous zone has lessened in importance with the development of the exclusive economic zone (EEZ). The concept developed from the view that fishery resources are not inexhaustible and a widespread concern at the failure to deal adequately with resource management issues at UNCLOS I and II. The Fishing and Conservation of the Living Resources of the High Seas Convention 1958 (FC) had attempted to deal with the conservation of living marine resources but confirmed that all states had the right to engage in fishing on the high seas and only imposed a duty on states to co-operate in adopting such measures as may be necessary for the conservation of resources. The FC set down a procedure for settling disputes and only permitted states to take unilateral action where there was an urgent need for the application of conservation measures. In any event, such unilateral action could not discriminate against foreign fishermen.

In the meantime many states had been seeking to establish exclusive fishing zones outside their territorial waters. In 1945 US President Truman had issued two declarations one of which related to the continental shelf which will be discussed at 10.6; the other, the Proclamation with Respect to Coastal Fisheries in Certain Areas of the High Seas, proposed the establishment of fishery conservation zones in waters beyond the US territorial sea. In fact, this proclamation was never applied but a number of other states developed their own fishing limits, and the twelve-mile fishing zone was recognised as a rule of customary law by the ICJ in the *Fisheries Jurisdiction* case (1974). Many states were claiming much larger exclusive fishing areas and the ICJ left unanswered in that case whether Iceland's 50-mile claim was legitimate. On the particular facts it held that Iceland's unilateral extension was contrary to international law.

Negotiation at UNCLOS III led to fairly widespread acceptance of the concept of a maximum 200-mile EEZ and the ICJ in the *Continental Shelf* case

(1985) and the arbitral tribunal in the *Guinea/Guinea-Bissau* case (1985) have indicated that the EEZ now forms part of customary international law.

11.5.1 Rights within the EEZ

Article 57 of the LOSC provides that the EEZ can extend to a distance of up to 200 miles from the baseline. The regime of the EEZ provides that coastal states do not enjoy full sovereign rights but only sovereign rights for the purpose of exploiting and exploring, conserving and managing the natural resources, whether living or non-living, of the sea bed and subsoil and the superjacent waters. So, for example, a coastal state can set fishing quotas within its EEZ with a view to conserving resources. If the coastal state is unable to catch the amount of fish allowed by the quota then other states will be allowed access to take the remaining amount. The coastal state is not the owner, but rather the guardian of the natural resources of the EEZ. Within the EEZ the coastal state can construct artificial islands and other installations for the purpose of exploring and exploiting the zone which are subject to the coastal state's exclusive jurisdiction. Although such installations are not to be regarded as islands and do not therefore possess territorial seas of their own, it is permissible for the coastal state to establish reasonable safety exclusion zones around them. Other states enjoy the right of free navigation, overflight, pipe-laying and cable-laying provided they respect the rights of the coastal state, which is under a duty to ensure the safety of navigation.

It should be noted that the EEZ has to be specifically claimed; it is not inherent in statehood. At the present time over 70 states have claimed an EEZ. There is further reference to the issue of marine resource management and conservation in Chapter 17.

11.6   The continental shelf

Strictly speaking the continental shelf is a geographical term to describe the sea bed, which is covered by shallow water of generally less than 200 metres, projecting from the coast before a relatively steep descent (the continental slope) to the deep sea bed. The breadth of the continental shelf varies enormously: off some parts of the Pacific coast of the USA the continental shelf extends for less than five miles, while in contrast the whole of the North Sea constitutes continental shelf.

The traditional freedom of the high seas meant that all states enjoyed the rights to explore the sea bed. Disputes began to arise as the oil reserves of the continental shelf became exploitable. In 1945 President Truman claimed exclusive rights to the resources of the contiguous continental shelf in the Proclamation with respect to the natural resources of the subsoil and sea bed of the Continental Shelf. No outer limit to the claim was specified in the Proclamation although an accompanying press release indicated that the continental shelf was only considered to exist to a depth of 200 metres. A large number of similar claims followed and it became clear that there was an urgent need for the law to be clarified and settled.

The outcome of discussion in the 1950s was the Continental Shelf Convention (CSC) agreed at UNCLOS I in 1958. This provides in Article 1 a definition of the continental shelf which includes the sea bed and subsoil to a depth of 200 metres or beyond that limit to where the depth of superjacent waters admits the possibility of exploitation. Part VI LOSC gives an amended definition in terms of maximum distance of 200 miles from the baseline or, exceptionally, to the geophysical limit of the continental shelf up to a maximum of 350 miles.

11.6.1 Continental shelf rights

Part VI LOSC proved to be the least controversial sections of the convention and for the most part is generally regarded as being a codification of customary international law. This point appeared to be confirmed by the ICJ in the *Continental Shelf* case (1985). The rights of the coastal state over the continental shelf are inherent and, unlike in the case of the EEZ, do not have to be expressly claimed. The coastal state has exclusive rights to the exploitation and exploration of the natural resources of the continental shelf, although it may permit other states to undertake exploitation or exploration. Natural resources are defined in Article 2 of the CSC and Article 77(4) of the LOSC.

At UNCLOS I sedentary species were said to include, 'coral, sponges, oysters, including pearl oysters, pearl shell, the sacred chank of India and Ceylon, the trocus and plants'. Disputes have arisen over the status of lobsters and crabs, and in 1963 Brazil raised protests over French fishing of *langoustes* on the Brazilian continental shelf. Adult *langoustes* are normally sedentary but will swim if pursued. The dispute was eventually settled by a compromise which allowed the French limited access to the *langoustes*. Both the UK and the USA have indicated that they consider lobsters but not crabs to be sedentary species. What are excluded are species generally referred to as fish. Of course, rights to fish are dealt with in the EEZ regime. The rights pertaining to the continental shelf do not affect the status of superjacent waters.

As with the EEZ the coastal state is permitted to establish artificial islands and other structures on the continental shelf and to authorise and regulate drilling. Safety zones up to a maximum of 5,000 metres can be established around such structures. Article 79 of the LOSC retains the right of all states to lay submarine cables and pipelines on the continental shelf, although they should not impede the coastal state's right to explore and exploit the area and the course of such pipelines and cables requires the consent of the coastal state.

One aspect of Part VI LOSC which has proved controversial and does not reflect customary law is Article 82 which provides that the coastal state must make payment to the International Sea-bed Authority in respect of exploitation of non-living resources of the continental shelf beyond the 200-mile limit. The role of the International Sea bed Authority and the precise nature of charges will be discussed at 11.8.

11.6.2 Delimitation of the continental shelf and the EEZ

Given the areas of sea and sea bed involved it is not uncommon for two or more states, either opposite or adjacent, to share the continental shelf and the EEZ.

Many issues of delimitation have been dealt with by agreement but there have been a number of disputes which have required settlement by international tribunal. Through looking at the agreements and the decisions of tribunals a number of principles governing delimitation can be ascertained.

Under Article 6 of the CSC delimitation was to be by agreement or failing that in the case of an opposite state the boundary should be the median line, every point of which is equidistant from the nearest point of the baselines of each state. This rule could be departed from if there were special circumstances. In the case of adjacent states, in the absence of an agreement, the boundary should be determined by application of the principle of equidistance from the nearest point of the baselines of each state, unless special circumstances justify some other boundary. In the *North Sea Continental Shelf* cases (1969)[6] the ICJ refused to accept that the equidistance principle was a rule of customary international law and thus it was not binding on West Germany which was not at the time a party to CSC. Instead the Court seemed to favour the application of equitable principles to ensure that each state had a fair allocation of continental shelf which reflected the general configuration and length of the coastlines of the claimant states.

In the *Anglo-French Continental Shelf Arbitration* (1979)[7] an *ad hoc* Court of Arbitration was called upon to consider the delimitation of the continental shelf between France and the UK. Both states were parties to CSC but were unable to reach an agreement. The Court accepted that Article 6 formulated a single special circumstances-equidistance rule rather than two separate rules. This meant that there was no requirement to prove special circumstances, the Court was only obliged to apply the equidistance principle if no other boundary were justified by special circumstances. The Court understood this to require it to ensure an equitable delimitation. It stated that:

> Even under Article 6 it is the geographical and other circumstances of any given case which indicate and justify the use of the equidistance method as the means of achieving an equitable solution rather than the inherent quality of the method as a legal norm of delimitation.

In both the *Continental Shelf* cases (1982[8] and 1985[9]) involving Libya the ICJ stressed the principles of equity and recognised that there should be a reasonable degree of proportionality between the area of shelf appertaining to a state and the length of its coastline. The customary law requirement, simply that an equitable result is achieved in the delimitation of continental shelf and EEZ boundaries, was confirmed in both the *Gulf of Maine* case (1984)[10] and the *Guinea/Guinea-Bissau Maritime Delimitation* case (1985).[11] The most recent case concerning delimitation of the continental shelf and the EEZ involved Denmark and Norway (*Case Concerning Maritime Delimitation in the Area Between Greenland*

---

6   [1969] *ICJ Rep* at p 3.

7   (1979) 53 ILR 6.

8   {1982] *ICJ Rep* at p 18.

9   [1985] *ICJ Rep* at p 1.

10 [1984] *ICJ Rep* at p 246.

11 [1985] *ICJ Rep* at p 127.

and Jan Mayen (1993))[12] where the ICJ again confirmed the need for delimitation to be made according to equitable principles. The case is notable for the separate opinion of Judge Weeramantry who discussed the role of equity in international law at some length. Article 83 of the LOSC provides that delimitation of the continental shelf between opposite or adjacent states shall be achieved by agreement on the basis of international law in order to achieve equitable principles. If no agreement can be reached states are required to seek peaceful settlement of the dispute according to Part XV of the Convention. It seems therefore that the main rule of international law regarding the delimitation of the continental shelf and the EEZ is that an equitable distribution shall be achieved. It therefore follows that each case will depend upon its particular facts although factors such as length and configuration of coastline will be significant.

11.7 High seas

Traditionally, the high seas were defined as 'all parts of the sea not included in the territorial sea or in the internal waters of a state' (Article 1 of the HSC). With the advent of the EEZ and the concept of archipelagic waters, this definition has now to be modified. Article 86 of the LOSC states that the high seas rules apply to: '... all parts of the sea that are not included in the EEZ, in the territorial sea or in the internal waters of a State, or in the archipelagic waters of an archipelagic state.' The dominant principle on the high seas is the presumption of the exclusiveness of flag-state jurisdiction. The legal concept of the high seas also extends to the superjacent air space. It used to extend also to the sea bed, but the emergence of special regimes for the continental shelf and the sea bed beyond national jurisdiction has eroded this wider definition.

The high seas are open to all states and no state may validly purport to subject any part of them to its sovereignty (Article 2 of the HSC, Articles 87 and 89 of the LOSC). This is a fundamental rule of customary international law, although it has not always been so. In the 15th and 16th centuries, national claims were made to sovereignty over extensive areas of the oceans. In 1493, for example, Pope Alexander VI divided the Atlantic Ocean between Spain and Portugal. It was during the great period of maritime exploration in the 17th century that the present rules began to emerge. Grotius in his book *Mare Liberum* argued for the importance of freedom of navigation and by the 19th century it was settled that the high seas were juridically distinct from territorial waters and were not susceptible to appropriation by any state.

11.7.1 Freedom of the high seas

From the rule that no state can subject areas of the high seas to its sovereignty or jurisdiction, it follows that no state has the right to prevent ships of other states from using the high seas for any lawful purpose. Article 2 of the HSC listed the freedoms of navigation, fishing, laying of submarine cables and pipelines and overflight as examples of high seas freedoms but accepted that the list was not

---

12   [1993] *ICJ Rep* at p 1.

exhaustive. All exercise of such freedoms shall be with reasonable regard to the interests of other states, for example, the stringing out of long fishing lines across busy shipping lanes would not be permissible. The exercise of the freedom of the high seas is of course subject to the general rules of international law, such as those governing the use of force. The list in Article 2 has been extended by Article 87 of the LOSC to include the freedom to construct artificial islands and other installations and freedom of scientific research. But LOSC also places greater restrictions on some of the freedoms, particularly in relation to the sea bed and continental shelf. The fact that both conventions give non-exhaustive lists of freedoms means that arguments do ensue over what other freedoms exist. It is generally accepted that some naval manoeuvres and conventional weapons testing may be carried out on the high seas despite the fact that Article 88 of the LOSC provides that the high seas should be used for peaceful purposes. Mariners are notified of the areas and times at which these take place, and although they are not usually forbidden to enter the areas and care is taken to avoid busy areas of the sea, there is a clear expectation that foreign vessels should keep out of such areas. The position with regard to nuclear weapons testing is slightly different. At UNCLOS I the Soviet Union had proposed that nuclear tests should be expressly prohibited by HSC but the conference agreed to refer the matter to the UN General Assembly. In 1963 the Nuclear Test Ban Treaty came into force which expressly prohibits nuclear testing on the high seas. An opportunity to establish whether such testing was contrary to international law was missed in the *Nuclear Tests* cases (1974).[13] France, which was not a party to the Nuclear Test Ban Treaty, had been carrying out tests in the South Pacific to which New Zealand and Australia and a number of other states objected. New Zealand and Australia sought a declaration from the ICJ that such tests were unlawful but before the case was heard France announced it would henceforth cease such tests. The ICJ therefore decided that there was no longer a case to hear. The use of nuclear weapons in armed conflict will be discussed in Chapter 14.

11.7.2 Jurisdiction on the high seas

In general, the flag state, the state which has granted to a ship the right to sail under its flag, has the exclusive right to exercise legislative and enforcement jurisdiction over its ships on the high seas (Article 6 of the HSC and Article 92 of the LOSC). The fiction that a ship is a floating piece of territory is not now approved. The exclusiveness of the flag state's jurisdiction is not, however, absolute. It admits of several exceptions, in which other states share legislative or enforcement jurisdiction, or both, with the flag state.

11.7.2.1 The flagging of ships

Traditionally it has been up to each state to decide itself the grounds on which it will grant the right to fly its flag to a ship. The only restriction on this right was that a state could not confer its 'nationality' on a vessel already under the flag of another state except in consequence of a change of registration. This position

---

13   [1974] *ICJ Rep* at p 253.

was confirmed in Articles 5 and 6 of the HSC. However, in addition to the traditional doctrine HSC attempted to impose a requirement that there be a genuine link between ships and the flag state. The requirement of a genuine link was repeated in Article 91 of the LOSC. The practice of states, however, has not always followed the conventions and there is still widespread use of 'flags of convenience' resulting in there being an absence of any genuine link between flag state and ship. The requirement of a genuine link was also questioned during the Iran-Iraq war and the run up to the Gulf War when the practice of 're-flagging' oil tankers was used to bring the tankers of smaller states under the protection of the US, UK and Soviet navies. Both HSC and LOSC require that ships sail under the flag of one state only and ships which sail under more than one flag are considered to be without nationality.

11.7.2.2 Collisions at sea

Collisions at sea may involve two states, each of which considers the collision and those responsible for it to be within its jurisdiction. The existence of concurrent jurisdiction was upheld by the PCIJ in the *Lotus* case (1927).[14] The rule was much criticised and the position is now set out in Article 11 of the HSC and Article 97 LOSC which provide that penal and disciplinary jurisdiction in cases of collision or other navigational incidents may only be exercised by authorities of the state in whose ship the defendant served or the state of which he is a national.

11.7.2.3 Exceptions to the flag state's exclusive jurisdiction

Piracy: all states have the right and duty to act against piracy (Article 14 of the HSC and Article 100 of the LOSC). Piracy is defined in both conventions (Article 15 of the HSC and Article 101 of the LOSC) as consisting of the following:

(a) any illegal acts of violence or detention, or any act of depredation, committed for private ends by the crew or the passengers of a private ship or aircraft, and directed:

    (i) on the high seas, against another ship or aircraft, or against persons or property on board such ship or aircraft;

    (ii) against a ship, aircraft, persons or property in a place outside the jurisdiction of any state;

(b) any act of voluntary participation in the operation of a ship or of an aircraft with knowledge of facts making it a pirate ship or aircraft;

(c) any act of inciting or of intentionally facilitating an act described in sub-para (a) or (b).

The conventions allow the visiting and boarding of any ship, flying whatever flag, reasonably suspected of being engaged in piracy. If the suspicions prove to be correct the ship may be seized and those engaged in piracy may be arrested and tried in the courts of the seizing state. If the suspicions of piracy prove to be unfounded and unjustified by any action of the ship boarded compensation must be paid for any loss or damage that is sustained.

---

14 PCIJ Ser A, No 9 (1927).

Unlawful acts against maritime safety: following the *Achille Lauro* incident (1985), which was discussed in Chapter 7, the International Maritime Organisation adopted the Convention for the Suppression of Unlawful Acts against the Safety of Maritime Navigation 1988 together with a Protocol for the Suppression of Unlawful Acts against the Safety of Fixed Platforms Located on the Continental Shelf 1988. Neither convention nor protocol is yet in force but they aim to deal with the issue of acts of violence or detention committed on board ships or oil rigs carried out for non-private ends. Such acts would not come within the definition of piracy and the convention and protocol therefore create the specific offence and provide for the jurisdiction of states other than the flag state.

Slavery and drug trafficking: all states are under a duty to suppress the trade and transport of slaves and narcotic and psychotropic drugs and ships suspected of being engaged in such activities may be visited and boarded but it is the right and responsibility of the flag state to proceed with action against those involved in such activities.

Unauthorised broadcasting: Unauthorised broadcasting refers to any radio or television transmission from the high seas which is intended for reception by the general public contrary to international regulations. It is more commonly known as pirate broadcasting. HSC contained no provisions relating to so-called pirate radio broadcasting and there are no clear customary law rules on the subject although reference should be made to the general rules relating to protective and security jurisdiction discussed at 7.4. Article 109(3)(4) of the LOSC does give wide powers of enforcement jurisdiction over pirate radio stations and allows the flag state, the defendant's state, and any state which can receive transmissions or suffer interference to authorised broadcasts to exercise jurisdiction. This jurisdiction includes the right to prosecute offences together with the right to exercise powers of arrest and seizure.

Ships of uncertain nationality: states may visit and enforce their laws against their own ships on the high seas. Consequently where a ship, though flying a foreign flag, is reasonably suspected of being of the same nationality as a warship it may be visited and boarded. If the suspicions prove to be unfounded and unjustified by action of the ship boarded then compensation must be paid.

11.7.3 Hot pursuit

The right of hot pursuit, recognised at customary international law in cases such as the *I'm Alone* case (1933)[15] and in Article 23 of the HSC, allows a coastal state's warships or military aircraft to pursue a foreign ship which has violated the coastal state's laws within internal or territorial waters and to arrest it on the high seas. Pursuit must begin while the foreign ship is within territorial waters (or, in the case of customs, fiscal, immigration or sanitary laws, within the contiguous zone). Article 111 of the LOSC extends the right of hot pursuit to cover offences committed within archipelagic waters and the EEZ. The foreign ship must first be given a visual or auditory signal, within range, to stop. Pursuit must be immediate and continuous upon refusal to stop. Hot pursuit

---

15   (1933) RIAA 1609.

cannot be continued into the foreign ship's own territorial waters or the territorial waters of a third state. The pursuing vessel may use reasonable force to effect the arrest, but compensation is due for unjustifiable hot pursuit.

11.7.4 Safety of shipping

Article 110 of the HSC provides that every state shall take such measures for its vessels as are necessary to ensure safety at sea with regard to communications, the prevention of collisions, crew conditions and seaworthiness of ships. A slightly tougher regime is spelt out in LOSC. Additionally, there are some specific conventions mostly the work of the International Maritime Organisation, the principle one being the International Convention for the Safety of Life at Sea 1974 (SOLAS). This convention is the latest version of a line of treaties dating back to the sinking of *The Titanic*. SOLAS lays down minimum crewing standards and deals with such things as provision of life-rafts, fire-fighting equipment, navigational and broadcasting aids. Responsibility for enforcement lies with the flag state, but port states do also have some measure of control. The port state is entitled to check that ships in port have a valid certificate as required by SOLAS. In 1978 a protocol to SOLAS was adopted dealing with tanker safety and pollution prevention – which covers such things as inert gas systems and emergency steering.

In addition to the SOLAS Conventions there have been a series of regulations for preventing collisions at sea. The current regulations are annexed to the Convention on the International Regulations for Preventing Collisions at Sea 1972. The regulations deal with matters of signalling, conduct on the seas, and use of sea lanes.

The issue of marine pollution will be discussed in Chapter 17.

11.8 International sea bed

Sovereignty over the deep sea bed, that is to say the area of the sea bed beyond the continental shelf, has become a topic of conflict as technology has developed. The discovery of important mineral resources in the deep sea bed was made 100 years ago but it has only comparatively recently become technically and commercially viable to exploit such resources. The main resources are the manganese nodules which are composed of high grade metal ores such as manganese, iron, nickel, copper and cobalt. It is only a handful of rich nations who are at present capable of exploiting the resources and such exploitation has the added advantage for the state concerned of lessening dependence on foreign land-based deposits. For the mineral exporting countries the effect could be disastrous.

Once deep-sea mining became a possibility, the few mining states sought legal justification for their actions. Three principal arguments were put forward:

1 Exploitation could be justified on the basis of a continuation of the regime of the continental shelf by defining the continental shelf in terms of the ability to exploit its resources.

2 Exploitation could be justified on the application of the principle of the freedom of the high seas.

3   Title to the deep sea bed area could be gained by occupation through use.

Many of the potential exploiters of the deep sea bed favoured the second argument. By the late 1960s many of the newly independent states were expressing concern at the possibility of the exploitation of the resources of the sea bed for the benefit of a few rich nations. In 1969 the General Assembly of the UN passed a resolution by 62 votes to 28 with 28 abstentions calling for a moratorium on sea bed activities and in 1970 the Declaration of Principles Governing the Sea Bed and Ocean Floor was passed (108:0 with 14 abstentions) which declared the area to be 'the common heritage of mankind' and therefore not susceptible to any territorial claim. The Declaration further proposed the establishment of an international regime to govern all activities in the area. The Group of 77, made up of over a hundred states, have argued that this declaration is binding and that it prohibits unilateral sea bed mining. The Western states have argued that the resolution is merely one of principle. The topic was fully discussed at UNCLOS III and proved to be the major area of disagreement.

11.8.1 *The LOSC regime*

Part XI and Annexes II and IV to the Convention (Part XI) and the Agreement Relating to the Implementation of Part XI of the United Nations Convention on the Law of the Sea of 10 December 1982 (Agreement) establish the legal regime governing exploration and exploitation of mineral resources of the deep sea bed beyond coastal state jurisdiction (sea bed mining regime).

Flaws in Part XI caused the United States and other industrialised states not to become parties to the Convention. The unwillingness of industrialised states to adhere to the Convention unless its sea bed mining provisions were reformed led the Secretary General of the United Nations, in 1990, to initiate informal consultations aimed at achieving such reform and thereby promoting widespread acceptance of the Convention. These consultations resulted in the Agreement, which was adopted by the United Nations General Assembly on 28 July 1994 by a vote of 121 (including the United States) in favour with 0 opposed and 7 abstentions. As of 8 September 1994, 50 countries had signed the Agreement including the United States (subject to ratification). More are expected to follow.

The objections of the United States and other industrialised States to Part XI were that:

- it established a structure for administering the sea bed mining regime that did not accord with industrialised states' influence in the regime commensurate with their interests;

- it incorporated economic principles inconsistent with free market philosophy; and

- its specific provisions created numerous problems from an economic and commercial policy perspective that would have impeded access by the United States and other industrialised countries to the resources of the deep sea bed beyond national jurisdiction.

The decline in commercial interest in deep sea bed mining, due to relatively low metals prices over the last decade, created an opening for reform of Part XI. This waning interest and resulting decline in exploration activity led most states to recognise that the large bureaucratic structure and detailed provisions on commercial exploitation contained in Part XI were unnecessary. This made possible the negotiation of a scaled down regime to meet the limited needs of the present, but one capable of evolving to meet those of the future, coupled with general principles on economic and commercial policy that will serve as the basis for more detailed rules when interest in commercial exploitation re-emerges.[16]

CONVENTION OF THE TERRITORIAL SEA AND THE CONTIGUOUS ZONE

The States Parties to this Convention

Have agreed as follows:

PART I
TERRITORIAL SEA

SECTION I
GENERAL

Article 1

1   The sovereignty of a state extends, beyond its land territory and its internal waters, to a belt of sea adjacent to its coast, described as the territorial sea.

2   This sovereignty is exercised subject to the provisions of these Articles and to other rules of international law.

Article 2

The sovereignty of a coastal state extends to the air space over the territorial sea as well as to its bed and subsoil.

SECTION II
LIMITS OF THE TERRITORIAL SEA

Article 3

Except where otherwise provided in these articles, the normal baseline for measuring the breadth of the territorial sea is the low-water line along the coast marked on large-scale charts officially recognised by the coastal state.

Article 4

1   In localities where the coastline is deeply indented and cut into, or if there is a fringe of islands along the coast in its immediate vicinity, the method of straight baselines joining appropriate points may be employed in drawing the baseline from which the breadth of the territorial sea is measured.

2   The drawing of such baselines must not depart to any appreciable extent from the general direction of the coast, and the sea areas lying within the lines must be sufficiently closely linked to the land domain to be subject to the regime of internal waters.

3   Baselines shall not be drawn to and from low-tide elevations, unless lighthouses or similar installations which are permanently above sea level have been built on them.

---

16   *US Commentary on the Law of the Sea Convention*, US State Department, 1996.

4   Where the method of straight baselines is applicable under the provisions of para 1, account may be taken, in determining particular baselines, of economic interests peculiar to the region concerned, the reality and importance of which are clearly evidenced by a long usage.

5   The system of straight baselines may not be applied by a state in such a manner as to cut off from the high seas the territorial sea of another state.

6   The coastal state must clearly indicate straight baselines on charts, to which due publicity must be given.

Article 5

1   Waters on the landward side of the baseline of the territorial sea form part of the internal waters of the state.

2   Where the establishment of a straight baseline in accordance with Article 4 has the effect of enclosing as internal waters areas which previously had been considered as part of the territorial sea or of the high seas, a right of innocent passage, as provided in Articles 14 to 23, shall exist in those waters.

Article 6

The outer limit of the territorial sea is the line every point of which is at a distance from the nearest point of the baseline equal to the breadth of the territorial sea.

Article 7

1   This article relates only to bays the coasts of which belong to a single state.

2   For the purposes of these articles, a bay is a well-marked indentation whose penetration is in such proportion to the width of its mouth as to contain land-locked waters and constitute more than a mere curvature of the coast. An indentation shall not, however, be regarded as a bay unless its area is as large as, or larger than, that of the semi-circle whose diameter is a line drawn across the mouth of that indentation.

3   For the purpose of measurement, the area of an indentation is that lying between the low-water mark around the shore of the indentation and a line joining the low-water mark of its natural entrance points. Where, because of the presence of islands, an indentation has more than one mouth, the semi-circle shall be drawn on a line as long as the sum total of the lengths of the lines across the different mouths. Islands within an indentation shall be included as if they were part of the water area of the indentation.

4   If the distance between the low-water marks of the natural entrance points of a bay does not exceed twenty-four miles, a closing line may be drawn between these two low-water marks, and the waters enclosed thereby shall be considered as internal waters.

5   Where the distance between the low-water marks of the natural entrance points of a bay exceeds 24 miles, a straight baseline of twenty-four miles shall be drawn within the bay in such a manner as to enclose the maximum area of water that is possible with a line of that length.

6   The foregoing shall not apply to so-called 'historic' bays, or in any case where the straight baseline system provided for in Article 4 is applied.

Article 8

For the purpose of delimiting the territorial sea, the outermost permanent harbour works which form an integral part of the harbour system shall be regarded as forming part of the coast.

Article 9

Roadsteads which are normally used for the loading, unloading, and anchoring of ships, and which would otherwise be situated wholly or partly outside the outer limit of the territorial sea, are included in the territorial sea. The coastal state must clearly demarcate such roadsteads and indicate them on charts together with their boundaries, to which due publicity must be given.

Article 10

1   An island is a naturally-formed area of land, surrounded by water which is above water at high tide.

2   The territorial sea of an island is measured in accordance with the provisions of these articles.

Article 11

1   A low-tide elevation is a naturally-formed area of land which is surrounded by and above water at low-tide but submerged at high tide. Where a low-tide elevation is situated wholly or partly at a distance not exceeding the breadth of the territorial sea from the mainland or an island, the low-water line on that elevation may be used as the baseline for measuring the breadth of the territorial sea.

2   Where a low-tide elevation is wholly situated at a distance exceeding the breadth of the territorial sea from the mainland or an island, it has no territorial sea of its own .

Article 12

1   Where the coasts of two states are opposite or adjacent to each other, neither of the two states is entitled, failing agreement between them to the contrary, to extend its territorial sea beyond the median line every point of which is equidistant from the nearest points on the baselines from which the breadth of the territorial sea of each of the two states is measured. The provisions of this paragraph shall not apply, however, where it is necessary by reason of historic title or other special circumstances to delimit the territorial seas of the two states in a way which is at variance with this provision.

2   The line of delimitation between the territorial seas of two states lying opposite to each other or adjacent to each other shall be marked on large-scale charts officially recognised by the coastal states.

Article 13

If a river flows directly into the sea, the baseline shall be a straight line across the mouth of the river between points on the low-tide line of its banks.

SECTION III

RIGHT OF INNOCENT PASSAGE

Sub-section A   Rules applicable to all ships

Article 14

1   Subject to the provisions of these articles, ships of all states, whether coastal or not, shall enjoy the right of innocent passage through the territorial sea.

2   Passage means navigation through the territorial sea for the purpose either of traversing that sea without entering internal waters, or of proceeding to internal waters, or of making for the high seas from internal waters.

3   Passage includes stopping and anchoring, but only in so far as the same are incidental to ordinary navigation or are rendered necessary by *force majeure* or by distress.

4   Passage is innocent so long as it is not prejudicial to the peace, good order or security of the coastal state. Such passage shall take place in conformity with these articles and with other rules of international law.

5   Passage of foreign fishing vessels shall not be considered innocent if they do not observe such laws and regulations as the coastal state may make and publish in order to prevent these vessels from fishing in the territorial sea.

6   Submarines are required to navigate on the surface and to show their flag.

Article 15

1   The coastal state must not hamper innocent passage through the territorial sea.

2   The coastal state is required to give appropriate publicity to any dangers of navigation, of which it has knowledge, within its territorial sea.

Article 16

1   The coastal state may take the necessary steps in its territorial sea to prevent passage which is not innocent.

2   In the case of ships proceeding to internal waters, the coastal state shall also have the right to take the necessary steps to prevent any breach of the conditions to which admission to those waters is subject.

3   Subject to the provisions of para 4, the coastal state may, without discrimination amongst foreign ships, suspend temporarily in specified areas of the territorial sea the innocent passage of foreign ships if such suspensions is essential for the protection of its security. Such suspensions shall take effect only after having been duly publicised.

4   There shall be no suspension of the innocent passage of foreign ships through straits which are used for international navigation between one part of the high seas and another part of the high seas or the territorial sea of a foreign state.

Article 17

Foreign ships exercising the right of innocent passage shall comply with the laws and regulations enacted by the coastal state in conformity with these articles and other rules of international law and, in particular, with such laws and regulations relating to transport and navigation.

Sub-section B   Rules applicable to merchant ships

Article 18

1   No charge may be levied upon foreign ships by reason only of their passage through the territorial sea.

2   Charges may be levied upon a foreign ship passing through the territorial sea as payment only for specific services rendered to the ship. These charges shall be levied without discrimination.

Article 19

1   The criminal jurisdiction of the coastal state should not be exercised on board a foreign ship passing through the territorial sea to arrest any person or to conduct any investigation in connection with any crime on board the ship during its passage, save only in the following cases:

(a) If the consequences of the crime extend to the coastal state; or

(b) If the crime is of a kind to disturb the peace of the country or the good order of the territorial sea; or

(c) If the assistance of the local authorities has been requested by the captain of the ship or by the consul of the country whose flag the ship flies; or

(d) If it is necessary for the suppression of illicit traffic in narcotic drugs.

2   The above provisions do not affect the right of the coastal state to take any steps authorised by its laws for the purpose of an arrest or investigation on board a foreign ship passing through the territorial sea after leaving internal waters.

3   In the cases provided for in paras 1 and 2 of this article, the coastal state shall, if the captain so requests, advise the consular authority of the flag state before taking any steps, and shall facilitate contact between such authority and the ship's crew. In cases of emergency this notification may be communicated while the measures are being taken.

4   In considering whether or how an arrest should be made, the local authorities shall pay due regard to the interests of navigation.

5   The coastal state may not take any steps on board a foreign ship passing through the territorial sea to arrest any person or to conduct any investigation in connection with any crime committed before the ship entered the territorial sea, if the ship, proceeding from a foreign port, is only passing through the territorial sea without entering internal waters.

Article 20

1   The coastal state should not stop or divert a foreign ship passing through the territorial; sea for the purpose of exercising civil jurisdiction in relation to a person on board the ship.

2   The coastal state may not levy execution against or arrest the ship for the purpose of any civil proceedings, save only in respect of obligations or liabilities assumed or incurred by the ship itself in the course or for the purpose of its voyage through the waters of the coastal state.

3   The provisions of the previous paragraph are without prejudice to the right of the coastal state, in accordance with its laws, to levy execution against or to arrest, for the purpose of any civil proceedings, a foreign ship lying in the territorial sea, or passing though the territorial sea after leaving internal waters.

Sub-section C   Rules applicable to government ships other than warships

Article 21

The rules contained in sub-ss A and B shall also apply to government ships operated for commercial purposes.

Article 22

1   The rules contained in sub-s A and in Article 18 shall apply to government ships operated for non-commercial purposes.

2   With such exceptions as are contained in the provisions referred to in the preceding paragraph, nothing in these articles affects the immunities which such ships enjoy under these articles or other rules of international law.

Sub-section D   Rule applicable to warships

Article 23

If any warship does not comply with the regulations of the coastal State concerning passage through the territorial sea and disregards any request for compliance which is made to it, the coastal state may require the warship to leave the territorial sea.

PART II
CONTIGUOUS ZONE

Article 24

1   In a zone of the high seas contiguous to its territorial sea, the coastal state may exercise the control necessary to:

(a) Prevent infringement of its customs, fiscal, immigration or sanitary regulations within its territorial or territorial sea;

(b) Punish infringement of the above regulations committed within its territory or territorial sea.

2   The contiguous zone may not extend beyond twelve miles from the baseline from which the breadth of the territorial sea is measured.

3   Where the coasts of two states are opposite or adjacent to each other, neither of the two states is entitled, failing agreement between them to the contrary, to extend its contiguous zone beyond the median line every point of which is equidistant from the nearest points on the baselines from which the breadth of the territorial seas of the two states is measured.

PART III
FINAL ARTICLES

Article 25

The provisions of this Convention shall not affect conventions or other international agreements already in force, as between States Parties to them.

Article 26

This Convention shall, until 31 October 1958, be open for signature by all States Members of the United Nations or of any of the specialised agencies, and by any other state invited by the General Assembly of the United Nations to become a party to the Convention.

Article 27

This Convention is subject to ratification. The instruments of ratification shall be deposited with the Secretary General of the United Nations.

Article 28

This Convention shall be open for accession by any states belonging to any of the categories mentioned in Article 26. The instrument of accession shall be deposited with the Secretary General of the United Nations.

Article 29

1   This Convention shall come into force on the thirtieth day following the date of deposit of the twenty-second instrument of ratification or accession with the Secretary General of the United Nations.

2　For each state ratifying or acceding to the Convention after the deposit of the twenty-second instrument of ratification or accession, the Convention shall enter into force on the thirtieth day after deposit by such state of its instrument of ratification or accession.

Article 30

1　After the expiration of a period of five years from the date on which this Convention shall enter into force, a request for the revision of this Convention may be made at any time by any Contracting Party by means of a notification in writing addressed to the Secretary General of the United Nations.

2　The General Assembly of the United Nations shall decide upon the steps, if any, to be taken in respect of such request.

Article 31

The Secretary General of the United Nations shall inform all States Members of the United Nations and the other States referred to in Article 26:

    (a)　Of signatures to this Convention and of the deposit of instruments of ratification or accession, in accordance with Articles 26, 27 and 28;

    (b)　Of the date on which this Convention will come into force, in accordance with Article 29;

    (c)　Of requests for revision in accordance with Article 30.

Article 32

The original of this Convention, of which the Chinese, English, French, Russian, and Spanish texts are equally authentic, shall be deposited with the Secretary General of the United Nations, who shall send certified copies thereof to all States referred to in Article 26.

IN WITNESS WHEREOF the undersigned plenipotentiaries, being duly authorised thereto by their respective governments, have signed this Convention.

DONE AT GENEVA, this twenty-ninth day of April one thousand nine hundred and fifty-eight.

CONVENTION ON THE HIGH SEAS

The States Parties to this Convention,

Desiring to codify the rules of international law relating to the high seas,

Recognising that the United Nations Conference on the Law of the Sea, held at Geneva from 24 February to 27 April 1958, adopted the following provisions as generally declaratory of established principles of international law,

Have agreed as follows:

Article 1

The term 'high seas' means all parts of the sea that are not included in the territorial sea or in the internal waters of a state.

Article 2

The high seas being open to all nations, no state may validly purport to subject any part of them to its sovereignty. Freedom of the high seas is exercised under the conditions laid down by these articles and by the other rules of international law. It comprises, *inter alia*, both for coastal and non-coastal states:

(a) freedom of navigation;

(b) freedom of fishing;

(c) freedom to lay submarine cables and pipelines;

(d) freedom to fly over the high seas.

These freedoms, and others which are recognised by the general principles of international law, shall be exercised by all states with reasonable regard to the interests of other states in their exercise of the freedom of the high seas.

Article 3

1 In order to enjoy the freedom of the seas on equal terms with coastal states, states having no sea-coast should have free access to the sea. To this end states situated between the sea and a state having no sea-coast shall by common agreement with the latter and in conformity with existing international conventions accord:

(a) To the state having no sea-coast, on a basis of reciprocity, free transit through their territory; and

(b) To ships flying the flag of that state treatment equal to that accorded to their own ships, or to the ships of any other States, as regards access to seaports and the use of such ports.

2 States situated between the sea and a state having no sea-coast shall settle, by mutual agreement with the latter, and taking into account the rights of the coastal state having no sea-coast, all matters relating to freedom of transit and equal treatment in ports, in case such states are not already parties to existing international conventions.

Article 4

Every state, whether coastal or not, has the right to sail ships under its flag on the high seas.

Article 5

1 Each state shall fix conditions for the grant of its nationality to ships, for the registration of ships in its territory, and for the right to fly its flag. Ships have the nationality of the state whose flag they are entitled to fly. There must exist a genuine link between the state and the ship; in particular, the state must effectively exercise its jurisdiction and control in administrative, technical and social matters over ships flying its flag.

2 Each state shall issue to ships to which it has granted the right to fly its flag documents to that effect.

Article 6

1 Ships shall sail under the flag of one state only and, save in exceptional cases expressly provided for in international treaties or in these articles, shall be subject to its exclusive jurisdiction on the high seas. A ship may not change its flag during a voyage or while in a port of call, save in the case of a real transfer of ownership or change of registry.

2 A ship which sails under the flags of two or more states, using them according to convenience, may not claim any of the nationalities in question with respect to any other state, and may be assimilated to a ship without nationality.

Article 7

The provisions of the preceding articles do not prejudice the question of ships employed on the official service of an intergovernmental organisation flying the flag of that organisation.

Article 8

1   Warships on the high seas have complete immunity from the jurisdiction of any state other than the flag state.

2   For the purposes of these articles, the term 'warship' means a ship belonging to the naval forces of a state and bearing the external marks distinguishing warships of its nationality, under the command of an officer duly commissioned by the government and whose name appears in the Navy List, and manned by a crew who are under regular naval discipline.

Article 9

Ships owned or operated by a state and used only on government non-commercial service shall, on the high seas, have complete immunity from the jurisdiction of any state other than the flag state.

Article 10

1   Every state shall take such measures for ships under its flag as are necessary to ensure safety at sea with regard *inter alia* to:

   (a)   The use of signals, the maintenance of communications and the prevention of collisions;

   (b)   The manning of ships and labour conditions for crews taking into account the applicable international labour instruments;

   (c)   The construction, equipment, and seaworthiness of ships.

2   In taking such measures each state is required to conform to generally accepted international standards and to take any steps which may be necessary to ensure their observance.

Article 11

1   In the event of a collision or of any other incident of navigation concerning a ship on the high seas, involving the penal or disciplinary responsibility of the master or of any other persons in the service of the ship, no penal or disciplinary proceedings may be instituted against such persons except before the judicial or administrative authorities either of the flag state or of the state of which such person is a national.

2   In disciplinary matters, the state which has issued a master's certificate or a certificate of competence or licence shall alone be competent, after due legal process, to pronounce the withdrawal of such certificates, even if the holder is not a national of the state which issued them.

3   No arrest or detention of the ship, even as a measure of investigation, shall be ordered by any authorities other than those of the flag state.

Article 12

1   Every state shall require the master of a ship sailing under its flag, in so far as he can do so without serious danger to the ship, the crew, or the passengers:

   (a)   To render assistance to any person found at sea in danger of being lost;

   (b)   To proceed with all possible speed to the rescue of persons in distress if informed of their need of assistance, in so far as such action may reasonably be expected of him;

    (c)   After a collision, to render assistance to the other ship, her crew and her passengers and, where possible, to inform the other ship of the name of his own ship, her port of registry and the nearest port at which she will call.

2   Every coastal state shall promote the establishment and maintenance of an adequate and effective search and rescue service regarding safety on and over the sea and – where circumstances so require – by way of mutual regional arrangements co-operate with neighbouring States for this purpose.

Article 13

Every state shall adopt effective measures to prevent and punish the transport of slaves in ships authorised to fly its flag, and to prevent the unlawful use of its flag for that purpose. Any slave taking refuge on board any ship, whatever its flag, shall, *ipso facto*, be free.

Article 14

All states shall co-operate to the fullest possible extent in the repression of piracy on the high seas or in any other place outside the jurisdiction of any state.

Article 15

Piracy consists of any of the following acts:

1   Any illegal acts of violence, detention or any act of depredation committed for private ends by the crew or the passengers of a private ship or a private aircraft, and directed:

    (a)   On the high seas, against another ship or aircraft, or against persons or property on board such ship or aircraft;

    (b)   Against a ship, aircraft, persons, or property in a place outside the jurisdiction of any state;

2   Any act of voluntary participation in the operation of a ship or of an aircraft with knowledge of facts making it a pirate ship or aircraft;

3   Any act of inciting or of intentionally facilitating an act described in sub-para 1 or sub-para 2 of this article.

Article 16

The acts of piracy, as defined in Article 15, committed by a warship, government ship or government aircraft whose crew has mutinied and taken control of the ship or aircraft are assimilated to acts committed by a private ship.

Article 17

A ship or aircraft is considered a pirate ship or aircraft if it is intended by the persons in dominant control to be used for the purpose of committing one of the acts referred to in Article 15. The same applies if the ship or aircraft has been used to commit any such act, so long as it remains under the control of the persons guilty of that act.

Article 18

A ship or aircraft may retain its nationality although it has become a pirate ship or aircraft. The retention or loss of nationality is determined by the law of the state from which such nationality was derived.

Article 19

On the high seas, or in any other place outside the jurisdiction of any state, every state may seize a pirate ship or aircraft, or a ship taken by piracy and under the control of pirates, and arrest the persons and seize the property on board. The courts of the state which carried out the seizure may decide upon the penalties to be imposed, and may also determine the action to be taken with regard to the ships, aircraft or property, subject to the rights of third parties acting in good faith.

Article 20

Where the seizure of a ship or aircraft on suspicion of piracy has been effected without adequate grounds, the state making the seizure shall be liable to the state the nationality of which is possessed by the ship or aircraft, for any loss or damage caused by the seizure.

Article 21

A seizure on account of piracy may only be carried out by warships or military aircraft, or other ships or aircraft on government service authorised to that effect.

Article 22

1   Except where acts of interference derive from powers conferred by treaty, a warship which encounters a foreign merchant ship on the high seas is not justified in boarding her unless there is reasonable ground for suspecting:

    (a)   that the ship is engaged in piracy; or

    (b)   that the ship is engaged in the slave trade; or

    (c)   that, though flying a foreign flag or refusing to show its flag, the ship is, in reality, of the same nationality as the warship.

2   In the case provided for in sub-paras (a), (b) and (c) above, the warship may proceed to verify the ship's right to fly its flag. To this end, it may send a boat under the command of an officer to the suspected ship. If suspicion remains after the documents have been checked, it may proceed to a further examination on board the ship, which must be carried out with all possible consideration.

3   If the suspicions prove to be unfounded, and provided that the ship boarded has not committed any act justifying them, it shall be compensated for any loss or damage that may have been sustained.

Article 23

1   The hot pursuit of a foreign ship may be undertaken when the competent authorities of the coastal state have good reason to believe that the ship has violated the laws and regulations of that state. Such pursuit must be commenced when the foreign ship or one of its boats is within the internal waters or the territorial sea or the contiguous zone of the pursuing state, and may only be continued outside the territorial sea or the contiguous zone if the pursuit has not been interrupted. It is not necessary that, at the time when the foreign ship within the territorial sea or the contiguous zone receives the order to stop, the ship giving the order should likewise be within the territorial sea or the contiguous zone. If the foreign ship is within a contiguous zone, as defined in Article 24 of the Convention on the Territorial Sea and the Contiguous Zone, the pursuit may only be undertaken if there has been a violation of the rights for the protection of which the zone was established.

2   The right of hot pursuit ceases as soon as the ship pursued enters the territorial sea of its own country or of a third state.

3   Hot pursuit is not deemed to have begun unless the pursuing ship has satisfied itself by such practicable means as may be available that the ship pursued or one of its boats or other craft working as a team and using the ship pursued as a mother ship was within the limits or the territorial sea, or

as the case may be within the contiguous zone. The pursuit may only be commenced after a visual or auditory signal to stop has been given at a distance which enables it to be seen or heard by the foreign ship.

4 The right of hot pursuit may be exercised only by warships or military aircraft, or other ships or aircraft on government service specially authorised to that effect.

5 Where hot pursuit is effected by an aircraft:

(a) The provisions of paras 1 to 3 of this article shall apply *mutatis mutandis*;

(b) The aircraft giving the order to stop must itself actively pursue the ship until a ship or aircraft of the coastal state, summoned by the aircraft, arrives to take over the pursuit, unless the aircraft is itself able to arrest the ship. It does not suffice to justify an arrest on the high seas that the ship was merely sighted by the aircraft as an offender or suspected offender, if it was not both ordered to stop and pursued by the aircraft with itself or other aircraft or ships which continue the pursuit without interruption.

6 The release of a ship arrested within the jurisdiction of a state and escorted to a port of that state for the purposes of an inquiry before the competent authorities may not be claimed solely on the ground that the ship, in the course of its voyage, was escorted across a portion of the high seas, if the circumstances rendered this necessary.

7 Where a ship has been stopped or arrested on the high seas in circumstances which do not justify the exercise of the rights or hot pursuit, it shall be compensated for any loss or damage that may have been thereby sustained.

Article 24

Every state shall draw up regulations to prevent pollution of the seas by the discharge of oil from ships or pipelines or resulting from the exploitation and exploration of the sea bed and its subsoil, taking account of existing treaty provisions on the subject.

Article 25

1 Every state shall take measures to prevent pollution of the seas from the dumping of radioactive waste, taking into account any standards and regulations which may be formulated by the competent international organisations.

2 All states shall co-operate with the competent international organisations in taking measures for the prevention of pollution of the seas or air space above, resulting from any activities with the radioactive materials or other harmful agents.

Article 26

1 All states shall be entitled to lay submarine cables and pipelines on the bed of the high seas.

2 Subject to its right to take reasonable measures for the exploration of the continental shelf and the exploitation of its natural resources, the coastal state may not impede the laying or maintenance of such cables or pipelines.

3 When laying such cables or pipelines the state in question shall pay due regard to cables or pipelines already in position on the sea bed. In particular, possibilities of repairing existing cables or pipelines shall not be prejudiced.

Article 27

Every state shall take the necessary legislative measures to provide that the breaking or injury by a ship flying its flag or by a person subject to its jurisdiction of a submarine cable beneath the high seas done wilfully or through culpable negligence, in such a manner a to be liable to interrupt or obstruct telegraphic or telephonic communications, and similarly the breaking or injury of a submarine pipeline or high-voltage power cable shall be a punishable offence. This provision shall not apply to any break or injury caused by persons who acted merely with the legitimate object of saving their lives or their ships, after having taken all necessary precautions to avoid such break or injury.

Article 28

Every state shall take the necessary legislative measures to provide that, if persons subject to its jurisdiction who are the owners of a cable or pipeline beneath the high seas, in laying or repairing that cable or pipeline, cause a break or injury to another cable or pipeline, they shall bear the coast of the repairs.

Article 29

Every state shall take the necessary legislative measures to ensure that the owners of ships who can prove that they have sacrificed an anchor, a net or any other fishing gear, in order to avoid injuring a submarine cable or pipeline, shall be indemnified by the owner of the cable or pipeline, provided that the owner of the ship has taken all reasonable precautionary measures beforehand.

Article 30

The provisions of this Convention shall not affect conventions or other international agreements already in force, as between States Parties to them.

Article 31

This Convention shall, until 31 October 1958, be open for signature by all States Members of the United Nations or of any of the specialised agencies, and by any other state invited by the General Assembly of the United Nations to become a Party to the Convention.

Article 32

This Convention is subject to ratification. The instruments of ratification shall be deposited with the Secretary General of the United Nations.

Article 33

This Convention shall be open for accession by any states belonging to any of the categories mentioned in Article 31. The instrument of accession shall be deposited with the Secretary General of the United Nations.

Article 34

1   This Convention shall come into force on the thirtieth day following the date of deposit of the twenty-second instrument of ratification or accession with the Secretary General of the United Nations.

2   For each state ratifying or acceding to the Convention after the deposit of the twenty-second instrument of ratification or accession, the Convention shall enter into force on the thirtieth day after deposit by such states of its instrument of ratification or accession.

Article 35

1   After the expiration of a period of five years from the date on which this Convention shall enter into force, a request for the revision of this Convention may be made at any time by any Contracting Party by means of a

notification in writing addressed to the Secretary General of the United Nations.

2   The General Assembly of the United Nations shall decide upon the steps, if any, to be taken in respect of such request.

Article 36

The Secretary General of the United Nations shall inform all States Members of the United Nations and the other states referred to in Article 31:

    (a)   Of signatures to this Convention and of the deposit of instruments of ratification or accession, in accordance with Articles 31, 32, and 33;

    (b)   Of the date on which this Convention will come into force, in accordance with Article 34;

    (c)   Of requests for revision in accordance with Article 35.

Article 37

The original of this Convention, of which the Chinese, English, French, Russian, and Spanish texts are equally authentic, shall be deposited with the Secretary General of the United Nations, who shall send certified copies thereof to all States referred to in Article 31.

IN WITNESS WHEREOF the undersigned plenipotentiaries, being duly authorised thereto by their respective governments, have signed this Convention.

DONE AT GENEVA, this twenty-ninth day of April one thousand nine hundred and fifty-eight.

CONVENTION ON FISHING AND CONSERVATION OF THE LIVING RESOURCES OF THE HIGH SEAS

The States Parties to this Convention

Considering that the development of modern techniques for the exploitation of the living resources of the sea, increasing man's ability to meet the need of the world's expanding population for food, has exposed some of these resources to the danger of being over-exploited.

Considering also that the nature of the problems involved in the conservation of the living resources of the high seas is such that there is a clear necessity that they be solved, wherever possible, on the basis of international co-operation through the concerted action of all the states concerned,

Have agreed as follows:

Article 1

1   All states have the right for their nationals to engage in fishing on the high seas, subject:

    (a)   to their treaty obligations;

    (b)   to the interests and rights of coastal states as provided for in this Convention;

    (c)   to the provisions contained in the following articles concerning conservation of the living resources of the high seas.

2   All states have the duty to adopt, or to co-operate with other states in adopting, such measures for their respective nationals as may be necessary for the conservation of the living resources of the high seas.

Article 2

As employed in this Convention, the expression 'conservation of the living resources of the high seas' means the aggregate of the measures rendering possible the optimum sustainable yield from those resources so as to secure a maximum supply of food and other marine products. Conservation programmes should be formulated with a view to securing in the first place a supply of food for human consumption.

Article 3

A state whose nationals are engaged in fishing any stock or stocks of fish or other living marine resources in any area of the high seas where the nationals of other states are not thus engaged shall adopt, for its own nationals, measures in that area when necessary for the purpose of the conservation of the living resources affected.

Article 4

1   If the nationals of two or more states are engaged in fishing the same stock or stocks of fish or other living marine resources in any area of areas of the high seas, these states shall, at the request of any of them, enter into negotiations with a view to prescribing by agreement for their nationals the necessary measures for the conservation of the living resources affected.

2   If the states concerned do not reach agreement within 12 months, any of the parties may initiate the procedure contemplated by Article 9.

Article 5

1   If, subsequent to the adoption of the measures referred to in Articles 3 and 4, nationals of other states engage in fishing the same stock or stocks of fish or other living marine resources in any area or areas of the high seas, the other states shall apply the measure, which shall not be discriminatory in form or in fact, to their own nationals not later than seven months after the date on which the measures shall have been notified to the Director General of the Food and Agriculture Organisation of the United Nations. The Director General shall notify such measures to any state which so requests and, in any case, to any state specified by the state initiating the measure.

2   If these other states do not accept the measures so adopted and if no agreement can be reached within twelve months, any of the interested parties may initiate the procedure contemplated by Article 9. Subject to para 2 of Article 10, the measures adopted shall remain obligatory pending the decision of the special commission.

Article 6

1   A coastal state has a special interest in the maintenance of the productivity of the living resources in any area of the high seas adjacent to its territorial sea.

2   A coastal state is entitled to take part on an equal footing in any system of research and regulation for purposes of conservation of the living resources of the high seas in that area, even though its nationals do not carry on fishing there.

3   A state whose nationals are engaged in fishing in any area of the high seas adjacent to the territorial sea of a state shall, at the request of that coastal state, enter into negotiations with a view to prescribing by agreement the

measures necessary for the conservation of the living resources of the high seas in that area.

4   A state whose nationals are engaged in fishing in any area of the high seas adjacent to the territorial sea of a coastal state shall not enforce conservation measures in that area which are opposed to those which have been adopted by the coastal state, but may enter into negotiations with the coastal state with a view to prescribing by agreement the measures necessary for the conservation of the living resources of the high seas in that area.

5   If the states concerned do not reach agreement with respect to conservation measures within 12 months, any of the parties may initiate the procedure contemplated by Article 9.

Article 7

1   Having regard to the provisions of para 1 of Article 6, any coastal state may, with a view to the maintenance of the productivity of the living resources of the sea, adopt unilateral measures of conservation appropriate to any stock of fish or other marine resources in nay area of the high seas adjacent to its territorial sea, provided that negotiations to that effect with the other states concerned have not lead to an agreement within six months.

2   The measures which the coastal state adopts under the previous paragraph shall be valid as to other states only if the following requirements are fulfilled:

(a)   That there is a need for urgent application of conservation measures in the light of the existing knowledge of the fishery;

(b)   That the measures adopted are based on appropriate scientific findings;

(c)   That such measures do not discriminate in form or in fact against foreign fisherman.

3   These measures shall remain in force pending the settlement, in accordance with the relevant provisions of this Convention, of any disagreement as to their validity.

4   If the measures are not accepted by the other states concerned, any of the parties may initiate the procedure contemplated by Article 9. Subject to para 2 of Article 10, the measures adopted shall remain obligatory pending the decision of the special commission.

5   The principles of geographical demarcation as defined in Article 12 of the Convention on the Territorial Sea and the Contiguous Zone shall be adopted when coasts of different states are involved.

Article 8

1   Any state which, even if its nationals are not engaged in fishing in an area of the high seas not adjacent to its coast, has a special interest in the conservation of the living resources of the high seas in that area, may request the state or states whose nationals are engaged in fishing there to take the necessary measures of conservation under Articles 3 and 4 respectively, at the same time mentioning the scientific reasons which in its opinion make such measures necessary, and indicating its special interest.

2   If no agreement is reached within 12 months, such state may initiate the procedure contemplated by Article 9.

Article 9

1   Any dispute which may arise between states under Articles 4, 5, 6, 7, and 8 shall, at the request of any of the parties, be submitted for settlement to a

special commission of five members, unless the parties agree to seek a solution by another method of peaceful settlement, as provided for in Article 33 of the Charter of the United Nations.

2   The members of the commission, one of whom shall be designated as chairman, shall be named by agreement between the states in dispute within three months of the request for settlement in accordance with the provisions of this Article. Failing agreement they shall, upon the request of any state party, be named by the Secretary General of the United Nations, within a further three month period, in consultation with the States in dispute and with the President of the International Court of Justice and the Director General of the Food and Agriculture Organisation of the United Nations, from amongst well-qualified persons being nationals of States not involved in the dispute and specialising in legal, administrative or scientific questions relating to fisheries, depending upon the nature of the dispute to be settled. Any vacancy arising after the original appointment shall be filled in the same manner as provided for the initial selection.

3   Any States Party to proceedings under these articles shall have the right to name one of its nationals to the special commission, with the right to participate fully in the proceedings on the same footing as a member of the commission, but without the right to vote or take part in the writing of the commission's decision.

4   The commission shall determine its own procedure, assuring each party to the proceedings a full opportunity to be heard and to present its case. It shall also determine how the costs and expenses shall be divided between the parties to the dispute, failing agreement by the parties on this matter.

5   The special commission shall render its decision within a period of five months from the time it is appointed unless it decides, in case of necessity, to extend the time limit for a period not exceeding three months.

6   The special commission shall, in reaching its decisions, adhere to these articles and to any special agreements between the disputing parties regarding settlement of the dispute.

7   Decisions of the commission shall be by majority vote.

Article 10

1   The special commission shall, in disputes arising under Article 7, apply the criteria listed in para 2 of that article. In disputes under Articles 4, 5, 6, and 8, the commission shall apply the following criteria, according to the issues involved in the dispute:

(a)   Common to the determination of disputes arising under Articles 4, 5 and 6 are the requirements:

(i)   that scientific findings demonstrate the necessity of conservation measures;

(ii)   that the specific measures are based on scientific findings and are practicable; and

(iii)   that the measures do not discriminate in form or in fact, against fishermen of other states;

(b)   Applicable to the determination of disputes arising under Article 8 is the requirement that scientific findings demonstrate the necessity for conservation measures, or that the conservation programme is adequate, as the case may be.

2 The special commission may decide that pending its award the measures in dispute shall not be applied, provided that, in the case of disputes under Article 7, the measures shall only be suspended when it is apparent to the commission on the basis of *prima facie* evidence that the need for the urgent application of such measures does not exist.

Article 11

The decisions of the special commission shall be binding on the states concerned and the provisions of para 2 of Article 94 of the Charter of the United nations shall be applicable to those decisions. If the decisions are accompanied by any recommendations, they shall receive the greatest possible consideration.

Article 12

1 If the factual basis of the award of the special commission is altered by substantial changes in the conditions of the stock or stocks of fish or other living marine resources or in the methods of fishing, any of the states concerned may request the other states to enter into negotiations with a view to prescribing by agreement the necessary modifications in the measures of conservation.

2 If no agreement is reached within a reasonable period of time, any of the states concerned may again resort to the procedure contemplated by Article 9 provided that at least two years have elapsed from the original award.

Article 13

1 The regulation of fisheries conducted by means of equipment embedded in the floor of the sea in areas of the high seas adjacent to the territorial sea of a state may be undertaken by that state where such fisheries have long been maintained and conducted by its nationals, provided that non-nationals are permitted to participate in such activities on an equal footing with nationals except in areas where such fisheries have by long usage been exclusively enjoyed by such nationals. Such regulations will not, however, affect the general status of the areas as high seas.

2 In this article, the expression 'fisheries conducted by means of equipment embedded in the floor of the sea' means those fisheries using gear with supporting members embedded in the sea floor, constructed on a site and left there to operate permanently or, if removed, restored each season on the same site.

Article 14

In Articles 1, 3, 4, 5, 6 and 8, the terms 'nationals' means fishing boats or craft of any size having the nationality of the state concerned according to the law of that state, irrespective of the nationality of the members of the crews.

Article 15

This Convention shall, until 31 October 1958, be open for signature by all States Members of the United Nations or of any of the specialised agencies, and by any other state invited by the General Assembly of the United Nations to become a Party to the Convention.

Article 16

This Convention is subject to ratification. The instruments of ratification shall be deposited with the Secretary General of the United Nations.

Article 17

This Convention shall be open for accession by any states belonging to any of the categories mentioned in Article 15. The instrument of accession shall be deposited with the Secretary General of the United Nations.

Article 18

1   This Convention shall come into force on the thirtieth day following the date of deposit of the twenty-second instrument of ratification or accession with the Secretary General of the United Nations.

2   For each state ratifying or acceding to the Convention after the deposit of the twenty-second instrument of ratification or accession, the Convention shall enter into force on the thirtieth day after deposit by such States of its instrument of ratification or accession.

Article 19

1   At the time of signature, ratification or accession, any state may make reservations to articles of the Convention other than to Articles 6, 7, 9, 10, 11 and 12.

2   Any contracting state making a reservation in accordance with the preceding paragraph may at any time withdraw the reservation by a communication to that effect addressed to the Secretary General of the United Nations.

Article 20

1   After the expiration of a period of five years from the date on which this Convention shall enter into force, a request for the revision of this Convention may be made at any time by any Contracting Party by means of a notification in writing addressed to the Secretary General of the United Nations.

2   The General Assembly of the United Nations shall decide upon the steps, if any, to be taken in respect of such request.

Article 21

The Secretary General of the United Nations shall inform all States Members of the United Nations and the other States referred to in Article 15:

(a)   of signatures to this Convention and of the deposit of instruments of ratification or accession, in accordance with Articles 15, 16 and 17;

(b)   of the date on which this Convention will come into force, in accordance with Article 18;

(c)   of requests for revision in accordance with Article 20.

(d)   of reservations to this Convention in accordance with Article 19.

Article 22

The original of this Convention, of which the Chinese, English, French, Russian, and Spanish texts are equally authentic, shall be deposited with the Secretary General of the United Nations, who shall send certified copies thereof to all States referred to in Article 15.

IN WITNESS WHEREOF the undersigned plenipotentiaries, being duly authorised thereto by their respective governments, have signed this Convention.

DONE AT GENEVA, this twenty-ninth day of April one thousand nine hundred and fifty-eight.

CONVENTION ON THE CONTINENTAL SHELF

The States Parties to this Convention
Have agreed as follows:

Article 1

For the purpose of these Articles, the term 'continental shelf' is used as referring

(a) To the sea bed and subsoil of the submarine areas adjacent to the coast but outside the area of the territorial sea, to a depth of 200 metres or, beyond that limit, to where the depth of the superjacent waters admits of the exploitation of the natural resources of the said areas;

(b) To the sea bed and subsoil of similar submarine areas adjacent to the coasts of islands.

Article 2

1 The coastal state exercises over the continental shelf sovereign rights for the purpose of exploring it and exploiting its natural resources.

2 The rights referred to in para 1 of this article are exclusive in the sense that if the coastal state does not explore the continental shelf or exploit its natural resources, no one may undertake these activities, or make a claim to the continental shelf, without the express consent of the coastal state.

3 The rights of the coastal state over the continental shelf do not depend on occupation, effective or notional, or on any express proclamation.

4 The natural resources referred to in these articles consist of the mineral and other non-living resources of the sea bed and subsoil together with living organisms belonging to sedentary species, that is to say, organisms which, at the harvestable state, either are immobile on or under the sea bed or are unable to move expect in constant physical contact with the sea bed or the subsoil.

Article 3

The rights of the coastal state over the continental shelf do not affect the legal status of the superjacent waters as high seas, or that of the air space above those waters.

Article 4

Subject to its right to take reasonable measures for the exploration of the continental shelf and the exploitation of its natural resources, the coastal state may not impede the laying or maintenance of submarine cables or pipelines on the continental shelf.

Article 5

1 The exploration of the continental shelf and the exploitation of its natural resources must not result in any unjustifiable interference with navigation, fishing or the conservation of the living resources of the sea, nor result in any interference with fundamental oceanographic or other scientific research carried out with the intention of open publication.

2 Subject to the provisions of paras 1 and 6 of this article, the coastal state is entitled to construct and maintain or operate on the continental shelf installations and other devices necessary for its exploration and the exploitation of its natural resources, and to establish safety zones around such installations and devices and to take in those zones measures necessary for their protection.

3   The safety zones referred to in para 2 of this article may extend to a distance of 500 metres around the installations and other devices which have been erected, measured from each point of their outer edge. Ships of all nationalities must respect these safety zones.

4   Such installations and devices, though under the jurisdiction of the coastal state, do not possess the status of islands. They have no territorial sea of their own, and their presence does not affect the delimitation of the territorial sea of the coastal state.

5   Due notice must be given of the construction of any such installations, and permanent means for giving warning of their presence must be maintained. Any installations which are abandoned or disused must be entirely removed.

6   Neither the installations or devices, nor the safety zones around them, may be established where interference may be caused to the use of recognised sea lanes essential to international navigation.

7   The coastal state is obliged to undertake, in the safety zones, all appropriate measures for the protection of the living resources of the sea from harmful agents.

8   The consent of the coastal state shall be obtained in respect of any research concerning the continental shelf and undertaken there. Nevertheless, the coastal state shall not normally withhold its consent if the request is submitted by a qualified institution with a view to purely scientific research into the physical or biological characteristics of the continental shelf, subject to the proviso that the coastal state shall have the right, if it so desires, to participate or to be represented in the research, and that in any event the results shall be published.

Article 6

1   Where the same continental shelf is adjacent to the territories of two or more states whose coasts are opposite each other, the boundary of the continental shelf appertaining to such states shall be determined by agreement between them. In the absence of agreement, and unless another boundary line is justified by special circumstances, the boundary is the median line, every point of which is equidistant from the nearest point of the baselines from which the breadth of the territorial sea of each state is measured.

2   Where the same continental shelf is adjacent to the territories of two adjacent states, the boundary of the continental shelf shall be determined by agreement between them. In the absence of agreement, and unless another boundary line is justified by special circumstances, the boundary shall be determined by application of the principle of equidistance from the nearest point of the baseline from which the breadth of the territorial sea of each state is measured.

3   In delimiting the boundaries of the continental shelf, any lines which are drawn in accordance with the principles set out in paras 1 and 2 of this article should be defined with reference to charts and geographical features as they exist at a particular date, and reference should be made to fixed permanent identifiable points on the land.

Article 7

The provisions of these articles shall not prejudice the right of the coastal state to exploit the subsoil by means of tunnelling irrespective of the depth of water above the subsoil.

Article 8

This Convention shall, until 30 October 1958, be open for signature by all States Members of the United Nations or of any of the specialised agencies, and by any other state invited by the General Assembly of the United Nations to become a Party to the Convention.

Article 9

This Convention is subject to ratification. The instruments of ratification shall be deposited with the Secretary General of the United Nations.

Article 10

This Convention shall be open for accession by any states belonging to any of the categories mentioned in Article 8. The instrument of accession shall be deposited with the Secretary General of the United Nations.

Article 11

1   This Convention shall come into force on the thirtieth day following the date of deposit of the twenty-second instrument of ratification or accession with the Secretary General of the United Nations.

2   For each state ratifying or acceding to the Convention after the deposit of the twenty-second instrument of ratification or accession, the Convention shall enter into force on the thirtieth day after deposit by such States of its instrument of ratification or accession.

Article 12

1   At the time of signature, ratification or accession, any state may make reservations to articles of the Convention other than to Articles 1 to 3 inclusive.

2   Any contracting state making a reservation in accordance with the preceding paragraph may at any time withdraw the reservation by a communication to that effect addressed to the Secretary General of the United Nations.

Article 13

1   After the expiration of a period of five years from the date on which this Convention shall enter into force, a request for the revision of this Convention may be made at any time by any Contracting Party by means of a notification in writing addressed to the Secretary General of the United Nations.

2   The General Assembly of the United Nations shall decide upon the steps, if any, to be taken in respect of such request.

Article 14

The Secretary General of the United Nations shall inform all States Members of the United Nations and the other States referred to in Article 8:

(a)   of signatures to this Convention and of the deposit of instruments of ratification or accession, in accordance with Articles 8, 9 and 10;

(b)   of the date on which this Convention will come into force, in accordance with Article 11;

(c)   of requests for revision in accordance with Article 13;

(d)   of reservations to this Convention, in accordance with Article 12.

Article 15

The original of this Convention, of which the Chinese, English, French, Russian, and Spanish texts are equally authentic, shall be deposited with the Secretary

General of the United Nations, who shall send certified copies thereof to all States referred to in Article 31.

IN WITNESS WHEREOF the undersigned plenipotentiaries, being duly authorised thereto by their respective governments, have signed this Convention.

DONE AT GENEVA, this twenty-ninth day of April one thousand nine hundred and fifty-eight.

UNITED NATIONS CONVENTION ON THE LAW OF THE SEA

Signed at Montego Bay, Jamaica, 10 December 1982

The States Parties to this Convention,

Prompted by the desire to settle, in a spirit of mutual understanding and co-operation, all issues relating to the law of the sea and aware of the historic significance of this Convention as an important contribution to the maintenance of peace, justice and progress for all peoples of the world,

Noting that developments since the United Nations Conferences on the Law of the Sea held at Geneva in 1958 and 1960 have accentuated the need for a new and generally acceptable Convention on the law of the sea,

Conscious that the problems of ocean space are closely interrelated and need to be considered as a whole,

Recognising the desirability of establishing through this Convention, with due regard for the sovereignty of all states, a legal order for the seas and oceans which will facilitate international communication, and will promote the peaceful uses of the seas and oceans, the equitable and efficient utilisation of their resources, the conservation of their living resources, and the study, protection and preservation of the marine environment,

Bearing in mind that the achievement of these goals will contribute to the realisation of a just and equitable international economic order which takes into account the interests and needs of mankind as a whole and, in particular, the special interests and needs of developing countries, whether coastal or land-locked,

Desiring by this Convention to develop the principles embodied in Resolution 2749 (XXV) of 17 December 1970 in which the General Assembly of the United Nations solemnly declared *inter alia* that the area of the sea bed and ocean floor and the subsoil thereof, beyond the limits of national jurisdiction, as well as its resources, are the common heritage of mankind, the exploration and exploitation of which shall be carried out for the benefit of mankind as a whole, irrespective of the geographical location of States,

Believing that the codification and progressive development of the law of the sea achieved in this Convention will contribute to the strengthening of peace, security, co-operation and friendly relations among all nations in conformity with the principles of justice and equal rights and will promote the economic and social advancement of all peoples of the world, in accordance with the Purposes and Principles of the United Nations as set forth in the Charter,

Affirming that matters not regulated by this Convention continue to be governed by the rules and principles of general international law,

Have agreed as follows:

PART I
INTRODUCTION

Article 1 Use of terms and scope

1 For the purposes of this Convention:

(1) 'Area' means the sea bed and ocean floor and subsoil thereof beyond the limits of national jurisdiction;

(2) 'Authority' means the International Sea Bed Authority;

(3) 'activities in the Area' means all activities of exploration for, and exploitation of, the resources of the Area;

(4) 'pollution of the marine environment' means the introduction by man, directly or indirectly, of substances or energy into the marine environment, including estuaries, which results or is likely to result in such deleterious effects as harm to living resources and marine life, hazards to human health, hindrance to marine activities, including fishing and other legitimate uses of the sea, impairment of quality for use of sea water and reduction of amenities;

(5) (a) 'dumping' means:

    (i) any deliberate disposal of wastes or other matter from vessels, aircraft, platforms or other man-made structures at sea;

    (ii) any deliberate disposal of vessels, aircraft, platforms or other man-made structures at sea

(b) 'dumping' does not include:

    (i) the disposal of wastes or other matter incidental to, or derived from the normal operations of vessels, aircraft, platforms or other man-made structures at sea and their equipment, other than wastes or other matter transported by or to vessels, aircraft, platforms or other man-made structures at sea, operating for the purpose of disposal of such matter or derived from the treatment of such wastes or other matter on such vessels, aircraft, platforms or structures;

    (ii) placement of matter for a purpose other than the mere disposal thereof, provided that such placement is not contrary to the aims of this Convention.

2 (1) 'States Parties' means states which have consented to be bound by this Convention and for which this Convention is in force.

(2) This Convention applies *mutatis mutandis* to the entities referred to in Article 305, para 1(b), (c), (d), (e) and (f), which become parties to this Convention in accordance with the conditions relevant to each, and to that extent 'States Parties' refers to those entities.

PART II
TERRITORIAL SEA AND CONTIGUOUS ZONE
SECTION 1 GENERAL PROVISIONS

Article 2 Legal status of the territorial sea, of the air space over the territorial sea and of its bed and subsoil

1 The sovereignty of a coastal state extends, beyond its land territory and internal waters and, in the case of an archipelagic state, its archipelagic waters, to an adjacent belt of sea, described as the territorial sea.

2   This sovereignty extends to the air space over the territorial sea as well as to its bed and subsoil.

3   The sovereignty over the territorial sea is exercised subject to this Convention and to other rules of international law.

SECTION 2   LIMITS OF THE TERRITORIAL SEA

Article 3   Breadth of the territorial sea

Every state has the right to establish the breadth of its territorial sea up to a limit not exceeding 12 nautical miles, measured from baselines determined in accordance with this Convention.

Article 4   Outer limit of the territorial sea

The outer limit of the territorial sea is the line every point of which is at a distance from the nearest point of the baseline equal to the breadth of the territorial sea.

Article 5   Normal baseline

Except where otherwise provided in this Convention, the normal baseline for measuring the breadth of the territorial sea is the low-water line along the coast as marked on large-scale charts officially recognised by the coastal state.

Article 6   Reefs

In the case of islands situated on atolls or of islands having fringing reefs, the baseline for measuring the breadth of the territorial sea is the seaward low-water line of the reef, as shown by the appropriate symbol on charts officially recognised by the coastal state.

Article 7   Straight baselines

1   In localities where the coastline is deeply indented and cut into, or if there is a fringe of islands along the coast in its immediate vicinity, the method of straight baselines joining appropriate points may be employed in drawing the baseline from which the breadth of the territorial sea is measured.

2   Where because of the presence of a delta and other natural conditions the coastline is highly unstable, the appropriate points may be selected along the furthest seaward extent of the low-water line and, notwithstanding subsequent regression of the low-water line, the straight baselines shall remain effective until changed by the coastal state in accordance with this Convention.

3   The drawing of straight baselines must not depart to any appreciable extent from the general direction of the coast, and the sea areas lying within the lines must be sufficiently closely linked to the land domain to be subject to the regime of internal waters.

4   Straight baselines shall not be drawn to and from low-tide elevations, unless lighthouses or similar installations which are permanently above sea level have been built on them or except in instances where the drawing of baselines to and from such elevations has received general international recognition.

5   Where the method of straight baselines is applicable under para 1, account may be taken, in determining particular baselines, of economic interests peculiar to the region concerned, the reality and the importance of which are clearly evidenced by long usage.

6   The system of straight baselines may not be applied by a state in such a manner as to cut off the territorial sea of another state from the high seas or an exclusive economic zone.

Article 8   Internal waters

1   Except as provided in Part IV, waters on the landward side of the baseline of the territorial sea form part of the internal waters of the state.

2   Where the establishment of a straight baseline in accordance with the method set forth in Article 7 has the effect of enclosing as internal waters areas which had not previously been considered as such, a right of innocent passage as provided in this Convention shall exist in those waters.

Article 9   Mouths of rivers

If a river flows directly into the sea, the baseline shall be a straight line across the mouth of the river between points on the low-water line of its banks.

Article 10   Bays

1   This article relates only to bays the coasts of which belong to a single state.

2   For the purposes of this Convention, a bay is a well-marked indentation whose penetration is in such proportion to the width of its mouth as to contain land-locked waters and constitute more than a mere curvature of the coast. An indentation shall not, however, be regarded as a bay unless its area is as large as, or larger than, that of the semi-circle whose diameter is a line drawn across the mouth of that indentation.

3   For the purpose of measurement, the area of an indentation is that lying between the low-water mark around the shore of the indentation and a line joining the low-water mark of its natural entrance points. Where, because of the presence of islands, an indentation has more than one mouth, the semicircle shall be drawn on a line as long as the sum total of the lengths of the lines across the different mouths. Islands within an indentation shall be included as if they were part of the water area of the indentation.

4   If the distance between the low-water marks of the natural entrance points of a bay does not exceed 24 nautical miles, a closing line may be drawn between these two low-water marks, and the waters enclosed thereby shall be considered as internal waters.

5   Where the distance between the low-water marks of the natural entrance points of a bay exceeds 24 nautical miles, a straight baseline of 24 nautical miles shall be drawn within the bay in such a manner as to enclose the maximum area of water that is possible with a line of that length.

6   The foregoing provisions do not apply to so-called 'historic' bays, or in any case where the system of straight baselines provided for in Article 7 is applied.

Article 11   Ports

For the purpose of delimiting the territorial sea, the outermost permanent harbour works which form an integral part of the harbour system are regarded as forming part of the coast. Off-shore installations and artificial islands shall not be considered as permanent harbour works.

Article 12   Roadsteads

Roadsteads which are normally used for the loading, unloading and anchoring of ships, and which would otherwise be situated wholly or partly outside the outer limit of the territorial sea, are included in the territorial sea.

Article 13   Low-tide elevations

1   A low-tide elevation is a naturally formed area of land which is surrounded by and above water at low tide but submerged at high tide. Where a low-tide elevation is situated wholly or partly at a distance not exceeding the breadth of the territorial sea from the mainland or an island, the low-water line on that elevation may be used as the baseline for measuring the breadth of the territorial sea.

2   Where a low-tide elevation is wholly situated at a distance exceeding the breadth of the territorial sea from the mainland or an island, it has no territorial sea of its own.

Article 14   Combination of methods for determining baselines

The coastal state may determine baselines in turn by any of the methods provided for in the foregoing articles to suit different conditions.

Article 15   Delimitation of the territorial sea between States with opposite or adjacent coasts

Where the coasts of two states are opposite or adjacent to each other, neither of the two states is entitled, failing agreement between them to the contrary, to extend its territorial sea beyond the median line every point of which is equidistant from the nearest points on the baselines from which the breadth of the territorial seas of each of the two states is measured. The above provision does not apply, however, where it is necessary by reason of historic title or other special circumstances to delimit the territorial seas of the two states in a way which is at variance therewith.

Article 16   Charts and lists of geographical co-ordinates

1   The baselines for measuring the breadth of the territorial sea determined in accordance with Articles 7, 9 and 10, or the limits derived therefrom, and the lines of delimitation drawn in accordance with Articles 12 and 15 shall be shown on charts of a scale or scales adequate for ascertaining their position. Alternatively, a list of geographical co-ordinates of points, specifying the geodetic datum, may be substituted.

2   The coastal state shall give due publicity to such charts or lists of geographical co-ordinates and shall deposit a copy of each such chart or list with the Secretary General of the United Nations.

SECTION 3   INNOCENT PASSAGE IN THE TERRITORIAL SEA

SUB-SECTION A   RULES APPLICABLE TO ALL SHIPS

Article 17   Right of innocent passage

Subject to this Convention, ships of all states, whether coastal or land-locked, enjoy the right of innocent passage through the territorial sea.

Article 18   Meaning of passage

1   Passage means navigation through the territorial sea for the purpose of:

    (a)   traversing that sea without entering internal waters or calling at a roadstead or port facility outside internal waters; or

    (b)   proceeding to or from internal waters or a call at such roadstead or port facility.

2   Passage shall be continuous and expeditious. However, passage includes stopping and anchoring, but only in so far as the same are incidental to

ordinary navigation or are rendered necessary by force majeure or distress or for the purpose of rendering assistance to persons, ships or aircraft in danger or distress.

Article 19   Meaning of innocent passage

1   Passage is innocent so long as it is not prejudicial to the peace, good order or security of the coastal state. Such passage shall take place in conformity with this Convention and with other rules of international law.

2   Passage of a foreign ship shall be considered to be prejudicial to the peace, good order or security of the coastal state if in the territorial sea it engages in any of the following activities:

(a)   any threat or use of force against the sovereignty, territorial integrity or political independence of the coastal state, or in any other manner in violation of the principles of international law embodied in the Charter of the United Nations;

(b)   any exercise or practice with weapons of any kind;

(c)   any act aimed at collecting information to the prejudice of the defence or security of the coastal state;

(d)   any act of propaganda aimed at affecting the defence or security of the coastal state;

(e)   the launching, landing or taking on board of any aircraft;

(f)   the launching, landing or taking on board of any military device;

(g)   the loading or unloading of any commodity, currency or person contrary to the customs, fiscal, immigration or sanitary laws and regulations of the coastal state;

(h)   any act of wilful and serious pollution contrary to this Convention;

(i)   any fishing activities;

(j)   the carrying out of research or survey activities;

(k)   any act aimed at interfering with any systems of communication or any other facilities or installations of the coastal state;

(l)   any other activity not having a direct bearing on passage.

Article 20   Submarines and other underwater vehicles

In the territorial sea, submarines and other underwater vehicles are required to navigate on the surface and to show their flag.

Article 21   Laws and regulations of the coastal state relating to innocent passage

1   The coastal state may adopt laws and regulations, in conformity with the provisions of this Convention and other rules of international law, relating to innocent passage through the territorial sea, in respect of all or any of the following:

(a)   the safety of navigation and the regulation of maritime traffic;

(b)   the protection of navigational aids and facilities and other facilities or installations;

(c)   the protection of cables and pipelines;

(d)   the conservation of the living resources of the sea;

(e)   the prevention of infringement of the fisheries laws and regulations of the coastal state;

(f) the preservation of the environment of the coastal state and the prevention, reduction and control of pollution thereof;

(g) marine scientific research and hydrographic surveys;

(h) the prevention of infringement of the customs, fiscal, immigration or sanitary laws and regulations of the coastal state.

2 Such laws and regulations shall not apply to the design, construction, manning or equipment of foreign ships unless they are giving effect to generally accepted international rules or standards.

3 The coastal state shall give due publicity to all such laws and regulations.

4 Foreign ships exercising the right of innocent passage through the territorial sea shall comply with all such laws and regulations and all generally accepted international regulations relating to the prevention of collisions at sea.

Article 22 Sea lanes and traffic separation schemes in the territorial sea

1 The coastal state may, where necessary having regard to the safety of navigation, require foreign ships exercising the right of innocent passage through its territorial sea to use such sea lanes and traffic separation schemes as it may designate or prescribe for the regulation of the passage of ships.

2 In particular, tankers, nuclear-powered ships and ships carrying nuclear or other inherently dangerous or noxious substances or materials may be required to confine their passage to such sea lanes.

3 In the designation of sea lanes and the prescription of traffic separation schemes under this article, the coastal state shall take into account:

(a) the recommendations of the competent international organisation;

(b) any channels customarily used for international navigation;

(c) the special characteristics of particular ships and channels; and

(d) the density of traffic.

4 The coastal state shall clearly indicate such sea lanes and traffic separation schemes on charts to which due publicity shall be given.

Article 23 Foreign nuclear-powered ships and ships carrying nuclear or other inherently dangerous or noxious substances

Foreign nuclear-powered ships and ships carrying nuclear or other inherently dangerous or noxious substances shall, when exercising the right of innocent passage through the territorial sea, carry documents and observe special precautionary measures established for such ships by international agreements.

Article 24 Duties of the coastal state

1 The coastal state shall not hamper the innocent passage of foreign ships through the territorial sea except in accordance with this Convention. In particular, in the application of this Convention or of any laws or regulations adopted in conformity with this Convention, the coastal state shall not:

(a) impose requirements on foreign ships which have the practical effect of denying or impairing the right of innocent passage; or

(b) discriminate in form or in fact against the ships of any state or against ships carrying cargoes to, from or on behalf of any state.

2 The coastal state shall give appropriate publicity to any danger to navigation, of which it has knowledge, within its territorial sea.

Article 25   Rights of protection of the coastal state

1   The coastal state may take the necessary steps in its territorial sea to prevent passage which is not innocent.

2   In the case of ships proceeding to internal waters or a call at a port facility outside internal waters, the coastal state also has the right to take the necessary steps to prevent any breach of the conditions to which admission of those ships to internal waters or such a call is subject.

3   The coastal state may, without discrimination in form or in fact among foreign ships, suspend temporarily in specified areas of its territorial sea the innocent passage of foreign ships if such suspension is essential for the protection of its security, including weapons exercises. Such suspension shall take effect only after having been duly published.

Article 26   Charges which may be levied upon foreign ships

1   No charge may be levied upon foreign ships by reason only of their passage through the territorial sea.

2   Charges may be levied upon a foreign ship passing through the territorial sea as payment only for specific services rendered to the ship. These charges shall be levied without discrimination.

SUBSECTION B   RULES APPLICABLE TO MERCHANT SHIPS AND GOVERNMENT SHIPS OPERATED FOR COMMERCIAL PURPOSES

Article 27   Criminal jurisdiction on board a foreign ship

1   The criminal jurisdiction of the coastal state should not be exercised on board a foreign ship passing through the territorial sea to arrest any person or to conduct any investigation in connection with any crime committed on board the ship during its passage, save only in the following cases:

(a)   if the consequences of the crime extend to the coastal state;

(b)   if the crime is of a kind to disturb the peace of the country or the good order of the territorial sea;

(c)   if the assistance of the local authorities has been requested by the master of the ship or by a diplomatic agent or consular officer of the flag state; or

(d)   if such measures are necessary for the suppression of illicit traffic in narcotic drugs or psychotropic substances.

2   The above provisions do not affect the right of the coastal state to take any steps authorised by its laws for the purpose of an arrest or investigation on board a foreign ship passing through the territorial sea after leaving internal waters.

3   In the cases provided for in paras 1 and 2, the coastal state shall, if the master so requests, notify a diplomatic agent or consular officer of the flag state before taking any steps, and shall facilitate contact between such agent or officer and the ship's crew. In cases of emergency this notification may be communicated while the measures are being taken.

4   In considering whether or in what manner an arrest should be made, the local authorities shall have due regard to the interests of navigation.

5   Except as provided in Part XII or with respect to violations of laws and regulations adopted in accordance with Part V, the coastal state may not take any steps on board a foreign ship passing through the territorial sea to arrest any person or to conduct any investigation in connection with any crime

committed before the ship entered the territorial sea, if the ship, proceeding from a foreign port, is only passing through the territorial sea without entering internal waters.

Article 28   Civil jurisdiction in relation to foreign ships

1   The coastal state should not stop or divert a foreign ship passing through the territorial sea for the purpose of exercising civil jurisdiction in relation to a person on board the ship.

2   The coastal state may not levy execution against or arrest the ship for the purpose of any civil proceedings, save only in respect of obligations or liabilities assumed or incurred by the ship itself in the course or for the purpose of its voyage through the waters of the coastal state.

3   Paragraph 2 is without prejudice to the right of the coastal state, in accordance with its laws, to levy execution against or to arrest, for the purpose of any civil proceedings, a foreign ship lying in the territorial sea, or passing through the territorial sea after leaving internal waters.

SUBSECTION C   RULES APPLICABLE TO WARSHIPS AND OTHER GOVERNMENT SHIPS OPERATED FOR NON-COMMERCIAL PURPOSES

Article 29   Definition of warships

For the purposes of this Convention, 'warship' means a ship belonging to the armed forces of a state bearing the external marks distinguishing such ships of its nationality, under the command of an officer duly commissioned by the government of the state and whose name appears in the appropriate service list or its equivalent, and manned by a crew which is under regular armed forces discipline.

Article 30   Non-compliance by warships with the laws and regulations of the coastal state

If any warship does not comply with the laws and regulations of the coastal state concerning passage through the territorial sea and disregards any request for compliance therewith which is made to it, the coastal state may require it to leave the territorial sea immediately.

Article 31   Responsibility of the flag state for damage caused by a warship or other government ship operated for non-commercial purposes

The flag state shall bear international responsibility for any loss or damage to the coastal state resulting from the non-compliance by a warship or other government ship operated for non-commercial purposes with the laws and regulations of the coastal state concerning passage through the territorial sea or with the provisions of this Convention or other rules of international law.

Article 32   Immunities of warships and other government ships operated for non-commercial purposes

With such exceptions as are contained in sub-s A and in Articles 30 and 31, nothing in this Convention affects the immunities of warships and other government ships operated for non-commercial purposes.

SECTION 4   CONTIGUOUS ZONE

Article 33   Contiguous zone

1   In a zone contiguous to its territorial sea, described as the contiguous zone, the coastal state may exercise the control necessary to:

(a) prevent infringement of its customs, fiscal, immigration or sanitary laws and regulations within its territory or territorial sea;

(b) punish infringement of the above laws and regulations committed within its territory or territorial sea.

2   The contiguous zone may not extend beyond 24 nautical miles from the baselines from which the breadth of the territorial sea is measured.

PART III
STRAITS USED FOR INTERNATIONAL NAVIGATION
SECTION 1   GENERAL PROVISIONS

Article 34   Legal status of waters forming straits used for international navigation

1   The regime of passage through straits used for international navigation established in this Part shall not in other respects affect the legal status of the waters forming such straits or the exercise by the states bordering the straits of their sovereignty or jurisdiction over such waters and their air space, bed and subsoil.

2   The sovereignty or jurisdiction of the states bordering the straits is exercised subject to this Part and to other rules of international law.

Article 35   Scope of this Part

Nothing in this Part affects:

(a) any areas of internal waters within a strait, except where the establishment of a straight baseline in accordance with the method set forth in Article 7 has the effect of enclosing as internal waters areas which had not previously been considered as such;

(b) the legal status of the waters beyond the territorial seas of states bordering straits as exclusive economic zones or high seas; or

(c) the legal regime in straits in which passage is regulated in whole or in part by long-standing international conventions in force specifically relating to such straits.

Article 36   High seas routes or routes through exclusive economic zones through straits used for international navigation

This Part does not apply to a strait used for international navigation if there exists through the strait a route through the high seas or through an exclusive economic zone of similar convenience with respect to navigational and hydrographical characteristics; in such routes, the other relevant Parts of this Convention, including the provisions regarding the freedoms of navigation and overflight, apply.

SECTION 2   TRANSIT PASSAGE

Article 37   Scope of this section

This section applies to straits which are used for international navigation between one part of the high seas or an exclusive economic zone and another part of the high seas or an exclusive economic zone.

Article 38   Right of transit passage

1   In straits referred to in Article 37, all ships and aircraft enjoy the right of transit passage, which shall not be impeded; except that, if the strait is formed by an island of a state bordering the strait and its mainland, transit

passage shall not apply if there exists seaward of the island a route through the high seas or through an exclusive economic zone of similar convenience with respect to navigational and hydrographical characteristics.

2   Transit passage means the exercise in accordance with this Part of the freedom of navigation and overflight solely for the purpose of continuous and expeditious transit of the strait between one part of the high seas or an exclusive economic zone and another part of the high seas or an exclusive economic zone. However, the requirement of continuous and expeditious transit does not preclude passage through the strait for the purpose of entering, leaving or returning from a state bordering the strait, subject to the conditions of entry to that state.

3   Any activity which is not an exercise of the right of transit passage through a strait remains subject to the other applicable provisions of this Convention.

Article 39   Duties of ships and aircraft during transit passage

1   Ships and aircraft, while exercising the right of transit passage, shall:

(a)   proceed without delay through or over the strait;

(b)   refrain from any threat or use of force against the sovereignty, territorial integrity or political independence of States bordering the strait, or in any other manner in violation of the principles of international law embodied in the Charter of the United Nations;

(c)   refrain from any activities other than those incident to their normal modes of continuous and expeditious transit unless rendered necessary by *force majeure* or by distress;

(d)   comply with other relevant provisions of this Part.

2   Ships in transit passage shall:

(a)   comply with generally accepted international regulations, procedures and practices for safety at sea, including the International Regulations for Preventing Collisions at Sea;

(b)   comply with generally accepted international regulations, procedures and practices for the prevention, reduction and control of pollution from ships.

3   Aircraft in transit passage shall:

(a)   observe the Rules of the Air established by the International Civil Aviation Organisation as they apply to civil aircraft; state aircraft will normally comply with such safety measures and will at all times operate with due regard for the safety of navigation;

(b)   at all times monitor the radio frequency assigned by the competent internationally designated air traffic control authority or the appropriate international distress radio frequency.

Article 40   Research and survey activities

During transit passage, foreign ships, including marine scientific research and hydrographic survey ships, may not carry out any research or survey activities without the prior authorisation of the states bordering straits.

Article 41   Sea lanes and traffic separation schemes in straits used for international navigation

1   In conformity with this Part, states bordering straits may designate sea lanes and prescribe traffic separation schemes for navigation in straits where necessary to promote the safe passage of ships.

2   Such states may, when circumstances require, and after giving due publicity thereto, substitute other sea lanes or traffic separation schemes for any sea lanes or traffic separation schemes previously designated or prescribed by them.

3   Such sea lanes and traffic separation schemes shall conform to generally accepted international regulations.

4   Before designating or substituting sea lanes or prescribing or substituting traffic separation schemes, states bordering straits shall refer proposals to the competent international organisation with a view to their adoption. The organisation may adopt only such sea lanes and traffic separation schemes as may be agreed with the states bordering the straits, after which the States may designate, prescribe or substitute them.

5   In respect of a strait where sea lanes or traffic separation schemes through the waters of two or more states bordering the strait are being proposed, the States concerned shall co-operate in formulating proposals in consultation with the competent international organisation.

6   States bordering straits shall clearly indicate all sea lanes and traffic separation schemes designated or prescribed by them on charts to which due publicity shall be given.

7   Ships in transit passage shall respect applicable sea lanes and traffic separation schemes established in accordance with this article.

Article 42   Laws and regulations of states bordering straits relating to transit passage

1   Subject to the provisions of this section, states bordering straits may adopt laws and regulations relating to transit passage through straits, in respect of all or any of the following:

   (a)   the safety of navigation and the regulation of maritime traffic, as provided in Article 41;

   (b)   the prevention, reduction and control of pollution, by giving effect to applicable international regulations regarding the discharge of oil, oily wastes and other noxious substances in the strait;

   (c)   with respect to fishing vessels, the prevention of fishing, including the stowage of fishing gear;

   (d)   the loading or unloading of any commodity, currency or person in contravention of the customs, fiscal, immigration or sanitary laws and regulations of states bordering straits.

2   Such laws and regulations shall not discriminate in form or in fact among foreign ships or in their application have the practical effect of denying, hampering or impairing the right of transit passage as defined in this section.

3   States bordering straits shall give due publicity to all such laws and regulations.

4   Foreign ships exercising the right of transit passage shall comply with such laws and regulations.

5   The flag state of a ship or the state of registry of an aircraft entitled to sovereign immunity which acts in a manner contrary to such laws and regulations or other provisions of this Part shall bear international responsibility for any loss or damage which results to states bordering straits.

Article 43 Navigational and safety aids and other improvements and the prevention, reduction and control of pollution

User States and States bordering a strait should by agreement co-operate:

(a) in the establishment and maintenance in a strait of necessary navigational and safety aids or other improvements in aid of international navigation; and

(b) for the prevention, reduction and control of pollution from ships.

Article 44 Duties of States bordering straits

States bordering straits shall not hamper transit passage and shall give appropriate publicity to any danger to navigation or overflight within or over the strait of which they have knowledge. There shall be no suspension of transit passage.

SECTION 3 INNOCENT PASSAGE

Article 45 Innocent passage

1 The regime of innocent passage, in accordance with Part II, section 3 shall apply in straits used for international navigation:

(a) excluded from the application of the regime of transit passage under Article 38, para 1; or

(b) between a part of the high seas or an exclusive economic zone and the territorial sea of a foreign state.

2 There shall be no suspension of innocent passage through such straits.

PART IV
ARCHIPELAGIC STATES

Article 46 Use of terms

For the purposes of this Convention:

(a) 'archipelagic state' means a state constituted wholly by one or more archipelagos and may include other islands;

(b) 'archipelago' means a group of islands, including parts of islands, interconnecting waters and other natural features which are so closely interrelated that such islands, waters and other natural features form an intrinsic geographical, economic and political entity, or which historically have been regarded as such.

Article 47 Archipelagic baselines

1 An archipelagic state may draw straight archipelagic baselines joining the outermost points of the outermost islands and drying reefs of the archipelago provided that within such baselines are included the main islands and an area in which the ratio of the area of the water to the area of the land, including atolls, is between 1 to 1 and 9 to 1.

2 The length of such baselines shall not exceed 100 nautical miles, except that up to 3% of the total number of baselines enclosing any archipelago may exceed that length, up to a maximum length of 125 nautical miles.

3 The drawing of such baselines shall not depart to any appreciable extent from the general configuration of the archipelago.

4 Such baselines shall not be drawn to and from low-tide elevations, unless lighthouses or similar installations which are permanently above sea level

have been built on them or where a low-tide elevation is situated wholly or partly at a distance not exceeding the breadth of the territorial sea from the nearest island.

5   The system of such baselines shall not be applied by an archipelagic state in such a manner as to cut off from the high seas or the exclusive economic zone the territorial sea of another state.

6   If a part of the archipelagic waters of an archipelagic state lies between two parts of an immediately adjacent neighbouring state, existing rights and all other legitimate interests which the latter state has traditionally exercised in such waters and all rights stipulated by agreement between those states shall continue and be respected.

7   For the purpose of computing the ratio of water to land under para 1, land areas may include waters lying within the fringing reefs of islands and atolls, including that part of a steep-sided oceanic plateau which is enclosed or nearly enclosed by a chain of limestone islands and drying reefs lying on the perimeter of the plateau.

8   The baselines drawn in accordance with this article shall be shown on charts of a scale or scales adequate for ascertaining their position. Alternatively, lists of geographical co-ordinates of points, specifying the geodetic datum, may be substituted.

9   The archipelagic state shall give due publicity to such charts or lists of geographical co-ordinates and shall deposit a copy of each such chart or list with the Secretary General of the United Nations.

Article 48 Measurement of the breadth of the territorial sea, the contiguous zone, the exclusive economic zone and the continental shelf

The breadth of the territorial sea, the contiguous zone, the exclusive economic zone and the continental shelf shall be measured from archipelagic baselines drawn in accordance with Article 47.

Article 49 Legal status of archipelagic waters, of the air space over archipelagic waters and of their bed and subsoil

1   The sovereignty of an archipelagic state extends to the waters enclosed by the archipelagic baselines drawn in accordance with Article 47, described as archipelagic waters, regardless of their depth or distance from the coast.

2   This sovereignty extends to the air space over the archipelagic waters, as well as to their bed and subsoil, and the resources contained therein.

3   This sovereignty is exercised subject to this Part.

4   The regime of archipelagic sea lanes passage established in this Part shall not in other respects affect the status of the archipelagic waters, including the sea lanes, or the exercise by the archipelagic state of its sovereignty over such waters and their air space, bed and subsoil, and the resources contained therein.

Article 50 Delimitation of internal waters

Within its archipelagic waters, the archipelagic state may draw closing lines for the delimitation of internal waters, in accordance with Articles 9, 10 and 11.

Article 51 Existing agreements, traditional fishing rights and existing submarine cables

1   Without prejudice to Article 49, an archipelagic state shall respect existing agreements with other States and shall recognise traditional fishing rights and other legitimate activities of the immediately adjacent neighbouring

states in certain areas falling within archipelagic waters. The terms and conditions for the exercise of such rights and activities, including the nature, the extent and the areas to which they apply, shall, at the request of any of the states concerned, be regulated by bilateral agreements between them. Such rights shall not be transferred to or shared with third states or their nationals.

2   An archipelagic state shall respect existing submarine cables laid by other states and passing through its waters without making a landfall. An archipelagic state shall permit the maintenance and replacement of such cables upon receiving due notice of their location and the intention to repair or replace them.

Article 52   Right of innocent passage

1   Subject to Article 53 and without prejudice to Article 50, ships of all states enjoy the right of innocent passage through archipelagic waters, in accordance with Part II, section 3.

2   The archipelagic state may, without discrimination in form or in fact among foreign ships, suspend temporarily in specified areas of its archipelagic waters the innocent passage of foreign ships if such suspension is essential for the protection of its security. Such suspension shall take effect only after having been duly published.

Article 53   Right of archipelagic sea lanes passage

1   An archipelagic state may designate sea lanes and air routes thereabove, suitable for the continuous and expeditious passage of foreign ships and aircraft through or over its archipelagic waters and the adjacent territorial sea.

2   All ships and aircraft enjoy the right of archipelagic sea lanes passage in such sea lanes and air routes.

3   Archipelagic sea lanes passage means the exercise in accordance with this Convention of the rights of navigation and overflight in the normal mode solely for the purpose of continuous, expeditious and unobstructed transit between one part of the high seas or an exclusive economic zone and another part of the high seas or an exclusive economic zone.

4   Such sea lanes and air routes shall traverse the archipelagic waters and the adjacent territorial sea and shall include all normal passage routes used as routes for international navigation or overflight through or over archipelagic waters and, within such routes, so far as ships are concerned, all normal navigational channels, provided that duplication of routes of similar convenience between the same entry and exit points shall not be necessary.

5   Such sea lanes and air routes shall be defined by a series of continuous axis lines from the entry points of passage routes to the exit points. Ships and aircraft in archipelagic sea lanes passage shall not deviate more than 25 nautical miles to either side of such axis lines during passage, provided that such ships and aircraft shall not navigate closer to the coasts than 10% of the distance between the nearest points on islands bordering the sea lane.

6   An archipelagic state which designates sea lanes under this article may also prescribe traffic separation schemes for the safe passage of ships through narrow channels in such sea lanes.

7   An archipelagic state may, when circumstances require, after giving due publicity thereto, substitute other sea lanes or traffic separation schemes for any sea lanes or traffic separation schemes previously designated or prescribed by it.

8   Such sea lanes and traffic separation schemes shall conform to generally accepted international regulations.

9   In designating or substituting sea lanes or prescribing or substituting traffic separation schemes, an archipelagic state shall refer proposals to the competent international organisation with a view to their adoption. The organisation may adopt only such sea lanes and traffic separation schemes as may be agreed with the archipelagic state, after which the archipelagic state may designate, prescribe or substitute them.

10   The archipelagic state shall clearly indicate the axis of the sea lanes and the traffic separation schemes designated or prescribed by it on charts to which due publicity shall be given.

11   Ships in archipelagic sea lanes passage shall respect applicable sea lanes and traffic separation schemes established in accordance with this article.

12   If an archipelagic state does not designate sea lanes or air routes, the right of archipelagic sea lanes passage may be exercised through the routes normally used for internal navigation.

Article 54 Duties of ships and aircraft during their passage, research and survey activities, duties of the archipelagic state and laws and regulations of the archipelagic state relating to archipelagic sea lanes passage

Articles 39, 40, 42 and 44 apply *mutatis mutandis* to archipelagic sea lanes passage.

PART V

EXCLUSIVE ECONOMIC ZONE

Article 55 Specific legal regime of the exclusive economic zone

The exclusive economic zone is an area beyond and adjacent to the territorial sea, subject to the specific legal regime established in this Part, under which the rights and jurisdiction of the coastal state and the rights and freedoms of other states are governed by the relevant provisions of this Convention.

Article 56 Rights, jurisdiction and duties of the coastal state in the exclusive economic zone

1   In the exclusive economic zone, the coastal state has:

(a) sovereign rights for the purpose of exploring and exploiting, conserving and managing the natural resources, whether living or non-living, of the waters superjacent to the sea bed and of the sea bed and its subsoil, and with regard to other activities for the economic exploitation and exploration of the zone, such as the production of energy from the water, currents and winds;

(b) jurisdiction as provided for in the relevant provisions of this Convention with regard to:

(i)   the establishment and use of artificial islands, installations and structures;

(ii) marine scientific research;

(iii) the protection and preservation of the marine environment;

(c) other rights and duties provided for in this Convention.

2   In exercising its rights and performing its duties under this Convention in the exclusive economic zone, the coastal state shall have due regard to the rights

and duties of other states and shall act in a manner compatible with the provisions of this Convention.

3   The rights set out in this article with respect to the sea bed and subsoil shall be exercised in accordance with Part VI.

Article 57   Breadth of the exclusive economic zone

The exclusive economic zone shall not extend beyond 200 nautical miles from the baselines from which the breadth of the territorial sea is measured.

Article 58   Rights and duties of other states in the exclusive economic zone

1   In the exclusive economic zone all states, whether coastal or land-locked, enjoy, subject to the relevant provisions of this Convention, the freedoms referred to in Article 87 of navigation and overflight and of the laying of submarine cables and pipelines, and other internationally lawful uses of the sea related to these freedoms, such as those associated with the operation of ships, aircraft and submarine cables and pipelines, and compatible with the other provisions of this Convention.

2   Articles 88 to 115 and other pertinent rules of international law apply to the exclusive economic zone in so far as they are not incompatible with this Part.

3   In exercising their rights and performing their duties under this Convention in the exclusive economic zone, states shall have due regard to the rights and duties of the coastal state and shall comply with the laws and regulations adopted by the coastal state in accordance with the provisions of this Convention and other rules of international law in so far as they are not incompatible with this Part.

Article 59   Basis for the resolution of conflicts regarding the attribution of rights and jurisdiction in the exclusive economic zone

In cases where this Convention does not attribute rights or jurisdiction to the coastal state or to other states within the exclusive economic zone, and a conflict arises between the interests of the coastal state and any other state or states, the conflict should be resolved on the basis of equity and in the light of all the relevant circumstances, taking into account the respective importance of the interests involved to the parties as well as to the international community as a whole.

Article 60   Artificial islands, installations and structures in the exclusive economic zone

1   In the exclusive economic zone, the coastal state shall have the exclusive right to construct and to authorise and regulate the construction, operation and use of:

(a)   artificial islands;

(b)   installations and structures for the purposes provided for in Article 56 and other economic purposes;

(c)   installations and structures which may interfere with the exercise of the rights of the coastal state in the zone.

2   The coastal state shall have exclusive jurisdiction over such artificial islands, installations and structures, including jurisdiction with regard to customs, fiscal, health, safety and immigration laws and regulations.

3   Due notice must be given of the construction of such artificial islands, installations or structures, and permanent means for giving warning of their presence must be maintained. Any installations or structures which are abandoned or disused shall be removed to ensure safety of navigation, taking

into account any generally accepted international standards established in this regard by the competent international organisation. Such removal shall also have due regard to fishing, the protection of the marine environment and the rights and duties of other states. Appropriate publicity shall be given to the depth, position and dimensions of any installations or structures not entirely removed.

4   The coastal state may, where necessary, establish reasonable safety zones around such artificial islands, installations and structures in which it may take appropriate measures to ensure the safety both of navigation and of the artificial islands, installations and structures.

5   The breadth of the safety zones shall be determined by the coastal state, taking into account applicable international standards. Such zones shall be designed to ensure that they are reasonably related to the nature and function of the artificial islands, installations or structures, and shall not exceed a distance of 500 metres around them, measured from each point of their outer edge, except as authorised by generally accepted international standards or as recommended by the competent international organisation. Due notice shall be given of the extent of safety zones.

6   All ships must respect these safety zones and shall comply with generally accepted international standards regarding navigation in the vicinity of artificial islands, installations, structures and safety zones.

7   Artificial islands, installations and structures and the safety zones around them may not be established where interference may be caused to the use of recognised sea lanes essential to international navigation.

8   Artificial islands, installations and structures do not possess the status of islands. They have no territorial sea of their own, and their presence does not affect the delimitation of the territorial sea, the exclusive economic zone or the continental shelf.

Article 61   Conservation of the living resources

1   The coastal state shall determine the allowable catch of the living resources in its exclusive economic zone.

2   The coastal state, taking into account the best scientific evidence available to it, shall ensure through proper conservation and management measures that the maintenance of the living resources in the exclusive economic zone is not endangered by over-exploitation. As appropriate, the coastal state and competent international organisations, whether subregional, regional or global, shall co-operate to this end.

3   Such measures shall also be designed to maintain or restore populations of harvested species at levels which can produce the maximum sustainable yield, as qualified by relevant environmental and economic factors, including the economic needs of coastal fishing communities and the special requirements of developing states, and taking into account fishing patterns, the interdependence of stocks and any generally recommended international minimum standards, whether subregional, regional or global.

4   In taking such measures the coastal state shall take into consideration the effects on species associated with or dependent upon harvested species with a view to maintaining or restoring populations of such associated or dependent species above levels at which their reproduction may become seriously threatened.

5   Available scientific information, catch and fishing effort statistics, and other
     data relevant to the conservation of fish stocks shall be contributed and
     exchanged on a regular basis through competent international organisations,
     whether subregional, regional or global, where appropriate and with
     participation by all states concerned, including states whose nationals are
     allowed to fish in the exclusive economic zone.

Article 62   Utilisation of the living resources

1   The coastal state shall promote the objective of optimum utilisation of the
     living resources in the exclusive economic zone without prejudice to Article
     61.

2   The coastal state shall determine its capacity to harvest the living resources of
     the exclusive economic zone. Where the coastal state does not have the
     capacity to harvest the entire allowable catch, it shall, through agreements or
     other arrangements and pursuant to the terms, conditions, laws and
     regulations referred to in para 4, give other states access to the surplus of the
     allowable catch, having particular regard to the provisions of Articles 69 and
     70, especially in relation to the developing states mentioned therein.

3   In giving access to other states to its exclusive economic zone under this
     article the coastal state shall take into account all relevant factors, including,
     inter alia, the significance of the living resources of the area to the economy of
     the coastal state concerned and its other national interests, the provisions of
     Articles 69 and 70, the requirements of developing states in the subregion or
     region in harvesting part of the surplus and the need to minimise economic
     dislocation in states whose nationals have habitually fished in the zone or
     which have made substantial efforts in research and identification of stocks.

4   Nationals of other states fishing in the exclusive economic zone shall comply
     with the conservation measures and with the other terms and conditions
     established in the laws and regulations of the coastal state. These laws and
     regulations shall be consistent with this Convention and may relate, *inter alia*,
     to the following:

     (a)   licensing of fishermen, fishing vessels and equipment, including
           payment of fees and other forms of remuneration, which, in the case of
           developing coastal States, may consist of adequate compensation in the
           field of financing, equipment and technology relating to the fishing
           industry;

     (b)   determining the species which may be caught, and fixing quotas of
           catch, whether in relation to particular stocks or groups of stocks or
           catch per vessel over a period of time or to the catch by nationals of any
           state during a specified period;

     (c)   regulating seasons and areas of fishing, the types, sizes and amount of
           gear, and the types, sizes and number of fishing vessels that may be
           used;

     (d)   fixing the age and size of fish and other species that may be caught;

     (e)   specifying information required of fishing vessels, including catch and
           effort statistics and vessel position reports;

     (f)   requiring, under the authorisation and control of the coastal state, the
           conduct of specified fisheries research programmes and regulating the
           conduct of such research, including the sampling of catches, disposition
           of samples and reporting of associated scientific data;

(g) the placing of observers or trainees on board such vessels by the coastal state;

(h) the landing of all or any part of the catch by such vessels in the ports of the coastal state;

(i) terms and conditions relating to joint ventures or other co-operative arrangements;

(j) requirements for the training of personnel and the transfer of fisheries technology, including enhancement of the coastal state's capability of undertaking fisheries research;

(k) enforcement procedures.

5 Coastal states shall give due notice of conservation and management laws and regulations.

Article 63 Stocks occurring within the exclusive economic zones of two or more coastal States or both within the exclusive economic zone and in an area beyond and adjacent to it

1. Where the same stock or stocks of associated species occur within the exclusive economic zones of two or more coastal states, these states shall seek, either directly or through appropriate subregional or regional organisations, to agree upon the measures necessary to co-ordinate and ensure the conservation and development of such stocks without prejudice to the other provisions of this Part.

2 Where the same stock or stocks of associated species occur both within the exclusive economic zone and in an area beyond and adjacent to the zone, the coastal state and the states fishing for such stocks in the adjacent area shall seek, either directly or through appropriate subregional or regional organisations, to agree upon the measures necessary for the conservation of these stocks in the adjacent area.

Article 64 Highly migratory species

1 The coastal state and other states whose nationals fish in the region for the highly migratory species listed in Annex I shall co-operate directly or through appropriate international organisations with a view to ensuring conservation and promoting the objective of optimum utilisation of such species throughout the region, both within and beyond the exclusive economic zone. In regions for which no appropriate international organisation exists, the coastal state and other states whose nationals harvest these species in the region shall co-operate to establish such an organisation and participate in its work.

2 The provisions of para 1 apply in addition to the other provisions of this Part.

Article 65 Marine mammals

Nothing in this Part restricts the right of a coastal state or the competence of an international organisation, as appropriate, to prohibit, limit or regulate the exploitation of marine mammals more strictly than provided for in this Part. States shall co-operate with a view to the conservation of marine mammals and in the case of cetaceans shall in particular work through the appropriate international organisations for their conservation, management and study.

Article 66 Anadromous stocks

1 States in whose rivers anadromous stocks originate shall have the primary interest in and responsibility for such stocks.

2   The state of origin of anadromous stocks shall ensure their conservation by the establishment of appropriate regulatory measures for fishing in all waters landward of the outer limits of its exclusive economic zone and for fishing provided for in para 3(b). The state of origin may, after consultations with the other states referred to in paras 3 and 4 fishing these stocks, establish total allowable catches for stocks originating in its rivers.

3   (a)   Fisheries for anadromous stocks shall be conducted only in waters landward of the outer limits of exclusive economic zones, except in cases where this provision would result in economic dislocation for a state other than the state of origin. With respect to such fishing beyond the outer limits of the exclusive economic zone, states concerned shall maintain consultations with a view to achieving agreement on terms and conditions of such fishing giving due regard to the conservation requirements and the needs of the state of origin in respect of these stocks.

    (b)   The state of origin shall co-operate in minimising economic dislocation in such other states fishing these stocks, taking into account the normal catch and the mode of operations of such states, and all the areas in which such fishing has occurred.

    (c)   States referred to in sub-para (b), participating by agreement with the state of origin in measures to renew anadromous stocks, particularly by expenditures for that purpose, shall be given special consideration by the state of origin in the harvesting of stocks originating in its rivers.

    (d)   Enforcement of regulations regarding anadromous stocks beyond the exclusive economic zone shall be by agreement between the state of origin and the other states concerned.

4   In cases where anadromous stocks migrate into or through the waters landward of the outer limits of the exclusive economic zone of a state other than the state of origin, such state shall co-operate with the state of origin with regard to the conservation and management of such stocks.

5   The state of origin of anadromous stocks and other states fishing these stocks shall make arrangements for the implementation of the provisions of this article, where appropriate, through regional organisations.

Article 67   Catadromous species

1   A coastal state in whose waters catadromous species spend the greater part of their life cycle shall have responsibility for the management of these species and shall ensure the ingress and egress of migrating fish.

2   Harvesting of catadromous species shall be conducted only in waters landward of the outer limits of exclusive economic zones. When conducted in exclusive economic zones, harvesting shall be subject to this article and the other provisions of this Convention concerning fishing in these zones.

3   In cases where catadromous fish migrate through the exclusive economic zone of another state, whether as juvenile or maturing fish, the management, including harvesting, of such fish shall be regulated by agreement between the state mentioned in para 1 and the other state concerned. Such agreement shall ensure the rational management of the species and take into account the responsibilities of the state mentioned in para 1 for the maintenance of these species.

Article 68   Sedentary species

This Part does not apply to sedentary species as defined in Article 77, para 4.

Article 69   Right of land-locked states

1   Land-locked states shall have the right to participate, on an equitable basis, in the exploitation of an appropriate part of the surplus of the living resources of the exclusive economic zones of coastal states of the same subregion or region, taking into account the relevant economic and geographical circumstances of all the states concerned and in conformity with the provisions of this article and of Articles 61 and 62.

2   The terms and modalities of such participation shall be established by the states concerned through bilateral, subregional or regional agreements taking into account, *inter alia*:

(a)   the need to avoid effects detrimental to fishing communities or fishing industries of the coastal state;

(b)   the extent to which the land-locked state, in accordance with the provisions of this article, is participating or is entitled to participate under existing bilateral, subregional or regional agreements in the exploitation of living resources of the exclusive economic zones of other coastal states;

(c)   the extent to which other land-locked states and geographically disadvantaged states are participating in the exploitation of the living resources of the exclusive economic zone of the coastal state and the consequent need to avoid a particular burden for any single coastal state or a part of it;

(d)   the nutritional needs of the populations of the respective states.

3   When the harvesting capacity of a coastal state approaches a point which would enable it to harvest the entire allowable catch of the living resources in its exclusive economic zone, the coastal state and other states concerned shall co-operate in the establishment of equitable arrangements on a bilateral, subregional or regional basis to allow for participation of developing land-locked states of the same subregion or region in the exploitation of the living resources of the exclusive economic zones of coastal states of the subregion or region, as may be appropriate in the circumstances and on terms satisfactory to all parties. In the implementation of this provision the factors mentioned in para 2 shall also be taken into account.

4   Developed land-locked states shall, under the provisions of this article, be entitled to participate in the exploitation of living resources only in the exclusive economic zones of developed coastal states of the same subregion or region having regard to the extent to which the coastal state, in giving access to other states to the living resources of its exclusive economic zone, has taken into account the need to minimise detrimental effects on fishing communities and economic dislocation in States whose nationals have habitually fished in the zone.

5   The above provisions are without prejudice to arrangements agreed upon in subregions or regions where the coastal states may grant to land-locked states of the same subregion or region equal or preferential rights for the exploitation of the living resources in the exclusive economic zones.

Article 70   Right of geographically disadvantaged States

1   Geographically disadvantaged states shall have the right to participate, on an equitable basis, in the exploitation of an appropriate part of the surplus of the living resources of the exclusive economic zones of coastal states of the same subregion or region, taking into account the relevant economic and geographical circumstances of all the states concerned and in conformity with the provisions of this article and of Articles 61 and 62.

2   For the purposes of this Part, 'geographically disadvantaged states' means coastal states, including states bordering enclosed or semi-enclosed seas, whose geographical situation makes them dependent upon the exploitation of the living resources of the exclusive economic zones of other states in the subregion or region for adequate supplies of fish for the nutritional purposes of their populations or parts thereof, and coastal states which can claim no exclusive economic zones of their own.

3   The terms and modalities of such participation shall be established by the states concerned through bilateral, subregional or regional agreements taking into account, *inter alia*:

(a)   the need to avoid effects detrimental to fishing communities or fishing industries of the coastal state;

(b)   the extent to which the geographically disadvantaged state, in accordance with the provisions of this article, is participating or is entitled to participate under existing bilateral, subregional or regional agreements in the exploitation of living resources of the exclusive economic zones of other coastal states;

(c)   the extent to which other geographically disadvantaged states and land-locked states are participating in the exploitation of the living resources of the exclusive economic zone of the coastal state and the consequent need to avoid a particular burden for any single coastal state or a part of it;

(d)   the nutritional needs of the populations of the respective states.

4   When the harvesting capacity of a coastal state approaches a point which would enable it to harvest the entire allowable catch of the living resources in its exclusive economic zone, the coastal state and other states concerned shall co-operate in the establishment of equitable arrangements on a bilateral, subregional or regional basis to allow for participation of developing geographically disadvantaged states of the same subregion or region in the exploitation of the living resources of the exclusive economic zones of coastal states of the subregion or region, as may be appropriate in the circumstances and on terms satisfactory to all parties. In the implementation of this provision the factors mentioned in para 3 shall also be taken into account.

5   Developed geographically disadvantaged states shall, under the provisions of this article, be entitled to participate in the exploitation of living resources only in the exclusive economic zones of developed coastal states of the same subregion or region having regard to the extent to which the coastal state, in giving access to other states to the living resources of its exclusive economic zone, has taken into account the need to minimise detrimental effects on fishing communities and economic dislocation in states whose nationals have habitually fished in the zone.

6   The above provisions are without prejudice to arrangements agreed upon in subregions or regions where the coastal states may grant to geographically disadvantaged states of the same subregion or region equal or preferential

rights for the exploitation of the living resources in the exclusive economic zones.

Article 71   Non-applicability of Articles 69 and 70

The provisions of Articles 69 and 70 do not apply in the case of a coastal state whose economy is overwhelmingly dependent on the exploitation of the living resources of its exclusive economic zone.

Article 72   Restrictions on transfer of rights

1   Rights provided under Articles 69 and 70 to exploit living resources shall not be directly or indirectly transferred to third states or their nationals by lease or licence, by establishing joint ventures or in any other manner which has the effect of such transfer unless otherwise agreed by the states concerned.

2   The foregoing provision does not preclude the states concerned from obtaining technical or financial assistance from third states or international organisations in order to facilitate the exercise of the rights pursuant to Articles 69 and 70, provided that it does not have the effect referred to in para 1.

Article 73   Enforcement of laws and regulations of the coastal state

1   The coastal state may, in the exercise of its sovereign rights to explore, exploit, conserve and manage the living resources in the exclusive economic zone, take such measures, including boarding, inspection, arrest and judicial proceedings, as may be necessary to ensure compliance with the laws and regulations adopted by it in conformity with this Convention.

2   Arrested vessels and their crews shall be promptly released upon the posting of reasonable bond or other security.

3   Coastal state penalties for violations of fisheries laws and regulations in the exclusive economic zone may not include imprisonment, in the absence of agreements to the contrary by the states concerned, or any other form of corporal punishment.

4   In cases of arrest or detention of foreign vessels the coastal state shall promptly notify the flag state, through appropriate channels, of the action taken and of any penalties subsequently imposed.

Article 74   Delimitation of the exclusive economic zone between states with opposite or adjacent coasts

1   The delimitation of the exclusive economic zone between states with opposite or adjacent coasts shall be effected by agreement on the basis of international law, as referred to in Article 38 of the Statute of the International Court of Justice, in order to achieve an equitable solution.

2   If no agreement can be reached within a reasonable period of time, the states concerned shall resort to the procedures provided for in Part XV.

3   Pending agreement as provided for in para 1, the states concerned, in a spirit of understanding and co-operation, shall make every effort to enter into provisional arrangements of a practical nature and, during this transitional period, not to jeopardise or hamper the reaching of the final agreement. Such arrangements shall be without prejudice to the final delimitation.

4   Where there is an agreement in force between the states concerned, questions relating to the delimitation of the exclusive economic zone shall be determined in accordance with the provisions of that agreement.

Article 75 Charts and lists of geographical co-ordinates

1   Subject to this Part, the outer limit lines of the exclusive economic zone and the lines of delimitation drawn in accordance with Article 74 shall be shown on charts of a scale or scales adequate for ascertaining their position. Where appropriate, lists of geographical co-ordinates of points, specifying the geodetic datum, may be substituted for such outer limit lines or lines of delimitation.

2   The coastal state shall give due publicity to such charts or lists of geographical co-ordinates and shall deposit a copy of each such chart or list with the Secretary General of the United Nations.

PART VI

CONTINENTAL SHELF

Article 76 Definition of the continental shelf

1   The continental shelf of a coastal state comprises the sea bed and subsoil of the submarine areas that extend beyond its territorial sea throughout the natural prolongation of its land territory to the outer edge of the continental margin, or to a distance of 200 nautical miles from the baselines from which the breadth of the territorial sea is measured where the outer edge of the continental margin does not extend up to that distance.

2   The continental shelf of a coastal state shall not extend beyond the limits provided for in paras 4 to 6.

3   The continental margin comprises the submerged prolongation of the land mass of the coastal state, and consists of the sea bed and subsoil of the shelf the slope and the rise. It does not include the deep ocean floor with its oceanic ridges or the subsoil thereof.

4   (a) For the purposes of this Convention, the coastal state shall establish the outer edge of the continental margin wherever the margin extends beyond 200 nautical miles from the baselines from which the breadth of the territorial sea is measured, by either:

   (i) a line delineated in accordance with para 7 by reference to the outermost fixed points at each of which the thickness of sedimentary rocks is at least 1% of the shortest distance from such point to the foot of the continental slope; or

   (ii) a line delineated in accordance with para 7 by reference to fixed points not more than 60 nautical miles from the foot of the continental slope.

   (b) In the absence of evidence to the contrary, the foot of the continental slope shall be determined as the point of maximum change in the gradient at its base.

5   The fixed points comprising the line of the outer limits of the continental shelf on the sea bed, drawn in accordance with para 4(a)(i) and (ii), either shall not exceed 350 nautical miles from the baselines from which the breadth of the territorial sea is measured or shall not exceed 100 nautical miles from the 2,500 metre isobath, which is a line connecting the depth of 2,500 metres.

6   Notwithstanding the provisions of para 5, on submarine ridges, the outer limit of the continental shelf shall not exceed 350 nautical miles from the baselines from which the breadth of the territorial sea is measured. This

paragraph does not apply to submarine elevations that are natural components of the continental margin, such as its plateaux, rises, caps, banks and spurs.

7   The coastal state shall delineate the outer limits of its continental shelf, where that shelf extends beyond 200 nautical miles from the baselines from which the breadth of the territorial sea is measured, by straight lines not exceeding 60 nautical miles in length, connecting fixed points, defined by co-ordinates of latitude and longitude.

8   Information on the limits of the continental shelf beyond 200 nautical miles from the baselines from which the breadth of the territorial sea is measured shall be submitted by the coastal state to the Commission on the Limits of the Continental Shelf set up under Annex II on the basis of equitable geographical representation. The Commission shall make recommendations to coastal states on matters related to the establishment of the outer limits of their continental shelf. The limits of the shelf established by a coastal state on the basis of these recommendations shall be final and binding.

9   The coastal state shall deposit with the Secretary General of the United Nations charts and relevant information, including geodetic data, permanently describing the outer limits of its continental shelf. The Secretary General shall give due publicity thereto.

10   The provisions of this article are without prejudice to the question of delimitation of the continental shelf between states with opposite or adjacent coasts.

Article 77   Rights of the coastal state over the continental shelf

1   The coastal state exercises over the continental shelf sovereign rights for the purpose of exploring it and exploiting its natural resources.

2   The rights referred to in para 1 are exclusive in the sense that if the coastal state does not explore the continental shelf or exploit its natural resources, no one may undertake these activities without the express consent of the coastal state.

3   The rights of the coastal state over the continental shelf do not depend on occupation, effective or notional, or on any express proclamation.

4   The natural resources referred to in this Part consist of the mineral and other non-living resources of the sea bed and subsoil together with living organisms belonging to sedentary species, that is to say, organisms which, at the harvestable stage, either are immobile on or under the sea bed or are unable to move except in constant physical contact with the sea bed or the subsoil.

Article 78   Legal status of the superjacent waters and air space and the rights and freedoms of other states

1   The rights of the coastal state over the continental shelf do not affect the legal status of the superjacent waters or of the air space above those waters.

2   The exercise of the rights of the coastal state over the continental shelf must not infringe or result in any unjustifiable interference with navigation and other rights and freedoms of other states as provided for in this Convention.

Article 79   Submarine cables and pipelines on the continental shelf

1   All states are entitled to lay submarine cables and pipelines on the continental shelf, in accordance with the provisions of this article.

2   Subject to its right to take reasonable measures for the exploration of the continental shelf, the exploitation of its natural resources and the prevention, reduction and control of pollution from pipelines, the coastal state may not impede the laying or maintenance of such cables or pipelines.

3   The delineation of the course for the laying of such pipelines on the continental shelf is subject to the consent of the coastal state.

4   Nothing in this Part affects the right of the coastal state to establish conditions for cables or pipelines entering its territory or territorial sea, or its jurisdiction over cables and pipelines constructed or used in connection with the exploration of its continental shelf or exploitation of its resources or the operations of artificial islands, installations and structures under its jurisdiction.

5   When laying submarine cables or pipelines, states shall have due regard to cables or pipelines already in position. In particular, possibilities of repairing existing cables or pipelines shall not be prejudiced.

Article 80   Artificial islands, installations and structures on the continental shelf

Article 60 applies *mutatis mutandis* to artificial islands, installations and structures on the continental shelf.

Article 81   Drilling on the continental shelf

The coastal state shall have the exclusive right to authorise and regulate drilling on the continental shelf for all purposes.

Article 82   Payments and contributions with respect to the exploitation of the continental shelf beyond 200 nautical miles

1   The coastal state shall make payments or contributions in kind in respect of the exploitation of the non-living resources of the continental shelf beyond 200 nautical miles from the baselines from which the breadth of the territorial sea is measured.

2   The payments and contributions shall be made annually with respect to all production at a site after the first five years of production at that site. For the sixth year, the rate of payment or contribution shall be 1% of the value or volume of production at the site. The rate shall increase by 1% for each subsequent year until the twelfth year and shall remain at 7% thereafter. Production does not include resources used in connection with exploitation.

3   A developing state which is a net importer of a mineral resource produced from its continental shelf is exempt from making such payments or contributions in respect of that mineral resource.

4   The payments or contributions shall be made through the Authority, which shall distribute them to States Parties to this Convention, on the basis of equitable sharing criteria, taking into account the interests and needs of developing states, particularly the least developed and the land-locked among them.

Article 83   Delimitation of the continental shelf between States with opposite or adjacent coasts

1   The delimitation of the continental shelf between states with opposite or adjacent coasts shall be effected by agreement on the basis of international law, as referred to in Article 38 of the Statute of the International Court of Justice, in order to achieve an equitable solution.

2   If no agreement can be reached within a reasonable period of time, the states concerned shall resort to the procedures provided for in Part XV.

3   Pending agreement as provided for in para 1, the states concerned, in a spirit of understanding and co-operation, shall make every effort to enter into provisional arrangements of a practical nature and, during this transitional period, not to jeopardise or hamper the reaching of the final agreement. Such arrangements shall be without prejudice to the final delimitation.

4   Where there is an agreement in force between the states concerned, questions relating to the delimitation of the continental shelf shall be determined in accordance with the provisions of that agreement.

Article 84 Charts and lists of geographical co-ordinates

1   Subject to this Part, the outer limit lines of the continental shelf and the lines of delimitation drawn in accordance with Article 83 shall be shown on charts of a scale or scales adequate for ascertaining their position. Where appropriate, lists of geographical co-ordinates of points, specifying the geodetic datum, may be substituted for such outer limit lines or lines of delimitation.

2   The coastal state shall give due publicity to such charts or lists of graphical co-ordinates and shall deposit a copy of each such chart or list with the Secretary General of the United Nations and, in the case of those showing the outer limit lines of the continental shelf, with the Secretary General of the Authority.

Article 85 Tunnelling

This Part does not prejudice the right of the coastal state to exploit the subsoil by means of tunnelling, irrespective of the depth of water above the subsoil.

PART VII

HIGH SEAS

SECTION 1 GENERAL PROVISIONS

Article 86 Application of the provisions of this Part

The provisions of this Part apply to all parts of the sea that are not included in the exclusive economic zone, in the territorial sea or in the internal waters of a state, or in the archipelagic waters of an archipelagic state. This article does not entail any abridgement of the freedoms enjoyed by all states in the exclusive economic zone in accordance with Article 58.

Article 87 Freedom of the high seas

1   The high seas are open to all states, whether coastal or land-locked. Freedom of the high seas is exercised under the conditions laid down by this Convention and by other rules of international law. It comprises, *inter alia*, both for coastal and land-locked states:

(a)   freedom of navigation;

(b)   freedom of overflight;

(c)   freedom to lay submarine cables and pipelines, subject to Part VI;

(d)   freedom to construct artificial islands and other installations permitted under international law, subject to Part VI;

(e)   freedom of fishing, subject to the conditions laid down in section 2;

(f)   freedom of scientific research, subject to Parts VI and XIII.

2   These freedoms shall be exercised by all states with due regard for the interests of other states in their exercise of the freedom of the high seas, and also with due regard for the rights under this Convention with respect to activities in the Area.

Article 88   Reservation of the high seas for peaceful purposes

The high seas shall be reserved for peaceful purposes.

Article 89   Invalidity of claims of sovereignty over the high seas

No state may validly purport to subject any part of the high seas to its sovereignty.

Article 90   Right of navigation

Every state, whether coastal or land-locked, has the right to sail ships flying its flag on the high seas.

Article 91   Nationality of ships

1   Every state shall fix the conditions for the grant of its nationality to ships, for the registration of ships in its territory, and for the right to fly its flag. Ships have the nationality of the state whose flag they are entitled to fly. There must exist a genuine link between the state and the ship.

2   Every state shall issue to ships to which it has granted the right to fly its flag documents to that effect.

Article 92   Status of ships

1   Ships shall sail under the flag of one state only and, save in exceptional cases expressly provided for in international treaties or in this Convention, shall be subject to its exclusive jurisdiction on the high seas. A ship may not change its flag during a voyage or while in a port of call, save in the case of a real transfer of ownership or change of registry.

2   A ship which sails under the flags of two or more states, using them according to convenience, may not claim any of the nationalities in question with respect to any other state, and may be assimilated to a ship without nationality.

Article 93   Ships flying the flag of the United Nations, its specialised agencies and the International Atomic Energy Agency

The preceding articles do not prejudice the question of ships employed on the official service of the United Nations, its specialised agencies or the International Atomic Energy Agency, flying the flag of the organisation.

Article 94   Duties of the flag state

1   Every state shall effectively exercise its jurisdiction and control in administrative, technical and social matters over ships flying its flag.

2   In particular every state shall:

   (a)   maintain a register of ships containing the names and particulars of ships flying its flag, except those which are excluded from generally accepted international regulations on account of their small size; and

   (b)   assume jurisdiction under its internal law over each ship flying its flag and its master, officers and crew in respect of administrative, technical and social matters concerning the ship.

3   Every state shall take such measures for ships flying its flag as are necessary to ensure safety at sea with regard, *inter alia*, to:

   (a)   the construction, equipment and seaworthiness of ships;

(b)   the manning of ships, labour conditions and the training of crews, taking into account the applicable international instruments;

(c)   the use of signals, the maintenance of communications and the prevention of collisions.

4   Such measures shall include those necessary to ensure:

(a)   that each ship, before registration and thereafter at appropriate intervals, is surveyed by a qualified surveyor of ships, and has on board such charts, nautical publications and navigational equipment and instruments as are appropriate for the safe navigation of the ship;

(b)   that each ship is in the charge of a master and officers who possess appropriate qualifications, in particular in seamanship, navigation, communications and marine engineering, and that the crew is appropriate in qualification and numbers for the type, size, machinery and equipment of the ship;

(c)   that the master, officers and, to the extent appropriate, the crew are fully conversant with and required to observe the applicable international regulations concerning the safety of life at sea, the prevention of collisions, the prevention, reduction and control of marine pollution, and the maintenance of communications by radio.

5   In taking the measures called for in paras 3 and 4 each state is required to conform to generally accepted international regulations, procedures and practices and to take any steps which may be necessary to secure their observance.

6   A state which has clear grounds to believe that proper jurisdiction and control with respect to a ship have not been exercised may report the facts to the flag state. Upon receiving such a report, the flag state shall investigate the matter and, if appropriate, take any action necessary to remedy the situation.

7   Each state shall cause an inquiry to be held by or before a suitably qualified person or persons into every marine casualty or incident of navigation on the high seas involving a ship flying its flag and causing loss of life or serious injury to nationals of another state or serious damage to ships or installations of another state or to the marine environment. The flag state and the other state shall co-operate in the conduct of any inquiry held by that other state into any such marine casualty or incident of navigation.

Article 95 Immunity of warships on the high seas

Warships on the high seas have complete immunity from the jurisdiction of any state other than the flag state.

Article 96 Immunity of ships used only on government non-commercial service

Ships owned or operated by a state and used only on government non-commercial service shall, on the high seas, have complete immunity from the jurisdiction of any state other than the flag state.

Article 97 Penal jurisdiction in matters of collision or any other incident of navigation

1   In the event of a collision or any other incident of navigation concerning a ship on the high seas, involving the penal or disciplinary responsibility of the master or of any other person in the service of the ship, no penal or disciplinary proceedings may be instituted against such person except before the judicial or administrative authorities either of the flag state or of the state of which such person is a national.

2   In disciplinary matters, the state which has issued a master's certificate or a certificate of competence or licence shall alone be competent, after due legal process, to pronounce the withdrawal of such certificates, even if the holder is not a national of the state which issued them.

3   No arrest or detention of the ship, even as a measure of investigation, shall be ordered by any authorities other than those of the flag state.

Article 98 Duty to render assistance

1   Every state shall require the master of a ship flying its flag, in so far as he can do so without serious danger to the ship, the crew or the passengers:

   (a)   to render assistance to any person found at sea in danger of being lost;

   (b)   to proceed with all possible speed to the rescue of persons in distress, if informed of their need of assistance, in so far as such action may reasonably be expected of him;

   (c)   after a collision, to render assistance to the other ship, its crew and its passengers and, where possible, to inform the other ship of the name of his own ship, its port of registry and the nearest port at which it will call.

2   Every coastal state shall promote the establishment, operation and maintenance of an adequate and effective search and rescue service regarding safety on and over the sea and, where circumstances so require, by way of mutual regional arrangements co-operate with neighbouring states for this purpose.

Article 99 Prohibition of the transport of slaves

Every state shall take effective measures to prevent and punish the transport of slaves in ships authorised to fly its flag and to prevent the unlawful use of its flag for that purpose. Any slave taking refuge on board any ship, whatever its flag, shall *ipso facto* be free.

Article 100 Duty to co-operate in the repression of piracy

All states shall co-operate to the fullest possible extent in the repression of piracy on the high seas or in any other place outside the jurisdiction of any state.

Article 101 Definition of piracy

Piracy consists of any of the following acts:

   (a)   any illegal acts of violence or detention, or any act of depredation, committed for private ends by the crew or the passengers of a private ship or a private aircraft, and directed:

      (i)   on the high seas, against another ship or aircraft, or against persons or property on board such ship or aircraft;

      (ii)   against a ship, aircraft, persons or property in a place outside the jurisdiction of any state;

   (b)   any act of voluntary participation in the operation of a ship or of an aircraft with knowledge of facts making it a pirate ship or aircraft;

   (c)   any act of inciting or of intentionally facilitating an act described in sub-para (a) or (b).

Article 102 Piracy by a warship, government ship or government aircraft whose crew has mutinied

The acts of piracy, as defined in Article 101, committed by a warship, government ship or government aircraft whose crew has mutinied and taken control of the ship or aircraft are assimilated to acts committed by a private ship or aircraft.

Article 103 Definition of a pirate ship or aircraft

A ship or aircraft is considered a pirate ship or aircraft if it is intended by the persons in dominant control to be used for the purpose of committing one of the acts referred to in Article 101. The same applies if the ship or aircraft has been used to commit any such act, so long as it remains under the control of the persons guilty of that act.

Article 104 Retention or loss of the nationality of a pirate ship or aircraft

A ship or aircraft may retain its nationality although it has become a pirate ship or aircraft. The retention or loss of nationality is determined by the law of the state from which such nationality was derived.

Article 105 Seizure of a pirate ship or aircraft

On the high seas, or in any other place outside the jurisdiction of any state, every state may seize a pirate ship or aircraft, or a ship or aircraft taken by piracy and under the control of pirates, and arrest the persons and seize the property on board. The courts of the state which carried out the seizure may decide upon the penalties to be imposed, and may also determine the action to be taken with regard to the ships, aircraft or property, subject to the rights of third parties acting in good faith.

Article 106 Liability for seizure without adequate grounds

Where the seizure of a ship or aircraft on suspicion of piracy has been effected without adequate grounds, the state making the seizure shall be liable to the state the nationality of which is possessed by the ship or aircraft for any loss or damage caused by the seizure.

Article 107 Ships and aircraft which are entitled to seize on account of piracy

A seizure on account of piracy may be carried out only by warships or military aircraft, or other ships or aircraft clearly marked and identifiable as being on government service and authorised to that effect.

Article 108 Illicit traffic in narcotic drugs or psychotropic substances

1   All states shall co-operate in the suppression of illicit traffic in narcotic drugs and psychotropic substances engaged in by ships on the high seas contrary to international conventions.

2   Any state which has reasonable grounds for believing that a ship flying its flag is engaged in illicit traffic in narcotic drugs or psychotropic substances may request the co-operation of other states to suppress such traffic.

Article 109 Unauthorised broadcasting from the high seas

1   All states shall co-operate in the suppression of unauthorised broadcasting from the high seas.

2   For the purposes of this Convention, 'unauthorised broadcasting' means the transmission of sound radio or television broadcasts from a ship or installation on the high seas intended for reception by the general public contrary to international regulations, but excluding the transmission of distress calls.

3   Any person engaged in unauthorised broadcasting may be prosecuted before the court of:

    (a)   the flag state of the ship;

    (b)   the state of registry of the installation;

    (c)   the state of which the person is a national;

LIVERPOOL JOHN MOORES UNIVERSITY
LEARNING & INFORMATION SERVICES

(d) any state where the transmissions can be received; or

(e) any state where authorised radio communication is suffering interference.

4 On the high seas, a state having jurisdiction in accordance with para 3 may, in conformity with Article 110, arrest any person or ship engaged in unauthorised broadcasting and seize the broadcasting apparatus.

Article 110 Right of visit

1 Except where acts of interference derive from powers conferred by treaty, a warship which encounters on the high seas a foreign ship, other than a ship entitled to complete immunity in accordance with Articles 95 and 96, is not justified in boarding it unless there is reasonable ground for suspecting that:

(a) the ship is engaged in piracy;

(b) the ship is engaged in the slave trade;

(c) the ship is engaged in unauthorised broadcasting and the flag state of the warship has jurisdiction under Article 109;

(d) the ship is without nationality; or

(e) though flying a foreign flag or refusing to show its flag, the ship is, in reality, of the same nationality as the warship.

2 In the cases provided for in para 1, the warship may proceed to verify the ship's right to fly its flag. To this end, it may send a boat under the command of an officer to the suspected ship. If suspicion remains after the documents have been checked, it may proceed to a further examination on board the ship, which must be carried out with all possible consideration.

3 If the suspicions prove to be unfounded, and provided that the ship boarded has not committed any act justifying them, it shall be compensated for any loss or damage that may have been sustained.

4 These provisions apply *mutatis mutandis* to military aircraft.

5 These provisions also apply to any other duly authorised ships or aircraft clearly marked and identifiable as being on government service.

Article 111 Right of hot pursuit

1 The hot pursuit of a foreign ship may be undertaken when the competent authorities of the coastal state have good reason to believe that the ship has violated the laws and regulations of that state. Such pursuit must be commenced when the foreign ship or one of its boats is within the internal waters, the archipelagic waters, the territorial sea or the contiguous zone of the pursuing state, and may only be continued outside the territorial sea or the contiguous zone if the pursuit has not been interrupted. It is not necessary that, at the time when the foreign ship within the territorial sea or the contiguous zone receives the order to stop, the ship giving the order should likewise be within the territorial sea or the contiguous zone. If the foreign ship is within a contiguous zone, as defined in Article 33, the pursuit may only be undertaken if there has been a violation of the rights for the protection of which the zone was established.

2 The right of hot pursuit shall apply *mutatis mutandis* to violations in the exclusive economic zone or on the continental shelf, including safety zones around continental shelf installations, of the laws and regulations of the coastal state applicable in accordance with this Convention to the exclusive economic zone or the continental shelf, including such safety zones.

3   The right of hot pursuit ceases as soon as the ship pursued enters the territorial sea of its own state or of a third state.

4   Hot pursuit is not deemed to have begun unless the pursuing ship has satisfied itself by such practicable means as may be available that the ship pursued or one of its boats or other craft working as a team and using the ship pursued as a mother ship is within the limits of the territorial sea, or, as the case may be, within the contiguous zone or the exclusive economic zone or above the continental shelf. The pursuit may only be commenced after a visual or auditory signal to stop has been given at a distance which enables it to be seen or heard by the foreign ship.

5   The right of hot pursuit may be exercised only by warships or military aircraft, or other ships or aircraft clearly marked and identifiable as being on government service and authorised to that effect.

6   Where hot pursuit is effected by an aircraft:

(a)   the provisions of paras 1 to 4 shall apply *mutatis mutandis*,

(b)   the aircraft giving the order to stop must itself actively pursue the ship until a ship or another aircraft of the coastal state, summoned by the aircraft, arrives to take over the pursuit, unless the aircraft is itself able to arrest the ship. It does not suffice to justify an arrest outside the territorial sea that the ship was merely sighted by the aircraft as an offender or suspected offender, if it was not both ordered to stop and pursued by the aircraft itself or other aircraft or ships which continue the pursuit without interruption.

7   The release of a ship arrested within the jurisdiction of a state and escorted to a port of that state for the purposes of an inquiry before the competent authorities may not be claimed solely on the ground that the ship, in the course of its voyage, was escorted across a portion of the exclusive economic zone or the high seas, if the circumstances rendered this necessary.

8   Where a ship has been stopped or arrested outside the territorial sea in circumstances which do not justify the exercise of the right of hot pursuit, it shall be compensated for any loss or damage that may have been thereby sustained.

Article 112 Right to lay submarine cables and pipelines

1   All states are entitled to lay submarine cables and pipelines on the bed of the high seas beyond the continental shelf.

2   Article 79, para 5, applies to such cables and pipelines.

Article 113 Breaking or injury of a submarine cable or pipeline

Every state shall adopt the laws and regulations necessary to provide that the breaking or injury by a ship flying its flag or by a person subject to its jurisdiction of a submarine cable beneath the high seas done wilfully or through culpable negligence, in such a manner as to be liable to interrupt or obstruct telegraphic or telephonic communications, and similarly the breaking or injury of a submarine pipeline or high-voltage power cable, shall be a punishable offence. This provision shall apply also to conduct calculated or likely to result in such breaking or injury. However, it shall not apply to any break or injury caused by persons who acted merely with the legitimate object of saving their lives or their ships, after having taken all necessary precautions to avoid such break or injury.

Article 114 Breaking or injury by owners of a submarine cable or pipeline of another submarine cable or pipeline

Every state shall adopt the laws and regulations necessary to provide that, if persons subject to its jurisdiction who are the owners of a submarine cable or pipeline beneath the high seas, in laying or repairing that cable or pipeline, cause a break in or injury to another cable or pipeline, they shall bear the cost of the repairs.

Article 115 Indemnity for loss incurred in avoiding injury to a submarine cable or pipeline

Every state shall adopt the laws and regulations necessary to ensure that the owners of ships who can prove that they have sacrificed an anchor, a net or any other fishing gear, in order to avoid injuring a submarine cable or pipeline, shall be indemnified by the owner of the cable or pipeline, provided that the owner of the ship has taken all reasonable precautionary measures beforehand.

SECTION 2   CONSERVATION AND MANAGEMENT OF THE
LIVING RESOURCES OF THE HIGH SEAS

Article 116 Right to fish on the high seas

All states have the right for their nationals to engage in fishing on the high seas subject to:

(a)   their treaty obligations;

(b)   the rights and duties as well as the interests of coastal states provided for, *inter alia*, in Article 63, para 2, and Articles 64 to 67; and

(c)   the provisions of this section.

Article 117 Duty of states to adopt with respect to their nationals measures for the conservation of the living resources of the high seas

All states have the duty to take, or to co-operate with other states in taking, such measures for their respective nationals as may be necessary for the conservation of the living resources of the high seas.

Article 118 Co-operation of states in the conservation and management of living resources

States shall co-operate with each other in the conservation and management of living resources in the areas of the high seas. States whose nationals exploit identical living resources, or different living resources in the same area, shall enter into negotiations with a view to taking the measures necessary for the conservation of the living resources concerned. They shall, as appropriate, co-operate to establish subregional or regional fisheries organisations to this end.

Article 119 Conservation of the living resources of the high seas

1   In determining the allowable catch and establishing other conservation measures for the living resources in the high seas, states shall:

(a)   take measures which are designed, on the best scientific evidence available to the states concerned, to maintain or restore populations of harvested species at levels which can produce the maximum sustainable yield, as qualified by relevant environmental and economic factors, including the special requirements of developing states, and taking into account fishing patterns, the interdependence of stocks and any generally recommended international minimum standards, whether subregional, regional or global;

(b) take into consideration the effects on species associated with or dependent upon harvested species with a view to maintaining or restoring populations of such associated or dependent species above levels at which their reproduction may become seriously threatened.

2   Available scientific information, catch and fishing effort statistics, and other data relevant to the conservation of fish stocks shall be contributed and exchanged on a regular basis through competent international organisations, whether subregional, regional or global, where appropriate and with participation by all states concerned.

3   States concerned shall ensure that conservation measures and their implementation do not discriminate in form or in fact against the fishermen of any state.

Article 120 Marine mammals

Article 65 also applies to the conservation and management of marine mammals in the high seas.

PART VIII
REGIME OF ISLANDS

Article 121 Regime of islands

1   An island is a naturally formed area of land, surrounded by water, which is above water at high tide.

2   Except as provided for in para 3, the territorial sea, the contiguous zone, the exclusive economic zone and the continental shelf of an island are determined in accordance with the provisions of this Convention applicable to other land territory.

3   Rocks which cannot sustain human habitation or economic life of their own shall have no exclusive economic zone or continental shelf.

PART IX
ENCLOSED OR SEMI-ENCLOSED SEAS

Article 122 Definition

For the purposes of this Convention, 'enclosed or semi-enclosed sea' means a gulf, basin or sea surrounded by two or more states and connected to another sea or the ocean by a narrow outlet or consisting entirely or primarily of the territorial seas and exclusive economic zones of two or more coastal states.

Article 123 Co-operation of states bordering enclosed or semi-enclosed seas

States bordering an enclosed or semi-enclosed sea should co-operate with each other in the exercise of their rights and in the performance of their duties under this Convention. To this end they shall endeavour, directly or through an appropriate regional organisation:

(a) to co-ordinate the management, conservation, exploration and exploitation of the living resources of the sea;

(b) to co-ordinate the implementation of their rights and duties with respect to the protection and preservation of the marine environment;

(c) to co-ordinate their scientific research policies and undertake where appropriate joint programmes of scientific research in the area;

(d) to invite, as appropriate, other interested states or international organisations to co-operate with them in furtherance of the provisions of this article.

PART X
RIGHT OF ACCESS OF LAND-LOCKED STATES TO AND FROM THE SEA AND FREEDOM OF TRANSIT

Article 124 Use of terms

1 For the purposes of this Convention:

(a) 'land-locked state' means a state which has no sea-coast;

(b) 'transit state' means a state, with or without a sea-coast, situated between a land-locked state and the sea, through whose territory traffic in transit passes;

(c) 'traffic in transit' means transit of persons, baggage, goods and means of transport across the territory of one or more transit states, when the passage across such territory, with or without trans-shipment, warehousing, breaking bulk or change in the mode of transport, is only a portion of a complete journey which begins or terminates within the territory of the land-locked state;

(d) 'means of transport' means:

   (i) railway rolling stock, sea, lake and river craft and road vehicles;

   (ii) where local conditions so require, porters and pack animals.

2 Land-locked states and transit states may, by agreement between them, include as means of transport pipelines and gas lines and means of transport other than those included in para 1.

Article 125 Right of access to and from the sea and freedom of transit

1 Land-locked states shall have the right of access to and from the sea for the purpose of exercising the rights provided for in this Convention including those relating to the freedom of the high seas and the common heritage of mankind. To this end, land-locked states shall enjoy freedom of transit through the territory of transit states by all means of transport.

2 The terms and modalities for exercising freedom of transit shall be agreed between the land-locked states and transit states concerned through bilateral, subregional or regional agreements.

3 Transit states, in the exercise of their full sovereignty over their territory, shall have the right to take all measures necessary to ensure that the rights and facilities provided for in this Part for land-locked states shall in no way infringe their legitimate interests.

Article 126 Exclusion of application of the most-favoured-nation clause

The provisions of this Convention, as well as special agreements relating to the exercise of the right of access to and from the sea, establishing rights and facilities on account of the special geographical position of land-locked states are excluded from the application of the most-favoured-nation clause.

Article 127 Customs duties, taxes and other charges

1 Traffic in transit shall not be subject to any customs duties, taxes or other charges except charges levied for specific services rendered in connection with such traffic.

2   Means of transport in transit and other facilities provided for and used by land-locked states shall not be subject to taxes or charges higher than those levied for the use of means of transport of the transit state.

Article 128 Free zones and other customs facilities

For the convenience of traffic in transit, free zones or other customs facilities may be provided at the ports of entry and exit in the transit states, by agreement between those states and the land-locked states.

Article 129 Co-operation in the construction and improvement of means of transport

Where there are no means of transport in transit states to give effect to the freedom of transit or where the existing means, including the port installations and equipment, are inadequate in any respect, the transit states and land-locked states concerned may co-operate in constructing or improving them.

Article 130 Measures to avoid or eliminate delays or other difficulties of a technical nature in traffic in transit

1   Transit states shall take all appropriate measures to avoid delays or other difficulties of a technical nature in traffic in transit.

2   Should such delays or difficulties occur, the competent authorities of the transit States and land-locked states concerned shall co-operate towards their expeditious elimination.

Article 131 Equal treatment in maritime ports

Ships flying the flag of land-locked states shall enjoy treatment equal to that accorded to other foreign ships in maritime ports.

Article 132 Grant of greater transit facilities

This Convention does not entail in any way the withdrawal of transit facilities which are greater than those provided for in this Convention and which are agreed between States Parties to this Convention or granted by a state Party. This Convention also does not preclude such grant of greater facilities in the future.

PART XI

THE AREA

SECTION 1   GENERAL PROVISIONS

Article 133 Use of terms

For the purposes of this Part:

(a)   'resources' means all solid, liquid or gaseous mineral resources *in situ* in the Area at or beneath the sea bed, including polymetallic nodules;

(b)   resources, when recovered from the Area, are referred to as 'minerals'.

Article 134 Scope of this Part

1   This Part applies to the Area.

2   Activities in the Area shall be governed by the provisions of this Part.

3   The requirements concerning deposit of, and publicity to be given to, the charts or lists of geographical co-ordinates showing the limits referred to in Article 1, para 1 (1), are set forth in Part VI.

4   Nothing in this article affects the establishment of the outer limits of the continental shelf in accordance with Part VI or the validity of agreements relating to delimitation between states with opposite or adjacent coasts.

Article 135 Legal status of the superjacent waters and air space

Neither this Part nor any rights granted or exercised pursuant thereto shall affect the legal status of the waters superjacent to the Area or that of the air space above those waters.

SECTION 2 PRINCIPLES GOVERNING THE AREA

Article 136 Common heritage of mankind

The Area and its resources are the common heritage of mankind.

Article 137 Legal status of the Area and its resources

1   No state shall claim or exercise sovereignty or sovereign rights over any part of the Area or its resources, nor shall any state or natural or juridical person appropriate any part thereof. No such claim or exercise of sovereignty or sovereign rights nor such appropriation shall be recognised.

2   All rights in the resources of the Area are vested in mankind as a whole on whose behalf the Authority shall act. These resources are not subject to alienation. The minerals recovered from the Area, however, may only be alienated in accordance with this Part and the rules, regulations and procedures of the Authority.

3   No state or natural or juridical person shall claim, acquire or exercise rights with respect to the minerals recovered from the area except in accordance with this Part. Otherwise, no such claim, acquisition or exercise of such rights shall be recognised.

Article 138 General conduct of states in relation to the Area

The general conduct of states in relation to the Area shall be in accordance with the provisions of this Part, the principles embodied in the Charter of the United Nations and other rules of international law in the interests of maintaining peace and security and promoting international co-operation and mutual understanding.

Article 139 Responsibility to ensure compliance and liability for damage

1   States Parties shall have the responsibility to ensure that activities in the Area, whether carried out by States Parties, or state enterprises or natural or juridical persons which possess the nationality of States Parties or are effectively controlled by them or their nationals, shall be carried out in conformity with this Part. The same responsibility applies to international organisations for activities in the Area carried out by such organisations.

2   Without prejudice to the rules of international law and Annex III, Article 22, damage caused by the failure of a state Party or international organisation to carry out its responsibilities under this Part shall entail liability, States Parties or international organisations acting together shall bear joint and several liability. A state Party shall not however be liable for damage caused by any failure to comply with this Part by a person whom it has sponsored under Article 153, para 2(b), if the state Party has taken all necessary and appropriate measures to secure effective compliance under Article 153, para 4, and Annex III, Article 4, para 4.

3   States Parties that are members of international organisations shall take appropriate measures to ensure the implementation of this article with respect to such organisations.

Article 140 Benefit of mankind

1   Activities in the Area shall, as specifically provided for in this Part, be carried out for the benefit of mankind as a whole, irrespective of the geographical location of states, whether coastal or land-locked, and taking into particular consideration the interests and needs of developing states and of peoples who have not attained full independence or other self-governing status recognised by the United Nations in accordance with General Assembly Resolution 1514 (XV) and other relevant General Assembly resolutions.

2   The Authority shall provide for the equitable sharing of financial and other economic benefits derived from activities in the Area through any appropriate mechanism on a non-discriminatory basis, in accordance with Article 160, para 2 (f)(i).

Article 141 Use of the Area exclusively for peaceful purposes

The Area shall be open to use exclusively for peaceful purposes by all states, whether coastal or land-locked, without discrimination and without prejudice to the other provisions of this Part.

Article 142 Rights and legitimate interests of coastal states

1   Activities in the Area, with respect to resource deposits in the Area which lie across limits of national jurisdiction, shall be conducted with due regard to the rights and legitimate interests of any coastal state across whose jurisdiction such deposits lie.

2   Consultations, including a system of prior notification, shall be maintained with the state concerned, with a view to avoiding infringement of such rights and interests. In cases where activities in the Area may result in the exploitation of resources lying within national jurisdiction, the prior consent of the coastal state concerned shall be required.

3   Neither this Part nor any rights granted or exercised pursuant thereto shall affect the rights of coastal states to take such measures consistent with the relevant provisions of Part XII as may be necessary to prevent, mitigate or eliminate grave and imminent danger to their coastline, or related interests from pollution or threat thereof or from other hazardous occurrences resulting from or caused by any activities in the Area.

Article 143 Marine scientific research

1   Marine scientific research in the Area shall be carried out exclusively for peaceful purposes and for the benefit of mankind as a whole in accordance with Part XIII.

2   The Authority may carry out marine scientific research concerning the Area and its resources, and may enter into contracts for that purpose. The Authority shall promote and encourage the conduct of marine scientific research in the Area, and shall co-ordinate and disseminate the results of such research and analysis when available.

3   States Parties may carry out marine scientific research in the Area. States Parties shall promote international co-operation in marine scientific research in the Area by:

(a)   participating in international programmes and encouraging co-operation in marine scientific research by personnel of different countries and of the Authority;

(b) ensuring that programmes are developed through the Authority or other international organisations as appropriate for the benefit of developing states and technologically less developed states with a view to:

    (i) strengthening their research capabilities;

    (ii) training their personnel and the personnel of the Authority in the techniques and applications of research;

    (iii) fostering the employment of their qualified personnel in research in the Area;

(c) effectively disseminating the results of research and analysis when available, through the Authority or other international channels when appropriate.

Article 144 Transfer of technology

1 The Authority shall take measures in accordance with this Convention:

    (a) to acquire technology and scientific knowledge relating to activities in the Area; and

    (b) to promote and encourage the transfer to developing states of such technology and scientific knowledge so that all States Parties benefit therefrom.

2 To this end the Authority and States Parties shall co-operate in promoting the transfer of technology and scientific knowledge relating to activities in the Area so that the Enterprise and all States Parties may benefit therefrom. In particular they shall initiate and promote:

    (a) programmes for the transfer of technology to the Enterprise and to developing states with regard to activities in the Area, including, *inter alia*, facilitating the access of the Enterprise and of developing states to the relevant technology, under fair and reasonable terms and conditions;

    (b) measures directed towards the advancement of the technology of the Enterprise and the domestic technology of developing states, particularly by providing opportunities to personnel from the Enterprise and from developing states for training in marine science and technology and for their full participation in activities in the Area.

Article 145 Protection of the marine environment

Necessary measures shall be taken in accordance with this Convention with respect to activities in the Area to ensure effective protection for the marine environment from harmful effects which may arise from such activities. To this end the Authority shall adopt appropriate rules, regulations and procedures for *inter alia*:

    (a) the prevention, reduction and control of pollution and other hazards to the marine environment, including the coastline, and of interference with the ecological balance of the marine environment, particular attention being paid to the need for protection from harmful effects of such activities as drilling, dredging, excavation, disposal of waste, construction and operation or maintenance of installations, pipelines and other devices related to such activities;

    (b) the protection and conservation of the natural resources of the Area and the prevention of damage to the flora and fauna of the marine environment.

Article 146 Protection of human life

With respect to activities in the Area, necessary measures shall be taken to ensure effective protection of human life. To this end the Authority shall adopt appropriate rules, regulations and procedures to supplement existing international law as embodied in relevant treaties.

Article 147 Accommodation of activities in the Area and in the marine environment

1   Activities in the Area shall be carried out with reasonable regard for other activities in the marine environment.

2   Installations used for carrying out activities in the Area shall be subject to the following conditions:

(a)   such installations shall be erected, emplaced and removed solely in accordance with this Part and subject to the rules, regulations and procedures of the Authority. Due notice must be given of the erection, emplacement and removal of such installations, and permanent means for giving warning of their presence must be maintained;

(b)   such installations may not be established where interference may be caused to the use of recognised sea lanes essential to international navigation or in areas of intense fishing activity;

(c)   safety zones shall be established around such installations with appropriate markings to ensure the safety of both navigation and the installations. The configuration and location of such safety zones shall not be such as to form a belt impeding the lawful access of shipping to particular maritime zones or navigation along international sea lanes;

(d)   such installations shall be used exclusively for peaceful purposes;

(e)   such installations do not possess the status of islands. They have no territorial sea of their own, and their presence does not affect the delimitation of the territorial sea, the exclusive economic zone or the continental shelf.

3   Other activities in the marine environment shall be conducted with reasonable regard for activities in the Area.

Article 148 Participation of developing states in activities in the Area

The effective participation of developing states in activities in the Area shall be promoted as specifically provided for in this Part, having due regard to their special interests and needs, and in particular to the special need of the land-locked and geographically disadvantaged among them to overcome obstacles arising from their disadvantaged location, including remoteness from the Area and difficulty of access to and from it.

Article 149 Archaeological and historical objects

All objects of an archaeological and historical nature found in the Area shall be preserved or disposed of for the benefit of mankind as a whole, particular regard being paid to the preferential rights of the state or country of origin, or the state of cultural origin, or the state of historical and archaeological origin.

SECTION 3 DEVELOPMENT OF RESOURCES OF THE AREA

Article 150 Policies relating to activities in the Area

Activities in the Area shall, as specifically provided for in this Part, be carried out in such a manner as to foster healthy development of the world economy and balanced growth of international trade, and to promote international co-operation for the overall development of all countries, especially developing states, and with a view to ensuring:

(a) the development of the resources of the Area;

(b) orderly, safe and rational management of the resources of the Area, including the efficient conduct of activities in the Area and, in accordance with sound principles of conservation, the avoidance of unnecessary waste;

(c) the expansion of opportunities for participation in such activities consistent in particular with Articles 144 and 148;

(d) participation in revenues by the Authority and the transfer of technology to the Enterprise and developing states as provided for in this Convention;

(e) increased availability of the minerals derived from the Area as needed in conjunction with minerals derived from other sources, to ensure supplies to consumers of such minerals;

(f) the promotion of just and stable prices remunerative to producers and fair to consumers for minerals derived both from the Area and from other sources, and the promotion of long-term equilibrium between supply and demand;

(g) the enhancement of opportunities for all States Parties, irrespective of their social and economic systems or geographical location, to participate in the development of the resources of the Area and the prevention of monopolisation of activities in the Area;

(h) the protection of developing countries from adverse effects on their economies or on their export earnings resulting from a reduction in the price of an affected mineral, or in the volume of exports of that mineral, to the extent that such reduction is caused by activities in the Area, as provided in Article 151;

(i) the development of the common heritage for the benefit of mankind as a whole; and

(j) conditions of access to markets for the imports of minerals produced from the resources of the Area and for imports of commodities produced from such minerals shall not be more favourable than the most favourable applied to imports from other sources.

Article 151 Production policies

1 (a) Without prejudice to the objectives set forth in Article 150 and for the purpose of implementing sub-para (h) of that article, the Authority, acting through existing forums or such new arrangements or agreements as may be appropriate, in which all interested parties, including both producers and consumers, participate, shall take measures necessary to promote the growth, efficiency and stability of markets for those commodities produced from the minerals derived from the Area, at prices remunerative to producers and fair to consumers. All States Parties shall co-operate to this end.

(b) The Authority shall have the right to participate in any commodity conference dealing with those commodities and in which all interested parties including both producers and consumers participate. The Authority shall have the right to become a party to any arrangement or agreement resulting from such conferences. Participation of the Authority in any organs established under those arrangements or agreements shall be in respect of production in the Area and in accordance with the relevant rules of those organs.

(c) The Authority shall carry out its obligations under the arrangements or agreements referred to in this paragraph in a manner which assures a uniform and non-discriminatory implementation in respect of all production in the Area of the minerals concerned. In doing so, the Authority shall act in a manner consistent with the terms of existing contracts and approved plans of work of the Enterprise.

2 (a) During the interim period specified in para 3, commercial production shall not be undertaken pursuant to an approved plan of work until the operator has applied for and has been issued a production authorisation by the Authority. Such production authorisations may not be applied for or issued more than five years prior to the planned commencement of commercial production under the plan of work unless, having regard to the nature and timing of project development, the rules, regulations and procedures of the Authority prescribe another period.

(b) In the application for the production authorisation, the operator shall specify the annual quantity of nickel expected to be recovered under the approved plan of work. The application shall include a schedule of expenditures to be made by the operator after he has received the authorisation which are reasonably calculated to allow him to begin commercial production on the date planned.

(c) For the purposes of sub-paras (a) and (b), the Authority shall establish appropriate performance requirements in accordance with Annex III, Article 17.

(d) The Authority shall issue a production authorisation for the level of production applied for unless the sum of that level and the levels already authorized exceeds the nickel production ceiling, as calculated pursuant to para 4 in the year of issuance of the authorisation, during any year of planned production falling within the interim period.

(e) When issued, the production authorisation and approved application shall become a part of the approved plan of work.

(f) If the operator's application for a production authorisation is denied pursuant to sub-para (d), the operator may apply again to the Authority at any time.

3 The interim period shall begin five years prior to 1 January of the year in which the earliest commercial production is planned to commence under an approved plan of work. If the earliest commercial production is delayed beyond the year originally planned, the beginning of the interim period and the production ceiling originally calculated shall be adjusted accordingly. The interim period shall last 25 years or until the end of the Review Conference referred to in Article 155 or until the day when such new arrangements or agreements as are referred to in para 1 enter into force, whichever is earliest. The Authority shall resume the power provided in this article for the remainder of the interim period if the said arrangements or agreements should lapse or become ineffective for any reason whatsoever.

4 (a) The production ceiling for any year of the interim period shall be the sum of:

   (i)   the difference between the trend line values for nickel consumption as calculated pursuant to sub-para (b), for the year immediately prior to the year of the earliest commercial production and the year immediately prior to the commencement of the interim period; and

   (ii) 60% of the difference between the trend line values for nickel consumption, as calculated pursuant to sub-para (b), for the year for which the production authorisation is being applied for and the year immediately prior to the year of the earliest commercial production.

   (b) For the purposes of sub-para (a):

   (i)   trend line values used for computing the nickel production ceiling shall be those annual nickel consumption values on a trend line computed during the year in which a production authorisation is issued. The trend line shall be derived from a linear regression of the logarithms of actual nickel consumption for the most recent 15-year period for which such data are available, time being the independent variable. This trend line shall be referred to as the original trend line;

   (ii) if the annual rate of increase of the original trend line is less than 3%, then the trend line used to determine the quantities referred to in sub-para (a) shall instead be one passing through the original trend line at the value for the first year of the relevant 15-year period, and increasing at 3% annually; provided however that the production ceiling established for any year of the interim period may not in any case exceed the difference between the original trend line value for that year and the original trend line value for the year immediately prior to the commencement of the interim period.

5 The Authority shall reserve to the Enterprise for its initial production a quantity of 38,000 metric tonnes of nickel from the available production ceiling calculated pursuant to para 4.

6 (a) An operator may in any year produce less than or up to 8 per cent more than the level of annual production of minerals from polymetallic nodules specified in his production authorisation, provided that the overall amount of production shall not exceed that specified in the authorisation. Any excess over 8% and up to 20% in any year, or any excess in the first and subsequent years following two consecutive years in which excesses occur, shall be negotiated with the Authority, which may require the operator to obtain a supplementary production authorisation to cover additional production.

   (b) Applications for such supplementary production authorisations shall be considered by the Authority only after all pending applications by operators who have not yet received production authorisations have been acted upon and due account has been taken of other likely applicants. The Authority shall be guided by the principle of not exceeding the total production allowed under the production ceiling in any year of the interim period. It shall not authorise the production under any plan of work of a quantity in excess of 46,500 metric tonnes of nickel per year.

7   The levels of production of other metals such as copper, cobalt and manganese extracted from the polymetallic nodules that are recovered pursuant to a production authorisation should not be higher than those which would have been produced had the operator produced the maximum level of nickel from those nodules pursuant to this article. The Authority shall establish rules, regulations and procedures pursuant to Annex III, Article 17, to implement this paragraph.

8   Rights and obligations relating to unfair economic practices under relevant multilateral trade agreements shall apply to the exploration for and exploitation of minerals from the Area. In the settlement of disputes arising under this provision, States Parties which are parties to such multilateral trade agreements shall have recourse to the dispute settlement procedures of such agreements.

9   The Authority shall have the power to limit the level of production of minerals from the Area, other than minerals from polymetallic nodules, under such conditions and applying such methods as may be appropriate by adopting regulations in accordance with Article 161, para 8.

10   Upon the recommendation of the Council on the basis of advice from the Economic Planning Commission, the Assembly shall establish a system of compensation or take other measures of economic adjustment assistance including co-operation with specialised agencies and other international organisations to assist developing countries which suffer serious adverse effects on their export earnings or economies resulting from a reduction in the price of an affected mineral or in the volume of exports of that mineral, to the extent that such reduction is caused by activities in the Area. The Authority on request shall initiate studies on the problems of those states which are likely to be most seriously affected with a view to minimising their difficulties and assisting them in their economic adjustment.

Article 152 Exercise of powers and functions by the Authority

1   The Authority shall avoid discrimination in the exercise of its powers and functions, including the granting of opportunities for activities in the Area.

2   Nevertheless, special consideration for developing states, including particular consideration for the land-locked and geographically disadvantaged among them, specifically provided for in this Part shall be permitted.

Article 153 System of exploration and exploitation

1   Activities in the Area shall be organised, carried out and controlled by the Authority on behalf of mankind as a whole in accordance with this article as well as other relevant provisions of this Part and the relevant Annexes, and the rules, regulations and procedures of the Authority.

2   Activities in the Area shall be carried out as prescribed in para 3:

   (a) by the Enterprise, and

   (b) in association with the Authority by States Parties, or state enterprises or natural or juridical persons which possess the nationality of States Parties or are effectively controlled by them or their nationals, when sponsored by such states, or any group of the foregoing which meets the requirements provided in this Part and in Annex III.

3   Activities in the Area shall be carried out in accordance with a formal written plan of work drawn up in accordance with Annex III and approved by the Council after review by the Legal and Technical Commission. In the case of

activities in the Area carried out as authorised by the Authority by the entities specified in para 2(b), the plan of work shall, in accordance with Annex III, Article 3, be in the form of a contract. Such contracts may provide for joint arrangements in accordance with Annex III, Article 11.

4   The Authority shall exercise such control over activities in the Area as is necessary for the purpose of securing compliance with the relevant provisions of this Part and the Annexes relating thereto, and the rules, regulations and procedures of the Authority, and the plans of work approved in accordance with para 3. States Parties shall assist the Authority by taking all measures necessary to ensure such compliance in accordance with Article 139.

5   The Authority shall have the right to take at any time any measures provided for under this Part to ensure compliance with its provisions and the exercise of the functions of control and regulation assigned to it thereunder or under any contract. The Authority shall have the right to inspect all installations in the Area used in connection with activities in the Area.

6   A contract under para 3 shall provide for security of tenure. Accordingly, the contract shall not be revised, suspended or terminated except in accordance with Annex III, Articles 18 and 19.

Article 154 Periodic review

Every five years from the entry into force of this Convention, the Assembly shall undertake a general and systematic review of the manner in which the international regime of the Area established in this Convention has operated in practice. In the light of this review the Assembly may take, or recommend that other organs take, measures in accordance with the provisions and procedures of this Part and the Annexes relating thereto which will lead to the improvement of the operation of the regime.

Article 155 The Review Conference

1   Fifteen years from 1 January of the year in which the earliest commercial production commences under an approved plan of work, the Assembly shall convene a conference for the review of those provisions of this Part and the relevant Annexes which govern the system of exploration and exploitation of the resources of the Area. The Review Conference shall consider in detail, in the light of the experience acquired during that period:

(a)   whether the provisions of this Part which govern the system of exploration and exploitation of the resources of the Area have achieved their aims in all respects, including whether they have benefited mankind as a whole;

(b)   whether, during the 15-year period, reserved areas have been exploited in an effective and balanced manner in comparison with non-reserved areas;

(c)   whether the development and use of the Area and its resources have been undertaken in such a manner as to foster healthy development of the world economy and balanced growth of international trade;

(d)   whether monopolisation of activities in the Area has been prevented;

(e)   whether the policies set forth in Articles 150 and 151 have been fulfilled; and

(f)   whether the system has resulted in the equitable sharing of benefits derived from activities in the Area, taking into particular consideration the interests and needs of the developing states.

2   The Review Conference shall ensure the maintenance of the principle of the common heritage of mankind, the international regime designed to ensure equitable exploitation of the resources of the Area for the benefit of all countries, especially the developing states, and an Authority to organise, conduct and control activities in the Area. It shall also ensure the maintenance of the principles laid down in this Part with regard to the exclusion of claims or exercise of sovereignty over any part of the Area, the rights of states and their general conduct in relation to the Area, and their participation in activities in the Area in conformity with this Convention, the prevention of monopolisation of activities in the Area, the use of the Area exclusively for peaceful purposes, economic aspects of activities in the Area, marine scientific research, transfer of technology, protection of the marine environment, protection of human life, rights of coastal states, the legal status of the waters superjacent to the Area and that of the air space above those waters and accommodation between activities in the Area and other activities in the marine environment.

3   The decision-making procedure applicable at the Review Conference shall be the same as that applicable at the Third United Nations Conference on the Law of the Sea. The Conference shall make every effort to reach agreement on any amendments by way of consensus and there should be no voting on such matters until all efforts at achieving consensus have been exhausted.

4   If, five years after its commencement, the Review Conference has not reached agreement on the system of exploration and exploitation of the resources of the Area, it may decide during the ensuing 12 months, by a three-fourths majority of the States Parties, to adopt and submit to the States Parties for ratification or accession such amendments changing or modifying the system as it determines necessary and appropriate. Such amendments shall enter into force for all States Parties 12 months after the deposit of instruments of ratification or accession by three-fourths of the States Parties.

5   Amendments adopted by the Review Conference pursuant to this article shall not affect rights acquired under existing contracts.

SECTION 4   THE AUTHORITY SUBSECTION A. GENERAL PROVISIONS

Article 156   Establishment of the Authority

1   There is hereby established the International Sea Bed Authority, which shall function in accordance with this Part.

2   All States Parties are *ipso facto* members of the Authority.

3   Observers at the Third United Nations Conference on the Law of the Sea who have signed the Final Act and who are not referred to in Article 305, para 1(c), (d), (e) or (f), shall have the right to participate in the Authority as observers, in accordance with its rules, regulations and procedures.

4   The seat of the Authority shall be in Jamaica.

5   The Authority may establish such regional centres or offices as it deems necessary for the exercise of its functions.

Article 157   Nature and fundamental principles of the Authority

1   The Authority is the organisation through which States Parties shall, in accordance with this Part, organise and control activities in the Area, particularly with a view to administering the resources of the Area.

2   The powers and functions of the Authority shall be those expressly conferred upon it by this Convention. The Authority shall have such incidental powers, consistent with this Convention, as are implicit in and necessary for the exercise of those powers and functions with respect to activities in the Area.

3   The Authority is based on the principle of the sovereign equality of all its members.

4   All members of the Authority shall fulfil in good faith the obligations assumed by them in accordance with this Part in order to ensure to all of them the rights and benefits resulting from membership.

Article 158 Organs of the Authority

1   There are hereby established, as the principal organs of the Authority, an Assembly, a Council and a Secretariat.

2   There is hereby established the Enterprise, the organ through which the Authority shall carry out the functions referred to in Article 170, para 1.

3   Such subsidiary organs as may be found necessary may be established in accordance with this Part.

4   Each principal organ of the Authority and the Enterprise shall be responsible for exercising those powers and functions which are conferred upon it. In exercising such powers and functions each organ shall avoid taking any action which may derogate from or impede the exercise of specific powers and functions conferred upon another organ.

SUBSECTION B THE ASSEMBLY

Article 159 Composition, procedure and voting

1   The Assembly shall consist of all the members of the Authority. Each member shall have one representative in the Assembly, who may be accompanied by alternates and advisers.

2   The Assembly shall meet in regular annual sessions and in such special sessions as may be decided by the Assembly, or convened by the Secretary General at the request of the Council or of a majority of the members of the Authority.

3   Sessions shall take place at the seat of the Authority unless otherwise decided by the Assembly.

4   The Assembly shall adopt its rules of procedure. At the beginning of each regular session, it shall elect its President and such other officers as may be required. They shall hold office until a new President and other officers are elected at the next regular session.

5   A majority of the members of the Assembly shall constitute a quorum.

6   Each member of the Assembly shall have one vote.

7   Decisions on questions of procedure, including decisions to convene special sessions of the Assembly, shall be taken by a majority of the members present and voting.

8   Decisions on questions of substance shall be taken by a two-thirds majority of the members present and voting, provided that such majority includes a majority of the members participating in the session. When the issue arises as to whether a question is one of substance or not, that question shall be treated as one of substance unless otherwise decided by the Assembly by the majority required for decisions on questions of substance.

9　　When a question of substance comes up for voting for the first time, the President may, and shall, if requested by at least one fifth of the members of the Assembly, defer the issue of taking a vote on that question for a period not exceeding five calendar days. This rule may be applied only once to any question, and shall not be applied so as to defer the question beyond the end of the session.

10　　Upon a written request addressed to the President and sponsored by at least one fourth of the members of the Authority for an advisory opinion on the conformity with this Convention of a proposal before the Assembly on any matter, the Assembly shall request the Sea Bed Disputes Chamber of the International Tribunal for the Law of the Sea to give an advisory opinion thereon and shall defer voting on that proposal pending receipt of the advisory opinion by the Chamber. If the advisory opinion is not received before the final week of the session in which it is requested, the Assembly shall decide when it will meet to vote upon the deferred proposal.

Article 160　Powers and functions

1　　The Assembly, as the sole organ of the Authority consisting of all the members, shall be considered the supreme organ of the Authority to which the other principal organs shall be accountable as specifically provided for in this Convention. The Assembly shall have the power to establish general policies in conformity with the relevant provisions of this Convention on any question or matter within the competence of the Authority.

2　　In addition, the powers and functions of the Assembly shall be:

(a)　to elect the members of the Council in accordance with Article 161;

(b)　to elect the Secretary General from among the candidates proposed by the Council;

(c)　to elect, upon the recommendation of the Council, the members of the Governing Board of the Enterprise and the Director General of the Enterprise;

(d)　to establish such subsidiary organs as it finds necessary for the exercise of its functions in accordance with this Part. In the composition of these subsidiary organs due account shall be taken of the principle of equitable geographical distribution and of special interests and the need for members qualified and competent in the relevant technical questions dealt with by such organs;

(e)　to assess the contributions of members to the administrative budget of the Authority in accordance with an agreed scale of assessment based upon the scale used for the regular budget of the United Nations until the Authority shall have sufficient income from other sources to meet its administrative expenses;

(f)　(i)　to consider and approve, upon the recommendation of the Council the rules, regulations and procedures on the equitable sharing of financial and other economic benefits derived from activities in the Area and the payments and contributions made pursuant to Article 82, taking into particular consideration the interests and needs of developing states and peoples who have not attained full independence or other self-governing status. If the Assembly does not approve the recommendations of the Council, the Assembly shall return them to the Council for reconsideration in the light of the views expressed by the Assembly;

    (ii)   to consider and approve the rules, regulations and procedures of the Authority, and any amendments thereto, provisionally adopted by the Council pursuant to Article 162, para 2 (o)(ii). These rules, regulations and procedures shall relate to prospecting, exploration and exploitation in the Area, the financial management and internal administration of the Authority, and, upon the recommendation of the Governing Board of the Enterprise, to the transfer of funds from the Enterprise to the Authority;

(g)   to decide upon the equitable sharing of financial and other economic benefits derived from activities in the Area, consistent with this Convention and the rules, regulations and procedures of the Authority;

(h)   to consider and approve the proposed annual budget of the Authority submitted by the Council;

(i)   to examine periodic reports from the Council and from the Enterprise and special reports requested from the Council or any other organ of the Authority;

(j)   to initiate studies and make recommendations for the purpose of promoting international co-operation concerning activities in the Area and encouraging the progressive development of international law relating thereto and its codification;

(k)   to consider problems of a general nature in connection with activities in the Area arising in particular for developing states, as well as those problems for states in connection with activities in the Area that are due to their geographical location, particularly for land-locked and geographically disadvantaged states;

(l)   to establish, upon the recommendation of the Council, on the basis of advice from the Economic Planning Commission, a system of compensation or other measures of economic adjustment assistance as provided in Article 151, para 10;

(m)   to suspend the exercise of rights and privileges of membership pursuant to Article 185;

(n)   to discuss any question or matter within the competence of the Authority and to decide as to which organ of the Authority shall deal with any such question or matter not specifically entrusted to a particular organ, consistent with the distribution of powers and functions among the organs of the Authority.

SUBSECTION C THE COUNCIL

Article 161 Composition, procedure and voting

1   The Council shall consist of 36 members of the Authority elected by the Assembly in the following order:

(a)   four members from among those States Parties which, during the last five years for which statistics are available, have either consumed more than 2% of total world consumption or have had net imports of more than 2% of total world imports of the commodities produced from the categories of minerals to be derived from the Area, and in any case one state from the Eastern European (Socialist) region, as well as the largest consumer;

    (b)   four members from among the eight States Parties which have the largest investments in preparation for and in the conduct of activities in the Area, either directly or through their nationals, including at least one state from the Eastern European (Socialist) region;

    (c)   four members from among States Parties which on the basis of production in areas under their jurisdiction are major net exporters of the categories of minerals to be derived from the Area, including at least two developing states whose exports of such minerals have a substantial bearing upon their economies;

    (d)   six members from among developing States Parties, representing special interests. The special interests to be represented shall include those of states with large populations, states which are land-locked or geographically disadvantaged, states which are major importers of the categories of minerals to be derived from the Area, states which are potential producers of such minerals, and least developed states;

    (e)   eighteen members elected according to the principle of ensuring an equitable geographical distribution of seats in the Council as a whole, provided that each geographical region shall have at least one member elected under this sub-paragraph. For this purpose, the geographical regions shall be Africa, Asia, Eastern European (Socialist), Latin America and Western European and Others.

2   In electing the members of the Council in accordance with para 1, the Assembly shall ensure that:

    (a)   land-locked and geographically disadvantaged states are represented to a degree which is reasonably proportionate to their representation in the Assembly;

    (b)   coastal states, especially developing states, which do not qualify under para 1(a), (b), (c) or (d) are represented to a degree which is reasonably proportionate to their representation in the Assembly;

    (c)   each group of States Parties to be represented on the Council is represented by those members, if any, which are nominated by that group.

3   Elections shall take place at regular sessions of the Assembly. Each member of the Council shall be elected for four years. At the first election, however, the term of one half of the members of each group referred to in para 1 shall be two years.

4   Members of the Council shall be eligible for re-election, but due regard should be paid to the desirability of rotation of membership.

5   The Council shall function at the seat of the Authority, and shall meet as often as the business of the Authority may require, but not less than three times a year.

6   A majority of the members of the Council shall constitute a quorum.

7   Each member of the Council shall have one vote.

8   (a)   Decisions on questions of procedure shall be taken by a majority of the members present and voting.

    (b)   Decisions on questions of substance arising under the following provisions shall be taken by a two-thirds majority of the members present and voting, provided that such majority includes a majority of the members of the Council: Article 162, para 2, sub-paras (f); (g); (h); (i); (n); (p); (v); Article 191.

(c) Decisions on questions of substance arising under the following provisions shall be taken by a three-fourths majority of the members present and voting, provided that such majority includes a majority of the members of the Council: Article 162, para 1; Article 162, para 2, sub-paras (a); (b); (c); (d); (e); (I); (q); (r); (s); (t); (u) in cases of non-compliance by a contractor or a sponsor; (w) provided that orders issued thereunder may be binding for not more than 30 days unless confirmed by a decision taken in accordance with sub-para (d); Article 162, para 2, sub-paras (x); (y); (z); Article 163, para 2; Article 174, para 3; Annex IV, Article 11.

(d) Decisions on questions of substance arising under the following provisions shall be taken by consensus: Article 162, para 2(m) and (o); adoption of amendments to Part XI.

(e) For the purposes of sub-paras (d), (f) and (g), 'consensus' means the absence of any formal objection. Within 14 days of the submission of a proposal to the Council, the President of the Council shall determine whether there would be a formal objection to the adoption of the proposal. If the President determines that there would be such an objection, the President shall establish and convene, within three days following such determination, a conciliation committee consisting of not more than nine members of the Council, with the President as chairman, for the purpose of reconciling the differences and producing a proposal which can be adopted by consensus. The committee shall work expeditiously and report to the Council within 14 days following its establishment. If the committee is unable to recommend a proposal which can be adopted by consensus, it shall set out in its report the grounds on which the proposal is being opposed.

(f) Decisions on questions not listed above which the Council is authorised to take by the rules, regulations and procedures of the Authority or otherwise shall be taken pursuant to the sub-paragraphs of this paragraph specified in the rules, regulations and procedures or, if not specified therein, then pursuant to the sub-paragraph determined by the Council if possible in advance, by consensus.

(g) When the issue arises as to whether a question is within sub-para (a), (b), (c) or (d), the question shall be treated as being within the sub-para requiring the higher or highest majority or consensus as the case may be, unless otherwise decided by the Council by the said majority or by consensus.

9 The Council shall establish a procedure whereby a member of the Authority not represented on the Council may send a representative to attend a meeting of the Council when a request is made by such member, or a matter particularly affecting it is under consideration. Such a representative shall be entitled to participate in the deliberations but not to vote.

Article 162 Powers and functions

1 The Council is the executive organ of the Authority. The Council shall have the power to establish, in conformity with this Convention and the general policies established by the Assembly, the specific policies to be pursued by the Authority on any question or matter within the competence of the Authority.

2 In addition, the Council shall:

(a) supervise and co-ordinate the implementation of the provisions of this Part on all questions and matters within the competence of the Authority and invite the attention of the Assembly to cases of non-compliance;

(b) propose to the Assembly a list of candidates for the election of the Secretary General;

(c) recommend to the Assembly candidates for the election of the members of the Governing Board of the Enterprise and the Director General of the Enterprise;

(d) establish, as appropriate, and with due regard to economy and efficiency, such subsidiary organs as it finds necessary for the exercise of its functions in accordance with this Part. In the composition of subsidiary organs, emphasis shall be placed on the need for members qualified and competent in relevant technical matters dealt with by those organs provided that due account shall be taken of the principle of equitable geographical distribution and of special interests;

(e) adopt its rules of procedure including the method of selecting its president;

(f) enter into agreements with the United Nations or other international organisations on behalf of the Authority and within its competence, subject to approval by the Assembly;

(g) consider the reports of the Enterprise and transmit them to the Assembly with its recommendations;

(h) present to the Assembly annual reports and such special reports as the Assembly may request;

(i) issue directives to the Enterprise in accordance with Article 170;

(j) approve plans of work in accordance with Annex III, Article 6. The Council shall act upon each plan of work within 60 days of its submission by the Legal and Technical Commission at a session of the Council in accordance with the following procedures:

  (i) if the Commission recommends the approval of a plan of work, it shall be deemed to have been approved by the Council if no member of the Council submits in writing to the President within 14 days a specific objection alleging non-compliance with the requirements of Annex III, Article 6. If there is an objection, the conciliation procedure set forth in Article 161, para 8(e), shall apply. If, at the end of the conciliation procedure, the objection is still maintained, the plan of work shall be deemed to have been approved by the Council unless the Council disapproves it by consensus among its members excluding any state or states making the application or sponsoring the applicant;

  (ii) if the Commission recommends the disapproval of a plan of work or does not make a recommendation, the Council may approve the plan of work by a three-fourths majority of the members present and voting, provided that such majority includes a majority of the members participating in the session;

(k) approve plans of work submitted by the Enterprise in accordance with Annex IV, Article 12, applying, *mutatis mutandis*, the procedures set forth in sub-para (j);

(l)   exercise control over activities in the Area in accordance with Article 153, para 4, and the rules, regulations and procedures of the Authority;

(m) take, upon the recommendation of the Economic Planning Commission, necessary and appropriate measures in accordance with Article 150, sub-para (h), to provide protection from the adverse economic effects specified therein;

(n) make recommendations to the Assembly, on the basis of advice from the Economic Planning Commission, for a system of compensation or other measures of economic adjustment assistance as provided in Article 151, para 10;

(o) (i)   recommend to the Assembly rules, regulations and procedures on the equitable sharing of financial and other economic benefits derived from activities in the Area and the payments and contributions made pursuant to Article 82, taking into particular consideration the interests and needs of the developing states and peoples who have not attained full independence or other self-governing status;

      (ii) adopt and apply provisionally, pending approval by the Assembly, the rules, regulations and procedures of the Authority, and any amendments thereto, taking into account the recommendations of the Legal and Technical Commission or other subordinate organ concerned. These rules, regulations and procedures shall relate to prospecting, exploration and exploitation in the Area and the financial management and internal administration of the Authority. Priority shall be given to the adoption of rules, regulations and procedures for the exploration for and exploitation of polymetallic nodules. Rules, regulations and procedures for the exploration for and exploitation of any resource other than polymetallic nodules shall be adopted within three years from the date of a request to the Authority by any of its members to adopt such rules, regulations and procedures in respect of such resource. All rules, regulations and procedures shall remain in effect on a provisional basis until approved by the Assembly or until amended by the Council in the light of any views expressed by the Assembly;

(p) review the collection of all payments to be made by or to the Authority in connection with operations pursuant to this Part;

(q) make the selection from among applicants for production authorisations pursuant to Annex III, Article 7, where such selection is required by that provision;

(r) submit the proposed annual budget of the Authority to the Assembly for its approval;

(s) make recommendations to the Assembly concerning policies on any question or matter within the competence of the Authority;

(t) make recommendations to the Assembly concerning suspension of the exercise of the rights and privileges of membership pursuant to Article 185;

(u) institute proceedings on behalf of the Authority before the Sea Bed Disputes Chamber in cases of non-compliance;

(v) notify the Assembly upon a decision by the Sea Bed Disputes Chamber in proceedings instituted under sub-para (u), and make any recommendations which it may find appropriate with respect to measures to be taken;

(w) issue emergency orders, which may include orders for the suspension or adjustment of operations, to prevent serious harm to the marine environment arising out of activities in the Area;

(x) disapprove areas for exploitation by contractors or the Enterprise in cases where substantial evidence indicates the risk of serious harm to the marine environment;

(y) establish a subsidiary organ for the elaboration of draft financial rules, regulations and procedures relating to:

    (i) financial management in accordance with Articles 171 to 175; and

    (ii) financial arrangements in accordance with Annex III, Article 13 and Article 17, para 1(c);

(z) establish appropriate mechanisms for directing and supervising a staff of inspectors who shall inspect activities in the Area to determine whether this Part, the rules, regulations and procedures of the Authority, and the terms and conditions of any contract with the Authority are being complied with.

Article 163 Organs of the Council

1   There are hereby established the following organs of the Council:

(a) an Economic Planning Commission;

(b) a Legal and Technical Commission.

2   Each Commission shall be composed of 15 members, elected by the Council from among the candidates nominated by the States Parties. However, if necessary, the Council may decide to increase the size of either Commission having due regard to economy and efficiency.

3   Members of a Commission shall have appropriate qualifications in the area of competence of that Commission. States Parties shall nominate candidates of the highest standards of competence and integrity with qualifications in relevant fields so as to ensure the effective exercise of the functions of the Commissions.

4   In the election of members of the Commissions, due account shall be taken of the need for equitable geographical distribution and the representation of special interests.

5   No state Party may nominate more than one candidate for the same Commission. No person shall be elected to serve on more than one Commission.

6   Members of the Commissions shall hold office for a term of five years. They shall be eligible for re-election for a further term.

7   In the event of the death, incapacity or resignation of a member of a Commission prior to the expiration of the term of office, the Council shall elect for the remainder of the term, a member from the same geographical region or area of interest.

8   Members of Commissions shall have no financial interest in any activity relating to exploration and exploitation in the Area. Subject to their responsibilities to the Commissions upon which they serve, they shall not disclose, even after the termination of their functions, any industrial secret, proprietary data which are transferred to the Authority in accordance with

Annex III, Article 14, or any other confidential information coming to their knowledge by reason of their duties for the Authority.

9   Each Commission shall exercise its functions in accordance with such guidelines and directives as the Council may adopt.

10   Each Commission shall formulate and submit to the Council for approval such rules and regulations as may be necessary for the efficient conduct of the Commission's functions.

11   The decision-making procedures of the Commissions shall be established by the rules, regulations and procedures of the Authority. Recommendations to the Council shall, where necessary, be accompanied by a summary on the divergencies of opinion in the Commission.

12   Each Commission shall normally function at the seat of the Authority and shall meet as often as is required for the efficient exercise of its functions.

13   In the exercise of its functions, each Commission may, where appropriate, consult another commission, any competent organ of the United Nations or of its specialised agencies or any international organisations with competence in the subject matter of such consultation.

Article 164 The Economic Planning Commission

1   Members of the Economic Planning Commission shall have appropriate qualifications such as those relevant to mining, management of mineral resource activities, international trade or international economics. The Council shall endeavour to ensure that the membership of the Commission reflects all appropriate qualifications. The Commission shall include at least two members from developing states whose exports of the categories of minerals to be derived from the Area have a substantial bearing upon their economies.

2   The Commission shall:

(a)   propose, upon the request of the Council, measures to implement decisions relating to activities in the Area taken in accordance with this Convention;

(b)   review the trends of and the factors affecting supply, demand and prices of materials which may be derived from the Area, bearing in mind the interests of both importing and exporting countries, and in particular of the developing states among them;

(c)   examine any situation likely to lead to the adverse effects referred to in Article 150, sub-para (h), brought to its attention by the state Party or States Parties concerned, and make appropriate recommendations to the Council;

(d)   propose to the Council for submission to the Assembly, as provided in Article 151, para 10, a system of compensation or other measures of economic adjustment assistance for developing states which suffer adverse effects caused by activities in the Area. The Commission shall make the recommendations to the Council that are necessary for the application of the system or other measures adopted by the Assembly in specific cases.

Article 165 The Legal and Technical Commission

1   Members of the Legal and Technical Commission shall have appropriate qualifications such as those relevant to exploration for and exploitation and processing of mineral resources, oceanology, protection of the marine

environment, or economic or legal matters relating to ocean mining and related fields of expertise. The Council shall endeavour to ensure that the membership of the Commission reflects all appropriate qualifications.

2 The Commission shall:

(a) make recommendations with regard to the exercise of the Authority's functions upon the request of the Council;

(b) review formal written plans of work for activities in the Area in accordance with Article 153, para 3, and submit appropriate recommendations to the Council. The Commission shall base its recommendations solely on the grounds stated in Annex III and shall report fully thereon to the Council;

(c) supervise, upon the request of the Council, activities in the Area, where appropriate, in consultation and collaboration with any entity carrying out such activities or state or states concerned and report to the Council;

(d) prepare assessments of the environmental implications of activities in the Area;

(e) make recommendations to the Council on the protection of the marine environment, taking into account the views of recognised experts in that field;

(f) formulate and submit to the Council the rules regulations and procedures referred to in Article 162, para 2(o) taking into account all relevant factors including assessments of the environmental implications of activities in the Area;

(g) keep such rules, regulations and procedures under review and recommend to the Council from time to time such amendments thereto as it may deem necessary or desirable;

(h) make recommendations to the Council regarding the establishment of a monitoring programme to observe, measure, evaluate and analyse by recognised scientific methods, on a regular basis, the risks or effects of pollution of the marine environment resulting from activities in the Area, ensure that existing regulations are adequate and are complied with and co-ordinate the implementation of the monitoring programme approved by the Council;

(i) recommend to the Council that proceedings be instituted on behalf of the Authority before the Sea Bed Disputes Chamber, in accordance with this Part and the relevant Annexes taking into account particularly Article 187;

(j) make recommendations to the Council with respect to measures to be taken, upon a decision by the Sea Bed Disputes Chamber in proceedings instituted in accordance with sub-para (i);

(k) make recommendations to the Council to issue emergency orders, which may include orders for the suspension or adjustment of operations, to prevent serious harm to the marine environment arising out of activities in the Area. Such recommendations shall be taken up by the Council on a priority basis;

(l) make recommendations to the Council to disapprove areas for exploitation by contractors or the Enterprise in cases where substantial evidence indicates the risk of serious harm to the marine environment;

(m) make recommendations to the Council regarding the direction and supervision of a staff of inspectors who shall inspect activities in the

Area to determine whether the provisions of this Part, the rules, regulations and procedures of the Authority and the terms and conditions of any contract with the Authority are being complied with;

(n) calculate the production ceiling and issue production authorisations on behalf of the Authority pursuant to Article 151, paras 2 to 7, following any necessary selection among applicants for production authorisations by the Council in accordance with Annex III, Article 7.

3 The members of the Commission shall, upon request by any state Party or other party concerned, be accompanied by a representative of such state or other party concerned when carrying out their function of supervision and inspection.

SUBSECTION D THE SECRETARIAT

Article 166 The Secretariat

1 The Secretariat of the Authority shall comprise a Secretary General and such staff as the Authority may require.

2 The Secretary General shall be elected for four years by the Assembly from among the candidates proposed by the Council and may be re-elected.

3 The Secretary General shall be the chief administrative officer of the Authority, and shall act in that capacity in all meetings of the Assembly, of the Council and of any subsidiary organ, and shall perform such other administrative functions as are entrusted to the Secretary General by these organs.

4 The Secretary General shall make an annual report to the Assembly on the work of the Authority.

Article 167 The staff of the Authority

1 The staff of the Authority shall consist of such qualified scientific and technical and other personnel as may be required to fulfil the administrative functions of the Authority.

2 The paramount consideration in the recruitment and employment of the staff and in the determination of their conditions of service shall be the necessity of securing the highest standards of efficiency, competence and integrity. Subject to this consideration, due regard shall be paid to the importance of recruiting the staff on as wide a geographical basis as possible.

3 The staff shall be appointed by the Secretary General. The terms and conditions on which they shall be appointed, remunerated and dismissed shall be in accordance with the rules, regulations and procedures of the Authority.

Article 168 International character of the Secretariat

1 In the performance of their duties the Secretary General and the staff shall not seek or receive instructions from any government or from any other source external to the Authority. They shall refrain from any action which might reflect on their position as international officials responsible only to the Authority. Each state Party undertakes to respect the exclusively international character of the responsibilities of the Secretary General and the staff and not to seek to influence them in the discharge of their responsibilities. Any violation of responsibilities by a staff member shall be submitted to the appropriate administrative tribunal as provided in the rules, regulations and procedures of the Authority.

2   The Secretary General and the staff shall have no financial interest in any activity relating to exploration and exploitation in the Area. Subject to their responsibilities to the Authority, they shall not disclose, even after the termination of their functions, any industrial secret, proprietary data which are transferred to the Authority in accordance with Annex III, Article 14, or any other confidential information coming to their knowledge by reason of their employment with the Authority.

3   Violations of the obligations of a staff member of the Authority set forth in para 2 shall, on the request of a state Party affected by such violation, or a natural or juridical person, sponsored by a state Party as provided in Article 153, para 2(b), and affected by such violation, be submitted by the Authority against the staff member concerned to a tribunal designated by the rules, regulations and procedures of the Authority. The Party affected shall have the right to take part in the proceedings. If the tribunal so recommends, the Secretary General shall dismiss the staff member concerned.

4   The rules, regulations and procedures of the Authority shall contain such provisions as are necessary to implement this article.

Article 169 Consultation and co-operation with international and non-governmental organisations

1   The Secretary General shall, on matters within the competence of the Authority, make suitable arrangements, with the approval of the Council, for consultation and co-operation with international and non-governmental organisations recognised by the Economic and Social Council of the United Nations.

2   Any organisation with which the Secretary General has entered into an arrangement under para 1 may designate representatives to attend meetings of the organs of the Authority as observers in accordance with the rules of procedure of these organs. Procedures shall be established for obtaining the views of such organisations in appropriate cases.

3   The Secretary General may distribute to States Parties written reports submitted by the non-governmental organisations referred to in para 1 on subjects in which they have special competence and which are related to the work of the Authority.

SUBSECTION E   THE ENTERPRISE

Article 170 The Enterprise

1   The Enterprise shall be the organ of the Authority which shall carry out activities in the Area directly, pursuant to Article 153, para 2(a), as well as the transporting, processing and marketing of minerals recovered from the Area.

2   The Enterprise shall, within the framework of the international legal personality of the Authority, have such legal capacity as is provided for in the Statute set forth in Annex IV. The Enterprise shall act in accordance with this Convention and the rules, regulations and procedures of the Authority, as well as the general policies established by the Assembly, and shall be subject to the directives and control of the Council.

3   The Enterprise shall have its principal place of business at the seat of the Authority.

4   The Enterprise shall, in accordance with Article 173, para 2, and Annex IV, Article 11, be provided with such funds as it may require to carry out its functions, and shall receive technology as provided in Article 144 and other relevant provisions of this Convention.

SUB-SECTION F FINANCIAL ARRANGEMENTS OF THE AUTHORITY

...

SUB-SECTION G LEGAL STATUS, PRIVILEGES AND IMMUNITIES

Article 176 Legal status

The Authority shall have international legal personality and such legal capacity as may be necessary for the exercise of its functions and the fulfilment of its purposes.

...

SUB-SECTION H SUSPENSION OF THE EXERCISE OF RIGHTS AND PRIVILEGES OF MEMBERS

...

SECTION 5 SETTLEMENT OF DISPUTES AND ADVISORY OPINIONS

Article 186 Sea Bed Disputes Chamber of the International Tribunal for the Law of the Sea

The establishment of the Sea Bed Disputes Chamber and the manner in which it shall exercise its jurisdiction shall be governed by the provisions of this section, of Part XV and of Annex VI.

Article 187 Jurisdiction of the Sea Bed Disputes Chamber

The Sea Bed Disputes Chamber shall have jurisdiction under this Part and the Annexes relating thereto in disputes with respect to activities in the Area falling within the following categories:

(a) disputes between States Parties concerning the interpretation or application of this Part and the Annexes relating thereto;

(b) disputes between a state Party and the Authority concerning:

    (i) acts or omissions of the Authority or of a state Party alleged to be in violation of this Part or the Annexes relating thereto or of rules, regulations and procedures of the Authority adopted in accordance therewith; or

    (ii) acts of the Authority alleged to be in excess of jurisdiction or a misuse of power;

(c) disputes between parties to a contract, being States Parties, the Authority or the Enterprise, state enterprises and natural or juridical persons referred to in Article 153, para 2(b), concerning:

    (i) the interpretation or application of a relevant contract or a plan of work; or

    (ii) acts or omissions of a party to the contract relating to activities in the Area and directed to the other party or directly affecting its legitimate interests;

(d) disputes between the Authority and a prospective contractor who has been sponsored by a state as provided in Article 153, para 2(b), and has duly fulfilled the conditions referred to in Annex III, Article 4, para 6, and Article 13, para 2, concerning the refusal of a contract or a legal issue arising in the negotiation of the contract;

(e) disputes between the Authority and a state Party, a state enterprise or a natural or juridical person sponsored by a state Party as provided for in Article 153, para 2(b), where it is alleged that the Authority has incurred liability as provided in Annex III, Article 22;

(f) any other disputes for which the jurisdiction of the Chamber is specifically provided in this Convention.

Article 188 Submission of disputes to a special chamber of the International Tribunal for the Law of the Sea or an *ad hoc* chamber of the Sea Bed Disputes Chamber or to binding commercial arbitration

1 Disputes between States Parties referred to in Article 187, sub-para (a), may be submitted:

(a) at the request of the parties to the dispute, to a special chamber of the International Tribunal for the Law of the Sea to be formed in accordance with Annex VI, Articles 15 and 17; or

(b) at the request of any party to the dispute, to an *ad hoc* chamber of the Sea Bed Disputes Chamber to be formed in accordance with Annex VI, Article 36.

2 (a) Disputes concerning the interpretation or application of a contract referred to in Article 187, sub-para (c)(i), shall be submitted, at the request of any party to the dispute, to binding commercial arbitration, unless the parties otherwise agree. A commercial arbitral tribunal to which the dispute is submitted shall have no jurisdiction to decide any question of interpretation of this Convention. When the dispute also involves a question of the interpretation of Part XI and the Annexes relating thereto, with respect to activities in the Area, that question shall be referred to the Sea Bed Disputes Chamber for a ruling.

(b) If, at the commencement of or in the course of such arbitration, the arbitral tribunal determines, either at the request of any party to the dispute or *proprio motu*, that its decision depends upon a ruling of the Sea Bed Disputes Chamber, the arbitral tribunal shall refer such question to the Sea Bed Disputes Chamber for such ruling. The arbitral tribunal shall then proceed to render its award in conformity with the ruling of the Sea Bed Disputes Chamber.

(c) In the absence of a provision in the contract on the arbitration procedure to be applied in the dispute, the arbitration shall be conducted in accordance with the UNCITRAL Arbitration Rules or such other arbitration rules as may be prescribed in the rules, regulations and procedures of the Authority, unless the parties to the dispute otherwise agree.

Article 189 Limitation on jurisdiction with regard to decisions of the Authority

The Sea Bed Disputes Chamber shall have no jurisdiction with regard to the exercise by the Authority of its discretionary powers in accordance with this Part; in no case shall it substitute its discretion for that of the Authority. Without prejudice to Article 191, in exercising its jurisdiction pursuant to Article 187, the Sea Bed Disputes Chamber shall not pronounce itself on the question of whether any rules, regulations and procedures of the Authority are in conformity with this Convention, nor declare invalid any such rules, regulations and procedures. Its jurisdiction in this regard shall be confined to deciding claims that the application of any rules, regulations and procedures of the Authority in individual cases would be in conflict with the contractual obligations of the parties to the dispute or their obligations under this Convention, claims concerning excess of jurisdiction or misuse of power, and to claims for damages to be paid or other remedy to be given to the party concerned for the failure of the other party to comply with its contractual obligations or its obligations under this Convention.

Article 190 Participation and appearance of sponsoring States Parties in proceedings

1   If a natural or juridical person is a party to a dispute referred to in Article 187, the sponsoring state shall be given notice thereof and shall have the right to participate in the proceedings by submitting written or oral statements.

2   If an action is brought against a state Party by a natural or juridical person sponsored by another state Party in a dispute referred to in Article 187, sub-para (c), the respondent state may request the state sponsoring that person to appear in the proceedings on behalf of that person. Failing such appearance, the respondent state may arrange to be represented by a juridical person of its nationality.

Article 191 Advisory opinions

The Sea Bed Disputes Chamber shall give advisory opinions at the request of the Assembly or the Council on legal questions arising within the scope of their activities. Such opinions shall be given as a matter of urgency.

PART XII
PROTECTION AND PRESERVATION OF THE MARINE ENVIRONMENT[17]

...

PART XIII
MARINE SCIENTIFIC RESEARCH

...

PART XIV
DEVELOPMENT AND TRANSFER OF MARINE TECHNOLOGY

...

PART XV
SETTLEMENT OF DISPUTES
SECTION 1   GENERAL PROVISIONS

Article 279 Obligation to settle disputes by peaceful means

States Parties shall settle any dispute between them concerning the interpretation or application of this Convention by peaceful means in accordance with Article 2, para 3, of the Charter of the United Nations and, to this end, shall seek a solution by the means indicated in Article 33, para 1, of the Charter.

Article 280 Settlement of disputes by any peaceful means chosen by the parties

Nothing in this Part impairs the right of any States Parties to agree at any time to settle a dispute between them concerning the interpretation or application of this Convention by any peaceful means of their own choice.

---

17 See Chapter 18.

Article 281 Procedure where no settlement has been reached by the parties

1   If the States Parties which are parties to a dispute concerning the interpretation or application of this Convention have agreed to seek settlement of the dispute by a peaceful means of their own choice, the procedures provided for in this Part apply only where no settlement has been reached by recourse to such means and the agreement between the parties does not exclude any further procedure .

2   If the parties have also agreed on a time limit, para 1 applies only upon the expiration of that time-limit.

Article 282 Obligations under general, regional or bilateral agreements

If the States Parties which are parties to a dispute concerning the interpretation or application of this Convention have agreed, through a general, regional or bilateral agreement or otherwise, that such dispute shall, at the request of any party to the dispute, be submitted to a procedure that entails a binding decision, that procedure shall apply in lieu of the procedures provided for in this Part, unless the parties to the dispute otherwise agree.

Article 283 Obligation to exchange views

1   When a dispute arises between States Parties concerning the interpretation or application of this Convention, the parties to the dispute shall proceed expeditiously to an exchange of views regarding its settlement by negotiation or other peaceful means.

2   The parties shall also proceed expeditiously to an exchange of views where a procedure for the settlement of such a dispute has been terminated without a settlement or where a settlement has been reached and the circumstances require consultation regarding the manner of implementing the settlement.

Article 284 Conciliation

1   A state Party which is a party to a dispute concerning the interpretation or application of this Convention may invite the other party or parties to submit the dispute to conciliation in accordance with the procedure under Annex V, section 1, or another conciliation procedure.

2   If the invitation is accepted and if the parties agree upon the conciliation procedure to be applied, any party may submit the dispute to that procedure.

3   If the invitation is not accepted or the parties do not agree upon the procedure, the conciliation proceedings shall be deemed to be terminated.

4   Unless the parties otherwise agree, when a dispute has been submitted to conciliation, the proceedings may be terminated only in accordance with the agreed conciliation procedure.

Article 285 Application of this section to disputes submitted pursuant to Part XI

This section applies to any dispute which pursuant to Part XI, section 5, is to be settled in accordance with procedures provided for in this Part. If an entity other than a state Party is a party to such a dispute, this section applies *mutatis mutandis*.

SECTION 2   COMPULSORY PROCEDURES ENTAILING BINDING DECISIONS

Article 286 Application of procedures under this section

Subject to section 3, any dispute concerning the interpretation or application of this Convention shall, where no settlement has been reached by recourse to section 1, be submitted at the request of any party to the dispute to the court or tribunal having jurisdiction under this section.

Article 287 Choice of procedure

1   When signing, ratifying or acceding to this Convention or at any time thereafter, a state shall be free to choose, by means of a written declaration, one or more of the following means for the settlement of disputes concerning the interpretation or application of this Convention:

  (a) the International Tribunal for the Law of the Sea established in accordance with Annex VI;

  (b) the International Court of Justice;

  (c) an arbitral tribunal constituted in accordance with Annex VII;

  (d) a special arbitral tribunal constituted in accordance with Annex VIII for one or more of the categories of disputes specified therein.

2   A declaration made under para 1 shall not affect or be affected by the obligation of a state Party to accept the jurisdiction of the Sea Bed Disputes Chamber of the International Tribunal for the Law of the Sea to the extent and in the manner provided for in Part XI, section 5.

3   A state Party, which is a party to a dispute not covered by a declaration in force, shall be deemed to have accepted arbitration in accordance with Annex VII.

4   If the parties to a dispute have accepted the same procedure for the settlement of the dispute, it may be submitted only to that procedure, unless the parties otherwise agree.

5   If the parties to a dispute have not accepted the same procedure for the settlement of the dispute, it may be submitted only to arbitration in accordance with Annex VII, unless the parties otherwise agree.

6   A declaration made under para 1 shall remain in force until three months after notice of revocation has been deposited with the Secretary General of the United Nations.

7   A new declaration, a notice of revocation or the expiry of a declaration does not in any way affect proceedings pending before a court or tribunal having jurisdiction under this article, unless the parties otherwise agree.

8   Declarations and notices referred to in this article shall be deposited with the Secretary General of the United Nations, who shall transmit copies thereof to the States Parties.

Article 288 Jurisdiction

1   A court or tribunal referred to in Article 287 shall have jurisdiction over any dispute concerning the interpretation or application of this Convention which is submitted to it in accordance with this Part.

2   A court or tribunal referred to in Article 287 shall also have jurisdiction over any dispute concerning the interpretation or application of an international agreement related to the purposes of this Convention, which is submitted to it in accordance with the agreement.

3   The Sea Bed Disputes Chamber of the International Tribunal for the Law of the Sea established in accordance with Annex VI, and any other chamber or arbitral tribunal referred to in Part XI, section 5, shall have jurisdiction in any matter which is submitted to it in accordance therewith.

4   In the event of a dispute as to whether a court or tribunal has jurisdiction, the matter shall be settled by decision of that court or tribunal.

Article 289 Experts

In any dispute involving scientific or technical matters, a court or tribunal exercising jurisdiction under this section may, at the request of a party or *proprio motu*, select in consultation with the parties no fewer than two scientific or technical experts chosen preferably from the relevant list prepared in accordance with Annex VIII, Article 2, to sit with the court or tribunal but without the right to vote.

Article 290 Provisional measures

1   If a dispute has been duly submitted to a court or tribunal which considers that *prima facie* it has jurisdiction under this Part or Part XI, section 5, the court or tribunal may prescribe any provisional measures which it considers appropriate under the circumstances to preserve the respective rights of the parties to the dispute or to prevent serious harm to the marine environment, pending the final decision.

2   Provisional measures may be modified or revoked as soon as the circumstances justifying them have changed or ceased to exist.

3   Provisional measures may be prescribed, modified or revoked under this article only at the request of a party to the dispute and after the parties have been given an opportunity to be heard.

4   The court or tribunal shall forthwith give notice to the parties to the dispute, and to such other States Parties as it considers appropriate, of the prescription, modification or revocation of provisional measures.

5   Pending the constitution of an arbitral tribunal to which a dispute is being submitted under this section, any court or tribunal agreed upon by the parties or, failing such agreement within two weeks from the date of the request for provisional measures, the International Tribunal for the Law of the Sea or, with respect to activities in the Area, the Sea Bed Disputes Chamber, may prescribe, modify or revoke provisional measures in accordance with this article if it considers that *prima facie* the tribunal which is to be constituted would have jurisdiction and that the urgency of the situation so requires. Once constituted, the tribunal to which the dispute has been submitted may modify, revoke or affirm those provisional measures, acting in conformity with paras 1 to 4.

6   The parties to the dispute shall comply promptly with any provisional measures prescribed under this article.

Article 291 Access

1   All the dispute settlement procedures specified in this Part shall be open to States Parties.

2   The dispute settlement procedures specified in this Part shall be open to entities other than States Parties only as specifically provided for in this Convention.

Article 292 Prompt release of vessels and crews

1   Where the authorities of a state Party have detained a vessel flying the flag of another state Party and it is alleged that the detaining state has not complied with the provisions of this Convention for the prompt release of the vessel or its crew upon the posting of a reasonable bond or other financial security, the

question of release from detention may be submitted to any court or tribunal agreed upon by the parties or, failing such agreement within 10 days from the time of detention, to a court or tribunal accepted by the detaining state under Article 287 or to the International Tribunal for the Law of the Sea, unless the parties otherwise agree.

2   The application for release may be made only by or on behalf of the flag state of the vessel.

3   The court or tribunal shall deal without delay with the application for release and shall deal only with the question of release, without prejudice to the merits of any case before the appropriate domestic forum against the vessel, its owner or its crew. The authorities of the detaining state remain competent to release the vessel or its crew at any time.

4   Upon the posting of the bond or other financial security determined by the court or tribunal, the authorities of the detaining state shall comply promptly with the decision of the court or tribunal concerning the release of the vessel or its crew.

Article 293 Applicable law

1   A court or tribunal having jurisdiction under this section shall apply this Convention and other rules of international law not incompatible with this Convention.

2   Paragraph 1 does not prejudice the power of the court or tribunal having jurisdiction under this section to decide a case *ex aequo et bono*, if the parties so agree.

Article 294 Preliminary proceedings

1   A court or tribunal provided for in Article 287 to which an application is made in respect of a dispute referred to in Article 297 shall determine at the request of a party, or may determine *proprio motu*, whether the claim constitutes an abuse of legal process or whether *prima facie* it is well founded. If the court or tribunal determines that the claim constitutes an abuse of legal process or is *prima facie* unfounded, it shall take no further action in the case.

2   Upon receipt of the application, the court or tribunal shall immediately notify the other party or parties of the application, and shall fix a reasonable time limit within which they may request it to make a determination in accordance with para 1.

3   Nothing in this article affects the right of any party to a dispute to make preliminary objections in accordance with the applicable rules of procedure.

Article 295 Exhaustion of local remedies

Any dispute between States Parties concerning the interpretation or application of this Convention may be submitted to the procedures provided for in this section only after local remedies have been exhausted where this is required by international law.

Article 296 Finality and binding force of decisions

1   Any decision rendered by a court or tribunal having jurisdiction under this section shall be final and shall be complied with by all the parties to the dispute.

2   Any such decision shall have no binding force except between the parties and in respect of that particular dispute.

SECTION 3   LIMITATIONS AND EXCEPTIONS TO APPLICABILITY OF
SECTION 2

...

PART XVI
GENERAL PROVISIONS

...

PART XVII
FINAL PROVISIONS

...

CHAPTER 12

AIR AND SPACE LAW

12.1 Air space

Up until the early part of this century the law relating to air space was not settled. Certain writers suggested that there should be a territorial air space above a state's territory with a similar regime to that of the territorial sea. Through the territorial air space there would be a right of innocent passage for foreign civilian aircraft and above it there would be freedom of navigation. Another school of thought advocated complete freedom of the air. The law came to be settled during the First World War and the customary law was codified in the Paris Convention on the Regulation of Aerial Navigation 1919. The approach adopted at Paris was that states should have complete and exclusive sovereignty over the air space above their land and territorial sea. Sovereignty was understood to extend upwards to an unlimited distance. As far as the air space above the high seas and other areas not subject to national jurisdiction was concerned it was accepted that there was complete freedom of navigation.

12.2 The Chicago Convention

The present regime concerning aerial navigation was developed at the 1944 Chicago Conference and is reflected in the conventions adopted there. The Chicago Convention on International Civil Aviation (the Chicago Convention) entered into force in January 1945.

CHICAGO CONVENTION ON INTERNATIONAL CIVIL AVIATION 1944[1]

Article 1

The contracting states recognise that every state has complete and exclusive sovereignty over the air space above its territory.

Article 2

For the purposes of this Convention the territory of a state shall be deemed to be the land areas and territorial waters adjacent thereto under the sovereignty, suzerainty, protection or mandate of such state.

Article 3

(a) This Convention shall be applicable only to civil aircraft, and shall not be applicable to state aircraft.

(b) Aircraft used in military, customs and police services shall be deemed to be state aircraft.

---

1 UKTS 8 (1953) Cmd 8742; 15 UNTS 295 – entered into force in 1947.

(c) No state aircraft of a contracting state shall fly over the territory of another state or land thereon without authorisation by special agreement or otherwise, and in accordance with the terms thereof.

(d) The contracting states undertake, when issuing regulations for their state aircraft, that they will have due regard for the safety of navigation of civil aircraft.

Article 3 *bis*

(a) The contracting states recognise that every state must refrain from resorting to the use of weapons against civil aircraft in flight and that, in case of interception, the lives of persons on board and the safety of aircraft must not be endangered. This provision shall not be interpreted as modifying in any way the rights and obligations of state set forth in the Charter of the United Nations.

(b) The contracting states recognise that every state, in the exercise of its sovereignty, is entitled to require the landing at some designated airport of a civil aircraft flying above its territory without authority or if there are reasonable grounds to conclude that it is being used for any purpose inconsistent with the aims of this Convention; it may also give such aircraft any other instructions to put an end to such violations. For this purpose, the contracting states may resort to any appropriate means consistent with relevant rules of international law, including the relevant provisions of this Convention, specifically para (a) of this article. Each contracting state agrees to publish regulations in force regarding the interception of civil aircraft.

(c) Every civil aircraft shall comply with an order given in conformity with para (b) of this article. To this end each contracting state shall establish all necessary provisions in its national laws or regulations to make such compliance mandatory for any civil aircraft registered in that state or operated by a person having his principal place of business in that state or permanent residence in that state. Each contracting state shall make any violation of such applicable laws or regulations punishable by severe penalties and shall submit the case to its competent authorities in accordance with its laws or regulations.

(d) Each contracting state shall take appropriate measures to prohibit the deliberate use of any civil aircraft registered in that state or operated by an operator who has his principal place of business or permanent residence in that state for any purpose inconsistent with the aims of this Convention. This provision shall not affect para (a) or derogate from paras (b) and (c) of this article.

Article 5

Each contracting state agrees that all aircraft of the other contracting states, being aircraft not engaged in scheduled international air service, shall have the right, subject to the observance of the terms of this Convention, to make flights into or in transit non-stop across its territory and to make stops for non-traffic purposes without the necessity of obtaining prior permission, and subject to the right of the state flown over to require landing. Each contracting state nevertheless reserves the right, for reasons of safety of flight, to require aircraft desiring to proceed over regions which are inaccessible or without adequate air navigation facilities to follow prescribed routes, or to obtain special permission for such flights.

Such aircraft, if engaged in the carriage of passengers, cargo, or mail for remuneration or hire other than scheduled international air services, shall also, subject to the provisions of Article 7, have the privilege of taking on or discharging passengers, cargo or mail, subject to the right of any state where such embarkation or discharge takes place to impose such regulations, conditions or limitations as it may consider desirable.

Article 6

No scheduled international air service may be operated over or into the territory of a contracting state, except with the special permission or other authorisation of that state, and in accordance with the terms of such permission or authorisation.

...

Article 17

Aircraft have the nationality of the state in which they are registered.

Article 18

An aircraft cannot be validly registered in more than one state, but its registrations may be changed from one state to another.

Article 19

The registration or transfer of registration of aircraft in any contracting state shall be made in accordance with its laws and regulations.

A scheduled air service is defined as 'a series of flights that possesses all the following characteristics:

(a) it passes through the air space over the territory of more than one state;

(b) it is performed by aircraft for the transport of passengers, mail or cargo for remuneration, in such a manner that each flight is open to use by members of the public;

(c) it is operated, so as to serve traffic between the same two or more points, either:

(i) according to a published timetable; or

(ii) with flights so regular and frequent that they constitute a recognisably systematic series.

CHICAGO INTERNATIONAL AIR SERVICES TRANSIT AGREEMENT 1944[2]

Article 1

1   Each contracting state grants to the other contracting states the following freedoms of the air in respect of scheduled international air services.

(1)   The privilege to fly across its territory without landing;

(2)   The privilege to land for non-traffic purposes ...

---

2   UKTS 8 (1953) Cmd 8742; 171 UNTS 387.

12.3 Unauthorised aerial intrusion

A question that flows from the fact that states possess sovereignty over the air space above their territory is what action can be taken against 'trespassing' aircraft. As far as military aircraft are concerned the international law position appears to be clear. Unauthorised intrusion by military aircraft (with the exception of military transport aircraft) may be met by the use of force without warning. The most famous example occurred in the U-2 incident. In May 1960 a U-2 (an American reconnaissance aircraft) was shot down by USSR fighters over Soviet territory. The aircraft had been engaged in the aerial reconnaissance of the Soviet Union. The USSR protested at the flight and the USA made no attempt to justify its action in terms of international law or protest at the shooting down or the subsequent trial of the pilot.

As far as civilian aircraft are concerned, Harris estimates that since 1945 trespassing civil aircraft have been shot down at the rate of nearly one a year. The international law position has become more clear following the shooting down of Korean Airlines Flight 007 by Soviet aircraft in 1983. A scheduled flight from Alaska to South Korea had strayed into Soviet air space and was shot down. All 169 passengers and crew were killed. An ICAO inquiry concluded that the aircraft had strayed off course as a result of the negligence of the crew. They found that the Soviet aircraft had made insufficient efforts to intercept the Boeing 747. It was accepted by all parties that at the time of the shooting there was a US military intelligence aircraft in the area, but in spite of this the inquiry felt that the Soviet aircrew should have made greater effort to establish whether or not the 747 was an intelligence aircraft before shooting it down. As a consequence of the shooting, in 1984 ICAO adopted a new Article 3 *bis* of the Chicago Convention.

12.4 Jurisdiction over aircraft

The nationality of civil aircraft is governed by the Chicago Convention which provides that they shall have the nationality of the state in which they are registered and that they cannot be validly registered in more than one state. The registering state does have a valid claim to exercise jurisdiction while the aircraft is in flight over the high seas or other territory not belonging to any state. As for aircraft within the territory of a state, jurisdiction will be primarily territorial, although the registering state may make express provision for claiming jurisdiction over acts committed on board the aircraft in its own legislation.

12.4.1 Threats to aviation security

The use of hijacking and other acts of terrorism involving aircraft from the early 1960s onwards proved the general rules on jurisdiction inadequate. The nature and situation of the offence meant it was not always easy for the registering state to assert jurisdiction nor was it always clear over whose territory the offence was committed. Furthermore, even if the offenders could be located the limitations of extradition treaties meant that it was often not possible to bring them to trial.

TOKYO CONVENTION ON OFFENCES AND CERTAIN OTHER ACTS COMMITTED ON BOARD AIRCRAFT 1963

CHAPTER I
SCOPE OF THE CONVENTION

Article 1

1   This Convention shall apply in respect of:

   (a)   offences against penal law;

   (b)   acts which, whether or not they are offences, may or do jeopardise the safety of the aircraft or of persons or property therein or which jeopardise good order and discipline on board.

2   Except as provided in Chapter III, this Convention shall apply in respect of offences committed or acts done by a person on board any aircraft registered in a contracting state while that aircraft is in flight or on the surface of the high seas or of any other area outside the territory of any state.

3   For the purposes of this Convention, an aircraft is considered to be in flight from the moment when the power is applied for the purpose of take-off until the moment when the landing run ends.

4   This Convention shall not apply to aircraft used in military, customs or police services.

CHAPTER II
JURISDICTION

Article 3

1   The state of registration of the aircraft is competent to exercise jurisdiction over offences and acts committed on board.

2   Each contracting state shall take such measures as may be necessary to establish its jurisdiction as the state of registration over offences committed on board aircraft registered in such state.

3   This Convention does not exclude any criminal jurisdiction exercised in accordance with national law.

Article 4

A contracting state which is not the state of registration may not interfere with an aircraft in flight in order to exercise its criminal jurisdiction over an offence committed on board except in the following cases:

   (a)   the offence has effect on the territory of such state;

   (b)   the offence has been committed by or against a national or permanent resident of such state;

   (c)   the offence is against the security of such state;

   (d)   the offence consists of a breach of any rules or regulations relating to the flight or manoeuvre of aircraft in such state;

   (e)   the exercise of jurisdiction is necessary to ensure the observance of any obligation of such state under a multilateral international agreement.

CHAPTER III
POWERS OF THE AIRCRAFT COMMANDER

Article 5

1   The provisions of this chapter shall not apply to offences and acts committed or about to be committed by a person on board an aircraft in flight in the air space of the state of registration or over the high seas or any other area outside the territory of any state unless the last point of take-off or the next point of intended landing is situated in a state other than that of registration, or the aircraft subsequently flies in the air space of a state other than that of registration with such person still on board.

2   Notwithstanding the provisions of Article 1, para 3, an aircraft shall, for the purposes of this chapter, be considered to be in flight at any time from the moment when all its external doors are closed following embarkation until the moment when any such door is opened for disembarkation. In the case of a forced landing, the provisions of this chapter shall continue to apply with respect to offences and acts committed on board until competent authorities of a state take over responsibility for the aircraft and for the persons and property on board.

Article 6

1   The aircraft commander may, when he has reasonable grounds to believe that a person has committed, or is about to commit, on board the aircraft, an offence or act contemplated by Article 1, para 1, impose upon such person reasonable measures including restraint which are necessary:

(a)   to protect the safety of the aircraft, or of persons or property therein; or

(b)   to maintain good order and discipline on board; or

(c)   to enable him to deliver such person to competent authorities or to disembark him in accordance with the provisions of this chapter.

2   The aircraft commander may require or authorise the assistance of other crew members and may request or authorise, but not require, the assistance of passengers to restrain any person whom he is entitled to restrain. Any crew member or passenger may also take reasonable preventive measures without such authorisation when he has reasonable grounds to believe that such action is immediately necessary to protect the safety of the aircraft, or of persons or property therein.

Article 7

1   Measures of restraint imposed upon a person in accordance with Article 6 shall not be continued beyond any point at which the aircraft lands unless:

(a)   such point is in the territory of a non-contracting state and its authorities refuse to permit disembarkation of that person or those measures have bee imposed in accordance with Article 6, para 1(c) in order to enable his delivery to competent authorities;

(b)   the aircraft makes a forced landing and the aircraft commander is unable to deliver that person to competent authorities; or

(c)   that person agrees to onward carriage under restraint.

2   The aircraft commander shall as soon as practicable, and if possible before landing in the territory of a state with a person on board who has been placed under restraint in accordance with the provisions of Article 6, notify the authorities of such state of the fact that a person on board is under restraint and of the reason for such restraint.

Article 8

1   The aircraft commander may, in so far as it is necessary for the purpose of sub-para (a) or (b) of para 1 of Article 6, disembark in the territory of any state in which the aircraft lands any person who he has reasonable grounds to believe has committed, or is about to commit, on board the aircraft an act contemplated in Article 1 para 1(b).

2   The aircraft commander shall report to the authorities of the state in which he disembarks any person pursuant to this article, the fact of, and the reasons for, such disembarkation.

Article 9

1   The aircraft commander may deliver to the competent authorities of any Contracting state in the territory of which the aircraft lands any person who he has reasonable grounds to believe has committed on board the aircraft an act which, in his opinion, is a serious offence according to the penal law of the state of registration of the aircraft.

2   The aircraft commander shall as soon as practicable and if possible before landing in the territory of a contracting state with a person on board whom the aircraft authorities of such state of his intention to deliver such person and the reason therefor.

3   The aircraft commander shall furnish the authorities to whom any suspected offender is delivered in accordance with the provisions of this article with evidence and information which, under the law of the state of registration of the aircraft, are lawfully in his possession.

Article 10

For actions taken in accordance with this Convention, neither the aircraft commander, any other member of the crew, any passenger, the owner or operator of the aircraft, nor the person on whose behalf the flight was performed shall be held responsible in any proceeding on account of the treatment undergone by the person against whom the actions were taken.

CHAPTER IV
UNLAWFUL SEIZURE OF AIRCRAFT

Article 11

1   When a person on board has unlawfully committed by force or threat thereof an act of interference, seizure, or other wrongful exercise of control of an aircraft in flight or when such an act is about to be committed, contracting states shall take all appropriate measures to restore control to the aircraft to its lawful commander or to preserve his control of the aircraft.

2   In the cases contemplated in the preceding paragraph, the contracting state in which the aircraft lands shall permit its passengers and crew to continue their journey as soon as practicable, and shall return the aircraft and its cargo to the persons lawfully entitled to possession.

CHAPTER V
POWERS AND DUTIES OF STATES

Article 12

Any contracting state shall allow the commander of an aircraft registered in another contracting state to disembark any person pursuant to Article 8, para 1.

Article 13

1   Any contracting state shall take delivery of any person whom the aircraft commander delivers pursuant to Article 9, para 1.

2   Upon being satisfied that the circumstances so warrant, any contracting state shall take custody or other measures to ensure the presence of any person suspected of an act contemplated in Article 11, para 1, and of any person of whom it has taken delivery. The custody and other measures shall be as provided in the law of that state but may only be continued for such time as is reasonably necessary to enable any criminal or extradition proceedings to be instituted.

3   Any person in custody pursuant to the previous paragraph shall be assisted in communicating immediately with the nearest appropriate representative of the state of which he is a national.

4   Any contracting state, to which a person is delivered pursuant to Article 9, para 1 or in whose territory an aircraft lands following the commission of an act contemplated in Article 11, para 1, shall immediately make a preliminary enquiry into the facts.

5   When a state, pursuant to this article, has taken a person into custody, it shall immediately notify the state of registration of the aircraft and the state of nationality of the detained person and, if it considers it advisable, any other interested state of the fact that such person is in custody and of the circumstances which warrant his detention. The state which makes the preliminary enquiry contemplated in para 4 of this article shall promptly report its finding to the said states and shall indicate whether it intends to exercise jurisdiction.

Article 14

1   When any person has been delivered in accordance with Article 8, para 1, or delivered in accordance with Article 9, para 1, or has disembarked after committing an act contemplated in Article 11, para 1, and when such person cannot or does not desire to continue his journey and the state of landing refuses to admit him, that state may, if the person in question is not a national or permanent resident of that state, return him to the territory of the state of which he is a national or permanent resident or to the territory of the state in which he began his journey by air.

2   Neither disembarkation, nor delivery, nor the taking of custody or other measures contemplated in Article 13, para 2, nor the return of the person concerned, shall be considered as admission to the territory of the contracting states concerned for the purpose of its law relating to entry or admission of persons and nothing in this Convention shall affect the law of a contracting state relating to the expulsion of persons from its territory.

Article 15

1   Without prejudice to Article 14, any person who has been disembarked in accordance with Article 8, para 1, or delivered in accordance with Article 9, para 1, or has disembarked after committing an act contemplated in Article 11, para 1, and who desires to continue his journey shall be at liberty as soon as practicable to proceed to any destination of his choice unless his presence is required by the law of the state of landing for the purpose of extradition or criminal proceedings.

2   Without prejudice to its law as to entry and admission to, and extradition and expulsion from its territory, a contracting state in whose territory a person

has been disembarked in accordance with Article 8, para 1, or delivered in accordance with Article 9, para 1, or has disembarked and is suspected of having committed an act contemplated in Article 11, para 1, shall accord to such person treatment which is no less favourable for his protection and security than that accorded to nationals of such contracting state in like circumstances.

The principal weakness of the Tokyo Convention is that there is no obligation on states to recognise an offence of unlawful seizure of aircraft. During the later 1960s the number of hijackings dramatically increased reaching a peak of 89 separate incidents in 1969. Where hijackers were caught most states were unable to prosecute for hijacking and instead, where they had jurisdiction, prosecuted for the constituent acts of assault, etc. The ICAO, concerned at the increase in hijackings and recognising the deficiencies in the Tokyo Convention, called for the re-enforcement of the law. The problem was highlighted by the Dawson's Field incident.

On 6 September 1970 Palestinian commandos belonging to the Popular Front for the Liberation of Palestine attacked four aircraft. One attack was on an El Al aircraft in London, but three other aircraft belonging to Pan American, TWA and Swissair were captured in flight. The Pan American plane was taken to Cairo where, after the passengers were allowed to leave, it was blown up. The TWA and Swissair flight together with a BOAC plane which had been seised on 9 September were eventually flown to Dawson's Field in Jordan and the 400 passengers on board were held hostage while negotiations continued and US military intervention seemed imminent. As Jordanian troops began attacking Palestinian refugee camps in what came to be known as Black September the hostages were gradually released in return for the release of a number of Palestinian prisoners held around the world (including Leila Khaled who had led the attack on the El Al plane). The three aircraft were blown up.

The hijackings received world-wide publicity and focused attention on the need to reform the law. On 16 December 1970 the ICAO convened an international conference which resulted in the Hague Convention for the Suppression of Unlawful Seizure of Aircraft 1970.

HAGUE CONVENTION FOR THE SUPPRESSION OF UNLAWFUL SEIZURE OF AIRCRAFT 1970

Article 1
Any person who on board an aircraft in flight:
   (a) unlawfully, by force or threat thereof, or by any other form of intimidation, seises, or exercises control of, that aircraft, or attempts to perform any such act; or
   (b) is an accomplice of a person who performs or attempts to perform any such act commits an offence (hereinafter referred to as 'the offence').

Article 2
Each contracting state undertakes to make the offence punishable by severe penalties.

Article 3

1   For the purpose of this Convention, an aircraft is considered to be in flight at any time from the moment when all its external doors are closed following embarkation until the moment when any such door is opened for disembarkation. In the case of a forced landing, the flight shall be deemed to continue until the competent authorities take over the responsibility for the aircraft and for persons and property on board.

2   This Convention shall not apply to aircraft used in military, customs or police services.

3   This Convention shall apply only if the place of take-off or the place of actual landing of the aircraft on board which the offence is committed is situated outside the territory of the state of registration of that aircraft; it shall be immaterial whether the aircraft is engaged in an international or domestic flight.

4   In the cases mentioned in Article 5, this Convention shall not apply if the place of take-off and the place of actual landing of the aircraft on board which the offence is committed are situated within the territory of the same state where that state is one of those referred to in that article.

5   Notwithstanding the paras 3 and 4 of this article, Articles 6, 7, 8 and 100 shall apply whatever the place of take-off or the place of actual landing of the aircraft, if the offender or the alleged offender is found in the territory of a state other than the state of registration of that aircraft.

Article 4

1   Each contracting state shall take such measures as may be necessary to establish its jurisdiction over the offence and any other act of violence against passengers or crew committed by the alleged offender in connection with the offence in the following cases:

   (a)   when the offence is committed on board an aircraft registered in that state;

   (b)   when the aircraft on board which the offence is committed lands in its territory with the alleged offender still on board;

   (c)   when the offence is committed on board an aircraft leased without crew to a lessee who has his principal place of business, or if the lessee has no such place of business, his permanent residence, in that state.

2   Each contracting state shall likewise take such measures as may be necessary to establish its jurisdiction over the offence in the case where the alleged offender is present in its territory and it does not extradite him pursuant to Article 8 to any of the states mentioned in para 1 of this article.

3   The Convention does not exclude any criminal jurisdiction exercised in accordance with national law.

Article 5

The contracting states which establish joint air transport operating organisations or international operating agencies, which operate aircraft which are subject to joint or international registration shall, by appropriate means, designate for each aircraft the state among them which shall exercise the jurisdiction and have the attributes of the state of registration for the purpose of this Convention and shall give notice thereof to the International Civil Aviation Organisation which shall communicate the notice to all State Parties to this Convention.

Article 6

1   Upon being satisfied that the circumstances so warrant, any contracting state in the territory of which the offender or the alleged offender is present, shall take him into custody or take other measures to ensure his presence. The custody and other measures shall be as provided in the law of that state but may only be continued for such time as is necessary to enable any criminal or extradition proceedings to be instituted.

2   Such state shall immediately make a preliminary enquiry into the facts.

3   Any person in custody pursuant to para 1 of this article shall be assisted in communicating immediately with the nearest appropriate representative of the state of which he is a national.

4   When a state, pursuant to this article, has taken a person into custody, it shall immediately notify the state of registration of the aircraft, the state mentioned in Article 4, para 1(c), the state of nationality of the detained person and, if it considers it advisable, any other interested state of the fact that such person is in custody and of the circumstances which warrant his detention. The state which makes the preliminary enquiry contemplated in para 2 of this article shall promptly report its findings to the said states and shall indicate whether it intends to exercise jurisdiction.

Article 7

The contracting state in the territory of which the alleged offender is found, if it does not extradite him, shall be obliged, without exception whatsoever and whether or not the offence was committed in its territory, to submit the case to its competent authorities for the purpose of prosecution. Those authorities shall take their decision in the same manner as in the case of any ordinary offence of a serious nature under the law of that state.

Article 8

1   The offence shall be deemed to be included as an extraditable offence in any extradition treaty existing between contracting states. contracting states undertake to include the offence as an extraditable treaty to be concluded between them.

2   If a contracting state which makes extradition conditional on the existence of a treaty receives a request for extradition from another contracting state with which it has no extradition treaty, it may at its option consider this Convention as the legal basis for extradition in respect of the offence. Extradition shall be subject to the other conditions provided by the law of the requested state.

3   contracting states which do not make extradition conditional on the existence of a treaty shall recognise the offence between themselves subject to the conditions provided by the law of the requested state.

4   The offence shall be treated, for the purpose of extradition between contracting states, as if it had been committed not only in the place in which it occurred but also in the territories of the states required to establish their jurisdiction in accordance with Article 4, para 1.

Article 9

1   When any of the acts mentioned in Article 1(a) has occurred or is about to occur, contracting states shall take all appropriate measures to restore control of aircraft to its lawful commander or to preserve his control of the aircraft.

2   In the cases contemplated by the preceding paragraph, any contracting state in which the aircraft or its passengers or crew are present shall facilitate the continuation of the journey of the passengers and crew as soon as practicable, and shall without delay return the aircraft and its cargo to the persons lawfully entitled to possession.

Article 10

1   contracting states shall afford one another the greatest measure of assistance in connection with criminal proceedings brought in respect of the offence and other acts mentioned in Article 4. The law of the state requested shall apply in all cases.

2   The provisions of para 1 of this article shall not affect obligations under any other treaty, bilateral or multilateral, which governs or will govern, in whole or in part, mutual assistance in criminal matters.

Article 11

Each contracting state shall in accordance with its national law report to the Council of the International Civil Aviation Organisation as promptly as possible any relevant information in its possession concerning:

(a)   the circumstances of the offence;

(b)   the action taken pursuant to Article 9;

(c)   the measures taken in relation to the offender or the alleged offender, and, in particular, the results of any extradition proceedings or other legal proceedings.

The Hague Convention did not deal with the problem of aircraft sabotage. The ICAO convened a conference in 1971 to remedy this deficiency and the conference adopted the Montreal Convention for the Suppression of Unlawful Acts Against the Safety of Civil Aviation 1971. Following a series of attacks at airports a protocol to the Convention was agreed in 1988 – the Montreal Protocol for the Suppression of Unlawful Acts of Violence at Airports Serving International Civil Aviation 1988.

MONTREAL CONVENTION FOR THE SUPPRESSION OF UNLAWFUL ACTS AGAINST THE SAFETY OF CIVIL AVIATION 1971

Article 1

1   Any person commits an offence if he unlawfully and intentionally:

(a)   performs an act of violence against a person on board an aircraft in flight if that act is likely to endanger the safety of that aircraft; or

(b)   destroys an aircraft in service or causes damage to such an aircraft which renders it incapable of flight or which is likely to endanger its safety in flight; or

(c)   places or causes to be placed on an aircraft in service, by any means whatsoever, a device or substance which is likely to destroy that aircraft, or to cause damage to it which renders it incapable of flight, or to cause damage to it which is likely to endanger its safety in flight; or

(d) destroys or damages air navigation facilities or interferes with their operation, if any such act is likely to endanger the safety of aircraft in flight; or

(e) communicates information which he knows to be false, thereby endangering the safety of an aircraft in flight.

2 Any person also commits an offence if he:

(a) attempts to commit any of the offences mentioned in para 1 of this article; or

(b) is an accomplice of a person who commits or attempts to commit any such offence.

Article 2

For the purpose of this Convention:

(a) an aircraft is considered to be in flight at any time from the moment when all its external doors are closed following embarkation until the moment when any such door is opened for disembarkation; in the case of a forced landing, the flight shall be deemed to continue until the competent authorities take over the responsibility for the aircraft and for persons and property on board;

(b) an aircraft is considered to be in service from the beginning of the preflight preparation of the aircraft by ground personnel or by the crew for a specific flight until twenty-four hours after any landing; the period of service shall, in any event, extend for the entire period during which the aircraft is in flight as defined in para (a) of this article.

Article 3

Each contracting state undertakes to make the offences mentioned in Article 1 punishable by severe penalties.

Article 4

1 This Convention shall not apply to aircraft used in military, customs or police services.

2 In the cases contemplated in sub-paras (a), (b), (c) and (e) of para 1 of Article 1, this Convention shall apply irrespective of whether the aircraft is engaged in an international or domestic flight, only if:

(a) the place of take-off or landing, actual or intended, of the aircraft is situated outside the territory of the state of registration of the aircraft;

(b) the offence is committed in the territory of a state other than the state of registration of the aircraft.

3 Notwithstanding para 2 of this article, in the cases contemplated in sub-paras (a), (b), (c) and (e) of para 1 of Article 1, this Convention shall also apply if the offender or the alleged offender is found in the territory of a state other than the state of registration of the aircraft.

4 With respect to the states mentioned in Article 9 and in the cases mentioned in sub-paras (a), (b), (c) and (e) of para 1 of Article 1, this Convention shall not apply if the places referred to in sub-para (a) of para 2 of this article are situated within the territory of the same state where that state is one of those referred to in Article 9, unless the offence is committed or the offender or alleged offender is found in the territory of a state other than that state.

5   In the cases contemplated in sub-para (d) of para 1 of Article 1, this Convention shall apply only if the air navigation facilities are used in international air navigation.

6   The provisions of paras 2, 3, 4 and 5 of this article shall also apply in the cases contemplated in para 2 of Article 1.

Article 5

1   Each contracting state shall take such measures as may be necessary to establish its jurisdiction over the offences in the following cases:

(a)   when the offence is committed in the territory of that state;

(b)   when the offence is committed against or on board an aircraft registered in that state;

(c)   when the aircraft on board which the offence is committed lands in its territory with the alleged offender still on board;

(d)   when the offence is committed against or on board an aircraft leased without crew to a lessee who has his principal place of business or, if the lessee has no such place of business, his permanent residence, on that state.

2   Each contracting state shall likewise take such measures as may be necessary to establish its jurisdiction over the offences mentioned in Article 1, para 1(a), (b) and (c), and in Article 1, para 2, in so far as that paragraph relates to those offences, in the case where the alleged offender is present in its territory and it does not extradite him pursuant to Article 8 to any of the states mentioned in para 1 of this article.

3   This Convention does not exclude any criminal jurisdiction exercised in accordance with national law.

Article 6

1   Upon being satisfied that the circumstances so warrant, any contracting state in the territory of which the offender or the alleged offender is present, shall take him into custody or take other measures to ensure his presence. The custody and other measures shall be as provided in the law of that state but may only be continued for such time as is necessary to enable any criminal or extradition proceedings to be instituted.

2   Such state shall immediately make a preliminary enquiry into the facts.

3   Any person in custody pursuant to para 1 of this article shall be assisted in communicating immediately with the nearest appropriate representative of the state of which he is a national.

4   When a state, pursuant to this article, has taken a person into custody, it shall immediately notify the state of registration of the aircraft, the state mentioned in Article 5, para 1, the state of nationality of the detained person and, if it considers it advisable, any other interested state of the fact that such person is in custody and of the circumstances which warrant his detention. The state which makes the preliminary enquiry contemplated in para 2 of this article shall promptly report its findings to the said states and shall indicate whether it intends to exercise jurisdiction.

Article 7

The contracting state in the territory of which the alleged offender is found, if it does not extradite him, shall be obliged, without exception whatsoever and whether or not the offence was committed in its territory, to submit the case to its competent authorities for the purpose of prosecution. Those authorities shall take their decision in the same manner as in the case of any ordinary offence of a serious nature under the law of that state.

Article 8

1 The offence shall be deemed to be included as an extraditable offence in any extradition treaty existing between contracting states. contracting states undertake to include the offence as an extraditable offence in any extradition treaty to be concluded between them.

2 If a contracting state which makes extradition conditional on the existence of a treaty receives a request for extradition from another contracting state with which it has no extradition treaty, it may at its option consider this Convention as the legal basis for extradition in respect of the offence. Extradition shall be subject to the other conditions provided by the law of the requested state.

3 Contracting states which do not make extradition conditional on the existence of a treaty shall recognise the offence between themselves subject to the conditions provided by the law of the requested state.

4 The offence shall be treated, for the purpose of extradition between contracting states, as if it had been committed not only in the place in which it occurred but also in the territories of the states required to establish their jurisdiction in accordance with Article 5, paras 1(b), (c) and (d).

Article 9

The contracting states which establish joint air transport operating organisations or international operating agencies, which operate aircraft which are subject to joint or international registration shall, by appropriate means, designate for each aircraft the state among them which shall exercise the jurisdiction and have the attributes of the state of registration for the purpose of this Convention and shall give notice thereof to the International Civil Aviation Organisation which shall communicate the notice to all State Parties to this Convention.

Article 10

1 Contracting states shall, in accordance with international and national law, endeavour to take all practicable measures for the purpose of preventing the offences mentioned in Article 1.

2 When, due to the commission of one of the offences mentioned in Article 1, a flight has been delayed or interrupted, any contracting state in whose territory the aircraft or passengers or crew are present shall facilitate the continuation of the journey as soon as practicable, and shall without delay return the aircraft and its cargo to the persons lawfully entitled to possession.

Article 11

1 Contracting states shall afford one another the greatest measure of assistance in connection with criminal proceedings brought in respect of the offence and other acts mentioned in Article 4. The law of the state requested shall apply in all cases.

2 The provisions of para 1 of this article shall not affect obligations under any other treaty, bilateral or multilateral, which governs or will govern, in whole or in part, mutual assistance in criminal matters.

Article 12

Any contracting state having reason to believe that one of the offences mentioned in Article 1 will be committed shall, in accordance with its national law, furnish any relevant information in its possession to those states which it believes would be the states mentioned in Article 5, para 1.

Article 13

Each contracting state shall in accordance with its national law report to the Council of the International Civil Aviation Organisation as promptly as possible any relevant information in its possession concerning:

    (a)   the circumstances of the offence;

    (b)   the action taken pursuant to Article 10, para 2;

    (c)   the measures taken in relation to the offender or the alleged offender, and, in particular, the results of any extradition proceedings or other legal proceedings.

Article 14

1   Any dispute between two or more contracting states concerning the interpretation or application of this Convention which cannot be settled through negotiation shall, at the request of one of them, be submitted to arbitration. If within six months from the date of the request for arbitration the Parties are unable to agree on the organisation of the arbitration, any one of those Parties may refer the dispute to the International Court of Justice by request in conformity with the Statute of the Court.

2   Each state may at the time of signature or ratification of this Convention or accession thereto, declare that it does not consider itself bound by the preceding paragraph. The other contracting states shall not be bound by the preceding paragraph with respect to any contracting state having made such a reservation.

3   Any contracting states having made a reservation in accordance with the preceding paragraph may at any time withdraw this reservation by notification to the Depositary Governments.

PROTOCOL OF THE MONTREAL CONVENTION FOR THE SUPPRESSION OF UNLAWFUL ACTS OF VIOLENCE AT AIRPORTS SERVING INTERNATIONAL CIVIL AVIATION 1971

Article I

This Protocol supplements the Convention for the Suppression of Unlawful Acts against the Safety of Civil Aviation, done at Montreal on 23 September 1971 (hereinafter referred to as 'the Convention'), and, as between the parties to this Protocol, the Convention and the Protocol shall be read and interpreted together as one single instrument.

Article II

1   In Article 1 of the Convention, the following shall be added as new para 1 *bis*:

'1 *bis* Any person commits an offence if he unlawfully and internationally, using any device, substance or weapon:

    (a)   performs and act of violence against a person at an airport serving international civil aviation which causes serious injury or death; or

    (b)   destroys or seriously damages the facilities of an airport serving international civil aviation or aircraft not in service located thereon or disrupts the services of the airport, if such an act endangers or is likely to endanger safety at that airport.'

2   In para 2(a) of Article 1 of the Convention, the following words shall be inserted after the words 'para 1': 'or para 1 *bis*'.

One of the problems with the conventions on aviation and airport security is they provide no enforcement measures which can be used against defaulting states. The Bonn Declaration on International Terrorism 1978 which was signed by Canada, France, the Federal Republic of Germany, Italy, Japan, the UK and the US provided that where a state refused to extradite or prosecute those who have hijacked an aircraft, action should be taken to cease all flights to and from that state and all flights by its airlines. The Tokyo, Hague and Montreal Conventions merely provide that in the case of a dispute arising over interpretation and application of the conventions resort should be had to international arbitration and, failing that, the ICJ.

12.5   The liability of airline companies

An issue of major importance as far as air law is concerned relates to the liability of civil airline companies for death or injury suffered by passengers. The Warsaw Convention for the Unification of Certain Rules relating to International Carriage by Air 1929 (Warsaw Convention) as amended at the Hague in 1955 establishes upper limits for liability and deals with issues of responsibility and insurance. Article 20 of the Convention provides that the airline is not liable if it proves that it and its agents have taken all necessary measures to avoid the damage or that it was impossible to take such measures. Article 22 puts a financial ceiling on compensation available, unless it can be proved that the damage resulted from wilful misconduct of the airline in which case liability is unlimited. As far as flights flying into and out of the USA are concerned, the position for passengers is much improved by the Montreal Agreement which was concluded in 1966. But for all other international flights the present law is heavily weighted in favour of the airlines, and this has resulted in passengers suffering loss or injury suing the manufacturers of the aircraft or the maintenance crew rather than going for the airline itself.

It is worth noting that the question of liability for damage caused by aircraft to persons and property on the surface is covered by the Rome Convention 1952 and the Montreal Protocol 1978. It is the aircraft operator, presumed to be the registered owner, who is responsible for damage caused by an aircraft in flight or by any person or thing falling from it. The Convention provides for strict liability but the amount of compensation available in such situations is limited.

12.6   Outer space

New problems of international law have been created by the increase of activity in the upper strata of the atmosphere and beyond. The launching of the first satellite orbiting the earth by the Soviet Union in 1957 heralded the beginning of outer space exploration which has since rapidly expanded with landings on the moon and other planets and the possibility of permanent space stations all giving rise to territorial and jurisdictional problems.

It will be remembered that the traditional view of sovereignty over air space is that it extends above the territory of a state without limit. A strict application of this rule would mean that orbiting satellites would require prior authorisation for flight over the territory of foreign states. This would clearly be impractical and thus it has been accepted that satellites may pass above territory and such overflight does not constitute a violation of air space sovereignty. It follows from this that national sovereignty does cease at some upper limit. Where that limit is remains uncertain but what is clear is that outer space constitutes *res communis* or part of the common heritage of mankind.

In 1958 the UN Committee on the Peaceful Uses of Outer Space was established and it has been responsible for a number of measures adopted regulating outer space activity. All such measures recognise that outer space must be used for peaceful means and is the common heritage of mankind. Treaties governing use of outer space include:

The Treaty on Principles Governing the Activities of states in the Exploration and Use of Outer Space including the Moon and other Celestial Bodies (Space Treaty) which was signed in 1967 and affirms that space shall be the province of all mankind. No area of space may be appropriated by any state and exploration is to be conducted according to international law and the principles of the Charter of the UN. Under the Space Treaty jurisdiction over items launched into space remains with the registering state.

The Space Treaty has been revised and clarified by the Agreement Governing the Activities of states on the Moon and other Celestial Bodies 1979 (Moon Treaty) which provides that the natural resources of the moon and other celestial bodies should be exploited as the common heritage of mankind. The treaty entered into force in 1984.

The Space Treaty has been further supplemented by two further agreements – the Agreement on the Rescue of Astronauts, the Return of Astronauts and the Return of Objects Launched into Space 1968 (Astronauts Treaty) and the Convention on International Liability for Damages Caused by Space Objects 1972 (Liability Convention). The latter convention is concerned with damage caused by space objects on the surface of the earth or to aircraft in flight. There is a strict liability imposed on the launching state. As regards damage caused in outer space fault liability applies. The nature of liability for damage caused by space objects was discussed in the Cosmos 954 Claim (1979) which arose after a Soviet satellite, which had a nuclear reactor, disintegrated through Canadian air space and crashed onto Canadian territory. Canada claimed six million dollars in compensation from the USSR although the dispute was settled by the Soviet Union making an *ex gratia* payment of three million dollars.

The Registration of Objects Launched into Space Convention 1975 provides that every launch of a space craft must be public and its purpose must be registered on a public register maintained by the UN Secretary General. The use of satellite communications is further governed by the various international telecommunications agreements and overseen by a UN Agency, the International Telecommunications Union.

OUTER SPACE

TREATY ON PRINCIPLES GOVERNING THE ACTIVITIES OF STATES IN THE EXPLORATION AND USE OF OUTER SPACE, INCLUDING THE MOON AND OTHER CELESTIAL BODIES 1967[3]

The States Parties to this Treaty,

Inspired by the great prospects opening up before mankind as a result of man's entry into outer space,

Recognising the common interest of all mankind in the progress of the exploration and use of outer space for peaceful purposes,

Believing that the exploration and use of outer space should be carried on for the benefit of all peoples irrespective of the degree of their economic or scientific development,

Desiring to contribute to broad international co-operation in the scientific as well as the legal aspects of the exploration and use of outer space for peaceful purposes,

Believing that such co-operation will contribute to the development of mutual understanding and to the strengthening of friendly relations between states and peoples,

Recalling Resolution 1962 (XVIII), entitled 'Declaration of Legal Principles Governing the Activities of states in the Exploration and Use of Outer Space', which was adopted unanimously by the United Nations General Assembly on 13 December 1963,

Recalling Resolution 1884 (XVIII), calling upon states to refrain from placing in orbit around the earth any objects carrying nuclear weapons or any other kinds of weapons of mass destruction or from installing such weapons on celestial bodies, which was adopted unanimously by the United Nations General Assembly on 17 October 1963,

Taking account of United Nations General Assembly Resolution 110 (II) of 3 November 1947, which condemned propaganda designed or likely to provoke or encourage any threat to the peace, breach of the peace or act of aggression, and considering that the aforementioned Resolution is applicable to outer space,

Convinced that a Treaty on Principles Governing the Activities of States in the Exploration and Use of Outer Space, including the Moon and Other Celestial Bodies, will further the Purposes and Principles of the Charter of the United Nations,

Have agreed on the following:

Article 1

The exploration and use of outer space, including the moon and other celestial bodies, shall be carried out for the benefit and in the interests of all countries, irrespective of their degree of economic or scientific development, and shall be the province of all mankind.

---

3   UKTS 10 (1968) 3519; 610 UNTS 205.

Outer space, including the moon and other celestial bodies, shall be free for exploration and use by all states without discrimination of any kind, on a basis of equality and in accordance with international law, and there shall be free access to all areas of celestial bodies.

There shall be freedom of scientific investigation in outer space, including the moon and other celestial bodies, and states shall facilitate and encourage international co-operation in such investigation.

Article 2

Outer space, including the moon and other celestial bodies, is not subject to national appropriation by claim of sovereignty, by means of use or occupation, or by any other means.

Article 3

States Parties to the Treaty shall carry on activities in the exploration and use of outer space, including the moon and other celestial bodies, in accordance with international law, including the Charter of the United Nations, in the interest of maintain international peace and security and promoting international co-operation and understanding.

Article 4

States Parties to the Treaty undertake not to place in orbit around the Earth any objects carrying nuclear weapons or any other kinds of weapons of mass destruction, install such weapons on celestial bodies, or station such weapons in outer space in any other manner.

The moon and other celestial bodies shall be used by all States Parties to the Treaty exclusively for peaceful purposes. The establishment of military bases, installations and fortifications, the testing of any type of weapons and the conduct of military manoeuvres on celestial bodies shall be forbidden. The use of military personnel for scientific research or for any other peaceful purposes shall not be prohibited. The use of any equipment or facility necessary for peaceful exploration of the moon and other celestial bodies shall also not be prohibited.

Article 5

States Parties to the Treaty shall regard astronauts as envoys of mankind in outer space and shall render to them all possible assistance in the event of accident, distress, or emergency landing on the territory of another State Party or on the high seas. When astronauts make such a landing, they shall be safely and promptly returned to the state of registry of their space vehicle.

In carrying on activities in outer space and on celestial bodies, the astronauts of one State Party shall render all possible assistance to the astronauts of other State Parties.

State Parties to the Treaty shall immediately inform the other States Parties to the Treaty or the Secretary General of the United Nations of any phenomena they discover in outer space, including the moon and other celestial bodies, which could constitute a danger to the life or health of astronauts.

Article 6

States Parties to the Treaty shall bear international responsibility for national activities in outer space, including the moon and other celestial bodies, whether such activities are carried on by governmental agencies or by non-governmental entities, and for assuring that national activities are carried out in conformity with the provisions set forth in the present Treaty. The activities of non-governmental entities in outer space, including the moon and other celestial bodies, shall require authorisation and continuing supervision by the appropriate State Party to the Treaty. When activities are carried on in outer space, including the moon and other celestial bodies, by an international organisation, responsibility for compliance with this Treaty shall be borne both by the international organisation and by the States Parties to the Treaty participating in such organisation.

Article 7

Each State Party to the Treaty that launches or procures the launching of an object into outer space, including the moon and other celestial bodies, and each State Party from whose territory or facility an object is launched, is internationally liable for damage to another State Party to the Treaty or to its natural or judicial persons by such object or its component parts on the Earth, in air space or in outer space, including the moon and other celestial bodies.

Article 8

A State Party to the Treaty on whose registry an object launched into outer space is carried shall retain jurisdiction and control over such object, and over any personnel thereof, while in outer space or on a celestial body. Ownership of objects launched into outer space, including objects landed or constructed on a celestial body, and of their component parts, is not affected by their presence in outer space or on a celestial body or by their return to the Earth. Such objects or component parts found beyond the limits of the State Party to the Treaty on whose registry they are carried shall be returned to that State Party, which shall, upon request, furnish identifying data prior to their return.

Article 9

In the exploration and use of outer space, including the moon and other celestial bodies, State Parties to the Treaty shall be guided by the principle of co-operation and mutual assistance and shall conduct all their activities in outer space, including the moon and other celestial bodies, with due regard to the corresponding interests of all other States Parties to the Treaty. States Parties to the Treaty shall pursue studies of outer space, including the moon and other celestial bodies, and conduct exploration of them so as to avoid heir harmful contamination and also adverse changes in the environment of the Earth resulting from the introduction of extraterrestrial matter and, where necessary, shall adopt appropriate measures for this purpose. If a State Party to the Treaty has reason to believe that an activity or experiment planned by it or its nationals in outer space, including the moon and other celestial bodies, would cause potentially harmful interference with activities of other States Parties in the peaceful exploration and use of outer space, including the moon and other celestial bodies, it shall undertake appropriate international consultations before proceeding with any such activity or experiment. A State Party to the Treaty which has reason to believe that an activity or experiment planned by another State Party in outer space, including the moon and other celestial bodies, would cause potentially harmful interference with activities in the peaceful exploration and use of outer space, including the moon and other celestial bodies, may request consultation concerning the activity or experiment.

Article 10

In order to promote international co-operation in the exploration and use of outer space, including the moon and other celestial bodies, in conformity with the purposes of this Treaty, the States Parties to the Treaty shall consider on a basis of equality any requests by other States Parties to the treaty to be afforded an opportunity to observe the flight of space objects launched by those states.

The nature of such an opportunity for observation and the conditions under which it could be afforded shall be determined by agreement between the states concerned.

Article 11

In order to promote international co-operation in the peaceful exploration of outer space, States Parties to the Treaty conducting activities in outer space, including the moon and other celestial bodies, agree to inform the Secretary General of the United Nations as well as the public and the international scientific community, to the greatest extent feasible and practicable, of the nature, conduct, locations and results of such activities. On receiving the said information, the Secretary General of the United Nations should be prepared to disseminate it immediately and effectively.

Article 12

All stations, installations, equipment and space vehicles on the moon and other celestial bodies shall be open to representatives of other States Parties to the Treaty on a basis of reciprocity. Such representatives shall give reasonable advance notice of a projected visit, in order that appropriate consultations may be held and that maximum precautions may be taken to assure safety and to avoid interference with normal operations in the facility to be visited.

Article 13

The provisions of this Treaty shall apply to the activities of States Parties to the Treaty in the exploration and use of outer space, including the moon and other celestial bodies, whether such activities are carried on by a single State Party to the Treaty or jointly with other states, including cases where they are carried on within the framework of international inter-governmental organisations.

Any practical questions arising in connexion with activities carried on by international inter-governmental organisations in the exploration and use of outer space, including the moon and other celestial bodies, shall be resolved by the States Parties to the Treaty either with the appropriate international organisation or with one or more states members of that international organisation, which are Parties to this Treaty.

Article 14

1   This Treaty shall be open to all states for signature. Any state which does not sign this Treaty before its entry into force in accordance with para 3 of this article may accede to it at any time.

2   This Treaty shall be subject to ratification by signatory states. Instruments of ratification and instruments of accession shall be deposited with the governments of the United Kingdom of Great Britain and Northern Ireland, the Union of Soviet Socialist Republics and the United States of America, which are hereby designated the Depositary Governments.

3   This Treaty shall enter into force upon the deposit of instruments of ratification by five governments including the governments designated as Depositary Governments under this Treaty.

4   For states whose instruments of ratification or accession are deposited subsequent to the entry into force of this Treaty, it shall enter into force on the date of the deposit of their instruments of ratification or accession.

5   The Depositary Governments shall promptly inform all signatory and acceding states of the date of each signature, the date of deposit of each

instrument of ratification of and accession to this Treaty, the date of its entry into force and other notices.

6 This Treaty shall be registered by the Depositary Governments pursuant to Article 102 of the Charter of the United Nations.

Article 15

Any State Party to the Treaty may propose amendments to this Treaty. Amendments shall enter into force for each State Party to the Treaty accepting the amendments upon their acceptance by a majority of the States Parties to the Treaty and thereafter for each remaining State Party to the Treaty on the date of acceptance by it.

Article 16

Any State Party to the Treaty may give notice of its withdrawal from the Treaty one year after its entry into force by written notification to the Depositary Governments. Such withdrawal shall take effect one year from the date of receipt of this notification.

Article 17

This Treaty, of which the English, Russian, French, Spanish and Chinese texts are equally authentic, shall be deposited in the archives of the Depositary Governments. Duly certified copies of this Treaty shall be transmitted by the Depositary Governments to the governments of the signatory and acceding states.

In witness whereof the undersigned, duly authorised, have signed this Treaty.

Done in triplicate, at the cities of London, Moscow and Washington, the twenty-seventh day of January, one thousand nine hundred and sixty-seven.

AGREEMENT ON THE RESCUE OF ASTRONAUTS, THE RETURN OF ASTRONAUTS AND THE RETURN OF OBJECTS LAUNCHED INTO OUTER SPACE (1968)

ENTERED INTO FORCE: 3 December 1968

The Contracting Parties,

Noting the great importance of the Treaty on Principles Governing the Activities of states in the Exploration and Use of Outer Space, including the Moon and Other Celestial Bodies, which calls for the rendering of all possible assistance to astronauts in the event of accident, distress or emergency landing, the prompt and safe return of astronauts, and the return of objects launched into outer space,

Desiring to develop and give further concrete expression to these duties,

Wishing to promote international co-operation in the peaceful exploration and use of outer space,

Prompted by sentiments of humanity,

Have agreed on the following:

Article 1

Each Contracting Party which receives information or discovers that the personnel of a spacecraft have suffered accident or are experiencing conditions of distress or have made an emergency or unintended landing in territory under its jurisdiction or on the high seas or in any other place not under the jurisdiction of any state shall immediately:

(a) notify the launching authority or, if it cannot identify and immediately communicate with the launching authority, immediately make a public announcement by all appropriate means of communication at its disposal;

(b) notify the Secretary General of the United Nations, who should disseminate the information without delay by all appropriate means of communication at his disposal.

Article 2

If, owing to accident, distress, emergency or unintended landing, the personnel of a spacecraft land in territory under the jurisdiction of a Contracting Party, it shall immediately take all possible steps to rescue them and render them all necessary assistance. It shall inform the launching authority and also the Secretary General of the United Nations of the steps it is taking and of their progress. If assistance by the launching authority would help to effect a prompt rescue or would contribute substantially to the effectiveness of search and rescue operations, the launching authority shall co-operate with the Contracting Party with a view to the effective conduct of search and rescue operations. Such operations shall be subject to the direction and control of the Contracting Party, which shall act in close and continuing consultation with the launching authority.

Article 3

If information is received or it is discovered that the personnel of a spacecraft have alighted on the high seas or in any other place not under the jurisdiction of any state, those Contracting Parties which are in a position to do so shall, if necessary, extend assistance in search and rescue operations for such personnel to assure their speedy rescue. They shall inform the launching authority and the Secretary General of the United Nations of the steps they are taking and of their progress.

Article 4

If, owing to accident, distress, emergency or unintended landing, the personnel of a spacecraft land in territory under the jurisdiction of a Contracting Party or have been found on the high seas or in any other place not under the jurisdiction of any state, they shall be safely and promptly returned to representatives of the launching authority.

Article 5

1   Each Contracting Party which receives information or discovers that a space object or its component parts has returned to Earth in territory under its jurisdiction or on the high seas or in any other place not under the jurisdiction of any state, shall notify the launching authority and the Secretary General of the United Nations.

2   Each Contracting Party having jurisdiction over the territory on which a space object or its component parts has been discovered shall, upon the request of the launching authority and with assistance from that authority if requested, take such steps as it finds practicable to recover the object or component parts.

3   Upon request of the launching authority, objects launched into outer space or their component parts found beyond the territorial limits of the launching authority shall be returned to or held at the disposal of representatives of the

launching authority, which shall, upon request, furnish identifying data prior to their return.

4   Notwithstanding paras 2 and 3 of this article, a Contracting Party which has reason to believe that a space object or its component elsewhere, is of a hazardous or deleterious nature may so notify the launching authority, which shall immediately take effective steps, under the direction and control of the said Contracting Party, to eliminate possible danger of harm.

5   Expenses incurred in fulfilling obligations to recover and return a space object or its component parts under paras 2 and 3 of this article shall be borne by the launching authority.

Article 6

For the purposes of this Agreement, the term 'launching authority' shall refer to the state responsible for launching, or, where an international intergovernmental organisation is responsible for launching, that organisation, provided that that organisation declares its acceptance of the rights and obligations provided for in this Agreement and a majority of the states members of that organisation are Contracting Parties to this Agreement and to the Treaty on Principles Governing the Activities of states in the Exploration and Use of Outer Space, including the Moon and Other Celestial Bodies.

Article 7

1   This Agreement shall be open to all states for signature. Any state which does not sign this Agreement before its entry into force in accordance with para 3 of this Article may accede to it at any time.

2   This Agreement shall be subject to ratification by signatory states. Instruments of ratification and instruments of accession shall be deposited with the governments of the United Kingdom of Great Britain and Northern Ireland, the Union of Soviet Socialist Republics and the United States of America, which are hereby designated the Depositary Governments.

3   This Agreement shall enter into force upon the deposit of instruments of ratification by five governments including the governments designated as Depositary Governments under this Agreement.

4   For states whose instruments of ratification or accession are deposited subsequent to the entry into force of this Agreement, it shall enter into force on the date of the deposit of their instruments of ratification or accession.

5   The Depositary Governments shall promptly inform all signatory and acceding states of the date of each signature, the date of deposit of each instrument of ratification of and accession to this Agreement, the date of its entry into force and other notices.

6   This Agreement shall be registered by the Depositary Governments pursuant to Article 102 of the Charter of the United Nations.

Article 8

Any State Party to the Agreement may propose amendments to this Agreement. Amendments shall enter into force for each State Party to the Agreement accepting the amendments upon their acceptance by a majority of the States Parties to the Agreement and thereafter for each remaining State Party to the Agreement on the date of acceptance by it.

Article 9

Any State Party to the Agreement may give notice of its withdrawal from the Agreement one year after its entry into force by written notification to the

Depositary Governments. Such withdrawal shall take effect one year from the date of receipt of this notification.

Article 10

This Agreement, of which the English, Russian, French, Spanish and Chinese texts are equally authentic, shall be deposited in the archives of the Depositary Governments. Duly certified copies of this Agreement shall be transmitted by the Depositary Governments to the governments of the signatory and acceding states.

In witness whereof the undersigned, duly authorised, have signed this Agreement.

Done in triplicate, at the cities of London, Moscow and Washington, the twenty-second day of April, one thousand nine hundred and sixty-eight.

AGREEMENT GOVERNING THE ACTIVITIES OF STATES ON THE MOON AND OTHER CELESTIAL BODIES (1979)

ENTERED INTO FORCE: 11 July 1984

The States Parties to this Agreement,

Noting the achievements of states in the exploration and use of the moon and other celestial bodies,

Recognising that the moon, as a natural satellite of the earth, has an important role to play in the exploration of outer space,

Determined to promote on the basis of equality the further development of co-operation among states in the exploration and use of the moon and other celestial bodies,

Desiring to prevent the moon from becoming an area of international conflict,

Bearing in mind the benefits which may be derived from the exploitation of the natural resources of the moon and other celestial bodies,

Recalling the Treaty on Principles Governing the Activities of States in the Exploration and Use of Outer Space, including the Moon and Other Celestial Bodies, the Agreement on the Rescue of Astronauts, the Return of Astronauts and the Return of Objects Launched into Outer Space, the Convention on International Liability for Damage Caused by Space Objects, and the Convention on Registration of Objects Launched into Outer Space,

Taking into account the need to define and develop the provisions of these international instruments in relation to the moon and other celestial bodies, having regard to further progress in the exploration and use of outer space,

Have agreed on the following:

Article 1

1   The provisions of this Agreement relating to the moon shall also apply to other celestial bodies within the solar system, other than the earth, except in so far as specific legal norms enter into force with respect to any of these celestial bodies.

2   For the purposes of this Agreement reference to the moon shall include orbits around or other trajectories to or around it.

3   This Agreement does not apply to extraterrestrial materials which reach the surface of the earth by natural means.

Article 2

All activities on the moon, including its exploration and use, shall be carried out in accordance with international law, in particular the Charter of the United Nations, and taking into account the Declaration on Principles of International Law concerning Friendly Relations and Co-operation Among states in accordance with the Charter of the United Nations, adopted by the General Assembly on 24 October 1970, in the interests of maintaining international peace and security and promoting international co-operation and mutual understanding, and with due regard to the corresponding interests of all other States Parties.

Article 3

1   The moon shall be used by all States Parties exclusively for peaceful purposes.

2   Any threat or use of force or any other hostile act or threat of hostile act on the moon is prohibited. It is likewise prohibited to use the moon in order to commit any such act or to engage in any such threat in relation to the earth, the moon, spacecraft, the personnel of spacecraft or man-made space objects.

3   States Parties shall not place in orbit around or other trajectory to or around the moon objects carrying nuclear weapons or any other kinds of weapons of mass destruction or place or use such weapons on or in the moon.

4   The establishment of military bases, installations and fortifications, the testing of any type of weapons and the conduct of military manoeuvres on the moon shall be forbidden. The use of military personnel for scientific research or for any other peaceful purposes shall not be prohibited. The use of any equipment or facility necessary for peaceful exploration and use of the moon shall also not be prohibited.

Article 4

1   The exploration and use of the moon shall be the province of all mankind and shall be carried out for the benefit and in the interests of all countries, irrespective of their degree of economic or scientific development. Due regard shall be paid to the interests of present and future generations as well as to the need to promote higher standards of living and conditions of economic and social progress and development in accordance with the Charter of the United Nations.

2   States Parties shall be guided by the principle of co-operation and mutual assistance in all their activities concerning the exploration and use of the moon. International co-operation in pursuance of this Agreement should be as wide as possible and may take place on a multilateral basis, on a bilateral basis or through international intergovernmental organisations.

Article 5

1   States Parties shall inform the Secretary General of the United Nations as well as the public and the international scientific community, to the greatest extent feasible and practicable, of their activities concerned with the exploration and use of the moon. Information on the time, purposes, locations, orbital parameters and duration shall be given in respect of each mission to the moon as soon as possible after launching, while information on the results of each mission, including scientific results, shall be furnished upon completion of the mission. In the case of a mission lasting more than thirty days, information on conduct of the mission, including any scientific results, shall be given periodically at thirty days' intervals. For missions lasting more than

six months, only significant additions to such information need be reported thereafter.

2   If a State Party becomes aware that another State Party plans to operate simultaneously in the same area of or in the same orbit around or trajectory to or around the moon, it shall promptly inform the other state of the timing of and plans for its own operations.

3   In carrying out activities under this Agreement, States Parties shall promptly inform the Secretary General, as well as the public and the international scientific community, of any phenomena they discover in outer space, including the moon, which could endanger human life or health, as well as of any indication of organic life.

Article 6

1   There shall be freedom of scientific investigation on the moon by all States Parties without discrimination of any kind, on the basis of equality and in accordance with international law.

2   In carrying out scientific investigations and in furtherance of the provisions of this Agreement, the States Parties shall have the right to collect on and remove from the moon samples of its mineral and other substances. Such samples shall remain at the disposal of those States Parties which caused them to be collected and may be used by them for scientific purposes. States Parties shall have regard to the desirability of making a portion of such samples available to other interested States Parties and the international scientific community for scientific investigation. States Parties may in the course of scientific investigations also use mineral and other substances of the moon in quantities appropriate for the support of their missions.

3   States Parties agree on the desirability of exchanging scientific and other personnel on expeditions to or installations on the moon to the greatest extent feasible and practicable.

Article 7

1   In exploring and using the moon, States Parties shall take measures to prevent the disruption of the existing balance of its environment whether by introducing adverse changes in that environment, by its harmful contamination through the introduction of extra-environmental matter or otherwise. States Parties shall also take measures to avoid harmfully affecting the environment of the earth through the introduction of extraterrestrial matter or otherwise.

2   States Parties shall inform the Secretary General of the United Nations of the measures being adopted by them in accordance with para 1 of this article and shall also, to the maximum extent feasible, notify him in advance of all placements by them of radio-active materials on the moon and of the purposes of such placements.

3   States Parties shall report to other States Parties and to the Secretary General concerning areas of the moon having special scientific interest in order that, without prejudice to the rights of other States Parties, consideration may be given to the designation of such areas as international scientific preserves for which special protective arrangements are to be agreed upon in consultation with the competent bodies of the United Nations.

Article 8

1   States Parties may pursue their activities in the exploration and use of the moon anywhere on or below its surface, subject to the provisions of this Agreement.

2   For these purposes States Parties may, in particular:

(a)   land their space objects on the moon and launch them from the moon;

(b)   place their personnel, space vehicles, equipment, facilities, and installations anywhere on or below the surface of the moon.

Personnel, space vehicles, equipment, facilities, stations and installations may move or be moved freely over or below the surface of the moon.

3   Activities of States Parties in accordance with paras 1 and 2 of this article shall not interfere with the activities of other States Parties on the moon. Where such interference may occur, the States Parties concerned shall undertake consultations in accordance with Article 15, paras 2 and 3 of this Agreement.

Article 9

1   States Parties may establish manned and unmanned stations on the moon. A State Party establishing a station shall use only that area which is required for the needs of the station and shall immediately inform the Secretary General of the United Nations of the location and purposes of that station. Subsequently, at annual intervals that state shall likewise inform the Secretary General whether the station continues in use and whether its purposes have changed.

2   Stations shall be installed in such a manner that they do not impede the free access to all areas of the moon by personnel, vehicles and equipment of other States Parties conducting activities on the moon in accordance with the provisions of this Agreement or of Article I of the Treaty on Principles Governing the Activities of states in the Exploration and Use of Outer Space, including the Moon and Other Celestial Bodies.

Article 10

1   States Parties shall adopt all practicable measures to safeguard the life and health of persons on the moon. For this purpose they shall regard any person on the moon as an astronaut within the meaning of Article V of the Treaty on Principles Governing the Activities of states in the Exploration and Use of Outer Space, including the Moon and Other Celestial Bodies and as part of the personnel of a spacecraft within the meaning of the Agreement on the Rescue of Astronauts, the Return of Astronauts and the Return of Objects Launched into Outer Space.

2   States Parties shall offer shelter in their stations, installations, vehicles and other facilities to persons in distress on the moon.

Article 11

1   The moon and its natural resources are the common heritage of mankind, which finds its expression in the provisions of this Agreement and in particular in para 5 or this article.

2   The moon is not subject to national appropriation by any claim of sovereignty, by means of use or occupation, or by any other means.

3   Neither the surface nor the subsurface of the moon, nor any part thereof or natural resources in place, shall become property of any state, international intergovernmental or non-governmental organisation, national organisation or non-governmental entity or of any natural person. The placement of personnel, space vehicles, equipment, facilities, stations and installations on or below the surface of the moon, including structures connected with its surface or subsurface, shall not create a right of ownership over the surface or the subsurface of the moon or any areas thereof. The foregoing provisions are without prejudice to the international regime referred to in para 5 of this article.

4   States Parties have the right to exploration and use of the moon without discrimination of any kind, on a basis of equality and in accordance with international law and the terms of this Agreement.

5   States Parties to this Agreement hereby undertake to establish an international regime, including appropriate procedures, to govern the exploitation of the natural resources of the moon as such exploitation is about to become feasible. This provision shall be implemented in accordance with Article 18 of this Agreement.

6   In order to facilitate the establishment of the international regime referred to in para 5 of this article, States Parties shall inform the Secretary General of the United Nations as well as the public and the international scientific community, to the greatest extent feasible and practicable, of any natural resources they may discover on the moon.

7   The main purposes of the international regime to be established shall include:

(a) the orderly and safe development of the natural resources of the moon;

(b) the rational management of those resources;

(c) the expansion of opportunities in the use of those resources;

(d) an equitable sharing by all States Parties in the benefits derived from those resources, whereby the interests and needs of the developing countries, as well as the efforts of those countries which have contributed either directly or indirectly to the exploration of the moon, shall be given special consideration.

8   All the activities with respect to the natural resources of the moon shall be carried out in a manner compatible with the purposes specified in para 7 of this article and the provisions of Article 6, para 2, of this Agreement.

Article 12

1   States Parties shall retain jurisdiction and control over their personnel, vehicles, equipment, facilities, stations and installations on the moon. The ownership of space vehicles, equipment, facilities, stations and installations shall not be affected by their presence on the moon.

2   Vehicles, installations and equipment or their component parts found in places other than their intended location shall be dealt with in accordance with Article 5 of the Agreement on Rescue of Astronauts, the Return of Astronauts and the Return of Objects Launched into Outer Space.

3   In the event of an emergency involving a threat to human life, States Parties may use the equipment, vehicles, installations, facilities or supplies of other States Parties on the moon. Prompt notification of such use shall be made to the Secretary General of the United Nations or the State Party concerned.

Article 13

A State Party which learns of the crash landing, forced landing or other unintended landing on the moon of a space object, or its component parts, that were not launched by it, shall promptly inform the launching State Party and the Secretary General of the United Nations.

Article 14

1   States Parties to this Agreement shall bear international responsibility for national activities on the moon, whether such activities are carried on by governmental agencies or by non-governmental entities, and for assuring that national activities are carried out in conformity with the provisions set forth in this Agreement. States Parties shall ensure that non-governmental entities under their jurisdiction shall engage in activities on the moon only under the authority and continuing supervision of the appropriate State Party.

2   States Parties recognise that detailed arrangements concerning liability for damage caused on the moon, in addition to the provisions of the Treaty on Principles Governing the Activities of states in the Exploration and Use of Outer Space, including the Moon and Other Celestial Bodies and the Convention on International Liability for Damage Caused by Space Objects, may become necessary as a result of more extensive activities on the moon. Any such arrangements shall be elaborated in accordance with the procedure provided for in Article 18 of this Agreement.

Article 15

1   Each State Party may assure itself that the activities of other States Parties in the exploration and use of the moon are compatible with the provisions of this Agreement. To this end, all space vehicles, equipment, facilities, stations and installations on the moon shall be open to other States Parties. Such States Parties shall give reasonable advance notice of a projected visit, in order that appropriate consultations may be held and that maximum precautions may be taken to assure safety and to avoid interference with normal operations in the facility to be visited. In pursuance of this article, any State Party may act on its own behalf or with the full or partial assistance of any other State Party or through appropriate international procedures within the framework of the United Nations and in accordance with the Charter.

2   A State Party which has reason to believe that another State Party is not fulfilling the obligations incumbent upon it pursuant to this Agreement or that another State Party is interfering with the rights which the former state has under this Agreement may request consultations with that State Party. A State Party receiving such a request shall enter into such consultations without delay. Any other State Party which requests to do so shall be entitled to take part in the consultations. Each State Party participating in such consultations shall seek a mutually acceptable resolution of any controversy and shall bear in mind the rights and interests of all States Parties. The Secretary General of the United Nations shall be informed of the results of the consultations and shall transmit the information received to all States Parties concerned.

3   If the consultations do not lead to a mutually acceptable settlement which has due regard for the rights and interests of all States Parties, the parties concerned shall take all measures to settle the dispute by other peaceful means of their choice appropriate to the circumstances and the nature of the dispute. If difficulties arise in connexion with the opening of consultations or if consultations do not lead to a mutually acceptable settlement, any State

Party may seek the assistance of the Secretary General, without seeking the consent of any other State Party concerned, in order to resolve the controversy. A State Party which does not maintain diplomatic relations with another State Party concerned shall participate in such consultations, at its choice, either itself or through another State Party or the Secretary General as intermediary.

Article 16

With the exception of Articles 17 to 21, references in this Agreement to states shall be deemed to apply to any international intergovernmental organisation which conducts space activities if the organisation declares its acceptance of the rights and obligations provided for in this Agreement and if a majority of the states members of the organisation are States Parties to this Agreement and to the Treaty on Principles Governing the Activities of states in the Exploration and Use of Outer Space, including the Moon and Other Celestial Bodies. states members of any such organisation which are States Parties to this Agreement shall take all appropriate steps to ensure that the organisation makes a declaration in accordance with the foregoing.

Article 17

Any State Party to this Agreement may propose amendments to the Agreement. Amendments shall enter into force for each State Party to the Agreement accepting the amendments upon their acceptance by a majority of the States Parties to the Agreement and thereafter for each remaining State Party to the Agreement on the date of acceptance by it.

Article 18

Ten years after the entry into force of this Agreement, the question of the review of the Agreement shall be included in the provisional agenda of the General Assembly of the United Nations in order to consider, in the light of past application of the Agreement, whether it requires revision. However, at any time after the Agreement has been in force for five years, the Secretary General of the United Nations, as depository, shall, at the request of one third of the States Parties to the Agreement and with the concurrence of the majority of the States Parties, convene a conference of the States Parties to review this Agreement. A review conference shall also consider the question of the implementation of the provisions of Article 11, para 5, on the basis of the principle referred to in para 1 of that article and taking into account in particular any relevant technological developments.

Article 19

1   This Agreement shall be open for signature by all states at United Nations Headquarters in New York.

2   This Agreement shall be subject to ratification by signatory states. Any state which does not sign this Agreement before its entry into force in accordance with para 3 of this article may accede to it at any time. Instruments of ratification or accession shall be deposited with the Secretary General of the United Nations.

3   This Agreement shall enter into force on the thirtieth day following the date of deposit of the fifth instrument of ratification.

4   For each state depositing its instrument of ratification or accession after the entry into force of this Agreement, it shall enter into force on the thirtieth day following the date of deposit of any such instrument.

5   The Secretary General shall promptly inform all signatory and acceding states of the date of each signature, the date of deposit of each instrument of ratification or accession to this Agreement, the date of its entry into force and other notices.

Article 20

Any State Party to this Agreement may give notice of its withdrawal from the Agreement one year after its entry into force by written notification to the Secretary General of the United Nations. Such withdrawal shall take effect one year from the date of receipt of this notification.

Article 21

The original of this Agreement, of which the Arabic, Chinese, English, French, Russian and Spanish texts are equally authentic, shall be deposited with the Secretary General of the United Nations, who shall send certified copies thereof to all signatory and acceding states.

In witness whereof the undersigned, being duly authorised thereto by their respective governments, have signed this Agreement, opened for signature at New York on 18 December 1979.

CONVENTION ON REGISTRATION OF OBJECTS LAUNCHED INTO OUTER SPACE (1975)

The States Parties to this Convention,

Recognising the common interest of all mankind in furthering the exploration and use of outer space for peaceful purposes,

Recalling that the Treaty on Principles Governing the Activities of States in the Exploration and Use of Outer Space, including the Moon and Other Celestial Bodies of 27 January 1967 affirms that states shall bear international responsibility for their national activities in outer space and refers to the state on whose registry an object launched into outer space is carried,

Recalling also that the Agreement on the Rescue of Astronauts, the Return of Astronauts and the Return of Objects Launched into Outer Space of 22 April 1968 provides that a launching authority shall, upon request, furnish identifying data prior to the return of an object it has launched into outer space found beyond the territorial limits of the launching authority,

Recalling further that the Convention on International Liability for Damage Caused by Space Objects of 29 March 1972 establishes international rules and procedures concerning the liability of launching states for damage caused by their space objects,

Desiring, in the light of the Treaty on Principles Governing the Activities of States in the Exploration and Use of Outer Space, including the Moon and Other Celestial Bodies, to make provision for the national registration by launching states of space objects launched into outer space,

Desiring further that a central register of objects launched into outer space be established and maintained, on a mandatory basis, by the Secretary General of the United Nations,

Desiring also to provide for States Parties additional means and procedures to assist in the identification of space objects,

Believing that a mandatory system of registering objects launched into outer space would, in particular, assist in their identification and would contribute to the application and development of international law governing the exploration and use of outer space,

Have agreed on the following:

Article I

For the purposes of this Convention:

(a) The term 'launching state' means:

(i) a state which launches or procures the launching of a space object;

(ii) a state from whose territory or facility a space object is launched;

(b) The term 'space object' includes component parts of a space object as well as its launch vehicle and parts thereof;

(c) The term 'state of registry' means a launching state on whose registry a space object is carried in accordance with Article II.

Article II

1 When a space object is launched into earth orbit or beyond, the launching state shall register the space object by means of an entry in an appropriate registry which it shall maintain. Each launching state shall inform the Secretary General of the United Nations of the establishment of such a registry.

2 Where there are two or more launching states in respect of any such space object, they shall jointly determine which one of them shall register the object in accordance with para 1 of this article, bearing in mind the provisions of Article VIII of the Treaty on principles governing the activities of states in the exploration and use of outer space, including the moon and other celestial bodies, and without prejudice to appropriate agreements concluded or to be concluded among the launching states on jurisdiction and control over the space object and over any personnel thereof.

3 The contents of each registry and the conditions under which it is maintained shall be determined by the state of registry concerned.

Article III

1 The Secretary General of the United Nations shall maintain a Register in which the information furnished in accordance with Article IV shall be recorded.

2 There shall be full and open access to the information in this Register.

...

CONVENTION ON INTERNATIONAL LIABILITY FOR DAMAGE CAUSED BY SPACE OBJECTS (1972)

ENTERED INTO FORCE: 1 September 1972

The States Parties to this Convention,

Recognising the common interest of all mankind in furthering the exploration and use of outer space for peaceful purposes,

Recalling the Treaty on Principles Governing the Activities of States in the Exploration and Use of Outer Space, including the Moon and Other Celestial Bodies,

Taking into consideration that, notwithstanding the precautionary measures to be taken by states and international intergovernmental organisations involved in the launching of space objects, damage may on occasion be caused by such objects,

Recognising the need to elaborate effective international rules and procedures concerning liability for damage caused by space objects and to ensure, in particular, the prompt payment under the terms of this Convention of a full and equitable measure of compensation to victims of such damage,

Believing that the establishment of such rules and procedures will contribute to the strengthening of international co-operation in the field of the exploration and use of outer space for peaceful purposes,

Have agreed on the following:

Article I

For the purposes of this Convention:

(a) The term 'damage' means loss of life, personal injury or other impairment of health; or loss of or damage to property of states or of persons, natural or juridical, or property of international intergovernmental organisations;

(b) The term 'launching' includes attempted launching;

(c) The term 'launching state' means:

  (i) a state which launches or procures the launching of a space object;

  (ii) a state from whose territory or facility a space object is launched;

(d) The term 'space object' includes component parts of a space object as well as its launch vehicle and parts thereof.

Article II

A launching state shall be absolutely liable to pay compensation for damage caused by its space object on the surface of the earth or to aircraft in flight.

Article III

In the event of damage being caused elsewhere than on the surface of the earth to a space object of one launching state or to persons or property on board such a space object by a space object of another launching state, the latter shall be liable only if the damage is due to its fault or the fault of persons for whom it is responsible.

Article IV

1 In the event of damage being caused elsewhere than on the surface of the earth to a space object of one launching state or to persons or property on board such a space object by a space object of another launching state, and of damage thereby being caused to a third state or to its natural or juridical persons, the first two states shall be jointly and severally liable to the third state, to the extent indicated by the following:

  (a) if the damage has been caused to the third state on the surface of the earth or to aircraft in flight, their liability to the third state shall be absolute;

  (b) if the damage has been caused to a space object of the third state or to persons or property on board that space object elsewhere than on the surface of the earth, their liability to the third state shall be based on the fault of either of the first two states or on the fault of persons for whom either is responsible.

2   In all cases of joint and several liability referred to in para 1 of this Article, the burden of compensation for the damage shall be apportioned between the first two states in accordance with the extent to which they were at fault; if the extent of the fault of each of these states cannot be established, the burden of compensation shall be apportioned equally between them. Such apportionment shall be without prejudice to the right of the third state to seek the entire compensation due under this Convention from any or all of the launching states which are jointly and severally liable.

Article V

1   Whenever two or more states jointly launch a space object, they shall be jointly and severally liable for any damage caused.

2   A launching state which has paid compensation for damage shall have the right to present a claim for indemnification to other participants in the joint launching. The participants in a joint launching may conclude agreements regarding the apportioning among themselves of the financial obligation in respect of which they are jointly and severally liable. Such agreements shall be without prejudice to the right of a state sustaining damage to seek the entire compensation due under this Convention from any or all of the launching states which are jointly and severally liable.

3   A state from whose territory or facility a space object is launched shall be regarded as a participant in a joint launching.

Article VI

1   Subject to the provisions of para 2 of this Article, exoneration from absolute liability shall be granted to the extent that a launching state establishes that the damage has resulted either wholly or partially from gross negligence or from an act or omission done with intent to cause damage on the part of a claimant state or of natural or juridical persons it represents.

2   No exoneration whatever shall be granted in cases where the damage has resulted from activities conducted by a launching state which are not in conformity with international law including, in particular, the Charter of the United Nations and the Treaty on Principles Governing the Activities of States in the Exploration and Use of Outer Space, including the Moon and Other Celestial Bodies.

Article VII

The provisions of this Convention shall not apply to damage caused by a space object of a launching state to:

(a)   nationals of that launching state;

(b)   foreign nationals during such time as they are participating in the operation of that space object from the time of its launching or at any stage thereafter until its descent, or during such time as they are in the immediate vicinity of a planned launching or recovery area as the result of an invitation by that launching state.

Article VIII

1   A state which suffers damage, or whose natural or juridical persons suffer damage, may present to a launching state a claim for compensation for such damage.

2   If the state of nationality has not presented a claim, another state may, in respect of damage sustained in its territory by any natural or juridical person, present a claim to a launching state.

3   If neither the state of nationality nor the state in whose territory the damage was sustained has presented a claim or notified its intention of presenting a claim, another state may, in respect of damage sustained by its permanent residents, present a claim to a launching state.

Article IX

A claim for compensation for damage shall be presented to a launching state through diplomatic channels. If a state does not maintain diplomatic relations with the launching state concerned, it may request another state to present its claim to that launching state or otherwise represent its interests under this Convention. It may also present its claim through the Secretary General of the United Nations, provided the claimant state and the launching state are both Members of the United Nations.

Article X

1   A claim for compensation for damage may be presented to a launching state not later than one year following the date of the occurrence of the damage or the identification of the launching state which is liable.

2   If, however, a state does not know of the occurrence of the damage or has not been able to identify the launching state which is liable, it may present a claim within one year following the date on which it learned of the aforementioned facts; however, this period shall in no event exceed one year following the date on which the state could reasonably be expected to have learned of the facts through the exercise of due diligence.

3   The time-limits specified in paras 1 and 2 of this article shall apply even if the full extent of the damage may not be known. In this event, however, the claimant state shall be entitled to revise the claim and submit additional documentation after the expiration of such time limits until one year after the full extent of the damage is known.

Article XI

1   Presentation of a claim to a launching state for compensation for damage under this Convention shall not require the prior exhaustion of any local remedies which may be available to a claimant state or to natural or juridical persons it represents.

2   Nothing in this Convention shall prevent a state, or natural or juridical persons it might represent, from pursuing a claim in the courts or administrative tribunals or agencies of a launching state. A state shall not, however, be entitled to present a claim under this Convention in respect of the same damage for which a claim is being pursued in the courts or administrative tribunals or agencies of a launching state or under another international agreement which is binding on the states concerned.

Article XII

The compensation which the launching state shall be liable to pay for damage under this Convention shall be determined in accordance with international law and the principles of justice and equity, in order to provide such reparation in respect of the damage as will restore the person, natural or juridical, state or international organisation on whose behalf the claim is presented to the condition which would have existed if the damage had not occurred.

Article XIII

Unless the claimant state and the state from which compensation is due under this Convention agree on another form of compensation, the compensation shall be paid in the currency of the claimant state or, if that state so requests, in the currency of the state from which compensation is due.

Article XIV

If no settlement of a claim is arrived at through diplomatic negotiations as provided for in Article IX, within one year from the date on which the claimant state notifies the launching state that it has submitted the documentation of its claim, the parties concerned shall establish a Claims Commission at the request of either party.

Article XV

1   The Claims Commission shall be composed of three members: one appointed by the claimant state, one appointed by the launching state and the third member, the Chairman, to be chosen by both parties jointly. Each party shall make its appointment within two months of the request for the establishment of the Claims Commission.

2   If no agreement is reached on the choice of the Chairman within four months of the request for the establishment of the Commission, either party may request the Secretary General of the United Nations to appoint the Chairman within a further period of two months.

Article XVI

1   If one of the parties does not make its appointment within the stipulated period, the Chairman shall, at the request of the other party, constitute a single-member Claims Commission.

2   Any vacancy which may arise in the Commission for whatever reason shall be filled by the same procedure adopted for the original appointment.

3   The Commission shall determine its own procedure.

4   The Commission shall determine the place or places where it shall sit and all other administrative matters.

5   Except in the case of decisions and awards by a single-member Commission, all decision and awards of the Commission shall be by majority vote.

Article XVII

No increase in the membership of the Claims Commission shall take place by reason of two or more claimant states or launching states being joined in any one proceeding before the Commission. The claimant states so joined shall collectively appoint one member of the Commission in the same manner and subject to the same conditions as would be the case for a single claimant state. When two or more launching states are so joined, they shall collectively appoint one member of the Commission in the same way. If the claimant states or the launching states do not make the appointment within the stipulated period, the Chairman shall constitute a single-member Commission.

Article XVIII

The Claims Commission shall decide the merits of the claim for compensation and determine the amount of compensation payable, if any.

Article XIX

1   The Claims Commission shall act in accordance with the provisions of Article XII.

2   The decision of the Commission shall be final and binding if the parties have so agreed; otherwise the Commission shall render a final and

recommendatory award, which the parties shall consider in good faith. The Commission shall state the reasons for its decision or award.

3   The Commission shall give its decision or award as promptly as possible and no later than one year from the date of its establishment, unless an extension of this period is found necessary by the Commission.

4   The Commission shall make its decision or award public. It shall deliver a certified copy of its decision or award to each of the parties and to the Secretary General of the United Nations.

Article XX

The expenses in regard to the Claims Commission shall be borne equally by the parties, unless otherwise decided by the Commission.

Article XXI

If the damage caused by a space object presents a large-scale danger to human life or seriously interferes with the living conditions of the population or the functioning of vital centres, the States Parties, and in particular the launching state, shall examine the possibility of rendering appropriate and rapid assistance to the state which has suffered the damage, when it so requests. However, nothing in this article shall affect the rights or obligations of the States Parties under this Convention.

Article XXII

1   In this Convention, with the exception of Articles XXIV to XXVII, references to states shall be deemed to apply to any international intergovernmental organisation which conducts space activities if the organisation declares its acceptance of the rights and obligations provided for in this Convention and if a majority of the states members of the organisation are State Parties to this Convention and to the Treaty on Principles Governing the Activities of States in the Exploration and Use of Outer Space, including the Moon and Other Celestial Bodies.

2   States Members of any such organisation which are States Parties to this Convention shall take all appropriate steps to ensure that the organisation makes a declaration in accordance with the preceding paragraph.

3   If an international intergovernmental organisation is liable for damage by virtue of the provisions of this Convention, that organisation and those of its members which are States Parties to this Convention shall be jointly and severally liable; provided, however, that:

(a)   any claim for compensation in respect of such damage shall be first presented to the organisation;

(b)   only where the organisation has not paid, within a period of six months, any sum agreed or determined to be due as compensation for such damage, may the claimant state invoke the liability of the members which are States Parties to this Convention for the payment of that sum.

4   Any claim, pursuant to the provisions of this Convention, for compensation in respect of damage caused to an organisation which has made a declaration in accordance with para 1 of this Article shall be presented by a state member of the organisation which is a State Party to this Convention.

Article XXIII

1   The provisions of this Convention shall not affect other international agreements in force in so far as relations between the States Parties to such agreements are concerned.

2   No provision of this Convention shall prevent states from concluding international agreements reaffirming, supplementing or extending its provisions.

Article XXIV

1   This Convention shall be open to all states for signature. Any state which does not sign this Convention before its entry into force in accordance with para 3 of this article may accede to it at any time.

2   This Convention shall be subject to ratification by signatory states. Instruments of ratification and instruments of accession shall be deposited with the governments of the United Kingdom of Great Britain and Northern Ireland, the Union of Soviet Socialist Republics and the United States of America, which are hereby designated the Depositary Governments.

3.   This Convention shall enter into force on the deposit of the fifth instrument of ratification.

4   For states whose instruments of ratification or accession are deposited subsequent to the entry into force of this Convention, it shall enter into force on the date of the deposit of their instruments of ratification or accession.

5   The Depositary Governments shall promptly inform all signatory and acceding states of the date of each signature, the date of deposit of each instrument of ratification of and accession to this Convention, the date of its entry into force and other notices.

6   This Convention shall be registered by the Depositary Governments pursuant to Article 102 of the Charter of the United Nations.

Article XXV

Any State Party to this Convention may propose amendments to this Convention. Amendments shall enter into force for each State Party to the Convention accepting the amendments upon their acceptance by a majority of the States Parties to the Convention and thereafter for each remaining State Party on the date of acceptance by it.

Article XXVI

Ten years after the entry into force of this Convention, the question of the review of this Convention shall be included in the provisional agenda of the United Nations General Assembly in order to consider, in the light of past application of the Convention, whether it requires revision. However, at any time after the Convention has been in force for five years, and at the request of one third of the States Parties to the Convention, and with the concurrence of the majority of the States Parties, a conference of the States Parties shall be convened to review this Convention.

Article XXVII

Any State Party to this Convention may give notice of its withdrawal from the Convention one year after its entry into force by written notification to the Depositary Governments. Such withdrawal shall take effect one year from the date of receipt of this notification.

Article XXVIII

This Convention, of which the English, Russian, French, Spanish and Chinese texts are equally authentic, shall be deposited in the archives of the Depositary Governments. Duly certified copies of this Convention shall be transmitted by the Depositary Governments to the governments of the signatory and acceding states.

In witness whereof the undersigned, duly authorised thereto, have signed this Convention.

Done in triplicate, at the cities of London, Moscow and Washington, this twenty-ninth day of March, one thousand nine hundred and seventy-two.

CHAPTER 13

THE PEACEFUL SETTLEMENT OF DISPUTES

13.1 Introduction

I. PRINCIPLE OF THE PEACEFUL SETTLEMENT OF DISPUTES BETWEEN STATES

A   Charter of the United Nations

1   The Charter of the United Nations provides in its Chapter I (Purposes and Principles) that the Purposes of the United Nations are:

> To maintain international peace and security, and to that end, to take effective collective measures for the prevention and removal of threats to the peace, and for the suppression of acts of aggression or other breaches of the peace, and to bring about by peaceful means, and in conformity with the principles of justice and international law, adjustment or settlement of international disputes or situations which might lead to a breach of the peace (Article 1, para 1).

The Charter also provides in the same Chapter that the Organisation and its Members, in pursuit of the Purposes stated in Article 1, shall act in accordance with, among others, the following principle: 'All Members shall settle their international disputes by peaceful means in such a manner that international peace and security, and justice, are not endangered' (Article 2, para 3). It furthermore, in Chapter VI (Pacific Settlement of Disputes), states that:

> The parties to any dispute, the continuance of which is likely to endanger the maintenance of international peace and security, shall, first of all, seek a solution by negotiation, inquiry, mediation, conciliation, arbitration, judicial settlement, resort to regional agencies or arrangements, or other peaceful means of their own choice (Article 33, para 1).

B   Declarations and Resolutions of the General Assembly

2   The principle of the peaceful settlement of disputes has been reaffirmed in a number of General Assembly Resolutions, including Resolutions 2627 (XXV) of 24 October 1970, 2734 (XXV) of 16 December 1970 and 40/9 of 8 November 1985. It is dealt with comprehensively in the Declaration on Principles of International Law concerning Friendly Relations and Co-operation among States in accordance with the Charter of the United Nations (Resolution 2625 (XXV), annex), in the section entitled 'The principle that states shall settle their international disputes by peaceful means in such a manner that international peace and security and justice are not endangered', as well as in the Manila Declaration on the Peaceful Settlement of International Disputes (Resolution 37/10, annex), in the Declaration on the Prevention and Removal of Disputes and Situations Which May Threaten International Peace and Security and on the Role of the United Nations in this field (Resolution 43/51, annex) and in the Declaration on Fact-finding by the United Nations in the Field of the Maintenance of International Peace and Security (Resolution 46/59, annex).

C   Corollary and related principles

3   The principle of the peaceful settlement of international disputes is linked to various other principles of international law. It may be recalled in this connection that under the Declaration on Friendly Relations, the principles dealt with in the Declaration – namely, the principle that states shall refrain in their international relations from the threat or use of force against the territorial

integrity or political independence of any state, or in any other manner inconsistent with the purposes of the United Nations; the principle that states shall settle their international disputes by peaceful means in such a manner that international peace and security and justice are not endangered; the principle concerning the duty not to intervene in matters within the domestic jurisdiction of any state, in accordance with the Charter; the duty of states to co-operate with one another in accordance with the Charter; the principle of equal rights and self-determination of peoples; the principle of sovereign equality of states; and the principle that states shall fulfil in good faith the obligations assumed by them in accordance with the Charter – are interrelated in their interpretation and application and each principle should be construed in the context of other principles.

4   The Final Act of the Conference on Security and Co-operation in Europe, adopted at Helsinki on 1 August 1975, states that all the principles set forth in the Declaration on Principles Guiding Relations between Participating states – ie, sovereign equality, respect for the rights inherent in sovereignty; refraining from the threat or use of force; inviolability of frontiers; territorial integrity of states; peaceful settlement of disputes; non-intervention in internal affairs; respect for human rights and fundamental freedoms, including the freedom of thought, conscience, religion or belief; equal rights and self-determination of peoples; co-operation among states; and fulfilment in good faith of obligations under international law – 'are of primary significance and, accordingly, they will be equally and unreservedly applied, each of them being interpreted taking into account the others.'

5   The links between the principle of the peaceful settlement of disputes and other specific principles of international law are highlighted both in the Friendly Relations Declaration and in the Manila Declaration as follows:

1   *Principle of non-use of force in international relations*

6   The interrelation between this principle and the principle of peaceful settlement of disputes is highlighted in the fourth preambular paragraph of the Manila Declaration and is also referred to in section I, para 13, thereof, under which neither the existence of a dispute nor the failure of a procedure of peaceful settlement of disputes shall permit the use of force or threat or force by any of the states parties to the dispute.

7   The links between the principle of peaceful settlement of disputes and the principle of non-use of force are also highlighted in a number of other international instruments, including the 1945 Pact of the League of Arab States (art 5), the 1948 American Treaty on Pacific Settlement (Pact of Bogota) (art I), the 1947 Inter-American Treaty of Reciprocal Assistance (arts 1 and 2) and the last paragraph of section II of the Declaration on Principles Guiding Relations between Participating states contained in the Final Act of the Conference on Security and Co-operation in Europe.

2   *Principle of non-intervention in the internal or external affairs of states*

8   The interrelation between this principle and the principle of the peaceful settlement of disputes is highlighted in the fifth preambular paragraph of the Manila Declaration.

9   The links between the principle of peaceful settlement of disputes and the principle of non-intervention are also highlighted in Article V of the 1948 Pact of Bogota.

3   *Principle of equal rights and self-determination of peoples*

10   The links between this principle and the principle of peaceful settlement of disputes are highlighted in the Manila Declaration which (1) reaffirms in its

eighth preambular paragraph the principle of equal rights and self-determination as enshrined in the Charter and referred to in the Friendly Relations Declaration and in other relevant Resolutions of the General Assembly; (2) stresses in its ninth preambular paragraph the need for all states to desist from any forcible action which deprives peoples, particularly peoples under colonial and racist regimes or other forms of alien domination, of their inalienable right to self-determination, freedom and independence; (3) refers in section I, para 12, to the possibility for parties to a dispute to have recourse to the procedures mentioned in the Declaration 'in order to facilitate the exercise by the peoples concerned of the right to self-determination'; and (4) declares in its penultimate paragraph that 'nothing in the present Declaration could in any way prejudice the right to self-determination, freedom and independence, as derived from the Charter, of peoples forcibly deprived of that right and referred to in the Declaration on Principles of International Law concerning Friendly Relations and Co-operation among states in accordance with the Charter of the United Nations, particularly peoples under colonial or racist regimes or other forms of alien domination; nor the right of these peoples to struggle to that end and to seek and receive support, in accordance with the principles of the Charter and in conformity with the above-mentioned Declaration'.

4 Principle of the sovereign equality of states

11 The links between this principle and the principle of the peaceful settlement of disputes are highlighted in the fifth paragraph of the relevant section of the Friendly Relations Declaration which provides that 'International disputes shall be settled on the basis of the sovereign equality of states' as well as in section I, para 3 of the Manila Declaration.

5 Principles of international law concerning the sovereignty, independence and territorial integrity of states

12 Paragraph 4 of section I of the Manila Declaration enunciates the duty of states parties to a dispute to continue to observe in their mutual relations their obligations under the fundamental principles of international law concerning the sovereignty, independence and territorial integrity of states.

6 Good faith in international relations

13 The Manila Declaration enunciates in its section I, para 1, the duty of states to 'act in good faith', with a view to avoiding disputes among themselves likely to affect friendly relations among states. Other references to good faith are to be found in para 5, under which good faith and a spirit of co-operation are to guide states in their search for an early and equitable settlement of their disputes; in para 11, which provides that states shall in accordance with international law implement in good faith all the provisions of agreements concluded by them for the settlement of their disputes; in para 2 of section II, under which Member states shall fulfil in good faith the obligations assumed by them in accordance with the Charter of the United Nations; and in one of the concluding paragraphs of the declaration, whereby the General Assembly urges all states to observe and promote in good faith the provisions of the declaration in the peaceful settlement of their international disputes.

14 A provision similar to para 5 of section I of the Manila Declaration is to be found in the third paragraph of section V of the Declaration on Principles Guiding Relations between Participating states contained in the Final Act of the Conference on Security and Co-operation in Europe.

7 Principles of justice and international law

15 The 'principles of international law' are mentioned together with the principles of justice in Article 1, para 1 of the Charter under which one of the

purposes of the United Nations is 'to bring about, by peaceful means, and in conformity with the principles of justice and international law, adjustment or settlement of international disputes or situations which might lead to a breach of the peace'. The principles of international law are also mentioned jointly with the principles of justice in section I, para 3 of the Manila Declaration under which 'international disputes shall be settled on the basis of the sovereign equality of states and in accordance with the principle of free choice of means in conformity with obligations under the Charter of the United Nations and with the principles of justice and international law'.

16   Paragraph 4 of section I of the Manila Declaration provides that 'States Parties to a dispute shall continue to observe in their mutual relations ... generally recognised principles and rules of contemporary international law'.

17   'Justice' is referred to in Article 2, para 3, of the Charter and in the first paragraph of the relevant section of the Friendly Relations Declaration, both of which provide for the settlement of international disputes 'by peaceful means in such a manner that international peace and security and justice are not endangered'.

8   Other corollary and related principles and rules

18   In its tenth preambular paragraph, the Manila Declaration singles out among 'respective principles and rules concerning the peaceful settlement of international disputes', 'the exhaustion of local remedies whenever applicable'. Article VII of the 1948 Pact of Bogota contains a similar provision.

D   Free choice of means

19   The principle of free choice of means is laid down in Article 33, para 1, of the Charter of the United Nations and reiterated in the fifth paragraph of the relevant provisions of the Friendly Relations Declaration and in section I, paras 3 and 10, of the Manila Declaration. As indicated above, both the Friendly Relations Declaration and the Manila Declaration make it clear that recourse to, or acceptance of, a settlement procedure freely agreed to with regard to existing or future disputes shall not be regarded as incompatible with the sovereign equality of states. The principle of free choice of means has also found expression in a number of other international instruments, including the Pact of Bogota (art III) and the Declaration on Principles Guiding Relations between Participating States contained in the Final Act of the Conference on Security and Co-operation in Europe (third paragraph of section V).

20   The following means are listed in Article 33 of the Charter, in the second paragraph of the relevant section of the Friendly Relations Declaration and in para 5 of section I of the Manila declaration: negotiation, inquiry, mediation, conciliation, arbitration, judicial settlement, resort to regional arrangements or agencies or other peaceful means of the parties' own choice. Among those 'other peaceful means', the Manila Declaration singles out good offices. Under the Friendly Relations Declaration (second paragraph of the relevant section) and the Manila Declaration (para 5 of section I), it is for the parties to agree on such peaceful means as may be appropriate to the circumstances and the nature of their dispute.[1]

---

1   United Nations, Office of Legal Affairs, *Handbook on the Peaceful Settlement of Disputes between States*, 1992, New York: United Nations at pp 3–7.

DECLARATION ON PRINCIPLES OF INTERNATIONAL LAW CONCERNING FRIENDLY RELATIONS AND CO-OPERATION AMONG STATES IN ACCORDANCE WITH THE CHARTER OF THE UNITED NATIONS

ANNEX TO RESOLUTION 2625 (XXV) OF THE UNITED NATIONS GENERAL ASSEMBLY ADOPTED WITHOUT A VOTE 24 OCTOBER 1970

PREAMBLE

The General Assembly

Reaffirming in the terms of the Charter that the maintenance of international peace and security and the development of friendly relations and co-operation between nations are among the fundamental purposes of the United Nations,

Recalling that the peoples of the United Nations are determined to practise tolerance and live together in peace with one another as good neighbours,

Bearing in mind the importance of maintaining and strengthening international peace founded upon freedom, equality, justice and respect for fundamental human rights and of developing friendly relations among nations irrespective of their political, economic and social systems or the levels of their development,

Bearing in mind also the paramount importance of the Charter of the United Nations in the promotion of the rule of law among nations.

Considering that the faithful observance of the principles of international law concerning friendly relations and co-operation among states and the fulfilment in good faith of the obligations assumed by states, in accordance with the Charter, is of the greatest importance for the maintenance of international peace and security and for the implementation of the other purposes of the United Nations,

Noting that the great political, economic and social changes and scientific progress which have taken place in the world since the adoption of the Charter of the United Nations give increased importance to these principles and to the need for their more effective application in the conduct of states wherever carried on,

Recalling the established principle that outer space, including the moon and other celestial bodies, is not subject to national appropriation by claims of sovereignty, by means of use or occupation, or by any other means, and mindful of the fact that consideration is being given in the United Nations to the question of establishing other appropriate provisions similarly inspired,

Convinced that the strict observance by states of the obligation not to intervene in the affairs of any other state is an essential condition to ensure that nations live together in peace with one another, since the practice of any form of intervention not only violates the spirit and letter of the Charter, but also leads to the creation of situations which threaten international peace and security,

Recalling the duty of states to refrain in their international relations from military, political, economic or any other form of coercion aimed against the political independence or territorial integrity of any state,

Considering it essential that all states shall refrain in their international relations from the threat or use of force against the territorial integrity or political independence of any state, or in any other manner inconsistent with the purposes of the United Nations,

Considering it equally essential that all states shall settle their international disputes by peaceful means in accordance with the Charter,

Reaffirming, in accordance with the Charter, the basic importance of sovereign equality and stressing that the purposes of the United Nations can be implemented only if states enjoy sovereign equality and comply fully with the requirements of this principle in their international relations,

Convinced that the subjection of peoples to alien subjugation, domination and exploitation constitutes a major obstacle to the promotion of international peace and security,

Convinced that the principle of equal rights and self-determination of peoples constitutes a significant contribution to contemporary international law, and that its effective application is of paramount importance for the promotion of friendly relations among states, based on respect for the principle of sovereign equality,

Convinced in consequence that any attempt aimed at the partial or total disruption of the national unity and territorial integrity of a state or country or at its political independence is incompatible with the purposes and principles of the Charter,

Considering the provisions of the Charter as a whole and taking into account the role of the relevant Resolutions adopted by the competent organs of the United Nations relating to the content of the principles,

Considering that the progressive development and codification of the following principles:

(a) The principle that states shall refrain in their international relations from the threat or use of force against the territorial integrity or political independence of any state, or in any other manner inconsistent with the purposes of the United Nations;

(b) The principle that states shall settle their international disputes by peaceful means in such a manner that international peace and security and justice are not endangered;

(c) The duty not to intervene in matters within the domestic jurisdiction of any state, in accordance with the Charter;

(d) The duty of states to co-operate with one another in accordance with the Charter;

(e) The principle of equal rights and self-determination of peoples;

(f) The principle of sovereign equality of states;

(g) The principle that states shall fulfil in good faith the obligations assumed by them in accordance with the Charter;

so as to secure their more effective application within the international community would promote the realisation of the purposes of the United Nations,

Having considered the principles of international law relating to friendly relations and co-operation among states,

1   *Solemnly proclaims* the following principles:

The principle that states shall refrain in their international relations from threat or use of force against the territorial integrity or political independence of any state, or in any other manner inconsistent with the purposes of the United Nations

Every state has the duty to refrain in its international relations from the threat or use of force against the territorial integrity or political independence of any state, or in any other manner inconsistent with the purposes of the United Nations. Such a threat or use of force constitutes a violation of international law and the Charter of the United Nations and shall never be employed as a means of settling international issues.

A war of aggression constitutes a crime against the peace, for which there is responsibility under international law.

In accordance with the Purposes and Principles of the United Nations, states have the duty to refrain from propaganda for wars of aggression.

Every state has the duty to refrain from the threat or use of force to violate the existing international boundaries of any state or as a means of solving international disputes, including territorial disputes and problems concerning frontiers of states.

Every state likewise has the duty to refrain from the threat or use of force to violate international lines of demarcation, such as armistice lines, established by or pursuant to an international agreement to which it is a party or which it is otherwise bound to respect. Nothing in the foregoing shall be construed as prejudicing the positions of the parties concerned with regard to the status and effects of such lines under their special regimes or as affecting their temporary character.

States have a duty to refrain from acts of reprisal involving the use of force.

Every state has the duty to refrain from any forcible action which deprives peoples referred to in the elaboration of the principle of equal rights and self-determination and freedom and independence.

Every state has the duty to refrain from organising or encouraging the organisation of irregular forces or armed bands, including mercenaries, for incursion into the territory of another state.

Every state has the duty to refrain from organising, instigating, assisting or participating in acts of civil strife or terrorist acts in another state or acquiescing in organised activities within its territory directed towards the commission of such acts, when the acts referred to in the present paragraph involve a threat or use of force.

The territory of a state shall not be the object of military occupation resulting from the use of force in contravention of the provisions of the Charter. The territory of a state shall not be the object of acquisition by another state resulting from the threat or use of force. No territorial acquisition resulting from the threat or use of force shall be recognised as legal. Nothing in the foregoing shall be construed as affecting:

   (a)   provisions of the Charter or any international agreement prior to the Charter regime and valid under international law; or

   (b)   the powers of the Security Council under the Charter.

All states shall pursue in good faith negotiations for the early conclusion of a universal treaty on general and complete disarmament under effective international control and strive to adopt appropriate measures to reduce international tensions and strengthen confidence among states.

All states shall comply in good faith with their obligations under the generally recognised principles and rules of international law with respect to the maintenance of international peace and security, and shall endeavour to make the United Nations security system based on the Charter more effective.

Nothing in the foregoing paragraphs shall be construed as enlarging or diminishing in any way the scope of the provisions of the Charter concerning cases in which the use of force is lawful.

The principle that states shall settle their international disputes by peaceful means in such a manner that international peace and security and justice are not endangered

Every state shall settle its international disputes with other states by peaceful means, in such a manner that international peace and security and justice are not endangered.

States shall accordingly seek early and just settlement of their international disputes by negotiation, inquiry, mediation, conciliation, arbitration, judicial settlement, resort to regional agencies or arrangements or other peaceful means of their choice. In seeking such a settlement the parties shall agree upon such peaceful means as may be appropriate to the circumstances and nature of the dispute.

The parties to a dispute have the duty, in the event of failure to reach a solution by any one of the above peaceful means, to continue to seek a settlement of the dispute by other peaceful means agreed upon by them.

State parties to an international dispute, as well as other states, shall refrain from any action which may aggravate the situation so as to endanger the maintenance of international peace and security, and shall act in accordance with the purposes and principles of the United Nations.

International disputes shall be settled on the basis of the sovereign equality of states and in accordance with the principle of free choice of means. recourse to, or acceptance of, a settlement procedure freely agreed to by states with regard to existing or future disputes to which they are parties shall not be regarded as incompatible with sovereign equality.

Nothing in the foregoing paragraphs prejudices or derogates from the applicable provisions of the Charter, in particular those relating to the pacific settlement of international disputes.

The principle concerning the duty not to intervene in matters within the domestic jurisdiction of any state, in accordance with the Charter

No state or group of states has the right to intervene, directly or indirectly, for any reason whatsoever, in the internal or external affairs of any other state. Consequently, armed intervention and all other forms of interference or attempted threats against the personality of the state or against its political, economic and cultural elements, are in violation of international law.

No state may use or encourage the use of economic, political or any other types of measures to coerce another state in order to obtain from it the subordination of the exercise of its sovereign rights and to secure from it advantages of any kind. Also, no state shall organise, assist, foment, finance, incite or tolerate subversive, terrorist or armed activities directed towards the violent overthrow of the regime of another state, or interfere in civil strife in another state.

The use of force to deprive peoples of their national identity constitutes a violation of their inalienable rights and of the principle of non-intervention.

Every state has an inalienable right to choose its political, economic, social and cultural systems, without interference in any form by another state.

Nothing in the foregoing paragraphs shall be construed as affecting the relevant provisions of the Charter relating to the maintenance of international peace and security.

The duty of states to co-operate with one another in accordance with the Charter

States have the duty to co-operate with one another, irrespective of the differences in their political, economic and social systems, in the various spheres of international relations, in order to maintain international peace and security and to promote international economic stability and progress, the general welfare of nations and international co-operation free from discrimination based on such differences.

To this end:

(a) states shall co-operate with other states in the maintenance of international peace and security;

(b) states shall co-operate in the promotion of universal respect for and observance of human rights and fundamental freedoms for all, and in the elimination of all forms of racial discrimination and all forms of religious intolerance;

(c) states shall conduct their international relations in the economic, social, cultural, technical and trade fields in accordance with the principles of sovereign equality and non-intervention;

(d) states Members of the United Nations have the duty to take joint and separate action in co-operation with the United Nations in accordance with the relevant provisions of the Charter.

States should co-operate in the economic, social and cultural fields as well as in the field of science and technology and for the promotion of international cultural and educational progress. states should co-operate in the promotion of economic growth throughout the world, especially that of the developing countries.

The principle of equal rights and self-determination of peoples

By virtue of the principle of equal rights and self-determination of peoples enshrined in the Charter of the United Nations, all peoples have the right freely to determine, without external interference, their political status and to pursue their economic, social and cultural development, and every state has the duty to respect this right in accordance with the provisions of the Charter.

Every state has the duty to promote, through joint and separate action, realisation of the principle of equal rights and self-determination of peoples, in accordance with the provisions of the Charter, and to render assistance to the United Nations in carrying out the responsibilities entrusted to it by the Charter regarding the implementation of the principle, in order:

(a) to promote friendly relations and co-operation among states; and

(b) to bring a speedy end to colonialism, having due regard to the freely expressed will of the peoples concerned;

and bearing in mind that subjection of peoples to alien subjugation, domination and exploitation constitutes a violation of the principle, as well as a denial of fundamental human rights, and is contrary to the Charter.

Every state has the duty to promote through joint and separate action universal respect for and observance of human rights and fundamental freedoms in accordance with the Charter.

The establishment of a sovereign and independent state, the free association or integration with an independent state or the emergence into any other political status freely determined by a people constitute modes of implementing the right of self-determination by that people.

Every state has the duty to refrain from any forcible action which deprives peoples referred to above in the elaboration of the present principle of their right to self-determination and freedom and independence. In their actions against, and resistance to, such forcible action in pursuit of the exercise of their right to self-determination, such peoples are entitled to seek and to receive support in accordance with the purposes and principles of the Charter.

The territory of a colony or other non-self-governing territory has, under the Charter, a status separate and distinct from the territory of the state administering it; and such separate and distinct status under the Charter shall exist until the people of the colony or non-self-governing territory have exercised their right of self-determination in accordance with the Charter, and particularly its Purposes and Principles.

Nothing in the foregoing paragraphs shall be construed as authorising or encouraging any action which would dismember or impair, totally or in part, the territorial integrity or political unity of sovereign and independent states conducting themselves in compliance with the principles of equal rights and self-determination of peoples as described above and thus possessed of a government representing the whole people belonging to the territory without distinction as to race, creed, or colour.

Every state shall refrain from any action aimed at the partial or total disruption of the national unity and territorial integrity of any other state or country.

The principle of sovereign equality of states

All states enjoy sovereign equality. They have equal rights and duties and are equal members of the international community, notwithstanding differences of an economic, social, political or other nature.

In particular, sovereign equality includes the following elements:

(a) states are juridically equal;

(b) each state enjoys the rights inherent in full sovereignty;

(c) each state has the duty to respect the personality of other states;

(d) the territorial integrity and political independence of the state are inviolable;

(e) each state has the right freely to choose and develop its political, social, economic and cultural systems;

(f) each state has the duty to comply fully and in good faith with its international obligations and to live in peace with other states.

The principle that states shall fulfil in good faith the obligations assumed by them in accordance with the Charter

Every state has the duty to fulfil in good faith the obligations assumed by it in accordance with the Charter of the United Nations.

Every state has the duty to fulfil in good faith its obligations under the generally recognised principles and rules of international law.

Every state has the duty to fulfil in good faith its obligations under international agreements valid under the generally recognised principles and rules of international law.

Where obligations arising under international agreements are in conflict with the obligations of Members of the United Nations under the Charter of the United Nations, the obligations under the Charter shall prevail.

2   *Declares that:*

In their interpretation and application the above principles are interrelated and each principle should be construed in the context of the other principles.

Nothing in this Declaration shall be construed as prejudicing in any manner the provisions of the Charter or the rights of peoples under the Charter, taking into account the elaboration of these rights in this Declaration,

3   *Declares further that:*

The principles of the Charter which are embodied in this Declaration constitute basic principles of international law, and consequently appeals to all states to be guided by these principles in their international conduct and to develop their mutual relations on the basis of the strict observance of these principles.

The peaceful methods of international dispute settlement that exist can be divided into diplomatic and legal settlement. Legal settlement refers to modes of dispute settlement which result in binding decisions and will involve either arbitration or judicial settlement. The following can be identified as forms of diplomatic settlement:

- negotiation and consultation;
- good offices;
- mediation;
- conciliation;
- inquiry.

What constitutes an 'international dispute' is a matter for objective determination. In the *Mavrommatis Palestine Concessions (Jurisdiction)* case (1924) the PCIJ stated that a dispute could be regarded as 'a disagreement over a point of law or fact, a conflict of legal views or of interests between two persons'. In the *Interpretation of Peace Treaties* case (1950) the ICJ, in an Advisory Opinion, confirmed that the existence of an international dispute was a matter of objective determination stating:

> The mere denial of the existence of a dispute does not prove its non-existence ... There has thus arisen a situation in which two sides hold clearly opposite views concerning the question of the performance or non-performance of treaty obligations. Confronted with such a situation, the Court must conclude that international disputes have arisen.

13.2 Negotiation and consultation

Negotiation is by far the most popular means of dispute settlement and consists of discussions between the interested parties. It is distinguished from other diplomatic means of settlement in that there is no third party involvement. Negotiations are normally conducted through 'normal diplomatic channels' (foreign ministers, ambassadors, etc),[2] although some states have set up semi-permanent 'mixed commissions' consisting of an equal number of representatives of both parties which can deal with disputes as and when they arise, for example the Canadian-US Joint Commission. Negotiation is used to try and prevent disputes arising in the first place and will also often be used at the start of other dispute Resolution procedures. In the *Mavrommatis Palestine Concessions (Jurisdiction)* case (1924) the PCIJ indicated that negotiation should be a preliminary to bringing a case before the Court in order that the subject matter of a dispute be clearly defined. In the *Free Zones of Upper Savoy* case (1932) the PCIJ stated that:

> Before a dispute can be made the subject of an action at law, its subject matter should have been clearly defined by diplomatic negotiations.[3]

It is clear that states are under a general obligation to negotiate in good faith:

> The parties are under an obligation to enter into negotiations with a view to arriving at an agreement, and not merely to go through a formal process of negotiation of a sort of prior condition for the automatic application of a certain method of delimitation in the absence of agreement; they are under an obligation so to conduct themselves that the negotiations are meaningful, which will not be the case when either of them insists upon its own position without contemplating any modification of it.[4]

13.3 Good offices

'Good offices' involves the involvement of a third party, with the consent of the states in dispute, to help them establish direct contacts or to take up negotiations. The person providing the 'good offices' will usually be a neutral party who is trusted by both sides. The UN Secretary General is often used in this role to facilitate communication between contending parties, and he may, on behalf of a concerned international community, play an active role in encouraging negotiations and promoting a successful outcome.

> Furthermore, the Security Council and other organs of the United Nations have entrusted the Secretary General with various tasks which broadly entail the exercise of good offices. This is a very flexible term as it may mean very little or very much. But, in an age in which negotiations have to replace confrontation, I feel that the Secretary General's good offices can significantly help in encouraging member states to bring their disputes to the negotiating table. Negotiations today have a character quite different from what they had in the past. Talleyrand called negotiations *'l'art de laisser les autres suivre votre propre*

---

2 Negotiation, consultation, diplomacy, 'through the usual diplomatic channels' tend to be used interchangeably to mean the same thing.

3 *PCIJ* Ser A, No 22, p 13.

4 *North Sea Continental Shelf* case [1969] *ICJ Rep* at p 47, para 85 (a).

voie'. That, however, was true of a world which no longer exists. Today, negotiations need to take account of the great political and economic changes of our world. In order to succeed, and if the vital interests of all concerned are taken sufficiently into consideration, no party will consider it a sign of weakness to listen to a cogent argument, and accept a demonstrably reasonable outcome. The parties may retain their different outlooks, but wherever they confront one another, life imposes upon them the obligation to seek all possible means of *rapprochement* and try to reduce the elements of contention and conflict. The task of the United Nations and the purpose of good offices of the Secretary General is to make the discharge of this obligation easier. In view of the complexity of the issues which arise in our dynamic world, traditional diplomacy can no longer suffice. New methods and devices have become important.

The process involved contributes to the growth of international law, for every Resolution of a dispute, every new agreement, adds a new building stone to the edifice of law. More immediately, it answers the need of peace-making. It is a very complex task, requiring great discretion. One of my predecessors rightly remarked that, 'while the Secretary General is working privately with the parties in an attempt to resolve a delicate situation, he is criticised publicly for his inaction or even lack of interest'. In situations of confrontation, the parties to a dispute are extremely sensitive and this makes it important that they should have confidence in the impartiality or the objectivity of the United Nations and its Secretary General. The only instrument I can use is persuasion. When successful, it is a more powerful weapon that constraint, for it makes the persuaded party an ally of the solution. But to be able to persuade, you must prove the virtues of a solution, demonstrate the need to compromise and convince the party concerned that an agreement today is much more advantageous for it than a doubtful victory tomorrow. It is here that inventiveness is essential. We have to stretch our imagination to discern points of potential agreement even where at first sight they look non-existent. Even more important is patience, the refusal to give up in the face of apparently hopeless odds. Patience is greatly helped by the realisation that in so many areas some of the great problems of today reflect the accumulation of violations, mistakes and passivity stretching over long periods. Hence, the difficulty of reconciling different positions, and hence also, its acute urgency.

As Secretary General of the United Nations, I am encouraged when states respond positively to the offer of my services. if two parties are unable or unwilling to sit down at the same table, action from some third quarter – such as the United Nations – is indispensable. But, in such a situation, each party must feel that it will not incur a disadvantage by responding to my good offices. And in making my good offices available, timing is of critical importance.[5]

13.4 Mediation

Whereas in good offices the third party is doing little more than providing a channel for communication, in mediation the third party plays a more active role by offering advice and proposals for a solution of the dispute. In practice it is often hard to establish a clear distinction between the two. What may begin as provision of good offices may end up as mediation.

---

5   Statement of the UN Secretary General, SG/SM/3525, pp 4–5.

13.5 Conciliation

Conciliation also involves the use of third parties, but the third party plays a more detached role. Rather than becoming involved in the negotiations, the conciliator will investigate the dispute and present formal proposals for a solution. Conciliation is often undertaken by a commission of conciliation acting as a formal body. In 1922 the League of Nations adopted a Resolution encouraging states to submit their disputes to conciliation commissions which would undertake both a mediation and an inquiry role.

GENERAL ACT ON PACIFIC SETTLEMENT OF INTERNATIONAL DISPUTES[6]
CHAPTER 1 CONCILIATION

Article 1

Disputes of every kind between two or more Parties to the present General Act which it has not been possible to settle by diplomacy shall, subject to such reservations as may be made under Article 39, be submitted, under the conditions laid down in the present Chapter, to the procedure of conciliation.

Article 2

The disputes referred to in the preceding article shall be submitted to a permanent or special Conciliation Commission constituted by the parties to the dispute.

Article 3

On a request to that effect being made by one of the Contracting Parties to another Party, a permanent Conciliation Commission shall be constituted within a period of six months.

Article 4

Unless the parties concerned agree otherwise, the Conciliation Commission shall be constituted as follows:

1   The Commission shall be composed of five members. The parties shall each nominate one commissioner, who may be chosen from among their respective nationals, the three other commissioners shall be appointed by agreement from among the nations of third Powers. These three commissioners must be of different nationalities and must not be habitually resident in the territory nor be in the service of the parties. The parties shall appoint the President of the Commission from among them.

2   The commissioners shall be appointed for three years. They shall be re-eligible. The commissioners appointed jointly may be replaced during the course of their mandate by agreement between the parties. Either party may however, at any time replace a commissioner whom it has appointed. Even if replaced, the

---

6   93 LNTS 345. Done at Geneva on 26 September 1928, entered into force on 16 August 1929. The following states are parties: Australia, Belgium, Canada, Denmark, Ethiopia, Finland, France, Greece, India, Ireland, Italy, Luxembourg, Netherlands, New Zealand, Norway, Pakistan, Peru, Spain (denunciation, 8 April 1934), Switzerland, Turkey, United Kingdom (denunciation, 8 February 1974).

commissioners shall continue to exercise their functions until the termination of the work in hand.

3   Vacancies which may occur as a result of death, resignation or any other cause shall be filled within the shortest possible time in the manner fixed for the nominations.

Article 5

If, when a dispute arises, no permanent Conciliation Commission appointed by the parties is in existence, a special commission shall be constituted for the examination of the dispute within a period of three months from the date at which a request to that effect is made in the manner laid down in the preceding article, unless the parties shall decide otherwise.

Article 6

1   If the appointment of the commissioners to be designated jointly is not made within the periods provided for in Articles 3 and 5, the making of the necessary appointments shall be entrusted to a third Power, chosen by agreement between the parties, or on the request of the parties, to the Acting President of the Council of the League of Nations.

2   If no agreement is reached on either of these procedures, each party shall designate a different Power, and the appointment shall be made in concert by the Powers thus chosen.

3   If, within a period of three months, the two Powers have been unable to reach an agreement, each of them shall submit a number of candidates equal to the number of members to be appointed. It shall then be decided by lot which of the candidates thus designated shall be appointed.

Article 7

1   Disputes shall be brought before the Conciliation Commission by means of an application addressed to the President by the two parties acting in agreement, or in default thereof by one or other of the parties.

2   The application, after giving a summary account of the subject of the dispute, shall contain the invitation to the Commission to take all necessary measures with a view to arriving at an amicable solution.

3   If the application emanates from only one of the parties, the other party shall, without delay, be notified of it.

Article 8

1   Within 15 days from the date on which a dispute has been brought by one of the parties before a permanent Conciliation Commission, either party may replace its own commissioner, for the examination of the particular dispute, by a person possessing special competence in the matter.

2   The party making use of this right shall immediately notify the other party; the latter shall, in such case, be entitled to take similar action within 15 days from the date on which it received the notification.

Article 10

The work of the Conciliation Commission shall not be conducted in public unless a decision to that effect is taken by the Commission with the consent of the parties.

Article 11

1   In the absence of agreement to the contrary between the parties, the Conciliation Commission shall lay down its own procedure, which in any case

must provide for both parties being heard. In regard to inquiries, the Commission, unless it decides unanimously to the contrary, shall act in accordance with the provisions of Part III of the Hague Convention of 18 October 1907, for the Pacific Settlement of International Disputes.

2   The parties shall be represented before the Conciliation Commission by agents, whose duties shall be to act as intermediaries between them and the Commission; they may, moreover, be assisted by counsel and experts appointed by them for that purpose and may request that all persons whose evidence appears to them desirable shall be heard.

3   The Commission, for its part, shall be entitled to request oral explanations from the agents, counsel and experts of both parties, as well as from all persons it may think desirable to summon with the consent of their governments.

Article 12

In the absence of agreement to the contrary between the parties, the decisions of the Conciliation Commission shall be taken by a majority vote, and the Commission may only take decisions on the substance of the dispute if all its members are present.

Article 13

The parties undertake to facilitate the work of the Conciliation Commission, and particularly to supply it to the greatest possible extent with all relevant documents and information as well as to use the means at their disposal to allow it to proceed in their territory, and in accordance with their law, to the summoning and hearing of witnesses or experts and to visit the localities in question.

Article 14

1   During the proceedings of the Commission, each of the commissioners shall receive emoluments the amount of which shall be fixed by agreement between the parties, each of which shall contribute an equal share.

2   The general expenses arising out of the working of the Commission shall be divided in the same manner.

Article 15

1   The task of the Conciliation Commission shall be to elucidate the questions in dispute, to collect with that object all necessary information by means of inquiry or otherwise, and to endeavour to bring the parties to an agreement. It may, after the case has been examined, inform the parties of the terms of settlement which seem suitable to it and lay down the period within which they are to make their decision.

2   At the close of the proceedings the Commission shall draw up a *procès-verbal* stating, as the case may be, either that the parties have come to an agreement and, if need arises, the terms of the agreement, or that it h as been impossible to effect a settlement. No mention shall be made in the *procès-verbal* of whether the Commission's decisions were taken unanimously or by a majority vote.

3   The proceedings of the Commission must, unless the parties otherwise agree, be terminated within six months from the date on which the Commission shall have been given cognisance of the dispute.

Article 16

The Commission's *procès-verbal* shall be communicated without delay to the parties. The parties shall decide whether it shall be published.

13.6 Inquiry

Inquiries prove useful where a dispute is largely concerned with issues of fact. The need for some independent inquiry procedures was illustrated by events leading to the Spanish-American War of 1898. In February 1898 a US warship, at anchor in Cuba, was destroyed by an explosion which killed large numbers of US sailors. Relations between Spain and the US were already strained and the US quickly blamed Spain for the explosion. Spain held a commission of inquiry which found that the explosion was caused by factors present on the ship whilst a US inquiry found that the ship had been destroyed by a mine. The conflicting findings of the two inquiries only served to exacerbate the situation.

At the Hague Peace Conference 1899 the Russians proposed the establishment of international commissions of inquiry which would be able, impartially, to decide disputes of fact and which would put an end to the type of dispute between the US and Spain. The proposals were accepted and formed the basis for Articles 9 to 14 of the Hague Convention for the Pacific Settlement of Disputes 1899. In 1904 a Committee of Inquiry, established under the provisions of the Hague Convention, was held to look into the sinking of a number of UK trawlers by Russian warships. The Committee consisted of representatives from the UK and Russia and also France, the US and Austro-Hungary. The inquiry made a finding of fact and the dispute between Russia and the UK was settled amicably.

The rules relating to inquiries were further refined by the Hague Convention for the Pacific Settlement of Disputes 1907 (Articles 9–35).

> In disputes of an international nature involving neither honour nor essential interests, and arising from a difference of opinion on points of fact, the Contracting Parties deem it expedient and desirable that the parties who have not been able to come to an agreement by means of diplomacy should, as far as circumstances allow, institute an international commission of inquiry, to facilitate a solution of these disputes by elucidating the facts by means of an impartial and conscientious investigation.[7]

There has been little use of inquiries as a means of settling disputes since the establishment of a World Court which can decide questions of both law and fact. The last international inquiry to be held was the *Red Crusader Inquiry* (1962) which investigated an incident involving a UK trawler and a Danish fisheries protection vessel. The *Red Crusader Inquiry* itself was the first to be held for 40 years. There has been much greater use of slightly less formal 'fact-finding missions', particularly under the auspices of the United Nations, in the context of dispute prevention and Resolution.

13.7 Arbitration

> 168 The 1899 and 1907 Hague Conventions for the Pacific Settlement of International Disputes described the object of international arbitration as the settlement of disputes between states by judges chosen by the parties themselves

---

7 Hague Convention for the Pacific Settlement of International Disputes 1907 article 9.

and on the basis of respect for law.[8] They further provided that recourse to the procedure implied submission in good faith to the award of the tribunal. Accordingly, one of the basic characteristics of arbitration is that it is a procedure which results in binding decisions upon the parties to the dispute.

169   The power to render binding decisions is, therefore, a characteristic which arbitration shares with the method of judicial settlement by international courts whose judgments are not only binding but also, as in the case of the International Court of Justice, final and without appeal, as indicated in Article 60 of the ICJ Statute. For this reason arbitration and judicial settlement are both usually referred to as compulsory means of settlement of disputes.

170   However, while both arbitration and judicial settlement are similar in that respect, the two methods are nevertheless structurally different from each other. Arbitration, in general, is constituted by mutual consent of the states parties to a specific dispute where such parties retain considerable control over the process through the power of appointing arbitrators of their own choice.[9, 10]

The modern history of international arbitration is traced back to the Treaty of Ghent 1814 between the US and the UK whereby the two states agreed that certain disputes should be arbitrated by national commissioners with reference to a disinterested third party. The earlier Jay Treaty 1794 between the two states had made provision for arbitration by national commissioners. Throughout the 19th century arbitration was frequently used, its popularity increasing markedly following the successful *Alabama Claims Arbitration* (1872) between the UK and the US in which both sides nominated a member of the arbitration tribunal as did Brazil, Italy and Switzerland.

The Hague Convention on Pacific Settlement of Disputes 1899 marked the beginning of a new era of arbitration by establishing a Permanent Court of Arbitration (PCA) which began functioning in 1902 and is still in existence. The Permanent Court of Arbitration is a bit of a misnomer since it is neither a court nor is it permanent. The PCA consists of a panel of 300 members (four nominated by each contracting party to the Hague Conventions 1899 and 1907) from whom each disputant can select one or more arbitrators (normally two, one of whom can be a national). The selected arbitrators then choose an umpire who presides over the arbitration. Decision of the arbitration panel is by majority vote. Of course, states do not have to use the PCA procedures and can establish *ad hoc* arbitration tribunals of their own such as the one set up to deal with the *Guinea/Guinea Bissau Maritime Delimitation* case (1985).

Arbitration depends on consent. The law to be applied, the make up of the tribunal, any time limits must all be mutually agreed before the arbitration starts. The mutual agreement under which the parties agree to submit their

---

8   See articles 15 and 37 respectively of the 1899 and 1907 Hague Conventions for the Pacific Settlement of International Disputes.

9   Sometimes the parties may agree in advance to appoint arbitrators from among a pre-existing list. For example, the Hague Convention provides such a list. Similarly the 1982 United Nations Convention on the Law of the Sea provides for a list of arbitrators in accordance with article 2 of annex VII on 'Arbitration' and article VIII on 'Special arbitration'.

10   United Nations, Office of Legal Affairs, *Handbook on the Peaceful Settlement of Disputes between States*, 1992, New York: United Nations at p 55.

dispute to arbitration and under which they agree the procedures and rules to be applied is known as the *compromis*. The *compromis* should also provide that the arbitration decision will be binding on the parties. There do exist model rules of procedure, for example, the Model Rules on Arbitral Procedures which were drawn up by the ILC and adopted by the UN General Assembly in 1958.

Between 1900 and 1932 some 20 disputes went through the PCA procedure, but since then only 3 cases have been heard. Arbitration has revived in popularity more recently especially since the coming into force of the Convention on the Settlement of Investment Disputes 1964 which set up an international arbitration centre in Washington to deal with disputes between states arising out of the expropriation of foreign owned property. Arbitration is most favoured in commercial and technical disputes in which arbitrators can be appointed who have specialist knowledge. It also has the advantage over judicial settlement in that it is usually less expensive.

One question which has been raised recently is whether the decision of an arbitration tribunal is capable of review. It has already been seen that the decisions of such tribunals are to be regarded as final and this would seem to rule out the possibility of review or appeal unless there is a clear error of law. However in *Guinea Bissau v Senegal* (1991)[11] the ICJ was willing to consider whether or not it should declare an arbitration award to be void. Guinea-Bissau alleged that the arbitration tribunal had exceeded its powers, that there was no true majority in favour of the decision, and that the award was based on insufficient reasoning. The Court did not uphold Guinea-Bissau's claims but the fact that it was prepared to investigate the claims would indicate that arbitration awards are susceptible to review by the ICJ. The decision has been criticised by a number of writers on the grounds that it undermines arbitration as a means of achieving final settlement of disputes.

13.8 Judicial settlement

By judicial settlement is meant a settlement brought about by a properly constituted international judicial tribunal, applying rules of law. The most well known of the international judicial tribunals is the International Court of Justice. There are also a number of regional international tribunals and also tribunals with jurisdiction over particular disputes. For example, the Law of the Sea Convention 1982 provides arrangements for the establishment of an International Tribunal for the Law of the Sea and the Sea Bed Disputes Chamber for dealing with disputes arising from the Convention. There is no absolute distinction between arbitration and judicial settlement, although judicial settlement generally involves reference of the dispute to a permanent tribunal which applies fixed rules of procedure.

13.8.1 The World Court

The World Court refers to both the Permanent Court of International Justice (PCIJ) and its successor, the International Court of Justice (ICJ).

---

11   [1991] *ICJ Rep* at p 53.

The PCIJ sat for the first time in the Hague on 15 February 1922 and between 1922 and 1939 it dealt with 79 cases. The PCIJ was dissolved together with the League of Nations in April 1946. It was succeeded by the ICJ which is the principal judicial organ of the UN. The ICJ is an integral part of the UN established under Article 92 of the UN Charter. The Statute of the ICJ, which broadly follows the text of the Statute of the PCIJ, contains the basic rules of the Court which are supplemented by the Rules of the Court adopted by the court under Article 30. The present rules were adopted on 14 April 1978 and represent a major revision of the original 1946 rules. The Rules govern the procedure of the Court.

STATUTE OF THE INTERNATIONAL COURT OF JUSTICE

Article 1

The International Court of Justice established by the Charter of the United Nations as the principal judicial organ of the United Nations shall be constituted and shall function in accordance with the provisions of the present Statute.

CHAPTER I
ORGANISATION OF THE COURT

Article 2

The Court shall be composed of a body of independent judges, elected regardless of their nationality from among persons of high moral character, who possess the qualifications required in their respective countries for appointment to the highest judicial offices, or are jurisconsults of recognised competence in international law.

Article 3

1   The Court shall consist of 15 members, no two of whom may be nationals of the same state.

2   A person who for the purposes of membership in the Court could be regarded as a national of more than one state shall be deemed to be a national of the one in which he ordinarily exercises civil and political rights.

Article 4

1   The members of the Court shall be elected by the General Assembly and by the Security Council from a list of persons nominated by the national groups in the Permanent Court of Arbitration, in accordance with the following provisions.

2   In the case of Members of the United Nations not represented in the Permanent Court of Arbitration, candidates shall be nominated by national groups appointed for this purpose by their Governments under the same conditions as those prescribed for members of the Permanent Court of Arbitration by Article 44 of the Convention of The Hague of 1907 for the pacific settlement of international disputes.

3   The conditions under which a state is a party to the present Statute but is not a Member of the United Nations may participate in electing the members of the Court shall, in the absence of a special agreement, be laid down by the General Assembly upon recommendation of the Security Council.

Article 5

1   At least three months before the date of the election, the Secretary General of the United Nations shall address a written request to the members of the Permanent Court of Arbitration belonging to the states which are parties to the present Statute, and to the members of the national groups appointed under Article 4, para 2, inviting them to undertake, within a given time, by national groups, the nomination of persons in position to accept the duties of a member of the Court.

2   No group may nominate more than four persons, not more than two of whom shall be of their own nationality. In no case may the number of candidates nominated by a group be more than double the number of seats to be filled.

Article 6

Before making these nominations, each national group is recommended to consult its highest court of justice, its legal faculties and schools of law, and its national academies and national sections of international academies devoted to the study of law.

Article 7

1   The Secretary General shall prepare a list in alphabetical order of all the persons thus nominated. Save as provided in Article 12, para 2, these shall be the only persons eligible.

2   The Secretary General shall submit this list to the General Assembly and the Security Council.

Article 8

The General Assembly and the Security Council shall proceed independently of one another to elect the members of the Court.

Article 9

At every election, the electors shall bear in mind not only that the persons to be elected should individually possess the qualifications required, but also that in the body as a whole the representation of the main forms of civilisation and of the principal legal systems of the world should be assured.

Article 10

1   Those candidates who obtain an absolute majority of votes in the General Assembly and in the Security Council shall be considered as elected.

2   Any vote of the Security Council, whether for the election of judges or for the appointment of members of the conference envisaged in Article 12, shall be taken without any distinction between permanent and non-permanent members of the Security Council.

3   In the event of more than one national of the same state obtaining an absolute majority of the votes both of the General Assembly and of the Security Council, the eldest of these only shall be considered as elected.

Article 11

If, after the first meeting held for the purpose of the election, one or more seats remain to be filled, a second and, if necessary, a third meeting shall take place.

Article 12

1   If, after the third meeting, one or more seats still remain unfilled, a joint conference consisting of six members, three appointed by the General Assembly and three by the Security Council, may be formed at any time at the request of either the General Assembly or the Security Council, for the purpose of choosing by the vote of an absolute majority one name for each seat still vacant, to submit to the General Assembly and the Security Council for their respective acceptance.

2   If the joint conference is unanimously agreed upon any person who fulfils the required conditions, he may be included in its list, even though he was not included in the list of nominations referred to in Article 7.

3   If the joint conference is satisfied that it will not be successful in procuring an election, those members of the Court who have already been elected shall, within a period to be fixed by the Security Council, proceed to fill the vacant seats by selection from among those candidates who have obtained votes either in the General Assembly or in the Security Council.

4   In the event of an equality of votes among the judges, the eldest judge shall have a casting vote.

Article 13

1   The members of the Court shall be elected for nine years and may be re-elected; provided, however, that of the judges elected at the first election, the terms of five judges shall expire at the end of three years and the terms of five more judges shall expire at the end of six years.

2   The judges whose terms are to expire at the end of the above-mentioned periods of three and six years shall be chosen by lot to be drawn by the Secretary General immediately after the fist election has been completed.

3   The members of the Court shall continue to discharge their duties until their places have been filled. Though replaced, they shall finish any cases which they may have begun.

4   In the case of the resignation of a member of the Court, the resignation shall be addressed to the President of the Court for transmission to the Secretary General. This last notification makes the place vacant.

Article 14

Vacancies shall be filled by the same method as that laid down for the first election, subject to the following provision: the Secretary General shall, within one month of the occurrence of the vacancy, proceed to issue invitations provided for in Article 5, and the date of the election shall be fixed by the Security Council.

Article 15

A member of the Court elected to replace a member whose term of office has not expired shall hold office for the remainder of his predecessor's term.

Article 16

1   No member of the Court may exercise any political or administrative function, or engage in any other occupation of a professional nature.

2   Any doubt on this point shall be settled by the decision of the Court.

Article 17

1   No member of the Court may act as agent, counsel, or advocate in any case.

2   No member may participate in the decision of any case in which he has previously taken part as agent, counsel, or advocate for one of the parties, or as a member of a national or international court, or of a commission of inquiry, or in any other capacity.

3   Any doubt on this point shall be settled by a decisions of the Court.

Article 18

1   No member of the Court can be dismissed unless, in the unanimous opinion of the other members, he has ceased to fulfil the required conditions.

2   Formal notification thereof shall be made to the Secretary General by the Registrar.

3   This notification makes the place vacant.

Article 19

The membership of the Court, when engaged on the business of the Court, shall enjoy diplomatic privileges and immunities.

Article 20

Every member of the Court shall, before taking up his duties, make a solemn declaration in open court that he will exercise his powers impartially and conscientiously.

Article 21

1   The Court shall elect its President and Vice-President for three years; they may be re-elected.

2   The Court shall appoint its Registrar and may provide for the appointment of such other officers as may be necessary.

Article 22

1   The seat of the Court shall be established at The Hague. This, however, shall not prevent the Court from sitting and exercising its functions elsewhere whenever the Court considers it desirable.

2   The President and the Registrar shall reside at the seat of the Court.

Article 23

1   The Court shall remain permanently in session, except during the judicial vacations, the dates and durations of which shall be fixed by the Court.

2   Members of the Court are entitled to periodic leave, the dates and duration of which shall be fixed by the Court, having in mind the distance between The Hague and the home of each judge.

3   Members of the Court shall be bound, unless they are on leave or prevented from attending by illness or serious reasons duly explained to the President, to hold themselves permanently at the disposal of the Court.

Article 24

1   If, for some special reason, a member of the Court considers that he should not take part in the decision of a particular case, he shall so inform the President.

2   If the President considers that for some special reason one of the members of the Court should not sit in a particular case, he shall give him notice accordingly.

3   If in any such case the member of the Court and the President disagree, the matter shall be settled by the decision of the Court.

Article 25

1   The full Court shall sit except when it is expressly provided otherwise in the present Statute.

2   Subject to the condition that the number of judges available to constitute the Court is not thereby reduced below eleven, the Rules of the Court may provide for allowing one or more judges, according to circumstances and in rotation, to be dispensed from sitting.

3   A quorum of nine judges shall suffice to constitute the Court.

Article 26

1   The Court may from time to time form one or more chambers, composed of three or more judges as the Court may determine, for dealing with particular categories of cases; for example, labour cases and cases relating to transit and communications.

2   The Court may at any time form a chamber for dealing with a particular case. The number of judges to constitute such a chamber shall be determined by the Court with the approval of the parties.

3   Cases shall be heard and determined by the chambers provided for in this article if the parties so request.

Article 27

A judgment given by any of the chambers provided for in Articles 26 and 29 shall be considered by the Court.

Article 28

The chambers provided for in Articles 26 and 29 may, with the consent of the parties, sit and exercise their functions elsewhere than at The Hague.

Article 29

With a view to the speedy dispatch of business, the Court shall form annually a chamber composed of five judges which, at the request of the parties, may hear and determine cases by summary procedure. In addition, two judges shall be selected for the purpose of replacing judges who find it impossible to sit.

Article 30

1   The Court shall frame rules for carrying out its functions. In particular, it shall lay down rules of procedure.

2   The Rules of the Court may provide for assessors to sit with the Court or with any of its chambers, without the right to vote.

Article 31

1   Judges of the nationality of each of the parties shall retain their right to sit in the cases before the Court.

2   If the Court includes upon the Bench a judge of the nationality of one of the parties any other party may choose a person to sit as judge. Such person shall be chosen preferably from among those persons who have been nominated as candidates as provided for in Articles 4 and 5.

3   If the Court includes upon the Bench no judge of the nationality of the parties, each of these parties may proceed to choose a judge as provided in para 2 of this article.

4   The provisions of this article shall apply to the case of Articles 26 and 29. In such cases, the President shall request one or, if necessary, two of the members of the Court forming the chamber to give place to the members of

the Court of the nationality of the parties concerned, and, failing such or if they are unable to be present, to the judges specially chosen by the parties.

5   Should there be several parties in the same interest, they shall, for the purposes of the preceding provisions, be reckoned as one party only. Any doubt upon this point shall be settled by the decision of the Court.

6   Judges chosen as laid down in paras 2, 3, and 4 of this article shall fulfil the conditions required by Articles 2, 17 (para 2), 20 and 24 of the present Statute. They shall take part in the decision on terms of complete equality with their colleagues.

Article 32

1   Each member of the Court shall receive an annual salary.

2   The President shall receive a special annual allowance.

3   The Vice-President shall receive a special allowance for every day on which he acts as President.

4   The judges chosen under Article 31, other than members of the Court, shall receive compensation for each day on which they exercise their functions.

5   These salaries, allowances, and compensation shall be fixed by the General Assembly. They may not be decreased during the term of office.

6   The salary of the Registrar shall be fixed by the General Assembly on the proposal of the Court.

7   Regulations made by the General Assembly shall fix the conditions under which retirement pensions may be given to members of the Court and to the Registrar, and the conditions under which members of the Court and the Registrar shall have their travelling expenses refunded.

8   The above salaries, allowances, and compensation shall be free of all taxation.

Article 33

The expenses of the Court shall be borne by the United Nations in such a manner as shall be decided by the General Assembly.

CHAPTER II
COMPETENCE OF THE COURT

Article 34

1   Only states may be parties in cases before the Court.

2   The Court, subject to and in conformity with its Rules, may request of public international organisations information relevant to cases before it, and shall receive such information presented by such organisations on their own initiative.

3   Whenever the construction of the constituent instrument of a public international organisation or of an international convention adopted thereunder is in question in a case before the Court, the Registrar shall so notify the public international organisation concerned and shall communicate to it copies of all the written proceedings.

Article 35

1   The Court shall be open to the States Parties to the present Statute.

2   The conditions under which the Court shall be open to other states shall, subject to the special provisions contained in treaties in force, be laid down

by the Security Council, but in no case shall such conditions place the parties in a position of inequality before the Court.

3   When a state which is not a Member of the United Nations is a party to a case, the Court shall fix the amount which that party shall contribute towards the expenses of the Court. This provision shall not apply if such state is bearing a share of the expenses of the Court.

Article 36

1   The jurisdiction of the Court comprises all cases which the parties refer to it and all matters specially provided for in the Charter of the United Nations or in treaties or conventions in force.

2   The States Parties to the present Statute may at any time declare that they recognise as compulsory *ipso facto* and without special agreement, in relation to any other state accepting the same obligation, the jurisdiction of the Court in all legal disputes concerning:

(a)   the interpretation of a treaty;

(b)   any question of international law;

(c)   the existence of any fact which, if established, would constitute a breach of an international obligation;

(d)   the nature or extent of the reparation to be made for the breach of an international obligation.

3   The declarations referred to above may be made unconditionally or on condition of reciprocity on the part of several or certain states, or for a certain time.

4   Such declarations shall be deposited with the Secretary General of the United Nations, who shall transmit copies thereof to the parties to the Statute and to the Registrar of the Court.

5   Declarations made under Article 36 of the Statute of the Permanent Court of International Justice and which are still in force shall be deemed, as between the parties to the present Statute, to be acceptance of the compulsory jurisdiction of the International Court of Justice for the period which they still have to run and in accordance with their terms.

6   In the event of a dispute as to whether the Court has jurisdiction, the matter shall be settled by the decision of the Court.

Article 37

Whenever a treaty or convention in force provides for reference of a matter to a tribunal to have been instituted by the League of Nations, or to the Permanent Court of International Justice, the matter shall, as between the parties to the present Statute, be referred to the International Court of Justice.

Article 38

1   The Court, whose function it is to decide in accordance with international law such disputes as are submitted to it, shall apply:

(a)   international conventions, whether general or particular, establishing rules expressly recognised by the contesting states;

(b)   international custom, as evidence of a general practice accepted as law;

(c)   the general principles of law recognised by civilised nations;

(d)   subject to the provisions of Article 59, judicial decisions and the teachings of the most highly qualified publicists of the various nations, as subsidiary means for the determination of rules of law.

2   This provision shall not prejudice the power of the Court to decide a case *ex aequo et bono*, if the parties agree thereto.

CHAPTER III
PROCEDURE

Article 39

1   The official languages of the Court shall be French and English. If the parties agree that the case shall be conducted in French, the judgment shall be delivered in French. If the parties agree that the case shall be conducted in English, the judgment shall be delivered in English.

2   In the absence of an agreement as to which language shall be employed, each party may, in the pleadings, use the language which it prefers; the decision of the Court shall be given in French and English. In this case the Court shall at the same time determine which of the two texts shall be considered as authoritative.

3   The Court shall, at the request of any party, authorise a language other than French or English to be used by that party.

Article 40

1   Cases are brought before the Court, as the case may be, either by the notification of the special agreement or by a written application addressed to the Registrar. In either case the subject of the dispute and the parties shall be indicated.

2   The Registrar shall forthwith communicate the application to all concerned.

3   He shall also notify the Members of the United Nations through the Secretary General, and also any other states entitled to appear before the Court.

Article 41

1   The Court shall have the power to indicate, if it considers that circumstances so require, any provisional measures which ought to be taken to preserve the respective rights of either party.

2   Pending the final decision, notice of the measure suggested shall forthwith be given to the parties and to the Security Council..

Article 42

1   The parties shall be represented by agents.

2   They may have the assistance of counsel or advocates before the Court.

3   The agents, counsel and advocates of parties before the Court shall enjoy the privileges and immunities necessary to the independent function of the Court.

Article 43

1   The procedure shall consist of two parts: written and oral.

2   The written proceedings shall consist of the communication to the Court and to the parties of memorials, counter-memorials, and if necessary, replies; also all papers and documents in support.

3   These communications shall be made through the Registrar, in the order and within the time fixed by the Court.

4   A certified copy of every document produced by one party shall be communicated to the other party.

5   The oral proceedings shall consist of the hearing by the Court of witnesses, experts, agents, counsel, and advocates.

Article 44

1   For the service of all notices upon persons other than agents, counsel, and advocates, the Court shall apply direct to the government of the state upon whose territory the notice has to be served.

2   The same provision shall apply whenever steps are taken to procure evidence on the spot.

Article 45

The hearing shall be under the control of the President or, if he is unable to preside, of the Vice-President; if neither it able to preside, the senior judge present shall preside.

Article 46

The hearing in Court shall be public, unless the Court shall decide otherwise, or unless the parties demand that the public be not admitted.

Article 47

1   Minutes shall be made at each hearing, and signed by the Registrar and the President.

2   These minutes alone shall be authentic.

Article 48

The Court shall make orders for the conduct of the case, shall decide the form and time in which each party must conclude its arguments, and make all arrangements connected with the taking of evidence.

Article 49

The Court may, even before the hearing begins, call upon the agents to produce any document or to supply any explanations. Formal note shall be taken of any refusal.

Article 50

The Court may, at any other time, entrust any individual body, bureau, commission, or other organisation that it may select, with the task of carrying out an inquiry or giving an expert opinion.

Article 51

During the hearing any relevant questions are to be put to the witnesses and experts under the conditions laid down by the Court in the rules of procedure referred to in Article 30.

Article 52

After the Court has received the proofs and evidence within the time specified for the purpose, it may refuse to accept any further oral or written evidence that one party may desire to present unless the other side consents.

Article 53

1   Whenever one of the parties does not appear before the Court, or fails to defend his case, the other party may call upon the Court to decide in favour of its claim.

2   The Court must, before doing so, satisfy itself, not only that it has jurisdiction in accordance with Articles 36 and 37, but also that the claim is well founded in fact and law.

Article 54

1   When, subject to the control of the Court, the agents, counsel, and advocates have completed their presentation of the case, the President shall declare the hearing closed.

2   The Court shall withdraw to consider the judgment.

3   The deliberations of the Court shall take place in private and remain secret.

Article 55

1   All questions shall be decided by a majority of the judges present.

2   In the event of an equality of votes, the President or the judge who acts in his place shall have a casting vote.

Article 56

1   The judgment shall state the reasons on which it is based.

2   It shall contain the names of the judges who have taken part in the decision.

Article 57

If the judgment does not represent in whole or in part the unanimous opinion of the judges, any judge shall be entitled to deliver a separate opinion.

Article 58

The judgment shall be signed by the President and by the Registrar. It shall be read in open court, due notice having been given to the agents.

Article 59

The decision of the Court has no binding force except between the parties and in respect of that particular case.

Article 60

The judgment is final and without appeal. In the event of dispute as to the meaning or scope of the judgment, the Court shall construe it upon the request of any party.

Article 61

1   An application for revision of a judgment may be made only when it is based upon the discovery of some fact of such a nature as to be a decisive factor, which fact was, when the judgment was given, unknown to the Court and also to the party claiming revision, always provided that such ignorance was not due to negligence.

2   The proceedings for revision shall be opened by a judgment of the Court expressly recording the existence of the new fact, recognising that it has such a character as to lay the case open for revision, and declaring the application admissible on this ground.

3   The Court may require previous compliance with the terms of the judgment before it admits proceedings in revision.

4   The application for revision must be made at latest within six months of the discovery of the new fact.

5   No application for revision may be made after the lapse of ten years from the date of the judgment.

Article 62

1   Should a state consider that it has an interest of a legal nature which may be affected by the decision in the case, it may submit a request to the Court to be permitted to intervene.

2   It shall be for the Court to decide upon this request.

Article 63

1   Whenever the construction of a convention to which states other than those concerned in the case are parties is in question, the Registrar shall notify all such states forthwith.

2   Every state so notified has the right to intervene in the proceedings, but if it uses this right, the construction given by the judgment will be equally binding upon it.

Article 64

Unless otherwise decided by the Court, each party shall bear its own costs.

CHAPTER IV
ADVISORY OPINIONS

Article 65

1   The Court may give an advisory opinion on any legal question at the request of whatever body may be authorised by or in accordance with the Charter of the United Nations to make such a request.

2   Questions upon which the advisory opinion of the Court is asked shall be laid before the Court by means of a written request containing an exact statement of the question upon which an opinion is required, and accompanied by all documents likely to throw light upon the question.

Article 66

1   The Registrar shall forthwith give notice of the request for an advisory opinion to all states entitled to appear before the Court.

2   The Registrar shall also, by means of a special and direct communication, notify any state entitled to appear before the Court or international organisation considered by the Court or, should it not be sitting, by the President, as likely to be able to furnish information on the question, that the Court will be prepared to receive, within a time limit to be fixed by the President, written statements, or to hear, at a public sitting to be held for the purpose, oral statements relating to the question.

3   Should any such state entitled to appear before the Court have failed to receive the special communication referred to in para 2 of this article, such state may express a desire to submit a written statement or to be hear; and the Court will decide.

4   states and organisations having presented written and oral statements or both shall be permitted to comment on the statements made by other states or organisations in the form, to the extent, and within the time limits which the Court or, should it not be sitting, the President, shall decide in each particular case. Accordingly, the Registrar shall in due time communicate any such written statement to states and organisations having submitted similar statements.

Article 67

The Court shall deliver its advisory opinions in open court, notice having been given to the Secretary General and to the representatives of Members of the United Nations, of other states and of international organisations immediately concerned.

Article 68

In the exercise of its advisory functions the Court shall further be guided by the provisions of the present Statute which apply in contentious cases to the extent to which it recognises them to be applicable.

CHAPTER V

AMENDMENT

Article 69

Amendments to the present Statute shall be effected by the same procedure as is provided by the Charter of the United Nations for amendments to that Charter, subject, however, to any provisions which the General Assembly upon recommendation of the Security Council may adopt concerning the participation of states which are parties to the present Statute but are not Members of the United Nations.

Article 70

The Court shall have the power to propose such amendments to the present Statute as it may deem necessary, through written communications to the Secretary General, for consideration in conformity with the provisions of Article 69.

13.8.2 Composition of the Court

The Court is composed of 15 judges nominated by the national groups on the panel of the Permanent Court of Arbitration. No two judges may be of the same nationality. The judges are elected by absolute majority by secret ballot at meetings of the Security Council and General Assembly held simultaneously in an attempt to avoid fixing. In practice there is much disagreement and political bargaining. Those eligible are persons of high moral character who possess the qualifications required in their country for appointment to high judicial office or, alternatively, are recognised international jurists (Article 2 of the ICJ Statute). Judges are to be elected without regard to nationality, although under a current 'understanding' the regional distribution of judges to be elected is as follows:

Africa	3
Asia	3
Latin America	2
Eastern Europe	2
Western Europe + others	5

and in general the five permanent members of the UN Security Council are represented (US, UK, Russia, China, and France). Judges are appointed for a period of nine years which is renewable. Elections are staggered and five judges are elected every three years. The judges themselves elect a President and Vice-President who serve for a three-year term. Presidents and Vice-Presidents can be re-elected. The current composition of the Court is as follows (term expires on 5 February of the year in parentheses):

Mohammed Badjaoui (Algeria) (2006)

Carl-August Fleischhauer (Germany) (2003)

Gilbert Guillaume (France) (2000)

Geza Herczegh (Hungary) (2003

Rosalyn Higgins (United Kingdom) (2000)

Sui Jiuyong (China) (2003)

Pieter H Kooijmans (Netherlands) (2006)

Abdul G Koroma (Sierra Leone) (2003)

Shigeru Oda (Japan) (2003)

Gonzalo Parra-Aranguren (Venezuela) (2000)

Raymond Ranjeva (Madagascar) (2000)

Jose Francisco Rezek (Brazil) (2006)

Stephen M Schwebel (United States) (2006)

Christopher G Weeramantry (Sri Lanka) (2000)

Vladlen S Vereshchetin (Russian Federation) (2006)

On 6 February 1997 Stephen M Schwebel was elected President of the Court for a three-year term. Christopher G Weeramantry was elected Vice-President. The Registrar of the Court is Eduardo Valencia-Ospina (Colombia) and the Deputy Registrar is Jean-Jacques Arnaldez (France).

Although the nationality of judges may be significant in their selection, once appointed they are expected to be impartial and not subject to control by the states of which they are nationals. A judge is not prohibited from sitting in a case in which his national state is a party, although a President should not act as President in such a case. A party not represented on the bench can be represented by an *ad hoc* judge. This is to provide equality of the parties – the alternative would be to exclude judges from hearing cases about their own national state. Article 17(2) of the Statute provides that no member of the court should participate in the decision of any case in which he has previously acted as a representative for one of the parties although this rule has not always been observed in practice. For example, in the *Namibia* case (1971) members of the Court had previously been involved in UN discussions as national representatives on the Security Council and had played an active part in Resolutions directly relevant to the case. South Africa challenged the court's jurisdiction on this basis but the challenge was rejected.

The cases are heard in either English or French and are decided by majority vote. If it is necessary the President has a casting vote in addition to his own vote. The Court delivers a single judgment, but individual judges can add their own judgment whether or not they are dissenting. The cases can be heard by the full court (quorum = nine) or by a Chamber of three or more for a particular case (Article 26 of the ICJ Statute). The composition of the Chamber is decided by the Court after the parties have been consulted. In the *Gulf of Maine* case (1982) the US and Canada threatened to withdraw their case if their wishes as to the composition of the Chamber were not respected. Since then a number of other cases have been heard by a Chamber of the Court and this has led to the expression of some concern on the possible effects on the reputation of the Court as a whole. The apparent ability of states to choose the composition of the

Chamber may have an adverse effect on the Court's ability to develop a universally applicable body of international law.

13.8.3 Jurisdiction of the Court

13.8.3.1 Jurisdiction in contentious cases

Article 34 of the Statute of the Court declares that only states may be parties before the ICJ and the court is open to all members of the UN (who are automatically parties to the Statute).[12] states which are not UN members may become parties to the Statute on conditions set by the UN General Assembly (Article 93 of the UN Charter) and two states, Switzerland and Nauru, have taken advantage of this provision. Access to the Court is also available to non-parties to the Statute if they lodge a declaration with the court accepting the obligations of the Statute and Article 94 of the UN Charter. Declarations can be particular to a particular dispute, or they can be general.

In contentious cases, in principle, the exercise of the court's jurisdiction is conditional on the consent of the parties to the dispute. This was confirmed in the separate opinion of Judge Lauterpacht given in the *Case Concerning the Application of the Genocide Convention* (1993) where he stated:

> The Court can only act in a case if the parties, both applicant and respondent, have conferred jurisdiction upon it by some voluntary act of consent ...

and he indicated that consent could be given in one of three ways:

(i) under the provisions of a treaty;

(ii) by acceptance of the court's compulsory jurisdiction under Article 36(2) of the Statute;

(iii) by acceptance of jurisdiction by the respondent through its conduct following the unilateral initiation of proceedings by the applicant.

A joint decision to make reference to the court will usually be drawn up in a special agreement (*compromis*). A unilateral reference by one state will be sufficient to vest the court with jurisdiction if the other state subsequently consents under the doctrine known as *forum prorogatum*. Such a situation arose in the *Corfu Channel* case (1947). If there is no consent, then the court cannot hear the case. Nor can the court hear a case in the absence of a materially interested state.

The most usual method of conferring jurisdiction under Article 36(1) is by treaty. A treaty may be one providing for the reference of specific disputes, or it may be couched in more general terms. For example, Article 16(1) Convention on Unlawful Acts Against Maritime Navigation 1988 provides that:

> Any dispute between two or more State Parties concerning the interpretation or application of this Convention which cannot be settled through negotiation within a reasonable time shall, at the request of one of them, be submitted to arbitration. If within six months from the date of the request for arbitration, the parties are unable to agree on the organisation of the arbitration any one of those

---

12　There are currently 185 members of the United Nations – see Appendix 1.

parties may refer the dispute to the International Court of Justice by request in conformity with the Statute of the Court.

In the *US Diplomatic and Consular Staff in Tehran* case (1980) the ICJ founded jurisdiction on Article 1 of the Optional Protocols concerning the Compulsory Settlement of Disputes which accompany both the Vienna Convention on Consular Relations 1963 and the Vienna Convention on Diplomatic Relations 1961.

Although it is true to state that the jurisdiction of the ICJ is conditional on the consent of the parties, matters are slightly confused by Article 36(2) of the Statute. Under this provision states may make a declaration recognising as compulsory the jurisdiction of the court in a number of defined disputes. Such declarations obviate the need for special agreement. Making the declaration is optional, but once it has been made acceptance of the court's jurisdiction is compulsory. The effectiveness of Article 36(2) depends on many, if not all, states making such a declaration. So far fewer than 50 states have done so. Declarations are lodged with the UN Secretary General, and once a state has made the declaration it has the right to bring to the Court any other state accepting the same obligation, providing the subject matter of the dispute falls within the specified categories. Article 36(3) provides that declarations may be made unconditionally or on condition of reciprocity on the part of several or certain states or for a certain time. Reservations are to be found in most declarations and the Court's jurisdiction over a case is restricted to those disputes that states have not excluded from its 'compulsory' jurisdiction. Declarations can also be made subject to a reservation permitting withdrawal at any time. They may be made indefinitely or for a fixed term of years.

The majority of declarations made according to Article 36(2) operate on the basis of reciprocity. This means that the ICJ will only have jurisdiction to the extent that the two declarations of the parties to the dispute coincide. This point was confirmed by the ICJ in the *Norwegian Loans* case (1957) where France sought to rely on the fact that both it and Norway had made declarations accepting the compulsory jurisdiction of the court. The ICJ found that:

> A comparison between the two declarations shows that the French declaration accepts the Court's jurisdiction within narrower limits than the Norwegian declaration; consequently, the common will of the parties, which is the basis of the Court's jurisdiction, exists within these narrower limits indicated by the French reservation.

As a result, Norway was entitled to invoke the French reservation and the ICJ found itself without jurisdiction to hear the case.

The type of reservation which was found in the French case, often known as a self-judging or automatic reservation, has caused particular problems. The French reservation was worded as follows:

> This declaration does not apply to differences relating to matters which are essentially within the national jurisdiction as understood by the government of the Republic of France.

Article 36(6) of the Statute provides it is the ICJ which must ultimately decide any dispute about its jurisdiction and it would therefore appear that such automatic reservations usurp the powers of the Court by allowing the reserving state to have the final say as to what constitutes a matter within national jurisdiction. Judge Lauterpacht, in a separate opinion in the *Norwegian Loans* case, stated that the French declaration did conflict with Article 36(6) and was therefore invalid. He went on to consider what the effect of the invalid reservation was. He suggested two alternatives: either the invalid reservation could be severed from the declaration, or the reservation could be regarded as invalidating the entire declaration. Judge Lauterpacht favoured the latter option and was supported in this view by the dissenting opinion of Judge Guerrero. Judge Lauterpacht repeated his view in the *Interhandel* case (1959) where the Court was faced with an automatic reservation contained in the US optional declaration. However, in that case the Court itself did not find it necessary to comment on the validity of such reservations. It would seem to be settled that automatic or self-judging reservations are themselves invalid. As to the effect of such invalidity on the rest of the declaration the position is less clear, although the view preferred by the majority of writers is that the invalid reservation can be severed from the rest of the declaration thus leaving the amended declaration effective.

States are free to modify and withdraw their declarations and the question of the extent of notice required has created some problems. The declaration made by the USA in 1946 provided for termination after a six-month notice period. When it became clear that Nicaragua was going to bring proceedings against it in the ICJ, the US sought to modify, with immediate effect, its declaration so as to exclude the Court's jurisdiction. In considering the question of jurisdiction in the *Nicaragua* case (1984) the ICJ held that Nicaragua (whose declaration contained no reservation) was entitled to invoke against the US the six-month notice requirement and that this requirement would apply to modifications to the declaration. The US's modification, which was made on 6 April 1984, three days before the Court became seised of the case, would therefore only take effect on 6 October 1984, by which time the Court would already have begun to hear the case.

A final point to note in respect of reservations to optional declarations made under Article 36(2) is that they only relate to the Court's jurisdiction under Article 36(2). Even if a reservation provides an effective bar to Article 36(2) jurisdiction, the Court may be able to base jurisdiction on some other manifestation of a common will of the parties. In practice, jurisdiction in very few cases is based solely on the optional declaration.

13.8.3.2 Incidental jurisdiction

The ICJ may be called upon to exercise an incidental jurisdiction, independently of the main case: hearing preliminary objections, applications to intervene, and taking interim measures.

Preliminary objections: often, before it looks at the merits of the case, the Court will be asked to consider objections to jurisdiction. These jurisdictional issues are decided first. As has already been stated, it is the Court itself which has authority to settle disputes about jurisdiction by virtue of Article 36(6) of the Statute of the ICJ.

Intervention: a state not a party to the dispute may intervene under Article 62 and 63 of the Statute if it considers it has an interest in the case and it is for the ICJ to decide as a preliminary matter whether or not such an interest exists. In the *Continental Shelf* case (1982) the Court rejected Malta's application to intervene. While Malta did have an interest similar to other states in the area in the case in question, the Court said that in order to intervene under Article 62 it had to have an interest of a legal nature which may be affected by the Court's decision in the instant case. In the *Land, Island and Maritime Frontier* case (1992) the ICJ gave permission to Nicaragua to intervene in the dispute between Honduras and El Salvador. In doing so it suggested a number of general principles which would apply with regard to any application to intervene. First, the intervening state has the burden of proving it has an interest of a legal nature which may, rather than will, be affected by the dispute. Secondly, the court can grant permission to intervene even if one or both of the other parties object. Thirdly, if permission is granted, the intervening state does not become a party to the dispute and no binding determination of its rights will occur. The purpose of intervention is to allow the intervening state to remind the Court of rights that may be affected by Resolution of the dispute between the two parties.

Interim measures: under Article 41 of the Statute the Court may grant provisional measures of protection in order to preserve the respective rights of the parties. These are awarded to assist the Court to ensure the integrity of the proceedings and are not to be regarded as judgments on the merits of the case. Interim measures have been awarded in a number of cases but compliance with such orders has been poor. In making interim indications, which are heard first, the court has to be satisfied that there is a *prima facie* basis for jurisdiction. In the *Lockerbie* case (1992) the ICJ refused Libya's requests for interim measures of protection from the use of sanctions and possible use of force against it. The principal ground for refusal was that the sanctions and possible use of force were being effected by a UN Security Council Resolution and the Court drew back at the interim stage from ruling such a Resolution *ultra vires*. The Court was therefore unable to find that there was a risk of Libya's interests in the case suffering irreparable damage. The Court was also required to consider the effect of a conflict between treaty obligations and Security Council Resolutions and Judge Lachs, in a separate opinion, expressly stated his view that treaty obligations could be overridden by Resolutions passed by the Security Council. It seems likely that when the court considers the merits of the case it will have to consider the relationship between itself and other organs of the UN and the extent to which it can rule on the validity of Resolutions passed under provisions of the UN Charter.

In the *Case Concerning the Land and Maritime Boundary between Cameroon and Nigeria*, the Court issued an Order indicating the following provisional measures:

(1) Unanimously,

Both Parties should ensure that no action of any kind, and particularly no action by their armed forces, is taken which might prejudice the rights of the other in respect of whatever judgment the Court may render in the case, or which might aggravate or extend the dispute before it;

(2) By 16 votes to 1,

Both Parties should observe the agreement reached between the Ministers for Foreign Affairs in Kara, Togo, on 17 February 1996, for the cessation of all hostilities in the Bakassi Peninsula;

IN FAVOUR: President Bedjaoui; Vice-President Schwebel; Judges Oda, Guillaume, Shahabuddeen, Weeramantry, Ranjeva, Herczegh, Shi, Fleischhauer, Koroma, Vereshchetin, Ferrari Bravo, Higgins, Parra-Aranguren; Judge *ad hoc* Mbaye;

AGAINST: Judge *ad hoc* Ajibola.

(3) By 12 votes to 5,

Both Parties should ensure that the presence of any armed forces in the Bakassi Peninsula does not extend beyond the positions in which they were situated prior to 3 February 1996;

IN FAVOUR: President Bedjaoui; Vice-President Schwebel; Judges Oda, Guillaume, Ranjeva, Herczegh, Fleischhauer, Koroma, Ferrari Bravo, Higgins, Parra-Aranguren;

Judge *ad hoc* Mbaye;

AGAINST: Judges Shahabuddeen, Weeramantry, Shi, Vereshchetin;

Judge *ad hoc* Ajibola.

(4) By 16 votes to 1,

Both Parties should take all necessary steps to conserve evidence relevant to the present case within the disputed area;

IN FAVOUR: President Bedjaoui; Vice-President Schwebel; Judges Oda, Guillaume, Shahabuddeen, Weeramantry, Ranjeva, Herczegh, Shi, Fleischhauer, Koroma, Vereshchetin, Ferrari Bravo, Higgins, Parra-Aranguren; Judge *ad hoc* Mbaye;

AGAINST: Judge *ad hoc* Ajibola.

(5) By 16 votes to 1,

Both Parties should lend every assistance to the fact-finding mission which the Secretary General of the United Nations has proposed to send to the Bakassi Peninsula;

IN FAVOUR: President Bedjaoui; Vice-President Schwebel; Judges Oda, Guillaume, Shahabuddeen, Weeramantry, Ranjeva, Herczegh, Shi, Fleischhauer, Koroma, Vereshchetin, Ferrari Bravo, Higgins, Parra-Aranguren; Judge *ad hoc* Mbaye;

AGAINST: Judge *ad hoc* Ajibola.[13]

The Court goes on to observe that the power conferred upon it by Articles 41 of the Statute of the Court and 73 of the Rules of Court to indicate provisional measures has as its object to preserve the respective rights of the Parties, pending a decision of the Court, and presupposes that irreparable prejudice shall not be caused to rights which are the subject of dispute in judicial proceedings; that it follows that the Court must be concerned to preserve by such measures the rights which may subsequently be adjudged by the Court to belong either to the Applicant or to the Respondent; and that such measures are only justified if there is urgency.

---

13 *Case Concerning the Land and Maritime Boundary between Cameroon and Nigeria (Cameroon v Nigeria)* (Provisional Measures) Order of 15 March 1996.

LIVERPOOL JOHN MOORES UNIVERSITY
LEARNING & INFORMATION SERVICES

The Court finds that the mediation conducted by the President of the Republic of Togo and the ensuing communiqué announcing the cessation of all hostilities published on 17 February 1996 do not deprive the Court of the rights and duties pertaining to it in the case brought before it. It is clear from the submissions of both Parties to the Court that there were military incidents and that they caused suffering, occasioned fatalities – of both military and civilian personnel – while causing others to be wounded or unaccounted for, as well as causing major material damage. The rights at issue in these proceedings are sovereign rights which the Parties claim over territory, and these rights also concern persons; and armed actions have regrettably occurred on territory which is the subject of proceedings before the Court.

Independently of the requests for the indication of provisional measures submitted by the Parties to preserve specific rights, the Court possesses by virtue of Article 41 of the Statute the power to indicate provisional measures with a view to preventing the aggravation or extension of the dispute whenever it considers that circumstances so require.

The Court finds that the events that have given rise to the request, and more especially the killing of persons, have caused irreparable damage to the rights that the Parties may have over the Peninsula; that persons in the disputed area and, as a consequence, the rights of the Parties within that area are exposed to serious risk of further irreparable damage; and that armed actions within the territory in dispute could jeopardise the existence of evidence relevant to the present case. From the elements of information available to it, the Court takes the view that there is a risk that events likely to aggravate or extend the dispute may occur again, thus rendering any settlement of that dispute more difficult.

The Court here observes that, in the context of the proceedings concerning the indication of provisional measures, it cannot make definitive findings of fact or of imputability, and that the right of each Party to dispute the facts alleged against it, to challenge the attribution to it of responsibility for those facts, and to submit arguments, if appropriate, in respect of the merits, must remain unaffected by the Court's decision.

The Court draws attention to the fact that the decision given in the present proceedings in no way prejudges the question of the jurisdiction of the Court to deal with the merits of the case, or any questions relating to the admissibility of the Application, or relating to the merits themselves and leaves unaffected the right of the governments of Cameroon and Nigeria to submit arguments in respect of those questions.[14]

13.8.3.3 Advisory opinions

In addition to having contentious jurisdiction, Article 65(1) of the Statute allows the ICJ to give advisory opinions on any legal question at the request of any body so authorised by or in accordance with the UN Charter. The General Assembly and the Security Council are authorised by Article 96 of the UN Charter to request advisory opinions and a large proportion of the specialised agencies of the UN have been authorised in accordance with the Charter. states are not able to request advisory opinions themselves. Although advisory opinions are not binding in law on the requesting body, they have generally

---

14 *Case Concerning the Land and Maritime Boundary between Cameroon and Nigeria (Cameroon v Nigeria)* (Provisional Measures) Order of 15 March 1996.

been accepted and acted upon by any state concerned. In exercising jurisdiction to give advisory opinions the ICJ is keen to avoid situations where an answer to a question would have the effect of deciding a specific dispute between two states since to do so would infringe the general requirement of the consent of states to the Resolution of contentious cases. Thus, in the *Eastern Carelia* case (1923) the PCIJ declined to give an opinion which would have directly affected a dispute between Finland and the USSR.

10   The Court must first consider whether it has the jurisdiction to give a reply to the request of the General Assembly for an advisory opinion and whether, should the answer be in the affirmative, there is any reason it should decline to exercise any such jurisdiction.

The Court draws its competence in respect of advisory opinions from Article 65, para 1, of its Statute. Under this article, the Court

> ... may give an advisory opinion on any legal question at the request of whatever body may be authorised by or in accordance with the Charter of the United Nations to make such a request.

11   For the Court to be competent to give an advisory opinion, it is thus necessary at the outset for the body requesting the opinion to be 'authorised by or in accordance with the Charter of the United Nations to make such a request'. The Charter provides in Article 96, para 1, that:

> The General Assembly or the Security Council may request the International Court of Justice to give an advisory opinion on any legal question.

Some states which oppose the giving of an opinion by the Court argued that the General Assembly and Security Council are not entitled to ask for opinions on matters totally unrelated to their work. They suggested that, as in the case of organs and agencies acting under Article 96, para 2, of the Charter, and notwithstanding the difference in wording between that provision and para 1 of the same article, the General Assembly and Security Council may ask for an advisory opinion on a legal question only within the scope of their activities.

In the view of the Court, it matters little whether this interpretation of Article 96, para 1, is or is not correct; in the present case, the General Assembly has competence in any event to seise the Court. Indeed, Article 10 of the Charter has conferred upon the General Assembly a competence relating to 'any questions or any matters' within the scope of the Charter. Article 11 has specifically provided it with a competence to 'consider the general principles ... in the maintenance of international peace and security, including the principles governing disarmament and the regulation of armaments'. Lastly, according to Article 13, the General Assembly 'shall initiate studies and make recommendations for the purpose of ... encouraging the progressive development of international law and its codification'.

12   The question put to the Court has a relevance to many aspects of the activities and concerns of the General Assembly including those relating to the threat or use of force in international relations, the disarmament process, and the progressive development of international law. The General Assembly has a long-standing interest in these matters and in their relation to nuclear weapons. This interest has been manifested in the annual First Committee debates, and the Assembly Resolutions on nuclear weapons; in the holding of three special sessions on disarmament (1978, 1982 and 1988) by the General Assembly, and the annual meetings of the Disarmament Commission since 1978; and also in the commissioning of studies on the effects of the use of nuclear weapons. In this

context, it does not matter that important recent and current activities relating to nuclear disarmament are being pursued in other fora.

Finally, Article 96, para 1, of the Charter cannot be read as limiting the ability of the Assembly to request an opinion only in those circumstances in which it can take binding decisions. The fact that the Assembly's activities in the above-mentioned field have led it only to the making of recommendations thus has no bearing on the issue of whether it had the competence to put to the Court the question of which it is seised.

13   The Court must furthermore satisfy itself that the advisory opinion requested does indeed relate to a 'legal question' within the meaning of its Statute and the United Nations Charter.

The Court has already had occasion to indicate that questions:

> ... framed in terms of law and rais[ing] problems of international law ... are by their very nature susceptible of a reply based on law ... [and] appear ... to be questions of a legal character (Western Sahara, Advisory Opinion [1975] *ICJ Rep* at p 18, para 15).

The question put to the Court by the General Assembly is indeed a legal one, since the Court is asked to rule on the compatibility of the threat or use of nuclear weapons with the relevant principles and rules of international law. To do this, the Court must identify the existing principles and rules, interpret them and apply them to the threat or use of nuclear weapons, thus offering a reply to the question posed based on law.

The fact that this question also has political aspects, as, in the nature of things, is the case with so many questions which arise in international life, does not suffice to deprive it of its character as a 'legal question' and to 'deprive the Court of a competence expressly conferred on it by its Statute' (Application for Review of Judgment No 158 of the United Nations Administrative Tribunal, Advisory Opinion [1973] *ICJ Rep* at p 172, para 14). Whatever its political aspects, the Court cannot refuse to admit the legal character of a question which invites it to discharge an essentially judicial task, namely, an assessment of the legality of the possible conduct of states with regard to the obligations imposed upon them by international law (*cf* Conditions of Admission of a state to Membership in the United Nations (Article 4 of the Charter), Advisory Opinion [1947–48] *ICJ Rep* at pp 61–62; Competence of the General Assembly for the Admission of a state to the United Nations, Advisory Opinion [1950] *ICJ Rep* at pp 6–7; Certain Expenses of the United Nations (Article 17, para 2, of the Charter), Advisory Opinion [1962] *ICJ Rep* at p 155).

Furthermore, as the Court said in the Opinion it gave in 1980 concerning the Interpretation of the Agreement of 25 March 1951 between the WHO and Egypt:

> Indeed, in situations in which political considerations are prominent it may be particularly necessary for an international organisation to obtain an advisory opinion from the Court as to the legal principles applicable with respect to the matter under debate ... (Interpretation of the Agreement of 25 March 1951 between the WHO and Egypt, Advisory Opinion [1980] *ICJ Rep* at p 87, para 33.)

The Court moreover considers that the political nature of the motives which may be said to have inspired the request and the political implications that the opinion given might have are of no relevance in the establishment of its jurisdiction to give such an opinion.

14   Article 65, para 1, of the Statute provides: 'The Court may give an advisory opinion ...' This is more than an enabling provision. As the Court has repeatedly emphasised, the Statute leaves a discretion as to whether or not it will give an advisory opinion that has been requested of it, once it has established its competence to do so. In this context, the Court has previously noted as follows:

The Court's Opinion is given not to the states, but to the organ which is entitled to request it; the reply of the Court, itself an 'organ of the United Nations', represents its participation in the activities of the Organisation, and, in principle, should not be refused.' (Interpretation of Peace Treaties with Bulgaria, Hungary and Romania, First Phase, Advisory Opinion [1950] *ICJ Rep* at p 71; see also Reservations to the Convention on the Prevention and Punishment of the Crime of Genocide, Advisory Opinion [1951] *ICJ Rep* at p 19; Judgments of the Administrative Tribunal of the ILO upon Complaints Made against Unesco, Advisory Opinion [1956] *ICJ Rep* at p 86; Certain Expenses of the United Nations (Article 17, para 2, of the Charter), Advisory Opinion [1962] *ICJ Rep* at p 155; and Applicability of Article VI, Section 22, of the Convention on the Privileges and Immunities of the United Nations, Advisory Opinion [1989] *ICJ Reps* at p 189.)

The Court has constantly been mindful of its responsibilities as 'the principal judicial organ of the United Nations' (Charter, Art 92). When considering each request, it is mindful that it should not, in principle, refuse to give an advisory opinion. In accordance with the consistent jurisprudence of the Court, only 'compelling reasons' could lead it to such a refusal (Judgments of the Administrative Tribunal of the ILO upon Complaints Made against Unesco, Advisory Opinion [1956] *ICJ Rep* at p 86; Certain Expenses of the United Nations (Article 17, para 2, of the Charter), Advisory Opinion [1962] *ICJ Reps* at p 155; Legal Consequences for states of the Continued Presence of South Africa in Namibia (South West Africa) notwithstanding Security Council Resolution 276 (1970), Advisory Opinion [1971] *ICJ Rep* at p 27; Application for Review of Judgment No 158 of the United Nations Administrative Tribunal, Advisory Opinion [1973] *ICJ Rep* at p 183; Western Sahara, Advisory Opinion [1975] *ICJ Rep* at p 21; and Applicability of Article VI, Section 22, of the Convention on the Privileges and Immunities of the United Nations, Advisory Opinion [1989] *ICJ Rep* at p 191). There has been no refusal, based on the discretionary power of the Court, to act upon a request for advisory opinion in the history of the present Court; in the case concerning the Legality of the Use by a state of Nuclear Weapons in Armed Conflict, the refusal to give the World Health Organisation the advisory opinion requested by it was justified by the Court's lack of jurisdiction in that case. The Permanent Court of International Justice took the view on only one occasion that it could not reply to a question put to it, having regard to the very particular circumstances of the case, among which were that the question directly concerned an already existing dispute, one of the states parties to which was neither a party to the Statute of the Permanent Court nor a Member of the League of Nations, objected to the proceedings, and refused to take part in any way (*Status of Eastern Carelia*, PCIJ Ser B, No 5).

15   Most of the reasons adduced in these proceedings in order to persuade the Court that in the exercise of its discretionary power it should decline to render the opinion requested by General Assembly Resolution 49/75K were summarised in the following statement made by one state in the written proceedings:

The question presented is vague and abstract, addressing complex issues which are the subject of consideration among interested states and within other bodies of the United Nations which have an express mandate to address these matters. An opinion by the Court in regard to the question presented would provide no practical assistance to the General Assembly in carrying out its functions under the Charter. Such an opinion has the potential of undermining progress already made or being made on this sensitive subject and, therefore, is contrary to the interest of the United Nations Organisation (United States of America, Written statement, pp 1–2; *cf* pp 3–7, II. See also United Kingdom, Written statement, pp 9–20, paras 2.23–2.45; France, Written statement, pp 13–20, paras 5–9; Finland, Written statement, pp 1–2; Netherlands, Written statement, pp 3–4, paras 6–13; Germany, Written Statement, pp 3–6, para 2(b)).

In contending that the question put to the Court is vague and abstract, some states appeared to mean by this that there exists no specific dispute on the subject matter of the question. In order to respond to this argument, it is necessary to distinguish between requirements governing contentious procedure and those applicable to advisory opinions. The purpose of the advisory function is not to settle – at least directly – disputes between states, but to offer legal advice to the organs and institutions requesting the opinion (*cf* Interpretation of Peace Treaties [1950] *ICJ Rep* at p 71). The fact that the question put to the Court does not relate to a specific dispute should consequently not lead the Court to decline to give the opinion requested.

Moreover, it is the clear position of the Court that to contend that it should not deal with a question couched in abstract terms is 'a mere affirmation devoid of any justification', and that 'the Court may give an advisory opinion on any legal question, abstract or otherwise' (Conditions of Admission of a state to Membership in the United Nations (Article 4 of the Charter), Advisory Opinion [1947–48] *ICJ Rep* at p 61; see also Effect of Awards of Compensation Made by the United Nations Administrative Tribunal, Advisory Opinion [1954] *ICJ Rep* at p 51; and Legal Consequences for states of the Continued Presence of South Africa in Namibia (South West Africa) notwithstanding Security Council Resolution 276 (1970), Advisory Opinion [1971] *ICJ Reps* at p 27, para 40).

Certain states have however expressed the fear that the abstract nature of the question might lead the Court to make hypothetical or speculative declarations outside the scope of its judicial function. The Court does not consider that, in giving an advisory opinion in the present case, it would necessarily have to write 'scenarios', to study various types of nuclear weapons and to evaluate highly complex and controversial technological, strategic and scientific information. The Court will simply address the issues arising in all their aspects by applying the legal rules relevant to the situation.

16   Certain states have observed that the General Assembly has not explained to the Court for what precise purposes it seeks the advisory opinion. Nevertheless, it is not for the Court itself to purport to decide whether or not an advisory opinion is needed by the Assembly for the performance of its functions. The General Assembly has the right to decide for itself on the usefulness of an opinion in the light of its own needs.

Equally, once the Assembly has asked, by adopting a Resolution, for an advisory opinion on a legal question, the Court, in determining whether there are any compelling reasons for it to refuse to give such an opinion, will not have regard to the origins or to the political history of the request, or to the distribution of votes in respect of the adopted resolution.

17   It has also been submitted that a reply from the Court in this case might adversely affect disarmament negotiations and would, therefore, be contrary to the interest of the United Nations. The Court is aware that, no matter what might be its conclusions in any opinion it might give, they would have relevance for the continuing debate on the matter in the General Assembly and would present an additional element in the negotiations on the matter. Beyond that, the effect of the opinion is a matter of appreciation. The Court has heard contrary positions advanced and there are no evident criteria by which it can prefer one assessment to another. That being so, the Court cannot regard this factor as a compelling reason to decline to exercise its jurisdiction.

18   Finally, it has been contended by some states that in answering the question posed, the Court would be going beyond its judicial role and would be taking upon itself a law-making capacity. It is clear that the Court cannot legislate, and, in the circumstances of the present case, it is not called upon to do so. Rather its task is to engage in its normal judicial function of ascertaining the existence or otherwise of legal principles and rules applicable to the threat or use of nuclear weapons. The contention that the giving of an answer to the question posed would require the Court to legislate is based on a supposition that the present *corpus juris* is devoid of relevant rules in this matter. The Court could not accede to this argument; it states the existing law and does not legislate. This is so even if, in stating and applying the law, the Court necessarily has to specify its scope and sometimes note its general trend.

19   In view of what is stated above, the Court concludes that it has the authority to deliver an opinion on the question posed by the General Assembly, and that there exist no 'compelling reasons' which would lead the Court to exercise its discretion not to do so.

An entirely different question is whether the Court, under the constraints placed upon it as a judicial organ, will be able to give a complete answer to the question asked of it. However, that is a different matter from a refusal to answer at all.[15]

13.8.4 Law applied by the Court

It has already been pointed out that a major difference between arbitration and judicial settlement is that with judicial settlement the parties do not have a choice as to the law applied. Article 38(1) of the Statute provides that the ICJ must decide such disputes as are submitted to it in accordance with international law. Article 38(2), however, does provide that, if the parties to a dispute agree, the court can adopt a slightly more flexible approach and decide disputes *ex aequo et bono*.

13.8.5 Effect of judgment

The decision of the ICJ in contentious cases has no binding force except between the parties (Article 59 of the ICJ Statute), although the court does have regard to earlier decisions. According to Article 60 the decision is final and without appeal although the court can interpret its decision if there is any confusion. Article 61 allows the court to revise its judgment in the light of discovery of some new and decisive fact. Such revision must be requested within 10 years of judgment and the new fact must have been one which could not have been

---

15 *Legality of the Threat or Use of Nuclear Weapons* case, International Court of Justice, 8 July 1996.

discovered with due diligence at the time of the original case. The rate of compliance with judgments of the court is relatively high. A far greater problem is caused by non-appearance.

13.8.6 Non-appearance

There have been a number of cases in recent years where the court has had to have recourse to Article 53. Its effect is to require the court to advance the legal arguments of the absent party.

13.9 Settlement within the UN

By Article 24 of the UN Charter the UN Security Council is given primary responsibility for the maintenance of international peace and security and member states are under an obligation to carry out the decisions of the Security Council. Chapter VI of the Charter deals with the pacific settlement of disputes. Under Article 34 the Security Council has the power to investigate any dispute or potential dispute and can call upon the parties to seek a peaceful resolution of the dispute. If the parties to the dispute fail to settle it by peaceful means they should refer it to the Security Council which can then recommend appropriate action, including terms of settlement. Under Chapter VI the Security Council can only make non-binding recommendations. However, if the Security Council determines that the continuance of the dispute constitutes a threat to the peace, or that the situation involves a breach of the peace or act of aggression it can take action under Chapter VII of the Charter. Chapter VII gives the Security Council the power to make decisions which are binding on member states, once it has determined the existence of a threat to the peace, breach of the peace, or act of aggression. Security Council action under Chapter VII of the Charter will be discussed in Chapter 14.

Although the Security Council has primary responsibility for maintaining peace and security, under Article 14 the General Assembly may recommend measures for the peaceful adjustment of any situation which 'it deems likely to impair the general welfare or friendly relations among nations'.

The role of regional organisations in maintaining the peace is recognised by Article 52 of the UN Charter and a number of regional organisations and groupings of states, such as the Organisation of American states and the Organisation for Security and Co-operation in Europe, have created their own machinery for the settlement of disputes.

CHARTER OF THE UNITED NATIONS

[AMENDMENTS ARE IN ITALICS]

WE THE PEOPLES OF THE UNITED NATIONS DETERMINED

to save succeeding generations from the scourge of war, which twice in our lifetime has brought untold sorrow to mankind, and

to reaffirm faith in fundamental human rights, in the dignity and worth of the human person, in the equal rights of men and women and of nations large and small, and to establish conditions under which justice and respect for the obligations arising form treaties and other sources of international law can be maintained, and

to promote social progress and better standards of life in larger freedom,

AND FOR THESE ENDS

to practise tolerance and live together in peace with one another as good neighbours, and

to unite our strength to maintain international peace and security, and

to ensure, by the acceptance of principles and the institution of methods, that armed force shall not be used, save in the common interest, and

to employ international machinery for the promotion of the economic and social advancement of all peoples,

HAVE RESOLVED TO COMBINE OUR EFFORTS TO ACCOMPLISH THESE AIMS

Accordingly, our respective Governments, through representatives assembled in the City of San Francisco, who have exhibited their full powers found to be in good and due form, have agreed to the present Charter of the United Nations and do hereby establish an international organisation to be known as the United Nations.

CHAPTER I
PURPOSES AND PRINCIPLES

Article 1

The Purposes of the United Nations are:

1   To maintain international peace and security, and to that end: to take effective collective measures for the prevention and removal of threats to the peace, and for the suppression of acts of aggression or other breaches of the peace, and to bring about by peaceful means, and in conformity with the principles of justice and international law, adjustment or settlement of international disputes or situations which might lead to a breach of the peace;

2   To develop friendly relations among nations based on respect for the principle of equal rights and self-determination of peoples, and to take other appropriate measures to strengthen universal peace;

3   To achieve international co-operation in solving international problems of an economic, social, cultural or humanitarian character, and in promoting and encouraging respect for human rights and for fundamental freedoms for all without distinction as to race, sex, language, or religion; and

4   To be a centre of harmonising the actions of nations in the attainment of these common ends.

Article 2

The Organisation and its Members, in pursuit of the Purposes stated in Article 1, shall act in accordance with the following Principles:

1   The Organisation is based on the principle of the sovereign equality of all its Members.

2   All Members, in order to ensure to all of them the rights and benefits resulting from membership, shall fulfil in good faith the obligations assumed by them in accordance with the present Charter.

3   All Members shall settle their international disputes by peaceful means in such a manner that international peace and security, and justice, are not endangered.

4   All Members shall refrain in their international relations from the threat or use of force against the territorial integrity or political independence of any state, or in any other manner inconsistent with the Purposes of the United Nations.

5   All Members shall give the United Nations every assistance in any action it takes in accordance with the present Charter, and shall refrain from giving assistance to any state against which the United Nations is taking preventive or enforcement action.

6   The Organisation shall ensure that states which are not Members of the United Nations act in accordance with these Principles so far as may be necessary for the maintenance of peace and security.

7   Nothing contained in the present Charter shall authorise the United Nations to intervene in matters which are essentially within the domestic jurisdiction of any state or shall require the Members to submit such matters to settlement under the present Charter; but this principle shall not prejudice the application of enforcement measures under Chapter VII.

CHAPTER II
MEMBERSHIP

Article 3

The original Members of the United Nations shall be the states which, having participated in the United Nations Conference on International Organisation at San Francisco, or having previously signed the Declaration by United Nations of 1 January 1942, sign the present Charter and ratify it in accordance with Article 110.

Article 4

1   Membership in the United Nations is open to all other peace-loving states which accept the obligations contained in the present Charter and, in the judgment of the Organisation, are able and willing to carry out these obligations.

2   The admission of any such state to membership in the United Nations will be effected by a decision of the General Assembly upon the recommendation of the Security Council.

Article 5

A member of the United Nations against which preventive or enforcement action has been taken by the Security Council may be suspended from the exercise of the rights and privileges of membership by the General Assembly upon the recommendation of the Security Council. The exercise of these rights and privileges may be restored by the Security Council.

Article 6

A member of the United Nations which has persistently violated the Principles contained in the present Charter may be expelled from the Organisation by the General Assembly upon the recommendation of the Security Council.

CHAPTER III
ORGANS

Article 7

1   There are established as the principal organs of the United Nations: a General Assembly, a Security Council, an Economic and Social Council, a Trusteeship Council, an International Court of Justice, and a Secretariat.

2   Such subsidiary organs as may be found necessary may be established in accordance with the present Charter.

Article 8

The United Nations shall place no restrictions on the eligibility of men and women to participate in any capacity and under conditions of equality in its principal and subsidiary organs.

CHAPTER IV
THE GENERAL ASSEMBLY
Composition

Article 9

1   The General Assembly shall consist of all the Members of the United Nations.

2   Each member shall have not more than five representatives in the General Assembly.

Functions and Powers

Article 10

The General Assembly may discuss any questions or any matters within the scope of the present Charter or relating to the powers and functions of any organs provided for in the present Charter, and, except as provided in Article 12, may make recommendations to the Members of the United Nations or to the Security Council or to both on any such questions or matters.

Article 11

1   The General Assembly may consider the general principles of co-operation in the maintenance of international peace and security, including the principles governing disarmament and the regulation of armaments, and may make recommendations with regard to such principles to the Members or to the Security Council or to both.

2   The General Assembly may discuss any questions relating to the maintenance of international peace and security brought before it by any Member of the United Nations, or by the Security Council, or by a state which is not a member of the United Nations in accordance with Article 35, para 2, and, except as provided in Article 12, may make recommendations with regard to any such questions to the state or states concerned or to the Security Council or to both. Any such question, on which action is necessary, shall be referred to the Security Council by the General Assembly either before or after discussion.

3   The General Assembly may call the attention of the Security Council to situations which are likely to endanger international peace and security.

4   The powers of the General Assembly set forth in this article shall not limit the general scope of Article 10.

Article 12

1   While the Security Council is exercising in respect of any dispute or situation the functions assigned to it in the present Charter, the General Assembly shall not make any recommendation with regard to that dispute or situation unless the Security Council so requests.

2   The Secretary General, with the consent of the Security Council, shall notify the General Assembly at each session of any matters which are being dealt with by the Security Council and shall similarly notify the General Assembly, or the members of the United Nations if the General Assembly is not in session, immediately the Security Council ceases to deal with such matters.

Article 13

1   The General Assembly shall initiate studies and make recommendations for the purpose of:

(a)   Promoting international co-operation in the political field and encouraging the progressive development of international law and its codification;

(b)   Promoting international co-operation in the economic, social, cultural, educational, and health fields, and assisting in the realisation of human rights and fundamental freedoms for all without distinction as to race, sex, language or religion.

2   The further responsibilities, functions, and powers of the General Assembly with respect to matters mentioned in para 1(b) above are set forth in Chapters IX and X.

Article 14

Subject to the provisions of Article 12, the General Assembly may recommend measures for the peaceful adjustment of any situation, regardless of origin, which it deems likely to impair the general welfare or friendly relations among nations, including situations resulting from a violation of the provisions of the present Charter setting forth the Purposes and Principles of the United Nations.

Article 15

1   The General Assembly shall receive and consider annual and special reports from the Security Council; these reports shall include an account of the measures that the Security Council has decided upon or taken to maintain international peace and security.

2   The General Assembly shall receive and consider reports from the other organs of the United Nations.

Article 16

The General Assembly shall perform such functions with respect to the international trusteeship system as are assigned to it under Chapters XII and XIII, including the approval of the trusteeship agreements for areas not designated as strategic.

Article 17

1   The General Assembly shall consider and approve the budget of the Organisation.

2   The expenses of the Organisation shall be borne by the Members as apportioned by the General Assembly.

3   The General Assembly shall consider and approve any financial and budgetary arrangements with specialised agencies referred to in Article 57

and shall examine the administrative budgets of such specialised agencies with a view to making recommendations to the agencies concerned.

Voting

Article 18

1   Each Member of the General Assembly shall have one vote.

2   Decisions of the General Assembly on important questions shall be made by a two-thirds majority of the Members present and voting. These questions shall include: recommendations with respect to the maintenance of international peace and security, the election of the non-permanent members of the Security Council, the election of the members of the Economic and Social Council, the election of the members of the Trusteeship Council in accordance with para 1(c) of Article 86, the admission of new Members to the United Nations, the suspension of the rights and privileges of membership, the expulsion of Members, questions relating to the operation of the Trusteeship system, and budgetary questions.

3   Decision on other questions, including the determination of additional categories of questions to be decided by a two-thirds majority, shall be made by a majority of the Members present and voting.

Article 19

A Member of the United Nations which is in arrears in the payment of its financial contributions to the Organisation shall have no vote in the General Assembly if the amount of its arrears equals or exceeds the amount of the contributions due form it for the preceding two full years. The General Assembly may, nevertheless, permit such a Member to vote if it is satisfied that the failure to pay is due to conditions beyond the control of the Member.

Procedure

Article 20

The General Assembly shall meet in regular annual sessions and in such special sessions as occasion may require. Special sessions shall be convoked by the Secretary General at the request of the Security Council or of a majority of the Members of the United Nations.

Article 21

The General Assembly shall adopt its own rules of procedure. It shall elect its President for each session.

Article 22

The General Assembly may establish such subsidiary organs as it deems necessary for the performance of its functions.

CHAPTER V

THE SECURITY COUNCIL

Composition

Article 23

1   The Security Council shall consist of 15 Members of the United Nations. The Republic of China, France, the Union of Soviet Socialist Republics, the United Kingdom of Great Britain and Northern Ireland, and the United States of America shall be permanent members of the Security Council. The General Assembly shall elect 10 other Members of the United Nations to be non-

permanent members of the Security Council, due regard being specially paid, in the first instance, to the contribution of Members of the United Nations to the maintenance of international peace and security and to the other purposes of the organisation, and also to equitable geographical distribution.

[GENERAL ASSEMBLY RESOLUTION 1991 (XVIII), A, PARA 3, REQUIRES ELECTION ACCORDING TO THE FOLLOWING PATTERN: (A) FIVE FROM AFRICAN AND ASIAN STATES; (B) ONE FROM EASTERN EUROPEAN STATES; (C) TWO FROM LATIN-AMERICAN STATES; (D) TWO FROM WESTERN EUROPEAN AND OTHER STATES]

2   The non-permanent members of the Security Council shall be elected for a term of two years. *In the first election of the non-permanent members after the increase of the membership of the Security Council from 11 to 15 two of the four additional members shall be chosen for a term of one year.*

3   Each member of the Security Council shall have one representative.

Functions and Powers

Article 24

1   In order to ensure prompt and effective action by the United Nations, its Members confer on the Security Council primary responsibility for the maintenance of international peace and security, and agree that in carrying out its duties under this responsibility the Security Council acts on their behalf.

2   In discharging these duties the Security Council shall act in accordance with the Purposes and Principles of the United Nations. The specific powers granted to the Security Council for the discharge of these duties are laid down in Chapters VI, VII VIII, and XII

3   The Security Council shall submit annual and, when necessary, special reports to the General Assembly for its consideration.

Article 25

The Members of the United Nations agree to accept and carry out the decisions of the Security Council in accordance with the present Charter.

Article 26

In order to promote the establishment and maintenance of international peace and security with the least diversion for armaments of the world's human and economic resources, the Security Council shall be responsible for formulating, with the assistance of the Military Staff Committee referred to in Article 47, plans to be submitted to the Members of the United Nations for the establishment of a system for the regulation of armaments.

Voting

Article 27

1   Each member of the Security Council shall have one vote.

2   Decisions of the Security Council on procedural matters shall be made by an affirmative vote of *nine* members.

3   Decisions of the Security Council on all other matters shall be made by an affirmative vote of *nine* members including the concurring votes of the permanent members; provided that, in decisions under Chapter VI, and under para 3 of Article 52, a party to a dispute shall abstain from voting.

Procedure

Article 28

1   The Security Council shall be so organised as to be able to function continuously. Each member of the Security Council shall for this purpose be represented at all times at the seat of the Organisation.

2   The Security Council shall hold periodic meetings at which each of its members may, if it so desires, be represented by a member of the government of by some other specially designated representative.

3   The Security Council may hold meetings at such places other than the seat of the organisation as in its judgment will best facilitate its work.

Article 29

The Security Council may establish such subsidiary organs as it deems necessary for the performance of its functions.

Article 30

The Security Council shall adopt its own rules of procedure, including the method of electing its President.

Article 31

Any Member of the United nations which is not a member of the Security Council may participate, without vote, in the discussion of any question brought before the Security Council whenever the latter consider that the interests of that Member are specially affected.

Article 32

Any Member of the United Nations which is not a member of the Security Council or any state which is not a Member of the United nations, if it is a party to a dispute under consideration by the Security Council, shall be invited to participate, without vote, in the discussion relating to the dispute. The Security Council shall lay down such conditions as it deems just for the participation of a state which is not a Member of the United Nations.

CHAPTER VI
PACIFIC SETTLEMENT OF DISPUTES

Article 33

1   The parties to any dispute, the continuance of which is likely to endanger the maintenance of international peace and security, shall, first of all, seek a solution by negotiation, enquiry, mediation, conciliation, arbitration, judicial settlement, resort to regional agencies or arrangements, or other peaceful means of their own choice.

2   The Security Council shall, when it deems necessary, call upon the parties to settle their dispute by such means.

Article 34

The Security Council may investigate any dispute, or any situation which might lead to international friction or give rise to a dispute, in order to determine whether the continuance of the dispute or situation is likely to endanger the maintenance of international peace and security.

Article 35

1   Any Member of the United Nations may bring any dispute, or any situation of the nature referred to in Article 34, to the attention of the Security Council or of the General Assembly.

2   A state which is not a Member of the United Nations may bring to the attention of the Security Council or of the General Assembly any dispute to which it is a party if it accepts in advance, for the purposes of the dispute, the obligations of pacific settlement provided in the present Charter.

3   The proceedings of the General Assembly in respect of matters brought to its attention under this article will be subject to the provisions of Articles 11 and 12.

Article 36

1   The Security Council may, at any stage of a dispute of the nature referred to in Article 33 or of a situation of like nature, recommend appropriate procedures or methods of adjustment.

2   The Security Council should take into consideration any procedures for the settlement of the dispute which have already been adopted by the parties.

3   In making recommendations under this article the Security Council should also take into consideration that legal disputes should as a general rule be referred by the parties to the International Court of Justice in accordance with the provisions of the Statute of the Court.

Article 37

1   Should the parties to a dispute of the nature referred to in Article 33 fail to settle it by the means indicated in that article, they shall refer it to the Security Council.

2   If the Security Council deems that the continuance of the dispute is in fact likely to endanger the maintenance of international peace and security, it shall decide whether to take action under Article 36 or to recommend such terms of settlement as it may consider appropriate.

Article 38

Without prejudice to the provisions of Articles 33 to 37, the Security Council may, if all the parties to any dispute so request, make recommendation to the parties with a view to a pacific settlement of the dispute.

CHAPTER VII
ACTION WITH RESPECT TO THREATS TO THE PEACE, BREACHES OF THE PEACE, AND ACTS OF AGGRESSION

Article 39

The Security Council shall determine the existence of any threat to the peace, breach of the peace, or act of aggression and shall make recommendations, or decide what measures shall be taken in accordance with Articles 41 and 42, to maintain or restore international peace and security.

Article 40

In order to prevent an aggravation of the situation, the Security Council may, before making the recommendations or deciding upon the measures provided for in Article 39, call upon the parties concerned to comply with such provisional measures as it deems necessary or desirable. Such provisional measures shall be without prejudice to the rights, claims or position of the parties concerned. The

Security Council shall duly take account of failure to comply with such provisional measures.

Article 41

The Security Council may decide what measures not involving the use of armed force are to be employed to give effect to its decisions, and it may call upon the Members of the United Nations to apply such measures. These may include complete or partial interruption of economic relations and of rail, sea, air, postal, telegraphic, radio, and other means of communication, and the severance of diplomatic relations.

Article 42

Should the Security Council consider that measures provided for in Article 41 would be inadequate or have proved to be inadequate, it may take such action by air, sea, or land forces as may be necessary to maintain or restore international peace and security. Such action may include demonstrations, blockade, and other operations by air, sea, or land forces of Members of the United Nations.

Article 43

1　All Members of the United Nations, in order to contribute to the maintenance of international peace and security, undertake to make available to the Security Council, on its call and in accordance with a special agreement or agreements, armed forces, assistance, and facilities, including rights of passage, necessary for the purpose of maintaining peace and security.

2　Such agreement or agreements shall govern the numbers and types of forces, their degree of readiness and general location, and the nature of the facilities and assistance to be provided.

3　The agreement or agreements shall be negotiated as soon as possible on the initiative of the Security Council. They shall be concluded between the Security Council and Members or between the Security Council and groups of Members and shall be subject to ratification by the signatory states in accordance with their respective constitutional processes.

Article 44

When the Security Council has decided to use force it shall, before calling upon a Member not represented on it to provide armed forces in fulfilment of the obligations assumed under Article 43, invite that Member, if the Member so desires, to participate in the decisions of the Security Council concerning the employment of contingents of that Member's armed forces.

Article 45

In order to enable the United Nations to take urgent military measures, Members shall hold immediately available national air-force contingents for combined international enforcement action. The strength and degree of readiness of these contingents and plans for their combined action shall be determined, within the limits laid down in the special agreement or agreements referred to in Article 43, by the Security Council with the assistance of the Military Staff Committee.

Article 46

Plans for the application of armed force shall be made by the Security Council with the assistance of the Military Staff Committee.

Article 47

1　There shall be established a Military Staff Committee to advise and assist the Security Council on all questions relating to the Security Council's military requirements for the maintenance of international peace and security, the employment and command of forces placed at its disposal, the regulation of armaments, and possible disarmament.

2   The Military Staff Committee shall consist of the Chiefs of Staff of the permanent members of the Security Council or their representatives. Any Member of the United Nations not permanently represented on the Committee shall be invited by the Committee to be associated with it when the efficient discharge of the Committee's responsibilities requires the participation of that Member in its work.

3   The Military Staff Committee shall be responsible under the Security Council for the strategic direction of any armed forces placed at the disposal of the Security Council. Questions relating to the command of such forces shall be worked out subsequently.

4   The Military Staff Committee, with the authorisation of the Security Council and after consultation with appropriate regional agencies, may establish regional sub-committees.

Article 48

1   The action required to carry out the decisions of the Security Council for the maintenance of international peace and security shall be taken by all the Members of the United Nations or by some of them, as the Security Council may determine.

2   Such decisions shall be carried out by the Members of the United Nations directly and through their action in the appropriate international agencies of which they are members.

Article 49

The Members of the United Nations shall join in affording mutual assistance in carrying out the measures decided upon by the Security Council.

Article 50

If preventive or enforcement measures against any state are taken by the Security Council, any other state, whether a Member of the United Nations or not, which finds itself confronted with special economic problems arising from the carrying out of those measures shall have the right to consult the Security Council with regard to the solution of those problems.

Article 51

Nothing in the present Charter shall impair the inherent right of individual or collective self-defence if an armed attack occurs against a Member of the United Nations, until the Security Council has taken measures necessary to maintain international peace and security. Measures taken by members in the exercise of this right of self-defence shall be immediately reported to the Security Council and shall not in any way affect the authority and responsibility of the Security Council under the present Charter to take at any time such action as it deems necessary in order to maintain or restore international peace and security.

CHAPTER VII
REGIONAL ARRANGEMENTS

Article 52

1   Nothing in the present Charter precludes the existence of regional arrangements or agencies for dealing with such matters relating to the maintenance of international peace and security as are appropriate for

regional action, provided that such arrangements or agencies and their activities are consistent with the Purposes and Principles of the United Nations.

2   The Members of the United Nations entering into such arrangements or constituting such agencies shall make every effort to achieve pacific settlement of local disputes through such regional arrangements or by such regional agencies before referring them to the Security Council.

3   The Security Council shall encourage the development of pacific settlement of local disputes through such regional arrangements or by such regional agencies either on the initiative of the states concerned or by reference from the Security Council.

4   This Article in no way impairs the application of Articles 34 and 35.

Article 53

1   The Security Council shall, where appropriate, utilise such regional arrangements or agencies for enforcement action under its authority. But no enforcement action shall be taken under regional arrangements or by regional agencies without the authorisation of the Security Council, with the exception of measures against any enemy state, as defined in para 2 of this article, provided for pursuant to Article 107 or in regional arrangements directed against renewal of aggressive policy on the part of any such state, until such time as the Organisation may, on request of the Governments concerned, be charged with the responsibility for preventing aggression by such a state.

2   The term 'enemy state' as used in para 1 of this article applies to any state which during the Second World War has been an enemy of any signatory of the present Charter.

Article 54

The Security Council shall at all times be kept fully informed of activities undertaken or on contemplation under regional arrangements or by regional agencies for the maintenance of international peace and security.

CHAPTER IX
INTERNATIONAL ECONOMIC AND SOCIAL CO-OPERATION

Article 55

With a view to the creation of conditions of stability and well-being which are necessary for peaceful and friendly relations among nations based on respect for the principle of equal rights and self-determination of peoples, the United Nations shall promote:

(a)   higher standards of living, full employment, and conditions of economic and social progress and development;

(b)   solutions of international economic, social, health, and related problems; and international cultural and educational co-operation; and

(c)   universal respect for, and observance of, human rights and fundamental freedoms for all without distinction as to race, sex, language, or religion.

Article 56

All Members pledge themselves to take joint and separate action in co-operation with the Organisation for the achievement of the purposes set forth in Article 55.

Article 57

The various specialised agencies, established by inter-governmental agreement and having wide international responsibilities, as defined in their basic instruments, in economic, social, cultural, educational, health, and related fields, shall be brought into relationship with the United Nations in accordance with the provisions of Article 63.

Article 58

The Organisation shall make recommendations for the co-ordination of the policies and activities of the specialised agencies.

Article 59

The Organisation shall, where appropriate, initiate negotiations among the states concerned for the creation of any new specialised agencies required for the accomplishment of the purposes set forth in Article 55.

Article 60

Responsibility for the discharge of the functions of the Organisation set forth in this Chapter shall be vested in the General Assembly and, under the authority of the General Assembly, in the Economic and Social Council, which shall have for this purpose the powers set forth in Chapter X.

CHAPTER X
THE ECONOMIC AND SOCIAL COUNCIL
Composition

Article 61

1   *The Economic and Social Council shall consist of 54 Members of the United Nations elected by the General Assembly.*

2   *Subject to the provisions of para 3, nine members of the Economic and Social Council shall be elected each year for a term of three years. [GENERAL ASS RES. 1991(XVIII), B, PARA 3 'FURTHER DECIDES THAT, WITHOUT PREJUDICE TO THE PRESENT DISTRIBUTION OF SEATS IN THE ECONOMIC AND SOCIAL COUNCIL THE NINE ADDITIONAL MEMBERS SHALL BE ELECTED ACCORDING TO THE FOLLOWING PATTERN: (A) SEVEN FROM AFRICAN AND ASIAN STATES; (B) ONE FROM LATIN AMERICAN STATES; (C) ONE FROM WESTERN EUROPE AND OTHER STATES] A retiring member shall be eligible for immediate re-election.*

3   *At the first election after the increase in the membership of the Economic and Social Council from 18 to 27 members, in addition to the members elected in pace of the six members whose term of office expires at the end of that year, nine additional members shall be elected. Of these nine additional members, the term of office of three members so elected shall expire at the end of one year, and of three other members at the end of two years, in accordance with arrangements made by the General Assembly.*

4   *Each member of the Economic and Social Council shall have one representative.*

Functions and Powers

Article 62

1   The Economic and Social Council may make or initiate studies and reports with respect to international economic, social, cultural, educational, health, and related matters and may make recommendations with respect to any

such matters to the General Assembly, to the Members of the United Nations, and to the specialised agencies.

2   It may make recommendations for the purpose of promoting respect for, and observance of, human rights and fundamental freedoms for all.

3   It may prepare draft conventions for submission to the General Assembly, with respect to matters falling within its competence.

4   It may call, in accordance with the rules prescribed by the United Nations, international conferences on matters falling within its competence.

Article 63

1   The Economic and Social Council may enter into agreements with any of the agencies referred to in Article 57, defining the terms on which the agency concerned shall be brought into relationship with the United Nations. Such agreements shall be subject to approval by the General Assembly.

2   It may co-ordinate the activities of the specialised agencies through consultation with and recommendations to such agencies and through recommendations to the General Assembly and to the Members of the United Nations.

Article 64

1   The Economic and Social Council may take appropriate steps to obtain regular reports from the specialised agencies. It may make arrangements with the Members of the United Nations and with the specialised agencies to obtain reports on the steps being taken to give effect to its own recommendations and to recommendations on matters falling within its competence made by the General Assembly.

2   It may communicate its observations on these reports to the General Assembly.

Article 65

The Economic and Social Council may furnish information to the Security Council and shall assist the Security Council upon its request.

Article 66

1   The Economic and Social Council shall perform such functions as fall within its competence in connection with the carrying out of the recommendations of the General Assembly.

2   It may, with the approval of the General Assembly, perform services at the request of Members of the United Nations and at the request of specialised agencies.

3   It shall perform such other functions as are specified elsewhere in the present Charter or as may be assigned to its by the General Assembly.

Voting

Article 67

1   Each member of the Economic and Social Council shall have one vote.

2   Decisions of the Economic and Social Council shall be made by a majority of the members present and voting.

Procedure

Article 68

The Economic and Social Council shall set up commissions in economic and social fields and for the promotion of human rights, and such other commissions as may be required for the performance of its functions.

Article 69

The Economic and Social Council shall invite any Member of the United Nations to participate, without a vote, in its deliberations on any matter of particular concern to that Member.

Article 70

The Economic and Social Council may make arrangements for representatives of the specialised agencies to participate, without vote, in its deliberations and in those of the commissions established by it and for its representatives to participate in the deliberations of the specialised agencies.

Article 71

The Economic and Social Council may make suitable arrangements for consultation with non-governmental organisations which are concerned with matters within its competence.

Such arrangements may be made with international organisations and, where appropriate, with national organisations after consultation with the Members of the United Nations concerned.

Article 72

1   The Economic and Social Council shall adopt its own rules of procedure, including the method of electing a President.

2   The Economic and Social Council shall meet as required in accordance with its rules, which shall include provisions for the convening of meetings on the request of a majority of its members.

CHAPTER XI
DECLARATION REGARDING NON-SELF-GOVERNING TERRITORIES

Article 73

Members of the United Nations which have or assume responsibilities for the administration of territories whose peoples have not yet attained a full measure of self-government recognise the principle that the interests of the inhabitants of these territories are paramount, and accept as a sacred trust the obligation to promote to the utmost, within the system of international peace and security established by the present Charter, the well-being of the inhabitants of these territories, and to this end:

(a)   to ensure, with due respect for the culture of the peoples concerned, their political, economic, social and educational advancement, their just treatment, and their protection against abuses;

(b)   to develop self-government, to take due account of the political aspirations of the peoples, and to assist them in the progressive development of their free political institutions, according to the particular circumstances of each territory and its peoples and their varying stages of advancement;

(c)   to promote international peace and security;

(d)   to promote constructive measures of development, to encourage research, and to co-operate with one another and, when and where appropriate, with specialised international bodies with a view to the practical achievement of the social, economic, and scientific purposes set forth in this article; and

    (e)   to transmit regularly to the Secretary General for information purposes, subject to such limitation as security and constitutional considerations may require, statistical and other information of a technical nature relating to economic, social, and educational conditions in the territories for which they are respectively responsible other than those territories to which Chapters XII and XIII apply.

Article 74

Members of the United Nations also agree that their policy in respect of the territories to which this Chapter applies, no less than in respect of their metropolitan areas, must be based on the general principle of good neighbourliness, due account being taken of the interests and well-being of the rest of the world, in social, economic, and commercial matters.

CHAPTER XII[16]
INTERNATIONAL TRUSTEESHIP SYSTEM

Article 75

The United Nations shall establish under its authority an international trusteeship system for the administration and supervision of such territories as may be placed thereunder by subsequent individual agreements. These territories are hereinafter referred to as Trust Territories.

Article 76

The basic objectives of the trusteeship system, in accordance with the Purposes of the United Nations laid down in Article 1 of the present Charter, shall be:

    (a)   to further international peace and security;

    (b)   to promote the political, economic, social, and educational advancement of the inhabitants of the trust territories, and their progressive development towards self-government or independence as may be appropriate to the particular circumstances of each territory and its peoples and the freely expressed wishes of the people concerned, and as may be provided by the terms of each trusteeship agreement;

    (c)   to encourage respect for human rights and for fundamental freedoms of all without distinction as to race, sex, language, or religion, and to encourage recognition of the interdependence of the peoples of the world; and

    (d)   to ensure equal treatment in social, economic, and commercial matters for all Members of the United Nations and their nationals, and also equal treatment for the latter in the administration of justice, without prejudice to the attainment of the foregoing objectives and subject to the provisions of Article 80.

Article 77

1   The trusteeship system shall apply to such territories in the following categories as may be placed thereunder by means of trusteeship agreements:

    (a)   territories now held under mandate;

---

16 In November 1994 the Security Council terminated the UN Trusteeship Agreement for the last of the original 11 Trustee Territories – the Trust Territory of the Pacific islands (Palau), administered by the United States. The Trusteeship Council (made up of the five permanent members of the Security Council) has amended its rules of procedure and will now meet as and when the occasion demands it.

(b)　territories which may be detached from enemy states as a result of the Second World War; and

(c)　territories voluntarily placed under the system by states responsible for their administration.

2　It will be a matter for subsequent agreement as to which territories in the foregoing categories will be brought under the trusteeship system and upon what terms.

Article 78

The trusteeship system shall not apply to territories which have become Members of the United Nations, relationship among which shall be based on respect for the principle of sovereign equality.

Article 79

The terms of trusteeship for each territory to be placed under the trusteeship system, including any alteration or amendment, shall be agreed upon by the states directly concerned, including the mandatory power in the case of territories held under mandate by a Member of the United Nations, and shall be approved as provided for in Articles 83 and 85.

Article 80

1　Except as may be agreed upon individual trusteeship agreements, made under Articles 77, 79, and 81, placing each territory under the trusteeship system, and until such agreements have been concluded, nothing in this Charter shall be construed in or of itself to alter in any manner the rights whatsoever of any states or any peoples or the terms of existing international instruments to which Members of the United Nations may respectively be parties.

2　Paragraph 1 of this article shall not be interpreted as giving grounds for delay or postponement of the negotiation and conclusion of agreements for placing mandated and other territories under the trusteeship system as provided for in Article 77.

Article 81

The trusteeship agreement shall in each case include the terms under which the trust territory will be administered and designate the authority which will exercise the administration of the Trust Territory. Such authority, hereinafter called the administering authority, may be one or more states or the Organisation itself.

Article 82

There may be designated, in any trusteeship agreement, a strategic area or areas which may include part or all of the Trust Territory to which the agreement applies, without prejudice to any special agreement or agreements made under Article 43.

Article 83

1　The functions of the United Nations relating to strategic areas, including the approval of the terms of the trusteeship agreements and of their alteration or amendment, shall be exercised by the Security Council.

2　The basic objectives set forth in Article 76 shall be applicable to the people of each strategic area.

3　The Security Council shall, subject to the provisions of the trusteeship agreements and without prejudice to security considerations, avail itself of the assistance and the Trusteeship Council to perform those functions of the United Nations under the trusteeship system relating to political, economic, social, and educational matters in the strategic area.

Article 84

It shall be the duty of the administering authority to ensure that the trust territory shall play its part in the maintenance of international peace and security. To this end the administering authority may make use of volunteer forces, facilities, and assistance from the trust territory in carrying out the obligations towards the Security Council undertaken in this regard by the administering authority, as well as for local defence and the maintenance of law and order within the Trust Territory.

Article 85

1   The functions of the United Nations with regard to trusteeship agreements for all areas not designated as strategic, including the approval of the terms of the trusteeship agreements and of their alteration or amendment, shall be exercised by the General Assembly.

2   The Trusteeship Council, operating under the authority of the General Assembly, shall assist the General Assembly in carrying out these functions.

CHAPTER XII
THE TRUSTEESHIP COUNCIL
Composition

Article 86

1   The Trusteeship Council shall consist of the following Members of the United Nations:

(a)   those Members administering trust territories;

(b)   such of those Members mentioned by name in Article 23 as are not administering Trust Territories; and

(c)   as many other Members elected for three-year terms by the General Assembly as may be necessary to ensure that the total number of members of the Trusteeship Council is equally divided between those Members of the United Nations which administer trust territories and those which do not.

2   Each member of the Trusteeship Council shall designate one specially qualified person to represent it therein.

Functions and Powers

Article 87

The General Assembly and, under its authority, the Trusteeship Council, in carrying out their functions, may:

(a)   consider reports submitted by the administering authority;

(b)   accept petitions and examine them in consultation with the administration authority;

(c)   provide for periodic visits to the respective trust territories at times agreed upon with the administering authority; and

(d)   take these and other actions in conformity with the terms of the trust agreements.

Article 88

The Trusteeship Council shall formulate a questionnaire on the political, economic, social, and educational advancement of the inhabitants of each trust territory, and the administering authority for each trust territory within the competence of the General Assembly shall make an annual report to the General Assembly upon the basis of such questionnaire.

Voting

Article 89

1   Each member of the Trusteeship Council shall have one vote.

2   Decisions of the Trusteeship Council shall be made by a majority of the members present and voting.

Procedure

Article 90

1   The Trusteeship Council shall adopt its own rules of procedure, including the method of selecting its President.

2   The Trusteeship Council shall meet as required in accordance with its rules, which shall include provision for the convening of meetings on the request of a majority of its members.

Article 91

The Trusteeship Council shall, when appropriate, avail itself of the assistance of the Economic and Social Council and of the specialised agencies in regard to matters with which they are respectively concerned.

CHAPTER XIV
THE INTERNATIONAL COURT OF JUSTICE

Article 92

The International Court of Justice shall be the principal judicial organ of the United Nations. It shall function in accordance with the annexed Statute, which is based upon the Statute of the Permanent Court of International Justice and forms an integral part of the present Charter.

Article 93

1   All Members of the United Nations are *ipso facto* parties to the Statute of the International Court of Justice.

2   A state which is not a Member of the United Nations may become a party to the Statute of the International Court of Justice on conditions to be determined in each case by the General Assembly upon the recommendation of the Security Council.

Article 94

1   Each Member of the United Nations undertakes to comply with the decision of the International Court in any case to which it is a party.

2   If any party to a case fails to perform the obligations incumbent upon it under a judgment rendered by the Court, the other party may have recourse to the Security Council, which may, if it deems necessary, make recommendations or decide upon measures to be taken to give effect to the judgment.

Article 95

Nothing in the present Charter shall prevent Members of the United Nations from entrusting the solution of their differences to other tribunals by virtue of agreements already in existence or which may be concluded in the future.

Article 96

1   The General Assembly or the Security Council may request the International Court of Justice to give an advisory opinion on any legal question.

2   Other organs of the United Nations and specialised agencies, which may at any time be so authorised by the General Assembly, may also request advisory opinions of the Court on legal questions arising within the scope of their activities.

CHAPTER XV

THE SECRETARIAT

Article 97

The Secretariat shall comprise a Secretary General and such staff as the Organisation may require. The Secretary General shall be appointed by the General Assembly upon the recommendation of the Security Council. He shall be the chief administrative officer of the Organisation.

Article 98

The Secretary General shall act in that capacity in all meetings of the General Assembly, of the Security Council, of the Economic and Social Council, and of the Trusteeship Council, and shall perform such other functions as are entrusted to him by these organs. The Secretary General shall make an annual report to the General Assembly on the work of the Organisation.

Article 99

The Secretary General may bring to the attention of the Security Council any matter which in his opinion may threaten the maintenance of international peace and security.

Article 100

1   In the performance of their duties the Secretary General and the staff shall not seek or receive instructions from any Government or from any other authority external to the Organisation. They shall refrain from any action which might reflect on their position as international officials responsible only to the Organisation.

2   Each Member of the United Nations undertakes to respect the exclusively international character or the responsibilities of the Secretary General and the staff and not to seek to influence them in the discharge of their responsibilities.

Article 101

1   The staff shall be appointed by the Secretary General under regulations established by the General Assembly.

2   Appropriate staffs shall be permanently assigned to the Economic and Social Council, the Trusteeship Council, and, as required, to other organs of the United Nations. These staffs shall form a part of the Secretariat.

3   The paramount consideration in the employment of the staff and in the determination of the conditions of service shall be the necessity of securing

the highest standard of efficiency, competence, and integrity. Due regard shall be paid to the importance of recruiting the staff on as wide a geographical basis as possible.

CHAPTER XVI
MISCELLANEOUS PROVISIONS

Article 102

1   Every treaty and every international agreement entered into by any Member of the United Nations after the present Charter comes into force shall as soon as possible be registered with the Secretariat and published by it.

2   No party to any such treaty or international agreement which has not been registered in accordance with the provision of para 1 of this article may invoke that treaty or agreement before any organ of the United Nations.

Article 103

In the event of a conflict between the obligations of the Members of the United Nations under the present Charter and their obligations under any other international agreement, their obligations under the present Charter shall prevail.

Article 104

The Organisation shall enjoy in the territory of each of its Members such legal capacity as may be necessary for the exercise of its functions and the fulfilment of its purposes.

Article 105

1   The Organisation shall enjoy in the territory of each of its Members such privileges and immunities as are necessary for the fulfilment of its purposes.

2   Representatives of the Members of the United Nations and officials of the Organisation shall similarly enjoy such privileges and immunities as are necessary for the independent exercise of their functions in connection with the Organisation.

3   The General Assembly may make recommendations with a view to determining the details of the application of paras 1 and 2 of this article or may propose conventions to the Members of the United Nations for this purpose.

CHAPTER XVII
TRANSITIONAL SECURITY ARRANGEMENTS

Article 106

Pending the coming into force of such special agreements referred to in Article 43 as in the opinion of the Security Council enable it to begin the exercise of its responsibilities under Article 42, the parties to the Four-Nation Declaration, signed at Moscow, 30 October 1943, and France shall, in accordance with the provisions of para 5 of that Declaration, consult with one another and as occasion requires with other Members of the United Nations with a view to such joint action on behalf of the Organisation as may be necessary for the purpose of maintaining international peace and security.

Article 107

Nothing in the present Charter shall invalidate or preclude action, in relation to any state which during the Second World War has been an enemy of any signatory to the present Charter, taken or authorised as a result of that war by the Governments having responsibility for such action.

CHAPTER XVIII
AMENDMENTS

Article 108

Amendments to the present Charter shall come into force for all Members of the United Nations when they have been adopted by a vote of two-thirds of the members of the General Assembly and ratified in accordance with their respective constitutional processes by two-thirds of the Members of the United Nations, including all the permanent members of the Security Council.

Article 109

1   A General Conference of the Members of the United Nations for the purpose of reviewing the present Charter may be held at a date and place to be fixed by a two-thirds vote of the members of the General Assembly and by a vote of any *nine [AMENDED TO READ THUS IN 1968]* members of the Security Council. Each Member of the United Nations shall have one vote in the conference.

2   Any alteration of the present Charter recommended by a two-thirds vote of the conference shall take effect when ratified in accordance with their respective constitutional processes by two-thirds of the Members of the United Nations including all the permanent members of the Security Council.

3   If such a conference has not been held before the tenth annual session of the General Assembly following the coming into force of the present Charter, the proposal to call such a conference shall be placed on the agenda of that session of the General Assembly, and the conference shall be held if so decided by a majority vote of the members of the General Assembly and by a vote of any seven members of the Security Council.

CHAPTER XIX
RATIFICATION AND SIGNATURE

Article 110

1   The present Charter shall be ratified by the signatory states in accordance with their respective constitutional processes.

2   The ratifications shall be deposited with the Government of the United States of America, which shall notify all the signatory states of each deposit as well as the Secretary General of the Organisation when he has been appointed.

3   The present Charter shall come into force upon the deposit of ratifications by the Republic of China, France, the Union of Soviet Socialist Republics, the United Kingdom of Great Britain and Northern Ireland, and the United States of America, and by a majority of the other signatory states. A protocol of the ratifications deposited shall thereupon be drawn up by the Government of the United States of America which shall communicate copies thereof to all the signatory states.

4   The states signatory to the present Charter which ratify it after it has come into force will become original Members of the United Nations on the date of the deposit of their respective ratifications.

Article 111

The present Charter, of which the Chinese, French, Russian, English and Spanish texts are equally authentic, shall remain deposited in the archives of the Government of the United States of America. Duly certified copies thereof shall be transmitted by that Government to the Governments of the other signatory states.

IN FAITH WHEREOF the representatives of the Governments of the United Nations have signed the present Charter.

DONE at the City of San Francisco the twenty-sixth day of June, one thousand nine hundred and forty-five.

CHAPTER 14

THE USE OF FORCE

14.1 Introduction

The corollary of the requirement of any effective legal system to provide a fair and adequate means of peacefully settling disputes is a prohibition on the unlawful use of force. The obligation not to use unlawful force can be said to be one of the most fundamental rules of international law and has the status of *jus cogens*. However, the actual use of force remains one of the most contentious areas of international law. While every state agrees that, *prima facie*, the use of force is impermissible, there is considerable disagreement over the precise definition of force and the circumstances in which it may lawfully be used. It is convenient to divide consideration of the international rules governing the use of force into two main areas:

- the unilateral use of force which encompasses the use of force by individual states or groups of states acting on their own initiative;
- the collective use of force which refers to force used by or under the auspices of a competent international organisation.

14.2 The law before 1945

In the early days of international law the question of a state's right to resort to the use of force was judged in terms of the criteria for the *just war*. The 16th century writers asserted that war could only be *just* when used as a defence against attack or for the purpose of righting a great wrong. A state should first try to find a peaceful solution and only if attempts failed could it resort to war, and only then if consideration had been given to whether the war might produce more harm than good. However, with the growth of positivism, international law abandoned efforts to judge right from wrong in this area and in effect accepted the use of force as a legitimate instrument of state policy. The use of force was not *per se* prohibited, although the European states recognised the right of the victors of armed conflict to exact reparations from the state judged by the victor to be responsible for causing the war. The main concern of international law at this time was with the actual conduct of hostilities through the development of the laws of war. The laws of war and other armed conflicts will be discussed in Chapter 15.

A change in the attitude of international law towards the use of force began with the advent of the League of Nations in 1920. Although the Covenant of the League of Nations did not specifically prohibit the use of force it did restrict its use by placing a duty on states to try to reach peaceful settlement first.

COVENANT OF THE LEAGUE OF NATIONS

Article 10

The Members of the League undertake to respect and preserve as against external aggression the territorial integrity and existing political independence of all Members of the League. In the case of any such aggression or in case of any threat or danger of such aggression the Council[1] shall advise upon the means by which this obligation shall be fulfilled.

Article 11

Any war or threat of war, whether immediately affecting any of the Members of the League or not, is hereby declared a matter of concern to the whole League, and the League shall take any action that may be deemed wise and effectual to safeguard the peace of nations. In case any such emergency should arise the Secretary General shall on the request of any Member of the League forthwith summon a meeting of the Council.

It is also declared to be the friendly right of each Member of the League to bring to the attention of the Assembly or of the Council any circumstances whatever affecting international relations which threatens to disturb international peace or the good understanding between nations upon which peace depends.

Article 12

The Members of the League agree that, if there should be arise between them any dispute likely to lead to a rupture they will submit the matter either to arbitration or judicial settlement or to enquiry by the Council, and they agree in no case to resort to war until three months after the award by the arbitrators or the judicial decision, or the report by the Council. In any case under this article the award of the arbitrators or the judicial decision shall be made within a reasonable time, and the report of the Council shall be made within six months after the submission of the dispute.

Article 13

The Members of the League agree that whenever any dispute shall arise between them which they recognised to be suitable for submission to arbitration or judicial settlement and which cannot be satisfactorily settled by diplomacy, they will submit the whole subject-matter to arbitration or judicial settlement.

Disputes as to the interpretation of a treaty, as to any question of international law, as to the existence of any fact which if established would constitute a breach of any international obligation, or as to the extent and nature of the reparation to be made for any such breach, are declared to be among those which are generally suitable for submission to arbitration or judicial settlement.

For the consideration of any such dispute, the court to which the case is referred shall be the Permanent Court of International Justice, established in accordance with Article 14, or any tribunal agreed on by the parties to the dispute or stipulated in any convention existing between them.

The Members of the League agree that they will carry out in good faith any award or decision that may be rendered, and that they will not resort to war against a Member of the League which complies therewith. In the event of any

---

1   The Council was established under the provisions of articles 2 and 4. Article 4 provides that 'The Council shall consist of Representatives of the Principal Allied and Associated Powers, together with representatives of four other Members of the League'.

failure to carry out such an award or decision, the Council shall propose what steps should be taken to give effect thereto.

Article 14

The Council shall formulate and submit to the Members of the League for adoption plans for the establishment of a Permanent Court of International Justice. The Court shall be competent to hear and determine any dispute of an international character which the parties thereto submit to it. The Court may also give an advisory opinion upon any dispute or question referred to it by the Council or by the Assembly.

Article 15

If there should arise between Members of the League any dispute likely to lead to a rupture, which is not submitted to arbitration or judicial settlement in accordance with Article 13, the Members of the League agree that they will submit the matter to the Council. Any party to the dispute may effect such submission by giving notice of the existence of the dispute to the Secretary General, who will make all necessary arrangements for a full investigation and consideration thereof.

For this purpose the parties to the dispute will communicate to the Secretary General, as promptly as possible, statements of their case with all relevant facts and papers, and the Council may forthwith direct the publication thereof.

The Council shall endeavour to effect a settlement of the dispute, and if such efforts are successful, a statement shall be made public giving such facts and explanations regarding the dispute and the terms of settlement thereof as the Council may deem appropriate.

If the dispute is not thus settled, the Council either unanimously or by a majority vote shall make and publish a report containing a statement of the facts of the dispute and the recommendations which are deemed just and proper in regard thereto.

Any Member of the League represented on the Council may make public a statement of the facts of the dispute and of its conclusions regarding the same.

If a report by the Council is unanimously agreed to by the members thereof other than the Representatives of one or more of the parties to the dispute, the Members of the League agree that they will not go to war with any party to the dispute which complies with the recommendations of the report.

If the Council fails to reach a report which is unanimously agreed to by the members thereof, other than the Representatives of one or more of the parties to the dispute, the Members of the League reserve to themselves the right to take such action as they shall consider necessary for the maintenance of right and justice.

If the dispute between the parties is claimed by one of them, and is found by the Council, to arise out of a matter which by international law is solely within the domestic jurisdiction of that party, the Council shall so report, and shall make no recommendation as to its settlement.

The Council may in any case under this article refer the dispute to the Assembly. The dispute shall be so referred at the request of either party to the dispute, provided that such request be made within fourteen days after the admission of the dispute to the Council.

In any case referred to the Assembly, all the provisions of this article and Article 12 relating to the action and powers of the Council shall apply to the action and powers of the Assembly, provided that a report made by the Assembly, if concurred in by the Representatives of those Members of the League represented on the Council and of a majority of the other members of the League, exclusive in each case of the Representatives of the parties to the dispute, shall have the same force as a report by the Council concurred in by all the members thereof other than the Representatives of one or more of the parties to the dispute.

Article 16

Should any Member of the League resort to war in disregard of its covenants under Articles 12, 13 or 15, it shall *ipso facto* be deemed to have committed an act of war against all other Members of the League, which hereby undertake immediately to subject it to the severance of all trade or financial relations, the prohibition of all intercourse between their nationals and the nationals of the covenant-breaking state, and the prevention of all financial, commercial or personal intercourse between the nations of the covenant-breaking state and the nationals of any other state, whether a Member of the League or not.

It shall be the duty of the Council in such cases to recommend to the several governments concerned what effective military, naval or air force the Members of the League shall severally contribute to the armed forces to protect the covenants of the League.

The Members of the League agree, further, that they will mutually support one another in the financial and economic measures which are taken under this article, in order to minimise the loss and inconvenience resulting from the above measures, and that they will mutually support one another in resisting any special measures aimed at one of their number by the covenant-breaking state, and that they will take the necessary steps to afford passage through their territory to the forces of any of the Members of the League which are co-operating to protect the Covenants of the League.

Any Member of the League which has violated nay covenant of the League may be declared to be no longer a Member of the League by a vote of the Council concurred in by the Representatives of all the other members of the League represented thereon.

The provisions contained in the Covenant were subsequently reinforced by the Treaty Providing for the Renunciation of War as an Instrument of National Policy 1928 (also known as the Kellogg-Briand Pact and the Pact of Paris). Sixty-three states signed the treaty which remains in force today. The parties to the treaty renounced war as an instrument of national policy and committed themselves to peaceful settlement of disputes.

GENERAL TREATY FOR THE RENUNCIATION OF WAR 1928[2]

The Signatory states ...

Persuaded that the time has now come when a frank renunciation of war as an instrument of national policy should be made to the end that the peaceful and friendly relations now existing between their peoples may be perpetuated;

Convinced that all changes in their relations with one another should be sought only by pacific means and be the result of a peaceful and orderly process, and that

---

2   UKTS 29 (1929) Cmnd 3410; 94 LNTS 57.

any signatory Power which shall hereafter seek to promote its national interests by resort to war should be denied the benefits furnished by this Treaty ...

Have decided to conclude a Treaty ...

Article I

The High Contracting Parties solemnly declare in the names of their respective peoples that they condemn recourse to war for the solution of international controversies, and renounce it as an instrument of national policy in their relations with one another.

Article II

The High Contracting Parties agree that the settlement or solution of all disputes or conflicts of whatever nature or of whatever origin they may be, which arise among them, shall never be sought except by pacific means.

Two problems arose in relation to the Kellogg-Briand Pact. First, given that in the international law of the period 'war' applied only to the legal state existing between nations following an official declaration of war, there was some question whether the parties' undertakings applied also to use of force other than declared war and to the threat of war without actual hostilities. In 1934 the International Law Association, a private organisation of lawyers, suggested that the Pact did cover armed force and threat of war but such an interpretation was not supported by state practice. Secondly, it was unclear whether the Pact permitted war used in self-defence. The prevailing view was that it did.

14.3   The law after 1945: Article 2(4) of the UN Charter

Those responsible for drafting the UN Charter were much motivated by a desire to correct the inadequacies in the law which events after 1920 had revealed. Consequently the Charter emphasises in Article 1 that it is a purpose of the United Nations to 'maintain international peace and security' which may involve collective measures to prevent and remove threats to the peace, the suppression of acts of aggression or other breaches of the peace, and the settlement or adjustment of international disputes, or situations which might lead to a breach of the peace, by peaceful means. Article 2(3) obliges members to settle disputes by peaceful means in such a manner that international peace and security, and justice, are not endangered. The principal prohibition on the use of force is contained in Article 2(4) which states:

> All members shall refrain in their international relations from the threat or use of force against the territorial integrity or political independence of any state, or in any other manner inconsistent with the purposes of the United Nations.

It is generally acknowledged that Article 2(4) is declaratory of customary international law. In 1970 the General Assembly adopted by consensus the Declaration on Principles of International Law Concerning Friendly Relations and Co-operation among States in Accordance with the Charter of the United Nations.[3] This Declaration reaffirmed the commitment to outlawing the use of force. Further evidence for the customary law prohibition on the use of force is to be found in the ICJ decision in the *Nicaragua* case (1986).

---

3   See Chapter 13.

Customary law prohibition of use of force.

Nicaragua Case (Merits) Nicaragua v United States[4]

Judgment of the court

188   The Court ... finds that both Parties take the view that the principles as to the use of force incorporated in the United Nations Charter correspond, in essentials to those found in customary international law ... The Court has however to be satisfied that there exists in customary international law an *opinio juris* ... This *opinio juris* may, though with all due caution, be deduced from, *inter alia*, the attitude of the Parties and the attitude of states towards certain General Assembly resolutions, and particularly Resolution 2625 (XXV).[5] The effect of consent to the text of such resolutions ... may be understood as an acceptance of the validity of the rule or set of rules declared by the resolution by themselves. The principles of non-use of force, for example, may thus be regarded as a principle of customary international law, not as such conditioned by provisions relating to collective security, or to the facilities or armed contingent to be provided under Article 43 of the Charter ...

190   A further confirmation of the validity as customary international law of the principle of the prohibition of the use of force expressed in Article 2, para 4, of the Charter of the United Nations may be found in the fact that it is frequently referred to in statements by state representatives as being not only a principle of customary international law but also a fundamental or cardinal principle of such law. The International law Commission, in the course of its work on the codification or the law of treaties, expressed the view that 'the law of the Charter concerning the prohibition of the use of force in itself constitutes a conspicuous example of a rule in international law having the character of *jus cogens*'.[6]

191   As regards certain particular aspects of the principle in question it will be necessary to distinguish the most grave forms of the use of force (those constituting an armed attack) from other less grave forms. In determining the legal rule which applies to these latter forms, the Court can again draw on the formulations contained in ... General Assembly Resolution 2625 (XXV) ...

193   The general rule prohibiting force allows for certain exceptions ... the Court must express a view on the content of the right of self-defence, and more particularly the right of collective self-defence. First, with regard to the existence of this right, it notes that in the language of Article 51 of the United Nations Charter, the inherent right (or *'droit naturel'*) which any state possesses in the event of an armed attack, covers both collective and individual self-defence. Thus, the Charter itself testifies to the existence of the right of collective self-defence in customary international law. Moreover ... [in Resolution 2625 (XXV)] the reference to the prohibition of force is followed by a paragraph stating that:

> Nothing in the foregoing paragraphs shall be construed as enlarging or diminishing in any way the scope of the provisions of the Charter concerning cases in which the use of force is lawful.

This resolution demonstrates that the states represented in the General Assembly regard the exception to the prohibition of force constituted by the right of

---

4   [1986] *ICJ Rep* at p 14.

5   Declaration on Principles of International Law Concerning Friendly Relations and Co-operation among states in accordance with the Charter of the United Nations 1970.

6   *YBILC* 1966, II, p 247.

individual or collective self-defence as already a matter of customary international law.

194 With regard to the characteristics governing the right of self-defence, ... reliance is placed by the Parties only on the right of self-defence in the case of an armed attack which has already occurred, and the issue of the lawfulness of a response to the imminent threat of armed attack has not been raised. Accordingly the Court expresses no view on that issue. The parties also agree in holding that whether the response to the attack is lawful depends on observance of the criteria of the necessity and the proportionality of the measures taken in self-defence ...

195 In the case of individual self-defence, the exercise of this right is subject to the state concerned having been the victim of an armed attack. Reliance on collective self-defence of course does not remove the need for this. There appears now to be general agreement on the nature of the acts which can be treated as constituting armed attacks. In particular, it may be considered to be agreed that an armed attack must be understood as including not merely action by regular armed forces across an international border, but also 'the sending by or on behalf of a state of armed bands, groups, irregulars or mercenaries, which carry out acts of armed force against another state of such gravity as to amount to' (*inter alia*) an actual armed attack conducted by regular forces, 'or its substantial involvement therein'. This description, contained in Article 3, para (g), of the Definition of Aggression annexed to General Assembly Resolution 3314 (XXIX), may be taken to reflect customary international law. The Court sees no reason to deny that, in customary law, the prohibition of armed attacks may apply to the sending by a state of armed bands to the territory of another state, if such an operation, because of its scale and effects, would have been classified as an armed attack rather than a mere frontier incident has it been carried out by regular armed forces. But the Court does not believe the concept of 'armed attack' includes not only acts by armed bands where such acts occur on a significant scale but also assistance to rebels in the form of the provision of weapons or logistical or other support. Such assistance may be regarded as a threat or use of force, or amount to intervention in the internal or external affairs of other states. It is also clear that it is the state which is the victim of an armed attack which must form and declare the view that it has been so attacked. There is no rule in customary international law permitting its own assessment of the situation ...

199 At all events ... the Court [also] finds that in customary international law, whether of a general kind or that particular to the inter-American legal system, there is no rule permitting the exercise of collective self-defence in the absence of a request by the state which regards itself as the victim of an armed attack. The Court concludes that the requirement of a request by the state which is the victim of the alleged attack is additional to the requirement that such a state should have declared itself to have been attacked.

200 ... Article 51 of the United Nations Charter requires that measures taken by states in exercise of this right of self-defence must be 'immediately reported' to the Security Council. As the Court has observed above (paragraph ... 188), a principle enshrined in a treaty, or reflected in customary international law, may well be so unencumbered with the conditions and modalities surrounding it in the treaty. Whatever the influence the Charter may have had on customary international law it is not a condition of the lawfulness of the use of force in self-defence that a procedure so clearly dependent on the content of a treaty commitment and of the institutions established by it, should have been followed.

On the other hand, if self-defence is advanced as a justification for measures which would otherwise be in breach both of the principle of customary international law and of that contained in the Charter, it is to be expected that the conditions of the Charter should be respected. Thus for the purpose of enquiry into the customary law position, the absence of a report may be one of the factors indicating whether the state in question was itself convinced that it was acting in self-defence ...

202   The principle of non-intervention involves the right of every sovereign state to conduct its affairs without outside interference; though examples of trespass against this principle are not infrequent, the Court considers that it is part and parcel of customary international law. As the Court has observed [in the *Corfu Channel* case]: 'Between independent states, respect for territorial sovereignty is an essential foundation of international relations' ([1949] *ICJ Rep* at p 35), and international law requires political integrity also to be respected ... This principle [of non-intervention] is not, as such, spelt out in the Charter. But is was never intended that the Charter should embody written confirmation of every essential principle of international law in force. The existence in the *opinio juris* of states of the principle of non-intervention is backed by established and substantial practice. It has moreover been presented as a corollary of the principle of the sovereign equality of states ...

203   The principle has since been reflected in numerous declarations adopted by international organisations and conferences in which the United States and Nicaragua have participated, eg General Assembly Resolution 2131 (XX).[7] It is true that the United States, while it voted in favour of General Assembly Resolution 2131 (XX), also declared at the time of its adoption in the First Committee that it considered the declaration in that resolution to be 'only a statement of political intention and not a formulation of law' ... However, the essentials of Resolution 2131 (XX) are repeated in the Declaration approved by Resolution 2625 (XXV) which set out principles which the General Assembly declared to be 'basic principles' of international law, and on the adoption of which no analogous statement was made by the United States representative.

204   ... In a different context, the United States expressly accepted the principles set forth in the declaration, to which reference has already been made, appearing in the Final Act of the Conference on Security and Co-operation in Europe (Helsinki, 1 August 1975), including an elaborate statement of the principle of non-intervention; while these principles were presented as applying to the mutual relations among the participating states, it can be inferred that the text testifies to the existence, and the acceptance by the United States, of a customary principle which has universal application.

205   ... As regards the ... content of the principle of non-intervention – the Court will define only those aspects of the principle which appear to be relevant to the resolution of the dispute. In this respect it notes that, in view of the generally accepted formulations, the principle forbids all states or groups of states to intervene directly or indirectly in internal or external affairs of other states. A prohibited intervention must accordingly be one bearing on matters in which each state is permitted, by the principle of state sovereignty, to decide freely. One of these is the choice of political, economic, social and cultural system, and the

---

7   Declaration on the Inadmissibility of Intervention in the Domestic Affairs of States and the Protection of their Independence and Sovereignty 1965 – adopted by 109 votes to nil with one abstention (the UK).

formulation of foreign policy. Intervention is wrongful when it uses methods of coercion in regard to such choices, which must remain free ones. The element of coercion, which defines, and indeed forms the very essence of, prohibited intervention, is particularly obvious in the case of an intervention which uses force, either in the direct form of military action, or in the indirect form of support for subversive or terrorist armed activities within another state ... General Assembly Resolution 2625 (XXV) equates assistance of this kind with the use of force by the assisting state when the acts committed in another state 'involve threat or use of force'. These forms of action are therefore wrongful in the light of both the principle of non-use of force, and that of non-intervention ...

206   ... There have been in recent years a number of instances of foreign intervention for the benefit of forces opposed to the government of another state. The Court is not here concerned with the process of decolonisation; this question is not an issue in the present case. It has to consider whether there might be indications of a practice illustrative of belief in a kind of general right for states to intervene, directly or indirectly, with or without armed force, in support of internal opposition in another state, whose cause appeared particularly worthy by reason of the political and moral values with which it was identified. For such a general right to come into existence would involve a fundamental modification of the customary law principle of non-intervention.

207   In considering the instances of the conduct above described, the Court has to emphasise that, as was observed in the *North Sea Continental Shelf* cases, for a new customary rule to be formed, not only must the acts concerned 'amount to a settled practice' but they must be accompanied by the *opinio juris sive necessitatis* ... The significance for the Court of cases of state conduct *prima facie* inconsistent with the principle of non-intervention lies in the nature of the ground offered as justification. Reliance by a state on a novel right or any unprecedented exception to the principle might, if shared in principle by other states, tend towards a modification of customary international law. In fact, however, the Court finds that states have not justified their conduct by reference to a new right of intervention or a new exception to the principle of its prohibition ...

209   The Court therefore finds that no such general right of intervention in support of an opposition within another state, exists in contemporary international law ... The Court concludes that acts constituting a breach of the customary principle of non-intervention will also, if they directly or indirectly involve the use of force, constitute a breach of the principle of non-use of force in international relations.

210   ... [I]f one state acts towards another in breach of the principle of non-intervention, may a third state lawfully take such action by way of counter-measures against the first state as would otherwise constitute an intervention in its internal affairs? A right to act in this way in the case of intervention would be analogous to the right of collective self-defence in the case of armed attack, but both the act which gives rise to the reaction, and the reaction itself, would in principle be less grave. Since the Court is here dealing with a dispute in which a wrongful use of force is alleged, it has primarily to consider whether a state has a right to respond to intervention with intervention going so far as to justify a use of force in reaction to measures which do not constitute an armed attack but may nevertheless involve a use of force. The question is itself undeniably relevant from the theoretical viewpoint. However, since the Court is bound to confine its decisions to those points which are essential to the settlement of the dispute before it, it is not for the Court here to determine what direct reactions are lawfully open to a state which considers itself the victim of another state's act of

intervention, possibly involving the use of force. Hence it has not determine whether, in the event of Nicaragua's having committed any such acts against El Salvador, the latter was lawfully entitled to take any particular counter-measure. It might however be suggested that, in such a situation, the United States might have been permitted to intervene in Nicaragua in the exercise of some right analogous to the right of collective self-defence, one which might be resorted to in a case of intervention short of armed attack.

211   The Court has recalled above ... that for one state to use force against another, on the ground that that state has committed a wrongful act of force against a third state, is regarded as lawful, by way of an exception, only when the wrongful act provoking the response was an armed attack ... In the view of the Court, under international law in force today – whether customary international law or that of the United Nations system – states do not have a right of 'collective' armed response to acts which do not constitute an 'armed attack' ...

Judge Jennings (dissenting opinion): ... Another matter which seems to call for brief comment, is the treatment of collective self-defence taken by the Court. The passages beginning with para 196 seem to take a somewhat formalistic view of the conditions for the exercise of collective self-defence. Obviously the notion of collective self-defence is open to abuse and it is necessary to ensure that it is not employable as a mere cover for aggression disguised as protection, and the Court is therefore right to define it somewhat strictly. Even so, it may be doubted whether it is helpful to suggest that the attacked state must in some more or less formal way have 'declared' itself the victim of an attack and then have, as an additional requirement, made a formal request to a particular third state for assistance ... It may readily be agreed that the victim state must both be in real need of assistance and must want it and that the fulfilment of both these conditions must be shown. But to ask that these requirements take the form of some sort of formal declaration and request might sometimes be unrealistic.

But there is another objection to this way of looking at collective self-defence. It seems to be based almost upon the idea of vicarious defence by champions: that a third state may lawfully come to the aid of an authenticated victim of armed attack provided that the requirements of a declaration of attack and a request for assistance are complied with. But whatever collective self-defence means, it does not mean vicarious defence; for that way the notion is indeed open to abuse. The assisting state is not an authorised champion, permitted under certain conditions to go to the aid of a favoured state. The assisting state surely must, by going to the victim state's assistance, be also, and in addition to the other requirements, in some measure defending itself. There should even in 'collective self-defence' be some real element of 'self' involved with the notion of 'defence' ... (It may be objected that the very term 'self-defence' is a common law notion, and that, for instance, the French equivalent of *'legitime defense'* does not mention 'self'. Here, however, the French version is for once, merely unhelpful; it does no more than beg the question of what is *'legitime'*.)

14.4   The definition of force

It can immediately be noted that Article 2(4) is not concerned with outlawing 'war' but prohibits the use of 'force'. The problem is then to define what is meant by 'force'. Use of armed force is certainly covered, but the position as regards threats or action short of actual use of armed force is less clear. There has been dispute as to whether only armed force should be covered or whether the prohibition should extend to economic force. In the *travaux préparatoires* of the UN Charter Brazil proposed that a prohibition on the use of economic force should be included in Article 2(4). The proposal was rejected although the significance of the rejection is disputed, some writers arguing that it indicated a desire not to outlaw economic force, others suggesting that the proposal was rejected because 'force' would encompass all forms of force including economic force. No further definition was provided by the 1970 Declaration, although the section dealing with the prohibition on intervention in the domestic affairs of foreign states provides that:

> No state may use or encourage the use of economic, political or any other type of measures to coerce another state in order to obtain from it the subordination of the exercise of its sovereign rights and to secure from it advantages of any kind.

There is also some argument over whether Article 2(4) is absolute in its prohibition on the use of force or whether it only prohibits force directed against territorial integrity, political independence or force that is contrary to the purposes of the UN. Brownlie argues that territorial integrity and political independence constitute the sum total of legal rights which a state has, and thus all force is prohibited unless specifically allowed by the UN Charter. This view is often referred to as the *restrictive view of force*. But others, for example Bowett, argue for a *permissive view of force*, suggesting that the use of force which does not result in the loss or permanent occupation of territory, does not compromise a state's ability to make independent decisions and which is not contrary to the purposes of the United Nations is not unlawful. state practice since 1945 would appear to favour the restrictive view and no state has relied solely upon the permissive view to justify its use of force. In the *Corfu Channel* case (1949) the UK sought to argue that its mine-sweeping operation in Albanian territorial waters was not unlawful since it did not threaten the territorial integrity or political independence of Albania, but the argument was rejected by the ICJ.

14.5 The justifications for the unilateral use of force

14.5.1 Self-defence

Although Article 2(4) of the UN Charter prohibits the use of force, the prohibition has to be read in the light of Article 51 which states that:

> Nothing in the present Charter shall impair the inherent right of individual or collective self-defence if an armed attack occurs against a Member of the United Nations, until the Security Council has taken measures necessary to maintain international peace and security.

> The UN Charter is intended to provide a watertight scheme for the contemporary reality on the use of force. Article 2(4) explains what is prohibited, Article 51 what is permitted. But almost every phrase in Article 2(4) and Article 51 is open to more than one interpretation. Further, what happens if Articles 2(4) and 51 are not in fact a watertight system, are not entirely opposite sides of the same coin? Can there be, for example, a use of force that is *not* against the territorial integrity or political independence of a state (and thus not, on the face of it, violative of Article 2(4)) – but is also not individual or collective self-defence (and thus manifestly permitted under Article 51)? It is unlikely – most uses of force, no matter how brief, limited or transitory, do violate a state's territorial

integrity. A simple aerial military incursion will do so. So, too, will an attempt to exercise self-help even if in international straits. Self-help is the use of force to obtain legal rights improperly denied. In the *Corfu Channel* case[8] the United Kingdom engaged in mine-sweeping in the Corfu Straits (an international strait but also Albanian territorial waters) in order to make effective its legal right to free passage. The Court found such action unlawful – the action violated Albanian territorial sovereignty and legal rights were not to be vindicated through the manifestation of a policy of force.

It has been generally accepted, ever since this clear finding by the Court on the question, that self-help is unlawful under the Charter, notwithstanding the failure of the UN system to ensure that states do get the legal rights to which they are entitled. But, where the physical security of states is concerned, no matter has been more contested. So the inability of the United Nations to provide for the collective security of states has led to a rather more prolonged debate on the legal status of reprisal under the Charter. Reprisals consist of action in response to a prior unlawful military attack, aimed not at defending oneself against an attack as it happens, but rather at delivering a message of deterrence against the initial attack being repeated. Under customary international law, reprisals were lawful if certain criteria were met. These criteria, traditionally attributed to the *Naulilaa Arbitration*,[9] were that there must have been a prior deliberate violation of international law; that an unsuccessful attempt must have been made at redress; and that the action taken in reprisal be proportionate to the injury suffered. Reprisals would necessarily involve a violation of Article 2(4), however, and, not being in self-defence, are not brought within the permissive use of force in Article 51. It is undeniable that post-war state practice has seen a substantial amount of military activity that has been frankly characterised as reprisals – that has been particularly true of the Arab-Israeli conflict in the Middle East. At times it has seemed as if there is an expectation of reprisals in the face of attack, and that the major concern has been as to the proportionality of the reprisals. But the Security Council has repeatedly condemned reprisals (albeit while often failing to condemn equally the prior illegal acts that led to them); and they are condemned in terms in the General Assembly's Declaration of Principles of International Law Concerning Friendly Relations[10] (which *does* clearly also condemn the organisation or encouragement by one state of irregular forces for hostile conduct in another). The text of Articles 2(4) and 51 clearly do not allow reprisals; and the study of other instruments and practices and judicial decisions does not allow one to conclude that there has been any *de facto* amendment of the Charter on this point – notwithstanding the fact that, in the absence of effective means of self-protection, reprisals may be expected to continue.

When a state is not able to engage immediately in action to defend itself, subsequent action can (wrongly) take on the appearance of reprisals, though it is still action in self-defence. Let us imagine that a state is not in a position immediately to resist an invasion; provided that it does not repel the invasion as soon as it is able, or as soon as all attempts to secure a peaceful withdrawal have failed, the action will still be in self-defence. The position of the United Kingdom in respect of the Falklands/Malvinas, and of Kuwait in respect of Iraq, illustrates the point. In the former, a period of several weeks elapsed between the Argentine invasion and the arrival in the area of the UK task force. In the latter, nearly five

---

8   [1949] *ICJ Rep* at p 3.

9   *Naulilaa* case (*Germany v Portugal*) 2 RIAA 1011.

10 GA Res 2625 (XXV) 1970 A/8028 (1970).

months elapsed between the invasion of Kuwait by Iraq, and the military response by a coalition of UN members.

A particularly acute variation of this problems occurs when the United Nations secures a cease-fire, perhaps with a UN force to oversee the cease-fire – but does not succeed in obtaining the withdrawal of the invading forces. Does the UN cease-fire, and the passage of time (during which the position of the intervening forces becomes entrenched) really preclude the invaded country from liberating its territory? The decision of the Croatian troops on 22 January 1993 to march across UN lines into Serb-held territory within Croatia graphically illustrates the dilemma. it is hard to see that the United Nations' inability to secure the objectives of its agreed plan[11] after a year should extinguish a suspended right of self-defence.[12]

The US Secretary of State, Daniel Webster, gave the classic definition of self-defence in the *Caroline* case (1841)[13] following a British military raid on a US port to seize and destroy a ship, *The Caroline*, which had been used to supply anti-British rebels in Canada. The raid took place at night and without warning; The Caroline was set on fire and allowed to drift over the Niagara Falls. Following the attack, the US authorities arrested the British leader of the raid, McLeod, and charged him with murder and arson. The UK sought the release of McLeod arguing that the action had been one of self-defence. In the course of an exchange of diplomatic notes between the USA and the UK Webster wrote:

.... it will be for Her Majesty's government to show upon what state of facts, and upon what rules of national law, the destruction of the Caroline is to be defended. It will be for that government to show a necessity of self-defence, instant, overwhelming, leaving no choice of means, and no moment for deliberation. It will be for it to show, also, that the local authorities of Canada, even supposing the necessity of the moment authorised them to enter the territories of the United States at all, did nothing unreasonable or excessive; since the act, justified by the necessity of self-defence, must be limited by that necessity, and kept clearly within it. It must be shown that admonition or remonstrance to the person on board the Caroline was impracticable or would have been unavailing; it must be shown that day-light could not be waited for; that there could be no attempt at discrimination between the innocent and the guilty; that it would not have been enough to seize and detain the vessel; but that there was a necessity, present and inevitable, for attacking her in the darkness of night, while moored to the shore, and while unarmed men were asleep on board, killing some and wounding others, and then drawing her into the current, above the cataract, setting her on fire, and, careless to know whether there might not be in her the innocent with the guilty, or the living with the dead, committing her to a fate which fill the imagination with horror. A necessity for all this, the government of the United States cannot believe to have existed.

---

11 Return of certain lands to Croatia, demilitarisation of Krajina and its placing under UN supervised autonomy; and the return of refugees to their homes. See SC Res 743 (1992) establishing UNPROFOR, and approval of the associated UN plan in SC Res 740 (1992).

12 Rosalyn Higgins, *Problems and Processes: International Law and How We Use It*, 1994, Oxford: Clarendon Press at pp 239–41.

13 29 *British and Foreign State Papers* 1137–38; 30 *British and Foreign State Papers* 195–96.

The test for self-defence proposed by Webster was accepted by the UK and has since been regularly referred to as an articulation of the conditions under which the customary law right of self-defence can be exercised.

> It is, of course, the case that the doctrine of self-defence in international law is a very restrictive one. The classic formulation ... is that self-defence is justified where there is 'a necessity of self-defence instant, overwhelming, leaving no choice of means and no moment for deliberation'. In more modern parlance, we would take the view that the right to resort to self-defence arises where there is a serious threat or actual danger, where there is no other means of averting it or bringing it to an end, and that the action taken in self-defence must be limited to what is necessary and what is proportionate.[14]

Clearly, if a crisis can be avoided by diplomatic representations, or if the 'danger' is so remote as to be nothing more than a feeling or suspicion, self-defence is not justified. Similarly, an attack on a naval vessel cannot be used as an excuse for a full-scale occupation of the territory of the offending state, for this would not be a proportionate response. However if these flexible conditions are satisfied, the customary right of self-defence permits the use of force in any of the following circumstances:

(a) force is lawful in self-defence against an ongoing armed attack against state territory;

(b) force is lawful in anticipatory self-defence, so that a state may strike first, with force, to neutralise an immediate but potential threat to its security;

(c) force is lawful in self-defence in response to an attack (threatened or actual) against state interests, such as territory, nationals, property and rights guaranteed under international law. If any such interests are threatened, then the state may use force to protect them;

(d) force is lawful in self-defence even if the 'attack' does not itself involve measures of armed force, such as economic aggression and propaganda. All that is required is that there is an instant and overwhelming necessity for forceful action.

It can be seen that the customary right of self-defence is not a narrow exception to the general ban on use of force. It allows the use of force in a variety of situations, so long as there is some element of 'defence' of the 'state'. Importantly, customary self-defence may go beyond the right guaranteed by the Charter and for this reason it is important to determine whether customary self-defence has survived the Charter. In many of the recent examples of the use of force, the invasion of Grenada in 1983 by the US, the bombing of Libya by the US in 1986 and the destruction of the Iraqi nuclear reactor at Osarik by the Israeli airforce in 1981, the customary right of self-defence has been in part used as a justification by the state resorting to force.

However, under the restrictive approach to the use of force, it is argued that this wide right of self-defence is no longer available. Article 51 stipulates that

---

14 Sir John Freeland (then Legal Adviser to the Foreign and Commonwealth Office) to the Foreign Affairs Committee of the House of Commons, quoted in Mann, 'Inviolability' and the Vienna Convention' in Mann, *Further Studies in International Law*, 1990, Oxford: Oxford University Press at p 334.

nothing 'shall impair the inherent right of individual or collective self-defence if an armed attack occurs against a member of the United Nations'. If Article 2(4) prohibits all armed force, then the only right of self-defence available if the right found in Article 51. Customary law is superseded and a state may only resort to self-defence 'if an armed attack occurs' but not otherwise. Specifically, the right of anticipatory self-defence is not available, of the four situations outlined above, only (a) remains lawful.

Many states argue, however, that the customary right of self-defence still exists. It is argued that Article 51 was never intended to be a conclusive statement of the right to self-defence. Indeed, the *travaux préparatoires* of the San Francisco Conference suggest that Article 51 was included in order to clarify the relationship of regional organisations to the Security Council, rather than to define self-defence. Thus, regional organisations may take armed action, without Security Council authorisation, if it is a matter of self-defence and not 'enforcement action' (discussed at 14.6.2). It is also argued that the customary rights are specifically retained by the use of the word 'inherent'. This is taken to mean 'pre-existing in customary law'. It is also pointed out that Article 51 does not say that self-defence is available *only* if armed attack occurs. This permissive view of self-defence is supported by writers such as Bowett, McDougal and Stone.

One aspect of the right of self-defence which was discussed in the *Nicaragua* case (1986) was the question of what constitutes an 'armed attack'. The ICJ, quoting with approval the Declaration of Principles of International Law 1970, found that it included:

> ... not only action by the regular armed forces of a foreign state across an international border but also 'the sending by or on behalf of a state of armed bands, groups, irregulars, or mercenaries, which carry out acts of armed force against another state of such gravity as to amount to an actual armed attack carried out by regular forces' or its substantial involvement therein.

Writers favouring the restrictive view have argued that 'armed attack' carries a clear and specific meaning which is distinct from a 'use or threat of force' or a 'threat to the peace, breach of the peace or act of aggression' that falls short of actual armed attack.

The major area of controversy surrounding the use of self-defence concerns so-called anticipatory self-defence. Those supporting the restrictive view argue that it no longer exists and they are opposed by advocates of the permissive view. The matter has not been considered by any authoritative international tribunal. In the *Nicaragua* case (1986) the ICJ noted that the issue of a response to an imminent threat of armed attack had not been raised and therefore did not discuss the issue. Judge Schwebel, who gave a dissenting opinion, did express support for the permissive view of self-defence, although some allowance may be made for the fact that he was and is the US judge at the ICJ giving an opinion in a case in which the USA was the defendant. state practice on the issue is divided. Israel claimed the anticipatory right of self-defence when attacking the Iraqi nuclear reactor in 1981 which it claimed was to be used to produce nuclear weapons that could be used against Israel. In the debate which took place at the UN Security Council following the attack the majority of delegates condemned the attack and a number discussed the right of anticipatory self-defence in more general terms. Opinion as to whether such a right existed was divided, delegates from Pakistan, Guyana, Syria, Spain and Yugoslavia clearly supporting the restrictive view; delegates from Sierra Leone, Uganda, Malaysia, Niger, and the UK supporting the permissive view. Other examples follow a similar pattern. It seems to be correct to state that while there is no consensus among state practice recognising a right of anticipatory self-defence, there is certainly no consensus supporting the restrictive view. Given the general principle that the subjects of international law are free to do everything that is not specifically prohibited it would seem correct to state that the right of anticipatory self-defence remains pending the introduction of an authoritative rule prohibiting it.

Two final points should be noted with regard to the right of anticipatory self-defence. Firstly, the general rules applicable to self-defence still apply. In other words the threat of attack must be imminent and overwhelming and the action taken in self-defence must be proportionate to the perceived threat. Secondly, it should be noted that an attack may occur before troops actually cross the border, as when a missile is launched or aircraft deployed. Action taken in such circumstances would clearly fall within Article 51.

14.5.2 Invitation and civil wars

In traditional international law it was quite clear that the principle *volenti non fit injuria* applied to the effect that a state was free to allow another to use force in any form in its own territory. The question arises as to whether the principle survives the UN Charter. In other words, is consent one of the exceptions to the prohibition on use of force? There seems little doubt from state practice and interpreting Article 51 that international law permits states to use armed force to assist another state to assert its rights to self-defence if an express request is made. Thus Kuwait was able to ask for assistance from outside states in asserting its rights to self-defence against Iraq. The only rationale for such organisations as NATO is that an attack on one member state constitutes an attack on all members.

The more problematic area is where armed assistance is requested by a state in the putting down of an internal insurrection. A large number of states have argued that use of armed force is legitimate if requested by a government even if it is to put down an insurrection. In 1958, the UK sent troops to Jordan to assist the Jordanian government to put down a rebellion. However, a number of writers have argued that international law has been gradually restricting such rights of intervention. First, it was not always easy to be certain that assistance had genuinely been asked for, and secondly, where intervention resulted in armed force being used against an insurrection which had widespread popular support, there were possible conflicts with rights of self-determination. Examples of intervention besides the Jordanian illustration are: USSR interventions in Hungary (1956), Czechoslovakia (1968), Afghanistan (1979); USA intervention in Lebanon (1958), in the Dominican Republic (1965) and Grenada (1983).

Arend and Beck[15] in their study of the use of force suggest that the following four types of internal unrest can be identified and distinguished, each of which will give rise to different rights of foreign intervention:

Low Intensity Unrest: this is the least serious form of internal conflict and would be characterised by scattered riots or limited terrorist action. Organised opposition groups may exist but the objectively viewed purpose of such groups would not be the complete overthrow of the state.

Civil War: a civil war is characterised by the existence of a group or groups that seeking to overthrow the existing government and establish themselves in its place. The classic example would be the Spanish Civil War of the 1930s and more recent examples are provided by Afghanistan, Iran and Sri Lanka. In the case of civil wars a further distinction is often drawn between a state of insurgency and a state of belligerency. The distinction is principally based on the degree of recognition accorded to the rebels. A situation of insurgency exists when the rebels have received little international recognition and becomes a state of belligerency when it is acknowledged that both rebels and government have a similar degree of legitimacy and exercise a similar degree of authority over the population of the territory. Such a situation may well give rise to recognition of separate *de facto* and *de jure* governments.

Wars of Secession: such wars occur when a particular ethnic, religious or racial group seeks to break away and form a new separate state. The two main examples of a war of secession are the Biafran war in the late 1960s and the Bangladesh war in 1971. To some extent recent events in former Yugoslavia have had the characteristics of a war of secession.

Wars of Unification: such wars may be characterised as double wars of secession. They arise where a particular group lays claim to an area of territory which crosses international borders. The particular group wishes to unite to form its own new state. The principal examples of potential wars of unification are provided by the situation of the Kurds (who at present live in Turkey, Iraq and Iran) and the Armenians (who live in Iran and the territory of the former USSR).

In practice, of course, situations do not always neatly fit into one of the four categories. For example, how is the situation with respect to actions taken by the IRA in Northern Ireland and the British mainland to be categorised? Often the particular categorisation given to a particular situation of internal unrest will depend upon the political allegiance of the one carrying out the categorisation. Nevertheless, the four categories provide some assistance in identifying the degree of foreign intervention that is permitted.

The traditional view was that states had a wide liberty to provide armed assistance to foreign governments but that has been changed with the recognition of the right to self-determination. The use of force to support assertions of self-determination is discussed at 14.5.4. The position with regard to intervention would seem to be as follows: states may now only intervene to

---

15   Anthony Clark Arend and Robert J Black, *International Law and the Use of Force: Beyond the UN Charter Paradigm*, 1993, London: Routledge.

assist a foreign government experiencing low level civil strife and only in such situations where the consent of the foreign government is freely given. Subject to the rules relating to self-determination, states may never give assistance to rebels since to do so would contravene the prohibition on interference in the domestic affairs of another state.

Declaration on the Inadmissibility of Intervention in the Domestic Affairs of States and the Protection of Their Independence and Sovereignty 1965[16]

The General Assembly ... solemnly declares: ...

1 No state has the right to intervene, directly or indirectly, for any reason whatever, in the internal or external affairs of any other state. Consequently, armed intervention and all other forms of interference or attempted threats against the personality of the state or against its political, economic and cultural elements, are condemned.

2 No state may use or encourage the use of economic, political or any other type of measures to coerce another state in order to obtain from it the subordination of the exercise of its sovereign rights or to secure from it advantages of any kind. Also, no state shall organise, assist, foment, finance, incite or tolerate subversive, terrorist or armed activities directed towards the violent overthrow of the regime of another state, or interfere in civil strife in another state.

3 The use of force to deprive peoples of their national identity constitutes a violation of their inalienable rights and the principle of non-intervention.

4 The strict observance of these obligations is an essential condition to ensure that nations live together in peace with one another, since the practice of any form of intervention not only violates the spirit and letter of the Charter of the United Nations but also leads to the creation of situations which threaten international peace and security.

5 Every state has an inalienable right to choose its political, economic, social and cultural systems, without interference in any form by another state.

There was discussion of the question of intervention in the *Nicaragua* case (1986). In that case Nicaragua argued that the US was in breach of international law by providing armed support for the *contras*. The US argument, although not formally presented to the ICJ, was that it was using force in the collective self-defence of El Salvador, since Nicaragua had previously been providing armed assistance to rebels in El Salvador. The Court discussed the principle of non-intervention in the internal affairs of another state and found that customary international law:

---

16 Declaration on the Inadmissibility of Intervention in the Domestic Affairs of States and the Protection of their Independence and Sovereignty 1965 – adopted by 109 votes to nil with 1 abstention (the UK – which accepted the fundamental propositions set out in the Declaration).

... forbids all states or groups of states to intervene directly or indirectly in the internal or external affairs of other states. A prohibited intervention must accordingly be one bearing on matters in which each state is permitted, by the principle of state sovereignty, to decide freely. One of these is the choice of political, economic, social and cultural system, and the formulation of foreign policy. Intervention is wrongful when it uses methods of coercion in regard to such choices, which must remain free ones. The element of coercion ... is particularly obvious in the case of intervention which uses force, either in the direct form of military action, or in the indirect form of support for subversive or terrorist armed activities within another state.

It went on to state:

The Court therefore finds no such general right of intervention, in support of an opposition within another state, exists in contemporary international law.

The Court did, however, recognise a right of third states to intervene where one state has unlawfully intervened in the affairs of another state. The situation was said to be analogous to the right of collective self-defence with the attendant requirement of proportionality.

14.5.3 Protection of nationals and property abroad

On several occasions since the Second World War states have used armed force without the consent of the territorial state to protect their nationals and property in danger in the foreign territory. One of the earliest examples is the Anglo-French invasion of Egypt in 1956. UK and French troops occupied positions along the Suez Canal. France did not seek to justify its actions on the basis of a right to protect nationals abroad, but the UK government repeatedly asserted that nothing in the UN Charter abrogated the right of governments to use force to protect the lives of nationals abroad. In the debate in the House of Lords that followed the invasion the Lord Chancellor, Viscount Kilmuir, argued that the right to protect nationals abroad was an extension of the right of self-defence stating:

Self-defence undoubtedly includes a situation in which the lives of a state's nationals abroad are threatened and it is necessary to intervene on that territory for their protection.

Viscount Kilmuir then set down three conditions for the use of such protective action to be legitimate:

(1) the nationals must be in imminent danger of injury;

(2) there must be a failure or inability on the part of the territorial sovereign to protect the nationals in question;

(3) the measures taken must be strictly limited to the object of protecting the nationals against injury.

The invasion was heavily criticised by other states and in fact in the UN debates which followed, the UK relied little on a right to protect nationals and instead sought to justify the action on the basis of the need to safeguard international navigation through the Canal.

Since 1956 there have been a number of other examples of action taken to protect nationals. In 1960, Belgian paratroopers landed in the Congo, purportedly to protect foreign nationals on the grounds that the legitimate government of the Congo was no longer capable of affording protection. In fact, Belgium argued it was acting to protect the lives not only of Belgian nationals but of 'human lives in general' which would seem to bring it within a humanitarian intervention (discussed at 14.5.4).

In 1976 Israeli forces landed at Entebbe airport in Uganda to free 96 Israelis who had been taken hostage when the aircraft in which they were flying had been hijacked. The Israelis did not seek the prior approval of Uganda for the action, during the course of which 10 Ugandan military aircraft were destroyed and a number of Ugandan soldiers were killed. The Israeli action was discussed by the UN Security Council in which Uganda condemned the action and demanded full compensation from Israel. The Israeli delegate argued that Uganda was itself in breach of international law for failing to protect foreign nationals on its territory. Furthermore he stated:

> The right of a state to take military action to protect its nationals in mortal danger is recognised by all legal authorities in international law.

He quoted with approval a passage from Brierly's *Law of Nations* which suggests that normally action should be taken by the UN but where the UN is unable to act in time, unilateral action taken by a state would be legitimate. The reaction of other states was mixed, with only the USA positively supporting the right to protect nationals abroad. Interestingly, two years after the Entebbe raid Egypt intervened at Larnaca airport in Cyprus to protect Egyptian nationals taken hostage by Palestinian commandos. The Egyptians had prior permission from Cyprus to land but they had been forbidden from using force. The Egyptians did use force to free the hostages and during the fighting a number of Cypriot nationals were injured. The Cypriot authorities captured and detained the Palestinian commandos and a number of Egyptian soldiers whom they refused to hand over to Egypt, claiming a violation of its sovereignty.

Some of the more recent examples of intervention have involved the USA. In April 1980 US forces entered Iran in an unsuccessful attempt to release US nationals held hostage in the US Embassy in Tehran. In 1983, following a coup in Grenada, President Reagan authorised an invasion partly to protect US nationals who were believed to be at risk. The invasion was also carried out 'to restore democracy' and at the request of the Organisation of Eastern Caribbean States. Nevertheless, on 2 November 1983 the UN General Assembly voted 108 to nine to condemn the US action as a violation of international law. In December 1989 10,000 US forces entered Panama following General Noriega's decision to annul the elections which had been held there. The US seized Noriega and he was subsequently charged with drug trafficking offences in the USA. USA President Bush stated that the action was taken 'to safeguard the lives of Americans, to defend democracy in Panama, to combat drug trafficking and to protect the integrity of the Panama Canal Treaty': as such, the USA argued, it was consistent with international law. Most other states, however, condemned the invasion as a violation of international law. Finally, in 1990 the USA intervened to protect its nationals in Liberia in August 1990 a day after the rebel leader had ordered the arrest of all foreigners in Monrovia, the capital city.

Contrary to the claim made by the Israeli UN delegate following the Entebbe incident, the majority of writers seem to believe that use of force to protect nationals abroad is not permissible under present day international law. This view is consistent with statements made by the majority of states and two major UN resolutions: the Declaration on the Inadmissibility of Intervention in the Domestic Affairs of States (1965) and the Declaration of Principles of International Law (1970). However, one point which should be remembered here relates to the formation of customary international law. As was discussed in Chapter 3, in evaluating state practice 'actions speak louder than words'. The interventions that have taken place have been carried out by those states which have the military power to do so. It might be argued that statements of the law made by states which are unable to mount intervention carry less weight than the actions of states which have the necessary power. This point is stressed by those writers who adhere to the permissive view of the use of force. Writers such as Bowett, McDougal, Reisman and Waldock argue that intervention can be justified by an extension of the right of self-defence on the basis that an injury to a national in a foreign state which does not or cannot afford adequate protection is tantamount to an injury to the state itself. Such writers accept that use of force to protect nationals abroad is restricted by the three conditions outlined by Viscount Kilmuir following the Suez invasion.

14.5.4 Humanitarian intervention

Humanitarian intervention can be distinguished from action taken to protect nationals in that it applies to action taken to protect non-nationals. As has already been seen the distinction is not always a clear one in practice and states often claim to be protecting both their own and other nationals when intervening in foreign states. The topic being discussed here must also be distinguished from humanitarian intervention authorised by the organs of the UN which will be discussed at 14.6.3. What is to be discussed here is the situation where a state or group of states use armed force to protect the inhabitants of the target state from large-scale human rights violations.

There are a number of cases where states have partly justified their use of force on the grounds of humanitarian intervention. The most cited example is India's invasion of East Pakistan in December 1971. In elections held in 1970 a party pledged to achieving autonomous status for the region gained the majority of seats in East Pakistan. The Pakistan government responded to the result by imposing martial law and subsequently East Pakistan announced its intention to secede from Pakistan. In March 1971 the Pakistan army attacked Dacca, the capital of East Pakistan and there followed a period of intense fighting during which the population of East Pakistan was subject to indiscriminate killing and torture. Up to ten million refugees crossed into India and in December 1971 Indian forces moved in. After 12 days of fighting the Pakistan army surrendered and the new state of Bangladesh was recognised. At first India justified its actions on the basis of humanitarian intervention but subsequently claimed that the invasion was in response to a Pakistan attack on India. Many writers have attached significance to the fact that India changed the basis of its justification and argue that this was because India recognised that no right to humanitarian intervention existed in international law. Some writers have suggested, however, that India changed its argument more on the basis that a claim of humanitarian intervention would be difficult to sustain on the facts given India's own self-interest in seeing the emergence of an independent Bangladesh.

Indeed the bulk of state practice seems to deny a right of humanitarian intervention. When Biafra attempted to secede from Nigeria in the late 1960s the Nigerian army acted with considerable brutality that received world-wide condemnation yet no state felt it had the right to intervene. In 1979 Tanzania intervened in Uganda, following several years of atrocities committed against the population by the Amin regime, yet Tanzania did not seek to justify its action on the basis of humanitarian intervention but rather based its action on somewhat spurious claims to be acting in self-defence. When Vietnam invaded Cambodia in 1979 to overthrow the Pol Pot regime which had been responsible for acts of genocide, the invasion was condemned and little support was found for the right of humanitarian intervention that was asserted by Vietnam

More recently military action taken to provide humanitarian assistance has been authorised by the UN, the main examples being the protection of the Kurds in northern Iraq and action taken in Bosnia, although in the case of northern Iraq the extent of the authority given was not completely clear. It would appear that it is for regional and international organisations to intervene on humanitarian grounds and that no right exists for individual states to act on their own.

14.5.5 Self-determination

The use of force to achieve self-determination and for the assistance of national liberation movements has increasingly been claimed as legitimate in recent years, on the ground that it furthers the principles of the UN Charter.

The issue may arise in three ways. First, may the colonial power use force to suppress self-determination movements? This would seem to be unlawful being contrary to customary and to Charter law. According to the Declaration of Principles of International Law, 'every state has the duty to refrain from any forcible action which deprives peoples of their right to self-determination and freedom and independence'. Similarly, Article 2(4) prohibits the use of force in any manner inconsistent with the purposes of the UN and this may have been designed specifically to protect peoples who have not yet achieved statehood.

Secondly, may national liberation movements use force to overthrow the colonial power and thereby achieve self determination? This is more problematic, although many developing countries argue that such a right is implicit in the Declaration on Principles of International Law. Generally speaking the use of force within a state will remain an internal matter and will thus not be a concern of international law, although as will be seen in Chapter 15, there are now rules of international law governing the actual conduct of hostilities in non-international conflicts.

Thirdly, can an established state use force to assist a national liberation movement in its fight for self-determination, as was partly claimed by India in respect of its invasion of East Pakistan. Once again, several states have argued that the obligation in Article 2(4) does not prohibit force for this beneficial purpose and further that it is implicitly recognised in a number of UN resolutions. Yet, as has already been seen at 14.5.2 and 14.5.4, if the struggle for self-determination is an internal affair states are generally under a duty not to intervene.

14.6 Collective use of force

14.6.1 The United Nations – a brief introduction

The term 'United Nations' was first used shortly after the USA entered World War Two in 1941. On 14 August 1941 Churchill and Roosevelt met in mid-Atlantic and issued a declaration of common principles known as the Atlantic Charter on which was based their hopes for a better future for the world. These included the eventual abandoning of the use of force, territorial changes and forms of government to be based on the expressed wishes of the peoples concerned and economic co-operation between all nations with the object of securing for all improved labour standards, economic advancement and social security. On 1 January 1942 a Declaration by the United Nations was made and adhered to by all those states at war with the Axis Powers. This was followed by the Moscow Declaration of 30 October 1943 in which the USA, the USSR and the UK committed themselves to forming a new world organisation for the maintenance of international peace and security. Proposals for its Charter were drawn up in 1944 at Dumbarton Oaks in the USA, by the USA, USSR, UK and China and the following year the three major powers agreed on voting procedures for the Security Council at the Yalta Conference. The amended Dumbarton Oaks Proposals formed the basis of the 50-nation conference held on 25 April in San Francisco and on 26 June 1945 the Charter of the United Nations was formally signed. It contained 111 articles which defined the purposes, principles and methods of the new organisation and set up its structure. The main purposes of the UN are set out in Article 1, and Article 2 sets down the fundamental obligations of member states. Membership of the UN is open to all peace-loving states which accept the obligations contained in the Charter and which, in the opinion of the UN, are able and willing to carry them out.

The UN has six principal organs – the General Assembly, the Security Council, the Economic and Social Council, the Trusteeship Council, the International Court of Justice and the Secretariat. The General Assembly consists of all members of the UN, each of which has equal voting rights. It may discuss any matter within the scope of the Charter unless it is already under discussion in the Security Council and it may make recommendations. It has no mandatory powers. Major decisions are taken by a two-thirds majority, less important ones by a simple majority. Amendments to the Charter require a two-thirds majority including the concurrent votes of the five Permanent members of the Security Council. The Assembly meets once annually in regular session from September to December. Special sessions and emergency sessions may be called by the Security Council or a majority of members to discuss particular issues. The work of the Assembly continues all year, however, through the special committees and subsidiary organs such as the United Nations Conference on Trade and Development.

The UN Security Council has primary responsibility for maintaining international peace and security. It has five permanent members (the USA,

Russia, the UK, China, and France) and 10 non-permanent members who are elected for a two-year term (five are elected each year). Decisions of the Security Council must have the affirmative vote of nine members including the permanent members, except on procedural matters where voting is by majority. The question of whether something is or is not a procedural matter is itself a non-procedural matter. Any permanent member can therefore veto a decision; abstention, however, is not taken as a veto. According to the Charter no member should vote on a matter in which it is involved, but this rule is not observed in practice.

14.6.2 The UN and collective use of force – the Security Council

Under the UN collective security system as originally envisaged, the Security Council was to be the organ through which international peace and security were to be maintained. It is given specific powers in Chapter VII of the Charter to act on behalf of all states, even if this means using force itself. Resolutions passed under Chapter VII provisions are binding on all states.

Article 39 of the Charter provides that:

> The Security Council shall determine the existence of any threat to the peace, breach of the peace, or act of aggression and shall make recommendations, or decide what measures shall be taken in accordance with Articles 41 and 42 to maintain or restore international peace and security.

Under Article 40 the Security Council may indicate provisional measures pending a determination under Article 39. It is therefore important to determine what type of behaviour might fall within Article 39.

Resolution on the Definition of Aggression 1974[17]

The General Assembly adopts the following definition of aggression:

Article 1

Aggression is the use of armed force by a state against the sovereignty, territorial integrity or political independence of another state, or in any other manner inconsistent with the Charter of the United Nations, as set out in this Definition.

Explanatory note: In this Definition the term 'state':

(a) is used without prejudice to questions of recognition or to whether a state is a Member of the United Nations;

(b) includes the concept of a 'group of states' where appropriate.

Article 2

The first use of armed force by a state in contravention of the Charter shall constitute *prima facie* evidence of an act of aggression although the Security Council may, in conformity with the Charter, conclude that a determination that an act of aggression has been committed would not be justified in the light of other relevant circumstances, including the fact that the acts concerned or their consequences are not of sufficient gravity.

---

17 General Assembly Resolution 3314 (XXIX), 14 December 1974.

Article 3

Any of the following acts, regardless of a declaration of war, shall, subject to and in accordance with the provisions of Article 2, qualify as an act of aggression:

    (a)   the invasion or attack by the armed forces of a state of the territory of another state, or any military occupation, however temporary, resulting from such invasion or attack, or an annexation by the use of force of the territory of another state or part thereof;

    (b)   bombardment by the armed forces of a state against the territory of another state or the use of any weapons by a state against the territory of another state;

    (c)   the blockade of the ports or coasts of a state by the armed forces of another state; ...

    (e)   the use of armed forces of one state which are within the territory of another state with the agreement of the receiving state, in contravention of the conditions provided for in the agreement or any extension of their presence in such a territory beyond the termination of the agreement;

    (f)   the action of a state in allowing its territory, which it has placed at the disposal of another state, to be used by that other state for perpetrating an act of aggression against a third state;

    (g)   the sending by or on behalf of a state of armed bands, groups, irregulars, or mercenaries, which carry out acts of armed force against another state of such gravity as to amount to the acts listed above, or its substantial involvement therein.

Article 4

The acts enumerated above are not exhaustive and the security Council may determine that other acts constitute aggression under the provisions of the Charter.

Article 5

1   No consideration of whatever nature, whether political, economic, military or otherwise, may serve as a justification for aggression.

2   A war of aggression is a crime against international peace. Aggression gives rise to international responsibility.

3   No territorial acquisition or special advantage resulting from aggression is or shall be recognised as lawful.

Article 6

Nothing in this Definition shall be construed as in any way enlarging or diminishing the scope of the Charter including its provisions concerning cases in which the use of force is lawful.

Article 7

Nothing in this Definition, and in particular Article 3, could in any way prejudice the right to self-determination, freedom and independence, as derived from the Charter, of peoples forcibly deprived of that right and referred to in the Declaration on Principles of International law concerning Friendly Relations and Co-operation among states in accordance with the Charter of the United Nations, particularly peoples under colonial and racist regimes or other forms of alien domination; nor the right of these peoples to struggle to that end and to seek and receive support, in accordance with the principles of the Charter and in conformity with the above-mentioned Declaration.

The measures envisaged by Article 41 involve non-military sanctions, such as trade boycotts or arms embargoes. Decisions taken under Article 41 are binding on member states. In the event of the measures available under Article 41 being considered inadequate Article 42 enables the Security Council to take such military action as may be necessary to maintain or restore international peace and security. Under the original scheme the use of force by the Security Council under Article 42 depended upon satisfactory agreements having been concluded under Article 43 which envisaged an organised military force being permanently at the Council's disposal. No such agreements have ever been concluded. There is no indication that Article 42 is dependent upon agreements reached under Article 43 and Article 42 does state that enforcement action 'may include demonstrations, blockade, and other operations by air, sea, or land forces of members of the UN'.

Enforcement action taken under Chapter VII of the UN Charter must be distinguished from the peace-keeping role exercised by the UN under Chapter VI and often carried out through the use of the so-called 'blue helmets'. This peacekeeping role will be discussed at 14.6.4.

14.6.3 Enforcement action under Chapter VII

In the history of the UN, the Security Council has authorised the use of force under Chapter VII on six occasions and these will be looked at in turn. In addition the UN has on a number of occasions imposed measures falling short of the authorisation of the actual use of force. The use of Chapter VII enforcement action has dramatically increased since the collapse of the former Soviet Union and the ending of the Cold War.

14.6.3.1   Korea 1950

Before World War Two Korea had been under Japanese control. In 1943 its independence was guaranteed by the Allies but in 1945 Japan surrendered North Korea to the Soviet Union and surrendered South Korea (south of the 38th parallel) to the USA. Deadlock ensued and in June 1950 North Korean troops crossed the border into South Korea. At that time the USSR was boycotting meetings of the Security Council in protest against the fact that it was Nationalist China rather than the People's Republic which was the representative of China. The invasion was reported to the Security Council which determined that the action constituted a breach of the peace and called for an immediate cessation of hostilities. When this call went unheeded the Council passed a second resolution under Article 39 recommending that all states should provide such assistance to South Korea as was necessary to repel the armed attack and to restore international peace and security to the area. A third resolution established the UN unified command and recommended that member states should make military force and other assistance available to the unified command under the USA. The USA provided the commander of such forces and was in overall control. Subsequently the USSR returned to the Security Council and the matter passed into the hands of the General Assembly because agreement was no longer possible in the Security Council.

There have been arguments put forward that the Korean action was not legitimate under the UN Charter on the basis that USSR's absence should not be counted as a concurring vote. A similar argument was mounted against Security Council Resolution 678 (1990) which imposed a deadline on Iraq to withdraw from Kuwait or face military action. In that case it was China that abstained. The majority of opinion seems to suggest that an abstention should not be considered to be a veto. It was also disputed as to whether the Security Council could instigate the use of armed force outside the Article 42 and Article 43 procedure. The action in Korea has therefore been characterised by some commentators as an example of the collective self-defence of South Korea.

14.6.3.2 Rhodesia 1965

Following the unilateral declaration of independence by Southern Rhodesia in November 1965 the Security Council passed a resolution calling upon all states to refrain from any action which would assist and encourage the illegal regime and in particular to desist from providing it with arms, equipment and military material and to do their utmost to break all economic relations with Southern Rhodesia including an embargo on oil and petroleum products. In April 1966 in Resolution 221 the Security Council made a determination that the situation in Southern Rhodesia constituted a threat to peace and the voluntary sanctions were replaced by mandatory sanctions under Article 41. The resolution passed authorised the UK to use force if necessary to uphold the oil embargo imposed upon Southern Rhodesia. The UK made use of this authority when it threatened to use force against a Greek registered oil tanker in April 1966 although the actual use of force was not necessary.

14.6.3.3 Iraq

On 2 August 1990 Iraqi forces invaded Kuwait after a period of growing tension between the two states. The invasion was almost universally condemned and the Security Council passed a series of resolutions relating to the situation. On the day of the invasion the Security Council passed Resolution 660 which determined that the situation constituted a breach of international peace and security and demanded immediate Iraqi withdrawal. Following Iraq's failure to withdraw, Resolution 661 was passed which imposed comprehensive economic sanctions on Iraq. Resolution 665, passed on 25 August 1990, authorised those member states co-operating with the government of Kuwait to 'use such measures commensurate to the specific circumstances as may be necessary under the authority of the Security Council' to enforce the sea blockade of Iraq. Colombia and Cuba both questioned whether it was permissible for the Security Council to authorise the use of force without the agreements necessary under Article 43, but no conclusive answer was given. The USA and the UK announced that they would use force to uphold the sanctions but their main justification for doing so was based on the right of collective self-defence of Kuwait. The USA and the UK continued to maintain that use of force against Iraq was permitted under rights of self-defence although it was recognised that politically it would be better to act under UN authorisation. Accordingly, Security Resolution 678 which was passed by 12 votes to two (with the Yemen and China abstaining) on 20 November 1990 authorised member states 'to use all necessary means' in co-operation with the government of Kuwait to implement Resolution 660 unless Iraq withdrew by 15 January 1991. What was never completely clear was whether the resolution amounted to Chapter VII enforcement action or was merely a recognition of the Kuwaiti right to collective self-defence. The majority of writers seem to support the view that Resolution 678 amounted to enforcement action and thus military force was not confined purely to the liberation of Iraq as it would have been if restricted by the conditions applicable to self-defence.

14.6.3.4 Somalia, Bosnia and Haiti

Within the last two years the use of Chapter VII procedures has taken on a new aspect raising questions of humanitarian intervention by the UN. In both Bosnia and Somalia the UN Security Council recognised that the situations there constituted a threat to peace and security. However, the main concern in both cases was the provision of humanitarian relief to the local population rather than a response to the use of aggression by another state. In spite of the fact that there was no outside aggressor the UN Security Council has authorised the use of force in both situations. In the case of Bosnia, member states were authorised under Security Council resolution 816 (1993) to take 'all necessary measures' to enforce the no-fly zone above the territory of Bosnia-Herzegovina.

Perhaps the greatest extension of UN powers has come in respect of Haiti. Following the overthrow of the democratically elected government of President Aristide concern was expressed by the Organisation of American States at the worsening situation in Haiti. In June 1993 the Security Council determined that the situation constituted a threat to international peace and security, called for the re-instatement of President Aristide and imposed a number of economic sanctions pending his re-instatement. The sanctions were lifted in August 1993 but stronger sanctions were re-imposed following a new Article 39 determination in October. In Resolution 875 (1993) the Security Council authorised the use of force to enforce the sanctions. Thus for the first time, the UN has authorised the use of force in a situation of civil unrest and in an attempt to bring about a return to democracy. While the use of such action in respect of the particular situation in Haiti might be welcomed the general principle operating gives rise for some concern. If, as seems possible, the ICJ finds in the *Lockerbie* case that it has no power to review the legitimacy of Security Council Resolutions then the use of the Security Council to bring about changes in the government of states is open to considerable abuse.

> When Saddam Hussein invaded Kuwait on 2 August 1990 the security Council reacted with unusual speed and decisiveness. Between 2 August and 29 November it adopted, under Chapter VII of the Charter, 12 resolutions on different aspects of the Kuwait crisis.[18] It imposed sanctions;[19] a naval embargo;[20] and then, on 29 November, it finally authorised the use of force if Iraq did not comply with its resolutions by 15 January 1991.[21]
>
> While the Council's unprecedented sense of urgency and determination in dealing with aggression were widely praised, it was not acting precisely

---

18 The first was SC Res 660 of 2 August 1990 condemning the Iraqi invasion of Kuwait which had taken place earlier the same day.

19 SC Res 661 of 6 August 1990.

20 SC Res 665 of 25 August 1990.

21 SC Res 678 of 29 November 1990.

according to Chapter VII of the Charter. Articles 46 and 47 clearly imply that enforcement measures under Chapter VII will be under the control of the Security Council and its Military Staff Committee. Thus, already on 25 August, when it asked the states with maritime forces in the Gulf area to monitor shipping, the Council had begun to depart from the precise terms of Chapter VII of the Charter. On 29 November, in Resolution 678, the Council diverged still further from the terms of Chapter VII when it authorised 'member states co-operating with the government of Kuwait ... to use all necessary means' (ie the use of force) if Iraq had not withdrawn by 15 January 1991. A comparable departure from the course envisaged in Chapter VII had also occurred in the Korean war (1950–3) in which there was also US control of military operations.[22]

The tendency to diverge from the Charter was inherent from the beginning of the 1990–1 Gulf crisis, and for a very good reason. In the 40 years of the Cold War the Security Council has made none of the preparations necessary to meet a crisis of this kind in the way suggested in the Charter. The Military Staff Committee had held no substantive meetings since 1948, and had done no preparatory work or contingency planning. No agreements with member states had been concluded under Article 43. Thus, when the Council denounced Iraq's aggression in August 1990, it was not in a position to assure the security of other states in the region – most notably Saudi Arabia – against a possible attack by Iraq.

Instead, a parallel operation was mounted under US leadership to protect Saudi Arabia. This was justified primarily under Article 51 of the Charter, which provides for the inherent right of individual or collective self-defence. When this operation, involving a massive deployment of forces, began, its name, Operation Desert Shield, gave the impression that it was defensive, and that UN sanctions and embargoes were to be the means of eventually forcing Iraq to withdraw from Kuwait. Later on, however, when the US build-up became so large as to have offensive capacity, and sanctions seemed to be having little effect on Saddam Hussein's determination to hold on to Kuwait, the choice of the main instrument to reverse Iraq's aggression shifted from sanctions to the use of force.

The wisdom of the change from sanctions to force was a matter of much debate at the time, more particularly since the enforcement operation would be under the command of the USA rather than of a command structure designated by the Security Council. Moreover, the goal of Chapter VII is action short of force if possible. Article 42 states: 'Should the Security Council consider that measures provided for in Article 41 [sanctions] would be inadequate, it may take such action by air, sea, or land forces as may be necessary to maintain or restore international peace and security.'

No formal determination as to the inadequacy of sanctions was ever made by the Security Council was ever made by the Security Council before Operation Desert Storm was launched. In retrospect, it seems that sanctions, even when rigorously applied, are unlikely, in the short run at any rate, to force a dictatorial and unscrupulous leader to reverse his course. Saddam Hussein may well also have believed that the Security Council's threat of force was a bluff which would never become a reality. When he had invaded Iran in 1980, the Security Council had sat on its hands, neither demanding withdrawal nor imposing sanctions. His assessment of the determination of the Security Council to reverse aggression was certainly influenced by this experience.

---

22   SC Res 678 of 29 November 1990.

The USA and its coalition partners commenced the major military operation on the night of 16-17 January 1991 with Operation Desert Storm, an air offensive against Iraqi targets in Iraq and Kuwait. The main coalition land offensive began on 24 February. A suspension of coalition offensive combat operations came into effect on 28 February after coalition forces had taken over all of Kuwait and parts of southern Iraq.

After the end of this war, Saddam Hussein was required to carry out the terms of a monumental cease-fire resolution.[23] This requires, among other things, the destruction or removal of all weapons of mass destruction, including chemical and nuclear weapons, as well as missiles with a greater range than 150 kilometres. It also requires reparations and the return of all Kuwaiti property, and maintains the sanctions on Iraq until these and other provisions are fulfilled. Sanctions also provided the background for international efforts to protect the Kurdish population of northern Iraq and the Shiites of the south from the tender mercies of the central government. 'Safe havens', 'no-fly zones', a UN guard force, and massive relief operations are all part of the complex aftermath of Desert Storm. Iraq resisted many of the conditions imposed on it by the UN and by some of the coalition powers, who responded with air attacks on targets in Iraq on 14 and 18 January 1993.

The forceful reaction in January-February 1991 to Saddam Hussein's Kuwait adventure may well prove something of a deterrent to future aggressors. However, such a clear case of aggression in a strategically sensitive region is unlikely to recur in the foreseeable future; and the long-term impact of that reaction was inevitably weakened by the fact that Saddam Hussein remained firmly in power in Iraq. At all events, the episode shed much light on the capacity of the UN as an instrument of collective security.

In the existing state of international leadership and military preparedness, an operation of the size and strength of Desert Storm could not be undertaken without the leadership and military commitment of the USA. That fact has already contributed to negative interpretations, in some quarters, of the Security Council's conduct over Kuwait. It has also, partly due to the unfortunate use of the phrase 'new world order', created much speculation as to the US government's conception of the future role of the USA, the sole surviving superpower, *vis-à-vis* the rest of the world.

As far as the Security Council is concerned, there seems little or no will to make a literal reality of the articles in Chapter VII of the Charter. There is no inclination at the present time to resuscitate the Military Staff Committee even in a contingency-planning role. Nor is there any sign of a governmental response to Secretary General Boutros-Ghali's urging that governments conclude agreements under Article 43 to make forces available to the Security Council.[24]

On the other hand, Chapter VII, the enforcement chapter – used partially, and only on rare occasions, to impose sanctions during the Cold War – is far more freely invoked in the post-Cold War era. This tendency is causing considerable concern in the developing world as a harbinger of a new great power hegemony. For this, among other reasons, the vexed questions of the structure of the

---

23 SC Res 687 of 3 April 1991; 'the mother of all resolutions'. This had been preceded by Res 686 of 2 March 1991, outlining necessary measures by Iraq which would permit a definitive end to the hostilities.

24 Boutros Boutros-Ghali, *An Agenda for Peace*, June 1992, para 43.

Security Council and the anachronistic present structure of Permanent Members are becoming pressing political issues.

In spite of the recommendations in Boutros-Ghali's 'Agenda for Peace', there seems little concern at present to put the UN and the Security Council in a better position to respond in full accordance with the terms of Chapter VII of the Charter to a new and serious act of aggression – nor indeed to give the organisation the capacity to deal with more limited challenges. The deterrent to major acts of aggression – and to disastrous disruptions of civil order – thus remain largely the military power of the USA and one or two of its allies, and the determining factor in responding to future emergencies will be the interest and concern of the USA and its allies in a given situation. There is no guarantee that forceful action can, or will, be taken against acts of aggression wherever they may occur. However, there is still a practical possibility of the UN taking less extreme steps, such as interruption of diplomatic relations and communications, and sanctions. In May 1992, for example, although there was little support for major military intervention in former Yugoslavia, the Security Council adopted stringent sanctions against Serbia and Montenegro; these were toughened further in 1993.[25, 26]

14.6.4 Peace-keeping actions

The Security Council has also been involved in the use of force on other occasions which have not been considered enforcement actions under Chapter VII. In July 1960 the breakdown of law and order following Congo independence brought a request from the Congolese government requesting immediate military assistance. The Security Council passed a resolution authorising the Secretary General to take the necessary steps in consultation with the Congo government to provide such military assistance as was necessary. A multinational force under UN authority was assembled (ONUC) but the authority to use force from the Security Council was given in terms of preventing civil war. The legitimacy of the action was subsequently discussed in the *Expenses* case (1962) and the ICJ concluded that the use of force was not against a state which had committed an act of aggression and that the action did not involve any enforcement measures under Chapter VII. Under Chapter VI the Security Council is given general powers relating to the pacific settlement of disputes. Article 37 states that once the Council has deemed that a dispute is likely to endanger international peace and security it shall decide on appropriate measures to be taken. The terms are very wide and while the general intention is to encourage settlement by arbitration or the ICJ the words of Articles 36 and 37 do not rule out the creation of a peace-keeping force. Such peace-keeping forces have been used on a number of occasions but their presence in a state depends upon the consent of that state. It should be noted that, unlike Chapter VII, resolutions passed under the provisions of Chapter VI are not legally binding on states.

---

25 SC Res 757 of 30 May 1992; SC Res 820 of 19 April 1993.

26 Brian Urquhart, 'The UN and International Security after the Cold War', in Roberts and Kingsbury (eds), *United Nations, Divided World*, 2nd edn, 1994, Oxford: Clarendon at pp 82–87.

Current peace-keeping operations:

UNTSO	United Nations Truce Supervision Organisation[27]
UNMOGIP	United Nations Military Observer Group in India and Pakistan
UNFICYP	United Nations Peace-keeping Force in Cyprus
UNDOF	United Nations Disengagement Observer Force[28]
UNIFIL	United Nations Interim Force in Lebanon[29]
UNIKOM	United Nations Iraq-Kuwait Observation Mission
UNAVEM III	United Nations Angola Verification Mission III
MINUSO	United Nations Mission for the Referendum in Western Sahara
UNPROFOR	United Nations Protection Force[30]
UNOMIG	United Nations Observer Mission in Georgia
UNOMIL	United Nations Observer Mission in Liberia
UNMIH	United Nations Mission in Haiti
UNMOT	United Nations Mission of Observers in Tajikistan

14.6.5 The General Assembly's role

The perceived failure of the original system and the widespread use of the veto during the Cold War eventually led the General Assembly to play a more active role in the maintenance of international peace and security. In 1950 the Assembly passed the Uniting for Peace Resolution. This provides that if the Security Council could not discharge its primary responsibility because of the veto, the General Assembly shall consider the matter immediately with a view to making appropriate recommendations to members for collective measures including, in the case of a breach of the peace or act of aggression, the use of armed force where necessary to restore peace and security. This landmark resolution has been used on many occasions to justify consideration of cases where force has been used. The resolution was passed in connection with the Korean crisis. It was used in 1956 as the basis for the formation of a multinational force (UNEF) which operated on Egyptian soil with Egyptian consent after the Suez crisis. Because it was there with Egypt's consent the ICJ stated in the *Expenses* case that the deployment of the force did not constitute enforcement action and did therefore not require the Security Council's authorisation. It is still argued that the Uniting for Peace Resolution does not authorise the General Assembly to carry out enforcement action – that would require a revision of the UN Charter. Multinational forces operating in Lebanon (UNIFIL) and on the Israeli-Syrian border (UNDOF) on the basis of General Assembly resolutions do not really operate under the UN Charter; like UNEF they only remain with the consent of the host state and they have limited

---

27 Supervises the truce which brought an end to them Arab-Israeli war of 1947–8.
28 Set up following the 1973 Six-Day War.
29 The 'interim' force has now been in place for six months short of 20 years.
30 Formed in three parts – UNCRO in Croatia, UNPROFOR in Bosnia-Herzegovina, UNPREDEP in the Former Yugoslavian Republic of Macedonia.

powers. Since the ending of the Cold War the need for the General Assembly to act in a peace-keeping role has diminished.

14.6.6 Regional organisations

Under Article 53 of the Charter the Security Council can utilise regional organisations such as the OAS and OAU for 'enforcement action'. However it is clearly stated in Article 53 that no enforcement action can be taken without the authorisation of the Security Council. Some states argue that regional organisations can take measures on their own decision to maintain the peace including use of armed force. For example, the USA argued that its invasions of the Dominican Republic in 1965 and Grenada in 1983 were partly justified as actions authorised by the relevant regional organisations taken to restore peace and security in the region. This view has obtained little widespread support and it is thought that action in the name of regional organisations is only legitimate if there has been a request from a sovereign state and the regional force operates within the requesting state or under the doctrine of collective self-defence.

CHAPTER 15

THE REGULATION OF ARMED CONFLICT

15.1 Introduction

Traditionally there has always been a distinction made between the law relating to the resort to war (the *jus ad bellum*) and the law governing the conduct of the war (the *jus in bello*). The law of war in classical international law was the regime that came into operation when the relations of particular countries with each other were no longer governed by the law of peace because a state of declared war existed between them. The law of war dealt with all aspects of the hostile relationship.

The modern development of legal restrictions on the resort to war and the use of armed force has caused a shift in attitude towards the law of war. For example, the traditional view was that treaties were annulled as soon as war broke out. That is now not the case and the position depends much more on the terms of the treaty and the intention of the parties. The law of war is now less regarded as an alternative to the law of peace and more regarded as a device for alleviating the suffering caused by war. Since the end of World War Two there has been a concerted attempt, led by the International Committee of the Red Cross, to strengthen that branch of the law of war which is now often referred to as International Humanitarian Law.

Another modern phenomenon has been the reluctance of states actually to admit that they are at war and the absence of international recognition of states of war. For example, in 1982 the UK Prime Minister made it clear that the UK was not at war with Argentina and the hostilities relating to the Falkland Islands was always officially referred to as the Falklands Conflict or the Falklands Crisis. Similarly the use of force in 1991 in response to Iraq's continued occupation of Kuwait is usually officially referred to as the Gulf Conflict. This reluctance to resort to war, so-called, has led to the development of what is known as the law of armed conflict. The scope of the law of armed conflict has been extended over the years to include not only hostilities between states but also civil wars and other 'non-international' conflicts. This has been necessary because traditionally the law of war did not come into operation until there was a recognised state of war.

The definition of war offered by Starke is that it is a hostile relationship between two or more states resulting in a contest which is primarily between the armed forces of either side. There has been some dispute as to whether a formal declaration of war was required before a state of war could exist. Certainly it is felt that a declaration, even a unilateral one, is sufficient evidence that a state of war exists. But it is now accepted today that the question of whether or not a war exists is an objective one and depends on the overall picture. It is also true that with the development of the law of armed conflict much of the importance of the distinction has gone.

15.2   The sources of the law of armed conflict

Throughout history there have been restrictions placed on those using armed force in respect of methods of combat, use of weapons and treatment of civilians and prisoners of war. Up until the middle of the last century the source of the law governing armed conflict was almost entirely customary law. However, over the last 140 years a significant number of treaties have been agreed, many of which codify previously existing rules of international law. Rules of customary international law still have an enormously important role to play and much of the evidence for specific rules is found in the manuals of military law which most states have promulgated.

One of the first treaties to be concluded was the Paris Declaration Respecting Maritime Law 1856. At the outbreak of the Crimean War in 1854 all belligerents agreed certain rules relating to neutral ships and the capture of property at sea. At the peace conference that ended the war the seven participants signed the Declaration which has since been acceded to by a large number of states and, strictly speaking, remains in force to this day. In 1864 the Red Cross was established by Henri Dunant and the first of the 'Red Cross' conventions, the Geneva Convention for the Amelioration of the Condition of the Wounded in Armies in the Field 1864, was adopted. Since that time a large number of treaties have been signed, among the most important of which are:

- Hague Declarations 1899;

- Hague Conventions 1907, in particular the Hague Convention IV Respecting the Laws and Customs of War on Land 1907 together with the annexed Hague Regulations on the Laws and Customs of War on Land;

- the four Geneva Conventions 1949 and their two additional Protocols 1977.

    Seeing that, while seeking means to preserve peace and prevent armed conflicts between nations, it is likewise necessary to bear in mind the case where the appeal to arms has been brought about by events which their care was unable to avert;

    Animated by the desire to serve, even in this extreme case, the interests of humanity and the ever progressive needs of civilisation;

    Thinking it important, with this object, to revise the general laws and customs of war, either with a view to defining them with greater precision or to confining them within such limits as would mitigate their severity as far as possible;

    Have deemed it necessary to complete and explain in certain particulars the work of the First Peace Conference, which, following on the Brussels Conference of 1874, and inspired by the ideas dictated by a wise and generous forethought, adopted provisions intended to define and govern the usages of war on land.

    According to the views of the High Contracting Parties, these provisions, the wording of which has been inspired by the desire to diminish the evils of war, as far as military requirements permit, are intended to serve as a general rule of conduct for the belligerents in their mutual relations and in their relations with the inhabitants.

    It has not, however, been found possible at present to concert regulations covering all the circumstances which arise in practice;

    On the other hand, the High Contracting Parties clearly do not intend that unforeseen cases should, in the absence of a written undertaking, be left to the arbitrary judgment of military commanders.

Until a more complete code of the laws of war has been issued, the High Contracting Parties deem it expedient to declare that, in cases not included in the Regulations adopted by them, the inhabitants and the belligerents remain under the protection and the rule of the principles of the law of nations, as they result from the usages established among civilised peoples, from the laws of humanity, and the dictates of the public conscience.[1]

15.3 Application of the law: international and non-international armed conflicts

As has already been stated, the law regulating armed conflict has developed from the laws of war. War was, by definition, a dispute between states and thus clearly within the ambit of international law. As the law was extended to cover situations which could not formally be referred to as war, debate occurred as to whether the law applied to situations of civil war and internal armed conflict. Applying international law to such situations could create problems in that it might be argued that it contravened the principle of non-interference in the domestic affairs of sovereign states. Historically, internal and civil wars were matters solely for the particular state involved. However, by the 1930s there existed a number of regional agreements concerned with the regulation of internal conflicts and customary international law had developed to the situation where the laws of war would apply where a recognised situation of belligerency existed. The need for such recognition has diminished since the end of World War Two and a growing acceptance that certain provisions of the law of armed conflict will apply to internal conflict. Article 3 which is repeated in all four Geneva Conventions 1949 provides that in the case of an armed conflict not of an international character occurring in the territory of one of the parties to the Conventions, certain fundamental humanitarian provisions relating to protection of civilians will apply to those participating in the conflict. The law has been further strengthened by the Geneva Protocol II Relating to the Protection of Victims of Non-International Armed Conflicts 1977. The provisions of Protocol II are much less extensive than those which relate to international armed conflicts. Nevertheless, the Protocol does provide certain protections for members of the civilian population and the wounded, sick and shipwrecked.

In addition to extending provisions of the law to non-international conflicts there has also been a broadening of the definition of international conflict to include 'armed conflicts in which peoples are fighting for self-determination against colonial and alien occupation and against racist regimes in the exercise of their rights of self-determination'. This broader definition was first included in General Assembly Resolution 3103 (1973) which was passed by a 82:13 vote with 19 states abstaining. Among those voting against or abstaining were the majority of Western states and the Resolution could not be considered to have the status of customary international law at the time. However, the definition was repeated in Article 1(4) Geneva Protocol I to which the majority of states

---

1   Convention (IV) Respecting the Laws and Customs of War on Land – signed at The Hague, 18 October 1907.

(including the Western states) are parties and it is submitted that it is now correct to include such national liberation struggles within the category of international armed conflict. Clearly, there remains a large number of actual and potential conflicts which still do not fall into the broader definition and these will be subject to the relatively more restricted provisions contained in Geneva Protocol II. The issue of the nature of the armed conflict has particular relevance in the current situation in Bosnia where the status of 'Serbian' troops is critical. At its simplest, the question can be posed thus: were the 'Serbian' forces operating in Bosnia members of the armed forces of the state of Serbia and Montenegro, or were they members of a Bosnian Serb militia? If the former is true, then the conflict must be defined as an international armed conflict since the armed forces of one state are operating without consent in the territory of another state; if the latter is true the conflict remains a non-international one. For the civilians who are suffering the question is perhaps purely an academic one, but it has important implications as to the rules of law which apply and in particular the degree of responsibility that can attach to those involved in some of the worst atrocities.

15.4 Effect of outbreaks of war and armed conflicts

The outbreak of war has far-reaching effects on the relations between the opponent belligerent states. The general rule of international law is that states are free to enact municipal legislation dealing with such matters as trading with the enemy, and provide for seizure of enemy property. This would seem to be true of war and any other armed conflict. As far as individuals are concerned state practice varies as to the exact nature of test of enemy character, but most states now effectively adopt one based on nationality.

On the outbreak of *war* diplomatic relations between the two states will cease although according to the Vienna Convention on Diplomatic Relations diplomatic agents must be enabled to leave. As has already been stated the effect on treaties is unsettled and the Vienna Convention on Treaties contains no provision dealing with effect of war.

15.5 Rules on belligerence

Much of the law relating to belligerency has the aim of minimising damage to civilians. Many prohibitions apply to non-military objectives. *Military objectives* usually means targets which by their nature, location, purpose or use make an effective contribution to military action and whose destruction, capture or neutralisation offer a definite military advantage.

15.5.1 Restrictions on weapons

Attempts to prohibit the use of particular types of weapons have been made in various civilisations over a long period of time. In the ancient Hindu codes there was a prohibition on the use of poisoned arrows. In 1132 the Lateran Council declared that the crossbow was an 'un-Christian weapon'. When the law of war began to be codified in the 19th century, the prohibition of certain weapons was an early objective. The St Petersburg Declaration 1868 is regarded as the first major international agreement prohibiting the use of particular weapons, in this case the prohibition of bullets under 400 grammes which exploded on impact – no states objected to exploding shells. Further development of the rules occurred at the Hague Conference in 1899 which resulted in the three Hague Declarations 1899. Declaration 2 prohibits the use of certain asphyxiating gases and Declaration 3 further prohibits the use of exploding bullets. The Declaration outlawed the use of so-called dum-dum bullets which were designed to expand in the body after impact. They were named dum-dum after the place in India where the UK first manufactured them.

A subsequent conference was held in the Hague in 1907 which resulted in a number of treaties relating to war. Hague Convention VIII Relative to the Laying of Automatic Submarine Mines 1907 remains applicable today: it regulates the use of naval mines (still relevant); and Hague Convention XIV attempted to regulate the use of bombing from balloons.

More progress was made after World War One and in 1925 the Geneva Gas Protocol was agreed.

PROTOCOL FOR THE PROHIBITION OF THE USE IN WAR OF ASPHYXIATING, POISONOUS OR OTHER GASES, AND OF BACTERIOLOGICAL METHODS OF WARFARE

ENTRY INTO FORCE: 8 February 1928

The undersigned Plenipotentiaries, in the name of their respective governments:

Whereas the use in war of asphyxiating, poisonous or other gases, and of all analogous liquids, materials or devices, has been justly condemned by the general opinion of the civilised world; and

Whereas the prohibition of such use has been declared in Treaties to which the majority of powers of the world are Parties; and

To the end that this prohibition shall be universally accepted as a part of International Law, binding alike the conscience and the practice of nations;

Declare:

That the High Contracting Parties, so far as they are not already Parties to Treaties prohibiting such use, accept this prohibition, agree to extend this prohibition to the use of bacteriological methods of warfare and agree to be bound as between themselves according to the terms of this declaration.

The High Contracting Parties will exert every effort to induce other states to accede to the present Protocol. Such accession will be notified to the government of the French Republic, and by the latter to all signatories and acceding Powers, and will take effect on the date of the notification by the government of the French Republic.

The present Protocol, of which the English and French texts are both authentic, shall be ratified as soon as possible. It shall bear today's date.

The ratifications of the present Protocol shall be addressed to the government of the French Republic, which will at once notify the deposit of such ratification to each of the signatory and acceding Powers.

The instruments of ratification of and accession to the present Protocol will remain deposited in the archives of the Government of the French Republic.

The present Protocol will come into force for each signatory power as from the date of deposit of its ratification, and, from that moment, each power will be bound as regards other powers which have already deposited their ratifications.

In witness whereof the Plenipotentiaries have signed the present Protocol.

Done at Geneva in a single copy, the seventeenth day of June, One Thousand Nine Hundred and Twenty-Five.

Since the Second World War there have been a number of attempts to modify further and strengthen the law relating to weapons. However, it sadly has to be admitted that the development of the law is usually one step behind the ingenuity of weapons manufacturers. As particular restrictions are introduced so states look for ways of evading the new law. An illustration of the problem is provided by examining the law relating to four particular categories of weapons:

* conventional weapons
* weapons of mass destruction
* biological and chemical weapons
* environmental weapons

15.5.1.1 Conventional weapons

'Conventional weapons' includes all weapons not included in the other four categories. The principal relevant treaty is the UN Convention on Prohibitions or Restrictions of Certain Conventional Weapons that Cause Unnecessary Suffering or Have Indiscriminate Effects 1981 (the Weaponry Convention) together with its three annexed protocols which entered into force in December 1983.

CONVENTION ON PROHIBITIONS OR RESTRICTIONS ON THE USE OF CERTAIN CONVENTIONAL WEAPONS WHICH MAY BE DEEMED TO BE EXCESSIVELY INJURIOUS OR TO HAVE INDISCRIMINATE EFFECTS AND PROTOCOLS (1980)

ENTRY INTO FORCE: 2 December 1983

The High Contracting Parties,

Recalling that every state has the duty, in conformity with the Charter of the United Nations, to refrain in its international relations from the threat or use of force against the sovereignty, territorial integrity or political independence of any state, or in any other manner inconsistent with the purposes of the United Nations,

Further recalling the general principle of the protection of the civilian population against the effects of hostilities,

Basing themselves on the principle of international law that the right of the parties to an armed conflict to choose methods or means of warfare is not unlimited, and on the principle that prohibits the employment in armed conflicts of weapons, projectiles and material and methods of warfare of a nature to cause superfluous injury or unnecessary suffering,

Also recalling that it is prohibited to employ methods or means of warfare which are intended, or may be expected, to cause widespread, long-term and severe damage to the natural environment,

Confirming their determination that in cases not covered by this Convention and its annexed Protocols or by other international agreements, the civilian population and the combatants shall at all times remain under the protection and authority of the principles of international law derived from established custom, from the principles of humanity and from the dictates of public conscience,

Desiring to contribute to international detente, the ending of the arms race and the building of confidence among states, and hence to the realisation of the aspiration of all peoples to live in peace,

Recognising the importance of pursuing every effort which may contribute to progress towards general and complete disarmament under strict and effective international control,

Reaffirming the need to continue the codification and progressive development of the rules of international law applicable in armed conflict,

Wishing to prohibit or restrict further the use of certain conventional weapons and believing that the positive results achieved in this area may facilitate the main talks on disarmament with a view to putting an end to the production, stockpiling and proliferation of such weapons,

Emphasising the desirability that all states become parties to this Convention and its annexed Protocols, especially the militarily significant states,

Bearing in mind that the General Assembly of the United Nations and the United Nations Disarmament Commission may decide to examine the question of a possible broadening of the scope of the prohibitions and restrictions contained in this Convention and its annexed Protocols,

Further bearing in mind that the Committee on Disarmament may decide to consider the question of adopting further measures to prohibit or restrict the use of certain conventional weapons,

Have agreed as follows:

Article 1   Scope of application

This Convention and its annexed Protocols shall apply in the situations referred to in Article 2 common to the Geneva Conventions of 12 August 1949 for the Protection of War Victims, including any situation described in para 4 of Article 1 of Additional Protocol I to these Conventions.

Article 2   Relations with other international agreements

Nothing in this Convention or its annexed Protocols shall be interpreted as detracting from other obligations imposed upon the High Contracting Parties by international humanitarian law applicable in armed conflict.

Article 3   Signature

This Convention shall be open for signature by all states at United Nations Headquarters in New York for a period of 12 months from 10 April 1981.

Article 4   Ratification, acceptance, approval or accession

1   This Convention is subject to ratification, acceptance or approval by the Signatories. Any state which has not signed this Convention may accede to it.

2   The instruments of ratification, acceptance, approval or accession shall be deposited with the Depositary.

3   Expressions of consent to be bound by any of the Protocols annexed to this Convention shall be optional for each state, provided that at the time of the deposit of its instrument of ratification, acceptance or approval of this Convention or of accession thereto, that state shall notify the Depositary of its consent to be bound by any two or more of these Protocols.

4   At any time after the deposit of its instrument of ratification, acceptance or approval of this Convention or of accession thereto, a state may notify the Depositary of its consent to be bound by any annexed Protocol by which it is not already bound.

5   Any Protocol by which a High Contracting Party is bound shall for that Party form an integral part of this Convention.

Article 5   Entry into force

1   This Convention shall enter into force six months after the date of deposit of the twentieth instrument of ratification, acceptance, approval or accession.

2   For any state which deposits its instrument of ratification, acceptance, approval or accession after the date of the deposit of the twentieth instrument of ratification, acceptance, approval or accession, this Convention shall enter into force six months after the date on which that state has deposited its instrument of ratification, acceptance, approval or accession.

3   Each of the Protocols annexed to this Convention shall enter into force six months after the date by which twenty states have notified their consent to be bound by it in accordance with para 3 or 4 of Article 4 of this Convention.

4   For any state which notifies its consent to be bound by a Protocol, annexed to this Convention after the date by which twenty states have notified their consent to be bound by it, the Protocol shall enter into force six months after the date on which that state has notified its consent so to be bound.

Article 6   Dissemination

The High Contracting Parties undertake, in time of peace as in time of armed conflict, to disseminate this Convention and those of its annexed Protocols by which they are bound as widely as possible in their respective countries and, in particular, to include the study thereof in their programmes of military instruction, so that those instruments may become known to their armed forces.

Article 7   Treaty relations upon entry into force of this Convention

1   When one of the parties to a conflict is not bound by an annexed Protocol, the parties bound by this Convention and that annexed Protocol shall remain bound by them in their mutual relations.

2   Any High Contracting Party shall be bound by this Convention and any Protocol annexed thereto which is in force for it, in any situation contemplated by Article 1, in relation to any state which is not a party to this Convention or bound by the relevant annexed Protocol, if the latter accepts and applies this Convention or the relevant Protocol, and so notifies the Depositary.

3   The Depositary shall immediately inform the High Contracting Parties concerned of any notification received under para 2 of this article.

4   This Convention, and the annexed Protocols by which a High Contracting Party is bound, shall apply with respect to an armed conflict against that High Contracting Party of the type referred to in Article 1, para 4, of Additional

Protocol I to the Geneva Conventions of 12 August 1949 for the Protection of War Victims:

(a) where the High Contracting Party is also a party to Additional Protocol I and an authority referred to in Article 96, para 3, of that Protocol has undertaken to apply the Geneva Conventions and Additional Protocol I in accordance with Article 96, para 3, of the said Protocol, and undertakes to apply this Convention and the relevant annexed Protocols in relation to that conflict; or

(b) where the High Contracting Party is not a party to Additional Protocol I and an authority of the type referred to in sub-para (a) above accepts and applies the obligations of the Geneva Conventions and of this Convention and the relevant annexed Protocols in relation to that conflict. Such an acceptance and application shall have in relation to that conflict the following effects:

    (i) the Geneva Conventions and this Convention and its relevant annexed Protocols are brought into force for the parties to the conflict with immediate effect;

    (ii) the said authority assumes the same rights and obligations as those which have been assumed by a High Contracting Party to the Geneva Conventions, this Convention and its relevant annexed Protocols; and

    (iii) the Geneva Conventions, this Convention and its relevant annexed Protocols are equally binding upon all parties to the conflict.

The High Contracting Party and the authority may also agree to accept and apply the obligations of Additional Protocol I to the Geneva Conventions on a reciprocal basis.

Article 8   Review and amendments

1

(a) At any time after the entry into force of this Convention any High Contracting Party may propose amendments to this Convention or any annexed Protocol by which it is bound. Any proposal for an amendment shall be communicated to the Depositary, who shall notify it to all the High Contracting Parties and shall see their views on whether a conference should be convened to consider the proposal. If a majority, that shall not be less than eighteen of the High Contracting Parties so agree, he shall promptly convene a conference to which all High Contracting Parties shall be invited. states not parties to this Convention shall be invited to the conference as observers.

(b) Such a conference may agree upon amendments which shall be adopted and shall enter into force in the same manner as this Convention and the annexed Protocols, provided that amendments to this Convention may be adopted only by the High Contracting Parties and that amendments to a specific annexed Protocol may be adopted only by the High Contracting Parties which are bound by that Protocol.

2

(a) At any time after the entry into force of this Convention any High Contracting Party may propose additional Protocols relating to other categories of conventional weapons not covered by the existing annexed Protocols. Any such proposal for an additional Protocol shall be communicated to the Depositary, who shall notify it to all the High Contracting Parties in accordance with sub-para 1(a) of this article. If a majority, that shall not be less than eighteen of the High Contracting Parties so agree, the Depositary shall promptly convene a conference to which all states shall be invited.

(b) Such a conference may agree, with the full participation of all states represented at the conference, upon additional protocols which shall be adopted in the same manner as this Convention, shall be annexed thereto and shall enter into force as provided in paras 3 and 4 of Article 5 of this Convention.

3

(a) If, after a period of 10 years following the entry into force of this Convention, no conference has been convened in accordance with sub-para 1(a) or 2(a) of this article, any High Contracting Party may request the Depositary to convene a conference to which all High Contracting Parties shall be invited to review the scope and operation of this Convention and the Protocols annexed thereto and to consider any proposal for amendments of this Convention or of the existing Protocols. states not Parties to this Convention shall be invited as observers to the conference. The conference may agree upon amendments which shall be adopted and enter into force in accordance with sub-para 1(b) above.

(b) At such conference consideration may also be given to any proposal for additional Protocols relating to other categories of conventional weapons not covered by the existing annexed Protocols. All states represented at the conference may participate fully in such consideration. Any additional protocols shall be adopted in the same manner as this Convention, shall be annexed thereto and shall enter into force as provided in paras 3 and 4 of Article 5 of this Convention.

(c) Such a conference may consider whether provision should be made for the convening of a further conference at the request of any High Contracting Party if, after a similar period to that referred to in sub-para 3(a) of this article, no conference has been convened in accordance with sub-para 1(a) or 2(a) of this Article.

Article 9   Denunciation

1   Any High Contracting Party may denounce this Convention or any of its annexed Protocols by so notifying the Depositary.

2   Any such denunciation shall only take effect one year after receipt by the Depositary of the notification of denunciation. If, however, on the expiry of that year the denouncing High Contracting Party is engaged in one of the situations referred to in Article 1, the Party shall continue to be bound by the obligations of this Convention and of the relevant annexed Protocols until the end of the armed conflict or occupation and, in any case, until the termination of operations connected with the final release, repatriation or re-establishment of the person protected by the rules of international law applicable in armed conflict, and in the case of any annexed Protocol containing provisions concerning situations in which peace-keeping, observation or similar functions are performed by United Nations forces or missions in the area concerned, until the termination of those functions.

3   Any denunciation of this Convention shall be considered as also applying to all annexed Protocols by which the denouncing High Contracting Party is bound.

4   Any denunciation shall have effect only in respect of the denouncing High Contracting Party.

5   Any denunciation shall not affect the obligations already incurred, by reason of an armed conflict, under this Convention and its annexed Protocols by such denouncing High Contracting Party in respect of any act committed before this denunciation becomes effective.

Article 10   Depositary

1   The Secretary General of the United Nations shall be the Depositary of this Convention and of its annexed Protocols.

2   In addition to his usual functions, the Depositary shall inform all states of:

(a) signatures affixed to this Convention under Article 3;

(b) deposits of instruments of ratification, acceptance or approval of or accession to this Convention deposited under Article 4;

(c) notifications of consent to be bound by annexed Protocols under Article 4;

(d) the dates of entry into force of this Convention and of each of its annexed Protocols under Article 5; and

(e) notifications of denunciation received under Article 9, and their effective date.

Article 11   Authentic texts

The original of this Convention with the annexed Protocols, of which the Arabic, Chinese, English, French, Russian and Spanish texts are equally authentic, shall be deposited with the Depositary, who shall transmit certified true copies thereof to all states.

PROTOCOL ON NON-DETECTABLE FRAGMENTS (PROTOCOL I)

It is prohibited to use any weapon the primary effect of which is to injure by fragments which in the human body escape detection by X-rays.

PROTOCOL ON PROHIBITIONS OR RESTRICTIONS ON THE USE OF MINES, BOOBY-TRAPS AND OTHER DEVICES (PROTOCOL II)

Article 1   Material scope of application

This Protocol relates to the use on land of the mines, booby-traps and other devices defined herein, including mines laid to interdict beaches, waterway crossings or river crossings, but does not apply to the use of anti-ship mines at sea or in inland waterways.

Article 2   Definitions

For the purpose of this Protocol:

1   'Mine' means any munition placed under, on or near the ground or other surface area and designed to be detonated or exploded by the presence, proximity or contact of a person or vehicle, and 'remotely delivered mine' means any mine so defined delivered by artillery, rocket, mortar or similar means or dropped from an aircraft.

2   'Booby-trap' means any device or material which is designed, constructed or adapted to kill or injure and which functions unexpectedly when a person disturbs or approaches an apparently harmless object or performs an apparently safe act.

3   'Other devices' means manually-emplaced munitions and devices designed to kill, injure or damage and which are actuated by remote control or automatically after a lapse of time.

4   'Military objective' means, so far as objects are concerned, any object which by its nature, location, purpose or use makes an effective contribution to military action and whose total or partial destruction, capture or neutralisation, in the circumstances ruling at the time, offers a definite military advantage.

5   'Civilian objects' are all objects which are not military objectives as defined in para 4.

6   'Recording' means a physical, administrative and technical operation designed to obtain, for the purpose of registration in the official records, all available information facilitating the location of minefields, mines and booby-traps.

Article 3   General restrictions on the use of mines, booby-traps and other devices

1   This article applies to:

(a)   mines;

(b)   booby-traps; and

(c)   other devices.

2   It is prohibited in all circumstances to direct weapons to which this article applies, either in offence, defence or by way of reprisals, against the civilian population as such or against individual civilians.

3   The indiscriminate use of weapons to which this article applies is prohibited. Indiscriminate use is any placement of such weapons:

(a)   which is not on, or directed at, a military objective; or

(b)   which employs a method or means of delivery which cannot be directed at a specific military objective; or

(c)   which may be expected to cause incidental loss of civilian life, injury to civilians, damage to civilian objects, or a combination thereof, which would be excessive in relation to the concrete and direct military advantage anticipated.

4   All feasible precautions shall be taken to protect civilians from the effects of weapons to which this article applies. Feasible precautions are those precautions which are practicable or practically possible taking into account all circumstances ruling at the time, including humanitarian and military considerations.

Article 4 Restrictions on the use of mines other than remotely delivered mines, booby-traps and other devices in populated areas

1   This article applies to:

(a)   mines other than remotely delivered mines;

(b)   booby-traps; and

(c)   other devices.

2   It is prohibited to use weapons to which this article applies in any city, town, village or other area containing a similar concentration of civilians in which combat between ground forces is not taking place or does not appear to be imminent, unless either:

(a)   they are placed on or in the close vicinity of a military objective belonging to or under the control of an adverse party; or (b)　measures are taken to protect civilians from their effects, for example, the posting of warning signs, the posting of sentries, the issue of warnings or the provision of fences.

Article 5　Restrictions on the use of remotely delivered mines

1　The use of remotely delivered mines is prohibited unless such mines are only used within an area which is itself a military objective or which contains military objectives, and unless:

(a)　their location can be accurately recorded in accordance with Article 7(1)(a); or

(b)　an effective neutralising mechanism is used on each such mine, that is to say, a self-actuating mechanism which is designed to render a mine harmless or cause it to destroy itself when it is anticipated that the mine will no longer serve the military purpose for which it was placed in position, or a remotely-controlled mechanism which is designed to render harmless or destroy a mine when the mine no longer serves the military purpose for which it was placed in position.

2　Effective advance warning shall be given of any delivery or dropping of remotely delivered mines which may affect the civilian population, unless circumstances do not permit.

Article 6　Prohibition on the use of certain booby-traps

1　Without prejudice to the rules of international law applicable in armed conflict relating to treachery and perfidy, it is prohibited in all circumstances to use:

(a)　any booby-trap in the form of an apparently harmless portable object which is specifically designed and constructed to contain explosive material and to detonate when it is disturbed or approached; or

(b)　booby-traps which are in any way attached to or associated with:

　(i)　internationally recognised protective emblems, signs or signals;

　(ii)　sick, wounded or dead persons;

　(iii)　burial or cremation sites or graves;

　(iv)　medical facilities, medical equipment, medical supplies or medical transportation;

　(v)　children's toys or other portable objects or products specially designed for the feeding, health, hygiene, clothing or education of children;

　(vi)　food or drink;

　(vii)　kitchen utensils or appliances except in military establishments, military locations or military supply depots;

　(viii)　objects clearly of a religious nature;

　(ix)　historic monuments, works of art or places or worship which constitute the cultural or spiritual heritage of peoples;

　(x)　animals or their carcasses.

2　It is prohibited in all circumstances to use any booby-trap which is designed to cause superfluous injury or unnecessary suffering.

Article 7　Recording and publication of the location of minefields, mines and booby-traps

1　The parties to a conflict shall record the location of:

(a)　all pre-planned minefields laid by them; and

(b)　all areas in which they have made large-scale and pre-planned use of booby-traps.

2   The parties shall endeavour to ensure the recording of the location of all other minefields, mines and booby-traps which they have laid or placed in position.

3   All such records shall be retained by the parties who shall:

(a)   immediately after the cessation of active hostilities:

    (i)   take all necessary and appropriate measures, including the use of such records, to protect civilians from the effects of minefields, mines and booby-traps; and either

    (ii)   in cases where the forces of neither party are in the territory of the adverse party, make available to each other and to the Secretary General of the United Nations all information in their possession concerning the location of minefields, mines and booby-traps in the territory of the adverse party; or

    (iii)   once complete withdrawal of the forces of the parties from the territory of the adverse party has taken place, make available to the adverse party and to the Secretary General of the United Nations all information in their possession concerning the location of minefields, mines and booby-traps in the territory of the adverse party;

(b)   when a United Nations force or mission performs functions in any area, make available to the authority mentioned in Article 8 such information as is required by that article;

(c)   whenever possible, by mutual agreement provide for the release of information concerning the location of minefields, mines and booby-traps, particularly in agreements governing the cessation of hostilities.

Article 8   Protection of United Nations forces and missions from the effects of minefields, mines and booby-traps

1   When a United Nations force or mission performs functions of peacekeeping, observation or similar functions in any area, each party to the conflict shall if requested by the head of the United Nations force or mission in that area, as far as it is able:

(a)   remove or render harmless all mines or booby-raps in that area;

(b)   take such measures as may be necessary to protect the force or mission from the effects of minefields, mines and booby-traps while carrying out its duties; and

(c)   make available to the head of the United Nations force or mission in that area, all information in the party's possession concerning the location of minefields, mines and booby-traps in that area.

2   When a United Nations fact-finding mission performs functions in any area, any party to the conflict concerned shall provide protection to that mission except where, because of the size of such mission, it cannot adequately provide such protection. In that case it shall make available to the head of the mission the information in its possession concerning the location of minefields, mines and booby-traps in that area.

Article 9   International co-operation in the removal of minefields, mines and booby-traps

After the cessation of active hostilities, the parties shall endeavour to reach agreement, both among themselves and, where appropriate, with other states and with international organisations, on the provision of information and technical and material assistance – including, in appropriate circumstances, joint operations necessary to remove or otherwise render ineffective minefields, mines and booby-traps placed in position during the conflict.

TECHNICAL ANNEX TO THE PROTOCOL ON PROHIBITIONS OR RESTRICTIONS ON THE USE OF MINES, BOOBY-TRAPS AND OTHER DEVICES (PROTOCOL II)

Whenever an obligation for the recording of the location of minefields, mines and booby-traps arises under the Protocol, the following guidelines shall be taken into account.

1 With regard to pre-planned minefields and large-scale and pre-planned use of booby-traps:

(a) maps, diagrams or other records should be made in such a way as to indicate the extent of the minefield or booby-trapped area; and

(b) the location of the minefield or booby-trapped area should be specified by relation to the co-ordinates of a single reference point and by the estimated dimensions of the area containing mines and booby-traps in relation to that single reference point.

2 With regard to other minefields, mines and booby-traps laid or placed in position:

In so far as possible, the relevant information specified in para 1 above should be recorded so as to enable the areas containing minefields, mines and booby-traps to be identified.

PROTOCOL ON PROHIBITIONS OR RESTRICTIONS ON THE USE OF INCENDIARY WEAPONS (PROTOCOL III)

Article 1 Definitions

For the purpose of this Protocol:

1 'Incendiary weapon' means any weapon or munition which is primarily designed to set fire to objects or to cause burn injury to persons through the action of flame, heat, or a combination thereof, produced by a chemical reaction of a substance delivered on the target.

(a) Incendiary weapons can take the form of, for example, flame throwers, fougasses, shells, rockets, grenades, mines, bombs and other containers of incendiary substances.

(b) Incendiary weapons do not include:

(i) Munitions which may have incidental incendiary effects, such as illuminants, tracers, smoke or signalling systems;

(ii) Munitions designed to combine penetration, blast or fragmentation effects with an additional incendiary effect, such as armour-piercing projectiles, fragmentation shells, explosive bombs and similar combined-effects munitions in which the incendiary effect is not specifically designed to cause burn injury to persons, but to be used against military objectives, such as armoured vehicles, aircraft and installations or facilities.

2 'Concentration of civilians' means any concentration of civilians, be it permanent or temporary, such as in inhabited parts of cities, or inhabited towns or villages, or as in camps or columns of refugees or evacuees, or groups of nomads.

3   'Military objective' means, so far as objects are concerned, any object which by its nature, location, purpose or use makes an effective contribution to military action and whose total or partial destruction capture or neutralisation, in the circumstances ruling at the time, offers a definite military advantage.

4   'Civilian objects' are all objects which are not military objectives as defined in para 3.

5   'Feasible precautions' are those precautions which are practicable or practically possible taking into account all circumstances ruling at the time, including humanitarian and military considerations.

Article 2   Protection of civilians and civilian objects

1   It is prohibited in all circumstances to make the civilian population as such, individual civilians or civilian objects the object of attack by incendiary weapons.

2   It is prohibited in all circumstances to make any military objective located within a concentration of civilians the object of attack by air-delivered incendiary weapons.

3   It is further prohibited to make any military objective located within a concentration of civilians the object of attack by means of incendiary weapons other than air-delivered incendiary weapons, except when such military objective is clearly separated from the concentration of civilians and all feasible precautions are taken with a view to limiting the incendiary effects to the military objective and to avoiding, and in any event to minimising, incidental loss of civilian life, injury to civilians and damage to civilian objects.

4   It is prohibited to make forests or other kinds of plant cover the object of attack by incendiary weapons except when such natural elements are used to cover, conceal or camouflage combatants or other military objectives, or are themselves military objectives.

15.5.1.2   Weapons of mass destruction

One of the first decisions taken by the UN General Assembly was made in January 1946 to establish a Commission for, *inter alia*, the 'elimination of major weapons adaptable to mass destruction'. The Commission for Conventional Armaments in 1948 defined weapons of mass destruction to include atomic explosive weapons, radio-active material weapons, as well as certain lethal chemical and biological weapons. The General Assembly later expanded the definition to include any weapons developed in the future which have characteristics comparable in destructive effect to those of the atomic bomb.

The main type of weapons of mass destruction are nuclear weapons and the international law on the subject operates on two levels. First, there are restrictions on the production and possession of nuclear weapons, for example, the Treaty on the Non-Proliferation of Nuclear Weapons 1963 which restricts the number of states which can build and possess nuclear weapons.

TREATY ON THE NON-PROLIFERATION OF NUCLEAR WEAPONS (1968)[2]

ENTERED INTO FORCE: 5 March 1970

The states concluding this Treaty, hereinafter referred to as the 'Parties to the Treaty',

Considering the devastation that would be visited upon all mankind by a nuclear war and the consequent need to make every effort to avert the danger of such a war and to take measures to safeguard the security of peoples,

Believing that the proliferation of nuclear weapons would seriously enhance the danger of nuclear war,

In conformity with resolutions of the United Nations General Assembly calling for the conclusion of an agreement on the prevention of wider dissemination of nuclear weapons,

Undertaking to co-operate in facilitating the application of International Atomic Energy Agency safeguards on peaceful nuclear activities,

Expressing their support for research, development and other efforts to further the application, within the framework of the International Atomic Energy Agency safeguards system, of the principle of safeguarding effectively the flow of source and special fissionable materials by use of instruments and other techniques at certain strategic points,

Affirming the principle that the benefits of peaceful applications of nuclear technology, including any technological by-products which may be derived by nuclear-weapon states from the development of nuclear explosive devices, should be available for peaceful purposes to all Parties to the Treaty, whether nuclear-weapon or non-nuclear-weapon states,

Convinced that, in furtherance of this principle, all Parties to the Treaty are entitled to participate in the fullest possible exchange of scientific information for, and to contribute alone or in co-operation with other states to, the further development of the applications of atomic energy for peaceful purposes,

Declaring their intention to achieve at the earliest possible date the cessation of the nuclear arms race and to undertake effective measures in the direction of nuclear disarmament,

Urging the co-operation of all states in the attainment of this objective,

Recalling the determination expressed by the Parties to the 1963 Treaty banning nuclear weapon tests in the atmosphere, in outer space and under water in its Preamble to seek to achieve the discontinuance of all test explosions of nuclear weapons for all time and to continue negotiations to this end,

Desiring to further the easing of international tension and the strengthening of trust between states in order to facilitate the cessation of the manufacture of nuclear weapons, the liquidation of all their existing stockpiles, and the elimination from national arsenals of nuclear weapons and the means of their delivery pursuant to a Treaty on general and complete disarmament under strict and effective international control,

Recalling that, in accordance with the Charter of the United Nations, states must refrain in their international relations from the threat or use of force against the

---

2   UNTS No 10485, Vol 729, pp 169–75.

territorial integrity or political independence of any state, or in any other manner inconsistent with the Purposes of the United Nations, and that the establishment and maintenance of international peace and security are to be promoted with the least diversion for armaments of the world's human and economic resources,

Have agreed as follows:

Article I

Each nuclear-weapon State Party to the Treaty undertakes not to transfer to any recipient whatsoever nuclear weapons or other nuclear explosive devices or control over such weapons or explosive devices directly, or indirectly; and not in any way to assist, encourage, or induce any non-nuclear-weapon state to manufacture or otherwise acquire nuclear weapons or other nuclear explosive devices, or control over such weapons or explosive devices.

Article II

Each non-nuclear-weapon State Party to the Treaty undertakes not to receive the transfer from any transferor whatsoever of nuclear weapons or other nuclear explosive devices or of control over such weapons or explosive devices directly or indirectly; not to manufacture or otherwise acquire nuclear weapons or other nuclear explosive devices; and not to seek or receive any assistance in the manufacture of nuclear weapons or other nuclear explosive devices.

Article III

1   Each non-nuclear-weapon State Party to the Treaty undertakes to accept safeguards, as set forth in an agreement to be negotiated and concluded with the International Atomic Energy Agency in accordance with the Statute of the International Atomic Energy Agency and the Agency's safeguards system, for the exclusive purpose of verification of the fulfilment of its obligations assumed under this Treaty with a view to preventing diversion of nuclear energy from peaceful uses to nuclear weapons or other nuclear explosive devices. Procedures for the safeguards required by this article shall be followed with respect to source or special fissionable material whether it is being produced, processed or used in any principal nuclear facility or is outside any such facility. The safeguards required by this article shall be applied on all source or special fissionable material in all peaceful nuclear activities within the territory of such state, under its jurisdiction, or carried out under its control anywhere.

2   Each State Party to the Treaty undertakes not to provide: (a) source or special fissionable material, or (b) equipment or material especially designed or prepared for the processing, use or production of special fissionable material, to any non-nuclear-weapon state for peaceful purposes, unless the source or special fissionable material shall be subject to the safeguards required by this article.

3   The safeguards required by this article shall be implemented in a manner designed to comply with Article IV of this Treaty, and to avoid hampering the economic or technological development of the Parties or international co-operation in the field of peaceful nuclear activities, including the international exchange of nuclear material and equipment for the processing, use or production of nuclear material for peaceful purposes in accordance with the provisions of this article and the principle of safeguarding set forth in the Preamble of the Treaty.

4   Non-nuclear-weapon States Party to the Treaty shall conclude agreements with the International Atomic Energy Agency to meet the requirements of this article either individually or together with other states in accordance with the Statute of the International Atomic Energy Agency. Negotiation of such

agreements shall commence within 180 days from the original entry into force of this Treaty. For states depositing their instruments of ratification or accession after the 180-day period, negotiation of such agreements shall commence not later than the date of such deposit. Such agreements shall enter into force not later than eighteen months after the date of initiation of negotiations.

Article IV

1   Nothing in this Treaty shall be interpreted as affecting the inalienable right of all the Parties to the Treaty to develop research, production and use of nuclear energy for peaceful purposes without discrimination and in conformity with Articles I and II of this Treaty.

2   All the Parties to the Treaty undertake to facilitate, and have the right to participate in, the fullest possible exchange of equipment, materials and scientific and technological information for the peaceful uses of nuclear energy. Parties to the Treaty in a position to do so shall also co-operate in contributing alone or together with other states or international organisations to the further development of the applications of nuclear energy for peaceful purposes, especially in the territories of non-nuclear-weapon States Party to the Treaty, with due consideration for the needs of the developing areas of the world.

Article V

Each Party to the Treaty undertakes to take appropriate measures to ensure that, in accordance with this Treaty, under appropriate international observation and through appropriate international procedures, potential benefits from any peaceful applications of nuclear explosions will be made available to non-nuclear-weapon States Party to the Treaty on a non-discriminatory basis and that the charge to such Parties for the explosive devices used will be as low as possible and exclude any charge for research and development. Non-nuclear-weapon States Party to the Treaty shall be able to obtain such benefits, pursuant to a special international agreement or agreements, through an appropriate international body with adequate representation of non-nuclear-weapon states. Negotiations on this subject shall commence as soon as possible after the Treaty enters into force. Non-nuclear-weapon States Party to the Treaty so desiring may also obtain such benefits pursuant to bilateral agreements.

Article VI

Each of the Parties to the Treaty undertakes to pursue negotiations in good faith on effective measures relating to cessation of the nuclear arms race at an early date and to nuclear disarmament, and on a treaty on general and complete disarmament under strict and effective international control.

Article VII

Nothing in this Treaty affects the right of any group of states to conclude regional treaties in order to assure the total absence of nuclear weapons in their respective territories.

Article VIII

1   Any Party to the Treaty may propose amendments to this Treaty. The text of any proposed amendment shall be submitted to the Depositary Governments which shall circulate it to all Parties to the Treaty. Thereupon, if requested to do so by one-third or more of the Parties to the Treaty, the Depositary Governments shall convene a conference, to which they shall invite all the Parties to the Treaty, to consider such an amendment.

2   Any amendment to this Treaty must be approved by a majority of the votes of all the Parties to the Treaty, including the votes of all nuclear-weapon States

Party to the Treaty and all other Parties which, on the date the amendment is circulated, are members of the Board of Governors of the International Atomic Energy Agency. The amendment shall enter into force for each Party that deposits its instrument of ratification of the amendment upon the deposit of such instruments of ratification by a majority of all the Parties, including the instruments of ratification of all nuclear-weapon States Party to the Treaty and all other Parties which, on the date the amendment is circulated, are members of the Board of Governors of the International Atomic Energy Agency. Thereafter, it shall enter into force for any other Party upon the deposit of its instrument of ratification of the amendment.

3   Five years after the entry into force of this Treaty, a conference of Parties to the Treaty shall be held in Geneva, Switzerland, in order to review the operation of this Treaty with a view to assuring that the purposes of the Preamble and the provisions of the Treaty are being realised. At intervals of five years thereafter, a majority of the Parties to the Treaty may obtain, by submitting a proposal to this effect to the Depositary Governments, the convening of further conferences with the same objective of reviewing the operation of the Treaty.

Article IX

1   This Treaty shall be open to all states for signature. Any state which does not sign the Treaty before its entry into force in accordance with para 3 of this article may accede to it at any time.

2   This Treaty shall be subject to ratification by signatory states. Instruments of ratification and instruments of accession shall be deposited with the governments of the United Kingdom of Great Britain and Northern Ireland, the Union of Soviet Socialist Republics and the United States of America, which are hereby designated the Depositary Governments.

3   This Treaty shall enter into force after its ratification by the states, the governments of which are designated Depositaries of the Treaty, and 40 other states signatory to this Treaty and the deposit of their instruments of ratification. For the purposes of this Treaty, a nuclear-weapon state is one which has manufactured and exploded a nuclear weapon or other nuclear explosive device prior to 1 January, 1967.

4   For states whose instruments of ratification or accession are deposited subsequent to the entry into force of this Treaty, it shall enter into force on the date of the deposit of their instruments of ratification or accession.

5   The Depositary Governments shall promptly inform all signatory and acceding states of the date of each signature, the date of deposit of each instrument of ratification or of accession, the date of the entry into force of this Treaty, and the date of receipt of any requests for convening a conference or other notices.

6   This Treaty shall be registered by the Depositary Governments pursuant to Article 102 of the Charter of the United Nations.

Article X

1   Each Party shall in exercising its national sovereignty have the right to withdraw from the Treaty if it decides that extraordinary events, related to the subject matter of this Treaty, have jeopardised the supreme interests of its country. It shall give notice of such withdrawal to all other Parties to the Treaty and to the United Nations Security Council three months in advance. Such notice shall include a statement of the extraordinary events it regards as having jeopardised its supreme interests.

2   Twenty-five years after the entry into force of the Treaty, a conference shall be convened to decide whether the Treaty shall continue in force indefinitely, or shall be extended for an additional fixed period or periods. This decision shall be taken by a majority of the Parties to the Treaty.

Article XI

This Treaty, the English, Russian, French, Spanish and Chinese texts of which are equally authentic, shall be deposited in the archives of the Depositary Governments. Duly certified copies of this Treaty shall be transmitted by the Depositary Governments to the governments of the signatory and acceding states.

IN WITNESS WHEREOF the undersigned, duly authorised, have signed this Treaty.

DONE in triplicate, at the cities of London, Moscow and Washington, the first day of July, one thousand nine hundred and sixty-eight.

In addition, there are treaties which prohibit the testing and use of nuclear weapons in particular locations, for example, the Space Treaty 1967 and the Antarctic Treaty 1959.

The use of nuclear weapons, along with the use of all other weapons, is subject to three basic principles: the necessity to use them; the proportionality of their use; and the obligation not to cause unnecessary suffering. Nuclear weapons cause, by their very nature, indiscriminate suffering and destruction and, as such, it could be argued that their use is contrary to the rules of international law. It has also been argued that the use of nuclear weapons would contravene the Genocide Convention and could also contravene the Hague Regulations which prohibit poisonous weapons. Those who argue in favour of a right to use nuclear weapons have suggested that the rules prohibiting indiscriminate suffering relate to conventional weapons only and that the use of nuclear weapons would be permissible in the absence of any positive law to the contrary. What does seem to be accepted is that the first use of nuclear weapons is acceptable although state practice seems to suggest that the possession and production of such weapons is not, providing there is no breach of the Non-Proliferation Treaty, in itself a breach of international law. In 1994 the United Nations General Assembly requested an advisory opinion from the ICJ on the question of the legality of the use by a state of nuclear weapons in armed conflict:

LEGALITY OF THE THREAT OR USE OF NUCLEAR WEAPONS CASE[3]

20   The Court must next address certain matters arising in relation to the formulation of the question put to it by the General Assembly. The English text asks: 'Is the threat or use of nuclear weapons in any circumstance permitted under international law?' The French text of the question reads as follows: '*Est-il permis en droit international de recourir à la menace ou à l'emploi d'armes nucléaires en*

---

3   [1996] *ICJ Rep* at p 90.

toute circonstance?' It was suggested that the Court was being asked by the General Assembly whether it was permitted to have recourse to nuclear weapons in every circumstance, and it was contended that such a question would inevitably invite a simple negative answer.

The Court finds it unnecessary to pronounce on the possible divergences between the English and French texts of the question posed. Its real objective is clear: to determine the legality or illegality of the threat or use of nuclear weapons.

21 The use of the word 'permitted' in the question put by the General Assembly was criticised before the Court by certain states on the ground that this implied that the threat or the use of nuclear weapons would only be permissible if authorisation could be found in a treaty provision or in customary international law. Such a starting point, those states submitted, was incompatible with the very basis of international law, which rests upon the principles of sovereignty and consent; accordingly, and contrary to what was implied by use of the word 'permitted', states are free to threaten or use nuclear weapons unless it can be shown that they are bound not to do so by reference to a prohibition in either treaty law or customary international law. Support for this contention was found in *dicta* of the Permanent Court of International Justice in the *Lotus* case that 'restrictions upon the independence of states cannot ... be presumed' and that international law leaves to states 'a wide measure of discretion which is only limited in certain cases by prohibitive rules' (*PCIJ*, Ser A, No 10, pp 18 and 19). Reliance was also placed on the *dictum* of the present Court in the case concerning Military and Paramilitary Activities in and against Nicaragua (*Nicaragua v United States of America*) that:

> in international law there are no rules, other than such rules as may be accepted by the state concerned, by treaty or otherwise, whereby the level of armaments of a sovereign state can be limited ([1986] *ICJ Rep* at p 135, para 269).

For other states, the invocation of these *dicta* in the *Lotus* case was inapposite; their status in contemporary international law and applicability in the very different circumstances of the present case were challenged. It was also contended that the above-mentioned *dictum* of the present Court was directed to the possession of armaments and was irrelevant to the threat or use of nuclear weapons.

Finally, it was suggested that, were the Court to answer the question put by the Assembly, the word 'permitted' should be replaced by 'prohibited'.

22 The Court notes that the nuclear-weapon states appearing before it either accepted, or did not dispute, that their independence to act was indeed restricted by the principles and rules of international law, more particularly humanitarian law (see below, para 86), as did the other states which took part in the proceedings.

Hence, the argument concerning the legal conclusions to be drawn from the use of the word 'permitted', and the questions of burden of proof to which it was said to give rise, are without particular significance for the disposition of the issues before the Court.

23 In seeking to answer the question put to it by the General Assembly, the Court must decide, after consideration of the great corpus of international law norms available to it, what might be the relevant applicable law.

24 Some of the proponents of the illegality of the use of nuclear weapons have argued that such use would violate the right to life as guaranteed in Article 6 of

the International Covenant on Civil and Political Rights, as well as in certain regional instruments for the protection of human rights. Article 6, para 1, of the International Covenant provides as follows:

> Every human being has the inherent right to life. This right shall be protected by law. No one shall be arbitrarily deprived of his life.

In reply, others contended that the International Covenant on Civil and Political Rights made no mention of war or weapons, and it had never been envisaged that the legality of nuclear weapons was regulated by that instrument. It was suggested that the Covenant was directed to the protection of human rights in peacetime, but that questions relating to unlawful loss of life in hostilities were governed by the law applicable in armed conflict.

25   The Court observes that the protection of the International Covenant of Civil and Political Rights does not cease in times of war, except by operation of Article 4 of the Covenant whereby certain provisions may be derogated from in a time of national emergency. Respect for the right to life is not, however, such a provision. In principle, the right not arbitrarily to be deprived of one's life applies also in hostilities. The test of what is an arbitrary deprivation of life, however, then falls to be determined by the applicable *lex specialis*, namely, the law applicable in armed conflict which is designed to regulate the conduct of hostilities. Thus whether a particular loss of life, through the use of a certain weapon in warfare, is to be considered an arbitrary deprivation of life contrary to Article 6 of the Covenant, can only be decided by reference to the law applicable in armed conflict and not deduced from the terms of the Covenant itself.

26   Some states also contended that the prohibition against genocide, contained in the Convention of 9 December 1948 on the Prevention and Punishment of the Crime of Genocide, is a relevant rule of customary international law which the Court must apply. The Court recalls that, in Article II of the Convention genocide is defined as:

> ... any of the following acts committed with intent to destroy, in whole or in part, a national, ethnical, racial or religious group, as such:
>
> (a)   killing members of the group;
>
> (b)   causing serious bodily or mental harm to members of the group;
>
> (c)   deliberately inflicting on the group conditions of life calculated to being about its physical destruction in whole or in part;
>
> (d)   imposing measures intended to prevent births within the group;
>
> (e)   forcibly transferring children of the group to another group.

It was maintained before the Court that the number of deaths occasioned by the use of nuclear weapons would be enormous; that the victims could, in certain cases, include persons of a particular national, ethnic, racial or religious group; and that the intention to destroy such groups could be inferred from the fact that the user of the nuclear weapon would have omitted to take account of the well-known effects of the use of such weapons.

The Court would point out in that regard that the prohibition of genocide would be pertinent in this case if the recourse to nuclear weapons did indeed entail the element of intent, towards a group as such, required by the provision quoted above. In the view of the Court, it would only be possible to arrive at such a conclusion after having taken due account of the circumstances specific to each case.

27   In both their written and oral statements, some states furthermore argued that any use of nuclear weapons would be unlawful by reference to existing

norms relating to the safeguarding and protection of the environment, in view of their essential importance.

Specific references were made to various existing international treaties and instruments. These included Additional Protocol I of 1977 to the Geneva Conventions of 1949, Article 35, para 3, of which prohibits the employment of 'methods or means of warfare which are intended, or may be expected, to cause widespread, long-term and severe damage to the natural environment'; and the Convention of 18 May 1977 on the Prohibition of Military or Any Other Hostile Use of Environmental Modification Techniques, which prohibits the use of weapons which have 'widespread, long-lasting or severe effects' on the environment (Art 1). Also cited were Principle 21 of the Stockholm Declaration of 1972 and Principle 2 of the Rio Declaration of 1992 which express the common conviction of the states concerned that they have a duty 'to ensure that activities within their jurisdiction or control do not cause damage to the environment of other states or of areas beyond the limits of national jurisdiction'. These instruments and other provisions relating to the protection and safeguarding of the environment were said to apply at all times, in war as well as in peace, and it was contended that they would be violated by the use of nuclear weapons whose consequences would be widespread and would have transboundary effects.

28   Other states questioned the binding legal quality of these precepts of environmental law; or, in the context of the Convention on the Prohibition of Military or Any Other Hostile Use of Environmental Modification Techniques, denied that it was concerned at all with the use of nuclear weapons in hostilities; or, in the case of Additional Protocol I, denied that they were generally bound by its terms, or recalled that they had reserved their position in respect of Article 35, para 3, thereof.

It was also argued by some states that the principal purpose of environmental treaties and norms was the protection of the environment in time of peace. It was said that those treaties made no mention of nuclear weapons. It was also pointed out that warfare in general, and nuclear warfare in particular, were not mentioned in their texts and that it would be destabilising to the rule of law and to confidence in international negotiations if those treaties were now interpreted in such a way as to prohibit the use of nuclear weapons.

29   The Court recognises that the environment is under daily threat and that the use of nuclear weapons could constitute a catastrophe for the environment. The Court also recognises that the environment is not an abstraction but represents the living space, the quality of life and the very health of human beings, including generations unborn. The existence of the general obligation of states to ensure that activities within their jurisdiction and control respect the environment of other states or of areas beyond national control is now part of the corpus of international law relating to the environment.

30   However, the Court is of the view that the issue is not whether the treaties relating to the protection of the environment are or not applicable during an armed conflict, but rather whether the obligations stemming from these treaties were intended to be obligations of total restraint during military conflict.

The Court does not consider that the treaties in question could have intended to deprive a state of the exercise of its right of self-defence under international law because of its obligations to protect the environment. Nonetheless, states must take environmental considerations into account when assessing what is necessary and proportionate in the pursuit of legitimate military objectives. Respect for the environment is one of the elements that go to assessing whether an action is in conformity with the principles of necessity and proportionality.

This approach is supported, indeed, by the terms of Principle 24 of the Rio Declaration, which provides that:

> Warfare is inherently destructive of sustainable development. states shall therefore respect international law providing protection for the environment in times of armed conflict and cooperate in its further development, as necessary.

31 The Court notes furthermore that Articles 35, para 3, and 55 of Additional Protocol I provide additional protection for the environment. Taken together, these provisions embody a general obligation to protect the natural environment against widespread, long-term and severe environmental damage; the prohibition of methods and means of warfare which are intended, or may be expected, to cause such damage; and the prohibition of attacks against the natural environment by way of reprisals.

These are powerful constraints for all the states having subscribed to these provisions.

32 General Assembly Resolution 47/37 of 25 November 1992 on the Protection of the Environment in Times of Armed Conflict, is also of interest in this context. It affirms the general view according to which environmental considerations constitute one of the elements to be taken into account in the implementation of the principles of the law applicable in armed conflict: it states that 'destruction of the environment, not justified by military necessity and carried out wantonly, is clearly contrary to existing international law'. Addressing the reality that certain instruments are not yet binding on all states, the General Assembly in this resolution '[a]ppeals to all states that have not yet done so to consider becoming parties to the relevant international conventions'.

In its recent Order in the Request for an Examination of the Situation in Accordance with Paragraph 63 of the Court's Judgment of 20 December 1974 in the *Nuclear Tests (New Zealand v France)* case, the Court stated that its conclusion was 'without prejudice to the obligations of states to respect and protect the natural environment' (Order of 22 September 1995; [1995] *ICJ Rep* at p 306, para 64). Although that statement was made in the context of nuclear testing, it naturally also applies to the actual use of nuclear weapons in armed conflict.

33 The Court thus finds that while the existing international law relating to the protection and safeguarding of the environment does not specifically prohibit the use of nuclear weapons, it indicates important environmental factors that are properly to be taken into account in the context of the implementation of the principles and rules of the law applicable in armed conflict.

34 In the light of the foregoing the Court concludes that the most directly relevant applicable law governing the question of which it was seised, is that relating to the use of force enshrined in the United Nations Charter and the law applicable in armed conflict which regulates the conduct of hostilities, together with any specific treaties on nuclear weapons that the Court might determine to be relevant.

35 In applying this law to the present case, the Court cannot however fail to take into account certain unique characteristics of nuclear weapons.

The Court has noted the definitions of nuclear weapons contained in various treaties and accords. It also notes that nuclear weapons are explosive devices whose energy results from the fusion or fission of the atom. By its very nature, that process, in nuclear weapons as they exist today, releases not only immense quantities of heat and energy, but also powerful and prolonged radiation. According to the material before the Court, the first two causes of damage are vastly more powerful than the damage caused by other weapons, while the phenomenon of radiation is said to be peculiar to nuclear weapons. These characteristics render the nuclear weapon potentially catastrophic. The destructive power of nuclear weapons cannot be contained in either space or time. They have the potential to destroy all civilisation and the entire ecosystem of the planet.

The radiation released by a nuclear explosion would affect health, agriculture, natural resources and demography over a very wide area. Further, the use of nuclear weapons would be a serious danger to future generations. Ionising radiation has the potential to damage the future environment, food and marine ecosystem, and to cause genetic defects and illness in future generations.

36   In consequence, in order correctly to apply to the present case the Charter law on the use of force and the law applicable in armed conflict, in particular humanitarian law, it is imperative for the Court to take account of the unique characteristics of nuclear weapons, and in particular their destructive capacity, their capacity to cause untold human suffering, and their ability to cause damage to generations to come.

37   The Court will now address the question of the legality or illegality of recourse to nuclear weapons in the light of the provisions of the Charter relating to the threat or use of force.

38   The Charter contains several provisions relating to the threat and use of force. In Article 2, para 4, the threat or use of force against the territorial integrity or political independence of another state or in any other manner inconsistent with the purposes of the United Nations is prohibited. That paragraph provides:

> All Members shall refrain in their international relations from the threat or use of force against the territorial integrity or political independence of any state, or in any other manner inconsistent with the Purposes of the United Nations.

This prohibition of the use of force is to be considered in the light of other relevant provisions of the Charter. In Article 51, the Charter recognises the inherent right of individual or collective self-defence if an armed attack occurs. A further lawful use of force is envisaged in Article 42, whereby the Security Council may take military enforcement measures in conformity with Chapter VII of the Charter.

39   These provisions do not refer to specific weapons. They apply to any use of force, regardless of the weapons employed. The Charter neither expressly prohibits, nor permits, the use of any specific weapon, including nuclear weapons. A weapon that is already unlawful *per se*, whether by treaty or custom, does not become lawful by reason of its being used for a legitimate purpose under the Charter.

40   The entitlement to resort to self-defence under Article 51 is subject to certain constraints. Some of these constraints are inherent in the very concept of self-defence. Other requirements are specified in Article 51.

41   The submission of the exercise of the right of self-defence to the conditions of necessity and proportionality is a rule of customary international law. As the Court stated in the case concerning Military and Paramilitary Activities in and against Nicaragua (*Nicaragua v United States of America*) ([1986] *ICJ Rep* at p 94, para 176): 'there is a specific rule whereby self-defence would warrant only measures which are proportional to the armed attack and necessary to respond to it, a rule well established in customary international law'. This dual condition

applies equally to Article 51 of the Charter, whatever the means of force employed.

42 The proportionality principle may thus not in itself exclude the use of nuclear weapons in self-defence in all circumstances. But at the same time, a use of force that is proportionate under the law of self-defence, must, in order to be lawful, also meet the requirements of the law applicable in armed conflict which comprise in particular the principles and rules of humanitarian law.

43 Certain states have in their written and oral pleadings suggested that in the case of nuclear weapons, the condition of proportionality must be evaluated in the light of still further factors. They contend that the very nature of nuclear weapons, and the high probability of an escalation of nuclear exchanges, mean that there is an extremely strong risk of devastation. The risk factor is said to negate the possibility of the condition of proportionality being complied with. The Court does not find it necessary to embark upon the quantification of such risks; nor does it need to enquire into the question whether tactical nuclear weapons exist which are sufficiently precise to limit those risks: it suffices for the Court to note that the very nature of all nuclear weapons and the profound risks associated therewith are further considerations to be borne in mind by states believing they can exercise a nuclear response in self-defence in accordance with the requirements of proportionality.

44 Beyond the conditions of necessity and proportionality, Article 51 specifically requires that measures taken by states in the exercise of the right of self-defence shall be immediately reported to the Security Council; this article further provides that these measures shall not in any way affect the authority and responsibility of the Security Council under the Charter to take at any time such action as it deems necessary in order to maintain or restore international peace and security. These requirements of Article 51 apply whatever the means of force used in self-defence.

45 The Court notes that the Security Council adopted on 11 April 1995, in the context of the extension of the Treaty on the Non-Proliferation of Nuclear Weapons, Resolution 984 (1995) by the terms of which, on the one hand, it:

> ... [t]akes note with appreciation of the statements made by each of the nuclear-weapon states (S/1995/261, S/1995/262, S/1995/263, S/1995/264, S/1995/265), in which they give security assurances against the use of nuclear weapons to non-nuclear-weapon states that are Parties to the Treaty on the Non-Proliferation of Nuclear Weapons,

and, on the other hand, it:

> ... [w]elcomes the intention expressed by certain states that they will provide or support immediate assistance, in accordance with the Charter, to any non-nuclear-weapon State Party to the Treaty on the Non-Proliferation of Nuclear Weapons that is a victim of an act of, or an object of a threat of, aggression in which nuclear weapons are used.

46 Certain states asserted that the use of nuclear weapons in the conduct of reprisals would be lawful. The Court does not have to examine, in this context, the question of armed reprisals in time of peace, which are considered to be unlawful. Nor does it have to pronounce on the question of belligerent reprisals save to observe that in any case any right of recourse to such reprisals would, like self-defence, be governed *inter alia* by the principle of proportionality.

47 In order to lessen or eliminate the risk of unlawful attack, states sometimes signal that they possess certain weapons to use in self-defence against any state violating their territorial integrity or political independence. Whether a signalled

intention to use force if certain events occur is or is not a 'threat' within Article 2, para 4, of the Charter depends upon various factors. If the envisaged use of force is itself unlawful, the stated readiness to use it would be a threat prohibited under Article 2, para 4. Thus it would be illegal for a state to threaten force to secure territory from another state, or to cause it to follow or not follow certain political or economic paths. The notions of 'threat' and 'use' of force under Article 2, para 4, of the Charter stand together in the sense that if the use of force itself in a given case is illegal – for whatever reason – the threat to use such force will likewise be illegal. In short, if it is to be lawful, the declared readiness of a state to use force must be a use of force that is in conformity with the Charter. For the rest, no state – whether or not it defended the policy of deterrence – suggested to the Court that it would be lawful to threaten to use force if the use of force contemplated would be illegal.

48 Some states put forward the argument that possession of nuclear weapons is itself an unlawful threat to use force. Possession of nuclear weapons may indeed justify an inference of preparedness to use them. In order to be effective, the policy of deterrence, by which those states possessing or under the umbrella of nuclear weapons seek to discourage military aggression by demonstrating that it will serve no purpose, necessitates that the intention to use nuclear weapons be credible. Whether this is a 'threat' contrary to Article 2, para 4, depends upon whether the particular use of force envisaged would be directed against the territorial integrity or political independence of a state, or against the Purposes of the United Nations or whether, in the event that it were intended as a means of defence, it would necessarily violate the principles of necessity and proportionality. In any of these circumstances the use of force, and the threat to use it, would be unlawful under the law of the Charter.

49 Moreover, the Security Council may take enforcement measures under Chapter VII of the Charter. From the statements presented to it the Court does not consider it necessary to address questions which might, in a given case, arise from the application of Chapter VII.

50 The terms of the question put to the Court by the General Assembly in Resolution 49/75K could in principle also cover a threat or use of nuclear weapons by a state within its own boundaries. However, this particular aspect has not been dealt with by any of the states which addressed the Court orally or in writing in these proceedings. The Court finds that it is not called upon to deal with an internal use of nuclear weapons.

51 Having dealt with the Charter provisions relating to the threat or use of force, the Court will now turn to the law applicable in situations of armed conflict. It will first address the question whether there are specific rules in international law regulating the legality or illegality of recourse to nuclear weapons *per se*; it will then examine the question put to it in the light of the law applicable in armed conflict proper, ie the principles and rules of humanitarian law applicable in armed conflict, and the law of neutrality.

52 The Court notes by way of introduction that international customary and treaty law does not contain any specific prescription authorising the threat or use of nuclear weapons or any other weapon in general or in certain circumstances, in particular those of the exercise of legitimate self-defence. Nor, however, is there any principle or rule of international law which would make the legality of the threat or use of nuclear weapons or of any other weapons dependent on a specific authorisation. State practice shows that the illegality of the use of certain weapons as such does not result from an absence of authorisation but, on the contrary, is formulated in terms of prohibition.

53   The Court must therefore now examine whether there is any prohibition of recourse to nuclear weapons as such; it will first ascertain whether there is a conventional prescription to this effect.

54   In this regard, the argument has been advanced that nuclear weapons should be treated in the same way as poisoned weapons. In that case, they would be prohibited under:

(a)   the Second Hague Declaration of 29 July 1899, which prohibits 'the use of projectiles the object of which is the diffusion of asphyxiating or deleterious gases';

(b)   Article 23(a) of the Regulations respecting the laws and customs of war on land annexed to the Hague Convention IV of 18 October 1907, whereby 'it is especially forbidden ... to employ poison or poisoned weapons'; and

(c)   the Geneva Protocol of 17 June 1925 which prohibits 'the use in war of asphyxiating, poisonous or other gases, and of all analogous liquids, materials or devices'.

55   The Court will observe that the Regulations annexed to the Hague Convention IV do not define what is to be understood by 'poison or poisoned weapons' and that different interpretations exist on the issue. Nor does the 1925 Protocol specify the meaning to be given to the term 'analogous materials or devices'. The terms have been understood, in the practice of states, in their ordinary sense as covering weapons whose prime, or even exclusive, effect is to poison or asphyxiate. This practice is clear, and the parties to those instruments have not treated them as referring to nuclear weapons.

56   In view of this, it does not seem to the Court that the use of nuclear weapons can be regarded as specifically prohibited on the basis of the above-mentioned provisions of the Second Hague Declaration of 1899, the Regulations annexed to the Hague Convention IV of 1907 or the 1925 Protocol (see para 54 above).

57   The pattern until now has been for weapons of mass destruction to be declared illegal by specific instruments. The most recent such instruments are the Convention of 10 April 1972 on the Prohibition of the Development, Production and Stockpiling of Bacteriological (Biological) and Toxin Weapons and on their destruction – which prohibits the possession of bacteriological and toxic weapons and reinforces the prohibition of their use – and the Convention of 13 January 1993 on the Prohibition of the Development, Production, Stockpiling and Use of Chemical Weapons and on Their Destruction – which prohibits all use of chemical weapons and requires the destruction of existing stocks. Each of these instruments has been negotiated and adopted in its own context and for its own reasons. The Court does not find any specific prohibition of recourse to nuclear weapons in treaties expressly prohibiting the use of certain weapons of mass destruction.

58   In the last two decades, a great many negotiations have been conducted regarding nuclear weapons; they have not resulted in a treaty of general prohibition of the same kind as for bacteriological and chemical weapons. However, a number of specific treaties have been concluded in order to limit:

(a)   the acquisition, manufacture and possession of nuclear weapons (Peace Treaties of 10 February 1947; State Treaty for the Re-establishment of an Independent and Democratic Austria of 15 May 1955; Treaty of Tlatelolco of 14 February 1967 for the Prohibition of Nuclear Weapons in Latin America, and its Additional Protocols; Treaty of 1 July 1968 on the Non-Proliferation of Nuclear Weapons; Treaty of Rarotonga of 6 August 1985 on the Nuclear-

Weapon-Free Zone of the South Pacific, and its Protocols; Treaty of 12 September 1990 on the Final Settlement with respect to Germany);

(b) the deployment of nuclear weapons (Antarctic Treaty of 1 December 1959; Treaty of 27 January 1967 on Principles Governing the Activities of States in the Exploration and Use of Outer Space, including the Moon and Other Celestial Bodies; Treaty of Tlatelolco of 14 February 1967 for the Prohibition of Nuclear Weapons in Latin America, and its Additional Protocols; Treaty of 11 February 1971 on the Prohibition of the Emplacement of Nuclear Weapons and Other Weapons of Mass Destruction on the Sea Bed and the Ocean Floor and in the Subsoil Thereof; Treaty of Rarotonga of 6 August 1985 on the Nuclear-Weapon-Free Zone of the South Pacific, and its Protocols); and

(c) the testing of nuclear weapons (Antarctic Treaty of 1 December 1959; Treaty of 5 August 1963 Banning Nuclear Weapon Tests in the Atmosphere, in Outer Space and under Water; Treaty of 27 January 1967 on Principles Governing the Activities of States in the Exploration and Use of Outer Space, including the Moon and Other Celestial Bodies; Treaty of Tlatelolco of 14 February 1967 for the Prohibition of Nuclear Weapons in Latin America, and its Additional Protocols; Treaty of Rarotonga of 6 August 1985 on the Nuclear-Weapon-Free Zone of the South Pacific, and its Protocols).

59 Recourse to nuclear weapons is directly addressed by two of these Conventions and also in connection with the indefinite extension of the Treaty on the Non-Proliferation of Nuclear Weapons of 1968:

(a) the Treaty of Tlatelolco of 14 February 1967 for the Prohibition of Nuclear Weapons in Latin America prohibits, in Article 1, the use of nuclear weapons by the Contracting Parties. It further includes an Additional Protocol II open to nuclear-weapon states outside the region, Article 3 of which provides:

The governments represented by the undersigned Plenipotentiaries also undertake not to use or threaten to use nuclear weapons against the Contracting Parties of the Treaty for the Prohibition of Nuclear Weapons in Latin America.

The Protocol was signed and ratified by the five nuclear-weapon states. Its ratification was accompanied by a variety of declarations. The United Kingdom government, for example, stated that 'in the event of any act of aggression by a Contracting Party to the Treaty in which that Party was supported by a nuclear-weapon state', the United Kingdom government would 'be free to reconsider the extent to which they could be regarded as committed by the provisions of Additional Protocol II'. The United States made a similar statement. The French government, for its part, stated that it 'interprets the undertaking made in Article 3 of the Protocol as being without prejudice to the full exercise of the right of self-defence confirmed by Article 51 of the Charter'. China reaffirmed its commitment not to be the first to make use of nuclear weapons. The Soviet Union reserved 'the right to review' the obligations imposed upon it by Additional Protocol II, particularly in the event of an attack by a State Party either 'in support of a nuclear-weapon state or jointly with that state'. None of these statements drew comment or objection from the parties to the Treaty of Tlatelolco.

(b) the Treaty of Rarotonga of 6 August 1985 establishes a South Pacific Nuclear Free Zone in which the Parties undertake not to manufacture, acquire or possess any nuclear explosive device (Art 3). Unlike the Treaty of Tlatelolco, the Treaty of Rarotonga does not expressly prohibit the use of such weapons. But such a prohibition is for the States Parties the necessary consequence of the prohibitions stipulated by the Treaty. The Treaty has a number of protocols. Protocol 2, open to the five nuclear-weapon states, specifies in its Article 1 that:

> Each Party undertakes not to use or threaten to use any nuclear explosive device against:
>
> (a) Parties to the Treaty; or
>
> (b) any territory within the South Pacific Nuclear Free Zone for which a state that has become a Party to Protocol 1 is internationally responsible.

China and Russia are parties to that Protocol. In signing it, China and the Soviet Union each made a declaration by which they reserved the 'right to reconsider' their obligations under the said Protocol; the Soviet Union also referred to certain circumstances in which it would consider itself released from those obligations. France, the United Kingdom and the United States, for their part, signed Protocol 2 on 25 March 1996, but have not yet ratified it. On that occasion, France declared, on the one hand, that no provision in that Protocol 'shall impair the full exercise of the inherent right of self-defence provided for in Article 51 of the ... Charter' and, on the other hand, that 'the commitment set out in Article 1 of [that] Protocol amounts to the negative security assurances given by France to non-nuclear-weapon states which are parties to the Treaty on ... Non-Proliferation', and that 'these assurances shall not apply to states which are not parties' to that Treaty. For its part, the United Kingdom made a declaration setting out the precise circumstances in which it 'will not be bound by [its] undertaking under Article 1' of the Protocol.

(c) as to the Treaty on the Non-Proliferation of Nuclear Weapons, at the time of its signing in 1968 the United States, the United Kingdom and the USSR gave various security assurances to the non-nuclear-weapon states that were parties to the Treaty. In Resolution 255 (1968) the Security Council took note with satisfaction of the intention expressed by those three states to:

> ... provide or support immediate assistance, in accordance with the Charter, to any non-nuclear-weapon State Party to the Treaty on the Non-Proliferation ... that is a victim of an act of, or an object of a threat of, aggression in which nuclear weapons are used.

On the occasion of the extension of the Treaty in 1995, the five nuclear-weapon states gave their non-nuclear-weapon partners, by means of separate unilateral statements on 5 and 6 April 1995, positive and negative security assurances against the use of such weapons. All the five nuclear-weapon states first undertook not to use nuclear weapons against non-nuclear-weapon states that were parties to the Treaty on the Non-Proliferation of Nuclear Weapons. However, these states, apart from China, made an exception in the case of an invasion or any other attack against them, their territories, armed forces or allies, or on a state towards which they had a security commitment, carried out or sustained by a non-nuclear-weapon State Party to the Non-Proliferation Treaty in association or alliance with a nuclear-weapon state. Each of the nuclear-weapon states further undertook, as a permanent Member of the Security Council, in the event of an attack with the use of nuclear weapons, or threat of such attack, against a non-nuclear-weapon state, to refer the matter to the Security Council without delay and to act within it in order that it might take immediate measures with a view to supplying, pursuant to the Charter, the necessary assistance to the victim state (the commitments assumed comprising minor variations in wording). The Security Council, in unanimously adopting Resolution 984 (1995) of 11 April 1995, cited above, took note of those statements with appreciation. It also recognised:

> ... that the nuclear-weapon state permanent members of the Security Council will bring the matter immediately to the attention of the Council and seek Council action to provide, in accordance with the Charter, the necessary assistance to the state victim;

and welcomed the fact that:

> ... the intention expressed by certain states that they will provide or support immediate assistance, in accordance with the Charter, to any non-nuclear-weapon State Party to the Treaty on the Non-Proliferation of Nuclear Weapons that is a victim of an act of, or an object of a threat of, aggression in which nuclear weapons are used.

60 Those states that believe that recourse to nuclear weapons is illegal stress that the conventions that include various rules providing for the limitation or elimination of nuclear weapons in certain areas (such as the Antarctic Treaty of 1959 which prohibits the deployment of nuclear weapons in the Antarctic, or the Treaty of Tlatelolco of 1967 which creates a nuclear-weapon-free zone in Latin America), or the conventions that apply certain measures of control and limitation to the existence of nuclear weapons (such as the 1963 Partial Test-Ban Treaty or the Treaty on the Non-Proliferation of Nuclear Weapons) all set limits to the use of nuclear weapons. In their view, these treaties bear witness, in their own way, to the emergence of a rule of complete legal prohibition of all uses of nuclear weapons.

61 Those states who defend the position that recourse to nuclear weapons is legal in certain circumstances see a logical contradiction in reaching such a conclusion. According to them, those Treaties, such as the Treaty on the Non-Proliferation of Nuclear Weapons, as well as Security Council Resolutions 255 (1968) and 984 (1995) which take note of the security assurances given by the nuclear-weapon states to the non-nuclear-weapon states in relation to any nuclear aggression against the latter, cannot be understood as prohibiting the use of nuclear weapons, and such a claim is contrary to the very text of those instruments. For those who support the legality in certain circumstances of recourse to nuclear weapons, there is no absolute prohibition against the use of such weapons. The very logic and construction of the Treaty on the Non-Proliferation of Nuclear Weapons, they assert, confirm this. This Treaty, whereby, they contend, the possession of nuclear weapons by the five nuclear-weapon states has been accepted, cannot be seen as a treaty banning their use by those states; to accept the fact that those states possess nuclear weapons is tantamount to recognising that such weapons may be used in certain circumstances. Nor, they contend, could the security assurances given by the nuclear-weapon states in 1968, and more recently in connection with the Review and Extension Conference of the Parties to the Treaty on the Non-Proliferation of Nuclear Weapons in 1995, have been conceived without its being supposed that there were circumstances in which nuclear weapons could be used in a lawful manner. For those who defend the legality of the use, in certain circumstances, of nuclear weapons, the acceptance of those instruments by the different non-nuclear-weapon states confirms and reinforces the evident logic upon which those instruments are based.

62 The Court notes that the treaties dealing exclusively with acquisition, manufacture, possession, deployment and testing of nuclear weapons, without specifically addressing their threat or use, certainly point to an increasing

concern in the international community with these weapons; the Court concludes from this that these treaties could therefore be seen as foreshadowing a future general prohibition of the use of such weapons, but they do not constitute such a prohibition by themselves. As to the treaties of Tlatelolco and Rarotonga and their Protocols, and also the declarations made in connection with the indefinite extension of the Treaty on the Non-Proliferation of Nuclear Weapons, it emerges from these instruments that:

(a) a number of states have undertaken not to use nuclear weapons in specific zones (Latin America; the South Pacific) or against certain other states (non-nuclear-weapon states which are parties to the Treaty on the Non-Proliferation of Nuclear Weapons);

(b) nevertheless, even within this framework, the nuclear-weapon states have reserved the right to use nuclear weapons in certain circumstances; and

(c) these reservations met with no objection from the parties to the Tlatelolco or Rarotonga Treaties or from the Security Council.

63   These two treaties, the security assurances given in 1995 by the nuclear-weapon states and the fact that the Security Council took note of them with satisfaction, testify to a growing awareness of the need to liberate the community of states and the international public from the dangers resulting from the existence of nuclear weapons. The Court moreover notes the signing, even more recently, on 15 December 1995, at Bangkok, of a Treaty on the Southeast Asia Nuclear-Weapon-Free Zone, and on 11 April 1996, at Cairo, of a treaty on the creation of a nuclear-weapons-free zone in Africa. It does not, however, view these elements as amounting to a comprehensive and universal conventional prohibition on the use, or the threat of use, of those weapons as such.

64   The Court will now turn to an examination of customary international law to determine whether a prohibition of the threat or use of nuclear weapons as such flows from that source of law. As the Court has stated, the substance of that law must be 'looked for primarily in the actual practice and *opinio juris* of states' (*Continental Shelf (Libyan Arab Jamahiriya/Malta) Judgment*, [1985] *ICJ Rep* at p 29, para 27).

65   States which hold the view that the use of nuclear weapons is illegal have endeavoured to demonstrate the existence of a customary rule prohibiting this use. They refer to a consistent practice of non-utilisation of nuclear weapons by states since 1945 and they would see in that practice the expression of an *opinio juris* on the part of those who possess such weapons.

66   Some other states, which assert the legality of the threat and use of nuclear weapons in certain circumstances, invoked the doctrine and practice of deterrence in support of their argument. They recall that they have always, in concert with certain other states, reserved the right to use those weapons in the exercise of the right to self-defence against an armed attack threatening their vital security interests. In their view, if nuclear weapons have not been used since 1945, it is not on account of an existing or nascent custom but merely because circumstances that might justify their use have fortunately not arisen.

67   The Court does not intend to pronounce here upon the practice known as the 'policy of deterrence'. It notes that it is a fact that a number of states adhered to that practice during the greater part of the Cold War and continue to adhere to it. Furthermore, the members of the international community are profoundly divided on the matter of whether non-recourse to nuclear weapons over the past fifty years constitutes the expression of an *opinio juris*. Under these circumstances the Court does not consider itself able to find that there is such an *opinio juris*.

68   According to certain states, the important series of General Assembly resolutions, beginning with Resolution 1653 (XVI) of 24 November 1961, that deal with nuclear weapons and that affirm, with consistent regularity, the illegality of nuclear weapons, signify the existence of a rule of international customary law which prohibits recourse to those weapons. According to other states, however, the resolutions in question have no binding character on their own account and are not declaratory of any customary rule of prohibition of nuclear weapons; some of these states have also pointed out that this series of resolutions not only did not meet with the approval of all of the nuclear-weapon states but of many other states as well.

69   States which consider that the use of nuclear weapons is illegal indicated that those resolutions did not claim to create any new rules, but were confined to a confirmation of customary law relating to the prohibition of means or methods of warfare which, by their use, overstepped the bounds of what is permissible in the conduct of hostilities. In their view, the resolutions in question did no more than apply to nuclear weapons the existing rules of international law applicable in armed conflict; they were no more than the 'envelope' or instrumentum containing certain pre-existing customary rules of international law. For those states it is accordingly of little importance that the instrumentum should have occasioned negative votes, which cannot have the effect of obliterating those customary rules which have been confirmed by treaty law.

70   The Court notes that General Assembly resolutions, even if they are not binding, may sometimes have normative value. They can, in certain circumstances, provide evidence important for establishing the existence of a rule or the emergence of an *opinio juris*. To establish whether this is true of a given General Assembly resolution, it is necessary to look at its content and the conditions of its adoption; it is also necessary to see whether an *opinio juris* exists as to its normative character. Or a series of resolutions may show the gradual evolution of the *opinio juris* required for the establishment of a new rule.

71   Examined in their totality, the General Assembly resolutions put before the Court declare that the use of nuclear weapons would be 'a direct violation of the Charter of the United Nations'; and in certain formulations that such use 'should be prohibited'. The focus of these resolutions has sometimes shifted to diverse related matters; however, several of the resolutions under consideration in the present case have been adopted with substantial numbers of negative votes and abstentions; thus, although those resolutions are a clear sign of deep concern regarding the problem of nuclear weapons, they still fall short of establishing the existence of an *opinio juris* on the illegality of the use of such weapons.

72   The Court further notes that the first of the resolutions of the General Assembly expressly proclaiming the illegality of the use of nuclear weapons, Resolution 1653 (XVI) of 24 November 1961 (mentioned in subsequent resolutions), after referring to certain international declarations and binding agreements, from the Declaration of St Petersburg of 1868 to the Geneva Protocol of 1925, proceeded to qualify the legal nature of nuclear weapons, determine their effects, and apply general rules of customary international law to nuclear weapons in particular. That application by the General Assembly of general rules of customary law to the particular case of nuclear weapons indicates that, in its view, there was no specific rule of customary law which prohibited the use of nuclear weapons; if such a rule had existed, the General Assembly could simply have referred to it and would not have needed to undertake such an exercise of legal qualification.

73   Having said this, the Court points out that the adoption each year by the General Assembly, by a large majority, of resolutions recalling the content of Resolution 1653 (XVI), and requesting the member states to conclude a convention prohibiting the use of nuclear weapons in any circumstance, reveals the desire of a very large section of the international community to take, by a specific and express prohibition of the use of nuclear weapons, a significant step forward along the road to complete nuclear disarmament. The emergence, as *lex lata*, of a customary rule specifically prohibiting the use of nuclear weapons as such is hampered by the continuing tensions between the nascent *opinio juris* on the one hand, and the still strong adherence to the practice of deterrence on the other.

74   The Court not having found a conventional rule of general scope, nor a customary rule specifically proscribing the threat or use of nuclear weapons *per se*, it will now deal with the question whether recourse to nuclear weapons must be considered as illegal in the light of the principles and rules of international humanitarian law applicable in armed conflict and of the law of neutrality.

75   A large number of customary rules have been developed by the practice of states and are an integral part of the international law relevant to the question posed. The 'laws and customs of war' – as they were traditionally called – were the subject of efforts at codification undertaken in The Hague (including the Conventions of 1899 and 1907), and were based partly upon the St Petersburg Declaration of 1868 as well as the results of the Brussels Conference of 1874. This 'Hague Law' and, more particularly, the Regulations Respecting the Laws and Customs of War on Land, fixed the rights and duties of belligerents in their conduct of operations and limited the choice of methods and means of injuring the enemy in an international armed conflict. One should add to this the 'Geneva Law' (the Conventions of 1864, 1906, 1929 and 1949), which protects the victims of war and aims to provide safeguards for disabled armed forces personnel and persons not taking part in the hostilities. These two branches of the law applicable in armed conflict have become so closely interrelated that they are considered to have gradually formed one single complex system, known today as international humanitarian law. The provisions of the Additional Protocols of 1977 give expression and attest to the unity and complexity of that law.

76   Since the turn of the century, the appearance of new means of combat has – without calling into question the long-standing principles and rules of international law – rendered necessary some specific prohibitions of the use of certain weapons, such as explosive projectiles under 400 grammes, dum-dum bullets and asphyxiating gases. Chemical and bacteriological weapons were then prohibited by the 1925 Geneva Protocol. More recently, the use of weapons producing 'non-detectable fragments', of other types of 'mines, booby-traps and other devices', and of 'incendiary weapons', was either prohibited or limited, depending on the case, by the Convention of 10 October 1980 on Prohibitions or Restrictions on the Use of Certain Conventional Weapons Which May Be Deemed to Be Excessively Injurious or to Have Indiscriminate Effects. The provisions of the Convention on 'mines, booby-traps and other devices' have just been amended, on 3 May 1996, and now regulate in greater detail, for example, the use of anti-personnel land mines.

77   All this shows that the conduct of military operations is governed by a body of legal prescriptions. This is so because 'the right of belligerents to adopt means of injuring the enemy is not unlimited' as stated in Article 22 of the 1907 Hague Regulations relating to the laws and customs of war on land. The St Petersburg Declaration had already condemned the use of weapons 'which uselessly

aggravate the suffering of disabled men or make their death inevitable'. The aforementioned Regulations relating to the laws and customs of war on land, annexed to the Hague Convention IV of 1907, prohibit the use of 'arms, projectiles, or material calculated to cause unnecessary suffering' (Article 23).

78 The cardinal principles contained in the texts constituting the fabric of humanitarian law are the following. The first is aimed at the protection of the civilian population and civilian objects and establishes the distinction between combatants and non-combatants; states must never make civilians the object of attack and must consequently never use weapons that are incapable of distinguishing between civilian and military targets. According to the second principle, it is prohibited to cause unnecessary suffering to combatants: it is accordingly prohibited to use weapons causing them such harm or uselessly aggravating their suffering. In application of that second principle, states do not have unlimited freedom of choice of means in the weapons they use.

The Court would likewise refer, in relation to these principles, to the Martens Clause, which was first included in the Hague Convention II with Respect to the Laws and Customs of War on Land of 1899 and which has proved to be an effective means of addressing the rapid evolution of military technology. A modern version of that clause is to be found in Article 1, para 2, of Additional Protocol I of 1977, which reads as follows:

> In cases not covered by this Protocol or by other international agreements, civilians and combatants remain under the protection and authority of the principles of international law derived from established custom, from the principles of humanity and from the dictates of public conscience.

In conformity with the aforementioned principles, humanitarian law, at a very early stage, prohibited certain types of weapons either because of their indiscriminate effect on combatants and civilians or because of the unnecessary suffering caused to combatants, that is to say, a harm greater than that unavoidable to achieve legitimate military objectives. If an envisaged use of weapons would not meet the requirements of humanitarian law, a threat to engage in such use would also be contrary to that law.

79 It is undoubtedly because a great many rules of humanitarian law applicable in armed conflict are so fundamental to the respect of the human person and 'elementary considerations of humanity' as the Court put it in its Judgment of 9 April 1949 in the *Corfu Channel* case ([1949] *ICJ Rep* at p 22), that the Hague and Geneva Conventions have enjoyed a broad accession. Further these fundamental rules are to be observed by all states whether or not they have ratified the conventions that contain them, because they constitute intransgressible principles of international customary law.

80 The Nuremberg International Military Tribunal had already found in 1945 that the humanitarian rules included in the Regulations annexed to the Hague Convention IV of 1907 'were recognised by all civilised nations and were regarded as being declaratory of the laws and customs of war' (*International Military Tribunal, Trial of the Major War Criminals, 14 November 1945: 1 October 1946*, Nuremberg, 1947, Vol 1, p 254).

81 The Report of the Secretary General pursuant to para 2 of Security Council Resolution 808 (1993), with which he introduced the Statute of the International Tribunal for the Prosecution of Persons Responsible for Serious Violations of International Humanitarian Law Committed in the Territory of the Former Yugoslavia since 1991, and which was unanimously approved by the Security Council (Resolution 827 (1993)), stated:

In the view of the Secretary General, the application of the principle *nullum crimen sine lege* requires that the international tribunal should apply rules of international humanitarian law which are beyond any doubt part of customary law ...

The part of conventional international humanitarian law which has beyond doubt become part of international customary law is the law applicable in armed conflict as embodied in: the Geneva Conventions of 12 August 1949 for the Protection of War Victims; the Hague Convention (IV) Respecting the Laws and Customs of War on Land and the Regulations annexed thereto of 18 October 1907; the Convention on the Prevention and Punishment of the Crime of Genocide of 9 December 1948; and the Charter of the International Military Tribunal of 8 August 1945.

82   The extensive codification of humanitarian law and the extent of the accession to the resultant treaties, as well as the fact that the denunciation clauses that existed in the codification instruments have never been used, have provided the international community with a corpus of treaty rules the great majority of which had already become customary and which reflected the most universally recognised humanitarian principles. These rules indicate the normal conduct and behaviour expected of states.

83   It has been maintained in these proceedings that these principles and rules of humanitarian law are part of *jus cogens* as defined in Article 53 of the Vienna Convention on the Law of Treaties of 23 May 1969. The question whether a norm is part of the *jus cogens* relates to the legal character of the norm. The request addressed to the Court by the General Assembly raises the question of the applicability of the principles and rules of humanitarian law in cases of recourse to nuclear weapons and the consequences of that applicability for the legality of recourse to these weapons. But it does not raise the question of the character of the humanitarian law which would apply to the use of nuclear weapons. There is, therefore, no need for the Court to pronounce on this matter.

84   Nor is there any need for the Court elaborate on the question of the applicability of Additional Protocol I of 1977 to nuclear weapons. It need only observe that while, at the Diplomatic Conference of 1974–77, there was no substantive debate on the nuclear issue and no specific solution concerning this question was put forward, Additional Protocol I in no way replaced the general customary rules applicable to all means and methods of combat including nuclear weapons. In particular, the Court recalls that all states are bound by those rules in Additional Protocol I which, when adopted, were merely the expression of the pre-existing customary law, such as the Martens Clause, reaffirmed in the first article of Additional Protocol I. The fact that certain types of weapons were not specifically dealt with by the 1974–77 Conference does not permit the drawing of any legal conclusions relating to the substantive issues which the use of such weapons would raise.

85   Turning now to the applicability of the principles and rules of humanitarian law to a possible threat or use of nuclear weapons, the Court notes that doubts in this respect have sometimes been voiced on the ground that these principles and rules had evolved prior to the invention of nuclear weapons and that the Conferences of Geneva of 1949 and 1974–77 which respectively adopted the four Geneva Conventions of 1949 and the two Additional Protocols thereto did not deal with nuclear weapons specifically. Such views, however, are only held by a small minority. In the view of the vast majority of states as well as writers there can be no doubt as to the applicability of humanitarian law to nuclear weapons.

86   The Court shares that view. Indeed, nuclear weapons were invented after most of the principles and rules of humanitarian law applicable in armed conflict had already come into existence; the Conferences of 1949 and 1974–77 left these weapons aside, and there is a qualitative as well as quantitative difference between nuclear weapons and all conventional arms. However, it cannot be concluded from this that the established principles and rules of humanitarian law applicable in armed conflict did not apply to nuclear weapons. Such a conclusion would be incompatible with the intrinsically humanitarian character of the legal principles in question which permeates the entire law of armed conflict and applies to all forms of warfare and to all kinds of weapons, those of the past, those of the present and those of the future. In this respect it seems significant that the thesis that the rules of humanitarian law do not apply to the new weaponry, because of the newness of the latter, has not been advocated in the present proceedings. On the contrary, the newness of nuclear weapons has been expressly rejected as an argument against the application to them of international humanitarian law:

> In general, international humanitarian law bears on the threat or use of nuclear weapons as it does of other weapons.
>
> International humanitarian law has evolved to meet contemporary circumstances, and is not limited in its application to weaponry of an earlier time. The fundamental principles of this law endure: to mitigate and circumscribe the cruelty of war for humanitarian reasons. (New Zealand, Written Statement, p 15, paras 63–64.)

None of the statements made before the Court in any way advocated a freedom to use nuclear weapons without regard to humanitarian constraints. Quite the reverse; it has been explicitly stated,

> Restrictions set by the rules applicable to armed conflicts in respect of means and methods of warfare definitely also extend to nuclear weapons (Russian Federation, CR 95/29, p 52);
>
> So far as the customary law of war is concerned, the United Kingdom has always accepted that the use of nuclear weapons is subject to the general principles of the *jus in bello* (United Kingdom, CR 95/34, p 45); and
>
> The United States has long shared the view that the law of armed conflict governs the use of nuclear weapons – just as it governs the use of conventional weapons (United States of America, CR 95/34, p 85).

87   Finally, the Court points to the Martens Clause, whose continuing existence and applicability is not to be doubted, as an affirmation that the principles and rules of humanitarian law apply to nuclear weapons.

88   The Court will now turn to the principle of neutrality which was raised by several states. In the context of the advisory proceedings brought before the Court by the WHO concerning the Legality of the Use by a State of Nuclear Weapons in Armed Conflict, the position was put as follows by one state:

> The principle of neutrality, in its classic sense, was aimed at preventing the incursion of belligerent forces into neutral territory, or attacks on the persons or ships of neutrals. Thus: 'the territory of neutral powers is inviolable' (Article 1 of the Hague Convention (V) Respecting the Rights and Duties of Neutral Powers and Persons in Case of War on Land, concluded on 18 October 1907); 'belligerents are bound to respect the sovereign rights of neutral powers ...' (Article 1 to the Hague Convention (XIII) Respecting the Rights and Duties of Neutral Powers in Naval War, concluded on 18 October 1907), 'neutral states have equal interest in having their rights respected by

belligerents ...' (Preamble to Convention on Maritime Neutrality, concluded on 20 February 1928). It is clear, however, that the principle of neutrality applies with equal force to transborder incursions of armed forces and to the transborder damage caused to a neutral state by the use of a weapon in a belligerent state (Legality of the Use by a State of Nuclear Weapons in Armed Conflict, Nauru, Written Statement (I), p 35, IV E).

The principle so circumscribed is presented as an established part of the customary international law.

89 The Court finds that as in the case of the principles of humanitarian law applicable in armed conflict, international law leaves no doubt that the principle of neutrality, whatever its content, which is of a fundamental character similar to that of the humanitarian principles and rules, is applicable (subject to the relevant provisions of the United Nations Charter), to all international armed conflict, whatever type of weapons might be used.

90 Although the applicability of the principles and rules of humanitarian law and of the principle of neutrality to nuclear weapons is hardly disputed, the conclusions to be drawn from this applicability are, on the other hand, controversial.

91 According to one point of view, the fact that recourse to nuclear weapons is subject to and regulated by the law of armed conflict does not necessarily mean that such recourse is as such prohibited. As one state put it to the Court:

> Assuming that a state's use of nuclear weapons meets the requirements of self-defence, it must then be considered whether it conforms to the fundamental principles of the law of armed conflict regulating the conduct of hostilities (United Kingdom, Written Statement, p 40, para 3.44);

> the legality of the use of nuclear weapons must therefore be assessed in the light of the applicable principles of international law regarding the use of force and the conduct of hostilities, as is the case with other methods and means of warfare' (United Kingdom, Written Statement, p 75, para 4.2(3)); and

> The reality ... is that nuclear weapons might be used in a wide variety of circumstances with very different results in terms of likely civilian casualties. In some cases, such as the use of a low yield nuclear weapon against warships on the High Seas or troops in sparsely populated areas, it is possible to envisage a nuclear attack which caused comparatively few civilian casualties. It is by no means the case that every use of nuclear weapons against a military objective would inevitably cause very great collateral civilian casualties' (United Kingdom, Written Statement, p 53, para 3.70; see also United States of America, Oral Statement, CR 95/34, pp 89–90).

92 Another view holds that recourse to nuclear weapons could never be compatible with the principles and rules of humanitarian law and is therefore prohibited. In the event of their use, nuclear weapons would in all circumstances be unable to draw any distinction between the civilian population and combatants, or between civilian objects and military objectives, and their effects, largely uncontrollable, could not be restricted, either in time or in space, to lawful military targets. Such weapons would kill and destroy in a necessarily indiscriminate manner, on account of the blast, heat and radiation occasioned by the nuclear explosion and the effects induced; and the number of casualties which would ensue would be enormous. The use of nuclear weapons would therefore be prohibited in any circumstance, notwithstanding the absence of any explicit conventional prohibition. That view lay at the basis of the assertions by

certain states before the Court that nuclear weapons are by their nature illegal under customary international law, by virtue of the fundamental principle of humanity.

93   A similar view has been expressed with respect to the effects of the principle of neutrality. Like the principles and rules of humanitarian law, that principle has therefore been considered by some to rule out the use of a weapon the effects of which simply cannot be contained within the territories of the contending states.

94   The Court would observe that none of the states advocating the legality of the use of nuclear weapons under certain circumstances, including the 'clean' use of smaller, low yield, tactical nuclear weapons, has indicated what, supposing such limited use were feasible, would be the precise circumstances justifying such use; nor whether such limited use would not tend to escalate into the all-out use of high yield nuclear weapons. This being so, the Court does not consider that it has a sufficient basis for a determination on the validity of this view.

95   Nor can the Court make a determination on the validity of the view that the recourse to nuclear weapons would be illegal in any circumstance owing to their inherent and total incompatibility with the law applicable in armed conflict. Certainly, as the Court has already indicated, the principles and rules of law applicable in armed conflict – at the heart of which is the overriding consideration of humanity – make the conduct of armed hostilities subject to a number of strict requirements. Thus, methods and means of warfare, which would preclude any distinction between civilian and military targets, or which would result in unnecessary suffering to combatants, are prohibited. In view of the unique characteristics of nuclear weapons, to which the Court has referred above, the use of such weapons in fact seems scarcely reconcilable with respect for such requirements. Nevertheless, the Court considers that it does not have sufficient elements to enable it to conclude with certainty that the use of nuclear weapons would necessarily be at variance with the principles and rules of law applicable in armed conflict in any circumstance.

96   Furthermore, the Court cannot lose sight of the fundamental right of every state to survival, and thus its right to resort to self-defence, in accordance with Article 51 of the Charter, when its survival is at stake.

Nor can it ignore the practice referred to as 'policy of deterrence', to which an appreciable section of the international community adhered for many years. The Court also notes the reservations which certain nuclear-weapon states have appended to the undertakings they have given, notably under the Protocols to the Treaties of Tlatelolco and Rarotonga, and also under the declarations made by them in connection with the extension of the Treaty on the Non-Proliferation of Nuclear Weapons, not to resort to such weapons.

97   Accordingly, in view of the present state of international law viewed as a whole, as examined above by the Court, and of the elements of fact at its disposal, the Court is led to observe that it cannot reach a definitive conclusion as to the legality or illegality of the use of nuclear weapons by a state in an extreme circumstance of self-defence, in which its very survival would be at stake.

98   Given the eminently difficult issues that arise in applying the law on the use of force and above all the law applicable in armed conflict to nuclear weapons, the Court considers that it now needs to examine one further aspect of the question before it, seen in a broader context.

In the long run, international law, and with it the stability of the international order which it is intended to govern, are bound to suffer from the continuing difference of views with regard to the legal status of weapons as deadly as nuclear weapons. It is consequently important to put an end to this state of affairs: the long-promised complete nuclear disarmament appears to be the most appropriate means of achieving that result.

99 In these circumstances, the Court appreciates the full importance of the recognition by Article VI of the Treaty on the Non-Proliferation of Nuclear Weapons of an obligation to negotiate in good faith a nuclear disarmament. This provision is worded as follows:

> Each of the Parties to the Treaty undertakes to pursue negotiations in good faith on effective measures relating to cessation of the nuclear arms race at an early date and to nuclear disarmament, and on a treaty on general and complete disarmament under strict and effective international control.

The legal import of that obligation goes beyond that of a mere obligation of conduct; the obligation involved here is an obligation to achieve a precise result – nuclear disarmament in all its aspects – by adopting a particular course of conduct, namely, the pursuit of negotiations on the matter in good faith.

100 This twofold obligation to pursue and to conclude negotiations formally concerns the 182 States Parties to the Treaty on the Non-Proliferation of Nuclear Weapons, or, in other words, the vast majority of the international community.

Virtually the whole of this community appears moreover to have been involved when resolutions of the United Nations General Assembly concerning nuclear disarmament have repeatedly been unanimously adopted. Indeed, any realistic search for general and complete disarmament, especially nuclear disarmament, necessitates the co-operation of all states.

101 Even the very first General Assembly resolution, unanimously adopted on 24 January 1946 at the London session, set up a commission whose terms of reference included making specific proposals for, among other things, 'the elimination from national armaments of atomic weapons and of all other major weapons adaptable to mass destruction'. In a large number of subsequent resolutions, the General Assembly has reaffirmed the need for nuclear disarmament. Thus, in Resolution 808 A (IX) of 4 November 1954, which was likewise unanimously adopted, it concluded:

> that a further effort should be made to reach agreement on comprehensive and co-ordinated proposals to be embodied in a draft international disarmament convention providing for: ... (b) the total prohibition of the use and manufacture of nuclear weapons and weapons of mass destruction of every type, together with the conversion of existing stocks of nuclear weapons for peaceful purposes.

The same conviction has been expressed outside the United Nations context in various instruments.

102 The obligation expressed in Article VI of the Treaty on the Non-Proliferation of Nuclear Weapons includes its fulfilment in accordance with the basic principle of good faith. This basic principle is set forth in Article 2, para 2, of the Charter. It was reflected in the Declaration on Friendly Relations between States (Resolution 2625 (XXV) of 24 October 1970) and in the Final Act of the Helsinki Conference of 1 August 1975. It is also embodied in Article 26 of the Vienna Convention on the Law of Treaties of 23 May 1969, according to which '[e]very treaty in force is binding upon the parties to it and must be performed by them in good faith'.

Nor has the Court omitted to draw attention to it, as follows:

One of the basic principles governing the creation and performance of legal obligations, whatever their source, is the principle of good faith. Trust and confidence are inherent in international co-operation, in particular in an age when this co-operation in many fields is becoming increasingly essential (*Nuclear Tests (Australia v France)*, Judgment of 20 December 1974; [1974] *ICJ Rep* at p 268, para 46).

103 In its Resolution 984 (1995) dated 11 April 1995, the Security Council took care to reaffirm 'the need for all States Parties to the Treaty on the Non-Proliferation of Nuclear Weapons to comply fully with all their obligations' and urged:

> ... all states, as provided for in Article VI of the Treaty on the Non-Proliferation of Nuclear Weapons, to pursue negotiations in good faith on effective measures relating to nuclear disarmament and on a treaty on general and complete disarmament under strict and effective international control which remains a universal goal.

The importance of fulfilling the obligation expressed in Article VI of the Treaty on the Non-Proliferation of Nuclear Weapons was also reaffirmed in the final document of the Review and Extension Conference of the parties to the Treaty on the Non-Proliferation of Nuclear Weapons, held from 17 April to 12 May 1995.

In the view of the Court, it remains without any doubt an objective of vital importance to the whole of the international community today.

104 At the end of the present Opinion, the Court emphasises that its reply to the question put to it by the General Assembly rests on the totality of the legal grounds set forth by the Court above (paras 20 to 103), each of which is to be read in the light of the others. Some of these grounds are not such as to form the object of formal conclusions in the final paragraph of the Opinion; they nevertheless retain, in the view of the Court, all their importance.

105 For these reasons,

THE COURT,

(1) By 13 votes to one,

Decides to comply with the request for an advisory opinion;

IN FAVOUR: President Bedjaoui; Vice-President Schwebel; Judges Guillaume, Shahabuddeen, Weeramantry, Ranjeva, Herczegh, Shi, Fleischhauer, Koroma, Vereshchetin, Ferrari Bravo, Higgins;

AGAINST: Judge Oda.

(2) Replies in the following manner to the question put by the General Assembly:

A   Unanimously,

There is in neither customary nor conventional international law any specific authorisation of the threat or use of nuclear weapons;

B   By 11 votes to three,

There is in neither customary nor conventional international law any comprehensive and universal prohibition of the threat or use of nuclear weapons as such;

IN FAVOUR: President Bedjaoui; Vice-President Schwebel; Judges Oda, Guillaume, Ranjeva, Herczegh, Shi, Fleischhauer, Vereshchetin, Ferrari Bravo, Higgins;

AGAINST: Judges Shahabuddeen, Weeramantry, Koroma.

C   Unanimously,

A threat or use of force by means of nuclear weapons that is contrary to Article 2, para 4, of the United Nations Charter and that fails to meet all the requirements of Article 51, is unlawful;

D   Unanimously,

A threat or use of nuclear weapons should also be compatible with the requirements of the international law applicable in armed conflict, particularly those of the principles and rules of international humanitarian law, as well as with specific obligations under treaties and other undertakings which expressly deal with nuclear weapons;

E   By seven votes to seven, by the President's casting vote,

It follows from the above-mentioned requirements that the threat or use of nuclear weapons would generally be contrary to the rules of international law applicable in armed conflict, and in particular the principles and rules of humanitarian law;

However, in view of the current state of international law, and of the elements of fact at its disposal, the Court cannot conclude definitively whether the threat or use of nuclear weapons would be lawful or unlawful in an extreme circumstance of self-defence, in which the very survival of a state would be at stake;

IN FAVOUR: President Bedjaoui; Judges Ranjeva, Herczegh, Shi, Fleischhauer, Vereschetin, Ferrari Bravo;

AGAINST: Vice-President Schwebel; Judges Oda, Guillaume, Shahabuddeen, Weeramantry, Koroma, Higgins.

F   Unanimously,

There exists an obligation to pursue in good faith and bring to a conclusion negotiations leading to nuclear disarmament in all its aspects under strict and effective international control.

A specific aspect of nuclear weapons that has been considered is the use of radiological weapons. Such weapons are designed to utilise the radio-active fallout which follows a nuclear explosion. Radiological weapons fall into two categories: those which use separate radio-active agents which act independently of the nuclear explosion itself, and so-called dirty nuclear weapons which are designed to maximise the amount of fallout from the nuclear explosion. The use and possession of such weapons has for some time been considered by the UN Conference on Disarmament.

15.5.1.3   Biological and chemical weapons

Biological and chemical weapons can be distinguished from other weapons in that they exercise their effect solely on living matter and are aimed at large groups rather than individual soldiers. The use of poisoned weapons is not new. Historically much use has been made during sieges of the tactic of poisoning water supplies and in medieval times plague victims proved effective weapons when thrown over city walls.

The first treaty reference to such weapons appeared in Article 23 of the Hague Regulations Respecting the Laws and Custom of War on Land which prohibits the use of poison or poisoned weapons. The Regulations are generally regarded as constituting customary international law but it remains unclear whether the prohibition on the use of poison covers the use of gas. Gas was used in both World Wars, in Vietnam and in the Iran-Iraq war. The peace treaties concluded after World War One all prohibited the possession by Germany of all 'asphyxiating, poisonous and other gases and analogous liquids, material and devices' but it was unclear whether this prohibition applied to all states. The Geneva Protocol for the Prohibition of the Use in War of Asphyxiating, Poisonous or Other Gases, and of Bacteriological Methods of Warfare 1925 (the Geneva Gas Protocol) expressly recognised that the prohibition of asphyxiating, poisonous and other gases and analogous liquids, materials and devices was part of international law and extended the prohibition to the use in war of bacteriological weapons. However, problems have remained over the interpretation of the Protocol's provisions. In particular there has been dispute over whether the prohibition covers only lethal weapons or extends to such things as tear gas and other non-lethal materials such as herbicides. The problem is partly caused by the fact that the French text, which is equally authentic to the English text of the Protocol, refers to 'similaires' rather than 'other' gases and analogous liquids, etc.

In 1986 a UN Security Council resolution condemned the use by Iraq of chemical weapons which was stated to be in clear violation of the Geneva Gas Protocol. The prevailing view today seems to be that the provisions of the Protocol have become customary international law and that consequently the first use of lethal chemical and biological weapons is prohibited. There is less agreement on the use of non-lethal chemical and biological weapons.

There now exist a Biological Weapons Convention 1972 and a Chemical Weapons Convention 1992, both of which prohibit the production and stockpiling of specific weapons, although they do not deal with the use in armed conflict of such weapons.

15.5.1.4 Environmental weapons

The widespread use of defoliants by the USA during the Vietnam War and growing concern about the environment generally led to calls for regulation of weapons which have a particular effect on the environment. During the Vietnam War there were press reports that the USA was attempting to artificially produce rain in the war zone to flood North Vietnamese supply routes. This provoked international discussions aimed at prohibiting the use of environmental modification techniques as weapons of war. The result of the discussions was the UN Convention on the Prohibition of Military Use of Environmental Modification Techniques 1977. This Convention prohibits the hostile use of any technique for changing 'the dynamics, composition or structure of the Earth, including its biota, lithosphere, hydrosphere and atmosphere, or of outer space'. It is arguable that the Convention would cover the use of nuclear weapons.

In addition to the 1977 Convention, Article 55 of the Geneva Protocol I Additional to the Geneva Conventions of 1949 and Relating to the Protection of Victims of International Armed Conflicts 1977 places an obligation on states in warfare to minimise widespread, long-term and severe damage to the natural environment and prohibits the use of weapons and methods of warfare which 'may be expected to cause' such damage and thereby to prejudice the health and survival of the population. It has been suggested that the deliberate spillage by Iraq of quantities of oil into the Persian Gulf during the 1991 Gulf Conflict contravened these provisions.

15.5.2 Restrictions on methods of warfare

A basic distinction in the law of armed conflict must be drawn between combatants and civilians. Combatants are those under command, having fixed visible and distinctive emblems, carrying arms openly, and observing the laws of war. The basis of the law of armed conflict is that it is the combatants who fight the war, and if they are captured they are entitled to Prisoner of War (POW) status. The civilian, in turn, should be protected from attack. The distinction between combatant and civilian is crucial to the question of legitimate targets: combatant or military targets are legitimate, civilian targets are not. The rule is one of customary international law binding on all states. The problem is then one of establishing what is a military target and what is a civilian target. Clearly some objects can be defined without problem, for example, a tank is a military target, a nursery school is not. However, not all targets can be so clearly distinguished.

An attempt was made at a distinction in the Hague Draft Rules of Aerial Warfare 1923 which were never fully adopted but which are now considered declaratory of customary international law. The Draft Rules prescribed that attacks from the air would only be permitted if directed against a military objective, the total or partial destruction of which presented a 'distinct military advantage to the attacker'. Article 24 contained a list of targets which were to be classed as military targets:

> ... military forces, military works, military establishments or depots, factories constituting important and well-known centres engaged in the manufacture of arms, ammunition or distinctively military supplies, lines of communication or transportation used for military purposes.

The Rules provided that compensation was payable for any breach of the prohibition. As can be seen, the list leaves considerable scope for interpretation and raises problems where targets are used for both military and civilian purposes, for example, railways or roads. The problem was further compounded by the fact that the rules were produced in three languages, French, German and English, all of which were equally authentic and valid and none of which said completely the same thing. The German text, for example, makes more clear reference to radio stations and other news media, not expressly included in the English text 'lines of communication'.

Some writers in the 1930s suggested that a subjective approach should be adopted based on the dominant purpose. Further development of the definition occurred during and immediately after the Second World War. It became more clear that bombing exclusively directed at civilian population is prohibited. Both the UK and the US governments condemned such bombing in December 1939 in the context of German tactics during the Spanish Civil War and at the beginning of World War Two and the Charter of the Nuremberg Tribunal 1946 included such indiscriminate bombing in its definition of war crimes. It has to be noted, however, that UK and US practice, particularly in respect of the 'carpet' bombing of Dresden, did not accord with the statements made in 1939. The prohibition on attacks on civilian targets has been re-iterated in a series of UN Resolutions and the most recent example comes from the Iran-Iraq war when Iraqi bombing of civilian areas in Iran drew widespread condemnation and led to an agreement between the two sides to cease military attacks on purely civilian targets.

The present law can be found in the Geneva Protocol I 1977 which is widely considered to represent a codification of customary international law. The Protocol defines military targets as those objects which by their nature, location, purpose or use make effective contribution to military action as well as those whose total or partial destruction, capture or neutralisation in the circumstances at the time, offers a definite military advantage. Article 52 of the Protocol then goes on to outlaw attacks on civilian objects and Article 57 imposes a duty on those planning or deciding upon an attack to take all feasible precautions to verify that the objectives to be attacked are military objectives and to refrain from attack which might cause incidental loss of civilian life which would be excessive in relation to the military advantage gained (the proportionality principle). Part II of the Protocol contains provisions relating to the protection of the sick, wounded and shipwrecked and Article 12 specifically states that medical units shall not be the object of attack. Medical units includes any establishment, military or civilian, which is organised for the search for, collection, transportation, diagnosis or treatment of the wounded, sick or shipwrecked. Such units should be clearly identified by the red cross (lion, star or crescent) emblem. Linked to the protection given to medical units is the obligation on states not to site them close to legitimate military targets. During the Gulf Conflict 1991 there were allegations that Iraq had deliberately sited anti-aircraft batteries close to hospitals in Baghdad. Such deliberate siting and the misuse of the red cross emblem will result in the protection given under the Protocol being withdrawn and constitutes a breach of treaty obligations. Part IV of the Protocol deals with the civilian population and states clearly that civil defence installations, such as air raid shelters, shall be protected. However, Article 65 states that the protection shall cease if they are used to commit acts harmful to the enemy. The chapter goes on to provide that shelters should be identifiable. The internationally recognised symbol for such installations is a blue triangle on an orange background.

The question of legitimate targets was much discussed during the Gulf Conflict specifically in the context of Coalition attacks on bridges that were used for both civilian and military transport and one particular attack on a building that Iraq claimed was an air-raid shelter but which the Coalition forces argued was being used as a military communications headquarters. The discussions confirmed the existence of binding rules regarding legitimate and non-legitimate targets but showed the immense difficulties encountered in clearly distinguishing between the two in practice. A term which was much used during the war and which has continued to have a high currency is collateral damage. This was used to refer to damage caused to non-legitimate targets during the carrying out of attacks on military targets. Clearly there is a limit to the amount of collateral damage that can be caused before it becomes wholly disproportionate to the military advantage gained.

In addition to the question of targets of attack, there are four methods of warfare which are specifically prohibited under international law:

- *No quarter*: this refers to methods of warfare which admit of no limit. An order to leave no survivors and take no prisoners would amount to no quarter and it has long been prohibited by international law. The Geneva Protocol I specifically forbids such orders given in relation to enemy combatants (Article 40);

- *Starvation*: deliberately subjecting the civilian population to starvation as a means of defeating the enemy. Article 54 of the Geneva Protocol I expressly prohibits the use of starvation as a method of warfare and also prohibits attacks on foodstuffs and other objects and areas indispensable to the survival of the population, for example, drinking water installations. Articles 69 to 71 further provide protection to those engaged in humanitarian relief operations;

- *Belligerent reprisals*: acts of victimisation or vengeance directed against civilians, POWs or others *hors de combat* in response to attacks by non-combatants are prohibited by international law.

- *Perfidy*: international law draws a distinction, which is not always easy to make in practice, between a general level of deception which is an integral part of warfare and the deliberate use of certain specific acts of treachery and 'impermissible ruses' such as the improper use of the white flag of surrender, the use of false flags, and such things as disguising missile sites as hospitals.

15.5.3 Humanitarian rules

Humanitarian law in the widest sense concerns the protection of individuals in war or armed conflict. What are discussed here are humanitarian rules in a narrower sense, that is to say, those rules which specifically protect the human person, rather than the general rules concerning means and methods of waging warfare. The majority of these humanitarian rules apply to both international and non-international armed conflicts.

15.5.3.1 Treatment of civilians

Civilians are non-combatants and combatants who are *hors de combat*. Most of the protection afforded to civilians is based on the system laid down in the Geneva Convention IV 1949 as supplemented by Geneva Protocols I and II of 1977. The Protocols actually state that anyone who is not a combatant is presumed to be a civilian. Article 75 Protocol I includes a catalogue of forbidden practices to which civilians and persons *hors de combat* must not be subjected:

(a) violence to life, health of physical or mental well-being of persons, in particular:
  (i) murder;
  (ii) torture of all kinds, whether physical or mental;
  (iii) corporal punishment;
  (iv) mutilation;

(b) outrages upon personal dignity, in particular humiliating and degrading treatment, enforced prostitution and any form of indecent assault;

    (c)   taking of hostages;

    (d)   collective punishments;

    (e)   threats to commit any of the above.

Civilians must not be subjected to any action which causes their physical suffering or their intimidation. Hostages must not be taken and civilians must not be used to protect military targets. These provisions were breached by Iraq during the Gulf Conflict. If civilians are interned they must be given adequate clothes, light and heat and must not be subjected to forced mass transfers. There have been many allegations of breaches of these rules during the conflict in former Yugoslavia.

15.5.3.2 Specially protected groups

Certain categories of persons are afforded specific protection by international law:

Wounded, sick and shipwrecked: the protections given to the wounded, sick and shipwrecked apply to both civilians and combatants. They must all be treated humanely and not subjected to murder, torture, or any biological experiments. There is an obligation on captors to search for and collect enemy wounded, sick and shipwrecked and to give them adequate care.

Women: special protection is given to women under Geneva Convention IV which prescribes that they must not be subjected to attacks on their honour, enforced prostitution, rape or any form of indecent assault. Further protection is given to pregnant women and those with new-born babies.

Children under 15: Geneva Convention IV imposes an obligation on belligerents to ensure the safety of those under 15 who have been orphaned or separated from their parents as a result of war.

Journalists: war correspondents receive some protection under Geneva Convention III in that they are to be accorded POW status if captured. They are given further protection under Geneva Protocol I Article 79.

Civil defence, medical and religious personnel: individuals falling within these categories are given extra protection under the Geneva Conventions and Protocols in that they must be allowed to carry on their work and medical personnel must not be made POWs.

Prisoners of war (POWs): there was early agreement on rudimentary protection of POWs in the Geneva Convention 1864. The essence of the obligations as far as POWs are concerned is that detaining them is not a sanction or punishment but is purely a precautionary measure. There is an overriding duty to treat POWs humanely. Those who can be accorded POW status are listed in Article 4 of the Geneva Convention III and Protocol I but there is still some doubt as to the ambit of protection. There is dispute about the status of those who commit war crimes prior to capture, and the exact status of guerrilla forces is unclear.

As has already been mentioned, POWs must be treated humanely. More specifically, POWs cannot be subjected to summary execution, medical experiments, torture, or interrogation. Article 17 of the Geneva Convention III provides that POWs are only required to give their name, rank and number. POWs are to be given adequate food, clothing and health care and adequate hygiene standards must be observed. Escapees may be disciplined within the limits imposed by Article 89. Non-officers may be compelled to undertake work of a type authorised by the Convention. POWs are allowed to receive and send up to two letters and four postcards per month. At the end of hostilities all POWs must be repatriated and those who are seriously wounded should be repatriated during hostilities.

15.6 Responsibility and enforcement

Violations of the laws of armed conflict involve state responsibility (discussed in Chapter 9) and the duty to make reparation. Yet as the International Military Tribunal at Nuremberg stated:

> Crimes against international law are committed by men, not abstract entities, and only by punishing individuals who commit such crimes can the provisions of international law be enforced.

The problem for international law has therefore been to identify the individuals responsible for breaches of the laws of armed conflict and to ensure that they are effectively punished. The issue of enforcement has often shown up weaknesses in international law. Partly this has been because of the procedural difficulties encountered in bringing to trial those responsible for breaches but more particularly it is because the enforcement of the law has usually been seen as little more than the application of the principle of *vae victis*: it only ever appears to be members of the defeated side who bear responsibility for breaches of the law. The legitimacy of war criminal trials is always adversely effected by the fact that the tribunal itself is seen as having a major interest in the result since generally it is made up of representatives of the victorious states. The alternative is for trials to take place within the municipal courts of the defendant's state. The drawback with this option is that the defendant's state often has little interest in pursuing the trial with any real conviction.

One aspect of individual responsibility that was established at Nuremberg that should be noted is that the fact that an individual was acting pursuant to the orders of his or her government or of a superior does not automatically absolve him or her from responsibility. It may only be considered in mitigation of punishment. This seemed to confirm a view that had been held for some time that 'superior orders' does not constitute a defence to breaches of the laws of armed conflict. The one exception to this is where it can be shown that the subordinate individual could not reasonably have been expected to be aware of the illegality of the superior orders given. Of course, in such a situation, the individual giving the order will bear responsibility for the action carried out.

Following the end of the First World War the Allied Commission upon the Responsibility of the Authors of the War and on the Enforcement of Penalties prepared a list of 896 alleged war criminals, including the German Kaiser Wilhelm II, and the intention was to try the leading members before an international tribunal. However, difficulties in actually bringing any of the principal defendants to trial and criticism that the whole process was motivated by a spirit of vindictiveness led to the proposal's failure. In 1920 an Advisory Commission of Jurists investigated the possibilities of establishing an international criminal court with powers to try crimes constituting a breach of international public order or against the universal law of nations. The League of Nations rejected the proposal on the grounds that there was not sufficient agreement among nations on the content of an international penal code.

The events of World War Two led to repeated demands for the trial of those responsible for war crimes and crimes against peace. By 1943 there were discussions among the Allies as to what to do with the leaders of the Axis powers at the end of the war. The American Secretary of State proposed that they should be hanged after a summary trial or court martial. But Churchill, Roosevelt and Eden favoured an international trial. Subsequent discussion led to the London Conference in August 1945 at which basic agreement was reached on a trial of German leaders by an international military tribunal. There remained considerable differences of opinion, not least because of different conceptions of criminal justice between those used to an Anglo-American system and those used to the Continental system. The Charter of the International Military Tribunal 1945 that was agreed by the USA, UK, USSR and France therefore represents a considerable compromise. The Charter established the International Military Tribunal although it was not a truly international tribunal since the four allies were acting in the capacity of occupying powers in place of the dissolved Nazi regime in Germany. There have therefore been arguments that the Tribunal operated in some way as a municipal court under the authority of the national government of occupation. This would deal with the difficulty posed by the fact that, certainly at the time, individuals could not be considered the subjects of international law and could therefore not come within the jurisdiction of true international tribunals. Article 6 of the Charter gave the Tribunal jurisdiction over three types of offence:

- *Crimes against peace*: planning, preparation, initiation, or waging a war of aggression, or a war in violation of international treaties, or conspiracy to commit the foregoing;

- *War crimes*: violations of the laws or customs of war including murder, ill-treatment of civilian population, plunder of public or private property, wanton destruction of cities, towns or villages, or devastation not justified by military necessity;

- *Crimes against humanity*: namely murder, extermination, enslavement, deportation or other inhumane acts committed against any civilian population before or during a war and genocide whether or not in violation of the domestic law of the country where perpetrated.

The Tribunal began its proceedings in November 1945. A similar charter was agreed with respect to Japanese War Criminals and an International Military Tribunal for the Far East sat in Tokyo. The judgment of the Nuremberg Tribunal in 1946 and of the Tokyo Tribunal in 1948 affirmed the principle of direct individual responsibility in international law.

The ILC subsequently drew up a Draft Code of Principles Recognised in the Tribunal's judgment which was the start of attempts to establish an international criminal law. The code reiterated the principle of individual responsibility which is repeated in the Genocide Convention.

The definition of war crimes has implications for the individual jurisdiction of states and may involve application of the universality principle (discussed at

7.7). A number of serious violations of the laws of armed conflict were identified in the Charter of the International Military Tribunal as constituting war crimes but the list contained in Article 6 was not intended to be exhaustive. The Geneva Conventions 1949 referred to certain 'grave breaches' of the provisions of the conventions which would constitute war crimes and imposed a duty on states 'to provide effective penal sanctions for persons committing or ordering to be committed, any grave breaches of the Convention'. Every state party to the conventions was further obliged to search for offenders and to bring them, irrespective of their nationality, to trial before its municipal courts or to hand them over for trial in the courts of another contracting party. The definition of grave breaches is further extended in Protocol I which repeats the obligation on states to bring offenders to trial but in addition places an obligation on states to take 'all measures necessary' for the suppression of all acts contrary to the conventions and protocols other than grave breaches. Protocol I also provides for the establishment of an International Fact-Finding Commission to investigate grave breaches of the Conventions or the Protocol.

CONVENTION ON THE PREVENTION AND PUNISHMENT OF THE CRIME OF GENOCIDE 1948

[Signed on 11 December 1948 – entered into force 12 January 1951]

The Contracting Parties,

Having considered the declaration made by the General Assembly of the United Nations in its Resolution 96 (I) dated 11 December 1946 that genocide is a crime under international law, contrary to the spirit and aims of the United Nations and condemned by the civilised world,

Recognising that at all periods of history genocide has inflicted great losses on humanity, and

Being convinced that, in order to liberate mankind form such an odious scourge, international co-operation is required,

Hereby agreed as hereinafter provided:

Article I

The Contracting Parties confirm that genocide, whether committed in time of peace or in time of war, is a crime under international law which they undertake to prevent and to punish.

Article II

In the present Convention, genocide means any of the following acts committed with intent to destroy, in whole or part, a national, ethnical, racial or religious group, as such:

- (a) killing members of the group;
- (b) causing serious bodily or mental harm to members of the groups;
- (c) deliberately inflicting on the group conditions of life calculated to bring about its physical destruction in whole or in part;

  (d) imposing measures intended to prevent births within the group;

  (e) forcibly transferring children of the group to another group.

Article III

The following acts shall be punishable:

  (a) genocide;

  (b) conspiracy to commit genocide;

  (c) direct and public incitement to commit genocide;

  (d) attempt to commit genocide;

  (e) complicity in genocide.

Article IV

Persons committing genocide or any of the other acts enumerated in Article III shall be punished, whether they are constitutionally responsible rulers, public officials or private individuals.

Article V

The Contracting Parties undertake to enact, in accordance with their respective Constitutions, the necessary legislation to give effect to the provisions of the present Convention and, in particular, to provide effective penalties for persons guilty of genocide or of any of the other acts enumerated in Article III.

Article VI

Persons charged with genocide or any of the other acts enumerated in Article III shall be tried by a competent tribunal of the state in the territory of which the act was committed, or by such international penal tribunal as may have jurisdiction with respect to those Contracting Parties which shall have accepted its jurisdiction.

Article VII

Genocide and the other acts enumerated in Article III shall not be considered as political crimes for the purposes of extradition.

The Contracting Parties pledge themselves in such cases to grant extradition in accordance with their laws and treaties in force.

Article VIII

Any Contracting Party may call upon the competent organs of the United Nations to take such action under the Charter of the United Nations as they consider appropriate for the prevention and suppression of acts of genocide or any of the other acts enumerated in Article III.

Article IX

Disputes between the Contracting Parties relating to the interpretation, application or fulfilment of the present Convention, including those relating to the responsibility of a state for genocide or for any of the other acts enumerated in Article III, shall be submitted to the International Court of Justice at the request of any of the parties to the dispute.

Article X

The present Convention, of which the Chinese, English, French, Russian and Spanish texts are equally authentic, shall bear the date of 9 December 1948.

Article XI

The present Convention shall be open until 31 December 1949 for signature on behalf of any Member of the United Nations and of any non-member state to which an invitation to sign has been addressed by the General Assembly.

The present Convention shall be ratified, and the instruments of ratification shall be deposited with the Secretary General of the United Nations.

After 1 January 1950 the present Convention may be acceded to on behalf of any Member of the United Nations and of any non-member state which has received an invitation as aforesaid.

Instruments of accession shall be deposited with the Secretary General of the United Nations.

Article XII

Any Contracting Party may at any time, by notification addressed to the Secretary General of the United Nations, extend the application of the present Convention to all or any of the territories for the conduct of whose foreign relations that Contracting Party is responsible.

Article XIII

On the day when the first twenty instruments of ratification or accession have been deposited, the Secretary General shall draw up a *proces-verbal* and transmit a copy thereof to each member of the United Nations and to each of the non-member states contemplated in Article XI.

The present Convention shall come into force on the ninetieth day following the date of deposit of the twentieth instrument of ratification or accession.

Any ratification or accession effected subsequent to the latter date shall become effective on the ninetieth day following the deposit of the instrument of ratification or accession.

Article XIV

The present Convention shall remain in effect for a period of ten years as from the date of its coming into force.

It shall thereafter remain in force for successive periods of five years for such Contracting Parties as have not denounced it at least six months before the expiry of the current period.

Denunciation shall be effected by a written notification addressed to the Secretary General of the United Nations.

Article XV

If, as a result of denunciations, the number of Parties to the present Convention should become less than 16, the Convention shall cease to be in force as from the date on which the last of these denunciations shall become effective.

Article XVI

A request for the revision of the present Convention may be made at any time by any Contracting Party by means of a notification in writing addressed to the Secretary General.

The General Assembly shall decided upon the steps, if any, to be taken in respect of such a request.

Article XVII

The Secretary General of the United Nations shall notify all Members of the United Nations and the non-member states contemplated in Article XI of the following:

(a) signatures, ratifications and accessions received in accordance with Article XI;

(b) notifications received in accordance with Article XII;

(c)   the date upon which the present Convention comes into force in accordance with Article XIII;

(d)   denunciations received in accordance with Article XIV;

(e)   the abrogation of the Convention in accordance with Article XV;

(f)   notifications received in accordance with Article XVI.

Article XVIII

The original of the present Convention shall be deposited in the archives of the United Nations.

A certified copy of the Convention shall be transmitted to each Member of the United Nations and to each of the non-member states contemplated in Article XI.

Article XIX

The present Convention shall be registered by the Secretary General of the United Nations on the date of its coming into force.

CHAPTER 16

HUMAN RIGHTS

16.1 Introduction

As was stated in Chapter 1, the present system of international law has developed from the law of nations that governed the relations between sovereign states. Prior to World War One it was a clear principle of international law that a state's treatment of its own nationals was a matter exclusively within its domestic jurisdiction. The only exception to this was the concept of humanitarian intervention to prevent large scale atrocities but as was shown in Chapter 13, the concept is one of dubious legality. As has already been noted in Chapter 9, the mistreatment of aliens can give rise to state responsibility.

Following World War One, and with the establishment of the League of Nations, widespread concern was expressed about the protection of 'minorities'. However, the emphasis was very much on protection rather than enforceable rights.

Covenant of the League of Nations

Article 22

1 To those colonies and territories which as a consequence of the late war have ceased to be under the sovereignty of the states which formerly governed them and which are inhabited by peoples not yet able to stand by themselves under the strenuous conditions of the modern world, there should be applied the principle that the well-being and development of such peoples form a sacred trust of civilisation and that securities for the performance of this trust should be embodied in the Covenant.

2 The best method of giving practical effect to this principle is that the tutelege of such peoples should be entrusted to advanced nations who by reason of their resources, their experience or their geographical position can best undertake this responsibility, and who are willing to accept it, and that this tutelage should be exercised by them as Mandatories on behalf of the League.

3 The character of the mandate must differ according to the stage of development of the people, the geographical situation of the territory, its economic conditions and other similar circumstances.

4 Certain communities formerly belonging to the Turkish Empire have reached a stage of development where their existence as independent nations can be provisionally recognised subject to the rendering of administrative advice and assistance by a Mandatory until such time as they are able to stand alone. The wishes of these communities must be a principal consideration in the selection of the Mandatory.

5 Other peoples, especially those of Central Africa, are at such a stage that the Mandatory must be responsible for the administration of the territory under conditions which will guarantee freedom of conscience and religion, subject only to the maintenance of public order and morals, the prohibition of abuses such as the slave trade, the arms traffic and the liquor traffic, and the prevention of fortifications or military and naval bases and of military training of the natives

for other than police purposes and the defence of territory, and will also secure equal opportunities for the trade and commerce of other Members of the League.

6   There are territories, such as South-West Africa and certain of the South Pacific Islands which, owing to the sparseness of their population, or their small size, or their remoteness from the centres of civilisation, or their geographical contiguity to the territory of the Mandatory, and other circumstances, can be best administered under the laws of the Mandatory as integral portions of its territory, subject to the safeguard above mentioned in the interests of the indigenous population.

7   In every case of mandate, the Mandatory shall render to the Council an annual report in reference to the territory committed to its charge.

8   The degree of authority, control, or administration to be exercised by the Mandatory shall, if not previously agreed upon by the Members of the League, be explicitly defined in each case by the Council.

9   A permanent Commission shall be constituted to receive and examine the annual reports of the Mandatories and to advise the Council on all matters relating to the observance of the mandates.

Article 23

Subject to and in accordance with the provisions of international conventions existing or hereafter to be agreed upon, the Members of the League:

(a)   will endeavour to secure and maintain fair and humane conditions of labour for men, women, and children, both in their own countries and in all countries to which their commercial and industrial relations extend, and for that purpose will establish and maintain the necessary international organisations;

(b)   undertake to secure just treatment of the native populations of territories under their control;

(c)   will entrust the League with the general supervision over the execution of agreements with regard to the traffic in women and children, and the traffic in opium and other dangerous drugs;

(d)   will entrust the League with the general supervision of the trade in arms and ammunition with the countries in which the control of this traffic is necessary in the common interest;

(e)   will make provision to secure and maintain freedom of communications and of transit and equitable treatment for the commerce of all Members of the League. In this connection the special necessities of the regions devastated during the war of 1914-18 shall be borne in mind;

(f)   will endeavour to take steps in matters of international concern for the prevention and control of disease.

In addition to the provisions of the Covenant the League of Nations also established a system protecting specific minorities in the new Eastern European and Baltic states which emerged following the break-up of the Austro-Hungarian Empire.[1] The League of Nations Council was given the task of monitoring the rights of minorities and there was also a right of petition procedure by minorities to the League of Nations. However such protections

---

1   Among the specific treaties was one dealing with the Serbo-Croat-Slovene State.

only applied to the minorities expressly mentioned and there was no attempt at the creation of any binding obligations of general application.

The atrocities committed before and during World War Two exposed the need for some comprehensive system of protection of fundamental human rights and this was recognised in the Preamble to the Charter of the United Nations which states:

> We the Peoples of the United Nations determined to save succeeding generations from the scourge of war ... and to reaffirm faith in fundamental human rights, in the dignity and worth of the human person, in the equal rights of men and women and of nations large and small ... have resolved to combine out efforts to accomplish these aims.

Article 1(3) of the Charter pledged member states to achieve international co-operation in promoting and encouraging respect for 'human rights and for fundamental freedoms for all without distinction as to race, sex, language, or religion'. The obligation to promote respect for and observance of human rights and fundamental freedoms is made express in Articles 55 and 56 of the Charter:

Article 55

With a view to the creation of conditions of stability and well-being which are necessary for peaceful and friendly relations among nations based on respect for the principle of equal rights and self-determination of peoples, the United Nations shall promote:

(a) higher standards of living, full employment, and conditions of economic and social progress and development;

(b) solutions of international economic, social, health, and related problems; and international cultural and educational co-operation; and

(c) universal respect for, and observance of, human rights and fundamental freedoms for all without distinction as to race, sex, language, or religion.

Article 56

All members pledge themselves to take joint and separate action in co-operation with the Organisation for the achievement of the purposes set forth in Article 55.

Since 1945 a considerable number of rules of international law, both customary and treaty, have been developed with the aim of protecting human rights and fundamental freedoms. Of course the effectiveness of such rules is open to doubt. The mere existence of rules does not ensure observance of them and over the years it has proved far easier to identify particular rights than to provide effective enforcement mechanisms. More has been achieved on a regional basis rather than at a global level and many human rights experts look to developments regionally as the way forward rather than hoping for great things on the global plane. It is worth noting, however, that the mere existence of human rights agreements can have a beneficial role by giving publicity to abuses and by raising expectations and standards of behaviour and treatment. The role of publicity in the sphere of human rights enforcement should not be underestimated

One final introductory point can be made. Human rights are extremely difficult to define. Generally speaking, they are regarded as those fundamental and inalienable rights which are essential for life as a human being. Put another way, they are those rights which inherent in that they exist by virtue of the human condition. However, the view of what specific rights exist and more importantly the interpretation of the extent of such rights may well differ according to the particular economic, social and cultural society in which they are being defined. Thus, while it may be comparatively easy to obtain global agreement that human rights are 'a good thing' the task of reaching consensus on the articulation of particular rights has proved, and is still proving, far more difficult.

16.2 The sources of the law

International human rights law is a combination of customary international law and treaty law. The treaties may be global or regional and general or specialised.

16.2.1 General international agreements

At the inaugural conference of the United Nations held in San Francisco in April 1946 the representatives of Cuba, Mexico and Panama had proposed that the conference should adopt a Declaration on the Essential Rights of Man. However, there was insufficient time available to discuss the proposal, and so, at the first session of the UN General Assembly, Panama submitted a Draft Declaration on Fundamental Human Rights and Freedoms. On 11 December 1946 the General Assembly decided to refer the draft to the Economic and Social Council (ECOSOC) for detailed consideration by its Commission on Human Rights. The Commission had been established by ECOSOC under Article 68 of the UN Charter and it spent two years working on a draft International Bill of Rights with the instructions that the bill should be acceptable to all, short, simple and easy to understand. The draft bill was presented to the Third session of the UN General Assembly, and on 10 December 1948 Resolution 217A was adopted: the Universal Declaration of Human Rights (UDHR). There was no opposition to the resolution although eight States did abstain, primarily because of the effect that such obligations could have on State sovereignty. The Declaration contains a list of economic, social, cultural and political rights. Since it was only a resolution of the General Assembly, it could not create binding legal obligations, nor was it intended to do so. Rather the UDHR serves to provide a standard for States to aim at. The precise effect of the resolution was to urge States to establish procedures for the future protection of human rights. The Declaration has, however, provided the impetus for the development of customary law (which is discussed at 16.2.4, below). Commitment to the provisions of UDHR and other instruments relating to human rights was recently reaffirmed in Vienna Declaration and Programme of Action 1993, made by States at the UN World Conference on Human Rights held in Vienna in June 1993.

UNIVERSAL DECLARATION OF HUMAN RIGHTS[2]

PREAMBLE

Whereas recognition of the inherent dignity and of the equal and inalienable rights of all members of the human family is the foundation of freedom, justice and peace in the world,

Whereas disregard and contempt for human rights have resulted in barbarous acts which have outraged the conscience of mankind, and the advent of a world in which human beings shall enjoy freedom of speech and belief and freedom from fear and want has been proclaimed as the highest aspiration of the common people,

Whereas it is essential, if man is not to be compelled to have recourse, as a last resort, to rebellion against tyranny and oppression, that human rights should be protected by the rule of law,

Whereas it is essential to promote the development of friendly relations between nations,

Whereas the peoples of the United Nations have in the Charter reaffirmed their faith in fundamental human rights, in the dignity and worth of the human person and in the equal rights of men and women and have determined to promote social progress and better standards of life in larger freedom,

Whereas Member States have pledged themselves to achieve, in co-operation with the United Nations, the promotion of universal respect for and observance of human rights and fundamental freedoms,

Whereas a common understanding of these rights and freedoms is of the greatest importance for the full realisation of this pledge.

Now, Therefore,

THE GENERAL ASSEMBLY

Proclaims

The universal declaration of human rights as a common standard of achievement for all peoples and all nations, to the end that every individual and every organ of society, keeping this Declaration constantly in mind, shall strive by teaching and education to promote respect for these rights and freedoms and by progressive measures, national and international, to secure their universal and effective recognition and observance, both among the peoples of member states themselves and among the peoples of territories under their jurisdiction.

Article 1

All human beings are born free and equal in dignity and rights. They are endowed with reason and conscience and should act towards one another in a spirit of brotherhood.

Article 2

Everyone is entitled to all the rights and freedoms set forth in this Declaration, without distinction of any kind, such as race colour, sex, language, religion, political or other opinion, national or social origin, property, birth or other status.

---

2   Adopted by the UN General Assembly on 10 December 1948 (UN Doc A/811. Voting was 48 for and nil against – Byelorussian SSR, Czechoslovakia, Poland, Saudi Arabia, Ukrainian SSR, USSR, Union of South Africa, and Yugoslavia abstained.

Article 3

Everyone has a right to life, liberty and security of person.

Article 4

No one shall be held in slavery or servitude; slavery and the slave trade shall be prohibited in all their forms.

Article 5

No one shall be subjected to torture or to cruel, inhuman or degrading treatment or punishment.

Article 6

Everyone has the right to recognition everywhere as a person before the law.

Article 7

All are equal before the law and are entitled without any discrimination to equal protection of the law. All are entitled to equal protection against any discrimination in violation of this Declaration and against any incitement to such discrimination.

Article 8

Everyone has the right to an effective remedy by the competent national tribunals for acts violating the fundamental rights granted by the constitution or by law.

Article 9

No one shall be subjected to arbitrary arrest, detention or exile.

Article 10

Everyone is entitled in full equality to a fair and public hearing by an independent and impartial tribunal, in the determination of his rights and obligations and of any criminal charge against him.

Article 11

(1) Everyone charged with a penal offence has the right to be presumed innocent until proved guilty according to law in a public trial at which he has had all the guarantees necessary for his defence.

(2) No one shall be held guilty of any penal offence on account of any act or omission which did not constitute a penal offence, under national or international law, at the time when it was committed. Nor shall a heavier penalty be imposed than the one that was applicable at the time the penal offence was committed.

Article 12

No one shall be subjected to arbitrary interference with his privacy, family, home or correspondence, nor to attacks upon his honour and reputation. Everyone has the right to the protection of the law against such interference or attacks.

Article 13

(1) Everyone has the right to freedom of movement and residence within the borders of each state.

(2) Everyone has the right to leave any country, including his own, and to return to his country.

Article 14

(1) Everyone has the right to seek and to enjoy in other countries asylum from persecution.

(2)   This right may not be invoked in the case of prosecutions genuinely arising from non-political crimes or from acts contrary to the purposes and principles of the United Nations.

Article 15

(1   Everyone has the right to a nationality.

(2)   No one shall be arbitrarily deprived of his nationality nor denied the right to change his nationality.

Article 16

(1)   Men and women of full age, without any limitation due to race, nationality or religion, have the right to marry and to found a family. They are entitled to equal rights as to marriage, during marriage and at its dissolution.

(2)   Marriage shall be entered into only with the free and full consent of the intending spouses.

(3)   The family is the natural and fundamental group unit of society and is entitled to protection by society and the State.

Article 17

(1)   Everyone has the right to own property alone as well as in association with others.

(2)   No one shall be arbitrarily deprived of his property.

Article 18

Everyone has the right to freedom of thought, conscience and religion; this includes freedom to change his religion or belief, either alone or in community with others and in public or private to manifest his religion or belief in teaching, practice, worship and observance.

Article 19

Everyone has the right to freedom of opinion and expression; this right includes the freedom to hold opinions without interference and to seek, receive and impart information and ideas through any media and regardless of frontiers.

Article 20

(1)   Everyone has the right to freedom of peaceful assembly and association.

(2)   No one may be compelled to belong to an association.

Article 21

(1)   Everyone has the right to take part in the government of his country, directly or through freely chosen representatives.

(2)   Everyone has the right of equal access to public service in his country.

(3)   The will of the people shall be the basis of the authority of government; this will shall be expressed in periodic and genuine elections which shall be by universal and equal suffrage and shall be held by secret vote or by equivalent free voting procedures.

Article 22

Everyone, as a member of society, has the right to social security and is entitled to realisation, through national effort and international co-operation and in accordance with the organisation and resources of each State, of the economic, social and cultural rights indispensable for his dignity and the free development of his personality.

Article 23

(1) Everyone has the right to work, to free choice of employment, to just and favourable conditions of work and to protection against unemployment.

(2) Everyone, without any discrimination, has the right to equal pay for equal work.

(3) Everyone who works has the right to just and favourable remuneration ensuring for himself and his family an existence worthy of human dignity, and supplemented, if necessary, by other means of social protection.

(4) Everyone has the right to form and to join trade unions for the protection of his interests.

Article 24

Everyone has the right to rest and leisure, including reasonable limitation of working hours and periodic holidays with pay.

Article 25

(1) Everyone has the right to a standard of living adequate for the health and well-being of himself and of his family, including food, clothing, housing and medical care and necessary social services, and the right to security in the event of unemployment, sickness, disability, widowhood, old age or other lack of livelihood in circumstances beyond his control.

(2) Motherhood and childhood are entitled to special care and assistance. All children, whether born in or out of wedlock, shall enjoy the same social protection.

Article 26

(1) Everyone has the right to education. Education shall be free, at least in the elementary and fundamental stages. Elementary education shall be compulsory. Technical and professional education shall be made generally available and higher education shall be equally accessible to all on the basis of merit.

(2) Education shall be directed to the full development of the human personality and to the strengthening of respect for human rights and fundamental freedoms. It shall promote understanding, tolerance and friendship among all nations, racial and religious groups, and shall further the activities of the United Nations for the maintenance of peace.

(3) Parents have a prior right to choose the kind of education that shall be given to their children.

Article 27

(1) Everyone has the right freely to participate in the cultural life of the community, to enjoy the arts and to share in the scientific advancement and its benefits.

(2) Everyone has the right to protection of the moral and material interests resulting from any scientific, literary or artistic production of which he is the author.

Article 28

Everyone is entitled to a social and international order in which the rights and freedoms set forth in this Declaration can be fully realised.

Article 29

(1) Everyone has duties to the community in which alone the free and full development of his personality is possible.

(2) In the exercise of his rights and freedoms, everyone shall be subject only to such limitations as are determined by law solely for the purpose of securing due recognition and respect for the rights and freedoms of others and of meeting the just requirements of morality, public order and the general welfare in a democratic society.

(3) These rights and freedoms may in no case be exercised contrary to the Purposes and Principles of the United Nations.

Article 30

Nothing in this Declaration may be interpreted as implying for any state, group or person any right to engage in any activity or to perform any act aimed at the destruction of any of the rights and freedoms set forth herein.

INTERNATIONAL COVENANT ON ECONOMIC, SOCIAL AND CULTURAL RIGHTS[3]

PREAMBLE

The States Parties to the present Covenant,

Considering that, in accordance with the principles proclaimed in the Charter of the United Nations, recognition of the inherent dignity and of the equal and inalienable rights of all members of the human family is the foundation of freedom, justice and peace in the world,

Recognising that these rights derive from the inherent dignity of the human person,

Recognising that, in accordance with the Universal Declaration of Human Rights, the ideal of free human beings enjoying freedom from fear and want can only be achieved if conditions are created whereby everyone may enjoy his economic, social and cultural rights, as well as his civil and political rights,

Considering the obligation of States under the Charter of the United Nations to promote universal respect for, and observance of, human rights and freedoms,

Realising that the individual, having duties to other individuals and to the community to which he belongs is, under a responsibility to strive for the promotion and observance of the rights recognised in the present Covenant,

Agree on the following articles:

PART I

Article 1

1   All peoples have the right of self-determination. By virtue of that right they freely determine their political status and freely pursue their economic, social and cultural development.

2   All peoples may, for their own ends, freely dispose of their natural wealth and resources without prejudice to any obligations arising out of international economic co-operation, based upon the principle of mutual benefit, and international law. In no case may a people be deprived of its own means of subsistence.

---

3   Adopted by the UN General Assembly on 16 December 1966 – entered into force on 3 January 1976.

3   The States Parties to the present Covenant, including those having responsibility for the administration of Non-Self-Governing and Trust Territories, shall promote the realisation of the right of self-determination, and shall respect that right, in conformity with the provisions of the Charter of the United Nations.

PART II

Article 2

1   Each State Party to the present Covenant undertakes to take steps, individually and through international assistance and co-operation, especially economic and technical, to the maximum of its available resources, with a view to achieving progressively the full realisation of the rights recognised in the present Covenant by all appropriate means, including particularly the adoption of legislative measures.

2   The States Parties to the present Covenant undertake to guarantee that the rights enunciated in the present Covenant will be exercised without discrimination of any kind as to race, colour, sex, language, religion, political or other opinion, national or social origin, property, birth or other status.

3   Developing countries, with due regard to human rights and their national economy, may determine to what extent they would guarantee the economic rights recognised in the present Covenant to non-nationals.

Article 3

The States Parties to the present Covenant undertake to ensure the equal right of men and women to the enjoyment of all economic, social and cultural rights set forth in the present Covenant.

Article 4

The States Parties to the present Covenant recognise that, in the enjoyment of those rights provided by the state in conformity with the present Covenant, the State may subject such rights only to such limitations as are determined by law only in so far as this may be compatible with the nature of these rights and solely for the purpose of promoting the general welfare in a democratic society.

Article 5

1   Nothing in the present Covenant may be interpreted as implying for any state, group or person any right to engage in any activity or to perform any act aimed at the destruction of any of the rights or freedoms recognised herein, or at their limitation to a greater extent than is provided for in the present Covenant.

2   No restriction upon or derogation from any of the fundamental human rights recognised or existing in any country in virtue of law, conventions, regulations or custom shall be admitted on the pretext that the present Covenant does not recognise such rights or that it recognises them to a lesser extent.

PART III

Article 6

1   The States Parties to the present Covenant recognise the right to work, which includes the right of everyone to the opportunity to gain his living by work which he freely chooses or accepts, and will take appropriate steps to safeguard this right.

2   The steps to be taken by a State Party to the present Covenant to achieve the full realisation of this right shall include technical and vocational guidance and training programmes, policies and techniques to achieve steady economic, social and cultural development and full and productive employment under conditions safeguarding fundamental political and economic freedoms to the individual.

Article 7

The States Parties to the present Covenant recognise the right of everyone to the enjoyment of just and favourable conditions of work, which ensure, in particular:

(a)   Remuneration which provides all workers, as a minimum with:

    (i)   Fair wages and equal remuneration for work of equal value without distinction of any kind, in particular women being guaranteed conditions of work not inferior to those enjoyed by men, with equal pay for equal work;

    (ii)   A decent living by themselves and their families in accordance with the provisions of the present Covenant;

(b)   Safe and healthy working conditions;

(c)   Equal opportunity for everyone to be promoted in his employment to an appropriate higher level, subject to no considerations other than those of seniority and competence;

(d)   Rest, leisure and reasonable limitation of working hours and periodic holidays with pay, as well as remuneration for public holidays.

Article 8

1   The States Parties to the present Covenant undertake to ensure:

(a)   The right of everyone to form trade unions and join the trade union of his choice, subject only to the rules of the organisation concerned, for the promotion and protection of his economic and social interests. No restrictions may be placed on the exercise of this right other than those prescribed by law and which are necessary in a democratic society in the interests of national security or public order or for the protection of the rights and freedoms of others;

(b)   The right of trade unions to establish national federations or confederations and the right of the latter to form or join international trade union organisations;

(c)   The right of trade unions to function freely subject to no limitations other than those prescribed by law and which are necessary in a democratic society in the interests of national security or public order or for the protection of the rights and freedoms of others;

(d)   The right to strike, provided that it is exercised in conformity with the laws of the particular country.

2   This article shall not prevent the imposition of lawful restrictions on the exercise of these rights by members of the armed forces or of the police or of the administration of the state.

3   Nothing in this article shall authorise States Parties to the International Labour Organisation of 1948 concerning Freedom of Association and Protection of the Right to Organise to take legislative measures which would prejudice, or apply the law in such a manner as would prejudice, the guarantees provided for in that Convention.

Article 9

The States Parties to the present Covenant recognise the right of everyone to social security, including social insurance.

Article 10

The States Parties to the present Covenant recognise that:

1   The widest possible protection and assistance should be accorded to the family, which is the natural and fundamental group unit of society, particularly for its establishment and while it is responsible for the care and education of dependent children. Marriage must be entered into with the free consent of the intending spouses.

2   Special protection should be accorded to mothers during a reasonable period before and after childbirth. During such period working mothers should be accorded pair leave or leave with adequate social security benefits.

3   Special measures of protection and assistance should be taken on behalf of all children and young persons without any discrimination for reasons of parentage or other conditions. Children and young persons should be protected from economic and social exploitation. Their employment in work harmful to their morals or health or dangerous to life or likely to hamper their normal development should be punishable by law. States should also set their limits below which the paid employment of child labour should be prohibited and punishable by law.

Article 11

1   The States Parties to the present Covenant recognise the right of everyone to an adequate standard of living for himself and his family, including adequate food, clothing and housing, and to the continuous improvement of living conditions. The States Parties will take appropriate steps to ensure the realisation of this right, recognising to this effect the essential importance of international co-operation based on free consent.

2   The States Parties to the present Covenant, recognising the fundamental right of everyone to be free from hunger, shall take, individually and through international co-operation, the measures, including specific programmes, which are needed:

(a)   To improve methods of production, conservation and distribution of food by making full use of technical and scientific knowledge by disseminating knowledge of the principles of nutrition and by developing or reforming agrarian systems in such a way as to achieve the most efficient development and utilisation of natural resources;

(b)   Taking into account the problems of both food-importing and food-exporting countries, to ensure an equitable distribution of world food supplies in relation to need.

Article 12

1   The States Parties to the present Covenant recognise the right of everyone to the enjoyment of the highest standard of physical and mental health.

2   The steps to be taken by the States Parties to the present Covenant to achieve the fuller realisation of this right shall include those necessary for:

(a)   The provision for the reduction of the stillbirth-rate and of infant mortality and for the healthy development of the child;

(b)   The improvement of all aspects of environmental and industrial hygiene;

(c) The prevention, treatment and control of epidemic, endemic, occupational and other diseases;

(d) The creation of conditions which would assure to all medical service and medical attention in the event of sickness.

Article 13

1   The States Parties to the present Covenant recognise the right of everyone to education. They agree that education shall be directed to the full development of the human personality and the sense of its dignity, and shall strengthen respect for human rights and fundamental freedoms. They further agree that education shall enable all persons to participate effectively in a free society, promote understanding, tolerance and friendship among all nations and all racial, ethnic or religious groups, and further the activities of the United Nations for the maintenance of peace.

2   The States Parties to the present Covenant recognise that, with a view to achieving the full realisation of this right:

(a) Primary education shall be compulsory and available free to all:

(b) Secondary education in its different forms, including technical and vocational secondary education, shall be made generally available and accessible to all by every appropriate means, and in particular by the progressive introduction of free education;

(c) Higher education shall be made equally accessible to all, on the basis of capacity, by every appropriate means, and in particular by the progressive introduction of free education;

(d) Fundamental education shall be encouraged or intensified as afar as possible for those persons who have not received or completed the whole period of their primary education;

(e) The development of a system of schools at all levels shall be actively pursued, an adequate fellowship system shall be established, and the material conditions of teaching staff shall be continuously improved.

3   The States Parties to the present Covenant undertake to have respect for the liberty of parents and, when applicable, legal guardians, to choose for their children schools, other than those established by the public authorities, which conform to such minimum educational standards as may be laid down or approved by the state and to ensure the religious and moral education of their children in conformity with their own convictions.

4   No part of this article shall be construed so as to interfere with the liberty of individuals and bodies to establish and direct educational institutions, subject always to the observance of the principles set forth in para 1 of this article and to the requirement that the education given in such institutions shall conform to such minimum standards as may be laid down by the state.

Article 14

Each State Party to the present Covenant which, at the time of becoming a party, has not been able to secure in its metropolitan territory or other territories under its jurisdiction compulsory primary education, free of charge, undertakes, within two years, to work out and adopt a detailed plan of action for the progressive implementation, within a reasonable number of years, to be fixed in the plan, of the principle of compulsory education free of charge for all.

Article 15

1   The States Parties to the present Covenant recognise the right of everyone:

(a)   To take part in cultural life;

(b)   To enjoy the benefits of scientific progress and its applications;

(c)   To benefit from the protection of the moral and material interests resulting from any scientific, literary or artistic production of which he is the author.

2   The steps to be taken by the States Parties to the present Covenant to achieve the full realisation of this right shall include those necessary for the conservation, the development and the diffusion of science and culture.

3   The States Parties to the present Covenant undertake to respect the freedom indispensable for scientific research and creative activity.

4   The States Parties to the present Covenant recognise the benefits to be derived from the encouragement and development of international contacts and co-operation in the scientific and cultural fields.

PART IV

Article 16

1   The States Parties to the present Covenant undertake to submit in conformity with this part of the Covenant reports on the measures which they have adopted and the progress made in achieving the observance of the rights recognised herein.

2

(a)   All reports shall be submitted to the Secretary General of the United Nations, who shall transmit copies to the Economic and Social Council for consideration in accordance with the provisions of the present Covenant.

(b)   The Secretary General of the United Nations shall also transmit to the specialised agencies copies of the reports, or any relevant parts therefrom, from States Parties to the present Covenant which are also members of these specialised agencies in so far as these reports, or parts therefrom, relate to any matters which fall within the responsibilities of the said agencies in accordance with their constitutional instruments.

Article 17

1   The States Parties to the present Covenant shall furnish their reports in stages, in accordance with a programme to be established by the Economic and Social Council within one year of the entry into force of the present Covenant after consultation with the States Parties and the specialised agencies involved.

2   Reports may indicate factors and difficulties affecting the degree of fulfilment of obligations under the present Covenant.

3   Where relevant information has previously been furnished to the United Nations or to any specialised agency by any State Party to the present Covenant, it will not be necessary to reproduce that information, but a precise reference to the information so furnished will suffice.

Article 18

Pursuant to its responsibilities under the Charter of the United Nations in the field of human rights and fundamental freedoms, the Economic and Social Council may make arrangements with the specialised agencies in respect of their reporting to it on the progress made in achieving the observance of the provisions of the present Covenant falling within the scope of their activities.

These reports may include particulars of decisions and recommendations on such implementation adopted by their competent organs.

Article 19

The Economic and Social Council may transmit to the Commission on Human Rights for study and general recommendation or as appropriate for information the reports concerning human rights as submitted by States in accordance with Articles 16 and 17, and those concerning human rights submitted by the specialised agencies in accordance with Article 18.

Article 20

The States Parties to the present Covenant and the specialised agencies concerned may submit comments to the Economic and Social Council on any general recommendation under Article 19 or reference to such general recommendation in any report of the Commission on Human Rights or any documentation referred to therein.

Article 21

The Economic and Social Council may submit from time to time to the General Assembly reports with recommendations of a general nature and a summary of the information received form the States Parties to the present Covenant and the specialised agencies on the measures taken and the progress made in achieving general observance of the rights recognised in the present Covenant.

Article 22

The Economic and Social Council may bring to the attention of other organs of the United Nations, their subsidiary organs and specialised agencies concerned with furnishing technical assistance any matters arising out of the reports referred to in this part of the present Covenant which may assist such bodies in deciding, each within its field of competence, on the advisability of international measures likely to contribute to the effective progressive implementation of the present Covenant.

Article 23

The States Parties to the present Covenant agree that international action for the achievement of the rights recognised in the present Covenant includes such methods as the conclusion of conventions, the adoption of recommendations, the furnishing of technical assistance and the holding of regional meetings and technical meetings for the purpose of consultation and study organised in conjunction with the governments concerned.

Article 24

Nothing in the present Covenant shall be interpreted as impairing the provisions of the Charter of the United Nations and of the constitutions of the specialised agencies which define the respective responsibilities of the various organs of the United Nations and of the specialised agencies in regard to the matters dealt with in the present Covenant.

Article 25

Nothing in the present Covenant shall be interpreted as impairing the inherent right of all peoples to enjoy and utilise fully and freely their natural wealth and resources.

PART V

Article 26

1   The present Covenant is open for signature by any State Member of the United Nations or members of any of its specialised agencies, by any State Party to the Statute of the International Court of Justice, and by any other State which has been invited to the General Assembly of the United Nations to become a party to the present Covenant.

2   The present Covenant is subject to ratification. Instruments of ratification shall be deposited with the Secretary General of the United Nations.

3   The present Covenant shall be open to accession by any state referred to in para 1 of this article.

4   Accession shall be effected by the deposit of an instrument of accession with the Secretary General of the United Nations.

5   The Secretary General of the United Nations shall inform all states which have signed the present Covenant or acceded to it of the deposit of each instrument of ratification or accession.

Article 27

1   The present Covenant shall enter into force three months after the date of the deposit with the Secretary General of the United Nations of the thirty-fifth instrument of ratification or instrument of accession.

2   For each state ratifying the present Covenant or acceding to it after the deposit of the thirty-fifth instrument of ratification or instrument of accession, the present Covenant shall enter into force three months after the date of the deposit of its own instrument of ratification or instrument of accession.

Article 28

The provisions of the present Covenant shall extend to all parts of federal states without any limitations or exceptions.

Article 29

1   Any State Party to the present Covenant may propose an amendment and file it with the Secretary General of the United Nations. The Secretary General shall thereupon communicate any proposed amendments to the State Parties to the present Covenant with a request that they notify him whether they favour a conference of States Parties for the purpose of considering and voting upon the proposals. In the event that at least one third of the States Parties favours such a conference, the Secretary General shall convene the conference under the auspices of the United Nations. Any amendments adopted by a majority of the States Parties present and voting at the conference shall be submitted to the General Assembly of the United Nations for approval.

2   Amendments shall come into force when they have been approved by the General Assembly of the United Nations and accepted by a two-thirds majority of the States Parties to the present Covenant in accordance with their respective constitutional processes.

3 When amendments come into force they shall be binding on those States Parties which have accepted them, other States Parties still being bound by the provisions of the present Covenant and any earlier amendment which they have accepted.

Article 30

Irrespective of the notifications made under Article 26, para 5, the Secretary General of the United Nations shall inform all States referred to in para 1 of the same article of the following particulars:

(a)   Signatures, ratifications and accessions under Article 26;

(b)   The date of the entry into force of the present Covenant under Article 27 and the date of the entry into force of any amendments under Article 29.

Article 31

1   The present Covenant, of which the Chinese, English, French, Russian and Spanish texts are equally authentic, shall be deposited in the archives of the United Nations.

2   The Secretary General of the United Nations shall transmit certified copies of the present Covenant to all states referred to in Article 26.

Following the adoption of the UDHR the UN Commission on Human Rights began work on drafting two international covenants on human rights: one on economic, social and cultural rights and one on civil and political rights. Initially a single treaty had been envisaged, but in consequence of continued revision and debate, the Commission requested that two separate instruments should be prepared. The two conventions, the International Covenant on Civil and Political Rights and the International Covenant on Economic, Social and Cultural Rights, were completed by the mid 1950s and they were adopted by the UN General Assembly and opened for signature in 1966. The two conventions recognise different sets of rights but they do contain some common provisions. However, the machinery for enforcement differs as between the two documents and is discussed at 16.4.1 (below).

The International Covenant on Civil and Political Rights 1966 entered into force in January 1976 and at present there are over 100 states party to it, including the UK. ICPR is a treaty binding on the parties, and each state is obliged to give effect to the provisions. In particular, each state should adopt legislative measures to give effect to the Covenant and provide effective remedies for violations. The Covenant establishes a code of civil and political rights similar to those found in the UDHR. Derogation in times of emergency is allowed with respect to some rights, but not with respect to those rights expressed to be fundamental, such as the right to life (Article 6) and the right to freedom from torture (Article 7).

The International Covenant on Economic, Social and Cultural Rights 1966 entered into force in 1976 and there are now over 100 states that are party to it, including the UK. Obligations under the ICESCR are less specific than those under the ICPR, and the tone of the whole covenant is more promotional than mandatory.

INTERNATIONAL COVENANT ON CIVIL AND POLITICAL RIGHTS

PREAMBLE

The States Parties to the present Covenant,

Considering that, in accordance with the principles proclaimed in the Charter of the United Nations, recognition of the inherent dignity and of the equal and inalienable rights of all members of the human family is the foundation of freedom, justice and peace in the world,

Recognising that these rights derive from the inherent dignity of the human person,

Recognising that, in accordance with the Universal Declaration of Human Rights, the ideal of free human beings enjoying freedom from fear and want can only be achieved if conditions are created whereby everyone may enjoy his civil and political rights, as well as his economic, social and cultural rights,

Considering the obligation of States under the Charter of the United Nations to promote universal respect for, and observance of, human rights and freedoms,

Realising that the individual, having duties to other individuals and to the community to which he belongs is, under a responsibility to strive for the promotion and observance of the rights recognised in the present Covenant,

Agree on the following articles:

PART I

Article 1

1   All peoples have the right of self-determination. By virtue of that right they freely determine their political status and freely pursue their economic, social and cultural development.

2   All peoples may, for their own ends, freely dispose of their natural wealth and resources without prejudice to any obligations arising out of international economic co-operation, based upon the principle of mutual benefit, and international law. In no case may a people be deprived of its own means of subsistence.

3   The States Parties to the present Covenant, including those having responsibility for the administration of Non-Self-Governing and Trust Territories, shall promote the realisation of the right of self-determination, and shall respect that right, in conformity with the provisions of the Charter of the United Nations.

PART II

Article 2

1   Each State Party to the present Covenant undertakes to respect and to ensure to all individuals within its territory and subject to its jurisdiction the rights recognised in the present Covenant, without distinction of any kind, such as race, colour, sex, language, religion, political or other opinion, national or social origin, property, birth or other status.

2   Where not already provided for by existing legislative or other measures, each State Party to the present Covenant undertakes to take the necessary steps,

in accordance with its constitutional processes and with the provisions of the present Covenant, to adopt such legislative or other measures as may be necessary to give effect to the rights recognised in the present Covenant.

3   Each State Party to the present Covenant undertakes:

(a)   To ensure that any person whose rights or freedoms as herein recognised are violated shall have an effective remedy, notwithstanding that the violation has been committed by persons acting in an official capacity;

(b)   To ensure that any person claiming such a remedy shall have his right thereto determined by competent judicial, administrative or legislative authorities, or by any other competent authority provided for by the legal system of the State, and to develop the possibilities of judicial remedy;

(c)   To ensure that the competent authorities shall enforce such remedies when granted.

Article 3

The States Parties to the present Covenant undertake to ensure the equal right of men and women to the enjoyment of all civil and political rights set forth in the present Covenant.

Article 4

1   In times of public emergency which threatens the life of the nation and the existence of which is officially proclaimed, the States Parties to the present Covenant may take measures derogating from their obligations under the present Covenant to the extent strictly required by the exigencies of the situation, provided that such measures are not inconsistent with their other obligations under international law and do not involve discrimination solely on the ground of race, colour, sex, language, religion or social origin.

2   No derogation from Articles 6, 7, 8 (paras 1 and 2), 11, 15, 16 and 18 may be made under this provision.

3   Any State party to the present Covenant availing itself of the right of derogation shall immediately inform the other State Parties to the present Covenant, through the intermediary of the Secretary General of the United Nations, of the provisions from which it has derogated and of the reasons by which it was actuated. A further communications shall be made, through the same intermediary, on the date on which it terminates such derogation.

Article 5

1   Nothing in the present Covenant may be interpreted as implying for any state, group or person any right to engage in any activity or to perform any act aimed at the destruction of any of the rights or freedoms recognised herein, or at their limitation to a greater extent than is provided for in the present Covenant.

2   There shall be no restriction upon or derogation from any of the fundamental human rights recognised or existing in any State Party to the present Covenant pursuant to law, conventions, regulations or custom on the pretext that the present Covenant does not recognise such rights or that it recognises them to a lesser extent.

PART III

Article 6

1   Every human being has the inherent right to life. This right shall be protected by law. No one shall be arbitrarily deprived of his life.

2   In countries which have not abolished the death penalty, sentence of death may be imposed only for the most serious crimes in accordance with the law in force at the time of the commission of the crime and not contrary to the provisions of the present Covenant and to the Convention on the Prevention and Punishment of the Crime of Genocide. This penalty can only be carried out pursuant to a final judgment rendered by a competent court.

3   When deprivation of life constitutes the crime of genocide, it is understood that nothing in this article shall authorise any State Party to the present Covenant to derogate in any way from any obligation assumed under the provisions of the Convention on the Prevention and Punishment of the Crime of Genocide.

4   Anyone sentenced to death shall have the right to seek pardon or commutation of the sentence. Amnesty, pardon or commutation of the sentence of death may be granted in all cases.

5   Sentence of death shall not be imposed for crimes committed by persons below 18 years of age and shall not be carried out on pregnant women.

6   Nothing in this article shall be invoked to prevent the abolition of capital punishment by any State Party to the present Covenant.

Article 7

No one shall be subjected to torture or to cruel, inhuman or degrading treatment or punishment. In particular, no one shall be subjected without his free consent to medical or scientific experimentation.

Article 8

1   No one shall be held in slavery; slavery and the slave-trade in all their forms shall be prohibited.

2   No one shall be held in servitude.

3

(a)   No on shall be required to perform forced or compulsory labour;

(b)   Paragraph 3(a) shall not be held to preclude, in countries where imprisonment with hard labour may be imposed as a punishment for a crime, the performance of hard labour in pursuance of a sentence to such punishment by a competent court;

(c)   For the purpose of this paragraph the termed 'forced or compulsory labour' shall not include:

   (i)   Any work or service, not referred to in sub-para (b), normally required of a person who is under detention in consequence of a lawful order of a court, or of a person during conditional release from such detention;

   (ii)   Any service of a military character and, in countries where conscientious objection is recognised, any national service required by law of conscientious objectors;

   (iii)   Any service exacted in cases of emergency or calamity threatening the life or well-being of the community;

   (iv)   Any work or service which forms part of normal civil obligations.

Article 9

1   Everyone has the right to liberty and security of person. No one shall be subjected to arbitrary arrest or detention. No one shall be deprived of his liberty except on such grounds and in accordance with such procedures as are established by law.

2   Anyone who is arrested shall be informed, at the time of arrest, of the reasons for his arrest and shall be promptly informed of any charges against him.

3   Anyone arrested or detained on a criminal charge shall be brought promptly before a judge or other officer authorised by law to exercise judicial power and shall be entitled to trial within a reasonable time or to release. It shall not be the general rule that persons awaiting trial shall be detained in custody, but release may be subject to guarantees to appear for trial, at any other stage of the judicial proceedings, and, should occasion arise, for execution of the judgment.

4   Anyone who is deprived of his liberty by arrest or detention shall be entitled to take proceedings before a court, in order that that court may decide without delay on the lawfulness of his detention and order his release if the detention is not lawful.

5   Anyone who has been the victim of unlawful arrest or detention shall have an enforceable right to compensation.

Article 10

1   All persons deprived of their liberty shall be treated with humanity and with respect for the inherent dignity of the human person.

2

(a)   Accused persons shall, save in exceptional circumstances, be segregated form convicted persons and shall be subject to separate treatment appropriate to their status as unconvicted persons;

(b)   Accused juvenile persons shall be separated from adults and brought as speedily as possible for adjudication.

3   The penitentiary system shall comprise treatment of prisoners the essential aim of which shall be their reformation and social rehabilitation. Juvenile offenders shall be segregated from adults and be accorded treatment appropriate to their age and legal status.

Article 11

No one shall be imprisoned merely on the ground of the inability to fulfil a contractual obligation.

Article 12

1   Everyone lawfully within the territory of a state shall, within that territory, have the right to liberty of movement and freedom to choose his residence.

2   Everyone shall be free to leave any country, including his own.

3   The above-mentioned rights shall not be subject to any restrictions except those which are provided by law, are necessary to protect national security, public order (*ordre public*), public health or morals or the rights and freedoms of others, and are consistent with the other rights recognised in the present Covenant.

4   No one shall be arbitrarily deprived of the right to enter his own country.

Article 13

An alien lawfully in the territory of a State Party to the present Covenant may be expelled therefrom only in pursuance of a decision reached in accordance with law and shall, except where compelling reasons of national security otherwise require, be allowed to submit the reasons against his expulsion and to have his case reviewed by, and be represented for the purpose before, the competent authority or a person or persons especially designated by the competent authority.

Article 14

1 All persons shall be equal before the courts and tribunals. In the determination of any criminal charge against hum, or of his rights and obligations in a suit at law, everyone shall be entitled to a fair and public hearing by a competent, independent and impartial tribunal established by law. The Press and the public may be excluded from all or part of a trial for reasons of moral, public order (*ordre public*) or national security in a democratic society, or when the interest of the private lives of the parties so requires, or to the extent strictly necessary in the opinion of the court in special circumstances where publicity would prejudice the interests of justice; but any judgment rendered in a criminal case or in a suit at law shall be made public except where the interest of juvenile persons otherwise requires or the proceedings concern matrimonial disputes or the guardianship of children.

2 Everyone charged with a criminal offence shall have the right to be presumed innocent until proved guilty according to law.

3 In the determination of any criminal charge against him, everyone shall be entitled to the following minimum guarantees, in full equality:

(a) To be informed promptly and in detail in a language which he understands of the nature and cause of the charge against him:

(b) To have adequate time and facilities for the preparation of his defence and to communicate with counsel of his own choosing;

(c) To be tried without undue delay;

(d) To be tried in his presence, and to defend himself in person or through legal assistance of his own choosing; to be informed, if he does not have legal assistance, of this right; and to have legal assistance assigned to him, in any case where the interests of justice so require, and without payment by him in any such case if he does not have sufficient means to pay for it;

(e) To examine, or have examined, the witnesses against him and to obtain the attendance and examination of witnesses on his behalf under the same conditions as witnesses against him;

(f) To have the free assistance of an interpreter if he cannot understand or speak the language used in court;

(g) Not to be compelled to testify against himself or to confess guilt.

4 In the case of juvenile persons, the procedure shall be such as will take account of their age and the desirability of promoting their rehabilitation.

5 Everyone convicted of a crime shall have the right to his conviction and sentence being reviewed by a higher tribunal according to law.

6 When a person has by a final decision been convicted of a criminal offence and when subsequently his conviction has been reversed or he has been pardoned on the ground that a new or newly discovered fact shows conclusively that there has been a miscarriage of justice, the person who has suffered punishment as a result of such conviction shall be compensated according to law, unless it is proved that the non-disclosure of the unknown fact in time is wholly or partly attributable to him.

7 No one shall be liable to be tried or punished again for an offence for which he has already been finally convicted or acquitted in accordance with the law and penal procedure of each country.

Article 15

1 No one shall be held guilty of any criminal offence on account of any act or omission which did not constitute a criminal offence, under national or international law, at the time when it was committed. Nor shall a heavier penalty be imposed than the one that was applicable at the time when the criminal offence was committed. If, subsequent to the commission of the offence, provision is made by law for the imposition of a lighter penalty, the offender shall benefit thereby.

2 Nothing in this article shall prejudice the trial and punishment of any person for any act or omission which, at the time when it was committed, was criminal according to the general principles of law recognised by the community of nations.

Article 16

Everyone shall have the right to recognition everywhere as a person before the law.

Article 17

1 No one shall be subjected to arbitrary or unlawful interference with his privacy, family, home or correspondence, nor to unlawful attacks on his honour and reputation.

2 Everyone has the right to the protection of the law against such interference or attacks.

Article 18

1 Everyone shall have the right to freedom of thought, conscience and religion. This right shall include freedom to have or to adopt a religion or belief of his choice, and freedom, either individually or in community with others and in public or private, to manifest his religion or belief in worship, observance, practice and teaching.

2 No one shall be subject to coercion which would impair his freedom to have or to adopt a religion or belief of his choice.

3 Freedom to manifest one's religion or beliefs may be subject only to such limitations as are prescribed by law and are necessary to protect public safety, order, health, or morals or the fundamental rights and freedoms of others.

4 The States Parties to the present Covenant undertake to have respect for the liberty of parents and, when applicable, legal guardians to ensure the religious and moral education of their children in conformity with their own convictions.

Article 19

1 Everyone shall have the right to hold opinions without interference.

2 Everyone shall have the right to freedom of expression; this right shall include freedom to seek, receive and impart information and ideas of all kinds, regardless of frontiers, either orally, in writing or in print, in the form of art, or through any other media of his choice.

3 The exercise of the rights provided for in para 2 of this article carries with it special duties and responsibilities. It may therefore be subject to certain restrictions, but these shall only be such as are provided by law and are necessary:

(a) For respect of the rights or reputations of others;

(b) For the protection of national security or of public order (*ordre public*), or of public health or morals.

Article 20

1   Any propaganda for war shall be prohibited by law.

2   Any advocacy of national, racial or religious hatred that constitutes incitement to discrimination, hostility or violence shall be prohibited by law.

Article 21

The right of peaceful assembly shall be recognised. No restrictions may be placed on the exercise of this right other than those imposed in conformity with the law and which are necessary in a democratic society in the interests of national security or public safety, public order (*ordre public*), the protection of public health or morals or the protection of the rights and freedoms of others.

Article 22

1   Everyone shall have the right to freedom of association with others, including the right to form and join trade unions for the protection of his interests.

2   No restriction may be placed on the exercise of this right other than those which are prescribed by law and which are necessary in a democratic society in the interests of national security or public safety, public order (*ordre public*), the protection of public health or morals or the protection of the rights and freedoms of others. This article shall not prevent the imposition of lawful restrictions on members of the armed forces and of the police in their exercise of this right.

3   Nothing in this article shall authorise States Parties to the International Labour Organisation Convention of 1948 concerning Freedom of Association and Protection of the Right to Organise to take legislative measures which would prejudice, or to apply the law in such a manner as to prejudice, the guarantees provided for in that Convention.

Article 23

1   The family is the natural and fundamental group unit of society and is entitled to protection by society and the State.

2   The right of men and women of marriageable age to marry and to found a family shall be recognised.

3   No marriage shall be entered into without the free and full consent of the intending spouses.

4   States Parties to the present Covenant shall take appropriate steps to ensure equality of rights and responsibilities of spouses as to marriage, during marriage and at its dissolution. In the case of dissolution, provision shall be made for the necessary protection of any children.

Article 24

1   Every child shall have, without any discrimination as to race, colour, sex, language, religion, national or social origin, property or birth, the right to such measures of protection as are required by his status as a minor, on the part of his family, society and the state.

2   Every child shall be registered immediately after birth and shall have a name.

3   Every child has the right to acquire a nationality.

Article 25

Every citizen shall have the right and the opportunity, without any of the distinctions mentioned in Article 2 and without unreasonable restrictions:

(a)   To take part in the conduct of public affairs, directly or through freely chosen representative;

(b) To vote and to be elected at genuine periodic elections which shall be by universal and equal suffrage and shall be held by secret ballot, guaranteeing the free expression of the will of the electors;

(c) To have access, on general terms of equality, to public service in his country.

Article 26

All persons are equal before the law and are entitled without any discrimination to the equal protection of the law. In this respect, the law shall prohibit discrimination and guarantee to all persons equal and effective protection against discrimination on any ground such as race, colour, sex, language, religion, political or other opinion, national or social origin, property, birth or other status.

Article 27

In those states in which ethnic, religious or linguistic minorities exist, persons belonging to such minorities shall not be denied the right, in community with the other members of their group, to enjoy their own culture, to profess and practise their own religion, or to use their own language.

PART IV

Article 28

1   There shall be established a Human Rights Committee (hereafter referred to in the present Covenant as the Committee). It shall consist of eighteen members and shall carry out the functions hereinafter provided.

2   The Committee shall be composed of nationals of the States Parties to the present Covenant who shall be persons of high moral character and recognised competence in the field of human rights, consideration having been given to the usefulness of the participation of some persons having legal experience.

3   The members of the Committee shall be elected and shall serve in their personal capacity.

Article 29

1   The members of the Committee shall be elected by secret ballot from a list of persons possessing the qualifications prescribed in Article 28 and nominated for the purpose by the States Parties to the present Covenant.

2   Each State Party to the present Covenant may nominate not more than two persons. These persons shall be nationals of the nominating State.

3   A person shall be eligible for renomination.

Article 30

1   The initial election shall be held no later than six months after the date of the entry into force of the present Covenant.

2   At least four months before the date of each election to the Committee, other than an election to fill a vacancy declared in accordance with Article 34, the Secretary General of the United Nations shall address a written invitation to the States Parties to the present Covenant to submit their nominations for membership of the Committee within three months.

3   The Secretary General of the United Nations shall prepare a list in alphabetical order of all the persons thus nominated, with an indication of the States Parties which have nominated them, and shall submit it to the States Parties to the present Covenant no later than one month before the date of each election.

4   Elections of the members of the Committee shall be held at a meeting of the States Parties to the present Covenant convened by the Secretary General of the United Nations at the Headquarters of the United Nations. At that meeting, for which two thirds of the States Parties to the present Covenant shall constitute a quorum, the persons elected to the Committee shall be those nominees who obtain the largest number of votes and an absolute majority of the votes of the representatives of States Parties present and voting.

Article 31

1   The Committee may not include more than one national of the same state.

2   In the election of the Committee, consideration shall be given to equitable geographical distribution of membership and to the representation of the different forms of civilisation and of the principal legal systems.

Article 32

1   The members of the Committee shall be elected for a term of four years. They shall be eligible for re-election if renominated. However, the terms of nine of the members elected at the first election shall expire at the end of two years; immediately after the first election, the names of these nine members shall be chosen by lot by the Chairman of the meeting referred to in Article 30, para 4.

2   Elections at the expiry of office shall be held in accordance with the preceding articles of this part of the present Covenant.

Article 33

1   If, in the unanimous opinion of the other members, a member of the Committee has ceased to carry out his functions for any cause other than absence of a temporary character, the Chairman of the Committee shall notify the Secretary General of the United Nations, who shall then declare the seat of that member to be vacant.

2   In the event of the death or the resignation of a member of the Committee, the Chairman shall immediately notify the Secretary General of the United Nations, who shall declare the seat vacant from the date of death or the date on which the resignation takes effect.

Article 34

1   When a vacancy is declared in accordance with Article 33 and if the term of office of the member to be replaced does not expire within six months of the declaration of the vacancy, the Secretary General of the United Nations shall notify each of the States Parties to the present Covenant, which may within two months submit nominations in accordance with Article 29 for the purpose of filling the vacancy.

2   The Secretary General of the United Nations shall prepare a list in alphabetical order of the persons thus nominated and shall submit it to the States Parties to the present Covenant. The election to fill the vacancy shall then take place in accordance with the relevant provisions of this part of the present Covenant.

3   A member of the Committee elected to fill a vacancy declared in accordance with Article 33 shall hold office for the remainder of the term of the member who vacated the seat on the Committee under the provisions of that article.

Article 35

The members of the Committee shall, with the approval of the General Assembly of the United Nations, receive emoluments from United Nations resources on such terms and conditions as the General Assembly may decide, having regard to the importance of the Committee's responsibilities.

Article 36

The Secretary General of the United Nations shall provide the necessary staff and facilities for the effective performance of the functions of the Committee under the present Covenant.

Article 37

1 The Secretary General of the United Nations shall convene the initial meeting of the Committee at the Headquarters of the United Nations.

2 After its initial meeting, the Committee shall meet at such times as shall be provided in its rules of procedure.

3 The Committee shall normally meet at the Headquarters of the United Nations or at the United Nations Office at Geneva.

Article 38

Every member of the Committee shall, before taking up his duties, make a solemn declaration in open committee that he will perform his functions impartially and conscientiously.

Article 39

1 The Committee shall elect its officers for a term of two years. They may be re-elected.

2 The Committee shall establish its own rules of procedure but these rules shall provide, *inter alia*, that:

(a) Twelve members shall constitute a quorum;

(b) Decisions of the Committee shall be made by a majority vote of the members present.

Article 40

1 The States Parties to the present Covenant undertake to submit reports on the measures they have adopted which give effect to the rights recognised herein and on the progress made in the enjoyment of those rights:

(a) Within one year of the entry into force of the present Covenant for the States Parties concerned;

(b) Thereafter whenever the Committee so requests.

2 All reports shall be submitted to the Secretary General of the United Nations who shall transmit them to the Committee for consideration. Reports shall indicate the factors and difficulties, if any affecting the implementation of the present Covenant.

3 The Secretary General of the United Nations may, after consultation with the Committee, transmit to the specialised agencies concerned copies of such parts of the reports as may fall within their fields of competence.

4 The Committee shall study the reports submitted by the States Parties to the present Covenant. It shall transmit its reports, and such general comments as it may consider appropriate, to the States Parties. The Committee may also transmit to the Economic and Social Council their comments along with the copies of the reports it has received from States Parties to the present Covenant.

5 The States Parties to the present Covenant may submit to the Committee observations on any comments that may be made in accordance with para 4 of this article.

Article 41

1 A State Party to the present Covenant may at any time declare under this article that it recognises the competence of the Committee to receive and consider

communications to the effect that a State Party claims that another State Party is not fulfilling its obligations under the present Covenant. Communications under this article may be received and considered only if submitted by a State Party which has made a declaration recognising in regard to itself the competence of the Committee. No communication shall be received by the Committee if it concerned a State Party which has not made such a declaration. Communications received under this article shall be dealt with in accordance with the following procedure:

(a) If a State Party to the present Covenant considers that another State Party is not giving effect to the provisions of the present Covenant, it may, by written communication, bring the matter to the attention of that State Party. Within three months after the receipt of communication, the receiving state shall afford the state which sent the communication an explanation or any other statement in writing clarifying the matter, which should include, to the extent possible and pertinent, reference to domestic procedures and remedies taken, pending, or available in the matter.

(b) If the matter is not adjusted to the satisfaction of other States Parties concerned within six months after the receipt by the receiving state of the initial communication, either state shall have the right to refer the matter to the Committee, by notice given to the Committee and to the other state.

(c) The Committee shall deal with a matter referred to it only after it has ascertained that all available domestic remedies have been invoked and exhausted in the matter, in conformity with the generally recognised principles of international law. This shall not be the rule where the application of the remedies is unreasonably prolonged.

(d) The Committee shall hold closed meetings when examining communications under this article.

(e) Subject to the provisions of sub-para (c), the Committee shall make available its good offices to the State Parties concerned with a view to a friendly solution of the matter on the basis of respect for human rights and fundamental freedoms as recognised in the present Covenant.

(f) In any matter referred to it, the Committee may call upon the States Parties concerned, referred to in sub-para (b), to supply any relevant information.

(g) The States Parties concerned, referred to in sub-para (b), shall have the right to be represented when the matter is being considered in the Committee and to make submissions orally and/or in writing.

(h) The Committee shall, within 12 months after the date of receipt of notice under sub-para (b), submit a report:

(i) If a solution within the terms of sub-para (e) is reached, the Committee shall confine its report to a brief statement of the facts and of the solution reached;

(ii) If a solution within the terms of sub-para (e) is not reached the Committee shall confine its report to a brief statement of the facts; the written submissions and record of the oral submissions made by the State Parties concerned shall be attached to the report.

In every matter, the report shall be communicated to the States Parties concerned.

2 The provisions of this article shall come into force when ten States Parties to the present Covenant have made declarations under para 1 of this article. Such declarations shall be deposited by the States Parties with the Secretary General of

the United Nations, who shall transmit copies thereof to the other States Parties. A declaration may be withdrawn at any time by notification to the Secretary General. Such a withdrawal shall not prejudice the consideration of any matter which is the subject of a communication already transmitted under this article; no further communication by any State Party shall be received after the notification of withdrawal of the declaration has been received by the Secretary General, unless the State Party concerned has made a new declaration.

Article 42

1

(a) If a matter referred to the Committee in accordance with Article 41 is not resolved to the satisfaction of the States Parties concerned, the Committee may, with the prior consent of the States Parties concerned, appoint an ad hoc Conciliation Commission (hereinafter referred to as the Commission). The good offices of the Commission shall be made available to the States Parties concerned with a view to an amicable solution of the matter on the basis of respect for the present Covenant;

(b) The Commission shall consist of five persons acceptable to the States Parties concerned. If the States Parties concerned fail to reach agreement within three months on all or part of the composition of the Commission the members of the Commission concerning whom no agreement has been reached shall be elected by secret ballot by a two-thirds majority vote of the Committee from among its members.

2   The members of the Commission shall serve in their personal capacity. They shall not be nationals of the States Parties concerned, or of a State not party to the present Covenant, or of a State Party which has not made a declaration under Article 41.

3   The Commission shall elect its own Chairman and adopt its own rules of procedure.

4   The meetings of the Commission shall normally be held at the Headquarters of the United Nations or at the United Nations Office in Geneva. However, they may be held at such other convenient places as the Commission may determine in consultation with the Secretary General of the United Nations and the States Parties concerned.

5   The Secretariat provided in accordance with Article 36 shall also service the commissions appointed under this article.

6   The information received and collated by the Committee shall be made available to the Commission and the Commission may call upon the States Parties concerned to supply any other relevant information.

7   When the Commission has fully considered the matter, but in any event not later than 12 months after having been seized of the matter, it shall submit to the Chairman of the Committee a report for communication to the States Parties concerned.

(a) If the Commission is unable to complete its consideration of the matter within twelve months, it shall confine its report to a brief statement of the status of its consideration of the matter.

(b) If an amicable solution to the matter on the basis of respect for human rights as recognised in the present Covenant is reached, the Commission shall confine its report to a brief statement of the facts and of the solution reached.

(c) If a solution within the terms of sub-para (b) is not reached, the Commission's report shall embody its findings on all questions of fact relevant to the issues between the States Parties concerned, and its views on the possibilities of an amicable solution of the matter. This report shall also contain the written submissions and a record of the oral submissions made by the States Parties concerned.

(d) If the Commission's report is submitted under sub-para (c), the States Parties concerned shall, within three months of the receipt of the report, notify the Chairman of the Committee whether or not they accept the contents of the report of the Commission.

8   The provisions of this article are without prejudice to the responsibilities of the Committee under Article 41.

9   The States Parties concerned shall share equally all the expenses of the members of the Commission in accordance with estimates to be provided by the Secretary General of the United Nations.

10   The Secretary General of the United Nations shall be empowered to pay the expenses of the members of the Commission, if necessary, before reimbursement by the States Parties concerned, in accordance with para 9 of this article.

Article 43

The members of the Committee, and of the *ad hoc* conciliation commissions which may be appointed under Article 42, shall be entitled to the facilities, privileges and immunities of experts on mission for the United Nations as laid down in the relevant sections of the Convention on the Privileges and Immunities of the United Nations.

Article 44

The provisions for the implementation of the present Covenant shall apply without prejudice to the procedures prescribed in the field of human rights by or under the constituent instruments and the conventions of the United Nations and of the specialised agencies and shall not prevent the States Parties to the present Covenant from having recourse to other procedures for settling a dispute in accordance with general or special international agreements in force between them.

Article 45

The Committee shall submit to the General Assembly of the United Nations through the Economic and Social Council, an annual report on its activities.

PART V

Article 46

Nothing in the present Covenant shall be interpreted as impairing the provisions of the Charter of the United Nations and of the constitutions of the specialised agencies which define the respective responsibilities of the various organs of the United Nations and of the specialised agencies in regard to the matters dealt with in the present Covenant.

Article 47

Nothing in the present Covenant shall be interpreted as impairing the inherent right of all peoples to enjoy and utilise fully and freely their natural wealth and resources.

PART VI

Article 48

1   The present Covenant is open for signature by any State Member of the United Nations or members of any of its specialised agencies, by any State Party to the Statute of the International Court of Justice, and by any other state which has been invited to the General Assembly of the United Nations to become a party to the present Covenant.

2   The present Covenant is subject to ratification. Instruments of ratification shall be deposited with the Secretary General of the United Nations.

3   The present Covenant shall be open to accession by any state referred to in para 1 of this article.

4   Accession shall be effected by the deposit of an instrument of accession with the Secretary General of the United Nations.

5   The Secretary General of the United nations shall inform all states which have signed the present Covenant or acceded to it of the deposit of each instrument of ratification or accession.

Article 49

1   The present Covenant shall enter into force three months after the date of the deposit with the Secretary General of the United Nations of the thirty-fifth instrument of ratification or instrument of accession.

2   For each state ratifying the present Covenant or acceding to it after the deposit of the thirty-fifth instrument of ratification or instrument of accession, the present Covenant shall enter into force three months after the date of the deposit of its own instrument of ratification or instrument of accession.

Article 50

The provisions of the present Covenant shall extend to all parts of federal states without any limitations or exceptions.

Article 51

1   Any State Party to the present Covenant may propose an amendment and file it with the Secretary General of the United Nations. The Secretary General shall thereupon communicate any proposed amendments to the State Parties to the present Covenant with a request that they notify him whether they favour a conference of States Parties for the purpose of considering and voting upon the proposals. In the event that at least one third of the States Parties favours such a conference, the Secretary General shall convene the conference under the auspices of the United Nations. Any amendments adopted by a majority of the States Parties present and voting at the conference shall be submitted to the General Assembly of the United Nations for approval.

2   Amendments shall come into force when they have been approved by the General Assembly of the United Nations and accepted by a two-thirds majority of the States Parties to the present Covenant in accordance with their respective constitutional processes.

3   When amendments come into force they shall be binding on those States Parties which have accepted them, other States Parties still being bound by the provisions of the present Covenant and any earlier amendment which they have accepted.

Article 52

Irrespective of the notifications made under Article 48, para 5, the Secretary General of the United Nations shall inform all states referred to in para 1 of the same article of the following particulars:

(a)   Signatures, ratifications and accessions under Article 48;

(b)   The date of the entry into force of the present Covenant under Article 49 and the date of the entry into force of any amendments under Article 51.

Article 53

1   The present Covenant, of which the Chinese, English, French, Russian and Spanish texts are equally authentic, shall be deposited in the archives of the United Nations.

2   The Secretary General of the United Nations shall transmit certified copies of the present Covenant to all States referred to in Article 48.

Report of the United Nations High Commissioner for Human Rights 1996

1   As evidenced by all too many examples of constant threats to and violations of the basic rights of individuals around the world, the human rights situation continues to be a daunting challenge for the international community. Considerable progress must yet be made in order to secure the realisation of human rights standards and a firmly established human rights culture. The ideals that inspired the Universal Declaration of Human Rights are as relevant today as they were nearly half a century ago when the community of nations pledged to promote universal respect for and observance of human rights and fundamental freedoms. Bearing this in mind, collective efforts must be made on the part of all human rights actors to uphold these aspirations and to implement fully the mechanisms that ensure their effective realisation.

2   The United Nations human rights programme, under the direction of the United Nations High Commissioner for Human Rights, is making notable advances in promoting the objectives of the Vienna Declaration and Programme of Action (A/CONF.157/24 (Part I), Chapter III), which serves as a blueprint for action in the international efforts to promote and protect human rights. During the last year, important progress has been made in expanding the ratification of international human rights instruments, supporting the establishment or strengthening of human rights national institutions and broadening technical co-operation projects. These efforts have yielded positive and concrete results.

3   An important feature of the High Commissioner's agenda has been the strengthening of human rights work in the field. As governments increasingly seek human rights assistance *in situ*, the United Nations human rights programme is able to reach out to more people and bring tangible results to the numerous and urgent needs in this regard. This serves as further proof of the spirit of co-operation that more and more symbolises how human rights are being addressed today.

4   Similarly, the High Commissioner has assertively sought to secure that economic, social and cultural rights, and particularly the right to development, acquire a higher profile within the framework of United Nations human rights efforts, in the spirit of the Vienna Declaration and Programme of Action, which proclaimed that all human rights are universal, indivisible and interdependent and interrelated.

5   During his tenure, the High Commissioner has encouraged governments and other human rights actors to attach to the consideration of human rights greater prominence and stature. Through dialogue with member states, through co-ordination with the United Nations agencies that support human rights efforts, through permanent contact with regional forums, academic institutions

and the leadership of the main international financial institutions, the High Commissioner has sought to ensure that the issue of human rights become a constant in the thinking and actions of the political and economic forces that govern or influence events globally.

6   The United Nations human rights programme is indeed ambitious and must be implemented through partnership. Member states and others are aware of the various obstacles that have been surmounted to accomplish what thus far has been achieved. However, more needs to be done to achieve further progress. The High Commissioner is firmly determined to work closely with all partners in order to ensure these objectives.

7   It should be recalled that human rights, together with peace and security, and development, constitute the triad upon which the United Nations was founded. Member states should entrust the High Commissioner with invigorating the human rights programme in order to maintain the strength of this triad and to preserve the fundamental role envisioned for human rights by the founders of the United Nations. This should be carefully reflected upon as both the fiftieth anniversary of the Universal Declaration of Human Rights and the five-year review on the implementation of the Vienna Declaration and Programme of Action draw near.

8   The Vienna Declaration and Programme of Action provides the guidelines for the United Nations human rights programme. The methods and means being implemented are reflected throughout the present report. However, detailed information concerning the ways in which the recommendations adopted by the World Conference on Human Rights are being put into effect is also contained in other reports dealing with human rights submitted to the General Assembly at its fifty-first session.

9   The following fundamental principles continue to be the basis of the High Commissioner's activities aimed at enhancing international co-operation in the field of human rights: (a) the primary responsibility for the promotion and protection of human rights rests with governments; (b) the promotion and protection of all human rights is a legitimate concern of the international community; (c) the international community should foster processes leading towards a better implementation of human rights and the strengthening of democracy and the rule of law, and should take all necessary measures to prevent human rights abuses and to eradicate the gravest human rights violations; (d) the international protection and promotion of human rights is effective only if based on the principle of the indivisibility and equal value of all human rights – civil, cultural, economic, political and social, including the right to development; (e) the interdependence between democracy, development and respect for human rights, underlined by the World Conference on Human Rights, offers a prospect of harmonious national and international activity; (f) the international and regional systems of human rights protection are complementary and should support each other; and (g) national institutions, non-governmental organisations, academic institutions and grass-roots initiatives should be fully accepted as natural human rights advocates and partners in international co-operation for human rights.

...

33   The importance placed on strengthening the implementation of human rights world-wide by the General Assembly, the Commission on Human Rights, country and thematic special *rapporteurs*, working groups and treaty bodies has never been more clear. The globalisation of human rights as seen by their growing relevance for overall development trends world-wide, prompts the

international community to perceive making human rights a reality as one of its primary concerns. This attitude is strengthened by developments in countries that have recently chosen the challenging way to sustainable development through democracy and human rights. Already these countries are beginning to enjoy the benefits of this policy in the form of economic progress, political consolidation, and social stability. Although the adoption of legislation consistent with international standards is of utmost importance, it is the application of law which matters most.

34 The debate during the fifty-second session of the Commission on Human Rights has confirmed the overwhelming trend to human rights, democracy and development in the contemporary world. Adopted resolutions and decisions refer to positive developments in the current world human rights record. International exchange, promoted and facilitated by human rights organs and bodies, contributes to efforts made by governments and civil society. The value of the expertise of others, be it international organisations, governments, non-governmental organisations or local communities, cannot be overestimated.

35 However, as in previous years, the Commission continued to express its concern about (a) obstacles to the enjoyment of all human rights by all; (b) serious human rights violations, and (c) difficult human rights situations in a relatively large number of countries. Again, the Commission in its resolutions drew the attention of governments, the United Nations system and the general public to these issues. The Commission called for action with regard to impunity; racism and xenophobia; discrimination against women; ethnic and religious intolerance; mass exoduses and refugee flows; armed conflicts and terrorism and the lack of the rule of law as major obstacles to human rights. The Commission continued to alert the international community to extrajudicial, summary or arbitrary executions; torture and enforced disappearance; arbitrary detention; violence against women, children and vulnerable groups; the problem of internally displaced persons, extreme poverty and problems related to sustainable development, international debt, etc. Under the agenda item related to the question of violations of human rights and fundamental freedoms in any part of the world, with particular reference to colonial and other dependent countries and territories, the Commission expressed its concern about the human rights situation in Afghanistan, Burundi, Cyprus, Cuba, Equatorial Guinea, Haiti, the Islamic Republic of Iran, Iraq, Myanmar, Nigeria, the Papua New Guinea island of Bougainville, the Republic of Bosnia and Herzegovina, the Republic of Croatia and the Federal Republic of Yugoslavia (Serbia and Montenegro), Rwanda, southern Lebanon and the Western Bekaa, the Sudan and Zaire. Furthermore, the Commission adopted the Chairman's statements on the situation of human rights in Colombia, Liberia, East Timor and the Republic of Chechnya of the Russian Federation. Under agenda item 4, the Commission considered violations of human rights in the occupied Arab territories, including Palestine, human rights in the occupied Syrian Golan, and Israeli settlements in the occupied Arab territories, and under agenda item 9 the situation in occupied Palestine and the question of Western Sahara. In addition, various thematic procedures, in their reports to the Commission, pointed out serious human rights problems in a number of countries and made recommendations in that regard.

36 Concern continues to be expressed by the Commission on Human Rights when governments either deny or fail to lend their full co-operation to the Commission or its mechanisms. Similarly, the Commission expressed concern in its Resolution 1996/70 of 23 April 1996 with regard to continued reports of intimidation and reprisals against private individuals and groups who seek such co-operation. The High Commissioner shares those concerns.

37 Many human rights activists raise the problem of infringements upon their personal security and freedom of action. In this context, the High Commissioner supports endeavours aimed at the finalisation of the draft declaration on the right and responsibility of individuals, groups and organs of society to promote and protect universally recognised human rights and fundamental freedoms. The Commission on Human Rights, in its Resolution 1996/81 of 23 April 1996, urged an open-ended working group to make every effort to complete work on this draft declaration.

38 The High Commissioner raises issues related to the implementation of human rights in his dialogue with governments, stressing the need for consideration of the recommendations adopted by the Commission and made by its mechanisms. It is to be pointed out that in many cases the response of governments indicates their willingness to react constructively to the voice of the international community. The High Commissioner regrets that his appeals do not always bring expected results. In keeping with his mandate and guided by his responsibility to promote and protect human rights for everyone, the High Commissioner will continue to take up particular cases and, if appropriate, use direct contact with governments, and other relevant parties, in order to obtain concrete results.

...

V CHALLENGES TO HUMAN RIGHTS

A Equality and non-discrimination

1 Elimination of racial discrimination

71 In accordance with General Assembly Resolution 48/91 of 20 December 1993, in which the Assembly proclaimed the Third Decade to Combat Racism and Racial Discrimination, the High Commissioner/Centre for Human Rights organised a seminar to assess the implementation of the International Convention on the Elimination of All Forms of Racial Discrimination, with particular reference to Articles 4 and 6. The seminar was held at Geneva from 9 to 13 September 1996.

72 In his introductory statement, the High Commissioner focused on the discrimination of immigrants, refugees and ethnic minorities and the propaganda of racism and anti-semitism through the modern media, including the Internet. The participants expressed their concern about the use of media for the dissemination of racist ideas and incitement to acts of violence and stressed the necessity of a vigorous action, at the international and national levels, against such phenomena. In relation to the Internet, the seminar suggested that the High Commissioner/Centre for Human Rights hold a further seminar in co-operation with Internet service providers to discuss how to prevent racist information on the Internet. The seminar strongly underlined the importance of education as a significant means of preventing and eradicating racism and racial discrimination and of creating awareness of human rights principles, particularly among young people, and recommended to States parties that they take measures in that regard.

2 Women

73 In its Resolution 1996/22 of 19 April 1996, the Commission on Human Rights welcomed that the persons chairing the human rights treaty bodies had emphasised that the enjoyment of human rights by women should be closely monitored by each treaty body within the competence of its mandate, and recommended that the reporting guidelines adopted by each treaty body should be amended to identify gender-specific information that should be provided by

State parties in their reports. Subsequently, the treaty-based bodies are in the process of revising or preparing new sets of guidelines taking this recommendation into account. On the basis of analysis of gender-related data in State reports, the Division for the Advancement of Women is continuing to formulate methodologies by which the treaty-based bodies might systematically and routinely incorporate a gender perspective in their monitoring activities.

74 The Special *Rapporteur* on violence against women, Ms Radhika Coomaraswamy, visited Poland in May 1996, to study in depth the causes and consequences of the issue of trafficking and forced prostitution of women in the eastern European region. This visit was in accordance with para 7 of General Assembly Resolution 50/167 of 22 December 1995 on traffic in women and girls.

75 In July 1996 the Special *Rapporteur* on violence against women visited Brazil on the issue of domestic violence against women. The Special Rapporteur submitted to the Commission on Human Rights at its fifty-second session a framework for model legislation on domestic violence to be considered by governments (E/CN4/1996/53/Add 2).

76 The United Nations Population Fund (UNFPA), the High Commissioner/Centre for Human Rights and the Division for the Advancement of Women will jointly organise in December 1996 a round table on ways in which the recommendations of recent world conferences concerning women's reproductive and health rights might be integrated into the human rights monitoring and reporting procedures.

All six treaty bodies will be invited to be represented at the round table.

3   *Children*

77 The implementation of the Convention on the Rights of the Child represents the greatest hope for the future of children, particularly for the world's one billion poor children. The Convention, the most widely ratified human rights treaty, deserves great support as the clear expression of what the international community has adopted as standards for the treatment of children. Only a handful of countries have yet to ratify the Convention.

78 In 1995, the High Commissioner outlined a precise strategy to support the work of the Committee on the Rights of the Child. This strategy could serve as an example of how similar support to other treaty bodies could be provided, making it possible for them to carry out their own responsibilities more effectively. Through this plan of action, the High Commissioner is seeking to provide the Committee with the resources necessary to strengthen its monitoring activities and for the implementation of its recommendations: staff, database and information sharing, and co-operation with the relevant United Nations programmes and agencies, in particular UNICEF.

79 In his address to the World Congress against the Commercial Sexual Exploitation of Children, held at Stockholm from 26 to 30 August 1996, the High Commissioner expressed the hope that global awareness of crimes committed against children would strengthen action taken towards ending them. He proposed four concrete ways to achieve change: the participation of children themselves in campaigns to end their exploitation, thereby increasing the children's own awareness of their rights; making adults familiar with children's rights; legal reforms to protect children and to punish violators of children's rights; and co-operation at all levels to combat the problem of commercial sexual exploitation. The Special *Rapporteur* on the sale of children, child prostitution and child pornography, Ms Ofelia Calcetas-Santos, visited the Czech Republic on the issue of the sale of children and child prostitution and pornography.

80 In a follow-up to specific recommendations of the Committee on the Rights of the Child, a mission to formulate a project on the administration of juvenile justice was undertaken by the High Commissioner/Centre for Human Rights in Vietnam in March 1996, with the participation of a member of the Committee. A needs assessment mission on the same subject took place in July 1996 in the Philippines, also following a recommendation of the Committee on the Rights of the Child.

4   Minorities

81 At its meeting from 30 April to 3 May 1996, the Working Group on Minorities considered and adopted recommendations on the following issues: the promotion and practical realisation of the Declaration on the Rights of Persons Belonging to National or Ethnic, Religious and Linguistic Minorities; the examination of possible solutions to problems involving minorities, including the promotion of mutual understanding between and among minorities and governments; and the recommendation of further measures for the promotion and protection of the rights of persons belonging to national or ethnic, religious and linguistic minorities (see E/CN4/Sub 2/1996/28).

82 In his introductory statement, the High Commissioner welcomed the growing commitment of the international community to the protection of minorities. A programme of international activities should focus on the translation of international standards into domestic law and practice and embrace, inter alia, a world-wide campaign for the promotion of the Declaration on the Rights of Persons Belonging to National or Ethnic, Religious and Linguistic Minorities; education on rights of persons belonging to minorities and the creation of a climate of tolerance and understanding between different communities; setting up commissions for community relations to reinforce existing inter-group understanding.

83 The High Commissioner organised an inter-agency consultation on minorities on 21 August 1996 in Geneva. The rationale for the consultation was to exchange information on minority-related activities, to share ideas and to discuss future collaboration in the field of minority protection. Welcoming this initiative, the participants decided to continue their consultations on a regular basis.

5   Indigenous people

84 The international community renewed its commitment to the economic, social and cultural well-being of indigenous people and the full enjoyment of their rights by proclaiming the period 1995–2004 as the International Decade of the World's Indigenous People. Within the framework of the Programme of Activities as adopted by the General Assembly in the annex to its resolution 50/157 of 21 December 1995, the Advisory Group of the Co-ordinator of the Decade developed guidelines and a questionnaire for the submission of requests for financial assistance from the Voluntary Fund for the International Decade of the World's Indigenous People. It recommended that the High Commissioner/ Centre for Human Rights give priority to the following proposals: to organise a second international workshop on the establishment of a permanent forum for indigenous people within the United Nations; to develop a fellowship programme to provide indigenous people with training and practical experience in the field of human rights and the United Nations system; to sponsor, in conjunction with UNESCO, a human rights training programme for official delegates of the Governments of Peru and Ecuador and indigenous representatives from those countries; and to provide technical support for an information workshop on the draft declaration of the rights of indigenous peoples, as proposed by the Government of Fiji. Finally, it recommended that the necessary assistance should be provided to the implementation of an indigenous

project aimed at establishing a Central and East Africa regional office for indigenous peoples. The information workshop in Fiji has already taken place while the other projects are currently being developed.

85   From 24 to 28 March 1996, the government of Canada hosted a land rights seminar held at Whitehorse, Yukon, where a discussion on the negotiation process and legal arrangements for the demarcation, titling and protection of lands took place. It was recommended that the United Nations and its specialised agencies should consider providing technical assistance to states and indigenous people to contribute to the resolution of land claims.

86   The fourteenth session of the Working Group on Indigenous Populations was held from 29 July to 2 August 1996 and attracted 721 participants. It focused part of its deliberations on the issue of health and, in this regard, co-operated closely with WHO. The ideas and suggestions brought forward will, where possible, be incorporated in the WHO programme.

87   In its Resolution 50/157, the General Assembly recommended that, with regard to the issue of the establishment of a permanent forum for indigenous people within the United Nations, the Secretary General undertake a review of the existing mechanisms, procedures and programmes within the United Nations relating to indigenous people, and report to the Assembly at its fifty-first session. Although the findings of the review are encouraging (see A/51/493), it is clear that there is a lack of adequate procedures and mechanisms. The High Commissioner considers the question concerning the establishment of a permanent forum for indigenous people within the United Nations system to be one of the core issues in relation to the International Decade of the World's Indigenous People. The dialogue on this issue will continue during the second workshop that will be hosted by the government of Chile.

88   The High Commissioner calls upon the international community to recognise, protect and promote the rights of indigenous people in order to achieve full participation of this sector of the population in political, economic and social life at all levels of society. It is essential that this participation be based on full respect for languages, cultures, traditions and forms of social organisation of indigenous people.

6   *People infected by the human immunodeficiency virus*

89   The High Commissioner organised in conjunction with the Joint United Nations Programme on HIV/AIDS (UNAIDS) a Second International Consultation on HIV/AIDS and Human Rights at Geneva from 23 to 25 September 1996. The Consultation was attended by some 35 participants representing governments, human rights non-governmental organisations, AIDS service organisations, academia, networks of people living with HIV/AIDS, and United Nations system agencies and programmes.

90   The final document contains concrete, action-oriented strategy guidelines, intended primarily for governments, regarding the promotion of and the respect for human rights in the context of HIV/AIDS. The guidelines, set out in the framework of applicable international human rights standards, address areas of, *inter alia*, labour, education, immigration, law review and reform, and the empowerment of vulnerable groups. The Consultation also called for the creation of a Special *Rapporteur* of the Commission on Human Rights to monitor and receive communications regarding violations of human rights relating to AIDS.

B   Extrajudicial, summary or arbitrary executions

91   The eradication of extrajudicial, summary or arbitrary executions remains a matter of the highest priority in the protection of human rights. In its Resolution

1996/74 of 23 April 1996, the Commission on Human Rights reiterated its strong condemnation for the practice of such executions and demanded that all governments ensure that it be brought to an end. The High Commissioner pays particular attention to situations of serious concern in this context, and to situations where early action may have a preventive effect.

92   In his interim report to the General Assembly on extrajudicial, summary or arbitrary executions (A/51/457, annex), the Special *Rapporteur*, Mr Bacre Waly Ndiaye, offers an overview of the action undertaken during his years in office. The Special *Rapporteur* concludes that the number of violations of the right to life has not decreased in the last four years, and that women, children and the elderly have not been spared. Such violations have ranged from death threats, death in custody and due to attacks by security forces, death resulting from armed conflicts to executions imposed after unfair trials. In his report, the Special *Rapporteur* issues recommendations to strengthen respect for the right to life, calling upon all states to conduct exhaustive and impartial investigations into all allegations of violations of this right, and to bring to justice those responsible. Moreover, he considers that effective measures should be taken to avoid the recurrence of such violations.

C   Torture

93   In April 1996, only one month before the annual meeting of its Board of Trustees, the United Nations Voluntary Fund for Victims of Torture was facing an alarming financial situation. The total amount of contributions received by the fund was $333,000, whereas the amount requested for assistance was more than $5 million. The High Commissioner therefore made an appeal at the fifty-second session of the Commission on Human Rights urging all governments to contribute to the fund. Subsequently, over $2 million was received for the fund's activities.

94   The Board recommended that $2,535,500 be granted to 96 requests, corresponding to the total amount available. The projects scrutinised provide medical, psychological, social and legal assistance to victims of torture and their relatives. They are implemented by non-governmental organisations and specialised centres located in 60 countries world-wide.

D   Enforced disappearances

95   The systematic practice of acts of enforced disappearance became known in the early 1970s as a phenomenon prevalent in a relatively small number of countries. Since then, it has, unfortunately, spread to many regions of the world, occurring primarily in the context of internal armed conflict and ethnic strife. The Commission on Human Rights, in its Resolution 1996/30 of 19 April 1996, reiterated its deep concern about that phenomenon and called upon governments to establish appropriate structures and mechanisms aimed at preventing the occurrence of involuntary disappearances in their countries and at clarifying already existing cases. States should take effective measures to implement the principles of the Declaration on the Protection of All Persons from Enforced Disappearance, and to that end take action at the national and regional levels and in co-operation with the United Nations. The technical co-operation programme is available with regard to reform of legislation and training in this respect (see paras 43–47 above).

E   Internally displaced persons

96   A compilation and analysis of legal norms pertaining to the protection and assistance needs of internally displaced persons was presented to the Commission on Human Rights by the representative of the Secretary General on

internally displaced persons, Mr Francis Deng (E/CN4/1996/52/Add 2). This compilation examines the extent to which existing provisions of international human rights law and humanitarian law provide adequate coverage for the protection and assistance needs of the internally displaced, and also examines refugee law for purposes of analogy. In accordance with the recommendations by the General Assembly and the Commission, the representative is in the process of developing a body of guiding principles, based on the aforementioned compilation, with a view to addressing displacement in all its stages.

97   Ever since it started in January 1995, the High Commissioner and the Centre for Human Rights have participated in the overall process of the Conference on Refugees, Returnees, Displaced Persons and Related Migratory Movements in the Commonwealth of Independent States and Relevant Neighbouring States, which was organised by UNHCR, the International Organisation on Migration (IOM) and OSCE and held at Geneva on 30 and 31 May 1996. The High Commissioner/Centre maintained a close working relation with the Conference secretariat by sharing its expertise and providing background materials as well as contributions in the area of human rights and on the specific issues of forced displacement, with a view to ensuring that commitments undertaken under international human rights and humanitarian law standards were accurately reflected in the final document of the Conference. The United Nations human rights programme is contributing to the implementation of the programme of action adopted by the Conference.

...

122 The year 1998 will be important for human rights. Two years before the dawn of the next millennium, the international community will celebrate the fiftieth anniversary of its first-ever proclamation of rights and freedoms of the individual. In 1948, the international community agreed upon the Universal Declaration of Human Rights – a common standard of achievement for all peoples and all nations, which gave rise to a vigorous development of international promotion and protection of these rights. In order to respond to the hopes of the drafters of the Declaration and to generations of its advocates all over the world, the celebration of its fiftieth anniversary should be used for advancement of human rights.

123 The World Conference on Human Rights provided a means for reaching this objective by linking the fiftieth anniversary of the Universal Declaration with the five-year review of the implementation of the Vienna Declaration and Programme of Action. It requested the Secretary General: '... to invite on the occasion of the fiftieth anniversary of the Universal Declaration of Human Rights all States, all organs and agencies of the United Nations system related to human rights, to report to him on the progress made in the implementation of the present Declaration and to submit a report to the General Assembly at its fifty-third session, through the Commission on Human Rights and the Economic and Social Council. Likewise, regional, and as appropriate, national human rights institutions, as well as non-governmental organisations, may present their views to the Secretary General on the progress made in the implementation of the present Declaration.' The Commission on Human Rights, in its resolution 1996/42 of 19 April 1996 on the preparation for the 50th anniversary of the Universal Declaration of Human Rights, requested the High Commissioner to co-ordinate the preparations for the 50th anniversary of the Universal Declaration, bearing in mind provisions of the Vienna Declaration and Programme of Action for evaluation and follow-up.

124 The celebration of the 50th anniversary of the Universal Declaration and review of the implementation of the Vienna Declaration and Programme of

Action should provide the opportunity: (a) to strengthen the promotion and protection of human rights world-wide; (b) to review and assess the progress that has been made in the field of human rights since the adoption of the Universal Declaration; (c) to review the progress made in the implementation of the Vienna Declaration and Programme of Action; and (d) to outline or update human rights programmes to meet current and future challenges. This should be achieved through joint efforts of the international community. Let us call 1998 'Human Rights Year'.

125 All sectors of the human rights constituency, governments, United Nations agencies and programmes, international and regional organisations, academic institutions, non-governmental organisations and other parts of civil society, media and private enterprises, are called upon to take initiatives aimed at the commemoration of the fiftieth anniversary of the Universal Declaration of Human Rights. This should be a global movement giving evidence that human rights reflect not only hopes and aspirations but also essential interests and legitimate demands of all people on all continents. The international community should use 1998 to give new impetus to human rights, reflecting the vision of the next century.

126 The High Commissioner will facilitate co-operation between various initiatives aimed at the commemoration of the fiftieth anniversary of the Universal Declaration. To that end, the High Commissioner/Centre has initiated the United Nations inter-agency consultations that will provide a continuing forum throughout 1997 and 1998. In 1997, the High Commissioner intends to undertake sectoral consultations with regional organisations, non-governmental organisations, academic institutions, and others to discuss the preparations for the anniversary. In 1998, the Commission on Human Rights and the Economic and Social Council will be the United Nations focal points for the commemoration which should culminate on 10 December 1998. The General Assembly at its fifty-first session may wish to adopt a decision convening a ceremonial meeting for that day.

127 The review of the progress in the implementation of the Vienna Declaration and Programme of Action during the first five years since its adoption should include a profound analysis of achievements in and obstacles to the full realisation of the recommendations adopted at Vienna. A frank and open debate will be of paramount importance for future efforts aimed at the promotion and protection of human rights. It is useful to identify well in advance which role the Commission on Human Rights, the Economic and Social Council and the General Assembly should play in reviewing the implementation of the Vienna Declaration and Programme of Action. Governments, United Nations agencies and programmes, international organisations and non-governmental organisations are encouraged to launch preparations for the presentation of their reports and views on the progress made in the implementation of the Vienna Declaration and Programme of Action, in accordance with para 100 of that document (see para 123 above).

128 The Commission on Human Rights may wish to undertake in 1998 an initial evaluation of the implementation of the Vienna Declaration and Programme of Action. The results of that debate would provide input to the work of the Economic and Social Council and the General Assembly. This exchange would be enhanced considerably if held during a high-level segment of the Commission.

129 The Economic and Social Council, in its Decision 1996/283 of 24 July 1996, endorsed the recommendation of the Commission on Human Rights Resolution

1996/78 of 23 April 1996 to devote the co-ordination segment of its session in 1998 to the co-ordinated follow-up to, and implementation of the Vienna Declaration and Programme of Action as part of the overall co-ordinated follow-up to major United Nations conferences. This would be an excellent occasion to analyse the implementation of the Vienna Declaration and Programme of Action by the United Nations system.

130 The General Assembly may also wish to carry out in 1998 a comprehensive analysis of the progress achieved in the implementation of the Vienna Declaration and Programme of Action and to consider recommendations made by the Commission on Human Rights and the Economic and Social Council. Thus, the report of the Secretary General to the General Assembly concerning the implementation of the Vienna Declaration and Programme of Action will highlight the activities of all actors involved, including international and regional organisations, that are not parts of the United Nations system, and civil society.

131 A multifaceted and timely preparation of the celebration of the fiftieth anniversary of the Universal Declaration and of the review of the implementation of the Vienna Declaration and Programme of Action will produce an important contribution to the promotion and protection of human rights. A spirit of solidarity and co-operation should guide the international community in this endeavour.[4]

16.2.2 Specialised international agreements

The two Covenants adopted in 1966 set down a number of general rights which apply equally to all human beings. In addition to these two general agreements there exists an increasing number of specialised agreements either directed to the protection of particular rights or particular categories of individual. The specialised conventions have often been the work of the specialised agencies of the UN. For example, the International Labour Organisation has played an important role in addressing the issue of workers' rights and employment conditions and has been responsible for the adoption of a number of conventions dealing with such things as freedom of association.

One of the earliest specialised agreements actually pre-dates UDHR. The Slavery Convention 1926 outlaws slavery and the slave trade and makes such activities subject to the universal jurisdiction of states. The Slavery Convention was followed by the Forced Labour Convention 1930. Since 1948 there have been a considerable number of specialised agreements among the most significant of which are:

- Genocide Convention 1949, which was the first human rights treaty to be adopted under the auspices of the UN;
- Convention on the Status of Refugees 1951;
- Convention on the Suppression and Punishment of the Crime of Apartheid 1973;
- Convention against Torture and Other Cruel Inhuman or Degrading Treatment or Punishment 1984;
- Convention on the Rights of the Child 1989.

---

4   *Report of the United Nations High Commissioner for Human Rights* (A/51/36) 18 October 1996.

With regard to discrimination on grounds of sex, ECOSOC established a Commission on the Status of Women in 1946, which was largely responsible for the adoption of the Convention on the Political Rights of Women 1952 and the Convention on Elimination of all forms of Discrimination against Women 1979. The convention establishes a UN Committee on the Elimination of Discrimination against Women which is charged with monitoring the observance and implementation of the conventions provisions.

As far as racial discrimination is concerned, the Convention on the Elimination of all Forms of Racial Discrimination 1966, which entered into force in 1969, prohibits States from engaging in acts or practices which involve the 'distinction, exclusion, restriction or preference based on race, colour, descent, or national or ethnic origin' and which have the purpose or effect 'of nullifying or impairing the recognition, enjoyment or exercise, on an equal footing, of human rights and fundamental freedoms in the political, economic, social, cultural or any other field of public life'. The convention does not refer to discrimination on grounds of religion or nationality, which have been the subject of UN resolutions but regarding which there is no specific treaty. Article 1(4) of the convention expressly permits action taken to advance the interests of particular groups in order to secure their equal rights, and would cover instances of so-called 'affirmative action' or 'positive discrimination'. There exists a UN Committee on the Elimination of Racial Discrimination which monitors observance of the convention.

16.2.3 Regional agreements

16.2.3.1 European Convention for the Protection of Human Rights and Fundamental Freedoms 1950

The first regional agreement pertaining to the protection of human rights was the European Convention for the Protection of Human Rights and Fundamental Freedoms 1950 (ECHR), which was signed by the member states of the Council of Europe at Rome on 4 November 1950 and which entered into force in 1953.

ECHR went far beyond UDHR in that it imposed binding obligations on the parties to provide effective domestic remedies in regard to a number of rights, and it refined the definition of such rights. It also established the European Commission of Human Rights to investigate and report on violations of human rights at the instigation of State Parties, or, with the express prior consent of individual states, upon petition of any person, NGO, or groups of individuals within that state's jurisdiction. The Convention also provides for a European Court of Human Rights with compulsory jurisdiction. This was set up in 1959 after eight states had accepted its compulsory jurisdiction.

ECHR was followed later by the European Social Charter 1961, which entered into force in 1965. The Social Charter deals with the social, economic and cultural rights, including the right to work, the right to fair remuneration, the right to bargain collectively and the right to social security. The Social Charter puts claims rather than restrictions on States, and the enforcement machinery is very different from that created under ECHR. The European Social Charter 1961 must be distinguished from the Social Chapter of the Treaty on European Union (the Maastricht Treaty).

More recently the member states of the Council of Europe adopted the European Convention for the Prevention of Torture and Inhuman or Degrading Treatment or Punishment 1987, which entered into force in 1989. The convention establishes a European Committee for the Prevention of Torture which is charged with monitoring the treatment of those deprived of their liberty and envisages a system of inspections of prisons and other places of detention. The convention aims to encourage observance of its provisions rather than to provide formal enforcement mechanisms. Torture and other forms of degrading or inhuman treatment are already prohibited under Article 3 of the ECHR.

16.2.3.2 Other regional agreements

A number of other regional organisations have adopted conventions relating to human rights: The American Declaration of the Rights and Duties of Man of 1948, which was closely modelled on UDHR, was followed by the Protocol to the Charter of the Organisation of American States 1967, which established the Inter-American Commission on Human Rights as a principal organ of the OAS with the function of promoting respect for human rights. Two years later the Inter-American Convention on Human Rights 1969 was adopted, which details the rights to be observed and provides for an Inter-American Court of Human Rights.

The Organisation of African Unity has adopted the African Charter on Human and Peoples' Rights 1981. State parties are placed under an obligation to adopt measures to give effect to the rights contained in the charter rather than a strict obligation to observe the rights contained. The substantive provisions of this charter differ from other general human rights treaties in that far greater emphasis is placed on peoples' rights. The charter establishes an African Commission on Human and Peoples' Rights which is given responsibility for the promotion of such rights.

Discussions have also taken place with a view to establishing other regional agreements – for example, among the members of the Arab League and within the region of south Asia.

It is also worth noting here certain provisions of the Helsinki Declaration 1975, adopted by the Conference on Security and Co-operation in Europe. Although, as has previously been stated, this declaration was expressed not to be legally binding, Part VII of the declaration pledged respect for fundamental freedoms and human rights. Certain human rights are also dealt with in other more general treaties, for example, the Treaty of Rome 1957.

16.2.4 Customary rules

A significant number of the provisions contained in the various human rights treaties are now considered to be rules of customary international law. In particular, many of the provisions of UDHR, which as a UN resolution is not binding *per se*, have come to be regarded as expressing customary rules. An important case in this respect is *Filartiga v Pena-Irala* (1980), which was heard by a US court. The defendant in the case was a former chief of police in Asuncion, Paraguay, and the case was brought by two Paraguayan nationals who alleged that Pena-Irala had tortured to death a member of their family. In the course of giving judgment, the court had cause to consider whether the torture violated customary international law, and it cited with approval the view that UDHR had become, *in toto*, a part of binding, international customary law. The Third Restatement of US Foreign Relations Law (1987), which commands considerable respect as a statement of general international law, indicates in para 702 that the following practices, where carried out by or on behalf of states, constitute a violation of customary international law:

- genocide;
- slavery;
- murder or causing the disappearance of individuals (this would not include executions imposed following a fair trial);
- torture and other cruel, inhuman or degrading treatment;
- prolonged arbitrary detention;
- systematic racial discrimination.

It is suggested that such violations should be considered to be breaches of *jus cogens* and that the customary rules protecting human rights are binding *erga omnes*. Some support for this view is found in the judgment of the ICJ in the *Barcelona Traction* case (1970) in which the court indicated that certain obligations deriving from the outlawing of acts of aggression and genocide and 'from the principles and rules concerning basic rights of the human person including protection from slavery and racial discrimination' were owed to the international community as a whole and could be considered obligations *erga omnes*. In addition, the Restatement suggests that consistent gross violations of other generally recognised human rights would be contrary to customary international law even if isolated violations of such rights was not prohibited except by treaty. The Restatement suggests that a gross violation is one which is particularly shocking given its particular context.

16.3   Third generation human rights

It has already been indicated that international law distinguishes between civil and political rights and economic, social and cultural rights. The former are often referred to as 'first generation' rights and the latter as 'second generation' rights. According to the classical justification of human rights, which argued that such rights as existed were inherent in the existence of a human being, any rights belonging to entities other than human beings could not be considered as 'human rights' and their justification would have to be found elsewhere. However, with the development of rights such as those of assembly and association, which are possessed by individuals but which can only be asserted by collections of individuals, it has become clear that collective rights are recognised by the international community. From this, the idea of peoples' rights has followed. Such rights are seen as belonging to peoples rather than individuals, and the principal two such rights are the right to self-determination and the right to development. These rights are often referred to in the literature as 'third generation' rights. The right to development is discussed in Chapter 17 in the context of the international law governing economic relations. In this chapter, discussion is limited to the right of self-determination. In addition to these peoples' rights, there is a growing argument about the existence and nature of a right to a decent, viable, healthy and sustainable environment, and such argument will be discussed in Chapter 17.

16.3.1 The right to self-determination

Although the principle of self-determination has long been recognised as a political concept, it has only assumed the status of a legal right since 1945. It remains controversial because it is not always easy clearly to identify who possesses the right or what implementation of the right entails. The UN Charter refers to the principle of 'equal rights and self-determination of peoples' in Article 1(2), but UDHR make no specific mention of self-determination, although Article 21 provides that:

(1) everyone has the right to take part in the government of his country, directly or through freely chosen representatives; ...

(3) the will of the people shall be the basis of the authority of government ...

Events during the 1950s in colonial territories brought the issue of self-determination to the forefront of discussion, and in 1960 a UN General Assembly including a number of newly independent states adopted the Declaration on the Granting of Independence to Colonial Territories and Peoples which states that:

1 the subjection of peoples to alien subjugation, domination and exploitation constitutes a denial of fundamental human rights, is contrary to the Charter of the United Nations and is an impediment to the promotion of world peace and co-operation;

2 all peoples have the right to self determination; by virtue of that right they freely determine their political status and freely pursue their economic, social and cultural development;'

The provisions of para 2 were contained in the common Article 1 of both ICPR and ICESCR and, since 1966, recognition of the right of peoples to self-determination has been repeated in a number of resolutions and treaties. In the *Western Sahara* case (1975) the ICJ confirmed that the right was one recognised by international law.

The principle of self-determination certainly now seems to be a part of international law, but the problem remains as to who or what constitutes a people capable of possessing and asserting the right. The legal concept was developed during the period of de-colonisation, when it was easier to identify peoples who did not enjoy full rights to determine their own economic, social and cultural development because of the presence of the colonial government. From the 1970s onwards, the right has been asserted by groups wishing to establish a state in part of the territory of an existing state or states, and this has created problems which have yet to be resolved. Article 27 of the ICPR provides that:

In those states in which ethnic, religious or linguistic minorities exist, persons belonging to such minorities shall not be denied the right, in community with the other members of their group, to enjoy their own culture, to profess and practise their own religion, or to use their own language.

This article certainly appears to recognise a peoples' right and echoes some of the minority protection measures that were adopted after World War One, but it does not provide a full-blown right of self-determination.

The question of the existence of such a right in a non-colonial situation was considered by the Badinter Arbitration Committee, which was established by the European Union in August 1991 to consider various questions of law arising from events in former Yugoslavia. One of the questions presented was whether the Serbs living in Bosnia and Croatia had the right to self-determination. The Arbitration Committee, after making a study of the international law regarding the issue, came to four main conclusions:

1   The right to self-determination must not involve changes to existing frontiers at the time of independence except where the states concerned agree otherwise;

2   Where there are two or more groups within a state constituting one or more ethnic, religious or language communities, they have the right to recognition of their identity under international law;

3   Article 1 of the two 1966 Covenants establishes that the principle of the right of self-determination serves to safeguard human rights. By virtue of that right every individual may choose to belong to whatever ethnic, religious or language community he or she wishes;

4   The Serbian population in Croatia and Bosnia is entitled to the rights accorded minorities and such rights must be protected by the governments of Croatia and Bosnia.

The decision is important, as it is one of the few, if not the only, occasions in which an international tribunal has been called upon to consider whether a particular group has a right of self-determination and the consequence of that right. It would appear that, although all peoples have the right to self-determination, this should not be understood as a right to independent statehood. Where an identifiable group lives in an existing independent state, it is clear that they are entitled to minority rights; but it could be argued that 'the right to recognition of their identity' goes beyond this and suggests that such a group is entitled to some measure of autonomy as well. Certainly many of the peace proposals that have been made with regard to Bosnia have included recommendations that the Serbian population in Bosnia would possess powers in respect of their own government. However, such an interpretation of a limited right of self-determination in a non-colonial situation is not supported by the provisions of the Vienna Declaration 1993, adopted at the UN World Conference on Human Rights. Paragraph 2 re-affirms the right of all peoples to self-determination, but continues by stating that:

> This shall not be construed as authorising or encouraging any action which would dismember of impair, totally or in part, the territorial integrity or political unity of sovereign and independent states conducting themselves in compliance with the principle of equal rights and self-determination of peoples and thus possessed of a government representing the whole people belonging to the territory without distinction of any kind.

THE RIGHTS OF PEOPLES

From the perspective of international law, the key feature of the phrase 'rights of peoples' is not the term 'rights', but the term 'peoples'. From a philosophical point of view, no doubt, the term 'rights' is itself problematic. But lawyers, including international lawyers, are used to talking about rights, and so long as one accepts Hohfeld's point that one person's right must mean another person's duty, the term seems unremarkable even in the context of peoples' rights. Moreover, international law is familiar with the notion of 'collective' rights. References to the state, the basic unit of international law, involve a reference to the social fact of a territorial community of persons with a certain political organisation, in other words, a reference to a collectivity. In this sense, international law rules that confer rights on states confer collective rights. However, when international law attributes rights to states as social and political collectivities, it does so *sub modo* – that is to say, it does so subject to the rule that the actor on behalf of the state, and the agency to which other states are to look for the observation of the obligations of the state and which is entitled to activate its rights, is the government of the state. This basic rule drastically affects the point that the state *qua* community of persons has rights in international law, especially where the view or position taken by the government of a state diverges from the interests or wishes of the people of the state that the government represents. And it is, so far at least, axiomatic that international law does not guarantee representative, still less democratic, governments.

The proposition that the international law rights of states as communities of persons are moderated through a government (not necessarily representative, but legally the representative, of the people of the state) still represents the general rule. And it is that proposition which makes the term 'peoples' in the phrase 'rights of people' remarkable. Has international law taken up the task of conferring rights on groups or communities of people against the state which those people constitute, and against the government of the state? If so, it would be no great step for it to confer rights on those groups or communities as against other states and their governments. But the people of a state are – to put it mildly – at least as likely to have their rights violated by their own government as by the governments of other states. If the phrase 'rights of peoples' has any independent meaning, it must confer rights on peoples against their own governments. In other words, if the only rights of peoples are rights against other states, and if there is no change to the established position that the government of the state represents 'the state' (ie the people of the state) for all international purposes irrespective of its representativeness, then what is the point of referring to the rights in question as rights of peoples? Why not refer to them as the rights of states, in the familiar, well understood, though somewhat elliptical way?

I think it is more profitable to try to answer this question in the context of specific formulations of the 'rights of peoples'. Which of these rights are really rights of states in disguise? Which of them are really individual human rights – or aspirations to them? Which can properly be treated as rights of peoples, as distinct from individuals or states?[5]

---

5   James Crawford, 'The Rights of Peoples: "Peoples" or "Governments"?' in Crawford (ed), *The Rights of Peoples*, 1988, Oxford: Oxford University Press at pp 55–56.

THIRD-GENERATION RIGHTS

The emergence of third-generation or solidarity rights is closely identified with the rise of Third World nationalism and the perception of developing states that the existing international order is loaded against them. It may also be seen as a claim by developing states for fairer treatment and for the construction of a world system that will facilitate distributive justice in the broadest Rawlsian sense. The basis for these claims is not, however, simply moral, but can be identified as having a legal basis in a number of existing international instruments.

The UN Charter itself places human rights in a pivotal position to assist in the creation of a peaceful international order and economic development. Article 1(2) of the Charter provides that one of the purposes of the UN is 'to develop friendly relations among nations based on the principle of equal rights and self-determination of people'. Article 1(3) further provides that another purpose of the organisation is 'to achieve international co-operation in solving international problems of an economic, social, cultural or humanitarian character, and in promoting and encouraging respect for human rights and fundamental freedoms ...' These purposes are further reinforced by the substantive provisions of the Charter, particularly Articles 55 and 56, which clearly demonstrate that the creation of suitable international conditions is a prerequisite to the full social development of all individuals.

A number of other international instruments also support the view that the international community is obliged to establish a favourable global system for securing the better participation of developing states. The common Article 1 of the two International Covenants, for example, provide for both the political and economic right to self-determination. Article 1(2) provides:

> All peoples, may, for their own ends, freely dispose of their natural wealth and resources without any prejudice to any obligations arising out of international economic co-operation, based upon the principle of mutual benefit, and international law. In no case may a people be deprived of its own means of subsistence.

Article 2(1) of the ICESCR also provides that State Parties are 'to take steps individually and through international assistance and co-operation, especially economic and technical, to the maximum of available resources, with a view to achieving progressively the rights recognised in the present Covenant by all available means'. These provisions, it is argued by some jurists, provide a clear basis for a number of claims solidarity rights.

What, then, are these third-generation of solidarity rights? Burns Weston identifies at least six categories of solidarity rights:

1   the right to economic, political, social and cultural self-determination;
2   the right to economic and social development;
3   the right to participate in and benefit from the Common Heritage of Mankind and other information and progress;
4   the right to peace;
5   the right to a healthy environment;
6   the right to humanitarian relief.

It is immediately apparent that these rights have two dominant characteristics: first they are collective in nature and, second, they depend upon international co-operation for their achievement. It is also apparent that these rights build upon and develop existing categories of rights and in that sense they are, as Weston suggests, historically cumulative.

The fact that third-generation rights are collective in nature does not automatically mean that they should be thought of as less than 'real' rights for that reason alone. While traditional liberal conceptions of rights emphasise their individualistic quality, it is none the less apparent that even within the category of rights which might be described as civil and political, certain rights are collective in nature. These include the right to exercise one's religion in community with others, the right of peaceful assembly and the right to freedom of association. The rights categorised as economic, social and cultural, which are contained in a variety of international instruments, are also largely collectivist in nature, but are nevertheless recognised by the parties to those instruments as positive rights. The fact, however, that the new generation of rights depends for its implementation on international co-operation leads some authors to assert that they are little more than aspirational claims which do not possess the binding quality which is the hallmark of rights proper. Others, such as Alston, however, argue that there is no need to resort to claiming new rights which may be categorised as third generation, since by and large the problems which they seek to address are dealt with by existing instruments. Alston has also argued that claims for novel rights, such as the 'right to tourism,' obscure the need to properly develop existing rights, and more particularly, implementation programmes. He has also argued that there should be a system of procedures for granting a kind of approved origin mark to any 'new' rights proclaimed by the General Assembly.[6]

16.4 Enforcement

A survey of the implementation of international human rights law throughout the world could easily give the impression that the law is honoured more in its breach than its observance and that international agreements on human rights law are of little practical use. Such a view, it is submitted, would be wrong, since the very existence of international human rights law can serve to acknowledge that abuses are occurring and to set standards for future behaviour. A number of the conventions contain specific provision for their enforcement and, of course, as treaties, they are subject to the usual rules of observance discussed in Chapter 4. But any discussion of the enforcement of human rights law cannot ignore the prominent role played by publicity, both of abuses which occur and of the existence of the rights themselves. A number of organisations exist to monitor human rights violations, either in specific regions or States or throughout the world. A number of states also have introduced a formal system of monitoring, relying on information provided by their embassies abroad; for example, the US Congress prepares a fairly comprehensive annual report on the state of human rights throughout the world, which can have an important role to play in foreign policy decisions which are taken by the Executive.

---

6   Scott Davidson, *Human Rights*, 1933, Buckingham: Open University Press at pp 43–45.

16.4.1 UN mechanisms

Both ICPR and ICESCR establish enforcement machinery, although neither has proved to be extremely effective. Under Article 40 of the ICPR, every State Party is bound to submit periodic reports to a Human Rights Committee, which is established under Part VI of the Covenant. The Committee is made up of 18 members elected by the parties. Reports should indicate measures that have been taken to implement the Covenant, and the Committee can ask further questions about the report. The Committee itself produces a report on the state of human rights, but it has proved reluctant or unable to criticise States, and the reports submitted by individual states are unlikely to admit serious human rights violations.

Article 41 of the ICPR establishes a procedure for inter-State complaints, whereby a party may declare, at its option, and on the basis of reciprocity, that it recognises the competence of the Human Rights Committee to receive complaints from other states, subject to the requirement of exhaustion of local remedies. If an inter-state complaint is referred to the Committee, it will attempt to mediate and, if necessary, will refer the matter to an *ad hoc* Conciliation Commission: but the final report of such a commission is not binding on states. A limited number of states have made optional declarations under Article 41.

In addition, the Optional Protocol to the ICPR provides for the possibility of individual complaints to the Human Rights Committee, which can then carry out an investigation. The report of the Committee is not binding, although its publication may shame a state into action.

Enforcement mechanisms are much less strong under ICESCR. Under its provisions, parties must submit periodic reports are to a Group of Experts established by ECOSOC. The Group of Experts tends to be more open to political influence than the Human Rights Committee. There is also an 18-member Committee on Economic, Social and Cultural Rights set up by ECOSOC to assist in implementation of rights.

Aside from the provisions of the two covenants, the Human Rights Commission established by ECOSOC has an important role to play. The Commission is composed of 43 members representing their states, and it has jurisdiction to investigate allegations of widespread human rights violations and can establish independent working groups if necessary; for example, such a group investigated the state of Iranian prisons in 1990.

Since 1971, the UN Human Rights Commission has debated complaints submitted to it by the Sub-Commission on the Prevention of Discrimination and Protection of Minorities, which was authorised in 1970 to examine individual petitions relating to violations of human rights received by the Secretary General and reported to the Sub-Commission where they have revealed a consistent pattern of gross violation of human rights. It should be noted that the Sub-Commission has been subjected to immense political pressures and so has lacked effectiveness.

Recognising the problems of enforcement and realisation of human rights, the UN Conference on Human Rights at Vienna recommended a number of new measures, in particular the creation of the office of UN High Commissioner for Human Rights. The recommendation was acted upon by the UN General Assembly in December 1993 when it voted in favour of creating such a post. In February 1994, Jose Ayala Lasso from Ecuador was appointed the first UN High Commissioner for Human Rights, and he is to serve for an initial term of four years. The High Commissioner has responsibility for co-ordinating UN human rights activities and for promoting and protecting human rights. It remains to be seen what effect the appointment will have on international human rights.

16.4.2 European mechanisms

As has already been stated, ECHR was the first human rights treaty to provide mechanisms for enforcement, and to some extent it has served as a model for other regional agreements. In recent years, the system established under ECHR has been subject to considerable criticism, much of it related to the cost and time involved in bringing cases to conclusion. The Council of Europe has been debating changes, and in May 1994 the 32 members of the Council of Europe signed Draft Protocol 11. The Protocol replaces the present Articles 19–56 of the ECHR and establishes a new permanent European Court of Human Rights to replace the present Court and Commission. Under the Protocol, the court will have jurisdiction, and the right of individual petition will be mandatory. The Protocol requires ratification by all parties to ECHR before it will enter into force, although at the Vienna summit of the Council of Europe, the heads of government of the Member States pledged themselves to secure early ratification.

The present system contained in Articles 19-56 of the ECHR involves a two-stage process. Any State Party may refer a complaint involving allegations of breach of the convention to the European Commission of Human Rights. The Commission checks that the complaint is admissible. Claims will only be admissible if local remedies have been exhausted, if the claim is brought within six months of the date on which the final local decision was made, and providing the subject matter of the claim has not been settled by previous proceedings under the convention. If the claim is admissible, then the Commission will first attempt to bring about a friendly settlement. If this fails, a report is submitted to the Committee of Ministers of the Council of Europe, which can decide on the measures to be taken if there has been a breach, or refer the matter to the European Court of Human Rights for a full hearing. In addition to states being able to initiate proceedings under ECHR, Article 25 allows the Commission to receive petitions from any individual, non-governmental organisation or group of individuals claiming to be the victim of a violation by one of the State Parties of a right contained in the convention. This right only exists if the state against which the complaint has been made has lodged a prior declaration recognising the right to bring such petitions. The lodging of such declarations is optional, and such declarations may be made for a limited period. In spite of the recent criticisms that have been made of the enforcement machinery of ECHR, it has undoubtedly had an effect on the conduct of states. For example, the UK acted to end the use of corporal punishment in schools following the decision of the European Court of Human Rights in *Campbell and Cosans v UK*.[7] The Court has

---

7   (1982) 4 EHRR 293.

built up a considerable jurisprudence which is of use in defining and interpreting the nature and scope of a number of significant human rights. Among the landmark decisions are *Lawless v Ireland* (1961),[8] which raised the question of the situations in which a state would be able to depart from observance of human rights; *Ireland v UK* (1978),[9] which considered the definition of torture and inhuman and degrading treatment; and *Lingens v Austria* (1986),[10] which examined the extent of the right of freedom of expression.

---

8   (1961) 1 EHRR 1.
9   (1978) 58 ILR 190.
10   (1986) ECHR 407.

CHAPTER 17

ECONOMIC RELATIONS

17.1 Introduction

International economic law has tended to be marginalised in general works in English on public international law.[1] Clearly, any discussion of the law of the sea will need to consider the economic aspects of the management of the sea's resources and discussion of state responsibility will usually consider the issue of expropriation of foreign-owned property. But it is rare to find a chapter devoted solely to economic law. This is not to say it is not a valid subject of study nor should it be taken to suggest that there is no coherent body of international economic law. On the contrary, any effective legal system needs to provide some framework for the conduct of economic relations. If, as was suggested in Chapter 6, the majority of wars have had as their cause a dispute over territory, the desire to acquire territory has usually had an economic motive. With the realisation that the world's physical resources are not infinite there has developed a need for the existence of rules governing the exploitation and trade in such resources and the products of such resources. The attempts made by international law to conserve and manage the world's natural resources will be discussed in Chapter 18. This chapter will consider the rules of international law which pertain to trade and development. It will not refer to developments that have occurred within the European Union which can be studied in the textbooks of European law.

The rules regulating economic relations are of comparatively recent origin. During the 19th century most states operated a *laissez faire* policy towards their internal economies and accordingly there was little, if any, control of commercial and financial transactions involving foreigners. Such controls as existed were contained in provisions of municipal law and were largely confined to customs and import restrictions. A major impetus for change came with the emergence of the USSR in 1917 and its adoption of economic policies based on the state ownership of the means of production. Implementation of such policies involved the expropriation of foreign-owned property and at the Brussels Conference on Russia in 1921 a resolution was passed which stated that:

> The forcible expropriations and nationalisations without compensation or remuneration of property in which foreigners are interested is totally at variance with the practice of civilised states. Where such expropriation has taken place, a claim arises for compensation against the government of the country.

The current position regarding expropriation of foreign-owned property is discussed at 17.6.

An important aspect of international economic law is the emphasis placed on the need for free trade. During the 19th century many states had swung

---

1   This is not true of studies carried out in states other than Britain. The difference in approach may partly be explained by the fact that there is no real tradition within English law of studying economic law as a separate and independent subject.

between policies of free trade and polices of protectionism depending upon estimations of the relative strength of their own economies. Following the end of World War Two, with many economies in ruins, the USA saw the opportunity to expand its own economy by foreign investment. Such foreign investment undoubtedly helped in the recovery of local economies but to facilitate such investment it was necessary to keep trade barriers to a minimum. The international community also accepted the importance of international monetary stability. It was widely recognised that the extremely high inflation in Germany during the late 1920s and early 1930s had been one of the contributory factors in Hitler's rise to power. To assist in the maintenance of currency stability and the encouragement of free trade three international institutions were established. In July 1944 an international conference was held at Bretton Woods in the USA at which was established the International Monetary Fund (IMF) and the International Bank for Reconstruction and Development (IBRD). In 1947, 53 states met in Cuba and adopted the Havana Charter 1947 which established the International Trade Organisation (ITO). However the Charter was not signed by the USA and the ITO did not come into existence. Instead as a temporary measure the General Agreement on Tariffs and Trade 1947 (GATT) was signed. The role of the three institutions is discussed at 17.3 and 17.4.

The emergence of a large number of new independent states during the 1950s and 1960s resulted in new problems for international economic law. In particular, the new states argued for the recognition of a right to economic development which was not always compatible with the rules established through the work of the IMF, World Bank and GATT. Further, the principle of free trade conflicted with the new states desire to protect their own fledgling economies. In addition a number of the new states had strong reservations about foreign companies having control of important local industries and therefore adopted policies involving expropriation. In 1964 the first UN Conference on Trade and Development (UNCTAD) was attended by the overwhelming majority of states. The conference adopted a number of resolutions which set down guiding principles which should govern the law relating to economic development. The General Assembly subsequently established UNCTAD as one of its permanent institutions with a secretariat and executive body (the Trade and Development Board). The conference has met on a regular basis since then. The international law of development is discussed at 17.5.

17.1.1 The nature of international economic law and its definition

Perhaps more than is the case with other areas of international law, the definition of what should be included in the study of international economic law is itself problematic. It is heavily influenced by the role that is perceived for international law and, in a wider context, the role of states themselves:

> Let usa see how public international lawyers define their subject. Some definition is particularly essential to the English lawyer before embarking on the subject's study because he enjoys no background familiarity from national law with concepts of economic law.

Definitions fall into three groups; they may be determined by the source of legal authority, the content of the subject or the objective to be achieved. Once again, it must be borne in mind that the subject is under constant change; change in the international economy itself, and in the regulatory mechanisms adopted to deal with it. Definitions will inevitably alter to accommodate these changing facts.

A   Source of legal authority

Writers who adopt a definition on the origin of the rules governing the topic include Schwarzenberger, Carreau, Juillard, Flory, VerLoren van Thermat, and Seidl-Hohenveldern. For them international economic law is defined as public international rules for international economic relations. VerLoren van Thermat speaks of 'the total range of norms (directly or indirectly based on treaties) of public international law with regard to transnational economic transactions'.

B   Content of subject

The second group defines by reference to the content of the subject. Petersmann speaks for writers supporting this method, contrasting 'the international law of the economy' of the first method with his own preferred definition of 'the law of the international economy', 'a functional unity of the private, national and international regulations of the world economy' and consequently including private law, state law and public international law. Schwarzenberger offered, as early as 1966, a definition spanning both these methods:[2]

International economic law is the branch of public international law which is concerned with:

(i)   ownership and exploitation of natural resources;

(ii)   production and distribution of goods;

(iii)   invisible international transactions of an economic and financial nature, currency and finance, related services;

(iv)   status and organisation of those engaged in such activities.

Zamora also adopts a list approach: '... the main subject is international trade in goods and services, international financial transactions and monetary affairs, foreign investment.'[3]

Any definition on a list basis, however, can be criticised as open-ended, quickly becoming out of date and hence requiring continual additions.

C   Objective

The third group, that of the objective to be achieved, is best illustrated by proponents of the New International Economic Order who see the topic as one of regulation of the international economic order to give a proper place to Third World developing states. Flory equates international economic law with '*le droit du dévelopement*', the law of development, which, as Peller phrases, concerns the third stage of the three Ds: after decolonisation and (self-) determination of Third World states the law of development will enable these states to attain economic equality with Western industrialised states.

The economic advancement of developing states is not, however, the sole goal pursued by adherents of international economic law. Some see it as a mechanism

---

2   G Schwarzenberger, 'The Principles and Standards of International Economic Law' (1966-I) *Hague Recueil*.

3   S Zamora, 'Is There Customary International Economic Law?' (1990) 32 *German Yearbook of International Law* 9 at p 1.

to curb the domestic protectionism of their own states, the long-term interests of which, in their view, lie in liberalisation of world trade. Others emphasise the accountability of both state and international organisations in the management of world economy to the individual and the private trader and seek to develop procedures to protect the latter's interests. Yet another school of thought would emphasise the shared use of resources for the common good; the concept of the common heritage applied to outer space and the deep sea bed, the moratorium on minerals exploitation in Antarctica, the protection of the environment by restriction of economies to sustainable growth – all these concerns would be brought within the scope of international economic law.

D   Characteristics of international economic law

What are the characteristics of international economic law which these definitions seek to capture? Prosper Weil, in a well-argued paper, identified the original features of the subject. He wrote that it employed novel techniques of fact collection, monitoring of state conduct, and consultation; it abandoned the principle of equality of states in order to reflect the divergent weight which the economic policies of countries have on world development; rules of the GATT and regional economic free trade areas were applied with flexibility, hedged with safeguards and exceptions with their content expressed in vague, temporary and constantly modified terms; dispute settlement by third party adjudication was seen as too adversarial, rigid and slow to be resorted to – a convergence of viewpoints rather than a clarification of legal rights or a crystallisation of a rule, was sought. These features – lack of certainty, of formality or precision, impermanence of any general rule, absence of judicial sanctions – did not, however, in his view, entitle international economic law to qualify as an independent branch of law. They were more the marks of an immature legal system; and he explained them as due to a lack of cohesiveness in the international community which it was sought to regulate, inability to control or fully understand the economic factors at work resulting in consequent weakness in the community's sanctions, and non-justiciability of its rules.

V SOURCES OF INTERNATIONAL ECONOMIC LAW

Bearing these strictures in mind, let usa look at the definitions to see how they draw the boundaries of the subject and what source material they rely upon. All the definitions have to deal with the problems which the peculiar characteristics of the subject gave rise to. They can be dealt with by reference to the three elements which the title of the subject includes.

A   International

1   States and international organisations

Under 'international' we need to know who are the actors or subjects of this branch of law. Writers who define the subject by source of authority would reply states and international organisations. The study is consequently concerned with their acts, the agreements of states and the constitutions establishing international economic institutions. Source material will, therefore, include international agreements, universal, regional and bilateral: universal agreements include the General Agreement on Tariffs and Trade, international commodity agreements, regional agreements include the European Free Trade Area (EFTA), the Canada-USA Free Trade Area, ASEAN, ANDEAN and other agreements relevant to Central and South America and the Caribbean. (The decision to include these other regional arrangements may turn on whether the criterion is comprehensive coverage of attempts at economic co-operation or the effectiveness of that co-operation). Bilateral agreements would include treaties of friendship, navigation and commerce, investment protection treaties and lump sum agreements settling inter-state claims. There will be some overlap with the constitutions of international economic institutions; the universal group of these will include the articles of association of the IMF, of the World Bank and its ancillary bodies, the International Development Association (IDA), the International Finance Corporation (IFC), the Centre for Settlement of Investment Disputes (ICSID), the Bank for International Settlements (BIS); among the regional constitutions would be those relating to the Organisation for Economic Co-operation (OECD), and to the European Economic Community (EEC). A further category of functional arrangements might include on a world basis UN specialised agencies such as the Food and Agriculture Organisation (FAO) and ILO, the International Atomic Energy Agency (IAEA) and the World Intellectual Property Organisation (WIPO).

If we add to this body of international agreements secondary material relating to acts of states implementing the agreements or decisions of the financial institutions, and thus include the GATT codes, the Multifibre Arrangement, decisions of IMF relating to conditionality, the extended fund facility and general agreements to borrow, we will find that we have already a considerable corpus of material to study.

2   Other actors

But supporters of the other types of definition would extend the range of materials. Petersmann, for instance, sees one of the purposes of international economic regulation as the reduction of the unilateral power of the state to control trade matters. He would extend the study to other actors who have an impact on the international economy such as multinational corporations, agencies or sub-units of governments working together, such as the Committee of Central Bankers, the Basel-Mulhouse Airport project, non-governmental organisations such as ICC and IUCN. In doing so he would extend the scope of the materials, particularly in the field of foreign investment; thus documents relating to the conduct of transnational enterprises such as the ICC Guidelines for International Investment 1972, the ILO Tripartite Declaration of Principles relating to Multinational Enterprises and Social Policy 1977, the OECD Declaration on International Enterprises and Multinational Enterprises 1976, the UN ECOSOC Draft Code of Conduct on Multinational Corporations 1987, would all become relevant. Statements of intent in communiqués of political groupings such as G7 (Canada, France, Germany, Italy, Japan, UK and USA) would also be included.

3   Objectives of international law

Supporters of a policy-orientated definition would extend the material even further. Those who see international economic law in terms of a law of development would include UN General Assembly Resolutions such as Resolution 1803 (XVII) on Permanent Sovereignty over Natural Resources, the 1974 Declaration on the Establishment of a New International Economic Order, and the Charter of Economic Rights and Duties of States, the documentation relating to the regional and functional commissions of ECOSOC, UNCTAD's establishment in 1964 and work relating to commodities, UNCITRAL's programme from 1966 for the unification of the law of international trade. Not all collections of documents of international economic law include such material. For instance such documentation is notably absent from the American Society of International Law's database of basic materials set up by its interest group in international economic law. It is presumably excluded on the ground that it is policy not law. Its inclusion requires a consideration of the second element 'law' in the subject of our study.

B   Law

1   Treaty

International lawyers are already familiar with the distinction between 'hard' and 'soft' law, and the distinction needs to be examined in relation to international economic law. International agreements between states are clearly recognised as a source of law in Article 38 of the ICJ Statute; decisions of international organisations are not specifically mentioned; some derive their legal force expressly from their member states' agreements, others may be treated as evidence of state practice and hence evidence of custom or as themselves constituting international customary law.

2   Custom

International custom is not frequently invoked as a source of international economic law, it being widely accepted that this subject today remains largely treaty-based. The international law of expropriation is perhaps one instance of customary economic law.

3   Soft law

Recommendations of the UN General Assembly and other international organisations, guidelines and programmes for action vary in their authority. Some may rank as declaratory or interpretative of existing law; others' persuasive force will depend on the content, the wording of the text, the voting pattern by which they are adopted, subsequent repetition and practice of states and use by other international agencies – for example, the ICJ's use of the UN General Assembly Resolutions to interpret the UN Charter in the *Nicaragua v United States of America (Merits)* case lent the authority of that tribunal to those resolutions.[4] Lawyers engaged in the study of international economic law will need to assess their sources, to be aware that much may be models, optional standards, or tentative drafts of emerging law rather than crystallised law. They should keep in mind Sir Hersch Lauterpacht's words in the *Voting Procedure* case:

> The state ... while not bound to accept the recommendations is bound to give it due consideration. If ... it disregards it, it is bound to explain its reasons.[5]

4   Private and public law

We also need to understand what is meant by an international transaction. Does it cover any commercial act which takes place across frontiers? The Third restatement of the Foreign Relations of the United States seems to be of that view, declaring the law of international economic relations to cover 'all the international law and international agreements governing economic transactions that cross state boundaries or that otherwise have implications for more than one state'. There is a division of opinion among teachers and writers whether transnational private law transactions are to be totally excluded. On one view they do not involve international actors; they relate to bilateral commercial matters between private traders adjudicated by private law courts and even where the rules are internationally harmonised by treaty they remain of private law character to be applied by national courts with, in some exceptional cases,

---

4   [1986] *ICJ Rep* 14 at p 99–100.

5   Voting Procedures in Questions relating to reports and petitions concerning the territory of SW Afric [1955] *ICJ Rep* 67 at p 12.

the possibility of an appeal to a regional court to provide a uniform ruling. On this view national commercial laws relating to sale, supply and transport of goods and the financing of foreign sales, and the private international law rules governing such transactions are to be excluded as also is any *lex mercatoria* or customary rules followed by merchants or any international harmonisation of such substantive rules such as the UN Uniform International Sales Convention, or international harmonised private international law rules such as the Hague Conventions on Service Abroad of Judicial Documents and on Taking Evidence Abroad and international enforcement rules such as the New York Convention on the Recognition of Foreign Arbitral Awards and the Brussels Convention on Jurisdiction and Judgments 1982. On another view, which is the view frequently adopted in USA law courses on international trade and that followed in the database of basic documents set up by the ASIL interest group in international economic law, documents governing private law commercial transactions, international litigation and arbitration are relevant to the subject. This view approximates to that noted above as the English viewpoint which considers that if the rules governing transnational operation of these private law transactions are properly drawn, the unrestricted pursuit of these transactions will be the best means to achieve international economic prosperity.

C   Economic

However, to reduce the subject to manageable proportions for study, both in relating to the private law of international trade and to other branches of international law, we must remind ourselves of the third element in its title, 'economic'. Its inclusion does not require the fashioning of legal concepts to implement the latest economic theory, planned, mixed, privatised, federal, corporatist, or whatever. (Lawyers should follow Dean Collard's advice and beware of basic concepts, whether economic, mathematical or physical and confine their attention to the consequences of their application.) But it does mean that the subject is concerned with the direct legal regulation of the economy by international means. Indirect means through private law transactions or through other branches of international law which protect or balance economic interests of states as in the law of the sea, of the air, of neutrality, or as in international environmental law are therefore to be excluded.

VI   CONCLUSION

To sum up, international economic law may be defined as the law of regulation of the economy by states, international organisations and other international means. Its sources are primarily the treaties and constitutions of international economic institutions which have been referred to in the preceding pages and the consequential decisions and acts implementing the objectives of these treaties and constitutions. The extent to which other material is studied will depend on its classification as a source of law, on the type of definition applied to the subject, and above all, on its suitability for legal analysis and development of legal concepts. The student should never forget his role as a lawyer in handling such material.

As a conclusion ... let me offer some suggestions as to the areas which the subject may cover.

First, the identification, examination and testing by reference to the materials identified in the preceding pages of the fundamental assumptions on which the law must be based. Those assumptions will surely include economic sovereignty and mutual interdependence. The core of the problem lies in striking a balance between these two principles and in applying them in a uniform and fair way to the very different economic situations of large and small states, developed and developing, North and South. Account must also be taken of the position of the private individual or enterprise. This may call for recognition of freedoms of economic action exercisable by all and of internationally derived prohibitions to enforce such freedoms. Part of this enquiry will go to the extent to which such freedoms are to be vested in the state or directly in private enterprises and individuals, thereby bypassing the state.

Second, the subject must cover the manner in which the economic mechanisms and international economic institutions regulate the use of natural resources and investment. This may call for a comparative analysis of the major international economic institutions, their objectives, structure, the form and content of the legal means which they use, their co-ordination of action and resolution of disputes internally with member states, and externally with non-member states and other international institutions.

Finally, the subject will concern itself with the identification of legal values (often longer-term rather than transient economic targets) which should control the exercise of economic regulatory powers; such legal values include proper notification, record-keeping and transparency of any action taken, observance of jurisdictional limits, non-retroactivity, proportionality, equity, the recognition of the individual's right or reasonable expectations relating to the action regulated. The agenda is a lengthy one, but one which by reason of its application of legal techniques to a novel and uncharted territory offers a rewarding challenge to international lawyers entering the 21st century.[6]

17.2   The sources of international economic law

The international law governing economic relations differs from many other areas of law in that customary rules play a far more limited role. Although the majority of states may practise a capitalist form of economics and, in varying degrees, support the idea of a free market and free trade, there are a number of states that vehemently oppose such views. Even among the capitalist states there can exist considerable differences of view as to the rules that should be imposed. The bulk of the rules are contained in bilateral agreements made between states to regulate such things as import and export trade, shipping, foreign investment and banking. Many of these bilateral treaties display common characteristics but their nature has not given rise to a body of state practice and *opinio juris* sufficient to create binding customary rules. There are also a number of important multilateral treaties, for example, the Articles of Agreement of the International Monetary Fund 1944, the General Agreement on Tariffs and Trade 1947 and the various international commodity agreements. A third category of treaties relevant to the international economy would include those treaties which establish a regional body with powers relating to the economy, the best known example being the Treaty of Rome 1957.

In addition to treaty law there is an ever-growing body of resolutions and declarations which, while not constituting formal sources of law, do have an

---

6   Hazel Fox, 'The Defintion and Sources of International Economic Law', in Hazel Fox (ed), *International Economic Law and Developing States*, 1992, London: British Institute of International and Comparative Law.

enormous impact on the economic behaviour of states. The importance of such resolutions has led to arguments that they should be considered to constitute a body of quasi-law, not binding in themselves but representing a firm plan for future legal developments. Such quasi-law is generally referred to as soft law. Among the resolutions which are claimed as soft law are the UN General Assembly's Declaration on the Establishment of a New International Economic Order 1974 and the Charter of Economic Rights and Duties of States 1974. Additionally the declarations of institutions such as the Organisation for Economic Co-operation and Development (OECD) have an important role to play in the development of the law. The Organisation for European Economic Co-operation (OEEC) was established in 1948 to help implement the Marshall aid plan for European economic recovery and to provide a forum for the harmonisation of economic policies and the exchange of information and operates through the holding of regular meetings of government ministers. In 1961 the European members of OEEC were joined by the USA, Canada and Japan and the OECD was created.

17.3   Free trade and the WTO

The emergence at the end of World War Two of the USA as the world's most economically powerful state had the consequence that there was enormous pressure on international law to adopt and reflect principles of capitalist economics. Since USA economists stressed the need for a free market at home it is not surprising that free trade should become the guiding principle for the international economy. Until 1995 the institution principally charged with the development and encouragement of free trade was GATT. In fact, as has already been indicated, GATT was not created as an international organisation and it was only agreed after the failure to establish an International Trade Organisation. The abbreviation GATT is used in two senses: to indicate the actual treaty which was drafted in 1947, and to indicate the Geneva based institution which administers the agreement. In the latter sense GATT is hard to distinguish from an international organisation, although it is one without a separate international legal personality of its own. Over 100 states are now contracting parties to the agreement and their combined trade represents 80% of total world trade. The agreement provides a framework for developing international trade rules and sets down certain fundamental principles. Instead, GATT established a framework for discussion and set down a number of important guiding principles. The work of GATT is overseen by the GATT Council and there exists a procedure for settling trade disputes between states and the possibility of imposing sanctions on those state parties who do not abide by GATT rules. The agreement contains six principal obligations:

- commitment to most-favoured-nation trade;
- reduction of tariff barriers;
- non-discrimination between imported and domestic goods;
- elimination of import quotas;
- anti-dumping;
- restriction on export subsidies.

Most of the significant work of GATT has been achieved at the regular and sometimes protracted negotiations that are held between the parties to the agreement. In December 1993 the most recent such negotiation, the Uruguay Round, was concluded. The Uruguay Round achieved a number of important breakthroughs in the development of international law. The GATT rules were extended to several new areas of trade including agriculture, film and broadcasting and intellectual property rights. In addition, it was agreed to extend the life of the Multifibre Agreement (MFA) which regulates certain aspects of the international trade in textiles and clothing. Significantly the 117 participants at the concluding session agreed to establish the World Trade Organisation (WTO) as a true international organisation with a General Council and bi-annual ministerial meetings. The main functions of the WTO are:

- administering and implementing the multilateral and plurilateral trade agreements which together make up the WTO;

- acting as a forum for multilateral trade negotiations;

- seeking to resolve trade disputes;

- overseeing national trade policies; and

- co-operating with other international institutions in global economic policy-making.

The highest authority of the WTO is the Ministerial Conference which meets every two years – most recently in Singapore in December 1996. The day-to-day work of the WTO is carried out by the General Council which also convenes as the Dispute Settlement Body and the Trade Policy Review Body. The General Council delegates responsibility to three other major bodies – the Council for Trade in Goods; the Council for Trade in Services; and the Council for Trade-related Aspects of intellectual Property Rights. In addition there are three other bodies which report to the General Council: the Committee on Trade and Development, the Committee on Balance of Payments and the Committee on Budget, Finance and Administration.

THE WTO AGREEMENT

Marrakesh agreement establishing the World Trade Organisation 15 April 1994

The Parties to this Agreement,

Recognising that their relations in the field of trade and economic endeavour should be conducted with a view to raising standards of living, ensuring full employment and a large and steadily growing volume of real income and effective demand, and expanding the production of and trade in goods and services, while allowing for the optimal use of the world's resources in accordance with the objective of sustainable development, seeking both to protect and preserve the environment and to enhance the means for doing so in a manner consistent with their respective needs and concerns at different levels of economic development,

Recognising further that there is need for positive efforts designed to ensure that developing countries, and especially the least developed among them, secure a share in the growth in international trade commensurate with the needs of their economic development,

Being desirous of contributing to these objectives by entering into reciprocal and mutually advantageous arrangements directed to the substantial reduction of tariffs and other barriers to trade and to the elimination of discriminatory treatment in international trade relations,

Resolved, therefore, to develop an integrated, more viable and durable multilateral trading system encompassing the General Agreement on Tariffs and Trade, the results of past trade-liberalisation efforts, and all of the results of the Uruguay Round of Multilateral Trade Negotiations,

Determined to preserve the basic principles and to further the objectives underlying this multilateral trading system,

Agree as follows:

Article I   Establishment of the Organisation

The World Trade Organisation (hereinafter referred to as 'the WTO') is hereby established.

Article II   Scope of the WTO

1   The WTO shall provide the common institutional framework for the conduct of trade relations among its members in matters related to the agreements and associated legal instruments included in the Annexes to this Agreement.

2   The agreements and associated legal instruments included in Annexes 1, 2 and 3 (hereinafter referred to as 'Multilateral Trade Agreements') are integral parts of this Agreement, binding on all members.

3   The agreements and associated legal instruments included in Annex 4 (hereinafter referred to as 'Plurilateral Trade Agreements') are also part of this Agreement for those members that have accepted them, and are binding on those members. The Plurilateral Trade Agreements do not create either obligations or rights for members that have not accepted them.

4   The General Agreement on Tariffs and Trade 1994 as specified in Annex 1A (hereinafter referred to as 'GATT 1994') is legally distinct from the General Agreement on Tariffs and Trade, dated 30 October 1947, annexed to the Final Act Adopted at the Conclusion of the Second Session of the Preparatory Committee of the United Nations Conference on Trade and Employment, as subsequently rectified, amended or modified (hereinafter referred to as 'GATT').

Article III Functions of the WTO

1   The WTO shall facilitate the implementation, administration and operation, and further the objectives, of this Agreement and of the Multilateral Trade Agreements, and shall also provide the framework for the implementation, administration and operation of the Plurilateral Trade Agreements.

2   The WTO shall provide the forum for negotiations among its members concerning their multilateral trade relations in matters dealt with under the agreements in the Annexes to this Agreement. The WTO may also provide a forum for further negotiations among its members concerning their multilateral trade relations, and a framework for the implementation of the results of such negotiations, as may be decided by the Ministerial Conference.

3   The WTO shall administer the Understanding on Rules and Procedures Governing the Settlement of Disputes (hereinafter referred to as the 'Dispute Settlement Understanding' or 'DSU') in Annex 2 to this Agreement.

4   The WTO shall administer the Trade Policy Review Mechanism (hereinafter referred to as the 'TPRM') provided for in Annex 3 to this Agreement.

5   With a view to achieving greater coherence in global economic policy-making, the WTO shall co-operate, as appropriate, with the International Monetary Fund and with the International Bank for Reconstruction and Development and its affiliated agencies.

Article IV   Structure of the WTO

1   There shall be a Ministerial Conference composed of representatives of all the members, which shall meet at least once every two years. The Ministerial Conference shall carry out the functions of the WTO and take actions necessary to this effect. The Ministerial Conference shall have the authority to take decisions on all matters under any of the Multilateral Trade Agreements, if so requested by a member, in accordance with the specific requirements for decision-making in this Agreement and in the relevant Multilateral Trade Agreement.

2   There shall be a General Council composed of representatives of all the members, which shall meet as appropriate. In the intervals between meetings of the Ministerial Conference, its functions shall be conducted by the General Council. The General Council shall also carry out the functions assigned to it by this Agreement. The General Council shall establish its rules of procedure and approve the rules of procedure for the Committees provided for in para 7.

3   The General Council shall convene as appropriate to discharge the responsibilities of the Dispute Settlement Body provided for in the Dispute Settlement Understanding. The Dispute Settlement Body may have its own chairman and shall establish such rules of procedure as it deems necessary for the fulfilment of those responsibilities.

4   The General Council shall convene as appropriate to discharge the responsibilities of the Trade Policy Review Body provided for in the TPRM. The Trade Policy Review Body may have its own chairman and shall establish such rules of procedure as it deems necessary for the fulfilment of those responsibilities.

5   There shall be a Council for Trade in Goods, a Council for Trade in Services and a Council for Trade-Related Aspects of Intellectual Property Rights (hereinafter referred to as the 'Council for TRIPS'), which shall operate under the general guidance of the General Council. The Council for Trade in Goods shall oversee the functioning of the Multilateral Trade Agreements in Annex 1A. The Council for Trade in Services shall oversee the functioning of the General Agreement on Trade in Services (hereinafter referred to as 'GATS'). The Council for TRIPS shall oversee the functioning of the Agreement on Trade-Related Aspects of Intellectual Property Rights (hereinafter referred to as the 'Agreement on TRIPS'). These Councils shall carry out the functions assigned to them by their respective agreements and by the General Council. They shall establish their respective rules of procedure subject to the approval of the General Council. membership in these Councils shall be open to representatives of all members. These Councils shall meet as necessary to carry out their functions.

6   The Council for Trade in Goods, the Council for Trade in Services and the Council for TRIPS shall establish subsidiary bodies as required. These subsidiary bodies shall establish their respective rules of procedure subject to the approval of their respective Councils.

7   The Ministerial Conference shall establish a Committee on Trade and Development, a Committee on Balance of Payments Restrictions and a Committee on Budget, Finance and Administration, which shall carry out the functions assigned to them by this Agreement and by the Multilateral Trade

Agreements, and any additional functions assigned to them by the General Council, and may establish such additional Committees with such functions as it may deem appropriate. As part of its functions, the Committee on Trade and Development shall periodically review the special provisions in the Multilateral Trade Agreements in favour of the least-developed country members and report to the General Council for appropriate action. membership in these Committees shall be open to representatives of all members.

8   The bodies provided for under the Plurilateral Trade Agreements shall carry out the functions assigned to them under those Agreements and shall operate within the institutional framework of the WTO. These bodies shall keep the General Council informed of their activities on a regular basis.

Article V   Relations with Other Organisations

1   The General Council shall make appropriate arrangements for effective co-operation with other intergovernmental organisations that have responsibilities related to those of the WTO.

2   The General Council may make appropriate arrangements for consultation and co-operation with non-governmental organisations concerned with matters related to those of the WTO.

Article VI The Secretariat

1   There shall be a Secretariat of the WTO (hereinafter referred to as 'the Secretariat') headed by a Director General.

2   The Ministerial Conference shall appoint the Director General and adopt regulations setting out the powers, duties, conditions of service and term of office of the Director General.

3   The Director General shall appoint the members of the staff of the Secretariat and determine their duties and conditions of service in accordance with regulations adopted by the Ministerial Conference.

4   The responsibilities of the Director General and of the staff of the Secretariat shall be exclusively international in character. In the discharge of their duties, the Director General and the staff of the Secretariat shall not seek or accept instructions from any government or any other authority external to the WTO. They shall refrain from any action which might adversely reflect on their position as international officials. The members of the WTO shall respect the international character of the responsibilities of the Director General and of the staff of the Secretariat and shall not seek to influence them in the discharge of their duties.

Article VI Budget and Contributions

1   The Director General shall present to the Committee on Budget, Finance and Administration the annual budget estimate and financial statement of the WTO. The Committee on Budget, Finance and Administration shall review the annual budget estimate and the financial statement presented by the Director General and make recommendations thereon to the General Council. The annual budget estimate shall be subject to approval by the General Council.

2   The Committee on Budget, Finance and Administration shall propose to the General Council financial regulations which shall include provisions setting out:

(a)   the scale of contributions apportioning the expenses of the WTO among its members; and

(b)   the measures to be taken in respect of members in arrears.

The financial regulations shall be based, as far as practicable, on the regulations and practices of GATT 1947.

3   The General Council shall adopt the financial regulations and the annual budget estimate by a two-thirds majority comprising more than half of the members of the WTO.

4   Each member shall promptly contribute to the WTO its share in the expenses of the WTO in accordance with the financial regulations adopted by the General Council.

Article VIII   Status of the WTO

1   The WTO shall have legal personality, and shall be accorded by each of its members such legal capacity as may be necessary for the exercise of its functions.

2   The WTO shall be accorded by each of its members such privileges and immunities as are necessary for the exercise of its functions.

3   The officials of the WTO and the representatives of the members shall similarly be accorded by each of its members such privileges and immunities as are necessary for the independent exercise of their functions in connection with the WTO.

4   The privileges and immunities to be accorded by a member to the WTO, its officials, and the representatives of its members shall be similar to the privileges and immunities stipulated in the Convention on the Privileges and Immunities of the Specialised Agencies, approved by the General Assembly of the United Nations on 21 November 1947.

5   The WTO may conclude a headquarters agreement.

Article IX   Decision-making

1   The WTO shall continue the practice of decision-making by consensus followed under GATT 1947. Except as otherwise provided, where a decision cannot be arrived at by consensus, the matter at issue shall be decided by voting. At meetings of the Ministerial Conference and the General Council, each member of the WTO shall have one vote. Where the European Communities exercise their right to vote, they shall have a number of votes equal to the number of their member states which are members of the WTO. Decisions of the Ministerial Conference and the General Council shall be taken by a majority of the votes cast, unless otherwise provided in this Agreement or in the relevant Multilateral Trade Agreement.

2   The Ministerial Conference and the General Council shall have the exclusive authority to adopt interpretations of this Agreement and of the Multilateral Trade Agreements. In the case of an interpretation of a Multilateral Trade Agreement in Annex 1, they shall exercise their authority on the basis of a recommendation by the Council overseeing the functioning of that Agreement. The decision to adopt an interpretation shall be taken by a three-fourths majority of the members. This paragraph shall not be used in a manner that would undermine the amendment provisions in Article X.

3   In exceptional circumstances, the Ministerial Conference may decide to waive an obligation imposed on a member by this Agreement or any of the Multilateral Trade Agreements, provided that any such decision shall be taken by three-fourths of the members unless otherwise provided for in this paragraph.

(a)   A request for a waiver concerning this Agreement shall be submitted to the Ministerial Conference for consideration pursuant to the practice of decision-making by consensus. The Ministerial Conference shall establish a time period, which shall not exceed 90 days, to consider the request. If consensus is not reached during the time period, any decision to grant a waiver shall be taken by three-fourths of the members.

(b) A request for a waiver concerning the Multilateral Trade Agreements in Annexes 1A or 1B or 1C and their annexes shall be submitted initially to the Council for Trade in Goods, the Council for Trade in Services or the Council for TRIPS, respectively, for consideration during a time period which shall not exceed 90 days. At the end of the time period, the relevant Council shall submit a report to the Ministerial Conference.

4   A decision by the Ministerial Conference granting a waiver shall state the exceptional circumstances justifying the decision, the terms and conditions governing the application of the waiver, and the date on which the waiver shall terminate. Any waiver granted for a period of more than one year shall be reviewed by the Ministerial Conference not later than one year after it is granted, and thereafter annually until the waiver terminates. In each review, the Ministerial Conference shall examine whether the exceptional circumstances justifying the waiver still exist and whether the terms and conditions attached to the waiver have been met. The Ministerial Conference, on the basis of the annual review, may extend, modify or terminate the waiver.

5   Decisions under a Plurilateral Trade Agreement, including any decisions on interpretations and waivers, shall be governed by the provisions of that Agreement.

Article X Amendments

1   Any member of the WTO may initiate a proposal to amend the provisions of this Agreement or the Multilateral Trade Agreements in Annex 1 by submitting such proposal to the Ministerial Conference. The Councils listed in para 5 of Article IV may also submit to the Ministerial Conference proposals to amend the provisions of the corresponding Multilateral Trade Agreements in Annex 1 the functioning of which they oversee. Unless the Ministerial Conference decides on a longer period, for a period of 90 days after the proposal has been tabled formally at the Ministerial Conference any decision by the Ministerial Conference to submit the proposed amendment to the members for acceptance shall be taken by consensus. Unless the provisions of paras 2, 5 or 6 apply, that decision shall specify whether the provisions of paras 3 or 4 shall apply. If consensus is reached, the Ministerial Conference shall forthwith submit the proposed amendment to the members for acceptance. If consensus is not reached at a meeting of the Ministerial Conference within the established period, the Ministerial Conference shall decide by a two-thirds majority of the members whether to submit the proposed amendment to the members for acceptance. Except as provided in paras 2, 5 and 6, the provisions of para 3 shall apply to the proposed amendment, unless the Ministerial Conference decides by a three-fourths majority of the members that the provisions of para 4 shall apply.

2   Amendments to the provisions of this Article and to the provisions of the following Articles shall take effect only upon acceptance by all members:

Article IX of this Agreement;

Articles I and II of GATT 1994;

Article II:1 of GATS;

Article 4 of the Agreement on TRIPS.

3   Amendments to provisions of this Agreement, or of the Multilateral Trade Agreements in Annexes 1A and 1C, other than those listed in paras 2 and 6, of a nature that would alter the rights and obligations of the members, shall take effect for the members that have accepted them upon acceptance by two-thirds of the members and thereafter for each other member upon acceptance by it. The

Ministerial Conference may decide by a three-fourths majority of the members that any amendment made effective under this paragraph is of such a nature that any member which has not accepted it within a period specified by the Ministerial Conference in each case shall be free to withdraw from the WTO or to remain a member with the consent of the Ministerial Conference.

4   Amendments to provisions of this Agreement or of the Multilateral Trade Agreements in Annexes 1A and 1C, other than those listed in paras 2 and 6, of a nature that would not alter the rights and obligations of the members, shall take effect for all members upon acceptance by two-thirds of the members.

5   Except as provided in para 2 above, amendments to Parts I, II and III of GATS and the respective annexes shall take effect for the members that have accepted them upon acceptance by two-thirds of the members and thereafter for each member upon acceptance by it. The Ministerial Conference may decide by a three-fourths majority of the members that any amendment made effective under the preceding provision is of such a nature that any member which has not accepted it within a period specified by the Ministerial Conference in each case shall be free to withdraw from the WTO or to remain a member with the consent of the Ministerial Conference. Amendments to Parts IV, V and VI of GATS and the respective annexes shall take effect for all members upon acceptance by two-thirds of the members.

6   Notwithstanding the other provisions of this Article, amendments to the Agreement on TRIPS meeting the requirements of para 2 of Article 71 thereof may be adopted by the Ministerial Conference without further formal acceptance process.

7   Any member accepting an amendment to this Agreement or to a Multilateral Trade Agreement in Annex 1 shall deposit an instrument of acceptance with the Director General of the WTO within the period of acceptance specified by the Ministerial Conference.

8   Any member of the WTO may initiate a proposal to amend the provisions of the Multilateral Trade Agreements in Annexes 2 and 3 by submitting such proposal to the Ministerial Conference. The decision to approve amendments to the Multilateral Trade Agreement in Annex 2 shall be made by consensus and these amendments shall take effect for all members upon approval by the Ministerial Conference. Decisions to approve amendments to the Multilateral Trade Agreement in Annex 3 shall take effect for all members upon approval by the Ministerial Conference.

9   The Ministerial Conference, upon the request of the members parties to a trade agreement, may decide exclusively by consensus to add that agreement to Annex 4. The Ministerial Conference, upon the request of the members parties to a Plurilateral Trade Agreement, may decide to delete that Agreement from Annex 4.

10   Amendments to a Plurilateral Trade Agreement shall be governed by the provisions of that Agreement.

Article XI   Original membership

1   The contracting parties to GATT 1947 as of the date of entry into force of this Agreement, and the European Communities, which accept this Agreement and the Multilateral Trade Agreements and for which Schedules of Concessions and Commitments are annexed to GATT 1994 and for which Schedules of Specific Commitments are annexed to GATS shall become original members of the WTO.

2   The least-developed countries recognised as such by the United Nations will only be required to undertake commitments and concessions to the extent

consistent with their individual development, financial and trade needs or their administrative and institutional capabilities.

Article XII Accession

1 Any state or separate customs territory possessing full autonomy in the conduct of its external commercial relations and of the other matters provided for in this Agreement and the Multilateral Trade Agreements may accede to this Agreement, on terms to be agreed between it and the WTO. Such accession shall apply to this Agreement and the Multilateral Trade Agreements annexed thereto.

2 Decisions on accession shall be taken by the Ministerial Conference. The Ministerial Conference shall approve the agreement on the terms of accession by a two-thirds majority of the members of the WTO.

3 Accession to a Plurilateral Trade Agreement shall be governed by the provisions of that Agreement.

Article XIII Non-application of Multilateral Trade Agreements between particular members

1 This Agreement and the Multilateral Trade Agreements in Annexes 1 and 2 shall not apply as between any member and any other member if either of the members, at the time either becomes a member, does not consent to such application.

2 Paragraph 1 may be invoked between original members of the WTO which were contracting parties to GATT 1947 only where Article XXXV of that Agreement had been invoked earlier and was effective as between those contracting parties at the time of entry into force for them of this Agreement.

3 Paragraph 1 shall apply between a member and another member which has acceded under Article XII only if the member not consenting to the application has so notified the Ministerial Conference before the approval of the agreement on the terms of accession by the Ministerial Conference.

4 The Ministerial Conference may review the operation of this Article in particular cases at the request of any member and make appropriate recommendations.

5 Non-application of a Plurilateral Trade Agreement between parties to that Agreement shall be governed by the provisions of that Agreement.

Article XIV Acceptance, entry into force and deposit

1 This Agreement shall be open for acceptance, by signature or otherwise, by contracting parties to GATT 1947, and the European Communities, which are eligible to become original members of the WTO in accordance with Article XI of this Agreement. Such acceptance shall apply to this Agreement and the Multilateral Trade Agreements annexed hereto. This Agreement and the Multilateral Trade Agreements annexed hereto shall enter into force on the date determined by Ministers in accordance with para 3 of the Final Act Embodying the Results of the Uruguay Round of Multilateral Trade Negotiations and shall remain open for acceptance for a period of two years following that date unless the Ministers decide otherwise. An acceptance following the entry into force of this Agreement shall enter into force on the 30th day following the date of such acceptance.

2 A member which accepts this Agreement after its entry into force shall implement those concessions and obligations in the Multilateral Trade Agreements that are to be implemented over a period of time starting with the entry into force of this Agreement as if it had accepted this Agreement on the date of its entry into force.

3   Until the entry into force of this Agreement, the text of this Agreement and the Multilateral Trade Agreements shall be deposited with the Director General to the Contracting Parties to GATT 1947. The Director General shall promptly furnish a certified true copy of this Agreement and the Multilateral Trade Agreements, and a notification of each acceptance thereof, to each government and the European Communities having accepted this Agreement. This Agreement and the Multilateral Trade Agreements, and any amendments thereto, shall, upon the entry into force of this Agreement, be deposited with the Director General of the WTO.

4   The acceptance and entry into force of a Plurilateral Trade Agreement shall be governed by the provisions of that Agreement. Such Agreements shall be deposited with the Director General to the Contracting Parties to GATT 1947. Upon the entry into force of this Agreement, such Agreements shall be deposited with the Director General of the WTO.

Article XV Withdrawal

1   Any member may withdraw from this Agreement. Such withdrawal shall apply both to this Agreement and the Multilateral Trade Agreements and shall take effect upon the expiration of six months from the date on which written notice of withdrawal is received by the Director General of the WTO.

2   Withdrawal from a Plurilateral Trade Agreement shall be governed by the provisions of that Agreement.

Article XVI Miscellaneous provisions

1   Except as otherwise provided under this Agreement or the Multilateral Trade Agreements, the WTO shall be guided by the decisions, procedures and customary practices followed by the Contracting Parties to GATT 1947 and the bodies established in the framework of GATT 1947.

2   To the extent practicable, the Secretariat of GATT 1947 shall become the Secretariat of the WTO, and the Director General to the Contracting Parties to GATT 1947, until such time as the Ministerial Conference has appointed a Director General in accordance with para 2 of Article VI of this Agreement, shall serve as Director General of the WTO.

3   In the event of a conflict between a provision of this Agreement and a provision of any of the Multilateral Trade Agreements, the provision of this Agreement shall prevail to the extent of the conflict.

4   Each member shall ensure the conformity of its laws, regulations and administrative procedures with its obligations as provided in the annexed Agreements.

5   No reservations may be made in respect of any provision of this Agreement. Reservations in respect of any of the provisions of the Multilateral Trade Agreements may only be made to the extent provided for in those Agreements. Reservations in respect of a provision of a Plurilateral Trade Agreement shall be governed by the provisions of that Agreement.

6   This Agreement shall be registered in accordance with the provisions of Article 102 of the Charter of the United Nations.

DONE at Marrakesh this fifteenth day of April one thousand nine hundred and ninety-four, in a single copy, in the English, French and Spanish languages, each text being authentic.

SINGAPORE MINISTERIAL DECLARATION

Adopted on 13 December 1996 .

1   We, the Ministers, have met in Singapore from 9 to 13 December 1996 for the first regular biennial meeting of the WTO at Ministerial level, as called for in Article IV of the Agreement Establishing the World Trade Organisation, to further strengthen the WTO as a forum for negotiation, the continuing liberalisation of trade within a rule-based system, and the multilateral review and assessment of trade policies, and in particular to:

assess the implementation of our commitments under the WTO Agreements and decisions;

review the ongoing negotiations and work programme;

examine developments in world trade; and

address the challenges of an evolving world economy.

Trade and economic growth

2   For nearly 50 years members have sought to fulfil, first in the GATT and now in the WTO, the objectives reflected in the preamble to the WTO Agreement of conducting our trade relations with a view to raising standards of living worldwide. The rise in global trade facilitated by trade liberalisation within the rules-based system has created more and better-paid jobs in many countries. The achievements of the WTO during its first two years bear witness to our desire to work together to make the most of the possibilities that the multilateral system provides to promote sustainable growth and development while contributing to a more stable and secure climate in international relations.

Integration of economies; opportunities and challenges

3   We believe that the scope and pace of change in the international economy, including the growth in trade in services and direct investment, and the increasing integration of economies offer unprecedented opportunities for improved growth, job creation, and development. These developments require adjustment by economies and societies. They also pose challenges to the trading system. We commit ourselves to address these challenges.

Core labour standards

4   We renew our commitment to the observance of internationally recognised core labour standards. The International Labour Organisation (ILO) is the competent body to set and deal with these standards, and we affirm our support for its work in promoting them. We believe that economic growth and development fostered by increased trade and further trade liberalisation contribute to the promotion of these standards. We reject the use of labour standards for protectionist purposes, and agree that the comparative advantage of countries, particularly low-wage developing countries, must in no way be put into question. In this regard, we note that the WTO and ILO Secretariats will continue their existing collaboration.

Marginalisation

5   We commit ourselves to address the problem of marginalisation for least-developed countries, and the risk of it for certain developing countries. We will also continue to work for greater coherence in international economic policy-making and for improved co-ordination between the WTO and other agencies in providing technical assistance.

Role of WTO

6   In pursuit of the goal of sustainable growth and development for the common good, we envisage a world where trade flows freely. To this end we renew our commitment to:

a fair, equitable and more open rule-based system;

progressive liberalisation and elimination of tariff and non-tariff barriers to trade in goods;

progressive liberalisation of trade in services;

rejection of all forms of protectionism;

elimination of discriminatory treatment in international trade relations;

integration of developing and least-developed countries and economies in transition into the multilateral system; and

the maximum possible level of transparency.

Regional agreements

7   We note that trade relations of WTO members are being increasingly influenced by regional trade agreements, which have expanded vastly in number, scope and coverage. Such initiatives can promote further liberalisation and may assist least-developed, developing and transition economies in integrating into the international trading system. In this context, we note the importance of existing regional arrangements involving developing and least-developed countries. The expansion and extent of regional trade agreements make it important to analyse whether the system of WTO rights and obligations as it relates to regional trade agreements needs to be further clarified. We reaffirm the primacy of the multilateral trading system, which includes a framework for the development of regional trade agreements, and we renew our commitment to ensure that regional trade agreements are complementary to it and consistent with its rules. In this regard, we welcome the establishment and endorse the work of the new Committee on Regional Trade Agreements. We shall continue to work through progressive liberalisation in the WTO as we are committed in the WTO Agreement and Decisions adopted at Marrakesh, and in so doing facilitate mutually supportive processes of global and regional trade liberalisation.

Accessions

8   It is important that the 28 applicants now negotiating accession contribute to completing the accession process by accepting the WTO rules and by offering meaningful market access commitments. We will work to bring these applicants expeditiously into the WTO system.

Dispute settlement

9   The Dispute Settlement Understanding (DSU) offers a means for the settlement of disputes among members that is unique in international agreements. We consider its impartial and transparent operation to be of fundamental importance in assuring the resolution of trade disputes, and in fostering the implementation and application of the WTO agreements. The Understanding, with its predictable procedures, including the possibility of appeal of panel decisions to an Appellate Body and provisions on implementation of recommendations, has improved members' means of resolving their differences. We believe that the DSU has worked effectively during its first two years. We also note the role that several WTO bodies have played in helping to avoid disputes. We renew our determination to abide by the

rules and procedures of the DSU and other WTO agreements in the conduct of our trade relations and the settlement of disputes. We are confident that longer experience with the DSU, including the implementation of panel and appellate recommendations, will further enhance the effectiveness and credibility of the dispute settlement system.

Implementation

10 We attach high priority to full and effective implementation of the WTO Agreement in a manner consistent with the goal of trade liberalisation. Implementation thus far has been generally satisfactory, although some members have expressed dissatisfaction with certain aspects. It is clear that further effort in this area is required, as indicated by the relevant WTO bodies in their reports. Implementation of the specific commitments scheduled by members with respect to market access in industrial goods and trade in services appears to be proceeding smoothly. With respect to industrial market access, monitoring of implementation would be enhanced by the timely availability of trade and tariff data. Progress has been made also in advancing the WTO reform programme in agriculture, including in implementation of agreed market access concessions and domestic subsidy and export subsidy commitments.

Notifications and legislation

11 Compliance with notification requirements has not been fully satisfactory. Because the WTO system relies on mutual monitoring as a means to assess implementation, those members which have not submitted notifications in a timely manner, or whose notifications are not complete, should renew their efforts. At the same time, the relevant bodies should take appropriate steps to promote full compliance while considering practical proposals for simplifying the notification process.

12 Where legislation is needed to implement WTO rules, members are mindful of their obligations to complete their domestic legislative process without further delay. Those members entitled to transition periods are urged to take steps as they deem necessary to ensure timely implementation of obligations as they come into effect. Each member should carefully review all its existing or proposed legislation, programmes and measures to ensure their full compatibility with the WTO obligations, and should carefully consider points made during review in the relevant WTO bodies regarding the WTO consistency of legislation, programmes and measures, and make appropriate changes where necessary.

Developing countries

13 The integration of developing countries in the multilateral trading system is important for their economic development and for global trade expansion. In this connection, we recall that the WTO Agreement embodies provisions conferring differential and more favourable treatment for developing countries, including special attention to the particular situation of least-developed countries. We acknowledge the fact that developing country members have undertaken significant new commitments, both substantive and procedural, and we recognise the range and complexity of the efforts that they are making to comply with them. In order to assist them in these efforts, including those with respect to notification and legislative requirements, we will improve the availability of technical assistance under the agreed guidelines. We have also agreed to recommendations relative to the decision we took at Marrakesh concerning the possible negative effects of the agricultural reform programme on least-developed and net food-importing developing countries.

Least-developed countries

14   We remain concerned by the problems of the least-developed countries and have agreed to:

a Plan of Action, including provision for taking positive measures, for example duty-free access, on an autonomous basis, aimed at improving their overall capacity to respond to the opportunities offered by the trading system;

seek to give operational content to the Plan of Action, for example, by enhancing conditions for investment and providing predictable and favourable market access conditions for LDCs' products, to foster the expansion and diversification of their exports to the markets of all developed countries; and in the case of relevant developing countries in the context of the Global System of Trade Preferences; and

organise a meeting with UNCTAD and the International Trade Centre as soon as possible in 1997, with the participation of aid agencies, multilateral financial institutions and least-developed countries to foster an integrated approach to assisting these countries in enhancing their trading opportunities.

Textiles and clothing

15   We confirm our commitment to full and faithful implementation of the provisions of the Agreement on Textiles and Clothing (ATC). We stress the importance of the integration of textile products, as provided for in the ATC, into GATT 1994 under its strengthened rules and disciplines because of its systemic significance for the rule-based, non-discriminatory trading system and its contribution to the increase in export earnings of developing countries. We attach importance to the implementation of this Agreement so as to ensure an effective transition to GATT 1994 by way of integration which is progressive in character. The use of safeguard measures in accordance with ATC provisions should be as sparing as possible. We note concerns regarding the use of other trade distortive measures and circumvention. We reiterate the importance of fully implementing the provisions of the ATC relating to small suppliers, new entrants and least-developed country members, as well as those relating to cotton-producing exporting members. We recognise the importance of wool products for some developing country members. We reaffirm that as part of the integration process and with reference to the specific commitments undertaken by the members as a result of the Uruguay Round, all members shall take such action as may be necessary to abide by GATT 1994 rules and disciplines so as to achieve improved market access for textiles and clothing products. We agree that, keeping in view its quasi-judicial nature, the Textiles Monitoring Body (TMB) should achieve transparency in providing rationale for its findings and recommendations. We expect that the TMB shall make findings and recommendations whenever called upon to do so under the Agreement. We emphasise the responsibility of the Goods Council in overseeing, in accordance with Article IV:5 of the WTO Agreement and Article 8 of the ATC, the functioning of the ATC, whose implementation is being supervised by the TMB.

Trade and environment

16   The Committee on Trade and Environment has made an important contribution towards fulfilling its work programme. The Committee has been examining and will continue to examine, *inter alia*, the scope of the complementarities between trade liberalisation, economic development and environmental protection. Full implementation of the WTO Agreements will make an important contribution to achieving the objectives of sustainable development. The work of the Committee has underlined the importance of

policy co-ordination at the national level in the area of trade and environment. In this connection, the work of the Committee has been enriched by the participation of environmental as well as trade experts from member governments and the further participation of such experts in the Committee's deliberations would be welcomed. The breadth and complexity of the issues covered by the Committee's work programme shows that further work needs to be undertaken on all items of its agenda, as contained in its report. We intend to build on the work accomplished thus far, and therefore direct the Committee to carry out its work, reporting to the General Council, under its existing terms of reference.

Services negotiations

17 The fulfilment of the objectives agreed at Marrakesh for negotiations on the improvement of market access in services – in financial services, movement of natural persons, maritime transport services and basic telecommunications – has proved to be difficult. The results have been below expectations. In three areas, it has been necessary to prolong negotiations beyond the original deadlines. We are determined to obtain a progressively higher level of liberalisation in services on a mutually advantageous basis with appropriate flexibility for individual developing country members, as envisaged in the Agreement, in the continuing negotiations and those scheduled to begin no later than 1 January 2000. In this context, we look forward to full MFN agreements based on improved market access commitments and national treatment. Accordingly, we will:

achieve a successful conclusion to the negotiations on basic telecommunications in February 1997; and

resume financial services negotiations in April 1997 with the aim of achieving significantly improved market access commitments with a broader level of participation in the agreed time frame.

With the same broad objectives in mind, we also look forward to a successful conclusion of the negotiations on Maritime Transport Services in the next round of negotiations on services liberalisation.

In professional services, we shall aim at completing the work on the accountancy sector by the end of 1997, and will continue to develop multilateral disciplines and guidelines. In this connection, we encourage the successful completion of international standards in the accountancy sector by IFAC, IASC, and IOSCO. With respect to GATS rules, we shall undertake the necessary work with a view to completing the negotiations on safeguards by the end of 1997. We also note that more analytical work will be needed on emergency safeguards measures, government procurement in services and subsidies.

ITA and pharmaceuticals

18 Taking note that a number of members have agreed on a Declaration on Trade in Information Technology Products, we welcome the initiative taken by a number of WTO members and other states or separate customs territories which have applied to accede to the WTO, who have agreed to tariff elimination for trade in information technology products on an MFN basis as well as the addition by a number of members of over 400 products to their lists of tariff-free products in pharmaceuticals.

Work programme and built-in agenda

19 Bearing in mind that an important aspect of WTO activities is a continuous overseeing of the implementation of various agreements, a periodic examination and updating of the WTO Work Programme is a key to enable the WTO to fulfil

its objectives. In this context, we endorse the reports of the various WTO bodies. A major share of the work programme stems from the WTO Agreement and decisions adopted at Marrakesh. As part of these Agreements and decisions we agreed to a number of provisions calling for future negotiations on Agriculture, Services and aspects of TRIPS, or reviews and other work on Anti-Dumping, Customs Valuation, Dispute Settlement Understanding, Import Licensing, Preshipment Inspection, Rules of Origin, Sanitary and Phyto-Sanitary Measures, Safeguards, Subsidies and Countervailing Measures, Technical Barriers to Trade, Textiles and Clothing, Trade Policy Review Mechanism, Trade-Related Aspects of Intellectual Property Rights and Trade-Related Investment Measures. We agree to a process of analysis and exchange of information where provided for in the conclusions and recommendations of the relevant WTO bodies, on the Built-in Agenda issues, to allow members to better understand the issues involved and identify their interests before undertaking the agreed negotiations and reviews. We agree that:

the time frames established in the Agreements will be respected in each case;

the work undertaken shall not prejudge the scope of future negotiations where such negotiations are called for; and

the work undertaken shall not prejudice the nature of the activity agreed upon (ie negotiation or review).

Investment and competition

20   Having regard to the existing WTO provisions on matters related to investment and competition policy and the built-in agenda in these areas, including under the TRIMs Agreement, and on the understanding that the work undertaken shall not prejudge whether negotiations will be initiated in the future, we also agree to:

establish a working group to examine the relationship between trade and investment; and

establish a working group to study issues raised by members relating to the interaction between trade and competition policy, including anti-competitive practices, in order to identify any areas that may merit further consideration in the WTO framework. These groups shall draw upon each other's work if necessary and also draw upon and be without prejudice to the work in UNCTAD and other appropriate intergovernmental fora. As regards UNCTAD, we welcome the work under way as provided for in the Midrand Declaration and the contribution it can make to the understanding of issues. In the conduct of the work of the working groups, we encourage co-operation with the above organisations to make the best use of available resources and to ensure that the development dimension is taken fully into account. The General Council will keep the work of each body under review, and will determine after two years how the work of each body should proceed. It is clearly understood that future negotiations, if any, regarding multilateral disciplines in these areas, will take place only after an explicit consensus decision is taken among WTO members regarding such negotiations.

Transparency in government procurement

21   We further agree to:

establish a working group to conduct a study on transparency in government procurement practices, taking into account national policies, and, based on this study, to develop elements for inclusion in an appropriate agreement; and

direct the Council for Trade in Goods to undertake exploratory and analytical work, drawing on the work of other relevant international organisations, on the simplification of trade procedures in order to assess the scope for WTO rules in this area.

Trade facilitation

22 In the organisation of the work referred to in paras 20 and 21, careful attention will be given to minimising the burdens on delegations, especially those with more limited resources, and to co-ordinating meetings with those of relevant UNCTAD bodies. The technical co-operation programme of the Secretariat will be available to developing and, in particular, least-developed country members to facilitate their participation in this work.

23 Noting that the 50th anniversary of the multilateral trading system will occur early in 1998, we instruct the General Council to consider how this historic event can best be commemorated.

17.3.1 Commitment to most-favoured-nation trade

A guiding principle of GATT is non-discrimination. Accordingly Article I of the agreement provides that:

> Any advantage, favour, privilege, or immunity granted by any other contracting party to any product originating in or destined for any other country shall be accorded immediately and unconditionally to the like product originating in or destined for the territories of all other contracting parties.

In the late 19th century it was common for bilateral trade agreements to include a most-favoured-nation clause which committed each party to grant to the other all the trading rights and benefits that it accorded to the third state it treated best, in other words the states agreed to treat each other as well as their most favoured nations. Article I amounts to a most-favoured-nation (MFN) clause binding on and between all parties to the agreement. MFN treatment governs all import and export trade and applies to import and export customs duties and similar charges, all rules and formalities connected with import and export and to internal taxes or charges of any kind in excess of those applied to like domestic products. The commitment to immediate and unconditional MFN trade means that whenever a state party to GATT extends some privilege or right to one of its trading partners it will automatically extend to all other state parties. An important aspect of the unconditional nature of the rule is that it does not require reciprocity: if state A agrees to impose a reduced tariff on particular goods imported from state B that reduction will apply to state C and all other parties to GATT irrespective of whether state C and the other parties reduce tariffs on imports from state A. For this reason MFN status does not ensure that all GATT members trade on the basis of equality, although the multilateral and reciprocal basis of most trade agreements does help to avoid extreme imbalances.

17.3.2 Reduction of tariff barriers

Article II GATT commits the parties to co-operate on the lowering of tariffs. This is to be done through the tariff concession whereby a party promises to levy a tariff on a stated product no higher than that level agreed to at trade negotiations. GATT establishes the framework for regular negotiations between states to set tariff levels. These regular negotiations are known as 'rounds' and there have been eight such rounds. The early rounds tended to be conducted on a bilateral basis but gradually it became clear that more would be achieved by holding multilateral talks. The Kennedy Round (1962–67) resulted in a considerable lowering of tariffs and by the mid 1970s tariffs had been lowered to such an extent that they were no longer seen as the major barrier to international trade. Instead attention was turned to non-tariff barriers and a number of codes of practice were adopted at the Tokyo Round, for example the GATT Agreement on Technical Barriers to Trade which has the aim of harmonising product standards.

17.3.3 Non-discrimination

Article III GATT requires states to treat imported goods in the same way as domestically produced goods. Specifically, imported goods cannot be regulated or taxed in a manner different from that applying to domestic products. Article III(4) provides that:

> The products ... imported into the territory of any other contracting party shall be accorded treatment no less favourable than that accorded to like products of national origin in respect of all laws, regulations, and requirements affecting their internal sale.

Article VII does allow charges to be imposed on imports where they reflect services provided to the importer, for example, charging for the use of port facilities or for product inspection is permitted provided that it is reasonable and based on actual costs. Such charges cannot be used as an indirect import duty.

17.3.4 Import quotas

There is clearly little point in reducing import tariffs if states impose harsh restrictions on the number of imports allowed. Article XI GATT therefore prohibits states from imposing any restriction on imports other than duties, taxes and other charges. This prohibition is subject to a number of exceptions. Article XII allows states to impose import quotas where they are considered necessary to correct a severe balance of payments deficit which is resulting in the imminent threat or actual occurrence of 'a serious decline in its monetary reserves'.

17.3.5 Anti-dumping

Underlying GATT is the belief that everyone benefits from the existence of free trade and that obstacles to such trade should be kept to a minimum. However, this belief relies on trade being fair. Just as imposing high duties on imports is unfair to the importing country and adversely affects the flow of trade, so artificially reducing the price of exports is unfair to the importing country and can have a devastating effect on its economy. Dumping refers to the practice of selling goods in a foreign country for less than the price charged for the same goods in the producer's domestic market. Article VI GATT provides that where such a situation causes or threatens material injury to domestic industry or retards the development of such an industry, the importing state may impose an additional duty which reflects the difference between the price being charged for the goods and the price of the goods, or comparable goods, in the exporter's home market. Thus, for example, if a Japanese company were to market a machine in the UK at a price of £400 while the same machine was marketed at £800 in Japan, then the UK would be entitled to impose a £400 anti-dumping duty on the imported Japanese computer. The usual motivation behind the practice of dumping is an intention to drive competing companies in the importing state out of business. However, the intention of the exporter is not relevant to the imposition of anti-dumping duties. In 1979 the GATT Anti-Dumping Code was adopted in an attempt to further clarify Article VI. The code sets down a procedure for dealing with disputes arising out of allegations of dumping and establishes the Committee on Anti-Dumping Practices which is responsible for assisting in the settlement of such disputes.

17.3.6 Export subsidies

Just as dumping may distort international trade, so too can subsidies granted to exports since they too can make a product less expensive in the importing country which is likely to be to the detriment of foreign competitors. Export subsidies may take the form of export credit guarantees, favourable tax rates for income earned from export trade, or foreign exchange risk guarantees. Article XVI restricts the right of states to grant export subsidies where such subsidies threaten or cause material injury to an industry in the importing state. In such a situation, if export subsidies have been imposed, the importing state is entitled to offset the effect of the subsidies by imposing an additional tariff (countervailing duty). In 1979 GATT adopted the Subsidies Code which further refines the law and provides a mechanism for the settlement of disputes. One such dispute arose out of the development, manufacture and export of the European Airbus. Germany provided currency stabilisation guarantees to assist in the sale of the planes in the USA. The USA alleged that such guarantees violated the GATT code by threatening and causing injury to the American aviation industry. In 1992 a GATT panel of experts upheld the USA complaint.

17.4 Financial stability

At the end of World War Two the international community was faced with two major problems relating to international finance. An immediate problem concerned the need to finance the rebuilding of domestic economies devastated by six years of war. It was also recognised that there was a need to provide some system of regulation of currency exchange to help prevent the violent exchange rate fluctuations and associated hyper-inflation that had occurred during the 1920s and 1930s. These problems were addressed at the international conference held at Bretton Woods in 1944 which resulted in the establishment of the IMF and the International Bank for Reconstruction and Development.

17.4.1 The International Monetary Fund

The IMF was established to promote international monetary co-operation, to facilitate the growth of international trade and to promote foreign exchange stability. The IMF has a board of governors, 22 executive directors and a managing director. The Articles of Agreement of the IMF place a number of obligations on member states. Originally, the currency of each member was assigned a par value expressed in terms of gold and members were under a duty to maintain this value. Changes in par value could only be made to correct serious balance of payment crises and required the agreement of the IMF. By the late 1960s the fixed exchange rates were becoming increasingly difficult to maintain and in 1973 the Articles of Agreement were amended to allow for floating exchange rates. The IMF is financed through subscription by its members. Each member is allocated a subscription quota which is based on a number of criteria relating to the strength of its economy. The size of a state's quota affects its voting rights at meetings of the IMF. The IMF operates a system of weighted voting which gives those states with the strongest economies the biggest voice. As a result the IMF, which now has over 150 members, has always been heavily influenced by the Western industrialised nations. The size of the quota also influences a state's Special Drawing Rights. The Special Drawing Rights allow member states to draw currency from the IMF to correct temporary balance of payments problems. It amounts to a sort of overdraft facility for members. It was envisaged that the provision of Special Drawing Rights would remove the need for states to resort to protectionism in times of economic crisis. For the first 30 years of the IMF currency transactions and payments into the fund were calculated by reference to the official price of gold. In 1978 the Articles of Agreement were amended with the effect of abolishing this gold standard and since that time transactions have been valued on the basis of a 'weighted basket' of the five principal currencies (USA dollar, Deutschmark, yen, French franc, and pound sterling).

17.4.2 The International Bank for Reconstruction and Development

Traditionally states wishing to raise capital by resorting to the private financial markets or by borrowing from other states. As far as the private markets were concerned investors did not always see an adequate rate of return and also ran the risk that such investment might be wiped out by nationalisation or other measures adopted by the borrowing state. Borrowing from other states often led to problems involving the lending state interfering in the domestic affairs of the borrowing state. With the need for a massive injection of capital into the economies of many states after World War Two and with the desire to avoid some of the problems that had been encountered with the traditional methods the Bretton Woods conference agreed to establish the IBRD. membership of the bank is the same as that of the IMF and the two organisations work closely together. The capital of the bank is contributed by the members in proportion to their relative economic strength. Like the IMF voting is weighted according to contribution. The bank exists to lend money to states or to private enterprises where such loans are guaranteed by the government in whose territory the loan is to be used. Although initially the bank provided money to finance immediate post-war reconstruction, loans are now given only for projects which will enhance economic growth. Before any loan is made the bank will carry out a thorough investigation. Money is not lent for high-risk projects and the loans are generally provided on market terms.

It was soon realised that the IBRD's policies were aimed largely at industrialised nations experiencing short-term problems and were not really appropriate to the situation of a newly independent state attempting to establish its own economy. Developing states argued that a UN fund for development should be established but the Western states felt that this would not be in their own interests. As some sort of compromise the IBRD established the International Finance Corporation (IFC) in 1956. The aim of the IFC is to promote private investment in developing countries and to supplement such investment with its own funds. In 1960 the bank established the International Development Association (IDA). The IDA provides long-term low cost finance for the establishment of basic economic infrastructure, such as power supply and communications. The voting rights in the IDA are very heavily weighted in favour of the Western states which has led to criticisms of the organisation by a number of developing or under-developed states.

Together the IBRD, IFC and IDA are generally referred to as the World Bank.

17.5 Development

The basic objective of international economic law is to improve the situation of those developing countries most severely affected by the existing structure of world trade and the international division of labour. This emerging branch of law should nevertheless essentially be conceived as a tool for describing and regulating economic relations between all states. There is no question of establishing a branch of law consisting of rules applicable only to developing states. The basic purpose of international economic law is to establish a link between the industrialised countries and the developing countries, by means of a system of rights and obligations binding on all states together. The aim would be for the rich countries to treat the less developed countries more fairly, within the framework of a new system of rules covering all states. The universality of this branch of international law – in other words, the fact that it aims essentially to cover economic relations between all states in general – not only does not conflict, but is perfectly compatible, with its essential purpose, namely, to protect and to aid the less developed countries through the creation or reform of institutions and principles. This is not a new approach, neither is it alien to the law in general.

During the 19th century and at the beginning of the 20th it was thought that the existence of an objective, general system of laws, and equality before the law, were incompatible with the protection of particular social groups. Fortunately, this 19th century *laissez faire* concept no longer has a place in national legal systems. Sixty or 70 years ago at least, the more developed states realised that equality before the law did not prevent inequality and oppression, and consequently felt obliged to go beyond the purely formal concept of equality of all citizens before the law by creating a whole body of protective legislation to defend certain disadvantaged social groups against the economically powerful. This is precisely the reason and justification for the existence of a particular type of legislation, such as labour law and its institutions, which would have seemed unthinkable in the 19th century and which are now accepted by all. Social security is another example. It was realised with the passing of time that the creation of statutory institutions devised specifically to aid a social group had benefited society as a whole.

Likewise, the present international legal order cannot be based solely on the principle of the sovereign equality of states. The international community today can no longer remain satisfied with a legal order which merely ensures that the freedom of each one of its members is compatible with that of the others, which defends the territorial integrity of the state and provides machinery for the peaceful settlement of disputes. Observance of the principle of non-intervention is not enough.

International economic law must include the following two basic ingredients: on the one hand, a series of institutions, practices, methods and principles guaranteeing the effective protection of the natural resources of the developing countries. Examples of such principles and practices would be the principle of sovereignty over natural resources, equitable regulations of foreign investments and the establishment or recognition of appropriate regulations concerning nationalisation, expropriation, compensation and so on.

Its second basic ingredient would be the establishment of international economic co-operation as a legal institution within the general framework of international law. international co-operation in favour of the underprivileged countries should be more than a question of morality or good intentions and become an integral part of the law. The principles of solidarity and collective responsibility for the common good should be reflected in legal institutions, that is in a system of rights and obligations which, while protecting one section of the international community, will ultimately benefit that community as a whole.

Four phases of UN involvement in development

1   The first phase 1945–63

Four broad phases may be distinguished in the evolution of the UN's involvement with economic development since 1945. The first stretches from 1945 to 1963. One striking development at an early stage was the recognition by member states of the need for a measure of accountability to the international community in the economic and social domain. This development culminated in a report published in 1949 on national and international measures for full employment,[7] which led to a decision setting in motion a process of monitoring the progress of the world economy and the extent to which countries were meeting their employment commitments. The report also addressed the reduction of unemployment in the underdeveloped world, as it was then called, but only as an aspect of the broader question of world economic growth.

In this post-war colonial period systematic thinking on economic development was still in its infancy. The intellectual landmark of the period was a report prepared in 1950 by a group of five experts, which set the stage for UN development activity.[8] Curiously the report made no attempt to discuss the meaning of economic development, presumably because this was considered self-evident. Its main message was that underdeveloped countries should promote 'progressive attitudes and organisations', 'receptiveness to progressive technology', increased domestic capital formation, and reduced population growth. Thus development was essentially, indeed almost exclusively, a matter for 'measures requiring domestic action'. The report did, however, represent a departure from what was called 'colonial economics', in that it addressed the issue of the preconditions for economic development, in which were included the removal of relevant structural impediments through, for example, land reform. The report pointed to the administrative and legal actions, both in the public and private sectors, that were necessary for 'economic progress'. It also recognised a somewhat expanded role for government in the promotion of

---

7   *National and International Measures for Full Employment*, 1949, New York: UN.

8   *Measures for the Economic Development of Under-Developed Countries*, 1951, New York: UN.

economic development, going beyond the simple provision of physical infrastructure, social services, and administration.

These ideas bear a noticeable resemblance, in their essentials, to those advanced by Professor Arthur Lewis, who was actually a member of the expert group, in his book The Theory of Economic Growth, published a few years later.[9] (Interestingly, domestic measures and policies were to resurface in the 1980s, in some circles, as the new hallmark of development wisdom.) Measures by developed countries in support of development were limited to a show of self-restraint in refraining from subsidising certain products competing with the exports of underdeveloped countries. International action was restricted to increasing World Bank lending, and organising technical assistance through an international development authority.

The impact on UN development activity was to be seen in the spread of 'development planning', the techniques and priorities of which were spelled out in the expert group's report; in the sectoralising of international assistance, and the related evolution of technical assistance, and the related evolution of technical assistance programmes; and in the targeting of development resource transfers from developed countries. The UN First Development Decade, which was actually proclaimed in 1962, was in effect an operationalised version of basic ideas contained in the original expert group's report.

This first phase of the UN's involvement with economic development was also characterised by the absence of a collective presence on the part of the developing countries; by the implicit assertion of a wholly convergent process of world development; and by the assumption of an essentially benign external policy environment, and hence the irrelevance of negotiated policy reform addressing the structures and arrangements underpinning international economic relations.

2   The second phase: 1963–82

The second phase in the evolution of the UN's involvement with economic development extends from 1963 to about 1982. The impulses for new orientations in this period were many. They included the decolonisation process, the radical transformation this effected in the UN's membership, and the interest of many of the newly independent nations in socialist doctrines. As the period progressed a clearer perception emerged of the reality that political independence did not itself bring economic growth and development. These countries began to articulate the need for a framework of international economic relations that would be more conducive to the realisation of their economic aspirations. This perception, triggered by the more blatant abuses by transnational enterprises and reinforced by these countries' awareness of their potential power as a source of supply and as a market for the industrialised world, contributed to the evolution of a new outlook on relations between the developed and developing countries.

By the mid-1960s the UN was ripe for a major revision of its development philosophy. This time the intellectual underpinning was provided by the developing world itself, in the form of the doctrines of Raul Prebisch and his collaborators at the Economic Commission for Latin America. Although these ideas were being shaped from the latter part of the 1940s onwards,[10] they did

---

9   W Arthur Lewis, *The Theory of Economic Growth*, 1955, London: Allen & Unwin.

10   UN, Economic Commission for Latin America, *The Economic Development of Latin America and its Principal Problems*, 1950, New York: UN, Dept of Economic Affairs; and Hans Singer, 'The Distribution of Gains between Investing and Borrowing Countries', *Amercian Economic Review*, 40, no 2 (May 1950) at p 47.

not emerge in the form of specific propositions for North-South, or, as it was then called, centre-periphery, relationships until the first UN Conference on Trade and Development (UNCTAD) was held in 1964, with Prebisch as its Secretary General.[11]

The notions that informed the new approach to development theory and practice were radically different from those of the 1950s and the First Development Decade. The new approach asserted the existence of a process of inequalising exchange between the North and the South, as the latter's terms of trade of primary commodities exports for manufactured imports persistently deteriorated, as economic surplus was transferred from the South to the North through transnational enterprises, as mercantilist policies restricted access to technology, and as international capital limited structural change and constrained the potential for growth. A distinguishing feature of the new theories was that they ruled out the possibility of self-correcting forces operating spontaneously to restore equilibrium in the world economy. Persistent divergence between North and South was seen as the natural order. If these tendencies were to be corrected, deliberate policy actions would have to be taken, and thus international policy negotiations would become a special and continuing responsibility of the UN. There was accordingly a concentration on improving the international economic environment to promote development across a broad front. This was an attempt to rectify the gaps and shortcomings of the post-war system (encompassing IMF, IBRD, and GATT), which had given insufficient weight to the development issue. In this sense, the original, virtually exclusive, preoccupation with 'measures requiring domestic action' as the critical determinant of development was relegated to a less important place in the UN approach to economic development.

During this period therefore the focus of attention in the UN, and especially in UNCTAD, turned to the negotiation of international policies and principles, organised on the basis of four country groupings – the Group of 77 (developing countries), the developed market-economy countries, the socialist countries of eastern Europe, and China. The main areas of negotiation were commodity prices, trade in manufactures, the international monetary system, the transfer of technology, transnational corporations, restrictive business practices, international shipping, and, at a general level, the economic rights and duties of states. Many of these negotiations led to agreements, codes, and resolutions, some with greater legal significance than others.[12] Underlying these processes was a belief that market forces alone could not be relied upon to promote development, even if the policies of developing countries were optimal. Governmental intervention in cases of market failure was therefore necessary to support the development effort, and national strategies would have to be adjusted to one another with a view to a consistent set of international economic policies supportive of the development of the Third World.

---

11 *Towards a New Trade Policy for Development*: Report by the Secretary General of UNCTAD, 1964, New York: UN.

12 Examples include the International Commodity Agreements, the Agreement establishing the Common Fund for Commodities, the Code of Conduct on Liner Conferences, the Set of Principles and Rules on Restrictive Business Practices, the Generalised System of Preferences, the Resolution on Debt Relief for the Least-developed Countries, and the Charter on Economic Rights and Duties of States. Negotiations on proposals for Codes of Conduct on the Transfer of Technology, and on Transnational Corporations, ran into intractable difficulties which have yet to be resolved.

At the same time, it must be said, a difficult path was being pursued by the International Monetary Fund and the World Bank where, increasingly, access to their resources was being made conditional on the adoption of domestic measures and policies recommended by them. During this period too there was an impressive growth in technical and financial assistance to the various sectors of economic activity in developing countries, intended to enhance these countries' domestic capabilities. In the field of technical co-operation there was a considerable expansion in the range and volume of activity by the UN Development Programme (UNDP), which was formed in 1965 by a merger of the UN Expanded Programme of Technical Assistance and the UN Special Fund. This expansion was itself to give rise to continuing questions about the UNDP's priorities, coherence, and cost-effectiveness.

The action taken by OPEC in 1973 was seen by developing countries as a successful, even if painful, example of the assertion of endogenous control over national resources and as an inspiration to refashion the international economic system in the interests of efficiency and equity. This naturally gave a strong new impetus to the 'policy negotiation' approach to international economic co-operation for development. It lent credence to the possibility of fundamental change, and to the aspiration that a world of economic equity and justice, as envisaged by the developing countries, might actually be created. The 1974 Declaration on the Establishment of a New International Economic Order (NIEO) and its accompanying Programme of Action embodied this new message of strength and purpose.[13] The impulses for change deriving from this sense of commodity power were so strong that the period from 1973 might well be considered a distinct sub-phase, or even a new phase altogether. Essentially, they underscored the developing countries' conviction that change was needed in the structure and operation of the international economic system, and that such change could be effected through a process of global negotiation, in a context of the developing countries' strengthened bargaining power, and of the concrete realities of global interdependence. It is worth noting, for example, that the NIEO was ostensibly proclaimed to reassert and strengthen the 'spirit, purposes and principles of the Charter of the United Nations'.

Despite the language and the ambitiousness of the programme of international economic reform, as well as the more explicitly confrontational approach of the post-1973 period, many of the measures envisaged for their realisation dated back several years. However, in practical terms the new consciousness of and stress on 'permanent sovereignty over natural resources' gained in influence, while the notion of interdependence emerged more explicitly and with greater clarity as a rationale for international economic management. These approaches, together with the basic ideas associated with the founding of and developments in UNCTAD, merged with the older development currents of the 1950s to influence the shape of the International Development Strategy as proclaimed for the second and third UN Development Decades (which began respectively in 1971 and 1981).[14]

3   The third phase: the decade of the 1980s

The third phase dates from the early 1980s. The new strength and hopes inspired by the NIEO were to be relatively short-lived. By about 1982 the servicing of the massive petrodollar borrowing of developing countries ran into severe difficulty

---

13   General Assembly Resolution 3201 (S-VI) of 1 May 1974.
14   General Assembly Resolution 2626 (XXV) of 24 October 1970 and 35/56 of 5 December 1980.

as recession in the North, brought about by anti-inflationary monetary and fiscal policies, curtailed the export earnings of developing countries.[15] Besides this, a number of other influences had a modifying effect on the UN's development philosophy. There was much disappointment over the failure to negotiate or implement important aspects of the international agenda – international commodity agreements, the Common Fund for Commodities, the Code of Conduct for the Transfer of Technology, and the NIEO. The weakening of commodity power generally, including that of OPEC, diminished the Third World's bargaining power. The revival of the arms race, and continuing East-West tensions, put the North-South dialogue lower on the agenda of international concerns.

The period witnessed a return, primarily at the insistence of the developed market-economy countries, to a preoccupation with national measures and policies of developing countries, similar to that of the 1950s. In major Western economies, the ascendancy of neo-classical economics with its faith in market forces, together with the trend towards deregulation and privatisation, went hand in hand with a reduced interest and investment in forms of international management. These tendencies signalled a diminished concern with negotiated international policies for the promotion of international economic co-operation for development. They also pointed to a greater role for the private enterprise sector in the promotion of international co-operation and development.

Not surprisingly the period saw a weakening of the development consensus underlying the UN's work in this field. Fundamental differences became apparent in economic philosophies, and in perceptions of the capabilities of governments in national and international policy-making. The role of governments and of intergovernmental institutions, on the one hand, and of private market forces, on the other, became the subject of renewed controversy. Disagreement surfaced about the interplay of domestic policies and the external environment, and of the public and private sectors of economic activity. Indeed, governments came to hold divergent views even on how agreed common interests are best pursued in an international and multilateral context; such was the case, for example, on issues of global economic management, trade policies in the context of increasing protectionism, international monetary reform, the evolving international debt strategy, and resource flows to the developing world.

Yet there was no attempt to abrogate the goals and objectives of the International Development Strategy for the Third Development Decade.[16] On the contrary, member states registered their concern about the substantial deterioration of the situation of many developing countries, particularly in Africa, together with the disquieting dimensions that the problem of indebtedness had assumed for a larger number of them.

Meanwhile, increased interdependence within and among the different groups of countries through trade and production went hand in hand with, and was reinforced by, closer financial linkages. These, in turn, enhanced the influence of international finance over trade. Propelled by new developments in information and communications technologies, domestic financial markets increasingly became part of and subordinate to international markets; and the markets for

---

15 UNCTAD, *Trade and Development Report*, 1986, Geneva.

16 See the Agreed Conclusions section of *Report of the Committee on the Review and Appraisal of the Implementation of the International Development Strategy for the Third UN Development Decade*, UN doc A/40/48, New York, 1985.

different assets themselves became more intermeshed. The role of private international markets in the net flow of financial resources, particularly between developed and developing countries, assumed vast proportions. The international financial system as a whole became more sensitive to changes in the ability of developing countries to service their debts. Consequently, as countries became more exposed to international financial influences, the impact of fluctuations in world monetary and financial conditions on their output, employment, and price levels became more pronounced.

4   The fourth phase: from the turn of the decade

In the early 1990s the world community may be moving into a new, more mature phase of international economic co-operation for development. The shifts that have been under way for some years in approaches to economic and social organisation, and in perceptions of development policy, accelerated around the beginning of the decade. Much of the new momentum derived from the dramatic developments that took place in the central and eastern European countries, including the Soviet Union, leading to the introduction of democratic forms of government in place of existing regimes and the suppression of central planning systems by moves towards market-based economies. The challenges posed by the shifts just mentioned are described in the second part of this chapter, but they have laid bare many of the ingredients for a fresh development consensus.[17]

The retreat from multilateralism has come to a halt, prompted possibly by calculations of long-run self-interest on the part of the major industrialised countries – manifested, for instance, at the 1992 Conference on Environment and Development[18] – and partly by considerations of common interest and mutual benefit. Development itself is increasingly seen as a people-centred and equitable process whose ultimate goal must be the improvement of the human condition. Political arrangements are regarded as viable and important for the development process to the extent that they are based on consent, and the observance of human rights is widely accepted as a source of creativity, innovation, and initiative. A convergence of views has occurred on the necessity of supportive frameworks of broad economic policy, both national and international.

Reliance on market forces and competitiveness, and the fostering of entrepreneurial initiative, have become common features of the pursuit of economic efficiency. Approaches to sustainable growth are no longer confined to such criteria as the avoidance of high inflation, large payments imbalances, and sharp cyclical swings: they now encompass the improvement of medium-term growth potential through, for instance, policies that improve the functioning of markets, enlarge human capital, enhance labour mobility, promote openness to international trade, encourage competitiveness, and incorporate respect for the environment. The sharp rise in the level of concern for the health of the global environment and for the long-term security of the planet's ecology base has underscored the need to manage natural resources wisely and to evolve production and consumption patterns in ways consistent with the protection of the environment. Moreover, countries accept that high priority must be accorded to such aspects of the development process as the eradication of poverty and

---

17   General Assembly Resolution S-18/3 of 1 May 1990 entitled 'Declaration on International Economic Co-operation, in particular the Revitalisation of Economic Growth and Development of the Developing Countires'; and 'A New partnership for Development: the Cartegena Commitment' in *Report of UNCTAD on its Eighth Session*, February 1992, UN doc TD/364 of 6 July 1992, pp 6–60.

18   See Chapter 1.

hunger, human resources and institutional development, and improved population policies, as well as protection of the environment.

The proposition that, while the external economic environment is critical for small and open economies, developing countries have the primary responsibility for their own development remains unquestioned: there is no substitute for sustained national policies aimed at liberating and mobilising the latent energies and impulses for development within developing countries, at promising efficiency in the allocation and use of resources, and at taking advantage of the opportunities for trade, investment, and technological progress provided by the changing global environment. Indeed, it is these policies that have determined and will continue to determine how changes in external variables affect the pace of development.

Another factor now widely seen as inseparable from the success of development efforts is the quality of public management. The concept of good governance – or, less controversially, good management – has many dimensions, and it is ultimately defined by a wide variety of historical, cultural, social, and political considerations. As currently understood it encompasses governmental action to establish appropriate frameworks and rules of the game for the effective and proper functioning of markets, and a healthy climate for economic activity.[19] This purpose entails the provision of physical and social infrastructure, the pursuit of sound macroeconomic policies, the creation of a conducive policy environment, and the development of human resources required to support economic activity, as well as policies that promote efficiency in the use and allocation of resources. It also requires clear legal and regulatory frameworks, transparent processes for rule-setting and decision-making, and efficient institutions for the management of resources.

Good management should furthermore stimulate entrepreneurship and productivity growth; help to expand employment opportunities; and promote, or where necessary undertake, functions which cannot be adequately initiated or performed by the private sector. It calls, in addition, for the use of economic and regulatory instruments when markets left to themselves are unable to deal with the phenomenon of externalities and public goods, or to integrate environmental costs adequately into economic activities. Questions of income distribution also need to be addressed, including economic and social safety nets, and assistance to disadvantaged groups to gain access to market opportunities. Likewise, public intervention may be required to foster competition, particularly where concentrations of market power create excessive rents. Finally, strengthened systems of dispute settlement and conflict resolution, with an appropriate role for courts of law and guarantees of their independence, are essential.

As already indicated, the international aspects of good management are also important. Most governments acknowledge, in varying degrees, that the efforts of developing countries in particular to improve their domestic economic policy framework will not have the desired outcome without a supportive international economic environment. Such an environment is seen as depending critically on greater dynamism in the global economy, and on the loosening of such constrictions on development as external indebtedness, inadequate development finance, high trade barriers, depressed commodity prices, and adverse terms of

---

19 *Accelerating the Development Process*: Report by the Secretary General of UNCTAD to the Eighth Session of the Conference, part 2, Chap 1, *Market Forces, Public Policy and Good Management*; and *Report of UNCTAD on its Eighth Session*, 1992.

trade. The industrialised countries, it must be said, accept the importance of appropriate national macroeconomic growth and structural polices aimed at non-inflationary growth and structural adjustment and at avoiding undesired exchange-rate fluctuations and financial market disturbances. What would be even more helpful is a strong commitment to narrowing their imbalances in a manner that would benefit other countries, to stepping up their efforts to invigorate world economic growth, and bringing about a supportive and predictable international economic environment for development.

UN bodies have played a key role in the shaping of these common attitudes. They have also sought to encapsulate the guidelines stemming from them into such major texts as the resolution adopted at the 18th Special Session of the General Assembly in May 1990;[20] the International Development Strategy for the Fourth Development Decade, adopted in December 1990;[21] the Cartagena Commitment adopted by UNCTAD VIII in February 1992;[22] and, from a different vantage point, the final outcome of the 1992 Rio Conference on the Environment and Development.

In the short time that has passed since these texts were adopted, the results have been mixed. Perceptions of certain problems, particularly poverty eradication and environmental protection, have sharpened, and greater recognition of the paths to be followed has emerged. But the recession in the developing market economies, and the persistence of an unsupportive economic environment, not to speak of the 1991 Persian Gulf war and the dissolution of the Soviet Union, have weakened some of the basic premises of the guidelines these documents embody. The gap between international commitments made, and action taken by some of the key actors, has been large.

Effectively mobilised, the common attitudes just mentioned could evolve into a conviction that world economic stability and growth depend on higher levels of international co-operation for the management of interdependence. Interdependence could become a consistent vehicle of growth and development, bringing benefits for all in a positive sum game, on two conditions. One is that national policies, particularly those of the economically powerful, are formulated in a mutually reinforcing fashion to favour constructive adjustment and adaptation in the world economy. The other is that co-operative efforts are pursued to improve the systems, structures, and arrangements that have thus far underpinned international economic relations, particularly as regards trade, money, and finance.

Whether the necessary political determination among countries can be mustered to build on these perceptions so as to reactivate growth and development in the world economy is another matter. The vast enterprise that it entails requires countries both rich and poor to promote a new partnership for development based on the recognition of sovereign equality, mutual interests, and shared responsibilities. Its success depends crucially, of course, on the concerted efforts of the UN together with the family of organisations that has been built up around it.

---

20 GA Resolution 18/3 of 1 May 1990.
21 GA Resolution 45/199 of 21 December 1990, annex, 'International development Strategy for the Fourth UN Development Decade'.
22 *Report of UNCTAD on its Eighth Session*, 1992.

If the UN is effectively to address the challenges that these unprecedented changes pose for development, its capacity to deal with their various facets in an integrated manner – and within a coherent conceptual framework – will have to be enhanced. It is to be hoped that the current wave of reform in the UN, which follows closely upon far-reaching institutional reforms undertaken in UNCTAD, will make a stronger contribution to this objective.[23]

DECLARATION ON THE RIGHT TO DEVELOPMENT

The General Assembly,

Bearing in mind the purposes and principles of the Charter of the United Nations relating to the achievement of international co-operation in solving international problems of an economic, social, cultural or humanitarian nature, and in promoting and encouraging respect for human rights and fundamental freedoms for all without distinction as to race, sex, language or religion,

Recognising that development is a comprehensive economic, social, cultural and political process, which aims at the constant improvement of the well-being of the entire population and of all individuals on the basis of their active, free and meaningful participation in development and in the fair distribution of benefits resulting therefrom,

Considering that under the provisions of the Universal Declaration of Human Rights everyone is entitled to a social and international order in which the rights and freedoms set forth in that Declaration can be fully realised,

Recalling the provisions of the International Covenant on Economic, Social and Cultural Rights and the International Covenant on Civil and Political Rights,

Recalling further the relevant agreements, conventions, resolutions, recommendations and other instruments of the United Nations and its specialised agencies concerning the integral development of the human being, economic and social progress and development of all peoples, including those instruments concerning decolonisation, the prevention of discrimination, respect for, and observance of, human rights and fundamental freedoms, the maintenance of international peace and security and the further promotion of friendly relations and co-operation among states in accordance with the Charter,

Recalling the right of peoples to self-determination, by virtue of which they have the right freely to determine their political status and to pursue their economic, social and cultural development,

Recalling further the right of peoples to exercise, subject to relevant provisions of both International Covenants on Human Rights, their full and complete sovereignty over all their natural wealth and resources,

Mindful of the obligation of states under the Charter to promote universal respect for and observance of human rights and fundamental freedoms for all

---

23 Kenneth Dadzie, Secretary General of UNCTAD, 'The UN and the Problem of Economic Development', in Roberts and Kingsbury (eds), *United Nations, Divided World*, 1994, Oxford: Oxford University Press at pp 298–31.

without distinction of any kind such as race, colour, sex, language, religion, political or other opinion, national or social origin, property, birth or other status,

Considering that the elimination of the massive and flagrant violations of the human rights of the peoples and individuals affected by situations such as those resulting form colonialism, neo-colonialism, apartheid, all forms of racism and racial discrimination, foreign domination and occupation, aggression and threats against national sovereignty, national unity and territorial integrity and threats of war would contribute to the establishment of circumstances propitious to the development of a great part of mankind,

Concerned at the existence of serious obstacle to development, as well as to the complete fulfilment of human beings and of peoples, constituted, *inter alia*, by the denial of civil, political, economic, social and cultural rights, and considering that all human rights and fundamental freedoms are indivisible and interdependent and that, in order to promote development, equal attention and urgent consideration should be given to the implementation, promotion and protection of civil, political, economic, social and cultural rights and that, accordingly, the promotion of, respect for, and enjoyment of certain human rights and fundamental freedoms cannot justify the denial of other human rights and fundamental freedoms,

Considering that international peace and security are essential elements for the realisation of the right to development,

Reaffirming that there is a close relationship between disarmament and development and that progress in the field of development would considerably promote progress in the field of development and that resources released through disarmament measures should be devoted to the economic and social development and well-being of all peoples and, in particular, those of the developing countries,

Recognising that the human person is the central subject of the development process and that development policy should therefore make the human being the main participant and beneficiary of development,

Recognising that the conditions favourable to the development of peoples and individuals is the primary responsibility of their states,

Aware that efforts to promote and protect human rights at the international level should be accompanied by efforts to establish a new international economic order,

Confirming that the right to development is an inalienable human right and that equality of opportunity for development is a prerogative both of nations and of individuals who make up nations,

Proclaims the following Declaration on the right to development:

Article 1

1   The right to development is an inalienable human right by virtue of which every human person and all peoples are entitled to participate in, contribute to, and enjoy economic, social, cultural and political development, in which all human rights and fundamental freedoms can be fully realised.

2   The human right to development also implies the full realisation of the right of peoples to self-determination, which includes, subject to relevant provisions of both International Covenants on Human Rights, the exercise of their inalienable right to full sovereignty over all their natural wealth and resources.

Article 2

1   The human person is the central subject of development and should be the active participant and beneficiary of the right to development.

2   All human beings have a responsibility for development, individually and collectively, taking into account the need for full respect of their human rights and fundamental freedoms as well as their duties to the community, which alone can ensure the free and complete fulfilment of the human being, and they should therefore promote and protect an appropriate political, social and economic order for development.

3   States have the right and the duty to formulate appropriate national development policies that aim at the constant improvement of the well-being of the entire population and of all individuals, on the basis of their active, free and meaningful participation in development and in the fair distribution of the benefits resulting therefrom.

Article 3

1   States have the primary responsibility for the creation of national and international conditions favourable to the realisation of the right to development.

2   The realisation of the right to development requires full respect for the principles of international law concerning friendly relations and co-operation among states in accordance with the Charter of the United Nations.

3   States have the duty to co-operate with each other in ensuring development and eliminating obstacles to development. states should fulfil their rights and duties in such a manner as to promote a new international economic order based on sovereign equality, interdependence, mutual interest and co-operation among all states, as well as to encourage the observance and realisation of human rights.

Article 4

1   States have the duty to take steps, individually and collectively, to formulate international development policies with a view to facilitating the full realisation of the right to development.

2   Sustained action is required to promote more rapid development of developing countries. As a complement to the efforts of developing countries, effective international co-operation is essential in providing these countries with appropriate means and facilities to foster their comprehensive development.

Article 5

States shall take resolute steps to eliminate the massive and flagrant violations of the human rights of the peoples and individuals affected by situations such as those resulting form colonialism, neo-colonialism, apartheid, all forms of racism and racial discrimination, foreign domination and occupation, aggression and threats against national sovereignty, national unity and territorial integrity, threats of war and refusal to recognise the fundamental right of peoples to self-determination.

Article 6

1   All states should co-operate with a view to promoting, encouraging and strengthening universal respect for and observance of all human rights and fundamental freedoms for all without any distinction as to race, sex, language and religion.

2   All human rights and fundamental freedoms are indivisible and interdependent, equal attention and urgent consideration should be given to the

implementation, promotion and protection of civil, political, economic, social and cultural rights.

3   States should take steps to eliminate obstacles to development resulting from failure to observe civil and political rights as well as economic, social and cultural rights.

Article 7

All states should promote the establishment, maintenance and strengthening of international peace and security and, to that end, should do their utmost to achieve general and complete disarmament under effective international control as well as to ensure that the resources released by effective disarmament measures are used for comprehensive development, in particular that of the developing countries.

Article 8

1   States should undertake, at the national level, all necessary measures for the realisation of the right to development and shall ensure, *inter alia*, equality of opportunity for all in their access to basic resources, education, health services, food, housing, employment and the fair distribution of income. Effective measures should be undertaken to ensure that women have an active role in the development process. Appropriate economic and social reforms should be made with a view to eradicating all social injustices.

2   States should encourage popular participation in all spheres as an important factor in development and in the full realisation of all human rights.

Article 9

1   All the aspects of the right to development set forth in this Declaration are indivisible and interdependent and each of them should be considered in the context of the whole.

2   Nothing in this Declaration shall be construed as being contrary to the purposes and principles of the United Nations, or as implying that any state, group or person has a right to engage in any activity or to perform any act aimed at the violation of the rights set forth in the Universal Declaration of Human Rights and in the International Covenants on Human Rights.

Article 10

Steps should be taken to ensure the full exercise and progressive enhancement of the right to development, including the formulation, adopting and implementation of policy, legislative and other measures at the national and international level.

CHARTER OF ECONOMIC RIGHTS
AND DUTIES OF STATES[24]

The General Assembly,

Recalling that the United Nations Conference on Trade and Development, in its Resolution 45 (III) of 18 May 1972, stressed the urgency to establish generally accepted norms to govern international economic relations systematically and recognised that it is not feasible to establish a just order and a stable world as long as a Charter to protect the rights of all countries, and in particular the developing states, is not formulated,

Recalling further that in the same resolution it was decided to establish a Working Group of governmental representatives to draw up a draft Charter of Economic Rights and Duties of States, which the General Assembly, in its Resolution 3037 (XXVII) of 19 December 1972, decided should be composed of forty member states,

Noting that, in its Resolution 3082 (XXVIII) of 6 December 1973, it reaffirmed its conviction of the urgent need to establish or improve norms of universal application for the development of international relations on a just and equitable basis and urged the Working Group on the Charter of Economic Rights and Duties of States to complete, as the first step in the codification and development of the matter, the elaboration of a final draft Charter of Economic Rights and Duties of States, to be considered and approved by the General Assembly at its twenty-ninth session,

Bearing in mind the spirit and terms of its Resolutions 3201 (S-VI) and 3202 (S-VI) of 1 May 1974, containing the Declaration and the Programme of Action on the Establishment of a New International Economic Order, which underlined the vital importance of the Charter to be adopted by the General Assembly at its twenty-ninth session and stressed the fact that the Charter shall constitute an effective instrument towards the establishment of a new system of international economic relations based on equity, sovereign equality, and interdependence of the interests of developed and developing countries,

Having examined the report of the Working Group on the Charter of Economic Rights and Duties of States which, as a result of the task they performed in its four sessions held between February 1973 and June 1974, assembled the elements required for the completion and adoption of the Charter of Economic Rights and Duties of States at the twenty-ninth session of the General Assembly, as previously recommended,

Adopts and solemnly proclaims the following Charter:

PREAMBLE

The General Assembly,

Reaffirming the fundamental purposes of the United Nations, in particular the maintenance of international peace and security, the development of friendly relations among nations and the achievement of international co-operation in solving international problems in the economic and social fields,

---

24 Resolution 3281 (XXIX) adopted on 12 December 1974 by a vote of 120 in favour, six against (Belgium, Denmark, German Federal Republic, Luxembourg, UK, USA) and 10 abstentions.

Affirming the need for strengthening international co-operation in these fields,

Reaffirming further the need for strengthening international co-operation for development,

Declaring that it is a fundamental purpose of the present Charter to promote the establishment of the new international economic order, based on equity, sovereign equality, interdependence, common interest and co-operation among all states, irrespective of their economic and social systems,

Desirous of contributing to the creation of conditions for:

(a) The attainment of wider prosperity among all countries and of higher standards of living for all peoples;

(b) The promotion by the entire international community of the economic and social progress of all countries, especially developing countries;

(c) The encouragement of co-operation, on the basis of mutual advantage and equitable benefits for all peace-loving states which are willing to carry out the provisions of the present Charter, in the economic, trade, scientific and technical fields, regardless of political, economic or social systems;

(d) The overcoming of main obstacles in the way of the economic development of the developing countries;

(e) The acceleration of the economic growth of developing countries with a view to bridging the economic gap between developing and developed countries;

(f) The protection, preservation and enhancement of the environment,

Mindful of the need to establish and maintain a just and equitable economic and social order through:

(a) The achievement of more rational and equitable international economic relations and the encouragement of structural changes in the world economy;

(b) The creation of conditions which permit the further expansion of trade and intensification of economic co-operation among all nations;

(c) The strengthening of the economic independence of developing countries;

(d) The establishment and promotion of international economic relations, taking into account the agreed differences in development of the developing countries and their specific needs,

Determined to promote collective economic security for development, in particular of the developing countries, with strict respect for the sovereign equality of each state and through the co-operation of the entire community,

Considering that the genuine co-operation among states, based on joint consideration of and concerted action regarding international economic problems, is essential for fulfilling the international community's desire to achieve a just and rational development of all parts of the world,

Stressing the importance of ensuring appropriate conditions for the conduct of normal economic relations among all states, irrespective of differences in social and economic systems, and for the full respect of the rights of all peoples, as well as strengthening instruments of international economic co-operation as means for the consolidation of peace for the benefit of all,

Convinced of the need to develop a system of international economic relations on the basis of sovereign equality, mutual and equitable benefit and the close interrelationship of the interests of all states,

Reiterating that the responsibility for the development of every country rests primarily upon itself but that concomitant and effective international co-operation is an essential factor for the full achievement of its own development goals,

Firmly convinced of the urgent need to evolve a substantially improved system of international economic relations,

Solemnly adopts the present Charter of Economic Rights and Duties of States.

CHAPTER I
FUNDAMENTALS OF INTERNATIONAL ECONOMIC RELATIONS

Economic as well as political and other relations among states shall be governed, *inter alia*, by the following principles:

    (a) Sovereignty, territorial integrity and political independence of states;

    (b) Sovereign equality of all states;

    (c) Non-aggression;

    (d) Non-intervention;

    (e) Mutual and equitable benefit;

    (f) Peaceful coexistence;

    (g) Equal rights and self-determination of peoples;

    (h) Peaceful settlement of disputes;

    (i) Remedying of injustices which have been brought about by force and which deprive a nation of the natural means necessary for normal development;

    (j) Fulfilment in good faith of international obligations;

    (k) Respect for human rights and fundamental freedoms;

    (l) No attempt to seek hegemony and spheres of influence;

    (m) Promotion of international social justice;

    (n) International co-operation for development;

    (o) Free access to and from the sea by land-locked countries within the framework of the above principles.

CHAPTER II
ECONOMIC RIGHTS AND DUTIES OF STATES

Article 1

Every state has the sovereign and inalienable right to choose its economic system as well as its political, social and cultural systems in accordance with the will of its people, without outside interference, coercion or threat in any form whatsoever.

Article 2

1   Every state has and shall freely exercise full permanent sovereignty, including possession, use and disposal, over all its wealth, natural resources and economic activities.

2   Each state has the right:

   (a)   To regulate and exercise authority over foreign investment within its national jurisdiction in accordance with its laws and regulations and in conformity with its national objectives and priorities. No state shall be compelled to grant preferential treatment to foreign investment;

   (b)   To regulate and supervise the activities of transnational corporations within its national jurisdiction and take measures to ensure that such activities comply with its laws, rules and regulations and conform with its economic and social policies. Transnational corporations shall not intervene in the internal affairs of a host state. Every state should, with full regard for its sovereign rights, co-operate with other states in the exercise of the right set forth in this subparagraph;

   (c)   To nationalise, expropriate or transfer ownership of foreign property, in which case appropriate compensation should be paid by the state adopting such measures, taking into account its relevant laws and regulations and all circumstances that the state considers pertinent. In any case where the question of compensation gives rise to a controversy, it shall be settled under the domestic law of the nationalising state and by its tribunals, unless it is freely and mutually agreed by all states concerned that other peaceful means be sought on the basis of the sovereign equality of states and in accordance with the principle of free choice of means.

Article 3

In the exploitation of natural resources shared by two or more countries, each state must co-operate on the basis of a system of information and prior consultations in order to achieve optimum use of such resources without causing damage to the legitimate interest of others.

Article 4

Every state has the right to engage in international trade and other forms of economic co-operation irrespective of any differences in political, economic and social systems. No state shall be subjected to discrimination of any kind based solely on such differences. In the pursuit of international trade and other forms of economic co-operation, every state is free to choose the forms of organisation of its foreign economic relations and to enter into bilateral and multilateral arrangements consistent with its international obligations and with the needs of international economic co-operation.

Article 5

All states have the right to associate in organisations of primary commodity producers in order to develop their national economies, to achieve stable financing for their development and, in pursuance of their aims, to assist in the promotion of sustained growth of the world economy, in particular accelerating the development of developing countries. Correspondingly all states have the duty to respect that right by refraining from applying economic and political measures that would limit it.

Article 6

It is the duty of states to contribute to the development of international trade of goods, particularly by means of arrangements and by the conclusion of long-term multilateral commodity agreements, where appropriate, and taking into account the interests of producers and consumers. All states share the responsibility to promote the regular flow and access of all commercial goods trade at stable, remunerative and equitable prices, thus contributing to the equitable development of the world economy, taking into account, in particular, the interests of developing countries.

Article 7

Every state has the primary responsibility to promote the economic, social and cultural development of its people. To this end, each state has the right and responsibility to choose its means and goals of development, fully to mobilise and use its resources, to implement progressive economic and social reforms and to ensure the full participation of its peoples in the process and benefits of development. All states have the duty, individually and collectively, to co-operate in order to eliminate obstacles that hinder such mobilisation and use.

Article 8

States should co-operate in facilitating more rational and equitable international economic relations and in encouraging structural changes in the context of a balanced world economy in harmony with the needs and interests of all countries, especially developing countries, and should take appropriate measures to this end.

Article 9

All states have the responsibility to co-operate in the economic, social, cultural, scientific and technological fields for the promotion of economic and social progress throughout the world, especially that of the developing countries.

Article 10

All states are juridically equal and, as equal members of the international community, have the right to participate fully and effectively in the international decision-making process in the solution of world economic, financial and monetary problems, *inter alia*, through the appropriate international organisations in accordance with their existing and evolving rules, and to share equitably in the befits resulting therefrom.

Article 11

All states should co-operate to strengthen and continuously improve the efficiency of international organisations in implementing measures to stimulate the general economic progress of all countries, particularly of developing countries, and therefore should co-operate to adapt them, when appropriate, to the changing needs of international economic co-operation.

Article 12

1   States have the right, in agreement with the parties concerned, to participate in subregional, regional and interregional co-operation in the pursuit of their economic and social development. All states engaged in such co-operation have the duty to ensure that the policies of those groupings to which they belong correspond to the provisions of the present Charter and are outward-looking, consistent with their international obligations and with the needs of international economic co-operation, and have full regard for the legitimate interests of third countries, especially developing countries.

2   In the case of groupings to which the states concerned have transferred or may transfer certain competencies as regards matters that come within the scope of the present Charter, its provisions shall also apply to those groupings, in regard to such matters, consistent with the responsibilities of such states as members of such groupings. Those states shall co-operate in the observance by the groupings of the provisions of this Charter.

Article 13

1   Every state has the right to benefit from the advances and developments in science and technology for the acceleration of its economic and social development.

2   All states should promote international scientific and technological co-operation and the transfer of technology, with proper regard for all legitimate interests including, *inter alia*, the rights and duties of holders, suppliers and recipients of technology. In particular, all states should facilitate the access of developing countries to the achievements of modern science and technology, the transfer of technology and the creation of indigenous technology for the benefit of the developing countries in forms and in accordance with procedures which are suited to their economies and their needs.

3   Accordingly, developed countries should co-operate with the developing countries in the establishment, strengthening and development of their scientific and technological infrastructures and their scientific activities so as to help to expand and transform the economies of developing countries.

4   All states should co-operate in research with a view to evolving further internationally accepted guidelines or regulations for the transfer of technology, taking fully into account the interests of developing countries.

Article 14

Every state has the duty to co-operate in promoting a steady and increasing expansion and liberalisation of world trade and an improvement in the welfare and living standards of all peoples, in particular those of developing countries. Accordingly, all states should co-operate, *inter alia*, towards the progressive dismantling of obstacles to trade and the improvement of the international framework for the conduct of world trade and, to these ends, co-ordinated efforts shall be made to solve in an equitable way the trade problems of all countries, taking into account the specific trade problems of the developing countries. In this connection, states shall take measures aimed at securing additional benefits for the international trade of developing countries so as to achieve a substantial increase in their foreign exchange earnings, the diversification of their exports, the acceleration of the rate of growth of their trade, taking into account their development needs, an improvement in the possibilities for these countries to participate in the expansion of world trade and a balance more favourable to developing countries in the sharing of the advantages resulting from this expansion, through, in the largest possible measure, a substantial improvement in the conditions of access for the products of interests to the developing countries and, wherever appropriate, measures designed to attain stable, equitable and remunerative prices for primary products.

Article 15

All states have the duty to promote the achievement of general and complete disarmament under effective international control and to utilise the resources released by effective disarmament measures for the economic and social development of countries, allocating a substantial portion of such resources as additional means for the development needs of developing countries.

Article 16

1   It is the right and duty of all states, individually and collectively, to eliminate colonialism, *apartheid*, racial discrimination, neo-colonialism and all forms of foreign aggression, occupation and domination, and the economic and social consequences thereof, as a prerequisite for development. States which

practise such coercive policies are economically responsible to the countries, territories and peoples affected for the restitution and full compensation for the exploitation and depletion of, and damages to, the natural and all other resources of those countries, territories and peoples. It is the duty of all states to extend assistance to them.

2   No states has the right to promote or encourage investments that may constitute an obstacle to the liberation of a territory occupied by force.

Article 17

International co-operation for development is the shared goal and common duty of all states. Every state should co-operate with the efforts of developing countries to accelerate their economic and social development by providing favourable external conditions and by extending active assistance to them, consistent with their development needs and objectives, with strict respect for the sovereign equality of states and free of any conditions derogating from their sovereignty.

Article 18

Developed countries should extend, improve and enlarge the system of generalised non-reciprocal and non-discriminatory tariff preferences to the developing countries consistent with the relevant agreed conclusions and relevant decisions as adopted on this subject, in the framework of the competent international organisations. Developed countries should also give serious consideration to the adoption of other differential measures, in areas where this is feasible and appropriate and in ways which will provide special and more favourable treatment, in order to meet the trade and development needs of the developing countries. In the conduct of international economic relations the developed countries should endeavour to avoid measures having a negative effect on the development of the national economies of the developing countries, as promoted by generalised tariff preferences and other generally agreed differential measures in their favour.

Article 19

With a view to accelerating the economic growth of developing countries and bridging the gap between developed and developing countries, developed countries should grant generalised preferential, non-reciprocal and non-discriminatory treatment to developing countries in those fields of international economic co-operation where it may be feasible.

Article 20

Developing countries should, in their efforts to increase their overall trade, give due attention to the possibility of expanding their trade with socialist countries, by granting to these countries conditions for trade not inferior to those granted normally to the developed market economy countries.

Article 21

Developing countries should endeavour to promote the expansion of their mutual trade and to this end may, in accordance with the existing and evolving provisions and procedures of international agreements where applicable, grant trade preferences to other developing countries without being obliged to extend such preferences to developed countries, provided these arrangements do not constitute an impediment to general trade liberalisation and expansion.

Article 22

1   All states should respond to the generally recognised or mutually agreed development needs and objectives of developing countries by promoting

increased net flows of real resources to the developing countries from all sources, taking into account any obligations and commitments undertaken by the states concerned, in order to reinforce the efforts of developing countries to accelerate their economic and social development.

2   In this context, consistent with the aims and objectives mentioned above and taking into account any obligations and commitments undertaken in this regard, it should be their endeavour to increase the net amount of financial flows from official sources to developing countries and to improve the terms and conditions thereof.

3   The flow of development assistance resources should include economic and technical assistance.

Article 23

To enhance the effective mobilisation of their own resources, the developing countries should strengthen their economic co-operation and expand their mutual trade so as to accelerate their economic and social development. All countries, especially developed countries, individually as well as through the competent international organisations of which they are members, should provide appropriate and effective support and co-operation.

Article 24

All states have the duty to conduct their mutual economic relations in a manner which takes into account the interests of other countries. In particular, all states should avoid prejudicing the interests of developing countries.

Article 25

In furtherance of world economic development, the international community, especially its developed members, shall pay special attention to the particular needs and problems of the least developed among the developing countries, of land-locked developing countries and also island developing countries, with a view to helping them to overcome their particular difficulties and thus contribute to their economic and social development.

Article 26

All states have the duty to coexist in tolerance and live together in peace, irrespective of differences in political, economic, social and cultural systems, and to facilitate trade between states having difference economic and social systems. International trade should be conducted without prejudice to generalised non-discriminatory and non-reciprocal preferences in favour of developing countries, on the basis of mutual advantage, equitable benefits and the exchange of most-favoured-nation treatment.

Article 27

1   Every state has the right to enjoy fully the benefits of world invisible trade and to engage in the expansion of such trade.

2   World invisible trade, based on efficiency and mutual and equitable benefit, furthering the expansion of the world economy, is the common goal of all states. The role of developing countries in world invisible trade should be enhanced and strengthened consistent with the above objective, particular attention being paid to the special needs of developing countries.

3   All states should co-operate with developing countries in their endeavours to increase their capacity to earn foreign exchange from invisible transactions, in accordance with the potential and needs of each developing country and consistent with the objectives mentioned above.

Article 28

All states have the duty to co-operate in achieving adjustments in the prices of exports of developing countries in relation to prices of their imports so as to promote just and equitable terms of trade for them, in a manner which is remunerative for producers and equitable for producers and consumers.

CHAPTER III
COMMON RESPONSIBILITIES TOWARDS THE INTERNATIONAL COMMUNITY

Article 29

The sea-bed and ocean floor and the subsoil thereof, beyond the limits of national jurisdiction, as well as the resources of the area, are the common heritage of mankind. On the basis of the principles adopted by the General Assembly in Resolution 2749 (XXV) of 17 December 1970, all states shall ensure that the exploration of the area and the exploitation of its resources are carried out exclusively for peaceful purposes and that the benefits derived therefor are shared equitably by all states, taking into account the particular interests and needs of developing countries; an international regime applying to the area and its resources and including appropriate international machinery to give effect to its provisions shall be established by an international treaty of universal character, generally agreed upon.

Article 30

The protection, preservation and enhancement of the environment for the present and future generations is the responsibility of all states. All states shall endeavour to establish their own environmental and developmental policies in conformity with such responsibility. The environmental policies of all states should enhance and not adversely affect the present and future development potential of developing countries. All states have the responsibility to ensure that activities within their jurisdiction or control do not cause damage to the environment of other states or of areas beyond the limits of national jurisdiction. All states should co-operate in evolving international norms and regulations in the field of the environment.

CHAPTER IV
FINAL PROVISIONS

Article 31

All states have the duty to contribute to the balanced expansion of the world economy, taking duly into account the close interrelationship between the well-being of the developed countries and the growth and development of the developing countries, and the fact that the prosperity of the international community as a whole depends upon the prosperity of its constituent parts.

Article 32

No state may use or encourage the use of economic, political or any other type of measures to coerce another state in order to obtain from it the subordination of the exercise of its sovereign rights.

Article 33

1   Nothing in the present Charter shall be construed as impairing or derogating from the provisions of the Charter of the United Nations or actions taken in pursuance thereof.

2   In their interpretation and application, the provisions of the present Charter are interrelated and each provision should be construed in the context of the other provisions.

Article 34

An item on the Charter of Economic Rights and Duties of States shall be included in the agenda of the General Assembly at its thirtieth session, and thereafter on the agenda of every fifth session. In this way a systematic and comprehensive consideration of the implementation of the Charter, covering both progress achieved and any improvements and additions which might become necessary, would be carried out and appropriate measures recommended. Such consideration should take into account the evolution of all the economic, social, legal and other factors related to the principles upon which the present Charter is based and on its purpose.

DECLARATION ON THE ESTABLISHMENT OF A NEW INTERNATIONAL ECONOMIC ORDER[25]

The General Assembly

Adopts the following Declaration:

We, the members of the United Nations,

Having convened a special session of the General Assembly to study for the first time the problems of raw materials and development, devoted to the consideration of the most important economic problems facing the world community,

Bearing in mind the spirit, purposes and principles of the Charter of the United Nations to promote the economic advancement and social progress of all peoples,

Solemnly proclaim our united determination to work urgently for THE ESTABLISHMENT OF A NEW INTERNATIONAL ECONOMIC ORDER based on equity, sovereign equality, interdependence, common interest and co-operation among all states, irrespective of their economic and social systems which shall correct inequalities and redress existing injustices, make it possible to eliminate the widening gap between the developed and the developing countries and ensure steadily accelerating economic and social development and peace and justice for present and future generations, and, to that end, declare:

1   The greatest and most significant achievement during the last decades has been the independence from colonial and alien domination of a large number of peoples and nations which has enabled them to become members of the community of free peoples. Technological progress has also been made in all spheres of economic activities in the last three decades, thus providing a solid potential for improving the well-being of all peoples. However, the remaining vestiges of alien and colonial domination, foreign occupation, racial discrimination, apartheid and neo-colonialism in all its forms continue to be among the greatest obstacles to the full emancipation and progress of the developing countries and all the peoples involved. The benefits of technological

---

25   General Assembly Resolution 3201 (XXIX) of 1 May 1974 – adopted without a vote.

progress are not shared equitably by all members of the international community. The developing countries, which constitute 70% of the world's population, account for only 30% of the world's income. It has proved impossible to achieve an even and balanced development of the international community under the existing international economic order. The gap between the developed and developing countries continues to widen in a system which was established at a time when most of the developing countries did not even exist as independent states and which perpetuates inequality.

2   The present international economic order is in direct conflict with current developments in international political and economic relations. Since 1970, the world economy has experienced a series of grave crises which have had severe repercussions, especially on the developing countries because of their generally greater vulnerability to external economic impulses. The developing world has become a powerful factor that makes its influence felt in all fields of international activity. These irreversible changes in the relationship of forces in the world necessitate the active, full and equal participation of the developing countries in the formulation and application of all decisions that concern the international community.

3   All these changes have thrust into prominence the reality of interdependence of all members of the world community. Current events have brought into sharp focus the realisation that the interests of the developed countries and those of the developing countries can no longer be isolated from each other, that there is a close interrelationship between the prosperity of the developed countries and the growth and development of the developing countries, and that the prosperity of the international community as a whole depends upon the prosperity of its constituent parts. International co-operation for development is the shared goal and common duty of all countries. Thus the political, economic and social well-being of present and future generations depends more than ever on co-operation between all the members of the international community on the basis of sovereign equality and the removal of the disequilibrium that exists between them.

4   The new international economic order should be founded on full respect for the following principles:

(a)   Sovereign equality of all states, self-determination of all peoples, inadmissibility of the acquisition of territories by force, territorial integrity and non-interference in the internal affairs of other states;

(b)   The broadest co-operation of all the states members of the international community, based on equity, whereby the prevailing disparities in the world may be banished and prosperity secured for all;

(c)   Full and effective participation on the basis of equality of all countries in the solving of world economic problems in the common interest of all countries, bearing in mind the necessity to ensure the accepted development of all the developing countries, while devoting particular attention to the adoption of special measures in favour of the least developed, land-locked and island developing countries as well as those developing countries most seriously affected by economic crises and natural calamities, without losing sight of the interests of other developing countries;

(d)   The right of every country to adopt the economic and social system that it deems the most appropriate for its own development and not to be subjected to discrimination of any kind as a result;

(e) Full permanent sovereignty of every state over its natural resources and all economic activities. In order to safeguard these resources, each state is entitled to exercise effective control over them and their exploitation with means suitable to its own situation, including the right to nationalisation or transfer of ownership to its nationals, this right being an expression of the full permanent sovereignty of the state. No state may be subjected to economic, political or any other type of coercion to prevent the free and full exercise of this inalienable right;

(f) the right of all states, territories and peoples under foreign occupation, alien and colonial domination or apartheid to restitution and full compensation for the exploitation and depletion of, and damages to, the natural resources and all other resources of those states, territories and peoples;

(g) Regulation and supervision of the activities of transnational corporations by taking measures in the interest of the national economies of the countries where such transnational corporations operate on the basis of full sovereignty of those countries;

(h) The right of the developing countries and the peoples of territories under colonial and racial domination and foreign occupation to achieve their liberation and to regain effective control over their natural resources and economic activities;

(i) The extending of assistance to developing countries, peoples and territories which are under colonial and alien domination, foreign occupation, racial discrimination or apartheid or are subjected to economic, political or any other type of coercive measures to obtain from them the subordination of the exercise of their sovereign rights and to secure from them advantages of any kind, and to neo-colonialism in all its forms, and which have established or are endeavouring to establish effective control over their natural resources and economic activities that have been or are still under foreign control;

(j) Just and equitable relationship between the prices of raw materials, primary commodities, manufactured and semi-manufactured goods, exported by developing countries and the prices of raw materials, primary commodities, manufactures, capital goods and equipment imported by them with the aim of bringing about sustained improvement in their unsatisfactory terms of trade and the expansion of the world economy;

(k) Extension of active assistance to developing countries by the whole international community, free of any political or military conditions;

(l) Ensuring that one of the main aims of the reformed international monetary system shall be the promotion of the development of the developing countries and the adequate flow of real resources to them;

(m) Improving the competitiveness of natural materials facing competition from synthetic substitutes;

(n) Preferential and non-reciprocal treatment for developing countries wherever feasible, in all fields of economic co-operation whenever possible;

(o) Securing favourable conditions for the transfer of financial resources to developing countries;

(p) Giving to the developing countries access to the achievements of modern science and technology, and promoting the transfer of technology and the creation of indigenous technology for the benefit of the developing countries in forms and in accordance with procedures which are suited to their economies;

(q) The need for all states to put an end to the waste of natural resources, including food products;

(r) The need for developing countries to concentrate all their resources for the cause of development;

(s) The strengthening, through individual and collective actions, of mutual economic, trade, financial and technical co-operation among the developing countries, mainly on a preferential basis;

(t) Facilitating the role which producers' associations may play within the framework of international co-operation and, in pursuance of their aims, *inter alia*, assisting in the promotion of sustained growth of the world economy and accelerating the development of developing countries.

5   The unanimous adoption of the International Development Strategy for the Second United Nations Development Decade was an important step in the promotion of international economic co-operation on a just and equitable basis. The accelerated implementation of obligations and commitments assumed by the international community within the framework of the Strategy, particularly those concerning imperative development needs of developing countries, would contribute significantly to the fulfilment of the aims and objectives of the present Declaration.

6   The United Nations as a universal organisation should be capable of dealing with problems of international economic co-operation in a comprehensive manner and ensuring equally the interests of all countries. It must have an even greater role in the establishment of a new international economic order. The Charter of Economic Rights and Duties of States, for the preparation of which the present Declaration will provide an additional source of inspiration, will constitute a significant contribution in this respect. All the states members of the United Nations are therefore called upon to exert maximum efforts with a view to securing the implementation of the present Declaration, which is one of the principal guarantees for the creation of better conditions for all peoples to reach a life worthy of human dignity.

7   The present Declaration on the Establishment of a New International Economic Order shall be one of the most important bases of economic relations between all peoples and all nations.

17.6   Expropriation of foreign-owned property

GENERAL ASSEMBLY RESOLUTION ON PERMANENT SOVEREIGNTY OVER NATURAL RESOURCES 1962[26]

[RESOLUTION 1803 (XVII)]

The General Assembly,

Recalling its Resolutions 523 (VI) of 12 January 1952 and 626 (VII) of 21 December 1952,

Bearing in mind its Resolution 1314 (XII) of 12 December 1958, by which it established the Commission on Permanent Sovereignty over Natural Resources and instructed it to conduct a full survey of the status of permanent sovereignty

---

26 Adopted by the UN General Assembly on 14 December 1962: 87 states voted in favour, two against (France and South Africa) and the USSR abstained.

over natural wealth and resources as a basic constituent of the right to self-determination, with recommendations, where necessary, for its strengthening, and decided further that, in the conduct of the full survey of the status of the permanent sovereignty of peoples and nations over their natural wealth and resources, due regard should be paid to the rights and duties of states under international law and to the importance of encouraging international co-operation in the economic development of developing countries,

Bearing in mind its Resolution 1515 (XV) of 15 December 1960, in which it recommended that the sovereign right of every state to dispose of its wealth and natural resources should be respected,

Considering that any measure in this respect must be based on the recognition of the inalienable right of all states freely to dispose of their natural wealth and resources in accordance with their national interests, and on respect for the economic independence of states,

Considering that nothing in para 4 below in any way prejudices the position of any member state on any aspect of the question of the rights and obligations of successor states and governments in respect of property acquired before the accession to complete sovereignty of countries formerly under colonial rule,

Noting that the subject of succession of states and governments is being examined as a matter of priority by the International Law Commission,

Considering that it is desirable to promote international co-operation for the economic development of the developing countries, and that the economic and financial agreements between the developed and the developing countries must be based on the principles of equality and of the right of peoples and nations to self-determination,

Considering the benefits to be derived from exchanges of technical and scientific information likely to promote the development and use of such resources and wealth, and the important part which the United Nations and other international organisations are called upon to play in that connection,

Attaching particular importance to the question of promoting the economic development of developing countries and securing their economic independence,

Noting that the creation and strengthening of the inalienable sovereignty of states over their natural wealth and resources reinforces their economic independence,

Desiring that there should be further consideration by the United Nations of the subject of permanent sovereignty over natural resources in the spirit of international co-operation in the field of economic development, particularly that of the developing countries,

I

Declares that:

1   The right of peoples and nations to permanent sovereignty over their natural wealth and resources must be exercised in the interest of their national development and of the well-being of the people of the state concerned;

2   The exploration, development and disposition of such resources, as well as the import of the foreign capital required for these purposes, should be in conformity with the rules and conditions which the peoples and nations freely consider to be necessary or desirable with regard to the authorisation, restriction or prohibition of such activities;

3   In cases where authorisation is granted, the capital imported and the earnings on that capital shall be governed by the terms thereof, by the national legislation in force, and by international law. The profits derived must be shared in the proportions freely agreed upon, in each case, between the investors and the recipient state, due care being taken to ensure that there is no impairment, for any reason, of that state's sovereignty over its natural wealth and resources;

4   Nationalisation, expropriation or requisitioning shall be based on grounds or reasons of public utility, security or the national interest which are recognised as overriding purely individual or private interests, both domestic and foreign. In such cases the owner shall be paid appropriate compensation, in accordance with the rules in force in the state taking such measures in the exercise of its sovereignty and in accordance with international law. In any case where the question of compensation gives rise to a controversy, the national jurisdiction of the state taking such measures shall be exhausted. However, upon agreement by sovereign states and other parties concerned, settlement of the dispute should be made through arbitration or international adjudication;

5   The free and beneficial exercise of the sovereignty of peoples and nations over their natural resources must be furthered by the mutual respect of states based on their sovereign equality;

6   International co-operation for the economic development of developing countries, whether in the form of public or private capital investments, exchange of goods and services, technical assistance, or exchange of scientific information, shall be such as to further their independent national development and shall be based upon respect for their sovereignty over their natural wealth and resources;

7   Violation of the rights of peoples and nations to sovereignty over their natural wealth and resources is contrary to the spirit and principles of the Charter of the United Nations and hinders the development of international co-operation and the maintenance of peace;

8   Foreign investment agreements freely entered into by, or between, sovereign states shall be observed in good faith; states and international organisations shall strictly and conscientiously respect the sovereignty of peoples and nations over their natural wealth and resources in accordance with the Charter and the principles set forth in the present resolution.

II

Welcomes the decision of the International Law Commission to speed up its work on the codification of the topic of responsibility of states for the consideration of the General Assembly.

III

Requests the Secretary General to continue the study of the various aspects of permanent sovereignty over natural resources, taking into account the desire of member states to ensure the protection of their sovereign rights while encouraging international co-operation in the field of economic development, and to report to the Economic and Social Council and to the General Assembly, if possible at its eighteenth session.

GENERAL ASSEMBLY RESOLUTION ON PRMANENT SOVEREIGNTY OVER NATURAL RESOURCES[27]

1   Strongly reaffirms the inalienable rights of states to permanent sovereignty over all their natural resources, on land within their international boundaries as well as those in the sea bed and the subsoil thereof within their national jurisdiction and in the superjacent waters;

2   Supports resolutely the efforts of the developing countries and of the peoples of the territories under colonial and racial domination and foreign occupation in their struggle to regain effective control over their natural resources;

3   Affirms that the application of the principle of nationalisation carried out by states, as an expression of their sovereignty in order to safeguard their natural resources, implies that each state is entitled to determine the amount of possible compensation and the mode of payment, and that any disputes which might arise should be settled in accordance with the national legislation of each state carrying out such measures;

4   Deplores acts of states which use force, armed aggression, economic coercion or any other illegal or improper means in resolving disputes concerning the exercise of the sovereign rights mentioned in paras 1 to 3 above;

5   Re-emphasises that actions, measures or legislative regulations by states aimed at coercing, directly or indirectly, other states or peoples engaged in the reorganisation of their internal structure or in the exercise of their sovereign rights over their natural resources, both on land and in their coastal waters, are in violation of the Charter of the United Nations;

6   Emphasises the duty of all states to refrain in their international relations from military, political, economic or any other form of coercion aimed against the territorial integrity of any state and the exercise of its national jurisdiction;

7   Recognises that, as stressed in Economic and Social Council Resolution 1737 (LIV) of 4 May 1973, one of the most effective ways in which the developing countries can protect their natural resources is to establish, promote or strengthen machinery for co-operation among them which has as its main purpose to concert pricing policies, to improve conditions of access to markets, to co-ordinate production policies and, thus, to guarantee the full exercise of sovereignty by developing countries over their natural resources;

8   Requests the Economic and Social Council, at its fifty-sixth session, to consider the report of the Secretary General mentioned in the last preambular paragraph above and requests the Secretary General to prepare a supplement to that report, in the light of the discussion that are to take place at the fifty-sixth session of the Council and of any other relevant developments, and to submit that supplementary report to the General Assembly at its twenty-ninth session.

---

27   General Assembly Resolution 3171 (XXVIII) adopted on 17 December 1973: 108 states voted in favour, one against (UK) and 16 abstained (including France, FRG, Japan and the USA).

CHAPTER 18

ENVIRONMENTAL PROTECTION

18.1 Introduction

The development of modern international environmental law, starting essentially in the 1960s, has been one of the most remarkable exercises in international lawmaking, comparable only to the law of human rights in the scale and form it has taken. The system which has emerged from this process is neither primitive nor wholly without effect, though equally it has many weaknesses ... It is, of course, possible to argue that other approaches to environmental management may be more desirable, and more efficacious. But to say that economic models of control and assistance have as much or more to offer than international law is merely to observe that protecting the environmental is not exclusively a problem for lawyers. Similarly, it would be naive to expect international law to remedy problems of the complexity the world's environment now faces without an underlying political, scientific, and technical commitment on the part of states, and a corresponding response in national legal and political systems. It has not been the purpose of this book to explore the place of international law within this broader context; it will be sufficient to observe the reality that international environmental law has provided the framework for much political and scientific co-operation, for measures of economic assistance and distributive equity, fair resolution of international disputes, and for the adoption and harmonization of a great deal of national environmental law. These developments have clearly not been without considerable significance, and have laid the foundations of a new system of global environmental order.[1]

As Boyle and Birnie indicate, international environmental law is a comparatively new area of international law. This, of course, reflects changes in the general level of interest in protection and conservation of the environment. Although there is some early evidence of international concern with specific environmental matters[2] there was no general system of international environmental regulation until well into the second half of the 20th century. The sovereign equality of states has tended to mean that states are free to act as they chose, even if this is detrimental to the environment. The sovereignty possessed by states over their own territory, however, has long been limited by the obligation not to interfere in the rights of other states. States are under a duty not to act within their own territory in such a way as to cause harm in the territory of other states. The classic example of this point is provided by the *Trail Smelter Arbitration (USA v Canada)*.[3]

The Consolidated Mining and Smelting Company owned a smelting works at Trail, which is about 10 miles north of the Canadian-United States border on the Colombia River. As a result of the smelting process a large amount of sulphur dioxide was emitted, some of which was being carried down the Columbia River valley and across the border into the state of Washington where considerable

---

1 Boyle and Birnie, *International Law and the Environment*, 1992, Oxford: Oxford University Press at p 549.
2 See, for example, the 1885 Convention for the Uniform Regulation of Fishing in the Rhine and the Paris Convention for the protection of Birds Useful to Agriculture of 19 March 1902.
3 (1941) 3 RIAA 1905, 1965–66 (Arbitral Tribunal).

damage was caused. Canada and the United States agreed to refer the dispute to the International Joint Commission established by the Canadian-USA Boundary Waters Treaty 1909. In 1931 the Commission assessed the damage caused by the smelter at $350,000 and Canada agreed to pay the full amount. However, the pollution continued and the matter was referred to arbitration. Question 2 submitted to the arbitral tribunal was 'whether the Trail Smelter should be required to refrain from causing damage in the State of Washington in the future and, if so, to what extent?' The findings of the Tribunal are of general relevance to the question of liability and responsibility for pollution.

> The Tribunal ... finds that ... under the principles of international law, as well as of the law of the United States,[4] no state has the right to use or permit the use of its territory in such a manner as to cause injury by fumes in or to the territory of another or the properties or persons therein, when the case is of serious consequence and the injury is established by clear and convincing evidence.

> The decisions of the Supreme Court of the United States which are the basis of these conclusions are decisions in equity and a solution inspired by them, together with the regime hereinafter prescribed, will, in the opinion of the Tribunal, be 'just to all parties concerned', as long, at least, as the present conditions in the Columbia River Valley continue to prevail.

> Considering the circumstances of the case, the Tribunal holds that the Dominion of Canada is responsible in international law for the conduct of the Trail Smelter. Apart from the undertaking in the Convention, it is, therefore, the duty of the government of the Dominion of Canada to see to it that this conduct should be in conformity with the obligation of the Dominion under international law as herein determined.

> The Tribunal, therefore, answers Question No 2 as follows: (2) So long as the present conditions in the Columbia River Valley prevail, the Trail Smelter shall be required to refrain from causing any damage through fumes in the state of Washington; the damage herein referred to and its extent being such as would be recoverable under the decision of the courts of the United states in suits between private individuals. The indemnity for such damage should be fixed in such manner as the governments, acting under Article XI of the Convention, should agree upon.

Since World War Two there has been a growing realisation that the world's resources are not infinite and that the nature of industrial and agricultural practices adopted can have serious implications for future generations. The international community has come to accept that there is a need for common action to help sustain life, in all its forms, on this planet and that this need is incompatible with an absolute notion of state sovereignty.

One particular question that has been raised about international environmental law concerns the nature of the obligations imposed. Several writers have argued that the general obligation to preserve the environment constitutes a norm of *jus cogens* and that it is binding *erga omnes*. In the *Nuclear Tests* cases[5] the International Court of Justice doubted whether rights relating to

---

4   The parties to the dispute had instructed the tribunal to apply the relevant law and practice of the United States as well as international law.

5   [1974[*ICJ Rep* at p 253.

the high seas could be enforced as *erga omnes* obligations although the reasoning of the court has been criticised by some writers and conflicts with the ILC Draft Articles on State Responsibility 1980. Article 19(3)(d) provides that:

> ... a serious breach of an international obligation of essential importance for the safeguarding and preservation of the human environment, such as those prohibiting massive pollution of the atmosphere or of the seas ...

constitutes an international crime and therefore is the concern of all states and not just those suffering injury. The repetition of the obligation on states to safeguard and preserve the human environment in numerous international resolutions including the declaration made at the Rio Conference on the Environment and Development 1992 would seem to support the view that the obligation is indeed now one of *jus cogens*. The full extent of the obligation, however, remains to be clearly enunciated.

18.2 Sources

The bulk of international environmental law is contained in multilateral treaties and the important ones will be discussed in the subsequent sections. Such treaties may be designed to apply globally, such as the Convention on Long-Range Transboundary Air Pollution 1979 or may be concerned with protection of a specific region, for example the Antarctic Treaty 1959 and the Convention on Protection of the Mediterranean Sea 1976. In addition there are a number of treaties which, while not concerned exclusively with environmental matters, nevertheless contain provisions which have significance for the environment, for example the Law of the Sea Convention 1982.

Besides treaty law, there are also some important rules of customary international law affecting the environment. For example, reference has already been made to the prohibition on causing harm in or to the territory of another state. However, although states often make statements in support of environmental protection these statements are not always adhered to in practice. Furthermore it has often been difficult to prove the necessary accompanying *opinio juris* to be able to assert a binding rule of customary international law. Therefore, writers on international environmental law have made considerable use of the concept of soft law. It is often the case that states are unwilling to agree to legally binding obligations in particular areas of environmental protection because of the unavailability of relevant scientific information or knowledge. The concept of soft law allows there to be a statement of principle and intention and the soft law can gradually harden as scientific knowledge expands. Many of the international conventions dealing with environmental matters have been developed from broad statements of principle expressed in resolutions and declarations of the United Nations. Arguably, the declarations themselves could be considered soft law. A considerable amount of soft environmental law is to be found in the resolutions of various international organisations concerned with environmental matters such as the World Health Organisation, the International Atomic Energy Agency, the International Maritime Organisation and the Food and Agriculture Organisation.

If international protection of environmental resources requires an increasingly high degree of adaptability and responsiveness of the legal system to rapid and frequent change, a traditional, *ad hoc*, treaty-based approach to international environmental standard-setting, is evidently ill suited to meet the task. The disadvantages of the classic treaty approach are obvious: the drafting, adoption, and putting into effect of treaties as well as revisions or amendments involve elaborate and time-consuming exercises in diplomacy. In the aggregate, transaction costs of this approach become unacceptably high because, as legislative international intervention will be repeatedly required to respond to an evolving international environmental problem, this approach offers simply too many opportunities to states for 'opportunistic' behaviour.

The need to facilitate international environmental decision-making of a less cumbersome and time-consuming nature without sacrificing at the same time on the objective of broad state adherence to adequate environmental standards, has prompted the restructuring of multilateral legislative processes: diplomatic '*ad hocracy*' is being abandoned for institutionalised, periodic, and informal review of international regulatory regimes with simplified amendment procedures.

While there are other indications of this development in international environmental standard-setting (note, for example, the simplified amendment procedures of Article 313 of UNCLOS) it is only in the context of more recent environmental framework conventions and implementing Protocols that the trend has become conspicuous. For example, the Montreal Protocol on Substance that Deplete the Ozone Layer expressly provides for the periodic review and assessment of control measures taken and their adjustment or supplementation whenever deemed necessary ...

The resulting intrinsic flexibility or adaptability of the legislative process comes, as some might be apt to object, with a substantial price-tag. The framework-cum-implementation Protocols approach necessarily entails a significant degree of indeterminacy of the normative landscape thus being created: states tend to settle first broad policy outlines through the device of framework conventions and leave nettlesome international lawmaking within the individual environmental context as defined by the framework convention. By necessity, this approach also signals a certain open-endedness of the legislative enterprise.

More significantly still, states may leave the definition of key legal parameters regarding the scope and very nature of conventional obligations to which they contract to be settled at a later date ... international legislation under this guise is no longer a single well-defined product carried by expectations of stability for a foreseeable future. It is rather a fragile, temporary legal sign-post in an institutionalised process in which legal positions are subject to constant review and susceptible to frequent and speedy alteration ...

Some aspects of this development may be undesirable. For example, the institutional dynamics of multilateral regimes (with regard to both the setting and implementation of standards), may be such as to de-couple decision-making within the regime from traditional national processes of control and supervision. In this sense, the new type of environmental regime may signal an emerging 'democratic deficit'. Other implications of such regimes might be merely inconvenient. However, on balance, there can be little doubt that the evolving international legislative process represents progress towards better international legal management of increasingly demanding global environmental problems.

It is against the background of the special regulationary exigencies of international environmental problems, that so-called 'soft law' plays an important role in the evolution of international environmental law. 'Soft law' denotes international prescriptions that are deemed to lack the requisite characteristics of international legal norms proper, but which, notwithstanding this fact, are capable of producing certain effects. 'Soft law', of course, travels in tandem with 'hard law', its counterpart on the other side of the threshold of legal normativity.

There are international lawyers who harbour serious reservations about usage of the term, defining it as a 'pathological phenomenon' of international law; as introducing a graduated scale of normativity; as a practice that lends itself to legal pretension. The concept, so the argument goes, tends to blur the line between law and non-law, be that because merely aspirational norms are accorded 'legal' status, albeit of a secondary nature; be that because the effect of the usage of the term may be to undermine the status of an established legal norm.

On the other hand, 'soft law' can be a valuable instrument for enhancing or supplementing international law proper. In fact, frequently 'soft law' will capture emerging notions of international public order and thus help extend the realm of legitimate international concern to matters of previously exclusive national jurisdiction. This is especially true of the use of soft law with regard to the protection of the environment. In this sense, soft law is the thin end of the normative wedge of international environmental law, perhaps the 'Trojan Horse of environmentalists'.

There is, of course, abundant and well-known evidence of the effectiveness of soft law declarations as catalysts in the evolution of international environmental law proper. The so-called Helsinki Rules on the Uses of Waters of International Rivers, the 1972 Stockholm Declaration on the Human Environment, or the 1982 General Assembly Resolution entitled 'World Charter for Nature', to name only a few, all have proved to be agents in the 'legalisation of international environmental protection'.

In the final analysis, though, soft law concepts pose both a challenge for and an obligation on international lawyers. First, the declining reliability of formal criteria as guide-posts to what actually constitutes international law – a phenomenon that, as intimated, may be prevalent in the context of international environmental decision-making – requires an adequate theory about international law, namely as a process of communication, and thus sensitivity to those signals indicating international normativity and those that do not. Second, international environmental lawyers must heed the normative dividing line and avoid misrepresenting aspirational norms for 'hard law' and thereby rendering a disservice to the very cause that they purport to serve, namely the strengthening of the legal protection of the environment.'[6]

18.3 The Stockholm Conference

During the 1960s concern grew about the state of the human environment and manifested itself in Resolution 2398 (XXIII) which was passed by the General Assembly of the United Nations on 3 December 1968. The resolution noted that there was 'an urgent need for intensified action at national and international level to limit and, where possible, to eliminate the impairment of the human

6   Gunther Handl, 'Environmental Security and Global Change: The Challenge to International Law', in Lang, Neuhold and Zemanek (eds), *Environmental Protection and International Law*, 1991, London: Graham and Trotman at pp 61–64.

environment' and convened an international conference on the human environment to be held under the auspices of the United Nations. The Conference met in June 1972 in Stockholm and was attended by 113 states.[7] At the end of the conference agreement had been reached on four major areas of policy:

1   an Action Plan for environmental policy was agreed consisting of 106 recommendations, including the establishment of Earthwatch, which was charged with monitoring and providing information on the state of the environment;

2   an Environment Fund would be created, funded by voluntary contributions from states;[8]

3   the establishment of the UN Environment Programme (UNEP) with a Governing Council and Secretariat. UNEP is based in Nairobi, Kenya and has adopted a number of codes of practice and recommendations, many of which could be considered soft law;

4   a Declaration of principles on the human environment which would provide a focus for future binding rules of international law in a manner analogous to the Universal Declaration of Human Rights.

DECLARATION OF THE UNITED NATIONS CONFERENCE ON THE HUMAN ENVIRONMENT – THE STOCKHOLM DECLARATION[9]

The United Nations Conference on the Human Environment,

Having met at Stockholm from 5 to 16 June 1972,

Having considered the need for a common outlook and for common principles to inspire and guide the peoples of the world in the preservation and enhancement of the human environment,

I

Proclaims that:

1   Man is both creature and moulder of his environment, which gives him physical sustenance and affords him the opportunity for intellectual, moral, social and spiritual growth. In the long and tortuous evolution of the human race on this planet a stage has been reached when, through the rapid acceleration of science and technology, man has acquired the power to transform his

---

7   Significant absentees from the Conference were the USSR and a number of other Eastern-bloc states. This was due more to the fact that West Germany had been invited whilst East Germany (excluded from membership of the United Nations at that time) was not rather than any disagreement about the general aims of the Conference. Subsequently the USSR participated fully in the work of UNEP.

8   Unsurprisingly, states have proved extremely reluctant to contribute to the Fund and it has consequently not had the impact that might have been hoped in June 1972.

9   UN Doc A/Conf 48/14, Stockholm, 1972; (1972) 11 ILM 1416; *Report on the United Nations Conference on the Human Environment, Stockholm, 5–16 June 1972.*

environment in countless ways and on an unprecedented scale. Both aspects of man's environment, the natural and the man-made, are essential to his well-being and to the enjoyment of basic human rights – even the right to life itself.

2 The protection and improvement of the human environment is a major issue which affects the well-being of peoples and economic development throughout the world; it is the urgent desire of the peoples of the whole world and the duty of all governments ...

II

Principles

States the common conviction that:

Principle 1

Man has the fundamental right to freedom, equality and adequate conditions of life, in an environment that permits a life of dignity and well-being, and he bears a solemn responsibility to protect and improve the environment for present and future generations. In this respect, policies promoting or perpetuating apartheid, racial segregation, discrimination, colonial and other forms of oppression and foreign domination stand condemned and must be eliminated.

Principle 2

The natural resources of the earth, including the air, water, land, flora and fauna and especially representative samples of natural ecosystems, must be safeguarded for the benefit of present and future generations through careful planning or management, as appropriate.

Principle 3

The capacity of the earth to produce vital renewable resources must be maintained and, wherever practicable, restored or improved.

Principle 4

Man has a special responsibility to safeguard and wisely manage the heritage of wildlife and its habitat, which are now gravely imperilled by a combination of adverse factors. Nature conservation, including wildlife, must therefore receive importance in planning for economic development.

Principle 5

The non-renewable resources of the earth must be employed in such a way as to guard against the danger of their future exhaustion and to ensure that benefits from such employment are shared by all mankind.

Principle 6

The discharge of toxic substances or of other substances and the release of heat, in such quantities or concentrations as to exceed the capacity of the environment to render them harmless, must be halted in order to ensure that serious or irreversible damage is not inflicted upon ecosystems. The just struggle of the peoples of all countries against pollution should be supported.

Principle 7

States shall take all possible steps to prevent pollution of the seas by substances that are liable to create hazards to human health, to harm living resources and marine life, to damage amenities or to interfere with other legitimate uses of the sea.

Principle 8

Economic and social development is essential for ensuring a favourable living and working environment for man and for creating conditions on earth that are necessary for the improvement of the quality of life.

Principle 9

Environmental deficiencies generated by the conditions of underdevelopment and natural disasters pose grave problems and can best be remedied by accelerated development through the transfer of substantial quantities of financial and technological assistance as a supplement to the domestic effort of the developing countries and such timely assistance as may be required.

Principle 10

For the developing countries, stability of prices and adequate earnings for primary commodities and raw materials are essential to environmental management since economic factors as well as ecological processes must be taken into account.

Principle 11

The environmental policies of all states should enhance and not adversely affect the present or future development potential of developing countries, nor should they hamper the attainment of better living conditions for all, and appropriate steps should be taken by states and international organisations with a view to reaching agreement on meeting the possible national and international economic consequences resulting from the application of environmental measures.

Principle 12

Resources should be made available to preserve and improve the environment, taking into account the circumstances and particular requirements of developing countries and any costs which may emanate from their incorporating environmental safeguards into their development planning and the need for making available to them, upon their request, additional international technical and financial assistance for this purpose.

Principle 13

In order to achieve a more rational management of resources and thus to improve the environment, states should adopt an integrated and co-ordinated approach to their development planning so as to ensure that development is compatible with the need to protect and improve the environment for the benefit of their population.

Principle 14

Rational planning constitutes an essential tool for reconciling any conflict between the needs of development and the need to protect and improve the environment.

Principle 15

Planning must be applied to human settlements and urbanisation with a view to avoiding adverse effects on the environment and obtaining maximum social, economic and environmental benefits for all. In this respect, projects which are designed for colonialist and racist domination must be abandoned.

Principle 16

Demographic policies which are without prejudice to basic human rights and which are deemed appropriate by governments concerned should be applied in those regions where the rate of population growth or excessive population concentrations are likely to have adverse effects on the environment or development, or where low population density may prevent improvement of the human environment and impede development.

Principle 17

Appropriate national institutions must be entrusted with the task of planning, managing or controlling the environmental resources of states with a view to enhancing environmental quality.

Principle 18

Science and technology, as part of their contribution to economic and social development, must be applied to the identification, avoidance and control of environmental risks and the solution of environmental problems and for the common good of mankind.

Principle 19

Education in environmental matters, for the younger generation as well as adults, giving due consideration to the underprivileged, is essential in order to broaden the basis for an enlightened opinion and responsible conduct by individuals, enterprises and communities in protecting and improving the environment in its full human dimension. It is also essential that mass media of communications avoid contributing to the deterioration of the environment, but, on the contrary, disseminate information of an educational nature on the need to protect and improve the environment in order to enable man to develop in every respect.

Principle 20

Scientific research and development in the context of environmental problems, both national and multinational, must be promoted in all countries, especially the developing countries. In this connection, the free flow of up-to-date scientific information and transfer of experience must be supported and assisted, to facilitate the solution of environmental problems; environmental technologies should be made available to developing countries on terms which would encourage their wide dissemination without constituting an economic burden on the developing countries.

Principle 21

States have, in accordance with the Charter of the United Nations and the principles of international law, the sovereign right to exploit their own resources pursuant to their own environmental policies, and the responsibility to ensure that activities within their jurisdiction or control do not cause damage to the environment of other states or of areas beyond the limits of national jurisdiction.

Principle 22

States shall co-operate to develop further the international law regarding liability and compensation for the victims of pollution and other environmental damage caused by activities within the jurisdiction or control of such states to areas beyond their jurisdiction.

Principle 23

Without prejudice to such criteria as may be agreed upon by the international community, or to standards which will have to be determined nationally, it will be essential in all cases to consider the systems of values prevailing in each country, and the extent of the applicability of standards which are valid for the most advanced countries but which may be inappropriate and of unwarranted social cost for the developing countries.

Principle 24

International matters concerning the protection and improvement of the environment should be handled in a co-operative spirit by all countries, big and small, on an equal footing. Co-operation through multilateral or bilateral arrangements or other appropriate means is essential to effectively control, prevent, reduce and eliminate adverse environmental effects resulting from activities conducted in all spheres, in such a way that due account is taken of the sovereignty and interests of all states.

Principle 25

States shall ensure that international organisations play a co-ordinated, efficient and dynamic role for the protection and improvement of the environment.

Principle 26

Man and his environment must be spared the effects of nuclear weapons and all other means of mass destruction. States must strive to reach prompt agreement, in the relevant organs, on the elimination and complete destruction of such weapons.

18.4 The environment and development

Although concern about the environment was growing, during the 1960s the priority at the United Nations was economic development. The resolution on Permanent Sovereignty over Natural Resources[10] adopted in 1962 made no reference to conservation of resources or other environmental concerns and during the 1960s there were few voices in support of linking economic development issues to the environment. In fact, among developing states there was a significant number of people who viewed environmental concern with suspicion fearing that measures taken to protect and conserve the environment were simply a Western capitalist plot to prevent Third World development. Patricia Birnie identifies the preparations for the Stockholm Conference as marking a change in attitudes:

> A catalytic event, facilitating the success of UNCHE, was the convening of a meeting at Founex, Switzerland, in 1971, to consider a study (instigated by the UNCHE Prepcom) on environment and development. The study group brought together representatives of international development agencies and governments, including economists, bankers, planners, social scientists, and ecologists. Its conclusion that 'the kind of environmental problems that are of importance in developing countries are those that can be overcome by the process of development itself' reassured developing countries, which were wavering in their support for the conference. Twenty-five guidelines were laid down aimed at protecting their interests. This articulation of the symbiosis of environment and development was thus from the beginning central to the UN's work in the environmental field.[11]

The Stockholm Declaration acknowledged the link between the protection and improvement of the human environment and economic development although the emphasis of the Charter of Economic Rights and Duties of States,[12] adopted two years after the Stockholm Conference, was on optimum use of resources and full economic development with limited acknowledgment of environmental

---

10   GA Resolution 1803 (XVIII) of 14 December 1962.

11   Patricia Birnie, 'The UN and the Environment' in Roberts and Kingsbury (eds), *United Nations Divided World*, 2nd edn, 1993, Oxford: Oxford University Press at p 338.

12   GA Resolution 3202 (XXIX) of 1 May 1974.

concerns. It was not until 1983 that the link between environment and development started to attain practical significance. In that year the World Commission on Environment and Development (WCED) was created as a consequence of General Assembly Resolution 38/161 adopted at the 38th session of the UN in December 1983. That resolution called upon the Secretary General to appoint the Chairman and Vice Chairman of the Commission and in turn directed them jointly to appoint the remaining members, at least half of whom were to be selected from the developing world. The Secretary General appointed Mrs Brundtland, then leader of the Norwegian Labour Party, as Chairman and Dr Mansour Khalid, the former minister of Foreign Affairs from Sudan, as Vice Chairman. The WCED functioned as an independent body and its members served the Commission in their individual capacities not as state representatives. Its brief was to investigate the major environmental and development problems that faced the world and to formulate realistic proposals for their solution. The WCED reported back to the 42nd session of the General Assembly in the autumn of 1987. In her forward to the report Mrs Brundtland wrote:

> The environment does not exist as a sphere separate from human actions, ambitions, and needs, and attempts to defend it in isolation from human concerns have given the very word 'environment' a connotation of naiveté in some political circles. The word 'development' has also been narrowed by some into a very limited focus, along the lines of 'what poor nations should do to become richer', and thus again is automatically dismissed by many in the international arena as being a concern of specialists, of those involved in questions of 'development' assistance.
>
> But the 'environment' is where we all live; and 'development' is what we all do in attempting to improve our lot within that abode. The two are inseparable.[13]

The report itself acknowledged the important role that international law needed to play in protecting the environment:

> The international legal framework must also be significantly strengthened in support of sustainable development. Although international law related to environment has evolved rapidly since the 1972 Stockholm Conference, major gaps and deficiencies must still be overcome as part of the transition to sustainable development. Much of the evidence and conclusions presented in earlier chapters of this report calls into question not just the desirability but even the feasibility of maintaining an international system that cannot prevent one or several states from damaging the ecological basis for development and even the prospects for survival of any other or even all other states.[14]
>
> National and international law has traditionally lagged behind events. Today, legal regimes are being rapidly outdistanced by the accelerating pace and expanding scale of impacts on the environmental base of development. Human laws must be reformulated to keep human activities in harmony with the unchanging and universal laws of nature. There is an urgent need:

---

13 *Our Common Future*, Report of the World Commission on Environment and Development, 1987, Oxford: Oxford University Press at p xi.

14 *Our Common Future*, Report of the World Commission on Environment and Development, 1987, Oxford: Oxford University Press at pp 312–13.

- to recognise and respect the reciprocal rights and responsibilities of individuals and states regarding sustainable development;
- to establish and apply new norms for state and inter-state behaviour to achieve sustainable development;
- to strengthen and extend the application of existing laws and international agreements in support of sustainable development; and
- to reinforce existing methods and develop new procedures for avoiding and resolving environmental disputes.[15]

To assist it in its work the Commission had established a group of international legal experts chaired by Robert Munro of Canada. The WCED recommended to the General Assembly that it commit itself to preparing a universal declaration on environmental protection and sustainable development which could subsequently form the basis for an international convention. As a starting point for discussion the Commission submitted a number of legal principles prepared by the group of legal experts.

I GENERAL PRINCIPLES, RIGHTS, AND RESPONSIBILITIES

Fundamental human right

1   All human beings have the fundamental right to an environment adequate for their health and well-being.

Inter-generational equity

2   States shall conserve and use the environment and natural resources for the benefit of present and future generations.

Conservation and sustainable use

3   States shall maintain ecosystems and ecological processes essential for the functioning of the biosphere, shall preserve biological diversity, and shall observe the principles of optimum sustainable yield ion the use of living natural resources and ecosystems.

Environmental standards and monitoring

4   States shall establish adequate environmental protection standards and monitor changes in and publish relevant data on environmental quality and resource use.

Prior environmental assessments

5   States shall make or require prior environmental assessments of proposed activities which may significantly affect the environment or use of a natural resource.

Prior notification, access, and due process

6   States shall inform in a timely manner all persons likely to be significantly affected by a planned activity and grant them equal access and due process in administrative and judicial proceedings.

---

15 *Our Common Future*, Report of the World Commission on Environment and Development, 1987, Oxford: Oxford University Press at p 330.

Sustainable development and assistance

7   States shall ensure that conservation is treated as an integral part of the planning and implementation of development activities and provide assistance to other states, especially to developing countries, in support of environmental protection and sustainable development.

General obligation to co-operate

8   States shall co-operate in good faith with other states in implementing the preceding rights and obligations.

II PRINCIPLES, RIGHTS, AND OBLIGATIONS CONCERNING TRANSBOUNDARY NATURAL RESOURCES AND ENVIRONMENTAL INTERFERENCES

Reasonable and equitable use

9   States shall use transboundary resources in a reasonable and equitable manner.

Prevention and abatement

10   States shall prevent or abate any transboundary environmental interference which could cause or causes significant harm (but subject to certain exceptions provided for in Articles 11 and 12 below).

Strict liability

11   States shall take all reasonable precautionary measures to limit the risk when carrying out or permitting certain dangerous but beneficial activities and shall ensure that compensation is provided should substantial transboundary harm occur even when the activities were not known to be harmful at the time they were undertaken.

Prior agreements when prevention costs greatly exceed harm

12   States shall enter into negotiations with the affected state on the equitable conditions under which the activity could be carried out when planning to carry out or permit the activities causing transboundary harm which is substantial but far less than the cost of prevention. (If no agreement can be reached, see Article 22.)

Non-discrimination

13   States shall apply as a minimum at least the same standards for environmental conduct and impacts regarding transboundary natural resources and environmental interferences as are applied domestically (ie, do not do to others what you would not do to your own citizens).

General obligation to co-operate on transboundary environmental problems

14   States shall co-operate in good faith with other states to achieve optimal use of transboundary natural resources and effective prevention or abatement of transboundary natural resources or environmental interferences.

Exchange of information

15   States of origin shall provide timely and relevant information to the other concerned states regarding transboundary natural resources or environmental interferences.

Prior assessment and notification

16   States shall provide prior and timely notification and relevant information to the other concerned states and shall make or require an environmental assessment of planned activities which may have significant transboundary effects.

Prior consultations

17　States of origin shall consult at an early stage and in good faith with other concerned states regarding existing or potential transboundary interferences with their use of a natural resource or the environment.

Co-operation arrangements for environmental assessment and protection

18　States shall co-operate with the concerned states in monitoring, scientific research and standard setting regarding transboundary natural resources and environmental interferences.

Emergency situations

19　States shall develop contingency plans regarding emergency situations likely to cause transboundary environmental interferences and shall promptly warn, provide relevant information to and co-operate with concerned states when emergencies occur.

Equal access and treatment

20　States shall grant equal access, due process and equal treatment in administrative and judicial proceedings to all person who are or may be affected by transboundary interferences with their use of a natural resource or the environment.

III STATE RESPONSIBILITY

21　States shall cease activities which breach an international obligation regarding the environment and provide compensation for the harm caused.

IV PEACEFUL SETTLEMENT OF DISPUTES

22　States shall settle environmental disputes by peaceful means. If mutual agreement on a solution or on other dispute settlement arrangements is not reached within 18 months, the dispute shall be submitted to conciliation and , if unresolved, thereafter to arbitration or judicial settlement at the request of any of the concerned states.[16]

The immediate aim of establishing a universal declaration of economic rights was not realised but the recommendations of the WCED did have an impact on a number of specialised and regional environmental measures. The WCED Report also led directly to the General Assembly's decision to convene a UN Conference on Environment and Development (UNCED).

18.5 The 1992 Earth Summit

In June 1992 176 states met in Rio de Janeiro for the United Nations Conference on Environment and Development. The preparatory debates for the Conference revealed that there was still considerable dispute as to where the emphasis was

---

16　*Summary of proposed Legal Principles for Environmental Protection and Sustainable Development Adopted by the WCED Experts on Environmental Law reproduced in Annex 1 of Our Common Future*, Oxford University Press, 1987. The full Report of an Experts Group on Environmental Law was published separately as Munro and Lammers, *Environmental Protection and Sustainable Development*, London, 1987.

to be put: on environment or on development. Although the Conference had as its backdrop the ending of the Cold War, the recent successful international action against Iraq and President Bush's calls for the establishment of a new international order, the divisions between North and South on environmental and developmental issues were still very much apparent. Nonetheless, the Conference succeeded in producing five major documents:

1   Agenda 21 which is a 800-page document setting out an action plan for managing the various sectors of the environment in the 21st century;
2   the Climate Change Convention;
3   the Biological Diversity Convention;
4   a non-binding Statement of Consensus on Forest Principles; and
5   a Declaration on Environment and Development.

The Rio Declaration was adopted by consensus of those 176 states attending the Conference and, although not formally binding, is of major legal significance and can be seen as an example of soft law. In the preamble to the Declaration the Conference reaffirmed the Stockholm Declaration and expressed the desire to build upon it.

THE RIO DECLARATION ON ENVIRONMENT AND DEVELOPMENT[17]

Principle 1

Human beings are at the centre of concerns for sustainable development. They are entitled to a healthy and productive life in harmony with nature.

Principle 2

States have, in accordance with the Charter of the United Nations and the principles of international law, the sovereign right to exploit their own resources pursuant to their own environmental and developmental policies, and the responsibility to ensure that activities within their jurisdiction or control do not cause damage to the environment of other states or of areas beyond the limits of national jurisdiction.

Principle 3

The right to development must be fulfilled so as to equitably meet developmental and environmental needs of present and future generations.

Principle 4

In order to achieve sustainable development, environmental protection shall constitute an integral part of the development process and cannot be considered in isolation from it.

Principle 5

All states and all people shall co-operate in the essential task of eradicating poverty as an indispensable requirement for sustainable development, in order to decrease the disparities in standards of living and better meet the needs of the majority of the people of the world.

---

17   UN Doc A/CONF 151/5/Rev 1, 13 June 1992, reprinted at (1992) 31 *ILM* 874.

Principle 6

The special situation and needs of developing countries, particularly the least developed and those most environmentally vulnerable, shall be given special priority. International actions in the field of environment and development should also address the interests and needs of all countries.

Principle 7

States shall co-operate in a spirit of global partnership to conserve, protect and restore the health and integrity of the Earth's ecosystem. In view of the different contributions to global environmental degradation, States have common but differentiated responsibilities. The developed countries acknowledge the responsibility that they bear in the international pursuit of sustainable development in view of the pressures their societies place on the global environment and of the technologies and financial resources they command.

Principle 8

To achieve sustainable development and a higher quality of life for all people, states should reduce and eliminate unsustainable patterns of production and consumption and promote appropriate demographic policies.

Principle 9

States should co-operate to strengthen endogenous capacity-building for sustainable development by improving scientific understanding through exchanges of scientific and technological knowledge, and by enhancing the development, adaptation, diffusion and transfer of technologies, including new and innovative technologies.

Principle 10

Environmental issues are best handled with the participation of all concerned citizens, at the relevant level. At the national level, each individual shall have appropriate access to information on hazardous materials and activities in their communities, and the opportunity to participate in decision-making processes. States shall facilitate and encourage public awareness and participation by making information widely available. Effective access to judicial and administrative proceedings, including redress and remedy, shall be provided.

Principle 11

States shall enact effective environmental legislation. Environmental standards, management objectives and priorities should reflect the environmental and developmental context to which they apply. Standards applied by some countries may be inappropriate and of unwarranted economic and social cost to other countries, in particular developing countries.

Principle 12

States should co-operate to promote a supportive and open international economic system that would lead to economic growth and sustainable development in all countries, to better address the problems of environmental degradation. Trade policy measures for environmental purposes should not constitute a means of arbitrary or unjustifiable discrimination or a disguised restriction on international trade. Unilateral actions to deal with environmental challenges outside the jurisdiction of the importing country should be avoided. Environmental measures addressing transboundary or global environmental problems should, as far as possible, be based on an international consensus.

Principle 13

States shall develop national law regarding liability and compensation for the victims of pollution and other environmental damage. States shall also co-operate in an expeditious and more determined manner to develop further international law regarding liability and compensation for adverse effects of environmental damage caused by activities within their jurisdiction or control to areas beyond their jurisdiction.

Principle 14

States should effectively co-operate to discourage or prevent the relocation and transfer to other states of any activities and substances that cause severe environmental degradation or are found to be harmful to human health.

Principle 15

In order to protect the environment, the precautionary approach shall be widely applied by states according to their capabilities. Where there are threats of serious or irreversible damage, lack of full scientific certainty shall not be used as a reason for postponing cost-effective measures to prevent environmental degradation.

Principle 16

National authorities should endeavour to promote the internalisation of environmental costs and the use of economic instruments, taking into account the approach that the polluter should, in principle, bear the cost of pollution, with due regard to the public interest and without distorting international trade and investment.

Principle 17

Environmental impact assessment, as a national instrument, shall be undertaken for proposed activities that are likely to have a significant adverse impact on the environment and are subject to a decision of a competent national authority.

Principle 18

States shall immediately notify other states of any natural disasters or other emergencies that are likely to produce sudden harmful effects on the environment of those states. Every effort shall be made by the international community to help states so afflicted.

Principle 19

States shall provide prior and timely notification and relevant information to potentially affected states on activities that may have a significant adverse transboundary environmental effect and shall consult with those states at an early stage and in good faith.

Principle 20

Women have a vital role in environmental management and development. Their full participation is therefore essential to achieve sustainable development.

Principle 21

The creativity, ideas and courage of the youth of the world should be mobilised to forge a global partnership in order to achieve sustainable development and ensure a better future for all.

Principle 22

Indigenous people and their communities, and other local communities, have a vital role in environmental management and development because of their knowledge and traditional practices. States should recognise and duly support their identity, culture and interests and enable their effective participation in the achievement of sustainable development.

Principle 23

The environment and natural resources of people under oppression, domination and occupation shall be protected.

Principle 24

Warfare is inherently destructive of sustainable development. States shall therefore respect international law providing protection for the environment in times of armed conflict and co-operate in its further development, as necessary.[18]

Principle 25

Peace, development and environmental protection are interdependent and indivisible.

Principle 26

States shall resolve all their environmental disputes peacefully and by appropriate means in accordance with the Charter of the United Nations.

Principle 27

States and people shall co-operate in good faith and in a spirit of partnership in the fulfilment of the principles embodied in this Declaration and in the further development of international law in the field of sustainable development.

Subsequently the United Nations established the Commission on Sustainable Development[19] as a commission of ECOSOC. Its primary role is to monitor, review and consider progress in the implementation of international environmental policy and law. The following year, in acknowledgement of the seriousness attached now to environmental matters, the International Court of Justice established a 'Chamber of the Court for Environmental Matters' under the provisions of Article 26 of the Statute of the ICJ. The Constitution of a Chamber of the Court for Environmental Matters provides:

> ... in view of the developments in the field of environmental law and protection which have taken place in the last few years, and considering that it should be prepared to the fullest possible extent to deal with any environmental case falling within its jurisdiction, the Court has now deemed it appropriate to establish a seven-member Chamber for Environmental Matters.[20]

18.6 General principles

It should already be clear that it is not possible to maintain an absolute notion of territorial sovereignty. The freedom of states to act is necessarily constrained by the duty to have regard to the rights of other states and the environment in general. The principle of 'good neighbourliness' is a feature of international law.

---

18 The need for this principle was demonstrated by the recent Gulf Conflict. During their retreat from Kuwait in the spring of 1991 Iraqi forces set fire to 700 oil wells. In the nine months it took to bring the fires under control, a huge amount of hazardous gases was released into the atmosphere.

19 See UN General Assembly Resolution 47/191 (1992).

20 *ICJ Communiqué No 93/20* of 19 July 1993. The usual chamber consists of three judges.

In the sphere of environmental law this extremely general principle has been developed further and a number of more specific governing principles can be identified.

18.6.1 The duty to prevent, reduce and control environmental harm

Reference has already been made to the *Trail Smelter Arbitration*[21] in which the tribunal made it clear that states are under a duty not to use or permit the use of their territory in such a manner as to cause injury in or to the territory of another state. Similarly in the *Corfu Channel* case the International Court made reference to 'every state's obligation not to allow knowingly its territory to be used for acts contrary to the rights of other states'.[22] Principle 21 of the Stockholm Declaration, while affirming the sovereign right of states to exploit their own resources, re-affirms the duty incumbent on states 'to ensure that activities within their jurisdiction or control do not cause damage to the environment of other states or to areas beyond the limits of national jurisdiction'. A number of states made clear at the Stockholm Conference that they felt Principle 21 to be declaratory of existing customary international law. Its use in numerous conventions, declarations and resolutions since then only strengthens the view that it is indeed a rule of international law.

It should be noted that the principle involves more than the need to make reparation for damage caused. States are under a duty to prevent future harm occurring. This duty is often expressed as the need for states to exercise 'due diligence'. In deciding whether due diligence has been exercised it is legitimate to take into account a state's resources and capabilities, the effectiveness of territorial control and the nature of the specific activities under consideration. The more inherently dangerous the activity undertaken, the greater the amount of diligence required. Of course, such a formulation does not clearly provide what specific action is required of a state and there have been attempts to provide a more detailed minimum standard of care. Alternatively, a number of conventions have used the formulation of 'best available technology' or 'best practicable means'.[23] Increasingly, reference is made to the 'precautionary principle' according to which states have a duty undertake assessment of the likely consequences for the environment of planned activities and to take preventive measures where appropriate. However, the principle should be used with care:

> Despite its attractions, the great variety of interpretations given to the precautionary principle, and the novel and far-reaching effects of some applications, suggest that it is not yet a principle of international law. Difficult questions concerning the point at which it becomes applicable to any given activity remain unanswered and seriously undermine its normative character and practical utility, although support for it does indicate a policy of greater prudence on the part of those states willing to accept it.[24]

---

21 (1941) 3 RIAA 1905.

22 [1949] *ICJ Rep* 4 at p 22.

23 See, for example, Article 194(1) Law of the Sea Convention 1982; Article 4(3) Convention for the Prevention of Marine Pollution from Land Based Sources 1974.

24 Boyle and Birnie, *International Law and the Environment*, 1992, Oxford: Oxford Unitersity Press at p 98.

18.6.2 Consultation, co-operation and communication

An increasingly common provision in international conventions on the environment requires states to co-operate with other states likely to suffer environmental risks from proposed activities. In the *Lac Lanoux Arbitration*[25] Spain complained that France had violated a treaty by diverting a river which flowed through the territory of both states. Although the tribunal found no treaty violation it affirmed the requirement of prior notice and consultation:

> ... a state which is liable to suffer repercussions from work undertaken by a neighbouring state is the sole judge of its interests and if the neighbouring state has not taken the initiative the other state cannot be denied the right to insist on notification of works or concessions which are the object of a scheme.[26]

The tribunal made clear that consultations between the two states must be genuine and conducted in good faith.

Principle 24 of the Stockholm Declaration re-affirms the need for co-operation and the duty to notify and consult has been repeated in a number of conventions and draft conventions dealing with shared natural resources.[27] It is generally accepted that states are under a duty to give timely notification to states at risk following environmental accidents and emergencies. Thus it can be seen that while states are under a duty to prevent accidents, should an accident or emergency occur they have a continuing obligation to minimise its effects.

18.6.3 The polluter pays principle

A guiding principle that has found growing support in various measures taken to prevent pollution is that the polluter pays. The principle was endorsed by the OECD states in 1972 and adopted by the First Environmental Action Programme 1973 of the European Union. Article 25 of the Single European Act 1986 provides that action taken by the EU relating to the environment shall be based on the principles 'that environmental damage should as a priority be rectified at source and that the polluter should pay'. The principle was again endorsed, this time by the Conference on Security and Co-operation in Europe, in 1990. For long it was argued that the principle was only supported by the industrial states but Principle 16 of the Declaration on Environment and Development 1992 calls for national authorities to endeavour to internalise environmental costs by making the polluter 'in principle' bear the cost of pollution.

18.7 Pollution

Although the *Trail Smelter Arbitration*[28] illustrates that the discharge of toxic or other harmful substances in such a way as to cause harm on or to neighbouring

---

25 *Spain v France* (1957) 24 ILR 101.

26 (1957) 24 LIR at p 138.

27 Most notably in the ILC's Draft Articles on the Non-Navigational Uses of International watercourses, 1994 which are widely accepted as being generally declaratory on customary international law. See also the Convention on Transboundary Air Pollution 1979.

28 (1941) 3 RIAA 1905.

states would give rise to international liability, until the 1970s there was no real attempt to control pollution in other situations. The urgent need for action to be taken in respect of pollution was acknowledged by states at the Stockholm Conference in 1972.[29] After the conference UNEP, along with other concerned organisations, began investigating more specific measures that could be adopted to control pollution. One difficulty that was encountered early on was how best to define the level of pollution that would give rise to international responsibility. In 1974 the OECD adopted a definition of pollution that referred to:

> ... the introduction by man, directly or indirectly, of substances or energy into the environment resulting in deleterious effects of such a nature as to endanger human health, harm living resources and ecosystems, and impair or interfere with amenities and other legitimate uses of the environment.

This definition was subsequently included in Article 1 of the Convention on Long-Range Transboundary Air Pollution 1979 and has been used in a number of other conventions. The definition has two main implications. First, the term is confined to introduction of substances or energy by man into the environment and thus, over-use of resources, however harmful it might be, will not in itself constitute pollution. Secondly, the issue is raised of how harmful pollution needs to be before it will give rise to liability. Many conventions refer to harmful or deleterious effects, not just to property, but also to living resources and ecosystems. It would appear that some injury is necessary to establish responsibility subject to *de minimis* principles. Often the question of degree of harm is linked to the need to act with due diligence. Very often the allocation of responsibility will involve a balancing exercise between the harm caused and the practicable, available means to prevent such harm.

18.7.1 Atmospheric pollution

The municipal laws of industrialised states have long shown a concern with air pollution and have endeavoured to minimise the emission of noxious or other harmful gases. Unfortunately one of the methods often used to reduce the risk to the local population is to ensure that emissions are sent high into the atmosphere to disperse. It gradually came to be recognised that such actions did not irradiate the pollution but merely postponed and transferred the harmful effects. Today the major source of air pollution is the burning of fossil fuels in the course of energy production. Advances in scientific knowledge have meant that it has become more possible to track the spread of gases such as sulphur dioxide and nitrogen oxide to be able to establish both the source of the pollution and the location of its harmful effects. During the 1980s there was growing concern about the phenomena of acid rain, caused by the reaction of sulphur and nitrogen with water vapour in the air, and global warming. In addition the discovery was made that the ozone layer, which protects the earth from the sun's ultraviolet radiation, was being damaged by the release of high levels of chlorine-based substances.

One aspect of the law relating to air pollution has been the question of sovereign rights to air space (discussed in Chapter 12). It is accepted that for the

---

29 See in particular Principles 6 and 7 of the Stockholm Declaration.

purposes of control of pollution the transient physical characteristics of the atmosphere must be recognised. As a result there has been a tendency to treat the atmosphere as a shared resource for the purposes of pollution and other environmental protection. This approach was adopted by the Geneva Convention on Long-Range Transboundary Air Pollution 1979 which governs issues of air pollution within Europe and North America. The convention is largely an expression of broad principles and the parties agree to 'endeavour to limit' and gradually reduce air pollution. The important provisions relate to information exchange and the need to give notification of significant risks.

CONVENTION ON LONG-RANGE TRANSBOUNDARY AIR POLLUTION[30]

Definitions

Article 1

For the purposes of the present Convention:

(a) 'air pollution' means the introduction by man, directly or indirectly, of substances or energy into the air resulting in deleterious effects of such a nature as to endanger human health, harm living resources and ecosystems and material property and impair or interfere with amenities and other legitimate uses of the environment, and 'air pollutants' shall be construed accordingly;

(b) 'long-range transboundary air pollution' means air pollution whose physical origin is situated wholly or in part within the area under the national jurisdiction of one state and which has adverse effects in the area under the jurisdiction of another state at such a distance that it is not generally possible to distinguish the contribution of individual emission sources of groups of sources.

Fundamental principles

Article 2

The Contracting Parties, taking due account of the facts and problems involved, are determined to protect man and his environment against air pollution and shall endeavour to limit and, as far as possible, gradually reduce and prevent air pollution, including long-range transboundary air pollution.

Article 3

The Contracting Parties, within the framework or the present Convention, shall by means of exchanges of information, consultation, research and monitoring, develop without undue delay policies and strategies which shall serve as a means of combating the discharge of air pollutants, taking into account efforts already made at national and international levels.

Article 4

The Contracting Parties shall exchange information on and review their policies, scientific activities and technical measures which may have adverse effects,

---

30 Done at Geneva, 13 November 1979, entered into force 16 March 1983 – reproduced in (1979) 18 ILM 1442.

thereby contributing to the reduction of air pollution including long-range transboundary air pollution.

Article 5

Consultations shall be held, upon request, at an early stage between, on the one hand, Contracting Parties which are actually affected by or exposed to a significant risk of long-range transboundary air pollution and, on the other hand, Contracting Parties within which and subject to whose jurisdiction a significant contribution to long-range transboundary air pollution originates, in connection with activities carried on or contemplated therein.

Air quality management

Article 6

Taking into account Articles 2–5, the ongoing research, exchange of information and monitoring and the results therefor, the cost and effectiveness of local and other remedies and, in order to combat air pollution, in particular that originating from new or rebuilt installations, each Contracting Party undertakes to develop the best policies and strategies including air quality management systems and, as part of them, control measures compatible with balanced development, in particular by using the best available technology which is economically feasible and low- and non-waste technology.

Research and development

Article 7

The Contracting Parties, as appropriate to their needs, shall initiate and co-operate in the conduct of research into and/or development of:

(a) existing and proposed technologies for reducing emissions of sulphur compounds and other major air pollutants, including technical and economic feasibility, and environmental consequences;

(b) instrumentation and other techniques for monitoring and measuring emission rates and ambient concentrations of air pollutants;

(c) improved models for a better understanding of the transmission of long-range transboundary air pollutants;

(d) the effects of sulphur compounds and other major air pollutants on human health and the environment, including agriculture, forestry, materials, aquatic and other natural ecosystems and visibiiity, with a view to establishing a scientific basis for dose/effect relationships designed to protect the environment;

(e) the economic, social and environmental assessment of alternative measures for attaining environmental objectives including the reduction of long-range transboundary air pollution;

(f) education and training programmes related to the environmental aspects of pollution by sulphur compounds and other major air pollutants.

Exchange of information[31]

Article 8

The Contracting Parties, within the framework of the Executive Body referred to in Article 10 and bilaterally, shall, in their common interests, exchange available information on:

---

31 Provisions relating to exchange of information and publicity are increasingly common in treaties concerned with environmental issues. Adverse publicity and informed lobbying by the general public are seen as major sanctions against pollution.

(a) data on emissions at periods of time to be agreed upon, of agreed air pollutants, starting with sulphur dioxide, coming from grid-units of agreed size; or on the fluxes of agreed air pollutants, starting with sulphur dioxide, across national borders, at distances and at periods of time to be agreed upon;

(b) major changes in national policies and in general industrial development, and their potential impact, which would be likely to cause significant changes in long-range transboundary air pollution;

(c) control technologies for reducing air pollution relevant to long-range transboundary air pollution;

(d) the projected cost of the emission control of sulphur compounds and other major air pollutants on a national scale;

(e) meteorological and physico-chemical data relating to the processes during emission;

(f) physico-chemical and biological data relating to the effects of long-range transboundary air pollution and the extent of damage which these data indicate can be attributed to long-range transboundary air pollution;

(g) national, subregional and regional policies and strategies for the control of sulphur compounds and other major air pollutants.

Implementation and further development of the co-operative programme for the monitoring and evaluation of the long-range transmission of air pollutants in Europe

Article 9

The Contracting Parties stress the need for the implementation of the existing 'Co-operative programme for the monitoring and evaluation of the long-range transmission of air pollutants in Europe' (hereinafter referred to as EMEP) and, with regard to the further development of this programme, agree to emphasise:

(a) the desirability of Contracting Parties joining in and fully implementing EMEP which, as a first step, is based on the monitoring of sulphur dioxide and related substances;

(b) the need to use comparable or standardised procedures for monitoring whenever possible;

(c) the desirability of basing the monitoring programme on the framework of both national and international programmes. The establishment of monitoring stations and the collection of data shall be carried out under the national jurisdiction of the country in which the monitoring stations are located;

(d) the desirability of establishing a framework for a co-operative environmental monitoring programme, based on and taking into account present and future national, subregional, regional and other international programmes;

(e) the need to exchange data on emissions at periods of time to be agreed upon, of agreed air pollutants, starting with sulphur dioxide coming from grid-units of agreed size; or on the fluxes of agreed air pollutants, starting with sulphur dioxide, across national borders, at distances and at periods of time to be agreed upon. The method, including the model, used to determine the fluxes, as well as the method, including the model, used to determine the transmission of air pollutants based on the emissions per grid-unit, shall be made available and periodically reviewed, in order to improve the methods and the models;

(f)   their willingness to continue the exchange and periodic updating of national data on total emissions of agreed air pollutants, starting with sulphur dioxide;

(g)   the need to provide meteorological and physico-chemical data relating to processes during transmission;

(h)   the need to monitor chemical components in other media such as water, soil and vegetation, as well as a similar monitoring programme to record effects on health and environment;

(i)   the desirability of extending the national EMEP networks to make them operational for control and surveillance purposes.

Executive body

Article 10

1   The representatives of the Contracting Parties shall, within the framework of the Senior Advisors to ECE Governments on Environmental Problems, constitute the Executive Body of the present Convention, and shall meet at least annually in that capacity.

2   The Executive Body shall:

(a)   review the implementation of the present Convention;

(b)   establish, as appropriate, working groups to consider matters related to the implementation and development of the present Convention and to this end to prepare appropriate studies and other documentation and to submit recommendations to be considered by the Executive Body;

(c)   fulfil such other functions as may be appropriate under the provisions of the present Convention.

3   The Executive Body shall utilise the Steering Body for the EMEP to play an integral part in the operation of the present Convention, in particular with regard to data collection and scientific co-operation.

4   The Executive Body, in discharging its functions, shall, when it deems appropriate, also make use of information from other relevant international organisations.

Secretariat

Article 11

The Executive Secretary of the Economic Commission for Europe shall carry out, for the Executive Body, the following secretariat functions:

(a)   to convene and prepare the meetings of the Executive Body;

(b)   to transmit to the Contracting Parties reports and other information received in accordance with the provisions of the present Convention;

(c)   to discharge the functions assigned by the Executive Body.

Amendments to the Convention

Article 12

1   Any Contracting Party may propose amendments to the present Convention.

The text of proposed amendments shall be submitted in writing to the Executive Secretary of the Economic Commission for Europe, who shall communicate them to all Contracting Parties. The Executive Body shall discuss proposed amendments at its next annual meeting provided that such proposals have been circulated by the Executive Secretary of the Economic Commission for Europe to the Contracting Parties at least 90 days in advance.

3   An amendment to the present Convention shall be adopted by consensus of the representatives of the Contracting Parties, and shall enter into force for the Contracting Parties which have accepted it on the 90th day after the date on which two-thirds of the Contracting Parties have deposited their instruments of acceptance with the depositary. Thereafter, the amendment shall enter into force for any other Contracting Party on the 90th day after the date on which that Contracting Party deposits its instrument of acceptance of the amendment.

Settlement of disputes

Article 13

If a dispute arises between two or more Contracting Parties to the present Convention as to the interpretation or application of the Convention, they shall seek a solution by negotiation or by any other method of dispute settlement acceptable to the parties to the dispute.

Another major treaty dealing with atmospheric matters is the Vienna Convention for the Protection of the Ozone Layer 1985[32] which was largely the work of UNEP. The convention is supplemented by the Montreal Protocol on Substances that Deplete the Ozone Layer 1987[33] which sets targets for the gradual elimination of CFCs and other substances that have a deleterious effect on the ozone layer.[34]

VIENNA CONVENTION FOR THE PROTECTION OF THE OZONE LAYER[35]

Article 1   Definitions

For the purposes of this Convention:

1   'The ozone layer' means the layer of atmospheric ozone above the planetary boundary layer.

2   'Adverse effects' means changes in the physical environment or biota, including changes in the climate, which have significant deleterious effects on human health or on the composition, resilience and productivity of natural and managed ecosystems, or on materials useful to mankind.

3   'Alternative technologies or equipment' means technologies or equipment the use of which makes it possible to reduce or effectively eliminate emissions of substances which have or are likely to have adverse effects on the ozone layer.

4   'Alternative substances' means substances which reduce, eliminate or avoid adverse effects on the ozone layer.

---

32   Done at Vienna, 22 March 1985. Entered into force, 22 September 1988 – reprinted in (1987) 26 ILM 1529.

33   Done at Montreal, 16 September 1987. Entered into force 1 January 1989. Reproduced in (1987) 26 ILM 1550.

34   The international law relating to protection of the ozone layer provides a useful illustration of an increasingly popular form of law making and development. The original Convention is drafted in broad terms and essentially exists to provide a framework which can be filled in subsequently as and when more detailed agreement becomes possible.

35   Done at Vienna, 22 March 1985. Entered into force, 22 September 1988 – reprinted in (1987) 26 ILM 1529.

5   'Parties' means, unless the text otherwise indicates, parties to this Convention.

6   'Regional economic integration organisation' means an organisation constituted by sovereign states of a given region which has competence in respect of matters governed by this Convention or its Protocols and has been duly authorised, in accordance with its internal procedures, to sign, ratify, accept, approve or accede to the instruments concerned.

7   'Protocols' means Protocols to this Convention.

Article 2 General Obligations

1   The parties shall take appropriate measures in accordance with the provisions of this Convention and of those Protocols in force to which they are party to protect human health and the environment against adverse effects resulting or likely to result from human activities which modify or are likely to modify the ozone layer.

2   To this end the parties shall, in accordance with the means at their disposal and their capabilities:

(a)   Co-operate by means of systematic observations, research and information exchange in order to better understand and assess the effects of human activities on the ozone layer and the effects on human health and the environment from modification of the ozone layer.

(b)   Adopt appropriate legislative or administrative measures and co-operate in harmonising appropriate policies to control, limit, reduce or prevent human activities under their jurisdiction or control should it be found that these activities have or are likely to have adverse effects resulting from modification or likely modification of the ozone layer.

(c)   Co-operate in the formulation of agreed measures, procedures and standards for the implementation of this Convention, with a view to the adoption of Protocols and annexes.

(d)   Co-operate with competent international bodies to implement effectively this Convention and Protocols to which they are a party.

3   The provisions of this Convention shall in no way affect the right of parties to adopt, in accordance with international law, domestic measures additional to those referred to in paras 1 and 2 above, nor shall they affect additional domestic measures already taken by a party, provided that those measures are not incompatible with their obligations under this Convention.

4   The application of this article shall be based on relevant scientific and technical considerations.

In some ways linked to the question of depletion of the ozone layer is the issue of climatic change and in particular, global warming and the so-called greenhouse effect. Partly because of the limitations of universally accepted scientific knowledge in the area and also because of the strong economic interests that are connected with practices which are alleged to affect the climate adversely, it has proved difficult to obtain agreement on rules relating to climatic change. However, at the Rio Conference in 1992 the Convention on Global Climate Change 1992 was adopted. The Convention, which entered into force in March 1994, has been criticised for not going far enough to protect the global climate but it is at least a start from which further refinements may follow.

UNITED NATIONS FRAMEWORK CONVENTION ON CLIMATE CHANGE[36]

Article 1

For the purposes of this Convention:

1 'Adverse effects of climate change' means changes in the physical environment or biota resulting from climate change which have significant deleterious effects on the composition, resilience or productivity of natural and managed ecosystems or on the operation of socio-economic systems or on human health and welfare.

2 'Climate change' means a change of climate which is attributed directly or indirectly to human activity that alters the composition of the global atmosphere and which is in addition to natural climate variability observed over considerable time periods.

3 'Climate system' means the totality of the atmosphere, hydrosphere, biosphere and geosphere and their interactions.

4 'Emissions' means the release of greenhouse gases and/or their precursors into the atmosphere over a specified area and period of time.

5 'Greenhouse gases' means those gaseous constituents of the atmosphere, both natural and anthropogenic, that absorb and re-emit infra-red radiation.

6 'Regional economic integration organisation' means an organisation constituted by sovereign states of a given region which has competence in respect of matters governed by this Convention or its Protocols and has been duly authorised, in accordance with its internal procedures, to sign, ratify, accept, approve or accede to the instruments concerned.

7 'Reservoir' means a component or components of the climate system where a greenhouse gas or a precursor of a greenhouse gas is stored.

8 'Sink' means any process, activity or mechanism which removes a greenhouse gas, an aerosol or a precursor of a greenhouse gas from the atmosphere.

9 'Source' means any process or activity which releases a greenhouse gas, an aerosol or a precursor of a greenhouse gas into the atmosphere.

Article 2

The ultimate objective of this Convention and any related legal instruments that the Conference of the Parties may adopt is to achieve, in accordance with the relevant provisions of the Convention, stabilisation of greenhouse gas concentrations in the atmosphere at a level that would prevent dangerous anthropogenic interference with the climate system. Such a level should be achieved within a time-frame sufficient to allow ecosystems to adapt naturally to climate change, to ensure that food production is not threatened and to enable economic development to proceed in a sustainable manner.

Article 3

In their actions to achieve the objective of the Convention and to implement its provisions, the parties shall be guided, *inter alia*, by the following:

---

36 Adopted by the UN Conference on Environment and Development, Rio de Janeiro, 14 June 1992.

1   The parties should protect the climate system for the benefit of present and future generations of humankind, on the basis of equity and in accordance with their common but differentiated responsibilities and respective capabilities. Accordingly, the developed country Parties should take the lead in combating climate change and the adverse effects thereof.

2   The specific needs and special circumstances of developing country parties, especially those that are particularly vulnerable to the adverse effects of climate change, and of those parties, especially developing country parties, that would have to bear a disproportionate or abnormal burden under the Convention, should be given full consideration.

3   The parties should take precautionary measures to anticipate, prevent or minimise the causes of climate change and mitigate its adverse effects. Where there are threats of serious or irreversible damage, lack of full scientific certainty should not be used as a reason for postponing such measures, taking into account that policies and measures to deal with climate change should be cost-effective so as to ensure global benefits at the lowest possible cost. To achieve this, such policies and measures should take into account different socio-economic contexts, be comprehensive, cover all relevant sources, sinks and reservoirs of greenhouse gases and adaptation, and comprise all economic sectors. Efforts to address climate change may be carried out co-operatively by interested Parties.

4   The parties have a right to, and should, promote sustainable development. Policies and measures to protect the climate system against human-induced change should be appropriate for the specific conditions of each party and should be integrated with national development programmes, taking into account that economic development is essential for adopting measures to address climate change.

5   The parties should co-operate to promote a supportive and open international economic system that would lead to sustainable economic growth and development in all parties, particularly developing country parties, thus enabling them better to address the problems of climate change. Measures taken to combat climate change, including unilateral ones, should not constitute a means of arbitrary or unjustifiable discrimination or a disguised restriction on international trade.

18.7.2 Marine pollution

Marine pollution has long been an area of concern and as early as 1926 attempts were made to draw up an international convention to control pollution from ships.[37] However, the attempts were unsuccessful and for the next 40 years little was done to regulate the situation. For example, there was little discussion of marine pollution at either UNCLOS I or UNCLOS II apart from the expression of a general obligation on states to prevent pollution of the high seas by oil and by radioactive waste.[38] It was not until the late 1960s that it became clear that action needed to be taken to preserve the marine environment and reduce the level of pollution. This realisation of the need for action coincided with a rapid increase in the number of high tonnage oil tankers which posed the

---

37   See Boyle and Birnie, *International Law and the Environment* 1992, Oxford: Oxford University Press at p 251.

38   Articles 24 and 25 of the Convention on the High Seas, done at Geneva, 29 April 1958.

risk of massive environmental damage. In April 1967, the Liberian registered tanker, the *Torrey Canyon*, broke up off the coast of the UK spilling about 100,000 tons of crude oil into the sea. The environmental damage resulting from the spill and the high level publicity it received increased the pressure for new controls to be introduced. At the same time, it was discovered that mercury emissions from a Japanese factory were poisoning fish and it became clear that the threat to the marine environment came not just from ships. In fact, it is generally accepted that there are four main sources of marine pollution:

- shipping;
- dumping;
- sea bed activities;
- land-based pollution.

The *Torrey Canyon* disaster had an immediate effect on the law relating to liability for the effects of pollution. The International Convention on Civil Liability for Oil Pollution Damage 1969 (the Civil Liability Convention) and the International Convention on the Establishment of an International Fund for Compensation for Oil Pollution Damage 1971 (the Fund Convention) impose obligations on the shipowner to pay for pollution damage and the cost of any preventive measures taken. The Fund Convention establishes an International Oil Pollution Compensation Fund which will compensate victims in the event that the shipowner is not liable. The Fund is financed by a levy on oil imports. In addition to these measures two private schemes were adopted: the Tanker Owners' Voluntary Agreement concerning Liability for Oil Pollution (TOVALOP) and the Contract regarding an Interim Supplement to Tanker Liability for Oil Pollution (CRISTAL). These private schemes mirror the provisions of the conventions and still are of relevance to those states that are not parties to the conventions.

Aside from the question of compensation arrangements it was recognised that there was a need also for stricter controls on pollution. This was recognised at the Stockholm Conference and it was resolved that new controls would be introduced. In the same year as the conference the Convention on the Prevention of Marine Pollution by Dumping of Wastes and other Matters 1972 (the London Dumping Convention) was signed. Dumping is defined as the deliberate disposal of waste and the Convention prohibits the dumping of specific categories of waste. The Convention for the Prevention of Marine Pollution by Dumping from Ships and Aircraft 1972 (the Oslo Dumping Convention) imposes stricter rules in respect of the north-east Atlantic and the North Sea. There have since been a number of other similar regional conventions. The year after the adoption of the London and Oslo Conventions the International Convention for the Prevention of Pollution by Ships 1973 (MARPOL) was signed. Marine pollution was a major concern at UNCLOS III and the Law of the Sea Convention 1982 (LOSC) has a number of significant provisions relating to marine pollution. Most importantly LOSC gives the coastal state rights to make and enforce regulations protecting its territorial sea and the EEZ and continental shelf. More recently such regulations have been co-ordinated by regional agreements between neighbouring states and this can be particularly effective where the continental shelf and EEZs cover the major shipping lanes.

UNITED NATIONS CONVENTION ON THE LAW OF THE SEA 1982[39]

PART XII – PROTECTION AND PRESERVATION OF THE MARINE ENVIRONMENT

Section 1   General Provisions

Article 192   General Obligation

States have the obligation to protect and preserve the marine environment.

Article 193   Sovereign rights of states to exploit their natural resources

States have the sovereign right to exploit their natural resources pursuant to their environmental policies and in accordance with their duty to protect and preserve the marine environment.

Article 194   Measures to prevent, reduce and control pollution of the marine environment

1   States shall take, individually or jointly as appropriate, all measures consistent with this Convention that are necessary to prevent, reduce and control pollution of the marine environment from any source, using for this purpose the best practicable means at their disposal and in accordance with their capabilities, and they shall endeavour to harmonise their policies in this connection.

2   States shall take all measures necessary to ensure that activities under their jurisdiction or control are so conducted as not to cause damage by pollution to other states and their environment, and that pollution arising from incidents or activities under their jurisdiction or control does not spread beyond the areas where they exercise sovereign rights in accordance with this Convention.

3   The measures taken pursuant to this Part shall deal with all sources of pollution of the marine environment. These measures shall include, *inter alia*, those designed to minimise to the fullest possible extent:

(a)   the release of toxic, harmful or noxious substances, especially those which are persistent, from land-based sources, from or through the atmosphere by dumping;

(b)   pollution from vessels, in particular measures for preventing accidents and dealing with emergencies, ensuring the safety of operations at sea, preventing intentional and unintentional discharges, and regulating the design, construction, equipment, operation and manning of vessels;

(c)   pollution from installations and devices used in exploration or exploitation of the natural resources of the sea bed and subsoil in particular measures for preventing accidents and dealing with emergencies, ensuring the safety of operations at sea, and regulating the design, construction, equipment, operation and manning of such installations or devices;

(d)   pollution from other installations and devices operating in the marine environment, in particular measures for preventing accidents and dealing

---

39   Adopted at Montego Bay, 10 December 1982. Entered into force 16 November 1994. Reproduced in (1982) 21 *ILM* at 1261.

with emergencies, ensuring the safety of operations at sea, and regulating the design, construction, equipment, operation and manning of such installations or devices.

4   In taking such measures to prevent, reduce or control pollution of the marine environment, States shall refrain from unjustifiable interference with activities carried out by other states in the exercise of their rights and in pursuance of their duties in conformity with this Convention.

5   The measures taken in accordance with this Part shall include those necessary to protect and preserve rare and fragile ecosystems as well as the habitat of depleted, threatened or endangered species and other forms of marine life.

Section 2   Global and regional co-operation

Article 197 Co-operation on a global or regional basis

States shall co-operate on a global basis and, as appropriate, on a regional basis, directly or through competent international organisations, in formulating and elaborating international rules, standards and recommended practices and procedures consistent with this Convention, for the protection and preservation of the marine environment, taking into account characteristic regional features.

Article 198 Notification of imminent or actual damage

When a state becomes aware of cases in which the marine environment is in imminent danger of being damaged or has been damaged by pollution, it shall immediately notify other states it deems likely to be affected by such damage, as well as the competent international organisations.

Article 199 Contingency plans against pollution

In the cases referred to in Article 198, states in the area affected, in accordance with their capabilities, and the competent international organisations shall co-operate, to the extent possible, in eliminating the effects of pollution and preventing or minimising the damage. To this end, states shall jointly develop and promote contingency plans for responding to pollution incidents in the maritime environment.

Section 5   International rules and national legislation to prevent, reduce and control pollution of the marine environment

Article 207 Pollution from land-based sources

1   States shall adopt laws and regulations to prevent, reduce and control pollution of the marine environment from land-based sources, including rivers, estuaries, pipelines and outfall structures, taking into account internationally agreed rules, standards and recommended practices and procedures.

2   States shall take other measures as may be necessary to prevent, reduce and control such pollution.

3   States shall endeavour to harmonise their policies in this connection at the appropriate regional level.

4   States, acting especially through competent international organisations or diplomatic conference, shall endeavour to establish global and regional rules, standards and recommended practices and procedures to prevent, reduce and control pollution of the marine environment from land-based sources, taking into account characteristic regional features, the economic capacity of developing states and their need for economic development. Such rules, standards and recommended practices and procedures shall be re-examined from time to time as necessary.

5　Laws, regulations, measures, rules, standards and recommended practices and procedures referred to in paras 1, 2 and 4 shall include those designed to minimise, to the fullest extent possible, the release of toxic, harmful or noxious substances, especially those which are persistent, into the marine environment.

Article 208　Pollution from sea bed activities subject to national jurisdiction

1　Coastal states shall adopt laws and regulations to prevent, reduce and control pollution of the marine environment arising from or in connection with sea bed activities subject to their jurisdiction and from artificial islands, installations and structures under their jurisdiction, pursuant to Articles 60 and 80.

2　States shall take other measures as may be necessary to prevent, reduce and control such pollution.

3　Such laws, regulations and measures shall be no less effective than international rules, standards and recommended practices and procedures.

4　States shall endeavour to harmonise their policies in this connection at the appropriate regional level.

5　States, acting especially through competent international organisations or diplomatic conference, shall endeavour to establish global and regional rules, standards and recommended practices and procedures to prevent, reduce and control pollution of the marine environment referred to in para 1. Such rules, standards and recommended practices and procedures shall be re-examined from time to time as necessary.

Article 209　Pollution from activities in the Area[40]

Article 210　Pollution by dumping

1　States shall adopt laws and regulations to prevent, reduce and control pollution of the maritime environment by dumping.

2　States shall take other measures as may be necessary to prevent, reduce and control such pollution.

3　Such laws, regulations and measures shall ensure that dumping is not carried out without the permission of the competent authorities of states.

4　States, acting especially through competent international organisations or diplomatic conference, shall endeavour to establish global and regional rules, standards and recommended practices and procedures to prevent, reduce and control such pollution. Such rules, standards and recommended practices and procedures shall be re-examined from time to time as necessary.

5　Dumping within the territorial sea and the exclusive economic zone or onto the continental shelf shall not be carried out without the express prior approval of the coastal state, which has the right to permit, regulate and control such dumping after due consideration of the matter with other states which by reason of their geographical situation may be adversely affected thereby.

6　National laws, regulations and measures shall be no less effective in preventing, reducing and controlling such pollution than the global rules and standards.

Article 211　Pollution from vessels

1　States, acting through the competent international organisations or general diplomatic conference, shall establish international rules and standards to prevent, reduce and control pollution of the marine environment from vessels

---

40　See Chapter 11.

and promote the adoption, in the same manner, wherever appropriate, of routing systems designed to minimise the threat of accidents which might cause pollution of the marine environment, including the coastline, and pollution damage to the related interests of coastal states. Such rules and standards shall, in the same manner, be re-examined from time to time as necessary.

2   States shall adopt laws and regulations for the prevention, reduction and control of pollution of the marine environment from vessels flying their flag or of their registry. Such laws and regulations shall at least have the same effect as that of generally accepted international rules and standards established through the competent international organisation or general diplomatic conference.

3   States which establish particular requirements for the prevention, reduction and control of pollution of the marine environment as a condition for the entry of foreign vessels into their ports or internal waters or for a call at their off-shore terminals shall give due publicity to such requirements and shall communicate them to the competent international organisation. Whenever such requirements are established in identical form by two or more coastal states in an endeavour to harmonise policy, the communication shall indicate which states are participating in such co-operative arrangements. Every state shall require the master of a vessel flying its flag or of its registry, when navigating within the territorial sea of a state participating in such co-operative arrangements, to furnish, upon the request of that state, information as to whether it is proceeding to a state of the same region participating in such co-operative arrangements and, if so, indicate whether it complies with the port entry requirements of that state.

4   Coastal states may, in the exercise of their sovereignty within their territorial sea, adopt laws and regulations for the prevention, reduction and control of marine pollution from foreign vessels, including vessels exercising the right of innocent passage. Such laws and regulations shall, in accordance with Part XII, section 3, not hamper innocent passage of foreign vessels.

5   Coastal states, for the purpose of enforcement as provided for in section 6, may in respect of their exclusive economic zones adopt laws and regulations for the prevention, reduction and control of pollution from vessels conforming to and giving effect to generally accepted international rules and standards established through the competent international organisation or general diplomatic conference.

6 (a) Where the international rules and standards referred to in para 1 are inadequate to meet special circumstances and coastal states have reasonable grounds for believing that a particular, clearly defined area of their respective exclusive economic zones is an area where the adoption of special mandatory measures for the prevention of pollution from vessels is required for recognised technical reasons in relation to its oceanographical and ecological conditions, as well as its utilisation or the protection of its resources and the particular character of its traffic, the coastal states, after appropriate consultations through the competent international organisation with any other states concerned, may, for that area, direct a communication to that organization, submitting scientific and technical evidence in support and information on necessary reception facilities. Within 12 months after receiving such a communication, the organisation shall determine whether the conditions in that area correspond to the requirements set out above. If the organisation so determines, the coastal states may, for that area, adopt laws and regulations for the prevention, reduction and control of pollution from vessels implementing such international rules and standards or navigational practices as are made applicable, through the organisation, for

special areas. These laws and regulations shall not become applicable to foreign vessels until 15 months after the submission of the communication to the organisation.

(b) The coastal states shall publish the limits of any such particular, clearly defined area.

(c) If the coastal states intend to adopt additional laws and regulations for the same area for the prevention, reduction and control of pollution from vessels, they shall, when submitting the aforesaid communication, at the same time notify the organisation thereof. Such additional laws and regulations may relate to discharges or navigational practices but shall not require foreign vessels to observe design, construction, manning or equipment standards other than generally accepted international rules and standards; they shall become applicable to foreign vessels 15 months after the submission of the communication to the organisation, provided that the organisation agrees within 12 months after the submission of the communication.

7   The international rules and standards referred to in this article should include inter alia those relating to prompt notification to coastal states, whose coastline or related interests may be affected by incidents, including maritime casualties, which involve discharges or probability of discharges.

Article 212 Pollution from or through the atmosphere

1   States shall adopt laws and regulations to prevent, reduce and control pollution of the marine environment from or through the atmosphere, applicable to the air space under their sovereignty and to vessels flying their flag or vessels or aircraft of their registry, taking into account internationally agreed rules standards and recommended practices and procedures and the safety of air navigation.

2   States shall take other measures as may be necessary to prevent, reduce and control such pollution.

3   States, acting especially through competent international organisations or diplomatic conference, shall endeavour to establish global and regional rules, standards and recommended practices and procedures to prevent, reduce and control such pollution.

SECTION 6 ENFORCEMENT

Article 213 Enforcement with respect to pollution from land-based sources

States shall enforce their laws and regulations adopted in accordance with Article 207 and shall adopt laws and regulations and take other measures necessary to implement applicable international rules and standards established through competent international organisations or diplomatic conference to prevent, reduce and control pollution of the marine environment from land-based sources.

Article 214 Enforcement with respect to pollution from sea bed activities

States shall enforce their laws and regulations adopted in accordance with Article 208 and shall adopt laws and regulations and take other measures necessary to implement applicable international rules and standards established through competent international organisations or diplomatic conference to prevent, reduce and control pollution of the marine environment arising from or in connection with sea bed activities subject to their jurisdiction and from artificial islands, installations and structures under their jurisdiction, pursuant to Articles 60 and 80.

Article 215 Enforcement with respect to pollution from activities in the Area

Enforcement of international rules, regulations and procedures established in accordance with Part XI to prevent, reduce and control pollution of the marine environment from activities in the Area shall be governed by that Part.

Article 216 Enforcement with respect to pollution by dumping

1   Laws and regulations adopted in accordance with this Convention and applicable international rules and standards established through competent international organisations or diplomatic conference for the prevention, reduction and control of pollution of the marine environment by dumping shall be enforced:

(a)   by the coastal state with regard to dumping within its territorial sea or its exclusive economic zone or onto its continental shelf;

(b)   by the flag state with regard to vessels flying its flag or vessels or aircraft of its registry;

(c)   by any state with regard to acts of loading of wastes or other matter occurring within its territory or at its off-shore terminals.

2   No state shall be obliged by virtue of this article to institute proceedings when another state has already instituted proceedings in accordance with this article.

Article 217 Enforcement by flag states

1   States shall ensure compliance by vessels flying their flag or of their registry with applicable international rules and standards, established through the competent international organisation or general diplomatic conference, and with their laws and regulations adopted in accordance with this Convention for the prevention, reduction and control of pollution of the marine environment from vessels and shall accordingly adopt laws and regulations and take other measures necessary for their implementation. Flag states shall provide for the effective enforcement of such rules, standards, laws and regulations, irrespective of where a violation occurs.

2   States shall, in particular, take appropriate measures in order to ensure that vessels flying their flag or of their registry are prohibited from sailing, until they can proceed to sea in compliance with the requirements of the international rules and standards referred to in para 1, including requirements in respect of design, construction, equipment and manning of vessels.

3   States shall ensure that vessels flying their flag or of their registry carry on board certificates required by and issued pursuant to international rules and standards referred to in para 1. States shall ensure that vessels flying their flag are periodically inspected in order to verify that such certificates are in conformity with the actual condition of the vessels. These certificates shall be accepted by other states as evidence of the condition of the vessels and shall be regarded as having the same force as certificates issued by them, unless there are clear grounds for believing that the condition of the vessel does not correspond substantially with the particulars of the certificates.

4   If a vessel commits a violation of rules and standards established through the competent international organisation or general diplomatic conference, the flag state, without prejudice to Articles 218, 220 and 228, shall provide for immediate investigation and where appropriate institute proceedings in respect of the alleged violation irrespective of where the violation occurred or where the pollution caused by such violation has occurred or has been spotted.

5   Flag states conducting an investigation of the violation may request the assistance of any other state whose co-operation could be useful in clarifying the circumstances of the case. States shall endeavour to meet appropriate requests of flag states.

6   States shall, at the written request of any state, investigate any violation alleged to have been committed by vessels flying their flag. If satisfied that sufficient evidence is available to enable proceedings to be brought in respect of the alleged violation, flag states shall without delay institute such proceedings in accordance with their laws.

7   Flag states shall promptly inform the requesting state and the competent international organisation of the action taken and its outcome. Such information shall be available to all states.

8   Penalties provided for by the laws and regulations of states for vessels flying their flag shall be adequate in severity to discourage violations wherever they occur.

Article 218 Enforcement by port states

1   When a vessel is voluntarily within a port or at an off-shore terminal of a state, that state may undertake investigations and, where the evidence so warrants, institute proceedings in respect of any discharge from that vessel outside the internal waters, territorial sea or exclusive economic zone of that state in violation of applicable international rules and standards established through the competent international organisation or general diplomatic conference.

2   No proceedings pursuant to para 1 shall be instituted in respect of a discharge violation in the internal waters, territorial sea or exclusive economic zone of another state unless requested by that state, the flag state, or a state damaged or threatened by the discharge violation, or unless the violation has caused or is likely to cause pollution in the internal waters, territorial sea or exclusive economic zone of the state instituting the proceedings.

3   When a vessel is voluntarily within a port or at an off-shore terminal of a state, that state shall, as far as practicable, comply with requests from any state for investigation of a discharge violation referred to in para 1, believed to have occurred in, caused, or threatened damage to the internal waters, territorial sea or exclusive economic zone of the requesting state. It shall likewise, as far as practicable, comply with requests from the flag state for investigation of such a violation, irrespective of where the violation occurred.

4   The records of the investigation carried out by a port state pursuant to this article shall be transmitted upon request to the flag state or to the coastal state. Any proceedings instituted by the port state on the basis of such an investigation may, subject to section 7, be suspended at the request of the coastal state when the violation has occurred within its internal waters, territorial sea or exclusive economic zone. The evidence and records of the case, together with any bond or other financial security posted with the authorities of the port state, shall in that event be transmitted to the coastal state. Such transmittal shall preclude the continuation of proceedings in the port state.

Article 219 Measures relating to seaworthiness of vessels to avoid pollution

Subject to section 7, states which, upon request or on their own initiative, have ascertained that a vessel within one of their ports or at one of their offshore terminals is in violation of applicable international rules and standards relating to seaworthiness of vessels and thereby threatens damage to the marine environment shall, as far as practicable, take administrative measures to prevent the vessel from sailing. Such states may permit the vessel to proceed only to the nearest appropriate repair yard and, upon removal of the causes of the violation, shall permit the vessel to continue immediately.

Article 220 Enforcement by coastal states

1   When a vessel is voluntarily within a port or at an off-shore terminal of a state, that state may, subject to section 7, institute proceedings in respect of any violation of its laws and regulations adopted in accordance with this Convention or applicable international rules and standards for the prevention, reduction and control of pollution from vessels when the violation has occurred within the territorial sea or the exclusive economic zone of that state.

2   Where there are clear grounds for believing that a vessel navigating in the territorial sea of a state has, during its passage therein, violated laws and regulations of that state adopted in accordance with this Convention or applicable international rules and standards for the prevention, reduction and control of pollution from vessels, that state, without prejudice to the application of the relevant provisions of Part II, section 3, may undertake physical inspection of the vessel relating to the violation and may, where the evidence so warrants institute proceedings, including detention of the vessel, in accordance with its laws, subject to the provisions of section 7.

3   Where there are clear grounds for believing that a vessel navigating in the exclusive economic zone or the territorial sea of a state has, in the exclusive economic zone, committed a violation of applicable international rules and standards for the prevention, reduction and control of pollution from vessels or laws and regulations of that state conforming and giving effect to such rules and standards, that state may require the vessel to give information regarding its identity and port of registry, its last and its next port of call and other relevant information required to establish whether a violation has occurred.

4   States shall adopt laws and regulations and take other measures so that vessels flying their flag comply with requests for information pursuant to para 3.

5   Where there are clear grounds for believing that a vessel navigating in the exclusive economic zone or the territorial sea of a state has, in the exclusive economic zone, committed a violation referred to in para 3 resulting in a substantial discharge causing or threatening significant pollution of the marine environment, that state may undertake physical inspection of the vessel for matters relating to the violation if the vessel has refused to give information or if the information supplied by the vessel is manifestly at variance with the evident factual situation and if the circumstances of the case justify such inspection.

6   Where there is clear objective evidence that a vessel navigating in the exclusive economic zone or the territorial sea of a state has, in the exclusive economic zone, committed a violation referred to in para 3 resulting in a discharge causing major damage or threat of major damage to the coastline or related interests of the coastal state, or to any resources of its territorial sea or exclusive economic zone, that state may, subject to section 7, provided that the evidence so warrants, institute proceedings, including detention of the vessel, in accordance with its laws.

7   Notwithstanding the provisions of para 6, whenever appropriate procedures have been established, either through the competent international organisation or as otherwise agreed, whereby compliance with requirements for bonding or other appropriate financial security has been assured, the coastal state if bound by such procedures shall allow the vessel to proceed.

8   The provisions of paras 3, 4, 5, 6 and 7 also apply in respect of national laws and regulations adopted pursuant to Article 211, para 6.

Article 221 Measures to avoid pollution arising from maritime casualties

1   Nothing in this Part shall prejudice the right of states, pursuant to international law, both customary and conventional, to take and enforce measures beyond the territorial sea proportionate to the actual or threatened damage to protect their coastline or related interests, including fishing, from pollution or threat of pollution following upon a maritime casualty or acts relating to such a casualty, which may reasonably be expected to result in major harmful consequences.

2   For the purposes of this article, 'maritime casualty' means a collision of vessels, stranding or other incident of navigation, or other occurrence on board a vessel or external to it resulting in material damage or imminent threat of material damage to a vessel or cargo.

Article 222 Enforcement with respect to pollution from or through the atmosphere

States shall enforce, within the air space under their sovereignty or with regard to vessels flying their flag or vessels or aircraft of their registry, their laws and regulations adopted in accordance with Article 212, para 1, and with other provisions of this Convention and shall adopt laws and regulations and take other measures necessary to implement applicable international rules and standards established through competent international organisations or diplomatic conference to prevent, reduce and control pollution of the marine environment from or through the atmosphere, in conformity with all relevant international rules and standards concerning the safety of air navigation.

SECTION 7 SAFEGUARDS

Article 223 Measures to facilitate proceedings

In proceedings instituted pursuant to this Part, states shall take measures to facilitate the hearing of witnesses and the admission of evidence submitted by authorities of another state, or by the competent international organisation, and shall facilitate the attendance at such proceedings of official representatives of the competent international organisation, the flag state and any state affected by pollution arising out of any violation. The official representatives attending such proceedings shall have such rights and duties as may be provided under national laws and regulations or international law.

Article 224 Exercise of powers of enforcement

The powers of enforcement against foreign vessels under this Part may only be exercised by officials or by warships, military aircraft, or other ships or aircraft clearly marked and identifiable as being on government service and authorised to that effect.

Article 225 Duty to avoid adverse consequences in the exercise of the powers of enforcement

In the exercise under this Convention of their powers of enforcement against foreign vessels, states shall not endanger the safety of navigation or otherwise create any hazard to a vessel, or bring it to an unsafe port or anchorage, or expose the marine environment to an unreasonable risk.

Article 226 Investigation of foreign vessels

1 (a) States shall not delay a foreign vessel longer than is essential for purposes of the investigations provided for in Articles 216, 218 and 220. Any physical inspection of a foreign vessel shall be limited to an examination of such

certificates, records or other documents as the vessel is required to carry by generally accepted international rules and standards or of any similar documents which it is carrying; further physical inspection of the vessel may be undertaken only after such an examination and only when:

(i)   there are clear grounds for believing that the condition of the vessel or its equipment does not correspond substantially with the particulars of those documents;

(ii) the contents of such documents are not sufficient to confirm or verify a suspected violation; or

(iii) the vessel is not carrying valid certificates and records.

(b) If the investigation indicates a violation of applicable laws and regulations or international rules and standards for the protection and preservation of the marine environment, release shall be made promptly subject to reasonable procedures such as bonding or other appropriate financial security.

(c) Without prejudice to applicable international rules and standards relating to the seaworthiness of vessels, the release of a vessel may, whenever it would present an unreasonable threat of damage to the marine environment, be refused or made conditional upon proceeding to the nearest appropriate repair yard. Where release has been refused or made conditional, the flag state of the vessel must be promptly notified, and may seek release of the vessel in accordance with Part XV.

2   States shall co-operate to develop procedures for the avoidance of unnecessary physical inspection of vessels at sea.

Article 227 Non-discrimination with respect to foreign vessels

In exercising their rights and performing their duties under this Part, states shall not discriminate in form or in fact against vessels of any other state.

Article 228 Suspension and restrictions on institution of proceedings

1   Proceedings to impose penalties in respect of any violation of applicable laws and regulations or international rules and standards relating to the prevention, reduction and control of pollution from vessels committed by a foreign vessel beyond the territorial sea of the state instituting proceedings shall be suspended upon the taking of proceedings to impose penalties in respect of corresponding charges by the flag state within six months of the date on which proceedings were first instituted, unless those proceedings relate to a case of major damage to the coastal state or the flag state in question has repeatedly disregarded its obligation to enforce effectively the applicable international rules and standards in respect of violations committed by its vessels. The flag state shall in due course make available to the state previously instituting proceedings a full dossier of the case and the records of the proceedings, whenever the flag state has requested the suspension of proceedings in accordance with this article. When proceedings instituted by the flag state have been brought to a conclusion, the suspended proceedings shall be terminated. Upon payment of costs incurred in respect of such proceedings, any bond posted or other financial security provided in connection with the suspended proceedings shall be released by the coastal state.

2   Proceedings to impose penalties on foreign vessels shall not be instituted after the expiry of three years from the date on which the violation was committed, and shall not be taken by any state in the event of proceedings having been instituted by another state subject to the provisions set out in para 1.

3   The provisions of this article are without prejudice to the right of the flag state to take any measures, including proceedings to impose penalties, according to its laws irrespective of prior proceedings by another state.

Article 229 Institution of civil proceedings

Nothing in this Convention affects the institution of civil proceedings in respect of any claim for loss or damage resulting from pollution of the marine environment.

Article 230 Monetary penalties and the observance of recognised rights of the accused

1   Monetary penalties only may be imposed with respect to violations of national laws and regulations or applicable international rules and standards for the prevention, reduction and control of pollution of the marine environment, committed by foreign vessels beyond the territorial sea.

2   Monetary penalties only may be imposed with respect to violations of national laws and regulations or applicable international rules and standards for the prevention, reduction and control of pollution of the marine environment, committed by foreign vessels in the territorial sea, except in the case of a wilful and serious act of pollution in the territorial sea.

3   In the conduct of proceedings in respect of such violations committed by a foreign vessel which may result in the imposition of penalties, recognised rights of the accused shall be observed.

Article 231 Notification to the flag state and other states concerned

States shall promptly notify the flag state and any other state concerned of any measures taken pursuant to section 6 against foreign vessels, and shall submit to the flag state all official reports concerning such measures. However, with respect to violations committed in the territorial sea, the foregoing obligations of the coastal state apply only to such measures as are taken in proceedings. The diplomatic agents or consular officers and where possible the maritime authority of the flag state, shall be immediately informed of any such measures taken pursuant to section 6 against foreign vessels.

Article 232 Liability of states arising from enforcement measures

States shall be liable for damage or loss attributable to them arising from measures taken pursuant to section 6 when such measures are unlawful or exceed those reasonably required in the light of available information. States shall provide for recourse in their courts for actions in respect of such damage or loss.

Article 233 Safeguards with respect to straits used for international navigation

Nothing in sections 5, 6 and 7 affects the legal regime of straits used for international navigation. However, if a foreign ship other than those referred to in section 10 has committed a violation of the laws and regulations referred to in Article 42, para 1 (a) and (b), causing or threatening major damage to the marine environment of the straits, the states bordering the straits may take appropriate enforcement measures and if so shall respect *mutatis mutandis* the provisions of this section.

SECTION 8 ICE-COVERED AREAS

Article 234 Ice-covered areas

Coastal states have the right to adopt and enforce non-discriminatory laws and regulations for the prevention, reduction and control of marine pollution from vessels in ice-covered areas within the limits of the exclusive economic zone, where particularly severe climatic conditions and the presence of ice covering such areas for most of the year create obstructions or exceptional hazards to navigation, and pollution of the marine environment could cause major harm to or irreversible disturbance of the ecological balance. Such laws and regulations shall have due regard to navigation and the protection and preservation of the marine environment based on the best available scientific evidence.

SECTION 9 RESPONSIBILITY AND LIABILITY

Article 235 Responsibility and liability

1   States are responsible for the fulfilment of their international obligations concerning the protection and preservation of the marine environment. They shall be liable in accordance with international law.

2   States shall ensure that recourse is available in accordance with their legal systems for prompt and adequate compensation or other relief in respect of damage caused by pollution of the marine environment by natural or juridical persons under their jurisdiction.

3   With the objective of assuring prompt and adequate compensation in respect of all damage caused by pollution of the marine environment, states shall co-operate in the implementation of existing international law and the further development of international law relating to responsibility and liability for the assessment of and compensation for damage and the settlement of related disputes, as well as, where appropriate, development of criteria and procedures for payment of adequate compensation, such as compulsory insurance or compensation funds.

SECTION 10 SOVEREIGN IMMUNITY

Article 236 Sovereign immunity

The provisions of this Convention regarding the protection and preservation of the marine environment do not apply to any warship, naval auxiliary, other vessels or aircraft owned or operated by a state and used for the time being only on government non-commercial service. However, each state shall ensure, by the adoption of appropriate measures not impairing operations or operational capabilities of such vessels or aircraft owned or operated by it, that such vessels or aircraft act in a manner consistent, so far as is reasonable and practicable, with this Convention.

SECTION 11 OBLIGATIONS UNDER OTHER CONVENTIONS ON THE PROTECTION AND PRESERVATION OF THE MARINE ENVIRONMENT

Article 237 Obligations under other conventions on the protection and preservation of the marine environment

1   The provisions of this Part are without prejudice to the specific obligations assumed by states under special conventions and agreements concluded previously which relate to the protection and preservation of the marine environment and to agreements which may be concluded in furtherance of the general principles set forth in this Convention.

2   Specific obligations assumed by states under special conventions, with respect to the protection and preservation of the marine environment, should be carried out in a manner consistent with the general principles and objectives of this Convention.

18.7.3 Nuclear energy

In 1956 the International Atomic Energy Agency (IAEA) was established with the objective of encouraging the use of nuclear power. The Stockholm Conference 1972 indicated particular concern about nuclear waste and the dumping of radio-active waste at sea was outlawed by the London Dumping Convention 1972. Gradually too, the IAEA was given strongly enhanced powers with regard to the safety of nuclear installations including the right to carry out inspections. The basis of the legal regime pertaining to nuclear power is the requirement of publicity and notification, especially of significant risks, but also to encourage the spread of best practices with regard to safety.

Following the Chernobyl accident, when for some considerable time it was impossible to know exactly the extent of the disaster, the Convention on Assistance in Case of Nuclear Accident or Radiological Emergency 1986[41] and the Convention on Early Notification of Nuclear Accident 1986[42] were signed setting down some important provisions applicable should an accident or emergency occur.

18.8 Conservation of natural resources

Control of pollution is only one aspect of international environmental law. Principle 2 of the Stockholm Declaration proclaimed that the natural resources of the earth should be safeguarded for the benefit of present and future generations. The principle marks a shift away from ideas of absolute sovereignty over natural resources and has been followed by a number of conventions dealing both with general and specific aspects of conservation.

In 1980 the International Union for Conservation of Nature and Natural Resources (IUCN), a non-governmental organisation commissioned by UNEP to draw up a conservation action plan, published the 'World Conservation Strategy'. The aim of the strategy was to advance the achievement of sustainable development through the conservation of living resources. The strategy represents a consensus reached by the scientific community and those concerned with the environment. In the same year the General Assembly of the United Nations passed a resolution on conservation:

---

41 Convention on Assistance in Case of Nuclear Accident or Radiological Emergency, done at Vienna, 26 September 1986. Entered into force 26 February 1987. Reproduced in (1986) 25 *ILM* 1377.
42 Convention on Early Notification of a Nuclear Accident, done at Vienna, 26 September 1986. Entered into force 27 October 1986. Reproduced in (1986) 25 *ILM* 1370.

UN GENERAL ASSEMBLY RESOLUTION 35/8 (30 OCTOBER 1980) – HISTORICAL RESPONSIBILITY OF STATES FOR THE PRESERVATION OF NATURE FOR PRESENT AND FUTURE GENERATIONS

The General Assembly,

Having considered the item entitled 'Historical responsibility of states for the preservation of nature for present and future generations',

Conscious of the disastrous consequences which a war involving the use of nuclear weapons and other weapons of mass destruction would have on man and his environment,

Noting that the continuation of the arms race, including the testing of various types of weapons, especially nuclear weapons, and the accumulation of toxic chemicals are adversely affecting the human environment and damaging the vegetable and animal world,

Bearing in mind that the arms race is diverting material and intellectual resources from the solution of the urgent problems of preserving nature,

Attaching great importance to the development of planned, constructive international co-operation in solving the problems of preserving nature,

Recognising that the prospects for solving problems so universal as the preservation of nature are closely linked to the strengthening and development of international détente and the creation of conditions which would banish war from the life of mankind,

Noting with satisfaction the drafting and signature in recent years of a number of international agreements designed to preserve the environment,

Determined to preserve nature as a prerequisite for the normal life of man

1   Proclaims the historical responsibility of states for the preservation of nature for present and future generations;

2   Draws the attention of states to the fact that the continuing arms race has pernicious effects on the environment and reduces the prospects for the necessary international co-operation in preserving nature on our planet;

3   Calls upon states, in the interest of present and future generations, to demonstrate due concern and take the measures, including legislative measures, necessary for preserving nature, and also to promote international co-operation in this field;

4   Requests the Secretary General, with the co-operation of the United Nations Environment Programme, to prepare a report on the pernicious effects of the arms race on nature and to seek the views of states on possible measures to be taken at the international level for the preservation of nature;

5   Decides to include in the provisional agenda of its thirty-sixth session an item entitled 'Historical responsibility of states for the preservation of nature for present and future generations: report of the Secretary General'.

Two years later a more strongly worded document was adopted:

WORLD CHARTER FOR NATURE[43]

I   GENERAL PRINCIPLES

1   Nature shall be respected and its essential processes shall not be impaired.

2   The genetic viability on the earth shall not be compromised; the population levels of all life forms, wild and domesticated, must be at least sufficient for their survival, and to this end necessary habitats shall be safeguarded.

3   All areas of the earth, both land and sea, shall be subject to these principles of conservation; special protection shall be given to unique areas, to representative samples of all the different types of ecosystems and to the habitats of rare or endangered species.

4   Ecosystems and organisms, as well as the land, marine and atmospheric resources that are utilised by man, shall be managed to achieve and maintain optimum sustainable productivity, but not in such a way as to endanger the integrity of those other ecosystems or species with which they coexist.

5   Nature shall be secured against degradation caused by warfare or other hostile activities.

II   FUNCTIONS

6   In the decision-making process it shall be recognised that man's needs can be met only by ensuring the proper functioning of natural systems and by respecting the principles set forth in the present Charter.

7   In the planning and implementation of social and economic development activities, due account shall be taken of the fact that the conservation of nature is an integral part of those activities.

8   In formulating long-term plans for economic development, population growth and the improvement of standards of living, due account shall be taken of the long-term capacity of natural systems to ensure the subsistence and settlement of the populations concerned, recognising that this capacity may be enhanced through science and technology.

9   The allocation of areas of the earth to various uses shall be planned and due account shall be taken of the physical constraints, the biological productivity and diversity and the natural beauty of the areas concerned.

10   Natural resources shall not be wasted, but used with a restraint appropriate to the principles set forth in the present Charter, in accordance with the following rules:

(a)   living resources shall not be utilised in excess of their natural capacity for regeneration;

(b)   the productivity of soils shall be maintained or enhanced through measures which safeguard their long-term fertility and the process of organic decomposition, and prevent erosion and all other forms of degradation;

(c)   resources, including water, which are not consumed as they are used shall be reused or recycled;

(d)   non-renewable resources which are consumed as they are used shall be exploited with restraint, taking into account their abundance, the rational

---

43   Adopted by the UN General Assembly, 28 October 1982. UNGA Res 37/7, UN GAOR Supp (No 51) 21, UN Doc A/37/L4 and Add 1 (1982).

possibilities of converting them for consumption, and the compatibility of their exploitation with the functioning of natural systems.

11 Activities which might have an impact on nature shall be controlled, and the best available technologies that minimise significant risks to nature or other adverse effects shall be used; in particular:

(a) activities which are likely to cause irreversible damage to nature shall be avoided;

(b) activities which are likely to pose a significant risk to nature shall be preceded by an exhaustive examination; their proponents shall demonstrate that expected benefits outweigh potential damage to nature, and where potential adverse effects are not fully understood, the activities should not proceed;

(c) activities which may disturb nature shall be preceded by assessment of their consequences and environmental impact studies of development projects shall be conducted sufficiently in advance, and if they are to be undertaken, such activities shall be planned and carried out so as to minimise potential adverse effects;

(d) agriculture, grazing, forestry and fisheries practices shall be adapted to the natural characteristics and constraints of given areas;

(e) areas degraded by human activities shall be rehabilitated for purposes in accord with their natural potential and compatible with the well-being of affected populations.

12 Discharge of pollutants into natural systems shall be avoided and:

(a) where this is not feasible, such pollutants shall be treated at the source, using the best practicable means available;

(b) special precautions shall be taken to prevent discharge of radioactive or toxic wastes.

13 Measures intended to prevent, control or limit natural disasters, infestations and diseases shall be specifically directed to the causes of these scourges and shall avoid adverse side-effects on nature.

III IMPLEMENTATION

14 The principles set forth in the present Charter shall be reflected in the law and practice of each state, as well as at the international level.

15 Knowledge of nature shall be broadly disseminated by all possible means, particularly by ecological education as an integral part of general education.

16 All planning shall include, among its essential elements, the formulation of strategies for the conservation of nature, the establishment of inventories of ecosystems and assessments of the effects on nature of proposed policies and activities; all of these elements shall be disclosed to the public by appropriate means in time to permit effective consultation and participation.

17 Funds, programmes and administrative structures necessary to achieve the objective of the conservation of nature shall be provided.

18 Constant efforts shall be made to increase knowledge of nature by scientific research and to disseminate such knowledge unimpeded by restrictions of any kind.

19 The status of natural processes, ecosystems and species shall be closely monitored to enable early detection of degradation or threat, ensure timely intervention and facilitate the evaluation of conservation policies and methods.

20   Military activities damaging to nature shall be avoided, and in particular:

(a)   further development, testing and use of nuclear, biological, chemical or environmental modification methods of warfare shall be prohibited; and

(b)   protected areas, the Antarctic region and outer space shall be free of military activity.

21   States and, to the extent they are able, other public authorities, international organisations, individuals, groups and corporations shall:

(a)   co-operate in the task of conserving nature through common activities and other relevant actions, including information exchange and consultations;

(b)   establish standards for products and manufacturing processes that may have adverse effects on nature, as well as agreed methodologies for assessing these effects;

(c)   implement the applicable international legal provisions for the conservation of nature and the protection of the environment;

(d)   ensure that activities within their jurisdictions or control do not cause damage to the natural systems located within other states or in the areas beyond the limits of national jurisdiction;

(e)   safeguard and conserve nature in areas beyond national jurisdiction.

22   Taking fully into account the sovereignty of states over their natural resources, each state shall give effect to the provisions of the present Charter through its competent organs and in co-operation with other states.

23   All persons, in accordance with their national legislation, shall have the opportunity to participate, individually or with others, in the formulation of decisions of direct concern to their environment, and shall have access to means of redress when their environment has suffered damage of degradation.

24   Each person has a duty to act in accordance with the provisions of the present Charter; acting individually, in association with others or through participation in the political process, each person shall strive to ensure that the objectives of the present Charter are met.

As has already been seen, many of the provisions of the World Charter for Nature were re-affirmed and developed in the Rio Declaration 1992 and Agenda 21 also provided the framework for future action.

18.8.1 Conservation of migratory and land-based species

As far as existing conventional law is concerned, the emphasis has been on conservation of living resources. Some treaties refer to specific species, for example, the Agreement on the Conservation of Polar Bears 1973, while others impose rules of more general application. In addition there are a number of bilateral agreements relating to conservation. There are four multilateral treaties which are regarded as being particularly significant:

- Convention on Wetlands of International Importance 1971 (Ramsar Convention);

- Convention for the protection of the World Cultural and National Heritage 1972 (the World Heritage Convention);

- Convention on International Trade in Endangered Species of Wild Fauna and Flora 1973 (CITES);

- Convention on the Conservation of Migratory Species of Wild Animals 1980 (Bonn Convention).

All four adopt different approaches to the problem of conservation. The Ramsar Convention and the Bonn Convention make provision for the protection of habitats and the Ramsar Convention refers to sustainable utilisation of wetland areas. The World Heritage Convention is concerned with identifying natural sites of particular importance and imposing specific obligations in respect of such sites. The convention also establishes a trust fund to be administered through UNESCO for assisting in the protection of such sites. The Bonn Convention, in addition to providing habitat protection, also seeks to protect migratory species during the course of their migration. The convention is particularly concerned to encourage co-operation between states for the protection of migratory species. CITES has been the most successful of the four Conventions; it attempts to encourage conservation by outlawing commercial trade in endangered species, the view being that the ending of commercial trade will result in the ending of endangered status of many species. The Convention lists two categories of endangered species: those seriously threatened with extinction in which all trade is prohibited, and those which are not yet threatened with extinction but which may become so if trade continues uncontrolled. Trade in the latter category is permitted but is subject to stringent controls.

CONVENTION ON WETLANDS OF INTERNATIONAL IMPORTANCE[44]

The Contracting Parties,

Recognising the interdependence of man and his environment;

Considering the fundamental ecological functions of wetlands as regulators of water regimes and as habitats supporting a characteristic flora and fauna, especially waterfowl;

Being convinced that wetlands constitute a resource of great economic, cultural, scientific and recreational value, the loss of which would be irreparable;

Desiring to stem the progressive encroachment on and loss of wetlands now and in the future;

Recognising that waterfowl in their seasonal migrations may transcend frontiers and so should be regarded as an international resource;

Being confident that the conservation of wetlands and their flora and fauna can be ensured by combining far-sighted national policies with co-ordinated international action;

Have agreed as follows:

Article 1

1   For the purpose of this Convention wetlands are areas of marsh, fen, peatland or water, whether natural or artificial, permanent or temporary, with

---

44   Done at Ramsar, Iran on 2 February 1971, entered into force 21 December 1975.

water that is static or flowing, fresh, brackish or salt, including areas of marine water the depth of which at low tide does not exceed six metres.

2   For the purpose of this Convention waterfowl are birds ecologically dependent on wetlands.

Article 2

1   Each Contracting party shall designate suitable wetlands within its territory for inclusion in a List of Wetlands of International Importance, hereinafter referred to as 'the List' which is maintained by the bureau established under Article 8. The boundaries of each wetland shall be precisely described and also delimited on a map and they may incorporate riparian and coastal zones adjacent to the wetlands, and islands or bodies of marine water deeper than six metres at low tide lying within the wetlands, especially where these have an importance as waterfowl habitat.

2   Wetlands should be selected for the List on account of their international significance in terms of ecology, botany, zoology, limnology or hydrology. In the first instance, wetlands of international importance to waterfowl at any season should be included.

3   The inclusion of a wetland in the List does not prejudice the exclusive sovereign rights of the Contracting Party in whose territory the wetland is situated.

4   Each Contracting Party shall designate at least one wetland to be included in the List when signing this Convention or when depositing its instrument of ratification or accession, as provided in Article 9.

5   Any Contracting Party shall have the right to add to the List further wetlands situated within its territory, to extend the boundaries of those wetlands already included by it in the List and shall, at the earliest possible time, inform the organisation or government responsible for the continuing bureau duties specified in Article 8 of such changes.

6   Each Contracting Party shall consider its international responsibilities for the conservation, management and wise use of migratory stocks of waterfowl, both when designating entries for the List and when exercising its right to change entries in the List relating to wetlands within its territory.

Article 3

1   The Contracting Parties shall formulate and implement their planning so as to promote the conservation of the wetlands included in the List, and as far as possible the wise use of wetlands in their territory.

2   Each Contracting Party shall arrange to be informed at the earliest possible time if the ecological character of any wetland in its territory and included in the List has changed, is changing or is likely to change as the result of technological developments, pollution or other human interference. Information on such changes shall be passed without delay to the organisation or government responsible for the continuing bureau duties specified in Article 8.

Article 4

1   Each Contracting Party shall promote the conservation of wetlands and waterfowl by establishing nature reserves on wetlands, whether they are included in the List or not, and provide adequately for their wardening.

2   When a Contracting Party in its urgent national interest, deletes or restricts the boundaries of a wetland included in the List, it should as far as possible compensate for any loss of wetland resources, and in particular it should create

additional reserves for waterfowl and for the protection, either in the same area or elsewhere, of an adequate portion of the original habitat.

3   The Contracting Parties shall encourage research and the exchange of data and publications regarding wetlands and their flora and fauna.

4   The Contracting Parties shall endeavour through management to increase waterfowl populations on appropriate wetlands.

5   The Contracting Parties shall promote the training of personnel competent in the fields of wetland research, management and wardening.

Article 5

The Contracting Parties shall consult with each other about implementing obligations arising from the Convention especially in the case of a wetland extending over the territories of more than one Contracting Party or where a water system is shared by Contracting Parties.

They shall at the same time endeavour to co-ordinate and support present and future policies and regulations concerning the conservation of wetlands and their flora and fauna.

CONVENTION FOR THE PROTECTION OF THE WORLD CULTURAL AND NATIONAL HERITAGE 1972 (THE WORLD HERITAGE CONVENTION)[45]

I   Definitions of the cultural and the natural heritage

Article 1

For the purposes of this Convention, the following shall be considered as 'cultural heritage':

monuments: architectural works, works of monumental sculpture and painting, elements or structures of an archaeological nature, inscriptions, cave dwellings and combinations of features, which are of outstanding universal value from the point of view of history, art or science;

groups of buildings: groups of separate or connected buildings which, because of their architecture, their homogeneity or their place in the landscape, are of outstanding universal value from the point of view of history, art or science;

sites: works of man or the combined works of nature and of man, and areas including archaeological sites which are of outstanding universal value from the historical, aesthetic, ethnological or anthropological points of view.

Article 2

For the purposes of this Convention, the following shall be considered as 'natural heritage':

natural features consisting of physical and biological formations or groups of such formations, which are of outstanding universal value from the aesthetic or scientific point of view;

---

45   Convention for the Protection of the World Cultural and National Heritage 1972 (the World Heritage Convention), done at Paris, 23 November 1972. Entered into force 17 December 1975.

geological and physiographical formations and precisely delineated areas which constitute the habitat of threatened species of animals and plants of outstanding universal value from the point of view of science or conservation;

natural sites or precisely delineated areas of universal value from the point of view of science, conservation or natural beauty.

Article 3

It is for each State Party to this Convention to identify and delineate the different properties situated on its territory mentioned in Articles 1 and 2 above.

II   National protection and international protection of the cultural and natural heritage

Article 4

Each State Party to this Convention recognises that the duty of ensuring the identifications, protection, conservation, preservation and transmission to future generations of the cultural and natural heritage referred to in Articles 1 and 2 and situated on its territory, belongs primarily to that state. It will do all it can to this end, to the utmost of its own resources and, where appropriate, with any international assistance and co-operation, in particular, financial, artistic, scientific and technical, which it may be able to obtain.

Article 5

To ensure that effective and active measures are taken for the protection, conservation and preservation of the cultural and natural heritage situated on its territory, each State Party to this Convention shall endeavour, in so far as possible, and as appropriate for each country:

(a) to adopt a general policy which aims to give the cultural and natural heritage a function in the life of the community and to integrate the protection of that heritage into comprehensive planning programmes;

(b) to set up within its territories, where such services do not exist, one or more services for the protection, conservation and presentation of the cultural and natural heritage with an appropriate staff and possessing the means to discharge their functions;

(c) to develop scientific and technical studies and research and to work out such operating methods as will make the state capable of counteracting the dangers that threaten its cultural or natural heritage;

(d) to take the appropriate legal, scientific, technical, administrative and financial measures necessary for the identification, protection, conservation, presentation and rehabilitation of this heritage; and

(e) to foster the establishment or development of national or regional centres for training in the protection, conservation and presentation of the cultural and natural heritage and to encourage scientific research in this field.

Article 6

1   While fully respecting the sovereignty of the states on whose territory the cultural and natural heritage mentioned in Articles 1 and 2 is situated, and without prejudice to property rights provided by national legislation, the States Parties to this Convention recognise that such heritage constitutes a world heritage for whose protection it is the duty of the international community as a whole to co-operate.

2   The States Parties undertake, in accordance with the provisions of this Convention, to give their help in the identification, protection, conservation and preservation of the cultural and natural heritage referred to in paras 2 and 4 of Article 11 if the state on whose territory it is situated so request.

3   Each State Party to this Convention undertakes not to take any deliberate measures which might damage directly or indirectly the cultural and natural heritage referred to in Articles 1 and 2 situated on the territory of other States Parties to this Convention.

Article 7

For the purposes of this Convention, international protection of the world cultural and natural heritage shall be understood to mean the establishment of a system of international co-operation and assistance designed to support States Parties to the Convention in their efforts to conserve and identify that heritage.

II   Intergovernmental committee for the protection of the world cultural and natural heritage

Article 8

1   An intergovernmental committee for the protection of the cultural and natural heritage of outstanding universal value, called 'the World Heritage Committee', is hereby established within the United Nations Educational, Scientific and Cultural Organisation. It shall be composed of 15 States Parties to the Convention, elected by States Parties to the Convention meeting in general assembly during the ordinary session of the General Conference of the United Nations Educational, Scientific and Cultural Organisation. The number of States members of the Committee shall be increased to 21 as from the date of the ordinary session of the General Conference following the entry into force of this Convention for at least 40 states.

2   Election of members of the Committee shall ensure an equitable representation of the different regions and cultures of the world.

...

Article 11

1   Every State Party to this Convention shall, in so far as possible, submit to the World Heritage Committee an inventory of property forming part of the cultural and natural heritage, situated in its territory and suitable for inclusion in the list provided for in para 2 of this article. This inventory, which shall not be considered exhaustive, shall include documentation about the location of the property in question and its significance.

2   On the basis of the inventories submitted by states in accordance with para 1, the Committee shall establish, keep up to date and publish, under the title of 'World Heritage List', a list of properties forming part of the cultural and natural heritage, as defined in Articles 1 and 2 of this Convention, which it considers as having outstanding universal value in terms of such criteria as it shall have established. An updated list shall be distributed at least every two years.

3   The inclusion of a property in the World Heritage List requires the consent of the state concerned ...

...

IV   Fund for the protection of the world cultural and natural heritage

Article 15

1   A Fund for the Protection of the World Cultural and Natural Heritage of Outstanding Universal Value, called 'the World Heritage Fund', is hereby established.

2   The Fund shall constitute a trust fund, in conformity with the provisions of the Financial Regulations of the United Nations Educational, Scientific and Cultural Organisation.

3   The resources of the Fund shall consist of:

(a)   compulsory and voluntary contributions made by the States Parties to this Convention;

(b)   contributions, gifts or bequests;

(c)   any interest due on the resources of the Fund;

(d)   funds raised by collections and receipts from events organised for the benefit of the Fund; and

(e)   all other resources authorised by the Fund's regulations, as drawn up by the World Heritage Committee.

CONVENTION ON INTERNATIONAL TRADE IN ENDANGERED SPECIES OF WILD FAUNA AND FLORA[46]

The Contracting States,

Recognising that wild fauna and flora in their many beautiful and varied forms are an irreplaceable part of the natural systems of the earth which must be protected for this and the generations to come;

Conscious of the ever-growing value of wild fauna and flora from aesthetic, scientific, cultural, recreational and economic points of view;

Recognising that peoples and states are and should be the best protectors of their own wild fauna and flora;

Recognising, in addition, that international co-operation is essential for the protection of certain species of wild fauna and flora against over-exploitation through international trade;

Convinced of the urgency of taking appropriate measures to this end;

Have agreed as follows:

Article I   Definitions

For the purpose of the present Convention, unless the context otherwise requires:

(a)   'Species' means any species, subspecies, or geographically separate population thereof;

(b)   'Specimen' means:

(i)   any animal or plant, whether alive or dead;

(ii)   in the case of an animal: for species included in Appendices I and II, any readily recognisable part or derivative thereof; and for species included in Appendix III, any readily recognisable part or derivative thereof specified in Appendix III in relation to the species; and

(iii)   in the case of a plant: for species included in Appendix I, any readily recognisable part or derivative thereof; and for species included in Appendices II and III, any readily recognisable part or derivative thereof specified in Appendices II and III in relation to the species;

---

46   Convention on International Trade in Endangered Species of Wild Fauna and Flora (CITES) done at Washington, 3 March 1973. Entered into force 1 July 1975, 993 UNTS 243 – reprinted in (1973) 12 *ILM* 1085.

(c) 'Trade' means export, re-export, import and introduction from the sea;

(d) 'Re-export' means export of any specimen that has previously been exported;

(e) 'Introduction from the sea' means transportation into a state of specimens of any species which were taken in the marine environment not under the jurisdiction of any state;

(f) 'Scientific Authority' means a national scientific authority designated in accordance with Article IX;

(g) 'Management Authority' means a national management authority designated in accordance with Article IX;

(h) 'Party' means a state for which the present Convention has entered into force.

Article II Fundamental principles

1   Appendix I shall include all species threatened with extinction which are or may be affected by trade. Trade in specimens of these species must be subject to particularly strict regulation in order not to endanger further their survival and must only be authorised in exceptional circumstances.

2   Appendix II shall include:

(a) all species which although not necessarily now threatened with extinction may become so unless trade in specimens of such species is subject to strict regulation in order to avoid utilisation incompatible with their survival; and

(b) other species which must be subject to regulation in order that trade in specimens of certain species referred to in sub-para (a) of this paragraph may be brought under effective control;

3   Appendix III shall include all species which any Party identifies as being subject to regulation within its jurisdiction for the purpose of preventing or restricting exploitation, and as needing the co-operation of other parties in the control of trade.

4   The Parties shall not allow trade in specimens of species included in Appendices I, II and III except in accordance with the provisions of the present Convention.

Article III Regulation of trade in specimens of species included in Appendix I

1   All trade in specimens of species included in Appendix I shall be in accordance with the provisions of this Article.

2   The export of any specimen of a species included in Appendix I shall require the prior grant and presentation of an export permit. An export permit shall only be granted when the following conditions have been met:

(a) a Scientific Authority of the state of export has advised that such export will not be detrimental to the survival of that species;

(b) a Management Authority of the state of export is satisfied that the specimen was not obtained in contravention of the laws of that state for the protection of fauna and flora;

(c) a Management Authority of the state of export is satisfied that any living specimen will be so prepared and shipped as to minimise the risk of injury, damage to health or cruel treatment; and

(d) a Management Authority of the state of export is satisfied that an import permit has been granted for that specimen.

3   The import of any specimen of a species included in Appendix I shall require the prior grant and presentation of an import permit and either an export

permit or a re-export certificate. An import permit shall only be granted when the following conditions have been met:

(a) a Scientific Authority of the state of import has advised that the import will be for purposes which are not detrimental to the survival of the species involved;

(b) a Scientific Authority of the state of import is satisfied that the proposed recipient of a living specimen is suitably equipped to house and care for it; and

(c) a Management Authority of the state of import is satisfied that the specimen is not to be used for primarily commercial purposes.

4   The re-export of any specimen of a species included in Appendix I shall require the prior grant and presentation of a re-export permit. A re-export permit shall only be granted when the following conditions have been met:

(a) a Management Authority of the state of re-export is satisfied that the specimen was imported into that state in accordance with the provisions of the present Convention;

(b) a Management Authority of the state of re-export is satisfied that any living specimen will be so prepared and shipped as to minimise the risk of injury, damage to health or cruel treatment; and

(c) a Management Authority of the state of re-export is satisfied that an import permit has been granted for any living specimen.

5   The introduction from the sea of any specimen of a species included in Appendix I shall require the prior grant of a certificate from a Management Authority of the state of introduction. A certificate shall only be granted when the following conditions have been met:

(a) a Scientific Authority of the state of introduction advises that the introduction will not be detrimental to the survival of the species involved;

(b) a Management Authority of the state of introduction is satisfied that the proposed recipient of a living specimen is suitably equipped to house and care for it; and

(c) a Management Authority of the state of introduction is satisfied that the specimen is not to be used for primarily commercial purposes.

Article IV Regulation of trade in specimens of species included in Appendix II

1   All trade of species included in Appendix II shall be in accordance with the provisions of this article.

2   The export of any specimen of a species included in Appendix II shall require the prior grant and presentation of an export permit. An export permit shall only be granted when the following conditions have been met:

(a) a Scientific Authority of the state of export has advised that such export will not be detrimental to the survival of that species;

(b) a Management Authority of the state of export is satisfied that the specimen was not obtained in contravention of the laws of that state for the protection of fauna and flora; and

(c) a Management Authority of the state of export is satisfied that any living specimen will be so prepared and shipped as to minimise the risk of injury, damage to health or cruel treatment.

3   A Scientific Authority in each party shall monitor both the export permits granted by that state for specimens of species included in Appendix II and the

actual export of such specimens. Whenever a Scientific Authority determines that the export of such specimens of any such species should be limited in order to maintain that species throughout its range at a level consistent with its role in the ecosystems in which it occurs and well above the level at which that species might become eligible for inclusion in Appendix I, the Scientific Authority shall advise the appropriate Management Authority of suitable measures to be taken to limit the grant of export permits for specimens of that species.

4   The import of any specimen of a species included in Appendix II shall require the prior presentation of either an export permit or a re-export certificate.

5   The re-export of any specimen of a species included in Appendix II shall require the prior grant and presentation of a re-export certificate. A re-export certificate shall only be granted when the following conditions have been met:

(a)   a Management Authority of the state of re-export is satisfied that the specimen was imported into that state in accordance with the provisions of the present Convention; and

(b)   a Management Authority of the state of re-export is satisfied that any living specimen will be so prepared and shipped as to minimise the risk of injury, damage to health or cruel treatment.

6   The introduction from the sea of any specimen of a species included in Appendix II shall require the prior grant of a certificate from a Management Authority of the state of introduction. A certificate shall only be granted when the following conditions have been met:

(a)   a Scientific Authority of the state of introduction advises that the introduction will not be detrimental to the survival of the species involved; and

(b)   a Management Authority of the state of introduction is satisfied that any living specimen will be so handled as to minimise the risk of injury, damage to health or cruel treatment.

7   Certificates referred to in para 6 of this Article may be granted on the advice of a Scientific Authority, in consultation with other national scientific authorities or, when appropriate, international scientific authorities, in respect of periods not exceeding one year for total numbers of specimens to be introduced in such periods.

Article V   Regulation of trade in specimens of species included in Appendix III

1   All trade in specimens of species included in Appendix II shall be in accordance with the provisions of this article.

2   The export of any specimen of a species included in Appendix III from any state which has included that species in Appendix III shall require the prior grant and presentation of an export permit. An export permit shall only be granted when the following conditions have been met:

(a)   a Management Authority of the state of export is satisfied that the specimen was not obtained in contravention of the laws of that state for the protection of fauna and flora; and

(b)   a Management Authority of the state of export is satisfied that any living specimen will be so prepared and shipped as to minimise the risk of injury, damage to health or cruel treatment.

3   The import of any specimen of a species included in Appendix III shall require, except in circumstances to which para 4 of this article applies, the prior presentation of a certificate of origin and, where the import is from a state which has included that species in Appendix III, an export permit.

4 In the case of re-export, a certificate granted by the Management Authority of the state of re-export that the specimen was processed in that state or is being re-exported shall be accepted by the state of import as evidence that the provisions of the present Convention have been complied with in respect of the specimen concerned.

Article VI   Permits and Certificates

Article VII   Exemptions and Other Special Provisions Relating to Trade

Article VIII Measures to be Taken by the Parties

1   The Parties shall take appropriate measures to enforce the provisions of the present Convention and to prohibit trade in specimens in violation thereof. These shall include measures:

(a)   to penalise trade in, or possession of, such specimens, or both; and

(b)   to provide for the confiscation or return to the state of export of such specimens.

2   In addition to the measures taken under para 1 of this article, a party may, when it deems it necessary, provide for any method of internal reimbursement for expenses incurred as a result of the confiscation of a specimen traded in violation of the measures taken in the application of the provisions of the present Convention.

3   As far as possible, the parties shall ensure that specimens shall pass through any formalities required for trade with a minimum of delay. To facilitate such passage, a party may designate ports of exit and ports of entry at which specimens must be presented for clearance. The parties shall ensure further that all living specimens, during any period of transit, holding or shipment, are properly cared for so as to minimise the risk of injury, damage to health or cruel treatment.

4   Where a living specimen is confiscated as a result of measures referred to in para 1 of this Article:

(a)   the specimen shall be entrusted to a Management Authority of the state of confiscation;

(b)   the Management Authority shall, after consultation with the state of export, return the specimen to that state at the expense of that state, or to a rescue centre or such other place as the Management Authority deems appropriate and consistent with the purposes of the present Convention; and

(c)   the Management Authority may obtain the advice of a Scientific Authority, or may, whenever it considers it desirable, consult the Secretariat in order to facilitate the decision under sub-para (b) of this paragraph, including the choice of a rescue centre of other place.

5   A rescue centre as referred to in para 4 of this article means an institution designated by a Management Authority to look after the welfare of living specimens, particularly those that have been confiscated.

6   Each Party shall maintain records of trade in specimens of species included in Appendices I, II and III which shall cover:

(a)   the names and addresses of exporters and importers; and

(b)   the number and type of permits and certificate granted; the states with which such trade occurred; the numbers or quantities and types of specimens, names of species as included in Appendices I, II and III and, where applicable, the size and sex of the specimens in question.

7   Each party shall prepare periodic reports on its implementation of the present Convention and shall transmit to the Secretariat:

(a) an annual report containing a summary of the information specified in sub-para (b) of para 6 of this article; and

(b) a biennial report on legislative, regulatory and administrative measures taken to enforce the provisions of the present Convention.

8 The information referred to in para 7 of this article shall be available to the public where this is not inconsistent with the law of the Party concerned.

Article IX   Management and Scientific Authorities

1   Each party shall designate for the purposes of the present Convention:

(a) one or more Management Authorities competent to grant permits or certificates on behalf of that party; and

(b) one or more Scientific Authorities.

2   A state depositing an instrument of ratification, acceptance, approval or accession shall at that time inform the Depositary Government of the name and address of the Management Authority authorised to communicate with other parties and with the Secretariat.

3   Any changes in the designations or authorisations under the provisions of this Article shall be communicated by the party concerned to the Secretariat for transmission to all other parties.

4   Any Management Authority referred to in para 2 of this article shall if so requested by the Secretariat or the Management Authority of another party, communicate to it impression of stamps, seals or other devices used to authenticate permits or certificates.

Article X   Trade with states not party to the Convention

Where export or re-export is to, or import is from, a state not a party to the present Convention, comparable documentation issued by the competent authorities in that state which substantially conforms with the requirements of the present Convention for permits and certificates may be accepted in lieu thereof by any party.

CONVENTION ON THE CONSERVATION OF MIGRATORY SPECIES OF WILD ANIMALS[47]

Article II   Fundamental principles

1   The parties acknowledge the importance of migratory species[48] being conserved and of Range states[49] agreeing to take action to this end whenever possible and appropriate, paying special attention to migratory species the

---

47 Done at Bonn, Germany, 23 June 1979.

48 Defined in Article I as 'the entire population or any geographically separate part of a population of any species or lower taxon of wild animals, a significant proportion of whose members cyclically and predictably cross one or more national jurisdictional boundaries'.

49 Defined in Article I as 'any state that exercises jurisdiction over any part of the range of that migratory species, or a sState, flag vessels of which are engaged outside national jurisdictional limits in [taking, hunting, fishing, capturing, harassing, deliberately killing, or attempting to engage in any such conduct] that migratory species'.

conservation status of which is unfavourable, and taking individually or in co-operation appropriate and necessary steps to conserve such species and their habitat.

2   The parties acknowledge the need to take action to avoid any migratory species becoming endangered.

3   In particular, the parties:

(a)   should promote, co-operate in and support research relating to migratory species;

(b)   shall endeavour to provide immediate protection for migratory species included in Appendix I; and

(c)   shall endeavour to conclude agreements covering the conservation and management of migratory species included in Appendix II.[50]

In 1992 the Convention on Biological Diversity was signed at the Rio Conference. This takes the law relating to conservation a stage further by requiring states to take positive action in many key areas. The force of the Convention is however slightly undermined by the fact that many of the provisions are qualified with words such as 'as far as possible and appropriate' and it remains unclear what specific action the Convention will promulgate.

CONVENTION ON BIOLOGICAL DIVERSITY[51]

Article 1

The objectives of this Convention, to be pursued in accordance with its relevant provisions, are the conservation of biological diversity, the sustainable use of its components and the fair and equitable sharing of the benefits arising out of the utilisation of genetic resources, including by appropriate access to genetic resources and by appropriate transfer of relevant technologies, taking into account all rights over those resources and to technologies, and by appropriate funding.

Article 2

For the purposes of this Convention:

'Biological diversity' means the variability among living organisms from all sources including, *inter alia*, terrestrial, marine and other aquatic ecosystems and the ecological complexes of which they are part; this includes diversity within species, between species and of ecosystems.

'Biological resources' includes genetic resources, organisms or parts thereof, populations, or any other biotic component of ecosystems with actual or potential use or value for humanity.

'Biotechnology' means any technological application that uses biological systems, living organisms, or derivatives thereof, to make or modify products or processes for specific use.

---

50   Appendix I lists endangered species; Appendix II lists those species with an unfavourable conservation status.

51   Convention on Biological Diversity – adopted at the UN Conference on Environment and Development, 5 June 1992, reprinted (1992) 31 *ILM* 818.

'Country of origin of genetic resources' means the country which possesses those genetic resources in *in-situ* conditions.

'Country providing genetic resources' means the country supplying genetic resources collected from *in-situ* sources, including populations of both wild and domesticated species, or taken from *ex-situ* sources, which may or may not have originated in that country.

'Domesticated or cultivated species' means species in which the evolutionary process has been influenced by humans to meet their needs.

'Ecosystem' means a dynamic complex of plant, animal and micro-organism communities and their non-living environment interacting as a functional unit.

'*Ex-situ* conservation' means the conservation of components of biological diversity outside their natural habitat.

'Genetic material' means any material of plant, animal, microbial or other origin containing functional units of heredity.

'Genetic resources' means genetic material of actual or potential value.

'Habitat' means the place or type of site where an organisms or population naturally occurs.

'*In-situ* conditions' means conditions where genetic resources exist within ecosystems and natural habitats, and, in the case of domesticated or cultivated species, in the surroundings where they have developed their distinctive properties.

'*In-situ* conservation' means the conservation of ecosystems and natural habitats and the maintenance and recovery of viable populations of species in their natural surroundings and, in the case of domesticated or cultivated species, in the surroundings where they have developed their distinctive properties.

'Protected area' means a geographically defined area which is designated or regulated and managed to achieve specific conservation objectives.

'Regional economic integration organisation' means an organisation constituted by sovereign states of a given region, to which its member states have transferred competence in respect of matters governed by this Convention and which has been duly authorised, in accordance with its internal procedures, to sign, ratify, accept, approve or accede to it.

'Sustainable use' means the use of components of biological diversity in a way and at a rate that does not lead to the long-term decline of biological diversity, thereby maintain its potential to meet the needs and aspirations of present and future generations.

'Technology' includes biotechnology.

Article 3

States have, in accordance with the Charter of the United Nations and the principles of international law, the sovereign right to exploit their own resources pursuant to their own environmental policies, and the responsibility to ensure that activities within their jurisdiction or control do not cause damage to the environment of other states or of areas beyond the limits of national jurisdiction.

Article 4   Jurisdictional scope

Article 5

Each Contracting Party shall, as far as possible and as appropriate, co-operate with other Contracting Parties, directly or, where appropriate, through competent international organisations, in respect of areas beyond national jurisdiction and on other matters of mutual interest, for the conservation and sustainable use of biological diversity.

Article 6

Each Contracting Party shall, in accordance with its particular conditions and capabilities:

(a) develop national strategies, plans or programmes for the conservation and sustainable use of biological diversity or adapt for this purpose existing strategies, plans or programmes which shall reflect, *inter alia*, the measures set out in this Convention relevant to the Contracting Party concerned; and

(b) integrate, as far as possible and as appropriate, the conservation and sustainable use of biological diversity into relevant sectoral or cross-sectoral plans, programmes and policies.

18.8.2 Conservation of marine resources

The conservation regime governing living marine resources has a slightly different history since it has largely developed as an integral part of the law of the sea and the main concern has been with fishing rights and the need to avoid over-fishing. The first treaties regulating fishing rights were agreed before World War One and since that time there have been a number of treaties governing such things as fishing quotas and fishing rights. The UN Food and Agriculture Organisation has had an important role in encouraging co-operation between coastal states. Many groups of coastal states have made agreements setting a total allowable catch and very often attempting to exclude other states from fishing grounds. The first truly global attempt to regulate the conservation of marine resources was the Convention on Fishing and Conservation of the Living Resources of the High Seas 1958 which imposes only limited duties of conservation. Conservation provisions are considerably strengthened in LOSC although concerns continue to be expressed about the extent to which such provisions will prove effective.

In addition to the general rules relating to marine resources there are a number of specific agreements which relate to single species or groups of species, the best known of which is probably the International Convention for the Regulation of Whaling 1946.

18.8.3 Antarctica

Antarctica constitutes the largest area of land not subject to the jurisdiction of a single state. The special nature of the region has meant that it has been the subject of specific attention by international law. The region is important from an environmental point of view but it also has an economic importance since the discovery in the 1980s of significant quantities of manganese nodules. Historically, Antarctica had been the subject of completing claims to sovereignty by a number of different states. However in the late 1950s pressure from the scientific community resulted in the suspension of such claims and the signing of the Antarctic Treaty 1959 by the main claimant states. The treaty provides that the region shall only be used for peaceful purposes. Subsequently, the Convention for the Conservation of Antarctic Seals 1972 and the Convention on the Conservation of Antarctic Marine Living Resources 1980 were signed.

The discovery of the manganese deposits led to renewed discussions and a 50-year ban on mining was agreed in April 1991. In the same year a Protocol to the Antarctic Treaty, the Protocol on Environmental Protection 1991, was signed. The Protocol would have the effect of establishing Antarctica as a world park, thus putting a permanent end to the individual claims of sovereignty, and significantly strengthen the conservation provisions of the Antarctic regime.

18.9 A right to a decent environment

As was discussed in Chapter 1, traditionally international law was only concerned with the rights and obligations of states. It has already been seen in Chapter 16 that significant changes occurred with the establishment of rules governing human rights. Arguments have since been raised about the existence of people's rights additional to and different from the rights of individual human beings. The growth of environmental law has now led to discussion about whether there exists a right to a decent environment. Such a right might not only be possessed by individuals and peoples but raises the connected question of whether future generations, animals or even the environment itself have recognisable rights. Clearly, much depends on the concept of 'right' that is employed. Some would argue that rights which are not capable of legal enforcement should not properly be called rights. Jeremy Bentham expressed such a view when he referred to claims of the existence of rights as 'nonsense on stilts'. Others argue that no right can exist without a corresponding clearly defined duty.

It seems clear that the existence of recognised human rights has implications for environmental law. For example, the right to life must in some part be dependent on the existence of an environment capable of sustaining life. Principle 1 of the Stockholm Declaration provides that:

> Man has the fundamental right to freedom, equality and adequate conditions of life, in an environment of a quality that permits a life of dignity and well-being ...

and imposes a corresponding duty to protect and improve the environment for present and future generations. Article 24 of the African Charter on Human and Peoples' Rights 1981 provides:

> All peoples shall have the right to a general satisfactory environment favourable to their development.

No other treaty appears expressly to recognise an individual right to a decent environment and it is submitted that the right operates at the level of a general principle, in a manner similar to the right of self-determination, rather than as an individually enforceable human right.

APPENDIX

UNITED NATIONS MEMBER STATES[1]

With the admission of Palau, there are now 185 member states of the United Nations. The member states and the dates on which they joined the Organisation are listed below:

Member – (date of admission)

Afghanistan – (19 November 1946)

Albania – (14 December 1955)

Algeria – (8 October 1962)

Andorra – (28 July 1993)

Angola – (1 December 1976)

Antigua and Barbuda – (11 November 1981)

Argentina – (24 October 1945)

Armenia – (2 March 1992)

Australia – (1 November 1945)

Austria – (14 December 1955)

Azerbaijan – (9 March 1992)

Bahamas – (18 September 1973)

Bahrain – (21 September 1971)

Bangladesh – (17 September 1974)

Barbados – (9 December 1966)

Belarus – (24 October 1945)[2]

Belgium – (27 December 1945)

Belize – (25 September 1981)

Benin – (20 September 1960)

Bhutan – (21 September 1971)

Bolivia – (14 November 1945)

Bosnia and Herzegovina – (22 May 1992)

Botswana – (17 October 1966)

Brazil – (24 October 1945)

Brunei Darussalam – (21 September 1984)

Bulgaria – (14 December 1955)

Burkina Faso – (20 September 1960)

---

1 Source: UN Press Release ORG/1190 (15 December 1994). Updated 24 June 1997 from http://www.un.org/Overview/unmember.html.

2 On 19 September 1991, Byelorussia informed the United Nations that it had changed its name to Belarus.

Burundi – (18 September 1962)

Cambodia – (14 December 1955)

Cameroon – (20 September 1960)

Canada – (9 November 1945)

Cape Verde – (16 September 1975)

Central African Republic – (20 September 1960)

Chad – (20 September 1960)

Chile – (24 October 1945)

China – (24 October 1945)

Colombia – (5 November 1945)

Comoros – (12 November 1975)

Congo – (20 September 1960)

Costa Rica – (2 November 1945)

Côte d'Ivoire – (20 September 1960)

Croatia – (22 May 1992)

Cuba – (24 October 1945)

Cyprus – (20 September 1960)

Czech Republic – (19 January 1993)[3]

Democratic People's Republic of Korea – (17 September 1991)

Democratic Republic of the Congo – (20 September 1960)

Denmark – (24 October 1945)

Djibouti – (20 September 1977)

Dominica – (18 December 1978)

Dominican Republic – (24 October 1945)

Ecuador – (21 December 1945)

Egypt – (24 October 1945)[4]

El Salvador – (24 October 1945)

Equatorial Guinea – (12 November 1968)

Eritrea – (28 May 1993)

---

3   Czechoslovakia was an original member of the United Nations from 24 October 1945. In a letter dated 10 December 1992, its Permanent Representative informed the Secretary General that the Czech and Slovak Federal Republic would cease to exist on 31 December 1992 and that the Czech Republic and the Slovak Republic, as successor states, would apply for membership in the United Nations. Following the receipt of its application, the Security Council, on 8 January, recommended to the General Assembly that the Czech Republic be admitted to United Nations membership. The Czech Republic was thus admitted on 19 January as a member state.

4   Egypt and Syria were original members of the United Nations from 24 October 1945. Following a plebiscite on 21 February 1958, the United Arab Republic was established by a union of Egypt and Syria and continued as a single member. On 13 October 1961, Syria, having resumed its status as an independent state, resumed its separate membership in the United Nations. On 2 September 1971, the United Arab Republic changed its name to the Arab Republic of Egypt.

Estonia – (17 September 1991)

Ethiopia – (13 November 1945)

Federated States of Micronesia – (17 September 1991)

Fiji – (13 October 1970)

Finland – (14 December 1955)

France – (24 October 1945)

Gabon – (20 September 1960)

Gambia – (21 September 1965)

Georgia – (31 July 1992)

Germany – (18 September 1973)[5]

Ghana – (8 March 1957)

Greece – (25 October 1945)

Grenada – (17 September 1974)

Guatemala – (21 November 1945)

Guinea – (12 December 1958)

Guinea-Bissau – (17 September 1974)

Guyana – (20 September 1966)

Haiti – (24 October 1945)

Honduras – (17 December 1945)

Hungary – (14 December 1955)

Iceland – (19 November 1946)

India – (30 October 1945)

Indonesia – (28 September 1950)[6]

Iran – (24 October 1945)

Iraq – (21 December 1945)

Ireland – (14 December 1955)

Israel – (11 May 1949)

Italy – (14 December 1955)

Jamaica – (18 September 1962)

Japan – (18 December 1956)

Jordan – (14 December 1955)

---

5   The Federal Republic of Germany and the German Democratic Republic were admitted to membership in the United Nations on 18 September 1973. Through the accession of the German Democratic Republic to the Federal Republic of Germany, effective from 3 October 1990, the two German States have united to form one sovereign state.

6   By letter of 20 January 1965, Indonesia announced its decision to withdraw from the United Nations 'at this stage and under the present circumstances'. By telegram of 19 September 1966, it announced its decision 'to resume full co-operation with the United Nations and to resume participation in its activities'. On 28 September 1966, the General Assembly took note of this decision and the President invited representatives of Indonesia to take seats in the Assembly.

Kazakstan – (2 March 1992)

Kenya – (16 December 1963)

Kuwait – (14 May 1963)

Kyrgyz Republic – (2 March 1992)

Lao People's Democratic Republic – (14 December 1955)

Latvia – (17 September 1991)

Lebanon – (24 October 1945)

Lesotho – (17 October 1966)

Liberia – (2 November 1945)

Libya – (14 December 1955)

Liechtenstein – (18 September 1990)

Lithuania – (17 September 1991)

Luxembourg – (24 October 1945)

Madagascar – (20 September 1960)

Malawi – (1 December 1964)

Malaysia – (17 September 1957)[7]

Maldives – (21 September 1965)

Mali – (28 September 1960)

Malta – (1 December 1964)

Marshall Islands – (17 September 1991)

Mauritania – (7 October 1961)

Mauritius – (24 April 1968)

Mexico – (7 November 1945)

Monaco – (28 May 1993)

Mongolia – (27 October 1961)

Morocco – (12 November 1956)

Mozambique – (16 September 1975)

Myanmar – (19 April 1948)

Namibia – (23 April 1990)

Nepal – (14 December 1955)

Netherlands – (10 December 1945)

New Zealand – (24 October 1945)

Nicaragua – (24 October 1945)

Niger – (20 September 1960)

Nigeria – (7 October 1960)

---

7   The Federation of Malaya joined the United Nations on 17 September 1957. On 16 September 1963, its name was changed to Malaysia, following the admission to the new federation of Singapore, Sabah (North Borneo) and Sarawak. Singapore became an independent state on 9 August 1965 and a member of the United Nations on 21 September 1965.

Norway – (27 November 1945)

Oman – (7 October 1971)

Pakistan – (30 September 1947)

Palau – (15 December 1994)

Panama – (13 November 1945)

Papua New Guinea – (10 October 1975)

Paraguay – (24 October 1945)

Peru – (31 October 1945)

Philippines – (24 October 1945)

Poland – (24 October 1945)

Portugal – (14 December 1955)

Qatar – (21 September 1971)

Republic of Korea – (17 September 1991)

Republic of Moldova – (2 March 1992)

Romania – (14 December 1955)

Russian Federation – (24 October 1945)[8]

Rwanda – (18 September 1962)

Saint Kitts and Nevis – (23 September 1983)

Saint Lucia – (18 September 1979)

Saint Vincent and the Grenadines – (16 September 1980)

Samoa – (15 December 1976)

San Marino – (2 March 1992)

Sao Tome and Principe – (16 September 1975)

Saudi Arabia – (24 October 1945)

Senegal – (28 September 1960)

Seychelles – (21 September 1976)

Sierra Leone – (27 September 1961)

Singapore – (21 September 1965)

Slovak Republic – (19 January 1993)[9]

---

8   The Union of Soviet Socialist Republics was an original member of the United Nations from 24 October 1945. In a letter dated 24 December 1991, Boris Yeltsin, the President of the Russian Federation, informed the Secretary General that the membership of the Soviet Union in the Security Council and all other United Nations organs was being continued by the Russian Federation with the support of the 11 member countries of the Commonwealth of Independent States.

9   Czechoslovakia was an original member of the United Nations from 24 October 1945. In a letter dated 10 December 1992, its Permanent Representative informed the Secretary General that the Czech and Slovak Federal Republic would cease to exist on 31 December 1992 and that the Czech Republic and the Slovak Republic, as successor sStates, would apply for membership in the United Nations. Following the receipt of its application, the Security Council, on 8 January, recommended to the General Assembly that the Slovak Republic be admitted to United Nations membership. The Slovak Republic was thus admitted on 19 January as a member state.

Slovenia – (22 May 1992)

Solomon Islands – (19 September 1978)

Somalia – (20 September 1960)

South Africa – (7 November 1945)

Spain – (14 December 1955)

Sri Lanka – (14 December 1955)

Sudan – (12 November 1956)

Suriname – (4 December 1975)

Swaziland – (24 September 1968)

Sweden – (19 November 1946)

Syria – (24 October 1945)[10]

Tajikistan – (2 March 1992)

Thailand – (16 December 1946)

The former Yugoslav Republic of Macedonia – (8 April 1993)[11]

Togo – (20 September 1960)

Trinidad and Tobago – (18 September 1962)

Tunisia – (12 November 1956)

Turkey – (24 October 1945)

Turkmenistan – (2 March 1992)

Uganda – (25 October 1962)

Ukraine – (24 October 1945)

United Arab Emirates – (9 December 1971)

United Kingdom – (24 October 1945)

United Republic of Tanzania – (14 December 1961)[12]

United States of America – (24 October 1945)

Uruguay – (18 December 1945)

Uzbekistan – (2 March 1992)

Vanuatu – (15 September 1981)

---

10 Egypt and Syria were original members of the United Nations from 24 October 1945. Following a plebiscite on 21 February 1958, the United Arab Republic was established by a union of Egypt and Syria and continued as a single member. On 13 October 1961, Syria, having resumed its status as an independent State, resumed its separate membership in the United Nations.

11 The General Assembly decided on 8 April 1993 to admit to United Nations membership the state being provisionally referred to for all purposes within the United Nations as 'The former Yugoslav Republic of Macedonia' pending settlement of the difference that had arisen over its name.

12 Tanganyika was a member of the United Nations from 14 December 1961 and Zanzibar was a member from 16 December 1963. Following the ratification on 26 April 1964 of Articles of Union between Tanganyika and Zanzibar, the United Republic of Tanganyika and Zanzibar continued as a single member, changing its name to the United Republic of Tanzania on 1 November 1964.

Venezuela – (15 November 1945)
Viet Nam – (20 September 1977)
Yemen – (30 September 1947)[13]
Yugoslavia – (24 October 1945)
Zambia – (1 December 1964)
Zimbabwe – (25 August 1980)

Membership of the Security Council

Permanent members

China
France
Russian Federation
United Kingdom
United States of America

Elected members (membership term ends)

Chile (31 December 1997)
Costa Rica (31 December 1998)
Egypt (31 December 1997)
Guinea-Bissau (31 December 1997)
Japan (31 December 1998)
Kenya (31 December 1998)
Poland (31 December 1997)
Portugal (31 December 1998)
Republic of Korea (31 December 1997)
Sweden (31 December 1998)

---

13 Yemen was admitted to membership in the United Nations on 30 September 1947 and Democratic Yemen on 14 December 1967. On 22 May 1990, the two countries merged and have since been represented as one member with the name 'Yemen'.

INDEX

LIVERPOOL JOHN MOORES UNIVERSITY
Aldham Robarts L.R.C.
TEL. 0151 231 3701/3634